THE MOST
TRUSTED NAME
IN TRAVEL

ITALY 2024

16th Edition

By Donald Strachan, Stephen Brewer, Michelle Schoenung, Elizabeth Heath, Stephen Keeling

FrommerMedia LLC

Frommer's Italy 2024, 16th Edition

Published by:
Frommer Media LLC

Copyright © 2023 by Frommer Media LLC, New York City, New York. All rights reserved. No part of this publication may be reproduced, stored in a retrieval system, or transmitted in any form or by any means, electronic, mechanical, photocopying, recording, scanning or otherwise, except as permitted under Sections 107 or 108 of the 1976 United States Copyright Act, without the prior written permission of the Publisher. Requests to the Publisher for permission should be addressed to Support@FrommerMedia.com.

Frommer's is a registered trademark of Arthur Frommer. Frommer Media LLC is not associated with any product or vendor mentioned in this book.

ISBN 978-1-62887-563-8 (paper), 978-1-62887-564-5 (ebk)

Editorial Director: Pauline Frommer
Editor: Alexis Lipsitz Flippin
Production Editor: Erin Geile
Compositor: Lissa Auciello-Brogan
Cartographer: Andy Dolan
Photo Editor: Meghan Lamb
Indexer: Kelly Henthorne
Cover Designer: Dave Riedy

For information on our other products or services, see www.frommers.com.

FrommerMedia LLC also publishes its books in a variety of electronic formats. Some content that appears in print may not be available in electronic formats.

Manufactured in Malaysia

5 4 3 2 1

HOW TO CONTACT US

In researching this book, we discovered many wonderful places—hotels, restaurants, shops, and more. We're sure you'll find others. Please tell us about them, so we can share the information with your fellow travelers in upcoming editions. If you were disappointed with a recommendation, we'd love to know that, too. Please write to: Support@FrommerMedia.com

FROMMER'S STAR RATINGS SYSTEM

Every hotel, restaurant and attraction listed in this guide has been ranked for quality and value. Here's what the stars mean:

★ Recommended
★★ Highly Recommended
★★★ A must! Don't miss!

AN IMPORTANT NOTE

The world is a dynamic place. Hotels change ownership, restaurants hike their prices, museums alter their opening hours, and buses and trains change their routings. And all of this can occur in the several months after our authors have visited, inspected, and written about these hotels, restaurants, museums, and transportation services. Though we have made valiant efforts to keep all our information fresh and up-to-date, some few changes can inevitably occur in the periods before a revised edition of this guidebook is published. So please bear with us if a tiny number of the details in this book have changed. Please also note that we have no responsibility or liability for any inaccuracy or errors or omissions, or for inconvenience, loss, damage, or expenses suffered by anyone as a result of assertions in this guide.

CONTENTS

Via dei Corridori
St. Peter's
Piazza di San Pietro
Piazza Pio XII
Via della Conciliazione
Sant'Angelo
Ponte Sant'Angelo
Piazza di Ponte Sant'Angelo

LIST OF MAPS

ABOUT THE AUTHORS

Donald Strachan is a travel journalist who has written about Italy for publications worldwide, including *National Geographic Traveler, The Guardian, Sunday Telegraph,* CNN.com, and many others. He has also written several Italy guidebooks for Frommer's, including *Frommer's EasyGuide to Rome, Florence & Venice.* He lives in London, England. For more, see www.donaldstrachan.com.

Stephen Brewer has been savoring Italian pleasures ever since he sipped his first cappuccino while a student in Rome many, many years ago (togas had just gone out of fashion). He has written about Italy for many magazines and guidebooks and remains transported in equal measure by Bolognese cooking, Tuscan hillsides, the Bay of Naples, and the streets of Palermo.

Michelle Schoenung is an American journalist and translator in Milan who relocated to the Belpaese in 2000 for what was to be a yearlong adventure. More than 2 decades later, she is pleased that Milan has evolved into a much more international and cosmopolitan city and has shed its image of merely being a foggy northern Italian business hub. Her writings and translations have appeared in magazines and books in the United States and Italy. In her free time, she likes to read, run, travel, and explore the city with her two rambunctious Italian-American *ragazzi.*

Elizabeth Heath, a long-time contributor to Frommer's, is a writer and editor based in Umbria, central Italy, from where she writes about travel and adventures in Italy, Europe and farther afield. Her work appears in *The Washington Post, Travel & Leisure, Huffpost, Reader's Digest,* and many other outlets. Read more of her writings at www.elizabethfheath.com.

Stephen Keeling has been traveling to Italy since 1985 and covering his favorite nation for Frommer's since 2007. He has written for *The Independent, Daily Telegraph,* various magazines, and numerous travel guides as well as the award-winning *Frommer's Florence, Tuscany & Umbria.* Stephen resides in New York City.

1

THE BEST OF ITALY

By Donald Strachan

As the post-pandemic world began to travel again, Italy was right at the top of many a wanderlust wish list. It's easy to understand why: Just think the word "Italy" and you can already see it. The noble stones of Ancient Rome and the Greek temples of Sicily. The wine hills of Piedmont and Tuscany, the ruins of Pompeii, the secret canals and crumbling palaces of Venice. For centuries, visitors have come here looking for their own slice of *La Dolce Vita.* For the most part, they have found it.

Nowhere in the world felt the impact of the Renaissance more than its birthplace, **Florence,** whose vast repository of art includes works left by Masaccio, Botticelli, Leonardo da Vinci, Michelangelo, and many, many others. Much of the "known world" was once ruled from **Rome,** a city supposedly founded by twins Romulus and Remus in 753 B.C. There is no place with more artistic treasures—not even **Venice,** an impossible floating city whose beauty and history were shaped by trade with Byzantine and Islamic empires to the east.

Of course, there's more. Long before Italy was a country, it was a loose grouping of city-states. Centuries of alliance and rivalry left a legacy of art and architecture in **Verona,** where Shakespearean romance rubs alongside an intact Roman arena; and in **Mantua,** which blossomed during the Renaissance under the Gonzaga dynasty. **Padua**'s revolutionary Giotto paintings are within easy reach of Venice, too. In **Siena,** ethereal art and Gothic palaces survive, barely altered since their 1300s heyday.

A millennium earlier, the eruption of Vesuvius in A.D. 79 preserved **Pompeii** and **Herculaneum** under volcanic ash. They remain the best places to conjure up everyday Roman life. The buildings of Ancient Greece still stand at **Paestum,** in Campania, and at sites on **Sicily,** the Mediterranean's largest island. Cave dwellings, frescoed rupestrian churches, and even a rock cathedral honeycomb the rocks of **Matera,** in the unspoiled Basilicata region.

The corrugated, vine-clad hills of the **Chianti** and the cypress-studded, emerald-green expanses of the **Val d'Orcia** serve up iconic images of **Tuscany.** Adventurous walkers of all ages can hike between the coastal villages of the **Cinque Terre,** where you can roam untroubled by the 21st century. Whether it's Sicilian seafood, pizza in **Naples,** pasta in **Bologna,** pesto in **Genoa,** or the red Barolo and Barbaresco wines of **Piedmont,**

PREVIOUS PAGE: **Basilica Santa Maria della Salute with Canal Grande in Venice.**

your tastebuds enjoy their own adventure. For shoppers, **Milan** and Florence are centers of world fashion. Welcome to *La Bella Italia.*

ITALY'S best AUTHENTIC EXPERIENCES

- **Dining Italian style:** There is no pastime here more cherished than eating—even better, eating outdoors with a view of a medieval church or vineyard. And forget any idea of a single "Italian" cuisine: Each region and city has its own beloved recipes, handed down over generations. *Buon appetito!*
- **Exploring Rome's working food markets:** Testaccio's reborn historic market is a culinary and cultural treat, where local chefs and feisty *signore* compete for the best *pomodori, mozzarella di bufala,* and *trippa* (tripe). Savor delicious street food as you soak up a genuine neighborhood south of the Aventine. See p. 153.
- **Catching an opera at Verona's Arena:** In summer, Italians enjoy opera under the stars. The setting for Italy's largest and most famous outdoor festival is the ancient Arena di Verona, a site grand enough to accommodate as many elephants as *Aïda* needs. See p. 460.

Exploring a tiny harbor in Riomaggiore, one of the Cinque Terre towns.

- **Feeling the modern pulse of historic Bologna:** The youthful exuberance of Bologna, Europe's oldest university town, reveals itself amid medieval palaces and squares; 25 miles of portico-covered sidewalks; and best of all, markets, shops, and restaurants that dish up arguably Italy's best food. See chapter 8.
- **Slowing down to Italy pace:** Nothing happens quickly here: Linger over a glass of wine from the Tuscan hills, slurp a gelato made with seasonal Sicilian fruit, enjoy the evening *passeggiata* (ritual walk) just like the locals. They call it Slow Food for a reason.

Strolling through the portico-covered sidewalks of Bologna.

ITALY'S most memorable RESTAURANTS

- **L'Ottava Nota** (Palermo): Palermo's old Arab quarter, the Kalsa, buzzes these days, especially at this sleek restaurant with its creative spin on Sicilian cuisine. Ingredients come straight from the city's produce markets. See p. 763.
- **Osteria dell'Enoteca** (Florence): When successful wine-bar owners open a restaurant, you know the *vino* will be first-rate. Osteria dell'Enoteca doesn't disappoint, but also serves food that unites the best of Tuscany's traditional ingredients with a light, contemporary style. The stone-and-slate dining room is an atmospheric spot for any occasion. See p. 219.
- **Taverna San Giuseppe** (Siena): A brick-vaulted room from the 12th century is a characterful setting for hand-rolled *pici* with a *ragù* of *cinghiale* (wild boar), ricotta-filled *gnudi,* and other expert takes on Tuscan comfort food. It's a place that travelers long remember. See p. 243.
- **Wistèria** (Venice): Part of a new wave of contemporary restaurants opening in Venice, this place features innovative riffs on traditional *cicchetti* and seafood from the lagoon and farther out in the Adriatic. See p. 445.

- **Mimì alla Ferrovia** (Naples): Veteran waiters in bow ties and white jackets augment the old-fashioned charm at this beloved institution. Mimì elevates fried street food, market-fresh fish, and other Neapolitan favorites to high art. See p. 612.

ITALY'S most charming HOTELS

- **Villa Spalletti Trivelli** (Rome): Recent upgrades have only enhanced the unique experience of staying in a neoclassical mansion in the middle of the capital. Opulence plus impeccable, understated service comes at a price, of course. When our lottery numbers come up, we will be booking a stay here. See p. 132.
- **Santa Caterina** (Amalfi): Amid fragrant citrus groves above the sea, Santa Caterina is not outrageously posh, just magically transporting. Ceramic tiles, a smattering of antiques, sea-view terraces, a garden path leading to a private beach—it's worth the splurge. Shoulder-season rates and special offers bring prices down out of the stratosphere. See p. 671.
- **Palazzo Tolomei** (Florence): A palace where Raphael once stayed—perhaps even giving its owners a painting to make rent—sounds grand indeed. You won't be disappointed. A Renaissance layout and baroque redecoration from the 1600s are intact. See p. 208.
- **Fra I Sassi Residence** (Matera): Staying in a cave is an experience in itself, especially when accommodations are as stylish and comfortable as these. All open onto a meandering, sunny terrace with a front-row seat on a sculpted cluster of cave dwellings that tumble down surrounding cliffs. See p. 716.
- **Hotel Mediterraneo** (Rome): Upscale Art Deco Hotel Mediterraneo is the flagship of a trio of hotels near Termini Station run by the Bettoja family. Others are even more budget-friendly, but all offer vintage charm, old-school comforts, and warm service from a loyal, longtime staff. They don't make 'em like this anymore. See p. 134.
- **Agriturismo La Bruciata** (Montepulciano): All the ingredients of a perfect Tuscan stay come together in these stone houses on a sunny hillside. Accommodations are spacious; breakfasts and dinners are homemade and homegrown; and the welcome is as bright as the flower garden. See p. 251.

ITALY'S best FOR FAMILIES

- **Climbing Pisa's wonky tower** (Tuscany): Are we walking up or down? Pleasantly disoriented kids are bound to ask as you spiral your way to a rooftop-viewing balcony atop one of the world's most famous pieces of botched engineering. See p. 299.

The crazy tilt of Pisa's cathedral bell tower.

- **The beaches of Puglia and Basilicata:** Many of Italy's best sands are in the southeast, often reached via an easy, signposted hike through coastal forest. Even the prettiest may be empty outside high season. Try Torre Guaceto, north of Brindisi; Porto Selvaggio or Punta della Suina, close to Gallipoli; or coves along the remote Maratea coast. See chapter 14.
- **Exploring below Naples:** There's more to Naples than you can see at ground level. Head under its maze of streets to explore remains of ancient Greek and Roman cities, creepy catacombs used for early Christian burials, and tunnels where Neapolitans hid from an 1884 cholera epidemic and World War II bombing raids. See p. 602.
- **Taste-testing every artisan gelateria:** When it comes to Italian ice cream, choose carefully—Smurf-blue or bubblegum-pink flavors are a sure sign of color enhancers, and beware ice crystals and fluffy heaps that betray additives and pumped-in air. Authentic *gelaterie* produce good stuff from scratch daily, with fresh seasonal produce; look for a short, all-natural ingredient list posted proudly for all to see. Check "Where to Eat" and "Gelato" sections in individual chapters.

ITALY'S quietest LANDSCAPES

- **Gran Paradiso National Park** (Valle d'Aosta): Outside the August peak season, you could wander here for hours without seeing a soul. With the region's four towering peaks constantly in view, trek for miles up valleys and across wildflower meadows, then linger over steaming bowls of the local specialty, *carbonada con polenta* (beef stewed with juniper berries and red wine, served with cornmeal). See p. 543.

- **Umbria:** With fine wines, fêted produce (including game and olive oil), and centuries-old art and architecture, Tuscany's under-visited neighbor is often called "Italy's green heart." Wander off the beaten track to unspoiled Spello; explore vine-carpeted hillsides on the Strada del Sagrantino wine trail; or find solitude in medieval Gubbio, where St. Francis himself lodged in peace. See chapter 7.
- **Sicily's west coast:** Beyond the clamor of Palermo's markets and the glamour of Taormina, there is another Sicily. Go west, where salt marshes are a stopover for migrating birds: The maquis and coastline in the Zingaro reserve are off-limits to motor vehicles. Quieter still, the Egadi Archipelago is a place to detach yourself—from everyone and everything. See chapter 15.

ITALY'S unforgettable FLAVORS

- **Sicilian sweets:** Italy's largest island is a haven for sweet tooths. Begin the day with a granita-filled brioche; liven up your mid-morning espresso with a ricotta-stuffed *cannolo;* end a meal with a *biancomangiare.* Sicily's *pasticcerie* are justly famous.
- **Bistecca alla fiorentina:** The ultimate carnivores' sharing plate is usually at least 1.2kg (almost 3 lb.) of prime Chianina cattle on the bone. It's flame-grilled—briefly—and best accompanied by simple sides such as stewed Tuscan beans or potatoes roasted with rosemary.
- **The humble artichoke:** One of the joys of visiting Italy—especially Rome—in winter and early spring is great as a pizza topping; in traditional Roman dishes like *carciofi alla romana* or *alla guidia;* or carpaccio style, with just a splash of oil, a grind of pepper, and some shavings of hard cheese. *Delizioso!*
- **Cicchetti and a spritz:** Tapas-like small plates, usually at a bar, are a Venetian tradition. A spritz made with Aperol and sparkling Prosecco wine from Veneto completes the *cicchetti* experience.
- **Vino rosso:** If you are not by a lake or the sea, chances are the wine you're sipping is red. There is so much variety: near-black Primitivo from Puglia, robust reds from the Langhe in Piedmont, or the elegance of a great Tuscan Chianti Classico or Brunello di Montalcino.
- **Neapolitan pizza:** Leaving aside whether it was really invented in Naples, pizza Margherita finds its ultimate expression around Spaccanapoli. Prepared dough spends a few seconds in wood-burning furnaces—enough to aerate doughy crusts around a gorgeous puddle of molten mozzarella and San Marzano tomato.

- **A coffee al banco:** Italians—especially city dwellers—don't linger in a piazza sipping their morning cappuccino. For them, *un caffè* is a pit stop: They stand at the counter *(al banco)*, throw back the bitter elixir, and continue on their way, reinforced by a hit of caffeine. Drinking Italian-style costs less, maybe half of the sit-down price. See p. 155.

ITALY'S best MUSEUMS

- **Vatican Museums** (Rome): The 100 galleries of the Musei Vaticani are loaded with papal treasures accumulated over centuries. Musts include the Sistine Chapel, ancient Greek and Roman sculptures like "Laocoön" and "Belvedere Apollo," room upon room of Raphael frescoes (among them his "School of Athens"), Greco-Roman antiquities, and European Renaissance art. See p. 80.
- **Galleria degli Uffizi** (Florence): This U-shaped High Renaissance building designed by Giorgio Vasari—once administrative headquarters, or *uffizi* (offices), for Tuscany's dukes—is now the crown jewel of Europe's fine-art museums. It holds the world's greatest collection of Renaissance paintings, including iconic works by Botticelli, Leonardo da Vinci, and Michelangelo. See p. 179.
- **Accademia** (Venice): One of Europe's great museums houses an unequaled array of Venetian paintings, exhibited chronologically from the 13th to the 18th century. Walls are hung with works by Bellini, Carpaccio, Giorgione, Titian, and Tintoretto. See p. 417.

Michelangelo's Sistine Chapel, Vatican Museums.

The sun rising over the Roman Forum.

- **Museo Archeologico Nazionale** (Naples): Come here to see mosaics and frescoes from Pompeii and Herculaneum—the original "Cave Canem" ("Beware of the Dog") mosaic, the Villa of the Papyri frescoes—and much else, including the "Farnese Bull," which once decorated Rome's Terme di Caracalla. See p. 600.
- **Museo Egizio** (Turin): With a dazzling refit, Turin's Egyptology museum has doubled in size, with more space than ever for the finest collection of Egyptian artifacts outside Cairo. See p. 524.
- **Museo dell'Opera del Duomo** (Florence): With icons of sculpture in marble and bronze, modern multimedia curation, and a creative layout, this collection is the homage that two Florentine greats—Ghiberti and Brunelleschi—fully deserve. See p. 178.

ITALY'S best FREE THINGS TO DO

- **Watching the sun rise over the Roman Forum:** A short stroll from the Capitoline Hill down Via del Campidoglio to Via di Monte Tarpeo brings you to a perfect outlook: a terrace behind the Michelangelo-designed square, an ideal photo op when the sun rises behind the Temple of Saturn, illuminating the archaeological complex below in pink-orange light. Early risers should reward themselves with breakfast from one of the Jewish Ghetto's excellent bakeries. See p. 90.
- **Basking in the lights of the Renaissance:** At dusk, make the steep climb to the ancient church of San Miniato al Monte, Florence. Sit down on the steps and watch the city begin to twinkle. See p. 200.
- **Discovering you're hopelessly lost in Venice:** You haven't experienced Venice until you have turned a corner, convinced you're on the way to somewhere, only to find yourself smack against a canal with

no bridge. Shrug, smile, and give the maze of city streets another try, because getting lost here is a pleasure. See chapter 9.

- **Driving the Amalfi Coast:** The SS163, "road of a thousand bends," hugs cliffs and deep gorges, cutting through olive groves, lemon terraces, and whitewashed villages—against a background of the bluest ocean you can picture. One of the world's classic drives, it provokes fear, nausea, and wonder in equal doses. The secret? Make sure someone else is at the wheel, perhaps one of the steely-nerved bus drivers who ply the route daily. See p. 640.
- **Surrendering to the madness of a Palermo market:** In Sicily's capital—a crossroads between Europe, Africa, and Asia for 2,000 years—the colorful street theater is a vignette of a culture which often feels more Middle Eastern than European. See p. 766.

ITALY'S iconic ARCHITECTURAL LANDMARKS

- **Brunelleschi's dome** (Florence): It took the genius of Filippo Brunelleschi to raise a vast dome over the gaping hole in Florence's cathedral roof. Although rejected for a commission to cast the Baptistery doors, Filippo didn't sulk: He went away and became the city's greatest architect, creating one of Europe's most recognizable landmarks. See p. 178.
- **Beehive towns of the southeast** (Puglia): In the hinterlands of the Adriatic coast, storybook *trulli* dwellings enchant travelers to Alberobello and the Valle d'Itria. Once you're here, a bonus: the mazelike "white cities" of Ostuni, Martina Franca, Locorotondo, and Cisternino. See chapter 14.
- **The Gothic center of Siena** (Tuscany): Shell-shaped Piazza del Campo stands at the heart of one of Europe's best-preserved medieval cities. Steep, canyon-like streets, icons of Gothic architecture like the Palazzo

Detail of a preserved ancient fresco from Pompeii.

Pubblico, and Madonnas painted on gilded altarpieces transport you back to a time before the Renaissance. See p. 232.

- **Pompeii** (Campania): When Mt. Vesuvius blew its top in A.D. 79, Pompeii was buried under molten lava and ash, ending the lives of perhaps 35,000 citizens and suspending the city in a time capsule. Today, still in the menacing shadow of the volcano, you can coax this poignant ghost town into life with very little imagination. See p. 630.
- **Valley of the Temples, Agrigento** (Sicily): Seven Greek temples by the sea were built to impress, and their honey-colored columns and pediments still do. Seeing these romantic ruins—some, like the Temple of Concordia, beautifully preserved; others like the Temple of Juno, timeworn but proud—is an experience never forgotten. See p. 799.

best UNDISCOVERED ITALY

- **Byzantine art up close:** Unless you plan on living for another century or two, you will never again have the chance to see the 10 million mosaics of the Florence Baptistery ceiling from just a few inches away. While a major restoration is underway, small groups can ascend the scaffolding for this closer look. Book now. See p. 172.
- **Genoa's UNESCO center:** Don't be fooled by the rough, industrial exterior: Genoa has Italy's largest *centro storico,* with architecture to rival Venice. A restored old port, the Palazzo Reale, and the palaces of Strada Nuova are just a few highlights of a trading city made rich by the sea. See chapter 11.
- **The canals of Treviso:** Venice's near-neighbor has canals of its own, and much thinner crowds, even in peak season. Visit an atmospheric old fish market and churches decorated by Tommaso da Modena. See p. 461.
- **The old, old stones of Puglia:** Remains of a once-thriving Roman trading center are scattered across Puglia's coastal plains. Notable spots include a segment of the Trajan Way and the Tomb of the Pomegranates, its huge doors bearing ancient handles and hinges that still function. "Built to last," and then some. See p. 734.

ITALY'S best ACTIVE ADVENTURES

- **Flying in the Lucanian Dolomites** (Basilicata): Villagers in Castelmezzano and Pietrapertosa, perched on adjacent mountainsides, have linked themselves in a novel way: You can glide, via zipline, from one village to another. The "Flight of the Angel" is a thrill or a heartstopper, depending on your taste. See p. 718.

Ziplining town-to-town in the Dolomite mountains.

- **Touring Ferrara on two wheels:** Join bike-mad *Ferraresi* as they zip along narrow, cycle-friendly lanes that snake through the old center, past Castello Estense and the Renaissance elegance of Palazzo Schifanoia. You can even bike a circuit around the medieval walls. See p. 369.
- **Walking from the Monte Bianco Skyway:** In Italy's far northwestern corner, a revolving cable car scales Europe's tallest mountain: Monte Bianco ("Mont Blanc" to the French), flanked by perilous glaciers and jagged granite peaks, standing 4,810m (15,780 ft.) tall on the border between France and Italy. Departing from the mountain resort of Courmayeur, the cableway is pricey, but unforgettable. See p. 544.
- **Hiking the Cinque Terre** (Liguria): For sheer beauty, we love the 3-mile path from Corniglia to Vernazza and a 2-mile section from Vernazza to Monterosso, but the entire Cinque Terre area is rewarding to hike, especially off-season. Narrow paths skirt terraced vineyards. Olive and lemon groves hover over the sapphire Mediterranean Sea. See p. 576.

ITALY'S best NEIGHBORHOODS

- **Monti, Rome:** Between Termini Station and the Forum, the area now called Monti was once known as *Suburra*—the source of our word "suburbs." A slum and redlight district during the Roman Empire, today it's a colorful neighborhood that retains its working-class roots, with a lively dining and bar scene. See chapter 4.

- **San Frediano, Florence:** Most Florentines have abandoned their *centro storico* to the visitors, but the Arno's Left Bank in San Frediano has plenty of local action after dark. Dine at **iO** (p. 218), slurp a gelato by the river at **La Carraia** (p. 220), and sip cocktails at **Libreria-Café La Cité** (p. 223).
- **Navigli, Milan:** Nowhere exudes Milanese confidence more than the Navigli neighborhood, around the Darsena, once Milan's canal port. Locals come here after dark for summer concerts, shops and seasonal markets, or to watch a game on the big screen. See chapter 10.
- **Spaccanapoli, Naples:** It's sometimes said that Naples is Italy on overdrive, and the city goes up another gear in the narrow, laundry-strung lanes of its *centro storico.* Forget about a map—just plunge in and enjoy. Small stores sell everything from limoncello and carved nativity scenes to fried snacks and the world's best pizza. See chapter 12.
- **Sasso Barisano and Sasso Caveoso, Matera:** Inhabited for more than 3,000 years, clusters of cave dwellings carved into limestone cliffs create one of Italy's weirdest urban spectacles. The primitive, earth-hued assemblage of homes, churches, and monasteries pile one atop the other along a jumble of stepped streets. You can stay or dine here, too. See p. 713.

The sun sets on Naviglio Grande canal in Milan.

2

ITALY IN CONTEXT

By Donald Strachan

Many stereotypes you hear about this extraordinary country are accurate. Children are fussed over wherever they go; food and soccer are a religion; the north–south divide is alive and well; and (alas) bureaucracy is a frustrating feature of daily life for families and businesses—much less so for visitors. Some stereotypes, however, are wide of the mark: Not every Italian you meet will be open and effusive. Every now and then—but rarely in the South—they do taciturn pretty well, too. This chapter provides a little historical and cultural background to help you understand what makes Italy tick.

One important fact to remember is that, for a land so steeped in history—three millennia and counting—Italy has not been *a country* for long. In 2021 Italy celebrated its 160th birthday. Prior to 1861, the political map of the peninsula was in constant flux. War, alliance, invasion, and disputed successions caused that map to change color as often as a chameleon in a bag of M&Ms. Republics, city-states, emirates, dukedoms, kingdoms, and theocracies roll on and off the pages of Italian history with regularity. In many regions, you'll hear languages and dialects other than Italian. Identities are often more regional than national.

This confusing history explains why your Italian experience will differ wildly if you visit, say, Turin rather than Matera. (And why you should visit both if you can.) The architecture is different; the food is different; the legends and important historical figures are different. And the people are different: While the north–south schism is most often written about, cities as close together as Florence and Siena can feel very dissimilar. Milan to Naples is just over 4 hours by train, but you will experience them like two different worlds. This chapter helps you understand why.

ITALY TODAY: PANDEMIC & RECOVERY

Daily life in hill-towns, olive groves, wine cellars, and medieval city streets was profoundly impacted by the novel coronavirus (SARS-CoV-2) and the disease it causes, Covid-19. Italians are a friendly, tactile people; the virus hit at the heart of their social and sociable culture. Italy also has

FACING PAGE: **Photo ops at Pompeii, an ancient Roman town tragically preserved by volcanic ash.**

one of the world's oldest populations, and its elderly were hit especially hard.

And yet the Italian people fought back. On/off national and local lockdowns, mask mandates bolstered by stiff fines, strict enforcement of social distancing in shops and businesses, quarantines, and a national test-and-trace regime were deployed. Virus peaks in 2021 and 2022 grew progressively smaller, while vaccine rollout kept pace with European neighbors—driven both by altruism and by a growing realization that the return of treasured rituals like eating indoors, *aperitivo* hour, social events, inbound and outbound travel, even entering museums, depended on it.

The post-Covid bounce-back has been marked and rapid. Walking the streets of Florence or Rome today, you could be forgiven for forgetting the pandemic ever happened. Bars and restaurants are full; hotels have enjoyed a booking boom that shows no sign of relenting. Cafe chatter has returned to favored topics like football—the plight of the local team, or how the Azzurri national team somehow won football's 2021 European Championship, then failed to even qualify for the 2022 World Cup.

Yet pandemic aftershocks are still visible—in politics, especially. Covid-19 caused repeated government crises, which culminated in the collapse of a unity government in 2022. The election that followed was a triumph for the Fratelli d'Italia (FdI), a socially conservative, anti-immigrant political party. FdI's controversial leader, Giorgia Meloni, became Italy's first female prime minister at the head of an occasionally fractious right-wing coalition. Early government moves have been a mixed bag, of clampdown on protest combined with re-emphasizing Italy's commitment to fighting climate change and a close alliance with the U.S. on Ukraine.

The country's main challenges, as ever, remain economic. In a very difficult international climate, the outlook for Italy appears moderately optimistic. Italy has taken the first steps on a bumpy road to recovery—and bouncing back is critical for an economy that needs and draws visitors from every corner of the globe.

THE MAKING OF ITALY

Prehistory to the Rise of Rome

Among early inhabitants of the Italian peninsula, the **Etruscans** left the most extensive legacy. Archaeologists debate exactly where they came from; inscriptions they left behind (often on graves in *necropoli*) are too bland to be of much help. Whatever their origins, within 2 centuries of appearing around 800 B.C., they had subjugated the lands now known as Tuscany (so named to reflect that heritage), northern Lazio, and Campania, and the so-called **"Villanovan"** tribes who already lived there.

The **Latins,** who were based at Rome, were eventually conquered by the Etruscans around 600 B.C. These new overlords introduced gold tableware and jewelry, bronze urns and terra-cotta statuary, and the art and culture of Greece and Asia Minor; they also made Rome the government seat of Latium. "Roma" is an Etruscan name, and Rome's early, perhaps mythical kings had Etruscan names: Numa, Ancus, even Romulus.

Etruscan rule began to wane after the **Roman Revolt** around 509 B.C., which expelled Rome's Etruscan kings: By 250 B.C. Romans and their allies had vanquished or assimilated the Etruscans, wiping out their language and religion. However, many of the former rulers' manners and beliefs remained and became integral to what we now understand as "Roman culture."

Meanwhile, the **Greeks**—who predated both the Etruscans and the Romans—had built powerful colonial outposts in the south, notably in Naples, founded as Greek "Neapolis." Remains of a Greek *agora,* or market square, survive below **San Lorenzo Maggiore** (p. 601) in the old center of the city. The Greeks also left stone monuments above ground, including at the **Valley of the Temples,** Agrigento, Sicily (p. 799).

To see remnants of Etruscan civilization, Rome's **Museo Nazionale Etrusco** (p. 112) and the Etruscan collection in Rome's **Vatican Museums** (p. 80) are a logical starting point. Florence's **Museo Archeologico** (p. 193) houses one of the greatest Etruscan bronzes yet unearthed, the "Arezzo Chimera." Further fine Etruscan collections are in **Volterra,**

At Florence's Museo Archeologico, the Arezzo Chimera is possibly the most famous artwork surviving from the Etruscan period.

cuisine AROUND THE COUNTRY

Italians know how to cook—just ask any Italian. But be sure to leave plenty of time: Once Italians start talking food, they do not pause for breath. Yet Italy doesn't have one national "Italian" cuisine; it's more a loose grouping of regional cuisines that share a few staples, notably pasta, bread, tomatoes, and pig meat cured in many ways. On a **Rome** visit, you'll encounter authentic local specialties such as *saltimbocca alla romana* (literally "jump-in-the-mouth"—thin slices of veal with sage, cured ham, and cheese) and *carciofi alla romana* (artichokes cooked with herbs, such as mint and garlic), plus a dish that's become ubiquitous, *spaghetti alla carbonara*—pasta coated in a silky sauce made with egg, *Pecorino Romano* (ewe's milk cheese), and cured pork (*guanciale*, or cheek, if it's authentic). For reasons of historical migration, a strong current of Jewish cuisine also runs through Roman cooking.

To the north, in **Florence** and **Tuscany,** seasonal ingredients are served simply; it's the antithesis of French cooking, with its multiple processes. The main ingredient for almost any savory dish is the local olive oil, prized for low acidity. The typical Tuscan pasta is wide, flat *pappardelle,* generally tossed with a game sauce such as *lepre* (hare) or *cinghiale* (boar). Tuscans are fond of their own strong ewe's milk *pecorino* cheese, made most famously around the Val d'Orcia town of Pienza. Meat is usually the centerpiece of any *secondo:* A *bistecca alla fiorentina* is the classic main dish, a T-bone-like cut of meat. An authentic *fiorentina* should come only from the white Chianina breed of cattle. Sweet treats are also good here, particularly Siena's *panforte* (a dense sticky cake); *biscotti di Prato* (hard almond-flour biscuits for dipping in dessert wine, also known as *cantuccini*); and the *miele* (honey) of Montalcino.

Emilia-Romagna is the country's gastronomic center. Rich in produce, its school of cooking first created many pastas now common around Italy: tagliatelle, tortellini, and cappelletti (made in the shape of "little hats"). Pig also comes several ways, including in Bologna's mortadella (finely ground spiced pork) and deliciously sweet *prosciutto di Parma* (cured ham), served in paper-thin slices. The distinctive cheese Parmigiano Reggiano is made by hundreds of small producers in the provinces of Parma and Reggio Emilia.

Probably the most famous dish of **Lombardy** is *cotoletta alla milanese*

Tuscany (p. 281) and **Orvieto,** Umbria (p. 338). Tombs are scattered around the countryside of southern Tuscany and northern Lazio. Mary Beard's excellent book *SPQR* is packed with insight on the rise of Ancient Rome.

The Roman Republic: ca. 509–27 B.C.

After the Roman Republic was established around 509 B.C.—precise dating is impossible—the Romans continued to increase their power by conquering neighboring communities in the highlands and forming alliances with other Latins in the lowlands. They gave to their allies, and then to conquered peoples, partial or complete Roman citizenship with a corresponding obligation of military service. This further increased Rome's (veal cutlet dipped in egg and breadcrumbs and fried in olive oil)—German speakers call it *Wienerschnitzel. Osso buco* is another Lombard classic: braised shin of veal cooked in a ragout. **Piedmont** and Turin's iconic dish is *bagna càuda*—literally "hot bath" in the Piedmontese language, a sauce made with olive oil, garlic, butter, and anchovies, into which you dip raw vegetables. Piedmont is also the spiritual home of *risotto*, particularly Vercelli, a town surrounded by rice paddies.

Venice is rarely celebrated for its cuisine, but its fresh seafood is usually excellent and figures heavily in the Venetian diet. Grilled fish is often served with red radicchio, a bitter leaf that thrives around nearby Treviso. Two more classic Venetian dishes are *fegato alla veneziana* (liver and onions) and *risi e bisi* (rice and peas). **Liguria** also turns toward the sea for its inspiration, as reflected by its version of bouillabaisse, *burrida*. The region's most famous food is pesto *alla genovese*, made with fresh basil, hard cheese, olive oil, and crushed pine nuts, and used to dress pasta, fish, and many more local dishes.

So many Neapolitans moved to the New World that the cookery of **Campania**—including pizza and spaghetti with clam sauce—is familiar to North Americans. Mozzarella is the local cheese, the best being *mozzarella di bufala*, made with milk from water buffalo (first introduced to Campania from Asia in the Middle Ages). Mixed fish fries (a *fritto misto*) are a staple of many a lunch table, and genuine Neapolitan pizza is in a class of its own. The cuisine of **Basilicata** and **Puglia** is founded on peasant simplicity: pasta, often made without egg, tossed with oil and seasonal vegetables such as broccoli rabe (*cime di rapa*) or garbanzo beans (*ceci*). The region is known for sweet, piquant Senise peppers and spicy or fennel-spiked Lucanica sausage. A whole *burrata* (an unctuous sphere of young mozzarella cheese and cream) is one indulgent Puglian starter.

Sicily's distinctive cuisine features strong flavors and aromatic sauces influenced by North Africa. One staple is *pasta con le sarde* (with pine nuts, wild fennel, spices, chopped sardines, and olive oil). Fish is good and fresh almost everywhere (local swordfish is a standout). Classic desserts include *cannoli*, sweet cylindrical pastry cases filled with ricotta and candied fruit or chocolate. Sicilian *gelato* and homemade pastries are among the best in Italy.

power and reach. Citizen colonies were set up as settlements of Roman farmers or military veterans, including both **Florence** and **Siena.**

The stern culture of the Roman Republic was characterized by belief in the gods, the necessity of learning from the past, strength of the family, education through reading and public service, and most importantly, obedience. The all-powerful Senate presided as Rome defeated rival powers one after another and came to rule the Mediterranean. The Punic Wars with **Carthage** (in modern-day Tunisia) in the 3rd century B.C. were a temporary stumbling block, as Carthaginian general **Hannibal** (247–182 B.C.) conducted a devastating campaign across the Italian peninsula, crossing the Alps with elephants and winning bloody battles by the shore of

Lago Trasimeno, in Umbria, and at Cannae, in Puglia. Ultimately, however, Rome prevailed.

No figure was more towering during the late Republic, or more instrumental in its morphing into the Empire (see below), than **Julius Caesar,** the charismatic conqueror of Gaul—"the wife of every husband and the husband of every wife," according to scurrilous rumors reported by 1st-century historian Suetonius. After defeating the last resistance of the Pompeiians in 45 B.C., he came to Rome and was made dictator and consul for 10 years. Conspirators, led by Marcus Junius Brutus, stabbed him to death at the Theater of Pompey on March 15, 44 B.C., the "Ides of March." The site, now Largo di Torre Argentina, is an Instagram hotspot these days. (Not for the history; its ruins are home to a photogenic feral cat colony.)

The conspirators' motivation was to restore the power of the Republic and topple dictatorship. But they failed: **Mark Antony,** a Roman general, assumed control. He made peace with Caesar's willed successor, **Octavian,** and after the Treaty of Brundisium dissolved the Republic, found himself married to Octavian's sister, Octavia. This marriage, however, didn't prevent him from also marrying Cleopatra in 36 B.C. A furious Octavian gathered the legions and defeated Antony at the **Battle of Actium** on September 2, 31 B.C. Cleopatra fled to Egypt, followed by

A statue of Julius Caesar, charismatic leader of Rome.

Antony, who committed suicide in disgrace a year later. Cleopatra, unable to seduce his successor and retain her rule of Egypt, reputedly followed suit with the help of an asp (Egyptian cobra). The permanent end of the Republic was nigh.

Many standing buildings around ancient Rome date to periods after the Republic fell, but parts of the **Forum** (p. 90) were built during the Republic, including the **Temple of Saturn.** The adjacent **Capitoline Hill** and **Palatine Hill** have been sacred religious and civic places since the earliest days of Rome. Rome's best artifacts from the Republican era are inside the **Musei Capitolini** (p. 94).

The Roman Empire in Its Pomp: 27 B.C.–A.D. 395

Born Gaius Octavius in 63 B.C., and later known as Octavian, **Augustus** became the first Roman emperor in 27 B.C. and reigned until A.D. 14. His autocratic rule ushered in the so-called "*Pax Romana,*" 2 centuries of peace. In Rome you can still see the remains of the **Forum of Augustus** (p. 90) and admire his statue in the **Vatican Museums** (p. 80).

By now, Rome ruled the entire Mediterranean world, either directly or indirectly. All political, commercial, and cultural pathways led to Rome, a sprawling city set on seven hills: the Capitoline, Palatine, Aventine, Caelian, Esquiline, Quirinal, and Viminal. It was during this period **Virgil** wrote his epic poem *The Aeneid,* which supplied a grandiose founding myth for the great city and its empire; in this era **Ovid** also composed erotic poetry and **Horace** wrote his *Odes.*

Emperors brought Rome to new heights. Yet without the checks and balances once provided by the Senate and legislatures, success led to corruption. These centuries witnessed a steady decay in ideals and traditions on which the Empire was founded. The army became a fifth column of unruly mercenaries, and for every good emperor (Augustus, Claudius, Trajan, Vespasian, and Hadrian, to name a few), there were several cruel, debased, or incompetent tyrants (Caligula, Nero, Caracalla, and many others).

After Augustus died (by poison, perhaps), his widow, **Livia**—a shrewd operator who had divorced her first husband to marry Augustus—used intrigues and poisonings to set up her son, **Tiberius,** as ruler. A series of murders and purges ensued, and Tiberius, who ruled during Pontius Pilate's trial and crucifixion of Christ, was eventually murdered in his late seventies. Top-level murders were common; a short time later, **Domitian** (ruled A.D. 81–96) became so obsessed with the possibility of assassination, he had his palace walls covered in reflective mica to see behind himself at all times. (He was killed anyway.)

Excesses ruled the day—at least, if you believe tracts written by biased contemporary chroniclers: **Caligula** supposedly committed incest with his sister, Drusilla, appointed his horse to the Senate, lavished money on egotistical projects, and proclaimed himself a god. Caligula's successor, his uncle **Claudius,** was poisoned by his final wife—who was also his

EARLY ROMAN emperors

Caligula (r. A.D. 37–41): Young emperor whose reign of cruelty and terror ended when he was assassinated by his own Praetorian guard.

Nero (r. A.D. 54–68): The last emperor of the Julio-Claudian dynasty and another cruel megalomaniac. He killed his own mother and was blamed—probably inaccurately—for starting the Great Fire of Rome (A.D. 64).

Vespasian (r. A.D. 69–79): First emperor of the Flavian dynasty, who built the Colosseum (p. 88) and lived as husband-and-wife with a freed slave, Caenis.

Domitian (r. A.D. 81–96): Increasingly paranoid authoritarian and populist who fixated on the idea he would be assassinated—and was proved right.

Trajan (r. A.D. 98–117): Virtuous soldier–ruler who presided over the moment when Rome was at its geographically grandest scale; he also rebuilt much of the city.

Hadrian (r. A.D. 117–138): Humanist, general, and builder who redesigned the Pantheon (p. 102) and added the Temple of Venus and Roma to the Forum.

Marcus Aurelius (r. A.D. 161–180): Philosopher-king, and last of the so-called "Five Good Emperors," whose statue is in the Musei Capitolini (p. 94).

niece, Agrippina the Younger—to secure the succession of **Nero,** her son by a previous marriage. Nero's thanks were to later murder not only his mother but also his own wife (Claudius's daughter) and his rival, Claudius's 13-year-old son, Britannicus. An enthusiastic persecutor of Christians, Nero committed suicide with the cry, "What an artist I destroy!"

By the 3rd century, rivalry and corruption had become so prevalent that 23 emperors ruled in 73 years. Few, however, were as twisted as **Caracalla,** who, to secure control, had his brother Geta slashed to pieces while Geta was in the arms of their mother, former empress Julia Domna.

Constantine the Great, who became emperor in A.D. 306, made Constantinople (or Byzantium) the new capital of the Empire in 330, moving administrative functions away from Rome altogether, partly because of the growing menace of barbarian attacks. Constantine was the first Christian emperor, allegedly converting after he saw the "True Cross" in a dream, accompanied by the words, "in this sign shall you conquer." He defeated rival emperor Maxentius and his followers at the **Battle of the Milvian Bridge** (A.D. 312), a victory memorialized in Rome's triumphal **Arco di Costantino** (p. 87). Constantine formally ended the persecution of Christians with the **Edict of Milan** (A.D. 313).

During the Imperial period, Rome flourished in architecture—advancing in size and majesty far beyond earlier cities built by the Greeks. **Classical orders** were simplified into forms of column capital: **Doric** (a plain capital), **Ionic** (a capital with a scroll), and **Corinthian** (a capital with flowering acanthus). Much of this advance was thanks to a new form of concrete and fine-tuning of the arch, used with a logic, rhythm, and ease never before seen. Many of these monumental buildings still stand, notably **Trajan's Column** (p. 90), the **Colosseum** (p. 88), and Hadrian's **Pantheon** (p. 102). Elsewhere in Italy, Verona's massive **Arena** (p. 460) bears witness to crowds the brutal sport of gladiatorial combat would draw. Three **Roman cities** have been preserved, with street plans and, in some cases, even buildings intact: doomed **Pompeii** (p. 630) and its neighbor **Herculaneum** (p. 627), both buried by Vesuvius's cataclysmic A.D. 79 eruption, and Rome's ancient seaport, **Ostia Antica** (p. 158). At Herculaneum, one of Rome's greatest writers perished, **Pliny the Elder** (A.D. 23–79). It is thanks to him, his nephew **Pliny the Younger,** satirist **Juvenal,** and historians **Tacitus, Suetonius, Cassius Dio,** and **Livy** that knowledge of ancient Roman life and history was not lost.

Trajan's Column commemorates the soldier-emperor Trajan.

Surviving Roman **art** had a major influence on the painters and sculptors of the Renaissance (see p. 28). In Rome itself, look for the marble bas-reliefs (sculptures that project slightly from a flat surface) on the **Arco di Costantino** (p. 87), the sculpture and mosaic collections at the **Palazzo Massimo alle Terme** (p. 114), and the gilded equestrian statue of Marcus Aurelius at the **Musei Capitolini** (p. 94). In Florence, the **Uffizi** (p. 179) displays Medici rulers' vast collection of Roman statuary. Naples's **Museo Archeologico Nazionale** (p. 60) houses the world's most extraordinary collection of Roman art, preserved for centuries under the lava at Pompeii.

The Fall of the Empire through the "Dark Ages"

The Eastern and Western sections of the Roman Empire split in A.D. 395, leaving the Italian peninsula without support it once received from east of the Adriatic. When the **Goths** moved toward Rome in the early 5th century, citizens in the provinces, who had grown to hate the bureaucracy set up by **Emperor Diocletian,** initially welcomed the invaders. And then the pillage began.

Rome was first sacked by **Alaric I,** king of the Visigoths, in A.D. 410. The populace made no attempt to defend their city, other than trying in vain to buy him off (a tactic that worked 3 years earlier); most people fled

ALL ABOUT vino

Italy is the largest **wine**-producing country in the world; as early as 800 B.C. the Etruscans were vintners, and in 2021, the country produced about as much wine as the U.S., Australia, and Chile combined. However, only in 1965 were laws enacted to guarantee consistency in Italian winemaking. Quality wines are labeled **"DOC"** (Denominazione di Origine Controllata). If you see **"DOCG"** on a label (the "G" means *garantita*), this denotes an even higher-quality wine region (at least in theory). **"IGT"** (Indicazione Geografica Tipica) indicates a more general wine zone—for example, "Umbria"—but still with mandatory quality control.

Tuscany: Tuscan red wines rank with some of the world's finest. **Sangiovese** is the prince of grapes here, and **Chianti** from the hills south of Florence is the most widely known Sangiovese wine. The premium zone is **Chianti Classico,** where lively ruby-red wine develops a bouquet of violets. The Tuscan south houses two even finer DOCGs: mighty, robust **Brunello di Montalcino,** a garnet-colored red and ideal partner for roasts or game; and almost purple **Vino Nobile di Montepulciano,** which has a rich, velvet body. End a meal with the Tuscan dessert wine called **vin santo,** which is often accompanied by hard *biscotti* to dunk into your glass.

Veneto and Lombardy: Reds around Venice and the Lakes vary from light, lunchtime-friendly **Bardolino** to **Valpolicella,** which can be particularly intense if grapes are partly dried before fermentation to make an **Amarone.** White, Garganega-based **Soave** has a pale amber color and a velvety flavor; **Lugana** at its best has a sparkle of gold and a rich, dry structure. **Prosecco** is the classic Italian sparkling white, the base for both a Bellini and a Spritz—joints that use Champagne are doing it wrong!

Piedmont: The finest reds in Italy may hail from the vine-clad slopes of Piedmont, particularly those from the late-ripening **Nebbiolo** grape in the Langhe hills south of Alba. The big names—with big flavors and big price tags—are **Barbaresco** (brilliant ruby red with a delicate flavor) and **Barolo** (also brilliant ruby red, gaining finesse when it mellows into a velvety old age).

The South and Sicily: From the volcanic soil around Vesuvius, the wines of **Campania** have been admired for centuries: Homer praised **Falerno,** straw yellow in color. The key DOCG wines from Campania these days are **Greco di Tufo** (a mouth-filling, full white) and **Fiano di Avellino** (subtler and more floral). The wines of **Sicily**—once called a "paradise of the grape"—were also extolled by the ancients, and table wines here are improving rapidly. Sicily is the home of **Marsala,** a fortified golden wine often served with dessert; it also makes a great sauce for veal, chicken, or pork.

to the hills. The feeble Western emperor **Honorius** hid out the entire time in **Ravenna** (p. 376), which in A.D. 402 he'd declared the new capital of the Western Roman Empire.

More than 40 troubled years passed. Then **Attila the Hun** invaded Italy to besiege Rome. While Attila was dissuaded from attacking, thanks largely to a peace mission headed by Pope Leo I in A.D. 452, relief was short-lived: In A.D. 455, **Gaiseric,** king of the **Vandals,** sailed from Carthage in North Africa to carry out a 2-week sack of unparalleled thoroughness. The empire of the West lasted only another 20 years; finally, in

A walk along the ancient Appian Way illuminates the lives of early Christians in Rome.

A.D. 476, sacks and chaos ended a once-mighty city, and Rome itself was left to the popes, though still ruled nominally from Ravenna by an Exarch from Byzantium (aka Constantinople).

Although little detailed history of Italy in the immediate post-Roman period is known—and few buildings survive—the gradual spread of **Christianity** was certainly creating a new society. The religion was probably founded in Rome about a decade after the death of Jesus, and gained strength despite early (and enthusiastic) persecution by the Romans. The best way today to relive the early Christian era is to walk along the **Via Appia Antica** (p. 119), just outside Rome's ancient walls. A church on the Appian Way marks the spot where the disciple Peter, fleeing Roman persecution, is said to have received a pivotal vision of Christ; the nearby **Catacombs** (p. 120), the first cemeteries of the Christian community of Rome, house the remains of early popes and martyrs.

We have Christianity, along with the influence of Byzantium, to thank for Italy's next great artistic style: the **Byzantine.** Painting and mosaic work in this era were stylized and static, but also ornate and ethereal. The most accomplished examples of Byzantine art are found in the churches of **Ravenna** (p. 376). Later buildings in the Byzantine style include Venice's **Basilica di San Marco** (p. 406).

A Growing Taste for Beer

Italy will always be known, and adored, for its wine. But one gastronomic trend to watch for as you travel is the growth in popularity of **artisanal beer,** especially among the young. Although supermarket shelves are stacked with mainstream brands like Peroni and Moretti, smaller stores and bars increasingly offer craft microbrews (known as *birre artigianali*). Italy had fewer than 50 breweries in 2000; more than 1,250 were operating by 2021. Craft-beer consumption has more than tripled since 2012, according to brewers' association Unionbirrai. Look for Unionbirrai's official seal on the label of genuine craft brewery products. You'll even find these beers on the hallowed shelves of some wine vendors.

The Middle Ages: 9th Century to the 14th Century

A ravaged Rome entered the Middle Ages, its population scattered. A modest number of residents continued to live in the swamps of the **Campus Martius.** The Seven Hills—now without water because the aqueducts were cut—stood abandoned and crumbling.

The Pope turned toward Europe, where he found a powerful ally in **Charlemagne,** king of the Franks. In A.D. 800, Pope Leo III crowned him emperor. This didn't mark Rome's return to the big time, however: Charlemagne ruled his empire from Aachen, now northwest Germany. And although Charlemagne pledged allegiance to the Church and made the pope the final arbiter in most religious and cultural matters, he also set Western Europe on a course of bitter opposition to papal meddling in affairs of state.

The successor to Charlemagne's empire was a political entity known as the **Holy Roman Empire** (A.D. 962–1806). The new Empire defined the end of the Dark Ages but ushered in a long period of bloody warfare. Magyars from Hungary invaded northeastern Lombardy and, in turn, were defeated by increasingly powerful **Venice,** which, having defeated its naval rival **Genoa** in the 1380 Battle of Chioggia, reigned over most of the eastern Mediterranean. Venetian merchants ruled a republic that lasted a millennium and built a city of imposing architecture like the **Doge's Palace** (p. 410). The Lion of St. Mark—symbol of Venice's dominion—appears as far away as **Bergamo** (p. 493), close to Milan.

Meanwhile, **Rome** during the Middle Ages was a quaint backwater. Narrow lanes with overhanging buildings filled areas that were once showcases for imperial power. The forums, mercantile exchanges, temples, and theaters of the Imperial era slowly disintegrated. It remained the seat of the Roman Catholic Church, and its state was almost completely controlled by priests, who aggressively expanded church influence and acquisitions. An endless series of power struggles ensued. Between 1378 and 1417, competing popes—one in Rome, another **"antipope"** in Avignon—made simultaneous claims to St. Peter's legacy. In 1409–15, there were three—a third "pope" ruled from **Pisa.**

Down in **Sicily,** the **Normans** gained military control from the Arabs in the 11th century, dividing the island from the rest of Italy and altering forever its ethnic makeup. The reign of **Roger II of Sicily** (ruled A.D. 1130–54) was notable for religious tolerance, the multiracial nature of his court, and distinctive architecture. The **Palazzo dei Normanni** (p. 757) in Palermo, and nearby **Monreale** (p. 767), are just two of many great projects from Sicily's Norman era.

In the mid-14th century, the **Black Death** ravaged Europe. Western history's deadliest pandemic killed perhaps a third of Italy's population. The unique preservation of Tuscan towns like **San Gimignano** (p. 273) and **Siena** (p. 230) owes much to the fact they never fully recovered after

Hit hard by the Black Death in the mid-14th century, Siena fell into centuries of decline—and its grand Gothic architecture survived unaltered.

the devastation of the 1348–49 plague. Despite such setbacks, Italian **city-states** grew wealthy from Crusader booty, trade, and banking. The **Florin,** a gold coin minted in Florence, became the first truly international currency for centuries and dominated trade all over the European continent.

The medieval period marks the start of building in stone on a mass scale. Flourishing from A.D. 800 to 1300, **Romanesque** architecture took inspiration and rounded arches from Ancient Rome. Architects built large churches with wide aisles to accommodate the masses. Pisa's **Campo dei Miracoli** (1153–1360s; p. 296) is typical of the Pisan-Romanesque style, with stacked arcades of mismatched columns on the cathedral's facade (and wrapped around the **Leaning Tower of Pisa**) and blind arcading set with diamond-shaped lozenges. The influence of Arab architecture is obvious; Pisa was a city of seafaring merchants.

Romanesque **sculpture** was fluid but still far from naturalistic. Often wonderfully childlike in narrative simplicity, works frequently mix biblical scenes with the myths and motifs of local pagan traditions that were incorporated into medieval Christianity. Among Italy's greatest surviving examples of Romanesque sculpture are 48 relief panels on the bronze doors of the **Basilica di San Zeno Maggiore** in Verona (p. 460). The exterior of Parma's **Baptistery** (p. 386) has Romanesque friezes by Benedetto Antelami (1150–1230).

As the appeal of Romanesque and Byzantine faded, the **Gothic** style flourished from the 13th to the 15th centuries. In architecture, Gothic was characterized by flying buttresses, pointed arches, and delicate stained-glass windows. These engineering developments freed architecture from the heavy, thick walls of the Romanesque and allowed ceilings to soar, walls to thin, and windows to proliferate.

Although religion remained dominant in the Gothic age, many secular buildings arose, including palaces designed to show off the prestige of various ruling families. Siena's civic **Palazzo Pubblico** (p. 236) and many great buildings in **Venice** (see chapter 9) date from this period. **San Gimignano** (p. 273), in Tuscany, has a preserved Gothic center. Milan's **Duomo** (p. 474) is one of Europe's supreme Gothic cathedrals.

Painters such as **Cimabue** (1251–1302) and **Giotto** (1266–1337) in Florence, **Pietro Cavallini** (1259–ca. 1330) in Rome, and **Duccio di Buoninsegna** (ca. 1255–1319) in Siena lifted art from Byzantine rigidity and set it on the road to realism. Giotto's finest work is his fresco cycle at Padua's **Cappella degli Scrovegni** (p. 456); he was a harbinger of the approaching Renaissance, which would forever change art and architecture. Duccio's 1311 "Maestà," now in Siena's **Museo dell'Opera Metropolitana** (p. 237), influenced Sienese painters for centuries. Ambrogio Lorenzetti painted the greatest civic frescoes of the Middle Ages—his "Allegories of Good and Bad Government" in Siena's **Palazzo Pubblico** (p. 236)—before he succumbed to the Black Death, along with almost every significant Sienese artist of his generation.

The medieval period saw the birth of literature in the Italian language, which was a written version of the **Tuscan dialect**—primarily because the great writers of the age were Tuscans. Florentine **Dante Alighieri** wrote his "Divine Comedy" in the 1310s and Boccaccio's "Decameron"—a kind of Florentine "Canterbury Tales"—appeared in the 1350s.

Renaissance & Baroque Italy

The story of Italy from the dawn of the Renaissance in the early 15th century to the "Age of Enlightenment" in the 17th and 18th centuries is as fascinating and complicated as the rise and fall of the Roman Empire.

During this period, **Rome** underwent major physical change. The old centers of culture reverted to pastures and fields—cows grazed on the crumbling Forum—and great churches and palaces were built with the stones of Ancient Rome. The city's construction boom did more damage to ancient temples than any barbarian sack: Rare marbles were stripped from Imperial baths and used as altarpieces or sent to lime kilns for "recycling." So enthusiastic was the popes' destruction of Imperial Rome, it's a genuine miracle anything is left.

Milan (p. 466) was a glorious Renaissance capital, particularly under the Sforza dynasty and Ludovico "Il Moro" (1452–1508), patron of Leonardo da Vinci. Smaller but still significant centers of power included the Gonzaga family's **Mantua** (p. 497) and the Este clan's **Ferrara** (p. 369).

The entrance to the Uffizi Gallery in Florence, a treasure trove of Renaissance art.

Around 1400, however, the most significant power in Italy was the city where the Renaissance began: **Florence** (see chapter 5). Slowly but surely, the **Medici** family rose to become the most powerful of the city's ruling oligarchy, usurping the powers of trade guilds and republicans. They reformed law and commerce, expanded the city's power by taking control of neighbors such as **Pisa,** and sparked a "renaissance," or rebirth, in painting, sculpture, and architecture. Christopher Hibbert's *The Rise and Fall of the House of Medici* is the most readable account of the era. Netflix's "Medici: Masters of Florence" and "The Magnificent" serve up a sensationalized, fictionalized, but not entirely inaccurate "history" of power plays in the Renaissance city.

Under the patronage of the Medici (as well as other powerful Florentine families), innovative young painters and sculptors pursued expressiveness and naturalism. **Donatello** (1386–1466) cast the first freestanding nude since antiquity (a bronze now in Florence's **Museo Nazionale del Bargello,** p. 182). **Lorenzo Ghiberti** (1378–1455) labored for 50 years on two sets of doors for Florence's **Baptistery** (p. 172), the most famous of which were dubbed the "Gates of Paradise." **Masaccio** (1401–28) produced the first painting to realistically portray linear perspective, on a nave wall of **Santa Maria Novella** (p. 191).

Next followed a brief period known as the **High Renaissance.** The epitome of Renaissance Man, Florentine **Leonardo da Vinci** (1452–1519) painted his "Last Supper," now in Milan's **Santa Maria delle Grazie** (p. 481), and an "Annunciation" (1481), hanging in Florence's **Uffizi** (p. 179) alongside countless Renaissance masterpieces from such iconic painters as Paolo Uccello, Sandro Botticelli, and Piero della Francesca. **Raphael** (1483–1520) produced a sublime body of work in his 37 years. Skilled in sculpture, painting, and architecture, **Michelangelo** (1475–1564) marked the apogee of Renaissance: His giant "David" at the **Galleria dell'Accademia** (p. 193) in Florence is the world's most famous statue, and his **Sistine Chapel** frescoes lure millions to the **Vatican Museums** (p. 80) in Rome. The father of the Venetian High Renaissance was **Titian** (1485–1576), known for mastery of color and tone. Venice (see chapter 9) has a rich trove of Titian's work, along with works by earlier Venetian masters **Gentile Bellini** (1429–1507), **Giorgione** (1477–1510), and **Vittore Carpaccio** (1465–1525).

As in painting, Renaissance **architecture** stressed proportion, order, classical inspiration, and mathematical precision. **Filippo Brunelleschi** (1377–1446), in the early 1400s, grasped the concept of "perspective" and provided artists with ground rules for creating the illusion of 3-D on a flat surface. (Ross King's *Brunelleschi's Dome* tells the story of his greatest achievement, crowning Florence's cathedral with its massive dome.) Even **Michelangelo** took up architecture late in life, designing the Laurentian Library (1524) and New Sacristy (1524–34) at Florence's **Medici Chapel** (p. 188), then moving south to complete the soaring dome of Rome's **St. Peter's Basilica** (p. 78). The third great Renaissance architect—and most influential of them all—**Andrea Palladio** (1508–80) worked in a classical mode of columns, porticoes, pediments, and other ancient-temple-inspired features. His masterpieces include fine churches in Venice. The "Palladian" style of many U.S. capitol buildings is named for him.

In time, the High Renaissance evolved into the **baroque.** Stuccoes, sculptures, and paintings were designed to complement each other—and the space itself—to create a unified whole. The baroque movement's spiritual home was Rome, and its towering figure was **Gian Lorenzo Bernini** (1598–1680), the greatest baroque sculptor, an accomplished architect, and a more-than-decent painter, too. Among many fine, flowing sculptures, you'll find his best in Rome's **Galleria Borghese** (p. 110) and **Santa Maria della Vittoria** (p. 114). Baroque architecture is especially prominent in the South: in the churches and devotional architecture of **Naples** (p. 592) and in **Siracusa** (p. 782), Sicily. Under the Savoy dynasty, **Turin** (p. 519) was remodeled by the baroque architecture of **Guarino Guarini** (1624–83) and **Filippo Juvarra** (1678–1736). In music, the most famous of the baroque composers is Venetian **Antonio Vivaldi** (1678–1741), whose "Four Seasons" is among the most performed classical compositions of all time.

In painting, many baroque artists mixed a kind of super-realism, based on using everyday people as models and bold contrasts of light and dark—a technique called *chiaroscuro*—with compositional complexity and explosions of dynamic fury, movement, and color. The period produced many fine painters, notably **Caravaggio** (1571–1610). Among his masterpieces are a "St. Matthew" cycle (1599) in Rome's **San Luigi dei Francesi** (p. 100) and "The Acts of Mercy" in **Pio Monte della Misericordia** (p. 599), Naples. The baroque era also had an outstanding female painter in **Artemisia Gentileschi** (1593–1652): Her brutal "Judith Slaying Holofernes" (1620) hangs in Florence's **Uffizi** (p. 179).

Frothy and ornate, **rococo** art was the baroque taken to flamboyant extremes and had few serious proponents in Italy. **Giambattista Tiepolo**

A flamboyant fresco by Giambattista Tiepolo, perhaps Italy's finest rococo painter, in Milan's Palazzo Clerici.

(1696–1770), arguably the best of the rococo painters, specialized in ceiling frescoes and canvases with cloud-filled heavens of light. He worked extensively in Venice and the northeast. For rococo building—more a decorative than an architectural movement—look no further than Rome's **Spanish Steps** (p. 106) or the **Trevi Fountain** (p. 109).

At Last, a United Italy: The 1800s

By the 1800s, the glories of the Renaissance were a fading memory. From Turin to Naples, chunks of Italy had changed hands many, many times—between the Austrians, the Spanish, and the French, among autocratic thugs and enlightened princes, between the noble and the merchant classes. The 19th century witnessed the final collapse of many Renaissance city-states. The last of the Medici, Gian Gastone, had died in 1737, leaving Tuscany in the hands of foreign Lorraine and Habsburg princes.

French emperor **Napoleon** brought an end to a millennium of republican government in **Venice** in 1797 and installed puppet or client rulers across the Italian peninsula. During the **Congress of Vienna** (1814–15), which followed Napoleon's defeat by an alliance of British, Prussians, and Dutch, Italy was once again divided.

Political unrest became a fact of Italian life, some of it spurred by the industrialization of the north and some by the activity of insurrectionists like **Giuseppe Mazzini** (1805–72). Europe's year of revolutions, **1848,** rocked Italy, too, with violent uprisings in Lombardy and Sicily. After decades of political machination, nationalism, and intrigue, and thanks to the efforts of statesman **Camillo Cavour** (1810–61) and rebel general **Giuseppe Garibaldi** (1807–82), the Kingdom of Italy was proclaimed in 1861; **Vittorio Emanuele II** of Savoy became its first monarch. Initially the capital was **Turin** (1861–65), seat of the victorious Piedmontese, followed by **Florence** (1865–71).

The establishment of the kingdom, however, didn't signal a complete unification of Italy: Latium (including Rome) was still under papal control and Venetia was held by Austria. This was partially resolved in 1866, when Venetia joined the rest of Italy after the **Seven Weeks' War** between Austria and Prussia. Then, in 1871, Rome became the capital of this newly formed country, after the city was taken on September 20, 1870. Present-day **Via XX Settembre** is the very street up which patriots advanced after breaching the city gates. The **Risorgimento**—the "resurgence," Italian unification—was complete.

Political heights in Italy seemed to correspond to historic depths in art and architecture. Among few notable practitioners of this era, the most well-known is probably Venetian **Antonio Canova** (1757–1822), Italy's major neoclassical sculptor, who became notorious for portraying both Napoleon and his sister Pauline as mythical nudes. His best work is in Rome's **Galleria Borghese** (p. 110). Tuscany also bred a late-19th-century precursor to French Impressionism, the **Macchiaioli** movement; see their works in the "modern art" galleries at Florence's **Palazzo Pitti** (p. 198).

As art hit a low note, **music** was experiencing its Italian golden age. It's **opera** for which the 19th century is largely remembered. *Bel canto* composer **Gioachino Rossini** (1792–1868) was born in Pesaro, in the Marches, and found fame in 1816 with *The Barber of Seville*. The reputation of **Gaetano Donizetti** (1797–1848), a prolific native of Bergamo, was assured when his *Anna Bolena* premiered in 1830. Both were later

THE A-LIST OF italian novels IN ENGLISH

- Alessandro Manzoni, *The Betrothed* (1827)
- Alberto Moravia, *The Conformist* (1951)
- Giuseppe Tomasi di Lampedusa, *The Leopard* (1958)
- Elsa Morante, *History: A Novel* (1974)
- Italo Calvino, *If on a Winter's Night a Traveler* (1979)
- Umberto Eco, *Foucault's Pendulum* (1988)
- Niccolò Ammaniti, *I'm Not Scared* (2001)
- Elena Ferrante, *Neapolitan Quartet* (2012–15)
- Viola di Grado, *Hollow Heart* (2015)

overshadowed by **Giuseppe Verdi** (1813–1901), whose arias from such operas as *Rigoletto* and *La Traviata* took on profound national symbolism, and have since become some of the most whistled tunes on the planet. At the turn of the century, the dominant Romantic movement gave way to the *verismo* ("realism") of composer **Giacomo Puccini** (1858–1924), whose operas *La Bohème* (1896), *Tosca* (1900), *Madama Butterfly* (1904), and the unfinished *Turandot* (1924) still pack houses worldwide. He's celebrated with a museum and opera festival in **Lucca,** Tuscany (p. 285).

The 20th Century: Two World Wars & One Duce

In 1915, Italy entered **World War I** on the side of the Allies. Italy joined Britain, Russia, and France to help defeat Germany and the traditional enemy to the north—now known as the Austro-Hungarian Empire—and so to "reclaim" Trentino and Trieste. (Mark Thompson's *The White War* tells the story of Italy's catastrophic campaign.) In the aftermath of the wartime carnage, Italians suffered further with rising unemployment and horrendous inflation. As in Germany, deep political crisis led eventually to dictatorship.

On October 28, 1922, **Benito Mussolini,** who started his Fascist Party in 1919, knew the country was ripe for change. He gathered 30,000 Black Shirts for his **March on Rome.** Inflation was soaring and workers had called a general strike. Rather than recognize a state under siege, **King Victor Emmanuel III** (r. 1900–46) proclaimed Mussolini as the new leader. In 1929, "Il Duce"—a moniker Mussolini began using from 1925—defined the divisions between the Italian government and the pope by signing the Lateran Treaty, which granted political, territorial, and fiscal autonomy to the microstate of **Vatican City.** During the Spanish Civil War (1936–39), Mussolini's support for General Franco's Fascists, who had staged a coup against the elected government of Spain, helped seal the Axis alliance between Italy and Nazi Germany. Italy was inexorably and disastrously sucked into **World War II.**

Deeply unpleasant though their politics were, the Fascist regime did sponsor some remarkable **Rationalist architecture,** at its best in Rome's planned satellite community, **EUR** (p. 119). Important public buildings from the Fascist 1930s include the huge, ornate **Milano Centrale** train station (1931) and Florence's **Santa Maria Novella station** (1934), a striking modernist statement in local sandstone. Today memorials at both stations remember Jews who were sent from there to their deaths in Nazi Germany.

After defeat in World War II, Italy's people voted to end the monarchy and establish the First Republic—overwhelmingly so in northern and central Italy, which outvoted a southern royalist majority. Italy quickly succeeded in rebuilding its economy, in part because of U.S. aid under the **Marshall Plan** (1948–52). By the 1960s, as a member of the European Economic Community (founded by the **Treaty of Rome** in 1957), Italy had become one of the world's leading industrialized nations, and prominent in the manufacture of automobiles and office equipment. Fiat (from Turin), Ferrari (from Emilia-Romagna), and Olivetti (from northern Piedmont) were known around the world.

The postwar Italian **film industry** was celebrated for innovative directors. **Federico Fellini** (1920–93) burst onto the scene with a highly individual style, beginning with *La Strada* (1954) and later such classics as *The City of Women* (1980). His *La Dolce Vita* (1961) seems to define an era in Rome. The gritty "neorealism" of controversial **Pier Paolo Pasolini** (1922–75) is conveyed most vividly in *Accattone* (1961), which he wrote and directed.

The country was plagued, however, by economic inequality, including between an industrially prosperous North and the depressed South. During the late 1970s and early 1980s, it was also rocked by domestic terrorism: These were the so-called **Anni di Piombo** (Years of Lead), during which extremists of the left and right bombed and assassinated with impunity. Conspiracy theories became an Italian staple diet; everyone from a shadow state to Masonic lodges to the CIA was accused of involvement in what became, in effect, an undeclared civil war. The most notorious incidents were the kidnap and murder of Prime Minister **Aldo Moro** in 1978 and the **Bologna station bombing,** which killed 85 in 1980.

A tribute to the films of Federico Fellini at Cinecittà Studios in Rome.

You'll find a succinct account of these murky years in Tobias Jones's *The Dark Heart of Italy.*

Into the 21st Century

Resonant events in recent Italian history have touched on religion, too. As much of the world watched and prayed, Pope John Paul II died in April 2005, at the age of 84, ending a reign of 26 years. A doctrinal hardliner next took the papal throne as Pope Benedict XVI. He was succeeded by relatively liberal Pope Francis in 2013, after Benedict became the first pope since the 1400s to resign the office. The story of this extraordinary handover was fictionalized in the 2019 film, *The Two Popes.*

On the back of a severe economic crisis early in the 21st century—whose effects are still reflected in high levels of government debt—immigration has become a persistent national issue. Italy's population is aging, and the youth vacuum is filled by immigrants, especially those from Eastern Europe, notably Romania and Albania. The plight of migrant refugees from Syria and North Africa through the early 2020s added yet another layer of complexity to Italy's relationship with *stranieri* (foreigners). Italy had scant colonial experience and does not have a "melting pot" history. Tensions were inevitable, and discrimination is a daily fact of life for many minorities (although you are unlikely to experience it as a visitor). Change is coming: In 2013, Cécile Kyenge became Italy's first government minister of African descent. But it is coming too slowly for many, and anti-migrant sentiment is gleefully stoked by populist politicians.

While others arrive, a "brain drain" continues to push young Italians abroad to seek opportunity. The problem is especially ingrained in rural communities and on the islands, where the old maxim, "It's not what you know, it's who you know," applies more strongly than ever. It was in this unstable national context—and accompanying political turmoil—that the coronavirus pandemic hit in early 2020.

WHEN TO GO

The best months for traveling in much of Italy are from **April to June** and **mid-September to October:** Temperatures are usually comfortable, rural colors are rich, and crowds aren't too intense (except around Easter). Easter, May, and June usually usher in peak hotel prices in Rome and Florence. From July through early September the country's holiday spots teem with visitors. **August,** however, is the worst month in many places: Not only does it get uncomfortably hot and muggy, but seemingly the entire country goes on vacation for at least 2 weeks (many Italians take off the entire month). Family-run restaurants and shops are often shuttered, except at the spas, beaches, mountains, and islands, where most Italians head. Paradoxically, you will have many urban places almost to yourself if you visit in August—Turin and Milan in particular feel apocalyptically deserted, and even excellent hotels there are heavily discounted. (Florence and Rome are no longer as quiet as they once were, alas.) Be aware that many fashionable urban restaurants and nightspots close for the whole month.

From late October to Easter, many attractions operate on shorter winter hours and hotels occasionally close for renovation or redecoration, although this inconvenience is much less likely if you visit a city. Between November and February, beach resorts become padlocked ghost towns and family-run restaurants everywhere take a week or two off.

Weather

It's warm all over Italy in **summer;** it can be very hot in the south, and almost anywhere inland. Landlocked cities in Tuscany and Umbria, and on the plains of Veneto, Lombardy, and Emilia-Romagna, feel stifling during a July or August hot spell. Higher temperatures (measured in Italy in degrees Celsius) usually begin everywhere in May, often lasting until early October. **Winters** in the north of Italy are cold, with rain, fog, and snow. A biting wind whistles over the mountains into Milan, Turin, Venice, and sometimes even Florence. In Rome and the south, the weather is warm (or at least, warm-ish) almost all year, averaging 10°C (50°F) in winter. But even here chilly snaps are possible, including occasional freezing temperatures and snow. The rainiest months pretty much everywhere are October and November.

Italy's Average Daily High Temperature & Monthly Rainfall

ROME

	JAN	FEB	MAR	APR	MAY	JUNE	JULY	AUG	SEPT	OCT	NOV	DEC
TEMP. (°F)	55	56	59	63	71	77	83	83	79	71	62	57
TEMP. (°C)	12	13	15	17	21	25	28	28	26	21	16	13
RAINFALL (IN.)	3.2	2.8	2.7	2.6	2	1.3	.6	1	2.7	4.5	4.4	3.8

FLORENCE

	JAN	FEB	MAR	APR	MAY	JUNE	JULY	AUG	SEPT	OCT	NOV	DEC
TEMP. (°F)	49	53	60	68	75	84	89	88	81	69	58	50
TEMP. (°C)	9	11	15	20	23	28	31	31	27	20	14	10
RAINFALL (IN.)	1.9	2.1	2.7	2.9	3	2.7	1.5	1.9	3.3	4	3.9	2.8

VENICE

	JAN	FEB	MAR	APR	MAY	JUNE	JULY	AUG	SEPT	OCT	NOV	DEC
TEMP. (°F)	42	47	54	61	70	77	81	81	75	65	53	44
TEMP. (°C)	6	8	12	16	21	25	27	27	24	18	11	7
RAINFALL (IN.)	2.3	.1	2.2	2.5	2.7	3	2.5	3.3	2.6	2.7	3.4	2.1

Public Holidays

Offices, government buildings (but usually not tourist offices), and shops in Italy are generally closed on: January 1 (*Capodanno,* or New Year); January 6 (*La Befana,* or Epiphany); Easter Sunday *(Pasqua);* Easter Monday *(Pasquetta)*; April 25 (*Festa della Liberazione,* or Liberation Day); May 1 (*Festa del Lavoro,* or Labor Day); June 2 (*Festa della Repubblica,* or Republic Day); August 15 (*Ferragosto,* or the Assumption of the Virgin); November 1 (All Saints' Day); December 8 (*L'Immacolata,* or the Immaculate Conception); December 25 (*Natale,* Christmas Day); and December 26 (*Santo Stefano,* or St. Stephen's Day). Businesses often close also for an annual celebration day dedicated to the local patron saint (for example, on January 31 in San Gimignano, Tuscany).

3

SUGGESTED ITALY ITINERARIES

By Donald Strachan

Italy is so vast and treasure-filled, it's hard to resist the temptation to pack too much into your limited time. This is a dauntingly diverse destination. You can't even skim the surface in 1 or 2 weeks—so relax, and don't try. If you're a first-time visitor with little touring time, we suggest you zero in on the classic cities: Rome, Florence, and Venice could be packed into 1 very busy week, better yet in 2.

How can you accomplish that? Well, for starters, Italy has well-maintained highways (called *autostrade*). You'll pay a toll (p. 822), but it's much quicker to drive on them than to trust your limited time to minor roads, which can be *much* slower going.

The country also has one of the most efficient high-speed rail networks in Europe. Rome, Bologna, and Milan are key hubs of this 21st-century transportation empire—for example, from Rome's Termini station, Florence can be reached in only 95 minutes. If you're city-hopping between Rome, Florence, and Venice, you need never rent a car, because the key routes are served by comfortable, quick trains. Of course, you may feel more comfortable traveling in your own rented vehicle than a train carriage; see p. 820 for car rental tips.

Itineraries that follow introduce many of our favorite places. During the COVID-19 pandemic, many museums restricted visitor numbers with compulsory advance booking; some of these measures remain. You should certainly reserve ahead for any place your heart is set on. Organize the rest of each day around your must-sees.

Occasionally the pace of our itineraries may be a bit breathless for some visitors, so consider skipping a stop to take some chill-out time—after all, you're on vacation. You can also use any itinerary as a jumping-off point to develop your own custom-made adventure. *Buon viaggio!*

ITALY'S REGIONS IN BRIEF

Although bordered on the northwest by France, on the north by Switzerland and Austria, and on the northeast by Slovenia, Italy is mostly surrounded by sea. It isn't enormous; the peninsula's slender boot shape gives the impression of a much larger area. Here's a brief rundown of the cities and regions covered in this guide. See the inside front cover for a map of Italy by region.

ROME & LATIUM The region of **Latium** (**"Lazio"** in Italian) is dominated by **Rome,** capital of both an ancient empire and modern Italy. Much of the "civilized world" was once ruled from here, starting when Romulus

FACING PAGE: **The streets of Lucca in Tuscany.**

and Remus are said to have founded Rome, in 753 B.C. No place has more artistic monuments, or a bigger buzz.

FLORENCE, TUSCANY & UMBRIA **Tuscany** is one of Italy's most culturally and politically influential regions. The development of Italy without Tuscany is simply unthinkable. In fact, today's Italian language is essentially an update of the medieval Florentine dialect. Nowhere in the world is the impact of the Renaissance still felt more fully than in **Florence,** a repository of artworks by Masaccio, Leonardo da Vinci, Michelangelo, and many others. The main Tuscan destinations beyond Florence are the provincial cities of **Lucca, Pisa,** and especially **Siena,** Florence's great historical rival, as well as the **Chianti** winelands. Neighboring **Umbria** is a land of rolling green hills and olive groves, where the pace of life is sedate. It has outstanding art sights in **Perugia** and the former Etruscan capital of **Orvieto.**

The baroque Trevi Fountain, a tourist gathering spot in Rome.

BOLOGNA & EMILIA-ROMAGNA Italians don't agree on much, but one national consensus is that food in **Emilia-Romagna** is the best in Italy. The regional capital, **Bologna,** also has museums, churches, and a fine university founded in the Middle Ages. Among the region's other cities, none is nobler than Byzantine **Ravenna,** with mosaics dating to a time when it was capital of the Western Roman Empire in decline.

VENICE & THE VENETO Northeastern Italy is one of Europe's treasure troves, encompassing **Venice** (certainly the world's most unusual city) and the surrounding **Veneto** region. Aging, decaying, and sinking into the sea, Venice is so alluring we're tempted to say: Visit even if you have to skip everywhere else. Also recommended are the art cities of the Venetian Arc: **Verona,** with Shakespearean romance and an intact Roman amphitheater hosting a famous summer opera festival; and **Padua,** with Giotto paintings on the walls of its Cappella degli Scrovegni.

LOMBARDY, PIEDMONT & THE LAKES Flat, fertile, and prosperous, **Lombardy** is dominated by **Milan,** home to Leonardo's "Last Supper," the La Scala opera house, shopping, and some major museums. You'll also find nearby **Bergamo**—a charming small city—and **Mantua,** as well as the photogenic lakes of **Como** and **Garda.** In Piedmont's largest city,

Turin—home of the Fiat empire—the best-known sight is the Sacra Sindone (Holy Shroud), which some Christians believe is the cloth in which Christ's crucified body was wrapped.

LIGURIA Comprising most of the **Italian Riviera,** the region of **Liguria** incorporates the major historical seaport of **Genoa,** charming upscale resorts such as **Portofino,** and Italy's best coastal hiking, among the traditional villages of the **Cinque Terre.**

CAMPANIA, PUGLIA & BASILICATA **Campania** encompasses the fascinating anarchy of **Naples,** renowned ruins at **Pompeii** and **Herculaneum,** and the elegant beauty of **Capri** and the **Amalfi Coast.** In **Basilicata,** the city of **Matera** is peppered with cave dwellings—the *Sassi*—inhabited almost continuously since the Paleolithic Era. **Puglia** (sometimes called "Apulia" in English) is home to the conical *trulli* houses of **Alberobello** and the Valle d'Itria, and the baroque architecture of **Lecce**—sometimes nicknamed (ambitiously) "the Florence of the South."

SICILY The largest island in the Mediterranean Sea, **Sicily** has a unique mix of bloodlines and architecture from medieval Normandy, Aragónese Spain, Moorish North Africa, Ancient Greece, Phoenicia, and Rome. Cars, street markets, and fashionable people clog the lanes of its capital, **Palermo.** Areas of ravishing beauty and eerie historical interest include the coastal towns of **Syracuse** (Siracusa in Italian) and **Taormina,** and the ruins at **Agrigento** and **Selinunte.**

THE BEST OF ITALY IN 1 WEEK: ROME, FLORENCE & VENICE

Let's be realistic: It's impossible to see this country properly in a week. However, a fast, efficient, center-to-center rail network along the Rome–Florence–Venice line makes it surprisingly easy to see a handful of the best that these three elegant, art-stuffed cities have to offer. Our weeklong itinerary treads familiar highlights. But there's a reason these are the country's most visited sights: They're proven to provide memories that last a lifetime.

DAYS 1, 2 & 3: Rome: Capital, Ancient & Modern ★★★

You could spend forever in the Eternal City, but 3 days is enough to catch a flavor. There are two essential areas to focus on in a short visit. The first is the legacy of Imperial Rome, with the **Forum, Campidoglio,** and **Colosseum** (p. 87). Bookend **DAY 1** with the Forum and Colosseum (one first, the other last) to avoid the busiest times; the same ticket is good for both. Sights there are almost exclusively outdoors. On **DAY 2,** tackle **St. Peter's Basilica** and the **Vatican Museums** (p. 80), with a collection unlike any other in the world (including, of course, Michelangelo's **Sistine Chapel**). On **DAY 3,** it's a toss-up: Choose between visiting the underground catacombs of the **Via Appia Antica** (p. 119) or wandering the **Centro Storico** (p. 99) and the **Tridente** (p. 105) for Piazza Navona, the Pantheon, the Spanish Steps, the Trevi Fountain, and more. Spend your evenings in the bars of **Campo de' Fiori** or **Monti** (p. 156) and the restaurants of **Trastevere** (p. 147) or **Testaccio** (p. 149). Toward the end of your third day, catch a late train to Florence. ***Tip:*** You will save money if you book rail tickets in advance: Walk-up fares are much more expensive than advanced tickets on the high-speed network. However, only fully flexible fares are fully refundable. We suggest only booking (and paying upfront) when you are certain you will be traveling.

DAYS 4 & 5: Florence: Cradle of the Renaissance ★★★

You have 2 whole days to explore the city of Giotto, Leonardo, Botticelli, and Michelangelo. Start with their masterpieces at the **Uffizi** (p. 179; prebook tickets, weeks or even months ahead if possible), followed by the **Duomo** complex (p. 172): Scale Brunelleschi's dome (again, reservations are essential), and follow up with a visit to the nearby **Battistero di San Giovanni,** the revamped **Museo dell'Opera del Duomo,** and **Campanile di Giotto.** Start **DAY 5** with "David" at the **Accademia** (p. 193; another essential advance booking). For the

Piazza San Marco in Venice.

rest of your time, get to know the intimate murals of **San Marco** (p. 194), paintings hanging at the **Palazzo Pitti** (p. 198), and Masaccio's revolutionary frescoes in the **Cappella Brancacci** (p. 201). In the evenings, head south of the Arno, to San Frediano or San Niccolò, for lively wine bars and more creative restaurants than you generally find in the historic center. Leave on an early train for Venice on the morning of **DAY 6.**

DAYS 6 & 7: Venice: City that Defies the Sea ★★★

Ride into the heart of Venice on a *vaporetto* (water bus), taking the **Grand Canal,** the world's greatest thoroughfare. Begin the sightseeing at **Piazza San Marco** (p. 406). The **Basilica di San Marco** is right there, and after exploring it, visit the nearby **Palazzo Ducale** (Doge's Palace; p. 410) before walking over the **Bridge of Sighs.** Begin your evening with the classic Venetian *aperitivo,* an Aperol spritz, followed by *cicchetti* (Venetian tapas) before a late dinner. Make **DAY 7** all about the city's unique art: the **Gallerie dell'Accademia** (p. 417), the modern **Peggy Guggenheim Collection** (p. 419), and **San Rocco** (p. 423). Catch a late train back to Rome. Or add another night.... You can never stay too long in Venice.

THE BEST OF ITALY IN 2 WEEKS

It's still difficult to see the top sights of Italy—and to see them properly—in just 2 weeks. But in this itinerary, you get to see many of the best. We go beyond the well-trodden (and spectacular) Rome–Florence–Venice trail to include the southern region of Campania, notably Pompeii, which has Europe's most precious Roman ruins. Additional stops in the center and north are Pisa (for the Leaning Tower and more) and Verona (city of lovers since Romeo met Juliet).

DAYS 1, 2 & 3: Rome ★★★

Follow the itinerary suggested in "The Best of Italy in 1 Week," above. On your third day take a late afternoon train to Naples, where you'll be based for the next 2 nights.

DAY 4: Naples ★★

Spend a full day taking in the major attractions of urban Naples, the historic "capital" of southern Italy. Pore over an unparalleled collection of ancient artifacts at the **Museo Archeologico Nazionale** (p. 600), then see Titians and Caravaggios at the **Museo e Gallerie Nazionale di Capodimonte** (p. 604). After dark, wander **Spaccanapoli**—the old center's main east–west thoroughfare—then make a date with a **pizzeria:** Neapolitans claim pizza was invented here. It's certainly a Neapolitan artform. After dinner, stroll the **Mergellina** boardwalk for sea breezes and views across the Bay of Naples.

DAY 5: Pompeii ★★ & Sorrento ★

Take the Circumvesuviana train from Porta Nolana Station to spend a day wandering Europe's best-preserved Roman ruins at **Pompeii** (p. 625), 24km (15 miles) southeast of Naples. Pack water and lunch, because onsite services aren't great. Buried for almost 2,000 years after Vesuvius erupted in A.D. 79, Pompeii is one of the great archaeological treasures of Italy, including the patrician Casa dei Vettii and the frescoed Villa dei Misteri. Continue by local train to the pretty seaside town of **Sorrento,** where you will lodge for 2 nights (you

may leave luggage at Pompeii Station while you tour the ruins). This side trip (including **DAY 6**, below) is also straightforward by rental car: We recommend arranging pickup outside Naples' city center, where driving can be a hair-raising experience.

DAY 6: The Amalfi Coast ★★

On the morning of **DAY 6**, take a bus along the **Amalfi Drive,** of which Nobel laureate André Gide said: "[There is] nothing more beautiful on this earth." The drive twists around a precipitous coastline to the southern resorts of **Positano** and **Amalfi,** either of which would make an idyllic stopover to extend your stay. Allow at least 4 hours for a roundtrip back to Sorrento, because it can be slow-moving and you will want to linger.

DAYS 7 & 8: Florence ★★★

Connect from Sorrento by rail to Naples' Stazione Centrale (1 hr.), then onward via an early high-speed train to Florence (journey time: 3 hr.). Follow the itinerary suggested in "The Best of Italy in 1 Week," above. You'll be staying in Florence for the next 4 nights.

DAY 9: Siena ★★★

Terraced towns climb up coastal hillsides along the scenic Amalfi Coast.

It's just over an hour to Siena on the *rapida* bus from Florence (p. 230). Leave early and set out immediately on arrival for **Piazza del Campo,** the shell-shaped main square, including its art-filled **Museo Civico** (inside the **Palazzo Pubblico;** p. 236). Squeeze in a look at the **Duomo** (p. 235) and **Museo dell'Opera Metropolitana,** where you'll find Sienese master Duccio's giant "Maestà" painting. Pick an outdoor table on the Campo for an early evening drink and then head to a restaurant in Siena's atmospheric back streets. Eat an early dinner: The last bus back to Florence departs around 8:45pm (7:10pm on weekends).

DAY 10: Pisa ★★

Most trains between Florence and Pisa take around an hour. On arrival, hop aboard the LAM Rossa bus outside Pisa Centrale Station, alighting at the "Torre" stop for the **Campo dei Miracoli** ("Field of Miracles"). The set-piece piazza here is one of the most photographed slices of real estate on the planet—and home to the **Leaning Tower** (p. 299). Visit the **Duomo,** with its Arab-influenced Pisan-Romanesque facade; the **Battistero** with a carved pulpit and crazy acoustics; and the rest of the piazza's monuments and museums on the same combination ticket. Book a slot ahead of time if you want to climb the Leaning Tower. For dining *alla pisana,* head away from the touristy piazza to a warren of streets around the market square, **Piazza delle Vettovaglie.** Finish your visit with a stroll along a handsome promenade beside the **River Arno.** The last train back to Florence usually leaves at 10:30pm (though the 9:30pm train is quicker).

DAYS 11 & 12: Venice ★★★

Set your alarm clock for an early start: It takes around 2 hours to reach Venice from Florence aboard the high-speed train. Follow the itinerary suggested in "The Best of Italy in 1 Week," p. 43. You'll be staying in Venice for 3 nights.

DAY 13: Verona ★★★

Book roundtrip tickets ahead of time for a high-speed Frecciarossa train between Venice and Verona—the journey is just 1 hour, 10 minutes, compared with more than 2 hours for local train service. Although he likely never set foot in the place, Shakespeare placed the world's most famous love story, *Romeo and Juliet,* here. Wander **Piazza dei Signori** and take in another square, **Piazza delle Erbe,** before visiting the **Arena di Verona** (p. 460), the world's best-preserved gladiatorial arena, which hosts monumental open-air opera all summer. Head back to Venice for the night. Fast trains run until 10pm.

DAY 14: Milan ★★

Prebook a fast train connection between Venice and Milan, a journey of between 2¼ and 2½ hours. The most bustling city in Italy isn't only about industry and commerce. Milan has one of Europe's finest Gothic cathedrals, the **Duomo** (p. 474), two great art collections at the **Pinacoteca Ambrosiana** (p. 478) and the **Pinacoteca di Brera** (p. 479), and Leonardo's fading but still magnificent **"Last Supper"** (p. 481; prebook as far ahead as possible). Stay overnight here if you are flying home or onward: It is one of Europe's major airline hubs.

ITALY FOR FAMILIES

Italy is probably the friendliest family vacation destination in all Europe. Practically, it presents few challenges. If you're traveling by rental car with young children, be sure to request safety car seats ahead of time. Let the rental company know the age of your child and they will arrange for a seat to comply with EU regulations. Rail travelers should remember that reduced-price family fares are available on much of the high-speed network; ask when you buy your tickets or use a booking agent.

As you tour, don't go hunting for "child-friendly" restaurants or special kids' menus. There is always plenty available for little ones anywhere you dine, even dishes that aren't offered to grown-up patrons. Never be afraid to ask if you have a fussy eater in the family. Pretty much any request is met with a smile. Many of our favorite places to eat have outdoor tables—if that's your preference, don't hesitate to ask.

Perhaps the main issue for travelers with children is spacing your museum visits so you get to see the masterpieces without having young kids suffer a meltdown after one saint painting too many. You **often must book** major museum targets ahead of arrival; leave plenty of time between them if you are traveling with young children. And remember to punctuate every day with a **gelato** stop. Italy has the world's best ice cream, and soya milk flavors are available for anyone with an intolerance. End your trip in Venice, which for many kids is every bit as magical as a Disney theme park: It's a city. That floats. (Kinda.)

DAY 1: Rome's Ancient Outdoors ★★★

History is on your side here: The wonders of **Ancient Rome** (p. 87) should appeal as much to kids (of almost any age) as to adults. There are gory tales to tell at the **Colosseum** (p. 88), where the bookshop has guides aimed at kids. After that, they can let off steam wandering the **Roman Forum** and **Palatine Hill.** (The roadside ruins of the **Imperial Forums** can be viewed at any time.) Cap the afternoon by exploring the **Villa Borghese** (p. 110), a large park in the heart of Rome where you can rent bikes. At dinner, find crispy crusts at an authentic Roman **pizzeria.**

DAY 2: Rome: Living History ★★★

Head early to **St. Peter's Basilica** (p. 78). The kids will find it spooky wandering the Vatican grottoes, and few can resist climbing up to Michelangelo's dome at 114m (375 ft.). After a timeout for lunch, begin your assault on the **Vatican Museums** and **Sistine Chapel.** Even if your kids don't like museums, they will gawp at the grandeur. Later in the day, head for the **Spanish Steps** (a spot for upscale souvenir shopping; see p. 151) before wandering to the **Trevi Fountain.** Let the kids toss coins into the fountain, which is said to ensure a return to Rome—perhaps when they are older and can fully appreciate the city's many artistic attractions.

DAY 3: Rome: Underground ★★★

Literal layers of history survive below the city streets. Kids will love exploring the catacombs of the **Via Appia Antica** (p. 119), the first cemetery of Rome's Christian community, where the devout practiced their faith in secret during periods of persecution. After descending through the layers—and centuries—under **San Clemente** (p. 96), eat more **pizza** before you leave the city. Rome's pizzerias are matched only by those in Naples, to the south, and our next recommended stops all lie to the north. Leave on a late afternoon train to Florence.

DAYS 4 & 5: Florence ★★★

Florence is usually thought of as a grown-up city, but there's enough to fill two family days. A bonus: Much of the center is traffic-free.

With multiple nights here, renting an apartment gives you space to spread out—see p. 205 for apartment rental suggestions. Close to the Duomo, **Residence Hilda** (p. 212) is a small, family-friendly hotel with large, apartment-style rooms and kitchenettes.

Begin with the city's monumental main square, **Piazza della Signoria,** an open-air museum of statues. The **Palazzo Vecchio** (p. 185) dominates one side; you can all tour it with special family-friendly guides, including docents dressed as Cosimo I de' Medici and Eleonora di Toledo. Turn a visit to the famed **Uffizi Gallery** into a treasure trail by arriving with pictures or names of key artworks to hunt down. On the second morning, kids will delight in climbing to the top of Brunelleschi's dome on the **Duomo** for a classic panorama. Book an early slot, when the weather is cooler, because parts of the ancient staircase to the top are not well ventilated. If kids and adults have still more energy to burn, climb the 414 steps up to the **Campanile di Giotto,** run around in the **Giardino di Boboli,** and cross the **Ponte Vecchio** at dusk. With older, fit children, you could add another day here, to allow time to see the Chianti hills on two wheels (see p. 170 for bike rental info).

DAY 6: Pisa ★★

If your kids are age 7 or under, consider skipping **Pisa** (p. 293): Eight is the minimum age for the iconic ascent up the bell tower of Pisa's cathedral, aka the **Leaning Tower.** Older kids enjoy the hyperreal monuments of the **Campo dei Miracoli** and learning about the city's Galileo links: The scientist was born here, and supposedly discovered his law of pendulum motion while watching a swinging lamp inside the **Duomo.** Take the kids to taste a local specialty, *cecina,* a pizza-like garbanzo-bean flatbread served warm. Your daylong visit complete, whiz up the coast on the fast train to Genoa. There are luggage storage facilities *(deposito bagagli)* around Pisa Centrale Station.

DAYS 7 & 8: Genoa & the Riviera di Levante ★★

The industrial city-seaport of Genoa is home to one of Italy's most popular family attractions: The **Acquario di Genova** (p. 554) is Europe's largest aquarium, where you can all enjoy a trip around the world's oceans. It requires a half-day to see properly, so reserve an early entry slot, and then head out to the **Riviera di Levante** (p. 565), a coastline of pretty ports and rocky coves east of the city. Our favorite base around here is romantic **Portofino,** where you can easily kill a second day in Liguria beside the azure sea, dining on fish or filling up with *pesto al basilico,* a classic Ligurian dish. Nearby **Santa Margherita Ligure** is a budget-friendlier alternative to Portofino, with an easy rail link, a fine promenade, and a laid-back vibe.

DAYS 9 & 10: Lake Garda ★★

Slow down for a couple of days by Italy's biggest inland lake, perhaps basing yourself at photogenic **Sirmione** (p. 515). Take a ferry trip, hire a pedal boat or kayak, eat simple grilled lake fish, and ease into lakeside life. In Sirmione you can scramble on the ramparts of the **Castello Scaligero,** then ride the little train out to Roman ruins at the **Grotte di Catullo,** a villa supposedly inhabited by the poet Catullus (ca. 84 B.C.–ca. 54 B.C.). For active families with more time to spend, **Riva del Garda** (p. 516), close to the lake's northernmost point, is one of Europe's major windsurfing and sailboarding centers.

DAYS 11, 12 & 13: Venice ★★★

In Venice, the fun begins the moment you arrive and take a *vaporetto* along the **Grand Canal.** Head straight for **Piazza San Marco** (p. 406),

The beach at Riva del Garda is popular for windsurfing and sunbathing.

where children delight in riding the elevator up the great **Campanile.** Catch the mosaics inside the **Basilica di San Marco,** which dominates the square. At the **Palazzo Ducale** cross the infamous **Bridge of Sighs.** As in Florence, make time for some art: Prioritize the **Gallerie dell'Accademia** (p. 417) and **San Rocco,** where kids view the episodic Tintoretto paintings like a picture book or graphic novel. In summer, save time for the beach at **Lido** (p. 428) and perhaps for getting a different angle on Venice's canals, from the seat of a **gondola** (p. 404).

A WHISTLESTOP WEEK-OR-SO FOR FOOD & WINE LOVERS

Italy has one of Europe's great cuisines—or rather, make that *several* of Europe's great cuisines (some claim that Italy has maybe 50 distinct culinary traditions). This nation's history as a collection of independent city-states and noble fiefdoms left a diverse legacy in food. Each regional cuisine is committed to its own local produce and artisanal specialties, with treasured recipes handed down through generations. Fans of Stanley Tucci's CNN 2021–22 show *Searching for Italy* will be familiar with this backstory. (And if you haven't seen it, you certainly should.)

Italy is also the world's biggest wine producer. Although much is undistinguished (if perfectly drinkable) table wine, many icons of world wine hail from here. Our itinerary takes in three of the great Italian red wine zones: **Montepulciano,** whose noble wine was known to the Ancient Etruscans; **Chianti,** the first legally defined wine zone anywhere; and **Piedmont,** whose robust reds Barolo and Barbaresco command top prices at restaurants around the globe.

DAYS 1 & 2: Rome ★★★

The restaurants of Italy's capital offer a range of cuisines from pretty much everywhere on the peninsula. The **Trastevere, Monti,** and **Testaccio** neighborhoods are great for dining and drinks after dark (see p. 138 and pp. 147–151 for suggestions). While here, sample traditional Roman dishes like pasta with *cacio e pepe* (sheep's milk cheese and black pepper); *spaghetti alla carbonara* (similar but enriched with egg yolk plus added *guanciale,* cured pork cheek) or *alla gricia* (also with *guanciale* and *pecorino* cheese, but no egg); *saltimbocca alla romana*—literally, "jump in the mouth," a veal cutlet with prosciutto and sage; and *coda alla vaccinara* (stewed oxtail with tomatoes and celery). **Gelato** is either Florentine or Sicilian in origin, depending on who you ask, but in Rome you'll find lots of the country's tastiest (see p. 140). The city also has some of Italy's best craft beer bars (see p. 156). You'll need a rental car for your next leg.

Vineyards in Tuscany.

Collect it on your second afternoon and head north to Tuscany, to leave almost a full day at your next stop.

DAY 3: Montepulciano ★★

Begin with a walk up the handsome, steep Corso from the town gate to **Piazza Grande,** monumental heart of the *comune,* where you'll find the Palazzo Comunale (climb to the terrace for a panorama of the surrounding winelands) and Cattedrale. Oenophiles should head to the **Consorzio del Vino Nobile di Montepulciano** enoteca, where you can taste vintages from small producers and seek advice for nearby wineries to visit. Our favorite wine cellar in the center is **Gattavecchi**, where there's another scenic terrace. End the evening at **Acquacheta** (p. 253), with a menu that's all about beef—*"bistecca numero uno,"* is how Contucci winemaker Adamo once described it to us. Other local delicacies include sheep's milk cheese, *pecorino di Pienza.*

DAYS 4 & 5: The Chianti ★★★

Pick a base close to **Greve in Chianti** (p. 246) to lodge at the heart of Tuscany's largest quality wine region. Sangiovese grape–based Chianti is a diverse wine: Chianti Classico denotes grapes from the original (and best) growing zone, and tasting opportunities abound at wineries such as **Villa Vignamaggio** and **Castello di Volpaia.** Book ahead if you require a tour anywhere. The Chianti is also famed for its butchers, where you can buy everything from cuts of fresh beef (ideal if you're lodging in a villa) to salami made from a local breed of pig, the *Cinta Senese.* **Falorni,** in Greve, is outshone perhaps only by **Dario Cecchini,** in nearby Panzano. Also look for Tuscan extra virgin olive oil. Squeezed from the first pressing of olives harvested in November, this "green gold" is famed for its low acidity. It is among Italy's best.

DAYS 6 & 7: Bologna ★★

You have arrived in Italy's gastronomic capital. You can leave the rental car here; it's easy to continue onward by train, if you wish. The agricultural plains of Emilia-Romagna are Italy's breadbasket. So much of the produce we think of as typical "Italian food" hails from here: cured prosciutto and Parmigiano-Reggiano cheese from Parma and Reggio nell'Emilia; aged balsamic vinegar from Modena; mortadella sausage and tortellini (filled pasta) from Bologna itself. Foodies should browse Bologna's markets, the **Mercato delle Erbe** and the **Quadrilatero,** a warren of lanes with enticing food shops. Make a dinner reservation at a restaurant specializing in classic Bolognese cooking; see p. 361 for our picks.

DAYS 8 & 9: Turin ★

Snowcapped alpine peaks dot the horizon north and west of the Piedmontese capital. The cooking in Italy's northwest reflects the heartier and hardier mountain folk who live on the city's doorstep. Nearby **Vercelli** is Italy's rice capital—this town is ringed by paddy fields—and *risotto* tastes its creamy best here. There's also a noticeable Ligurian current in Torinese food: Basil-based pesto is superb, and the favorite slice-on-the-go isn't pizza but *farinata,* garbanzo bean–flour flatbread dusted with rosemary or pepper. The **Langhe Hills** (p. 539), south of the city, are famed for blockbuster red wines and white truffles. Sweet vermouth was also invented in Turin; the classic local labels are slightly bitter Punt e Mes ("point and a half" in Piedmontese) and vanilla-rich Carpano Antica Formula.

HISTORIC CITIES OF THE NORTH

Often overshadowed by blockbusters like Rome and Florence, the cities of northern Italy make an excellent itinerary for return visitors. Each city on our tour has a center with refined architecture and a history of independence—as well as struggle with, and eventual subjection to, the great regional powers, often Venice. The itinerary's logical starting point is Milan, gateway to Italy for flights from across the globe. Spend a day there, collect your rental car or rail tickets—all train connections on this

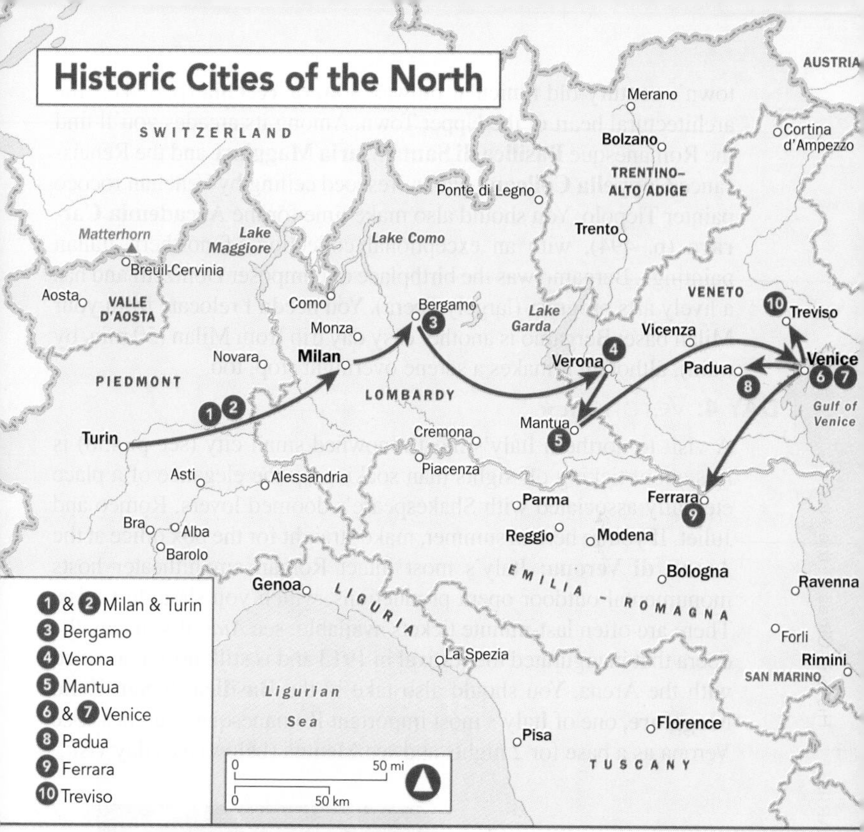

tour are easy—and set off early. The endpoint is Venice, where we recommend you extend your stay by as many days as you can; see chapter 9 for full coverage of the city.

DAYS 1 & 2: Milan ★★ & Turin ★★

See Milan under "The Best of Italy in 2 Weeks," p. 47. Spend **DAY 2** taking a day trip by train to **Turin** (p. 519). The city of Fiat and football (meaning soccer) has a handsome baroque center, the finest Egyptian collection outside of Cairo at the **Museo Egizio** (p. 524), and views of the Alps from the top of the **Mole Antonelliana** tower (p. 522). It also has a food culture every bit as refined as Bologna's; Turin is the city of vermouth and on the doorstep of the Piedmont wine-growing region, so you will not go thirsty. You can complete a rail journey between the cities in as little as 45 minutes: There's no need to relocate your base from Milan if you prefer not to change lodgings.

DAY 3: Bergamo ★★

Whether you arrive by train or car, alight in the **Lower Town** (Città Bassa) and ascend to the **Upper Town** (Città Alta) in style, on the town's century-old funicular railway. **Piazza Vecchia** (p. 494) is the architectural heart of the Upper Town. Among its arcades you'll find the Romanesque **Basilica di Santa Maria Maggiore** and the Renaissance **Cappella Colleoni,** with a frescoed ceiling by Venetian rococo painter Tiepolo. You should also make time for the **Accademia Carrara** (p. 494), with an exceptional collection of northern Italian paintings. Bergamo was the birthplace of composer Donizetti and has a lively arts program (largely opera). You needn't relocate from your Milan base: Bergamo is another easy day trip from Milan (50 min. by train), although it makes a serene overnight stop, too.

DAY 4: Verona ★★

A visit to northern Italy's most renowned small city (see p. 458) is less about ticking off sights than soaking up the elegance of a place eternally associated with Shakespeare's doomed lovers, Romeo and Juliet. If you're here in summer, make straight for the box office at the **Arena di Verona;** Italy's most intact Roman amphitheater hosts monumental outdoor opera productions, which you shouldn't miss. There are often last-minute tickets available; see *Aïda* if you can, the opera that inaugurated the festival in 1913 and is still most associated with the Arena. You should also take in the **Basilica di San Zeno Maggiore,** one of Italy's most important Romanesque churches. Use Verona as a base for 2 nights and see Mantua (below) as a day visit.

Juliet's Balcony in Verona.

DAY 5: Mantua ★★★

Landlocked it may be, but the Renaissance city of Mantua (Mantova in Italian; p. 497) is almost completely, romantically surrounded by lakes fed by the River Mincio. Just 45 minutes from Verona by train, Mantua owes its grandeur to the Gonzaga family, who filled piazzas and palaces with art by the greatest masters of the period, notably Mantegna. One day is just enough to visit architect L. B. Alberti's **Basilica di Sant'Andrea,** the frescoed **Palazzo Ducale,** and the Room of Giants inside **Palazzo Te.**

DAYS 6 & 7: Venice ★★★

Follow the itinerary suggested in "The Best of Italy in 1 Week," p. 43. Use Venice as a base for your last 5 nights, seeing Padua, Ferrara, and Treviso on day-trip excursions.

DAY 8: Padua ★★

At least 1 day before arrival, you should buy a PadovaCard, a discount ticket that includes entrance to almost everything in town plus free public transportation. Design your day around a prebooked time slot to see the most historically significant paintings in northern Italy, Giotto's frescoes in the **Cappella degli Scrovegni** (p. 456). The **Basilica di Sant'Antonio** is the final resting place of St. Anthony of Padua, the second-most eminent Franciscan saint after St. Francis himself.

DAY 9: Ferrara ★★

Like Mantua, this small, stately city owes its grandeur to one despotic family—in this case, the Este dukes, who held sway from the 1200s to the 1500s, ruling the city from their moated **Castello Estense** (p. 371). Elsewhere in the center, check out the elaborate exterior of a Gothic-Romanesque **Duomo;** the **Palazzo dei Diamanti,** another Este creation, named for 9,000 diamond-shaped stones adorning its facade; and **MEIS,** a new national museum dedicated to the long cultural history of Jews and Judaism in Italy. Ferrara is under an hour by high-speed train from Venice.

DAY 10: Treviso ★★

It's not far (half-hour by train) from Venice to its small northern neighbor, which the powerful Venetians dominated for over 450 years from the 14th century onward. They left a rich architectural legacy—plus canals, of course. The pace here is sedate. You'll have ample time to survey the greatest hits of painter **Tomaso da Modena,** at the churches of **Santa Lucia** and **San Nicoló,** and the **Museo di Santa Caterina** (pp. 461–462), before repairing to **Piazza dei Signori,** the medieval city's pretty heart, to enjoy a glass of local Prosecco sparkling wine.

ITALY'S ANCIENT RUINS

Italy itself isn't old—as a unified country, it only just passed the 160-year mark. But the peninsula is rightly considered a cradle of European civilization. Michelangelo and the Renaissance, Gothic architecture, even the Byzantine mosaics of Ravenna: These are relatively recent moments in Italian time. Even the Romans were not the first civilization to leave a mark here. Several ancient buildings still standing owe their construction to expatriates from Classical Greece. ***Note:*** Some ancient sites have cramped or poorly ventilated underground areas.

DAYS 1, 2, 3 & 4: Sicily ★★★

As Greek Syracuse, modern-day **Siracusa** (p. 781) was one of the cultural hotspots of the ancient Mediterranean: Dramatist Aeschylus was a visitor and lyric poet Sappho was exiled here toward the end of the 7th century B.C. A ruined Doric **Temple of Apollo** stands in town, and the **Parco Archeologico della Neapolis** (p. 786) has a Greek theater still used to stage dramas each summer. Our suggestion: Fly into Catania, 67km (41 miles) north of Siracusa, which is well connected by air with Rome (1 hr., 15 min. flight), then rent a car and make your base in Sicily's southwest for at least half your time on the island, to tour coastal **Selinunte** (p. 812), **Segesta** (p. 770), the Valley of the Temples at **Agrigento** (p. 799), and the mosaics of the **Villa Romana del Casale** in Piazza Armerina (p. 797). Return to Siracusa and fly back from Catania to Rome.

DAYS 5, 6 & 7: Rome ★★★

Rome is to archaeology as Coke is to fizzy brown liquids: This is the biggest brand when it comes to ancient ruins. Rome was the epicenter of a republic and empire which for centuries ruled most of Europe and Asia Minor, as well as much of North Africa and the Middle East. Spend **DAY 5** walking outdoors amid ancient Rome's civic and spiritual heart, the **Forum** (p. 90). The same ticket gets you into the **Colosseum** (p. 88). Between visits to those two, it makes sense to see the **Imperial Forums, Trajan's Markets,** and the city's best artifact

Ruins of the Temple of Apollo in Agrigento, Sicily.

collection, at the **Musei Capitolini** (p. 94). Rome's museums display an array of relics dug up over the centuries: Add the ancient collections of the **Vatican Museums** (p. 80) and the busts and Roman art at **Palazzo Massimo alle Terme** (p. 114) to your list for **DAY 6**. The outdoor ruins of Rome's former seaport, **Ostia Antica** (p. 158), stand a short train journey from the city—a comfortable half-day roundtrip for **DAY 7**. On the way back into the city, jump off at the Circo Massimo Metro stop to visit the **Terme di Caracalla** (p. 95) baths complex, and to admire for one last time the view of the **Palatine Hill** from the Circus Maximus. You could probably spend a month here just looking at the remnants of Ancient Rome.

DAYS 8, 9 & 10: Naples & Campania ★★

Ancient Naples—established as the fishing port of Parthenope, then re-founded as Neapolis in the 6th century B.C.—was a key settlement in Magna Graecia, or "Greater Greece." Reminders of the ancient world lie below Naples's *centro storico:* Visit the excavations under **San Lorenzo Maggiore** (p. 601) to see remains of the Greek *Ágora* (market) and a later Roman Forum. Day trips to the Roman towns of **Pompeii** and **Herculaneum** (p. 625) reveal haunting artifacts preserved for centuries under ash and lava after Vesuvius's cataclysmic eruption in A.D. 79; visit Naples' **Museo Archeologico Nazionale** (p. 600) to see wall art from Pompeii and Roman statuary, including the "Farnese Bull." Another day trip heads west of Naples to the amphitheater at **Pozzuoli** (p. 618), third-largest in the Roman world. Leave Naples on the high-speed Frecciarossa or Italo service late on **DAY 10** to get to Florence, just under 3 hours by rail.

DAYS 11 & 12: Florence ★★

Florence's Renaissance heyday, in the 1400s and 1500s, dominates much of the center's art and architecture. However, the **Museo Archeologico** (p. 193) displays relics from a civilization that predated the Romans: the Etruscans. While other visitors zero in on Michelangelo & co., you may have the "Arezzo Chimera" and many other precious Etruscan objects to yourself. You can also visit parts of a Roman theater uncovered below the **Palazzo Vecchio** (p. 185). A 20-minute bus journey from Florence gets you to **Fiesole** (p. 202), an outsized village with a preserved Roman theater, a stretch of Etruscan wall, and an archaeological area where visitors can roam freely among old stones.

DAY 13: Verona ★★

It seems harsh to label the **Arena di Verona** (p. 460) "a ruin." This city's enormous amphitheater is the best preserved in Italy and still in regular use. Come in summer—and book ahead—for the chance to experience one of Europe's most evocative outdoor opera festivals.

ROME

By Elizabeth Heath

4

With the devastating effects of the pandemic finally in its rearview mirror, the Eternal City is back to being the enchanting capital visitors know and love. Of course, some of that frustrating dysfunction is still there—and yes, you just have to roll with it. But on the whole, the city used its long pandemic pause to clean up, open new or long-shuttered archaeological sites, and—brace yourselves—modernize and automate ticketing and reservations systems. It's easier than ever to be a guest here, and Rome is ready to welcome visitors with open arms.

This is, after all, the city that once ruled the Western world, and even the partial, scattered ruins of Rome's empire are among the most overpowering sights on earth. To walk the Roman Forum, to view the Colosseum, the Pantheon, and the Appian Way: These are among the most memorable, instructive, and illuminating experiences in all of travel. Across the Tiber River, St. Peter's and the Holy See loom large—both for their physical imprint on the city and for how they shaped the history and culture of Rome, Italy, Europe, and much of the Western world.

As a visitor to Rome, you will be constantly reminded of its extraordinary history. Yet this is no city stuck in a time warp—Rome is a living, breathing metropolis whose residents just happen to live, work, dine out, and relax in and among ancient ruins, medieval piazzas, Renaissance palaces, and baroque fountains. Discover the city's ancient wonders, but don't just seek out old Rome—find the innovative bistro, the experimental gelateria, or the modern art exhibit. Get lost in the maze of streets of Rome's *centro storico,* and stumble upon its monuments, moments, and simpler pleasures.

Walk the streets of Rome, and the city will be yours.

DON'T LEAVE ROME WITHOUT . . .

Exploring the World's Smallest Country. Vatican City is just .2 square miles, but it packs a lot into that tiny space. From one of the finest museums on the planet, to its largest Catholic church, to the architectural masterwork that is St. Peter's Square, your trip isn't complete without at least a day spent here. See p. 75.

PREVIOUS PAGE: **Outdoor dining on the streets of Rome.**

Gazing over the Roman Forum and Palatine from the Capitoline Hill Terraces at Night. Yes, explore the ruins by day too, but after dark—as spotlights cast dramatic glows over solitary columns and crumbling arches—the view is truly, disarmingly spectacular. See p. 87.

Lingering over Dinner. Take time to unwind at a typical Roman trattoria, with a steady and wonderfully affordable flow of wine and delicious food. See p. 137.

Shopping like a Local at the Lively Mercato di Testaccio. No other market in the city has such a strong sense of community, coupled with the chance to sample real Roman street food. See p. 153.

Rome in the Post-Covid Era

We've always encouraged readers to buy tickets in advance for the attractions they really want to see; that advice is even more pertinent now. During the tentative days of post-lockdown re-openings and social distancing measures, many attractions switched to advanced-ticketing only in order to limit crowds. Many have retained these crowd control systems, which ultimately give visitors a better experience. We've indicated where advanced reservations are required or recommended as of press time.

ESSENTIALS

Arriving

BY PLANE Most flights arrive to Terminal 3 of Rome's **Leonardo da Vinci International Airport** (www.adr.it; ✆ **06-65951**), popularly known as **Fiumicino,** 30km (19 miles) from the city center. (If you're arriving from other European cities, you might land at Ciampino Airport, discussed below.) As you exit baggage claim, you'll see a **tourist information desk** to the right, staffed daily from 8:30am to 6pm. There are several ***cambio*** (currency exchange) desks in the pre- and post-security areas, but it's just as easy, and possibly less expensive, to withdraw cash from an ATM (*bancomat*) in the airport. See p. 828 for tips on using Italian ATMs.

Follow signs marked treni to find the **airport train station,** about a 10-minute walk from the arrivals area. **Pro tip:** If you have a lot of bags

Train or Taxi?

Whether to take the airport shuttle train or a taxi into Rome from FCO depends on your budget and your tolerance for schlepping. If you're traveling solo and/or traveling light, the train is the most economical option for getting into the city, and takes about the same time as a taxi. If you've got a lot of bags, however, bear in mind that the train is a bit of a long walk from the Arrivals terminal—and that, once your train arrives at Termini station, you'll still have to walk, or take Metro, bus, or taxi to your final destination. (See "By Train," p. 64, for more on Termini station options.) Bottom line? If there are three or more in your party or you're carrying lots of luggage, go for a taxi.

and opt for the train, grab a free luggage cart when you get to baggage claim. When you exit into the terminal, turn left instead of right, and take the elevator down to the train station level. If you go right, you have to take an escalator and ditch the luggage cart.

From there, catch the delightfully named **Leonardo Express** for a 32-minute shuttle ride to Rome's main station, **Stazione Termini.** The shuttle runs every 15 minutes (every 30 min. at off-peak hours) from 5:38am to 11:53pm for 14€ one-way (free kids 12 and under). You can buy tickets from one of several machines (machines take cash or credit, and you can opt for instructions in English) or at the Trenitalia window near the tracks. You can also buy e-tickets at www.trenitalia.com or use the Trenitalia mobile app.

A **taxi** from Fiumicino airport to the city costs a flat-rate 50€ for the 45-minute to 1-hour trip, depending on traffic (hotels tend to charge 50€–60€ for pickup service). Note that the flat rate is applicable from the airport to central Rome and vice versa, but only if your central Rome location is inside the Aurelian Walls (most hotels are). Otherwise, standard metered rates apply, which can bump the fare to 75€ or higher. There are also surcharges for large luggage, Sunday and holiday rides, more than four passengers, and rides after 10pm and before 6am.

If you arrive at **Ciampino Airport** (www.adr.it/ciampino; ✆ **06-65951**), you can take a **Terravision** bus (www.terravision.eu; ✆ **06-4880086;** first bus 8:45am, last bus 11:40pm) to Stazione Termini. This takes about 45 minutes and costs 6€. (Note that the timetable for buses fluctuates based on current flight schedules.) A **taxi** from Ciampino costs a flat rate of 30€, provided you're going to a destination within the old Aurelian Walls.

From either airport, ride-sharing service **Uber** is available—sort of. Because of licensing laws (and strong resistance from Rome's taxi drivers), only Uber Lux, Van, or Black services are offered, and they're much more expensive than a taxi.

BY TRAIN OR BUS Trains and buses (including trains from the airport) arrive in the center of old Rome at **Stazione Termini,** Piazza dei Cinquecento. This is the train, bus, and transportation hub for all of Rome, and it is surrounded by many hotels, especially budget choices.

The station is filled with services. Currency exchange windows and ATMs are located on the platform level, as well as on floor -1 (subway level). **Informazioni Ferroviarie** (in the outer hall) dispenses info on rail travel to other parts of Italy. There is also a **tourist information booth,** plus baggage services, newsstands, clean public toilets (they cost 1€), and snack bars.

To get from Termini to your final destination in Rome, you have several options. If you're taking the **Metropolitana** (subway), follow the illuminated red-and-white m signs. To catch a city bus, go straight through the outer hall and enter the sprawling bus lot of **Piazza dei Cinquecento.** (See p. 69 for more information about getting around Rome by public

ROMA & OMNIA passes

If you plan to do some serious sightseeing in Rome (and why else would you be here?), the **Roma Pass** (www.romapass.it) is worth considering. For 52€ per card, valid for 3 days, you get free entry to the first two museums or archaeological sites you visit; "express" entry to the Colosseum; discounted entry to all other museums and sites; free use of the city's public transport network (bus, Metro, tram, and railway lines, not including transfers to Fiumucino Airport), free use of P-Stop bathrooms (www.turismo-roma.it/en/page/pstop), and a free map.

If your stay in Rome is shorter, you may want to opt for the **Roma Pass 48 Hours** (32€), which offers the same benefits as the 3-day pass, except that only the first museum you visit is free and the ticket is valid for just 48 hours.

The free transportation perk with the Roma Pass is not insignificant, if only because it saves you the hassle of buying digital farecards or paper tickets. In any case, do some quick math; one major museum or attraction entrance costs 12€ to 16€, and each ride on public transportation is 1.50€. Discounts to other sites range from 20% to 50%. If you plan to visit lots of sites and dash around the city on public transport, it's probably worth the money.

A glaring disadvantage of the Roma Pass is that it does not include access to the Vatican Museums or the paid areas of St. Peter's. That's where the **OMNIA Card** comes to the rescue. The 72-hour card combines all the benefits of the Roma Pass with skip-the-line entry to the Vatican Museums and St. Peter's, an audioguide to St. Peter's, a hop-on-hop-off bus pass, and admission to other Vatican properties. At 129€ it's an investment, but worth it if you want to take in all the heavy hitters of Rome and the Vatican. If you just want express entrance to the Vatican Museums and St. Peter's, there's also a 24-hour Omnia Card (69€) that does not include Roma Pass benefits. The cards can be purchased online at www.omniavaticanrome.org and picked up at one of four Omnia Card offices in the city, including at St. Peter's Square.

You can buy Roma passes online (www.romapass.it) and pick them up at one of the Tourist Information Points (see p. 66); you can also order in advance by phone, with a credit card, at ✆ **06-060608.** Roma Passes are also sold directly at Tourist Information Point offices or at participating museums and ATAC subway ticket offices.

Note: Roma Pass holders intending to visit the Colosseum **must reserve timed entry.** We find the easiest way to do this is as follows: on the Roma Pass website, go to the FAQ page and scroll down to question 7.1. Follow the link to CoopCulture and buy your Roma Pass directly from that site, at the same time reserving entry to the Colosseum. Otherwise, Roma Pass holders can book the 2€-per-person timed-entry reservation directly on the CoopCulture website or by calling ✆ **06-39967575,** credit card in hand. Note that other sites included on the Roma Pass may also require advanced booking; check individual websites for the latest on opening hours and Roma Pass reservation requirements.

transportation.) You will also find a line of **taxis** parked out front. Note that taxis charge a 2€ supplement for any fares originating at Termini, plus 1€ for each bag in the trunk. Use the official taxi queue right in front of the station; don't go with a driver who approaches you or get into any cab where the meter is "broken." You should be able to pay with a credit or debit card in any official taxi, but confirm this before getting in.

BY CAR From the north or south, the main access route is the **Autostrada A1,** which runs from Milan to Naples via Bologna, Florence, and Rome. At 754km (469 miles), it is the longest Italian autostrada and the "spinal cord" of Italy's road network. All the autostrade connect with the **Grande Raccordo Anulare** (GRA), a ring road encircling Rome, channeling traffic into and around the congested city. ***Tip:*** Long before you reach the GRA, study your route carefully to see what part of Rome you plan to enter. Route signs along the ring road tend to be confusing.

Warning: If you must drive a car into Rome, return your rental car immediately on arrival, or at least get yourself to your hotel, park your car, and leave it there until you leave the city. Seriously think twice before driving in Rome—the traffic, as well as the parking options, are nightmarish. Plus most of central Rome is a **Zona Traffico Limitato** (ZTL), off-limits to nonresidents and rigorously enforced by cameras. You will almost certainly be fined; the ticket might arrive at your home address months after your trip.

Visitor Information

Information, maps, and the Roma Pass (p. 65) are available at six Tourist Information Points around the city maintained by **Roma Capitale** (for locations, go to www.turismoroma.it/en). Each kiosk keeps its own hours and none are exactly the same, but you can reliably find them open after 9:30am and before 6pm (some open earlier and stay open later). Note that the one at Termini (daily 8am–7pm), located next to platform 24, often has a long line.

City Layout

The bulk of what you'll want to visit—ancient, Renaissance, and baroque Rome (as well as the train station)—lies on the east side of the **Tiber River** (Fiume Tevere), which curls through the city. However, several important landmarks are on the other side: **St. Peter's Basilica** and the **Vatican, Castel Sant'Angelo,** and the colorful **Trastevere** neighborhood. Even if those last sights are slightly farther afield, Rome has one of the most compact and walkable city centers in Europe.

That doesn't mean you won't get lost from time to time (most newcomers do). Arm yourself with a detailed street map of Rome (or a smartphone with a hefty data plan). Most hotels hand out a pretty good version of a city map.

Rome's Neighborhoods in Brief

Much of Rome's historic core does not fall under distinct neighborhood classifications. Instead, when describing a location, the frame of reference is the name of the nearest large monument or square, like St. Peter's or Piazza di Spagna. Street numbers usually run consecutively, with odd numbers on one side of the street, evens on the other. However, in Centro, the numbers sometimes run up one side and then run back down on the other side (so #50 could potentially be opposite #308).

VATICAN CITY & PRATI **Vatican City** is technically a sovereign state, although in practice it is just another part of Rome. The **Vatican Museums, St. Peter's,** and the **Vatican Gardens** take up most of the land area; the popes have lived here for 7 centuries. If you plan to spend most of your time exploring Vatican City sights, or if you just want to stay outside the city center, **Prati,** a middle-class neighborhood east of the Vatican, has a smattering of affordable hotels and shopping streets, as well as some excellent places to eat.

CENTRO STORICO & THE PANTHEON One of the most desirable (and busiest) areas of Rome, the **Centro Storico** (historic center) is a maze of narrow streets and cobbled alleys dating from the Middle Ages, filled with churches and palaces built during the Renaissance and baroque eras, as well as countless hotels and Airbnb rentals. The only way to explore it is by foot. Its heart is elegant **Piazza Navona,** built over Emperor Domitian's stadium and bustling with overpriced sidewalk cafes and restaurants, street artists and musicians (licensed or otherwise), and milling crowds. Nearby, the area around the ancient Roman **Pantheon** is abuzz with crowds, a cafe scene, and nightlife. South of Corso Vittorio Emanuele is the lively square of **Campo de' Fiori,** home to the famous produce market. West of Via Arenula lies the old Jewish **Ghetto,** with several good restaurants and a few interesting hotels.

ANCIENT ROME, MONTI & CELIO Although no longer the heart of the city, this is where Rome began, with the **Colosseum, Palatine Hill, Roman Forum, Imperial Forums,** and **Circus Maximus.** This area offers only a few hotels, and many restaurants close to the Colosseum are tour-bus traps. Just beyond the Circus Maximus, the **Aventine Hill** is now a posh residential quarter with great city views. For more of a neighborhood feel, stay in **Monti** (Rome's oldest *rione,* or quarter, located north of the Colosseum) or **Celio** (southeast of the Colosseum). Monti especially has good dining and plenty of nightlife.

TRIDENTE & THE SPANISH STEPS The most upscale part of Rome, full of expensive hotels, designer boutiques, and chic restaurants, lies north of Rome's center. It's often called the Tridente, because Via di Ripetta, Via del Corso, and Via del Babuino form a trident leading down from **Piazza del Popolo.** The star here is unquestionably **Piazza di Spagna,** which attracts Romans and tourists alike (though mostly the latter) to linger at its celebrated **Spanish Steps** (just don't eat lunch on the steps! See p. 144). Some of Rome's most high-end shopping streets fan out from here, including **Via Condotti.**

VIA VENETO & PIAZZA BARBERINI In the 1950s and early 1960s, the tree-lined boulevard **Via Veneto** was the swinging place to be, the haunt of la Dolce Vita celebrities and paparazzi. Luxury hotels, cafes, and restaurants still cluster here, although the restaurants are mostly overpriced tourist traps. To the south, Via Veneto ends at **Piazza Barberini** and the magnificent **Palazzo Barberini,** begun in 1623 by Carlo Maderno and later completed by Bernini and Borromini.

VILLA BORGHESE & PARIOLI **Parioli** is Rome's most elegant residential section, a setting for excellent restaurants, hotels, museums, and public parks. Bordered by the green spaces of the **Villa Borghese** to the south and the **Villa Glori** and **Villa Ada** to the north, Parioli (and just to its south, Pinciano) is one of the city's safest districts, but it's not exactly central and not the best base if you plan to depend on public transportation.

AROUND STAZIONE TERMINI For many visitors, their first glimpse of Rome is the main train station and the unappealing **Piazza del Cinquecento** out front. There are a lot of affordable hotels in this area (as well as several less-affordable ones), and the location is convenient, near the city's transportation hub and not far from ancient Rome. Hotels on the Via Marsala side often occupy floors of a *palazzo* (palace), with clean and decent, sometimes even charming, rooms. The once-seedy neighborhoods on either side of Termini (Esquilino and Tiburtino) have slowly been cleaning up.

TRASTEVERE In a Roman shift of the Latin *Trans Tiber,* Trastevere means "across the Tiber." Since the 1970s, when expats and other bohemians discovered it, this once-medieval working-class district has been gentrified and is now most definitely on the tourist map. Yet Trastevere retains its colorful appeal, with dance clubs, offbeat shops, pubs, and little *trattorie* and wine bars. Trastevere has places to stay—mostly rather quaint rentals and Airbnbs—and excellent restaurants and bars, too. The

The Trastevere neighborhood is full of casual restaurants, great for alfresco dining.

area centers on the ancient churches of **Santa Cecilia** and **Santa Maria in Trastevere.**

TESTACCIO & SOUTHERN ROME Once home to slaughterhouses and Rome's port on the Tiber, the working-class neighborhood of **Testaccio** was built around one strange feature: a huge, compacted mound of broken amphorae and terracotta roof tiles, begun under Emperor Nero in A.D. 55 and added to over the centuries. Houses were built around the mound; caves were dug into its mass to store wine and foodstuffs. Now known for its authentic Roman restaurants, Testaccio is also one of Rome's liveliest areas after dark. Stay here if you want a taste of a real Roman neighborhood, but bear in mind that you're a bus, tram, or subway ride from most touristic sights.

THE APPIAN WAY Farther south and east, the 2,300-year-old **Via Appia Antica** road once extended from Rome to Brindisi on the southeast coast. This is one of the most historically rich areas of Rome, great for a day trip, but not a convenient place to stay. Its most famous sights are the **Catacombs,** the graveyards of early Christians and patrician families.

Getting Around Rome

Central Rome is perfect for exploring on foot, with sites of interest often clustered together. Much of the inner core is traffic-free, so you will need to walk whether you like it or not. ***Tip:*** Wear sturdy, comfortable walking shoes. In the most tourist-trod parts of the city, be ready to cope with crowds, uneven cobblestones, heavy traffic, and narrow (if any) sidewalks.

BY SUBWAY The **Metropolitana** (Metro) is managed by **ATAC** (www.atac.roma.it; ✆ **06-57003**), which also runs the city's buses, trams, and urban trains. The Metro operates daily from 5:30am to 11:30pm (until 1:30am on Sat). A big red **m** indicates the entrance to the subway. If your destination is close to a Metro stop, hop on, as your journey will be much faster than by taking surface transportation. There are three lines: **Line A** (orange) runs southeast to northwest via Termini, Barberini, Spagna, and several stations in Prati near the Vatican; **Line B** (blue) runs north to south via Termini and stops at the Colosseum; and a third, **Line C** (green), will ultimately run from Monte Compatri in the southeast to Clodio/Mazzini (just beyond the Ottaviano stop on Line A) and include several stops in the Centro Storico. While much of Line C is up and running, sections have been delayed for years, largely because crews working underground keep stumbling upon new archaeological finds that have to be researched and excavated.

Tickets are 1.50€ and are available from *tabacchi* (tobacco shops), many newsstands, and vending machines at all stations; booklets of tickets are also available at newsstands, *tabacchi,* and in some terminals. You can also buy a daily or weekly **pass** (see "By Bus & Tram" below). To open the subway barrier, insert your ticket. If you have a **Roma Pass** (p. 65), touch it against the yellow dot and the gates will open. Tickets,

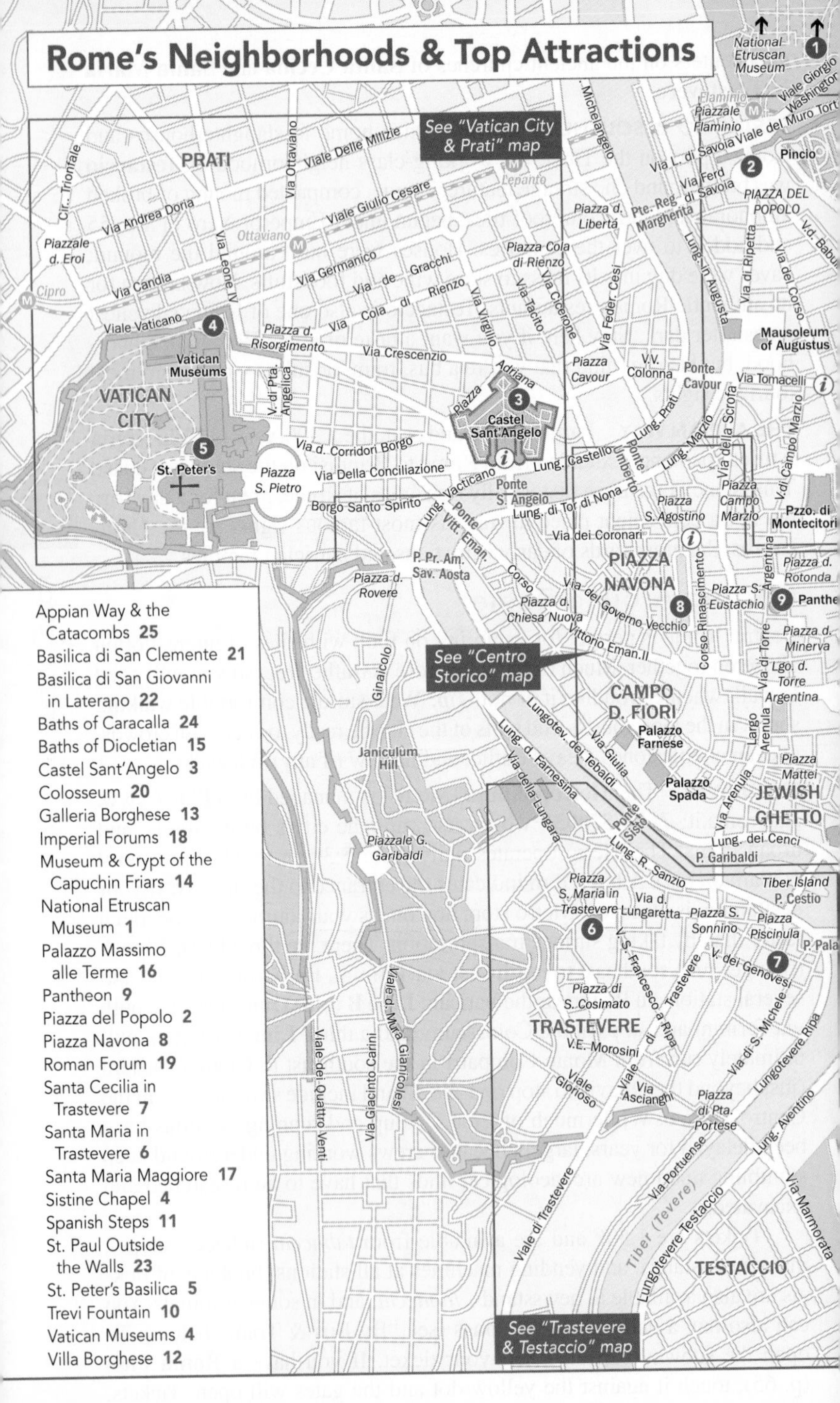
Rome's Neighborhoods & Top Attractions
National Etruscan Museum
Flaminio
Piazzale Flaminio
Viale Giorgio Washington
Viale del Muro Torto
Via L. di Savoia
Pincio
PIAZZA DEL POPOLO
See "Vatican City & Prati" map
Lepanto
PRATI
Cir. Trionfale
Viale Delle Millizie
Via Ottaviano
Viale Giulio Cesare
Via Andrea Doria
Piazzale d. Eroi
Ottaviano
Via Leone IV
Via Candia
Cipro
Via Germanico
Via de Gracchi
Via Cola di Rienzo
Viale Vaticano
Piazza d. Risorgimento
Via Crescenzio
Via Virgilio
Via Tacito
Via Cicerone
Piazza Cola di Rienzo
Via Michelangelo
Piazza d. Libertà
Pte. Reg. Margherita
Via Ferd di Savoia
Lung. in Augusta
Via di Ripetta
Via del Corso
V.d. Babuino
Mausoleum of Augustus
Via Feder. Cesi
Piazza Cavour
V.V. Colonna
Ponte Cavour
Via Tomacelli
Vatican Museums
VATICAN CITY
V. di Pta. Angelica
Piazza Adriana
Castel Sant'Angelo
St. Peter's
Piazza S. Pietro
Via d. Corridori Borgo
Via Della Conciliazione
Borgo Santo Spirito
Lung. Vacticano
Ponte S. Angelo
Lung. Castello
Lung. Prati
Ponte Umberto
Lung. Marzio
Lung. di Tor di Nona
Via della Scrofa
Piazza Campo Marzio
V. di Campo Marzio
Pzzo. di Montecitorio
Piazza S. Agostino
Via dei Coronari
Ponte Vitt. Eman.
P. Pr. Am. Sav. Aosta
Piazza d. Rovere
Corso Vittorio Eman. II
Piazza d. Chiesa Nuova
Via del Governo Vecchio
PIAZZA NAVONA
Corso Rinascimento
Piazza S. Eustachio
Piazza d. Rotonda
Pantheon
Argentina
Piazza d. Minerva
Via di Torre
Lgo. d. Torre Argentina
See "Centro Storico" map
Gianicolo
CAMPO D. FIORI
Palazzo Farnese
Lungotev. dei Tebaldi
Via Giulia
Largo Arenula
Piazza Mattei
Janiculum Hill
Lung. d. Farnesina
Via della Lungara
Palazzo Spada
Via Arenula
JEWISH GHETTO
Ponte Sisto
Lung. dei Cenci
P. Garibaldi
Piazzale G. Garibaldi
Lung. R. Sanzio
Tiber Island
P. Cestio
Piazza S. Maria in Trastevere
Via d. Lungaretta
Piazza S. Sonnino
Piazza Piscinula
P. Pala
V. dei Genovesi
V. S. Francesco a Ripa
Via di Trastevere
Piazza di S. Cosimato
Via di S. Michele
TRASTEVERE
V.E. Morosini
Lungotevere Ripa
Viale Glorioso
Via Ascianghi
Piazza di Pta. Portese
Lung. Aventino
Viale d. Mura Gianicolesi
Via Giacinto Carini
Viale dei Quattro Venti
Viale di Trastevere
Via Portuense
Via Marmorata
Tiber (Tevere)
Lungotevere Testaccio
TESTACCIO
See "Trastevere & Testaccio" map
Appian Way & the Catacombs 25
Basilica di San Clemente 21
Basilica di San Giovanni in Laterano 22
Baths of Caracalla 24
Baths of Diocletian 15
Castel Sant'Angelo 3
Colosseum 20
Galleria Borghese 13
Imperial Forums 18
Museum & Crypt of the Capuchin Friars 14
National Etruscan Museum 1
Palazzo Massimo alle Terme 16
Pantheon 9
Piazza del Popolo 2
Piazza Navona 8
Roman Forum 19
Santa Cecilia in Trastevere 7
Santa Maria in Trastevere 6
Santa Maria Maggiore 17
Sistine Chapel 4
Spanish Steps 11
St. Paul Outside the Walls 23
St. Peter's Basilica 5
Trevi Fountain 10
Vatican Museums 4
Villa Borghese 12

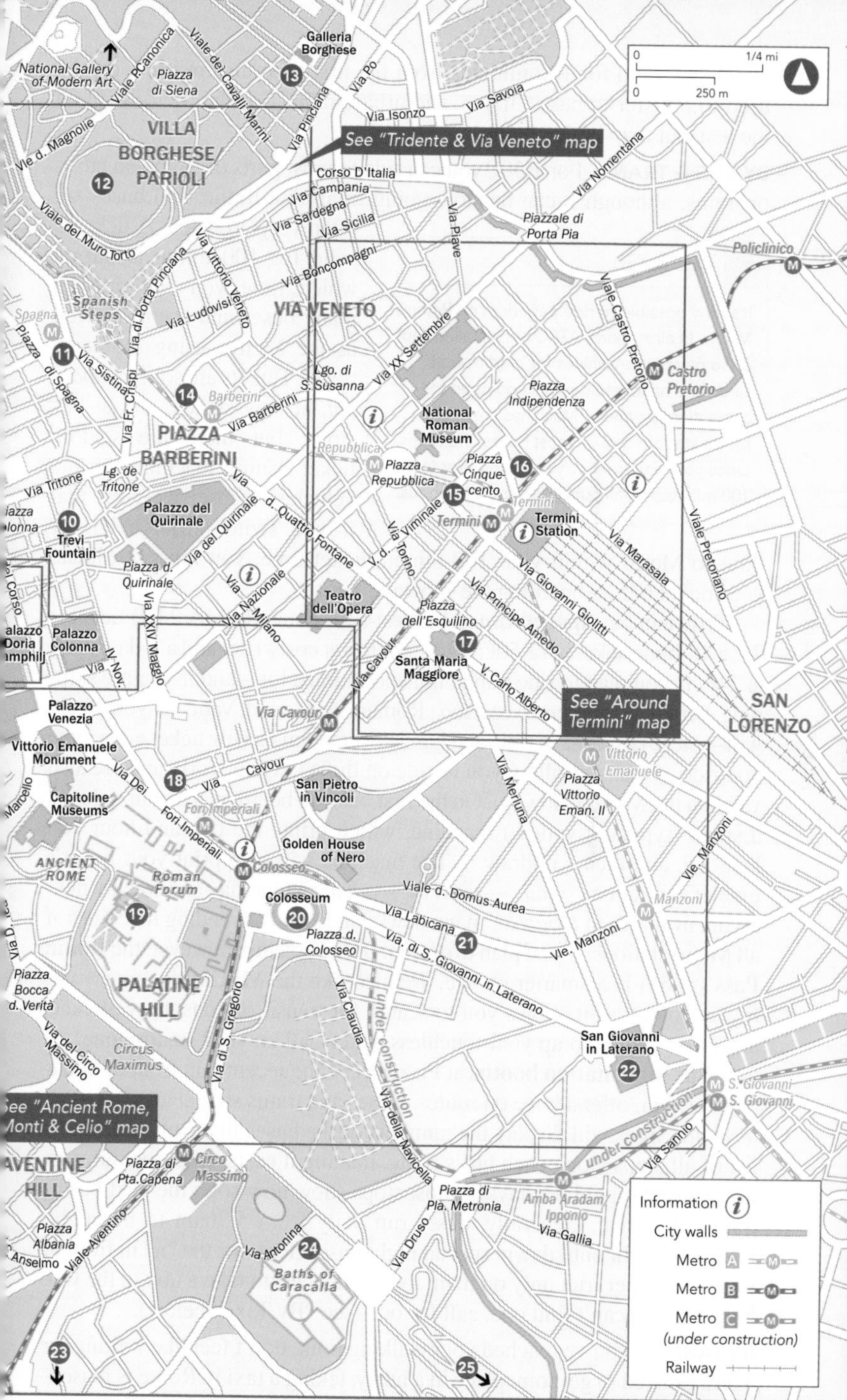

Galleria Borghese
National Gallery of Modern Art
Piazza di Siena
VILLA BORGHESE/PARIOLI
See "Tridente & Via Veneto" map
VIA VENETO
Spanish Steps
PIAZZA BARBERINI
Palazzo del Quirinale
Trevi Fountain
National Roman Museum
Termini Station
Teatro dell'Opera
Santa Maria Maggiore
See "Around Termini" map
SAN LORENZO
Palazzo Colonna
Palazzo Venezia
Vittorio Emanuele Monument
Capitoline Museums
San Pietro in Vincoli
Golden House of Nero
ANCIENT ROME
Roman Forum
Colosseum
PALATINE HILL
Circus Maximus
San Giovanni in Laterano
See "Ancient Rome, Monti & Celio" map
AVENTINE HILL
Baths of Caracalla
0 1/4 mi
0 250 m
Information
City walls
Metro A
Metro B
Metro C
(under construction)
Railway

which are valid for 100 minutes from the first time they're used, can be used to transfer to buses, trams, and urban trains. See the Metro map on the tear-out map in this guide.

BY BUS & TRAM For 1.50€ you can ride to most parts of Rome on buses or trams, although it can be slow going in all that traffic, and buses are often very crowded. A ticket is valid for 100 minutes, during which time you can ride on many buses and trams, as well as the Metro, using the same ticket. Tickets are sold in *tabacchi,* at newsstands, and at bus stops, but there are seldom ticket-issuing machines on the vehicles themselves. Note that if you switch from a bus or tram to Metro within your 100-minute ticket time, you must revalidate your ticket before boarding the subway.

Tap & Go

It's now possible to ride paperless on Rome's Metro. In all stations, ATAC has installed Tap & Go payment machines for credit/debit cards and handheld devices equipped for contactless payment. Machines are in all Metro stations and on most buses and trams. Once you're tapped in, you can ride for up to 100 minutes on all public transport methods.

You can buy **special timed passes:** a 24-hour (ROMA 24H) ticket is 7€; a 48-hour ticket is 12.50€; a 72-hour ticket costs 18€; and a 7-day ticket is 24€. If you plan to ride public transportation a lot—and if you are skipping between the *centro storico,* Roman ruins, and Vatican, you likely will—these passes save time and hassle over buying a new ticket every time you ride. All passes allow you to ride on the ATAC network, and are also valid on the Metro (subway). On the first bus you board, place your ticket in a small (typically yellow) machine, which prints the day and hour you boarded, and then withdraw it. The machine will also print your ticket's time of expiration ("*scad.*"—short for *scadenza*). One-day and weekly tickets are available at *tabacchi,* many newsstands, and at vending machines at all Metro stations. If you plan to do a lot of sightseeing, however, the **Roma Pass** (p. 65) is a smarter choice. We also like the **MyCicero** app (www.mycicero.eu), as it allows you to search for transit options, buy e-tickets and passes, and top up your touchless tickets, all on your smartphone.

Bus information booths at Piazza dei Cinquecento, in front of Stazione Termini, offer advice on routes. Buses and trams stop at areas marked *fermata.* Signs will display the numbers of the buses that stop there and a list of all stops along each bus's route, making it easier to scope out your destination; digital displays at most stops show how soon the next bus or tram will arrive. Generally, buses run daily from 5:30am to midnight. From midnight until dawn, special night buses (look for the "n" in front of the bus number) run only on main routes. It's best to take a taxi in the wee hours; if you can't find one, call for one (see "By Taxi," below).

BY TAXI If you've reached your walking limit, don't feel like waiting for a bus, or need to get someplace in a hurry, taking a taxi in Rome is reasonably affordable compared with other major world cities. Just don't count on hailing a taxi on the street. Instead, have your hotel call one, or if you're at a restaurant, ask the waiter or cashier to dial for you. If you want to phone for yourself, try the **city taxi service** at ✆ **06-0609** (Italian only) or one of the following **radio taxi numbers**, which may or may not have English-speaking operators on duty: ✆ **06-6645, 06-3570,** or **06-4994.** You can also text a taxi at ✆ **366-6730000** by typing the message "Roma [address]" (assuming you know the address in Italian). Taxis on call incur a surcharge of 3.50€. Larger taxi stands are at Piazza Venezia (east side), Piazza di Spagna, the Colosseum, Corso Rinascimento (Piazza Navona), Largo Argentina, the Pantheon, Piazza del Popolo, Piazza Risorgimento (near St. Peter's), and Piazza Belli (Trastevere). We always have luck finding a cab at Piazza di San Pantaleo on Corso Vittorio Emanuele II.

Many taxis accept credit cards, but it's best to check before getting in. Between 6am and 10pm, the meter begins at 3€ (4.50€ Sat–Sun); it starts at 6.50€ between 10pm and 6am. The meter adds 1.10€ per kilometer up to 11€, after which it's 1.30€ to 1.60€ per kilometer, depending on the length of the ride.

The main smartphone app for official city taxis is **it Taxi** (www.ittaxi.it), which is run by Rome's largest taxi company, **3570** (www.3570.it). It allows users to pay directly from the app using a credit card or PayPal. Popular throughout Europe, the **MyTaxi** app offers Uber-like convenience for ordering and prepaying a cab. **Uber** is currently available in Rome in a limited capacity only.

BY CAR All roads may lead to Rome, but you probably won't want to drive once you get here. If you do drive into the city, call or e-mail ahead to your hotel to find out the best route into Rome from wherever you are starting out. You will want to get rid of your rental car as soon as possible, or park it in a garage and leave it there until you depart Rome.

Rome's Key Bus Routes

First, know that any map of the Roman bus system will likely be outdated before it's printed. Second, take extreme caution when riding Rome's busiest buses—pickpockets abound! This is particularly true on bus no. 64, a favorite of visitors because of its route through the historic districts—and thus also a favorite of Rome's pickpocketing community. This bus has earned various nicknames, including the "Pickpocket Express" and "Wallet Eater."

Although routes may change, a few reliable bus routes have remained valid for years in Rome:

- **40 (Express):** Stazione Termini to the Vatican via Via Nazionale, Piazza Venezia and Piazza Pia, by Castel Sant'Angelo
- **64:** The "tourist route" from Termini, along Via Nazionale and through Piazza Venezia and along Via Argentina to Piazza San Pietro in the Vatican
- **75:** Stazione Termini to the Colosseum
- **H:** Stazione Termini via Piazza Venezia and the Ghetto to Trastevere via Ponte Garibaldi

If you want to **rent a car** to explore the countryside around Rome or drive to another city, you'll save money if you reserve before leaving home (see p. 820 in chapter 16). If you decide to book a car here, most major car rental companies have desks inside Stazione Termini. Note that rental cars in Italy may be smaller than what you're used to, particularly in trunk space. Make sure you consider both luggage size and the number of people when booking your vehicle.

[FastFACTS] ROME

Banks In general, banks are open Monday to Friday 8:30am to 1:30pm and 2:30 or 2:45 to 4pm. Note that many banks do not offer currency exchange.

Business Hours Most Roman shops open at 10am and close at 7pm from Monday to Saturday. Smaller shops close for 1 or 2 hours at lunch, and may remain closed Monday morning and Saturday afternoon. Many restaurants are closed for *riposo* (rest) 1 day per week, usually Sunday or Monday.

Dentists **American Dental Arts Rome,** Via del Governo Vecchio 73 (near Piazza Navona; www.adadentistsrome.com; ✆ **06-6832613**), uses the latest technology.

Doctors Call the U.S. Embassy at ✆ **06-46741** for a list of English-speaking doctors. You'll find English-speaking doctors at the privately run **Salvator Mundi International Hospital,** Viale delle Mura Gianicolensi 67 (in the Gianicolo neighborhood; www.salvatormundi.it; ✆ **06-588961**). The **International Medical Center** is on 24-hour duty at Via Firenze 47 (near Piazza della Repubblica; www.imc84.com; ✆ **06-4882371**). **Medi-Call Italia,** Via Cremera 8 (www.medi-call.it; ✆ **06-8840113**) can arrange for a qualified doctor to make a house call at your hotel or anywhere in Rome.

Emergencies To call the police, dial ✆ **113;** for an ambulance ✆ **118;** for a fire ✆ **115.**

Newspapers & Magazines The biweekly English-language expat magazine *Wanted in Rome* (www.wantedinrome.com) lists current events and shows.

Pharmacies Easily recognizable by their neon green or red cross signs, *farmacie* are generally open 8:30am to 1pm and 4 to 7:30pm, though some stay open later. **Farmacia Piram** at Via Nazionale 228 is open 24 hours. All closed pharmacies have signs in their windows indicating any open pharmacies nearby.

Police Dial ✆ **113.**

Safety Walking alone at night is usually fine anywhere in the *centro storico.* Violent crime is virtually nonexistent in Rome's touristed areas, though pickpocketing is common. Purse snatching happens on occasion, often by perps speeding by on scooters; keep your purse on the wall side of your body with the strap across your chest. Other pickpockets dress like typical businesspeople, so always be suspicious of anyone who tries to "befriend" you in a tourist area. Thieves will also strike where you may least expect it, such as in crowded paid areas like the Colosseum or Vatican Museums.

EXPLORING ROME

Rome's ancient monuments are a constant reminder that this was one of the greatest centers of Western civilization. In the heyday of the Empire, all roads led to Rome, with good reason. It was one of the first cosmopolitan cities, importing food, textiles, slaves, gladiators, great art, and even

St. Peter's Basilica and the Vatican, viewed from the Tiber River.

citizens from the far corners of the world. Despite its brutality and corruption, Rome left a legacy of law, art, architecture, and engineering—and a canny lesson in how to conquer enemies by absorbing their cultures.

But ancient Rome is only part of the spectacle. The Vatican has had a tremendous influence on making the city a tourism center. Although Vatican architects in the Renaissance stripped down much of the city's ancient glory, looting ruins (the Forum especially) for their precious marble, they created more treasures and occasionally incorporated the old into the new—as Michelangelo did when turning Diocletian's Baths complex into a church. And in the years that followed, Bernini adorned the city with baroque wonders, especially his glorious fountains.

Bypassing the Lines

It used to be that going to Rome's three biggest attractions—the Colosseum, the Vatican Museums, and St. Peter's Basilica—meant waiting in long, long lines. Now thanks to advance ticket sales for timed entry, there's no reason to wait in excessively long lines for the Colosseum or the Vatican Museums. (See individual listings for more details.) St. Peter's, however, still offers no skip-the-line perk. The only way to jump the line here is with the **Omnia Card** (see p. 65) or by booking a private or group tour (p. 122).

St. Peter's & the Vatican

VATICAN CITY

The world's smallest sovereign state, **Vatican City** is a truly tiny territory, comprising little more than St. Peter's Basilica, the Vatican Museums, and the walled headquarters of the Roman Catholic Church. While there are no border controls, the city-state's 800 inhabitants (essentially clergymen and Swiss Guards) have their own radio station, daily newspaper, tax-free pharmacy and petrol pumps, postal service, and head of state—the Pope. The Pope had always exercised a high degree of political independence from the rest of Italy, formalized by the 1929 Lateran Treaty between Pope Pius XI and the Italian government to create the Vatican. The city is still protected by the flamboyantly uniformed (allegedly their outfits were designed by Michelangelo) Swiss Guards, a tradition dating from when the Swiss, known as brave soldiers, were often hired out as mercenaries for foreign armies. Today the Vatican remains the center of the Roman Catholic world, the home of the Pope—and the resting place of St. Peter. **St. Peter's Basilica** is obviously one of the highlights, but the only part of the Apostolic Palace itself that you can visit independently is the **Vatican Museums,** the world's biggest and richest museum complex.

On the left side of Piazza San Pietro, the **Vatican Tourist Office** (www.vatican.va; ✆ **06-69882019;** Mon–Sat 8:30am–6:30pm) sells maps and guides that will help you make sense of the treasures in the museums; it also accepts reservations for tours of the Vatican Gardens. Adjacent to the information office, the **Vatican Post Office** sells special Vatican postage stamps (Mon–Sat 8:30am–6pm).

The only entrance to St. Peter's for tourists is through one of the glories of the Western world: Bernini's 17th-century **St. Peter's Square** (Piazza San Pietro). As you stand in the huge piazza, you are in the arms

Making the Most of a Day in Vatican City

Most Vatican visitors allot a day to see its two major sights, **St. Peter's Basilica** and the **Vatican Museums** (including the Sistine Chapel). We recommend starting with the museums. **Pre-order** tickets for the earliest time slot (from 9am) available the day you wish to visit. Plan to devote several hours to see the highlights of the museum collections (see p. 80).

Next, grab a quick late lunch, either in the museum cafeteria or at a nearby sandwich shop or pizza joint. The streets leading from the museum exit to St. Peter's Basilica are lined with cheap eateries—mostly mediocre, but they'll do in a pinch. (See p. 137 for some notably good options.)

Once you enter **St. Peter's Square,** head to the back of the line (always long, but it moves fairly quickly) to enter the basilica. From the time you enter the basilica, you'll need at least 1 hour for even the most cursory tour.

By now it'll be late afternoon, and you've got two options: Visit the **Vatican Grottoes,** burial place of dozens of popes, or climb the 551 steps (320 if you take the elevator) to the top of the **dome of St. Peter's.** Note that the dome and grottoes are open until 6pm April to September, 5pm October to March. If you've still got energy, head to nearby **Castel Sant'Angelo** (see p. 86)—the view of Rome from the castle's roof is a perfect way to cap off your marathon Vatican day.

Want more time at the Vatican Museums? Arrive at St. Peter's early in the morning to get in line before it opens at 7am; that way you can tour the basilica before the crowds show up. Then head to a late morning appointment at the museums and spend the rest of the day there.

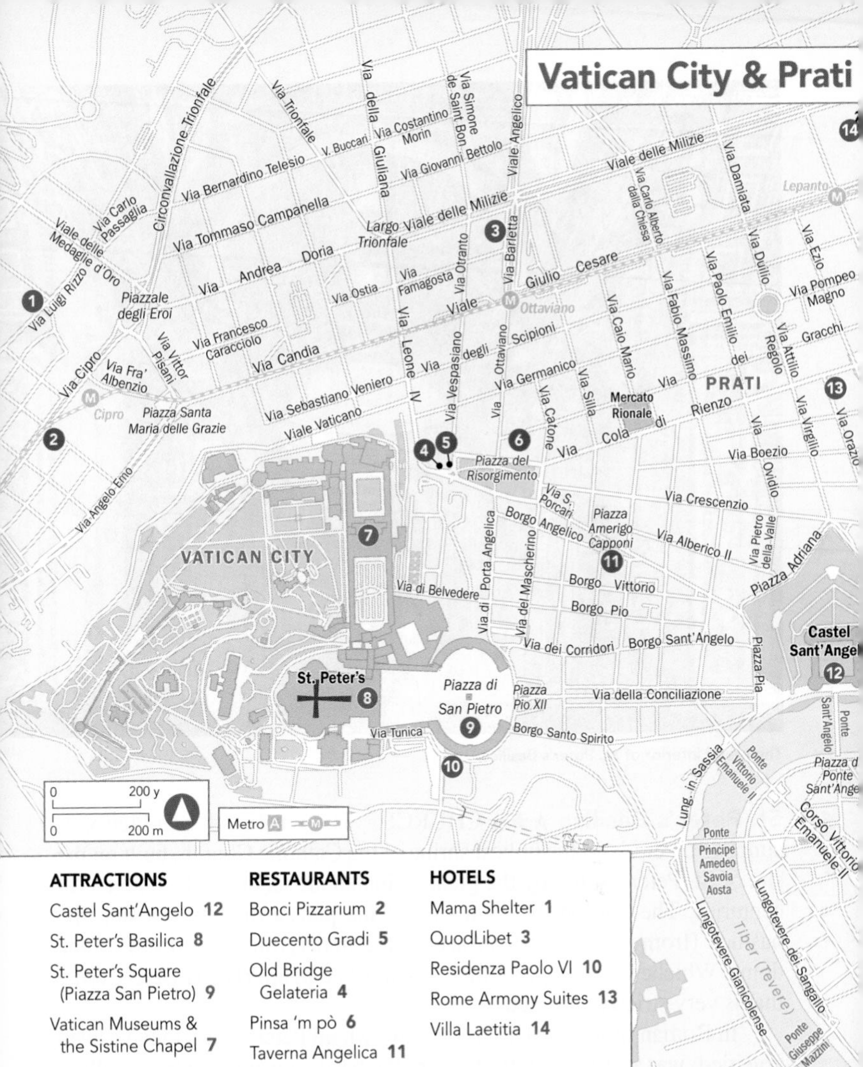

of an ellipse partly enclosed by a majestic **Doric-pillared colonnade.** Stand in the marked marble discs embedded in the pavement near the fountains to see all the columns lined up in a striking optical/geometrical play. Straight ahead is the facade of St. Peter's itself and to the right, above the colonnade, the dark brown buildings of the **papal apartments** and the Vatican Museums. In the center of the square stands a 4,000-year-old **Egyptian obelisk,** created in the ancient city of Heliopolis on the Nile Delta and appropriated by the Romans under Emperor Augustus. Flanking the obelisk are two 17th-century **fountains.** The one on the right (facing the basilica), by Carlo Maderno, who designed the facade of St. Peter's, was placed here by Bernini himself; the other is by Carlo Fontana.

The grand interior of St. Peter's Basilica.

St. Peter's Basilica ★★★ CHURCH The Basilica di San Pietro, or simply St. Peter's, is the holiest shrine of the Catholic Church, built on the site of St. Peter's tomb by the greatest Italian artists of the 16th and 17th centuries. The line on the right side of the piazza funnels you into the basilica (from where you can access the underground grottoes) or the dome. Whichever you opt for first, you must be **properly dressed**—a rule that is very strictly enforced.

In Roman times, the Circus of Nero, where Peter is said to have been crucified, was just to the left of where the basilica is today. He was allegedly buried here in A.D. 64, and in A.D. 324 Emperor Constantine commissioned a church to be built over Peter's tomb. That structure stood for more than 1,000 years. The present basilica, mostly completed in the 1500s and 1600s, is predominantly High Renaissance and baroque. Inside, the massive scale is almost too much to absorb, showcasing some of

A St. Peter's Warning

St. Peter's has a hard-and-fast dress code that makes no exceptions: **Men and women in shorts, above-the-knee skirts, or bare shoulders** are not admitted to the basilica, period, and **hats should be off.** I've occasionally seen guards handing out disposable cloaks for the scantily clad, but don't count on that: Cover up or bring a shawl. The same holds for the Roman Necropolis and the Vatican Museums.

Italy's greatest artists: Bramante, Raphael, and Michelangelo. In a church of such grandeur—overwhelming in its detail of gilt, marble, and mosaic—you can't expect much subtlety. It is meant to be overpowering.

Going straight into the basilica, the first thing you see on the right side of the nave—the longest nave in the world, as clearly marked in the floor along with other cathedral measurements—is the chapel containing Michelangelo's graceful **"Pietà" ★★★**. Created in the 1490s when the master was still in his 20s, it clearly shows his genius for capturing the human form. (The sculpture has been kept behind reinforced glass since an act of vandalism in the 1970s.) Note the lifelike folds of Mary's robes and her youthful features; although she would've been middle-aged at the time of the Crucifixion, Michelangelo portrayed her as a young woman to convey her purity. A few yards past the Pieta is a chapel housing the **tomb of Pope John Paul II.**

Further inside the nave, Michelangelo's dome is a mesmerizing space, rising high above the supposed site of St. Peter's tomb. With a diameter of 41.5m (136 ft.), the dome is Rome's largest, supported by four bulky piers decorated with reliefs depicting the basilica's key holy relics: St. Veronica's handkerchief (used to wipe the face of Christ); the lance of St. Longinus, which pierced Christ's side; and a piece of the True Cross. The fourth relic, St. Andrew's skull, is now in Patras, Greece. Under the dome, a twisty-columned **baldacchino ★★** by Bernini shelters the papal altar. The ornate 29m-high (96-ft.) canopy was created in part, so it is said, from bronze stripped from the Pantheon. Bernini sculpted the face of a woman on the base of each pillar; starting with the face on the left pillar (with your back to the entrance), circle the entire altar to see the progress of expressions from the agony of childbirth through to the fourth pillar, where the woman's face is replaced with that of her newborn baby.

Just before reaching the dome, on the right, the devout stop to touch or kiss the foot of the 13th-century **bronze of St. Peter ★**, attributed to Arnolfo di Cambio. Elsewhere the church is decorated by more of Bernini's lavish sculptures, including his monument to Pope Alexander VII in the south transept, its winged skeleton writhing under the heavy marble drapes.

An entrance off the nave leads to the Sacristy and the **Historical Museum** (Museo Storico) or **treasury ★**, which is chock-full of richly jeweled chalices, reliquaries, and copes, as well as the late-15th-century bronze tomb of Pope Sixtus IV by Pollaiuolo.

An entrance to the left of the baldacchino leads down to the **Vatican grottoes ★★**, with their tombs of the popes, both ancient and modern. There, behind a wall of glass, is what is considered to be the tomb of St. Peter.

After you leave the grottoes, you find yourself in a courtyard and ticket line for the grandest sight in the basilica: the climb to **Michelangelo's dome ★★★**, about 114m (375 ft.) high. You can walk all the way up or take the elevator as far as it goes (this saves you 171 steps). At this first stop, you can walk on the roof of the basilica (where there's also a restroom, a snack bar, and a gift shop) and also around the interior of the drum of the dome, which offers a bird's-eye view of the basilica below. After that, you *still* have 320 stairs to go to reach the very top. (Claustrophobes take note: The last part of the climb is up a very narrow spiral staircase.) At the top, you'll have a scintillating view over the rooftops of Rome and even the Vatican Gardens and papal apartments. The elevator back down drops you in the basilica interior, near the front entrance, or you can descend via a spiral ramp, its walls lined with inscriptions recalling famous visitors to the dome.

Visits to the **Necropolis Vaticana ★★** and St. Peter's tomb itself are restricted to 250 persons per day on guided tours (90 min.). You must send a fax or e-mail at least 3 weeks beforehand, or apply in advance in person at the Ufficio Scavi (✆/fax **06-69873017;** e-mail scavi@fsp.va; Mon–Fri 9am–6pm, Sat 9am–2pm), located through the arch to the left of the stairs up from the basilica. For details, check www.scavi.va/content/scavi/en/ufficio-scavi.html. Children 14 and under are not admitted to the Necropolis.

An Unofficial Assist

Though it's not an official portal for Vatican City, the independent website **stpeters basilica.info** offers a wealth of current, detailed, and helpful information for navigating your way through St. Peter's and its associated components.

Piazza San Pietro. www.vatican.va. ✆ **06-69881662.** Basilica (including grottoes) free. Necropolis Vaticana (St. Peter's tomb) 13€. Stairs to the dome 8€; elevator (partway) to the dome 10€; sacristy (with Historical Museum) 5€ adults, 3€ 12 and under. **Basilica** daily 7am–7pm (closes 6:30pm Oct–Mar). **Dome** daily 7:30am–6pm (closes 5pm Oct–Mar). ***Note:*** Basilica may not open until noon or 1pm on Wed when papal audience is in square. **Sacristy/museum** 9am–6:15pm (closes 5:15pm Oct–Mar). **Grottoes** 7am–6pm (closes 5pm Oct–Mar). Metro: Ottaviano/San Pietro, then a 10-min. walk; or bus 40, 46, or 62 to Piazza Pia/Traspontina, then a 10-min. walk.

Vatican Museums & the Sistine Chapel ★★★ MUSEUM Nothing else in Rome quite lives up to the awe-inspiring collections of the **Vatican Museums,** a 15-minute walk from St. Peter's out of the north side of Piazza San Pietro. It's a vast treasure store of art from antiquity and the Renaissance gathered by the Roman Catholic Church through the centuries, filling a series of ornate Papal palaces, apartments, and galleries leading to one of the world's most beautiful interiors, the justly celebrated **Sistine Chapel.** Obviously, one trip is not enough to see everything here. Below are previews of the main highlights, showstoppers, and masterpieces (in alphabetical order).

Note: the Vatican dress code also applies to its museums (no sleeveless blouses, no miniskirts, no shorts, no hats allowed), though it tends to be less rigorously enforced than at St. Peter's.

APPARTAMENTO BORGIA ★ Created for Pope Alexander VI (the infamous Borgia pope) between 1492 and 1494, these rooms were frescoed

Fontana Della Pigna in the courtyard of the Vatican Museum.

with biblical and allegorical scenes by Umbrian painter Pinturicchio and his assistants. Look for what is thought to be the earliest European depiction of Native Americans, painted little more than a year after Columbus returned from the New World and Alexander had "divided" the globe between Spain and Portugal.

COLLEZIONE D'ARTE CONTEMPORANEA ★ Spanning 55 rooms of almost 800 works, these galleries contain the Vatican's concession to modern art. There are some big names here, and the quality is high. Themes usually have a spiritual and religious component: Van Gogh's "Pietà, after Delacroix" is here, along with Francis Bacon's eerie "Study for a Pope II." You will also see works by Paul Klee ("City with Gothic Cathedral"), Siqueiros ("Mutilated Christ No. 467"), Otto Dix ("Road to Calvary"), Gauguin ("Religious Panel"), Chagall ("Red Pietà"), and a whole room dedicated to Georges Rouault.

MUSEI DI ANTICHITÀ CLASSICHE ★★★ The Vatican maintains four classical antiquities museums, the most important being the **Museo Pio Clementino ★★★**, crammed with Greek and Roman sculptures in the small Belvedere Palace of Innocent VIII. At the heart of the complex lies the Octagonal Court, where highlights include the sculpture of the Trojan priest **"Laocoön" ★★★** and his two sons locked in a doomed struggle with sea serpents, dating from around 40 B.C., and the exceptional

papal AUDIENCES

When the pope is in Rome, he gives a public audience every Wednesday beginning at 9:30am. If you want to get a good seat near the front, arrive early and prepare to wait—security begins to let people in between 7 and 7:30am, but the line starts much earlier. Audiences take place in the Paul VI Hall of Audiences, although sometimes St. Peter's Basilica and St. Peter's Square are used to accommodate a large attendance in the summer. You can check on Pope Francis's appearances and the ceremonies he presides over, including celebrations of Mass, on the Vatican website (www.vatican.va). Anyone is welcome, but you must first obtain a **free ticket;** without a reservation you can try the Swiss Guards by the Bronze Doors located just after security at St. Peter's (8am–8pm in summer and 8am–7pm in winter). You can pick up tickets here up to 3 days in advance, subject to availability.

If you prefer to reserve a place in advance, visit www.vatican.va/various/prefettura/index_en.html to download a request form, which must be submitted via fax (yes, really) to the **Prefecture of the Papal Household** at **✆ 06-69885863.** Tickets can be picked up at the office just inside the Bronze Doors from 3 to 7pm on the preceding day or on the morning of the audience from 7am.

At noon on Sundays, the pope speaks briefly from his study window and gives his blessing to visitors and pilgrims gathered in St. Peter's Square (no tickets are required for this). From about mid-July to mid-September, the Angelus and blessing historically takes place at the pope's summer residence at **Castel Gandolfo,** some 26km (16 miles) out of Rome. Under Pope Francis, the residence, gardens, and villas of the castle have been opened to visitors as a museum, accessible via Metro and bus as well as a new train service that leaves from the Roma San Pietro station. Visit biglietteriamusei.vatican.va for information on seeing Castel Gandolfo by train.

"Belvedere Apollo" ★★★ (a 2nd-c. Roman reproduction of a Greek work from the 4th c. B.C.), the symbol of classic male beauty and a possible inspiration for Michelangelo's "David." Look for the impressive gilded bronze statue of **"Hercules"** (late A.D. 2nd c.) in the Rotonda, and the **Hall of the Chariot,** containing a magnificent sculpture of a chariot combining Roman originals and 18th-century work by Francesco Antonio Franzoni.

The **Museo Chiaramonti** ★ occupies the long loggia that links the Belvedere Palace to the main Vatican palaces, jam-packed on both sides with more than 800 Greco-Roman works, including statues, reliefs, and sarcophagi. In the **Braccio Nuovo** ★ (New Wing), a handsome Neoclassical extension sumptuously lined with colored marble, lies the colossal statue of the **"Nile"** ★, the ancient river portrayed as an old man with his 16 children, most likely a reproduction of a long-lost Alexandrian Greek original.

The **Museo Gregoriano Profano** ★★, built in 1970, houses more Greek sculptures looted by the Romans (some from the Parthenon), mostly funerary steles and votive reliefs, as well as some choice Roman pieces, notably the restored mosaics from the floors of the public libraries in the **Baths of Caracalla** (p. 95).

MUSEO ETNOLOGICO ★★ Founded in 1926, the Ethnological Museum is an astounding assemblage of artifacts and artwork from cultures around the world, from ancient Chinese coins and notes to plaster sculptures of Native Americans and ceremonial art from Papua New Guinea.

MUSEO GREGORIANO EGIZIO ★★ Nine rooms are packed with plunder from Ancient Egypt, including sarcophagi, mummies, pharaonic statuary, votive bronzes, jewelry, cuneiform tablets from Mesopotamia, inscriptions from Assyrian palaces, and Egyptian hieroglyphics.

MUSEO GREGORIANO ETRUSCO ★★ The core of this collection is a cache of rare Etruscan art treasures dug up in the 19th century, dating from between the 9th and the 1st centuries B.C. The Romans learned a lot from the Etruscans, as the highly crafted ceramics, bronzes, silver, and gold on display attest. Don't miss the **Regolini-Galassi tomb** (7th c. B.C.), unearthed at Cerveteri. The museum is housed within the *palazzettos* of Innocent VIII (reigned 1484–92) and Pius IV (reigned 1559–65), the latter adorned with frescoes by Federico Barocci and Federico Zuccari.

PINACOTECA ★★★ The great painting collections of the popes are displayed in the Pinacoteca, including work from all the big names in Italian art, from Giotto and Fra Angelico to Perugino, Raphael, Veronese, and Crespi. Early medieval work occupies Room 1, with the most intriguing piece a keyhole-shaped wood panel of the "Last Judgment" by Nicolò e

Strategies for Visiting the Vatican Museums

The sheer size of the collections and vast crowds mean that seeing one of the greatest museums of art in the world isn't a leisurely, or even pleasant, experience. Visitors tend to get herded through room after room of galleries as they make their way to the Sistine Chapel, and lack of descriptive labels means they often don't know what they're looking at. Here are some tips to make sense of it all:

- Book **timed-entry** tickets in advance through the Vatican Museums website and avoid the risk of finding either a long entrance line or the museum at capacity.
- Do some advance research and decide which collections you most want to see.
- Once you're in the museum, take a few minutes to review the galleries map and map out your visit.
- If your priority is to see the Sistine Chapel, follow signs for the "Percorso Breve" (short route) to the Cappella Sistina.

For a deeper experience, consider a breakfast or after-hours visit (p. 86) or springing for a private tour of the collections. These are a great way to get the most out of a visit, especially if you have limited time. They're also the only way to visit the **Vatican Gardens.** Booking online is mandatory; visit **bigliettiamusei.vatican.va/musei/tickets** for information. See "Organized Tours" (p. 122) for info on private companies offering Vatican tours.

Giovanni, dated to the late 12th century. **Giotto** takes center stage in Room 2, with the "Stefaneschi Triptych" (six panels) painted for the old St. Peter's basilica between 1315 and 1320. **Fra Angelico** dominates Room 3, his "Stories of St. Nicholas of Bari" and "Virgin with Child" justly praised (check out the Virgin's microscopic eyes in the latter piece). Carlo Crivelli features in Room 6, and decent works by Perugino and Pinturicchio grace Room 7, but most visitors press on to the **Raphael salon ★★★** (Room 8), where you can view five paintings by the Renaissance master. The best are the "Coronation of the Virgin," the "Madonna of Foligno," and the vast "Transfiguration" (completed shortly before his death). Room 9 boasts Leonardo da Vinci's **"St. Jerome with the Lion" ★★**, as well as Giovanni Bellini's "Pietà." Room 10 is dedicated to Renaissance Venice, with Titian's "Madonna of St. Nicholas of the Frari" and Veronese's "Vision of St. Helen" being paramount. Don't skip the remaining galleries: Room 11 contains Barocci's "Annunciation," while Room 12 is really all about one of the masterpieces of the baroque, Caravaggio's **"Deposition from the Cross" ★★**.

STANZE DI RAFFAELLO ★★★ In the early 16th century, Pope Julius II hired the young Raphael and his workshop to decorate his personal apartments, on the second floor of the Pontifical Palace. Completed between 1508 and 1524, the **Raphael Rooms** now represent one of the great artistic spectacles inside the Vatican.

The **Stanza dell'Incendio** served as the Pope's high court room and later, under Leo X, a dining room. Most of its lavish frescoes have been attributed to Raphael's pupils. Leo X commissioned much of the work here, which explains the themes (past Popes named Leo). Note the intricate ceiling, painted by Umbrian maestro Perugino, Raphael's first teacher.

Raphael is the main focus in the **Stanza della Segnatura,** originally used as a Papal library and private office; here you'll find the awe-inspiring **"School of Athens" ★★★** fresco, depicting primarily Greek classical philosophers such as Aristotle, Plato, and Socrates. Many of the figures are thought to be based on portraits of Renaissance artists, including Bramante (on the right as Euclid, drawing on a chalkboard), Leonardo da Vinci (as Plato, the bearded man in the center), and Raphael himself (in the lower-right corner with a black hat). On the wall opposite stands the equally magnificent "Disputa del Sacramento," where Raphael used a similar technique; Dante Alighieri stands behind the pontiff on the right, and Fra Angelico poses as a monk (which in fact, he was) on the far left.

The **Stanza d'Eliodoro,** where the Pope held private audiences, was painted by Raphael immediately after he did the Segnatura. His aim here was to flatter his papal patron, Julius II: The pope is depicted driving Attila from Rome, symbolizing Julius II's mission to drive the French out of Italy. Finally, the **Sala di Costantino,** used for Papal receptions and official ceremonies, was completed by Raphael's students after his death, but based on his designs and drawings. It's a jaw-dropping space, commemorating four major episodes in the life of Emperor Constantine.

SISTINE CHAPEL ★★★ Michelangelo labored for 4 years (1508–12) to paint the ceiling of the Sistine Chapel; it is said he spent the entire time on his feet, paint dripping into his eyes. Could he have imagined that more than 500 years later, his magnum opus would still be considered one of the greatest accomplishments in Western art? Today, the world's most famous fresco is as vibrantly colorful and filled with roiling life as it was in 1512. And the chapel is still of central importance to the Catholic Church: This is where the Papal Conclave meets to elect new popes.

The "Creation of Adam," at the center of the ceiling, is one of the best known and most reproduced images in history, the outstretched hands of God and Adam—not quite touching—an iconic symbol of not just the Renaissance but the Enlightenment that followed. Nevertheless, it is somewhat ironic that this is Michelangelo's best-known work: The artist always regarded himself as a sculptor first and foremost.

Tip: The ceiling **frescoes** are obviously the main showstoppers, but staring up at them tends to take a heavy toll on the neck. To relieve your neck (and your tired feet), make your way to one of the benches that line both long sides of the gallery. As soon as someone gets up, grab a seat so you can gaze upward in relative comfort.

Commissioned by Pope Julius II in 1508 and completed in 1512, the ceiling frescoes primarily depict nine scenes from the Book of Genesis (including the famed "Creation of Adam"), from the "Separation of Light and Darkness" at the altar end to the "Great Flood" and "Drunkenness of Noah." Surrounding these main frescoes are paintings of 12 people who prophesied the coming of Christ, from Jonah and Isaiah to the Delphic Sibyl. Once you have admired the ceiling, turn your attention to the altar wall. At the age of 60, Michelangelo was summoned to finish the chapel decor 23 years after he finished the ceiling work. Apparently saddened by leaving Florence, and depressed by the morally bankrupt state of Rome at that time, he painted these dark moods in his "Last Judgment," where he included his own self-portrait on a sagging human hide held by St. Bartholomew (who was martyred by being flayed alive).

Yet the Sistine Chapel isn't all Michelangelo. The southern wall is covered by a series of astonishing paintings completed in the 1480s: "Moses Leaving to Egypt" by Perugino, the "Trials of Moses" by Botticelli, "The Crossing of the Red Sea" by Cosimo Rosselli (or Domenico Ghirlandaio), "Descent from Mount Sinai" by Cosimo Rosselli (or Piero di Cosimo), Botticelli's "Punishment of the Rebels," and Signorelli's "Testament and Death of Moses." On the right-hand northern wall are Perugino's "The Baptism of Christ," Botticelli's "The Temptations of Christ," Ghirlandaio's "Vocation of the Apostles," Perugino's "Delivery of the Keys," and Cosimo Rosselli's "The Sermon on the Mount" and "Last Supper." On the eastern wall, originals by Ghirlandaio and Signorelli

Seeing the Vatican After Hours...or for Breakfast

Vatican Museum visitors have an extraordinary opportunity to stroll through the galleries after closing time or before galleries open to the public, on guided tours that include the Raphael Rooms, the Sistine Chapel, and other areas. Morning visits begin or end with an American breakfast service, while evening visits conclude with happy hour, both served in the museum. There is a long menu of tour options on the museum website; be sure to read the tour descriptions in order to pick the right one. Prices for these special tours start at 40€ per person and include museum admission.

were painted over in the 1570s by Hendrik van den Broeck's "The Resurrection" and Matteo da Lecce's "Disputation over Moses."

Vatican City, Viale Vaticano (walk around Vatican walls from St. Peter's Sq.). www.museivaticani.va. ✆ **06-69884676. Advance booking with timed entrance is strongly recommended.** 17€ adults; 8€ ages 6–13; free for children 5 and under; 2-hr. tours of Vatican Gardens 34€ (no tours Wed or Sun). Advance tickets (reservation fee 5€) and guided tours (35€ per person) through biglietteriamusei.vatican.va. Mon–Sat 9am–6pm (ticket office closes 4pm), last Sun every month 9am–2pm (free admission). Closed Jan 1 and 6, Feb 11, Mar 19, Easter, May 1, June 29, Aug 15, Nov 1, Dec 8, and Dec 25–26. Metro: Ottaviano or Cipro–Musei Vaticani. Buses 23 and 492 to Bastioni di Michelangelo (3-min. walk from entrance), or buses 590, 982, and 19 tram to Piazza del Risorgimento (10-min. walk from entrance).

Castel Sant'Angelo ★★ CASTLE/PALACE Over the years, this bulky cylindrical fortress on the Vatican side of the Tiber has had many lives: as the mausoleum tomb of Emperor Hadrian in A.D. 138; as a papal residence in the 14th century; as a castle, where in 1527 Pope Clement VII hid from the looting troops of Charles V; and as a military prison from the 17th century on. Consider renting an audioguide at the entrance to fully appreciate its various manifestations.

From the entrance a stone ramp *(rampa elicoidale)* winds to the upper terraces, where you can see amazing views of the city and enjoy a coffee at the outdoor cafe. The sixth floor features the **Terrazza dell'Angelo,** crowned by a florid 18th-century statue of the Archangel Michael. It's famous to opera fans—the last act of Puccini's "Tosca" is set here.

From here you can walk back down through five floors. On levels 3 to 5 you'll see the Renaissance apartments used by some of Rome's most infamous popes, including Alexander VI, the Borgia pope. Below the apartments are the grisly dungeons **(Le Prigioni)** used as torture chambers in the medieval period (Cesare Borgia made great use of them). The castle is connected to St. Peter's Basilica by **Il Passetto di Borgo,** a walled passage built in 1277 by Pope Nicholas III, used by popes who needed to make a quick escape to the fortress in times of danger.

Lungotevere Castello 50. www.castelsantangelo.com. ✆ **06-32810.** 15€. Daily 9am–7:30pm. Bus: 23, 40, 62, 280, 982 (to Piazza Pia).

The Colosseum, Forum & Ancient Rome

THE MAJOR SIGHTS OF ANCIENT ROME

Your sightseeing experience will be enhanced if you know a little about the history and rulers of Ancient Rome: See p. 18 for a brief rundown.

Arco di Costantino ★★ MONUMENT The photogenic triumphal arch next to the Colosseum was erected by the Senate in A.D. 315 to honor Constantine's defeat of the pagan Maxentius at the Battle of the Milvian Bridge (A.D. 312). Many of the reliefs have nothing whatsoever to do with Constantine or his works, but they tell of the victories of earlier Antonine rulers (lifted from other, long-forgotten memorials).

The arch marks a period of great change in the history of Rome. Converted to Christianity by a vision on the eve of battle, Constantine ended the centuries-long persecution of the Christians, during which many followers of the new religion had been put to death in a gruesome manner. Although Constantine didn't ban paganism (which survived officially for another half century or so), he espoused Christianity himself and began the process that ended in the conquest of Rome by the Christian religion.
Btw. Colosseum and Palatine Hill. Metro: Colosseo. Bus: 51, 85, 87, 118. Tram: 3.

Circus Maximus ★ HISTORIC SITE Today mostly a long, oval-shaped field, the once-grand circus was pilfered by medieval and Renaissance builders in search of marble and stone—it's a far cry from its *Ben-Hur*-esque heyday. What the Romans called a "circus" was a large arena ringed by tiers of seats and used for sports or spectacles. At one time, 300,000 Romans could assemble here, while the emperor observed the games from his box high on the Palatine Hill. The last games were held in A.D. 549 on the orders of Totilla the Goth, who had seized Rome twice. Afterwards, the Circus Maximus was never used again, and the demand for building materials reduced it, like so much of Rome, to a great dusty field, now used mostly for big-name rock concerts. An archaeological area at its eastern end (closest to the Metro station) offers insights into how the space once functioned. A 40-minute virtual reality tour (12€, including site admission) is available at various times during the year; see www.circomaximoexperience.it for info. ***Tip:*** If you're crunched for time,

Strategies for Seeing Ancient Rome

Even though they're all included in the same admission fee, the ruins of the **Colosseum, Roman Forum,** and **Palatine Hill** are quite a lot to take in on a single day, particularly in the heat of the Roman summer. But if a day is all you have budgeted, buy your tickets well in advance so that you can choose the earliest morning entry to the Colosseum. Then you'll have the rest of the day for the Forum and Palatine Hill. If you've got a little more time (and interest), buy the 2-day Full Experience ticket (22€), which also gets you access to the S.U.P.E.R. sites (see p. 88).

bypass the Circus Maximus and instead take in the emperor's-eye-views of the arena from atop the Palatine Hill.

Btw. Via dei Cerchi and Via del Circo Massimo. www.sovraintendenzaroma.it (search "Circo Massimo" then translate). ✆ **060608**. Archaeological area 5€. Tues–Sun 9:30am–7pm summer (last entrance 6pm), to 5pm winter. Metro: Circo Massimo. Bus: 81, 118, 160.

Colosseum ★★★ ICON No matter how many pictures you've seen, your first view of the Flavian Amphitheater (the Colosseum's original name) is likely to amaze you with its sheer size and ruined grandeur. While you're still outside its massive walls, take time to walk completely around its 500m (1,640-ft.) circumference. It doesn't matter where you start, but do the circle. Look at the various stages of ruin; note the different column styles on each level. Mere photos could never convey its physical impact.

Vespasian ordered the construction of the elliptical bowl in A.D. 72; it was inaugurated by Titus in A.D. 80. Built for gladiatorial contests and wild animal fights, the stadium could hold as many as 87,000 spectators by some counts; seats were sectioned on three levels, dividing the people by social rank and gender. Some 80 entrances allowed the massive crowds to be seated and dispersed within a few minutes. When the Roman Empire fell, however, the abandoned arena was eventually overgrown. Much of the travertine that once sheathed its outside was used for palaces like the nearby Palazzo Venezia and Palazzo Cancelleria.

An ongoing conservation effort, funded in large part by the Italian design house Tod's, has scoured 2,000 years of soot from the monument's exterior and opened restored areas previously closed to the public, including the **Arena Floor and Underground,** which were formerly open only by guided or private tour. (The upper tier, called the **Belvedere,** is open periodically but is closed as of this writing.) The arena floor/underground area is ticketed separately from standard Colosseum admission and is *not* included with the RomaPass. There are a number of different options, but the two pertinent to most visitors are the Ordinary (also called Regular) and Full Experience tickets. Ordinary tickets (18€) are good for 24 hours from their first activation and include admission to the Colosseum, Roman Forum, and Palatine Hill. Full Experience tickets (24€, valid for 48 hours from first activation) add the Arena Floor and Underground (the latter visited only via a 40-minute guided tour), plus the S.U.P.E.R. sites of the Palatine (see p. 87). The Colosseum Underground tour includes explanations of the complex system of ramps, elevators, and trap doors that unleashed onto the arena floor the gladiators, wild animals, and array of theatrical effects that once thrilled and stunned audiences in the stands. These tours fill up very quickly. Though the pre-ticketing system has eliminated the long line to enter, you still must go through security screening, which can take up to an hour on busy days. **RomaPass holders** must reserve in advance a time to enter the Colosseum, either online or by

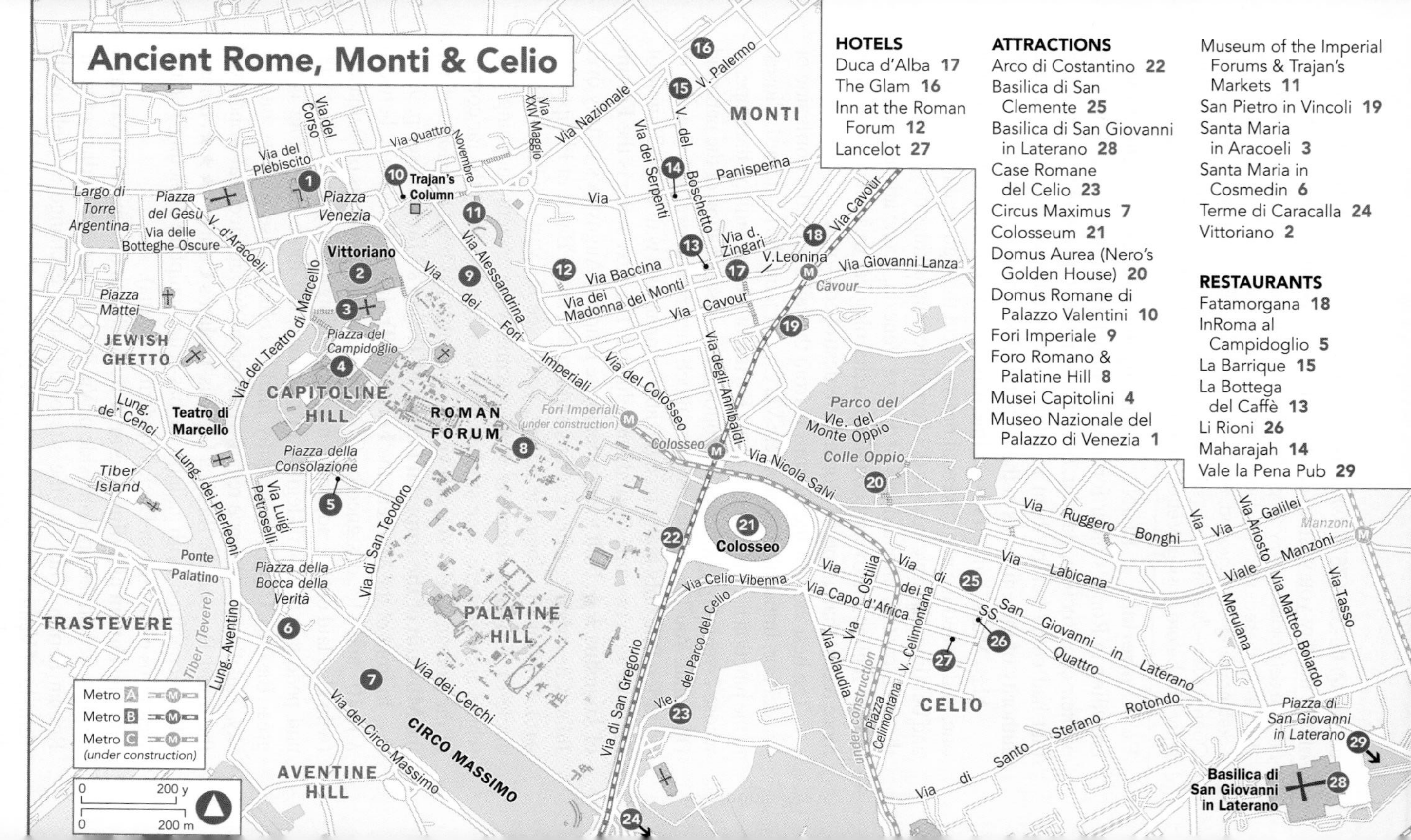
Ancient Rome, Monti & Celio
HOTELS
Duca d'Alba 17
The Glam 16
Inn at the Roman Forum 12
Lancelot 27
ATTRACTIONS
Arco di Costantino 22
Basilica di San Clemente 25
Basilica di San Giovanni in Laterano 28
Case Romane del Celio 23
Circus Maximus 7
Colosseum 21
Domus Aurea (Nero's Golden House) 20
Domus Romane di Palazzo Valentini 10
Fori Imperiale 9
Foro Romano & Palatine Hill 8
Musei Capitolini 4
Museo Nazionale del Palazzo di Venezia 1
Museum of the Imperial Forums & Trajan's Markets 11
San Pietro in Vincoli 19
Santa Maria in Aracoeli 3
Santa Maria in Cosmedin 6
Terme di Caracalla 24
Vittoriano 2
RESTAURANTS
Fatamorgana 18
InRoma al Campidoglio 5
La Barrique 15
La Bottega del Caffè 13
Li Rioni 26
Maharajah 14
Vale la Pena Pub 29
MONTI
CAPITOLINE HILL
ROMAN FORUM
PALATINE HILL
CIRCO MASSIMO
AVENTINE HILL
CELIO
TRASTEVERE
JEWISH GHETTO
Tiber Island
Vittoriano
Trajan's Column
Colosseo
Teatro di Marcello
Basilica di San Giovanni in Laterano
Parco del Colle Oppio
Via del Corso
Via del Plebiscito
Piazza Venezia
Via Quattro Novembre
Via XXIV Maggio
Via Nazionale
Via dei Serpenti
V. del Boschetto
V. Palermo
Via Panisperna
Via Cavour
Via d. Zingari
V. Leonina
Via Giovanni Lanza
Via Baccina
Via dei Madonna dei Monti
Via degli Annibaldi
Via Alessandrina
Via dei Fori Imperiali
Via del Colosseo
Fori Imperiali (under construction)
Cavour
Colosseo
Via Nicola Salvi
Vle. del Monte Oppio
Largo di Torre Argentina
Piazza del Gesù
V. d'Aracoeli
Via delle Botteghe Oscure
Piazza Mattei
Via del Teatro di Marcello
Piazza del Campidoglio
Lung. de' Cenci
Lung. dei Pierleoni
Piazza della Consolazione
Via Luigi Petroselli
Via di San Teodoro
Ponte Palatino
Piazza della Bocca della Verità
Tiber (Tevere)
Lung. Aventino
Via dei Cerchi
Via del Circo Massimo
Via di San Gregorio
Via Celio Vibenna
Vle. del Parco del Celio
Via Capo d'Africa
Via Ostilia
Via Claudia
V. Celimontana
Piazza Celimontana
under construction
Via di S.S. Quattro
Via dei SS.
Via di San Giovanni in Laterano
Via Labicana
Via Ruggero Bonghi
Via Galilei
Via Ariosto
Viale Manzoni
Manzoni
Via Merulana
Via Matteo Boiardo
Via Tasso
Via di Santo Stefano Rotondo
Piazza di San Giovanni in Laterano
Metro A
Metro B
Metro C (under construction)
0 200 y
0 200 m

calling ✆ **06-39967575,** *or* in person at one of the Forum/Palatine ticket offices the day you wish to enter. There's a 2€ per person reservation fee.

Piazzale del Colosseo. www.coopculture.it/en/colosseo-e-shop.cfm. ✆ **06-39967700.** 18€ pre-purchased online, includes Roman Forum & Palatine Hill; "Full Experience" ticket including Underground, Arena Floor, and S.U.P.E.R. sites of the Palatine 24€. Open 9:30am–dusk (as early as 4:30pm in winter, as late as 7:15pm Mar–Aug). Last entry 1 hr. before closing. Metro: Colosseo. Bus: 51, 75, 85, 87, 118. Tram: 3.

Fori Imperiale ★ RUINS Begun by Julius Caesar to relieve overcrowding in Rome's older forums, the Imperial Forums were, at the time of their construction, flashier, bolder, and more impressive than anything that had come before them in Rome. They conveyed the unquestioned authority of the emperors at the height of their absolute power.

Alas, Mussolini felt his regime was more important than the ancient one, and issued the controversial orders to cut through centuries of debris and buildings to carve out Via dei Fori Imperiali, linking the Colosseum to the 19th-century monuments of Piazza Venezia. Excavations under his Fascist regime uncovered countless archaeological treasures. Most ruins more recent than imperial Rome were destroyed—*argh!*

The best view of the Forums is from the railings on the north side of Via dei Fori Imperiali; begin where Via Cavour joins the boulevard. Closest to the junction are the remains of the **Forum of Nerva,** built by the emperor whose 2-year reign (A.D. 96–98) followed the assassination of the paranoid Domitian. You'll be struck by how much the ground level has risen in 19 centuries. The only really recognizable remnant is a wall of the Temple of Minerva with two fine Corinthian columns. The next along is the **Forum of Augustus** ★★, built to commemorate Emperor Augustus's victory over Julius Caesar's assassins, Cassius and Brutus, in the Battle of Philippi (42 B.C.). Continuing along the railing, you'll see the vast, multilevel semicircle of **Trajan's Markets** ★★, essentially an ancient shopping mall whose arcades were once stocked with merchandise from the far corners of the Roman world. You can visit the part that has been transformed into the **Museum of the Imperial Forum & Trajan's Markets** (see p. 95).

In front of the Markets, the **Forum of Trajan** ★★ was built between A.D. 107 and 113, designed by Greek architect Apollodorus of Damascus (who also laid out the adjoining market building). Many statue fragments and pedestals bear still-legible inscriptions, but more interesting is the great Basilica Ulpia, whose gray marble columns rise roofless into the sky. This forum was once regarded as one of the architectural wonders of the world. Beyond the Basilica Ulpia is **Trajan's Column** ★★★, in magnificent condition, with an intricate bas-relief sculpture depicting Trajan's victorious campaign in Dacia (modern Romania).

The **Forum of Julius Caesar** ★★, the first of the Imperial Forums to be built, lies on the opposite side of Via dei Fori Imperiali, adjacent to the Roman Forum. This was the site of the stock exchange as well as the Temple of Venus.

Along Via dei Fori Imperiali. Metro: Colosseo. Bus: 51, 75, 85, 87, 118.

three **FREE VIEWS** to savor for a lifetime

The Forum from the Campidoglio Standing on Piazza del Campidoglio, outside the Musei Capitolini (p. 94), walk around the right or left side of the Palazzo Senatorio to terraces overlooking the best panoramas of the Roman Forum, with the Palatine Hill and Colosseum as a backdrop. At night, the ruins look even more haunting when the Forum is dramatically floodlit.

The Whole City from the Janiculum Hill From many vantage points in the Eternal City, the views are panoramic. But one of the best spots for a memorable vista is the Janiculum Hill *(Gianicolo)* above Trastevere. Laid out before you are Rome's rooftops, peppered with domes ancient and modern. From up here, you will understand why Romans complain about the 19th-century Vittoriano (p. 99)—it's a gigantic white shock in a sea of rose- and honey-colored stone. Walk 50 yards north of the famous balcony (favored by tour buses) for a slightly better angle, from the Belvedere 9 Febbraio 1849. Views from the 1612 Fontana dell'Acqua Paola are also splendid, especially at night.

The Aventine Hill & the Priori dei Cavalieri di Malta The mythical site of Remus's original settlement, the Aventine *(Aventino)* is now a leafy, upscale residential neighborhood—but also blessed with some magical views. From Via del Circo Massimo walk through the gardens along Via di Valle Murcia, and keep walking in a straight line. Along your right side, the Giardino degli Aranci (Orange Tree Garden) offers views over the dome of St. Peter's. When you reach Piazza dei Cavalieri di Malta, look through the keyhole of the Priory gate (on the right) for a "secret" view of the Vatican.

Foro Romano & Palatine Hill ★★★ RUINS Traversed by the **Via Sacra ★** (Sacred Way), the main thoroughfare of ancient Rome, the Roman Forum flourished as the center of religious, social, and commercial life in the days of the Republic, before it gradually lost prestige (but never spiritual draw) to the Imperial Forums (see above). You'll see ruins and fragments, some partially intact columns, and monumental arches, and you'll feel the rush of history here. That any semblance of the Forum remains today is miraculous: It was used for years as a quarry (as was the Colosseum) and eventually became a *campo vaccino* (cow pasture). Excavations in the 19th century and later in the 1930s began to bring to light one of the world's most historic spots.

You can spend at least a morning wandering the ruins of the Forum. Enter via the gate on Via dei Fori Imperiali, at Via della Salara Vecchia. (Note that an access point in front of the Colosseum is also open from time to time.) Turn right at the bottom of the entrance slope to walk west along the old Via Sacra toward the arch. Just before it on your right is the large brick **Curia ★★**, the main seat of the Roman Senate, built by Julius Caesar, rebuilt by Diocletian, and consecrated as a church in A.D. 630.

The triumphal **Arch of Septimius Severus ★★** (A.D. 203), is the next important sight, displaying time-bitten reliefs of the emperor's victories in what are now Iran and Iraq. During the Middle Ages, Rome became a provincial backwater, and frequent flooding of the Tiber helped bury (and thus preserve) most of the Forum. Some bits did still stick out aboveground, including the top half of this arch, which was used to shelter a barbershop! Just to the left of the arch, you can make out the remains of a cylindrical lump of rock with some marble steps curving off it. That round stone was the **Umbilicus Urbus,** considered the center of Rome and of the entire Roman Empire; the curving steps are those of the **Imperial Rostra ★**, where great orators and legislators stood to speak and the people gathered to listen. Nearby, a much-photographed trio of fluted columns with Corinthian capitals supports a bit of architrave from the corner of the **Temple of Vespasian and Titus ★★**. (Emperors were routinely turned into gods upon dying.) Head to your left toward the eight Ionic columns marking the front of the **Temple of Saturn ★★** (rebuilt in 42 B.C.), which housed the first treasury of Republican Rome. It was also the site of one of the Roman year's biggest annual blowout festivals, the December 17 feast of Saturnalia, which, after a bit of tweaking, Christians now celebrate as Christmas. Turn left to start heading back east, past the worn steps and stumps of brick pillars outlining the enormous **Basilica Julia ★★**, built by Julius Caesar. Farther along, on the right, are the three Corinthian columns of the **Temple of the Dioscuri ★★★**, dedicated to the Gemini twins, Castor and Pollux. Forming one of the most photogenic sights of the Roman Forum, a trio of columns supports an architrave fragment. The founding of this temple dates from the 5th century B.C.

Beyond the bit of curving wall that marks the site of the little round **Temple of Vesta** (rebuilt several times after fires started by the sacred flame within), you'll find the reconstructed **House of the Vestal Virgins** (A.D. 3rd–4th c.), home of the consecrated young women who tended the sacred flame in the Temple of Vesta. These girls, chosen from patrician families to serve a 30-year-long priesthood, they were among Rome's most venerated citizens, with unique powers such as the ability to pardon condemned criminals. The cult was quite serious about the "virgin" part of the job description—if one of Vesta's earthly servants was found to have "misplaced" her virginity, the miscreant Vestal was buried alive, because it was forbidden to shed a Vestal's blood. (Her amorous accomplice was merely flogged to death.) The overgrown rectangle of their gardens is lined with broken, heavily worn statues of senior Vestals on pedestals.

Ancient Rome, with Dramatic License

We're fans of the new **Bardeum** app (www.bardeum.com), whose step-by-step audio walking tours of the Colosseum, Forum, Palatine Hill, and Circus Maximus combine meticulously researched historical details with riveting, fictionalized accounts of the ancient Romans who once trod these stones. The tours—each costing 4.50€ and lasting between 20 and 75 minutes—are written by noted authors and engagingly narrated by professional actors.

The path dovetails back to Via Sacra. Turn right, walk past the so-called Temple of Romulus, and then left to enter the massive brick remains of the 4th-century **Basilica of Constantine and Maxentius ★★** (Basilica di Massenzio). These were Rome's public law courts, and their architectural style was adopted by early Christians for their houses of worship (the reason so many ancient churches are called "basilicas").

Return to the path and continue toward the Colosseum. Veer right to the Forum's second great triumphal arch, the extensively rebuilt **Arch of Titus ★★** (A.D. 81), on which one relief depicts the carrying off of treasures from Jerusalem's temple. Look closely and you'll see a menorah among the booty. The war that this arch glorifies ended with the expulsion of Jews from the colonized Judea, signaling the beginning of the Jewish Diaspora throughout Europe. You can exit behind the Arch to continue on to the Colosseum, or head up to the Palatine Hill.

Access the **Palatine Hill ★★** (Palatino), where Romulus, after eliminating his twin brother Remus, founded Rome around 753 B.C. After climbing to the top of the hill, visitors are presented with a sprawling, mostly crowd-free archaeological garden, with some shady spots for cooling off in summer. The Palatine was where the first settlers built their huts under the direction of Romulus; in later years, it became a patrician residential district that attracted such citizens as Cicero. In time, however, the area was gobbled up by imperial palaces and drew an infamous roster of tenants, such as Livia (some of the frescoes in the House of Livia are in miraculous condition), Tiberius, Caligula (murdered here by members of his Praetorian Guard), Nero, and Domitian. A museum houses some of the most important finds from hill excavations. The elaborately decorated **houses of Livia and Augustus ★★** are open to those who purchase the Full Experience ticket, which also includes other sites not normally open to the public. Only the ruins of the Palatine's grandeur remain today, but it's worth the climb for the panoramic views of the Roman and Imperial Forums, as well as the Capitoline Hill, the Colosseum, and Circus Maximus. You can also enter from here, and do the entire tour in reverse.

Famine in the Forum

While you'll find a few water fountains on the Palatine and in the Forum, there is no place to eat—not even so much as a vending machine. If you're making a day of it, pack some snacks.

Note: In recent years, archaeological areas of the Palatine and Forum, called S.U.P.E.R. sites and normally closed to visitors, have become accessible via the Full Experience ticket.

Forum entrance on Via dei Fori Imperiali at Via della Salara Vecchia. Palatine Hill entrance at Via di San Gregorio 30 (south of the Colosseum). www.coopculture.it/en. ✆ **06-39967700.** 18€ prepurchased online (includes Colosseum); Full Experience ticket 24€. Daily 9:30am–dusk (as early as 4:30pm in winter and as late as 7:15pm Mar–Aug). Last entry 1 hr. before closing. Metro: Colosseo. Bus: 51, 75, 85, 87, 118. Tram: 3, 8.

The vast holdings of the Musei Capitolini (Capitoline Museums) include a wealth of classical statuary.

Musei Capitolini ★★ MUSEUM The Capitoline Museums' masterpieces are considered Rome's most valuable (recall that the Vatican Museums are *not* technically in Rome). They certainly were collected early: This is the oldest public museum *in the world.* So try and schedule adequate time, as there's much to see.

First stop is the courtyard of the **Palazzo dei Conservatori** (the building designed by Michelangelo, on the right of the piazza if you enter via the ramp from Piazza Venezia). It's scattered with gargantuan stone body parts—the remnants of a massive 12m (39-ft.) statue of the emperor Constantine, including his colossal head, hand, and foot. It's nearly impossible to resist posing for a photo next to the giant finger.

On the *palazzo*'s ground floor, the unmissable works are in the first series of rooms. These include "Lo Spinario" (Room 3), a lifelike bronze of a young boy digging a splinter out of his foot that was widely copied during the Renaissance; and the **"Lupa Capitolina"** (Room 4), a bronze statue of the famous she-wolf that suckled Romulus and Remus, the mythical founders of Rome. Scholars disagree on the date of the statue: It was long thought to be from around 500 B.C., but recent analysis suggests it may be from the 1100s. What is certain is that the twins were not on the original statue but were added in the 15th century. Room 5 has Bernini's famously pained portrait of "Medusa," even more compelling when you see its writhing serpent hairdo in person.

Before heading upstairs, go toward the newer wing at the rear, which houses the original equestrian **statue of Marcus Aurelius ★★★**, dating to around A.D. 180—the piazza outside, where it stood from 1538 until 2005, now has a copy. There's a giant bronze head from a statue of Constantine (ca. A.D. 337) and the foundations of the original Temple of Jupiter that stood on the Capitoline Hill since its inauguration in 509 B.C.

The second-floor **picture gallery** ★ is strong on baroque oil paintings. Masterpieces include Caravaggio's "John the Baptist" and "The Fortune Teller" (1595) and Guido Reni's "St. Sebastian" (1615).

A tunnel takes you under the piazza to the other part of the Capitoline Museums, the **Palazzo Nuovo,** via the **Tabularium** ★★. Built in 78 B.C. to house ancient Rome's city records, it was later used as a salt mine and then as a prison. Here, the moody *galleria lapidaria* houses a well-executed exhibit of ancient portrait tombstones and sarcophagi, many of their poignant epitaphs translated into English, and provides access to one of the best balcony **views** ★★★ in Rome: along the length of the Forum toward the Palatine Hill.

Much of the Palazzo Nuovo is dedicated to statues excavated from the forums below and brought in from outlying areas like Hadrian's Villa in Tivoli (p. 160). If you're running short on time, head straight for Room 3 and the 1st-century **"Capitoline Venus"** ★★ modestly covering up after a bath, and, in Rooms 4 and 5, a chronologically arranged row of distinct, expressive busts of Roman emperors and their families. Another favorite is the beyond handsome **"Dying Gaul"** ★★, a Roman copy of a lost ancient Greek work. Lord Byron considered the statue so lifelike and moving that he mentioned it in his poem "Childe Harold's Pilgrimage."

Piazza del Campidoglio 1. www.museicapitolini.org. © **060608.** 11.50€ (more during special exhibits); 13.50€ for 7-day ticket that includes Centrale Montemartini. Daily 9:30am–7:30pm. Last entry 1 hr. before closing. Bus: 40, 44, 60, 63, 64, 70, 118, 160, 170, 628, 716 or any bus that stops at Piazza Venezia.

Museum of the Imperial Forums & Trajan's Markets ★★ RUINS/MUSEUM Built on three levels, Emperor Trajan's Market housed 150 shops and commercial offices—think of it as the world's first shopping mall. Grooves still evident in the thresholds allowed merchants to slide doors shut and lock up for the night. You're likely to have the covered, tunnel-like market halls mostly to yourself—making the ancient past feel all the more present in this overlooked site. The Museum of the Imperial Forums occupies a converted section of the market, and excellent visual displays help you imagine what these grand public squares and temples used to look like. All in all, it's home to 172 marble fragments from the Fori Imperiali; there are also original remnants from the Forum of Augustus and Forum of Nerva.

Via IV Novembre 94. www.mercatiditraiano.it. © **060608.** 11.50€ (more during special exhibits). Daily 9:30am–7:30pm. Last admission 1 hr. before closing. Bus: 40, 60, 64, 70, 170.

Terme di Caracalla ★★ RUINS Named for Emperor Caracalla, a particularly unpleasant individual, the Baths of Caracalla were completed in A.D. 217 after his death. The richness of decoration has faded, but the massive brick ruins and the mosaic fragments that remain give modern visitors an idea of the complex's scale and grandeur. In their heyday, the baths sprawled over 11 hectares (27 acres) and included hot, cold, and tepid pools, as well as a *palestra* (gym) and changing rooms. A museum in the tunnels below the complex—built over an even more ancient *mithraem,* a worship site of an eastern cult—explores the hydraulic and heating systems (and slave power) needed to serve 8,000 or so Romans per day. Summer operatic performances here are an ethereal treat (see p. 155). For an extra 7€, a **virtual reality experience ★** brings the baths vividly to life.

Via delle Terme di Caracalla 52. www.coopculture.it/en. ✆ **06-39967702.** 8€ (10€ online). Virtual reality guide 7€. Tues–Sun 9am–dusk (as early as 4:30pm or as late as 7:15pm). Last entry 1 hr. before closing. Bus: 118 or 628.

OTHER ATTRACTIONS NEAR ANCIENT ROME

Basilica di San Clemente ★★ CHURCH A perfect example of how layers of history overlap in Rome, this 12-century Norman church, full of beautiful Byzantine mosaics, hides much more. Down in its eerie grottos (which you explore on your own) you'll find frescoes and mosaic floors from its previous incarnations as a 4th-century Christian church and a temple dedicated to the pagan deity Mithras—and below that, the foundations of a Roman house from the A.D. 1st century, where early Christians worshipped in secret. ***Note:*** Access to the underground area is limited to 30 minutes.

Via San Giovanni in Laterano (at Piazza San Clemente). www.basilicasanclemente.com. ✆ **06-7740021.** Basilica free; excavations 10€ (also bookable online). Mon–Sat 10am–12:30pm and 3–5:30pm; Sun noon–5:30pm. Last entry 30 min. before closing. Metro: Colosseo. Bus: 51, 85, 87, 117. Tram: 3.

NERO'S golden HOUSE

After the Great Fire of A.D. 64, charismatic, despotic Emperor Nero staged a land grab to facilitate construction of his *Domus Aurea,* or Golden House, a massive gilded villa complex covering all or parts of the Palatine, Esquiline, and Caelian hills, which displayed a level of ostentation and excess unheard of even among past emperors. After his death by noble suicide in A.D. 68, a campaign to erase all traces of Nero from the imperial city ensured that the palace was stripped of its gold, marble, jewels, mosaics, and statuary, then intentionally buried under millions of tons of rubble. It remained buried until the Renaissance, when young artists, including Raphael, descended into its "grottos" (actually the vaulted ceilings) to study the fanciful frescoes—the term grotesque (*grotto-esque*) was coined here. Later excavations revealed the scale and richness of the villa, but also subjected it to catastrophic moisture damage. The Domus Aurea is open for tours—but only if you time your trip well and plan ahead. Guided tours (16€; www.coopculture.it/en) of the scaffolded underground site (hardhats required) are currently offered on **Friday, Saturday,** and **Sunday,** only with advance reservations. The tour includes a spectacular **virtual reality experience ★★★** that in itself is worth the visit.

Basilica di San Giovanni in Laterano ★★ CHURCH This church, not St. Peter's, is officially the cathedral of the diocese of Rome; the pope celebrates Mass here on certain holidays. Though it was built in A.D. 314 by Constantine, only parts of the original baptistery remain; what you see today is an 18th-century facade by Alessandro Galilei (note signs of damage from a 1993 terrorist bomb) and an interior by Borromini, built for Pope Innocent X. In a misguided redecoration long ago, frescoes by Giotto were apparently destroyed; remains attributed to Giotto, discovered in 1952, are displayed against the first inner column on the right.

Across the street is the **Santuario della Scala Santa** (Palace of the Holy Steps), Piazza San Giovanni in Laterano 14 (✆ **06-7726641**), a set of 28 marble steps supposedly brought from Jerusalem by Constantine's mother, Helen. Though some historians say the stairs might date only from the 4th century, legend claims these were the stairs Christ climbed at Pontius Pilate's villa the day he was sentenced to death. Today pilgrims from the world over come here to climb the steps on their knees.

Piazza San Giovanni in Laterano 4. ✆ **06-69886433.** Free. Daily 7am–6:30pm. Metro: San Giovanni.

Case Romane del Celio ★ RUINS Beneath the 5th-century Basilica of SS. Giovanni e Paolo lies a fascinating archaeological site: A complex of Roman houses of different periods—a wealthy family's townhouse from the A.D. 2nd century and an A.D.-3rd-century apartment building for artisans. According to tradition, the latter was the home of two Roman officers, John and Paul (not the Apostles), who were beheaded during the reign of Julian the Apostate (361–63) for refusing to serve in a military campaign. They were later made saints, and their bones were said to have been buried here. The two-story construction also contains a small museum with finds from the site and fragmentary 12th-century frescoes.

Piazza Santi Giovanni e Paolo 13 (entrance on Clivo di Scauro). www.coopculture.it/en. ✆ **06-70454544.** 10€ adults. Fri–Mon and Wed 10am–4pm. Metro: Colosseo or Circo Massimo. Bus: 75, 81, 118. Tram: 3.

Domus Romane di Palazzo Valentini ★★★ RUINS/EXHIBIT All too often in Italy, archaeological sites are presented with little context, and it's difficult for untrained eyes to really understand what they're seeing. Not so at Palazzo Valentini, possibly Rome's best-presented ancient site. Visitors descend underneath a Renaissance palazzo and peer through a glass floor into the remains of several upscale Roman homes. With innovative use of 3-D projections, the walls, ceilings, floors. and fountains of these once-grand houses spring to life, offering a captivating look at lifestyles of the ancient rich and possibly famous.

Via Foro Traiano 85 (near Trajan's Column). www.palazzovalentini.it. ✆ **06-22761280.** 13.50€. Wed–Mon 10am–7pm timed entrance, with guided tours in English several times daily; reservations suggested. Metro: Colosseo. Bus: 40, 63, 70, 81, 83, 87, or any bus to Piazza Venezia. Tram: 8.

Museo Nazionale del Palazzo di Venezia ★ MUSEUM Best remembered today as Mussolini's Fascist headquarters in Rome, the palace was built in the 1450s as the Rome outpost of the Republic of Venice—hence the name. Today, several of its rooms house an eclectic mix of European paintings and decorative and religious objects spanning the centuries; highlights include Giorgione's enigmatic "Double Portrait" and some early Tuscan altarpieces.

Via del Plebiscito 118. www.museopalazzovenezia.beniculturali.it. ✆ **06-6780131.** 12€. Daily 9:30am–6:30pm, with guided entry admission at the bottom of every hour (English guides at 10:30am and 4:30pm). Bus: 30, 40, 46, 62, 64, 70, 87, or any bus to Piazza Venezia. Tram: 8.

San Pietro in Vincoli ★ CHURCH Founded in the 5th century to house the chains (*vincoli*) that supposedly bound St. Peter in Jerusalem (preserved under glass below the main altar), this lovely church is mainly worth visiting to see one of the world's most famous sculptures: **Michelangelo's "Moses" ★★**, carved for the tomb of Pope Julius II. Michelangelo never completed the 44 magnificent figures planned for the tomb, but this "minor" figure he did complete now numbers among his masterpieces.

Piazza San Pietro in Vincoli 4A. ✆ **06-97844952.** Free. Daily 8am–12:30pm and 3–7pm. Metro: Colosseo or Cavour. Bus: 75, 117.

Santa Maria in Aracoeli ★★ CHURCH This plain-on-the-outside church is worth the climb for its splendid interior. According to legend, Augustus ordered a temple erected on this spot on the Capitoline Hill, where a sibyl foretold the coming of Christ. The current church, built for the Franciscans in the 13th century, boasts a coffered Renaissance ceiling and the tomb of Giovanni Crivelli carved by the great Renaissance sculptor Donatello. The **Cappella Bufalini ★** (first chapel on the right) was frescoed by Pinturicchio with scenes of the life and death of St. Bernardino of Siena. A chapel behind the altar contains the **Santo Bambino,** a wooden figure of the Baby Jesus, which is venerated annually on Christmas Eve. The long flight of stairs leading up to the church was built in 1348 to celebrate the end of the Black Plague.

All Roads Lead to...Piazza Venezia

Love it or loathe it, the massive Vittoriano monument at Piazza Venezia is a helpful landmark for visitors to get their bearings, and almost every bus line convenient to tourists stops here. Streets fanning out from the piazza lead to Termini Station, the Colosseum, the Trevi Fountain, and across the Tiber to the Vatican and Trastevere.

Scala dell'Arcicapitolina 12. ✆ **06-69763838.** Free. Daily 7am–7pm. Bus: 30, 40, 46, 62, 64, 70, 87, or any bus to Piazza Venezia.

Santa Maria in Cosmedin ★ CHURCH People line up outside this ancient church not for great art treasures (though it's worth a peek inside), but for the **"Mouth of Truth,"** a large disk on the wall of the portico. As Gregory Peck demonstrated to Audrey Hepburn in the film *Roman*

Holiday, the mouth is supposed to chomp down on the hands of liars. It may have been an ancient drain cover, though one hypothesis says it was a so-called "talking statue," where anonymous notes were left to betray wrongdoers. Our take? Save this hokey photo op until you've seen everything else you want to see in Rome.

Piazza della Bocca della Verità 18. ✆ **06-6787759.** Free. Daily 9:30am–6pm (5pm winter). Bus: 30, 44, 81, 83, 85, 87, 118, 160, 628, 715.

Vittoriano (Altare della Patria) ★ MONUMENT It's impossible to miss the white marble Vittorio Emanuele monument dominating Piazza Venezia. Built in the late 1800s to honor the first king of a united Italy, this flamboyant (and widely disliked) landmark has been compared to everything from a wedding cake to a Victorian typewriter, its harsh white color glaring in a city of honey-gold tones. An eternal flame burns at the Tomb of the Unknown Soldier. For a panoramic city view, take a glass elevator to the **Terrazza delle Quadrighe** ★ (Terrace of the Chariots).

Piazza Venezia. vittoriano.beniculturali.it/en. ✆ **06-6780664.** Free. Elevator to panoramic terrace 15€ (includes admission to Palazzo Venezia; see p. 98). Daily 9:30am–7:30pm (last entry 6:45pm). Bus: 30, 40, 46, 62, 64, 70, 87, or any bus to Piazza Venezia.

Centro Storico & the Pantheon

CENTRO STORICO

Just across the Tiber from the Vatican and Castel Sant'Angelo lies the true heart of Rome, the **Centro Storico,** or "historic center," the triangular wedge of land that bulges into a bend of the river. Although the area lay outside the Roman city, it came into its own during the Renaissance, and today its streets and alleys are crammed with piazzas, elegant churches, and lavish fountains, all buzzing with scooters and people. It's a wonderful area in which to wander and get lost.

Fountain of the Four Rivers in Piazza Navona.

PIAZZA NAVONA & NEARBY ATTRACTIONS

Rome's most famous square, **Piazza Navona** ★★★, is a gorgeous baroque gem, lined with cafes and restaurants and often full of tourists, street artists, and pigeons. Its long, oval shape follows the contours of the old ruined Roman Stadium of Domitian, where chariot races once took place, made over in the mid-17th century by Pope Innocent X. The twin-towered facade of 17th-century **Sant'Agnese in Agone** lies on the piazza's western side, while the **Fontana dei Quattro Fiumi ★★★** (Fountain of the Four Rivers) opposite is one of three great fountains in the square, this one a typically exuberant creation by Bernini, topped with an Egyptian obelisk. The four stone personifications below symbolize the world's greatest rivers: the Ganges, Danube, de la Plata, and Nile. It's fun to try to figure out which is which. (***Hint:*** The figure with the shroud on its head is the Nile, so represented because the river's source was unknown at the time.) At the south end is Bernini's **Fontana del Moro** (Fountain of the Moor) and the 19th-century **Fontana di Nettuno** (Fountain of Neptune).

Art lovers should make the short walk from the piazza to **Santa Maria della Pace ★★** on Arco della Pace, a 15th-century church given the usual baroque makeover by Pietro da Cortona in the 1660s. The real gems are inside, beginning with Raphael's **"Four Sibyls" ★★** fresco, above the arch of the Cappella Chigi, and the **Chiostro del Bramante ★** (Bramante cloister), built between 1500 and 1504 and the Renaissance master's first work in the city. The church is normally open daily from 9:30am to 6:30pm, while the cloister opens daily 10am to 8pm (to 9pm Sat and Sun); admission to the church and cloister is free (www.chiostrodelbramante.it). ***Tip:*** Waiters from Piazza Navona's many overpriced restaurants lie in wait, hoping to woo passing tourists. While the setting is unmatchable, you'll have a far better meal on the side streets off the piazza.

Palazzo Altemps ★★ MUSEUM Inside this 15th-century *palazzo,* today a branch of the National Museum of Rome, is one of Rome's most charming museums housing some of the city's most famous private and public art collections. Much of it was once part of the famed **Boncompagni Ludovisi Collection,** created by Cardinal Ludovico Ludovisi (1595–1632) and sold at auction in 1901. Among the highlights is the **"Ludovisi Ares" ★★**, a handsome 2nd-century copy of an earlier Greek statue of Mars (Ares to the Greeks). Equally renowned is the **"Ludovisi Gaul" ★**, a marble depiction of a Gaulish warrior plunging a sword into his chest rather than become a slave of Rome; looking backward defiantly, he supports a dying woman with his left arm. Also worth a look is the **"Ludovisi Throne,"** a sculpted block of white marble, thought to date from the 5th century B.C., depicting Aphrodite rising from the sea.

Piazza di Sant'Apollinare 46. www.museonazionaleromano.beniculturali.it. ✆ **06-39967700.** 12€ for single museum, or 16€ for a 1-week pass that also includes Palazzo Massimo & Baths of Diocletian; free ages 17 and under. Tues–Sun 11am–6pm. Last entry 1 hr. before closing. Bus: 70, 81, 87, 492, 628.

San Luigi dei Francesi ★★ CHURCH For a painter of such stratospheric standards as Caravaggio, it is impossible definitively to name his "masterpiece." However, the **"Calling of St. Matthew" ★★**, in the far-left chapel of Rome's French church, must be a candidate. Done in

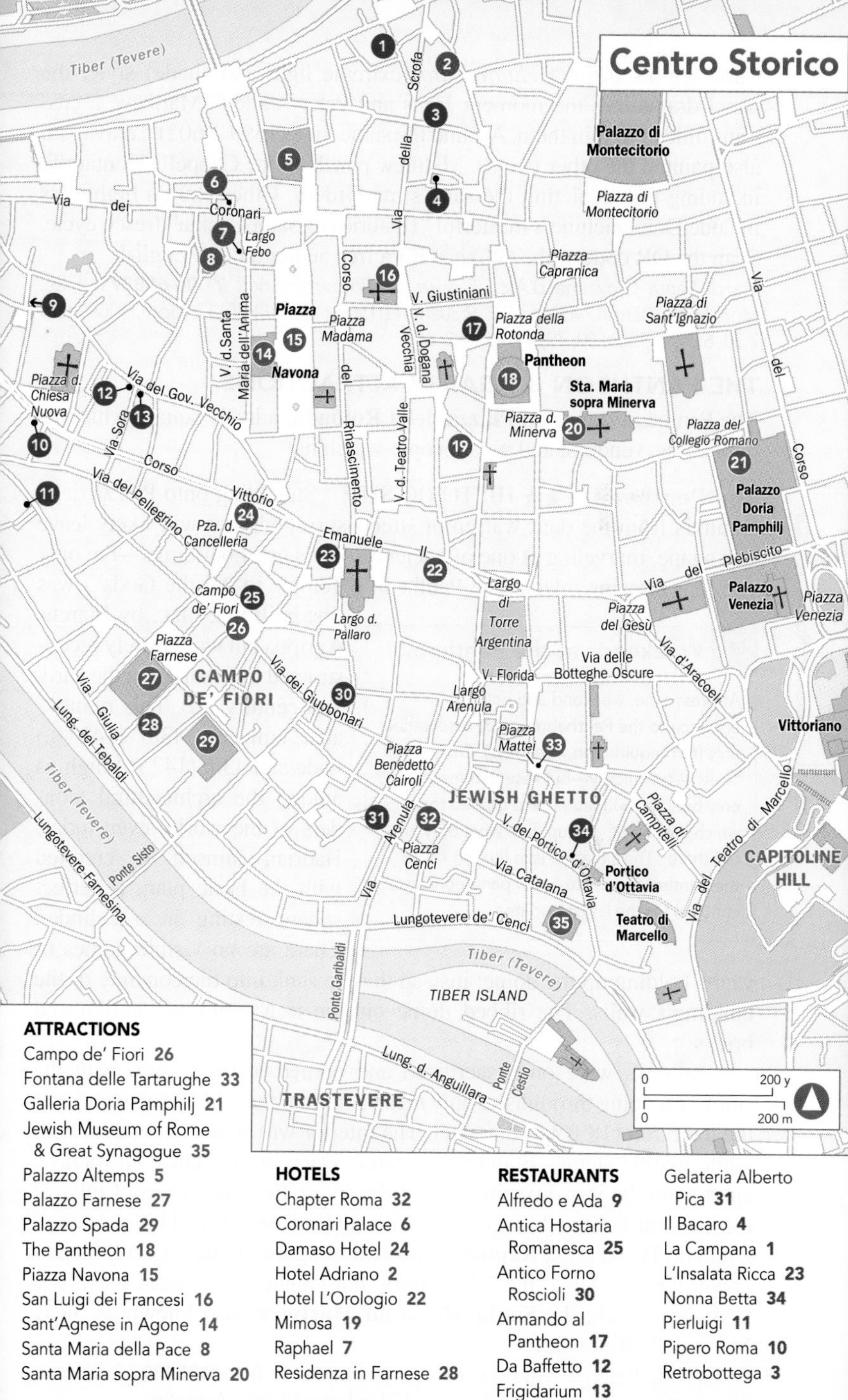
Centro Storico
Tiber (Tevere)
Via della Scrofa
Palazzo di Montecitorio
Piazza di Montecitorio
Via dei Coronari
Largo Febo
Piazza Capranica
Corso del Rinascimento
V. Giustiniani
Piazza di Sant'Ignazio
Via del Corso
V. d.Santa Maria dell'Anima
Piazza Navona
Piazza Madama
V. d. Dogana Vecchia
Piazza della Rotonda
Pantheon
Sta. Maria sopra Minerva
Piazza d. Chiesa Nuova
Via del Gov. Vecchio
Via Sora
Piazza d. Minerva
V. d. Teatro Valle
Piazza del Collegio Romano
Palazzo Doria Pamphilj
Corso Vittorio Emanuele II
Via del Pellegrino
Pza. d. Cancelleria
Via del Plebiscito
Largo di Torre Argentina
Largo d. Pallaro
Campo de' Fiori
Piazza del Gesù
Palazzo Venezia
Piazza Venezia
Piazza Farnese
Via d'Aracoeli
Via delle Botteghe Oscure
V. Florida
CAMPO DE' FIORI
Via dei Giubbonari
Largo Arenula
Via Giulia
Lung. dei Tebaldi
Vittoriano
Piazza Mattei
Piazza Benedetto Cairoli
JEWISH GHETTO
Piazza di Campitelli
Via del Teatro di Marcello
Via Arenula
V. del Portico d'Ottavia
Piazza Cenci
CAPITOLINE HILL
Lungotevere Farnesina
Ponte Sisto
Via Catalana
Portico d'Ottavia
Lungotevere de' Cenci
Teatro di Marcello
Ponte Garibaldi
TIBER ISLAND
Lung. d. Anguillara
Ponte Cestio
TRASTEVERE
0 200 y
0 200 m
ATTRACTIONS
Campo de' Fiori 26
Fontana delle Tartarughe 33
Galleria Doria Pamphilj 21
Jewish Museum of Rome & Great Synagogue 35
Palazzo Altemps 5
Palazzo Farnese 27
Palazzo Spada 29
The Pantheon 18
Piazza Navona 15
San Luigi dei Francesi 16
Sant'Agnese in Agone 14
Santa Maria della Pace 8
Santa Maria sopra Minerva 20
HOTELS
Chapter Roma 32
Coronari Palace 6
Damaso Hotel 24
Hotel Adriano 2
Hotel L'Orologio 22
Mimosa 19
Raphael 7
Residenza in Farnese 28
RESTAURANTS
Alfredo e Ada 9
Antica Hostaria Romanesca 25
Antico Forno Roscioli 30
Armando al Pantheon 17
Da Baffetto 12
Frigidarium 13
Gelateria Alberto Pica 31
Il Bacaro 4
La Campana 1
L'Insalata Ricca 23
Nonna Betta 34
Pierluigi 11
Pipero Roma 10
Retrobottega 3

Caravaggio's distinct *chiaroscuro* (extreme light and shade) style, the panel dramatizes the moment Jesus and Peter "called" Matthew, a customs officer, to join them. Around the same time (1599–1602) Caravaggio also painted the other two St. Matthew panels in the Cappella Contarelli, including one depicting the saint's martyrdom. Other church highlights include Domenichino's masterful "Histories of Saint Cecilia" fresco cycle. Scan the QR code at the entrance for a free audioguide in English.

Via di Santa Giovanna d'Arco 5. www.saintlouis-rome.net. ✆ **06-688271.** Free. Mon–Fri 9:30am–12:45pm; Sat 9:30am–12:15pm; Sun 11:30–12:45pm, plus daily 2:30–6:30pm. Bus: 30, 70, 81, 87, 492, 628.

THE PANTHEON & NEARBY ATTRACTIONS

The Pantheon stands on **Piazza della Rotonda,** a lively square with outdoor cafes, vendors, and great people-watching.

The Pantheon ★★★ HISTORIC SITE Stumbling onto Piazza della Rotunda from the dark warren of streets surrounding it will likely leave you agape, marveling at one of ancient Rome's great buildings—the only one that remains intact. The Pantheon ("Temple to All the Gods") was first built in 27 B.C. by Marcus Agrippa but was entirely reconstructed by Hadrian in the early 2nd century A.D. This remarkable building, 43m (142 ft.) wide and 43m (142 ft.) high, is among the architectural wonders of the world, even today. Hadrian himself is credited with the basic plan: a perfect sphere resting in a cylinder. There are no visible arches or vaults holding up the dome; instead they're sunk into the concrete of the building's walls. The ribbed dome outside is a series of cantilevered bricks.

Weekends at the Pantheon

At press time, weekend and holiday entrance to the Pantheon was by reservation only (not required on weekdays). Entry is still "free"—technically—but reservations are only bundled with audio and guided tours, which cost 8.50€ and up. See what they just did there? The situation is in flux, so check the Pantheon website (www.pantheonroma.com/en) for the latest updates.

Animals were once sacrificed and burned in the center, with the smoke escaping through the only means of light, the oculus, an opening at the top 5.5m (18 ft.) in diameter. The interior was richly decorated, with white marble statues ringing the central space in its niches. Nowadays, apart from the jaw-dropping size of the space, the main items of interest are the tombs of two Italian kings (Vittorio Emanuele II and his successor, Umberto I) and artist **Raphael** (fans still bring him flowers), with its poignant epitaph. Since the 7th century, the Pantheon has been used as a Catholic church, the **Santa Maria ad Martyres,** also known as Santa Maria della Rotonda.

Piazza della Rotonda. www.pantheonroma.com/en. ✆ **06-68300230.** Free. Daily 9am–7pm. Bus: 30, 40, 62, 64, 81, 87 or 492 to Largo di Torre Argentina.

Galleria Doria Pamphilj ★★ ART MUSEUM One of the city's finest rococo palaces, the Palazzo Doria Pamphilj is still privately owned by the aristocratic Doria Pamphilj family, but their stupendous art collection is open to the public. The *galleria* winds through the old apartments, their paintings displayed floor-to-ceiling among antique furniture and richly decorated walls. The strong Dutch and Flemish collection includes Pieter Brueghel the Elder's "Battle in the Port of Naples," and his son Jan Brueghel the Elder's "Earthly Paradise with Original Sin." Among the best Italian works are two Caravaggio paintings, the moving "Repentant Magdalene" and his wonderful "Rest on the Flight into Egypt," hanging near Titian's "Salome with the Head of St. John." There's also Raphael's "Double Portrait," an "Annunciation" by Filippo Lippi, and a "Deposition from the Cross" by Vasari. The gallery's real treasures occupy a special room: Bernini's bust of the Pamphilj **"Pope Innocent X"** ★, and Velázquez's **enigmatic painting** ★★ of the same man. Make sure you grab a free audioguide at the entrance—it's colorfully narrated by Prince Jonathan Doria Pamphilj himself, who recalls roller-skating in the palazzo as a child.

Via del Corso 305 (just N of Piazza Venezia). www.doriapamphilj.it. ✆ **06-6797323.** 15€ adults; 1€ 12 and under. Mon–Thurs 9am–7pm; Fri–Sun 10am–8pm; last entry 1 hr. before closing. Closed 3rd Wed of every month. Bus: 64 or any to Piazza Venezia.

Santa Maria sopra Minerva ★★★ CHURCH Just one block behind the Pantheon, Santa Maria sopra Minerva is Rome's most significant Dominican church and the only major Gothic church downtown. The facade is in Renaissance style (the church was begun in 1280 but worked on until 1725), but inside, the arched vaulting is pure Gothic. The main art treasures here are the "Statua del Redentore" (1521), a statue of Christ by **Michelangelo** (just to the left of the altar), and a wonderful fresco cycle in the **Cappella Carafa** (on the right before the altar), created by Filippino Lippi between 1488 and 1493 to honor St. Thomas Aquinas. Devout Catholics flock to the tomb of **Saint Catherine of Siena** under the high altar—the room where she died in 1380 was reconstructed by Antonio Barberini in 1637 (far left corner of the church). **Fra Angelico,** the Dominican friar and painter, also rests here, in the **Cappella Frangipane e Maddaleni-Capiferro.** In the piazza outside the church, a small obelisk sits on a delightful elephant statue by **Bernini.**

Piazza della Minerva 42. www.santamariasopraminerva.it/en. ✆ **06-69920384.** Free. Daily 9am–noon, 4–7pm.

CAMPO DE' FIORI

The southern section of the Centro Storico, **Campo de' Fiori** is another neighborhood of narrow streets, small piazzas, and ancient churches. Its main focus remains the piazza of **Campo de' Fiori** ★★ itself, where a touristy but delightful open-air market runs daily (with fewer vendors on

Sun) from early morning until midday, selling a dizzyingly colorful array of fruits, vegetables, and spices as well as cheap T-shirts and handbags. (Keep an eye on your valuables here.) From the center of the piazza rises a statue of the severe-looking monk **Giordano Bruno,** a reminder that heretics were occasionally burned at the stake here: Bruno was executed by the Inquisition in 1600. Curiously this is the only piazza in Rome that doesn't have a church in its perimeter.

Built from 1514 to 1589, the **Palazzo Farnese ★**, on Piazza Farnese just south of the Campo, was designed by Sangallo and Michelangelo, among others, and was an astronomically expensive project for the time. Its famous residents have included a 16th-century member of the Farnese family, plus Pope Paul III, Cardinal Richelieu, and the former Queen Christina of Sweden, who moved to Rome after abdicating. During the 1630s, when the heirs couldn't afford to maintain the *palazzo,* it was inherited by the Bourbon kings of Naples and purchased by the French government in 1874; the French Embassy is still located here, so the building is mostly closed to the general public. Tours are offered in English on Monday, Wednesday, and Friday afternoons and cost 12€. Reservations are mandatory (visite-palazzofarnese.it).

Palazzo Spada/Galleria Spada ★ MUSEUM Built around 1540 for Cardinal Gerolamo Capo di Ferro, Palazzo Spada was purchased by the eponymous Cardinal Spada in 1632, who then hired Borromini to restore it—most of what you see today dates from that period. Its ornate facade, covered in high-relief stucco decorations in the Mannerist style, is the finest of any building from 16th-century Rome. The State Rooms are closed (the Italian Council of State still meets here), but the richly decorated courtyard and corridor, where Borromini created a masterful illusion of perspective *(la prospettiva di Borromini)* ★★, and the four rooms of the **Galleria Spada** are open to the public. Inside you will find some absorbing paintings, such as the "Portrait of Cardinale Bernardino Spada" by Guido Reni, Titian's "Portrait of a Violinist," and minor works from Parmigianino, Pietro Testa, and Giambattista Gaulli.

Piazza Capo di Ferro 13. www.galleriaspada.beniculturali.it. ✆ **06-6874893.** 5€. Wed–Mon 8:30am–7:30pm. Bus: 23, 280, tram 8, or any bus to Largo di Torre Argentina.

THE JEWISH GHETTO

Across Via Arenula, Campo de' Fiori merges into the old **Jewish Ghetto ★★**, established near the River Tiber by a Papal Bull in 1555, which required that all the Jews in Rome live in one area. Walled in, overcrowded, prone to floods and epidemics, and set on some of the worst land in the city, it was an extremely grim place to live. After the Ghetto was abolished in 1882, its walls were finally torn down and the area was largely reconstructed. In the waning years of World War II, Nazis sent more than 1,000 Roman Jews to concentration camps; only a handful returned.

Today, the **Via Portico d'Ottavia** forms the heart of a flourishing Jewish Quarter, with Romans and tourists flocking here to sample the **Roman-Jewish** and **Middle Eastern food** for which the area is known. Head north on winding Via di S. Ambrogio to toss a coin in the **Fontana delle Tartarughe ★**, a beloved Renaissance fountain. The turtles, added in the 1600s, are thought to be by Bernini.

Jewish Museum of Rome ★★ MUSEUM On the premises of the Great Synagogue of Rome, the Museo Ebraico di Roma chronicles the history of not only Roman Jews but Jews from all over Italy. There are displays of works of 17th- and 18th-century Roman silversmiths, precious textiles from all over Europe, and a number of parchments and marble carvings that were saved when the Ghetto's original synagogues were demolished. Museum admission includes a guided English-language tour of the **Great Synagogue of Rome** (Tempio Maggiore), built from 1901 to 1904 in an eclectic style evoking Babylonian and Persian temples. Attacked by terrorists in 1982, the synagogue is now heavily guarded by *carabinieri,* a division of the Italian police, armed with machine guns.

Via Catalana. www.museoebraico.roma.it/en. ✆ **06-6840061.** 11€ adults; 5€ students; free for children 10 and under. Apr–Sept Sun–Thurs 10am–6pm and Fri 10am–4pm; Jan 21–Mar, Oct Sun–Thurs 10am–5pm and Fri 9am–2pm (Nov 1–Jan 20 closes 4 or 4:30pm Mon–Thurs; last entry 3:15pm). Closed on Jewish holidays.

The Tridente & the Spanish Steps

The northern half of central Rome is known as the **Tridente,** thanks to the trident shape formed by three roads—Via di Ripetta, Via del Corso, and Via del Babuino—leading down from **Piazza del Popolo.** The area around **Piazza di Spagna** and the **Spanish Steps** was once the artistic quarter of the city, attracting English poets Keats and Shelley, German author Goethe, and film director Federico Fellini (who lived on Via Margutta). Institutions such as **Antico Caffè Greco** and **Babington's Tea Rooms** are still here (see p. 144), but between the high rents and the throngs of tourists and shoppers, you're unlikely to see many artists left.

PIAZZA DEL POPOLO

Elegant **Piazza del Popolo ★★** is haunted with memories. Legend has it that the ashes of Nero were enshrined here, until 11th-century residents began complaining to the pope about his imperial ghost. The **Egyptian obelisk** dates from the 13th century B.C.; it was brought to Rome from Heliopolis during Augustus's reign (it once stood at the Circus Maximus).

The current piazza was designed in the early 19th century by Valadier, Napoleon's architect. Standing astride the three roads that form the "trident" are almost-twin baroque churches, **Santa Maria dei Miracoli** (1681) and **Santa Maria di Montesanto** (1679). The standout church, however, is at the piazza's northern curve: the 15th-century **Santa Maria del Popolo ★★**, with its splendid baroque facade modified by Bernini between 1655 and 1660. Inside, look for Raphael's mosaic series, the "Creation of the World" adorning the interior dome of the **Cappella Chigi** (second chapel on the left). Pinturicchio decorated the main choir vault with frescoes such as the "Coronation of the Virgin." The **Cappella Cerasi** (to the left of the high altar) contains gorgeous examples of baroque art: an altarpiece painting of "The Assumption of Mary" by Carracci, and on either side two great works by Caravaggio, "Conversion on the Road to Damascus" and "The Crucifixion of Saint Peter."

MAXXI (National Museum of the XXI Century Arts) ★ MUSEUM Ten minutes north of Piazza del Popolo by tram, leave the Renaissance far behind at MAXXI, a masterpiece of contemporary architecture designed by the late, great Zaha Hadid. The museum is divided into two sections, MAXXI art and MAXXI architecture, primarily serving as a venue for temporary exhibitions of contemporary work in both fields (although it does have a small permanent collection). Built in a dynamic design of bending and overlapping oblong tubes, the building is worth a visit in its own right.

Via Guido Reni 4a. www.maxxi.art/en. ✆ **06-3201954.** 12€ adults; 9€ ages 25 and under; free for children 13 and under. Tues–Sun 11am–7pm. Metro: Flaminio, then Tram 2.

Museo dell'Ara Pacis ★★ MUSEUM Set in a stunning ultra-modern building designed by American architect Richard Meier (long before his #MeToo contrition), the temple-like marble Altar of Peace was erected in 9 B.C. to honor soon-to-be-Emperor Augustus's success in subduing tribes north of the Alps. For centuries the monument was lost to memory; signs of its existence surfaced in the 16th century, but it wasn't until the 1930s that it was fully excavated. Even so, it lay virtually abandoned after World War II until a true restoration began in the 1980s. The exhibit complex provides context, with interactive displays in English.

Lungotevere in Augusta. www.arapacis.it/en. ✆ **06-060608.** 10.50€. Daily 9:30am–7:30pm (last entry 6:30pm). Metro: Spagna. Bus: 30, 70, 81, 87, 119, 280, 492, 628, 913.

PIAZZA DI SPAGNA

The undoubted highlight of Tridente is **Piazza di Spagna,** which attracts hordes of tourists to admire its celebrated **Spanish Steps ★★** (Scalinata della Trinità dei Monti), the widest stairway in Europe. The Steps are

No Swimming, Sitting, or Picnicking Allowed

In an effort to keep tourists from littering the city's monuments, or soaking their feet and even swimming (yes, it's happened) in its famous fountains, visitors are no longer permitted to picnic (or even sit) on the Spanish Steps or sit on the edge of the Trevi and other landmark fountains. You can stop long enough for a photo or coin toss, but don't plan on getting comfortable (or taking a dip).

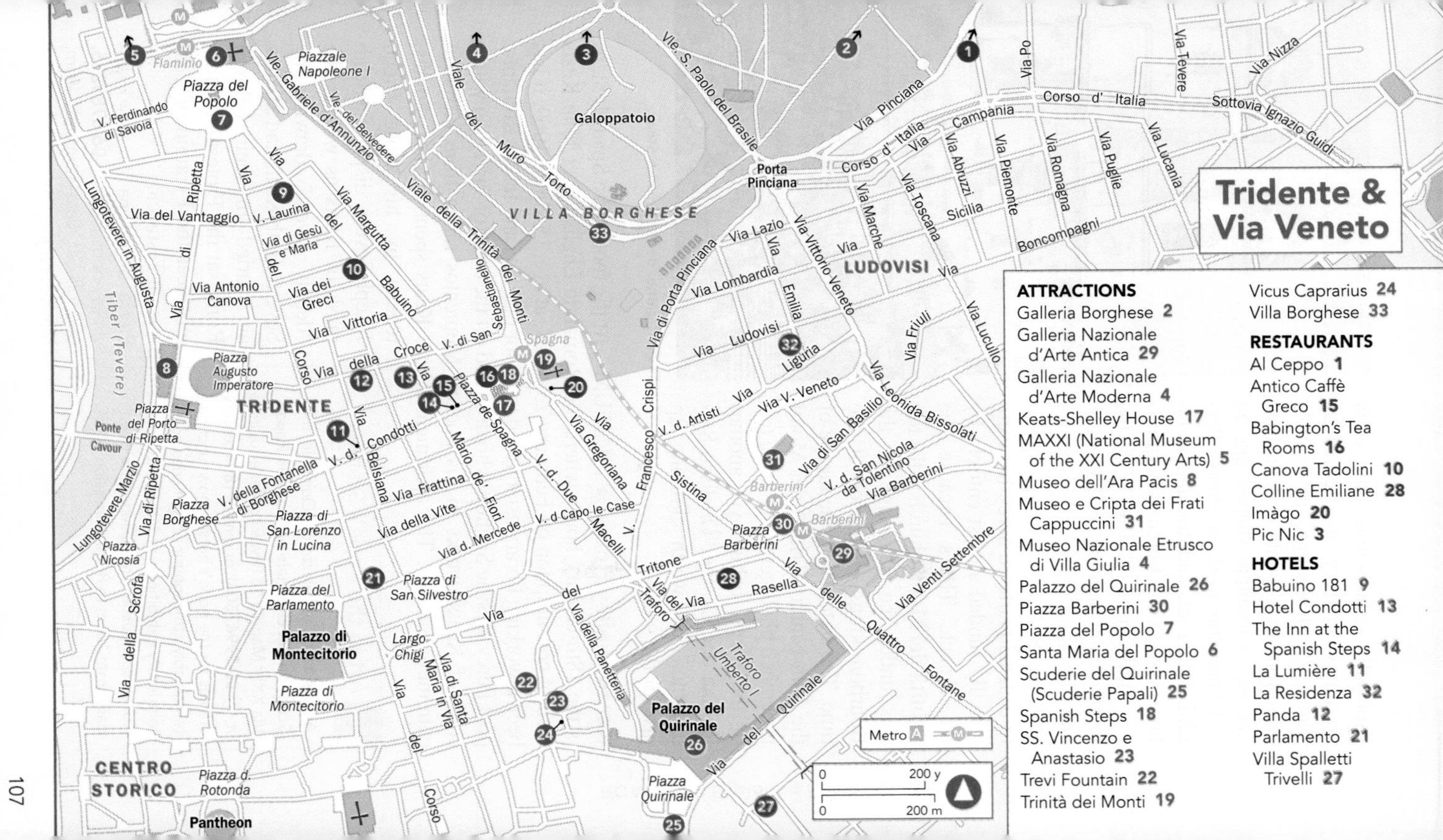
Tridente & Via Veneto
ATTRACTIONS
Galleria Borghese 2
Galleria Nazionale d'Arte Antica 29
Galleria Nazionale d'Arte Moderna 4
Keats-Shelley House 17
MAXXI (National Museum of the XXI Century Arts) 5
Museo dell'Ara Pacis 8
Museo e Cripta dei Frati Cappuccini 31
Museo Nazionale Etrusco di Villa Giulia 4
Palazzo del Quirinale 26
Piazza Barberini 30
Piazza del Popolo 7
Santa Maria del Popolo 6
Scuderie del Quirinale (Scuderie Papali) 25
Spanish Steps 18
SS. Vincenzo e Anastasio 23
Trevi Fountain 22
Trinità dei Monti 19
Vicus Caprarius 24
Villa Borghese 33
RESTAURANTS
Al Ceppo 1
Antico Caffè Greco 15
Babington's Tea Rooms 16
Canova Tadolini 10
Colline Emiliane 28
Imàgo 20
Pic Nic 3
HOTELS
Babuino 181 9
Hotel Condotti 13
The Inn at the Spanish Steps 14
La Lumière 11
La Residenza 32
Panda 12
Parlamento 21
Villa Spalletti Trivelli 27
Metro
0 200 y
0 200 m
VILLA BORGHESE
LUDOVISI
TRIDENTE
CENTRO STORICO
Galoppatoio
Piazza del Popolo
Piazzale Napoleone I
Porta Pinciana
Piazza Augusto Imperatore
Palazzo di Montecitorio
Palazzo del Quirinale
Piazza Barberini
Pantheon
Tiber (Tevere)
Via del Corso
Via Vittorio Veneto
Via Condotti
Via del Babuino
Via Margutta
Piazza de Spagna
Via del Tritone
Via delle Quattro Fontane
Via Sistina
Via Francesco Crispi
Via Veneto
Viale del Muro Torto
Viale della Trinità dei Monti
Via Ludovisi
Via Boncompagni
Corso d'Italia
Via Venti Settembre
Traforo Umberto I
Lungotevere in Augusta
Via di Ripetta

especially enchanting in early spring, when they are framed by thousands of blooming azaleas. At their foot lies "Fontana della Barcaccia," a fountain shaped like an old boat, the work of Pietro Bernini, father of sculptor and fountain-master Gian Lorenzo Bernini.

Built from 1723 to 1725, the monumental stairway of 135 steps and the square take their names from the Spanish Embassy (it used to be headquartered here), but were actually funded almost entirely by the French. That's because the **Trinità dei Monti** church at the top was under the patronage of the Bourbon kings of France at the time. The stately baroque facade of the 16th-century Trinità dei Monti is perched photogenically at the top of the Steps, behind yet another Roman obelisk, the "Obelisco Sallustiano." It's worth climbing up just for the views.

Tourists gather on the Spanish Steps.

Keats-Shelley House ★ MUSEUM At the foot of the Spanish Steps is the 18th-century house where the Romantic English poet John Keats died of consumption on February 23, 1821, at age 25. Since 1909, it has been a working library established in honor of Keats and fellow Romantic poet Percy Bysshe Shelley, who drowned off the coast of Viareggio with a copy of Keats' works in his pocket. Mementos range from kitsch to extremely moving. The apartment where Keats spent his last months, tended by his close friend Joseph Severn, displays a death mask of Keats as well as the "deadly sweat" drawing by Severn. Both Keats and Shelley are buried in their beloved Rome, at the Protestant cemetery near the Pyramid of Cestius, in Testaccio.

Piazza di Spagna 26. www.keats-shelley-house.org. ✆ **06-6784235.** 6€. Mon–Sat 10am–1pm and 2–6pm. Metro: Spagna.

Art in the Pope's Stables

Across from the Palazzo del Quirinale, the **Scuderie del Quirinale** or **Scuderie Papali,** Via XXIV Maggio 16 (www.scuderiequirinale.it; ✆ **06-39967500**), originally 18th-century stables for the pope's horses, now function as remarkably atmospheric art galleries hosting temporary exhibitions, including the occasional blockbuster. The galleries are open daily from 10am to 8pm. Admission is 15€.

Palazzo del Quirinale ★★ HISTORIC SITE Once the palace of popes and the king of Italy, since 1946 the Quirinale has been the official residence of the President of Italy, but parts of it are open to the public. Although it can't compare to Rome's major artistic showstoppers (there's little art or furniture in the rooms), the palace's baroque and neoclassical walls and ceilings are quite a spectacle. Few rooms anywhere are as impressive as the richly decorated 17th-century **Salone dei Corazzieri,** the **Sala d'Ercole** (once the apartments of Umberto I but completely rebuilt in 1940), and the tapestry-covered 17th-century **Sala dello Zodiaco.** Despite its Renaissance origins, this *palazzo* is rich in associations with ancient emperors and deities. The colossal statues of the "Dioscuri," Castor and Pollux, which now form part of the fountain in the piazza, were found in the nearby Baths of Constantine; in 1793 Pius VI had an ancient Egyptian obelisk moved here from the Mausoleum of Augustus. The sweeping view of the city from the piazza, which crowns the highest of the seven ancient hills of Rome, is itself worth the trip.

Coin Toss: Guaranteed Return to Rome?

The custom of tossing a coin into the Trevi Fountain to ensure your return to Rome apparently only works if you use correct form: With your back to the fountain, toss a coin with your right hand over your left shoulder. Works for me every time!

Piazza del Quirinale. palazzo.quirinale.it/palazzo.html. ✆ **06-39-96-7557.** 1.50€ for an 80-min. tour following one of three themed itineraries. Reservations must be made at least 5 days prior to visit. Tues–Wed and Fri–Sun 9:30am–4pm. Closed Aug. Metro: Barberini. Bus: 53, 60, 62-63, 70, 71, 80, 83, 85, 492.

Trevi Fountain ★★ MONUMENT As you elbow your way through the summertime crowds around the Trevi Fountain, it's hard to believe that this little piazza was nearly always deserted before 1950, when it began "starring" in films: *Roman Holiday* (1953), *Three Coins in the Fountain* (1954), and an iconic scene in Fellini's 1960 masterpiece *La Dolce Vita.* To this day, thousands of euro worth of coins are tossed into the fountain daily. The area is always jam-packed with tourists and selfie-stick hawkers, so keep your eye (and hands) on your belongings. Completed in 1762, this glorious baroque fountain centers on the triumphant figure of Neptune, standing on a shell chariot drawn by winged steeds and led by a pair of tritons. Allegorical figures in the side niches represent good health and fertility. On the southwestern corner of the piazza, the church of **SS. Vincenzo e Anastasio** has a strange claim to fame: Within it are the relics (hearts and intestines) of several popes. In an alley nearby, **Vicus Caprarius—the City of Water ★** (www.vicuscaprarius.com; ✆ **339-7786192;** 4€ admission; reservations suggested) is a privately run archaeological area comprised of several underground levels of ancient development, including an upscale home and part of the Acquedotto Vergine, the aqueduct that still feeds the Trevi.

Piazza di Trevi. Metro: Barberini. Bus: 52, 62-63, 80, 83, 85, 160, 492.

The Trevi Fountain.

Villa Borghese & Parioli

Villa Borghese ★★, just northeast of the Tridente, is not actually a villa but a large park, 6km (3¾ miles) in circumference. Cardinal Scipione Borghese created the park in the 1600s; Umberto I, king of Italy, acquired it in 1902 and presented it to the city of Rome. The greenbelt is crisscrossed by roads, but you can escape from the traffic and seek a shaded area under a tree to enjoy its landscaped vistas. On a sunny weekend, it's a pleasure to stroll here and see Romans at play, relaxing or inline skating. The park has a few casual cafes and food vendors (**Pic Nic** is a solid choice; see p. 145); you can also rent bikes or Segways here. In the northeast part of the park you'll find a **zoo** and the **Galleria Borghese** (see below). The neighborhoods to the north, Parioli and Pinciano, are elegant enclaves for those wishing to stay outside the crowded city center (see p. 68).

Galleria Borghese ★★★ ART MUSEUM On the far northeastern edge of the Villa Borghese, the Galleria Borghese occupies the former Villa Borghese Pinciana, built between 1609 and 1613 for Cardinal Scipione Borghese, an early patron of Bernini and an astute collector of work by Caravaggio. Today the gallery displays much of his collection and a lot more besides, making this one of Rome's great art treasures. It's also one of Rome's most pleasant sights to tour, thanks to the curators' mandate that only a limited number of people be allowed in at a time.

The ground floor is a **sculpture gallery** par extraordinaire, housing Canova's famously risqué statue of Paolina Borghese, sister of Napoleon and wife of the reigning Prince Camillo Borghese (when asked if she was uncomfortable posing nude, she reportedly replied, "No, the studio was heated."). The genius of Bernini reigns supreme in the following rooms, with his "David" (the face of which is thought to be a self-portrait) and **"Apollo and Daphne" ★★**, both seminal works of baroque sculpture. Look also for Bernini's Mannerist sculpture "The Rape of Persephone." Caravaggio is represented by several paintings: the "Madonna of the Grooms," the shadowy "St. Jerome," and the haunting **"David Holding the Head of Goliath" ★★**. Upstairs lies a rich collection of paintings, including Raphael's graceful "Deposition" and his sinuous "Lady with a Unicorn." There's also a series of self-portraits by Bernini, and his lifelike busts of Cardinal Scipione and Pope Paul V. One of Titian's best, **"Sacred and Profane Love" ★**, lies in one of the final rooms.

Important information: No more than 360 visitors at a time are allowed on the ground floor, and no more than 90 are allowed on the upper floor, during set 2-hour windows. **Reservations are essential** and can be made through the museum website. Roma Pass holders need to reserve an entry time by calling ✆ **06-32810** (Mon–Fri 9am–6pm; Sat 9am–1pm). English labeling in the museum is minimal. Guided tours of the galleries in English cost an extra 6.50€, or opt for an audioguide.

Piazzale del Museo Borghese 5 (off Via Pinciana). galleriaborghese.beniculturali.it. ✆ **06-32810.** 15€; 2€ ages 18 and under. Audio guides 5€. Tues–Sun 9am–7pm. Bus: 52, 53, 61, 89, 160, 490, 495, 590, 910. Tram: 3 or 19.

Bernini's "Rape of Persephone" in the Galleria Borghese.

Galleria Nazionale d'Arte Moderna ★ ART MUSEUM Housed in the monumental Bazzani Building constructed in 1911, this "modern" art collection ranges from unfashionable neoclassical and Romantic paintings and sculpture to better 20th-century works. Quality varies, but fans should seek out van Gogh's "Gardener" and "Portrait of Madame Ginoux" in Room 15, the handful of Impressionists in Room 14 (Cézanne, Degas, Monet, and Rodin), and Klimt's harrowing "Three Ages" in Room 16. Surrealist and Expressionist works by Miró, Kandinsky, and Mondrian appear in Room 22, and Pollock's "Undulating Paths" and Calder's "Mobile" hold court in Room 27. One of Warhol's "Hammer and Sickle" series is tucked away in Room 30.

Viale delle Belle Arti 131. lagallerianazionale.com/en. ✆ **06-322981.** 10€; free for ages 17 and under; 5€ for MAXXI ticket holders. Mon–Fri 9am–7pm. Metro: Flaminio. Bus: 61, 89, 160, 490, 495. Tram: 3 or 19.

Museo Nazionale Etrusco di Villa Giulia ★★★ MUSEUM The great Etruscan civilization was one of Italy's most advanced, although it remains relatively mysterious, in part because of its centuries-long rivalry with Rome. Rome definitively conquered the Etruscans by the 3rd century B.C., and though they adopted certain aspects of Etruscan culture, including religious practices, engineering innovations, and gladiatorial combat, gradual Romanization eclipsed virtually all the Etruscans' achievements.

The National Etruscan Museum, housed in the handsome Renaissance Villa Giulia, built by Pope Julius III between 1550 and 1555, is the best place in Italy to learn about the Etruscans, thanks to a cache of precious artifacts, sculptures, vases, monuments, tools, weapons, and jewels, the vast majority of it from tombs. Fans of ancient history could spend several hours here, but for those with less time, the most striking attraction is the stunning **Sarcofago degli Sposi** ★★ (Sarcophagus of the Spouses), a late-6th-century-B.C. terracotta funerary monument featuring a life-size bride and groom lounging at a banquet in the afterlife (Paris's Louvre has a similar monument). Equally fascinating are the **Pyrgi Tablets,** gold-leaf inscriptions in both Etruscan and Phoenician from the 5th century B.C., and the **Apollo of Veii,** a huge painted terracotta statue of Apollo dating to the 6th century B.C.

Piazzale di Villa Giulia 9. www.museoetru.it. ✆ **06-3226571.** 10€. Tues–Sun 8:30am–7:30pm; last entry 6:30pm. Bus: 982. Tram: 2, 19.

Via Veneto & Piazza Barberini

Piazza Barberini lies at the foot of several streets, among them Via Barberini, Via Sistina, and Via Vittorio Veneto. It would be a far more pleasant spot were it not for the traffic swarming around its principal feature, Bernini's **Fountain of the Triton** ★★ (Fontana del Tritone). For almost 4 centuries, this figure sitting in a vast open clam has been blowing water from his triton. To one side of the piazza is the aristocratic facade of the **Palazzo Barberini,** named for one of Rome's powerful families; inside is the **Galleria Nazionale d'Arte Antica** (see below). The Barberini reached their peak when a son was elected pope as Urban VIII; he encouraged Bernini and gave him patronage.

As you walk up **Via Vittorio Veneto,** look for the small fountain on the right corner of Piazza Barberini—it's another Bernini, the **Fountain of the Bees ★** (Fontana delle Api). At first they look more like flies, but they're the bees of the Barberini, the crest of that powerful family complete with the crossed keys of St. Peter above them. (Keys were always added to a family crest when a son was elected pope.)

Galleria Nazionale d'Arte Antica ★★★ ART MUSEUM On the southern side of Piazza Barberini, the grand **Palazzo Barberini** houses the Galleria Nazionale d'Arte Antica, which despite the "ancient" in its title is a trove of Italian art mostly from the early Renaissance to late baroque periods. Some of the art on display is wonderful, but the building itself is the main attraction, a baroque masterpiece begun by Carlo Maderno in 1627 and completed in 1633 by Bernini, with additional work by Borromini (notably a whimsical spiral staircase). The **Salone di Pietro da Cortona** in the center is the most captivating space, with a trompe l'oeil ceiling frescoed by da Cortona, a depiction of "The Triumph of Divine Providence." The museum's most intriguing works include Raphael's "La Fornarina," a baker's daughter thought to have been the artist's lover (look for Raphael's name on her bracelet); paintings by Tintoretto and Titian (Room 15); a Holbein portrait of English King Henry VIII (Room 16); and a couple of typically unsettling El Grecos in Room 17. Caravaggio dominates room 20 with the justly celebrated **"Judith and Holofernes" ★★★** and **"Narcissus" ★★.**

Via delle Quattro Fontane 13. www.barberinicorsini.org. ✆ **06-4814591.** 12€, valid for 20 days, also includes Palazzo Corsini; free ages 17 and under. Tues–Sun 10am–7pm; last entry 6pm. Metro: Barberini. Bus: 52, 53, 61–63, 80, 81, 83, 160, 492, 590.

Museum and Crypt of the Capuchin Friars ★★ RELIGIOUS SITE/MUSEUM One of the most mesmerizingly macabre sights in all Christendom, this otherwise restrained museum dedicated to the Capuchin order ends with a series of six chapels in the crypt, adorned with the skulls and bones of more than 3,700 Capuchin brothers, woven into mosaic works of art. Some of the skeletons are intact, draped with Franciscan habits; others form lamps and ceiling friezes. The tradition of the friars dates to a period when Christians had a richly creative cult of the dead and great spiritual masters meditated and preached with a skull in hand. Whatever you believe, the experience is a mix of spooky and meditative. The entrance is halfway up the first staircase on the right of the church of the Convento dei Frati Cappuccini, completed in 1630 and rebuilt in the early 1930s. ***Note:*** Because this site is located within a church, it maintains a strict dress code: no short pants or skirts and no bare arms—and no photos. We don't recommend this experience for kids under 10 or so.

Via Vittorio Veneto 27. www.cappucciniviaveneto.it. ✆ **06-88803695.** 8.50€; 5€ ages 17 and under. Daily 10am–7pm; last entry 6:30pm. Metro: Barberini. Bus: 52, 53, 61, 63, 80, 83, 160, 590.

Around Stazione Termini

Palazzo Massimo alle Terme ★★ MUSEUM A third of Rome's assortment of ancient art can be found at this branch of the Museo Nazionale Romano; among its treasures are a major coin collection, extensive maps of trade routes (with audio and visual exhibits on the network of traders over the centuries), and a vast sculpture collection that includes portrait busts of emperors and their families, as well as mythical figures like the Minotaur and Athena. But the real draw is on the second floor, where you can see some of the oldest of Rome's **frescoes ★★**; they depict an entire garden, complete with plants and birds, from the Villa di Livia a Prima Porta. (Livia was the wife of Emperor Augustus and was deified after her death in A.D. 29.)

Largo di Villa Peretti. www.museonazionaleromano.beniculturali.it. ✆ **06-39967700.** 12€ for single museum or 16€ for a 1-week pass that also includes Palazzo Altemps and the Baths of Diocletian; ages 17 and under free. Tues–Sun 11am–6pm; last entry 1 hr. before closing. Metro: Termini or Repubblica. Bus: 40, 64, or any bus that stops at Termini.

Santa Maria della Vittoria ★★ CHURCH A visit to this pretty little baroque church is all about one artwork: Gian Lorenzo Bernini's **"Ecstasy of St. Teresa" ★★★**. Crafted from marble between 1644 and 1647, it shows the Spanish saint at the moment of her ecstatic encounter with an angel (the so-called "Transverberation"), who gleefully pierces her with a spear. Bernini's depiction is deliciously erotic. Look for the Cornaro family, who sponsored the chapel's construction, watching the saint's ecstasy from their voyeuristic perch on the right.

Via XX Settembre 17 (at Largo S. Susanna). ✆ **06-42740571.** Free. Mon–Sat 9am–noon and 3:30–6pm; Sun 3:30–6pm. Metro: Repubblica. Bus: 61, 62, 85, 492, 590.

Santa Maria Maggiore ★★ CHURCH This imposing church, one of Rome's four papal basilicas, was founded by Pope Liberius in A.D. 358 and rebuilt on the orders of Pope Sixtus III from 432 to 440. Its 14th-century **campanile** is the city's loftiest. Don't be put off by the overdone 18th-century facade; there are treasures within, such as the 5th-century Roman mosaics in its nave, and the coffered ceiling, said to have been gilded with gold brought from the New World. The church also contains the **tomb of Bernini,** Italy's most important baroque sculptor–architect. The man who changed the face of Rome is buried in a tomb so simple that it takes a sleuth to track it down (to the right, near the altar).

Piazza di Santa Maria Maggiore. ✆ **06-69886800.** Free. Daily 7am–6:45pm. Metro: Termini or Cavour. Bus: 16, 70, 71, 75, 360, 590, 649, 714.

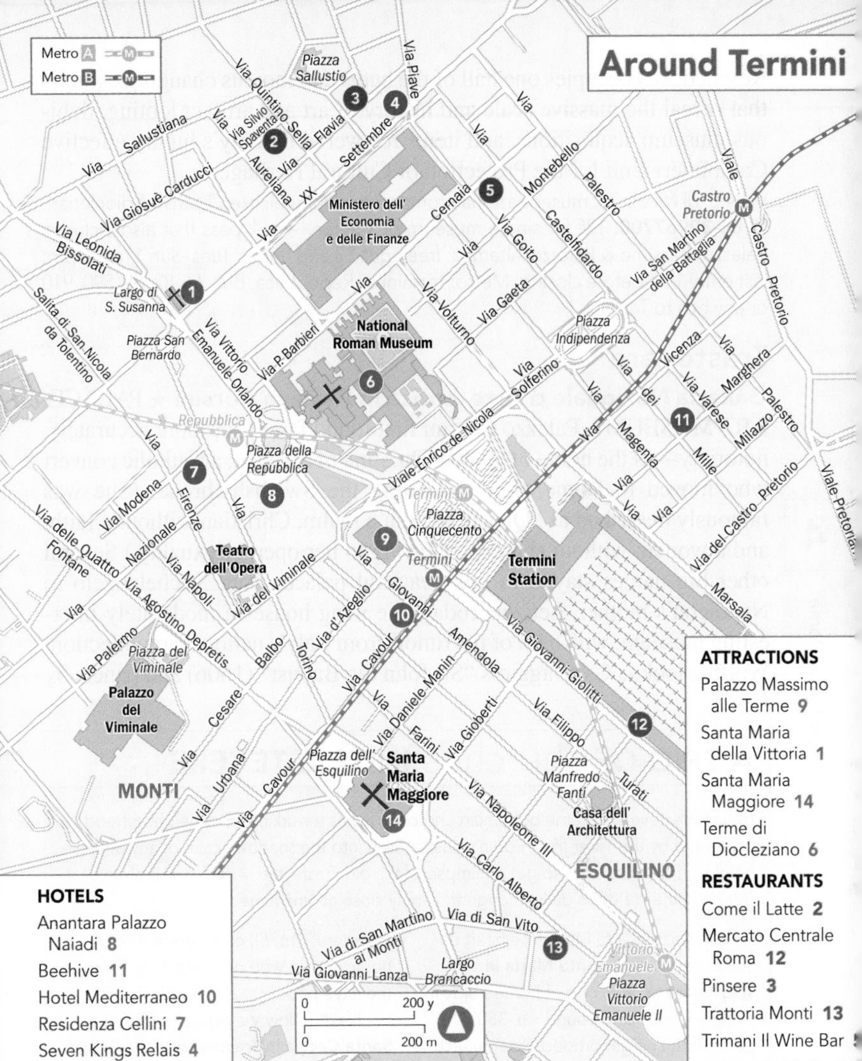

Terme di Diocleziano (Baths of Diocletian) ★★ MUSEUM/RUINS Originally this spot held the largest of Rome's baths, dating back to A.D. 298 and the reign of Emperor Diocletian. The vast baths, which once accommodated 3,000 at a time, were abandoned in the 6th century after the Goth invasions. During the Renaissance a church, cloister, and convent were built around the ruins—much of it designed by Michelangelo, no less. Today the entire hodgepodge is part of the Museo Nazionale Romano; it's a compelling museum stop that's usually quieter than the city's blockbusters. Exhibits include statuary and a large collection of inscriptions and other stone carvings from the Roman and pre-Roman eras. Since 2022, the new **Museo dell'Arte Salvata** ★★ (Museum for

Rescued Art) occupies one hall of the baths and mounts changing exhibits that reveal the massive scale and history of art and artifact looting, dubious museum acquisitions, and items recovered by Italy's highly effective Carabinieri Unit for the Protection of Cultural Heritage.

Viale E. di Nicola 78. museonazionaleromano.beniculturali.it/en/baths-of-diocletian. ✆ **06-39967700.** 12€ for single museum or 16€ for 1-week pass that also includes Palazzo Massimo & Palazzo Altemps; free ages 17 and under. Tues–Sun 11am–6pm; last entry 1 hr. before closing. Metro: Termini or Repubblica. Bus: 66, 82, 85, 590, 910 or any bus to Termini.

Trastevere

Galleria Nazionale d'Arte Antica in Palazzo Corsini ★ PALACE/ART MUSEUM Palazzo Corsini first found fame—or more accurately, notoriety—as the home of Queen Christina of Sweden, a Catholic convert who moved to Rome after abdicating the Swedish throne. (She was famously described as "Queen without a realm, Christian without a faith, and a woman without shame," referring to her open bisexuality.) Several other big names stayed in this beautiful palace, from Michelangelo to Napoleon's mother, Letizia. Today one wing houses a moderately interesting museum, with a lot of the runoff from Italy's national art collection. Worth a look is Caravaggio's "St. John the Baptist" (1606) and panels by

A TRIO OF churches IN TRASTEVERE

Before Trastevere became bohemian and cool, it was a working-class neighborhood, separated by the Tiber from Rome's bustle. Step into the shadowy calm of any of these neighborhood churches to get a glimpse of the old Trastevere. Admission is always free, and they're open daily, though they may close at lunchtime.

On Piazza Santa Maria, the heart of Trastevere, ornate **Santa Maria in Trastevere** ★★ is one of Rome's oldest churches, founded around A.D. 350. The pride of the neighborhood, it's spectacular inside and out, with a Romanesque brick bell tower, colorful frescoes, mosaics, and loads of recycled ancient marbles. Look for Cavallini's 1293 mosaics of the "Life of the Virgin Mary" in the apse.

From there, Via di San Francisco a Ripa angles southeast to the church of **San Francesco d'Assisi a Ripa** ★, so named because it's built over a convent where St. Francis stayed in 1219 when he came to Rome to see the pope (his simple cell is preserved inside). A Bernini treasure is tucked into the last chapel on the left: the "Tomb of Beata Ludovica Albertoni" (1675), commemorating a noblewoman who dedicated her life to the city's poor.

Next, follow Via Anicia northeast to **Santa Cecilia in Trastevere** ★★ (Piazza Santa Cecilia; www.benedettinesantacecilia.it), a still-functioning convent with a peaceful courtyard garden. Tradition holds that St. Cecilia herself once lived on this site; the church's altar has an exquisite marble sculpture of her (ca. 1600) carved by Stefano Maderno. The basilica and Roman-era ruins underneath can be visited daily (10am–12:30pm and 4–6pm; Sun opens at 11:30am). The partial remains of a "Last Judgment" by Pietro Cavallini (ca. 1293), a masterpiece of Roman medieval painting, can be visited only in the morning.

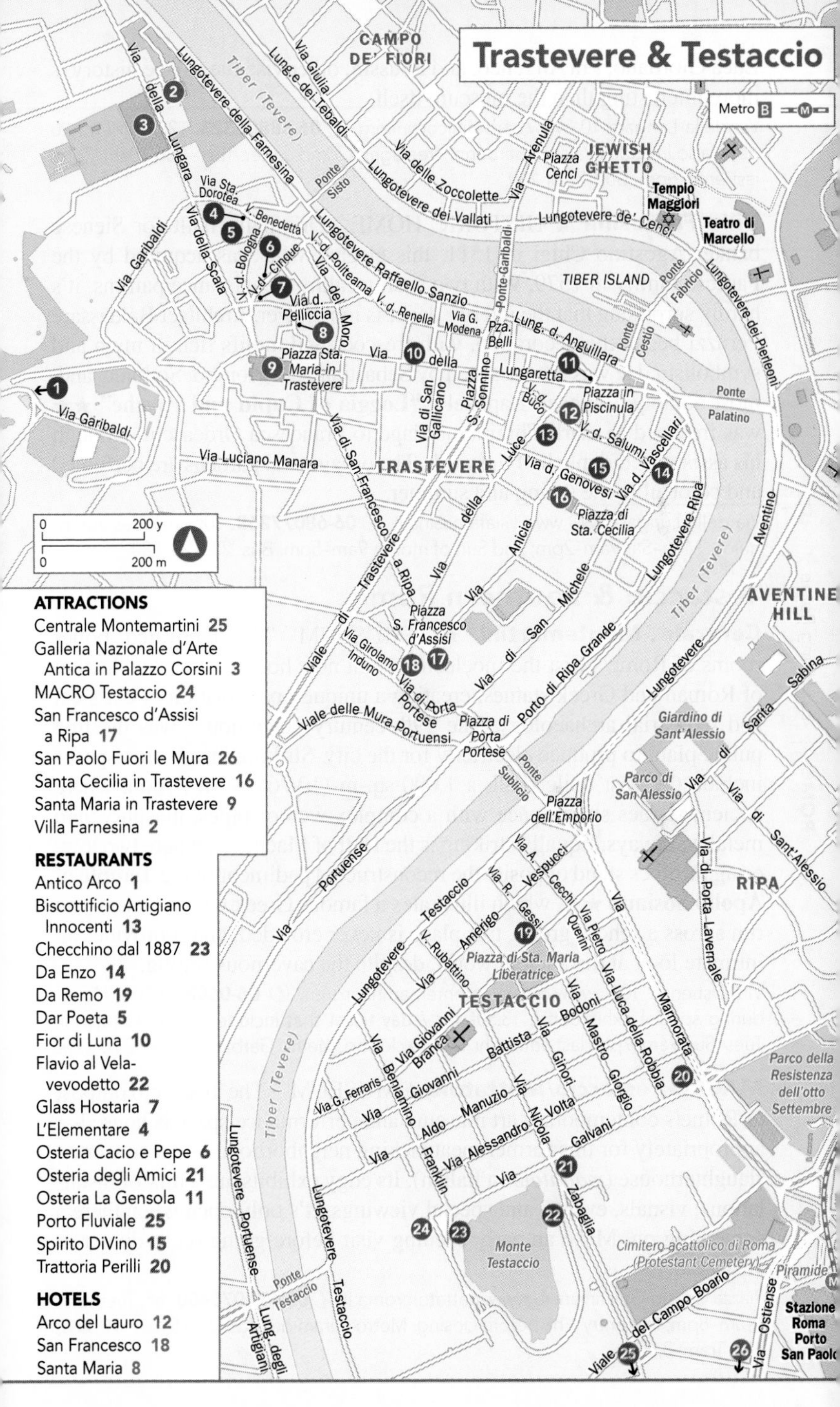

Trastevere & Testaccio
Metro B M
ATTRACTIONS
Centrale Montemartini 25
Galleria Nazionale d'Arte Antica in Palazzo Corsini 3
MACRO Testaccio 24
San Francesco d'Assisi a Ripa 17
San Paolo Fuori le Mura 26
Santa Cecilia in Trastevere 16
Santa Maria in Trastevere 9
Villa Farnesina 2
RESTAURANTS
Antico Arco 1
Biscottificio Artigiano Innocenti 13
Checchino dal 1887 23
Da Enzo 14
Da Remo 19
Dar Poeta 5
Fior di Luna 10
Flavio al Velavevodetto 22
Glass Hostaria 7
L'Elementare 4
Osteria Cacio e Pepe 6
Osteria degli Amici 21
Osteria La Gensola 11
Porto Fluviale 25
Spirito DiVino 15
Trattoria Perilli 20
HOTELS
Arco del Lauro 12
San Francesco 18
Santa Maria 8
0 200 y
0 200 m
CAMPO DE' FIORI
JEWISH GHETTO
Tempio Maggiori
Teatro di Marcello
TIBER ISLAND
TRASTEVERE
AVENTINE HILL
RIPA
TESTACCIO
Tiber (Tevere)
Via della Lungara
Lungotevere della Farnesina
Via Giulia
Lung.e dei Tebaldi
Via delle Zoccolette
Via Arenula
Piazza Cenci
Lungotevere dei Vallati
Lungotevere de' Cenci
Ponte Sisto
Via Sta. Dorotea
V. Benedetta
Via Garibaldi
Via della Scala
V. d. Bologna
V. d. Cinque
V. d. Politeama
Via del Moro
Via d. Pelliccia
Lungotevere Raffaello Sanzio
V. d. Renella
Via G. Modena
Ponte Garibaldi
Pza. Belli
Lung. d. Anguillara
Ponte Fabricio
Ponte Cestio
Lungotevere dei Pierleoni
Piazza Sta. Maria in Trastevere
Via della Lungaretta
Via di San Gallicano
Piazza S. Sonnino
V. d. Buco
Piazza in Piscinula
Ponte Palatino
V. d. Salumi
Via d. Vascellari
Via d. Genovesi
Piazza di Sta. Cecilia
Via della Luce
Via Luciano Manara
Via di San Francesco a Ripa
Viale di Trastevere
Via Anicia
Lungotevere Ripa
Aventino
Via di San Michele
Piazza S. Francesco d'Assisi
Via Girolamo Induno
Via di Porta Portese
Viale delle Mura Portuensi
Piazza di Porta Portese
Porto di Ripa Grande
Lungotevere Aventino
Giardino di Sant'Alessio
Parco di San Alessio
Via di Santa Sabina
Via di Sant'Alessio
Ponte Sublicio
Piazza dell'Emporio
Via Portuense
Via A. Vespucci
Via R. Gessi
Via A. Cecchi
Via Pietro Querini
Via di Porta Lavernale
Lungotevere Testaccio
Via Amerigo
V. Rubattino
Piazza di Sta. Maria Liberatrice
Via Luca della Robbia
Via Marmorata
Via Giovanni Branca
Via Beniamino Franklin
Via Giovanni Battista Bodoni
Via Mastro Giorgio
Via Ginori
Via G. Ferraris
Via Aldo Manuzio
Via Alessandro Volta
Via Nicola Zabaglia
Via Galvani
Parco della Resistenza dell'otto Settembre
Lungotevere Portuense
Monte Testaccio
Cimitero acattolico di Roma (Protestant Cemetery)
Piramide
Ponte Testaccio
Lung. degli Artigiani
Viale del Campo Boario
Via Ostiense
Stazione Roma Porto San Paolo

Luca Giordano, Fra Angelico, and Poussin; otherwise the palace history is more interesting than the museum itself.

Via della Lungara 10. www.barberinicorsini.org. ✆ **06-68802323.** 12€, valid for 20 days, also includes Palazzo Barberini; free ages 17 and under. Tues–Sun 10am–7pm; last entry 6pm. Bus: 23 or 280.

Villa Farnesina ★ HISTORIC HOME Originally built for Sienese banker Agostino Chigi in 1511, this elegant villa was acquired by the Farnese family in 1579. With two such wealthy Renaissance patrons, it's hardly surprising that the interior decor is top drawer. Architect Baldassare Peruzzi began the decoration, with frescoes and motifs rich in myth and symbolism. He was later assisted by Sebastiano del Piombo, Sodoma, and, most notably, Raphael. Raphael's **"Loggia of Cupid and Psyche"** ★★ was frescoed to mark Chigi's marriage to Francesca Ordeaschi—though his assistants did much of the work. The ornamental gardens are perfumed and colorful in the spring and summer.

Via della Lungara 230. www.villafarnesina.it. ✆ **06-68077268.** 10€, includes audioguide. Mon–Sat 9am–2pm; 2nd Sun of month 9am–5pm. Bus: 23, 125, 280.

Testaccio & Southern Rome

Centrale Montemartini ★★ MUSEUM The renovated boiler rooms of Rome's first thermoelectric plant now house a grand collection of Roman and Greek statues, creating a unique juxtaposition of classical and industrial archaeology. The 19th-century powerhouse was the first public plant to produce electricity for the city. Striking installation spaces include the vast boiler hall, a 1,000-sq.-m (10,764-sq.-ft.) room where ancient statues share space with a complex web of pipes, masonry, and metal walkways. Equally striking is the Hall of Machines, where two towering turbines stand opposite the reconstructed pediment of the **Temple of Apollo Sosiano** ★★, which illustrates a famous Greek battle. Unless you run across a school group, this place is never crowded, and it provides an intimate look at the ancient world, despite the cavernous setting.

Via Ostiense 106. www.centralemontemartini.org/en. ✆ **06-0608.** 7.50€ (higher during special exhibitions); 13.50€ for 7-day ticket that includes Musei Capitolini. Tues–Sun 9am–7pm; last entry 1 hr. before closing. Metro: Garbatella. Bus: 23 or 769.

MACRO Testaccio/Mattatoio ★ MUSEUM The Testaccio outpost of Rome's contemporary art museum and performance space is housed—appropriately for this former meatpacking neighborhood—in a converted slaughterhouse (*mattatoio* in Italian). Its edgy exhibits are a mix of installations, visuals, events, and special viewings. It's only open when there's something on. Make an early evening visit before going on to dinner in Testaccio.

Piazza Orazio Guistiniani 4. www.mattatoioroma.it. ✆ **06-671070400.** 8€. Tues–Sun 11am–8pm; last entry 1 hr. before closing. Metro: Piramide. Bus: 23, 75, 83, 170, 280, 716. Tram: 3, 8.

Mussolini's City of the Future

South of the city center, the outlying **EUR suburb ★** (the acronym stands for *Esposizione Universale Romana*) was designed and purpose-built by Mussolini in the Fascist era to stage the planned World Fair of 1942—canceled, thanks to World War II. Today, EUR's mix of rationalist and classical-inspired elements will enthuse anyone with a serious interest in architecture. Perfect symmetry and sleek marble-lined avenues house a number of museums, corporate headquarters, and office agglomerates, easily connected to the *centro storico* by Metro (Line B). We keep hoping that the **Museum of Roman Civilization,** closed indefinitely for renovation, will reopen one of these days (check status at www.museociviltaromana.it): It's known for its huge scale model of Rome at the time of Emperor Constantine.

San Paolo Fuori le Mura ★★ CHURCH The giant Basilica of St. Paul, whose origins date from the time of Constantine, is Rome's fourth great patriarchal church. It was erected over the tomb of St. Paul the Apostle and is the second-largest church in Rome after St. Peter's. The basilica fell victim to fire in 1823 and was subsequently rebuilt—hence the relatively modern look. Inside, translucent alabaster windows illuminate a forest of single-file columns and mosaic medallions (portraits of the various popes). Its most important artistic treasure is a 12th-century marble candelabrum by Vassalletto, who's also responsible for the remarkable cloisters containing twisted pairs of columns enclosing a rose garden. Miraculously, the baldacchino by Arnolfo di Cambio (1285) wasn't damaged in the fire; it now shelters the tomb of St. Paul.

Via Ostiense 190 (at Piazzale San Paolo). www.basilicasanpaolo.org. ✆ **06-69880800.** Basilica free; cloisters 4€. Basilica daily 7am–6:30pm; cloisters 9am–5:30pm. Metro: Basilica di San Paolo. Bus: 23, 769, 792.

The Via Appia (Appian Way) & the Catacombs

Of all the roads that led to Rome, **Via Appia Antica** (begun in 312 B.C.) was the most famous. It stretched all the way to the seaport of Brindisi, through which trade with Greece and the East was funneled. (According to Christian tradition, it was along the Appian Way that an escaping St. Peter encountered a vision of Christ, causing him to go back into the city to face martyrdom.) The road's initial stretch in Rome is lined with the monuments and ancient tombs of patrician Roman families—burials were forbidden within the city walls as early as the 5th century B.C.—and, below ground, miles of tunnels hewn out of the soft *tufa* stone, which hardens on exposure to the air.

These tunnels, or catacombs, were where early Christians buried their dead. A few are open to the public, so you can wander through tunnels whose walls are gouged out with tens of thousands of burial niches, now mostly empty, including small niches made for children. Early Christians referred to each chamber as a *dormitorio*—they believed the bodies were only sleeping, awaiting resurrection (which is why they could not observe the traditional Roman practice of cremation). In some you can still see the remains of early Christian art. The obligatory guided tours feature occasionally biased history, plus a dash of sermonizing, but the guides are very knowledgeable.

The **Appia Antica park** is a popular Sunday picnic site for Roman families, following the half-forgotten pagan tradition of dining in the presence of one's ancestors on holy days. Via Appia Antica is closed to cars on Sundays, left for the picnickers, walkers, and bicyclists. See **www.parcoappiaantica.it** for more, including downloadable maps.

To reach the catacombs area, take bus no. 218 from the San Giovanni Metro stop or the 118 from Colosseo or Circus Maximus. ***Tip:*** The 118 runs more frequently than the 218 and deposits you closer to the catacombs, but it runs less frequently on Sundays. If you are in a hurry to accommodate your visit to the catacombs, take a taxi (p. 72).

Catacombe di Domitilla ★★★ RELIGIOUS SITE/TOUR The oldest of the catacombs is the hands-down winner for most enjoyable experience. Groups are relatively small (in part because the site is not directly on the Appian Way), and guides are entertaining and personable. The catacombs—Rome's longest at 17km (11 miles)—were built below land donated by Domitilla, a noblewoman of the Flavian dynasty who was exiled from Rome for practicing Christianity. They were rediscovered in 1593, after a church abandoned in the 9th century collapsed. The visit begins in the sunken church founded in A.D. 380, the year Christianity became Rome's state religion.

There are fewer "sights" here than in the other catacombs, but this is the only catacomb where you'll still see bones; the rest have emptied their tombs to rebury the remains in inaccessible lower levels. Elsewhere in the tunnels, 4th-century frescoes contain some of the earliest representations of Saints Peter and Paul. Notice the absence of crosses: It was only later

A Noble Survivor

Of all the monuments on the Appian Way itself, the most impressive is the **Tomb of Cecilia Metella** ★, within walking distance of the catacombs. The cylindrical tomb, clad in travertine and topped with a marble frieze, honors the wife of one of Julius Caesar's military commanders from the republican era. Why such an elaborate tomb for a figure of relatively minor historical importance? Other mausoleums may have been even more elaborate, but Cecilia Metella's earned enduring fame simply because her tomb has remained while the others have decayed. Part of the reason is its symbiotic relationship with the early-14th-century **Castle Caetani** attached to the rear. For centuries, the tomb survived being plundered for building materials because of the castle, which was built to guard the road and collect tolls; in later eras, the castle was spared because it was attached to the romantic ruin of the tomb. Admission to the tomb (8€) includes access to other sites in the archaeological park. It's open from 9am to dusk. See www.parcoarcheologicoappiaantica.it for more info (Italian only).

that Christians replaced the traditional fish symbol with the cross. During this period, Christ's crucifixion was a source of shame to the community, as he'd been killed like a common criminal.

Via delle Sette Chiese 282. www.domitilla.info. ✆ **06-5110342.** 10€ adults; 7€ children 6–14. Wed–Mon 9am–noon and 2–5pm. Closed mid-Dec to mid-Jan. Bus: 30, 160, 714 (to Piazza dei Navigatori) or 218.

Catacombe di San Callisto ★★ RELIGIOUS SITE/TOUR "The most venerable and most renowned of Rome," said Pope John XXIII of the San Callisto funerary tunnels. These catacombs are often packed with tour-bus groups, but the tunnels are phenomenal. They're the first cemetery of Christian Rome, the burial place of 16 popes in the 3rd century. They bear the name of the deacon St. Callixtus, who served as pope from A.D. 217–22. The network of galleries is on four levels and reaches a depth of about 20m (65 ft.), the deepest in the area. There are many sepulchral chambers and almost half a million tombs of early Christians.

Entering the catacombs, you see the most important crypt, that of nine popes. Some of the original marble tablets of their tombs are preserved. Also commemorated is St. Cecilia, patron of sacred music (her relics were moved to her church in Trastevere during the 9th century; see p. 116). Farther on are the Cubicles of the Sacraments, with 3rd-century frescoes.

Via Appia Antica 110–26. www.catacombe.roma.it. ✆ **06-5130151.** 10€ adults; 7€ ages 7–15. Thurs–Tues 9am–noon and 2–5pm. Closed mid-Jan to mid-Feb. Bus: 118, 218.

Catacombe di San Sebastiano ★ RELIGIOUS SITE/TOUR Today the tomb and relics of St. Sebastian are in the ground-level basilica, but his original resting place was in the catacombs beneath it. Sebastian was a senior Milanese soldier in the Roman army who converted to Christianity and was martyred during Emperor Diocletian's persecutions, which were especially brutal in the first decade of the 4th century. From the reign of Valerian to that of Constantine, the bodies of Saints Peter and Paul were also hidden in the catacombs, which were dug from the soft volcanic rock (*tufa*). The church was built in the 4th century and remodeled in the 17th century. In the tunnels and mausoleums are mosaics and graffiti, along with many other pagan and Christian objects, as well as four Roman tombs with their frescoes and stucco fairly intact, found in 1922 after being buried for almost 2,000 years.

Via Appia Antica 136. www.catacombe.org. ✆ **06-7850350.** 10€ adults; 7€ ages 6–15. Daily 10am–5pm. Closed Dec. Bus: 118, 218.

New Ways to See Rome on Two Feet…or Four Wheels

We recently tried out two new tour options in Rome, and while they couldn't be more different from one another, we were wowed by both. Tour guide, art historian, and runner Isa Calidonna, the force behind **ArcheoRunning** (www.archeorunning.com), leads early-morning **running tours** of the city, including options that explore Trastevere, the

ORGANIZED tours

Forget the flag-waving guides leading a herd of dazed travelers around monuments. A better class of professionally guided tours delivers insider expertise, focused themes, and personal attention, plus perks such as skipping entry lines and visiting after hours. For **food tours and cooking classes** in Rome, see p. 139.

One of the leading tour operators in Rome, **Context Travel ★** (www.contexttravel.com; ✆ **800/691-6036** in the U.S., or 06-96727371) uses historians, art historians, and archaeologists to lead small-group walking tours around Rome's monuments, museums, and piazzas, as well as culinary walks and excellent family programs. Tour prices are high, beginning at about 100€ per person for 2 hours, but most participants consider them a highlight of their trip.

The affable team at **The Roman Guy** (www.theromanguy.com; ✆ **06-342-8761859**) provides knowledgeable guides who explain thousands of years of history in an engaging, informal way. They offer small-group (most about 15 people) tours of the Colosseum, Vatican Museums, and the Catacombs, food tours of Trastevere, and other options. Prices run from 60€ per person to much more for exclusive VIP access and/or private excursions.

Walks of Italy (www.walksofitaly.com; ✆ **06-95583331**) also runs excellent guided tours of Rome starting from 39€; more in-depth explorations of the Colosseum, Vatican Museums, and Forum go for 60€ to 125€.

Enjoy Rome (www.enjoyrome.com; ✆ **06-4451843**) offers a number of "greatest hits" walking tours, plus an early-evening tour of the Jewish Ghetto and Trastevere; their bus excursion to the catacombs and Appian Way visits an ancient aqueduct that most Romans, let alone tourists, never see. Tours start at 45€ per person; entrance fees are included with some, but not all tours.

The team at **Through Eternity** (www.througheternity.com; ✆ **06-7009336**) are art historians and architects; what sets them apart is their theatrical delivery, helped along by the dramatic scripts that many of the guides follow. It can be a lot of fun, but it's not for everyone. A 3½-hour tour of the Vatican is 69€; most other tours range from 39€ to 129€.

Tour broker **Get Your Guide** (www.getyourguide.com) offers a raft of options in Rome, including the usual ancient Roman suspects, as well as guided tours of Galleria Borghese and day trips to Pompeii and Tivoli.

For something completely different, artist Kelly Medford runs **Sketching Rome Tours** (www.sketchingrometours.com), 2½-hour small-group drawing and painting lessons in some of Rome's prettiest corners. Supplies are provided and no artistic talent is required (75€ per person).

Appian Way, and Villa Borghese. With frequent stops for Calidonna's engaging history lessons, there's time to catch your breath before setting off again. (She also offers walking tours.) Having the streets, bridges, and piazzas of Rome to yourself in the early morning hours is a glorious treat.

Golf-cart tours have existed in Rome for a few years, and we'll admit that we wrote them off as kind of a silly way to see the city—until we tried one. Our 2½-hour, fully narrated evening tour with **Wheel.Tours** (www.wheel.tours; ✆ **39/342-9812803;** 99€ per person) took in every major sight in the historic center and whisked us up the Janiculum Hill for an ethereal view of the Eternal City lit up below. Especially for those on a tight timeframe, there's simply no other way to cover so much ground in Rome—and absorb so much information—in such a short amount of time.

Especially for Kids

There's a real Jekyll-and-Hyde quality to exploring Rome with kids. On the one hand, it's a capital city, big, busy, and hot. On the other, the very best parts of the city for kids—Roman ruins, subterranean worlds, and *gelato*—are aspects you'd want to explore anyway. Seeing Rome with kids doesn't demand an itinerary redesign. And despite what you have heard about its famous seven hills, much of the center is mercifully flat, and pedestrian- (if not always stroller-) friendly.

Food is pretty easy too: Roman **pizzas** are some of the best in the world—see "Where to Eat" (p. 137) for our favorites. Ditto the ice cream, or *gelato* (p. 140). Restaurants in any price category will be happy to serve up a simple *pasta al pomodoro* (pasta with tomato sauce), and kids are welcomed virtually everywhere, including late in the evening.

The city is shorter on green spaces than many European cities, but the landscaped gardens of the **Villa Borghese** have plenty of room for kids to let off steam. Pack a picnic or rent some bikes (p. 110). The **Parco Appia Antica** (www.parcoappiaantica.it) is another favorite, especially on a Sunday or holiday when the old cobbled road is closed to traffic. The park's **catacombs** (p. 119) are eerie enough to intrigue young minds, but also fascinating Christian and historical sites in their own right.

Museums, of course, are trickier. My 8-year-old was enthralled by a small museum exhibit of gory Renaissance paintings depicting biblical murders and sacrifices, but could not get out of the crowded Vatican Museums fast enough—it's not much fun when you can't see over the backs of all those adults. You can probably get kids fired up more easily for the really ancient stuff. Make the bookshop at the **Colosseum** (p. 88) an early stop; it has a good selection of guides aimed at under-12s, themed on gladiators and featuring funny or cartoonish material. The **Musei Capitolini** (p. 94) invites kids to hunt down some of the collection's treasures, highlighted on a free leaflet—it'll buy you a couple of hours to admire the exhibits and perhaps see them from a new and unexpected angle. The multiple levels below **San Clemente** (p. 96) and the **Case Romane del Celio** (p. 97) are another draw for small visitors.

Also build in some time to throw a coin in the **Trevi Fountain** (p. 109), and to enjoy watching the feral cats relaxing amid the ruins of **Largo di Torre Argentina.** A cat sanctuary here provides basic health-care to Rome's many strays.

Aspiring young gladiators may want to spend 2 hours at the **Rome Gladiator School** (www.romegladiatorschool.com; 120€ per person), where they can prepare for a duel in a reasonably authentic way.

Several of the tour operators listed on page 122 offer family-oriented tours with special activities and perks for younger travelers.

WHERE TO STAY IN ROME

Hotels in Rome's *centro storico* are often overpriced and disappointing, and all too often the grand exteriors and lobbies of historic buildings give way to bland modern rooms. Our selections here made the cut because they offer unique experiences, highly personalized service, or extreme value—and in a few cases, all of the above.

Room rates vary wildly depending on the season, and last-minute deals are common. For example, a room at a hotel we classify as "expensive" might be had for as low as 99€ if it has empty beds to fill. Always **book directly with the hotel**—you'll usually get a better rate and the chance to build some rapport with reception staff.

Breakfast in all but the highest echelon of hotels is often a buffet with coffee, fruit, rolls, and cheese. It's not always included in the rate, so check the reservation options carefully. If you are budgeting and breakfast is a payable extra, skip it and go to a nearby cafe-bar, where a caffè and *cornetto* (espresso and croissant) will likely be much cheaper.

Though most Roman hotels now have **air-conditioning** (a must during the stifling summer months), some budget options still do not. If it's not listed as a room amenity, double-check.

Self-Catering Apartments

Rental apartments have some great virtues: They're often cheaper than standard facilities, and they let you save money by preparing at least some of your own meals.

Nearly every vacation rental in Rome—and there are tens of thousands of them—is owned and maintained by a third party (that is, not the rental agency). That means that the decor and flavor of the apartments, even in the same price range and neighborhood, can vary widely. Every reputable agency, however, puts multiple photos of each property they handle on its website, so you'll have a sense of what you're getting into. The photos should be accompanied by a list of amenities. Goliath booking sites **www.airbnb.com**, **Homeaway.com**, and **vrbo.com**, platforms that allow individuals to rent their own apartments to guests, have thousands of listings in Rome. These will often be cheaper than apartments rented through local agencies, but they won't be vetted, and sometimes you're on your own if something goes wrong.

If you decide to rent through one of the agencies below, know that it is standard practice for them to collect 30% of the total rental amount upfront to secure a booking. When you get to Rome and check in, the balance of your rental fee is often payable in cash only. Upon booking, the agency should provide you with detailed "check-in" procedures. ***Tip:*** Make sure you ask for a few numbers to call in case of an emergency.

Beyond that, most apartments come with information sheets that list neighborhood shops and services.

RECOMMENDED AGENCIES **Cross Pollinate** (www.cross-pollinate.com; ✆ **06-99369799**), a multi-destination agency, has a roster of apartments and B&Bs in Rome. Each property is inspected before it's listed. **Cities Reference** (www.citiesreference.com/en/rome; ✆ **06-48903612**) offers no-surprises property descriptions (with helpful and diplomatic tags like "better for young people") and even includes the eco-footprint for each apartment. You can expect transparency and responsiveness from the plain-dealing staff. **Rental in Rome** (www.rentalinrome.com; ✆ **06-3220068**) has the widest selection of midrange and luxury apartments in the *centro storico* zone (less expensive ones, too), plus an alluring website with video clips of the apartments.

Monasteries & Convents

Staying in a convent or a monastery can be a great bargain. But remember, these are religious houses, which means the decor is most often stark and the rules inflexible. Cohabitating is almost always frowned upon—though marriage licenses are rarely required—and unruly behavior is not tolerated (so no staggering in after too much vino at dinner). Plus, there's usually a curfew. Most rooms in convents and monasteries do not have private bathrooms; ask when making your reservation in case some are available. If, however, you're planning a low-key trip to Rome, and you can live with these parameters, convents and monasteries are an affordable and often fascinating option. The place to start is **www.monasterystays.com**, which lays out all your monastic options for the Eternal City.

A Note on a Notte in Rome

The Rome City Council applies a "sojourn" tax of 3€ to 7€ (depending on hotel class) per person, per night. Many hotels will request this fee in cash upon check-in or check-out; this is perfectly normal. Children ages 10 and under are exempt.

Around Vatican City & Prati

For many, this is a rather dull area to be based in. It's well removed from the ancient sites, and though Prati has some good restaurants, the area overall is not geared to nightlife. But if the main purpose of your visit centers on the Vatican, you'll be fine here, and you will be joined by thousands of other pilgrims, nuns, and priests (see map p. 77).

MODERATE

Mama Shelter Roma ★ The Rome installment of the trendy, affordable-ish design hotel chain is certainly the most interesting recent opening in this corner of the city—an otherwise nondescript residential area northwest of the Vatican Museums. Rooms are small, busy, and perhaps a little too self-consciously hip, but definitely on-brand. Buzzy perks include a

Views from the roof deck at Mama Shelter Roma.

roof deck, a restaurant, bar and pizzeria, and an indoor pool—the latter a real rarity in Rome.

Via Luigi Rizzo 20. mamashelter.com/roma. ✆ **06-94538900.** 217 units. 129€–289€ double. Metro: Cipro. **Amenities:** Restaurant; bar; pizzeria; roof terrace; indoor pool; fitness room; free Wi-Fi.

QuodLibet ★★★ The name is Latin for "what pleases," and we'll be frank: Everything pleases us here. This upscale B&B boasts spacious, colorful rooms, gorgeous artwork and furnishings, and generous breakfasts (served on the roof terrace, which also offers evening bar service). All the rooms are set on the fourth floor of an elegant building (with elevator and air-conditioning), so it's quieter than many places. It's located just a 10-minute walk from the Vatican Museums and a block from the Metro. Charming, conscientious hosts possess a deep knowledge of Rome and what will interest visitors. A top pick!

Via Barletta 29. www.quodlibetroma.com. ✆ **06-1222642.** 10 units. 89€–250€ double. Rates include breakfast. Minimum-stay rules may apply. Metro: Ottaviano. **Amenities:** Roof terrace; free Wi-Fi.

Residenza Paolo VI ★★ Literally across the street from Vatican City limits, Residenza Paolo can legitimately claim it's "steps from St. Peter's." Taking breakfast on the rooftop terrace is a special treat, as this narrow strip overlooks St. Peter's Square—if your timing's right, you'll see the pope blessing crowds on Sunday. (There's bar service on the terrace from 4pm onwards.) Old-worldy rooms feature tile or hardwood floors, heavy drapes, Oriental rugs, and quality beds, though standard guest rooms can be a bit "cozy."

Via Paolo VI 29. www.residenzapaolovi.com. ✆ **06-684870.** 35 units. 129€–229€ double. Rates include breakfast. Metro: Ottaviano (15-min. walk). Bus: 64. **Amenities:** Bar; room service; free Wi-Fi.

Villa Laetitia ★★★ This elegant hotel overlooking the River Tiber is the work of Anna Fendi of the Roman fashion dynasty. Thanks to her design aesthetic, the rooms are anything but traditional, despite the 1911 villa setting surrounded by tranquil gardens. The decor features bold patterns on the beds and floors, and modern art on the walls. Splurge for the black-and-white Giulio Cesare suite, with its round leather bed and blissful garden views. Standard rooms are on the snug side, but most have kitchenettes. It's worth noting that the hotel is a 20-minute walk to Centro and thus perhaps not the best choice for first-timers to Rome. **Enoteca la Torre** is the villa's two-Michelin-starred restaurant. ***Tip:*** Check for great last-minute rates on the hotel website.

Lungotevere delle Armi 22–23. www.villalaetitia.com. ✆ **06-3226776.** 20 units. 135€–400€ double. Rates include breakfast. Metro: Lepanto. **Amenities:** Restaurant; bar; babysitting; bike rentals; fitness room; room service; free Wi-Fi.

INEXPENSIVE

Rome Armony Suites ★★★ A warning: Rome Armony Suites is almost always booked up months in advance, so if you're interested, book early. Why so popular? The answer starts with service; owner Luca is a charming, sensitive host, especially helpful with first-time visitors to Rome. Rooms are big, clean, and modern, with private baths, minimalist decor, tea and coffee facilities, and a fridge in each unit. Final, major perk: free loaner smartphones loaded with maps and tourist info, to help guests get the most out of their visit; calls to the U.S. and Canada are included, too.

Via Orazio 3. www.romearmonysuites.com. ✆ **348-3305419.** 6 units. 95€–150€ double. Rates include breakfast (served at a nearby cafe). Metro: Lepanto. **Amenities:** Free Wi-Fi.

Ancient Rome, Monti & Celio

There aren't many hotel rooms on earth with a view of a 2,000-year-old amphitheater, so there's a definite "only in Rome" feeling to lodging on the edge of the ancient city (see map p. 89). The negative to staying in this area—and it's a big minus—is that the streets adjacent to those ancient monuments have little life outside tourism. There's a lot more going on in **Monti,** Rome's oldest "suburb" (only 5 min. from the Forum), which is especially lively after dark. **Celio** has more of a neighborhood vibe, a local, gentrified life quite separate from tourism.

EXPENSIVE

The Inn at the Roman Forum ★★ This small hotel is tucked down a medieval lane on the edge of Monti, with the forums of several Roman emperors as neighbors. Rooms are tastefully decadent, with colorful silks, rich textures, and spacious bathrooms. The posh fifth-floor Master Garden Rooms have private patios surrounded by flowers and greenery, ochre walls, and busts of emperors, and a plush apartment with a kitchen sleeps up to six people. The hotel's small **roof lounge** has views of the Campidoglio, and for archaeology buffs there's an ancient Roman *cryptoporticus* behind the lobby.

Via degli Ibernesi 30. www.theinnattheromanforum.com. ✆ **06-69190970.** 21 units. 180€–550€ double. Rates include breakfast. Metro: Cavour. **Amenities:** 2 bars; roof terrace; concierge; room service; free Wi-Fi.

MODERATE

Duca d'Alba ★★ Located on one of the main drags of hip Monti, with all the nightlife and authentic dining you'll need, Duca d'Alba strikes a fine balance between old-world gentility and 21st-century amenities. Rooms in the main building are snug and contemporary, with modern furniture and gadgetry and smallish bathrooms. If you want to spring for slightly higher rates, the spacious annex rooms next door have a *palazzo* character, with terracotta floors, oak and cherry furniture, and soundproofed street-facing rooms. Second-floor rooms are the brightest.

Via Leonina 14. www.hotelducadalba.com. ✆ **06-484471.** 27 units. 79€–230€ double. Some rates include breakfast. Metro: Cavour. **Amenities:** Bar; free Wi-Fi.

The Glam ★★ A decidedly modern vibe pervades at this superbly located, boutiquey hotel—right on Via Nazionale, within walking distance of Termini Station, the Colosseum and Forum, Trevi Fountain, and just about everything else you'll want to see in central Rome. Art-filled rooms are cool and functional, if a little impersonal, but a very friendly and welcoming staff more than compensates. A rooftop restaurant and glorious open-air bar and terrace are popular gathering spots for young Romans, and the bartender mixes a good cocktail.

Via Nazionale 82. www.theglamhotelroma.it. ✆ **06-99345430.** 59 units. 160€–305€ double. Some rates include breakfast. Metro: Repubblica or Cavour. **Amenities:** Bar; restaurant; roof terrace; free Wi-Fi.

Lancelot ★★★ Expect warmth and hospitality from the minute you walk in the door. The staff, all of whom have been here for years, are the heart and soul of Lancelot, and the reason why the hotel has so many repeat guests. The room decor is simple; most units are spacious, immaculately kept, and light-filled, thanks to large windows. Bathrooms are small but serviceable. Sixth-floor rooms have private terraces overlooking Ancient Rome—well worth springing for. The 1938 building retains vestiges of its Art Deco past, most felt in the genteel, chandelier-lit common areas for meeting other travelers, *Room With a View*–style. Unusual for

A sixth-floor terrace at Lancelot.

Rome, Lancelot also has limited private parking—but you'll need to book it in advance.

Via Capo d'Africa 47. c. ✆ **06-70450615.** 60 units. 130€–205€ double. Rates include breakfast. Metro: Colosseo. Bus: 53, 75, 85, 87, 118. Tram: 3. **Amenities:** Restaurant; bar; free Wi-Fi.

The Centro Storico & Pantheon

There's nothing like an immersion in the atmosphere of Rome's lively Renaissance heart, though you'll pay dearly for *location, location, location.* Since many of Centro's characteristic streets are pedestrian-only, expect to do a lot of walking, but that's a reason many visitors come here in the first place—to wander and discover the glory that was and is Rome. Many restaurants and cafes are an easy walk from the hotels here.

EXPENSIVE

Chapter Roma ★★ Stylish and irreverent, this design hotel is in step with the evolving character of the Rome Ghetto, where modern art galleries and concept stores are springing up next to traditional kosher restaurants. Rooms range from small to party-size, and all have wood floors, an industrial-chic vibe, original artworks, Marshall speakers, and bars stocked with booze and mixers. We appreciate the eco-friendly bath amenities and absence of tiny plastic bottles. The millennial vibe is strong in the lobby bar and adjacent **Market** cafe, which serves smoothies, wraps, and salads. A seasonal rooftop restaurant serves margaritas and Mexican food.

Via di S. Maria De' Calderari 47. www.chapter-roma.com. ✆ **06 89935351.** 42 units. 206€–600€ double. Bus: 40, 64 (to Largo Torre di Argentina). Tram: 8. **Amenities:** 2 restaurants; bar; cafe; free Wi-Fi.

Raphael ★★★ This ivy-covered palace just off Piazza Navona is an ideal choice for a special-occasion stay, with luxurious rooms, enthusiastic staff, and a roof terrace with spectacular views across Rome. It's a gorgeous hotel, highlighted by 20th-century artwork inside, including Picasso ceramics and paintings by Miró, Morandi, and De Chirico scattered around the property. The standard rooms are all decorated in Victorian style, with antique furnishings and hardwood floors. Some prefer staying in the Richard Meier–designed executive suites, which blend modern and Asian design and feature oak paneling, contemporary art, and Carrara marble. The haute organic vegetarian restaurant will leave even diehard carnivores sated.

Largo Febo 2, near Piazza Navona. www.raphaelhotel.com. ✆ **06-682831.** 51 units. 220€–680€ double. Bus: 40, 64, 70. **Amenities:** Restaurant; bar; babysitting; concierge; room service; free Wi-Fi.

MODERATE

Coronari Palace ★★ Extremely well located just a few steps from Piazza Navona, modernly equipped Coronari Palace offers six rooms featuring modular furnishings and wood laminate floors; three junior suites have terraces. While some bathrooms are on the snug side, they're sleek and well-designed, most with enough counter/sink space for a toiletry bag. The communal roof terrace invites guests to BYOB and enjoy a pleasant evening gazing over the terracotta rooftops of Rome. There are no surprises here, just clean, up-to-date facilities, good prices (for central Rome), and amicable staff.

Via dei Coronari 231. www.coronaripalace.com. ✆ **06-68309541.** 16 units. 198€–350€ double. Rates include breakfast. Bus: 40, 64. **Amenities:** Roof terrace; free Wi-Fi.

Damaso Hotel ★★ Consistently rated as one of the top hotels in Rome, this upscale three-star in a 19th-century palazzo punches above its weight class. Well-thought-out rooms and sleek marble bathrooms make the most of their small dimensions, though rooms overlooking busy Corso Vittorio Emanuele II may be a touch noisy. A decent breakfast buffet is offered in a woody dining room that converts to a cocktail bar at night, and the rooftop terrace brings the views.

Piazza della Cancelleria 62. www.hoteldamaso.it. ✆ **06-45503061.** 39 units. 120€–250€ double. Rates include breakfast. Bus: 42, 62, 64, 916. **Amenities:** Bar; roof terrace; lounge; free Wi-Fi.

Hotel Adriano ★★★ Just 5 minutes from the Pantheon, this stylish retreat occupies an elegant 17th-century *palazzo*. Rooms boast a chic and modern vibe, though standard rooms can be a tad utilitarian. A few deluxe rooms and suites have terraces with views of the Roman rooftops. In a crowded hotel market, Adriano stands out for its plush, well-designed common areas, including the **Gin Corner,** a trendy cocktail bar specializing in…you guessed it. The breakfast spread is generous. Rooms in the nearby Domus Adriani share a small kitchen and common area. ***Tip:*** E-mail the hotel directly for the lowest rates.

Via di Pallacorda 2. www.hoteladriano.com. ✆ **06-68802451.** 40 units. 200€–400€ double. Rates include breakfast. Bus: 70, 85. **Amenities:** Bar; babysitting; bikes; concierge; gym; free Wi-Fi.

Hotel L'Orologio ★★ Despite only opening in 2022, this sleek four-star feels like it's been here a long time—maybe because it occupies a historic palazzo just steps from the Largo Argentina archaeological site. The lovely midcentury modern lobby also lends a vintage air. Rooms are small and well-organized, if a little on the dark side, and showers have excellent water pressure. Two things stand out here: the extremely welcoming staff and a stunner of a rooftop terrace, where breakfast and evening *aperitivo* are served with a glorious view of the Rome skyline.

Corso Vittorio Emanuele II 110. www.hotelorologioroma.com. ✆ **06-6865019**. 43 units. 175€–450€ double. Rates include breakfast. Bus: 46, 62, 64, 81, 916. **Amenities:** Rooftop terrace, bar; free Wi-Fi.

Residenza in Farnese ★★ This little gem is set in a 15th-century mansion across the street from the Palazzo Farnese, within stumbling distance of Campo de' Fiori but still reasonably quiet. Rooms vary in size and are eclectic and artsy, with tiled floors and a vaguely Renaissance theme. Prices are usually on the low end of the range shown here, but a 2-night minimum may apply on weekends. The complimentary breakfast spread is downright generous. ***Tip:*** Last-minute rates are often much lower than those shown below.

Via del Mascherone 59. www.residenzafarneseroma.it. ✆ **06-68210980.** 31 units. 140€–240€ double. Rates include breakfast. Bus: 40, 64. **Amenities:** Bar; roof terrace; concierge; room service; free Wi-Fi.

INEXPENSIVE

Mimosa ★★ This budget stalwart in the heart of the *centro storico* enjoys great word of mouth, so book early. Recently renovated rooms are colorful and bright, with private bathrooms and air-conditioning—neither a given at this price point. Larger units are suitable for families with small children. A location this close to the Pantheon at these prices is hard to beat. Mention Frommer's for a 10% discount.

Via di Santa Chiara 61. www.hotelmimosa.net. ✆ **06-68801753.** 11 units. 89€–150€ double. Rates include breakfast. Bus: 40, 64, 70 to Largo di Torre Argentina. **Amenities:** Free Wi-Fi.

Tridente, the Spanish Steps & Via Veneto

The heart of the city is a great place to stay if you're a serious shopper or enjoy the romantic, somewhat nostalgic locales of the Spanish Steps and Trevi Fountain. But expect to part with a lot of extra euro for the privilege. Some of Rome's most legendary luxury hotels are in this area, including **Hotel Hassler** ★★★ (www.hotelhasslerroma.com), **Hotel d'Inghilterra** ★★★ (collezione.starhotels.com), and **Hotel de Russie** ★★★ (www.roccofortehotels.com), as well as sexy newcomer **W Rome** ★★★ (www.marriott.com)—any of which we heartily recommend if you've got the cash to splash. Here, we list some rare bargains in this most elegant area of Rome, plus a few worthy splurges.

EXPENSIVE

Babuino 181 ★★ Leave Renaissance and baroque Italy far behind at this sleek, contemporary hotel, with relatively spacious rooms and apartment-size suites outfitted with Frette bathrobes and Nespresso machines. Bathrooms are roomy and well laid out, and shuttered windows with hefty curtains provide a quiet and perfectly blacked-out environment for light sleepers. Onsite restaurant **EMME** offers a fine dining experience. A surcharged breakfast is served on the rooftop terrace, which doubles as a cocktail bar at night.

Via del Babuino 181. www.romeluxurysuites.com/babuino. ✆ **06-32295295.** 24 units. 225€–470€ double. Metro: Flaminio or Spagna. **Amenities:** Restaurant; bar; babysitting; concierge; roof terrace; room service; free Wi-Fi.

The Inn at the Spanish Steps ★★★ Set in one of Rome's most desirable locations on the famed Via dei Condotti shopping street, this hotel is the epitome of luxe. Rooms are fantasias of design and comfort, some with parquet floors and cherubim frescoes on the ceiling, others decked out with wispy fabrics draping canopied beds; upgraded units have swoon-worthy views of Piazza di Spagna. The rooftop garden provides beautiful views, to be enjoyed at breakfast—with its generous buffet spread—or for evening cocktails.

Via dei Condotti 85. www.atspanishsteps.com. ✆ **06-69925657.** 24 units. 200€–500€ double. Some rates include breakfast. Metro: Spagna. **Amenities:** Bar; babysitting; concierge; roof terraces; room service; free Wi-Fi.

Villa Spalletti Trivelli ★★★ This really is an experience rather than a hotel, an early-20th-century neoclassical villa remodeled into an exclusive 14-room guesthouse, where lodgers mingle in the gardens or the great hall, as if invited by an Italian noble for the weekend. There is no key for the entrance door; ring a bell and a staff member will open it for you, often offering you a glass of prosecco as a welcome. Rooms feature elegant antiques and embroidered bed linens, with sitting areas or separate lounges. And the minibar? All free, all day. A rooftop lounge boasts Jacuzzis, a complimentary bar, and light fare; onsite is a sizeable modern wellness oasis for those who want extra pampering.

Via Piacenza 4. www.villaspalletti.it. ✆ **06-48907934.** 14 units. 415€–750€ double. Rates include breakfast. Metro: Barberini. **Amenities:** Restaurant; bar; concierge; exercise room; roof terrace; room service; Jacuzzis; sauna; free Wi-Fi.

MODERATE

Hotel Condotti ★ This cozy hotel can be a tremendously good deal depending on when you stay and how far out you book. For your money you'll get a clean, unpretentious room, though the common areas aim higher, with marble floors, antiques, tapestries, and a Venetian-glass chandelier. Standard rooms are tight; you'll get a bit more space and modernity in the nearby annex rooms. Budget-priced "petite" rooms measure less than 9.3 sq. m (100 sq. ft). Overall it's worth considering for its proximity to the Spanish Steps.

Via Mario de' Fiori 37. www.hotelcondotti.com. ✆ **06-6794661.** 16 units. 135€–290€. Metro: Spagna. **Amenities:** Bar; babysitting; free Wi-Fi.

La Lumière ★ You won't be checking in for chic design or innovation—this traditional hotel just off Via dei Condotti smacks of old-school comfort, from rooms with matchy-matchy color schemes, wood floors, and warm lighting to the glassed-in roof terrace or open-air patio where breakfast and evening *aperitivo* are served. For all but highest season and holidays, it's a winner on the price/location ratio.

Via Belsiana 72. www.lalumieredipiazzadispagna.com. ✆ **06-69380806.** 10 units. 120€–350€ double. Rates include breakfast. Metro: Spagna. **Amenities:** Bar; roof terrace; free Wi-Fi.

La Residenza ★ Considering its location just off Via Veneto, this hotel—hosting guests since 1936—is a smart deal. Renovated, modern rooms retain a touch of Art Deco appeal, and are all relatively spacious, with a couple of easy chairs or a small couch in addition to a desk. Families with children are especially catered to—quad rooms and junior suites on the top floor feature a separate kids' alcove with two sofa beds, and there's an outdoor terrace with patio furniture. The excellent breakfast buffet includes quality charcuterie and cheeses, homemade breads, and pastries.

Via Emilia 22–24. www.hotel-la-residenza.com. ✆ **06-4880789.** 27 units. 150€–350€ double. Rates include breakfast. Metro: Barberini. **Amenities:** Bar; babysitting; cafe; terrace; room service; free Wi-Fi.

Parlamento ★★ Set on the top floors of a 17th-century *palazzo,* this is one of the best moderately priced deals in the area. Rooms are pleasantly fresh and modern, with wood floors and monochromatic color schemes. Breakfast is served on the rooftop terrace—where you can also chill with a glass of wine in the evening. The Trevi Fountain, Spanish Steps, and the Pantheon are all within a 5- to 10-minute walk.

Via delle Convertite 5 (at Via del Corso). www.hotelparlamento.it. ✆ **06-69921000.** 19 units. 165€–250€ double. Rates include breakfast. Metro: Spagna. **Amenities:** Bar; concierge; room service; free Wi-Fi.

INEXPENSIVE

Panda ★ Panda has long been popular among budget travelers, so it books up quickly. Rooms are spare, but not without some old-fashioned charm, like the characteristic Roman terracotta floor tiles, and the odd frescoed ceiling or exposed beam—and they do have air-conditioning. Most rooms are a bit cramped, but for these prices in this neighborhood they remain a very, very good deal. Outside your doorstep are several great cafes and wine bars where you can start the day with espresso and end with a nightcap. ***Tip:*** With its budget single rooms with shared baths, Panda is a fine pick for solo travelers. A 5€ breakfast voucher is good for the bar a couple of doors down.

Via della Croce 35. www.hotelpanda.it. ✆ **06-6780179.** 28 units (8 w/shared bath). 100€–130€ double w/bath. Metro: Spagna. **Amenities:** Free Wi-Fi.

Around Termini

Known for its concentration of cheap hotels, the Termini area (see map p. 115) is about the only part of the center where you can score a high-season double for under 100€. It's also seen a growing number of more upscale hotels, particularly in the zone northwest of the station. Streets close to the train station are hardly picturesque, and parts of the neighborhood are a little sketchy. Still, it's very convenient to most of Rome's top sights, and a hub for Metro lines, buses, and trams.

EXPENSIVE

Anantara Palazzo Naiadi ★★★ We won't sugarcoat it—this is one pricey palace. But in exchange for lots of dearly departed euro, guests are treated to a regal experience from the moment they approach the porticoed neoclassical facade, which wraps in a crescent around a quarter of Piazza della Repubblica. Rooms and suites are studies in rich textures and subtle color, with plush carpeting and marble baths. The lofty lobby bar serves fancy drinks and snacks, while the adjacent **Tazio** restaurant/bar swims in the ambiance of Fellini-era Rome. The hotel's spa is topnotch, and the summertime rooftop pool is a stunner.

Piazza della Repubblica 47. www.nh-hotels.com/hotel/anantara-palazzo-naiadi-rome-hotel. ✆ **06-489381.** 238 units. 340€–700€ double. Metro: Repubblica. **Amenities:** 2 restaurants (1 summer-only); 2 bars; concierge; rooftop pool; spa; fitness room; free Wi-Fi.

MODERATE

Hotel Mediterraneo ★★★ Within sight of Termini station, this surprisingly upscale hotel offers vintage Art Deco style, along with a team of long-time employees who warmly evoke the spirit of a bygone era of class and service. Freshly renovated rooms are large and well-equipped, with bathrooms of grand proportions; suites are downright palatial; and seven top-floor units have terraces with sweeping views. Read about the hotel's interesting World War II–era history as you linger over cocktails in its Wes Anderson-y bar. Sister properties **Atlantico** and **Massimo D'Azeglio,** located next door and across the street, respectively, offer lower room prices and share amenities with Mediterraneo. ***Tip:*** Check online for off-season or last-minute deals on those top-floor suites.

Via Cavour 15. www.romehotelmediterraneo.it. ✆ **06-4884051.** 245 units. 165€–250€ double. Most rates include breakfast. Metro: Termini. **Amenities:** Restaurant; bar; concierge; gym; roof terrace; room service; free Wi-Fi.

Residenza Cellini ★★ It's tradition all the way at Cellini, a modest, refined hotel around the corner from Piazza della Repubblica. Antique-styled rooms are proudly 19th century, with thick walls (so no noise from your neighbors), solid furnishings, and handsome parquet floors, yet also offer modern comforts like memory-foam mattresses and air-conditioning. Bathrooms come with Jacuzzi tubs or jetted showers. Service is topnotch and wonderfully personal.

Via Modena 5. www.residenzacellini.it. ✆ **06-47825204.** 18 units. 99€–199€ double. Rates do not include breakfast. Metro: Repubblica. **Amenities:** Concierge; room service; free Wi-Fi.

INEXPENSIVE

Beehive ★★★ Conceived as part hostel and part hotel, the Beehive is an utterly cheerful lodging experience, run by eco-minded American owners and offering rooms for a variety of budgets. Options range from fancy-for-the-price private rooms with ensuites and TVs to economical rooms with shared bathrooms, as well as both mixed and female-only dorms. All are decorated with flair, adorned with artwork or flea-market treasures, and they smell heavenly (go sniff for yourself). A garden offers trees and secluded space for reading and relaxing. A buzzy cafe offers breakfast a la carte, as well as occasional, budget-friendly vegan/vegetarian meals; there's also a concerted effort to maintain eco-conscious practices. Weekly pizza and pasta-making classes add to the fun.

Via Marghera 8. www.the-beehive.com. ✆ **06-44704553.** 20 units. 60€–100€ double; 20€–35€ dorm beds. Metro: Termini or Castro Pretorio. **Amenities:** Cafe; garden; lounge; free Wi-Fi.

Seven Kings Relais ★★ This unfussy hotel has a slightly retro feel, kitted out with dark wooden furniture, chocolate-brown bedspreads, and modern tiled floors. Despite its location right on one of Rome's busiest thoroughfares, street noise is minimal—an external courtyard and modern soundproofing see to that. "Breakfast" is a 24-hour self-service bar with tea, coffee, and packaged cookies, but the area has plenty of inexpensive dining options.

Via XX Settembre 58A. www.sevenkingsrelais.com. ✆ **06-42917784.** 11 units. 86€–180€ double. Metro: Repubblica. **Amenities:** Free Wi-Fi.

Trastevere

This was once an "undiscovered" neighborhood—but no longer. Being based here does give some degree of escape from the busy *centro storico,* though Trastevere's narrow streets can be packed to the gills in the evenings, as there are bars, shops, and restaurants galore in this boho section of Rome (see map p. 117). A preponderance of Airbnb-type rentals has also somewhat changed the character of the neighborhood.

MODERATE

Hotel San Francesco ★★ Lying at the edge of Trastevere, close to the Porta Portese gate in an area that hasn't (yet) been gentrified, this hotel has a local feel that has disappeared from much of the neighborhood. All rooms are bright, with color-washed walls and modern tiling. Doubles are fairly small, but the bathrooms are quite roomy. The grand piano in the lobby adds a touch of old-time charm; a top-floor garden with a cocktail bar overlooks terracotta rooftops and pealing church bell towers. A tasty cooked breakfast costs extra here. ***Tip:*** Book a "charity room," and the hotel will match your 2€ donation to help Rome's shelter dogs.

Via Jacopa de' Settesoli 7. www.hotelsanfrancesco.net. ✆ **06-48300051.** 24 units. 130€–199€ double. Bus: H, 44, or 75. Tram: 3 or 8. **Amenities:** Bar; free Wi-Fi.

Santa Maria ★★ Hidden behind an ivy-covered wall, the lovely Santa Maria is built around a 16th-century cloister, now a relaxing courtyard fragrant with orange trees. Cheerful rooms, some with exposed brick walls and beamed ceilings, are mostly on the ground floor. Free breakfast

The breakfast cafe at Arco del Lauro.

and loaner bikes, a roof garden, and a cocktail bar all make this charmer a standout in hotel-deprived Trastevere. ***Tip:*** Several spacious, multi-bed rooms make this a fine option for families.

Vicolo del Piede 2. www.htlsantamaria.com. ✆ **06-5894626.** 20 units. 106€–240€ double. Rates include breakfast. Tram: 8. Bus: 23, 280, H. **Amenities:** Bar; courtyard; loaner bikes; free Wi-Fi.

INEXPENSIVE

Arco del Lauro ★★ Hidden in Trastevere's snaking alleyways, this serene little B&B occupies the ground floor of a shuttered pink *palazzo.* Bright rooms have wood floors, plush beds, and simple decor, with a mix of modern and period furnishings. Rooms can't be defined as large, but they all feel spacious thanks to lofty wood ceilings. Breakfast is taken at a nearby cafe (with a 5€ surcharge); coffee and snacks are laid out around the clock. Minimum-stay rules may apply in high season.

Via Arco de' Tolomei 29. www.arcodellauro.it. ✆ **06-97840350.** 6 units. 85€–155€ double. Bus: 23, 280, H. Tram: 8. **Amenities:** Free Wi-Fi.

WHERE TO EAT IN ROME

Rome remains a top destination for food lovers and today offers more dining diversity than ever. Though many of its *trattorie* haven't changed their menus in a quarter of a century (for better or worse), the city has an increasing number of creative spots with chefs willing to revisit tradition.

Restaurants generally serve lunch between 12:30 and 2:30pm, and dinner between 7:30 and 10:30pm. At all other times, most restaurants are closed—though a new generation is moving toward all-day dining, with limited service at "in-between" mid-afternoon times.

If you have your heart set on any of these places below, we seriously recommend *reserving ahead of arrival.* Hot tables go quickly, especially on high-season weekends—often twice: once for the early-dining tourists, and then again for locals, who dine later, typically around 9pm.

A ***servizio*** (tip or service charge) is almost always added to your bill or included in the price. Sometimes it's marked on the menu as *coperto e servizio* or *pane e coperto* (bread, cover charge, and service). You can leave extra if you wish—a couple of euro as a token—but in general, big tipping is not the norm (although, contrary to advice on some travel blogs, Italian waitstaff will *not* be offended if you overtip). If you have questions about an item on your bill, don't hesitate to ask for an explanation.

Near Vatican City

For restaurant locations, see map p. 77. The path leading from the Vatican Museums to St. Peter's Basilica is something of a gauntlet of bad food—overpriced tourist traps preying on dazed crowds that have just wandered out of the museum and need sustenance before tackling the basilica.

Fortunately, a handful of very fine options for inexpensive fast food lie right near the Vatican—and no, we don't mean McDonald's (though it's here, too). For a quick, tasty sandwich before or after your Vatican safari, **Duecento Gradi ★★** is a topnotch *panino* joint with lots of yummy choices, right across from the Vatican walls at Piazza Risorgimento 3 (www.duecentogradi.it; ✆ **06-39754239;** Sun–Thurs 10am–2am; Fri–Sat 11am–5am). Around the corner, in a friendly hole-in-the-wall at Via Dei Gracchi 7, **Pinsa 'm pò! ★★** serves light and crispy "pinsa" pizzas with organic ingredients and gourmet toppings, most priced around 5€ (pinsampo.it; ✆ **06-88980716;** Mon–Sat 10:30am–9pm).

EXPENSIVE

Taverna Angelica ★★ MODERN ITALIAN/SEAFOOD In a sea of mediocre restaurants near St. Peter's, Angelica serves up surprisingly good and fairly priced (though not cheap) fare. Specialties include salted-cod-stuffed ravioli in spicy sauce, a divine risotto with blueberries and goat cheese, or baked turbot, roast pigeon, or a vegetarian Wellington. Save room for the delicious, non-run-of-the-mill dessert options. Reservations are required.

Piazza A. Capponi 6. tavernaangelica.com. ✆ **06-6874514.** Entrees 17€–38€; tasting menus from 50€. Fri–Sun 12:30–3:30pm, dinner Thurs–Sun 7:30pm–11pm. Closed 10 days in Aug. Metro: Ottaviano.

MODERATE

Bonci Pizzarium ★★★ PIZZA Celebrity chef Gabriele Bonci has always had a cult following in the Eternal City, and since he's been featured on TV shows overseas and written up by influential bloggers, you can expect long lines at his pizzeria. No matter—it's worth waiting (and walking 10 min. west of the Vatican Museums) for some of the best pizza you'll ever taste, sold by the slice or by weight. His ingredients are fresh and organic, the crust perfect, and toppings often experimental (try the mortadella and crumbled pistachio). There's also a good choice of Italian craft IPAs and wheat beers and wines by the glass. There's only a handful of stand-up tables inside and benches outside for seating, and reservations aren't taken.

Via della Meloria 43. www.bonci.it. ✆ **06-39745416.** Pizza 12€–40€ per kilo, depending on toppings. Mon–Sat 11am–10pm. Metro: Cipro.

Ancient Rome, Monti & Celio

For restaurant locations, see map p. 89. For a cappuccino, a quick bite, or *aperitivo* snacking, head to the epicenter of Monti, **La Bottega del Caffè ★★** (✆ **06-4741578**) on lively Piazza Madonna dei Monti, open from 8am to the wee hours. When we hanker for something other than Italian food, we head to **Maharajah ★★**, an elegant Northern Indian eatery at Via dei Serpenti 124 (www.maharajah.it; ✆ **06-4747144**).

deep dives INTO ROME'S CUISINE

Travel is inextricably linked to eating new and different foods, and nowhere is eating as important as it is in Italy. Numerous food tours and cooking classes offer a taste of Rome's culinary variety, from morning market tours to street food crawls to daylong cooking classes where you leave with new recipes and skills to try out at home. In addition to all that eating, drinking, and cooking, tours offer historical context and a more intimate look at Roman life as it relates to food. Here are two of our favorite ways to sample the vibrant, storied cuisine of the Eternal City:

Eating Europe (www.eatingeurope.com) offers in-depth small-group food and wine tours in Rome, particularly of Testaccio and Trastevere. Guides connect Rome's culinary culture to the city's history and traditions, and guests leave with their curiosity (and hunger) sated. Tours from 79€.

Run by a trio of food experts, including American **Eleonora Baldwin,** a TV foodie celebrity in Italy, **Casa Mia Tours** (www.casamiatours.com) offers private tours of Rome's markets and neighborhoods, with plenty of sampling along the way. They also do private cooking classes and dinners with locals. Prices range from 160€ per person for a cooking class to 390€ for a 3-hour private food tour for two. Mention this guidebook for a 10% discount.

Cheese tasting on a food tour with the Roman Guy (see p. 122).

MODERATE

InRoma al Campidoglio ★ ITALIAN Once a club for Rome's film industry, InRoma sits on a cobbled lane opposite the Palatine Hill. Though the place rests heavily on its cinematic laurels, it still serves up authentic Roman and regional cuisine. Meals might start with *caprese di bufala affumicata* (salad of tomatoes and smoked buffalo mozzarella) followed by classic pasta *carbonara*—they claim to do the best in Rome—or a main course of *saltimbocca* (veal cutlets wrapped with prosciutto and sage). Opt for a sidewalk table with a view to remember.

Via dei Fienili 56. www.inroma.eu. ✆ **06-69191024.** Entrees 10€–20€. Daily 12:30–3:30pm and 7–11pm. Bus: H, 81, 83, 160, 170, 628.

La Barrique ★★ MODERN ROMAN At this cozy, contemporary *enoteca* (wine bar with food), the kitchen knocks out fresh farm-to-table fare that complements the well-chosen wine list. The atmosphere is lively and informal, with rustic place settings and friendly service—as any proper *enoteca* should be. The menu offers classic comfort food, like meatballs in tomato sauce, and creative takes like a pumpkin tortino with Gorgonzola and amaretti cookies. Vegetarians will find plenty of options. Via del Boschetto 41B. labarriquevinoecucina.wordpress.com. ✆ **06-47825953.** Entrees 11€–17€. Mon–Sat 12:45–2:30pm, 7–11pm; Sun 12:30–11pm. Metro: Cavour.

INEXPENSIVE

Li Rioni ★★ PIZZA This fab neighborhood pizzeria is close enough to the Colosseum to be convenient, but just distant enough to avoid the dreaded "touristy" label that applies to so much dining in this part of town. Roman-style pizzas baked in the wood-stoked oven are among the

GETTING YOUR FILL OF gelato

Don't leave town without trying one (or several) of Rome's outstanding **ice cream parlors.** But choose your gelato carefully: Don't buy close to the tourist-packed piazzas, and don't be dazzled by vats of brightly (and artificially) colored, air-pumped gelato. The best gelato is made only from natural ingredients, which impart a natural color—if the pistachio gelato is bright green, move on. Take your cone *(cono)* or small cup *(coppetta)* and stroll as you eat—sitting down on the premises is usually more expensive. The recommended spots below are generally open mid-morning to late, sometimes after midnight on summer weekends. Cones and small cups cost between 2.50€ and 5€—at these prices you can eat it twice a day!

Near Campo de' Fiori, one of Rome's oldest artisan gelato makers, **Gelateria Alberto Pica** ★★★ (Via della Seggiola 12; ✆ **06-6868405;** bus H, 63 or 780; tram 8) produces top-quality gelato churned with local ingredients, including wild strawberries grown on the family's country estate. In Monti, fabulous (and gluten-free) **Fatamorgana** ★★★ (Piazza degli Zingari 5; www.gelateriafatamorgana.com; ✆ **06-86391589;** metro Cavour; other locations across Rome) is the place to try inventive flavors like delicate lavender and chamomile, or zingy avocado, lime, and white wine.

Two exceptions to the rule about avoiding gelato in touristy areas: venerable **Old Bridge Gelateria** ★ (Viale Bastioni di Michelangelo; gelateriaoldbridge.com; ✆ **328-411-9478**), which delights customers lined up for the Vatican Museums; and, near Piazza Navona, **Frigidarium** ★★★ (Via del Governo Vecchio 112; www.frigidarium-gelateria.com; ✆ **334-995-1184**), whose intense and creamy flavors will make you weep with joy. Have a *coppetta* of mango and coconut for me.

In the Termini area, tiny but sleek **Come il Latte** ★★★ (Via Silvio Spaventa 24; www.comeillatte.it; ✆ **06-42903882;** metro Repubblica or Castro Pretorio) turns out artisan gelatos in flavors ranging from salted caramel (yes, please!) to mascarpone and crumbled cookies; fruit flavors change according to season.

Trastevere's best artisan gelato, **Fior di Luna** ★★★ (Via della Lungaretta 96; www.fiordiluna.com; ✆ **06-64561314;** bus H or 780; tram 8), is made with natural and Fair Trade produce. Star flavors are the incredibly rich chocolates, spiked with fig or orange, and an absolutely perfect pistachio.

best in town, with perfect crisp crusts. There's also a bruschetta list (from around 4€) and a range of salads. Outside tables can be cramped, but there's plenty of room inside. If you want to eat late, booking is essential or you'll be fighting with hungry locals for a table. ***Tip:*** After visiting the Colosseum or the Basilica of San Clemente, stop for an *aperitivo,* then head here at 7 for an early (and cheap) pizza dinner.

Via SS. Quattro 24. www.lirioni.it. ✆ **06-70450605.** Pizzas 6€–9€. Wed–Mon 7pm–midnight. Closed 2 weeks Aug. Metro: Colosseo. Bus: 51, 85, 87. Tram: 3 or 8.

Centro Storico & the Pantheon

For restaurant locations, see map p. 101. Vegetarians (or anyone who just wants a break from meat and carbs) looking for big salads can find great food at the neighborhood branch of **L'Insalata Ricca,** Largo dei Chiavari 85 (www.linsalataricca.it; ✆ **06-68803656;** daily 11am–midnight).

EXPENSIVE

Pierluigi ★★ SEAFOOD There's a lot of pomp and circumstance at Pierluigi, a hallowed seafood restaurant near Piazza Farnese that's been in business since 1938. Fish that were swimming that morning and still-wriggling lobsters are brought tableside for inspection prior to being impeccably prepared to order. There's also an extensive raw bar menu and items for landlubbers. The wine list is encyclopedic; service is discreet and flawless. This is event dining, and the ambience—and prices—reflect it. ***Tip:*** Fresh fish is priced *per etto* (100 grams) and can add up fast.

Piazza de'Ricci 144. www.pierluigi.it. ✆ **06–6868717.** Entrees 32€–38€; fresh fish can go much higher. Daily noon–2:30pm and 7–11pm. Bus: 40, 64.

Pipero Roma ★★ MODERN ITALIAN This Michelin-starred, long-established foodie haven occupies chic digs opposite the Chiesa Nuova, in a setting that's as sophisticated as the plates paraded forth from the kitchen. While a la carte items are available, the focus here is on three-, six-, or eight-course tasting menus, with options like tagliolini pasta with yellow peppers and miso, and an exquisite dessert of almonds, lychee fruit, and rosewater. Everything is expensive, and the small, precious servings will either dazzle you or drive you nuts with their pretension—it's better to make that decision beforehand.

Corso Vittorio Emanuele II 250. www.piperoroma.it. ✆ **06-68139022.** Entrees 32€–45€; tasting menus 100€–160€. Tues–Fri noon–3pm and 7–11pm; Mon, Sat 7–11pm. Bus: 40, 46, 62, 64, 916.

MODERATE

Antica Hostaria Romanesca ★ ROMAN It's very easy to eat badly on Campo de' Fiori, which makes this authentic spot with ringside seats on the piazza such a pleasant surprise. Romanesca does dependable, old-school Roman fare at fair prices, including a gloriously juicy *pollo e* *peperoni* (stewed chicken with peppers) and *abbacchio scottadito,* lamb chops hot off the grill. Locals snatch up the tables after 9pm, so a reservation is advised.

Campo de' Fiori 40 (east side of square). ✆ **06-6864024.** Entrees 11€–16€. Daily noon–3pm and 7–11pm. Bus: 40, 64, 70. Tram: 8.

Armando al Pantheon ★★ ROMAN/VEGETARIAN Despite a location just a few steps from the Pantheon, this family-run trattoria serves as many locals as tourists. Chef Armando Gargioli took over the place in 1961, and his progeny now run the business. Roman favorites to look for include *cacio e pepe,* marinated artichokes, and spaghetti alla Gricia. Despite the preponderance of offal on the menu, there are many options suitable for vegetarians. Advance reservations are a must, via a booking link on their website (no e-mail).

Salita dei Crescenzi 31. www.armandoalpantheon.it. ✆ **06-68803034.** Entrees 10€–25€. Mon–Sat 12:30–3pm and 7–11pm. Closed Sun, all of Aug. Bus: 40, 64, 70. Tram: 8.

Il Bacaro ★★ MODERN ITALIAN Romantic and low-key, Il Bacaro's setting on a hidden backstreet near the Pantheon offers respite from the traffic and tourist crush. Delicious *primi* and *secondi* include white truffle tagliolini or a salted cod puttanesca. Desserts are of the creamy and fluffy variety, including the obligatory tiramisu. The wine list features well-priced varietals from all over Italy, including a couple dozen by the glass. Try to get a prized sidewalk table on a balmy summer evening.

Via degli Spagnoli 27 (near Piazza delle Coppelle). www.ilbacaroroma.com/en. ✆ **06-6872554.** Entrees 24€–32€. Daily noon–midnight. Bus: 70, 71.

La Campana ★★ ROMAN/ITALIAN Family atmosphere and a classic Roman elegance prevail in Rome's oldest restaurant (feeding guests since 1518!). The atmosphere is convivial yet refined, with a lovely mixture of regulars and locals. The broad selection of *antipasti* is displayed on a long table at the entrance, and the daily menu features authentic *cucina romana* that's heavy on offal—if you're not a fan, be sure to bring your Italian/English dictionary. You'll also find classics like *cacio e pepe,* plus myriad vegetarian choices. The wine list includes interesting local labels, and the staff and service are impeccable.

Vicolo della Campana 18/20. ✆ **06-6875273.** Entrees 12€–22€. Tues–Sun 12:30–3pm and 7:30–11pm. Metro: Spagna. Bus: 70.

Nonna Betta ★★ ROMAN/JEWISH The history is palpable at Nonna Betta's, where photos of the 19th-century Rome Ghetto line the walls. Traditional dishes include delicious *carciofi alla giudia:* deep-fried artichokes served with small morsels like battered cod filet, stuffed and fried zucchini flowers, carrot sticks, or whatever vegetable is in season. Don't forego the *baccalà* with onions and tomato or the zucchini carbonara. Middle Eastern specialties such as falafel and hummus are on the menu, and all desserts are homemade, including a stellar cake with pine nuts. In keeping with kosher law, meat and dairy are on separate menus and never combined in recipes.

Via del Portico d'Ottavia 16. www.nonnabetta.it. ✆ **06-68806263**. Entrees 12€–17€. Wed–Mon 12:15–3pm and 6:30–10pm. Bus: 40, 64, 170. Tram 8.

Retrobottega ★★ ROMAN Fresh, modern, and progressive, the somewhat misnamed Retrobottega is a nice contrast to the well-worn streets of the touristy heart of town. This culinary laboratory, founded by four young, accomplished chefs, is an intimate but convivial choice. Most seats surround the open kitchen, and customers interact directly with the chefs—there is no waitstaff. The day's offerings focus on local, seasonal, responsibly sourced ingredients and unexpected pairings, like risotto with malt and smoked ham, or pigeon with tamarind and artichokes. From the same owners, next-door **Pasta e Pane** serves dine-in and takeaway pasta.

Via della Stelletta 4. www.retro-bottega.com. ✆ **06-68136310.** Entrees 20€–28€, tasting menus 110€. Tues–Sun 1–2:30pm, 7:30pm–midnight. Adjacent pasta restaurant open Tues–Sun noon–4pm. Bus: 40, 70, 85.

INEXPENSIVE

Alfredo e Ada ★★ ROMAN A daily chalkboard menu is the norm here, which speaks to the freshness and simplicity of this ultimate comfort food destination, now in its third generation of family ownership. Look for classic trattoria fare like eggplant parmigiana, artichoke lasagna, excellent carbonara, or tripe. The whole place oozes character, with shared tables, scribbled walls, and the house wine poured into carafes from a tap in the wall. There are only five tables, so it's best to make a reservation or get here early. This sort of place is becoming rare in Rome—enjoy it while you can.

Via dei Banchi Nuovi 14. ✆ **06-6878842.** Entrees 8€–12€. Tues–Sat noon–3pm and 7–10:30pm. Closed Aug. Bus: 40, 64.

Antico Forno Roscioli ★★★ BAKERY The Rosciolis have been running this celebrated bakery for three generations since the 1970s, though bread has been made here since at least 1824. Today it's the home of the finest crusty sourdough in Rome, assorted cakes, and addictive pastries and biscotti, as well as exceptional Roman-style *pizza bianca* and *pizza rossa* sold by weight. This is largely a takeout joint, with limited seating—and the wider range of pizza toppings is only available from noon to 2:30pm. Around the corner is the wonderful **Roscioli restaurant and *salumeria* deli** at Via dei Giubbonari 21 and, at Piazza Benedetto Cairoli 16, **Roscioli Caffè,** the latest outpost of the family empire, which offers breakfast treats, cappuccini, and palate-pleasing panini.

Via dei Chiavari 34. www.anticofornoroscioli.it. ✆ **06-6864045.** Pizza from 5€ (sold by weight). Mon–Sat 7am–7:30pm, Sun 8am–6pm. Bus: 40, 85, 492. Tram: 8.

Da Baffetto ★★ PIZZA You don't come to Baffetto for cheerful service or even for comfort—tables are cramped and you might wind up sharing one with strangers—but for the gloriously authentic Roman pizza: crisp-crusted, oozing with toppings, and dispatched quickly from the wood oven. This place is dirt-cheap and immensely popular with locals. If there's a line out the door, take heart: They shuffle people in and out of here pretty fast, and a lot of folks are in line for takeaway. After dinner, pop next door to **Frigidarium** (p. 140) for a gelato.
Via del Governo Vecchio 114. www.pizzeriabaffetto.it. ✆ **06-6861617.** Pizza 6€–10€. Daily 12:30–3pm, 6:30pm–12:30am. Closed first 2 weeks of Aug. Bus: 40, 64, 70, 492.

Tridente, the Spanish Steps & Via Veneto

For restaurant locations, see map p. 107. The historic cafes near the Spanish Steps are saturated with history but, sadly, tend to be overpriced tourist traps, where mediocre slices of cake or even a cup of coffee or tea will cost 5€. Nevertheless, you may want to pop inside the two most celebrated institutions: **Babington's Tea Rooms** (www.babingtons.com; ✆ **06-6786027;** Wed–Mon noon–10pm), established in 1893 at the foot of the Spanish Steps by a couple of English *signore;* and **Antico Caffè Greco**, Via dei Condotti 86 (anticocaffegreco.eu; ✆ **06-6791700;** daily 9am–9pm), Rome's oldest bar, which opened in 1760 and has hosted Keats, Ibsen,

Homemade ravioli at Al Ceppo.

Goethe, and many other historical *cognoscenti.* In the heart of the Villa Borghese park, on Piazzale delle Canestre, **Pic Nic ★★** (✆ **06-855-7493;** daily 9am–7pm) is a great spot for lunch or a snack.

EXPENSIVE

Al Ceppo ★★ MARCHIGIANA/ROMAN The setting of this Parioli dining institution is an elegant 19th-century parlor, with dark wood furnishings, chandeliers, fresh flowers, family portraits on the walls, and an open kitchen with a wood-stoked hearth. The menu features regional dishes from the owners' home, the Le Marche region northeast of Rome: fish stews, fresh seafood, and grilled meats, all artfully prepared and presented, along with pastas both hearty and delicate. It's reason enough to head north to explore Parioli's many charms.

Via Panama 2 (near Piazza Ungheria). www.ristorantealceppo.com. ✆ **06-8419696.** Entrees 24€–32€. Tues–Sun 12:30–3pm and 7:30–11pm; Mon 7:30pm–11pm. Closed last 2 weeks Aug. Bus: 223, 360, 910. Tram: 3 or 19.

Imàgo ★★★ INTERNATIONAL The views of Rome from this sixth-floor hotel restaurant are jaw-dropping, the old city laid out before you, glowing pink as the sun goes down. The food is equally special, as chef Andrea Antonini reinterprets Italian cuisine, borrowing heavily from international culinary traditions. His Michelin-starred menu changes seasonally, but may include orecchiette pasta with sea urchin and turnip greens, deviled guinea fowl, or wild boar prepared with chocolate, cauliflower, and orange. Reservations are essential; jackets required for the gentlemen.

In Hotel Hassler, Piazza della Trinità dei Monti 6. www.imagorestaurant.com. ✆ **06-69934726.** Tasting menus 170€–200€. Tues–Sat 7–10:30pm. Closed most of Jan. Metro: Spagna.

MODERATE

Canova Tadolini ★★ ROMAN Few restaurants are as steeped in history as this place. Antonio Canova's sculpture studio was kept as a workshop by the descendants of his pupil Adamo Tadolini until 1967, and even today it's littered with tools and sculptures in bronze, plaster, and marble. The whole thing really does seem like a museum, with tables squeezed between models, casts, drapes, and bas-reliefs. Menus change from summer to winter, and always feature an interesting variety of traditional Roman pastas, plus meat, fish, and vegetarian dishes.

Via del Babuino 150A–B. www.canovatadolini.com. ✆ **06-32110702.** Entrees 18€–30€. Daily noon–11pm (bar/cafe 8am–midnight). Metro: Spagna.

Colline Emiliane ★★★ EMILIANA-ROMAGNOLA This family-owned restaurant tucked in an alley beside the Trevi Fountain has been serving traditional Emilia-Romagna dishes since 1931. Service is excellent and so is the food: Classics include *tortelli di zucca* (pumpkin ravioli in butter sauce) and magnificent *tagliatelle alla Bolognese,* the mother of all Italian comfort foods. The *secondi* menu is heavy on beef. Save room for the walnut-and-caramel cake or lemon meringue pie. Reservations are essential.

Via degli Avignonesi 22 (off Piazza Barberini). www.collineemiliane.com. ✆ **06-4817538.** Entrees 15€–19€. Tues–Sun 12:45–2:45pm; Tues–Sat 7:30–10:45pm. Closed Aug. Metro: Barberini.

Around Termini

For restaurant locations, see map p. 115. Mostly catering to dazed travelers toting wheeled suitcases, restaurants around Termini don't have to be good in order to bring in business. The following are some of our favorite exceptions to that norm.

MODERATE

Mercato Centrale Roma ★★ GOURMET MARKET This ambitious, three-story gourmet dining hall and street food hub is the best place to dine in Termini Station, with topnotch purveyors of everything from gourmet pizza to chocolate to truffles, plus a wine bar and a high-end restaurant. The space is inviting, if a little chaotic. Even if you don't have a train to catch, it's worth having lunch or a quick snack here. ***Tip:*** Walk through the hall and check out all the offerings, then snag a table and have members of your party take turns going to order their food.

Via Giovanni Giolitti 36 (in Termini Station). www.mercatocentrale.it/roma. ✆ **06-46202900.** Daily 8am–midnight. Metro: Termini.

Trattoria Monti ★★ REGIONAL/MARCHE Word is definitely out on this cozy, plain-Jane trattoria near Termini station. But that just means you need to reserve in advance to sample outstanding hearty pastas and meat and game dishes from the Marche region. You will remember for the rest of your life the *tortello al rosso d'uovo,* a large, delicate ravioli filled with spinach, ricotta, and egg yolk. You also may discover a few new favorites among the territory's underappreciated wines. Vegetarians take heart: There are always four or five non-meat entrees available.

Via di San Vito 13A (at Via Merulana). ✆ **06-4466573.** Entrees 12€–22€. Tues–Sat 1–2:45pm and 8–10:45pm; Sun 1–2:45pm. Metro: Cavour or Vittorio Emanuele. Bus: 360, 714. Tram: 5 or 14.

Trimani Il Wine Bar ★ MODERN ITALIAN This small bistro and well-stocked wine bar (with a 20-page wine list!) attracts white collars and wine lovers in a modern, relaxed ambience, accompanied by smooth jazz. The refined entrees might include rabbit stuffed with asparagus or Luganega sausage with a zucchini puree. The wines-by-the-glass list changes daily. If you just want a snack to accompany your vino, cheese and salami platters range from 9€ to 14€. The selection at Trimani's vast wine shop next door boggles the oenophilic mind.

Via Cernaia 37B. www.trimani.com. ✆ **06-4469630.** Entrees 12€–24€. Mon–Sat 11:30am–3pm and 5:30pm–midnight. Closed 2 weeks mid-Aug. Metro: Repubblica or Castro Pretorio.

INEXPENSIVE

Pinsere ★★ PIZZA *Pinsa* is an ancient Roman preparation: an oval focaccia made with a blend of four organic flours and olive oil that's left to rise for 2 to 3 days. The result is a crispy, feather-light, single-portion snack perfect for a light lunch. This friendly, small bakery always has an assortment of pies ready to pop in the oven. Favorites come with pureed pumpkin, smoked cheese, and pancetta; classic tomato, basil, and *bufala;* or the surprising combo of ricotta, fresh figs, raisins, pine nuts, and honey. Food to go only, or to eat standing up at one of the few small inside or outside counters. ***Note:*** Pinsere is closed Saturday and Sunday.

Via Flavia 98. ✆ **06-42020924.** Pinsa 4€–6€. Mon–Fri 10am–4pm. Metro: Castro Pretorio. Bus: 38, 66, 90, 223.

Trastevere

For restaurant locations, see map p. 117. The popular craft-beer bar Bir and Fud has been reimagined as **L'Elementare** (see p. 157), but still serves hungry drinkers pizzas and traditional snacks like *supplì* (fried stuffed rice croquettes). Hearts and tastebuds soar at **Biscottificio Artigiano Innocenti ★★** (Via della Luce 21; ✆ **06-5803926**), where Stefania and her family have been turning out delicate handmade cookies and cakes since the 1920s.

EXPENSIVE

Antico Arco ★★★ CREATIVE ITALIAN This well-known address for new Italian cuisine consistently delivers exquisite dishes made with the finest local and seasonal ingredients—like a beef fillet with buffalo mozzarella sauce and grilled eggplant, or amberjack with cauliflower, toasted hazelnuts, and lemon thyme, accompanied by excellent wine and topnotch service. A full meal here makes a special night out (reservations essential), but you can also just come to the restaurant's wine bar for *vino* and finger food—it pairs nicely with rapturous *centro storico* views from the nearby terraces of the Janiculum Hill. ***Tip:*** It's a 15-minute walk uphill from Trastevere, but the climb is gradual and pleasant.

Piazzale Aurelio 7 (at Via San Pancrazio). www.anticoarco.it. ✆ **06-5815274.** Entrees 32€–35€. Wed–Mon noon–midnight. Bus: 75, or tram 3 or 8, then 15-min. walk.

Glass Hostaria ★★ CONTEMPORARY ROMAN In an industrial-chic setting of exposed brick, stark white walls, and polished floors, Michelin-starred chef Cristina Bowerman serves refined food using high-quality ingredients. The menu changes seasonally, but expect carefully prepared shellfish, inventive pastas (such as linguine with pepper juice, cherries, mint, anchovies, and fish roe), and dishes like lamb with sumac, pecorino, and chicory). A vegetarian menu is available. Reservations are essential.

Vicolo del Cinque 58. glasshostaria.it. ✆ **06-58335903.** Entrees 38€–45€; tasting menu 125€. Wed–Sun 7:30–11pm; open for lunch Sat–Sun. Closed 2 weeks Jan, 2 weeks July. Bus: H, 75. Tram: 8.

Spirito DiVino ★★ ROMAN/SLOW FOOD In a medieval synagogue on a 2nd-century street (which you can visit on a cellar tour), the Catalani family does exceptional modern cuisine using only organic ingredients. Dishes such as an appetizer of raw sheep's cheese with cinnamon-pear compote, as well as ancient Roman cuisine (like *maiale alla mazio,* a favorite pork dish of Julius Caesar's), are as warm and comforting as the ambience. Finish with almond and chocolate cake served with banana and chile pepper.

Via dei Genovesi 31 (at Vicolo dell'Atleta). www.ristorantespiritodivino.com. ✆ **06-5896689.** Entrees 14€–26€. Mon–Sat 7–11:30pm. Bus: H, 75. Tram: 8.

MODERATE

Da Enzo ★★ ROMAN For traditional Roman cuisine, try this down-homey, non-touristy, family-run trattoria. *Cucina romana,* including classic carbonara, *amatriciana,* and *cacio e pepe,* win the gold, as do meat-heavy *secondi* like stewed tripe or meatballs braised in tomato sauce. Local wines can be ordered by the jug or glass, and desserts are worth the calories (try the mascarpone with wild strawberries). A few outdoor tables look out on some of Trastevere's characteristic alleyways.

Via dei Vascellari 29. www.daenzoal29.com. ✆ **06-5812260.** Entrees 12€–18€. Mon–Sat 12:15–3pm and 7–11pm. Bus: 75, 85, 170, H. Tram: 8.

Osteria Cacio e Pepe ★ ROMAN This neighborhood stalwart is an ultra-traditional trattoria, complete with paper tablecloths, a TV showing the game, the owner chatting up the ladies, and a bustling crowd of patrons waiting to be seated. Start with cheapo plates of fried tidbits, from rice *suppli* to cod to vegetables, then move on to the namesake pasta *cacio e pepe* or other classic Roman pasta dishes—and be ready for hearty portions. For *secondi*—if you have room left—consider *saltimbocca alla romana* (veal cutlets with sage and ham) or grilled meats, all reasonably priced. They even have pizza for the kids.

Vicolo del Cinque 15. ✆ **06-89572853.** Entrees 12€–22€. Daily 7:30pm–12:30am; Sat–Sun also noon–3pm. Bus: H. 75. Tram: 8.

Osteria La Gensola ★★★ SEAFOOD/ROMAN Considered one of the best seafood destinations in Rome, this warm and welcoming family-run restaurant feels like a true Trastevere home; decor is cozy, with soft lighting and a life-size wood-carved tree in the middle of the main dining room. Fish lovers come for heavenly spaghetti with fresh clams, *polpettine* (meatballs) made with tuna, and other traditional Roman cuisine with a marine twist. The grill churns out succulent beefsteaks, among non-fish dishes. Reservations are a must on weekends.

Piazza della Gensola 15. ✆ **06-58332758.** Entrees 15–20€. Daily 12:30–3pm and 7:30–11:30pm. Bus: 75, 85, 170, H. Tram: 8.

INEXPENSIVE

Dar Poeta ★ PIZZA Ranking among the best pizzerias in Rome, "the poet" is a fine place to enjoy a classic Roman pizza margherita (tomato sauce, mozzarella, and fresh basil) or a more creative combo like the *patataccia* (potatoes, creamed zucchini, and *speck* [a smoked prosciutto]). There are long lines to eat in, but you can also order takeout. The decadent dessert calzone is filled with fresh ricotta and Nutella.

Vicolo del Bologna 45. www.darpoeta.com. ✆ **06-5880516.** Pizzas 5€–9€. Daily noon–midnight. Bus: 75, H.

Testaccio

The slaughterhouses of Rome's old meatpacking district (see map p. 117) have been transformed into art venues, markets, and the museum **MACRO** (p. 118), but restaurants here still specialize in (though are not limited to) meats from the *quinto quarto* (the "fifth quarter")—the leftover parts of an animal after slaughter, typically offal like sweetbreads, tripe, tails, and other goodies you won't find on most American menus. This is an area to eat *cucina romana*—either in the restaurants below or from street-food stalls in the **Nuovo Mercato di Testaccio** (p. 153). Food-themed tours of Rome invariably end up here.

EXPENSIVE

Checchino dal 1887 ★★ ROMAN Often mischaracterized as an offal-only joint, this establishment, opened in 1887 across from Rome's now-defunct abattoir, is a special-night-out type of place, serving wonderful *bucatini all'amatriciana* and veal saltimbocca—as well as hearty plates of sweetbreads, intestines, and livers. Checchino is a pricier choice than most restaurants in this area, but Romans from all over the city keep coming back when they want the real thing. Despite its meat-centric leanings, Checchino has decent vegetarian options. They will also make gluten-free pasta.

Via di Monte Testaccio 30 (at Via Galvani). www.checchino-dal-1887.com. ✆ **06-5746316.** Entrees 12€–25€. Wed–Sun 12:30–3pm and 7:30–11pm. Closed Aug and part of Dec–Jan. Metro: Piramide.

MODERATE

Flavio al Velavevodetto ★ ROMAN Flavio's plain dining room is burrowed out of the side of Rome's most unusual "hill": a large mound made from amphorae discarded during the Roman era (see p. 69). Food-lovers come here for classic Roman pastas like *cacio e pepe* and *amatriciana,* plus *quinto quarto* (nose-to-tail) entrees at fair prices. Hearty dishes like *polpette al sugo* (meatballs in red sauce), *coda alla vaccinara* (oxtail), and fried calamari and anchovies are good for sharing. Flavio is justly famous, but may be coasting on its reputation just a wee bit.

Via di Monte Testaccio 97–99. www.ristorantevelavevodetto.it. ✆ **06-5744194.** Entrees 12€–16€. Daily noon–3pm and 7:30–11pm. Metro: Piramide.

Osteria degli Amici ★★ MODERN ROMAN On the corner of nightclub central and the hill of broken amphorae, this intimate, friendly *osteria* serves traditional Roman classics and creative variations. Claudio and Alessandro base their menu on their combined experience in famous kitchens around the world, with presentations that are more sophisticated than is typical for this part of town. Signature musts include fish- and seafood-based pastas and main courses, golden-fried mozzarella *in carrozza,* and a range of pastas from classic *carbonara* to *paccheri* tubes with squid, olives, and potatoes. Leave room for the apple tartlet with cinnamon gelato.

Via Nicola Zabaglia 25. www.osteriadegliamiciroma.it. ✆ **06-5781466.** Entrees 10€–20€. Wed–Mon 12:30–3pm and 8pm–midnight. Metro: Piramide.

Porto Fluviale ★ MODERN ITALIAN This multifunctional restaurant—part trattoria, part street-food stall, part pizzeria—can accommodate pretty much whatever you fancy. The decor is vaguely industrial, with a daytime clientele of families and professionals on lunch break; the vibe gets younger after dark. From the various menus, best bets are the 30 or so *cicchetti,* small plates that allow you to sample the kitchen's range. Several pastas and main courses are available in half-portions. Both the locale and the menus are highly kid-friendly.

Via del Porto Fluviale 22. www.portofluviale.com. ✆ **06-5743199.** Cicchetti 3€–5€; entrees 11€–28€. Daily 10:30am–2am. Metro: Piramide.

Trattoria Perilli ★★ ROMAN Dine elbow-to-elbow with locals and enjoy the old-school atmosphere at this beloved institution of Roman *ristorazione.* With zero pretense, Perilli's formally attired waitstaff serve unadulterated renditions of Roman classics. The menu is small and the dishes are reliable, from pasta standbys like *carbonara* and *cacio e pepe* to grilled meats and that most English of Italian desserts, *zuppa inglese* (literally "English soup," or trifle). It's a fun and reasonably affordable place for a four-course meal of *antipasto, primo, secondo,* and *dolce.* Reservations recommended.

Via Marmorata 39 (at Via Galvani). www.perilliatestaccio.com. ✆ **06-5742415.** Entrees 12€–24€. Thurs–Tues 12:15–3:15pm and 7:15–11:15pm. Metro: Piramide. Bus: 75. Tram: 3.

INEXPENSIVE

Da Remo ★★ PIZZA Mentioning "Testaccio" and "pizza" in the same sentence elicits one typical response from locals: Da Remo, a Roman institution. In the summer especially, come early or be prepared to wait for a table. Every crisp-crusted, perfectly foldable pizza is made for all to see behind open counters. The most basic ones (margherita and marinara) start at around 7€. If it's too crowded on a summer evening, order your pizza for takeout and eat it in the park across the street.

Piazza Santa Maria Liberatrice 44. © **06-5746270.** Most pizzas 6€–8€. Daily 7pm–1am. Bus: 75. Tram: 3, 8.

ROME SHOPPING

Of all the sectors of the Rome economy affected by the pandemic, traditional retail appears to have taken the hardest hit. Even businesses that had been around for decades weren't spared, and many now stand vacant or have been replaced by fast-fashion outlets or cheap souvenir stores. We expect that the retail scene will eventually bounce back, but it might take longer than anyone would like.

That said, Rome is still a magnet for high-end shoppers, foodies, and lovers of antiques. In our limited space below we've summarized streets and areas known for their shops. Keep in mind that the monthly rent on the famous streets is very high, and those costs are passed on to you. Note that **sales** usually run twice a year, starting in January and July.

Top Shopping Streets & Areas

AROUND PIAZZA DI SPAGNA Most of Rome's haute couture and seriously upscale shopping fans out from the bottom of the Spanish Steps. **Via Condotti** is probably Rome's poshest shopping street, where you'll find Prada, Gucci, Bulgari, and the like. A few more down-to-earth stores have opened, but it's still largely a playground for the super-rich. Neighboring **Via Borgognona** also has chic, ultra-expensive merchandise, but thanks to its pedestrian-only access and handsome baroque and neoclassical facades, it offers a nicer window-browsing experience. Shops are more densely concentrated on **Via Frattina,** the third of this trio of upscale streets. Chic boutiques for adults and kids rub shoulders with ready-to-wear fashion, high-end chains, and a few tourist tat vendors. It's usually crowded with shoppers who appreciate the lack of motor traffic.

VIA COLA DI RIENZO The commercial heart of the Prati neighborhood, this long street runs straight from the Tiber to Piazza Risorgimento. It's known for stores selling a variety of merchandise at reasonable prices, from jewelry to fashionable clothing, bags, and shoes. Among the most prestigious is the historic Roman perfume store (with products for

Upscale shopping on Via Condotti.

men and women), **Bertozzini Profumeria dal 1913,** at no. 192 (www.bertozzinidal1913.it). Department store **Coin** is at no. 173 (with a large supermarket in the basement); the largest branch of gourmet food store **Castroni** is at no. 196 (www.castronicoladirienzo.com); the smaller, more selective gourmet grocery **Franchi** is at no. 200 (www.franchi.it).

VIA DEL CORSO With less of a glamour quotient (and less stratospheric prices) than Via Condotti or Via Borgognona, Via del Corso boasts affordable styles aimed at younger consumers. Occasional gems are scattered amid international shops selling jeans and sportswear. The most interesting stores are toward the Piazza del Popolo end of the street (**Via del Babuino** has a similar profile). Or turn at Largo Chigi towards Via del Tritone, and run a retail gauntlet that includes **Altariva Shoes,** for high-quality, Made-in-Italy footwear (www.altarivashoes.it); **Rinascente**, a high-end department store; **Hugo BOSS;** and **Sephora.** The farther south you walk (towards the Vittoriano monument), the narrower the sidewalks—and generally, the tackier the stores.

VIA DEI CORONARI An antiques-lover's souk. If you're shopping, or just window-shopping for antiques, art, or vintage-style souvenir prints, then spend an hour walking the length of this pretty, pedestrian-only street.

CAMPO DE' FIORI Though the campo itself is now chockablock with restaurants, the streets leading up to it, notably **Via dei Giubbonari** and **Via Dei Baullari,** offer edgy and often one-of-a-kind fashions. Boutiques go in and out of business with dizzying frequency, but something interesting is always popping up.

VIA DEL GOVERNO VECCHIO It's Vintage Valhalla on this pretty street that winds parallel to Corso Vittorio Emanuele II. Lined with tiny resale shops that are stuffed to the gills with merchandise, Via del Governo Vecchio also has great places to eat and drink, particularly on the end closest to Piazza di San Pantaleo. Poke into vintage treasure trove **Omero e Cecilia** (at no. 110) or **Cinzia** (no. 45) before taking a restorative gelato break at **Frigidarium** (p. 140).

VIA MARGUTTA This beautiful, tranquil street is home to numerous art stalls and artists' studios—Federico Fellini used to live here—though a lot of stores these days tend to offer the same sort of antiques and mediocre paintings. You have to shop hard to find real quality. A definite highlight is **Bottega del Marmoraro** at no. 53b, the whimsical studio of master stone carver Sandro Fiorentini.

MONTI Rome's most fashion-conscious central neighborhood has a pleasing mix of artisan retailers, vintage boutiques, and honest, everyday stores frequented by locals, with not a brand name in sight. Roam the length of **Via del Boschetto** for one-off fashions, designer ateliers, and unique homewares. In fact, you can roam in every direction from the spot where Via del Boschetto meets **Via Panisperna.** Turn on nearby **Via Urbana** or **Via Leonina,** where boutiques jostle for space with cafes that are ideal for a break or light lunch.

Rome's Best Markets

Campo de' Fiori ★ Central Rome's food market, running since at least the 1800s, is no longer the place to find a produce bargain (though the fruit and veg displays are dazzling). It tends to attract more tourists than locals, but it's still a genuine slice of Roman life in one of its most attractive squares. The market runs daily 7am to 1 or 2pm, with fewer produce vendors on Sunday. Campo de' Fiori. No phone. Bus: 40, 64, 170. Tram: 8.

Nuovo Mercato di Testaccio ★★★ Traditional food and produce stalls meet street food central in this modernist, sustainably powered market building. It's the best place for produce shopping and a terrific stop for a lunch of *suppli* (fried rice balls) and craft beer (**Food Box ★★**, Box 66), meat and sauce-stuffed panini (**Mordi e Vai ★★**, Box 15, www.mordievai.it), or an espresso and something sweet (**Chicchi e Lettere ★**, Box 43). There are also clothes and kitchenware stalls. The market runs Monday to Saturday 7am to 3:30pm. Btw. Via Luigi Galvani and Via Aldo Manuzio (at Via Benjamin Franklin). www.mercatoditestaccio.it. No phone. Metro: Piramide.

Rome, Illuminated

When the sun goes down, Rome's palaces, ruins, fountains, and monuments are bathed in a theatrical white light. During your stay in Rome, be sure to make time for a memorable evening stroll past the solemn pillars of old temples or the cascading torrents of Renaissance fountains glowing under the blue-black sky. The **Fountain of the Naiads** (Fontana delle Naiadi) on Piazza della Repubblica, the **Fountain of the Tortoises** (Fontana della Tartarughe) on Piazza Mattei, the **Fountain of Acqua Paola** (Fontanone) at the top of the Janiculum Hill, and the **Trevi Fountain** (p. 109) are particularly beautiful at night. The **Capitoline Hill** (or Campidoglio) is magnificently lit after dark, its Renaissance facades glowing like jewel boxes. The view of the Roman Forum seen from the rear of Piazza del Campidoglio is perhaps the grandest in Rome (see "Three Free Views to Remember for a Lifetime," p. 91). Across the Tiber, the Vatican's **Piazza San Pietro** (p. 76) is impressive at night without the crowds. The combination of illuminated architecture, baroque fountains, and sidewalk shows makes **Piazza Navona** (p. 99) even more delightful at night.

Porta Portese ★ Trastevere's vast weekly flea market stretches all the way from the Porta Portese gate along Via di Porta Portese to Viale di Trastevere. You'll have to wade through a lot of junk (and a sea of humanity—hold tight to your belongings), but there are good stalls for vintage housewares, clothing, and collectibles. It runs Sundays from dawn until midafternoon. Via di Porta Portese. No phone. Tram: 8.

ENTERTAINMENT & NIGHTLIFE

Several English-language outlets offer current information about nightlife and cultural events in Rome. ***Wanted in Rome*** (www.wantedinrome.com) has listings of opera, rock, and English-language cinema showings, and gives an insider look at expat Rome. ***Romeing*** (www.romeing.it) is worth consulting, especially for contemporary arts and culture. As blogs go, we like the soup-to-nuts approach of Elyssa Bernard's **Romewise** (www.romewise.com) and expat Natalie Kennedy's honest assessments in **An American in Rome** (www.anamericaninrome.com).

Unless you're dead set on making the Roman nightclub circuit, try what might be a far livelier and less expensive option—sitting late into the evening on **Piazza della Rotonda** (the Pantheon), **Piazza del Popolo,** or one of Rome's other piazzas, all for the (admittedly inflated) cost of an espresso or a Campari and soda. If you're a clubber who likes it loud and late, jump in a cab to **Monte Testaccio** or **Via del Pigneto** and bar-hop wherever your fancy takes you. In Trastevere, there's always a bit of life on **Via del Politeama** where it meets **Piazza Trilussa.** In the *centro storico,* a nice *aperitivo-cena* scene unfolds along **Via del Governo Vecchio.**

Performing Arts & Live Music

Rome's music scene doesn't have the same vibrancy as Florence's (p. 222) nor the high-quality opera of Milan's **La Scala** (p. 493) or **La Fenice** in Venice (p. 413). Still, classical music fans are well catered to here. In addition to the major venues featured below, look for concerts and one-off events in churches and salons around the city. For a calendar of opera and ballet staged by the **Opera in Roma** association at enchanting venues across the city, check **www.operainroma.com**. The **Pontificio Instituto di Musica Sacra** regularly runs classical music and operatic evenings.

Outdoor cafes dot the streets of Rome.

Alexanderplatz Jazz Club ★★ Alexanderplatz has been the home of Rome's jazz scene since the early 1980s. If there's a good act in the city, you will find it here. Live music 7 nights a week. Via Ostia 9. www.alexanderplatzjazz.com. ✆ **06-39742171.** Cover usually 10€. Metro: Ottaviano.

Auditorium–Parco della Musica ★★ This multipurpose arts center, designed by Renzo Piano, brings a refreshing breath of modernity to Rome. The schedule features lots of aging rockers and eclectic singer-songwriter acts, as well as traditional orchestras. Great cafes and a bookstore on-site, too. Viale Pietro de Coubertin 30. www.auditorium.com. ✆ **06-80241281.** Metro: Flaminio, then Tram 2. Bus: 910.

Teatro dell'Opera di Roma ★★ Here you'll find marquee operas such as *Aida* and *Madame Butterfly;* classical concerts from top-rank orchestras; and such ballets as *Giselle, Swan Lake,* and *The Nutcracker.* In summer the action moves outdoors for unforgettable open-air operatic performances at the ruined **Baths of Caracalla** (p. 95). Piazza Beniamino Gigli 1 (at Via del Viminale). www.operaroma.it. ✆ **06-4817003** (box office). Tickets 25€–150€. Metro: Repubblica.

Cafes

Remember: In Rome and everywhere else in Italy, if you just want to drink a quick coffee and bolt, walk up to *il banco* (the bar), order *"un caffè, per favore"* or *"un cappuccino,"* and stay at the bar. They will make it for you to drink on the spot. It will usually cost more (at least double) to sit down to drink it—if you're in high-traffic, touristy areas, outdoor table service is the most expensive way to go. Even in the heart of the city center, a short coffee *al banco* should cost about 1€; add around .30€ for a *cappuccino.* Expect to pay up to five times that price if you sit outdoors on a marquee piazza. Most cafes in the city serve a decent cup of coffee, but here's a small selection of places worth hunting down.

With its shabby-chic interior and namesake fig tree backdrop to charming outdoor seating, **Bar del Fico** ★ (Piazza del Fico 26; www.bardelfico.com; ✆ **06-6880 8413**) is one of Rome's most beloved *aperitivo* spots and a coveted see-and-be-seen nightlife destination. **Sant'Eustachio il Caffè** ★★ (Piazza Sant'Eustachio 82; www.santeustachioilcaffe.it; ✆ **06-68802048**) roasts its own Fair Trade Arabica beans and draws a friendly crowd a few deep at the bar. (Unless you ask, the coffee comes with sugar.) Debate still rages among Romans as to whether the city's best cup of coffee is served at Sant'Eustachio or **Tazza d'Oro** ★, near the Pantheon (Via degli Orfani 84; www.tazzadorocoffeeshop.com; ✆ **06-6789792**) or **Spinelli** ★ (Via dei Mille 60; ✆ **06-31055552**), a no-nonsense locals' cafe near Termini station.

Wine Bars, Cocktail Bars & Craft Beer Bars

The mass social phenomenon of the *aperitivo* (happy hour) provides great insight into the particular ways of real Romans. It started in hard-working northern cities like Milan, where you'd go to a bar after leaving the office and, for the price of one drink, enjoy one or more plates of high-quality food—often with cheese, cured meats, bruschetta, and pasta salad. Luckily for Rome, the custom trickled down here, and now the city is filled with casual little places to drop in for a drink (from 6 or 7pm on) and eat to your heart's content. *Aperitivo* spreads vary in quantity and quality, but generally you'll pay anywhere from 8€ to 12€ per person for a drink and buffet. All the places listed here are fine for families, too—Italian kids love *aperitivo* (minus the alcohol)! Look for signs in the window and follow your nose. The **Monti** neighborhood is a good place to begin.

Ai Tre Scalini ★ This little *bottiglieria* (wine bar) is the soul of Monti. It has a traditional menu, as well as a wine list sourced from across Italy. Arrive early or call for a table: This place is usually jammed. Via Panisperna 251. www.aitrescalini.org. ✆ **06-48907495.** Metro: Cavour.

Cavour 313 ★★ As traditional and genuine as you will find this close to the ancient ruins, this wine bar serves over 30 wines by the glass (from 3.50€) as well as cold cuts, cheese, and vegetable platters, or excellent carpaccio. Closed Aug. Via Cavour 313. www.cavour313.it. ✆ **06-6785496.** Metro: Colosseo and Cavour.

Ex Circus ★ This convivial hub for digital nomads, hungry tourists on a budget, and *aperitivo* drinkers seeking an ample spread is just a few blocks from Piazza Navona. They also do great salads, smoothies, and Sunday brunch. Via della Vetrina 15. ex-circus.business.site. ✆ **06-97619258.** Bus: 40, 64, 70.

Freni e Frizioni ★★ Trastevere's "Brakes and Clutches" is a former mechanics garage turned nighttime hot spot, with an ethnic-inflected *aperitivo* spread (think curried risotto). On the adjacent square, an effervescent crowd lounges against stone walls and parked *motorini.* Via del Politeama 4–6 (near Piazza Trilussa). www.freniefrizioni.com. ✆ **06-45497499.** Bus: H. Tram: 8.

La Bottega del Caffè ★ Beers, wine, cocktails, *aperitivo*—there's a little of everything at one of Monti's busiest neighborhood bars. Piazza Madonna dei Monti 5. ✆ **06-64741578.** Metro: Cavour.

L'Elementare ★ Formerly called Bir and Fud, this Trastevere craft-beer watering hole has taken on a new name and devoted more attention to pizza and other snacky foods. But the beers are still here—most of them Italian craft brews, some as strong as 9%. It's 6€ for a small draft beer. Via Benedetta 23. pizzerialelementare.it. ✆ **06-5894016.** Bus: H. Tram: 8.

Open Baladin ★★ If anyone ever tells you that Italians don't do good beer, send them to this bar near the Ghetto. Forty taps line the bar, with beers from its own Piedmont brewery and across Italy. Via degli Specchi 5–6. www.baladin.it/en/open-baladin-roma. ✆ **06-6838989.** Bus: 40, 64, 70. Tram: 8.

Salotto42 ★★ It's all fancy cocktails and well-chosen wines at this über-hip bookbar opposite the columned facade of 2nd-century Hadrian's Temple (near the Pantheon). A classy after-dinner stop, it also does shared plates, fresh juices, smoothies, and infused teas. Piazza di Pietra 42 (off Via del Corso). www.salotto42.it. ✆ **06-6785804.** Bus: 64, 85, 492.

Stravinskij Bar ★ An evening at this award-winning cocktail bar inside one of Rome's most famous grand hotels is always a regal affair. Mixology, ingredients, and canapés are all topnotch. Inside Hotel de Russie, Via del Babuino 9. ✆ **06-32888874.** Metro: Spagna.

Vale la Pena Pub ★★ This way-casual, tongue-in-cheek beer pub, part of a nonprofit that works to reduce recidivism, offers beer from its own microbrewery, made by inmates from Rome's Rebibbia prison. It fits like a glove in the working-class Tuscolano district. Via Eurialo 22. ✆ **06-87606875.** Metro: Furio Camillo.

SIDE TRIPS FROM ROME

Ostia Antica ★★

24km (15 miles) SW of Rome

The ruins of Rome's ancient port are a must-see for anyone who can't make it to Pompeii (p. 630). It's an easier day trip on a similar theme: the chance to wander around the preserved ruins of an ancient Roman settlement that has been barely touched since its abandonment.

Ostia, at the mouth of the Tiber, was the port of Rome, the gateway for riches from the far corners of the Empire. Founded in the 4th century B.C., it became a major port and naval base under two later emperors, Claudius and Trajan. A prosperous city developed, full of temples, baths, theaters, and patrician homes. Flourishing between the 1st and 3rd centuries, Ostia survived until around the 9th century before it was abandoned, becoming little more than a malaria bed, a buried ghost city fading into history. A papal-sponsored commission launched a series of digs in the 19th century, but the major work of unearthing was carried out under Mussolini's orders from 1938 to 1942. The city is only partially dug out today, but it's believed that all the chief monuments have been uncovered. ***Note:*** Ostia is a mostly flat site, but the Roman streets underfoot are clad in giant basalt cobblestones—wear comfortable walking shoes. Archaeology enthusiasts, especially those with their own car, might want to visit some of the other sites in the area, including the remains of the Imperial Harbors and the vast Necropolis of Porto.

ESSENTIALS

ARRIVING Take the Metro to Piramide, changing lines there for the Lido train to Ostia Antica. Departures to Ostia run every half-hour; the trip is 25 minutes and included in the price of a Metro single-journey ticket or **Roma Pass** (see p. 65). It's just a 5-minute walk to the excavations from the Metro stop: Exit the station, walk over the footbridge, and continue straight until you reach the car park. The ticket booth is to the left.

VISITOR INFORMATION The site is open Tuesday to Sunday from 8:30am. Closing time is at dusk, which ranges from 7pm in spring/summer to 4:30pm in fall/winter; check at **www.ostiaantica.beniculturali.it** or call © **06-56350215.** The ticket office closes 1 hour before the ruins close. Admission costs 12€ (14€ if purchased online), free for ages 17 and under and 65 and over. The inexpensive map on sale at the ticket booth is a wise investment.

PARKING The car park, on Viale dei Romagnoli, costs a few euro per day, but it is fairly small. Arrive early if you're driving.

EXPLORING OSTIA ANTICA

The principal monuments are all labeled. On arrival, visitors first pass the *necropoli* (burial grounds, always outside the city gates in Roman towns and cities). The main route follows the giant cobblestones of the **Decumanus** ★ (the main street) into the heart of Ostia. The **Piazzale delle Corporazioni** ★★ is like an early version of Wall Street: This square contained nearly 75 corporations, the nature of their businesses identified by the patterns of preserved mosaics. Nearby, Greek dramas were performed at the **Teatro,** built in the early days of the Empire. The theater as it looks today is the result of much rebuilding. Every town the size of Ostia had a **Forum** ★, and its layout is still intact: A well-preserved **Capitolium** (once the largest temple in Ostia) faces the remains of the A.D.-1st-century **Temple of Roma and Augustus.** Elsewhere in the grid of streets are the ruins of the **Thermopolium** ★★, which was a bar; its name means "sale of hot drinks." An *insula* (a Roman block of apartments), **Casa Diana** ★, remains, its rooms arranged around an inner courtyard. The **Terme di Nettuno** ★ was a vast baths complex; climb the building at its entrance for an aerial view of its well-preserved mosaics.

WHERE TO EAT IN OSTIA ANTICA

There is no real need to eat by the ruins—a half-day here should suffice, and Ostia is within easy reach of Rome's city center. The obvious alternative is a picnic; the well-stocked food emporium **Eataly** is just a couple of minutes from the Lido platform at Piramide Metro station, making it easy to grab provisions when you change trains. There are perfect picnic spots beside fallen columns or old temple walls. If you crave a sit-down meal, trattoria **Allo Sbarco di Enea,** Viale dei Romagnoli 675 (allosbarcodienea.com; ✆ **06-5650034**), is right outside the archaeological park. There's also a snack and coffee bar on-site.

Tivoli & the Villas ★★

32km (20 miles) E of Rome

Perched high on a hill east of Rome, ancient Tivoli has always been a place of retreat from the city. In Roman times it was known as Tibur, a retirement town for the wealthy; during the Renaissance it again became the playground of the rich, who built their country villas here. You need a full day to do justice to the gardens and villas that remain—especially if Villa Adriana is on your list, as indeed it should be—so set out early.

ESSENTIALS

ARRIVING Tivoli is 32km (20 miles) east of Rome on Via Tiburtina, about an hour's drive with traffic (the Rome–L'Aquila *autostrada,* A24, is usually faster). If you don't have a car, you can take one of several daily trains from Termini or Tiburtina to Tivoli station. Villa d'Este is in Tivoli itself, close to the train station; to get to Villa Adriana you'll need to catch a regional bus from town. Or take the **Cotral** bus (www.cotralspa.it) that runs on Via Prenestina; this stops a short walk from the Villa Adriana entrance.

Another option is to take Metro Line B to Ponte Mammolo. After exiting the station, transfer to a Cotral bus for Tivoli. Cotral buses depart every 15 to 30 minutes during the day, and the trip will take less than an hour.

EXPLORING TIVOLI & THE VILLAS

Villa Adriana ★★★ HISTORIC SITE/RUINS Globe-trotting Emperor Hadrian spent the last 3 years of his life in grand style. Less than 6km (3¾ miles) from Tivoli, between A.D. 118 and 134 he built one of the greatest estates ever conceived, filling acre upon acre with architectural wonders he'd seen in his travels. Hadrian erected theaters, baths, temples, fountains, gardens, and canals, filling palaces and temples with sculpture, some of which now rest in the museums of Rome. In later centuries, barbarians, popes, and cardinals, as well as anyone who needed a slab of marble, carted off much that made the villa so spectacular. But enough of the fragmented ruins remain to inspire a real sense of awe. The most outstanding remnant is the **Canopo** ★★★, a re-creation of the Egyptian town of Canopus with its famous Temple of the Serapis. The ruins of a rectangular area, **Piazza d'Oro,** are still surrounded by a double portico. Likewise, the **Edificio con Pilastri Dorici** (Doric Pillared Hall) remains, its pilasters with bases and capitals holding up a Doric architrave. The apse and the ruins of some magnificent vaulting are found at the **Grandi Terme** (Great Baths), while only the north wall remains of the **Pecile ★**, known as the *Stoà Poikile di Atene* or Painted Porch, which Hadrian discovered in Athens and had reproduced here. The best is saved for last—the **Teatro Marittimo ★★★**, a circular theater in ruins, its central building enveloped by a canal spanned by small swing bridges.

Largo Marguerite Yourcenar 1, Tivoli. www.coopculture.it/en/poi/hadrians-villa. ✆ **0774-312070.** 12€. Daily 8:15am–sunset. Bus: 4 from Tivoli.

Villa d'Este ★★ PARK/GARDEN Like Hadrian centuries before, Cardinal Ippolito d'Este of Ferrara in the mid-16th century ordered this villa built on a Tivoli hillside. The dank Renaissance structure, with its second-rate paintings, is not that interesting; the big draw for visitors are the **spectacular gardens ★★★**, designed by Pirro Ligorio. As you descend the cypress-studded garden slope you're rewarded with everything from lilies to gargoyles spouting water, torrential streams, and waterfalls. The loveliest fountain is the **Fontana dell Ovato ★★**, by Ligorio. Nearby is the most spectacular engineering achievement: the **Fontana dell'Organo Idraulico ★★** (Fountain of the Hydraulic Organ), dazzling with music and water jets in front of a baroque chapel (the fountain "plays" every 2 hours from 10:30am). The moss-covered **Fontana dei Draghi** (Fountain of the Dragons), also by Ligorio, and the so-called **Fontana di Vetro** (Fountain of Glass), by Bernini, are also worth seeking out, as is the main promenade, lined with 100 spraying fountains. The garden is worth hours of exploration, but it involves a lot of walking, with some steep climbs.

The musical Fountain of the Hydraulic Organ and fishpond, Villa d'Este.

Piazza Trento 5, Tivoli. www.coopculture.it/en/poi/villa-deste. ✆ **0774-312070.** 10€. Tues–Sun 8:15am to 1 hr. before sunset; Mon from 2pm. Bus: Cotral service from Ponte Mammolo (Roma–Tivoli); bus stops near the entrance.

Villa Gregoriana ★ PARK/GARDEN Villa d'Este dazzles with artificial glamour, but the Villa Gregoriana relies more on nature. Originally laid out by Pope Gregory XVI in the 1830s, its main highlight is the panoramic waterfall of Aniene, with the trek to the bottom studded with grottoes and balconies that open onto the chasm. The only problem is that if you do make the full descent, you might need a helicopter to pull you up again (the climb back up is fierce). From one of the belvederes, there's a view of the **Temple of Vesta** on the hill.

Largo Sant'Angelo, Tivoli. www.fondoambiente.it/luoghi/parco-villa-gregoriana/visita. ✆ **0774-332650.** 8€. Late Apr to mid-Dec daily 10am–dusk (from 9am in summer); closed mid-Dec to late Apr. Bus: Cotral service from Ponte Mammolo (Roma–Tivoli); the bus stops near the entrance.

WHERE TO EAT IN TIVOLI

Tivoli's gardens make for a pleasant picnic place, but if you crave a sit-down meal, **Antica Trattoria del Falcone,** Via del Trevio 34 (✆ **0774-312358**), is a dependable option in Tivoli. Just off Largo Garibaldi, it's been open since 1918 and specializes in excellent pizza, Roman pastas, and roast meats. It's open daily lunch and dinner.

FLORENCE

By Donald Strachan

5

Florence may be small, but over the centuries it has packed a major punch in European history and culture. Its center—which you can easily cross on foot—evokes this illustrious past, packed as it is with monuments from the city's golden age. In the 15th and 16th centuries, Florence's achievements in art and architecture, science, literature, and even banking, were unmatched—and the rest of Europe knew it.

This was the center of the Renaissance movement and the hometown of its leading lights: Michelangelo, Brunelleschi, Leonardo da Vinci, Giotto, Galileo, Donatello, and many others. Florence built up a store of riches that still dazzles—including the **Uffizi Gallery,** heaving with masterpieces; an ingenious domed Cathedral; Michelangelo's **"David"**; and any number of decorated halls, palaces, and chapels. These treasures still represent the best humankind can achieve. Florence remains a must-visit for every first-time traveler to Italy and a must-return destination for anyone who cares about art and architecture.

DON'T LEAVE FLORENCE WITHOUT . . .

Seeing Michelangelo's "David." Rarely does an icon of art live up to its reputation as this one does. See p. 193.

Touring the Uffizi. Yes, everyone does it, but for good reason: The Uffizi has the best Renaissance art collection on earth. See p. 179.

Getting into Leather. A mecca for leather goods, Florence attracts hundreds of jacket-, boot-, and bag-makers. Browse the street stalls of San Lorenzo Market (p. 222) for a deal or the higher-end offerings at Santa Croce's leather school (p. 222) or Benheart (p. 221) for craftsmanship.

Roaming the Dome. Allot plenty of time to explore Piazza del Duomo, Florence's cathedral square dominated by Brunelleschi's dome—which you can experience from the inside, the outside, and up on top. See p. 172.

Feasting on Bistecca alla Fiorentina. Thick, juicy steak prepared over a wood-burning grill—the city's succulent signature dish makes carnivores very happy indeed.

Shopping and Dining on the Left Bank. Buy from fifth-generation artisans in family workshops around the Oltrarno neighborhood, then hit the restaurants and lively bars of San Frediano.

PREVIOUS PAGE: **View of Florence from Piazzale Michelangelo.**

ESSENTIALS

Arriving

BY PLANE Most international travelers reach Florence via the airports in Rome (see p. 63) or Milan (see p. 460), proceeding onward to Florence via train (see below). There are also direct international flights into Pisa's **Galileo Galilei Airport** (see p. 294), 97km (60 miles) west of Florence; several budget airlines fly here from European cities. Between four and eight daily **Sky Bus Lines** buses (www.caronnatour.com; ✆ **366/126-0651**) connect Florence with Pisa Airport in just over 1 hour (15€ adults; 7€ children 2–11). Florence drop-off/pick-up is at the Guidoni tram stop near Florence Airport (see below), except during the night, when the bus runs to/from Florence's main rail station. Enter your phone number during booking to confirm a seat booking via WhatsApp.

A growing number of European airlines, including British Airways, Air France, KLM, Lufthansa, and Vueling also serve Florence's super-convenient **Amerigo Vespucci Airport (FLR;** www.aeroporto.firenze.it/en; ✆ **055/306-15**), sometimes called **Peretola,** just 5km (3 miles) northwest of downtown. A modern **tram line (T2)** is the most cost-efficient way to reach the center from there (1.50€ each way). Trams depart every 5 to 11 minutes, 5am to midnight. Journey time to Florence's rail station is 20 minutes. **Taxis** line up outside the arrivals terminal: Exit and turn immediately to the right to find the rank. They charge a regulated flat rate of 22€ for the 15-minute journey to the city center (24€ holidays, 25.30€ after 10pm; extra 1€ per bag).

BY TRAIN Most travelers arrive in Florence by train. Luckily, this is Tuscany's rail hub, with regular connections to all Italy's major cities. To get here from Rome, take a high-speed **Frecciarossa** or **Frecciargento** train (1½ hr.; www.trenitalia.com) or rival high-speed trains operated by **Italo** (www.italotreno.it). High-speed trains run from Venice (2 hr.) via Padua and Bologna, and also direct from Rome's Fiumicino Airport. On high-speed trains, you must sit in your reserved seat.

Most Florence-bound trains roll into **Stazione Santa Maria Novella,** Piazza della Stazione, which you'll see abbreviated as **S.M.N.** The station is an architectural masterpiece, albeit one dating to Italy's Fascist period, rather than the Renaissance. It lies on the northwestern edge of the city's compact historic center, a 10-minute walk from the Duomo and a brisk 15-minute walk from Piazza della Signoria and the Uffizi.

BY CAR The **A1** ***autostrada*** runs north from Rome past Arezzo to Florence and continues to Bologna. Unnumbered **superhighways** run to and from Siena (the *SI-FI raccordo*) and Pisa (the so-called *FI-PI-LI*). To reach Florence from Venice, take the A13 southbound, then switch to the A1 at Bologna.

Advance Reservations for the Uffizi, Accademia & More

As soon as you set a date for your visit to Florence, consider making advance reservations for the **Uffizi** and the **Accademia** museums—it's the best way to avoid spending time in line, and walk-ups are either no longer allowed or strongly discouraged at some major museums. (Buying a cumulative ticket—see "Discount Tickets for Florence," p. 173—is your other smart strategy.) Book via **www.uffizi.it** or call Firenze Musei on ✆ **055/294-883** (English is spoken). This is the **only official ticketing agent for state museums:** Do not buy from elsewhere. There's a 4€ fee; you can pay by credit card. Reservations are also possible for the Galleria Palatina in the Pitti Palace, the Bargello, and several others. If you arrive in town without reservations, you can reserve in person at a kiosk in the facade of Orsanmichele, on Via dei Calzaiuoli (Mon–Sat); from Libreria My Accademia, Via Ricasoli 105R (Tues–Sun); at Opera Your Preview, Via Por Santa Maria 13R (www.operayourpreview.com); or for the Uffizi only, at Florence's Archaeological Museum (p. 193). For prebooking timed admission slots at city museums such as the Palazzo Vecchio or Cappella Brancacci, visit the ticketing hub at **ticketsmuseums.comune.fi.it**.

Driving *to* Florence is easy; the problems begin once you arrive. Almost all cars are banned from the historic center for much of the time; only residents or merchants with special permits are allowed into this clearly marked, camera-patrolled *zona a traffico limitato* (ZTL). You can enter the ZTL to drop off baggage at your hotel or go direct to a prebooked parking garage (either can organize a temporary ZTL permit when provided with your license plate). Usual ZTL hours are Monday to Friday 7:30am to 7:30pm, Saturday 7:30am to 6pm, but that extends to 3am on Thursday through Saturday evenings from May through September. It's a real hassle, so only rent a car if you're leaving town to visit somewhere off the rail network. **Day-trippers** by car should park and ride the tram: From the south, use the "Drive and Tramway" lot at the Villa Costanza terminus (A1 exit Villa Costanza; www.parcheggiovillacostanza.it); arriving from the north, head for Parcheggio Guidoni, beside the Guidoni stop on tram line T2. You can park all day at either car park for a few euro.

If you do drive into the center, your best bet for overnight or longer-term parking is one of the city-run garages. The best deal—better than most hotels' garage rates—is at the **Parterre parking lot** under Piazza Libertà at Via del Ponte Rosso 4 (✆ **055/5030-2209**). Open around the clock, it costs 2€ per hour or 15€ per day. Find more info on parking at **www.fipark.com**.

Don't park your car overnight on the street without local knowledge. If you're ticketed and towed, the fine is hefty and the headaches to retrieve the car are beyond description, and a near-impossible task on weekends. If this happens to you, start by calling the vehicle removal department **(Recupero Veicoli Rimossi)** at ✆ **055/422-4142.** One more reason **you should not drive in Florence.**

Visitor Information

TOURIST OFFICES The most convenient tourist office is opposite Florence's main rail terminus at Piazza della Stazione 4. With your back to the tracks, take the left exit and then bear right—it's across the tram tracks and road junction ahead. The office is open Monday through Saturday 9am to 7pm, Sunday 9am to 2pm, and provides useful free street maps. Another office, close to Santa Croce church at Borgo Santa Croce 29R, is open the same hours. A third central office, at Via Cavour 1R, two blocks north of the Duomo, is open Monday through Friday 9am to 1pm. An information kiosk in the Arrivals Hall at Florence airport is open daily 9am to 7pm. One central **phone number covers all tourist assistance: ✆ 055/000** (Mon–Sat 9am–7pm; Sun 9am–2pm). English is spoken.

WEBSITES The official Florence tourism website, **www.feelflorence.it**, contains a wealth of up-to-date information, including on local events. At the "Organize Your Trip" section of the site, you can download a printable PDF with opening hours for city sights; the document is updated daily. The **Feel Florence app** is available for Android and Apple mobile devices. For one-off exhibitions, inspiration, and culture, **Art Trav** (www.arttrav.com) is an essential English-language blog. For more Florence info, go to **www.frommers.com/destinations/florence**.

City Layout

Florence is a smallish city, sitting on the Arno River and petering out rather quickly to olive-planted hills to the north and south, but extending farther west and east along the Arno valley with suburbs and light industry. It has a compact center and is best negotiated on foot. No two major sights are more than a 25-minute walk apart, and most hotels and restaurants in this chapter are in a relatively small ***centro storico*** (historic center), a compact tangle of medieval streets and *piazze* (squares) where visitors spend most of their time. The bulk of Florence, including the majority of sights, is north of the river, with the **Oltrarno,** an old working artisans' neighborhood, hemmed in between the Arno and hills on the south side.

Locating Addresses: The Red & the Black

The address system in Florence has a split personality. Private homes, some offices, and hotels are numbered in black (or blue), but businesses, shops, and restaurants are numbered independently in red. (That's the theory anyway. In reality, the division between black and red numbers isn't so clear-cut.) The result is that 1, 2, 3 (black) addresses march up the block numerically oblivious to their 1R, 2R, 3R (red) neighbors. You might find doorways on one side of a street numbered 1R, 2R, 3R, 1, 4R, 2, 3, 5R. The color codes occur only in the *centro storico* and old sections of town. Outlying districts didn't bother with this confusing system.

Florence Neighborhoods in Brief

THE DUOMO The area surrounding Florence's gargantuan cathedral is as central as you can get. The Duomo itself is halfway between the two monastic churches of Santa Maria Novella and Santa Croce, as well as at the midpoint between the Uffizi Gallery and the Ponte Vecchio to the south and San Marco and the Accademia (home of Michelangelo's "David") to the north. A tangle of medieval streets south of the Duomo heads toward **Piazza della Signoria** (see below). Southwest of the Duomo, **Piazza della Repubblica** lies in an even older part of town, still laid out in its Roman-era grid, although the square itself, which was "modernized" in the 19th century, chafes architecturally with the rest of the center and has become a bit of a tourist trap. Overall, the Duomo neighborhood is one of the most hotel-heavy parts of town, with everything from luxury inns to student dives. But beware: Many hotels and restaurants here rely on location, rather than quality, for success.

The iconic red dome of Florence's Duomo lies at the city's heart.

PIAZZA DELLA SIGNORIA The city's civic heart is also prime territory for museum hounds—the Uffizi Gallery, Palazzo Vecchio, Bargello sculpture collection, and **Ponte Vecchio** are all nearby. A few blocks just north of the Ponte Vecchio have good shopping but unappealing modern buildings, thanks to post–World War II reconstruction. The neighborhood is stiflingly crowded in peak season—**Via Por Santa Maria** is one street to avoid—but in rare moments when it's empty of tour groups, this neighborhood's narrow lanes remain the romantic heart of medieval Florence. As in the Duomo neighborhood, be *very* choosy when picking a restaurant (or even an ice cream shop!) around here.

SAN LORENZO & THE MERCATO CENTRALE Centered on the Medici family church of **San Lorenzo,** this wedge of streets between the train station and the Duomo is market territory. The vast indoor **Mercato Centrale** food hall is here, along with the **San Lorenzo street market,** full of stalls hawking leather and other souvenirs. It's a colorful but rarely quiet area, with many budget hotels and some very good, affordable dining.

PIAZZA SANTA TRÍNITA This piazza is just north of the river at the south end of Florence's high-end shopping mecca, **Via de' Tornabuoni.** It's a quaint, well-to-do, and still medieval neighborhood—and if you're an upscale-shopping fiend, there's no better place to be.

SANTA MARIA NOVELLA Bounding the western edge of the *centro storico,* this neighborhood has two characters: a bland, busy zone around the train station and a nicer area south of it. In general, the rail-station area is noisy and lacks medieval atmosphere, but it does have more budget hotel options than any other quarter, especially along **Via Faenza** and its tributaries. Try to avoid staying on traffic-heavy **Via Nazionale.** The situation improves dramatically as you head south toward the river, where **Piazza Santa Maria Novella** and its tributary streets have several stylish hotels, many of them affordable.

SAN MARCO & SANTISSIMA ANNUNZIATA On the northern edge of the *centro storico,* you'll find **Piazza San Marco** and **Piazza Santissima Annunziata,** the most architecturally unified square in the city. The neighborhood is home to Florence's university, the **Accademia,** the San Marco paintings of Fra Angelico, and quiet streets with some hotel gems. It's not a bad walk from the heart of the action, yet just far enough to escape any crowds.

SANTA CROCE Few tourists roam east beyond **Piazza Santa Croce,** so if you want to feel like a local, head here. The streets around the **Mercato di Sant'Ambrogio** have an appealing feel and get lively after dark, especially **Via Pietrapiana** and the northern end of **Via de' Macci.** Some of the city's best restaurants and bars are in this area; *aperitivo* time is vibrant along **Via de' Benci.** There are fewer hotels over here, but affordable apartment rentals are everywhere.

THE OLTRARNO, SAN NICCOLÒ & SAN FREDIANO "Across the Arno" is an old artisans' neighborhood, still dotted with workshops. It began as working-class overflow from the medieval city and later became a chic area for aristocrats to build palaces with country views. The largest of these, the **Pitti Palace,** today houses a set of paintings second only to the Uffizi in scope. The Oltrarno's lively tree-shaded center, **Piazza Santo Spirito,** is lined with bars and close to great restaurants and nightlife. West of here, the neighborhood of **San Frediano** is ever more fashionable. **San Niccolò,** at the foot of Florence's southern hills, has popular bars. Oltrarno's hotel range isn't great, but here you can eat and drink better, at better prices, than in the *centro storico.* It's easily walkable to/from the center.

Getting Around Florence

Florence is a **walking** city. You can stroll between the two top sights, Piazza del Duomo and the Uffizi, in 5 minutes or so. The hike from the most northerly major sights, San Marco and the Accademia, to the most southerly, the Pitti Palace, takes less than 25 minutes for most. From Santa Maria Novella eastward to Santa Croce is a flat 20- to 30-minute walk. But beware: **Flagstones,** some of them uneven, are everywhere. Wear sensible shoes with good padding and foot support.

BY BUS & TRAM You will rarely need Florence's efficient **AT bus system** (www.at-bus.it; © **800/14-24-24** in Italy) since the center is so compact. Bus tickets cost 1.50€ (2.50€ on board) and are good for 90 minutes, irrespective of how many changes you make (even if you switch to a tram). Tickets are sold at *tabacchi* (tobacconists), automatic machines, some bars, and most newsstands. ***Note:*** Once on board, validate your paper ticket in the box to avoid a steep fine. Since traffic is restricted in most of the center, buses make runs on principal streets only, except for three tiny electric bus lines (C1–4), which trundle about the *centro storico* and Oltrarno. The most useful routes to outlying areas are no. 7 (for Fiesole) and nos. 12 and 13 (for Piazzale Michelangiolo). Buses run from 6am until 9:30 or 10pm daily, with a limited night service on a few key routes.

Tram lines (www.gestramvia.com) run from 5am until after midnight (until 2am Fri–Sat). Route T1 connects Careggi and the Fortezza via Santa Maria Novella station with the Opera di Firenze, Cascine Park, and Florence's southwestern suburbs. Line T2 connects the rail station with Peretola airport.

BY TAXI Taxis aren't cheap, and with the city so small and the one-way system forcing drivers to take convoluted routes, they aren't an economical way to get about the old center. They may be useful to get you and your bags between the train station and a hotel. It's 3.30€ to start the meter (which rises to 5.30€ on Sun, or to 6.60€ 10pm–6am), plus 1€ per bag or for a fourth passenger in the cab. There are taxi stands outside the train station, on Borgo San Jacopo, and in Piazza Santa Croce; otherwise, call **Radio Taxi SOCOTA** at © **055/4242** (hail a cab by WhatsApp on © **334/662-2550**) or **Radio Taxi COTAFI** at © **055/4390.**

BY BICYCLE Florence had already begun expanding its network of marked cycle lanes before the pandemic, and the project has accelerated since. The app-powered, dockless **bike-sharing** scheme **Movi by Mobike** (www.ridemovi.com) operates in Florence. When you've downloaded the app and registered, you're free to rent: Simply scan the QR code and ride. All payments are handled inside the app, which also displays prices for longer rentals (from 1€ per 20 min.). The Movi fleet includes standard city bikes and e-Bikes.

Fully electric, Italian-made e-scooters can also be rented by the minute, hour, or full day using a similar dockless sharing scheme. You can register for **Helbiz** (www.helbiz.com) at the website or using the app.

The surviving private bike-rental specialists are mostly located around San Lorenzo and San Marco, including **Florence by Bike ★**, Via

San Zanobi 54R (www.florencebybike.it; ✆ **055/488-992**), which rents city bikes and kids' bikes (15€ for the first day, then 10€/day), touring bikes (33€/25€), and e-Bikes (39€/35€). Advance reservations are essential (and sometimes discounted). They provide helmets, lights, and route maps for rides into the hills north and south of the center. Make sure to use a lock (one will be provided): Bike theft is depressingly common.

BY CAR Trying to drive in the *centro storico* is a frustrating, useless exercise, and unauthorized cars are usually fined if they enter the limited traffic zone (ZTL). You need a permit to do anything beyond dropping off and picking up bags at your hotel. **Park your vehicle in one of the lots** and pound the sidewalk. (See "By Car" under "Arriving," p. 165.)

[Fast FACTS] FLORENCE

Business Hours Hours mainly follow the Italian norm (see p. 829), although many larger and/or central shops stay open through the midday *riposo* or nap (note the sign *orario nonstop*).

Doctors & Dentists Tourist-oriented **Medical Service Firenze,** at Via Roma 4 (www.medicalservice.firenze.it; ✆ **055/475-411**) is generally open Monday to Friday 11am to noon, 1 to 3pm, and 5 to 6pm; and Saturday 11am to noon and 1 to 3pm. **All visits should be arranged in advance by phone;** call in the morning. A similar rule operates at **Dr. Stephen Kerr,** who has an office at Piazza Mercato Nuovo 1 (www.dr-kerr.com; ✆ **335/836-1682**), usually open Monday to Friday 10am to 12:20pm and 2 to 4:40pm. His consultation fee is 87€, or 55€ if you show a student ID card. The surgery also offers rapid, certified Covid antigen testing (50€).

Hospitals The most central hospital is **Santa Maria Nuova,** a block northeast of the Duomo on Piazza Santa Maria Nuova (www.uslcentro.toscana.it; ✆ **055/54-54-54**), with a 24-hour emergency room *(pronto soccorso).*

Left Luggage On platform 16 at Santa Maria Novella Station, you can leave luggage at **KiPoint** (www.kibag.it), open daily 7am to 9pm; the cost is 10€ per item for the day. Even cheaper (1€/hr.; 5€/day) is **Left Luggage Florence,** Via de' Boni 5R (www.leftluggageflorence.com).

Mail Florence's **main post office** at Via Pellicceria 3, off the southwest corner of Piazza della Repubblica, is open Monday to Friday 8:20am to 7:05pm and Saturday 8:20am to 12:30pm.

Pharmacies There is a 24-hour pharmacy (also open Sun and state holidays) in **Stazione Santa Maria Novella** (✆ **055/216-761;** ring the bell across from the taxi rank 11pm–7am). On holidays and at night, look for a sign in any pharmacy window telling you which ones are open locally or check www.feelflorence.it/en/farmacieh24.

Police To report a crime or passport problems, call the *questura* (police headquarters) at ✆ **055/49-771.** Lost property might find its way to the *Ufficio oggetti trovati:* ✆ **055/334-802.**

Safety As in any city, pickpockets are a risk in Florence, often light-fingered youngsters hanging around the train station. Otherwise it's a fairly safe city, but steer clear of the Cascine Park after dark. In the wee hours when nightlife is finished, avoid the area around Piazza Santo Spirito and the backstreets behind Santa Croce.

EXPLORING FLORENCE

Opening times can change without notice, especially at city churches. Tourist offices distribute a list of opening hours, updated daily at **www.feelflorence.it**. We **strongly advise** downloading this free PDF or collecting it from any tourist office (p. 167) on arrival. In the listings below we list opening times that *usually* apply. You should, alas, treat these as provisional. Note that last admission everywhere is usually between 30 and 45 minutes before the official closing time.

Italy's national **"First Sundays"** program (#domenicalmuseo), when state museums open doors gratis on the first Sunday of the month, usually operates in Florence between October and March. Check with the tourist office or individual museum websites. It can be both a blessing and a curse: Big-hitters like the Uffizi are mobbed, so aim for some of the many interesting niche state museums instead.

Piazza del Duomo

The cathedral square is always lively—filled with tourists and caricature artists during the day, strolling pedestrians in the early evening, and students strumming guitars on the Duomo's steps at night. The piazza's vivacity amid the glittering facades of the cathedral and the Baptistery doors keeps this an eternal Florentine sight.

Battistero ★★★ CHURCH In choosing a date to mark the beginning of the Renaissance, art historians often seize on 1401, the year Florence's powerful wool merchants' guild held a contest for the commission to design the **North Doors ★★** of the Baptistery to match its Gothic **South Doors ★★**, cast 65 years earlier by Andrea Pisano. The era's foremost Tuscan sculptors each cast a bas-relief bronze panel depicting their vision of the "Sacrifice of Isaac." Twenty-two-year-old Lorenzo Ghiberti, competing against Donatello, Jacopo della Quercia, and Filippo Brunelleschi, won. He spent the next 21 years casting 28 bronze panels and building his doors. The restored originals of all the Baptistery portals are now inside the **Museo dell'Opera del Duomo** (see p. 178).

The result so impressed the merchants' guild—not to mention the public and Ghiberti's fellow artists—that they asked him in 1425 to do the **East Doors ★★★**, facing the Duomo, this time giving him artistic freedom to realize his Renaissance ambitions. Twenty-seven years later, just before his death, Ghiberti finished 10 dramatic Old Testament scenes in gilded bronze, each a masterpiece of Renaissance sculpture and some of the finest examples of low-relief perspective in Italian art. Each illustrates episodes in the stories of Noah (second down on left), Moses (second up on left), Solomon (bottom right), and others. The panels mounted here are also copies, created using historically accurate techniques, with the originals displayed in the Museo dell'Opera del Duomo. Years later, Michelangelo was standing before these doors and someone asked his opinion.

discount TICKETS FOR FLORENCE

It may seem odd to label the **Firenzecard** (www.firenzecard.it) a "discount" ticket, since it costs a substantial 85€. Is it a good buy? For a busy, museum-packed trip, a Firenzecard is a good value. If you only expect to see a few highlights, skip it.

The details: This card (valid for 72 hr.) allows one-time entrance to 60-plus sites, including the Uffizi, Accademia, Cappella Brancacci, Palazzo Pitti, San Marco, and more. In fact, almost everything we recommend in this chapter *except the Duomo complex* is included with the card, even sites in Fiesole (p. 202). A Firenzecard gets you into "fast track" lines everywhere, and it includes prebooking fees—a savings of 3€ to 4€ for museums like the Uffizi and Accademia. However, many museums (including those two) **require Firenzecard holders to prebook** timed admission. The "Museums" section at www.firenzecard.it/en has an easy-to-follow traffic light system for tracking which places require prebooking.

Don't buy a Firenzecard for kids: With a full-priced card you can take family members ages 17 and under for free. Companions under 18 join the express queue with you and pay only the "reservation fee" at state-owned museums (4€ at the Uffizi, for example). Those under 18 also earn free admission to civic museums (such as the Palazzo Vecchio). Private museums and sights have their own payment rules, but this will not add up to 85€ per child. Not even close.

The Firenzecard excludes iconic sites on the cathedral square. The **Brunelleschi Pass** gets you into everything here—including climbing the dome—and costs 30€ (12€ ages 7–14), valid for 3 days. However, to ease crowding, only 1,800 of these comprehensive tickets are sold per day. If your heart is set on climbing the dome, **reserve a time slot as early as you can.** It is **obligatory** when you buy this pass. The cheaper **Giotto Pass** covers everything except the dome (Baptistery, Campanile, and revamped Museo dell'Opera; 20€/7€). The **Ghiberti Pass** excludes the Campanile (15€/5€). The cathedral is always free to visit. See **www.duomo.firenze.it/en** for details. In Florence, you can also buy from the ticket office opposite the cathedral's southern flank, at Piazza del Duomo 14, or inside the Museo dell'Opera. In peak season, it's unlikely that any of the 1,800 slots to climb the dome will be left: Plan ahead. **Do not buy "skip the line" or other tickets for Brunelleschi's dome on the street.** These are not valid and you will be turned away.

Another value option for art lovers is the **PassePartout 5 Days** ticket. It covers the Uffizi (including time slot), Pitti Palace, Boboli Garden, and Museo Archeologico (Mar–Oct 38€, Nov–Feb 18€). The Uffizi must be your first stop, after which you have 5 days to visit the others. You can combine this with a Piazza del Duomo ticket, above, for a shorter, yet still culture-packed visit at a lower cost than a Firenzecard.

His response sums up Ghiberti's accomplishment as no art historian could: "They are so beautiful that they would grace the entrance to Paradise." They've been nicknamed the Gates of Paradise ever since.

The octagonal building itself is ancient, first mentioned in city records in the 9th century but perhaps already 300 years old by then. Its exterior is clad in gleaming white Carrara and green Prato marble. Even the roof is marble, making this the world's only building completely covered in marble.

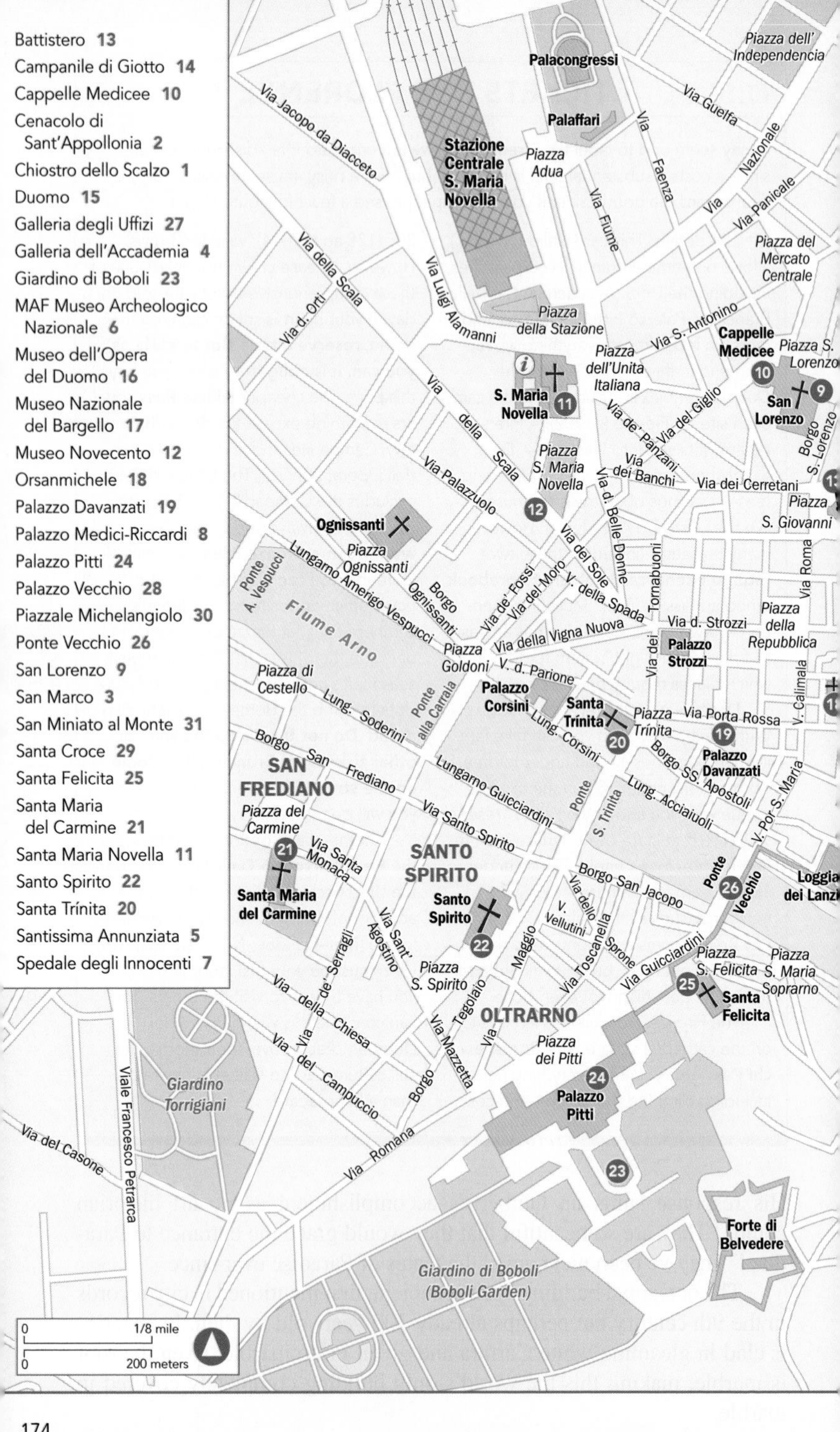
Battistero 13
Campanile di Giotto 14
Cappelle Medicee 10
Cenacolo di Sant'Appollonia 2
Chiostro dello Scalzo 1
Duomo 15
Galleria degli Uffizi 27
Galleria dell'Accademia 4
Giardino di Boboli 23
MAF Museo Archeologico Nazionale 6
Museo dell'Opera del Duomo 16
Museo Nazionale del Bargello 17
Museo Novecento 12
Orsanmichele 18
Palazzo Davanzati 19
Palazzo Medici-Riccardi 8
Palazzo Pitti 24
Palazzo Vecchio 28
Piazzale Michelangiolo 30
Ponte Vecchio 26
San Lorenzo 9
San Marco 3
San Miniato al Monte 31
Santa Croce 29
Santa Felicita 25
Santa Maria del Carmine 21
Santa Maria Novella 11
Santo Spirito 22
Santa Trínita 20
Santissima Annunziata 5
Spedale degli Innocenti 7
Palacongressi
Piazza dell' Independencia
Via Guelfa
Palaffari
Via Faenza
Via Nazionale
Via Jacopo da Diacceto
Stazione Centrale S. Maria Novella
Piazza Adua
Via Fiume
Via Panicale
Piazza del Mercato Centrale
Via della Scala
Via Luigi Alamanni
Via d. Orti
Piazza della Stazione
Via S. Antonino
Cappelle Medicee
Piazza S. Lorenzo
Piazza dell'Unita Italiana
S. Maria Novella
Via del Giglio
San Lorenzo
Borgo S. Lorenzo
Via de' Panzani
Via dei Banchi
Piazza S. Maria Novella
Via dei Cerretani
Piazza S. Giovanni
Via Palazzuolo
Via d. Belle Donne
Ognissanti
Piazza Ognissanti
Via del Sole
Via Roma
Ponte A. Vespucci
Lungarno Amerigo Vespucci
Borgo Ognissanti
Via de' Fossi
Via del Moro
V. della Spada
Via dei Tornabuoni
Piazza della Repubblica
Fiume Arno
Via d. Strozzi
Piazza Goldoni
Via della Vigna Nuova
Palazzo Strozzi
Piazza di Cestello
V. d. Parione
Palazzo Corsini
V. Calimala
Lung. Soderini
Ponte alla Carraia
Santa Trínita
Piazza Trínita
Via Porta Rossa
Lung. Corsini
Borgo San Frediano
SAN FREDIANO
Lungarno Guicciardini
Borgo SS. Apostoli
Palazzo Davanzati
Ponte S. Trinita
Lung. Acciaiuoli
Piazza del Carmine
Via Santo Spirito
V. Por S. Maria
Via Santa Monaca
SANTO SPIRITO
Borgo San Jacopo
Ponte Vecchio
Loggia dei Lanzi
Santa Maria del Carmine
Santo Spirito
V. Vellutini
Via dello Sprone
Via de' Serragli
Via Sant' Agostino
Maggio
Via Toscanella
Via Guicciardini
Piazza S. Felicita
Piazza S. Maria Soprarno
Piazza S. Spirito
Santa Felicita
Via della Chiesa
Via Tegolaio
OLTRARNO
Via Mazzetta
Piazza dei Pitti
Via del Campuccio
Borgo
Palazzo Pitti
Giardino Torrigiani
Viale Francesco Petrarca
Via del Casone
Via Romana
Forte di Belvedere
Giardino di Boboli (Boboli Garden)
0 1/8 mile
0 200 meters

Florence Attractions
San Marco
Santissima Annunziata
Galleria dell' Accademia
Museo Archeologico
Spedale degli Innocenti
Palazzo Medici-Riccardi
Palazzo Pucci
Ospedale S. Maria Nuova
Teatro d. Pergola
Santa Maria Maddalena dei Pazzi
Sinogoga (Museo Ebraico)
Duomo
Piazza del Duomo
Bargello
Badia
Teatro Verdi
Casa di Buonarroti
Carceri delle Murate
Archivo di Stato
Palazzo Vecchio
Uffizi
Santa Croce
Biblioteca Nazionale
SANTA CROCE
Fiume Arno
SAN NICCOLÒ
Piazzale Michelangiolo
Giardino dei Semplici
Giardino della Gherardesca
Piazza Donatello
Piazza d'Azeglio
Piazza San Marco
Piazza della SS. Annunziata
Piazza Brunelleschi
Piazza S. M. Nuova
Piazza Sant' Ambrogio
Piazza L. Ghiberti
Piazza Cesare Beccaria
Piazza della Signoria
Piazza S. Firenze
Piazza S. Croce
Piazza Mentana
Piazza dei Cavalleggeri
Piazza Piave
Piazza G. Poggi
Piazza F. Ferrucci
Via Cavour
Via della Dogana
Via G. Capponi
Via P. Cappone
Via G. La Farini
Via Giuseppe Giusti
Via della Colonna
Viale Antonio Gramsci
Via dell'Oriuolo
Via Ghibellina
Borgo degli Albizi
Lungarno delle Grazie
Lung. della Zecca Vecchia
Lungarno Serristori
Lungarno Torrigiani
Lungarno B. Cellini
Via di S. Niccolo
Via di Belvedere
Viale G. Poggi
Via del Monte alle Croci
Viale Michelangiolo
Viale Giovanni Amendola
Via dei Bastioni

The interior is ringed with columns pilfered from ancient Roman buildings, with a riot of mosaic-work above and below. The floor was inlaid in 1209, and between 1225 and the early 1300s the ceiling was covered with **mosaics ★★★**, most of approximately 10 *million* tiles crafted by Venetian or Byzantine-style workshops working off designs by the era's best artists. Coppo di Marcovaldo drew sketches for a 7.8m-high (26-ft.) "Christ in Judgment" and a "Last Judgment" that fills over a third of the ceiling. Four separate, concentric registers tell stories from the Old and New Testaments. Until the 1700s, this was the only place in Florence you could legally be baptized.

Tip: In 2023, a 6-year restoration project of the Baptistery ceiling began, which means its mosaics will not be fully visible from ground level. However, you now have a **once-in-a-lifetime opportunity**—literally—to ascend the scaffolding and see these incredible artworks up close. You get near enough to see mosaic fish and octopus swimming in the waters at Jesus' Baptism. That close. Groups are 10 people maximum; 65€ per person (usually Fri–Sat only); ages 14 and over only.

Piazza San Giovanni. www.duomo.firenze.it. ✆ **055/264-5789.** 30€/20€/15€ combo ticket. Daily 9am–7:30pm. Bus: C2.

Campanile di Giotto ★★ ARCHITECTURE In 1334, Giotto started the cathedral bell tower but completed only the first two levels before his death in 1337. A painter by trade, he was out of his league with the engineering aspect of architecture, and the tower was saved from falling by Andrea Pisano, who doubled the thickness of the walls. Pisano also changed the design to add statue niches—he even carved a few of the statues himself—before quitting the project in 1348. Francesco Talenti finished the job between 1350 and 1359. The **reliefs** and **statues** in the lower levels—by Andrea Pisano, Donatello, Luca della Robbia, and others—are all copies; weatherworn originals are housed in the Museo dell'Opera (p. 178). If you are fit, we recommend climbing the 414 steps to the top; the **view ★★** is memorable as you ascend and offers one of the city's best close-ups of Brunelleschi's dome. If dome tickets are sold out, the Campanile is a worthy substitute.

Piazza del Duomo. www.duomo.firenze.it. ✆ **055/264-5789.** 30€/20€ combo ticket. Daily 8:15am–7pm. Bus: C2, 14, 23.

Duomo (Cattedrale di Santa Maria del Fiore) ★★ CATHEDRAL By the late 13th century, Florence was feeling peevish. Archrivals Siena and Pisa had flamboyant new cathedrals while it was saddled with a tiny 5th- or 6th-century cathedral dedicated to St. Reparata. So, in 1296, the city hired Arnolfo di Cambio to design a new Duomo; he raised the facade and the first few bays before his death (around 1310). Work continued under the auspices of the Wool Guild and architect Francesco Talenti, who expanded the planned size and finished up to the drum of the dome. Over

The Duomo's ornate neo-Gothic facade.

the centuries, many designs for the unfinished facade were offered and rejected. For one lavish Medici wedding, the family even commissioned a temporary facade in papier-mâché. The permanent one is a neo-Gothic design by Emilio De Fabris, added from 1871 to 1887.

The Duomo's most distinctive feature is its enormous **dome ★★★** (or *cupola*), which dominates the skyline and has become the symbol of Florence itself. The raising of this dome was no mean architectural feat, tackled by Filippo Brunelleschi between 1420 and 1436 (see "A Man & His Dome," p. 178). The largest dome in the world in its time, it remains the widest ever built in brick. You can climb up between its two shells for one of the classic panoramas across the city—something not recommended for claustrophobes or anyone with no head for heights. Booking a time slot to climb the dome is **compulsory.** Book as far ahead as you can in peak seasons: Only 1,800 people may make the climb daily.

The cathedral interior is quite spartan, but one of the most dramatic episodes in the history of Florence played out here: The attempted assassination of the Medici brothers on Easter Sunday, 1478. The so-called Pazzi Conspiracy failed. Giuliano de' Medici was murdered, but a wounded Lorenzo barricaded himself into a sacristy (no one is certain which of the two) and escaped. Revenge was exacted in grisly fashion. Plotters including the powerful Pazzi family and the Archbishop of Pisa were found and hanged from the windows of the Palazzo Vecchio.

Restored in 2022, two optical-illusion **equestrian "statues" ★** decorate the north wall—of English soldier Sir John Hawkwood, painted in 1436 by Paolo Uccello, beside Niccolò da Tolentino by Andrea Del Castagno—elevating these two mercenaries to a status they perhaps did not deserve. The remains and mosaic floors of old **Santa Reparata ★** are in the crypt. English Mass is held Saturdays at 5pm.

Piazza del Duomo. www.duomo.firenze.it. ✆ **055/264-5789.** Church free; cupola via 30€ Brunelleschi Pass. Church Mon–Sat 10:15am–4:30pm. Cupola Mon–Fri 8:15am–6:45pm; Sat 8:15am–4:30pm; Sun 12:45–4:30pm. Bus: C1 or C2.

A MAN & HIS dome

Filippo Brunelleschi, a diminutive man whose ego was as big as his talent, managed in his arrogant, quixotic, and brilliant way to invent Renaissance architecture. Having been beaten by Lorenzo Ghiberti in the contest to cast the **Baptistery** doors (see p. 172), Brunelleschi decided he would rather be Florence's top architect than its second-best sculptor and took off for Rome to study its ancient buildings. On returning to his home city, he combined gray *pietra serena* stone, quarried near Fiesole, with smooth white plaster to create airy arches, vaults, and arcades of perfect classical proportions, in his own variant on the ancient orders of architecture. He designed **Santo Spirito** (p. 201), the elegant **Spedale degli Innocenti** (p. 196), a chapel at **Santa Croce** (p. 196), and a new sacristy for **San Lorenzo** (p. 190). But his greatest achievement was erecting the dome over Florence's cathedral.

The Duomo—at that time the world's largest church—had already been built, but nobody had figured out how to cover the daunting space over its crossing. No one was even sure they could create a dome that would hold up under its own weight. Brunelleschi insisted he knew how, and once granted the commission, revealed his ingenious plan, probably inspired by close study of Rome's **Pantheon** (p. 102). He built the dome in two shells, the inner one thicker than the outer, both shells thinning as they neared the top, thus leaving the center hollow and removing a good deal of the weight. He also planned to construct the dome from giant vaults with ribs crossing them, and dovetailed the stones making up the actual fabric of the dome. In this way, the walls of the dome would support themselves as they were erected. In the process of building, Brunelleschi found himself as much an engineer as an architect, designing winches and hoists to carry the materials (plus food and drink) faster and more efficiently up to the level of the construction work. Reputedly, only one person died during construction—a drunken worker who fell.

His finished work speaks for itself, 45m (148 ft.) wide at the base and 90m (295 ft.) high. The marble lantern—which Brunelleschi did not live to see dropped into place in 1446—serves as the structure's keystone. For his achievement, Brunelleschi was accorded the rare honor of burial inside Florence's cathedral.

Museo dell'Opera del Duomo ★★★ MUSEUM Florence's majestic, modern Cathedral Museum shows off Italy's second-largest collection of devotional art after the Vatican (p. 75). But at heart, it's an homage to two Florentine geniuses: Lorenzo Ghiberti and Filippo Brunelleschi.

The location is significant, as this was once the workshop where Michelangelo sculpted his "David." Today the prize exhibits are the original **Gates of Paradise** ★★★ cast by Lorenzo Ghiberti in the early 1400s (see Battistero, p. 172), displayed as the centerpiece of an extraordinary, life-sized re-creation of the early 1400s piazza, complete with a reimagined version of the cathedral's Gothic-era facade. Ghiberti's Baptistery **North Doors** ★★ have also been moved inside, scrubbed to reveal rose gold below years of soot and dirt. In 2019 Pisano's **South Doors** ★★ joined them to complete an unparalleled set of bronze relief sculpture.

Also on the ground floor, freshly restored in 2021, is Michelangelo's **"Bandini Pietà"** ★★ that nearly wasn't. Early in the process he told students this "Pietà" was to stand at his tomb, but when he found an imperfection in the marble, he began attacking it with a hammer (look at Christ's left arm). The master never returned to the work, but students later repaired the damage. The figure of Nicodemus was untouched, legend has it, because it was a self-portrait of the artist—a Michelangelo myth that, for once, is probably true.

In a **multimedia section** ★★ dedicated to Brunelleschi, films, displays, and models explain the engineering process behind his dome. Exhibits include some of the original equipment and machines he invented or used. A **roof terrace** ★ provides a photo op and a closeup of his extraordinary achievement.

Elsewhere are works by Donatello (including a restored **"Magdalen"** ★), Andrea del Verrocchio, and Luca della Robbia, and a restored early Giotto **"Madonna"** ★ damaged by the 1993 Uffizi car bomb.

Piazza del Duomo 9 (behind cathedral). www.duomo.firenze.it. ✆ **055/264-5789.** 30€/20€/15€ combo ticket. Daily 9am–7:30pm. Closed 1st Tues of month. Bus: C1.

Around Piazza della Signoria & Santa Trínita

Galleria degli Uffizi ★★★ ART MUSEUM There is no collection of Renaissance art on the planet to match the Uffizi Gallery. For this reason, **you must reserve a timed admission slot** as soon as you can. Despite its crowds and other inconveniences, the Uffizi remains a must-see. And what will you see? Some 60-plus rooms and marble corridors—built in the 16th century as the Medici's private offices, or *uffici*—packed with famous paintings, among them Botticelli's "Birth of Venus," Leonardo da Vinci's "Annunciation," Michelangelo's "Holy Family," and many, many more.

Initially, rooms are arranged chronologically. **Room A2** begins the pre-Renaissance, Gothic style of painting born in the Middle Ages. Compare Cimabue's "Santa Trínita Maestà," painted around 1290, with his student Giotto's **"Ognissanti Madonna"** ★★★, done in 1310. Both paintings have a similar subject and setting, but Giotto transformed Cimabue's iconlike Byzantine style into something human. Giotto's Madonna looks like she's sitting on a throne, her clothes emphasizing the curves of her body, whereas Cimabue's Madonna and angels float in space, like portraits on coins, with stiff positions. The room's third great Madonna, Duccio's sinuous, ethereal **"Rucellai Madonna"** ★ (1285), became a founding work for the Sienese School of painters.

Room A3 showcases the Sienese School at its peak, with Simone Martini's dazzling **"Annunciation"** ★★ (1333) slathered in gold ground and Ambrogio Lorenzetti's "Presentation at the Temple" (1342). Tragically, the Black Death of 1348 wiped out this entire generation of Sienese painters (along with half of Siena's population). **Rooms A5–A6** show

Florentine painting at its most decorative, in a style now termed International Gothic. The iconic work, Gentile da Fabriano's **"Procession of the Magi"** ★★★ (1423), depicts the line to see newborn Jesus, full of decorative and comic elements. It's even longer than the line waiting outside the Uffizi.

The unflattering profiles of the Duke Federico da Montefeltro of Urbino and his duchess, painted in oil by **Piero della Francesca** around 1473, are the centerpiece of **Room A8.** Piero's subjects are portrayed in a starkly realistic way—the duke exposes his warts and crooked nose, which was broken in a tournament. This focus on earthly, rather than Christian, elements recalls the secular teachings of Greek and Roman times and is made more vivid by a depiction (on the back) of the couple riding chariots driven by the humanistic virtues of faith, charity, hope, and modesty (for her) and prudence, temperance, fortitude, and justice (for him). The same room displays works by **Filippo Lippi** from the mid–15th century. The best backstory belongs to his **"Madonna and Child with Two Angels"** ★★, from around 1465. The work was a celebrity scandal. The woman who modeled for Mary was said to be Filippo's lover—would-be nun Lucrezia Buti, whom he spirited away from a convent before she took her vows—and the child looking toward the viewer, a product of their union. (That son, Filippino Lippi, would also become a painter of note.) Note the background, with distant mountains on one side and water on the other framing the portrait of a woman's face; Leonardo da Vinci stole the idea 40 years later for his "Mona Lisa." Also here is Paolo Uccello's **"Battle of San Romano"** (1435), essentially an experiment in painting perspective—with crazy results.

Rooms A10 to A14 (two linked spaces, despite the numbering) are devoted to the works of Filippo Lippi's student (and later Filippino's teacher) Sandro Filipepi, better known by his nickname "Little Barrels," or Botticelli. Botticelli's 1485 **"Birth of Venus"** ★★ hangs like a billboard you have seen a thousand times. Venus's pose is taken from classical statues, while the winds Zephyr and Aura blowing her to shore, and the muse welcoming her, are based on tales from Ovid's "Metamorphosis." Botticelli's 1478 **"Primavera"** ★★★, its dark, bold colors a stark contrast to filmy, pastel "Venus," defies definitive interpretation. But again it features Venus (center), alongside Mercury, with the winged boots, the Three Graces, and the goddess Flora. Botticelli had a phenomenal eye for botanical detail.

Next, the **Tribuna** ★★ is an architectural oddity, an ornate octagonal room added on the orders of Grand Duke Francesco I. Its centerpiece is the **"Medici Venus"** ★★, a Greek marble crafted in the 1st century B.C. Botticelli copied her pose for his Venus.

To cross to the Uffizi's west wing, you pass picture windows with views of the Arno River to one side and a perfect Renaissance perspective of the Uffizi piazza to the other—plus an often-overlooked Roman sculpture gallery most museums would kill for.

This wing showcases two true Renaissance heavyweights. **Room A35** displays Leonardo da Vinci's magnificent, unfinished **"Adoration of the Magi"** ★★★, with much of the artist's line drawing still visible, beside an **"Annunciation"** ★★. In the latter, completed in the early 1470s while Leonardo was still a student in Verrocchio's workshop, his ability to orchestrate the viewer's focus is already masterful: The line down the middle of the brick corner of the house draws your glance to Mary's delicate fingers, which themselves point along the top of a stone wall to the angel's two raised fingers. Those, in turn, draw attention to the mountain between the two parallel trees dividing Mary from the angel, representing the gulf between the worldly and the spiritual. Its apparently warped perspective was in fact painted intentionally, to be viewed from the lower right. (Test for yourself.)

Room A38 is dedicated to the other two Italian masters of the High Renaissance. In Michelangelo's 1505–08 **"Holy Family"** ★, the twisting shapes of Mary, Joseph, and Jesus recall those in the Sistine Chapel for their sculpted form and bright colors. Among several Uffizi Raphaels, his enchanting **"Madonna of the Goldfinch"** ★★ has a background landscape lifted from Leonardo and Botticelli.

The Uffizi Gallery displays an incredible collection of Renaissance art.

The torsion and tensions of Michelangelo's painting and sculpture inspired the next generation of Florentine painters, known as the **Mannerists ★★**. Andrea del Sarto (**Room D2**), Rosso Fiorentino, and Pontormo (**Room D4**) are the focus of a suite of rooms downstairs, inaugurated in 2021 and dedicated to the **Cinquecento** (1500s). **Room D22** shows off Titian's reclining nude, **"Venus of Urbino" ★★**. It is the highlight of a collection of Venetian Renaissance paintings that also includes Tintoretto and Giorgione. It's no coincidence that the edge of the curtain, the angle of her hand and leg, and the line splitting floor and bed all intersect at the forbidden part of Venus's body.

The final big-hitters hang in the **Sale Seicento** (1600s Rooms): paintings by Caravaggio, notably his crazed **"Medusa" ★** self-portrait and an enigmatic **"Bacchus" ★**. These rooms also explore 17th-century artists who aped his *chiaroscuro* (bright light and dark shadows) style. Greatest among them was Artemisia Gentileschi, a rare female painter from this period. Her **"Judith Slaying Holofernes" ★** (ca. 1612) is one of the bloodiest paintings in the gallery.

If you find yourself flagging (it happens to us all), there is a **coffee shop** at the far end of the upper floor's west wing. Prices are in line with the piazza below, plus you get a close-up of the Palazzo Vecchio's facade from the terrace. Fully refreshed, you can return to discover works by many great artists we haven't space to cover here: Cranach, Rembrandt, and Dürer; Velazquez, El Greco, and Goya; Bellini and Mantegna; Bernini and Barocci; and Masaccio, Bronzino, Parmigianino, and Veronese. In short, there is nowhere like the Uffizi—in Italy or anywhere else in the world.

Piazzale degli Uffizi. www.uffizi.it. ✆ **055/294-883.** Mar–Oct 25€ (before 9am 19€), Nov–Feb 12€ (includes entry to MAF, p. 193); free children 17 and under (booking fee still applies). Tues–Sun 8:15am–6:30pm; prebooking compulsory. Bus: C1 or C2.

Museo Nazionale del Bargello ★★ MUSEUM The Bargello Museum is the most important museum anywhere for Renaissance **sculpture**—yet it's often quieter than other museums in the city. Originally the city's prison, torture chamber, and execution site, the Bargello now stands as a three-story museum containing some of the best of Michelangelo, Donatello, and Ghiberti, as well as their most successful Mannerist successor, Giambologna.

In the ground-level Michelangelo room, scope out the variety of his craft, from a whimsical 1497 **"Bacchus" ★★** to a severe, unfinished "Brutus" of 1539. "Bacchus," created when Michelangelo was just 22, genuinely looks drunk, leaning back a little too far, his head off-kilter, with a cupid about to bump him over. Nearby is Giambologna's twisting **"Mercury" ★**, taking flight propelled by the breath of Zephyr. Cellini's **"Cosimo I" ★**, created about the same time as his "Perseus" (see below), casts this Florentine Grand Duke in the role of Imperial Roman general.

Upstairs, on an open-air loggia, is an "aviary" of bronze birds that once decorated the Medici family's Villa di Castello. Minutely observed and

PIAZZA DELLA signoria

When the Guelph party came out on top after a medieval political struggle with the Ghibellines, they razed part of Florence's old city center to build a new palace for civic government. It's reputed the Guelphs ordered architect Arnolfo di Cambio to build what we now call the **Palazzo Vecchio** (p. 185) in the corner of this space to make sure not an inch would sit on Ghibelline land. (This odd legend was probably fabricated to explain Arnolfo's off-center architecture.) At any rate, the L-shaped space around the *palazzo* became the new civic center of town, **Piazza della Signoria ★★**, named after the city's ruling oligarchy (the "Signoria"). Today, it's an outdoor sculpture gallery, teeming with tourists and ringed by outdoor cafes. If you want to catch the square at its serene best, arrive by 8am and have it to yourself.

The statuary on the piazza is particularly beautiful, starting on the left (as you face the Palazzo Vecchio) with Giambologna's 1594 equestrian statue of Grand Duke Cosimo I. To its right is one of Florence's favorite sculptures to hate, the **Fontana del Nettuno** (Neptune Fountain; 1560–75), created by Bartolomeo Ammannati as a tribute to Cosimo's naval ambitions. (Florentines have dubbed it "Il Biancone," or "Big Whitey.") A **porphyry plaque** on the ground in front of the fountain marks the site where puritanical monk Savonarola held the Bonfire of the Vanities. With fiery apocalyptic preaching, he whipped Florentines into a frenzy. Hundreds filed into this piazza, arms loaded with their "decadent" possessions to throw it all on the flames.

To the right of Neptune, a raised platform fronting the Palazzo Vecchio was known as the *arringheria*, from which soapbox speakers would lecture to crowds (and from where we get our word "harangue"). On its far left is a copy (original in the Bargello) of Donatello's "Marzocco," symbol of the city, a Florentine lion resting its raised paw on a shield emblazoned with the *giglio* (lily). To its right is another Donatello replica, "Judith Beheading Holofernes." Farther down is a man who needs little introduction, Michelangelo's **"David,"** a 19th-century copy of the famous original, now in the Accademia (p. 193). Near enough to David to look truly ugly in comparison is Baccio Bandinelli's lumpy "Hercules and Cacus" (1534).

At the piazza's south end, the **Loggia dei Lanzi ★★** (1376–82) is named after the Swiss Guard of lancers *(lanzi)* whom Cosimo de' Medici stationed here. (It's also called the Loggia della Signoria or the Loggia di Orcagna, after its designer Andrea Orcagna.) At front left stands Benvenuto Cellini's masterpiece in bronze, **"Perseus" ★★★** (1545), holding up the severed head of Medusa. On the far right is Giambologna's **"Rape of the Sabines" ★★**. You must walk all the way around to appreciate the dynamism, catching the action and artistry of its spiral design from different angles. The subject matter is a controversial tale from Roman mythology—a mass abduction—though this was only fixed after the sculpture was complete. Giambologna himself only intended to showcase his skill. Talk continues about moving the statue indoors, safe from the elements… but for now, it's still here.

intricately cast, they were completed in the mid–16th century by Giambologna, Ammannati, and others. An adjacent vaulted hall features some of Donatello's most accomplished sculpture, including his original "Marzocco" (from outside the Palazzo Vecchio; p. 185), and **"St. George" ★**, from a niche at Orsanmichele (p. 184). His bronze **"David" ★★** (which some think might actually be the god Mercury), done around 1440, was Italy's first freestanding nude sculpture after Roman times. The classical detail of Donatello's sculptures, as well as their naturalistic poses and reflective mood, is the essence of the Renaissance style.

Side by side on the back wall are contest entries submitted in 1401 by Ghiberti and Brunelleschi for the Baptistery doors commission. With the "Sacrifice of Isaac" as their biblical theme, both displayed innovative use of perspective. Ghiberti won, perhaps because his scene is more thematically unified. Brunelleschi could have ended up a footnote in art history, but instead he gave up the chisel and turned to architecture instead (see "A Man & His Dome," p. 178).

Faded 1330s frescoes by Giotto's workshop decorate the **Cappella della Maddalena,** the room where prisoners would wait before execution. Further extensive sections are dedicated to Italian majolica and Islamic art (carpets and ceramics).

Via del Proconsolo 4. www.bargellomusei.beniculturali.it. ✆ **055/064-9440.** 9€. Wed–Fri and Sun–Mon 8:45am–1:30pm; Sat 8:15am–6:50pm. Closed 2nd and 4th Sun of each month. Bus: C1 or C2.

Orsanmichele ★★ CHURCH This bulky structure halfway down Via dei Calzaiuoli looks more like a Gothic warehouse than a church—which is exactly what it was, built as a granary and grain market in 1337. After a

Miracles have been attributed to Bernardo Daddi's "Madonna and Child" icon in Orsanmichele church.

miraculous image of the Madonna appeared on a column inside, its lower level was turned into a shrine and chapel. The city's merchant guilds each decorated a Gothic tabernacle around the outside with a statue of their patron saint. Masters such as Ghiberti, Donatello, Verrocchio, and Giambologna all cast or carved masterpieces to set here (those remaining are mostly copies, including Donatello's "St. George"). Reopened after a 2023 restoration, the dark interior has an elaborate Gothic stone **Tabernacle ★** (1349–59) by Andrea Orcagna, which protects a luminous 1348 "Madonna and Child" painted by Giotto's student Bernardo Daddi, to which miracles were ascribed during the Black Death of 1348–50. Upstairs, the airy rooms of the **Museo di Orsanmichele ★** house many of the original sculptures that adorned the exterior niches. Among the treasures are a trio of bronzes: Ghiberti's "St. John the Baptist" (1412–16), the first life-size bronze of the Renaissance; Verrocchio's "Incredulity of St. Thomas" (1483); and Giambologna's "St. Luke" (1602). Climb up one more floor, to the top, for an unforgettable 360-degree **panorama ★★** of the city.

Via Arte della Lana 1. www.bargellomusei.beniculturali.it. ✆ **055/238-8610.** 4€. Hours vary; see website. Bus: C2.

Palazzo Davanzati ★★ HISTORIC HOME Reopened after a 2022 restoration, one of the city's best-preserved 14th-century palaces offers a glimpse of domestic life during the medieval and Renaissance period. It was originally built for the Davizzi family in the mid-1300s, then bought by the Davanzati clan in 1558; the latter's family tree, dating back to the 1100s, is emblazoned on ground-floor courtyard walls. Painted wooden ceilings and murals have aged well (even surviving World War II damage). The emphasis here is not on decor, however, but on insights into the medieval life of a noble Florentine family: feasts and festivities in the **Sala Madornale;** a private internal well that secured the water supply when things in Florence got sticky; and magnificent 14th-century bedchamber frescoes recounting, comic-strip style, "The Chatelaine of Vergy," a medieval morality tale. The palace has surprising North American connections: In 1916, a New York auction of its furnishings launched a "Florentine style" trend in U.S. interior design, and 2 years later, the set for the Met Opera premiere of Puccini's *Gianni Schicchi* was based on Palazzo Davanzati interiors.

Via Porta Rossa 13. www.bargellomusei.beniculturali.it. ✆ **055/064-9460.** 6€. Fri–Sun 1:15–6:50pm; Tues–Thurs 8:15am–1:50pm. Closed 1st, 3rd, and 5th Sun of each month. Bus: C2.

Palazzo Vecchio ★★ PALACE The core of this fortress-like town hall was built from 1299 to 1302 to designs by Arnolfo di Cambio, master builder of Gothic Florence. Home to centuries of Florentine government, the palace is still city hall. When Duke Cosimo I and his Medici family moved to the *palazzo* in 1540, they redecorated. Michelozzo's 1453

courtyard ★ was left architecturally intact but frescoed by Vasari with scenes of Austrian cities, to celebrate the 1565 marriage of Francesco I de' Medici and Joanna of Austria. A grand staircase leads up to the **Sala dei Cinquecento** ★, named for a 500-man assembly that met here in the pre-Medici days of the Florentine Republic. It's also the site of the greatest fresco cycle that ever wasn't: Leonardo da Vinci was commissioned in 1503–05 to paint one long wall with a scene celebrating Florence's victory at the 1440 Battle of Anghiari. Always trying new methods and materials, he decided to mix wax into his pigments. Leonardo had finished painting part of the wall, but it wasn't drying fast enough, so he brought in braziers stoked with hot coals to hurry the process. As onlookers watched in horror, wax in the fresco melted under the heat and colors ran to a puddle on the floor. The search for what remains of his work continues; some hope emerged in 2012 with discovery of pigments similar to those used by Leonardo in a cavity behind the current wall. Michelangelo was also supposed to paint a fresco on the opposite wall, but never got past preparatory drawings before Pope Julius II called him to Rome to paint the Sistine Chapel. Vasari and his assistants covered the bare walls from 1563 to 1565 with deferential frescoes exalting Cosimo I and his regime's military victories against Pisa (near wall) and Siena (far wall). Opposite the door you enter, Michelangelo's statue of **"Victory"** ★, carved from 1533 to 1534, was for Pope Julius II's tomb but later donated to the Medici.

Vasari's frescoes in the Palazzo Vecchio courtyard.

The first series of rooms on the upper floor is the **Quartiere degli Elementi,** frescoed with allegories and mythological characters, again by Vasari. Crossing the balcony overlooking the Sala dei Cinquecento, you enter the **Apartments of Eleonora di Toledo** ★, decorated for Cosimo's Spanish wife. Her **private chapel** ★★★ is a masterpiece of mid-16th-century fresco painting by Bronzino. Under the coffered ceiling of the **Sala dei Gigli** is Ghirlandaio's fresco of "St. Zenobius Enthroned," with figures from Republican and Imperial Rome, and Donatello's original **"Judith and Holofernes"** ★ bronze (1455), one of his last works. In the palace basement the **Scavi del Teatro Romano** ★ are remnants of Roman Florentia's theater, upon which the medieval palace was built.

Visitors can also climb the **Torre di Arnolfo** ★★, the palace's crenelated tower. If you can bear small spaces and 218 steps, views from the top of this medieval skyscraper and the palace battlements are sublime. The 95m (312-ft.) Torre is closed during bad weather. The minimum age to climb up is 6; ages 17 and under must be accompanied by an adult.

Piazza della Signoria. ticketsmuseums.comune.fi.it. ✆ **055/276-8325.** Palazzo 12.50€; Torre 12.50€; free children 17 and under. Palazzo: Fri–Wed 9am–7pm; Thurs 9am–2pm. Torre: Mon–Wed and Fri 9am–5pm; Thurs 9am–2pm. Bus: C1 or C2.

Ponte Vecchio ★ ARCHITECTURE The oldest and most famous bridge across the Arno, the Ponte Vecchio was built in 1345–50 by Taddeo Gaddi to replace an earlier version. Overhanging shops have lined a bridge here since at least the 12th century. In the 16th century, it was home to butchers, until Duke Ferdinand I moved into the Palazzo Pitti across the river. He couldn't stand the stench, so he evicted the meat cutters and moved in goldsmiths, silversmiths, and jewelers, who occupy it to this day.

In 1944 the Ponte Vecchio's fame saved it from the Nazis, who had orders to blow up all bridges before retreating as Allied forces advanced. They couldn't bring themselves to reduce this span to rubble, so instead blew up the ancient buildings on either end to block it off. Less discriminating was the **Great Arno Flood** of 1966, which severely damaged the stores. A private night watchman saw waters rising alarmingly and called many goldsmiths at home. They rushed to remove valuable stock before it was washed away. ***Tip:*** The Ponte Vecchio is a busy bottleneck for people crossing the river. If you are not comfortable in crowds, take another bridge, any of which will be much quieter.

Via Por Santa Maria/Via Guicciardini. Bus: C3 or C4.

Santa Trínita ★★ CHURCH Behind Bernardo Buontalenti's late-16th-century facade lies a dark church, rebuilt in the 1300s but originally founded by the Vallombrosan religious order before 1177. The third chapel on the right has remains of 14th-century frescoes of the "Madonna Enthroned" by Spinello Aretino, found beneath Lorenzo Monaco's 1424 "Scenes from the Life of the Virgin" frescoes in the next chapel along. This chapel's iron gate is contemporaneous (ca. 1420). In the right transept, Ghirlandaio frescoed the **Cappella Sassetti** ★ in 1485 with a cycle on the "Life of St. Francis," setting all the scenes against Florentine backdrops

Vasari's Corridor

An enclosed passage along the top of the Ponte Vecchio is part of the **Corridoio Vasariano** ★ (Vasari Corridor), a private elevated link between the Palazzo Vecchio (p. 185) and Palazzo Pitti (p. 198). Duke Cosimo I found the idea of mixing with the hoi polloi on his way to work distressing—and assassination was a real risk—so he commissioned Vasari to design his VIP route in 1565. His former secret passageway is now hung with the world's best collection of artists' self-portraits. The corridor has been closed since 2016 but is scheduled to open for public access by 2024. Inquire at the tourist office or check **www.uffizi.it/corridoio-vasariano** for updates.

peopled with portraits of contemporary notables. His "Francis Receiving the Order from Pope Honorius" (in the lunette) takes place under an arcade on the north side of Piazza della Signoria; you'll recognize the Loggia dei Lanzi in the middle, and on the left, the Palazzo Vecchio (the Uffizi hadn't yet been built). Take a 2€ coin for chapel lighting.

Tip: The south end of the piazza leads to the **Ponte Santa Trínita ★★**, Florence's most graceful bridge. In 1567, Ammannati built this span for the wedding of Cosimo II, and set it with four 16th-century statues of the seasons. After the Nazis blew up the bridge in 1944, it was rebuilt and everything was reset in place—save the head on Spring, which remained lost until a team dredging the river in 1961 found it by accident. If you want to photograph the Ponte Vecchio, head here at dusk.

Piazza Santa Trínita. ✆ **055/216-912.** Free. Mon–Sat 8am–noon and 4–6:15pm; Sun 8:15–10:45am and 4–6:15pm. Bus: C3, C4, 6, 11.

Catch an Exhibition at the Strozzi

The Renaissance **Palazzo Strozzi ★★**, Piazza Strozzi (www.palazzostrozzi.org; ✆ **055/264-5155**), Florence's major space for temporary and contemporary art, has been having a 21st-century rebirth of its own. Hit shows in recent years include Bill Viola's "Electronic Renaissance" in 2017 and Olafur Eliasson in 2023. There's usually plenty going on around each show, including talks, late opening nights, and downloadable activity kits for kids. Check the website. Admission to headline exhibitions is usually around 15€.

Around San Lorenzo & the Mercato Centrale

The church of San Lorenzo was once lost behind the leather and souvenir stalls of Florence's **San Lorenzo Street Market** (see p. 222), until a decade ago, when the carts were moved into adjacent streets. A bustle of commerce characterizes this whole neighborhood, centered on both this tourist market and the nearby **Mercato Centrale,** whose upper floor is a showcase for Italian street food (see p. 216).

Cappelle Medicee (Medici Chapels) ★ MONUMENT Michelangelo built San Lorenzo's **Sagrestia Nuova ★★** (New Sacristy), between 1519 and 1533 (finished by Vasari in 1556), as a monument to Lorenzo the Magnificent and his generation of relatively enlightened Medici; it was built in harmony with Brunelleschi's Old Sacristy inside San Lorenzo itself (see p. 190). (Architectural note: The dome's windows taper as they get near the top to fool you into thinking the dome is higher.) Michelangelo was supposed to produce three tombs here (perhaps four) but ironically finished only the two less important ones. So, Lorenzo de' Medici—wise ruler of the city, poet of note, grand patron of the arts, moneybags behind much of the Renaissance, and star of his own Netflix miniseries ("The Magnificent")—ended up with a mere inscription of his name next to his brother Giuliano's on a plain marble slab against the entrance wall. They did get one Michelangelo sculpture to decorate their slab, an unfinished

"Madonna and Child" ★. On the left wall of the sacristy, Michelangelo's **"Tomb of Lorenzo"** ★ commemorates the duke of Urbino (Lorenzo the Magnificent's grandson), whose seated statue symbolizes the contemplative life. Below him on the curves of the tomb stretch a pair of sculptures, "Dawn" (female) and "Dusk" (male). Observing them, one wonders if Michelangelo perhaps hadn't seen many naked women.

In contrast, when work got underway in 1604 on the adjacent **Cappella dei Principi** (Chapel of the Princes), it was to become one of Italy's most arrogant memorials, a mausoleum for the grand dukes, whose ranks include many decrepit tyrants. The Cappella dei Principi is a monolith of cut marble and semiprecious stones—jasper, alabaster, mother-of-pearl, agate, and the like—slathered onto walls and ceiling with little regard for composition or chromatic unity. Ducal funds poured into this monstrosity until Gian Gastone de' Medici drank himself to death in 1737, without an heir. Teams kept doggedly at the thing, and were still finishing the floor in 1962. It was restored in 2019; judge for yourself.

Piazza Madonna degli Aldobrandini (behind San Lorenzo, where Via Faenza and Via del Giglio meet). www.bargellomusei.beniculturali.it. ✆ **055/238-8602.** 9€; free children 17 and under. Mon and Wed–Sat 8:15am–6:50pm; Sun 8:15am–1:50pm. Bus: C1, C2, 22.

Palazzo Medici-Riccardi ★★ HISTORIC HOME Built by Michelozzo in 1444 for Medici "godfather" Cosimo il Vecchio, this is the

Courtyard of the Medici-Riccardi palace, the model for many a Florentine *palazzo*.

prototype Florentine *palazzo,* on which the more overbearing Strozzi and Pitti palaces were later modeled. It remained the Medici private home until Cosimo I (not the same guy) officially declared his power as duke by moving to the Palazzo Vecchio, Florence's civic nerve center. A door off Michelozzo's grand Renaissance courtyard leads up a staircase to the **Cappella dei Magi,** the oldest chapel to survive inside a private Florentine palace. Its walls are covered with dense and colorful Benozzo Gozzoli **frescoes** ★★ (1459–63), classics of the International Gothic style. The walls depict an extended "Journey of the Magi" to see the Christ child, who's being adored by Mary in the altarpiece.

Via Cavour 3. www.palazzomediciriccardi.it. ✆ **055/276-0552.** 7€ (10€ during exhibitions); free children 17 and under; free admission to courtyard and citrus garden. Thurs–Tues 9am–7pm. Bus: C1, 14, 23.

San Lorenzo ★★ CHURCH A rough brick anti-facade fronts what is most likely the oldest church in Florence, founded in A.D. 393. It was later the Medici family's parish church, and Cosimo il Vecchio, whose wise behind-the-scenes rule made him popular with Florentines, is buried in front of the high altar. A plaque marking the spot is inscribed pater patriae, "Father of the Homeland." Off the left transept, the **Sagrestia Vecchia** ★ (Old Sacristy) is one of Brunelleschi's purest pieces of early Renaissance architecture. The focal sarcophagus contains Cosimo il Vecchio's parents, Giovanni di Bicci de' Medici and Piccarda Bueri. A side chapel is decorated with a star map showing the night sky above Florence in 1442—a scene that also features, precisely, in Brunelleschi's Pazzi Chapel in Santa Croce; see p. 197.

On the wall of the main church's left aisle, Bronzino's 1568 fresco of the **"Martyrdom of San Lorenzo"** ★ depicts the poor saint being roasted on a grill in Rome. Two **bronze nave pulpits** ★★, depicting the "Passion" and "Resurrection," were Donatello's final works.

Piazza San Lorenzo. sanlorenzofirenze.it. ✆ **055/214-042.** 9€; free children 11 and under. Mon–Sat 10am–4pm. Bus: C1.

Near Piazza Santa Maria Novella

Two squat obelisks in **Piazza Santa Maria Novella** ★, resting on tortoises crafted by Giambologna, once served as turning posts for "chariot" races held here from the 16th to the mid–19th century. Down-at-heel just a couple of decades ago, this neighborhood now has some of Florence's priciest hotels.

Museo Novecento ★★ MUSEUM This 21st-century museum covers 20th-century Italian art in a multitude of media. Crowds are often sparse—let's face it, you're in Florence to experience the 1400s, not the 1900s. But this is no reflection on the collection's quality, which expertly spans 100 years of visual arts. Exhibits include works by major names such as De Chirico and Futurist Gino Severini; examinations of

Florence's role in fashion; and Italy's relationship with European avant-garde art. In a top-floor room, a 20-minute movie-clip montage shows Florence through the lens of the century's filmmakers, from Arnaldo Ginna's 1916 *Vita Futurista* to more recent hits like *Room with a View* and *Tea with Mussolini.*

Piazza Santa Maria Novella 10. www.museonovecento.it/en. ✆ **055/276-8224.** 9.50€; free children 17 and under. Fri–Wed 11am–8pm. Bus: 6 or 11.

Santa Maria Novella ★★★ CHURCH Of all Florence's major churches, this home of the Dominican order is the only one with a contemporaneous **facade ★★**. The lower Romanesque half was started in the 1300s by architect Fra Jacopo Talenti. Renaissance architect Leon Battista Alberti finished the facade, adding a classically inspired top that not only chimed seamlessly with the lower half, but also created a Cartesian plane of perfect geometry. Inside, Masaccio's **"Trinità" ★★★** (ca. 1425) was the first painting ever to use linear mathematical perspective. Florentine citizens and artists flooded in to see the fresco's unveiling, many in awe that it seemed to punch a hole into space, creating a chapel out of a flat wall. Frescoes by Filippino Lippi and others fill the **transept.** The **Sanctuary ★** behind the main altar was painted after 1485 by Ghirlandaio with the help of apprentices, probably including a young Michelangelo. The left wall is covered with a cycle on the "Life of the Virgin" and

A set of 14th-century frescoes in Santa Maria Novella's Spanish Chapel.

the right has a "Life of St. John the Baptist," works that are also snapshots of the era's fashions, stuffed with portraits of the Tornabuoni family who commissioned them.

The convent cloisters are accessible on the same admission ticket. The **Chiostro Verde ★★** (Green Cloister) was partly frescoed between 1431 and 1446 by Paolo Uccello, a Florentine painter who became obsessed with the mathematics behind perspective. His Old Testament scenes include a "Universal Deluge," which ironically was badly damaged by the Great Arno Flood of 1966. Off the cloister, the **Spanish Chapel ★★** is complex Dominican propaganda, frescoed in the 1360s by Andrea di Bonaiuto. One of the oldest parts, the **Chiostro dei Morti ★** (Cloister of the Dead), with low-slung vaults decorated by Andrea Orcagna and others, was also damaged in 1966. Visitors can access the **Chiostro Grande** (Florence's largest cloister) and papal apartments frescoed by Florentine Mannerist painter, Pontormo. Allow at least 90 minutes to explore this complex.

Piazza Santa Maria Novella/Piazza della Stazione 4. www.smn.it. ✆ **055/219-257.** 7.50€ (10€ during exhibition). Mon–Sat 9:30am–5pm (Fri opens 11am); Sun noon–5pm. Bus: C2, 6, 11, 22.

Near San Marco & Santissima Annunziata

Cenacolo di Sant'Apollonia ★ MUSEUM Andrea del Castagno (1421–57) learned his trade painting portraits of condemned men in city prisons, and the influence of this apprenticeship is apparent on the disciples' faces in his version of **"The Last Supper,"** the first of many painted in Florence during the Renaissance. This giant fresco, completed around 1447, covers an entire wall in this former convent refectory. Judas is banished to the far side of a communal table. Castagno's "Crucifixion," "Deposition," and "Entombment" complete the sequence.

Via XXVII Aprile 1. ✆ **055/238-8608.** Free. Daily 8:15am–1:50pm. Closed 1st, 3rd, and 5th Sat and Sun of each month. Bus: 1, 6, 11, 14, 17, 23.

Chiostro dello Scalzo ★ ART Opening here can be erratic, but for art lovers it is worth a short detour from San Marco. Between 1509 and 1526 painter Andrea del Sarto frescoed a cloister belonging to a religious fraternity dedicated to St. John the Baptist, who is the theme of an unusual monochrome *(grisaille)* fresco cycle. Follow the story counterclockwise from right of the main door. The cloister shines a light on del Sarto's development—work here spans almost his entire career. Compare the "Baptism of Christ" (1509) with the contorted, muscular Mannerism of his "Beheading of the Baptist" (1523), on your left as you walk in. The cloister is usually blissfully empty, too.

Via Cavour 69. ✆ **055/238-8604.** Free. Daily 8:15am–1:50pm; closed 1st, 3rd, and 5th Sun, and 2nd and 4th Mon of each month (same hours); may be closed temporarily during pandemic surges. Bus: C1, 1, 7, 25.

Galleria dell'Accademia ★★★ ART MUSEUM The Accademia's star exhibit, **"David" ★★★**—"Il Gigante"—is much larger than you imagine, looming 4.8m (16 ft.) on top of a 1.8m (6-ft.) pedestal. He hasn't faded with time, either; the marble still gleams as if it were unveiling day in 1504. Viewing the statue is a pleasure in the bright and spacious room custom-designed for him after his move to the Accademia in 1873, following 300 years of pigeons perching on his head in Piazza della Signoria. (Replicas now take the abuse there, and at Piazzale Michelangiolo; a spot high on the northern flank of the Duomo, for which he was originally commissioned, stands empty.)

But the Accademia is not only about "David"; you will be delighted to discover he is surrounded by a museum collection revamped with more space in 2022. Michelangelo's unfinished **"Prisoners" ★★** statues are a contrast to "David," their rough forms struggling to emerge from the raw stone. Michelangelo famously explained how he tried to free the sculpture within every block, and you can appreciate his technique here. New **Renaissance rooms** showcase devotional paintings by Perugino, Filippino Lippi, and Paolo Uccello, as well as a preparatory model for the **"Rape of the Sabines" ★** from the Loggia dei Lanzi (p. 183)—one of the world's oldest 1:1 scale models. Medieval rooms that extend upstairs showcase medieval Florentine art from 1370 onward, including Giotto and Andrea Orcagna. Also reopened after a 2-year restoration project, the **Plaster Cast Galllery (Gipsoteca) ★★** displays over 400 casts in a fresh, "studio" style, many by 19th-century sculptor Lorenzo Bartolini.

Via Ricasoli 60. www.galleriaaccademiafirenze.it. ✆ **055/294-883.** 12€; free children 17 and under (prebooking compulsory). Tues–Sun 8:15am–6:50pm. Bus: C1, 1, 6, 14, 19, 23, 31, 32.

MAF Museo Archeologico Nazionale ★ MUSEUM If you can force yourselves away from the Renaissance, rewind a millennium or two at one of the most important archaeology museums in central Italy, with particular strength in Etruscan art and artifacts. You'll need a little patience, however. The collection inside 17th-century Palazzo della Crocetta is not easy to navigate, although you will quickly find the **"Arezzo Chimera" ★★**, a bronze figure of a mythical lion–goat–serpent dating to the 4th century B.C., perhaps the most important bronze sculpture to survive from the Etruscan era. It is displayed alongside the "Arringatore," a life-sized bronze of an orator dating to the 1st century, just as Etruscan culture was being subsumed by Ancient Rome. On the top floor is the **"Idolino" ★**, a lithe and slightly mysterious bronze. The museum collection is strong on Etruscan-era *bucchero* pottery and funerary urns and Egyptian relics including several sarcophagi displayed in a series of eerie galleries. In 2018, the museum inaugurated a section dedicated to a vast collection of gems, cameos, and intaglio gathered by generations of Medici and Lorraine dukes. Some pieces date back many centuries B.C.

Florence's archaeological museum is rich in Etruscan artifacts, including the famous bronze figure known as the Arezzo Chimera.

With other travelers so focused on medieval and Renaissance sights in the city, you may have this museum almost to yourself.

Piazza Santissima Annunziata 9b. ✆ **055/23-575.** 8€ (free with Uffizi ticket). Mon, Wed, Fri, and Sat 8:30am–2pm; Tues and Thurs 8:30am–7pm; also open 1st Sun of month 8:30am–2pm. Bus: 6, 19, 31, 32.

San Marco ★★★ MUSEUM Showcasing the work of Fra Angelico, Dominican monk and Florentine painter in the International Gothic style, this is the most important collection in the world of his altarpieces and painted panels, residing in a deconsecrated 13th-century convent, once home to the multitasking artist-monk. Seeing it all in one place allows you to appreciate how his decorative impulses and the sinuous lines of his figures place his work right on the cusp of the Renaissance. The most moving and unusual is his **"Annunciation" ★★★**, a postcard favorite, but a close second are intimate frescoes of the life of Jesus—painted not on one giant wall, but scene by scene in monks' small cells that honeycomb the upper floor. The idea was that these scenes, painted by Fra Angelico and his assistants, would aid in prayer and contemplation. The final cell on the left corridor belonged to firebrand preacher Savonarola, who briefly incited the people of the most art-filled city in the world to burn their "decadent" paintings, illuminated manuscripts, and anything else he felt was a worldly betrayal of Jesus's ideals. (*Game of Thrones* fans will spot obvious parallels with the High Sparrow.) In Savonarola's cell are his rosary, chair, and what's left of the clothes he wore. An anonymous painted panel shows the day in 1498 when he was burned at the stake outside the Palazzo Vecchio, having run afoul of Signoria, pope, and populace.

There's much more Fra Angelico art secreted around Michelozzo-designed cloisters, including a **"Crucifixion"** ★ in the Chapter House. The former Pilgrims' Hospice is now a gallery dedicated to Fra Angelico and his contemporaries; look especially for his **"Tabernacolo dei Linaioli"** ★★, painted for the linen workers' guild, and a seemingly weightless **"Deposition"** ★★.

Piazza San Marco 3. ✆ **055/238-8608.** 8€; free children 17 and under. Daily 8:15am–1:50pm. Closed 1st, 3rd, and 5th Sun, and Mon after 2nd and 4th Sun of each month. Bus: C1, 1, 6, 7, 10, 11, 14, 17, 19, 20, 23, 25, 31, 32.

Santissima Annunziata ★★ CHURCH The story of this church begins humbly, in 1233, when seven Florentine nobles had a spiritual crisis, gave away their possessions, and retired to the forest to contemplate divinity. In 1250, they returned to what were fields outside the city walls and founded a small oratory, proclaiming themselves Servants of Mary (the "Servite Order"). Over the years, thanks to a miraculous painting (more on that later), the oratory grew into a grand basilica, enlarged by Michelozzo (1444–81) and later redecorated in unrestrained baroque style.

Visitors enter through the **Chiostro dei Voti** (Votive Cloister), which is today the church's main art draw, decorated with some of the city's finest **Mannerist frescoes** ★★ (1465–1515), once again vibrant after a 5-year restoration. Rosso Fiorentino provided an "Assumption" (1513) and Pontormo the "Visitation" (1515) just to the right of the door. Their master, Andrea del Sarto, contributed a "Birth of the Virgin" (1513), in the far-right corner, one of his finest works. To the right of the door into the church is a damaged but still fascinating "Procession of the Magi" (1514) by del Sarto, who included a giraffe and a self-portrait (front right, looking out from under his blue hat).

The church interior is a flamboyant affair, smothered in multicolored marble and topped with a gilded coffered ceiling. In a side chapel to the left of the entrance, an ornate tabernacle houses a small 14th-century painting of the "Annunciation." Why such a grandiose setting? According to legend, a friar who was painting the picture became vexed that he couldn't make the Madonna's face as beautiful as she should be, and went to take a nap. When he awoke, he found an angel had completed the face for him. This miraculous painting became an object of cult worship, and a once-humble church was changed forever.

On **Piazza Santissima Annunziata** ★★ outside, flanked by elegant Brunelleschi porticos, an equestrian statue of Grand Duke Ferdinand I was Giambologna's last work, cast in 1608 by his student Pietro Tacca after his death; Tacca also did the two fountains of fantastical mermonkey-monsters. ***Tip:*** You can stay right on this sublime piazza, at one of our favorite Florence hotels, the **Loggiato dei Serviti ★★** (p. 212).

Piazza Santissima Annunziata. ✆ **055/266-181.** Free. Cloister: Daily 7am–12:45pm and 4–5pm. Church: Daily 4–5pm. Bus: 6, 19, 31, 32.

Spedale degli Innocenti ★★ MUSEUM/ARCHITECTURE Originally funded by the silk guild, the "Nocenti" opened in 1419 and ever since has been one of the world's leading childcare organizations. (The Institute still works with UNICEF.) Its landmark building was designed by Brunelleschi himself, with elegant Renaissance loggias on the facade and surrounding its interior "Women's" and "Men's" **courtyards ★**. Inside, a three-floor museum has multimedia exhibits tracing the history of the place and the personal stories of many who benefited from its care. The Institute also has a fine **art collection,** including Renaissance works by Botticelli and Ghirlandaio, displayed in a top-floor gallery alongside original painted ceramic roundels by Della Robbia, which elegantly completed Brunelleschi's facade. As you leave, notice the little grated window on the north wall of the main loggia. Here, for centuries, babies were delivered anonymously to the orphanage's care.

Piazza Santissima Annunziata 13. www.museodeglinnocenti.it. ✆ **055/203-7122.** 8€. Daily 9am–7pm. Bus: 6, 19, 31, 32.

Around Piazza Santa Croce

Piazza Santa Croce is like any grand Florentine square—an open space ringed with souvenir and leather shops and thronged with tourists. Once a year (in late June) it's covered with dirt as violent Renaissance-style "soccer" is played on the piazza in a tournament known as **Calcio Storico Fiorentino.** In December, you'll also find Florence's main **Christmas market**—a fun, if boilerplate, German-style affair.

Santa Croce ★★ CHURCH The center of Florence's Franciscan universe was begun in 1294 by Gothic master Arnolfo di Cambio, to rival the Dominican church of Santa Maria Novella being raised across the city. The church wasn't consecrated until 1442, and even then it remained faceless until a neo-Gothic facade was added in 1857. This art-stuffed complex demands 2 hours of your time to see properly.

The vast Gothic interior is populated with the tombs of famous Florentines. Starting from the front door, immediately on the right is the tomb of the most venerated Renaissance master, **Michelangelo Buonarroti,** who died in Rome in 1564 at the age of 89. The pope wanted him buried in the Eternal City, but canny Florentines snuck his body home. Two berths along from Michelangelo's monument is a pompous 19th-century cenotaph for **Dante Alighieri,** one of history's great poets, whose *Divine Comedy* laid the basis for the modern Italian language. (Exiled from

Florence during his lifetime, Dante is actually buried in Ravenna—see p. 378.) Elsewhere are monuments to philosopher **Niccolò Machiavelli,** composer **Gioacchino Rossini,** sculptor **Lorenzo Ghiberti,** and scientist **Galileo Galilei.**

The church's right transept is richly decorated with frescoes. The **Cappella Castellani** was painted with stories of saints' lives by Agnolo Gaddi. His father, Taddeo Gaddi—one of Giotto's closest followers—decorated the **Cappella Baroncelli ★** (1328–30) at the transept's end. Its frescoes depict scenes from the "Life of the Virgin" and include an "Annunciation to the Shepherds," the first night scene in Italian fresco. Giotto himself painted the two chapels to the right of the high altar. Whitewashed over in the 17th century, they were uncovered in the 1800s and inexpertly restored. The more famous **Cappella Bardi ★★★** appeared in the movie *A Room with a View.* Key panels, featuring episodes in the life of St. Francis, include the "Trial by Fire Before the Sultan of Egypt" on the right wall; and one of Giotto's best-known works, the "Death of St. Francis," in which monks weep and wail with convincing pathos. Restoration work ongoing until 2025 obscures them from view.

Outside in the cloister is the **Cappella Pazzi ★★★**, one of Filippo Brunelleschi's architectural masterpieces, faithfully finished after his

Michelangelo's tomb in the church of Santa Croce.

5

FLORENCE | Exploring Florence

death in 1446, more than 30 years before every Pazzi would become *persona non grata* after a failed coup against the Medici (see p. 177). Giuliano da Maiano probably designed the chapel's porch, set with glazed terracottas by Luca della Robbia. The chapel is one of Brunelleschi's signature pieces, decorated with his trademark *pietra serena* gray stone. It is the defining example of early Renaissance architecture. Curiously, the ceiling of the smaller dome depicts the same night sky as his Old Sacristy in San Lorenzo (p. 190); it's not clear why.

Piazza Santa Croce. www.santacroceopera.it. ✆ **055/246-6105.** 8€; free children 17 and under. Mon–Sat 9:30am–5pm; Sun 12:30–5pm. Bus: C1, C2, C3.

The Oltrarno, San Niccolò & San Frediano

Giardino di Boboli ★★ PARK/GARDEN The statue-filled Boboli Garden behind the Pitti Palace is one of the earliest and finest Renaissance gardens, laid out mostly between 1549 and 1656 with box hedges in geometric patterns, groves of ilex (holm oak), dozens of statues, and rows of cypress. Just above the entrance through the courtyard of the Palazzo Pitti is an oblong **amphitheater** modeled on Roman circuses, with a **granite basin** from Rome's Baths of Caracalla and an **Egyptian obelisk** of Ramses II. In 1589 this was the setting for the wedding reception of Ferdinand de' Medici and Christine of Lorraine. For the occasion, the family commissioned entertainment from Jacopo Peri and Ottavio Rinuccini, who decided to set a classical story entirely to music and called it *Dafne*—the world's first opera. (Their follow-up hit, *Euridice,* performed here in 1600, is the earliest opera whose score survives.) At the south end of the park, the **Isolotto ★** is a dreamy island in a pond full of huge goldfish, with Giambologna's "L'Oceano" sculptural composition at its center. At the north end, around the end of the Pitti Palace, are fake caverns filled with statuary, attempting to invoke a classical sacred grotto. The most famous, the **Grotta Grande ★**, was created by Giorgio Vasari, Bartolomeo Ammannati, and Bernardo Buontalenti between 1557 and 1593. Dripping with phony stalactites, it's set with replicas of Michelangelo's unfinished "Prisoners" statues. You can usually get inside on the hour (but not every hour) for 15 minutes.

Entrance via Palazzo Pitti. www.uffizi.it. ✆ **055/238-8791.** Mar–Oct 10€, Nov–Feb 6€, includes Giardino Bardini. June–Aug daily 8:15am–7pm; Apr–May and Sept–Oct closes 6:30pm; Mar closes 5:30pm; Nov–Feb closes 4:30pm. Closed 1st and last Mon of month. Bus: C3, C4, 11, 36, 37.

Palazzo Pitti ★★ MUSEUM/PALACE Although built by and named after a rival of the Medici in the 1450s—the merchant Luca Pitti—the gigantic Pitti Palace soon came into Medici hands. It was the Medici family's principal home from the 1540s and continued to house Florence's rulers until 1919. The Pitti contains five museums, including one of the world's best collections of canvases by Raphael. Out back are elegant Renaissance gardens, the **Boboli** (see above).

In the art-crammed rooms of the Pitti's **Galleria Palatina ★★**, paintings are displayed like cars in a parking garage, stacked on walls above each other following the Enlightenment style of exhibition. Rooms are alternately dimly lit or garishly bright; this is how many great art treasures were once seen and enjoyed. For the casual browser, it can be a frustrating experience; but for art lovers, gems abound. One room here would be enough to build a museum around in many other cities, including some of the best efforts of Titian, Raphael, and Rubens.

Key works in the **Sala di Prometeo** (Prometheus Room) include Filippo Lippi's tondo (round painting) **"Madonna and Child" ★** (1452), which looks suspiciously like another portrait of Lippi's nun-turned-lover, Lucrezia Buti (see Uffizi, p. 179). Two giant canvasses of the "Assumption of the Virgin," both by Mannerist painter Andrea del Sarto, dominate the **Sala dell'Iliade** (Iliad Room). Here you will also find another Biblical woman painted by Artemisia Gentileschi, "Judith," and panels by Annibale Carracci and Rosso Fiorentino. The **Sala di Saturno ★** (Saturn Room) overflows with Raphaels; and in the **Sala di Giove** (Jupiter Room) is his sublime, naturalistic portrait of **"La Velata" ★★**, as well as **"The Three Ages of Man" ★**. The current attribution of the latter is awarded to Venetian Giorgione, though that has been disputed. Keep digging to unearth Allori, Bronzino, Rubens, and more.

At the **Appartamenti Reali** (Royal Apartments) you get a feeling for the conspicuous consumption of the Medici Grand Dukes and their Austrian and Belgian Lorraine successors—and see some notable paintings in their original, ostentatious setting. Italy's first king lived here for several years during the country's 19th-century unification process—when Florence was the second national capital after Turin, between 1865 and 1871, until Rome was finally conquered and the court moved there. Much of the gilded stucco, fabrics, and general decoration is in thunderously poor taste.

The Pitti's "modern" gallery, the **Galleria d'Arte Moderna ★**, has a good collection of 19th-century Italian paintings with a focus on Romanticism, Neoclassical works, and the **Macchiaioli,** a school of Italian painters who worked in an "impressionistic style" chronologically before the French Impressionists. Highlights hunters: Head straight for major works of the latter, in Sala 18 through 20, where Maremma landscapes by **Giovanni Fattori ★** (1825–1908) and Telemaco Signorini (1835–1901) hang. The Pitti's two lesser museums—the **Galleria del Costume** (Costume Gallery) and **Museo degli Argenti** (Museum of Silverware)—combine to prove that wealth and taste do not always go hand in hand. One thing you will notice in the Costume Gallery is how much smaller locals were a few centuries ago. In 2022, another Medici private collection was opened to the public as the **Museum of Russian Icons ★**, the oldest such collection in the Western world.

Piazza Pitti. www.uffizi.it. ✆ **055/294-883.** Mar–Oct 16€, Nov–Feb 10€; free children 17 and under. Tues–Sun 8:15am–6:50pm. Bus: C3, C4, 11, 36, 37.

Piazzale Michelangiolo ★★ SQUARE This pedestrianized, panoramic piazza is on the itinerary of every tour bus. The balustraded terrace was laid out in 1869 to give a sweeping **vista** ★★ of the Renaissance city, spread out in the valley below and backed by the hills of Fiesole beyond. You'll snap the classic shot of the Florence skyline from here. A bronze replica of "David" points directly at his original home, outside the Palazzo Vecchio.

Viale Michelangelo. Bus: 12 or 13.

San Miniato al Monte ★★ CHURCH High atop a hill, its gleaming white-and-green marble facade visible from the city below, San Miniato is one of few truly ancient churches of Florence to survive the centuries virtually intact. The current building took shape in 1013, under the auspices of the powerful Arte di Calimala guild, whose symbol, a bronze eagle clutching a bale of wool, perches on the **facade** ★★. Above the central window is a 13th-century mosaic of "Christ Between the Madonna and St. Minias" (a motif repeated in the apse). The interior has a few Renaissance additions, but they blend well with the overall medieval aspect—an airy, stony space with a raised choir at one end, painted wooden ceiling trusses, and tombs interspersed with inlaid marble zodiac symbols paving the floor.

Below the choir is an 11th-century **Crypt** ★ with remains of frescoes by Taddeo Gaddi. Off to the right of the raised choir is the sacristy, which Spinello Aretino covered in 1387 with elaborate frescoes depicting the **"Life of St. Benedict"** ★★. Off the left of the nave is the 15th-century **Cappella del Cardinale del Portogallo** ★★, a collaborative effort by Renaissance artists to honor a Portuguese humanist, Cardinal Jacopo di Lusitania. It's worth timing your visit to come here when the Benedictine monks are celebrating mass in Gregorian chant (usually 5:30pm). Around the back of the church is San Miniato's monumental **Cemetery** ★, whose paths are lined with tombs and mausoleums built in elaborate pastiches of every generation of Florentine architecture. It's a peaceful, often deserted spot, soundtracked only by birdsong and the occasional toll of church bells.

Via Monte alle Croci/Viale Galileo Galilei (behind Piazzale Michelangiolo). ✆ **055/234-2731.** Free. Mon–Sat 9:30am–12:30pm and 3pm until dusk; Sun 3–5:30pm. Bus: 12 or 13.

Santa Felicita ★ CHURCH Greek sailors who lived in this neighborhood in the 2nd century brought Christianity to Florence, and this little church was probably the second to be established in the city, its first iteration rising in the late 4th century. The current church was thoroughly remodeled in the 1730s. The star works are in the first chapel on the right, Brunelleschi-designed **Cappella Barbadori-Capponi** ★★, with paintings by Mannerist master Pontormo (1525–27). Pontormo's

"Deposition" ★★ and frescoed "Annunciation" are rife with his garish color palette of oranges, pinks, golds, lime greens, and sky blues, and exhibit his trademark surreal sense of figure.

Piazza Santa Felicita (off Via Guicciardini). ✆ **055/213-018.** Free (1€ to illuminate chapel lights). Mon–Sat 9:30am–12:30pm and 3:30–5:30pm. Bus: C3 or C4.

Santa Maria del Carmine ★★★ CHURCH Following a 1771 fire that destroyed everything but the transept chapels and sacristy, this Carmelite church was almost entirely reconstructed in high baroque style. To see the much older **Cappella Brancacci** ★★★ in the right transept, you enter through the cloisters and pay admission. The frescoes here were commissioned by an enemy of the Medici, Felice Brancacci, who in 1424 hired Masolino and his student Masaccio to decorate it with a "Life of St. Peter." Masolino probably worked out the cycle's scheme and painted a few scenes along with his pupil before taking off for 3 years to serve as court painter in Budapest. Masaccio kept painting, quietly creating the early Renaissance's greatest frescoes. Masaccio eventually left for Rome in 1428, where he died at age 27; the cycle was completed between 1480 and 1485 by Filippino Lippi.

Masolino painted "St. Peter Preaching," the upper panel to the left of the altar, and the two top scenes on the right wall, which shows his fastidious, decorative style in a long panel of "St. Peter Healing the Cripple" and "Raising Tabitha," and his "Adam and Eve." Contrast this first man and woman, about to take the snake's bait, with Masaccio's **"Expulsion from the Garden"** ★★★, opposite it. Masolino's figures are highly posed, expressionless models, while Masaccio's Adam and Eve burst with intense emotion. The top scene on the left wall, Masaccio's **"Tribute Money"** ★★, showcases his use of linear perspective. The scenes to the right of the altar are Masaccio's as well; the **"Baptism of the Neophytes"** ★★ is another of his masterpieces. Prebooking a timed entrance slot one day ahead is **essential**.

Piazza del Carmine. ticketsmuseums.comune.fi.it. ✆ **055/276-8224.** 10€; free children 17 and under; reservations essential. Mon and Fri–Sat 10am–5pm; Sun 1–5pm. Bus: C4.

Santo Spirito ★ CHURCH One of Filippo Brunelleschi's masterpieces of architecture, this 15th-century church doesn't look much from the outside (no proper facade was ever added). But the **interior** ★★ is a marvelous High Renaissance space—an expansive landscape of proportion and mathematics in classic Brunelleschi style, with coffered ceiling, lean columns with Corinthian capitals, and the stacked perspective of arched arcading. Late Renaissance and baroque paintings are scattered throughout, but the best stuff lies in the transepts, especially the **Cappella Nerli** ★, with a panel by Filippino Lippi (right transept). The church's extravagant baroque altar has a ciborium inlaid in *pietre dure* around

1607—and frankly, it looks a bit silly against the restrained elegance of Brunelleschi's architecture. A separate entrance admits you to the **Sacristy** to see a wooden "Crucifix" that has, controversially, been attributed to Michelangelo, as well as Santo Spirito's 17th-century cloister and refectory. ***Tip:*** Tree-shaded **Piazza Santo Spirito ★** is one of the focal points of the Oltrarno, lined with cafes and outdoor tables. Sometimes a few farmers sell fresh fruit and vegetables on the square.

Piazza Santo Spirito. www.basilicasantospirito.it. ✆ **055/210-030.** Church free; 2€ Sacristy and cloister. Mon–Tues and Thurs–Sat 10am–1pm and 3–6pm; Sun 11:30am–1:30pm and 3–6pm. Bus: C3, C4, 11, 36, 37.

A Side Trip to Fiesole

Although it's only a short distance from Florence, **Fiesole ★★** has a proud status as an independent municipality. In fact, this hilltop village high above Florence predates its big neighbor in the valley by centuries.

Etruscans from Arezzo probably founded a town here in the 6th century B.C., on the site of a Bronze Age settlement. *Faesulae* became the most important Etruscan center in the region, and although it eventually became a Roman town—conquered in 90 B.C., its inhabitants built a theater and adopted Roman customs—it retained a bit of otherness. Its place in late Roman history was assured when, in A.D. 406, Ostrogoth King Radagaisus was defeated and executed near Fiesole, after an unsuccessful siege of Florence. Following later barbarian invasions, it became part of Florence's administrative district in the 9th century, yet continued to struggle for self-government. Medieval Florence settled things in 1125 by attacking and razing the entire settlement, save the cathedral and bishop's palace.

An oasis of cultivated greenery still separates Fiesole from Florence. Even with the big city so close, Fiesole preserves the character of a Tuscan small town; it makes a perfect escape from the city's bustle. It stays relatively cool in summer, and while you sit at a sidewalk cafe on Piazza

Fiesole Essentials

To get to Fiesole, take bus no. 7 from Florence. It departs from Largo Fratelli Alinari, the station end of Via Nazionale. A scenic 25-minute ride through the greenery above Florence takes you to Fiesole's main square, **Piazza Mino.** The **tourist office** is at Via Portigiani 3 (www.fiesoleforyou.it; ✆ **055/596-1311**). Hours are changeable, but it's usually open daily from March to October (Apr–Sept 9am–7pm, Mar and Oct 10am–6pm). November through February is low season, when typical hours are weekends only from 10am to 3pm.

Fiesole's sights offer a single admission ticket, costing 12€ adults, 8€ ages 7 to 18; a family ticket (2+4) is 24€. Prices are 2€ per person lower without the Museo Bandini, which is missable for all but ardent art lovers, and anyway only opens Friday through Sunday. For more information, visit **www.museidifiesole.it** or call ✆ **055/596-1293.** The **Firenzecard** (p. 173) is valid in Fiesole.

Mino, sipping an iced cappuccino, the lines at the Uffizi seem distant indeed.

San Francesco ★ MONASTERY/MUSEUM The summit of the town is now occupied by a tiny monastery. Its 14th-century church has been largely overhauled, but at the end of a small nave hung with devotional works—Piero di Cosimo and Cenni di Francesco are both represented—is a fine "Crucifixion and Saints" altarpiece by Neri di Bicci. Off the cloisters is a quirky little **Ethnographic Museum,** stuffed with objects picked up by Franciscan missionaries, including an Egyptian mummy, Chinese jade, and ceramics. Entrance to the church's painted, vaulted **crypt** is through the museum. To reach San Francesco, you will climb a sharp hill. Pause close to the top, where a balcony provides perhaps the best **view** ★★★ of Florence and the wine hills of the Chianti beyond.

Via San Francesco 13. www.fratifiesole.it. ✆ **055/59-175.** Free (donation requested). Mon–Sat 10am–noon and 2–5pm; Sun 2–5pm. Bus: 7.

Teatro Romano ★★ RUINS Fiesole's archaeological area is romantically overgrown and scattered with sections of columns, broken friezes, and other ancient remnants. It is also dramatically sited, terraced into a hill with views over the olive groves and forests north of Florence. Beyond a **Roman Theater** ★★ (which seated 1,500 in its day), three rebuilt arches mark the remains of A.D.-1st-century **baths.** Near the arches, a cement balcony over the far edge of the archaeological park gives a good view of a remaining stretch of Fiesole's 4th-century-B.C. **Etruscan walls.** At the other end of the park from the baths, the floor and steps of a 1st-century-B.C. **Roman Temple** were built atop a 4th-century-B.C. Etruscan one dedicated to Minerva. To the left are oblong **Lombard tombs** from the A.D. 7th century, when this part of Fiesole was a necropolis. A small on-site **Archaeological Museum** displays finds uncovered around Fiesole.

Via Portigiani 1. ✆ **055/596-1293.** Apr–Sept daily 9am–7pm; Mar and Oct daily 10am–6pm; Nov–Feb Wed–Mon 10am–3pm. Bus: 7.

Organized Tours

To really get under Florence's surface, book an insightful culture tour with **Context Travel** ★★ (www.contexttravel.com/cities/florence). Led by academics and other experts on a variety of themes, from the gastronomic to the archaeological and artistic, these tours, limited to six people, generally cost around $110 per person. The quality of Context's walks is unmatched, well worth the above-average cost. Private tours start from around $400.

Food tours are booming. A few hours in city markets, or in the company of street vendors or a pro chef, gives you an insight into traditions and trends in Florentine cooking. The glass-fronted Arclinea kitchens upstairs at the Mercato Centrale host the **Lorenzo de' Medici Cooking**

School ★ (cucinaldm.com; ✆ **334/304-0551**), where 2-hour small-group courses (85€–140€; ages 14 and older) teach the skills to create dishes such as fresh pasta, seasonal dishes, or Italian meat and fish courses. **Eating Europe** (www.eatingeurope.com/florence) offers themed small-group tours (65€–85€) covering gelato-making, Oltrarno foodie haunts, and more. They can also customize a Florence food experience for you. Offbeat offerings from **Curious Appetite Travel ★** (curiousappetitetravel.com) include small-group street food market walks, a four-stop "dinner crawl," and artisan beer tastings. Prices range $135 to $185 per person, which includes food and drink. Offerings from **CAF Tours** (www.caftours.com; ✆ **055/283-200**) include themed walks and cooking classes costing from 20€ to more than 100€.

I Just Drive ★ (www.ijustdrive.us; ✆ **055/093-5928**) offers fully equipped cars (Wi-Fi, complimentary bottle of Prosecco) plus an English-speaking driver for various themed visits; for example, you can book a ride in a Bentley or Mercedes up to San Miniato al Monte at dusk to hear mass in Gregorian chant (1½ hr.; 129€). It also operates full-day and half-day private and group food and wine tours into the Chianti hills—by day or night—visits to the Ferrari factory, and even trips to the Cinque Terre.

Especially for Kids

You have to put in a bit of work (and reserve ahead) to reach some of Florence's best views. The climbs, up claustrophobic medieval staircases, are a favorite with many kids. The cupola of **Santa Maria del Fiore** (p. 176), the **Palazzo Vecchio**'s Torre di Arnolfo (p. 186), and the **Campanile di Giotto** (p. 176) are perfect for any youngster who has a head for heights.

The best activities with an educational component are run by **Mus.e ★★** (www.musefirenze.it; ✆ **055/276-8224**), a program that offers child's-eye tours in English around the Palazzo Vecchio, led by guides in period costumes. Lively, affordable activities focus on life at the ducal court, including "The Turtle and the Snail," pitched at children ages 4 to 7. Programs cost 5€ per person; book online or at the desk next to the Palazzo Vecchio ticket booth.

When youngsters need to escape the crowds, head for the **Biblioteca delle Oblate,** Via dell'Oriuolo 24 (www.biblioteche.comune.fi.it; ✆ **055/261-6526**), an air-conditioned library with a children's section on the ground floor (including books in English), as well as space to spread out, color, or draw. It's free and open 9am to 6:45pm, except for Monday morning and all day Sunday (closed 1 week mid-Aug). ***Tip:*** The Oblate's **cafeteria ★** is an excellent place to kick back, with fair prices and a view of Brunelleschi's dome that few visitors see.

Cycling is a pleasure in the riverside **Parco delle Cascine:** See p. 170 for bike rental advice. And remember you are in the **gelato** capital of the world. At least one multi-scoop gelato per day is the minimum recommended dose; see p. 219.

WHERE TO STAY IN FLORENCE

Even before Covid-19, a fast-growing stock of hotel beds had kept lodging prices stable in recent years. However, it remains difficult to find a high-season double you'd want to sleep in for much less than 100€.

Rates vary wildly by season: A room at 180€ in June might cost 50€ in February. Sadly, once-attractive August deals have mostly dried up; Florence no longer gets much quieter in its hottest month. Rooms almost everywhere tend to be smaller than most North Americans are used to.

Florence's city government adds a tourist levy of 3€ to 5€ **per person per night,** depending on the hotel's official star rating, for the first 7 nights of any stay. It is payable on departure and is not included in quoted rates. Children below age 12 are exempt from the tax. Airbnb and other holiday rentals are **not** exempt.

Peak hotel season is Easter through early July, September through October, and Christmas through January 6. May, June, and September are very popular; January and February are the months to grab a bargain—never be shy to haggle if you're coming then. **Booking direct** via phone, e-mail, or the hotel's own website is often key to unlocking the lowest rates or complimentary extras. Ask for a discount if you aim to stay more than 3 consecutive nights.

To help you decide in which area you'd like to base yourself, consult "Florence Neighborhoods in Brief," p. 168. For first-time visitors, there's no good reason to base yourself outside the center or Oltrarno. As indicated below, many hotels offer babysitting services, but almost always "on request"—at least a couple days' notice is advisable. Note we include parking information only for those places that offer it.

Apartment Rentals & Alternative Accommodations

Global players in apartment rental have overtaken most of the local specialists. **Vrbo.com**, TripAdvisor–owned **HolidayLettings.co.uk**, **Booking.com**, **Airbnb.com**, and others are well stocked.

A genuine alternative option, offering a unique perspective, is to stay in a **religious house ★★**. A few monasteries and convents in the center receive guests. For budget travelers, rates can be unbeatable. Our favorites are the **Suore di Santa Elisabetta,** Viale Michelangiolo 46 (near Piazza Ferrucci; ✆ **055/681-1884**), in a colonial villa just south of the Ponte San Niccolò; and close to Santa Croce, the **Istituto Oblate dell'Assunzione,** Borgo Pinti 15 (www.oblate.it; ✆ **055/2346-291**), which has simple, peaceful rooms in a Medici-era building ranged around a courtyard garden. The easiest way to build a monastery and convent itinerary in Florence and beyond is via agent **MonasteryStays.com ★★**. Most religious houses have a curfew, generally 11pm or midnight.

Tip: For basic grocery shopping in the center, try **PAM Local,** Via Cavour 66R (✆ **055/0944-672**), or any central branch of **Conad City**

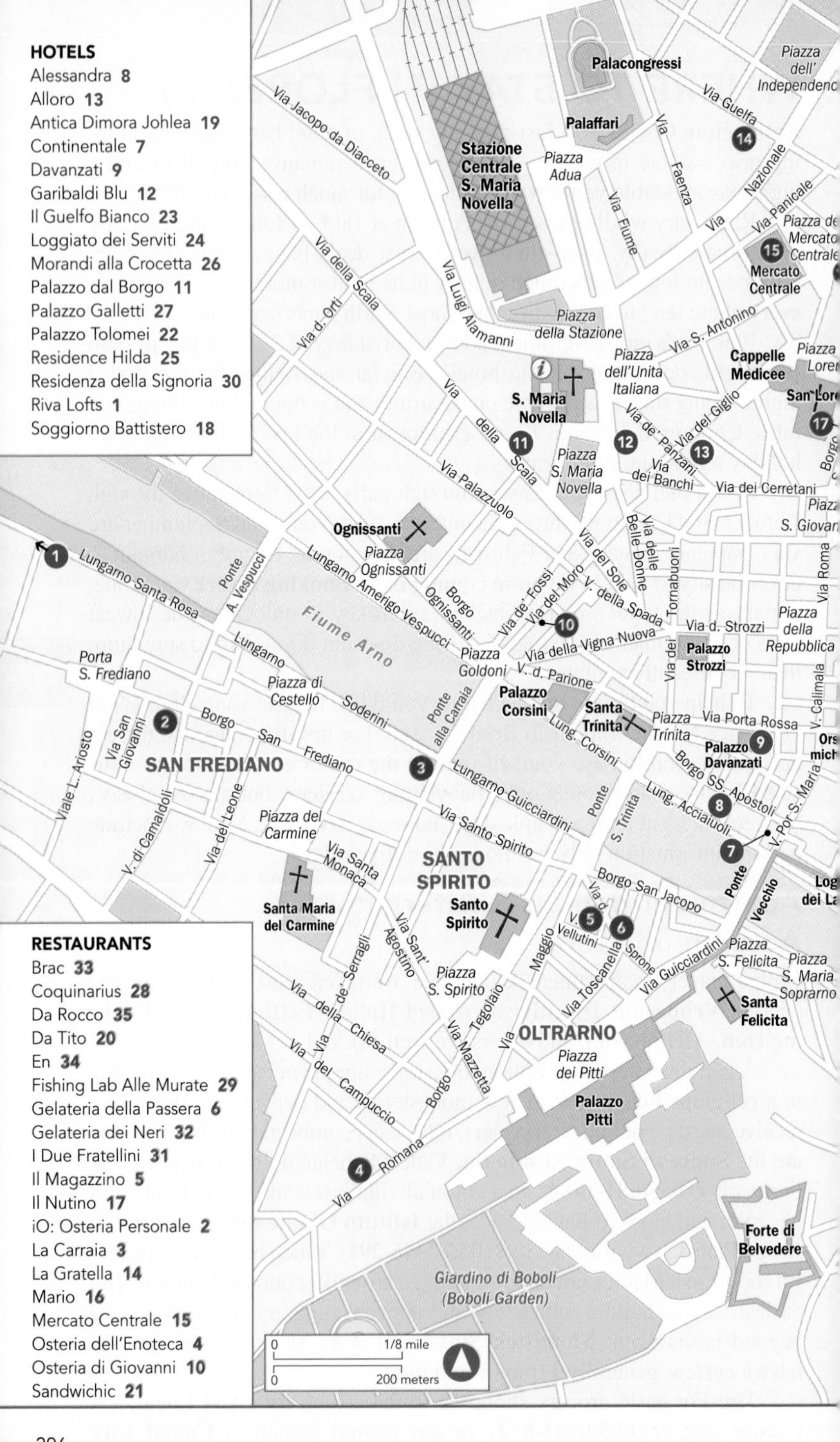
HOTELS
Alessandra 8
Alloro 13
Antica Dimora Johlea 19
Continentale 7
Davanzati 9
Garibaldi Blu 12
Il Guelfo Bianco 23
Loggiato dei Serviti 24
Morandi alla Crocetta 26
Palazzo dal Borgo 11
Palazzo Galletti 27
Palazzo Tolomei 22
Residence Hilda 25
Residenza della Signoria 30
Riva Lofts 1
Soggiorno Battistero 18
RESTAURANTS
Brac 33
Coquinarius 28
Da Rocco 35
Da Tito 20
En 34
Fishing Lab Alle Murate 29
Gelateria della Passera 6
Gelateria dei Neri 32
I Due Fratellini 31
Il Magazzino 5
Il Nutino 17
iO: Osteria Personale 2
La Carraia 3
La Gratella 14
Mario 16
Mercato Centrale 15
Osteria dell'Enoteca 4
Osteria di Giovanni 10
Sandwichic 21
Palacongressi
Palaffari
Stazione Centrale S. Maria Novella
Piazza Adua
Via Jacopo da Diacceto
Via Guelfa
Via Faenza
Via Fiume
Via Nazionale
Via Panicale
Mercato Centrale
Via della Scala
Via d. Orti
Via Luigi Alamanni
Piazza della Stazione
Via S. Antonino
Piazza dell'Unita Italiana
Cappelle Medicee
S. Maria Novella
Via de' Panzani
Via del Giglio
Via dei Banchi
Via dei Cerretani
Piazza S. Maria Novella
Via Palazzuolo
Ognissanti
Piazza Ognissanti
Borgo Ognissanti
Via delle Belle Donne
Via del Sole
V. della Spada
Via de' Fossi
Via del Moro
Via Tornabuoni
Via Roma
Piazza della Repubblica
Via d. Strozzi
Palazzo Strozzi
Via della Vigna Nuova
Lungarno Santa Rosa
Ponte A. Vespucci
Lungarno Amerigo Vespucci
Fiume Arno
Piazza Goldoni
V. d. Parione
Porta S. Frediano
Lungarno Soderini
Piazza di Cestello
Ponte alla Carraia
Palazzo Corsini
Santa Trínita
Piazza Trínita
Via Porta Rossa
V. Calimala
Palazzo Davanzati
Lung. Corsini
Borgo San Frediano
Via San Giovanni
Viale L. Ariosto
SAN FREDIANO
Borgo SS. Apostoli
V. Por S. Maria
Lungarno Guicciardini
Ponte S. Trinita
Lung. Acciaiuoli
V. di Camaldoli
Via del Leone
Piazza del Carmine
Via Santa Monaca
Via Santo Spirito
SANTO SPIRITO
Santo Spirito
Borgo San Jacopo
Ponte Vecchio
Santa Maria del Carmine
Via Sant' Agostino
Via de' Serragli
V. Vellutini
Via Maggio
Via dello Sprone
Via Toscanella
Via Guicciardini
Piazza S. Felicita
Piazza S. Maria Soprarno
Santa Felicita
Piazza S. Spirito
Via della Chiesa
Via Tegolaio
Via Mazzetta
OLTRARNO
Piazza dei Pitti
Palazzo Pitti
Via del Campuccio
Borgo
Via Romana
Forte di Belvedere
Giardino di Boboli (Boboli Garden)
0 1/8 mile
0 200 meters

Florence Hotels & Restaurants
Giardino dei Semplici
San Marco
Giardino della Gherardesca
Piazza Donatello
Piazza San Marco
Santissima Annunziata
Galleria dell' Accademia
Piazza della SS. Annunziata
Ospedale degli Innocenti
Museo Archeologico
Palazzo Medici-Riccardi
Palazzo Pucci
Piazza Brunelleschi
Ospedale S. Maria Nuova
Teatro d. Pergola
Santa Maria Maddalena dei Pazzi
Piazza d'Azeglio
Duomo
Piazza del Duomo
Piazza S. M. Nuova
Sinogoga (Museo Ebraico)
Piazza Sant' Ambrogio
Bargello
Badia
Piazza S. Firenze
Teatro Verdi
Casa di Buonarroti
Piazza L. Ghiberti
Piazza Cesare Beccaria
Carceri delle Murate
Archivio di Stato
Palazzo Vecchio
Piazza S. Croce
Santa Croce
SANTA CROCE
Biblioteca Nazionale
Piazza Mentana
Piazza dei Cavalleggeri
Piazza Piave
Fiume Arno
SAN NICCOLÒ
Piazza G. Poggi
Piazza F. Ferrucci
Piazzale Michelangiolo
Via S. Zanobi
Via XXVII Aprile
Via S. Gallo
Via V. S. Reparata
Via San Gallo
V. degli Arazzieri
Via G. Capponi
Via Cesare Battisti
Via G. La Farini
Via Guelfa
Via Cavour
Via Giuseppe Giusti
Pinti
Via J. Nardi
Via de' Ginori
Via Ricasoli
Via Laura
Borgo Pinti
Via degli Servi
Via della Colonna
Via L. C. Farini
Viale Antonio Gramsci
Via B. Varchi
Via dei Pucci
Via dei Martelli
Via M. Bufalini
Via della Pergola
Alfani
Via G. Carducci
Via della Colonna
Via dei Pilastri
Via de' Pepi
Via S. Egidio
Via dell'Oriuolo
Via Fiesolana
Via di Mezzo
Via della Mattonaia
Via A. Manzoni
V. d. Studio
Via del Proconsolo
Via del Corso
Borgo degli Albizi
Via Pietrapiana
Borgo la Croce
Via Dante Alighieri
Cimatori
Via de' Pandolfini
Via Ghibellina
V. d. Vigna Vecchia
Via G. Verdi
Via de' Pepi
V. M. Buonarroti
Allegri
Via F. Paolieri
Via dell' Agnolo
Via Ghibellina
Borgo de' Greci
Borgo Allegri
Via de' Macci
Via dei Neri
Borgo S. Croce
Via de' Benci
V. Magliabechi
Via di San Giuseppe
Via della Giovine Italia
Via Pietro Thouar
Viale della Giovine Italia
Viale Giovanni Amendola
Corso dei Tintori
Via de' Malcontenti
Lung. Gen. Diaz
Lungarno delle Grazie
Via Tripoli
Lung. della Zecca Vecchia
Lung. P. Giraldi
Ponte alle Grazie
Lungarno Torrigiani
Via de' Bardi
Lungarno Serristori
Via dei Renai
Via di S. Niccolo
Lungarno B. Cellini
Ponte A. Vespucci
Via dei Bastioni
Viale G. Poggi
Via di Belvedere
Via del Monte alle Croci
Viale Michelangiolo

or **Carrefour Express.** Both the **Mercato Centrale** and **Mercato di Sant'Ambrogio** sell an abundance of fresh produce (see "Florence's Best Markets," p. 222).

Near the Duomo

MODERATE/INEXPENSIVE

Palazzo Galletti ★★ Not many hotels within a sensible budget give you the chance to live like a Florentine noble. Rooms here have towering ceilings and an uncluttered arrangement of antiques; most have frescoed or painted-wood showpiece ceilings. Bathrooms, in contrast, have a contemporary design, decked out in travertine and marble. Aside from two street-facing suites, every room has a small balcony, ideal for a pre-dinner glass of wine. If you're here for a once-in-a-lifetime trip, spring for the large suites "Giove" or (especially) "Cerere"; the latter has walls covered in frescoes from the 1800s. Snag a free bottle of their organic estate wine when you book direct and show this Frommer's guide.

Via Sant'Egidio 12. www.palazzogalletti.it. ✆ **055/390-5750.** 11 units. 80€–199€ double. Rates include breakfast. Bus: C1, C2, 14, 23. **Amenities:** Free Wi-Fi.

Residenza della Signoria ★★ Location and value take center-stage at this small inn on the fourth floor of an old palace. It's right on Florence's main drag, but thanks to modern soundproofing you'd never know. Rooms are spacious with antique-styled furnishings and ceilings, parquet flooring, luscious drapes, and king-size beds with firm mattresses. Only the junior suites have a proper panorama of Brunelleschi's cathedral dome, but for a smaller outlay, room 6 has a view from its bathroom window. Continental breakfast is served next door at one of our favorite cafe-bars, **Cantinetta dei Verrazzano** (p. 224).

Via dei Tavolini 8. www.residenzadellasignoria.com. ✆ **055/493-3301.** 7 units. 99€–299€ double. Breakfast 10€. Parking 35€–45€. Bus: C2. **Amenities:** Free Wi-Fi.

Soggiorno Battistero ★★ The Baptistery is almost close enough to touch when you take a room with a view at this super-central B&B—a modest investment you'll remember forever. Location and value are hard to beat: You lodge mere paces from the Duomo steps. Rooms are simple, gently modernized, and spacious (although some bathrooms are a squeeze), with traditional decor of terracotta tiling and antique armoires. The square below can be noisy at night, but soundproofing keeps the racket out. Note the early checkout time: 10:30am.

Piazza San Giovanni 1. www.fortehospitality.it. ✆ **349/552-5398.** 6 units. 101€–295€ double. Rates include breakfast. Bus: C2. **Amenities:** Free Wi-Fi.

Near San Lorenzo

EXPENSIVE

Palazzo Tolomei Residenza d'Epoca ★★★ In its heyday, this palace was close to the epicenter of Medici power. In 1505 it welcomed the painter Raphael as a guest (probably in two rooms at the front, now Barocco 1 and 2). Guest rooms are large, with Renaissance wooden ceilings, terracotta floors, and Nespresso machines. Modern fittings—leather sofas, soft mattresses, and florid crystal chandeliers—chime perfectly with a 17th-century baroque redecoration, complete with ceiling frescoes by Alessandro Gherardini. The lower floor has opulent public rooms, just like when it was the *piano nobile* of the family palazzo. These days you'll find a music room, art books, a welcoming host, and probably an open bottle of Tuscan red wine. Book direct for deals—perhaps free late checkout or a discounted rate.

Via de' Ginori 19. www.palazzotolomei.it. ✆ **055/292-887.** 8 units. 159€–339€ double. Rates include breakfast (in nearby cafe). Bus: C1. **Amenities:** Concierge; free Wi-Fi.

MODERATE/INEXPENSIVE

Alloro ★★ Officially a "bed-and-breakfast," this feels more like a small hotel, whose modern rooms inside a Renaissance palace overlook a silent inner courtyard—neat soundproofing against a noisy neighborhood. Rooms offer an excellent value for the price and location, with high ceilings, color-washed walls, and air-conditioning. Breakfast is a traditional spread of fresh fruit and pastries. A friendly ghost from the Renaissance era reputedly roams part of the palace; you're unlikely to get a discount if you spot him, but there's no harm in asking.

Via del Giglio 8. www.allorobb.it. ✆ **055/211-685.** 5 units. 100€–195€ double. Rates include breakfast. Bus: C1. **Amenities:** Free Wi-Fi.

Il Guelfo Bianco ★★ Decor in this former noble Florentine home retains an authentic palazzo feel, although there's full hotel service and a thorough renovation of guestrooms and common areas was completed in 2023. No two units are the same—stone walls this thick cannot be knocked through—and several have antiques integrated into their schemes. Grand rooms at the front have Renaissance coffered ceilings and extra space. Sleep at the back and you'll wake to an unusual sound in Florence: birdsong.

Via Cavour 29. ilguelfobianco.it. ✆ **055/288-330.** 40 units. 70€–310€ double. Rates include breakfast. Parking 31€–39€. Bus: C1, 14, 23. **Amenities:** Restaurant; bar; babysitting; room service; free Wi-Fi.

Near the Ponte Vecchio

EXPENSIVE

Continentale ★★★ Everything about the Continentale is cool, and the effect is achieved without even a hint of frostiness. Rooms are uncompromisingly modern, decorated in bright white and bathed in natural light. Deluxe units, which are built into a medieval riverside tower, have mighty walls and medieval-sized windows (that is, small). Standard rooms are large (for Florence) and there's a retro-1950s feel to the overall styling.

Guest room at the Continentale.

Communal areas are a major hit, too: A relaxation room has a glass wall facing the Ponte Vecchio.

Vicolo dell'Oro 6R. www.lungarnocollection.com. ✆ **055/27-262.** 43 units. 292€–750€ double. Parking 39€. Bus: C3 or C4. **Amenities:** Bar; concierge; spa; free Wi-Fi.

MODERATE

Alessandra ★★ This typical Florentine *pensione* transports you back to the age of the gentleman and lady traveler. Decor has grown organically since it opened as a hotel in 1950; Alessandra is a place for evolution, not revolution. A pleasing mix of styles is the result—some rooms with carved headboards, gilt frames, and gold damask; others with eclectic postwar furniture, like a midcentury period movie set. A couple have views of the Arno, while front-side rooms overlook Borgo SS. Apostoli, one of the center's most atmospheric streets. Five other rooms with contemporary decor—including, across the street, two mezzanine mini-apartments with kitchenettes—have a separate website, **www.residenzaalessandra.com**.

Borgo SS. Apostoli 17. www.hotelalessandra.com. ✆ **055/283-438.** 27 units. 75€–189€ double. Rates include breakfast. Parking 25€. Bus: C3, C4, 6, 11, 36, 37. Closed a few days around Christmas. **Amenities:** Free Wi-Fi.

Davanzati ★★ Although installed inside a historic building, the Davanzati never rests on its medieval laurels: There is an iPad in every room with cellular data for free guest use, plus movies to stream to your TV. Rooms are decorated in the Tuscan style, with color-washed walls, cool tiled floors, and half-canopies over the beds. Room 100 is probably the best family hotel room in Florence, full of nooks, crannies, and split-levels that give the adults and the kids private space. A free daily afternoon tea and *aperitivo* daily from 6:30pm are all part of the Davanzati's family welcome.

Via Porta Rossa 5 (on Piazza Davanzati). www.hoteldavanzati.it. ✆ **055/286-666.** 27 units. 75€–303€ double. Rates include breakfast. Parking 26€. Bus: C2. **Amenities:** Bar; babysitting; concierge; use of nearby gym; free Wi-Fi.

Near Santa Maria Novella

EXPENSIVE/MODERATE

Garibaldi Blu ★★ The hotels of Piazza Santa Maria Novella are frequented by fashion models, rock stars, and blue-chip business folk. You can get a taste of that, for a fraction of the price, at this boutique hotel with attitude. Each of the mostly midsized rooms has a "warm denim" palette, with retro 1970s furniture, parquet floors, and marble bathrooms. It's well worth paying 30€ extra for a deluxe room at the front: These have more space and a view over Florence's prettiest church facade, Santa Maria Novella. Dotted around the hotel, life-sized models of superheroes like Captain America add a fun surreal touch.

Piazza Santa Maria Novella 21. www.hotelgaribaldiblu.com. ✆ **055/277-3001.** 21 units. 110€–446€ double. Rates include breakfast. Parking 35€–48€. Bus: C2, 6, 11, 22. **Amenities:** Bar; babysitting (prebooking essential); concierge; free Wi-Fi.

Palazzo dal Borgo ★★ High ceilings and spacious rooms—especially second-floor Superior units—are typical of a Florentine noble palace, which Palazzo dal Borgo was: Built in the 1500s, it was converted into a hotel in the early 1900s, leaving many original ceiling frescoes and architectural features intact. For an extra-silent night, request a room overlooking its interior courtyard or Santa Maria Novella, which is out back. A breakfast buffet is served in a quaint bar or outside among the citrus trees. The hotel's location is super-convenient for the rail station and airport tram.

Via della Scala 6. www.hotelpalazzodalborgo.it. ✆ **055/216-237.** 34 units. 99€–299€ double. Rates include breakfast. Parking 30€–35€. Bus: 6 or 11. **Amenities:** Bar; concierge; free Wi-Fi.

Near San Marco & Santissima Annunziata

MODERATE

Antica Dimora Johlea ★★ There's a neighborhood feel to the streets around this *dimora* (traditional Florentine home) guesthouse, which means evenings are lively and Sundays are quiet (although it's only a 7-min. walk to San Lorenzo). Standard-size rooms are snug; upgrade to an Executive if you need space, but there is no difference in the standard of decor, a mix of Florentine and earthy boho. The roof terrace has knockout views over terracotta rooftops to the dome and hills beyond. It is pure magic at dusk, when a scent of lavender floats in on the breeze. Breakfast is served a la carte.

Via San Gallo 80. www.antichedimorefiorentine.it. ✆ **055/463-3292.** 6 units. 100€–250€ double. Rates include breakfast. Bus: C1, 1, 6, 11, 14, 17, 23. **Amenities:** Bar; free Wi-Fi.

Loggiato dei Serviti ★★★ This city icon reopened in 2023, restyled under the new ownership of Rome's Del Sole at Pantheon. As it always did, a stay here evokes Florence as experienced by the gentleman and lady travelers of the Grand Tour. For starters, the building is a genuine Renaissance landmark, built by Sangallo the Elder in the 1520s. There is a sense of grandeur and unconventional luxury throughout, in common areas and inside rooms with writing desks and bags of vintage ambience. No unit is small. However, go up a grade from standard to enjoy a room with a view, of either Brunelleschi's dome or the perfect piazza outside.

Piazza Santissima Annunziata 3. www.loggiatodeiservitihotel.it. ✆ **055/289-592.** 37 units. 180€–350€ double. Rates include breakfast. Bus: C1, 6, 14, 19, 23, 31, 32. **Amenities:** Concierge; free Wi-Fi.

Morandi alla Crocetta ★★ Like many hotels in Florence, Morandi alla Crocetta was built in the shell of a convent. It has retained the original layout, meaning some rooms are snug. But what you lose in size, you more than gain in character: Every single one oozes *tipico fiorentino*—even the "new" breakfast room feels like you're on the Grand Tour. Rooms have parquet floors, throw rugs, and antique furniture. Original 1744 Zocchi prints of Florence are scattered around. Superior rooms have more space and either a private courtyard terrace or, in one, original frescoes decorating an entrance to the former convent chapel (the chapel itself is sealed off). The hotel is on a quiet street.

Via Laura 50. www.hotelmorandi.it. ✆ **055/234-4747.** 12 units. 80€–220€ double. Parking 25€. Bus: 6, 19, 31, 32. **Amenities:** Bar; babysitting; concierge; free Wi-Fi.

Residence Hilda ★★ With no hint of the Renaissance, these spacious, luxe mini-apartments are all bright-white decor and designer furnishings, with natural wood flooring, hypoallergenic mattresses, Starck chairs, and modern gadgetry. Each is spacious, cool in summer, and soundproofed against Florence's perma-noise. Every unit has a mini-kitchen, equipped for preparing a simple meal, ideal if you have kids in tow. Unusual for apartments, all are bookable by the single night—some guests stay for a year.

Via dei Servi 40. www.residencehilda.com. ✆ **055/288-021.** 12 units. 121€–360€ for 2–4-person apartment. Parking 31€. Bus: C1. **Amenities:** Airport transfer; babysitting; concierge; room service; free Wi-Fi.

West of the Center

MODERATE

Riva Lofts ★★★ The traditional Florentine alarm call—a morning mix of traffic and tourism—is replaced by birdsong when you awake in one of these stylish rooms by the banks of the Arno. A former artisan workshop, Riva had a refit to earn its "loft" label: mellow color schemes, laminate flooring, floating staircases, marble bathrooms with rainfall showers, and clever integration of natural materials such as original wooden ceilings. The center is a 30-minute walk or hop on one of Riva's vintage-style bikes and cycle to the Uffizi along the river. Further standout features are a shaded garden—where you can often dine on summer evenings—and an outdoor plunge pool. Staff also organize Tuscan cookery classes with a pro chef.

Plunge pool at Riva Lofts.

Via Baccio Bandinelli 98. www.rivalofts.com. ✆ **055/713-0272.** 12 units. 120€–400€ double. Rates include breakfast. Parking 15€. Tram: T1. **Amenities:** Restaurant (Tues–Fri evenings); bar; babysitting (on request); bike rental (free); outdoor pool; free Wi-Fi.

WHERE TO EAT IN FLORENCE

Florence is well supplied with restaurants, although in the most touristy areas (around the Duomo, Piazza della Signoria, Piazza della Repubblica, and the Ponte Vecchio), you must choose carefully—many eateries are of below-average quality or charge high prices; sometimes both. The highest concentrations of excellent *ristoranti* and *trattorie* are northeast of **Santa Croce** and across the river in the **Oltrarno** and **San Frediano.** There's also much improved dining around **San Lorenzo,** including street food counters on the top floor of the **Mercato Centrale** (p. 216). Bear in mind that menus at restaurants can change weekly or even daily. The city has become much more **gluten-savvy.** If you have a food intolerance, just ask.

Reservations are strongly recommended if you have set your heart on anywhere specific, especially at dinner on weekends. ***Tip:*** You can book at many Florence restaurants, including several of our favorites below, using **The Fork** (www.thefork.it) or **Quandoo** (www.quandoo.it) restaurant reservation services.

Near the Duomo

MODERATE

Coquinarius ★★ MODERN TUSCAN There is a regular menu here of pasta, main courses such as stuffed rabbit with creamed carrot, and traditional desserts. But it's equally pleasurable tucking into a couple of sharing plates and quaffing from an excellent wine list. Go for a swordfish carpaccio and maybe pair a *selezione di salumi e formaggi* (mixed Tuscan salami and cheeses) with a full-bodied red wine, to cut through the strong flavors of the fatty, salty pork and Tuscan sheep's milk cheese, pecorino.
Via delle Oche 11R. www.coquinarius.it/firenze. ✆ **055/230-2153.** Entrees 16€–24€. Mon–Sat noon–3pm and 7pm–midnight. Bus: C1 or C2.

Fishing Lab Alle Murate ★★ SEAFOOD This contemporary-style temple to seafood serves fish any way you like (almost) at fair prices. The range is safe—shrimp, tuna, bream, bass, and salmon dominate—but the fish are carefully sourced and preparation is modern. The raw bar has a selection of tartare and carpaccio, both super-fresh and dressed delicately with citrus fruit. Hot main courses include grilled filets, fishy pastas, and the ubiquitous poke bowl. Both clientele and staff are young and lively, matching the decor of urban furniture amid frescoes. Service is brisk. Reservations recommended.
Via del Proconsolo 16R. www.fishinglab.it. ✆ **055/240-618.** Entrees 12€–16€. Wed–Mon noon–11pm. Bus: C1 or C2.

INEXPENSIVE

I Due Fratellini ★★ SANDWICHES This hole-in-the-wall has been serving food to go since 1875 (and fed Conan O'Brien on his 2018 Italian gastronomic tour). The drill is simple: Choose a filling, pick a drink, then eat your fast-filled roll on the move. There are around 30 combos to choose from, including the usual Tuscan meats and cheeses—porchetta, pecorino, prosciutto—and more flamboyant options such as fennel-spiked salami with creamed cheese or *bresaola* (air-dried beef) and arugula. A glass of wine to wash it down costs from 2€. Lunchtime lines can be long.
Via dei Cimatori 38R (at corner of Via Calzaiuoli). ✆ **055/239-6096.** Sandwiches 5€. Daily 10am–7pm. Bus: C2.

Near Santa Trinita

MODERATE

Osteria di Giovanni ★★★ MODERN TUSCAN If only every Tuscan restaurant in town was this good. Family-run Osteria di Giovanni is a standout in the category and always buzzing: You should reserve even in low season. Meat is a specialty, both traditional (the *bistecca alla fiorentina* is legendary) and modern interpretations like *faraona all'arancia* (guinea hen stewed with a slightly sweet orange). Only the very brave should attempt a *primo/secondo/dolce* route, since portions are large. A steep cover charge (4€) is actually a good deal, because it includes a couple of tasty snacks and all the mineral water you can drink.

Via del Moro 22. www.osteriadigiovanni.com. ✆ **055/284-897.** Entrees 24€–28€. Daily 7–10:30pm; Sat–Sun also 12:30–2:30pm. Bus: 6, 11.

Near San Lorenzo

Florence's best sandwich bar, **SandwiChic ★★★**, Via San Gallo 3R (✆ **055/281-157**), keeps things simple, with freshly baked bread and expertly sourced ingredients including Tuscan-cured meats, preserved vegetables, and savory condiments. Try the likes of *finocchiona* (salami spiked with fennel), pecorino cheese, and *crema di porri* (a creamy leek relish). Sandwiches cost around 5€. It's open 11:30am to 6pm, but closed Saturdays.

MODERATE

Il Nutino ★★ TUSCAN/GRILL This tiny, traditional joint has been in business since 1955. It's our go-to for *bistecca alla fiorentina,* in both classic and marbled styles. Whichever you choose, it spends a short time on the flame grill and is best served simply with roasted potatoes and *fagioli al fiasco* (beans stewed in olive oil). There's also a full Tuscan menu of fresh pasta, *crostini,* soups, and the like—but the grill is the standout. Service is attentive and knowledgeable, especially when it comes to wine (Chianti Rufina Nipozzano is our choice to wash down the red meat). The location is one of Florence's most heavily touristed areas, but with 7 decades behind them, they are doing things the right way.

Borgo San Lorenzo 39R. www.ristoranteilnutino.it. ✆ **349/453-6035.** Entrees 17€–26€. Daily 8am–11:30pm. Bus: C1.

La Gratella ★★ FLORENTINE/GRILL It doesn't look much—a workers' canteen on a nondescript side street—but looks don't matter much when you can source and cook meat like they do here. With the market in such close proximity, the unsurprising star of the show is the

Talking Tripe

New York has the hot dog. London has pie and mash. Florence has…cow's intestine in a sandwich. The city's traditional street food, *lampredotto* (the cow's fourth stomach) stewed with tomatoes, made a big comeback over the last decade, including on the menus of some fine-dining establishments. The best places to sample it affordably are the city's *trippai,* tripe vendors who sell from food trucks around the center. The most convenient vendors are in **Piazza de' Cimatori** and on **Via de' Macci** at Piazza Sant'Ambrogio. A hearty, nutritious lunch should come in around 5€. Most are open Monday through Saturday, but close in August, when Florentines flee their city.

fiorentina steak. This large T-bone-like cut is grilled on the bone and brought to the table over coals. It is sold by weight and made for sharing; expect to pay about 70€ for enough to feed two or three. Pair this or any meat on the menu with simple Tuscan sides like *fagioli all'uccelletto* (beans ste-wed with tomato). They are happy to cater to celiacs and have child dishes, too.

Via Guelfa 81R. www.lagratella.it. ✆ **055/211-292.** Entrees 12€–24€. Daily noon–3pm and 7–11pm. Bus: 1, 6, 11, 14, 17, 23.

INEXPENSIVE

Mario ★★ FLORENTINE There is no doubt this market workers' trattoria is firmly on the tourist trail. But Mario's is utterly Florentine. It clings to the ethos it adopted when the burners first fired up 70 years ago: They even changed their brand of pasta when it began sponsoring Fiorentina's soccer archrivals, Juventus. Food is simple, hearty, and traditionally served at communal tables. If you don't reserve, arrive early, "check in," and you will be offered seats together wherever they come free. A typical meal might be *passato di fagioli* (bean puree soup) followed by traditional Tuscan beef pot roast, *stracotto,* or *maialino al forno* (roast piglet).

Via Rosina 2R. www.trattoriamario.com. ✆ **055/218-550.** Entrees 7.50€–20€. Mon–Sat noon–3pm; Thurs–Fri also 7–10pm. Closed Aug. Bus: C1.

Mercato Centrale ★★ MODERN ITALIAN The upper floor of Florence's produce market is a bustling shrine to modern street food. Counters sell dishes from all over Italy: pasta, vegetarian and vegan fare, authentic Neapolitan pizza, meats and cheeses, fresh fish, Chianina burgers or mixed grill from the butchers' counter, Florentine boiled beef dripping in its own juices, and much more. It works perfectly for families who can't agree on a dinner choice. Or just stop by for a drink and soak up the buzz: There's a beer bar and a superb enoteca where you can sip by the glass or bottle.

Piazza Mercato Centrale. www.mercatocentrale.it/firenze. ✆ **055/239-9798.** Dishes 5€–20€. Daily 9am–11pm. Bus: C1.

The bustling food stalls upstairs at Mercato Centrale.

Near San Marco

San Marco is the place to head for *schiacciata,* olive-oil flatbread loaded with savory toppings. You will find some of the best at **Pugi ★**, Piazza San Marco 9B (www.fornopugi.it; ✆ **055/280-981**), open Monday to Saturday 7:45am to 7:10pm, but closed most of August.

MODERATE

Da Tito ★★★ TUSCAN Every night feels like party at one of central Florence's rare genuine neighborhood trattorias. (For that reason, it's usually packed. Book ahead.) The dishes are classic Florentine, with a few modern Italian curveballs: Start, perhaps, with a seasonal treat like raw artichokes with shaved Grana Padano cheese or, in summer, *risotto con piselli e guanciale* (rice with fresh peas and cured pork cheek) before going on to a traditional grill such as *lombatina di vitella* (veal chop steak). The neighborhood location, a 10-minute walk north of San Lorenzo, and a mixed clientele keep quality very consistent. We've visited many times and never been disappointed.

Via San Gallo 112R. trattoriadatito.business.site. ✆ **055/472-475.** Entrees 12€–18€. Daily 12:30–3pm and 7–11pm. Bus: C1, 1, 7, 20, 25.

Near Santa Croce

MODERATE

Brac ★★ VEGETARIAN/VEGAN An artsy cafe-bookshop for most of the day, this is also one of Florence's best spots for vegetarian and

Vegetarians flock to the cafe-bookshop Brac.

vegan food. A *piatto unico* works out best for hungry diners: one combo plate with three different dishes from the menu, perhaps avocado carpaccio; *agnolotti* (pasta parcels) with red onion, plum, and a pine nut cream; plus a *pane carasau* (Sardinian flatbread) with datterini tomatoes and egg. The courtyard atmosphere is intimate, yet singletons won't feel out of place eating at the counter out front. Booking at dinner is a must.

Via dei Vagellai 18R. www.libreriabrac.net. ✆ **055/094-4877.** Entrees 10€–18€. Daily noon–midnight. Bus: C1, C3, 23.

En ★★ JAPANESE Japanese food is having a "moment" in Florence, and this izakaya-styled, informal place is tiny: You must reserve ahead at dinner. The menu features a range of well-executed comfort food classics, like *okonomiyaki* (egg, cabbage, prawn), *tonkatsu* (breaded pork cutlet), and *kara age* (deep-fried chicken thighs). The list of sake, shochu, and whiskey is chosen with love and expertise. In keeping with Japanese tradition, the filling lunchtime set is a steal (15€) and includes miso soup and tea.

Piazza Ghiberti 26R. ✆ **392/363-8449.** Entrees 9€–12€; dinner *omakase* 23€. Daily noon–3pm and 7:15–11pm. Bus: C2, C3, 14.

INEXPENSIVE

Da Rocco ★★ FLORENTINE This tiny trattoria inside Sant'Ambrogio Market is our favorite place for a bargain lunch. Behind a takeout counter is an enclosed seating area with snug booths. Hearty dishes of lasagne, roast meats like *coniglio* (rabbit), and *peposo* (spicy Tuscan beef stew) are plenty filling, especially if you pair one with a side like roast peppers or lightly fried spinach. The house wine is farmhouse Chianti; a bottle is left on your table and you pay for whatever you drink. Get here by 1pm if you want a table. Service is friendly but brisk: Lingering is gently discouraged.

Mercato di Sant'Ambrogio. No phone. Entrees 8€. Mon–Sat 10am–2:45pm. Bus: C2, C3, or 14.

In the Oltrarno & San Frediano

EXPENSIVE

iO: Osteria Personale ★★★ CONTEMPORARY TUSCAN There's a "grown-up hipster" atmosphere here, with the whitewashed brick and young, attentive, enthusiastic staff. But a fine dining ethos is ingrained, too. Many ingredients are familiar to Tuscan cooking but combined in a fresh way with global flavors. The menu is short, so iO is a better choice for adventurous rather than fussy eaters. There are always seafood, meat, and vegetarian dishes—perhaps guinea hen ravioli with roasted pumpkin and laurel followed by pork belly and roasted red pepper with a light tamarind and garam masala sauce. Reservations are advised; this place's reputation has only grown in more than a decade since we first championed it.

Borgo San Frediano 167R. www.io-osteriapersonale.it. ✆ **055/933-1341.** Entrees 24€–28€; tasting menus 45€–63€. Mon–Sat 7:30–10pm. Closed 10 days in Jan and all Aug. Bus: C4 or 6.

MODERATE

Il Magazzino ★ FLORENTINE A traditional value *osteria* that specializes in the flavors of old Florence, especially offal. It looks the part, too, with a terracotta tiled floor and barrel vault, chunky wooden furniture, and hanging lamps. If you dare, this is a place to try tripe or *lampredotto* (intestines), the traditional food of working Florentines, prepared expertly in ravioli or meatballs, boiled, or *alla fiorentina* (stewed with tomatoes and garlic). The rest of the menu is carnivore-friendly too. Follow *pici al ragù bianco* (thick spaghetti with a "white" veal sauce made with a little milk instead of tomatoes) with *guancia di vitello in agrodolce* (veal cheek stewed with baby onions in a sticky-sweet sauce).

Piazza della Passera 3. ✆ **055/215-969.** Entrees 12€–20€. Daily noon–3pm and 7:30–11pm. Bus: C3 or C4.

Osteria dell'Enoteca ★★★ MODERN TUSCAN Run by experienced wine bar owners, this place majors in reasonably priced, elegant dining. Traditional flavors dominate, although combinations are often modern, in such dishes as poached egg yolk "affogato," floating in a pecorino cheese cream with wild mushrooms, or roast pigeon with Swiss chard. Portions are not large, so cut loose and order three courses. There is no wine list; an English-speaking waiter leads you to a chiller stocked with boutique labels—strong on Tuscan as well as Langhe/Piedmont reds. The dining room itself is refined, with slate floors, stripped brick, and soft jazz. This is the place for a romantic meal that won't bust your budget. Reservations recommended.

Via Romana 70R. www.osteriadellenoteca.com. ✆ **055/228-6018.** Entrees 14€–24€. Wed–Mon 7–10:30pm; Fri–Sun also noon–2:30pm. Closed Feb. Bus: 11, 36, 37.

Gelato

Florence has a fair claim to being the birthplace of gelato, and has some of the world's best *gelaterie*—but many poor imitations, too. Steer clear of spots around major attractions with air-fluffed mountains of ice cream and flavors so full of artificial colors they glow in the dark. If you can see the Ponte Vecchio or Piazza della Signoria from the front door of the gelateria, you may want to move on. Walk a block, or duck down a side street, to find a genuine gelato artisan. Trust us, you'll taste the difference. Opening hours tend to be discretionary: On warm evenings, many places open beyond 11pm.

Gelateria della Passera ★★ The milk-free water ices here are intensely flavored, with moderate sweetness that doesn't overpower the flavor. Try the likes of pink grapefruit or jasmine tea gelato. Via Toscanella 15R (at Piazza della Passera). www.gelateriadellapassera.it. ✆ **055/291-882.** Cone from 2€. Bus: C3 or C4.

Gelateria dei Neri ★ It offers a large range of fruit, white, and chocolate flavors, but nothing overly elaborate. If the seasonal ricotta and fig flavor is offered, you are in luck. There's also a restroom. Via dei Neri 9R. www.gelateriadeineri.it. ✆ **055/210-034.** Cone from 2€. Closed Mon. Bus: C1, C3, 23.

La Carraia ★★ It's packed with locals late into the evening on summer weekends—for good reason. The range is vast, the quality high. Piazza N. Sauro 25R. www.gelaterialacarraia.it. ✆ **055/280-695.** Cone from 2€. Bus: C3, C4, 6, 11, 36, 37. Closed Jan. Also at: Via dei Benci 24R.

FLORENCE SHOPPING

After Milan, Florence is **Italy's top shopping city**—beating even Rome. Here's what to buy: leather, designer fashion, shoes, marbleized paper and other stationery, hand-embroidered linens, Tuscan wines, handmade jewelry, *pietre dure* (known also as "Florentine mosaic," inlaid semiprecious stones), and antiques. ***Note:*** It is illegal to knowingly buy fake goods anywhere in the city (and yes, a "Louis Vuitton" bag at 10€ counts as *knowingly*). You may be served a hefty on-the-spot fine if caught.

Traditionally, Florentine **shopping hours** are Monday through Saturday from 9:30am to noon or 1pm and 3 or 3:30 to 7:30pm. Increasingly, larger shops and those in tourist areas stay open on Sunday and through the midafternoon *riposo,* or "nap." Some small or family-run places close Monday mornings instead of Sundays.

Florence is known for its beautiful hand-tooled leather goods.

Top Shopping Streets & Areas

AROUND SANTA TRÍNITA The cream of the crop lines both sides of elegant **Via de' Tornabuoni,** with an extension along **Via della Vigna**

Nuova and other surrounding streets. Here you'll find the big Florentine fashion names like **Gucci** ★ (at no. 73R; www.gucci.com; ✆ **055/264-011**), **Pucci** ★ (at no. 22R; www.emiliopucci.com; ✆ **055/265-8082**), and **Ferragamo** ★★ (at no. 5R; www.ferragamo.com; ✆ **055/292-123**), ensconced in old palaces or minimalist boutiques. Florence-headquartered leather specialist **Benheart** ★★ (Via della Vigna Nuova 97R; www.benheart.it; ✆ **055/239-9483;** also at Via dei Calzaiuoli 78R) sells up-to-the-minute clothing, footwear, and accessories. You can even create your own belt with a choice of leather and buckles. Benheart isn't cheap, but the quality is first-rate. In 2022, a Florence branch of quality thrift store **Humana Vintage** ★ (Via delle Belle Donne 4R; humanavintage.it) added another dimension to the neighborhood.

AROUND VIA ROMA & VIA DEI CALZAIUOLI These are some of Florence's busiest streets, packed with mostly mainstream storefronts. Here you'll find major department store **La Rinascente** ★, Piazza della Repubblica (www.rinascente.it; ✆ **055/219-113**), alongside quality clothing labels such as Geox, Patrizia Pepe, and Zara. **La Feltrinelli RED,** Piazza della Repubblica 26 (www.lafeltrinelli.it; ✆ **199/151-173**), is the center's best bookstore. Online couture sales sensation **Luisa Via Roma** ★ (www.luisaviaroma.com) has its flagship physical store here, at Via Roma 21R.

AROUND SANTA CROCE One-of-a-kind stores flourish in the eastern part of the center, with an emphasis on young, independent fashions. **Borgo degli Albizi** and its tributary streets are worth roaming—**Sabatini** ★ (at no. 75R; ✆ **055/234-0240**) is an established go-to for affordable casual footwear. Across the street, **Marzotto** ★ (at 86R; cartafiorentinafirenze.com; ✆ **055/234-0726**), is a fabulous old treasure cave of affordable Florentine stationery. It's been in business here since 1890.

Crafts & Artisans

Florence has a longstanding reputation for craftsmanship. Although display windows along touristed streets are stuffed with cheap, mass-produced imports, if you search around you will find handmade, top-quality items.

Il Torchio ★★ This small Oltrarno workshop sells hand-bound notebooks and marbleized paper. Bespoke designs available. Via de' Bardi 17. www.legatoriailtorchio.com. ✆ **055/234-2862.** Closed weekends. Bus: C3 or C4.

Madova ★★ For over a century, this has been the city's best retailer of handmade leather gloves, lined with silk, cashmere, or lambswool. You'll pay between 50€ and 80€ for a pair. Madova is the real deal, even so close to the Ponte Vecchio. Closed Sundays. Via Guicciardini 1R. www.madova.com. ✆ **055/239-6526.** Bus: C3 or C4.

Marioluca Giusti ★ The boutique of this renowned Florentine designer sells only his trademark synthetic acrylic crystal. The range includes colorful reinventions of cocktail and wine glasses, jugs, and tumblers—every piece lightweight, tough, and chic. Via della Spada 20R. www.mariolucagiusti.it. ✆ **055/214-583.** Bus: 6 or 11. Also at: Via della Vigna Nuova 88R.

Officina Profumo-Farmaceutica di Santa Maria Novella ★★★ A shrine to scents and skincare, this is Florence's historic herbal pharmacy, with roots in the 17th century, when it was founded by the Dominican monks of Santa Maria Novella. Nothing is cheap, but the perfumes, cosmetics, moisturizers, and other products are handmade from the finest natural ingredients and packaged exquisitely. Via della Scala 16. www.smnovella.com. ✆ **055/216-276.** Bus: C2.

Parione ★ This traditional Florentine stationer celebrated its 100th birthday in 2023. It stocks notebooks, marbleized paper, fine pens, and souvenirs like wooden music boxes and playing cards with 17th-century designs. Closed Sundays. Via dello Studio 11R. www.parione.it. ✆ **055/215-030.** Bus: C1 or C2.

Scuola del Cuoio ★ Florence's leading leather school is open house for visitors. You can watch trainee leatherworkers and gilders at work (Mon–Fri), then visit the small store to buy portable items like wallets, belts, and bags. Closed Sundays in low season. Via San Giuseppe 5R (behind Santa Croce). www.scuoladelcuoio.com. ✆ **055/244-534.** Bus: C3.

Florence's Best Markets

Mercato Centrale ★★★ The center's main market stocks the usual fresh produce, but you can also browse (and taste) cheese, salami and cured hams, Tuscan wines, takeout food, sweets, and much more. This is picnic-making heaven; they'll also vacuum-pack items for taking home. It runs Monday to Saturday until 2pm (until 5pm Sat for most of the year). Upstairs is street-food nirvana, all day, every day; see p. 216. Btw. Piazza del Mercato Centrale and Via dell'Ariento. No phone. Bus: C1.

Mercato di San Lorenzo ★ The city's tourist street market is a fun place to pick up T-shirts, marbleized paper, a leather-bound notebook, or some other city souvenir. Wallets, purses, bags, and jackets are popular with international visitors—be sure to assess the workmanship, which can be variable, and haggle shamelessly. This busy market runs daily; watch for pickpockets. Via dell'Ariento and Via Rosina. No phone. Bus: C1.

ENTERTAINMENT & NIGHTLIFE

Florence has several listings publications, including **Informacittà** (www.informacitta.net), which is strong on theater, concerts, and one-off markets. Younger and hipper **Zero** (www.zero.eu/firenze) is hot on the latest eating, drinking, lifestyle, and edgy nightlife. ***Firenze Spettacolo,*** a 2€ Italian-language monthly sold at newsstands, is the most comprehensive listing of nightlife, arts, and entertainment.

If you prefer to wander and see what grabs you, you will find tourist-oriented action in bars around the city's main squares, many with outside piazza seating. For something livelier—and with a more local focus—visit **Borgo San Frediano, Piazza Santo Spirito,** or the northern end of **Via de' Macci,** close to where it meets Via Pietrapiana. **Via de' Benci** is popular with an expat crowd. **Via de' Renai** and the bars of San Niccolò around the **Porta San Miniato** are often lively too, with a mixed clientele of tourists and locals hovering around outdoor tables.

Arts & Live Music

Florence does not have the musical cachet of Milan, Venice, Naples, or Rome, but there are two symphony orchestras and a fine music school in Fiesole, as well as a modern opera house (see below). The city's theaters are respectable, and most major touring companies makes stops in town. Get tickets to all cultural events online, or buy in person at **Box Office,** Via delle Vecchie Carceri 1 (www.boxofficetoscana.it).

Many classical chamber music performances are sponsored by the **Amici della Musica** (www.amicimusicafirenze.it; ✆ **055/607-440**), so check their website to see what's on while you are here. The venue is often the historic **Teatro della Pergola;** prices range from 15€ to 30€.

Restored and reopened in 2023, the Art Deco **Odeon Firenze** ★ (Piazza Strozzi; www.odeonfirenze.com; ✆ **055/214-068**) theater shows the latest movies in their original language (10€).

Libreria-Café La Cité ★★ A relaxed cafe-bookshop by day, after dark this place becomes a bar and small-scale live music venue. The lineup is eclectic, with often offbeat or world music. One night, it's forrò or swing, the next Italian folk or chanteuse. Borgo San Frediano 20R. ✆ **055/210-387.** Bus: C3, C4, 6, 11, 36, 37.

Opera di Firenze ★★ This vast concert hall and arts complex seats up to 1,800 in daring postmodernist surrounds. Its program incorporates opera, ballet, and orchestral music. Each May and June it hosts the **Maggio Musicale Fiorentino,** one of Italy's most prestigious music festivals. Piazzale Vittorio Gui. www.operadifirenze.it. ✆ **055/277-9309.** Tickets 15€–200€. Tram: T1.

Volume ★ After nightly *aperitivo* from 6:30pm—indoors and out on the piazza—Volume becomes a buzzing cocktail bar with live acoustic sets. Piazza Santo Spirito 5R. www.volumefirenze.com. ✆ **055/238-1460.** Bus: C3, 11, 36, 37.

Cafes

Florence no longer has a glitterati or intellectuals' cafe scene, and when it did—from the 19th-century Risorgimento era through 1950s *Dolce Vita*—it was basically copying Paris. Although they're often overpriced tourist spots today (especially around **Piazza della Repubblica**), Florence's few remaining high-toned piazza cafes are fine if you want to sit outdoors and people-watch.

Cantinetta dei Verrazzano ★★ One of the coziest little cafe-bars in the center is decked out with antique wooden wine cabinets, in genuine *enoteca* style. Wines come from the first-rate Verrazzano estate, in Chianti (see p. 246). Light breakfast and morning cappuccino are a delight. Closed evenings. Via dei Tavolini 18R. www.verrazzano.com. ✆ **055/268-590.** Bus: C2.

Cantinetta dei Verrazzano.

Procacci ★ The second you walk in the door, you're hit with the perfume of Procacci's specialty: *panini tartufati,* brioche rolls spread with truffle butter. Via Tornabuoni 64R. www.procacci1885.it. ✆ **055/211-656.** Bus: C3.

Rivoire ★ If you want to pick one overpriced sidewalk cafe in Florence, make it this one. Steep prices (6€ a cappuccino) pay the rent for one of the prettiest slices of real estate on the planet. Piazza della Signoria 5R. www.rivoire.it. ✆ **055/214-412.** Bus: C2.

Tosca & Nino ★ The prices, like the rooftop perch, are a little elevated (3€–5€ for a coffee). But you get to enjoy your drink or light lunch on a hidden terrace in the sky, with just medieval towers and Brunelleschi's dome for company. 4th floor, La Rinascente, Piazza della Repubblica. www.toscanino.com. ✆ **055/4933-468.** Bus: C2.

Wine Bars, Cocktails & Craft Beer

Fermento ★ Opposite the Medici Chapels, this tiny bar with outside tables serves Italian and Belgian craft beers in every style from IPA to stout, simple cocktails like a spritz or Americano (9€), and carb-rich food to soak it up. Via Canto dei Nelli 38R. fermentofirenze.com. ✆ **055/013-8064.** Bus: C1.

Love Craft ★★ The bar is the star at this snazzy little spot dedicated to everything whiskey (and whisky). Global blends and single malts, cocktails, and flights are all well-priced. Borgo San Frediano 24R. www.lovecraftfirenze.it. No phone. Bus: C3, C4, 6, 11, 36, 37.

Manifattura ★★★ Clientele skews young and casual at this creative cocktail bar in the old center. Drinks are mixed with Italian spirits only, so expect plenty of invention—like a Sazerac without rye or bourbon (!)—and multiple seasonal takes on Florence's icon, the Negroni. Piazza San Pancrazio 1R. www.manifatturafirenze.it. No phone. Bus: 14, 37, 6A, 6B.

Mayday ★★ A Florence original, this laidback bar offers signature cocktails commemorating famous Tuscans and events in 20th-century history. It's delightfully decked out like a mismatched junk store, with everything from old school desks to low-watt lamps hanging from the ceiling. Via Dante Alighieri 16R. www.maydayclub.it. ✆ **055/238-1290.** Bus: C2.

Mostodolce ★ Burgers, pizza, snacks, Wi-Fi, and sports on the screen—so far, so good. And Mostodolce also has its own artisan beers on tap, brewed just outside Florence at Prato (some are very strong). Via Nazionale 114R. www.mostodolce.it. ✆ **055/230-2928.** Bus: 1, 6, 11, 14, 17, 23.

Sant'Ambrogio ★ In a lively part of the center, northeast of Santa Croce, this wine and cocktail bar is popular with locals without being too achingly hip. In summer, everyone spills out onto the little piazza and church steps outside. Piazza Sant'Ambrogio 7R. www.caffesantambrogio.it. ✆ **055/257-7277.** Bus: C2 or C3.

Santino ★★ This snug wine bar stocks niche labels from across Italy and serves exquisite "Florentine tapas" to munch while you sip. Via Santo Spirito 60R. ✆ **055/230-2820.** Bus: C4, 11, 36, 37.

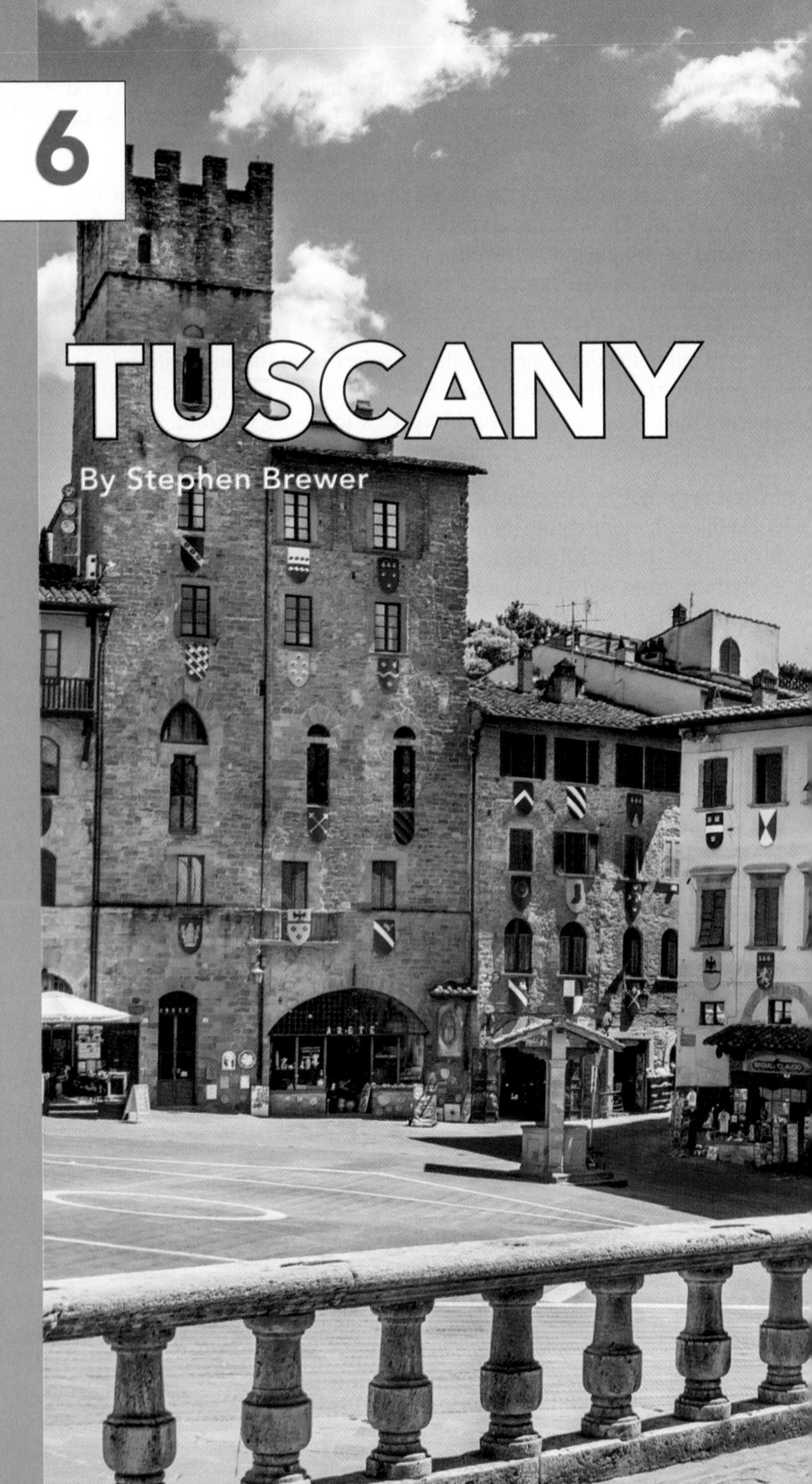

6

TUSCANY

By Stephen Brewer

Even for Italians from other parts of the peninsula, Tuscany is the epitome of everything that's good about their country: beguiling landscapes carpeted with cypresses and vineyards, delicious food and wine, evocative medieval churches and castles, and some of the greatest art and architecture of the Renaissance—the Leaning Tower of Pisa, Piero della Francesca's frescoes in Arezzo, Ambrogio Lorenzetti's "Allegories" in Siena's Palazzo Pubblico. Even a short visit inundates a traveler with an embarrassment of riches.

Soaking up culture is certainly part of the allure, and the pleasures of the palate are just as noted. Even a simple meal can seem like a work of art in places as bountiful as the Val di Chiana and Val d'Orcia. Somehow it only makes sense that full-bodied red wines should come from towns as appealing as Montepulciano and Montalcino, and character-filled whites from proud little San Gimignano. Then there's all that iconic scenery, in landscapes like the rolling fields and pointy cypresses of the Crete Sienese or the vineyards of Chianti. Art, scenery, food, wine—you may come to agree that all the good things in life come together in Tuscany.

DON'T LEAVE TUSCANY WITHOUT . . .

Getting into Hill Town Life. Panoramic views, cobblestone squares, friendly cafes: These are the charms of everyday life in a Tuscan hill town, ready to be savored in Cortona, Montepulciano, Volterra, San Gimignano, and Montalcino.

Fresco Gazing in Siena. Two masterpieces of medieval art bring the past to life in Siena: Ambrogio Lorenzetti's "Allegory of Good and Bad Government," in the Palazzo Pubblico, and depictions of the healing arts by Domenico di Bartolo and others in the former hospital Santa Maria della Scala. Linger over their storytelling scenes—the characters seem to reach across the centuries and speak to us.

Basking in Some of the World's Most Beautiful Landscapes. Open your senses to the beauties of the Tuscan countryside as you drive through the famous Chianti vineyards between Siena and Florence, or along the meandering roads of the Val d'Orcia between Pienza and Montalcino.

Enjoying Fine Wines. You've seen the vines; now sample the wines. Tuscany's bounty, of course, includes famous Chianti, Brunello di Montalcino, and Vino Nobile di Montepulciano, but don't stop there—almost every town has its own trademark vintages, from San Gimignano's Vernaccia to Cortona's Syrah.

FACING PAGE: **Piazza Grande in Arezzo.**

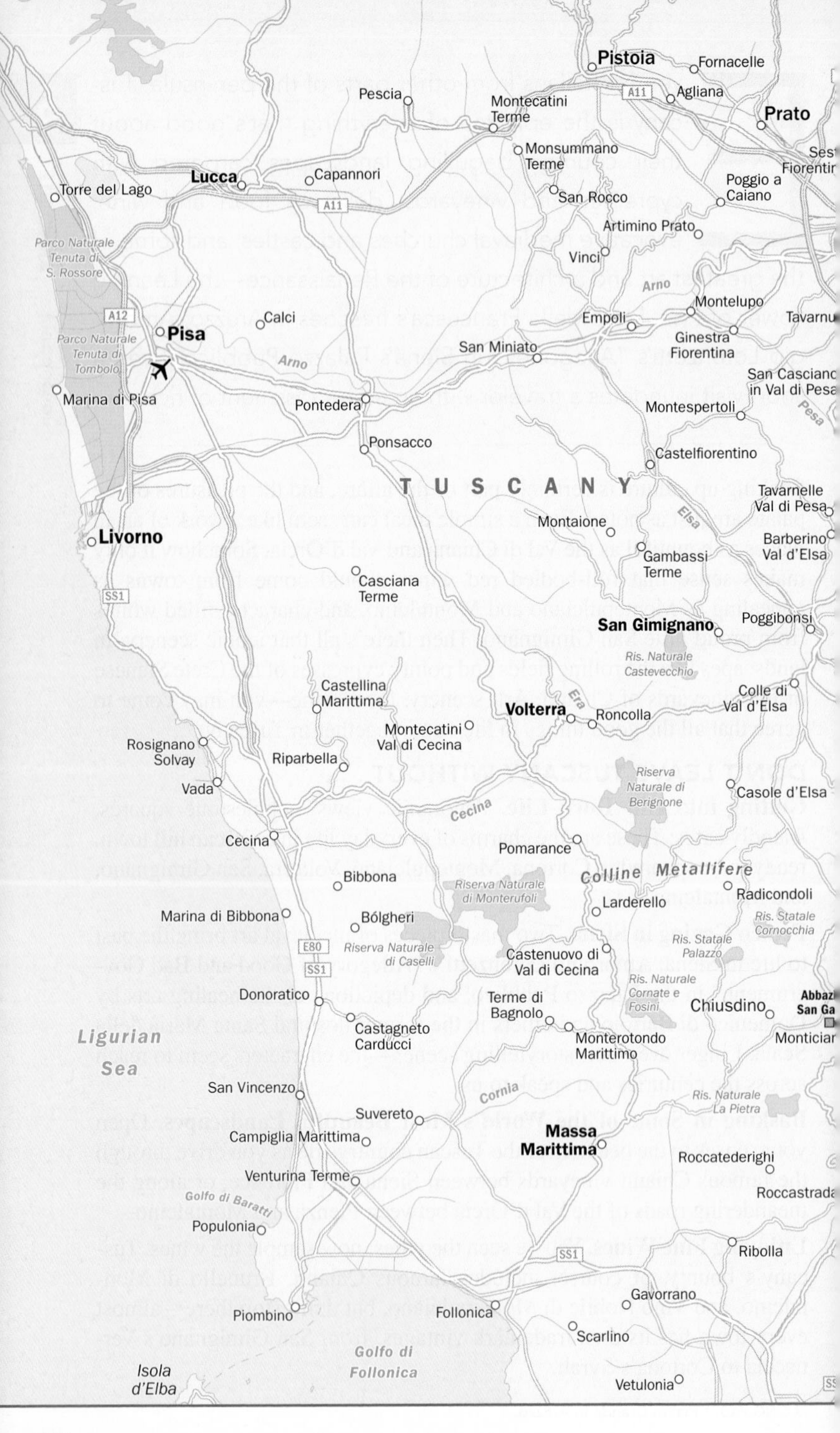

Pistoia
Fornacelle
Pescia
Montecatini Terme
A11
Agliana
Prato
Monsummano Terme
Sesto Fiorentino
Lucca
Capannori
Torre del Lago
A11
San Rocco
Poggio a Caiano
Artimino Prato
Parco Naturale Tenuta di S. Rossore
Vinci
Arno
A12
Calci
Empoli
Montelupo
Tavarnuzze
Pisa
Parco Naturale Tenuta di Tombolo
Arno
San Miniato
Ginestra Fiorentina
San Casciano in Val di Pesa
Marina di Pisa
Pontedera
Montespertoli
Pesa
Ponsacco
Castelfiorentino
TUSCANY
Tavarnelle Val di Pesa
Elsa
Livorno
Montaione
Barberino Val d'Elsa
Gambassi Terme
Casciana Terme
SS1
San Gimignano
Poggibonsi
Ris. Naturale Castevecchio
Castellina Marittima
Colle di Val d'Elsa
Era
Volterra
Roncolla
Montecatini Val di Cecina
Rosignano Solvay
Riparbella
Riserva Naturale di Berignone
Vada
Casole d'Elsa
Cecina
Cecina
Pomarance
Colline Metallifere
Bibbona
Riserva Naturale di Monterufoli
Radicondoli
Larderello
Marina di Bibbona
Bólgheri
Ris. Statale Cornocchia
E80
Riserva Naturale di Caselli
Ris. Statale Palazzo
Castenuovo di Val di Cecina
SS1
Ris. Naturale Cornate e Fosini
Donoratico
Terme di Bagnolo
Chiusdino
Abbazia San Ga
Ligurian Sea
Castagneto Carducci
Monterotondo Marittimo
Monticiano
San Vincenzo
Cornia
Ris. Naturale La Pietra
Suvereto
Campiglia Marittima
Massa Marittima
Roccatederighi
Venturina Terme
Roccastrada
Golfo di Baratti
Populonia
Ribolla
SS1
Gavorrano
Piombino
Follonica
Scarlino
Golfo di Follonica
Isola d'Elba
Vetulonia

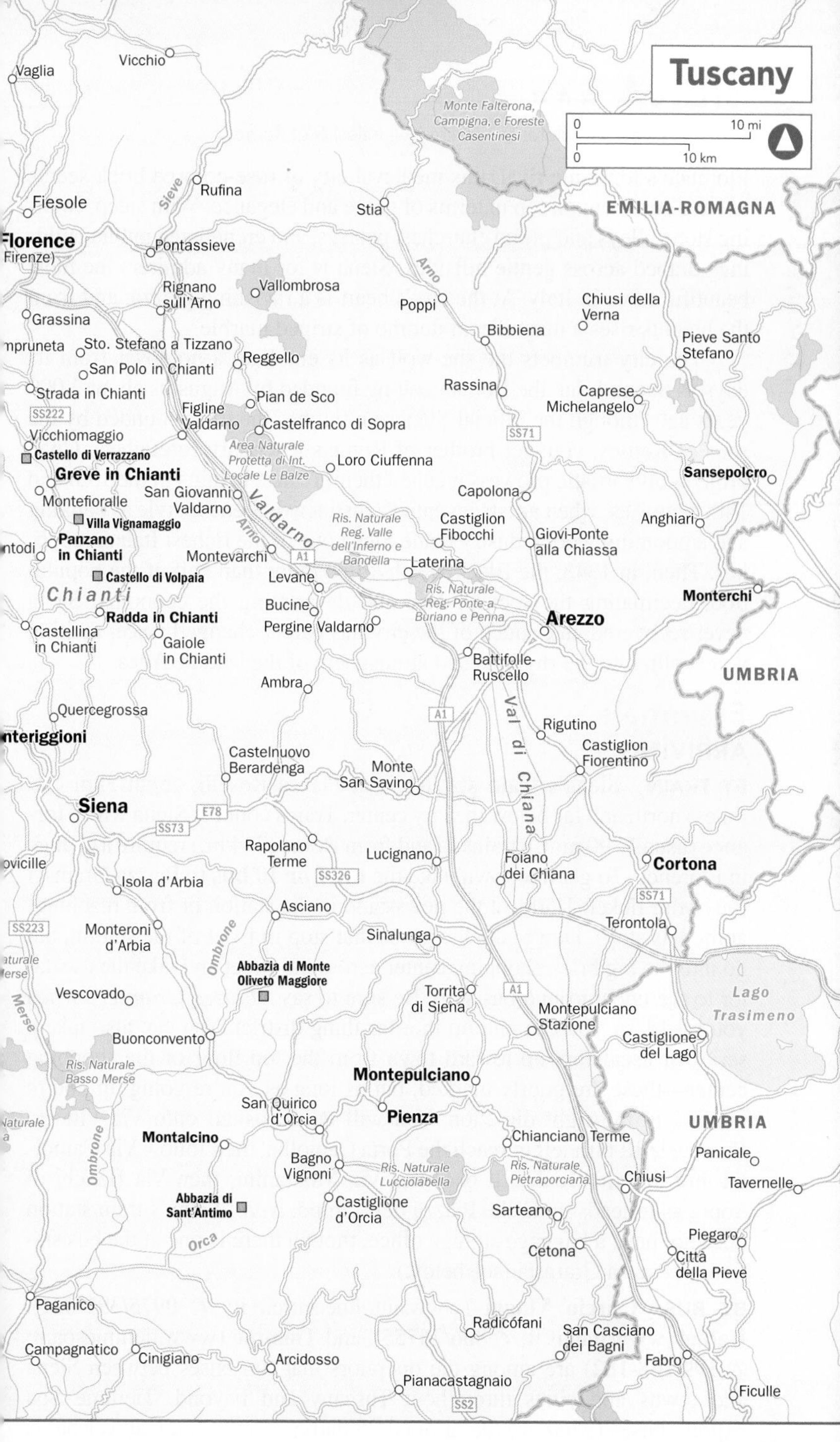
Tuscany
0
10 mi
0
10 km
EMILIA-ROMAGNA
UMBRIA
UMBRIA
Monte Falterona, Campigna, e Foreste Casentinesi
Vicchio
Vaglia
Rufina
Sieve
Fiesole
Stia
Florence
(Firenze)
Pontassieve
Arno
Rignano sull'Arno
Vallombrosa
Poppi
Chiusi della Verna
Grassina
Bibbiena
Sto. Stefano a Tizzano
Pieve Santo Stefano
San Polo in Chianti
Reggello
Strada in Chianti
Rassina
Caprese Michelangelo
Pian de Sco
SS222
Figline Valdarno
Castelfranco di Sopra
SS71
Vicchiomaggio
Area Naturale Protetta di Int. Locale Le Balze
Castello di Verrazzano
Loro Ciuffenna
Greve in Chianti
Sansepolcro
Montefioralle
San Giovanni Valdarno
Capolona
Valdarno
Villa Vignamaggio
Ris. Naturale Reg. Valle dell'Inferno e Bandella
Castiglion Fibocchi
Anghiari
Panzano in Chianti
Giovi-Ponte alla Chiassa
Montevarchi
A1
Laterina
Castello di Volpaia
Levane
Chianti
Ris. Naturale Reg. Ponte a Buriano e Penna
Monterchi
Bucine
Radda in Chianti
Arezzo
Castellina in Chianti
Pergine Valdarno
Gaiole in Chianti
Battifolle-Ruscello
Ambra
Val di Chiana
A1
Quercegrossa
Rigutino
Castiglion Fiorentino
Castelnuovo Berardenga
Monte San Savino
Siena
E78
SS73
Rapolano Terme
Lucignano
Foiano dei Chiana
Cortona
SS326
Isola d'Arbia
SS71
Asciano
Terontola
SS223
Monteroni d'Arbia
Sinalunga
Ombrone
Abbazia di Monte Oliveto Maggiore
Lago Trasimeno
Vescovado
Torrita di Siena
A1
Merse
Montepulciano Stazione
Buonconvento
Castiglione del Lago
Ris. Naturale Basso Merse
Montepulciano
San Quirico d'Orcia
Pienza
UMBRIA
Montalcino
Chianciano Terme
Ombrone
Bagno Vignoni
Ris. Naturale Lucciolabella
Ris. Naturale Pietraporciana
Panicale
Chiusi
Tavernelle
Abbazia di Sant'Antimo
Castiglione d'Orcia
Sarteano
Orca
Piegaro
Cetona
Città della Pieve
Paganico
Radicófani
San Casciano dei Bagni
Campagnatico
Cinigiano
Arcidosso
Fabro
Pianacastagnaio
Ficulle
SS2

SIENA ★★★

70km (43 miles) S of Florence, 232km (144 miles) N of Rome

Florence's longtime rival, this medieval city of rose-colored brick seems to have come out on top in terms of grace and elegance. With steep, twisting stone alleys and proud churches, palaces, and crenellated public buildings draped across gentle hillsides, Siena is for many admirers the most beautiful town in Italy. At the city's heart is a ravishing piazza, and from the heights rises a magnificent duomo of striped marble.

The city trumpets the she-wolf as its emblem, a holdover from its days as Saena Julia, the Roman colony founded by Augustus about 2,000 years ago (though the official Sienese myth has the town founded by the sons of Remus, younger brother of Rome's legendary forefather). Civic projects and artistic prowess reached their greatest heights in the 13th and 14th centuries, when artists invented a distinctive Sienese style as banking and a booming wool industry made Siena one of the richest Italian republics. Then, in 1348, the Black Death killed more than half of the population, decimating the social fabric and devastating the economy. Siena never recovered, and much of the city has barely changed since, inviting you to slip into the rhythms and atmosphere of the Middle Ages.

Essentials

ARRIVING

BY TRAIN Siena's **train station** is at Piazza Roselli, about 3km (1¾ miles) north and far below the city center. Trains connect Siena with **Florence** (usually 90 min.); trains to and from Rome (3–4 hr.) require a change in Florence. To get into town, take the **no. 7 or 10 bus** to Piazza Gramsci (buy your ticket, 1.50€, at the newsstand in the station or from machines at the bus stop). Don't take the buses that stop in front of the station, but go into the big brick shopping center across the street and take the escalator to the underground bus stop. Be sure to say *"Piazza Gramsci"* when you board, or you can end up in a far-flung district. You can also take a series of escalators up toward town from the top floor of the shopping center—these are poorly marked, but as long as you're going up you're moving in the right direction. You will be deposited onto Via Vittorio Emanuele II; turn left to reach the Porta Camollia, then follow Via Camollia into the city center. It becomes Via Montanini, then Via Banchi di Sopra as it heads up to the Piazza del Campo. ***Note:*** Siena's train station does not have a baggage storage office, though there is one at the bus station on Piazza Gramsci (see below).

BY BUS **Curcio Viaggi** (www.autolineecurcio.it; ✆ **0975/391-321**), **Itabus** (www.itabus.it; ✆ **866/76755**), and **Tiemme** (www.tiemmespa.it; ✆ **199/168-182**) are among the operators that run buses between Siena and towns and cities throughout Tuscany and beyond. Tiemme Spa express buses (*corse rapide;* around 25 daily; 75 min.) and slower buses

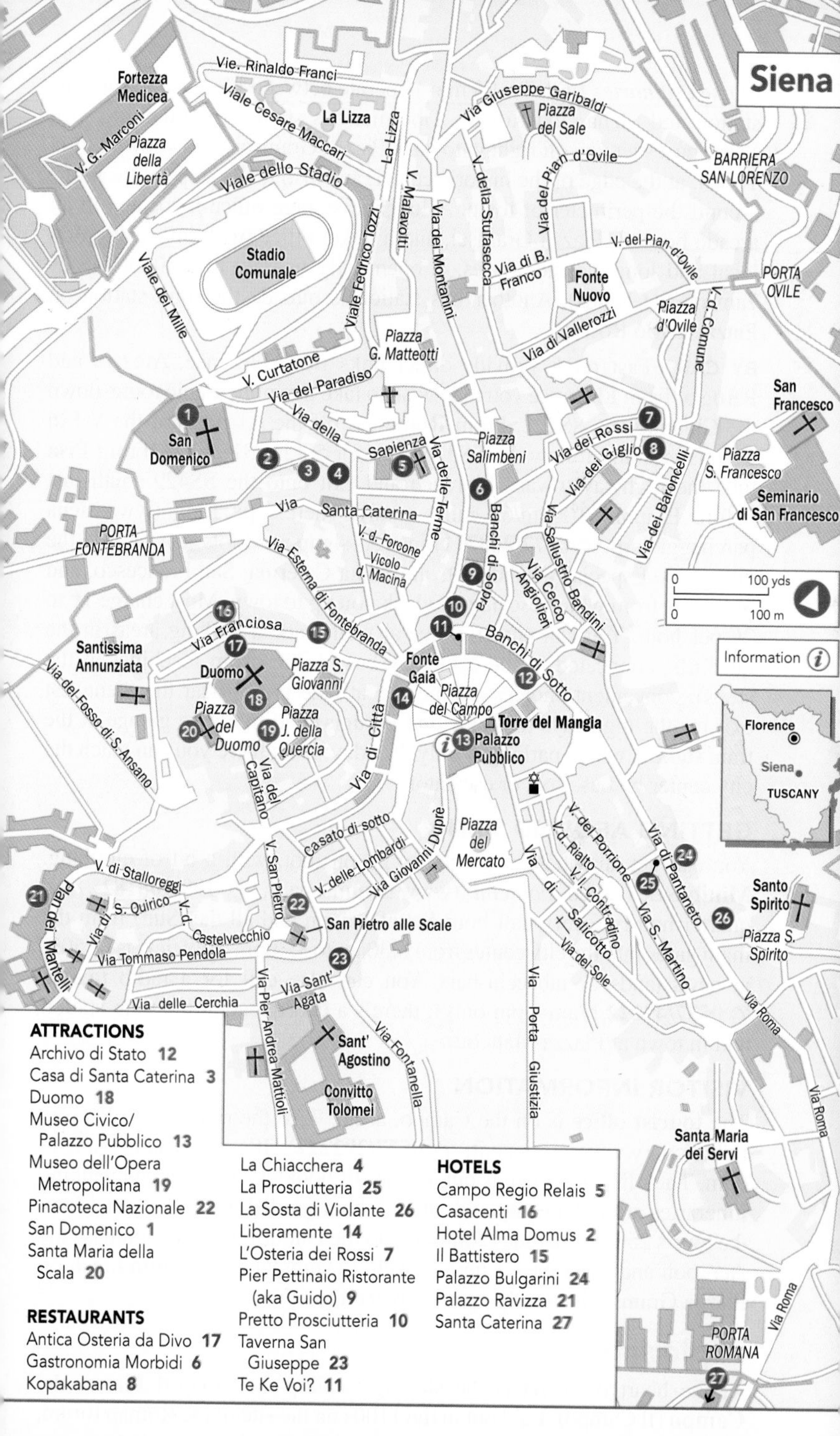
Siena
Fortezza Medicea
V. G. Marconi
Piazza della Libertà
Vie. Rinaldo Franci
Viale Cesare Maccari
La Lizza
Viale dello Stadio
Stadio Comunale
Viale dei Mille
Viale Fedrico Tozzi
La Lizza
V. Malavolti
Via dei Montanini
V. della Stufasecca
Via Giuseppe Garibaldi
Piazza del Sale
Via del Pian d'Ovile
BARRIERA SAN LORENZO
V. del Pian d'Ovile
Via di B. Franco
Fonte Nuovo
PORTA OVILE
Piazza d'Ovile
V. d. Comune
Via di Vallerozzi
Piazza G. Matteotti
V. Curtatone
Via del Paradiso
Via della Sapienza
San Domenico
San Francesco
Piazza Salimbeni
Via dei Rossi
Via dei Giglio
Piazza S. Francesco
Seminario di San Francesco
Via dei Baroncelli
Via delle Terme
Banchi di Sopra
Via Sallustrio Bandini
Via Santa Caterina
PORTA FONTEBRANDA
V. d. Forcone
Vicolo d. Macina
Via Esterna di Fontebranda
Via Cecco Angiolieri
0 100 yds
0 100 m
Information
Via Franciosa
Santissima Annunziata
Duomo
Piazza S. Giovanni
Fonte Gaia
Banchi di Sotto
Piazza del Campo
Torre del Mangia
Palazzo Pubblico
Via del Fosso di S. Ansano
Piazza del Duomo
Piazza J. della Quercia
Via del Capitano
Via di Città
Florence
Siena
TUSCANY
Casato di sotto
Piazza del Mercato
V. del Porrione
V. d. Rialto
V. I. Contradino
Via di Pantaneto
V. di Stalloreggi
V. San Pietro
V. delle Lombardi
Via Giovanni Duprè
Via di Salicotto
Via del Sole
Via S. Martino
Santo Spirito
Piazza S. Spirito
Pian dei Mantelli
Via di S. Quirico
V. d. Castelvecchio
San Pietro alle Scale
Via Tommaso Pendola
Via delle Cerchia
Via Sant' Agata
Via Pier Andrea Mattioli
Sant' Agostino
Convitto Tolomei
Via Fontanella
Via Porta Giustizia
Via Roma
Santa Maria dei Servi
PORTA ROMANA
ATTRACTIONS
Archivo di Stato 12
Casa di Santa Caterina 3
Duomo 18
Museo Civico/ Palazzo Pubblico 13
Museo dell'Opera Metropolitana 19
Pinacoteca Nazionale 22
San Domenico 1
Santa Maria della Scala 20
RESTAURANTS
Antica Osteria da Divo 17
Gastronomia Morbidi 6
Kopakabana 8
La Chiacchera 4
La Prosciutteria 25
La Sosta di Violante 26
Liberamente 14
L'Osteria dei Rossi 7
Pier Pettinaio Ristorante (aka Guido) 9
Pretto Prosciutteria 10
Taverna San Giuseppe 23
Te Ke Voi? 11
HOTELS
Campo Regio Relais 5
Casacenti 16
Hotel Alma Domus 2
Il Battistero 15
Palazzo Bulgarini 24
Palazzo Ravizza 21
Santa Caterina 27

(*corse ordinarie;* 14 daily; 95 min.) operate between Florence's main bus station and Siena, and Rome's Tiburtina bus station (5–9 daily; 3 hr.). Many buses let you off right in town at Piazza Gramsci (also known as Via Tozzi), at the edge of the historic center, and also make stops at locations around the perimeter of town. A luggage storage office is located in an arcade beneath Piazza Gramsci, and a ticket office, with information on local and long-distance buses, is open daily 6:30am to 7:30pm (opens 7am on weekends). Another bus station is outside the train station on Piazza Carlo Rossetti.

BY CAR Fast roads provide direct links from Florence, Arezzo, and Perugia; from **Florence** you may wish to take the more scenic route, down the Chiantigiana SS222. From **Rome** get off the A1 north at the Val di Chiana exit and follow the SS326 west for 50km (31 miles). From **Pisa** take the highway toward Florence and exit onto the SS429 south just before Empoli (100km/62 miles total). There's **parking** (www.siena parcheggi.com; ✆ **0577/228711**) in well-signposted lots just outside the city gates. Especially handy lots are Santa Caterina, San Francesco, and Stazione, from which escalators whisk you up to town. Most charge 1€ to 2€ per hour. You can park for free at well-marked parking areas in the outskirts, connected to the center by bus (1.20€, from machines at the stops); convenient choices are the one at Due Ponti (near the Siena Est exit for the highways to Rome and Perugia) and the large garage at the train station, where parking is only 2€ a day; from there you can reach the city center by bus, taxi, or escalator.

GETTING AROUND SIENA

You can get anywhere you want to go on foot, with a bit of climbing. **Minibuses,** called *pollicini* (www.tiemmespa.it; ✆ **199/168182**), run quarter-hourly (every half-hour Sat afternoon and all day Sun) from the main gates into the city center from 6:30am to 8:30pm. Buy tickets (1.50€) at newsstands or tabacchi-bars. You can also call for a radio **taxi** at ✆ **0577/49222** (7am–9pm only); there's a taxi queue at the train station and in town at Piazza Matteotti.

VISITOR INFORMATION

The **tourist office** is on the Campo, at no. 7, to the right of the Palazzo Pubblico (www.terresiena.it; ✆ **0577/292222**). It's open daily 9am to 6pm. The office staff hands out a series of booklets with themed walking itineraries around the city and offers 2-hour guided walks daily at 11am; the tour's 25€ fee includes admission to the Duomo. You can purchase the Acropoli and other passes here as well. In summer a small **info kiosk** on Piazza Gramsci is usually open daily 9am to 6pm.

Exploring Siena

At the heart of Siena is the sloping, scallop-shell-shaped **Piazza del Campo** (Il Campo). Laid out in the 1100s on the site of the Roman forum, the welcoming expanse is a testament to the city's civic achievements; it's anchored by a crenellated town hall, the **Palazzo Pubblico** (1297–1310), and the herringbone brick pavement is divided by white marble lines into nine sections representing the city's medieval ruling body, the Council of Nine. A 19th-century replica of Jacopo della Quercia's 14th-century fountain, the **Fonte Gaia,** is on one side of the square (some of the restored, but badly eroded, original panels are in Santa Maria della Scala; see p. 239). The dominant public monument is the slender 100m-tall (328-ft.) brick **Torre del Mangia** (1338–48), named for a slothful bell ringer nicknamed Mangiaguadagni, or "profit eater." (There's an armless statue of him in the courtyard of Palazzo Pubblico.) From the platform atop the tower's 503 steps, the undulating Tuscan hills seem to rise and fall to the ends of the earth (www.comune.siena.it; admission to tower 10€, family ticket 25€ for 2 adults & 2 children 11–18; Nov–Feb 10am–1pm and 1:45–4pm, Mar–Oct 10am–1pm and 1:45–7pm).

Siena's main streets run toward the Campo from seven gates in the old city walls. Enter through **Porta Camollia,** where the phrase cor magis tibi sena pandit ("Siena opens her heart to you") is carved over the arch. Medieval pilgrims stopped in Siena while walking the Via Francigena holy road between Canterbury and Rome; as you walk down narrow Via Camollia, note the simple-fronted church of **San Pietro alla Magione,** once a pilgrim's hospice. Farther down the street (now called Via Montanini) you'll

The Palio delle Contrade horse race in the Piazza del Campo in Siena.

pass the imposing Gothic **Palazzo Salimbeni,** the fortress-home of a wealthy banker-merchant clan and, since 1472, headquarters of the Monte die Paschi, one of the oldest banks in the world. On up the street (now called Banca di Sopra) is **Palazzo Tolomei,** home of the Salimbenis' bitterest banking rivals—the competition took a bloody turn when the Salimbenis stabbed 18 Tolomeis to death with roasting spits. Via di Citta flows to the right off Banca di Sopra and skirts the **Campo,** then rises toward the **Duomo,** passing the elegant arcaded **Palazzo Chigi Saracini** (Via di Citta 89). In September 1260, during the Battle of Montaperti—the bloodiest European skirmish of the Middle Ages—as the Sienese successfully fought Florentine forces on a ridge outside the city walls, a drummer in the palace tower tapped out ongoing reports to citizens inside the walls.

Archivio di Stato/Museo delle Biccherne ★ MUSEUM Tucked into the 1469 Florentine Renaissance-style Palazzo Piccolomini off the southeast corner of the Campo, this state archive displays such historic documents as Boccaccio's will and Jacopo della Quercia's contract for designing the Fonte Gaia fountain. The intriguing "Tavolette di Biccherna" is a remarkable set of wooden covers made in 1258 for the city's account books; they're painted with religious scenes, vignettes of daily working life, and important events in Siena's history. Note the Piccolomini family

A DAY AT THE races

On the evenings of July 2 and August 16, Siena's **Palio delle Contrade** transforms the Piazza del Campo into a racetrack, with spectators squeezing through the city's narrow alleyways to watch. This aggressive bareback horse race involves 10 of Siena's 17 *contrade* (districts), chosen by lot to participate, and is preceded by a showy flag-waving ceremony and parade. The race itself is over in just 2 minutes. Frenzied celebrations greet the winning rider, and the day is rounded off with communal feasts in each district.

To witness the event from the cordoned-off public view section in the middle of the Campo, you'll end up standing for hours in the sun—you'll need to arrive at least 5 hours before race time and, while vendors are on hand with refreshments, there are no toilet facilities. To view the Palio in relative comfort, reserve a spot in one of the temporary stands operated by the bars and shops in front of which they're erected. Getting a seat on one of these stands, for at least 200€, involves making arrangements with an establishment or a travel agent as long as a year in advance. Another option is to share a terrace or even a window with one of the aristocratic occupants of the apartments overlooking the campo—for one of these perches, expect to pay at least 400€ and as much as 700€ a person. Among the travel agents handling such arrangements is self-proclaimed Palio expert **Jacopo della Torre** (www.jacopodellatorre.com).

Otherwise, you may want to settle for the trial races, also held in the Campo (starting June 29 and Aug 13). Trial races aren't as fast and furious as the real thing, but they're just as photogenic and fun to watch. There are usually six in the mornings (9am) and evenings (7:45pm June, 7:15pm Aug).

coat of arms above the palace entrance; the papal tiara in the crest refers to the family's most illustrious member, Pope Pius II (served 1458–64). You'll see portraits of him in the Duomo's Libreria Piccolomini; he was also known for designing the town of Pienza (see p. 254), the first planned city in Europe.

Palazzo Piccolomini, Via Banchi di Sotto 52. www.archiviodistato.siena.it. ✆ **0577/247145.** Free. Fri–Sat 10am–1pm.

Duomo ★★★ CATHEDRAL Much of the artistic greatness of Siena comes together in this black-and-white-marble cathedral, a magnificent showcase of Italian Gothic architecture begun in the 12th century and completed in the 13th century. You're likely to come away with a great appreciation for the Pisanos, father and son. Nicola was the principal architect of the church, until he fell out of favor with the group overseeing construction; young Giovanni did much of the carving on the facade, where an army of prophets and apostles appears around three portals (most of the originals are now in the Museo dell'Opera Metropolitana; see p. 237). Both worked on the pulpit, with sumptuously sculpted scenes of the life of Christ and the prophets and evangelists.

Beneath the pulpit spreads a flooring mosaic of 59 etched and inlaid marble panels (1372–1547), a showpiece for 40 of Siena's medieval and Renaissance artistic luminaries. Most prolific among them was Domenico Beccafumi, born into a local peasant family and adopted by his lord, who saw the boy's talent for drawing. Beccafumi studied in Rome but returned to Siena and spent much of his career designing 35 scenes for the flooring (from 1517–47); his richly patterned images are a repository of Old Testament figures. Matteo di Giovanni, another Sienese, did a gruesome Slaughter of the Innocents—a favorite theme of the artist, whose fresco of the same scene is in Santa Maria della Scala (see p. 239). Many of the panels are protected by cardboard overlays and uncovered only from mid-August to early October in honor of the Palio.

Umbrian Renaissance master Bernardino di Betto (better known as Pinturicchio, or Little Painter, because of his stature) is the star in the **Libreria Piccolomini,** entered off the left aisle. Cardinal Francesco Piccolomini built the library in 1487 to house the illuminated manuscripts of his famous uncle, a popular Sienese bishop who later became Pope Pius II. (Cardinal Piccolomini himself later became Pope Pius III—for a mere 18 days, before dying in office.) Pinturicchio's frescoes depict 10 scenes from Pope Pius II's life, including an especially dramatic departure for the Council of Basel as a storm rages in the background.

In the **Baptistery** (not a separate building but beneath the choir), the great early Renaissance trio of Sienese and Florentine sculptors—Jacopo della Quercia, Lorenzo Ghiberti, and Donatello—crafted the gilded bronze panels of the baptismal font. Donatello wrought the dancing figure of Salome in the "Feast of Herod," and della Quercia did the statue of St. John that stands high above the marble basin. The subterranean **Cripta** displays fragments of colorful 13th-century frescoes discovered during excavation work beneath the Duomo in 1999.

Piazza del Duomo. www.operaduomo.siena.it. ✆ **0577/283048.** The **Opa Si pass** admits you to the Duomo, Libreria Piccolomini, Museo dell'Opera Metropolitana, Baptistery, Cripta, and the Gate of Heaven (cathedral rooftops). Mar–Oct 20€; Nov–Feb 18€. Apr–Oct Mon–Sat 10am–7pm, Sun 1:30–6pm; Nov–Mar Mon–Sat 10:30am–5:30pm, Sun 1:30–5:30pm.

Museo Civico/Palazzo Pubblico ★★★ MUSEUM Presiding over the Piazza del Campo, and topped by the soaring Torre del Mangia, this great Gothic-style townhall houses some of the city's finest artistic treasures. Siena's medieval governors, the Council of Nine, met in the **Sala della Pace,** and to help ensure they bore their duties responsibly, Ambrogio Lorenzetti frescoed the walls with what has become the most important piece of secular art to survive from medieval Europe. His 1338 "Allegory of Good and Bad Government and Their Effects on the Town and Countryside" provides not only a moral lesson but also a remarkable visual record of Siena and the nearby countryside as it appeared in the 14th century. Probably not by accident, the good-government frescoes are nicely illuminated by natural light, while scenes of bad government are cast in shadow (and have deteriorated over the years). In a panorama on the good side of the room, the towers, domes, and rooftops of Siena appear much as they do today, with horsemen, workers, and townsfolk going about their daily affairs; in the countryside, genteel lords on horseback overlook bountiful fields. On the bad-government side, streets are full of rubble, houses are collapsing, and soldiers pillage; beyond the walls, fields are barren and villages are ablaze. ***Note:*** Given recent closures for ongoing evaluation, check with the tourist office to make sure the Lorenzetti frescoes are on view when you plan to visit.

SIENA'S scholarly SAINT

Catherine di Benincasa (1347–1380), one of 25 children of a wealthy Sienese cloth dyer, had her first vision of Christ when she was 5 or 6 and vowed to devote her life to God. She took a nun's veil but not the vows when a teenager, was wed "mystically" to Christ when she was 21, and became known for helping the poor and infirm. She founded a woman's monastery outside Siena, and promoted "the total love for God" and a stronger church; she also acted as an envoy for the pope and wrote spiritual treatises. Frequent fasting eventually took such a toll on her health that she died at age 33. She was canonized as St. Catherine of Siena in 1461 by Pope Pius II—himself a native of the city.

The stark, cavernous church of **San Domenico** in Piazza San Domenico (free admission; 9am–6:30pm daily) houses Catherine's venerated head, preserved in a gold reliquary, and her thumb. Her family home, the **Casa di Santa Caterina,** Costa di Sant'Antonio (✆ **0577/44177;** free admission; daily 9am–6pm), has been preserved as a religious sanctuary; the former kitchen is now an oratory with a spectacular 16th-century majolica-tiled floor.

The Duomo of Siena.

Among other frescoes in these rooms is Sienese painter Simone Martini's greatest work, and his first, a "Maestà" (Majesty), finished in 1315 (he went over it again in 1321), in the **Sala del Mappamondo.** He shows the Virgin Mary as a medieval queen beneath a royal canopy, surrounded by a retinue of saints, apostles, and angels. The work not only introduces a secular element to a holy scene but also adds a sense of three-dimensional depth and perspective that came to the fore in Renaissance painting. Mary's presence here in the halls of civil power reinforces the idea of good government, with the Virgin presiding as a protector of the city. Just opposite is another great Martini work (though the attribution has been called into question), the "Equestrian Portrait of Guidoriccio da Fogliano," a depiction of a proud mercenary riding past a castle.

Palazzo Pubblico, Piazza del Campo. www.comune.siena.it. ✆ **0577/292226.** Museo Civico 6€ adult, 4.50€ students, free ages 11 and under; family ticket 22€ for 2 adults & 2 children 11–18. Cumulative ticket with Santa Maria della Scala 15€; with Torre del Mangia and Santa Maria della Scala 20€; with Torre del Mangia, Santa Maria della Scala, and Pinacoteca Nazionale 25€. Daily 10am–7pm (Nov–Feb closes 6pm). Bus: A (pink), B.

Museo dell'Opera Metropolitana ★★ MUSEUM Work on expanding the Duomo had just begun when the Black Death killed more than half the city's inhabitants in 1348. Work never resumed, partly because it was later discovered that the foundations could not support the massive structure. The aborted nave of the so-called "New Duomo" has now been repurposed to house many of the church's treasures. Here you can see the glorious-if-worse-for-wear statues by Giovanni Pisano that once adorned the facade, as well as a 30-sq.-m (323-sq.-ft.) stained-glass window made for the apse in the late 1280s, with nine colorful panels depicting the Virgin Mary, Siena's four patron saints, and the four Biblical Evangelists.

Upstairs is the "Maestà" by Duccio di Buoninsegna, an altarpiece that was declared a masterpiece when it was unveiled in 1311 and carried in a procession from the painter's workshop to the Duomo's altar. As a contemporary wrote, "all honorable citizens of Siena surrounded said panel with candles held in their hands, and women and children followed humbly behind." The front depicts the Madonna and Child surrounded by saints and angels, while the back once displayed 46 scenes from the lives of Mary and Christ. In 1711 the altarpiece was dismantled, and pieces are now in collections around the world. What remains here shows the genius of Duccio, who slowly broke away from a one-dimensional Byzantine style to imbue his characters with nuance, roundness, and emotion.

The **Facciatone,** a walkway atop the would-be facade of the "New Duomo," is the city's second-most popular viewpoint, with a stunning perspective of the cathedral across the piazza and sweeping views over the city's rooftops to Siena's favorite height, the Torre del Mangia towering over the Campo.

Piazza del Duomo 8. operaduomo.siena.it. ✆ **0577/283048.** The **Opa Si pass** admits you to the Duomo, Libreria Piccolomini, Museo dell'Opera Metropolitana, Baptistery, Cripta, and the Gate of Heaven (cathedral rooftops). Mar–Oct 20€; Nov–Feb 18€. Mar–Oct daily 10:30am–6pm; Nov–Feb daily 10:30am–5:30pm.

Pinacoteca Nazionale ★ ART MUSEUM While the greatest works of Sienese art have long since been dispersed to museums around the world, these adjoining palaces provide an overview of the city's major artists, especially those of the 12th through the 16th centuries. What you'll notice is that while the Renaissance was flourishing in Florence, Siena held to its old ways—these works are rich in Byzantine gold and Eastern styling. Duccio (of the famous "Maestà" in the Museo dell'Opera, p. 237) is represented by "Madonna and Child with Saints," in which a placid, otherworldly-looking Mary holds a very wise-looking infant Jesus. Simone Martini (painter of Siena's other great "Maestà," in the Museo Civico, p. 236) did the wonderful "Agostino Novello" altarpiece, depicting St. Augustine performing all sorts of heroic deeds, such as flying over boulders to save a monk trapped in a ravine. There are some charming landscapes by Ambrogio Lorenzetti (artist of the "Allegory of Good and Bad Government" in the Palazzo Pubblico, p. 236), including the almost surreal "Castle on the Lake," an architectural fantasy reminiscent of the 20th-century works of Giorgio di Chirico. His brother Pietro's "Madonna of the

Carmelites," an altarpiece created for the Carmelite church in Siena, shows the Virgin and Child in a distinctly medieval setting, in a Sienese landscape complete with horsemen and planted hillsides. Domenico Beccafumi's sketches for his Duomo floor panels are on the first floor.
Via San Pietro 29. pinacotecanazionale.siena.it. ✆ **0577/281-161.** 8€. Tues–Sat 9am–7pm; Sun–Mon 9am–1:30pm.

Santa Maria della Scala ★★★ MUSEUM One of Europe's first hospitals, probably founded around 1090, raised abandoned children, took care of the infirm, fed the poor, and lodged pilgrims who stopped in Siena on their way to and from Rome. These activities are recorded in scenes in the **Sala del Pellegrinaio** (Pilgrims' Hall), where colorful depictions of patients and healers from the Middle Ages looked down upon rows of hospital beds as recently as the 1990s. These are some of the finest secular works of the Middle Ages, color-rich 15th-century frescoes by Domenico di Bartolo and others, showing surgeons dressing a leg wound or holding a flask of urine to the light, or caregivers offering fresh clothing to an indigent young man. One of Bartolo's panels encapsulates an orphan's lifetime experience at the hospital, as he pictures infants being weaned, youngsters being taught by a stern-looking schoolmistress, and a young couple being wed (young women raised in the hospital were given dowries). As these activities transpire, a dog and cat scuffle, foundlings climb ladders toward the Virgin Mary, and wealthy benefactors stand on Oriental carpets.

You'll also see other frescoes and altarpieces commissioned by the hospital as it acquired considerable wealth over the centuries. One gallery houses some original panels from Jacopo della Quercia's 14th-century fountain in the Piazza del Campo, the Fonte Gaia. In the cellars is the dark and eerie **Oratorio di Santa Caterina della Notte,** where St. Catherine (see p. 236) allegedly passed her nights in prayer.
Piazza del Duomo 2. www.santamariadellascala.com. ✆ **0577/292-615.** 9€ adults; 8€ students; family ticket 20€ for 2 adults & 2 children 11–18. Cumulative ticket with Museo Civico 14€; with Torre del Mangia and Museo Civico 20€. Daily 10am–7pm.

Where to Stay in Siena

Many hotels have discount arrangements with garages outside the city center; 25€ per day is standard. If you plan on driving to a hotel to unload, check to make sure it is not in a restricted zone that is off-limits to nonresident drivers or for which you need written permission to enter.

EXPENSIVE

Campo Regio Relais ★★★ A "Room with a View" ambience pervades this stylish old house a 10-minute walk from the Campo. Two of the beautifully appointed rooms have spectacular views up a hillside crowned with the Duomo, one from its own sun-filled terrace, and all guests enjoy the same vista from an inviting sitting room/bar/breakfast room that also opens to a terrace. The old-fashioned *pensione* atmosphere is enhanced with modern updates that include lush fabrics and elegant furnishings. Amenities include an honesty bar, a library, attentive service, and excellent breakfast.

Via della Sapienza 25. www.camporegio.com. ✆ **0577/222073.** 6 units. 180€–220€ double. Rates include breakfast. Usually closed Jan to mid-Mar. **Amenities:** Library; free Wi-Fi.

MODERATE

Il Battistero ★★ Only a brief stroll from the Campo, this character-filled small palazzo, once home to a pope, adds quiet sophistication to Siena's medieval charm, blending old tilework and rough-hewn beams with contemporary furnishings and modern art. Individually designed rooms and suites—some with terraces—overlook the baptistery or across rooftops to San Domenico. As sophisticated as the surroundings are, the hospitality is warm, with a welcoming guest lounge/library, a wine shop at one end of the reception hall, and an atmospheric tasting cellar below.

Piazza San Giovanni 12. www.battisterosiena.com. ✆ **057/288921.** 7 units. 120€–160€ double. Rates include breakfast. **Amenities:** Free Wi-Fi.

Palazzo Ravizza ★★★ Generations of travelers have fallen under the spell of this 17th-century Renaissance *palazzo,* where high ceilings, oil paintings, highly polished antiques, and the gentle patina of age all suggest an era of grand travel. A large garden in the rear stretches towards green hills and can tempt anyone to give up sightseeing for a few hours and just relax; it's a popular cocktail spot for guests and Sienese alike. All the rooms are different, though most have wood beams and a surfeit of period detail, including some frescoes and coffered ceilings; furnishings throughout are comfortable and traditionally stylish. While this wonderful old place has the aura of a country hideaway, it's right in the city center, just a few streets below the Piazza del Campo—and it even has its own private parking lot, easily reached from Porta San Marco.

Pian dei Mantellini 34 (near Piazza San Marco). www.palazzoravizza.it. ✆ **0577/280462.** 35 units. 85€–150€ double. Rates include breakfast. Free parking. Closed early Jan–early Feb. Bus: A (green, yellow). **Amenities:** Bar; babysitting; concierge; room service; parking (free); free Wi-Fi.

Santa Caterina ★★ Just outside the Siena walls—literally so, as this is the first house after Porta Romana—this homey old inn feels as if it's in the countryside, yet it's only a 10-minute walk from Piazza del Campo. Have breakfast or a drink under the trees in good weather in the large, shady garden; inside, there's a snug little bar, a well-upholstered lounge, and a glass-enclosed breakfast room. Most of the cozy rooms, with wood-beamed ceilings, simple wood furnishings, and old prints on the walls, face the back, where wide-sweeping views of the green Val d'Orcia seem to go on forever. One choice room has a little balcony; a few others are bi-level, with bedrooms snuggled beneath the eaves. Ask for a rear-facing room or you'll miss that wonderful view.

Via Enea Silvio Piccolomini 7. www.hscsiena.it. ✆ **0577/221105.** 22 units. 70€–165€ double. Rates include breakfast. Bus: A (red) or 2. **Amenities:** Babysitting; bikes; concierge; free Wi-Fi.

INEXPENSIVE

Casacenti ★★★ Brothers Piero and Stefano have converted a family apartment into a welcoming bed-and-breakfast inn with the feel of a private home. Rooms are spacious, airy, and nicely furnished. All have hardwood floors, beamed ceilings, and beautifully done bathrooms, and several open to sweeping views across the rooftops to the rolling countryside beyond. The Duomo and other sights are just outside the door, as is the escalator to the Santa Caterina parking lot, making this an especially good choice if you're traveling by car.

Via di Vallepiatta 6, Siena. www.casacenti.it. ✆ **339/215-6827.** 4 units. 70€–90€ double. Rates include breakfast. Closed early Feb. **Amenities:** Free Wi-Fi.

Hotel Alma Domus ★★ This modern redo of the former drying rooms of a medieval wool works is run by the nuns of St. Catherine, who provide homey and spotless lodgings with a slightly contemporary flair. Set into the hillside below San Domenico church, near the Fontebranda (the oldest and most picturesque of the city's fountains), the place has the quiet air of a retreat, along with a great perk: city-view balconies in the more expensive rooms. Less expensive rooms do not come with views or air-conditioning. Breakfast is included, but it's a bit basic; you may prefer to walk up the hill and enjoy a cappuccino in the Campo.

Via Camporegio 37. www.hotelalmadomus.it. ✆ **0577/44177.** 28 units. 70€–95€ double. Rates include breakfast. Bus: A (red). **Amenities:** Free Wi-Fi.

Palazzo Bulgarini ★★ The converted *piano nobile* salons of an old palace aren't as opulent as they once were—furnishings are dated, and some better lighting would be welcome—but enough of the grandeur remains to elicit a gasp or two as you enter one of the six enormous guest rooms embellished with marble fireplaces and ceiling frescoes. Unchanged over the centuries are the stunning views from the rear rooms over the rolling hills beyond, a surprise given the city-center location. Prices are very reasonable, especially for accommodations so genuinely palatial.

Via Pantaneto. www.bbpalazzobulgarini.com. ✆ **0577/152-4466.** 6 units. 60€–90€ double. Rates include breakfast. Bus: A (pink). **Amenities:** Free Wi-Fi.

Where to Eat in Siena

While a drink or meal on the Campo can be an expensive and less-than-satisfying experience, a pleasant exception is friendly **Liberamente,** Piazza del Campo 7 (✆ **0577/274733**), where drinks are well-priced and usually come with generous nibbles. Siena's favorite fast-food stop, **Te Ke**

Voi? (tekevoi.com; ✆ **0577/40139**)—translation: Whaddaya Want?—is a pleasant, bustling room on Vicolo San Pietro, one of the narrow, sloping alleyways leading into the Campo; pasta, pizza, and burgers are dispensed from a self-service counter, along with wine and beer. For a quick meal, step into bright little **Pretto Prosciutteria** for sandwiches, delicious bruschetta, and generous platters of hams and cheeses, near the Campo at Via dei Termini 4 (www.prettoprosciutteria.it; ✆ **0577/289089**), or **La Prosciutteria,** on the corner of Via Magialotti and Via Pantaneto (www.laprosciutteria.com; ✆ **0577/42026**), where you can quite literally pig out on a platter of Tuscan hams or a *porchetta* sandwich, served on tables out front or in a series of small ornate rooms At **Gastronomia Morbidi,** Via Banca di Sopra 75, the city's busiest deli and gourmet shop, you can stock up on cheeses, hams, and pastries, enjoy a glass of wine or a cocktail, or partake of the buffet (www.morbidi.com; ✆ **0577/280268**).

Every Italian city has a favorite *gelateria,* and Siena's is **Kopakabana,** at Via de' Rossi 52–54 (www.gelateriakopakabana.it; ✆ **0577/284124;** mid-Feb to mid-Nov noon–8pm, later in warm weather), with flavors that include *panpepato,* based on the peppery Sienese cake.

Taste Siena (www.sienafoodtour.com) gives an excellent introduction to Sienese cuisine on walks with stops for breakfast, lunch, tastes of pianoforte, artisanal cheeses, wine, and other specialties, and a lot of lively insight into the history and cultural life of the city. Tours run daily, last 3 hours, and cost 85€, food and beverages included.

EXPENSIVE

Antica Osteria da Divo ★★ CONTEMPORARY SIENESE An almost-eerie assemblage of brick vaulting, exposed timbers, walls of bare rock, and even some Etruscan tombs is the setting for innovatively refined, uniquely Sienese dishes such as *pici alla lepre* (thick spaghetti in hare sauce), *sella di cinghiale* (saddle of wild boar braised in Chianti), or a breast of guinea fowl *(faraona)* roasted with balsamic vinegar. Service is outstanding, and the intimate spaces are beautifully candlelit at night.
Via Franciosa 25–29. www.osteriadadivo.com. ✆ **0577/284381.** Entrees 20€–30€. Wed–Mon noon–2:30pm and 7–10:30pm. Closed 2 weeks Jan–Feb. Bus: A (green, yellow).

MODERATE

La Sosta di Violante ★★★ SIENESE This warm, friendly, rose-hued room is only a 5-minute walk from Piazza del Campo but far enough off the beaten track to seem like a getaway (*sosta* means rest or break, as in "take a break"). The surroundings attract a mostly neighborhood crowd that has come to count on the kitchen for excellent preparations of *pappardelle, pici,* and other Tuscan pastas in rich sauces. Grilled Florentine steaks are another specialty, and so are many vegetarian choices, including delicious *frittelle di pecorino* (pecorino cheese fritters with pear sauce) and a cauliflower *(cavolfiore)* soufflé. The restaurant's name refers to Violante, the Bavarian-born 18th-century duchess who, after her Medici husband died from syphilis, became a beneficent governor of Siena; she divided the city into its famous present-day *contrade* (districts).

Via di Pantaneta 115. www.lasostadiviolante.it. ✆ **0577/43774.** Entrees 10€–17€. Mon–Sat 12:30–3pm and 7:15–10:30pm. Bus: A (pink).

Pier Pettinaio Ristorante (aka Guido) ★★ SIENESE Italian celebs whose photos hang among etchings and paintings are among generations of diners who have enjoyed this wonderfully old-world place, best known as Guido and radiating hospitality from every brick in the cavernous, vaulted dining room. Waiters in crisp jackets and ties make a special occasion of meals that might include one of the housemade pastas—*pici fatti al cacio e pepe* (with cheese and pepper) is a house classic—and one of several variations of grilled Tuscan beef.

Vicolo Beato Pier Pettinaio 7. www.ristorantepierpettinaio.com. ✆ **0577/280-042.** Entrees 9€–22€. Daily 12:30–2:30pm and 7:30–10:30pm.

Taverna San Giuseppe ★★★ TUSCAN/GRILL A long, brick vaulted room from the 12th century is the setting for meals many travelers long remember as among the best they've had in Italy. It's a testament to the warmth of the staff that, despite the popularity (reserve for dinner) and reputation among even discerning Sienese, they work so hard to make diners feel at home; they are justly proud of the Tuscan classics they bring out of the kitchen. *Pici,* the thick local pasta, with a ragu of *cinghiale* (wild boar), is surprisingly delicate, while ricotta-filled *gnudi* almost floats off the plate. Meals often begin with a complimentary glass of Prosecco and might end with a dessert on the house, bookends to an experience that in its entirety seems like a treat.

Via G. Dupré 132. www.tavernasangiuseppe.it. ✆ **0577/42286.** Entrees 15€–30€. Mon–Sat noon–2:30pm and 7–9:30pm. Bus: A (red).

INEXPENSIVE

La Chiacchera ★★ SIENESE This rustic room halfway along a steep alleyway is tiny but satisfies big appetites with large portions of *ribollita* (hearty bread and vegetable soup), *salsicce e fagioli* (sausage and white beans), or *tegamata di maiale* (a Sienese pork casserole). Good weather provides a unique dining experience on the street out front, where the legs of tables and chairs have been cut to accommodate the steep slope.

Costa di Sant'Antonio 4 (near San Domenico). www.osterialachiacchera.it. ✆ **0577/280-631.** Entrees 7€–14€. Daily noon–3:30pm and 7–11pm. Bus: A (red).

L'Osteria dei Rossi ★★ TUSCAN One of Siena's culinary treasures is this simple tile-floored, wood-beamed room where straightforward local cuisine is expertly prepared and served at extremely reasonable prices. Truffles occasionally appear in some special preparations, but for most of the year the short menu sticks to the classics—*pici al cinghiale* (pasta with wild boar sauce), tripe *(trippa)* stew, and thick steaks, accompanied by *fagioli bianchi* (white beans) and *patate fritte* (fried potatoes). Service can be brusque but efficient.

Via dei Rossi 79–81 (near San Francesco). ✆ **0577/287-592.** Entrees 8€–18€. Mon–Sat 12:30–3pm and 7–10:30pm and Sun 12:30–3pm. Bus: A (red).

Siena Shopping

Siena is famous for its *panforte,* a sweet, dense cake made from candied fruits, nuts, and honey that was created by city bakers in the Middle Ages and is still sold in shops all over town. Each shop has its own recipe, with the most popular varieties being sweet Panforte Margherita and bitter Panforte Nero. Try a slice at **Drogheria Manganelli,** Via di Città 71–73 (drogheriamanganelli.it; ✆ **0577/280002**), which has made its own *panforte* and soft *ricciarelli* almond cookies since the 19th century. Some Sienese would send you just as enthusiastically to the delectable and venerable **Pasticceria Nannini,** just off the Campo at Via Banchi di Sopra 24 (✆ **0577/236009**). The **Consorzio Agrario Siena,** Via Pianigiani 9 (www.capsi.it; ✆ **0577/2301**), showcases local wines, cheeses, pasta, even pastry, all from small Tuscan producers.

Authentic Sienese ceramics feature only three colors: black, white, and the reddish-brown "burnt sienna," or *terra di Siena.* **Ceramiche Artistiche Santa Caterina,** at Via di Città 74–76 (✆ **0577/283098**), sells high-quality pieces, courtesy of Maestro Marcello Neri, who trained at Siena's premier art and ceramics institutions, and his son, Fabio.

A Side Trip into the Chianti

For many visitors to Italy, heaven on earth is the 167 sq. km (64 sq. miles) of land between Florence and Siena, known as the Chianti. Traversing the gentle hillsides on the SR222, a twisting, picturesque route known as the Chiantigiana, is a classic drive, especially the stretch between Castellina in Chianti and Greve. Landscapes are smothered in vineyards and olive groves, punctuated by woodland and peppered with *case coloniche*—stone farmsteads with trademark square dovecotes protruding from the roofs. You'll need a car to get the most out of the route, but from Siena's train station you can get as far as Radda by four-times-a-day bus service, for a quick taste of the countryside; the trip takes an hour, and round-trip fare is about 10€; you'll find schedules at www.tiemmespa.it.

First stop for wine lovers is **Radda in Chianti,** 36km (22 miles) north of Siena; the turnoff is just north of Castellina. This important wine center retains its medieval street plan and a bit of its walls. The center of town is the 15th-century **Palazzo del Podestà,** studded with the mayoral coats of arms of past *podestà.* **Casa Porciatti** will give you a taste of traditional salami and cheeses at its *alimentari* on Piazza IV Novembre 1 at the gate into town (www.casaporciatti.it; ✆ **0577/738234**).

Seven kilometers (4⅓ miles) north of Radda on a secondary road is the **Castello di Volpaia ★★** (www.volpaia.com; ✆ **0577/738066**), a Florentine holding that was buffeted by Sienese attacks from the 10th to 16th

Main square in Radda in Chianti.

centuries. The still-impressive central keep is all that remains, but it's surrounded by a 13th-century *borgo* (village) containing the Renaissance La Commenda church. The central tower has an enoteca for tastings and sales, plus award-winning olive oils and farm-produced vinegars.

Back on the Chiantigiana (SR222), the next town is **Panzano in Chianti,** 12km (7 miles) north of Radda, known for its embroidery and a celebrity butcher, Dario Cecchini. At his shop **Antica Macelleria Cecchini,** Via XX Luglio 11 (www.dariocecchini.com; ✆ **055/852020**), the flamboyant Cecchini entertains visitors with classical music, product samples, sometimes even poetry recitations; in adjacent dining rooms he serves a five-course, beef-heavy tasting menu, 30€–50€ per person, including wine, at 1 and 8pm daily; reservations advised, vegetarian version available for noncarnivores.

Just north of Panzano, the SR222 takes you past the turnoff for Lamole. Along that road you'll find **Villa Vignamaggio ★★** (www.vignamaggio.com; ✆ **055/854661**), a russet-orange villa surrounded by elegant gardens where Lisa Gherardini, who grew up to pose for da Vinci's "Mona Lisa," spent time at what was then one of her family's farms. In 1404 the estate's wine was the first red wine to be referred to as "chianti." Book ahead at least a week to tour the cellar and gardens, sample the wines, or even stay overnight in atmosphere-laden rooms and farm cottages (from 220€ for a double; closed Nov–Mar).

Greve in Chianti, 8km (5 miles) north of Panzano on the SR222, is the center of the wine trade and the unofficial capital of Chianti. The central **Piazza Matteotti** is a rough triangle surrounded by a mismatched patchwork arcade—each merchant had to build the stretch in front of his own shop. Greve is the host of Chianti's annual September wine fair, and there are, naturally, dozens of wine shops in town. One of the best is the **Enoteca Bottega del Chianti Classico,** Piazzetta Santa Croce 8 (✆ **055/853297**). At **Antica Macelleria Falorni,** Piazza Matteotti 69–71 (www.falorni.it; ✆ **055/854363**), established in 1806, a cornucopia of *prosciutti* and dozens of other cured meats hang above display cases and tables where you can enjoy the products on tasting platters and in sandwiches and other light meals (shop and bistro open daily 9am–7:30pm).

The **Castello di Verrazzano** (www.verrazzano.com; ✆ **055/854243**), 6km (4 miles) northwest of Greve, is a significant stop for Americans: the ancestral home of the Verrazzano family, where Giovanni Verrazzano, who discovered New York, was born in 1485. The estate has been making wine since at least 1170; free tastings are offered daily at the roadside shop. Their "jewel" is a 100% Sangiovese called Sasello, while the Bottiglia Particolare (Particular [Special] Bottle) is a Super Tuscan wine, 70% Sangiovese and 30% cabernet. Tours of the gardens and cellars run Monday through Friday (prebooking essential); a rustic farmhouse inn, **Foresteria Casanova,** offers rooms from 100€.

From here it's 29km (17 miles) to Florence, or 50km (30 miles) back to Siena—allow a little over an hour without stops for the return trip.

WHERE TO STAY IN THE CHIANTI REGION

Castello Vicchiomaggio ★★ This 700-year-old storybook castle, complete with a crenellated tower, has hosted Renaissance nobles and such luminaries as Leonardo da Vinci and the poet-biologist Francesco Redi; modern-day visitors enjoy a stay on a working wine estate set amid world-acclaimed vineyards. Large, character-filled apartments in the castle are slipped into turrets and medieval salons along twisting staircases and corridors, each filled with old-fashioned furnishings that are more homey than grand. An adjacent priory has been converted into six comfortable suites that surround a communal lounge. All share a shady formal garden and a swimming pool that hangs over the vineyards.

Via Vicchiomaggio, Greve in Chianti. www.vicchiomaggio.it. ✆ **055/854079.** 12 units. 180€–230€ double. Rates include breakfast. Closed Nov to mid-Mar. **Amenities:** Restaurant; pool; free Wi-Fi.

Palazzo Leopoldo ★★ One of the grandest palaces in Radda in Chianti dates to the 15th century and was redone as a noble residence in the 18th century. Not much has changed since then. Guest rooms open off vaulted salons and have chunky beams, colorful frescoes, and comfy traditional furnishings to offer a satisfyingly historic, slightly regal ambience at very good value. Breakfast is served in the 18th-century kitchens, while

FEEL THE magic AROUND SIENA

If the Disney empire were to set up shop in Tuscany, it would have some ready-made stage sets near Siena. **Monteriggioni ★**, 14km (8½ miles) northwest of Siena along the SS2, is one of the most perfectly preserved fortified villages in all of Italy. The town was once a Sienese outpost, where soldiers were posted in towers to keep an eye out for Florentine troops—an image that Dante once likened to the circle of Titans guarding the lowest level of Hell. All 14 towers have survived, and you can climb up for a view (admission 4€; open Mar–Sept daily 9:30am–1:30pm and 2–7:30pm, Nov to early Jan Wed–Mon 10am–1:30pm and 2–4pm [until 4:30pm Sat], and late-Jan to Feb Sat–Sun 10am–1:30pm and 2–4:30pm). A walk from one end of Monteriggioni to the other takes about 5 minutes—as you pass, note the garden plots along the walls, which once kept townsfolk nourished in times of siege. The **tourist office** is at Piazza Roma 23, 53035 Monteriggioni (www.monteriggioniturismo.it; ✆ **0577/304810**). Siena city buses 130A and 130R run out to Monteriggioni every hour.

The enchanting **Abbey of San Galgano ★★**, in a grassy meadow on the banks of the River Merse, has a great "Sword in the Stone" back story. Galgano, born in Siena in 1148, was pursuing his career as a knight when he had a vision of the archangel Michael, who led him to a circular temple outside the village of Montesiepi, where he met the Twelve Apostles. Moved by the vision, Galgano went off to Montesiepi, drove his sword into a stone to renounce his knighthood, and built a round stone hermitage. After his death in 1182, his simple dwelling was expanded into a spectacular rotunda, which became the center of a community of Cistercian monks. Great church builders, they designed the cathedral in Siena as well as a Gothic abbey down the hill, now an evocative ruin—you can prowl around it, admiring its high arches, carved capitals, and stone settings for long-vanished stained-glass windows. The saint's tomb is up the hill in the hermitage; though his body long ago went missing, his sword remains in the stone, with only its handle protruding. The abbey and hermitage are outside the village of Chiusdino, about 40km (25 miles) southwest of Siena via S73 (www.comune.chiusdino.siena.it; ✆ **577/049305;** admission 5€; open daily 9am–6pm, until 8pm July–Aug and 7pm Sept and Oct).

a sunny terrace overlooks the nearby hills. A hedonistic **spa** is tucked beneath pleasant but slightly less atmospheric lodgings in an adjoining house.

Via Roma 33, Radda in Chianti. www.palazzoleopoldo.it. ✆ **0577/735605.** 22 units. 120€–140€ double. Most rates include breakfast. **Amenities:** Restaurant; bar; pool; spa; free Wi-Fi.

MONTEPULCIANO ★★

67km (41 miles) SE of Siena, 124km (77 miles) SE of Florence, 186km (116 miles) N of Rome

Sipping a delicious ruby wine in a friendly hill town is a good reason to trek across the beautiful Tuscan countryside. There are few better places to aim for than Montepulciano, with its medieval alleyways, Renaissance

Wine barrels in a Montepulciano cellar.

palaces, and famous violet-scented, orange-speckled Vino Nobile di Montepulciano. You'll earn your libation with some serious exercise, because Montepulciano's steep streets gives new meaning to the notion of a "hill town."

Montepulciano is also a good base for exploring other hill towns, especially nearby **Pienza** (see p. 254) and **Montalcino** (p. 257), and for excursions into the enchantingly beautiful **Val d'Orcia** region (p. 261).

Essentials

ARRIVING Driving is the best method: From Siena, the most scenic route is south through the Val d'Orcia on the SS2 to San Quirico d'Orcia, where you get the SS146 east through Pienza to Montepulciano. A dozen or so well-marked parking lots surround the town. Convenient lots are P8, at the top of the town next to the fortress, and P1, at the bottom of town just outside Porta al Prato. Rates are about 1.20€ an hour.

Tiemme **buses** (www.tiemmespa.it; ✆ **199/168182**) run from Siena 2 times a day (2½ hr.), with a change in Riomagno. Montepulciano is served by **train,** with frequent service from Siena and Florence, but the station is about 15km (9 miles) outside of town, with infrequent bus connections; a taxi into town will cost about 25€. Another option is to travel by train to Sinalunga, and to transfer there to one of the frequent buses operated by **Autolinee Toscane** (www.at-bus.it; ✆ **800/142242**), or to Chiusi with a transfer to a Tiemme bus.

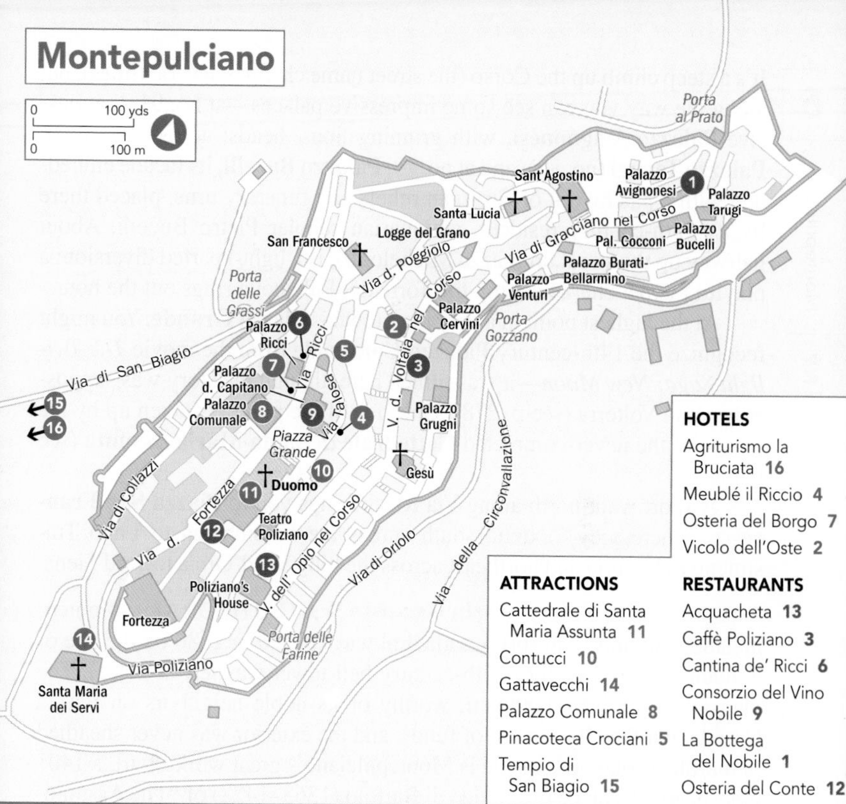

GETTING AROUND Montepulciano's Corso is very steep, but for those not up to the climb, little green electric *pollicini* buses connect the junction just below the Porta al Prato and Piazza Grande in about 8 minutes. Tickets cost 1.40€ each way (buy them on the bus or at tabacchi) and run every 20 minutes.

VISITOR INFORMATION Montepulciano's **tourist office** is in the P1 parking lot just below Porta al Prato at Piazza Don Mizzoni 1 (www.proloco montepulciano.it; ✆ **0578/757341**). It's open Monday through Saturday 10am to 1pm and 3pm to 6pm and Sundays 10am to 1pm. Another office, at Piazza Grande 7 (www.stradavinonobile.it; ✆ **0578/717484**) represents the Strada del Vino Nobile di Montepulciano e dei Sapori della Valdichiana Senese—that is, vineyards and other sights in the countryside around Montepulciano; it's a good place to learn about wine touring and smaller nearby towns. The office is open Monday to Friday 9:30am to 1:30pm and 2:30 to 6pm, Saturday 10am to 1pm and 2 to 5pm, and Sunday 10am to 1pm.

Exploring Montepulciano

It's all uphill from **Porta al Prato,** where the Medici crest (five balls) above the gate hint at Montepulciano's long association with Florence.

It's a steep climb up the Corso (the street name changes several times), but along the way you can see some impressive palaces—at no. 91, the massive **Palazzo Avignonesi,** with grinning lions' heads; across the street, **Palazzo Tarugi** (no. 82); and at no. 73, **Palazzo Bucelli,** its facade embedded with a patchwork of Etruscan reliefs and funerary urns, placed there by an 18th-century resident, antiquarian scholar Pietro Bucelli. About halfway up the street, in Piazza Michelozzo, is a light-hearted diversion: a playful puppet character atop the Torre del Pulcinella rings out the hour.

At the highest point in a very high town is **Piazza Grande.** You might recognize the 14th-century **Palazzo Comunale** from the movie *The Twilight Saga: New Moon*—it was filmed here, though the story was supposedly set in Volterra (see p. 278). One side of the piazza is taken up by the facade of the never-completed **Cattedrale di Santa Maria Assunta** (see below).

A short walk north along Via Ricci brings you to **Piazza San Francesco,** where views extend south across the Valdichiana to Lago Trasimeno in Umbria and northeast across the hilly Val d'Orcia toward Siena.

Cattedrale di Santa Maria Assunta ★★ CATHEDRAL Montepulciano's homely, bare-brick cathedral was erected in 1680 on the site of a much earlier church (a 15th-century bell tower was left in place). The plan was to build a landmark worthy of its noble neighbors on Piazza Grande, but the city ran out of funds, and the exterior was never sheathed in marble as planned. Inside is Montepulciano's great work of art, a 1401 gold-hued altarpiece by Taddeo di Bartolo (1363–1422) of "The Assumption of the Virgin with Saints." You can't get too close to the massive triptych soaring above the high altar, which is a shame, because the charm lies in the detail of its many various panels. The main sections show the death of the Virgin, with the apostles by her bedside; her ascension into Heaven, as the apostles survey her empty tomb; and the Virgin's coronation in heaven. The remnants of a marble sculptural group by Florentine architect and sculptor Michelozzo (1396–1472) were crafted for the tomb of papal secretary Bartolomeo Aragazzi. The tomb was disassembled in the 17th century (some pieces ended up in the Victoria and Albert Museum in London), but a few figures remain here—a reclining, hooded statue of Aragazzi himself, to the right of the central entrance door and, leaning against a nearby pillar, St. Bartholomew, Aragazzi's namesake.
Piazza Grande. No phone. Free. Daily 9am–12:30pm and 3:15–7pm.

Pinacoteca Crociani ★★ MUSEUM A few years ago this unassuming little collection found itself in possible possession of a blockbuster masterpiece when it was suggested that its painting "Portrait of a Gentleman" was done by Caravaggio, the wildly popular art star of the late 16th and early 17th centuries. Many art historians remain skeptical, though a nifty digital display next to the painting makes a compelling case for the provenance. Other showpieces are blue-and-white ceramic sculptures by Renaissance master Andrea della Robbia and a transcendently glowing

WINE TASTING IN montepulciano

The cellars of the **Gattavecchi** *cantine* (wineries), Via di Collazzi 74 (www.gattavecchi.it; ✆ **0578/757110**), have been in use since before 1200, originally by the friars of the adjacent church Santa Maria del Servi. Older still is the tiny room at the bottom, probably an Etruscan tomb. Gattavecchi's Vino Nobile is topnotch, as is the 100% Sangiovese Parceto. Tasting is free. Cavernous cellars at **Cantina de' Ricci,** Via di Collazzi 7 (www.cantinadericci.it; ✆ **0578/757166**), seem to spread beneath half of Montepulciano, with the main cellar, soaring 60 feet high, filled with centuries-old oak barrels. The cantina is open daily, with tastings (glasses from 2€) at the end of the tour. **Contucci** (www.contucci.it; ✆ **0578/757006**), in the 11th-century cellars of a historic palace in Piazza Grande, has a fine range of Vino Nobile wines; it's open for free tastings every day of the year. Opposite the cathedral, the **Palazzo del Capitano del Popolo** is another stop for wine buffs, with the **Consorzio del Vino Nobile di Montepulciano** (www.consorziovinonobile.it; ✆ **0578/757812;** Easter–Oct Mon–Fri 11:30am–1:30pm and 2–6pm, Sat 2–6pm) offering a rotating menu of tastings for a small fee. If you're heading into the country for some wine touring, staff here can provide maps. Across the corridor, the **Strada del Vino Nobile** office (www.stradavinonobile.it; ✆ **0578/717484**) will help you arrange a wine itinerary.

Tours of Tuscany (www.toursoftuscany.it; ✆ **3492/804365**) runs several enjoyable, informative daylong tours of the Tuscan wine regions, including one around Montalcino and Montepulciano, with tastings, lunch in a centuries-old wine cellar, a walk through Pienza, and other highlights; the price, 120€, includes pickup and drop-off in Siena or Florence or other points.

portrait of Montepulciano's patron saint, St. Agnes, by Domenico Beccafumi, who did much of the flooring in Siena's Duomo (see p. 235).

Via Ricci 10. www.museocivicomontepulciano.it. ✆ **0578/717300.** 6€. Apr Wed–Mon 10am–6pm; May–Oct Wed–Mon 10am–7pm; Nov–Mar Sat–Sun 10am–6pm.

Tempio di San Biagio ★ CHURCH This intriguing church just outside the town walls, completed in 1534, is the masterwork of Antonio da Sangallo the Elder. Best known for fortresses and other military defenses, here Sangallo broke out of the mold to create a beautiful travertine church on the plan of a Greek cross, with the four arms of equal length radiating from a central dome. Since the church is in the countryside with no other buildings nearby, it's easy to admire its classical unity. The interior is as refined as the exterior, but a bit dull on close inspection.

Via di San Biagio. No phone. Free. Apr–Sept daily 10:30am–1:30pm and 2–6:30pm; Oct and late Mar daily 10:30am–1:30pm and 2–6pm, Sun 11:30am–6pm; Nov to mid-Mar Sat–Sun 10:30am–1:30pm and 2–5pm (Dec 26–Jan 8 daily).

Where to Stay in Montepulciano

Agriturismo la Bruciata ★★★ A farmhouse poised on the edge of the Val d'Orcia just outside Montepulciano is an ideal base for a Tuscan getaway, a great spot for walking, touring wineries, or just lounging on the lawns next to the pools, soaking in the views and enjoying the hospitality of the Duchini family. Spacious, handsomely outfitted apartments have kitchens, terraces, and fireplaces for the chilly months, while fruits and vegetables from the family farm show up on the lavish breakfast buffet, at the welcome dinner (prepared weekly for guests and on request), and in the cooking classes that host Laura and her mother offer guests.

Via del Termine 9, Poggiano, 2km (1 mile) S of Montepulciano. www.agriturismolabruciata.it. ✆ **0578/757704.** 11 units. 650€–1,100€ a week, nightly rates on request. **Amenities:** Bar; dining room; kitchens; 2 pools; free Wi-Fi.

Meublé il Riccio ★★★ This atmospheric 800-year-old palazzo near Piazza Grande, passed down through the innkeeper's family, lays on the charm—in the arcaded, mosaic-tiled courtyard, the antiques-and-art-filled salon and breakfast room, the comfy lounge, and the rooftop terrace overlooking the landscapes of the Valdichiana far below. Some suites do justice to the surroundings with palatial expanses and terraces of their own, while other rooms are simpler and viewless but not without character. Carved wooden *ricci,* hedgehogs, which once emblazoned the 13th-century facade, make an appearance in all rooms. Ivana and Giorgio Caroti are on hand to dispense advice and make restaurant reservations, serving up delicious homemade pastries at breakfast and drinks throughout the day.

Via di Tolosa 21. www.ilriccio.net. ✆ **0578/757713.** 10 units. 110€–120€ double. Rates include breakfast. **Amenities:** Bar; free Wi-Fi.

Osteria del Borgo ★ Wood beams and exposed brickwork supply these bright, good-size rooms and apartments with rustic charm, while comfortably stylish furnishings and modern baths lend a bit of flair. The hilltop perch is just off Piazza Grande, so views from some rooms and the shared courtyard are expansive. A homey restaurant downstairs serves Tuscan specialties and spills out to a nice terrace in good weather.

Via Ricci. www.osteriadelborgo.it. ✆ **0578/716799.** 5 units. 120€–160€ double. Rates include breakfast and parking. **Amenities:** Restaurant; free Wi-Fi.

Vicolo dell'Oste ★★ Tuscan chic prevails in this house on a narrow lane off the Corso, just below Piazza Grande. Wood-beamed ceilings set off streamlined modern furnishings; some rooms have deluxe touches such as large Jacuzzis, and several include simple kitchens. While there are no communal spaces, breakfast is served in a nearby cafe, and innkeepers Giuseppe and Luisa seem always near at hand to take care of your needs.

Via delle Oste. www.vicolodelloste.it. ✆ **0578/758393.** 5 units. 95€–125€ double. Rates include breakfast. **Amenities:** Free Wi-Fi.

Where to Eat in Montepulciano

With a local wine that pairs especially well with hearty sauces and red meat, it's no accident that menus in Montepulciano rely heavily on game, beef from the Valdichiana, and thick pastas like hand-rolled *pici.* Aside from the town's many tasting rooms (see box p. 251), you can also drink wine and taste local salamis and cheeses in an atmospheric old cafe, the venerable, late-19th-century **Caffè Poliziano,** on the Corso (No. 27; www.caffepoliziano.it; ✆ **0578/758615**).

Acquacheta ★★★ SOUTHERN TUSCAN/GRILL If you're craving steak, head for this cellar eatery's rustic vaulted dining room, where meat is sold by weight and brought to your table for your approval by a cleaver-wielding chef before it goes onto the grill. A choice of pastas and sauces (mix and match as you please) are also available, as are hearty salads.
Via del Teatro 22. www.acquacheta.eu. ✆ **0578/717086.** Entrees 7€–40€ (steak by the weight). Wed–Mon 12:30–3pm and 7:30–10:30pm. Closed mid-Jan to mid-Mar.

La Bottega del Nobile ★★ TUSCAN It's a challenge to walk up the Corso without stopping at one of the many shops for a sip or two of wine. This appealing tasting room/restaurant satisfies that temptation and much more, serving food and drink throughout the day. The upper floor is part cafe and part wine shop, representing the region's best producers. In the snug, brick-walled cellars below, an affable young staff serves thick Tuscan steaks, pork roasts, and hearty sauces atop *pici,* and eagerly pairs just the right wine to complement each dish.
Corso 95. www.labottegadelnobile.it. ✆ **0578/757016.** Entrees 8€–16€. Thurs–Mon 12:30–2pm and 7:30–9:30pm.

Osteria del Conte ★★ SOUTHERN TUSCAN A trek to the top of town is rewarded with a delicious meal in this simple room off Piazza Grande, overseen by a mother-and-son team who are devoted to home cooking and warm hospitality. Put yourself in their hands with one of the set menus, which include several local specialties and wine, or choose from a nice a la carte selection—the *pici all'aglione* (handmade spaghetti with garlic sauce) is memorable, and lamb and steaks are grilled to order.
Via di San Donato 19. www.osteriadelconte.it. ✆ **0578/756062.** Entrees 10€–20€; set menus 28€ and 38€. Tues–Sun 12:30–2:30pm and 7:30–10pm.

Montepulciano Shopping

You may leave town with more than some wine in your shopping bags. The Mazzetti family has been crafting copper in Montepulciano since the

The Valdichiana: The Big Valley

Montepulciano, Cortona, and Arezzo nestle on the flanks of the Valdichiana (or Val di Chiana), a wide swath of farmland running north–south for some 100km (62 miles) through central Italy. Etruscans settled the valley 2,500 years ago, leaving behind remnants of their sophisticated civilization in Cortona, Chiusi, and other centers of their 12-city confederation. These days the valley supplies some of Italy's most prized beef, *bistecca alla fiorentina,* from Chianina cattle, along with stunning views from Cortona and other hill towns overlooking the green and golden landscape. You can shoot through the valley on the A1 *autostrada* or on fast trains between Rome and Florence, but for a nice close-up look, opt for the scenic 33km (20-mile) drive between Cortona and Montepulciano.

end of the 19th century, and Cesare and his craftspeople display their pots, pans, and other beautiful wares in the **Bottega del Rame** at Via dell'Opio nel Corso 64 (www.rameria.com; ✆ **0578/758753**); an adjacent museum shows off some of the family's prized pieces.

Side Trips from Montepulciano

Montepulciano, Montalcino, and Pienza are in the Crete Sienese, literally the "Sienese Clay Hills," a terrain of lone farmhouses and pointy cypress trees in a stark landscape of golden rolling hills, planted with wheat, fava beans, and sunflowers. You'll get a nice sense of the Crete Sienese on the drive between the three towns on SP 146. This is another face of Tuscany, quite different from the vineyard-clad hills of Chianti country, and at times the countryside seems forsaken.

PIENZA ★★

14km (9 miles) W of Montepulciano, 55km (34 miles) SE of Siena

A 20-minute drive west of Montepulciano on the SS146, this lovely hill town perches above the Val d'Orcia, with glorious landscapes of vineyards and wheat fields rising and falling in every direction. Narrow side streets are lined with shops selling the town's famous *pecorino* (sheep's milk cheese) and honey, but Pienza has a unique noble heritage, dating to the mid–15th century, when it was rebuilt by humanist Pope Pius II and

A tranquil courtyard in Pienza, designed to be the ideal Renaissance city.

architect Bernardo Rossellino to be the ideal Renaissance town. Piazzas and palaces, spaces and perspectives, were designed to reflect Renaissance ideals of rationality and humanism, and to instill the populace with notions of peace and harmony. Rossellino's budget was 10,000 florins and he spent 50,000, but Pius was so pleased with the transformation of his birthplace, he scrapped the town's name (Corsignano) and renamed it after himself. Pius died soon thereafter, and most of his plans for palaces, churches, piazzas, and well-ordered streets were never realized.

Park in one of the well-marked paid lots outside the town walls (1.25€ first hour, 1€ each following hour) and follow the main street, **Corso Rossellino,** through the center of the little town to the splendid **Piazza Pio II.** This focal point of Pius's town-planning dream is a Renaissance stage set of architectural perfection, flanked by the two main buildings of Pius's ambitious dream: The **Duomo** and the pope's residence, **Palazzo Piccolomini.** If you follow the little lane to the left of the square you'll come to a walkway with extensive views over the surrounding landscape. Pienza's **tourist office** is on Piazza Dante Alighieri (www.ufficioturisticodipienza.it; ✆ **0578/748359;** Mon, Tues, and Thurs 10am–1pm and Fri–Sun 10am–1pm and 3–6:30pm).

Duomo ★ CATHEDRAL This light-drenched *domus vitrea* (literally "house of glass") fulfilled Pius's notion that the church should symbolize enlightenment. The exterior represents Renaissance ideals of unity with a facade of three blind arches, atop which the pope immodestly placed his coat of arms. The interior was in part inspired by his travels in Germany, where he admired hall churches, lit by tall windows. For all of its perfection, the structure showed a serious flaw almost as soon as it was completed—the hillside on which it is built is unstable, and the foundations are slowly shifting (as you walk toward the rear, you'll notice the floor slightly slopes).
Piazza Pio II. ✆ **0578/749059.** Free. Daily 7am–1pm and 2:30–7pm.

Palazzo Piccolomini ★★ HISTORIC SITE Pope Pius had to have a residence worthy of his lofty status, of course, and his dining room, bedroom, library, and other chambers are appropriately regal. The stuffy rooms remained home to the pope's descendants until 1968. Linger in the palazzo's hanging garden and on the triple-decked loggia to take in the views south over the Val d'Orcia. With a setting like this, it's easy to see why Pius II—born Silvio Piccolomini into an impoverished branch of a noble Sienese family—wanted to return to this humble town of his birth after an event-filled life as a humanist scholar, itinerant diplomat, and pope from 1458 to 1464.
Piazza Pio II. www.palazzopiccolominipienza.it. ✆ **0578/74392.** 7€ adults; free children under 5. Wed–Mon 10am–4:30pm.

Where to Stay & Eat in Pienza

Fonte Berusi ★★★ Rural Tuscany doesn't get much more welcoming than it does at this enchanting olive estate just outside Pienza, where old farm buildings have been redone as eight large one- and two-room apartments. Color-rich, character-filled living and sleeping spaces open to vine-draped terraces and sunny patios; the Il Cortile apartment has a wood-burning stove, a nice amenity for an autumn or early-spring stay. Guests share the extensive grounds and a pool, along with a book-lined living room filled with artworks by Eduardo and his son Andrea, who, along with daughter-in-law Manuela, are the attentive resident proprietors.

Podere Fonte Bertusi. www.fontebertusi.it. ✆ **0578/748-077.** 8 units. 170€–290€ double. Rates include breakfast. Closed Jan to mid-Mar. **Amenities:** Pool; free Wi-Fi.

La Bandita Townhouse ★★ Pope Pius introduced Renaissance fashion to little Pienza, and this stylish guesthouse does the same with 21st-century style. Huge, loftlike guest quarters seem better suited to New York or Berlin (the elevator is the only one for miles around), but they certainly prove that contemporary chic can be comfortable. Amid design-magazine staples like steel frame beds, distressed leather armchairs, and slinky divans, you can enjoy such luxuries as slipping effortlessly from a supremely comfortable mattress into a deep tub perched right alongside. Timeless pleasures include honey-colored stone walls and garden views over the surrounding countryside. The dining room, decked out with retrofitted furnishings from a 1950s-era Florence school, sticks to straightforward takes on local cuisine, with innovations that include hamburgers made from the best Valdichiana beef.

Corso il Rossellino. www.la-bandita.com. ✆ **0578/749-005.** 12 units. 295€–350€ double. Rates include breakfast. **Amenities:** Restaurant; bar; free Wi-Fi.

La Casa di Adelina ★★★ Monticchiello, a walled village 10km (6 miles) east of Pienza, is an enchanting warren of piazzas and stone towers, and adding to the charm are these four rooms and an apartment in a grand old house on the central square. All are full of antiques, family heirlooms, and tasteful vintage-modern and contemporary pieces. Guests share a large beamed lounge where a fire burns in the stove on chilly evenings and a breakfast with homemade pastries is served by affable host Francesco. With a couple of shops and places to eat, the village is a good base for exploring the Val d'Orcia.

Piazza San Martina 3, Monticchiello. www.lacasadiadelina.eu. ✆ **0578/755167.** 5 units. 95€–130€ double. Rates include breakfast. Usually closed 2 weeks Feb. **Amenities:** Lounge; free Wi-Fi.

Trattoria da Fiorella ★★ TUSCAN An old stable is now an unusual and inviting dining room, with just eight or so tables on the main floor and a few on a balcony above. In this almost theatrical setting the two friendly proprietor-brothers give the town's famous pecorino cheese the star treatment: *crespelle al forno ripiene con zucchini e pecorino fresco,* baked crêpes filled with zucchini and young pecorino cheese; *verdure grigliata con pecorino,* a nice assortment of vegetables topped with shaved cheese; and mixed pecorinos with honey and walnuts. Several hearty homemade pastas, some with sauces of *cinghiale* (wild boar), and grilled steak and pork also show off the local bounty.

Via Condotti 11. © **0578/749045.** Entrees 8€–18€. Thurs–Tues noon–2:30pm and 7–9:30pm.

Trattoria Latte di Luna ★ TUSCAN Home-cooked meals are prepared by mom in the kitchen and served by dad and daughter in the yellow stucco dining room, off a little square at one end of the town's main street. *Pici all'aglione* (with spicy tomato-and-garlic sauce) or *zuppa di pane* (a local variant on *ribollita,* with more cabbage) are stellar starters, followed by wild boar or suckling pig in season or grilled steaks any time. The dessert of choice is the house-made *semifreddo* flavored with walnuts and seasonal fruits and berries.

Via San Carlo, next to Porta al Ciglio. © **0578/748606.** Entrees 7€–16€. Daily 11–4pm (sometimes open evenings).

MONTALCINO ★★

23km (14 miles) W of Pienza; 28km (17 miles) W of Montepulciano; 40km (25 miles) S of Siena

Montalcino presents a warm welcome on the approach from the Ombrone River valley below, its medieval houses clinging higgledy-piggledy to precipitous alleys beneath prickly towers. A circuit of walls encloses a warren of narrow streets that fan out from the Piazza del Popolo, where a slender clock tower soars above the Palazzo dei Priori and a Gothic loggia that at times still serves as a marketplace. Of course, if you know wine,

Sampling the Vino

Brunello di Montalcino is one of Italy's mightiest reds, a brawny wine that can hold its own with the rarest *bistecca alla fiorentina.* It's also the perfect accompaniment to game, pungent mushroom sauces, and aged cheeses. Brunello exudes the smell of mossy, damp earth and musky berries; it tastes of dark, sweet fruits and dry vanilla, and as the deep ruby liquid mellows to garnet, the wine takes on its characteristic complex and slightly tannic aspect. Although Montalcino has produced wine for centuries, its flagship Brunello is a recent development, born from late-19th-century Sangiovese experiments. Among the wine's 19th-century pioneers was Ferrucci Biondi Santi, who in 1888 also founded Montalcino's most popular drinking spot, **Fiaschetteria Italiana,** Piazza del Popolo 6 (www.caffefiaschetteriaitaliana.com; © **0577/849043**); patrons who've enjoyed the Brunellos on offer include England's King Charles. Most Brunellos are drinkable after about 4 to 5 years in the bottle; complex ones are best after 10 years or so (few last beyond 30 years). Montalcino's wine consortium **Consorzio del Vino Brunello di Montalcino** (www.consorziobrunellodimontalcino.it; © **0577/848246**), Piazza Cavour 8, can provide info on local wines and steer you to vineyards that are open to the public. **Poggio Antico** (www.poggioantico.com; © **0577/84804;** daily 10am–6pm), 4.5km (3 miles) south of Montalcino off SP14 toward Grosetto, gives free, informative tours in English, an excellent introduction to Brunello and other wines of the region. Tours with tastings begin at 30€.

you're aware that the scenery, fine as it is, is not the town's real calling card—that's Brunello di Montalcino, one of the world's most acclaimed reds, of which the town produces more than 3.5 million bottles a year, along with 3 million of its lighter-weight cousin, Rosso di Montalcino.

Montalcino was known as the "Republic of Siena at Montalcino" for housing Sienese refugees after Florence conquered Siena in 1555 (see **La Fortezza,** below); after Montalcino fell to Florence in 1559, it more or less languished until the 1960s, when the world began waking up to the fact that the local Sangiovese grosso grapes—known as "Brunello" to the locals—yielded a wine to be reckoned with.

The **tourist office** is at Costa del Municipio 1 (© **0578/757341;** daily 9am–1pm; and 2–6pm May–Sept).

La Fortezza ★★ HISTORIC SITE Built in 1361, this castle's moment arrived when the Sienese holed up here for 4 years after their city's final defeat by Florence in 1555 (ironically, the fortress had only recently been expanded and strengthened by Florence's Medici dukes). You can wander round the pentagonal walls and scale a ladder to the highest turret for a view across hills and dales all the way to Siena—but do so before you sample wine in the on-premise enoteca, perhaps the only tasting room in the world with ramparts.

Piazzale Fortezza. © **0577/849211.** 4€; 2€ ages 6–17. Tastings from 15€. Ramparts Tues–Sun 9am–6pm; enoteca daily 9am–8pm.

Museo Civico e Diocesano d'Arte Sacra ★ ART MUSEUM The cloisters of the church of Sant'Agostino house a trove of masterpieces you wouldn't expect in such a small town. Painting galleries are devoted largely to Sienese artists, who despite their static Byzantine influences were bold innovators in their times: The "Madonna dell'Unita" (Madonna of Humility), by Sano di Pietro (1406–1481), was quite shocking in its day, showing Mary kneeling on a cushion rather than seated on her traditional throne. Andrea della Robbia's terracotta statue of a refreshingly boyish St. Sebastian brings the collection into the full flower of the Renaissance.

Via Ricasoli 31. www.comunedimontalcino.it. © **0577/286300.** 4.50€; children 3€. Jan–Mar daily 10am–6pm; Apr–Dec Mon–Sat 10:30am–7pm, Sun noon–7pm.

Near Montalcino

Abbazia di Monte Oliveto Maggiore ★★★ RELIGIOUS SITE The most famous of Tuscany's rural monasteries is set in the scarred hills of the Crete Senesi, 22km (13 miles) northeast of Montalcino. The Olivetan order, founded by a group of wealthy Sienese businessmen who wanted to devote themselves to the contemplative life, built this redbrick monastic complex in the early 15th century. What draws most visitors today is one of the masterpieces of High Renaissance narrative painting: a 36-scene **fresco cycle** by Luca Signorelli and Sodoma illustrating the Life of St. Benedict. Signorelli started the job in 1497, before skipping town to work on Orvieto's Duomo, where he created his masterpiece

St. Benedict's life depicted in frescos inside the Great Cloister in the Abbazia di Monte Oliveto Maggiore.

"Last Judgment" (see p. 339). Antonio Bazzi, who arrived in 1505 and finished the cycle by 1508, is better known as "Il Sodoma," probably a reference to his predilection for young men, although he was married at least three times and had as many as 30 children. Look for his self-portrait in scene 3—he's the richly dressed fellow with flowing black hair, accompanied by two pet badgers, a chicken, and a raven. To follow the cycle's narrative, start in the back left-hand corner, with a scene of the young Benedict, astride a spirited white horse, leaving his parents' home to study in Rome. The scenes' precise details of medieval life are especially appealing: Check out the construction crews in scene 11, and the harlots smuggled into a monastery in scene 19 (allegedly, the abbot made Sodoma add clothing to the nudes he'd first painted). Also inside the church are gorgeous choir stalls crafted in intarsia in 1505 by the monk Giovanni da Verona, showing city scenes with remarkably detailed perspective.

SP 451, Strada di Monte Oliveto, Asciano. www.monteolivetomaggiore.it. ✆ **0577/707258.** Free. Daily 9:30am–12:30pm and 2:30–5:30pm. From Montalcino, follow SP14 north to Buonconvento, then head NE on SP451 to the abbey.

Abbazia di Sant'Antimo ★★★ RELIGIOUS SITE This exquisite Romanesque abbey of pale yellow travertine and alabaster nestles serenely in a valley amid vines and olive groves at the foot of the village of Castelnuovo dell'Abate, 9km (6 miles) south of Montalcino on SP55. Legend has it that the first stone here was laid on the order of Charlemagne in A.D. 781, after an angel cured his plague-stricken entourage on a journey from Rome. Near the entrance is a charming medieval relief of the Madonna and Child, and carvings of mythological animals and geometric designs surround the doors. Inside the columned interior, the carving continues; look on the right side for an intricate depiction of Daniel in the lion's den. In the chapel, 15th-century frescoes by Giovanni di Asciano show scenes from the life of St. Benedict, rich in earthy detail (one scene features two blatantly amorous pigs). A walk along the well-marked cross-country hiking trail from Montalcino to the monastery takes about 2 hours. For a quicker return, ask for a bus timetable at Montalcino's tourist office.

Via Della Badia di Sant'Antimo, Castelnuovo dell'Abate. www.antimo.it. ✆ **0577/286300.** Free; video guides 3€ and 6€. Apr–Sept daily 10am–6:30pm; Oct daily 10am–6pm; Nov–Mar daily 10:30am–5pm.

Where to Stay & Eat Near Montalcino

Albergo-Hotel Il Giglio ★★★ Here's just the sort of homey old-fashioned inn you'd expect to find along the medieval lanes of Montalcino. Tall, arched windows look across the Val d'Orcia, a fireplace glows in the cooler months, and the town's Brunello is dispensed from a small lobby bar and accompanies meals in the inhouse restaurant. In the rooms upstairs, armchairs are poised to take in the same sweeping views, and beds with wrought-iron headboards are tucked into alcoves.

Via Soccorso 5, Montalcino. www.gigliohotel.com. ✆ **0577/848167.** 12 units. 160€–170€ double. Rates include breakfast. **Amenities:** Restaurant; bar; free Wi-Fi.

Castello Banfi ★★ WINERY One of Tuscany's leading wine producers houses guests in stylish luxury, in a repurposed little *borgo* pressed against the castle walls. What were once peasant cottages are now extraordinarily luxurious suites and rooms fitted with stylish traditional furnishings, sumptuous fabrics, and rare antiques, plus the latest tech gadgetry. Along with polished, attentive service, guests enjoy such amenities as a swimming pool, a secluded rose garden, and two excellent restaurants. Also on the estate is a farmhouse where five large apartments provide a much more informal experience; furnishings are comfortably rustic, wide terraces overlook miles of vineyards, and the kitchens are well stocked with estate wines and provisions for a satisfying breakfast.

Castello di Poggio alle Mura, Montalcino. www.castellobanfiwineresort.it. ✆ **0577/877700.** 14 borgo units, 5 farmhouse apartments. Borgo units 580€–1,200€ double; apartments 220€–500€. Rates include breakfast. Contact the resort via the website about apartment rentals. Closed mid-Nov to mid-Mar. **Amenities:** 2 restaurants; bar; pool (borgo suites only); free Wi-Fi.

AREZZO ★

53km (32 miles) NE of Montepulciano

This lively little city on the eastern flanks of the Valdichiana is not as often visited as its more famous Tuscan neighbors, but get past that fairly

HOT SPOT: THE val d'orcia

If you're driving from Montalcino to Pienza, an easy side trip takes you into the rippling golden hills of the Val d'Orcia. First stop is **San Quirico d'Orcia,** about 15km (9 miles) east of Montalcino on SR2, where the honey-colored **Collegiata dei Santi Quirico e Giulitta** assaults you with a wealth of carved stone: capitals composed of animal heads, friezes of dueling fantasy creatures, and columns rising from the backs of stone lions. The church was once a popular stop for pilgrims on the Via Francigena from Canterbury to Rome. The namesake saints were 3-year-old Quirico, who inadvertently scratched the face of the pagan governor of Taurus and was thrown down a flight of stairs, and his mother, Giulitta, whose calm acceptance of her son's martyrdom so angered the governor that he had her ripped apart with hooks and beheaded. Just down the block in the main square, Piazza della Libertà, you'll find **Horti Leonini,** a Renaissance Italianate garden (1580) with geometric box-hedge designs and shady holm oaks, originally a resting spot for pilgrims, open daily sunrise to sunset. The town's **tourist office** is inside the Palazzo Chigi, Via Dante Alighieri 33 (✆ **0577/899726;** daily 10:30am–1pm and 3:30–6pm).

Five kilometers (3 miles) south and well signposted off the SS2 is **Bagno Vignoni,** little more than a group of houses surrounding one of the most memorable *piazze* in Tuscany. Instead of paving stones you'll find a steaming pool of mineral water, created when the Medici harnessed the hot sulfur springs percolating from the ground. Even St. Catherine of Siena (see p. 236) relaxed here with a sulfur cure. To see the springs in their more natural state, as Roman legionnaires did, take the second turnoff on the curving road into town and pull over after about a kilometer (½ mile), where on your right you see a tiny sulfurous mountain where the waters bubble up in dozens of tiny rivulets. You can also look down on the spectacle from the Parco di Mulino at the edge of town. From both vantage points, there's a fairy-tale view of the **Rocca d'Orcia,** the 11th-century stronghold of the Aldobrandeschi clan, formidable toll collectors along the Francigena pilgrim road. Should you wish to partake of the waters, head to the **Albergo de Terme,** Piazza del Moretto 12 (www.termedibagnovignoni.it; ✆ **0577/887150**), or the pools at the **Hotel Posta Marcucci** (www.postamarcucci.it; ✆ **0577/887112**) to soak away your cares.

unremarkable 20th-century perimeter—much of it built atop the rubble left by Allied bombings in World War II—and you'll find an enticing medieval city of cobbled streets. Arezzo's rich cultural life has left a number of art-filled churches; famous natives of Arezzo include not only Giorgio Vasari (author of the gossipy *Lives of the Artists*) but also painter Piero della Francesca (from nearby Sansepolcro), the poet Petrarch (1304–74), and actor and director Roberto Benigni, who filmed parts of his 1999 Oscar-winning *La Vita è Bella (Life Is Beautiful)* here.

Essentials

ARRIVING Arezzo is just off the A1 autostrada, putting it within easy reach of Florence and Rome by **car.** There's frequent **bus** service (www.at-bus.it) to and from Siena, and Arezzo is on a main north–south **train**

line, with frequent service to and from Florence and Rome. If you are just hopping off the train or bus to see the Piero della Francesco frescoes in the Basilica di San Francesco (well worth the stopover) you can leave your bags in the tobacco shop in the station by making reservations and paying in advance (7€) at **Kibag** (www.kibag.it). Two easy-to-reach underground parking garages near the historic center are **Parcheggio Piazza del Popolo,** at Piazza del Popolo 1, 2€ an hour, and **Parcheggio Piazza della Misericordia,** at Via Garibaldi 143, 1.50€ an hour (www.arezzoparcheggi.it; ✆ **393/921-3276**).

Antiques fair in the Tournament Square in Arezzo.

VISITOR INFORMATION The main **Arezzo Tourist Office** is on Piazza Grande at Via Giorgio Vassari 13 (www.discoverarezzo.com; ✆ **0575/377468**) and is usually open daily 10am to 6pm. The town also operates a smaller Discover Arezzo infopoint across from the Duomo on Piazza della Libertà, usually open 10am to 6pm.

Exploring Arezzo

Arezzo's medieval core centers on the charmingly lopsided **Piazza Grande.** An elegant loggia by Giorgio Vasari anchors one side of the piazza, while the rest of the space drapes casually across the slope, with slanting cobblestones and an irregular shape. The Duomo crowns the hilltop, while next to it the green expanse of the Parco del Prato, with airy views of the countryside, surrounds a ruined 16th-century fortress.

Basilica di San Francesco ★★★ CHURCH Piero della Francesca's "Legend of the True Cross" is reason enough to come to Arezzo. One of

Treasure Hunters & Knights

Arezzo's famous **antiques fair** takes over the Piazza Grande and adjoining streets the first Sunday of each month and the preceding Saturday. More than 500 vendors come from around Italy to sell an appealing array of old furniture, silver, oil paintings, and other wares, at very good prices.

The **Giostra del Saracino** (giostradelsaracinoarezzo.it), a jousting contest between the four districts of the town, turns the clock back to medieval times twice a year in June and September. A lively procession through the streets to the accompaniment of trumpets and drums ends in Piazza Grande, where jousters on colorfully bedecked horses wield their lances against armor-plated dummies.

LEGEND OF THE true cross

Piero della Francesca based his great Arezzo frescoes on a story from Jacopo da Varazze's 1260 *Golden Legend*, a compilation of saintly lore that was a wildly popular medieval bestseller. As the story goes, Seth, son of Adam, planted on his father's grave the seeds from the apple tree that had led to his parents' fall from Eden; timbers from the tree were eventually made into a bridge. Many years later, the much-mythologized Queen of Sheba recognized while crossing the bridge that its wood had special significance. She predicted to Solomon, king of Israel, that a savior would one day be hung from the timbers and cause the downfall of the Jewish nation. Solomon prudently had the wood buried but Romans inevitably discovered the beams and used them to crucify Christ.

Two centuries later, Roman emperor Constantine the Great saw the cross in a vision, emblazoned the image on his army's shields, defeated his co-emperor Maxentius, and converted to Christianity. His mother, Helen, went in search of the true cross in Jerusalem (her methods included torturing Jews to reveal the cross's whereabouts). Fragments of the Cross became popular medieval religious relics. It's a far-fetched story indeed, but in the hands of Piero della Francesca, the twists and turns become riveting.

the greatest artists of the Renaissance painted one of the world's greatest fresco cycles, in a league with the Sistine Chapel, between 1452 and 1466. The 10 panels are remarkable for their grace, narrative detail, compositional precision, perfect perspective, depth of humanity, and dramatic light effects—"the most perfect morning light in all Renaissance painting," wrote art historian Kenneth Clark. The full religious significance of the story may escape you, but with stalwart knights and fair ladies, the scenes seem like a medieval romance. The beauty is in the details: heaving bosoms, pouty lips, and dreamy eyes, along with some wonderful ancient and medieval finery. You may have seen these frescoes in the film *The English Patient,* when Kip hoists Hana up to the frescoes by means of ropes and pulleys; we see her expressions of delight and wonder as she comes face to face with Piero's colorful ladies and gents. You'll feel the same, even when earthbound and jostling for a good look with your co-viewers. Piazza San Francesco. www.polomusealetoscana.beniculturali.it. ✆ **0575/20059.** Church free. Della Francesca cycle: 9€, 5€ students and ages 16 and under; timed-entry tickets (30 min.) only; reservations required by phone, website, or in person. Mon, Thurs, and Fri 9am–6pm; Sat 9am–5:30pm; Sun 1–5:30pm.

Casa di Vasari ★★ HISTORIC HOUSE Giorgio Vasari was born in Arezzo in 1511, just as the Renaissance was flowering all around him. Though he never achieved the greatness of many of the other artists working around him, Vasari helped define the period in his writings and may have even coined the term "Renaissance" for the creative period that led Europe out of the Dark Ages. An architect as well an artist—he designed the Galleria degli Uffizi in Florence (see p. 179)—Vasari is best known for

Lives of the Most Excellent Painters, Sculptors and Architects, a rather juicy account of the great masters, many of whom Vasari knew personally. He settled down here in his hometown in 1540 and set about frescoing the walls and ceilings of his gracious house with classical themes and portraits. In the Room of Celebrities, Vasari painted portraits of Michelangelo, Andrea del Sarto, and other notable contemporaries, surrounding himself with the cultural greats of his day. Vasari's copious correspondence, including 17 letters from Michelangelo, is sometimes on view. Part of the beautiful garden remains, and like the rest of the house provides a glimpse of a cultured Renaissance lifestyle. The early Renaissance poet and scholar Francesco Petrarch was also a native of Arezzo, and his house near the Duomo is preserved as the **Casa Petrarca,** an academic institution that shows off a fine collection of medieval manuscripts and historic coins.

Casa di Vasari: Via XX Settembre 55. www.giorgiovasari-ticketoffice.it. ✆ **0575/409040.** 4€; 2€ students and children under 17. Mon and Wed–Fri 9am–7:30pm; Sun 9am–1:30pm; 1st and 3rd Sat of the month 2:15–7:30pm, 2nd and 4th Sat of the month 9am–1:30pm. **Casa Petrarca:** Via dell'Oro 28. www.arezzoturismo.it. ✆ **331/565-0036.** 4€; 2€ students and children under 17. Apr–Oct daily 9:30am–6:30pm; Nov–Mar Sat–Sun 10:30am–5:30pm.

Duomo di Arezzo (Cattedrale dei Santi Pietro e Donato) ★ CATHEDRAL First to catch your eye once you step inside the coldly stark interior of this big, austere Gothic barn, at the highest point in town will be the stained-glass windows by Guillaume de Marcillat (1470–1529), a French master summoned to Rome to work for the popes, who spent the last 10 years of his life in Arezzo creating these seven magnificent windows depicting Biblical scenes. Beneath this colorful tableaux are some other fine works: a robust Mary Magdalene portrayed in a fresco by Piero Della Francesca in an arch near the sacristy door; stone-carved battle scenes on the tomb of Guido Tarlati, an Aretine bishop who died in 1327; and in the chapel on the left near the entrance, a series of terracottas by della Robbia showing the Assumption, the Crucifixion, and a Madonna and Child.

Piazza del Duomo. ✆ **0575/23991.** Free. Daily 7am–12:30pm and 3–6:30pm.

Santa Maria della Pieve ★★ CHURCH Most great churches are intended to draw the eye heavenward, but few achieve the effect quite as dramatically as this 12th-century arched facade. Three stacked arcades of beige stone subtly narrow as they rise above a five-arched lower floor and the street below; above it all rises a bell tower with five rows of windows. The effect is all the more powerful since the church sits on a slope. Inside is an altarpiece by Pietro Lorenzetti, a Sienese artist who perished in the Black Death in 1348. Like the church's facade, his work here is multi-tiered, with figures getting smaller on each successive layer. Remains of the town's patron saint, Donato, a 4th-century bishop of Arezzo, are here, too, in a beautiful gold reliquary.

Corso Italia 7. ✆ **0575/377678.** Free. Daily 8am–12:30pm and 3–6:30pm.

Where to Stay in Arezzo

Antiche Mura ★★★ Tucked into the town walls just a few steps below the Duomo, this tall, narrow house dates from the 1200s. Rock outcroppings, stone walls, glass walkways over ancient foundations, and an old olive press celebrate the heritage, while sleek, simple furnishings, bright white walls, and splashes of color add a contemporary flair. Each room is named and styled after a famous woman in literature or the movies, from Madame Bovary's period decor to the sensual reds in the Marilyn Monroe room.

Piaggia di Murello 35. www.antichemura.info. ✆ **0575/20410.** 6 units. 90€–110€ double. Breakfast 5€. Free parking nearby. **Amenities:** Free Wi-Fi.

Graziella Patio Hotel ★★ Decor in this old palace a stone's throw from the church of San Francesco is based on the travel essays of the late Bruce Chatwin. The gimmick adds romance and drama without sacrificing comforts that include flourishes like huge bathtubs in the sitting/sleeping areas. The Colonial India room, with bright yellow walls and a four-poster bed, seems distinctly suited to the palatial surroundings, and the Moroccan room, with beautiful glazed-tile walls, is as colorful as the town's famous frescoes. Three especially extravagant rooms are on a lower floor that opens to a hidden garden: One has a hot tub the size of a small swimming pool, and another has a huge sunken bathtub reached by a staircase behind the bed. Guests have use of a MacBook for the duration of their stay.

Via Cavour 23. www.hotelpatio.it. ✆ **0575/401962.** 10 units. 135€–160€ double. Rates include breakfast. **Amenities:** Spa services; free Wi-Fi.

Vogue Hotel ★★ With a name like this, a hotel had better be stylish, and these good-size and gracious rooms deliver on the promise, bringing comfort and sophistication to centuries-old surroundings accented with rich fabrics, fine carpets, and handsome wood furnishings. Stone walls and beams accent rooms where huge soaking tubs are placed behind glass headboards, enormous showers have windows, and sitting areas are set into alcoves. Some rooms also provide a timeless view of the town's towers and rooftops, and all the sights are just steps away.

Via Guido Monaco 54. www.voguehotel.it. ✆ **0575/24361.** 26 units. 85€–110€ double. Rates include breakfast. **Amenities:** Bar; free Wi-Fi.

Where to Eat in Arezzo

In all but the worst weather, Aretines turn out for the evening *passeggiata.* A prime spot to sit on a terrace and enjoy a pre-dinner glass of wine or aperitif while watching the comings and goings is **Caffe Vasari** (✆ **0575/21945**) under the loggia overlooking Piazza Grande, a good place to perch even in the rain. A good stop for a quick bite is **Dal Moro,** Via Cavour 68 (✆ **0575/043-208**), with creative sandwiches and a huge selection of local cheeses and cold cuts. **Cremì,** Corso Italia 100 (✆ **333/976-6336**), dishes up the best artisan gelato in town, along with crepes with a choice of sweet fillings.

PAY HOMAGE TO piero

Piero della Francesco, whose Legend of the True Cross graces Arezzo's basilica di San Francesco, was a visionary whose figures appear as vivid, thriving beings even 500 years after he committed them to canvas. The master's "Madonna del Prato" hangs in the little museum in **Monterchi,** 28km (16 miles) east of Arezzo on SS73. The painting is rare in Italian art in that it depicts a heavily pregnant Virgin Mary—she holds her hand against her side to support her belly, and if you happen to be in the same condition, the 6.50€ admission fee is waived (www.madonnadelparto.it; ✆ **0575/70713;** daily 10am–1pm and 2–5pm). **Sansepolcro,** 15km (9 miles) farther north on SS73, houses another of Piero's great works, a 1468 "Resurrection of Christ" that British writer Aldous Huxley called "the greatest picture." In World War II a British officer demanded that shelling of the town cease lest the painting be damaged, and the transcendent work remains in the Museo Civico (www.museocivicosansepolcro.it; ✆ **0575/732218;** admission 8€; daily 10am–1pm and 2:30–6pm).

Antica Osteria l'Agania ★★★ TUSCAN Two floors of plain, brightly lit dining rooms bustle with locals. Pastas are homemade from organic ingredients, produce is market fresh, and the meat is from local farms. Daily specials include such local favorites as *trippa* (tripe) and *grifi e polenta* (chunks of veal stomach in polenta), but lighter fare is usually available, too, and specials often include eggs topped with fresh asparagus or *tartufo* (dried truffles), especially tasty when accompanied with a local Pinot Grigio. The house wine is excellent, and the house grappa puts the perfect finish on a meal.
Via Mazzini 10. www.facebook.com/anticaosterialagania. ✆ **0575/295-381.** Entrees 8€–12€. Tues–Sat noon–3pm and 7–10:30pm; Sun noon–3pm.

La Torre di Gnicche ★★ WINE BAR The emphasis here is on wine, with more than 30 choices available by the glass and hundreds by the bottle, accompanied by a choice of small plates and meals. A huge selection of local cheeses and salamis accompany many local favorites, such as *baccalà in umido* (salt-cod stew) and, in summer, *pappa al pomodoro* (a thick bread and tomato soup served at room temperature). The cluttered, bottle-lined room just off Piazza Grande is a nice hideaway on a chilly evening, and the few tables in the narrow lane outside are much in demand in warm weather.
Piaggia San Martino 8. www.latorredignicche.it. ✆ **0575/352035.** Entrees 7€–11€. Thurs–Tues noon–3pm and 6pm–1am. Closed 2 weeks in Jan.

CORTONA ★★

34km (22 miles) S of Arezzo; 31km (19 miles) NE of Montepulciano

Draped across a green mountainside above terraced olive groves, austere-looking Cortona is a steep medieval city, where cut-stone staircases take the place of many streets. In recent years, the book and film *Under the*

Palazzo Comunale in Cortona.

Tuscan Sun have brought more appreciative fans to town, but Cortona's somber lanes and stage-set piazzas have survived the wave of popularity. The appeal is as strong as ever, and among the attractions are the chance to enjoy Tuscan hill town life, some significant art treasures, and romantic, misty views over the wide Valdichiana.

Essentials

ARRIVING Cortona is on **rail** lines that run between Florence to the north and Perugia, Chiusi, and Rome to the south. The Camucia/Cortona train station (✆ **0575/603018**) is 5km (3 miles) below Cortona in the workaday town of Camucia, where many services are located as well. **Buses** run from here to Piazza Garibaldi in Cortona about hourly. You can include the bus trip up town when you buy a train ticket to Cortona-Camucia, or buy a ticket at Bar Stazione (1.50€) or pay on the bus.

VISITOR INFORMATION You'll find a **tourist office** at Piazza Signorelli 9, in the courtyard beyond the Museo dell'Accademia Etrusca ticket office (www.cortonaweb.net; ✆ **0575/637223**); it's open daily 10am to 6pm. Several paid-parking areas are located just outside the city walls, including ones at Piazzale del Mercato and Porta Colonia, where you'll pay about 1€ an hour, and you can park for free at designated spots around the city walls.

Exploring Cortona

Via Nazionale, known as the Rugapiana ("flat street," since it's the only one in town that even comes close to fitting that description), runs east-west through the medieval town to **Piazza della Repubblica,** presided over by a stern city hall loaded with towers, a stone staircase, and wooden balconies. On the northern corner the square opens into **Piazza Signorelli,** named for the town's famous Renaissance artist, Luca Signorelli (1445–1523). This piazza was once the headquarters of Cortona's Florentine governors, whose coats of arms adorn the Casali Palace (now home to the excellent Etruscan museum, see p. 269). From here, streets lead down to the **Piazza del Duomo** and a treasure trove of art in the **Museo Diocesano** (Diocesan Museum; p. 269). Other streets climb steeply uphill from Piazza Signorelli through the upper town to the **Basilica di Santa Margherita** (✆ **0575/605064**), where the embalmed body of the namesake patron—to which the centuries have not been terribly kind—lies in full view in a lavish 14th-century tomb above the main altar. Margaret, the former mistress of a lord from Montepulciano, was a follower of St. Francis who devoted her life to caring for the sick and poor. Admission is free; the church is open 8am to noon and 3 to 7pm (slightly shorter hours in winter). On the climb up, you can admire 15 modern mosaics depicting the Stations of the Cross by the Futurist artist Gino Severini (1883–1966), a Cortona native.

Basilica di Santa Margherita in Cortona.

Even higher is the hilltop **Fortezza di Girifalco** (www.fortezzadelgirifalco.it; ✆ **0575/637235;** admission 8€, 6€ seniors and students), defenses built over ancient foundations in 1556 on the orders of Duke Cosimo di Medici, under whom Cortona was a prosperous city; aside from housing a military garrison, the keep, bastions, and vaulted galleries have served as an orphanage and a World War II German radio headquarters and today host cultural events and an excellent wine bar that rewards the hike up. The fortress is open mid-April through mid-June daily 10am to 7pm; mid-June through early September daily 10am to 8pm; early September through early October daily 10am to 7pm; October 10am to 6pm, November through mid-April weekends only 10am–5pm (to 6pm early March to mid-Apr). From Piazza Signorelli you can stay on level ground and walk east along Via Nazionale to airy **Piazza Garibaldi,** which opens into public gardens with views south to Lago Trasimeno in Umbria and west across the Valdichiana to Montepulciano.

Church of San Francesco ★★ CHURCH This simple Romanesque church with its wood-raftered ceiling is the second Franciscan church ever built (the first, in St. Francis' hometown of Assisi, was begun around 1228, while this one dates to 1245). The church houses the tomb of Brother Elias of Cortona, who administered the Franciscan Order after Francis's death in 1226, as well as three precious relics of St. Francis himself—his tunic, his manuscript of the New Testament, and a cushion he often used. On the high altar is the Reliquary of the Holy Cross, an ornate 10th-century ivory tablet containing a fragment of Christ's cross, presented to Elias by the Byzantine Emperor in 1244. The artist Luca Signorelli, who died in Cortona in 1523, is believed to be buried in the crypt.

Via Berrettini. ✆ **0575/402-7226.** Free admission. Daily 9am–5:30pm.

Eremo le Celle ★★★ RELIGIOUS SITE St. Francis passed through Cortona in 1240, on his way to a mountainside hermitage 3km (2 miles) outside of town. Francis' companion Brother Elias then took up residence in one of the caves and redid the place into a bona fide monastery, which it remains to this day, home to a small community of monks and a place of solitary retreat for the religious. The honey-colored stone dwellings, forest paths, bubbling streams, and simple, rock-hewn chapels are bucolic and humbling, and the walk out from town is a delight. From Piazza Mazzini, outside Porta Colonia, walk northeast (to the right as you leave the gate) for about 500 feet to a gravel road on the left that skirts olive groves high above the baroque church of Santa Maria Nuova. At the entrance to a villa garden you will come to a fork; follow the road on the right to the Celle.

Localita Cappuccini 1. ✆ **0575/603362.** Donations welcome. Daily 7am–7pm (until 5pm in winter).

Museo dell'Accademia Etrusca ★★ MUSEUM Cortona was one of the 12 cities of the Etruscan confederation, and so many artifacts from that era were discovered nearby that an Etruscan Academy was founded in 1727. The collection is still housed in the Palazzo Casali, a 13th-century mansion built for the city's governors. The lower galleries tackle the Etruscan and Roman history of Cortona, with lots of gold from excavated tombs and the enigmatic Cortona Tablet, a 200-word document inscribed in bronze. On the sprawling upper floors, the most intriguing object is a one-of-a-kind oil lamp from the late 4th century B.C., decorated with human heads, allegorical figures, and a few virile Pans playing their pipes, all surrounding a leering Gorgon's head on the bottom. Several Etruscan tombs and the remains of a Roman villa, still being excavated, litter the Parco Archeologico, outside the hamlet of Sodo in the valley below town.

Piazza Signorelli 9. cortonamaec.org. ✆ **0575/637235.** Museum: 10€; 7€ children 6–12, free children under 6; 13€ and 8€ with Parco Archeologico. Apr–Oct daily 10am–7pm; Nov–Mar Tues–Sun 10am–5pm.

Museo Diocesano ★★★ MUSEUM Almost every work in this small collection in the former Gesù church is a masterpiece. Pride of place, however, belongs to Fra Angelico and Luca Signorelli. The Fra Angelico gem is a splendid 1436 altarpiece of "The Annunciation," graced by his mastery of perspective and command of detail—notice the angel's precious garment embroidered in gold, the Virgin's elaborate robes, and the carpet of wildflowers (the new Eden) on which her house sits. Luca Signorelli, who was born in Cortona around 1450 and whose masterpiece is the fresco cycle in Orvieto's duomo (see p. 339), is represented by a vividly detailed "Deposition" originally painted for Cortona's cathedral in 1502. The painter instilled his figure of Christ with so much realism and passion that legend claims he modeled it on his own son, who'd died of the plague that same year. Signorelli's "Communion of the Apostles" (1512) in the same room shows the artist's strong sense of architectural space. Notice Judas in the foreground, hiding the communion host in his purse—ashamed of his imminent betrayal, he can't swallow it.

Via Mura del Duomo. ✆ **0575/877-3610.** 6€. Apr–Oct daily 10:30am–6:30pm, Nov–Mar Fri–Sun 10am–5pm. Duomo (adjacent) open Apr–Oct daily 8am–7:30pm, Nov–Mar daily 8:30am–6:30pm.

Where to Stay in Cortona

Some of Cortona's most reasonably priced accommodations are in a convent and retreat house, **Villa Santa Margherita,** just a few minutes' walk from the town center at Viale Cesare Battisti 17 (www.villasantamargherita cortona.it; ✆ **0575/082440**). Spartan but pleasant doubles begin at about 80€.

Casa Zeni ★★★ You'll take to hill town life easily in one of these charming, stone-walled apartments in a meticulously restored medieval house in the center of town. Apartments sleep from three to six guests in great style, with contemporary furniture that blends well with rustic tile floors and wood-beamed ceilings. Amenities include kitchens, washers/dryers, superb beds, and beautifully equipped bathrooms. Hosts Silvia and Cristian provide caring hospitality and a wealth of handy advice.

Via Maccari 21. www.casazeni.com. ✆ **338/830-7737.** 3 units. 85€–110€ double. 2-night min. stay; discounts for stays of 1 week or longer. Rates include breakfast at nearby cafe. **Amenities:** Free Wi-Fi.

Hotel Italia ★★ This 15th-century palace is not as grand as the neighboring San Michele (see below), but the hospitality hits the same high notes. Piazza Signorelli is just steps away, and the relaxed ambience suits Cortona's small-town pace. Spacious rooms are plain but atmospheric, with tasteful rustic wood furnishings, beamed ceilings, and other architectural flourishes. Only a few have views, but all guests can enjoy panoramic vistas from the top-floor breakfast room or on the roof terrace.

Via Ghibellina 5–7. www.hotelitaliacortona.com. ✆ **0575/630254.** 17 units. 100€–125€ double. Rates include breakfast. **Amenities:** Free Wi-Fi.

Hotel San Michele ★★ In this 15th-century palazzo in the center of town, the salons and high-ceilinged guest rooms, a few frescoed and paneled, are reminders of Cortona's prosperous and noble past. Tile-floored rooms are appealingly, rather grandly furnished; some have views over the valley below, a choice few, including tower suites, from their own terraces. A roof terrace with the same vistas is open to all guests, as is a decidedly medieval-looking courtyard. The San Michele also operates **Villa Borgo San Pietro** (www.borgosanpietro.com; ✆ **0575/612402**), 4km (2½ miles) outside town in San Pietro a Cegliolo, with a countrified take on grand living—14 rooms and five apartments set amid 7 acres of olive trees and lavender, with a swimming pool (from 70€ a night).

Via Guelfa 15. www.hotelsanmichele.net. ✆ **0575/604348.** 42 units. 80€–135€ double. Rates include breakfast. Closed Nov to mid-Mar. **Amenities:** Bar; free Wi-Fi.

Relais Il Falconiere ★★ When Riccardo Baracchi inherited a farm from his grandmother, he and his wife, Sylvia, created a stylish and sophisticated retreat, with antiques-filled rooms scattered among a villa and stone farmhouses. Beamed ceilings and terracotta floors accompany the rural setting, with a pool and gardens amid 20 acres of olive groves and vineyards. A luxurious spa with a walled garden enhances the sense of relaxation. Sylvia oversees one of the best restaurants in the area, serving refined Tuscan food in the refitted lemon house.

San Martino (3km/2 miles N of Cortona). www.ilfalconiere.it. ✆ **0575/612616.** 15 units. 400€–600€ double. Rates include breakfast. Closed Mid-Nov to Mar. **Amenities:** Restaurant; bar; 2 swimming pools; spa; free Wi-Fi.

Relais la Corte dei Papi ★★ The hospitable David Papi has converted his family's country house, dating from 1770, into a quiet and luxurious retreat in the valley just below Cortona. The farm shows few traces of its humble rustic origins and is geared instead to a romantic getaway. Many of the enormous suites are set up as spas, with sumptuous, handcrafted furnishings surrounding pool-size soaking tubs and hydromassage showers that double as steam rooms. Enveloping the handsome stone buildings are lawns and flower gardens tended by David's lovely mom, Gabriella, and two outbuildings are set up as guest cottages. A well-regarded restaurant overlooks the swimming pool and its terraces.

Via la Dogana 12. www.lacortedeipapi.com. ✆ **0575/614109.** 15 units. 300€–450€ double. Rates include breakfast. Closed Jan–Feb. **Amenities:** Restaurant; bar; swimming pool; free Wi-Fi.

Where to Eat in Cortona

A walk through town usually includes a stop at **Molesini,** Piazza della Repubblica 3 (www.molesini-market.com; ✆ **0575/62544**), a local institution that will pour you a glass of wine and offer a big selection of cheese, olive oil, and other local products. The shop's selection features Cortona vineyards, where Syrah grapes are producing increasingly sophisticated yields. A standout is Usciòlo, from **Cantina Doveri,** in the outlying hamlet of Pergo (www.cantinadoveri.it; ✆ **388/614-5802**). **Caffe Tuscher,** Via Nazionale 43 (www.caffetuschercortona.com; ✆ **0575/62053**), is the most elegant spot in town for a cocktail, along with snacks and light meals throughout the day, served in a welcoming two-story space and on the street outside in good weather. **Enoteca Enotria,** Via Nazionale 81 (✆ **0575/603595**), sells wine by the glass and sandwiches, making the rustic room a popular hangout well into the late evening.

Chef Ryan Hanley (www.cookingclassestuscany.com; ✆ **388/100-3342**) teaches Tuscan cooking in his home kitchen just below Cortona in

Pergo; the 3- to 4-hour long lunch or dinner sessions end with a leisurely meal accompanied by local wines and a friendly take on local food, wine, and culture. Ryan and his Arezzo-born wife, Debora, also lead tours of vineyards around Cortona and across the valley near Montepulciano. Classes are 125€ a person; tour prices vary.

Osteria al Teatro ★★★ TUSCAN Chef Emiliano Rossi lays on the theatrics in three character-filled, candlelit rooms stuffed with antiques and old prints and in a charming summertime garden. All the good things of the palate come together in these amiable surroundings: excellent wines from a vast cellar, including many Cortona vintages, and a thoughtful and innovative menu, on which beef from the Valdichiana is presented many different ways (look for truffle pairings in season). End the meal with a carving board of house-made chocolate (not available in warmer months).

Via Maffei 2. www.osteria-del-teatro.it. ✆ **0575/630556.** Entrees 12€–22€. Thurs–Tues 12:30–2:30pm and 7–10pm.

Ristorante la Loggetta ★★ TUSCAN/GRILL You would probably be happy eating canned spaghetti while savoring the view over the Piazza della Repubblica from this restaurant's namesake loggia—or for that matter, dining under the enchanting stone-and-brick vaults inside. It's a moot point, however: The food here is very well done, and nicely served. The kitchen is acclaimed for its preparations of beef from the Valdichiana, often served with a rich red-wine reduction.

Piazza di Pescheria. www.laloggetta.com. ✆ **0575/630575.** Entrees 9€–28€. Thurs–Tues noon–3pm and 7–11pm. Closed Jan.

Trattoria Dardano ★★ TUSCAN/GRILL Cortonans come to this simple, brightly lit room for meat roasted over a charcoal fire, with the emphasis on *bistecca alla fiorentina* from cattle raised in the valley below town (generally considered the best beef in Italy). *Pollo* (chicken), *anatra* (duck), *miale* (pork) and *faraona* (guinea hen) also go onto the flames. The heaping platters are usually preceded by *crostini neri* (little black toasts), with chicken liver, some local salamis, and often *ribollita,* the thick Tuscan soup, all accompanied by local wine.

Via Dardano 24. www.trattoriadardano.com. ✆ **0575/601944.** Entrees 8€–13€. Thurs–Tues noon–3pm and 6:30–11pm.

Trattoria la Grotta ★★ TUSCAN For many regulars, any meal in this medieval, brick-vaulted dining room or in the tiny courtyard just off Piazza della Repubblica must include the light-as-a-feather house gnocchi. All the pastas are house-made and topped with rich, sweet sauces, while fresh locally grown zucchini and artichokes are a light antidote for the deftly grilled steaks. The house wine is delicious and reasonably priced.

Piazza Baldelli 3. trattorialagrotta.it. ✆ **0575/630271.** Entrees 8€–18€. Wed–Mon noon–2:30pm and 7–9:30pm.

Cortona Shopping

Cortona produces its own distinctive ceramics, in warm, creamy yellows and pleasant greens. You'll find handsome wares in pleasant surroundings at **Terrabruga,** Via Nazionale 54 (www.terrabruga.com; ✆ **0575/605099**), which ships its finely crafted tableware anywhere. **Il Pozzo** ("the Old Well") is a treasure trove of well-curated photography and art by local artists, alongside leather goods, handcrafted paper, and much more, shown off in historic surroundings at Via Nazionale 10/12 (✆ **0575/603730**). From a swanky showroom in a medieval olive mill at Vicolo Corazzi 17, off Piazza della Repubblica, **DelBrenna** (www.delbrennajewelry.com; ✆ **0575/630640**) sells distinctive jewelry, including signature chains embellished with gemstones and ancient coins, as well as handmade shoes.

SAN GIMIGNANO ★★

42km (26 miles) NW of Siena, 52km (32 miles) SW of Florence

In the 12th and 13th centuries, more than 70 towers rose above the tile roofs of San Gimignano, built partly to defend against outside invaders but mostly as status symbols for San Gimignano's powerful families. A dozen towers remain, and as you approach across the rolling countryside, they give the town the look of a fantasy kingdom—lending credence to such nicknames as "Manhattan of the Middle Ages" and "City of Beautiful Towers." Once inside the gates, the Manhattan reference seems all too apt, with visitors shoulder-to-shoulder in its narrow lanes, obliterating the medieval aura you've come to savor. Almost everyone traveling the hill town circuit makes a stop here, while bus tours pour in from Siena and Florence, and Italians arrive on weekend outings. If you want to be swept back to the Middle Ages, you're best visiting midweek in off-season, or late on weekday afternoons after the buses have pulled out.

Essentials

ARRIVING San Gimignano does not have a train station, but dozens of daily **trains** run between **Siena** and Florence and **Poggibonsi,** from where more than 30 buses make the 25-minute run to San Gimignano Monday through Saturday; only six buses run on Sunday.

It's more convenient to travel to San Gimignano by buses operated by **Autolinee Toscana** (www.at-bus.it). They run hourly (fewer on Sun) for most of the day from **Florence** (50 min.) to Poggibonsi and Colle di Val d'Elsa. Many immediately connect with buses to San Gimignano (20–25 min. farther). From **Siena** there are 10 daily direct buses (a 1¼ hr. journey) Monday through Saturday, with connections in Poggibonsi on Sunday

Arriving by **car,** take the Poggibonsi Nord exit off the **Florence-Siena** highway or the SS2. San Gimignano is 12km (7½ miles) from Poggibonsi. Parking is tight, and the *centro storico* is off-limits to most vehicles (including those of visitors). Read signs carefully, since many spots are reserved for residents, and some only allow parking for 1 hour.

The most convenient parking is at **Parcheggio Montemaggio,** outside the Porta San Giovanni (2€ an hour, 20€ a day). You can easily walk into town from here, but shuttle buses also take you up to Piazza della Cisterna (1€, tickets sold from parking-ticket machines).

VISITOR INFORMATION The **tourist office** at Piazza Duomo 1 (www.sangimignano.com; ✆ **0577/940008**) is open daily 10am to 1pm and 3 to 7pm (10am–1pm and 2–6pm Nov–Feb). Guided walks of the town depart from outside the office Monday through Saturday at 10:30am and 5pm (sometimes also 9:30pm in summer) and Sunday at 5pm; 15€. The office also leads walks in the hills around town at varying times, depending on demand, with fees from 15€ to 22€, depending on the walk. The office books accommodations.

Exploring San Gimignano

You'll see the town at its lively best if you come on a Thursday or Saturday morning, when the interlocking **Piazza della Cisterna** and **Piazza del Duomo** fill with market stalls. Piazza della Cisterna is named for the well at its center, a fairly ingenious device that for centuries was a repository for rainwater channeled from rooftops—a reliable and safe source of water that could not be tampered with or contaminated by events occurring outside the city walls. For a little more solitude, head up from the Duomo to the well-marked **Rocca e Parco di Montestaffoli,** filling the shell of the town's 14th-century fortress and providing greenery, quiet, and views over the town and countryside, all the better from the little tower in the far corner. Another refreshing vantage point, with views for miles across the rolling countryside, is a circuit around the top of the **town walls,** about 1½ miles in its entirety and accessed from any of the four gates; **Porta delle Fonti,** at the east end of town, is an especially scenic entry point, as just outside the portal are romantically arched medieval fountains. Step into **San Gimignano 1300** for an enchanting backward look at how the town appeared in medieval times—not much different actually. The detail of the ceramic to-scale model, with many more towers still standing, is fascinating (Via Costarella 3; www.sangimignano1300.com; ✆ **327/4395165;** free admission).

Festival of "Ferie delle Messi" in San Gimignano.

Basilica di Santa Maria Assunta (Il Duomo/Collegiata) ★★ CHURCH San Gimignano's main church is awash in frescoes. Around the main door, a gruesome "Last Judgment" by Sienese artist Taddeo di Bartolo (1410) shows mean-looking little devils taunting tortured souls. (Bartolo allegedly modeled some of the characters after townsfolk who rubbed him the wrong way.) Much of the nave is covered in flat, two-dimensional frescoes of the Sienese school—a comic-strip-like Poor Man's Bible, illustrating familiar stories for the illiterate faithful. The left wall is frescoed with scenes from the Old Testament (look for the panel showing the Pharaoh and his army being swallowed by the Red Sea), and the right wall features the New Testament (a very shifty-looking Judas receives his 30 pieces of silver for betraying Christ). The best frescoes in the church are in the tiny **Cappella di Santa Fina,** where Domenico Ghirlandaio decorated the walls with airy scenes of the life of Fina—a local girl who, though never officially canonized, is one of San Gimignano's patron saints. Little Fina was so devout that when she fell ill with paralysis, she refused a bed and lay instead on a board, never complaining even when worms and rats fed off her decaying flesh. As you'll see in one of the panels, St. Gregory foretold the exact day (his feast day, March 12) when Fina would die. She expired right on schedule and began working miracles immediately—all the bells in town rang spontaneously at the moment of her death.

Piazza del Duomo. ✆ **0577/286-300.** 5€ adults; 3€ ages 6–18. Apr–Oct Mon–Fri 10am–7:30pm, Sat 10am–5pm, Sun 12:30–7:30pm; Nov–Mar Mon–Sat 10am–5pm, Sun 12:30–5pm.

Palazzo Comunale & Torre Grossa ★★ MUSEUM The late-13th-century home of the city government, also known as Palazzo del Popolo, is topped with San Gimignano's tallest tower, the aptly named Torre Grossa (Big Tower), finished in 1311. Your reward for a climb to the top will be views of the cityscape and rolling countryside of the Val d'Elsa. (***Tip:*** Save your knees and enjoy the same outlook for free by making the gentler 5-minute climb uphill from Piazza del Duomo to the ruined Rocca.) Inside the palazzo's **Camera del Podestà** (Room of the Mayor) are San Gimignano's most famous frescoes, Memmo di Filippuccio's "Scenes of Married Life." In one scene, a couple takes a bath together, and in the other, the scantily-clad fellow climbs into bed beside his naked wife; on the opposite wall, a young man is seduced and robbed by several women and Aristotle cavorts with a courtesan, suggesting the cycle was meant to show the dangerous power of lust over reason and contentment. The "Coppo di Marcovaldo Crucifix," in the adjoining painting gallery, is an astonishingly touching work in which a vulnerably human figure of Christ is surrounded by six intricate little scenes of the Crucifixion. The artist Coppo, a Florentine soldier, was captured by the Sienese, who soon realized what a treasure they had in him; his masterpieces show a transition from flat Byzantine style to more varied texture and three-dimensionality. The head of St. Fina (see the Collegiata, p. 275) is kept in the

Tabernacle of Santa Fina (1402), painted with scenes of the teenage saint's miracles. Taddeo di Bartolo (see his terrifying "Last Judgment" in the Collegiata, p. 275) painted the "Life of St. Gimignano" for this room. St. Gimignano was a 5th-century bishop of Modena who miraculously spared the little town then known as Silvia from a barbarian attack. The grateful citizenry changed their town's name to honor the saint, who is depicted cradling his namesake town in his lap, towers and all.

Piazza del Duomo. www.sangimignanomusei.it. ✆ **0577/286300.** 9€; 7€ ages 6–17 (also includes church of San Lorenzo in Ponte). Nov–Mar Mon–Fri 11am–5:30pm, Sat–Sun 11am–6pm; Apr–Oct daily 10am–7:30pm.

Sant'Agostino ★★ CHURCH An especially appropriate presence in this 13th-century church at the north end of town is St. Sebastian, the "saint who was martyred twice." As a stop on trade and pilgrimage routes, San Gimignano was decimated by the plague time and again; this gave residents a special fondness for the 3rd-century saint Sebastian, who also was prone to repeated bad fortune. In 1464, after surviving yet another plague, the town hired Florentine painter Benozzo Gozzoli to paint a thankful scene. As the fresco shows, when Sebastian first proclaimed his faith, the emperor Diocletian ordered that he be taken to a field and shot full of arrows. Sebastian miraculously survived and was nursed back to health, but he tempted fate again by haranguing Diocletian as he passed in royal procession; the emperor had him bludgeoned to death on the spot. Gozzoli also frescoed the choir behind the main altar with scenes from the life of St. Augustine, a worldly scholar who, faced with the decision to give up his concubine, famously prayed, "Grant me continence and chastity but not just yet." The scenes are rich in landscape and architectural detail.

Piazza Sant'Agostino. ✆ **0577/907012.** Free. Apr–Oct daily 8am–noon and 3–7pm; Nov–Mar Mon–Fri 10am–noon and 3–6pm, Sat 4–6pm, Sun 8am–noon and 3–7pm.

Civic Art

Towers and medieval ambience aside, you'll also discover that San Gimignano is full of frescoes and other art—in churches, public buildings, and even outdoors. In **Piazza Pecori,** reached through the archway to the left of the Collegiata's facade, is a fresco of the "Annunciation," possibly painted in 1482 by the Florentine Domenico Ghirlandaio. The door to the right of the tourist office leads into a courtyard of the **Palazzo del Commune,** where Taddeo di Bartolo's 14th-century "Madonna and Child" is flanked by two works on the theme of justice by Sodoma. The simple 13th-century **church of San Lorenzo in Ponte** (Via Santo Stefano 8) features several frescoes depicting the life of St. Benedict (in one scene he almost gives in to temptation and accepts a loaf of poisoned bread); entry to this church is included in cumulative tickets that also include Santa Maria Assunta, the musei civici, and other sights; see p. 275. **Galleria Continua** introduces contemporary art to the town's medieval flavor, showcasing well-known and emerging artists in a former cinema, a tower, a cellar, and an old apartment (Via Del Castello 11; galleriacontinua.com; ✆ **0577/943134;** daily 10am–1pm and 2–7pm).

Where to Stay & Eat in San Gimignano

San Gimignano's slightly peppery, dry white wine, **Vernaccia di San Gimignano,** is the only DOCG white in Tuscany, and has quite a provenance, too: It's cited in Dante's *Divine Comedy*. A relaxing place to sip a glass or two is **diVinorum,** former stables with a small terrace at Via degli Innocenti 5 (www.divinorumwinebar.com; ✆ **0577/907192**). Combine a glass with a fine selection of panini and focaccia at **Dal Toscano Sapori e Tradizione,** in tranquil Vicolo dell'Oro (www.daltoscanosangimignano.it; ✆ **338/347-1107**). At the famous **Gelateria Dondoli,** Piazza della Cisterna 4 (www.gelateriadondoli.com; ✆ **0577/942244**), master gelato maker Sergio offers creative combinations like refreshing Champelmo, with sparkling wine and pink grapefruit, and *crema di Santa Fina,* made with saffron and pine nuts. The shop also conducts 2-hour gelato-making classes in the morning, booked through the website with prices on request.

Chiribiri ★★ ITALIAN This tiny, vaulted cellar, with a welcoming patio almost next to the walls, seems more serious about what it sends out of the kitchen than do many pricier spots in the center of town. Ravioli with pumpkin, white beans, and sage, beef in Chianti, wild boar stew, and other Tuscan classics are done well and served without fuss.

Piazzetta della Madonna 1. ✆ **0577/941948.** Entrees 8€–12€. Daily 11am–3pm and 7–11pm.

Dorandò ★★ TUSCAN Three stone-walled rooms with brick-vaulted ceilings are the setting for San Gimignano's most elegant dining, though there's nothing fussy about the cooking. Ingredients and recipes are decidedly local—beef is done in a sauce of Chianti classic, local pork comes with an apple puree, and *cibrèo,* a rich ragout, combines chicken livers and giblets scented with ginger and lemon. Reservations a must.

Vicolo dell'Oro 2. www.ristorantedorando.it. ✆ **0577/941862.** Entrees 20€–30€. Tues–Sun noon–2:30pm and 7–9:30pm (daily Easter–Sept).

Hotel l'Antico Pozzo ★★★ When this 15th-century palazzo was a convent, the namesake "ancient well" served a grim purpose—young novices were dangled over the depths when they resisted *droit de seigneur,* the feudal rights of noblemen to have their way with young women living on their lands. The present incarnation is more enlightened, being all about taste, elegance, and comfort. Reached by a broad stone staircase (or an elevator if you choose), many of the character-filled rooms are beamed and frescoed and have nice views of the town and Rocca. All are good-size and beautifully decorated, with classic furnishings that sometimes include canopied beds, along with fine prints and other appointments. A grassy garden is in the rear.

Via San Matteo 87. www.anticopozzo.com. ✆ **0577/942014.** 18 units. 100€–110€ double. Rates include breakfast. Closed 2 weeks In Jan. **Amenities:** Bar; free Wi-Fi.

La Cisterna ★★ The ivy-clad entrance on the town square has been a welcoming sight in San Gimignano for centuries, and quarters that once housed pilgrims now accommodate guests in rooms that vary considerably in size and outlook, some smaller ones overlooking a courtyard and many larger ones opening to balconies with views that extend for miles. Furnishings are simply and unobtrusively traditional Tuscan, with wrought-iron bedsteads and flourishes like arches, tile floors, and stone walls. The restaurant and terrace, along with a view-filled, glassed-in dining room upstairs, serve Tuscan food that's a lot better than you'd expect, given the presence of large tour groups that often pile in for lunch.
Piazza della Cisterna 24. www.hotelcisterna.it. ✆ **0577/940328.** 48 units. 80€–110€ double. Rates include breakfast. Closed Jan to mid-Mar. **Amenities:** Restaurant; bar; free Wi-Fi.

VOLTERRA ★★

29km (18 miles) SW of San Gimignano, 50km (31 miles) W of Siena

Volterra, in the words of British novelist D.H. Lawrence, perches "on a towering great bluff that gets all the winds and sees all the world." Volterra seems higher than any other Tuscan town, rising 540m (1,772 ft.) above the valley below. (You'll see the town long before you arrive.) Lawrence came here to study relics of the Etruscans for whom Volterra, then known as Velathri, was one of the largest cities in their Etruscan confederation.

A classic car race in the hill town of Volterra.

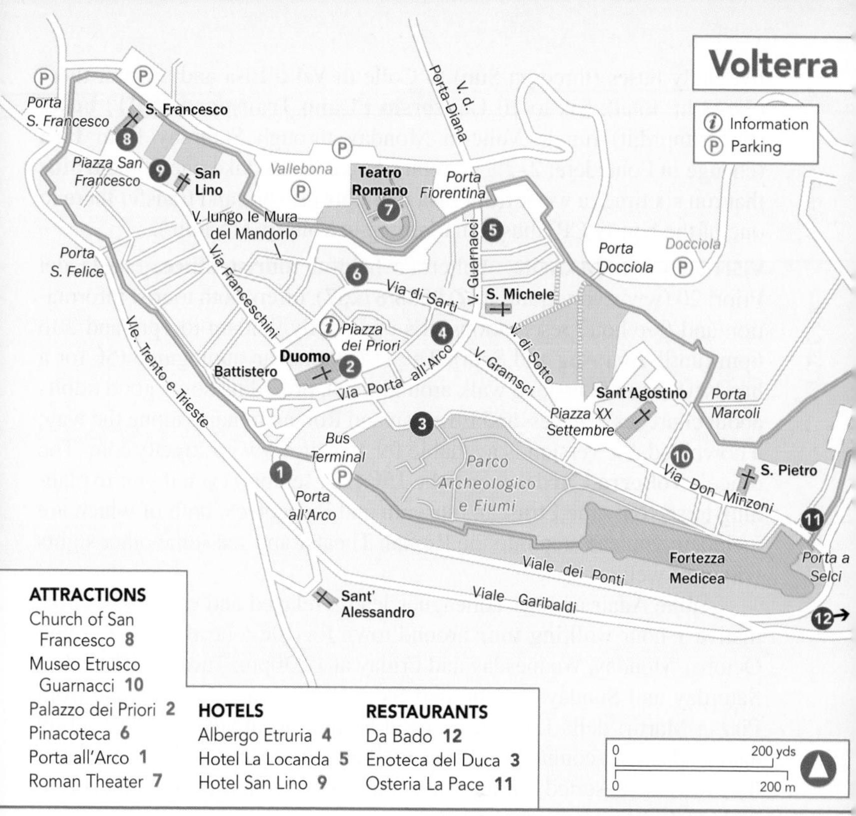

While many visitors come here to see Etruscan bronzes and alabaster urns, if you're a fan of Stephanie Meyer's teen vampire trilogy *Twilight,* you've probably also come to see the hometown of the Volturi vampire coven. Whatever brings you to Volterra, you'll soon find it's a pleasant place, more focused on day-to-day life than on plying the tourist trade.

Essentials

ARRIVING Driving is the easiest way to get here: Volterra is on the SS68 about 30km (19 miles) from the Colle di Val d'Elsa exit on the Florence-Siena highway. From San Gimignano, head southwest on the road to Castel di San Gimignano, where you can pick up the SS68. You can park for free in a large lot below Porta Fiorentina, but you will pay a price—a climb up 350 steps to town. The well-marked underground garage off Piazza Martiri della Libertà is handier, just a short walk from central Piazza dei Priori, and charges about 1€ an hour.

From **Siena,** some 16 daily **Tiemme buses** (www.tiemmespa.it; ✆ **199/168182**) make the 20- to 30-minute trip to **Colle di Val d'Elsa,** from which there are four daily buses to Volterra (50 min.). From **San Gimignano,** first take a bus to Poggibonsi (20 min.), then link up with those Colle di Val d'Elsa buses to Volterra. From **Florence,** take one of five daily buses (three on Sun) to Colle di Val d'Elsa and transfer there (2½–3 hr. total). Six to 10 **Consorsio Pisano Transporti (CPT) buses** (pisa.cttnord.it) run to Volterra Monday through Saturday from **Pisa** (change in Pontedera; 2–2½ hr. total). You can also take one of the **trains** that run six times a week from Pisa to Saline (1½ hr.) and transfer there to one of the hourly CPT buses that run up to Volterra (15 min.).

VISITOR INFORMATION Volterra's helpful **tourist office,** Piazza dei Priori 20 (www.volterratur.it; ✆ **0588/87257**), offers both tourist information and free hotel reservations. It's open daily 9:30am to 1pm and 2 to 6pm (until 7pm Aug and Sept). The office rents an audioguide (5€ for a handset) for an hour-long walk around town, providing some good tidbits about churches, palaces, and Etruscan and Roman remains along the way; a downloadable version is available for free at www.gpsmycity.com. The office's **Volterra Card** is worth the 15€ (12€ seniors) even if you're planning to see only the Etruscan museum and Pinacoteca, both of which are included; you can step into the Roman Theater and see some other sights with it as well.

Annie Adair and her colleagues lead a relaxed and extremely informative 1-hour **walking tour** around town for 10€ a head, April through October Monday, Wednesday and Friday at 12:30pm; Tuesday, Thursday, Saturday and Sunday at 6pm; and Saturday at 11am. Walks leave from Piazza Martiri della Libertà; no need to sign up in advance. The group also leads some country walks, as well as a fascinatingly bizarre tour of the town's deserted insane asylum (www.volterrawalkingtour.com; ✆ **0347/143-5004**).

Exploring Volterra

The most evocative way to enter Volterra is through **Porta all'Arco,** the main 4th-century-B.C. gateway to the Etruscan city. Via die Priori leads steeply uphill from there to Volterra's stony medieval heart, the **Piazza dei Priori,** where the Gothic **Palazzo dei Priori** (1208–57) is said to be the first city hall in Tuscany, and the model for Florence's Palazzo Vecchio; the frescoed council chamber is still a meeting place for the town government. A skull and crossbones outside the main hall handily sums up the medieval view of righteousness: "Remember divine judgement and you will not sin for all eternity." Magistrates meted out justice within the stately chamber, sometimes wasting no time in leveling sentences—guilty parties were promptly thrown from the mullioned windows. Two stone lions flanking the somber facade are symbols of the Florentines, who conquered Volterra in the early 14th century; inscribed in the stone are hatch marks marking the "canna votleranna," the city's medieval unit of measure with which goods were assessed and taxed. The squat tower in the eastern corner is festooned with a little pig *(porcellino)*, hence its name, **Torre del Porcellino.** The beast is actually a boar, a symbol of strength for medieval residents—not only because of its robust heft but also because boars were plentiful in the surrounding woods and the mainstay of their diet (pasta with *ragù di cinghiale* and grilled boar are still menu favorites). The council chamber and bell tower are open mid-March through mid-November daily 9am to 7pm, and mid-November through–mid-March daily 10am to 4:30pm; admission is 10€, 8€ seniors, included with the Volterra Card.

Inside the modest-looking **Duomo,** or Cattedrale di Santa Maria Assunta, around the corner (Piazza dei Priori; ✆ **0588/88261**) is a life-size "Deposition from the Cross," carved in wood around 1228 by anonymous Pisan masters and painted in bright colors. With their fluidity and emotional expressiveness, the figures look surprisingly contemporary. The Duomo is open Monday to Saturday 9am to 5pm, Sunday 1:30pm to 8pm; free admission.

Church of San Francesco ★★ CHURCH Volterra's 13th-century Franciscan church, just inside the Porta San Francesco, has one overwhelming reason to visit: Halfway up the right aisle is the **Cappella Croce del Giorno,** frescoed with the "Legend of the True Cross" in medieval Technicolor by Cenni di Francesco in 1410. While not nearly as beautifully executed as Piero della Francesca's telling of the same story in Arezzo (see p. 262), Cenni's version of this popular medieval tale is quite compelling, especially with his knack for reproducing the dress and architecture of his era. Though the artist worked for some of Florence's most important families, this is his only remaining signed work. It shows a unique style: golden backgrounds, flattened space, and elongated figures with elegant features.

Piazza San Francesco. No phone. Free. Daily 8:30am–6:30pm.

Museo Etrusco Guarnacci ★★★ MUSEUM Volterra's remarkable collection of Etruscan artifacts, reopened in 2022 after a cellar-to-attic refurbishment, is a joyful celebration of the farmers, seafarers, and miners who flourished between the Tiber and Arno rivers from about 800 B.C. until their assimilation by Rome in the A.D. 1st century (the name "Tuscany" is derived from "Etruscan"). The bulk of the holdings are on the ground floor, with row after row of **Etruscan funerary urns,** most from the 3rd century B.C., but some from as early as the 7th century B.C. Ashes were placed in these urns, which were topped with elaborately carved lids—finely dressed characters lounging with wine cups to offer to the gods, or horse and carriage rides into the underworld. One of the finest, the Urna degli Sposi, is a striking portrait of a husband and wife, somewhat dour-faced and full of wrinkles, together in death as in life. The Etruscans also crafted bronze sculptures, and one of the finest is a lanky young man with a beguiling smile known as the "Ombra della Sera" (Shadow of the Evening)—so called because the elongated shape looks like a shadow stretched in evening light.

Via Don Minzoni 15. volterratur.it. ✆ **0588/86347.** 8€, or with the Volterra Card. Mid-Apr to early Nov daily 9am–7pm; Nov to mid-Apr daily 10am–4:30pm.

Pinacoteca e Museo Civico ★ MUSEUM While much of Volterra preserves the Etruscan, Roman, and medieval past, the town's worthy painting gallery transports you to the Renaissance. Room 4 has a remarkably intact 1411 polyptych of the "Madonna with Saints" signed by Taddeo di Bartolo. (The fellow in the red cape and beard in the tiny left tondo is the original Santa Claus, St. Nicholas of Bari.) In room 11 is "Christ in Glory with Saints" (1492), the last great work of Florentine master Domenico Ghirlandaio. If you look hard, you can spot a giraffe being led along the road—an exotic animal that had only recently been acquired by the Medici for their menagerie. In room 12 hangs a remarkably colored "Annunciation" (1491) by Luca Signorelli—note the great rush of feeling as the archangel bursts through the doorway to announce the news to Mary. In the same room is a "Deposition" (1521) by 26-year-old Rosso Fiorentino, a red-headed (and reportedly hot-headed) Florentine painter, who ended up going to France to work at the Chateau Fontainebleau. Painted in his odd color palette of flat grays and reds, it unusually portrays this solemn scene of Christ being taken off the cross as a frantic swirl of action, with sashes flapping in the wind and workers scurrying up and down ladders.
Via del Sarti 1. volterratur.it. ✆ **0588/87580.** 8€, or with the Volterra Card. Mid-Apr to early Nov daily 9am–7pm; Nov to mid-Apr daily 10am–4:30pm.

Porta all'Arco ★★★ HISTORIC GATE Volterra's greatest landmark is this huge, magnificent gate built by the Etruscans as early as the 3rd century B.C. in their 7km (4 miles) circuit of city walls. The round arch contains a keystone that the Romans later incorporated into much of their architecture. On the outside are mounted three basalt heads—features worn away by well over 2,000 years of wind and rain—said possibly to represent the Etruscan gods Tinia (Jupiter), Uni (Juno), and Menrva (Minerva). The gateway almost didn't survive World War II, when retreating German troops decided to blow it up to block the Allied advance through the city. Volterrans dug up the surrounding paving stones and temporarily plugged the opening, convincing the Germans not to destroy a gate that no one could pass through anyway.
Porta all'Arco. No phone. Free.

Teatro Romano (Roman Theater) ★★ ARCHAEOLOGICAL SITE Take a stroll along Via Lungo le Mure, a walkway atop the medieval ramparts, to overlook the impressive remains of Volterra's Roman theater and baths, some of the best-preserved Roman remains in Tuscany. They remained buried for centuries, until the 1950s, when Enrico Fiumi of the Museo Etrusco Guarnacci unearthed them with the assistance of patients from the town's huge, now defunct insane asylum. The theater dates back to the 1st century B.C., though parts of it were torn up for building materials during the construction of the medieval walls. The view from up here is the best way to see it all, and for free, but if you do want to wander among the stones, there's an entrance down on Viale Francesco Ferrucci.

Viale Francesco Ferrucci. ✆ **0588/86050.** 8€, or with the Volterra Card. Mid-Apr to early Nov daily 9am–7pm; Nov to mid-Apr daily 10am–4:30pm.

Where to Stay in Volterra

Staying within Volterra's city walls can be a transporting experience, especially in the quiet of the evening when the city seems to drift back into the Middle Ages. Choices are fairly limited, so book ahead if you're planning a visit between May and September.

Albergo Etruria ★★ The lounge and guest kitchen are homey touches, but the real attraction of this cozy lodging is the roof garden, a leafy retreat where the greenery is backed by the town's brick towers and tile rooftops. Parts of an Etruscan wall enhance the historic character of the old house, yet rooms are up-to-date, filled with comfortable, attractive furniture handpicked by the friendly owners. The Piazza dei Priori is only a few steps from this stylish haven.

Via Matteotti 32. www.albergoetruria.it. ✆ **0588/87377.** 18 units. 100€–125€ double. Rates include breakfast. **Amenities:** Free Wi-Fi.

Hotel La Locanda ★★ A location just inside the town walls makes this converted convent a good choice if traveling by car, since parking is just steps away. High-ceilinged rooms are done in soothing pastels, a few have massage showers and whirlpool tubs, and most show off a patch or two of exposed stone and timber. The piazza and other sights are an easy walk away, and a quiet terrace in the back offers a breath of fresh air.

Via Guarnacci 24. www.hotel-lalocanda.com. ✆ **0588/81547.** 18 units. 90€–120€ double. Rates include breakfast. **Amenities:** Restaurant; bar; free Wi-Fi.

Hotel San Lino ★ There's a slightly utilitarian ring to the hallways and some guest rooms here, probably because for many centuries the 13th-century palazzo served as a cloistered convent. The enclosed gardens are still in place, and a little terrace looks across miles of countryside. There's also a small pool, the only one inside the city walls and reason enough to stay here in the summer. Some rooms are merely functional, while others are nicely turned out with a mix of modern and traditional furnishings. The best rooms overlook the garden and sweeping landscapes beyond.

Via San Lino 6 (near Porta San Francesco). www.hotelsanlino.net. ✆ **0588/85250.** 44 units. 85€–90€ double. Rates include breakfast. **Amenities:** Restaurant; bar; pool; free Wi-Fi.

Where to Eat in Volterra

Bar Trattoria Da Badò ★★★ TUSCAN Owner Giacomo's mom, Lucia, is in the kitchen of this favorite in the San Lazzero neighborhood, just outside the walls. She prepares a few daily choices that often include *zuppa volterrana* (bread and vegetable soup) and *baccalà rifatto* (pan-fried salted codfish stewed with tomatoes), along with *pappardelle alla lepre* (wide fettuccine with rabbit sauce) and other hearty pastas well suited to the homey, stone arched surroundings. Lucia also makes the jams that fill her delicious homemade tortes (cakes). A **cafe** in front serves coffee and pastries all day.

Da Bado. Borgo San Lazzero 9. ✆ **0588/80402.** Entrees 8€–13€. Thurs–Tues 12:30–2:30pm and 7:30–10pm.

Enoteca del Duca ★★ MODERN TUSCAN At Volterra's finest restaurant, you can choose either the elegant high-ceilinged dining room, a bottle-lined enoteca, or a pretty patio out back to enjoy innovative and refined takes on Tuscan classics. All the salamis and cheeses are from local producers, *lavagnette* (homemade egg pasta) comes with a sauce of celery and pecorino pesto, and local beef is grilled to perfection. Some of the wines come from the owners' vineyards.

Via di Castello 2. www.enoteca-delduca-ristorante.it. ✆ **0588/81510.** Entrees 15€–25€. Wed–Mon noon–3pm and 7–10pm (Fri–Sun only some winter months).

crafty VOLTERRANS

The Etruscans made good use of the easily mined local stone, a translucent calcium sulfate known as **alabaster**—witness the hundreds of alabaster sarcophagi in the Guarnacci museum (see p. 281). Alabaster became a major industry in Volterra again at the end of the 19th century, when the material was much in demand for lampshades, with the rise of electric lighting. Today local artisans work alabaster into a mind-boggling array of objects, from fine art pieces to some remarkable kitsch.

Plaques around town denote the workshops of some of the best traditional artisans, where you will find only hand-worked items. Via Porta all'Arco has several fine workshops, including internationally known **Paolo Sabatini,** at no. 45 (✆ **0588/81515**), whose alabaster sculptural pieces often combine wood and stone. The large **Rossi Alabastri** shop (www.rossialabastri.com; ✆ **0588/86133**) at Piazzetta della Pescheria shows off some especially distinctive lighting pieces, as well as alabaster bowls, fruits, and all sorts of other easily portable items. At **alab'Arte,** Via Don Minzoni 18 (www.alabarte.com; ✆ **340/718189** or 340/981-6908), Roberto Cini and Giorgio Finazzo create sculptural pieces of museum quality—in fact, they are often called upon to help restore sculpture in churches and museums around Italy. You'll find the work of many local artisans at the **Società Cooperativa Artieri Alabastro,** Piazza dei Priori 5 (www.artierialabastro.it; ✆ **0588/86135**), a sales showroom for smaller workshops. To learn more about the town's alabaster industry, visit the **Ecomuseo dell'Alabastro,** Piazzetta Minucci 2 (www.comune.volterra.pi.it; ✆ **0588/87580;** admission 8€ or with the Volterra Card; daily 9:30am–7pm).

Alabaster isn't the only craft in town. **Fabula Etrusca,** Via Lungo le Mura del Mandorlo 10 (www.fabulaetrusca.it; ✆ **0588/87401**), sells intricate handmade jewelry based on original Etruscan designs. For prints created from hand-engraved zinc plates—another local specialty—visit **L'Istrice,** Via Porta all'Arco 23 (www.laboistrice.it; ✆ **0347/726-9888**).

Osteria La Pace ★★ VOLTERRAN/TUSCAN No restaurant in Volterra can boast of such a long provenance, serving since 1600 and in the hands of the same family since 1939. The old brick walls and vaults look just as they must have 400 years ago, and the kitchen follows suit with perfectly prepared versions of such Volterra classics as tagliatelle with chestnuts and mushrooms and a hearty stew of wild boar.

Via Don Giovanni Minzoni 29. www.osteria-lapace.com. ✆ **0588/86511.** Entrees 10€–24€. Thurs–Tues 10am–3pm and 6:30–11pm.

LUCCA ★★

72km (45 miles) W of Florence

Lucca is the forgotten Tuscan town, just far enough off the beaten track to be left out of package tours. But travelers have been waxing poetic about the place for a long time. In the 19th century, novelist Henry James called Lucca "a charming mixture of antique character and modern inconsequence"—the "inconsequence" bit meaning that Lucca, beautifully preserved within 16th- and 17th-century walls (designed in part, allegedly, by Leonardo da Vinci), is much more a remnant of the past than a part of the modern world. The Etruscans were here as early as 700 B.C., and the Romans after them; the city flourished as a silk center in the Middle Ages. No doubt such a long and colorful history inspired the romantic operas of Lucca native son Giacomo Puccini (1858–1924), composer of *Tosca, Madame Butterfly,* and *La Bohème.* Lucca can seem like a stage set, and it's easy to look at the tiered facade of the church of San Michele and hear the strains of Puccini's aria "O Mio Bambino Caro."

Essentials

ARRIVING Lucca is on the Florence-Viareggio **train** line, with about 30 trains daily (fewer on Sun) connecting with **Florence** (75–90 min.). A similar number of trains make the short hop to/from **Pisa** (30 min.). The **station** is a short walk south of Porta San Pietro. You can stash your bags at **Tourist Center Lucca,** on the piazza in front of the station (www.touristcenterlucca.com; ✆ **0583/494401**), open daily 10am to 6m; the cost per bag is 3€ for 3 hours and 5€ a day. This is handy if you want to stop in Lucca on your way west to Pisa, the Cinque Terre, or Liguria.

By **car,** the A11 runs from Florence past Prato, Pistoia, and Montecatini before hitting Lucca. Inside the walls, you'll usually find a pay-parking space underground at **Mazzini** (enter from the east, through the Porta Elisa, and take an immediate right); aboveground parking areas surround the other gates as well, with rates from 1€ an hour.

Autolinee Toscana (www.at-bus.it; ✆ **800/142242**) service runs hourly from Florence (70 min.) and from Pisa (50 min.) to Lucca.

GETTING AROUND A set of *navette* (electric **minibuses**) whiz down the city's peripheral streets, but the flat center is easily traversed on foot. Taxis line up at the train station (✆ **0583/494-989**), Piazzale Verdi

Get in the Saddle

The popular way to get around Lucca, you'll soon learn, is via bike. Enjoy the medieval lanes and squares on foot, but equip yourself with two wheels for a ride on the **Passeggiata della Mura,** atop the medieval walls. You can do so in style on one of the neon-green or Barbie-pink models from **Antonio Poli** at Piazza Santa Maria 42 (www.biciclettepoli.com; ✆ **0583/493787;** daily 8:30am–7:30pm, closed Sun mid-Nov to Feb and Mon mornings year-round). On the same street, bikes are also available from **Cicli Bizzarri,** Piazza Santa Maria 32 (www.ciclibizzarri.net; ✆ **0583/496682;** daily 8:30am–12:30pm and 2–7:30pm, closed Sun mid-Sept to Feb). The going rates are 4€ an hour, 16€ for the day.

(✆ **0583/581305**), and Piazza Napoleone (✆ **0583/491-646**). To get around like a Lucchese, rent a bike—see box above for rental information.

VISITOR INFORMATION There's a **tourist office** on Piazzale Verdi next to Porta San Donato (www.turismo.lucca.it; ✆ **0583/538150;** daily 9:30am–6:30pm, closes at 4:30pm Nov–Mar). Another office is outside the train station on Piazza Curtatone (✆ **0583/442213;** Wed–Sat 9:30am–1:30pm, also Tues and Thurs 2:30–5:30pm). A walking tour of the city leaves from the Piazzale Verdi office daily at 2pm; the fee is 10€.

SPECIAL EVENTS For a few days at the end of October, the city is taken over by costumed attendees of the **Lucca Comics & Games** convention (www.luccacomicsandgames.com).

Exploring Lucca

Lucca has many remarkable architectural landmarks, but the first you'll notice are its incredibly intact city walls—more than 4km (2½ miles) of them, with 11 bastions and six gates; some stretches are 18m (59 ft.) wide. Topping the walls, the tree-shaded **Passeggiata delle Mura** can be circumnavigated on foot or by bike (see "Get in the Saddle," above), as you peer across Lucca's rooftops toward the hazy mountains. A stretch near the northeast corner of the walls overlooks the baroque gardens of the **Palazzo Pfanner,** a 17th-century nobleman's home; you can tour a few rooms of the palace and stroll in the gardens, but the formal plantings and an exquisite external staircase are just as impressive when viewed from above on the walls (www.palazzopfanner.it;

Cathedral San Michele in bike-loving Lucca.

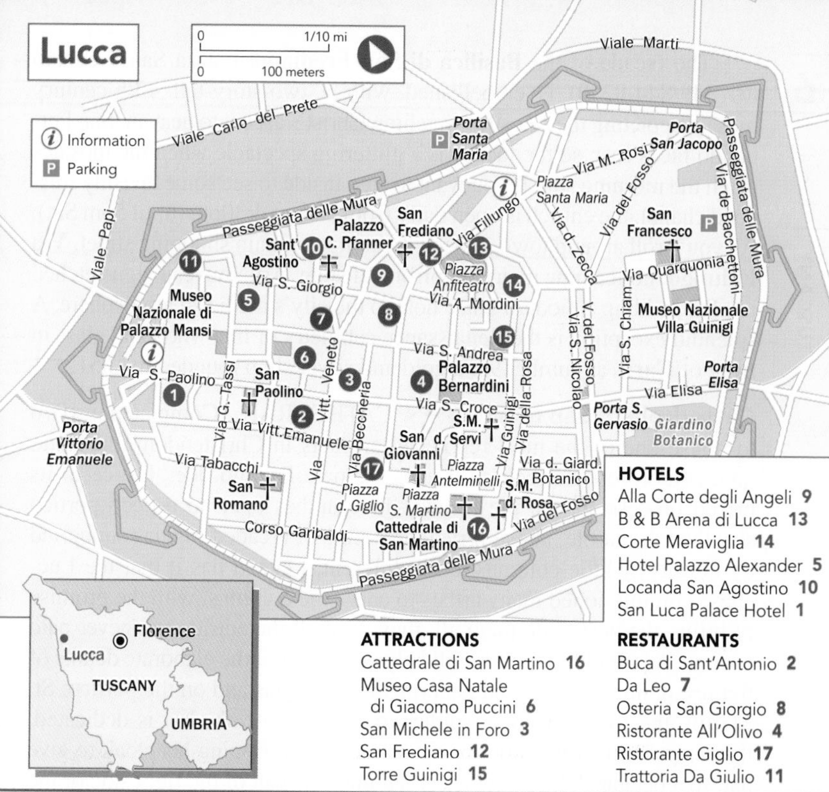

✆ **0583/95215;** 6.50€, 5.50€ seniors and children 12–16, under 12 free; house and garden 4.50€; house or garden 4€ seniors and children 12–16; Apr–Nov daily 10am–6pm).

The most curious feature of Lucca's street plan is **Piazza Anfiteatro,** near the north end of Via Fillungo, the main shopping street. This semicircle of handsome medieval houses stands atop what were once the grandstands of a 1st- or 2nd-century-A.D. Roman amphitheater; some of the little alleys leading into the square from surrounding, elliptical Via dell'Anfiteatro are the original entrances to the theater, with portions of their marble archways still visible. Nearby, **Torre Guinigi** (www.comune.lucca.it; ✆ **0583/48090**) rises from the 14th-century palace of one of Lucca's most powerful families at Via Sant'Andrea 41; the tower is topped with a little grove of seven holm oaks, typical of the gardens that once flourished atop hundreds of similar tower houses around the city. Climb the 230 steps for a spectacular view of Lucca's skyline, the snowcapped Apuan Alps, and the rolling green valley of the River Serchio (5€ adults, 4€ seniors and children 6–12; daily Jan–late-Mar and Oct–Dec 10am–4pm, late Mar–May 10am–6:30pm [until 7:30pm weekends], June–late Sept 10am–7:30pm [until 8pm weekends], and late Sept 10am–6:30pm).

The facade of the **Basilica di San Frediano,** Piazza San Frediano (✆ **349/844-0290**) is embellished with a two-story-tall 13th-century mosaic depicting the Apostles watching Christ's ascent to heaven. San Fernando faces east, so the facade is a glittering spectacle when the mosaics catch the morning sun. If you want to step inside to see some lavishly frescoed chapel, the church is open daily from 9am to 4:30pm (until 5pm Sat). As you stroll around town, especially along the main shopping street, **Via Fillungo,** notice how many shopfronts display Art Nouveau signs etched in glass, adding a modern grace note to the city's medieval atmosphere. A splendid exception is the Renaissance cabinetry of fine wood and glass in front of **Carli,** at number 95, a gold and silver shop founded in 1651.

Cattedrale di San Martino ★★ CATHEDRAL Completed in 1070 to house one of the most renowned artifacts in Christendom, the Volto Santo (more on that below), Lucca's ornate Duomo does justice to its prized procession. On the facade, three arches open to a deep portico sheathed in marble; above it rise three tiers of arcaded loggias supported by dozens of little columns, each different. Legend has it that the Lucchese commissioned many artists to carve the columns, with the promise of hiring the best to do them all; they used all the entries and never paid anyone. A pair of binoculars will help you pick out the elaborate details of figures, animals, vines, and patterns in the loggias and on the portico. St. Martin, the former Roman soldier to whom the cathedral is dedicated, figures prominently—look for the statue of him ripping his cloak to give half to a beggar. A labyrinth is carved into the wall of the right side of the portico, for the faithful to make a figurative pilgrimage to the center of the maze, as if to Jerusalem, before entering the church. A Latin inscription reads, "This is the labyrinth built by Daedalus of Crete; all who entered therein were lost, save Theseus, thanks to Ariadne's thread."

Inside, the handsome sweep of inlaid pavement and the high altar are the work of 15th-century Lucca native Matteo Civitali. He also designed the **Tempietto,** an octagonal, freestanding chapel of white and red marble in the left nave, where the famous **Volto Santo** is kept—a venerable crucifix said to have been carved by Nicodemus, the man who helped remove Christ's body from the cross. (See "A Crucifix with a Mind of Its Own," p. 289). The cathedral's other great treasure is the **Tomb of Ilaria Carretto Guinigi,** the wife of Lucca ruler Paolo Guinigi, who died in 1405 at the age of 26; she lives on, accompanied by a little dog (a sign of her faithfulness) in a beautiful image carved by Jacopo della Quercia, the Sienese sculptor whose work heavily influenced Michelangelo. An unseen presence is that of the great composer Giacomo Puccini, who was born nearby in 1858 and sang in the church choir.

Piazza San Martino. www.museocattedralelucca.it. ✆ **0583/490530.** 3€ adults; 2€ ages 6–14. Mon–Thurs 10am–5pm; Fri–Sat 10am–6pm; Sun noon–5pm.

A crucifix WITH A MIND OF ITS OWN

Throughout the medieval era, the legend of the **Volto Santo** attracted pilgrims to Lucca from throughout Europe. Tradition claimed that when Nicodemus, a follower of Christ, was carving this crucifix, he did not complete the face, fearing he could not do the holy visage justice. He fell asleep—and when he awoke, a beautiful face had miraculously been carved on the crucifix. Nicodemus stashed the Volto Santo crucifix in a cave for safekeeping; centuries later, an 8th-century Italian bishop on pilgrimage to the Holy Land discovered it (apparently the location had come to him in a dream). The bishop put the crucifix adrift in a boat, which magically washed up on the shores of northern Italy, where the relic somehow got into a driverless wagon pulled by two oxen, and arrived in Lucca. The crucifix was first placed in the basilica of San Frediano but had other ideas and transported itself to the cathedral. On May 3 and September 13 to 14, the Lucchese walk in a candlelit procession from San Frediano to the cathedral, where the famous statue awaits them, dressed in gold and wearing a gold crown.

Museo Casa Natale di Giacomo Puccini ★ MUSEUM Walking around Lucca, a Puccini aria could pop into your head at any moment—but the maestro comes most vividly to life in **Piazza Cittadella,** where in the guise of a bronze statue he sits, legs crossed, in an armchair. Puccini was born around the corner at 9 Corte San Lorenzo and lived there until he left for Milan in his early twenties. The modest-yet-comfortable rooms display some of his scores, random pieces of heavy furniture, and, most notably, the piano on which he often composed.

9 Corte San Lorenzo. www.puccinimuseum.org. ✆ **0583/584028.** 7€. Mar Wed–Mon 10am–6pm; Apr–Sept daily 10am–7pm; Oct Wed–Mon 10am–6pm; Nov to mid-Dec Mon and Wed–Fri 10am–2pm, Sat–Sun 10am–5pm; mid-Dec to mid-Jan Mon–Fri daily 10am–5pm; Jan–Feb Wed–Mon 10am–5pm.

San Michele in Foro ★★ CHURCH The magnificent facade of the Cattedrale di San Martino is matched, maybe even outdone, by the delicately stacked arches and arcades of this 12th-century church, which rises above the site of Lucca's Roman forum. The show begins just above the main portal, where St. Michael slays a dragon; above that two lions flank a rose window. Then begin four soaring tiers of little columns, inlaid with intricate carvings and topped with human heads, flowers, and animals; above each row is a frieze on which carved animals jump and run. The two narrow top tiers are capped by a bronze-winged statue of **St. Michael the Archangel,** flanked by two trumpeting cohorts. Lucchese claim to see a distinct glow emanating at sunset from St. Michael's right hand, created by a sapphire that, according to legend, he wears on his finger. The interior is rather dull by comparison, although in the right transept is a fine painting of "Sts. Roch, Sebastian, Jerome, and Helen" by Filippino Lippi. Born of a notorious relationship between the painter Fra Filippo Lippi and a young nun, Lucrezia Buti, Filippino became one of the most accomplished painters of the late 15th century.

Piazza San Michele. ✆ **0583/48459.** Free. Daily 9am–6pm.

Where to Stay in Lucca

Rentals in the countryside around Lucca include **Bertolli Villas** (www.bertollivillas.com; ✆ **335/776-7610**) in San Colombano Alto, 11km (7 miles north), where two stylishly comfortably houses on an olive estate are set in beautiful gardens and have private pools; 1,300€–3,300€ for six guests for 5 nights.

MODERATE

Alla Corte degli Angeli ★★ In this beautifully restored pink *palazzo* just off Via Fillungo, the main shopping street, colorful murals incorporate a different flower in each room, and rich draperies and upholstered headboards pick up on the themes. A scattering of antique pieces and excellent lighting enhance the stylish comfort. Bathrooms are good-sized, and some have both showers and hydromassage tubs. Rooms on an upper floor are filled with sunlight—third-floor Paolina, with two exposures, is an especially bright choice.

Via degli Angeli 23 (off Via Fillungo). www.allacortedegliangeli.com. ✆ **0583/469204.** 21 units. 120€–200€ double. Rates include breakfast. Closed 2 weeks Jan. **Amenities:** Bikes; concierge; free Wi-Fi.

Hotel Palazzo Alexander ★★ Stepping into this 12th-century palace tucked into medieval streets is like walking onto an operatic stage set, and the feeling certainly doesn't let up as you settle into rooms named after Puccini operas and done with gilded and polished wood, reproduction antiques, old prints, and plush fabrics. *Putti* (cherubs) grin down from frescoed ceilings, and some of the especially charming suites have vaulted and beamed ceilings that put a luxury spin on Rodolfo's *La Bohème* garret. Meanwhile, marble baths, Jacuzzi tubs in some rooms, excellent beds and fine linens, and other amenities are thoroughly up to date.

Via Santa Giustina 28. www.hotelpalazzoalexander.it. ✆ **0583/583571.** 9 units. 90€–175€ double. Rates include breakfast. Closed Jan. **Amenities:** Bar; free Wi-Fi.

Locanda Sant'Agostino ★★ Three large, stylish, and atmospheric guest rooms are set in a moody old palace. Four-poster beds, polished antiques, old oil paintings, and elegant wall coverings provide character and luxury, enhanced by a wisteria-shaded terrace and the raised hearth in the attractive lounge/breakfast room. The aptly named Teatro room comes with a big bonus: a private balcony with views over the ruins of a Roman theater.

Piazza San Agostino 3. www.locandasantagostino.it. ✆ **0583/572615.** 3 units. 120€–170€ double. Rates include breakfast. **Amenities:** Free Wi-Fi.

San Luca Palace Hotel ★★ A sense of tasteful, old-world comfort begins in the downstairs hall and sitting room and continues into the large guest rooms, with parquet floors and well-coordinated fabrics and draperies. Among the inviting flourishes are small "reading" alcoves with day beds in many rooms. This old palace just inside the walls also has plenty of practical conveniences, including an easy-to-reach location (parking is adjacent) just a short stroll from the sights and train station. There's no in-house restaurant, but a bar off the lobby serves light snacks.

Via San Paolino 103 (off Piazza Napoleone). www.sanlucapalace.com. ✆ **0583/317446.** 26 units. 120€–180€ double. Rates include breakfast. **Amenities:** Bar; free Wi-Fi.

INEXPENSIVE

B&B Arena di Lucca ★★★ Hosts Alex and Livia make sure the guests in their old apartment, a parcel of prime real estate overlooking the Arena, feel as if they have come for a stay in a family home. Terracotta floors, oil paintings, and comfy sofas and chairs fill the shared lounge, while two high-ceilinged rooms also face the lively scene below from small balconies; two other rooms look onto the atmospheric Via del Anfiteatro. The hosts serve a large breakfast by the kitchen hearth.

Via dell'Anfiteatro 16. www.bbarenalucca.com. ✆ **0389/948355.** 4 units. 65€–120€ double. Rates include breakfast. **Amenities:** Free Wi-Fi.

Corte Meraviglia ★★ Accommodations at this price rarely come with such atmospheric surroundings, a gracious old palace on the back lanes not far from the Piazza Anfiteatro. Decor in the lounge and well-equipped rooms tucked away on a couple of floors is comfortably shabby chic, and they share a shady terrace that opens to extensive gardens. Ceiling fans and thick walls stand in for air-conditioning, and they do the trick. Friendly host Paolo serves a light breakfast and is a welcoming presence.

Gia Via Nuova 63, Lucca. www.cortemeraviglia-lucca.com. ✆ **339/778-6914.** 4 units. 59€–115€ double. Rates include breakfast. **Amenities:** Garden; free Wi-Fi.

Where to Eat in Lucca

Lucca's extra-virgin olive oil appears on every restaurant table. An atmospheric 19th-century pastry shop, **Taddeucci,** Piazza San Michele 34 (www.buccellatotaddeucci.com; ✆ **0583/494933**), is famous for *buccellato,* a Lucca specialty—a ring-shaped sweet bread flavored with raisins and fennel seeds. For a fortifying snack, stop by **Amedo Giusti,** Via Santa Lucia 18 (✆ **0583/496285**), where focaccia with many different toppings emerges piping-hot from the oven. Sample Lucca's excellent DOC wines at **Enoteca Vanni,** Piazza San Salvatore 7 (www.enotecavanni.com; ✆ **0583/491902**). The atmospheric **Antica Bottega di Prospero,** Via Santa Lucia 13 (✆ **0583/494875**), will give you a deep appreciation of

Lucca's sophisticated palate—it's stocked with local olive oils, preserved vegetables, and an amazing array of dried beans and grains.

EXPENSIVE

Buca di Sant'Antonio ★ LUCCHESE Sitting in the atmospheric surroundings of Lucca's most venerable, 3½-centuries-old dining room is a terribly pleasant experience—and usually requires a dinnertime reservation. Quietly formal service (with waiters in bow ties) and a welcoming glass of Prosecco nicely accent a meal of traditional Lucchese dishes enjoyed beneath a canopy of hanging copper pots. The menu changes regularly but always includes fresh, house-made pastas and such local specialties as *farro alla garfagnana* (spelt, or barley, soup) and *coniglio in umido* (rabbit stew). A house dessert is the town's *buccellato,* the ring-shaped confection named for the bread that sustained Roman legionnaires.

Via della Cervia 3 (just W of Piazza San Michele). www.bucadisantantonio.com. ✆ **0583/55881.** Entrees 15€–25€. Tues–Sat 12:30–3pm and 7:30–10:30pm; Sun 12:30–3pm.

Ristorante Giglio ★★ LUCCHESE White tablecloths, fine china, and marble mantelpieces do justice to the setting in the 18th-century Palazzo Arnolfini, and the well-laid tables on the terrace add a splash of elegance to quietly refined Piazza Giglio out front. The food is reassuringly Old World and traditionally Tuscan. Many Lucchese regulars would not think of dining anywhere else, or wavering from a meal of the house specials: tagliatelle topped with shaved white truffles, perfectly grilled beef tenderloin with porcini mushrooms, and for dessert, Lucchese *buccellato* (sweet bread) filled with ice cream and berries.

Piazza del Giglio. ristorantegiglio.com. ✆ **0583/494058.** Entrees 20€–45€. Thurs–Mon 12:30–2:30pm and 7:30–10pm.

MODERATE

Osteria San Giorgio ★ LUCCHESE/TUSCAN On a quiet street near the Piazza Anfiteatro, this local favorite has a courtyard out front and comfortably informal rooms decorated with old photos. The menu is geared to neighbors looking for a home-cooked meal: hearty *farro alla luchesse* (beans and barley) soup, *coniglio stufato con olive taggiasche e uva* (rabbit stew with olives and grapes), and a local seafood favorite, *baccalà alla griglia con ceci* (grilled cod with chickpeas).

Via San Giorgio 26. ✆ **0583/953233.** Entrees 9€–13€. Daily noon–3pm and 7–10:30pm.

Ristorante All'Olivo ★★ LUCCHESE/SEAFOOD This is where the Lucchese come when they're in the mood for fish. Taking a seat in one of its four comfortable and elegant little rooms—one with a fireplace, another like a covered garden—definitely elevates a meal to a special occasion. Seafood is brought in daily from the nearby Tuscan port of Viareggio and

appears in a bounty of pastas, grilled platters, a nice choice of *antipasti di mare,* and a simply prepared catch of the day. Hearty roasts, grilled Tuscan steaks, and several vegetarian pasta dishes are also on the menu.
Piazza San Quirico 1. www.ristoranteolivo.it. ✆ **0583/493129.** Entrees 12€–25€. Fixed meat menu 55€; fixed seafood menu 65€. Daily 12:30–3:30pm and 7–11:30pm.

INEXPENSIVE

Da Leo ★★★ LUCCHESE/TUSCAN This pleasantly old-fashioned room with plastic-draped tablecloths has been serving local classics for 50 years, and the *arrosto di maialino con patate* (roast piglet and potatoes), *ontadin* (rabbit), and other authentic Lucchese fare remain as good as ever. This is the place to try the typically Luccan *zuppa di farro,* a soup made with spelt, a barley-like grain cooked al dente.
Via Tegrimi 1 (just N of Piazza San Salvatore). trattoriadaleo.webnode.it. ✆ **0583/492236.** Entrees 9€–12€. Mon–Sat noon–3pm and 7:30–10pm; Sun noon–3pm.

Trattoria Da Giulio ★★★ LUCCHESE/TUSCAN You may have to go out of your way to find this local favorite, tucked away on back streets near the northwest corner of the city walls. The family has been feeding the neighborhood since 1945, and it seems like everyone is on a first-name basis with the busy staff that dashes between the tables in the three brightly lit rooms. A long menu of local classics includes *salsicce con fagioli all'ucelletto,* sausage with beans in tomato sauce and sage; *tagliatelle alla ontadina,* with fresh tomatoes, basil and oregano; and a few variations of *cavallo* (horsemeat, served raw, *tartara,* and otherwise). Excellent house wines are available by the pitcher.
Via delle Conce 25. ✆ **0583/55948.** Entrees 8€–13€. Mon–Sat noon–2:30pm and 7–10:30pm.

Lucca Entertainment & Nightlife

Every evening at 7pm from April through October, the church of San Giovanni (Piazza di San Giovanni) hosts an opera recital or orchestral concert honoring hometown composer Giacomo Puccini, in a series called **Puccini e la sua Lucca** (www.puccinielasualucca.com). Tickets are 25€ (20€ for those 22 and under) and can be purchased all day inside San Giovanni. Just try listening to "Nessun Dorma" in this lovely church in the composer's hometown without chills running up your spine. Lago di Massaciuccoli is the backdrop for the summer **Puccini Festival** ★ in nearby Torre del Lago, where the composer built a villa (www.puccinifestival.it; ✆ **0584/359322**); tickets can be purchased online in advance (20€–125€).

PISA ★★

85km (53 miles) south of Lucca, 76km (47 miles) W of Florence

It's ironic that one of the most famous landmarks in a country that has given Western civilization much of its greatest art and architecture is in fact an engineering failure. Built on sandy soil too unstable to support so much heavy marble, Pisa's famous tower began to lean even while it was still under construction. Eight centuries later, however, the Leaning Tower puts Pisa on the map. Seeing the tower, maybe climbing it, and touring other landmarks on the Piazza del Duomo is probably why you come to this city near Tuscany's northwestern coast.

Pisa began as a seaside settlement around 1000 B.C. and was expanded into a naval trading port by the Romans in the 2nd century B.C. By the 11th century, the city had grown into one of the peninsula's most powerful maritime republics. In 1284, however, Pisa's battle fleet was destroyed by Genoa's navy at Meloria (off Livorno), forcing Pisa's long slide into twilight. Florence took control in 1406 and, despite a few small rebellions, stayed in charge until Italian unification in the 1860s.

Pisa is lively and cosmopolitan, home to a university founded in 1343, one of Europe's oldest. Once away from the Piazza del Duomo, however, there's not much to do other than soak in the city's medieval and Renaissance ambience—it's a quite doable day trip from Florence or nearby Lucca.

Essentials

ARRIVING Around 25 trains run every day between **Lucca** and Pisa (25–35 min.); from **Florence,** 50 daily trains make the trip (60–90 min.). On the Lucca line, day-trippers should get off at **San Rossore station,** a few blocks west of Piazza del Duomo and the Leaning Tower. All other trains pull into **Pisa Centrale** station (eventually the Lucca one will too). **Left Luggage Pisa,** at the east end of platform one (www.leftluggage tuscany.com), is open daily 8am to 7pm; the cost per bag is 10€ per day, 4€ an hour, 6€ for 2 hours, 8€ for 3 hours. This is handy if you want to stop in Pisa for a look at the tower on your way to somewhere else—if you're on the way from Genoa to Florence, for instance. The office also allows customers to recharge their electronic devices for free.

There's a Florence-Pisa fast **highway** along the Arno valley. Take the SS12 or SS12r from Lucca. Parking anywhere near the Duomo is not easy. Best bet is the Pietrasantina lot, in the northwest corner of the city and well-marked as you exit the autostrada at Pisa Nord; it's free, within walking distance of the Duomo, and also connected by frequent shuttle-bus service (1€ on the bus or at the I in the lot). For details on parking locations and charges, see **www.pisamo.it**.

Tuscany's main international airport, **Galileo Galilei (PSA;** www.pisa-airport.com), just 3km (2 miles) south of the center, is served by many European carriers, with service to and from London, Paris, Amsterdam, Frankfurt, and other international hubs. The automated **PisaMover** tram runs every 5 to 8 minutes between the airport terminal and Pisa

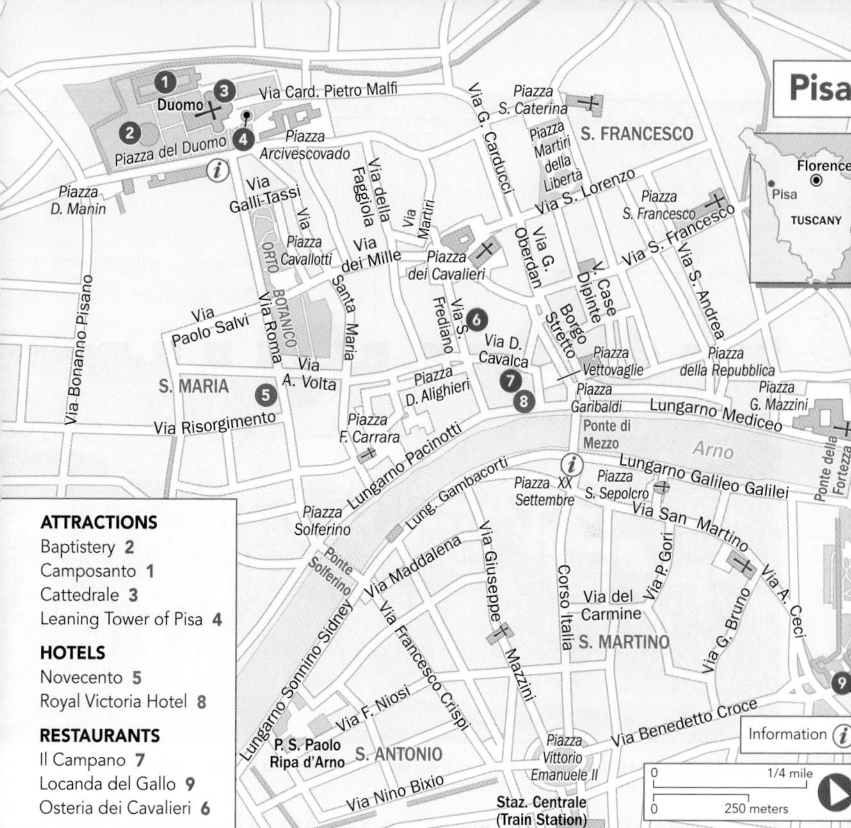

Centrale station; the fare is 5€ (pisa-mover.com). A metered **taxi** ride to the station or Piazza del Duomo costs 10€ to 15€ (drivers accept credit cards).

GETTING AROUND **CPT** (pisa.cttnord.it; ✆ **800/570-530** in Italy) runs the city's **buses.** The LAM Rossa bus run from Pisa Centrale station to the Piazza del Duomo (fare 1.80€; buy tickets at newsstands and tobacco shops or from machines at the stops). It's also an easy and pleasant 25-minute walk from the station to the Duomo on a route that will take you through the heart of the medieval city. Head north from the station on Corso Italia toward the river, and from the other bank follow Borgo Stretto to Via Dini and through Piazza Cavalieri toward the Piazza del Duomo.

Taxis can be found on Piazza della Stazione and Piazza del Duomo. Call a radio taxi at ✆ **050/541600.**

VISITOR INFORMATION The main **tourist office** is near the Leaning Tower on Piazza del Duomo (www.turismo.pisa.it; ✆ **050/550100**); it's open daily 10am to 6pm (until 4pm some winter months). Another office is near the river on Piazza XX Settembre and is open Monday through

Streets leading up to the Piazza dei Miracoli are lined with craft and souvenir sellers.

Friday 9am to 1pm, Tuesday also 2:30 to 5pm. This is where you can pick up a basic map (with few street names) for free or a detailed one for 3€. The offices also offer several insight-filled **walking tours** focusing on the medieval city, the banks of the Arno, and the design and history of the Piazza del Duomo. Tours leave around noon from outside the Piazza del Duomo office (times vary) on Friday, Saturday, and Sunday; the cost is 13€.

Exploring Pisa

On a grassy lawn wedged into the northwest corner of the city walls, medieval Pisans created one of the most dramatic squares in the world. Often dubbed **Piazza dei Miracoli** (Piazza of Miracles) or **Campo dei Miracoli** (Field of Miracles), Piazza del Duomo's elegant buildings epitomize the Pisan-Romanesque style. A subtle part of the appeal, aside from the beauty of the white marble-sheathed buildings, is the spatial geometry: If you were to look at an aerial photo of the square and draw connect-the-dot lines between the doors and other focal points, you'd come up with all sorts of perfect triangles and tangential lines. Less subtle are the visitors posing for photos angled to make it seem they're propping up the leaning tower.

Aside from immersing yourself in these spectacles, take a little time to see the rest of the city, where much of the historic center is a well-preserved slice of the Middle Ages and Renaissance. From the Duomo, walk south on Via Santa Maria and turn left onto Via dei Mille to reach **Piazza dei Cavalieri,** the seat of government when Pisa was one of the world's most powerful maritime republics. Dominating the square is a statue of Cosimo I Medici, a reminder that Florence conquered Pisa in the early 1500s and the city never regained its might or glory. Follow Via Ulisse Dini to **Borgo Stretto,** a lively shopping street; just off the street in **Piazza delle Vettovaglie,** a fish and vegetable market fills a Renaissance loggia every morning except Sunday. As you reach the river, pause in the middle of **Ponte di Mezzo** to look at the palazzo-lined banks; in the Middle Ages this graceful span, rebuilt many times, was lined with shops, like the Ponte Vecchio in Florence. Tidily wedged onto the south bank, downstream from the bridge, the exquisite **Chiesa di Santa Maria della Spina** was wrought by Pisa's leading Gothic sculptors, including Giovanni Pisano. From the south side of the bridge, shop-lined **Corso Italia** passes a graceful Florentine loggia and continues to the central train station. At Corso Vittorio Emanuele II, a slight detour to the west brings you to Via Zandonai and an unexpected sight: Shortly before his death in 1990, New York street artist Keith Haring painted the giant **Tuttomondo** mural on the theme of "peace and harmony," filling it with his trademark Pop Art figures.

Visiting the Campo dei Miracoli

Admission to the **Leaning Tower** and the **cathedral** is 20€. It costs 7€ to enter the cathedral and any one of the Campo's other sights: the **Baptistery, Camposanto,** the **Museo delle Sinopie,** or the **Museo Opera.** Admission to all these sights except the Tower is 10€, or 27€ with the Tower. Admission to the Tower is by timed entry only and space is limited; visitors are encouraged to purchase tickets in advance at **www.opapisa.it.**

Baptistery ★★ CHURCH Italy's largest baptistery (104m/341 ft. in circumference), begun in 1153 and capped with a Gothic dome in the 1300s, is built on the same unstable soil as the Leaning Tower—the first thing you notice is a decided tilt towards the cathedral. But it's the Baptistery's unadorned interior that is of greatest interest: Art historians consider this to be where the Renaissance, with its emphasis on classical style, first began to flower, in the pulpit created by sculptor Nicola Pisano (1255–60). Pisano had studied ancient Roman works that the Pisan navy brought back from Rome as booty, and the classical influence on his work is obvious—note the nude Roman god Hercules taking his place next to statues of St. Michael and St. John the Baptist (who is bathed in ethereal light on June 24, when the sun shines through a strategically placed opening in the walls to illuminate the saint on the feast of his birth). In scenes of the life of Christ, figures wear tunics and Mary wears the headdress of a Roman matron. Roughly once an hour or so, one of the guards will stand near the middle of the structure and sing, and the sound will reverberate melodically (the performer deserves a small tip). These acoustics are no accident—studies show that the baptistery was designed in such a way to amplify sounds to mimic a perfectly tuned pipe organ.

Piazza del Duomo. www.opapisa.it. ✆ **050/835-011.** For prices, see box p. 297. Daily Apr–Oct 9am–8pm; Nov–Mar 9am–6pm.

Camposanto ★ CEMETERY Pisa's cemetery, where the city's aristocracy was buried until the 1800s, was begun in 1278, when Crusaders began shipping back dirt from Golgotha (the mount where Christ was crucified). Giovanni di Simone (architect of the Leaning Tower) enclosed the field in a marble cloister, and the walls were covered by magnificent 14th- and 15th-century frescoes. Unfortunately, these were mostly destroyed by Allied bombings in World War II, but you can see renderings of them in the Museo delle Sinopie across the square. Roman sarcophagi, used as funerary monuments, fared better (84 of these survive), as did the huge chains that medieval Pisans used to protect their harbor, which now hang on the cemetery walls.

Piazza del Duomo. www.opapisa.it. ✆ **050/835011.** For prices, see box p. 297. Daily Apr–Oct 9am–8pm; Nov–Mar 9am–6pm.

Cattedrale ★★ CATHEDRAL Pisa's magnificent white marble cathedral will forever be associated with native son Galileo Galilei (1564–1642), a founder of modern physics. Bored during church services, he discovered the law of perpetual motion (a pendulum's swings always take the same amount of time) by watching the swing of a bronze chandelier now known as the "Lamp of Galileo." (It's also said that Galileo dropped two wooden balls of differing sizes from the Leaning Tower; they hit the ground at the same time, thus proving that gravity exerts the same force on objects no matter what they weigh.) The exuberant cathedral, with its intricate tiers of arches and columns, is remarkable in its own right as a prime example of Pisan Romanesque architecture, which was heavily influenced by Pisa's trading contact with the Arab world. Giovanni Pisano, whose father, Nicola, sculpted the pulpit in the Baptistery, created the pulpit here (1302–11), covering it with scenes from the New Testament. They're now considered a masterpiece of Gothic sculpture, but 16th-century restorers deemed them too old-fashioned and packed them away in crates; they were reassembled, rather clumsily, in 1926.

Piazza del Duomo. www.opapisa.it. ✆ **050/835011.** For prices, see box p. 297. Daily Apr–Oct 10am–8pm; Nov–Mar 10am–6pm.

Leaning Tower of Pisa ★★★ ICON Construction began on the bell tower of Pisa Cathedral in 1173. Three stories into the job, it became apparent the structure was leaning distinctly, whereupon architects Guglielmo and Bonnano Pisano called off the work. A century later, Giovanni di Simone resumed the job, having quite literally gone back to the drawing board—he tried to compensate for the tilt by making successive layers taller on one side than the other, thus giving the tower a slight banana-like curve. Over the centuries engineers have poured concrete into the foundations and tried other solutions, all in vain. By the late 20th century the tower was in such serious danger of collapse that it was closed and braced with cables. Crews removed more than 70 tons of earth from beneath the structure, allowing it to slightly right itself as it settled. With a lean of only 4m (13 ft.), compared to a precarious 4.6m (15 ft.) before the fix, the tower has been deemed stable for now and safe to climb once again. But before you do, take time to notice just how lovely the multicolor marble tower is, with eight arcaded stories that provide a mesmerizing sense of harmony as you look up its height.

The Leaning Tower of Pisa.

The only way to climb the tower is to book a visit in the office on the north side of the piazza—or, for peak season, book online well in advance. Visits are limited to 30 minutes, and you must be punctual for your slot or you'll lose your chance to climb the 293 steps. Children under 8 are not permitted to climb the tower, and those 8 to 18 need to be accompanied by an adult (children 8–12 must hold an adult's hand at all times).

Piazza del Duomo. www.opapisa.it. ✆ **050/835011.** 20€. Daily Apr–Oct 9am–10pm; Nov–Mar 9am–6pm.

Where to Stay & Eat in Pisa

Most visitors come to Pisa on a day trip, usually from Florence, which helps keep hotel prices down but also limits quality options. The low season for most hotels in Pisa is August. Any visit should include a stop for a coffee and pastry at **Caffè dell'Ussero ★★★**, one of Italy's oldest literary cafe-bars, doing a brisk business since 1775 from the ground floor of riverside Palazzo Agostini, Lungarno Pacinotti 27 (✆ **0338/727-2237**). For pizza or *cecina* (a flatbread made of garbanzo-bean flour and served warm), stop in at **Il Montino ★**, in the historic center a block or so west of Borgo Stretto at Vicolo del Monte 1 (✆ **050/598695**). At the end of Borgo Stretto, at number 11 in the riverside Piazza Garibaldi, is Pisa's most popular gelato shop, **Bottega del Gelato ★★** (bottegadelgelatopisa.it; ✆ **050/575467**).

Il Campano ★★ PISAN A meal in the simply furnished brick-and-stone rooms of an 18th-century tower house can be an evening-long event, as the kitchen makes everything to order. The *pappardelle alla lepre* (homemade pasta with hare sauce), *tagliata di scamerita di maiale* (grilled pork chops), Florentine steaks, and everything else on the menu is well worth waiting for.

Via Cavalca 19. www.ilcampano.com. ✆ **050/580585.** Entrees 10€–24€. Mon–Fri 7:30–11pm; Sat–Sun 12:30–3pm and 7:30–11pm.

Locanda del Gallo ★★★ TUSCAN Top off a country drive with a meal at this rural inn, where the home cooking is as welcoming as the farmhouse dining rooms or the terrace overlooking fields and vineyards. The house specialty is *peposi,* a velvety Tuscan pepper beef stew; pastas are made fresh daily and topped with hearty ragus and sauces of wild boar. The local wines are excellent, as are the house-made liqueurs. This is a good stop if you are driving between Pisa and Volterra and your trip happens to coincide with the locanda's limited opening hours.

Via Castellinese 10, Chianni, 46km (27 miles) SE of Pisa, 36km (21 miles) NW of Voterra. www.locandadelgallochianni.it. ✆ **0335/619-5858**. Entrees 8€–16€. Thurs 12:30–6pm; Sat 7:30pm–11pm; Sun noon–5pm.

Novecento ★★ These small, simple rooms set around a courtyard in an old villa are strictly contemporary, with Philippe Starck chairs and upholstered headboards set against colored accent walls. A lush garden is filled with lounge chairs; off to one side is the best room in the house, a self-contained, cottage-like unit. Pisa's Botanical Garden is just up the street, and the Duomo is a 10-minute walk.

Via Roma 37. www.hotelnovecento.pisa.it. ✆ **050/500323.** 14 units. 70€–100€ double. Rates include breakfast. **Amenities:** Free Wi-Fi.

Osteria dei Cavalieri ★★★ PISAN Set in stone rooms dating to the 12th century, the "Restaurant of the Knights" serves traditional Tuscan cooking that also honors the Slow Food principles of fresh and local. Being Pisa, this means seafood (*tagliolini* with razor clams or a classic *baccala,* dried cod lightly battered and fried), hearty meat choices such as grilled steaks or *pappardelle* with rabbit sauce, and robust vegetable soups.

Via San Frediano 16. www.osteriacavalieri.pisa.it. ✆ **050/580858.** Entrees 9€–18€. Thurs–Sat and Mon–Tues noon–2:15pm and 7:45–10:30pm; Wed 7:45–10:30pm.

Royal Victoria Hotel ★★★ The gracious Piegaga family has been hosting travelers since the days of the 19th-century Grand Tour, and their high-ceilinged guest rooms and fern-filled parlors ooze old-world charm. Little has changed since Charles Dickens stayed here—guests requiring spas, high-tech gadgetry, and chic designer style should look elsewhere. The rest of us will delight in front-room views of the Arno, an airy upper-floor terrace for cocktails, Art Deco tile work, marble mantelpieces, frescoes, and all the other trappings that only get better with age.

Lungarno Pacinotti 12. www.royalvictoria.it. ✆ **050/940111.** 75€–130€ double. Rates include breakfast. **Amenities:** Bar; free Wi-Fi.

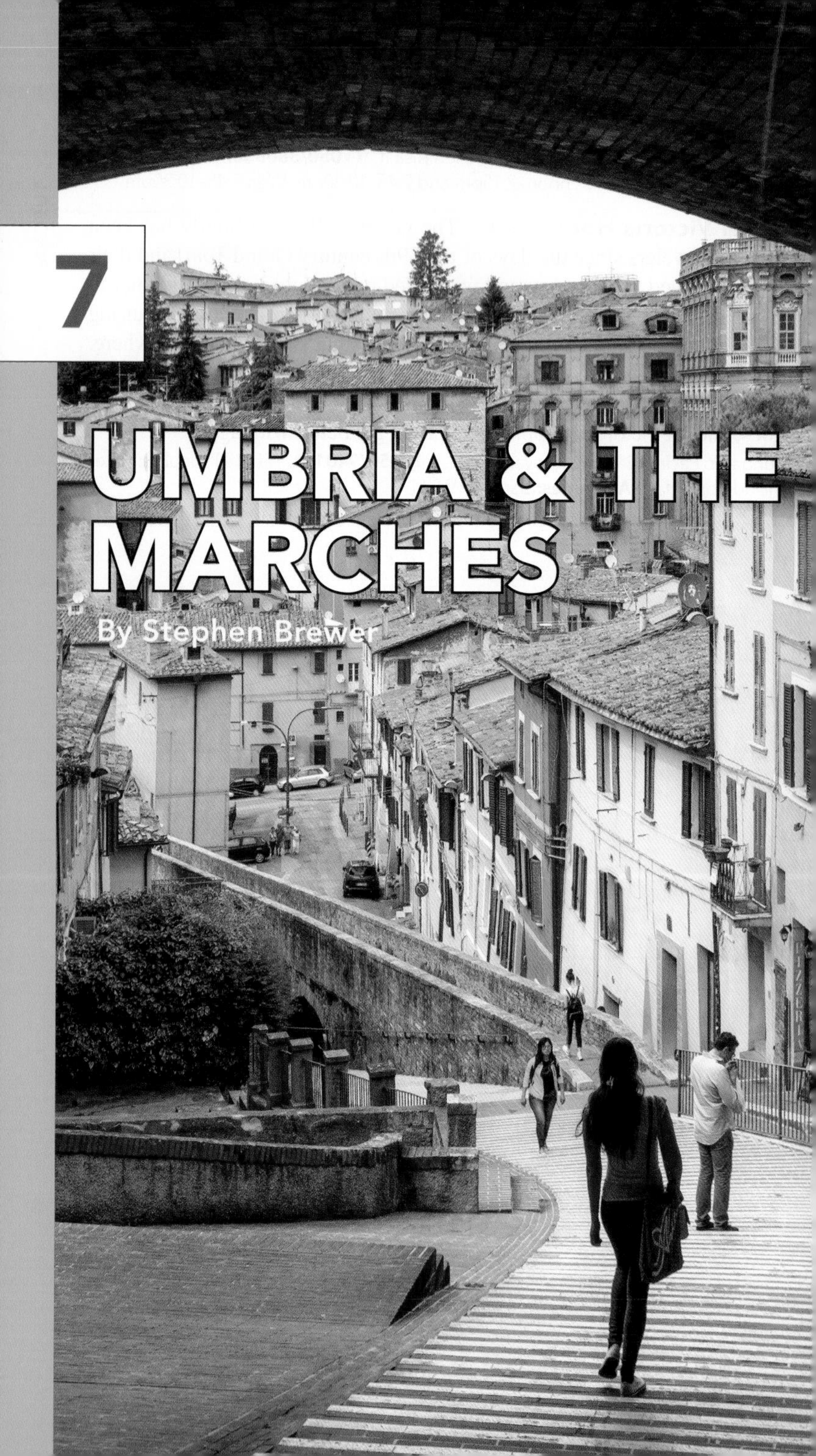

7

UMBRIA & THE MARCHES

By Stephen Brewer

It's easy for travelers to write off Umbria as second to Tuscany, its more-visited neighbor to the north, but that's a good thing—being slightly out of the limelight is one of the region's great assets. Perugia, Spoleto, Gubbio, and dozens of other noble hill towns are a little quieter than their Tuscan neighbors, a bit easier to enjoy, yet filled with rival-worthy art treasures, from Giotto's famous fresco cycle in Assisi to Signorelli's horrific view of Judgment Day in Orvieto. Even less visited are the rugged valleys of the Marches to the east, where charming towns like Urbino cling to hillsides in relative isolation.

Umbrian landscapes are most memorably green, a picturesque mix of vineyards and olive groves, fertile valleys, and deep forests, edged by the Apennine mountains. All this mellow scenery befits a region often called *la terra dei santi* (land of the saints), in homage to St. Francis of Assisi and his followers, reminders of whom are everywhere.

DON'T LEAVE UMBRIA WITHOUT . . .

Taking an Evening Passeggiata on Corso Vannucci in Perugia. Stop to admire the Fontana Maggiore and other landmarks, then wander up and down medieval lanes that traverse the city's many hills.

Communing with the Spirit of St. Francis. The kindly saint is still a presence in medieval Assisi and Gubbio, where he lived and performed miracles, as well as in the region's forested hills and mist-shrouded valleys.

Getting Vertigo While Crossing Spoleto's Ponte Delle Torre. High above the Tessino river gorge, this majestic medieval span leads off a scenic 4-mile walk through Umbrian forests and olive groves.

Scenting a Whiff of Brimstone in Orvieto. Luca Signorelli's masterpiece, his Last Judgment fresco cycle in the Duomo, delivers all the spine-tingling thrill of a horror movie—it may literally "put the fear of God in you!"

Finding Your Inner Renaissance Courtier in Urbino. As you stroll through the palace of the Duke da Montefeltro—model for Castiglione's 1507 bestseller *Book of the Courtier*—the ghosts of the Renaissance's highest ideals of art and thought still seem very much present.

FACING PAGE: **A classic hill town panorama in Perugia.**

PERUGIA ★★

164km (102 miles) SE of Florence, 176km (109 miles) N of Rome

Perugia may be Umbria's capital and the largest city between Florence and Rome, but this is still a medieval hill town at heart. In the historic center, strung out along ridges high above the Tiber valley, ancient alleys drop precipitously off **Corso Vannucci,** the cosmopolitan shopping promenade, and Gothic palaces rise above stony piazzas. The city produced and trained some of Umbria's finest artists, whose works fill the city's excellent art gallery. Thousands of students from Perugia's two universities impart a youthful energy, and Perugia's most famous product, chocolate, adds a sweet note to the city's appeal.

Essentials

ARRIVING Trains connect Perugia and **Rome** (2–3 hr.; many trains require a change at Terontola) and **Florence** (2¼ hr.; some trains also require a change at Terontola) every couple of hours. In addition, there are hourly trains to **Assisi** (20–30 min.), **Spoleto** (1¼ hr.), and other Umbrian towns. Limited high-speed Frecciarossa service connects Perugia with Florence (about 1½ hr.) and **Milan** (about 4 hr.). The main station, Perugia Fontivegge, is a few kilometers southwest and below the town center at Piazza Vittorio Veneto (✆ **147/888088**) but is well connected with buses

Piazza IV Novembre and Corso Vannucci, Perugia's main artery.

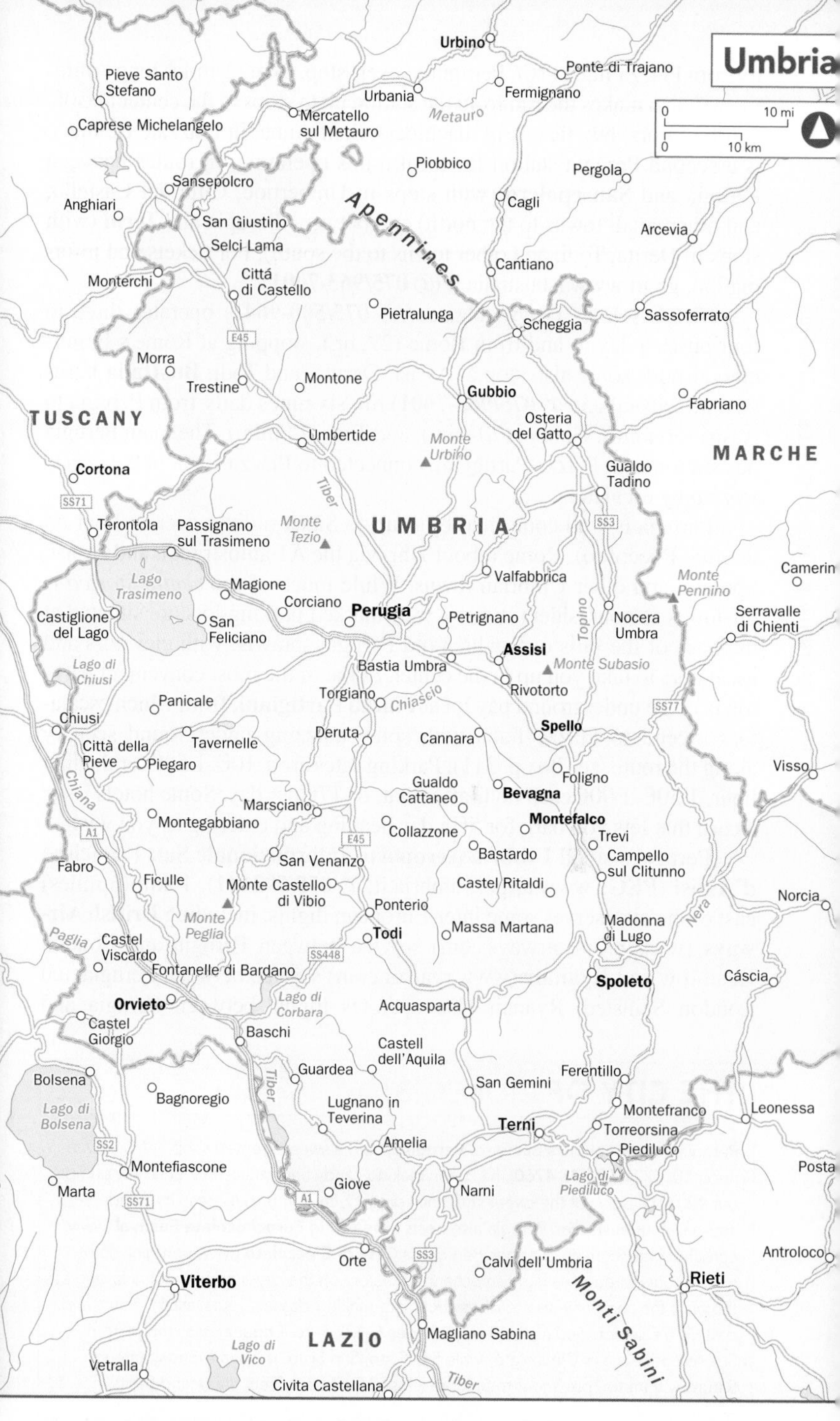
Umbria
0
10 mi
0
10 km
Urbino
Ponte di Trajano
Pieve Santo Stefano
Urbania
Fermignano
Mercatello sul Metauro
Metauro
Caprese Michelangelo
Piobbico
Pergola
Sansepolcro
Anghiari
San Giustino
Apennines
Cagli
Arcevia
Selci Lama
Monterchi
Città di Castello
Cantiano
Pietralunga
Sassoferrato
Scheggia
E45
Morra
Montone
Trestine
Gubbio
Fabriano
TUSCANY
Osteria del Gatto
Umbertide
Monte Urbino
MARCHE
Cortona
Tiber
Gualdo Tadino
SS71
Terontola
Passignano sul Trasimeno
Monte Tezio
UMBRIA
SS3
Valfabbrica
Camerin
Lago Trasimeno
Magione
Monte Pennino
Corciano
Perugia
Topino
Castiglione del Lago
San Feliciano
Petrignano
Nocera Umbra
Serravalle di Chienti
Assisi
Lago di Chiusi
Bastia Umbra
Monte Subasio
Rivotorto
Torgiano
Chiascio
Panicale
SS77
Chiusi
Spello
Deruta
Cannara
Tavernelle
Città della Pieve
Piegaro
Foligno
Visso
Chiana
Gualdo Cattaneo
Bevagna
Marsciano
Montefalco
Montegabbiano
A1
Collazzone
Trevi
E45
Bastardo
Fabro
San Venanzo
Campello sul Clitunno
Ficulle
Monte Castello di Vibio
Castel Ritaldi
Norcia
Ponterio
Nera
Monte Peglia
Paglia
Castel Viscardo
Todi
Massa Martana
Madonna di Lugo
SS448
Fontanelle di Bardano
Cáscia
Spoleto
Lago di Corbara
Orvieto
Acquasparta
Castel Giorgio
Baschi
Castell dell'Aquila
Bolsena
Guardea
Ferentillo
Tiber
Bagnoregio
San Gemini
Lago di Bolsena
Lugnano in Teverina
Montefranco
Leonessa
Terni
Torreorsina
Amelia
SS2
Piediluco
Montefiascone
Posta
Lago di Piediluco
Marta
Giove
Narni
SS71
A1
SS3
Antroloco
Orte
Calvi dell'Umbria
Monti Sabini
Viterbo
Rieti
LAZIO
Magliano Sabina
Lago di Vico
Vetralla
Tiber
Civita Castellana

to/from Piazza Italia (1€). Perugia's seven-stop, 3km (2-mile) long "minimetro" also makes the run from the station up to stops in the center (1.50€, 1.20€ seniors; buy tickets in machines). Sant'Anna, in Piazzale Bellucci, is a second Perugia station for local trains operating on routes between Perugia and **Sansepolcro** (with stops in Umbertide, Citta del Castello, and other small towns to the north) and between Perugia and **Terni** (with stops in Derita, Todi, and other towns to the south). For tickets and information, go to www.fsbusitalia.it (© **075/963-7001**).

SULGA lines (www.sulga.eu; © **075/500-9641**) operates three to four buses a day to and from Rome (2½ hr.), stopping at Rome's Fiumicino airport; some also stop at Assisi, Deruta, and Todi. **BusItalia** buses (www.fsbusitalia.it; © **075/963-7001**) run six times daily from Perugia to Assisi (50 min.), Gubbio (70 min.), and Todi (75 min.). The main Perugia bus station is in Piazza Partigiani, connected to Piazza Italia in the *centro storico* by escalator.

Perugia is well connected by **road** to Siena (a little over an hour on the free Raccordo), Rome (about 2 hr. via the A1 autostrada), and Assisi, Spoleto, and other Umbrian towns. While much of the *centro storico* is off-limits to nonresident drivers, well-marked parking lots are situated at the base of the hills over which old Perugia sprawls, with elevators and escalators to take you up to the center. Some of the most convenient parking is at the underground pay lot at **Piazza Partigiani,** from which escalators ascend to Piazza Italia with some amazing underground scenery along the route (see box p. 311). Parking rates are 1.10€–1.50€ for the first hour, 1.50€–1.90€ each hour after that, or 17€ per day. Some hotels issue a card that lets you park for 5€ a day, leaving and entering as you wish.

Perugia's small **Umbria Aeroporto Internazionale San Francisco d'Assisi (PEG;** www.airport.umbria.it; © **075/592141**), 10km (6 miles) east of the city, serves some inter-European flights, including **British Airways** (www.britishairways.com) service between Perugia and London Heathrow and **Ryanair** (www.ryanair.com) service between Perugia and London Stansted. Ryanair also operates flights between Perugia and

THE CITY OF cioccolato

Perugia is a chocoholic's paradise. **Perugina,** with a sweet-scented shop at Corso Vannucci 101 (© **075/573-4760**), has been making candy here since 1907 and now pumps out 120 tons a day of the sweet stuff, including 1½ million Baci (kisses), its gianduja-and-hazelnut bestseller. Perugia also hosts a weeklong **Eurochocolate Festival** (www.eurochocolate.com) in October. Perugina's **Casa di Cioccolato** (www.perugina.com) guides tours through its highly mechanized factory on the city outskirts, with a tasting at the end; the company also teaches chocolate-making classes. Tours last 1½ hours and cost 9€ (7€ seniors and ages 13–17, 4€ ages 6–12); 3- to 4-hour classes range from 30€ to 65€. Casa di Cioccolato, Viale San Sisto, San Sisto, is open Monday through Saturday 9am to 1pm and 2 to 5:30pm (closed Sat in Jan, Feb, June, and Sept).

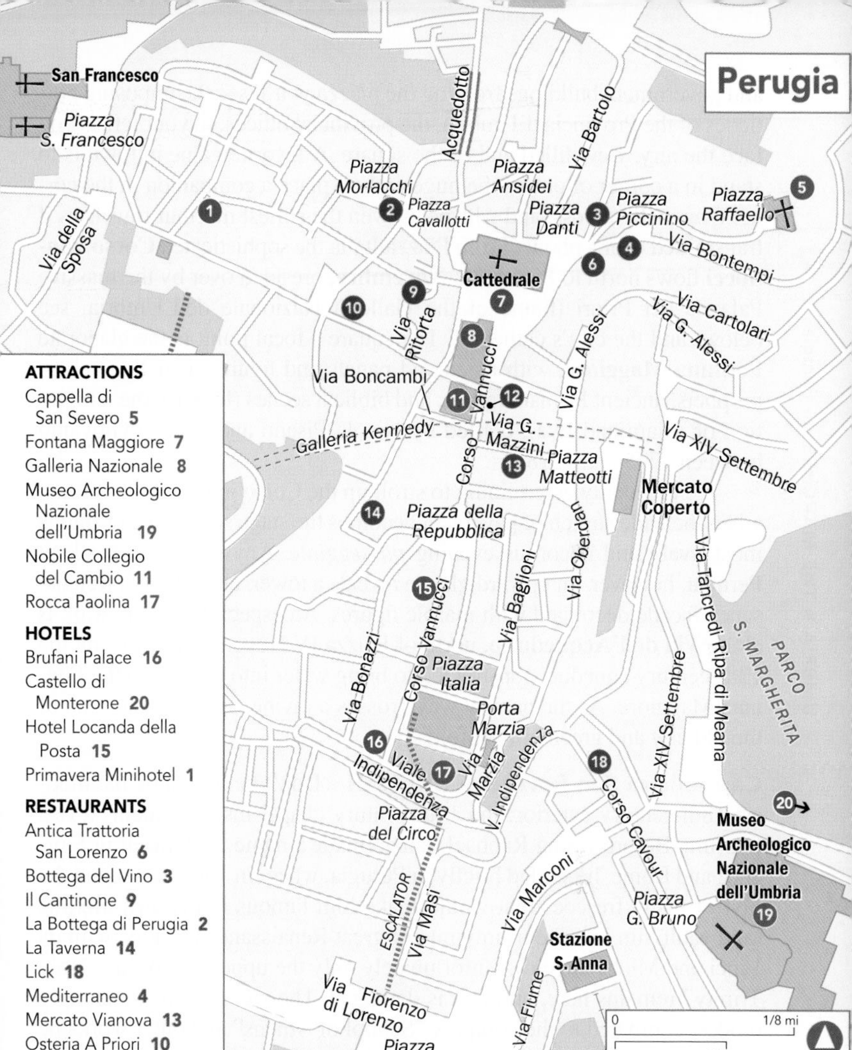

Malta, Palermo, and Catania, as well as many other European airports in summer. Buses connect the airport with the Perugia bus and train station and historic center (30–40 min.; 8€, 14€ roundtrip), but service is infrequent. Taxis to or from the airport cost around 25€.

VISITOR INFORMATION The **tourist office** at Piazza Matteotti 18 (turismo.comune.perugia.it; ✆ **075/573-6458**), open daily 9am to 6pm, provides a fairly useless map for free and a good one for 1€.

Exploring Perugia

Perugia's main public square, **Piazza Italia,** hangs like a balcony over the hillside at one end of the old town. Among the somber, formidable banks and government buildings fronting the piazza you'll see the imposing porticoes of the Provincia d'Umbria, the provincial offices, to your left as you face the airy, view-filled end of the square. A favorite game in town is to stand in a corner of one of the huge arches, place a companion in the corner diagonally across, and whisper—even the softest murmur travels as if transmitted over a phone. From Piazza Italia the sophisticated **Corso Vannucci** flows north to **Piazza IV Novembre,** presided over by the massive Palazzo dei Priori (home of the Galleria Nazionale dell'Umbria, see below) and the city's cathedral. The square's focal point is the elaborate **Fontana Maggiore,** with its carved panels and figures depicting saints, prophets, ancient Roman figures, and biblical scenes (look for the temptation of Adam and Eve), crafted by Nicola Pisano and his son Giovanni between 1275 and 1278.

It's especially entertaining to stroll up the Corso in the early evening, when the wide stretch of pavement becomes the stage set for one of Italy's most lively and decorous evening *passeggiate.* Anywhere you walk in Perugia, however, an upward glance reveals a tower, an arch, or a Renaissance facade decorated with marble figures. An especially scenic walk is along **Via dell'Acquedotto,** north of Piazza IV Novembre, following the 13th-century aqueduct constructed to bring water into the city to the Fontana Maggiore. As the narrow way crosses a ravine, an airy panorama of the old city and green hills unfolds.

Cappella di San Severo ★ CHURCH Don't be fooled by the modest 18th-century exterior; the 14th-century chapel inside contains a real treasure. Before young Raphael Sanzio made a name for himself in Florence and Rome, he settled briefly in Perugia, where in 1504 he painted the first of many frescoes that would make him famous in his own lifetime (and vault him into the triumvirate of great Renaissance masters, with da Vinci and Michelangelo). Unfortunately only the upper half of his "Holy Trinity" remains here, and that is damaged. The work seems touchingly modest compared to the complex "School of Athens" and other works he later did for the Vatican. As energetic in life as he was in his work, Raphael ran a huge workshop, had dozens of patrons, was in line to be a cardinal, and died on his 37th birthday, allegedly after a lustful session with his mistress. After Raphael's death, his then-septuagenarian teacher, Perugino, painted the six saints along the bottom of the fresco.

Piazza Raffaello. turismo.comune.perugia.it. ✆ **075/573/947-1766.** 4€ adults, 2€ ages 7–14, free for children 6 and under. Apr and Aug daily 10am–6pm; May–July and Sept–Oct Tues–Sun 10am–6pm; Nov–Mar Tues–Sun 11am–1:30pm and 2:30–5pm.

Galleria Nazionale dell'Umbria ★★★ MUSEUM Seven or so centuries of Umbrian art are housed on the top floors of the crenellated Palazzo dei Priori, where a ruling council of powerful merchants and guilds met in medieval times. It's only fitting that the museum spotlights native son Perugino, who was born nearby in Città della Pieve and spent

The Cappella di San Severo contains one of Raphael's first great frescoes.

much of his career working in Perugia (he also studied alongside Leonardo da Vinci in Florence and executed frescoes in the Sistine Chapel in Rome). Perugino's altarpieces are full of delicate landscapes, sweet Madonnas, and grinning Christ Childs that reveal his spare, precise style. Their divine beauty seems ironic, given that Perugino was openly anti-religion and had a fairly turbulent life—he was arrested in Florence for assault and barely escaped exile; he sued Michelangelo for defamation of character; and more than once he was censored for reusing images. He persevered, however, and worked prodigiously until his death at age 73, leaving a considerable fortune.

The museum's other showpiece is Piero della Francesca's "Polyptych of Perugia," painted for the city's church of Sant'Antonio in 1470. Its symmetry and realistic dimensions reflect the artist's other occupation as a mathematician; at the same time, his figures are robustly human. Della Francesca works sheer magic at the top of the piece, in a scene of the Annunciation, where an angel appears to Mary to tell her she will be the mother of the son of God. As she stands in a brightly lit cloister, the illusion of pillars leading off into the distance is regarded as one of the greatest examples of perspective in Renaissance art.

Palazzo dei Priori, Corso Vannucci 19. gallerianazionaledellumbria.it. ✆ **075/574-1247.** 10€ adults, free for ages 18 and under. Daily 8:30am–7:30pm (closed Mon Jan–Mar).

Museo Archeologico Nazionale dell'Umbria ★ MUSEUM Etruscans stand out as the stars of the National Archeological Museum of Umbria, set in the former church, convent, and cloisters of San Domenico. Most riveting are their large tombs, brought from around the Tuscan/Umbrian region, which 2,500 years ago was the heartland of a 12-city Etruscan confederation. To best appreciate the ancient masters' artistry, wander along the porticos of the vast cloisters and enjoy the stories of everyday life that emerge in stone on the tombs lining the walls. A man with scales in hand, perhaps an architect, stands in front of a town gate; a young couple kisses; workers harvest grapes. One of the most fascinating pieces, the Sarcophagus dello Sperandio, was discovered in 1843 in the tomb of a warrior, surrounded by iron weapons. On one side, three men recline on a divan, enjoying a banquet as a slave serves them; in another long relief, men, women, and animals (including heavily laden pack animals and collared dogs) follow one another in a procession, possibly a ceremonial parade or migration. It's believed the sarcophagus was fashioned in Chiusi and brought to Perugia by wagon along a rough ancient track. The Cippo di Perugia, from the 3rd century B.C., is the longest piece of Etruscan script ever found: It's a land contract between two families, proof that real estate has always been a sound investment.

Galleria Nazionale in the Palazzo dei Priori, Perugia.

Piazza Giordano Bruno 10. polomusealeumbria.beniculturali.it. ✆ **075/572-7141.** 5€. Daily 8:30am–7:30pm (closed third Sun of the month Sept–Nov).

Nobile Collegio del Cambio ★★ MUSEUM The cubicles and fluorescent lighting of modern office life will seem even more banal after you visit the frescoed meeting rooms of Perugia's Moneychanger's Guild, one of the best-preserved "office suites" of the Renaissance. Perugino was hired in 1496 to fresco the Sala dell'Udienza (Hearing Room), perhaps with the help of his young student Raphael. The images merge religion (scenes of the Nativity and Transfiguration) with classical references

Perugia's Medieval Pompeii

Beneath Piazza Italia, layers of history are displayed—literally. Around 1530, after the Perugians rebelled against Pope Paul III over a tax on salt (to this day, Perugian bread is salt-free), the Pope demolished more than a quarter of the city in retribution, and built his own castle, **Rocca Paolina,** atop the ruins. After Italian unification in 1860, locals ripped the castle to pieces and built Piazza Italia on top of that. Today, the vaults of the Pope's fort and even older relics of medieval dwellings and streets are in full view beneath the piazza. You can clamber through doorless entrances, climb the remains of stairways, walk through empty rooms, and wander at will through the brick maze. Enter the underground city (free; open daily 6:15am–1:45am) from the escalators that connect Piazza Italia to the lower town's Piazza Partigiani, with its car park and bus station. Guides lead half-hour-long tours of the underground departing from the cathedral four times a day; cost is 10€, under 16 6€ (isolasanlorenzo.it).

(female representations of the virtues) and, most riveting of all, glimpses of 15th-century secular life.

Palazzo dei Priori, Corso Vannucci 25. www.collegiodelcambio.it. ✆ **075/572-8599.** 6€. Tues–Sat 9am–1pm and 2:30–5:30pm, Sun–Mon 9am–1:30pm.

Where to Stay in Perugia

Brufani Palace ★★ Built in 1883 to host English travelers on the Grand Tour, Perugia's bastion of luxury commands one side of Piazza Italia and overlooks the valley below. The premises have not changed too much in the intervening years, except that the large, traditionally furnished rooms are now equipped with lavish marble bathrooms and lots of other amenities, including comfortable lounge chairs and sofas. Fires burn in big stone hearths in dining room and lounges; a swimming pool has been carved out of subterranean brick vaults, with see-through panels exposing Etruscan ruins beneath; and a large rooftop terrace is a perfect spot for a sunset glass of wine.

Piazza Italia 12. www.sinahotels.com. ✆ **075/573-2541.** 94 units. 190€–210€ double. Rates include breakfast. **Amenities:** Restaurant/bar; babysitting; concierge; small exercise room; indoor pool; room service; free Wi-Fi.

Castello di Monterone ★★★ It's surprising just how welcoming a medieval castle can be. That's partly because in the 19th century the Piceller family of musicians, artists, and archaeologists made this 13th-century stronghold their home, creating lounges surrounding massive fireplaces and a beautiful cloister garden dotted with ancient artifacts. These days the many nooks and crannies have been converted to utterly charming guest rooms embellished with wide beams, stone walls, handcrafted iron and wood furniture, and large marble bathrooms. Adding to the ambience is a library tucked off a landing, a cozy lounge bar in the old hall, a

GO jump IN THE LAKE

Lago Trasimeno, Italy's fourth-largest lake, washes up against the Tuscany-Umbria border between Cortona and Perugia. The shallow waters aren't quite a match for the beauty of Como and other lakes up north (see chapter 10), but Trasimeno is nonetheless a refreshing splash of blue amid olive groves and sunflower fields. **Passignano,** on the northern shore 30km (18 miles) northwest of Perugia, is the liveliest lakeshore town, with a shoreline promenade and a good stop for a gelato or a sunset aperitivo at **Bar del Sole,** Via Aganor Pompili (✆ **340/504-5309**). At **Castiglione del Lago,** on the western shore 50km (30 miles) west of Perugia, you can swim from a pebbly beach or cycle on shoreline paths; rent bikes (9€ half a day, 12€ a day) at Cicli Valentini, Via Firenze 68/B (ciclivalentini.it; ✆ **333/967-8327;** open Mon–Sat 9am–1pm and 3:30–8pm). An especially pleasant way to explore the lakeshore is on an e-bike (40€ a day).

From either town, 30-minute ferry trips run hourly across the lake to picturesque **Isola Maggiore,** an especially nice place to take a dip in the cool waters, or to buy lace from the few local women who carry on the longstanding tradition. Stepping ashore on Isola Maggiore, you'll be following in the footsteps of St. Francis, who spent Lent of 1213 here. Allegedly, the saint even charmed the local fish—when Francis threw a pike given to him by a fisherman back into the lake, the creature swam alongside his savior until the saint gave him a special blessing.

swimming pool surrounded by lawns, and a roof terrace on the old battlements. Though the castle nestles on a rural hillside, the center of Perugia is only 10 minutes away.

Strada Monteville 3. www.castellomonterone.com. ✆ **075/572-4214.** 14 units. 160€–170€ double. Rates include breakfast. **Amenities:** Restaurant; bar; pool; free Wi-Fi.

Hotel Locanda della Posta ★★ Perugia's oldest hotel has hosted the likes of Goethe and Hans Christian Anderson, and cherubs still smile down on modern guests from the frescoed ceilings in the lounges (as well as in one of the larger suites) as they did on them. Most guest rooms are surprisingly contemporary and minimalist, out of character with the surroundings but very well done, with views over the tile-roofed town taking center stage in most. Among modern touches are enormous marble showers, larger than the bathrooms in many hotels. Several rooms are in a similarly slick annex across the street.

Corso Pietro Vannucci 97, Perugia. www.locandadellapostahotel.it. ✆ **075/572-8925.** 24 units. 160€–200€ double. Rates include breakfast. **Amenities:** Room service; spa; parking (fee); free Wi-Fi.

Primavera Minihotel ★★ It's well worth the climb up three flights of stairs to this aerie-like retreat, where tall windows frame views of rooftops and the green valleys below. Rooms surround a welcoming lounge/breakfast room (breakfast costs extra), except for the best room in the house—a large rooftop double with a terrace. Some are furnished with Art

Nouveau pieces, others with traditional rustic furnishing and Deruta pottery; all have hardwood floors and lots of timber, stone, and other architectural details. Piazza della Repubblica and the center of town are just up some twisty streets, and an escalator puts the hotel within easy reach of Parking Pellini, with discounted rates for guests.

Via Vincioli 8. www.primaveraminihotel.it. ✆ **075/572-1657.** 8 units. 65€–90€ double. Closed mid-Jan to mid-Feb. **Amenities:** Free Wi-Fi.

Where to Eat in Perugia

Perugia's youthful student population ensures a wealth of pizza and *panini* (sandwiches). Most popular among cheap *pizzerie* is **Mediterranea,** at Piazza Piccinino 11 (✆ **075/572-4021**). Pizzas cost 6€ to 10€ (Mon–Sat 12:15–2:30pm and 7:15–11pm and Sun 9am–5pm). Top choice for a *panino* is **La Bottega di Perugia,** Piazza Francesco Morlacchi 4 (www.labottegadiperugia.it; ✆ **075/573–2965**), where the young proprietors pride themselves on using only local Umbrian hams, greens, and other ingredients; *panini* cost about 4€ and can be washed down with wine or beer (Mon–Sat 9am–9:30pm). Opened in 1860, the venerable **Sandri** is Perugia's oldest and most esteemed *pasticceria,* serving coffee, pastry, and light meals in Art Deco surrounds at Corso Vannucci 32 (✆ **075/572-4112;** Tues–Sun 7:30am–8pm). Sip stylish cocktails at the popular **Mercato Vianova,** Via Giuseppe Mazzini 15 (www.mercatovianova.it; ✆ **075/573-04450;** Tues–Sun 12:30–3pm and 6–11pm). The name says it all at **Lick,** Corso Cavour 40 (✆ **075/572-6917**), which dishes up gelato in such unusual variations as gorgonzola cheese and basil with Prosecco (Wed–Mon 11am–8:30; closed Jan).

Antica Trattoria San Lorenzo ★★ MODERN ITALIAN Everything here is local, right down to the Perugian-made pottery on the candlelit tables. Chef/owner Simone Ciccotti sources his ingredients from producers in the nearby countryside, then creates inventive dishes that emphasize those flavors, such as a "muffin" of caramelized onions and foie gras, or a *millefeuille* of grilled vegetables with smoked mozzarella. The restaurant's namesake, San Lorenzo, is a patron saint of Perugia—and also the patron saint of chefs.

Piazza Danti 19a. anticatrattoriasanlorenzo.business.site. ✆ **075/527-1956.** Entrees 15€–28€. Thurs–Tues 12:30–2:30pm and 7–10:30pm.

Bottega del Vino ★★ UMBRIAN A snug, vintage-photo-lined room right off Piazza IV Novembre serves wines by the glass along with a nice assortment of Umbrian hams and cheeses, perfect for an evening *aperitivo.* The small lunch and dinner menus include salads and a couple of pastas, as well as a dish or two of the day—such as a steak or roasted leg of lamb. Live jazz often plays into the wee hours.

Via del Sole 1. www.labottegadelvino.net. ✆ **075/571-6181.** Entrees 13€. Tues–Sat noon–3pm and 7pm–midnight. Closed Jan.

Il Cantinone ★★ UMBRIAN/PIZZA Even a pizza seems like a meal fit for a medieval courtier when you dine in this softly lit, stone-walled, and brick-vaulted 14th-century cantina in a hidden courtyard around the corner from Piazza Maggiore. The excellent Umbrian fare befits the distinctively Old Perugia surroundings, with such hearty choices as homemade tagliatelle with duck ragù or wild boar sauce and locally sourced beef from the Val di Chiana topped with black truffles, an Umbrian specialty.

Via Ritorta. ristoranteilcantinoneperugia.com. ✆ **075/573-4430.** Entrees 8€–18€. Wed–Mon 12:30–2:30pm and 7:30–10:30pm.

La Taverna ★★★ UMBRIAN A tiny courtyard down a flight of steps from Corso Vannucci fills with tables in warm weather, while inside, barrel-vaulted ceilings shimmer with candlelight in evening. The service and cooking are similarly warm and down-to-earth—everything, from bread to pasta to desserts, is made in-house and typically Umbrian: Pappardelle sauced with a hearty ragù, *caramelle rosse al gorgonzola* (beet ravioli with gorgonzola) made with local beets, and carefully selected meats seasoned with fresh herbs from the surroundings hillsides. Chef Claudio will make his way to your table at some point to ensure that everything is *tutto bene.*

Via delle Streghe 8 (near Piazza Repubblica). www.ristorantelataverna.com. ✆ **075/572-4128.** Entrees 12€–25€. Daily 12:30–2:30pm and 7:30–10:30pm.

Osteria A Priori ★★★ UMBRIAN You'll pass through a wine shop and climb a flight of stairs to reach this welcoming brick-vaulted room with contemporary wood furnishings, where the emphasis is on Umbrian products and age-old recipes. A portion of slowly cooked beans *(fagiolina)* is paired with eggs and onions and bread salad; *gnocconi* (large potato dumplings) are stuffed with fresh ricotta; slow-roasted pork shank *(stinco di maiale)* is served with crisp potatoes. The staff will eagerly walk you through the ever-changing menu and suggest wine pairings with each course.

Via dei Priori 39. www.osteriaapriori.it. ✆ **075/572-7098.** Entrees 9€–18€. Mon–Sat 12:30–2:30pm and 7:30–10pm.

Perugia Shopping

At **Museo Atelier Giuditta Brozzetti,** in a former church at Via Tiberio Berardi 5/6 (www.brozzetti.com; ✆ **075/40236**), Marta Cucchia oversees a centuries-old family weaving business, based on ages-old techniques. The studio/shop (Mon–Fri 8:30am–12:30pm, other times by appt.) offers pillows, runners, and other textiles for sale or to custom-order. One-day courses are available, in English, in hand-weaving, lacemaking, and embroidery. **Deruta,** a little hill town 20km (12 miles) south of Perugia via SS3bis, has been known for its ceramics since the Middle Ages; today some 300 studios line the streets. The Perugia tourist office can give you a list of shops; trains run frequently from Sant'Anna station (see above). Deruta products are showcased in Perugia on the overflowing shelves at **Bettini Ceramiche Maioliche Deruta Perugia**, Via Ulisse Rocchi (www.terrecottederuta.com; ✆ **075/971-0550;** Wed–Sat and Mon 10am–1pm and 2–7pm, Tues 10am–7pm).

GUBBIO ★★

39 km (24 miles) NE of Perugia

The most medieval-looking town in Italy, Gubbio presents itself to the world with a crenellated skyline backed by forest-covered mountains. At this old hill town's stony heart, the severe red-brick expanse of Piazza Grande dramatically drops away on its south side to soul-soothing views of misty hills and a sweeping valley.

When it comes to St. Francis lore, beautiful Gubbio gets overshadowed by **Assisi** (see p. 320), yet it was here that the saint performed one of his most popular miracles—taming a wolf that was terrorizing the citizens (see **Taverna del Lupo,** p. 318)—and it was here that the wealthy young Francis first cast off his finery and put on a rough monk's habit, forsaking his worldly goods. Gubbio is also associated with another holy presence, Don Matteo, the priest detective of a wildly popular Italian TV series set in the town, though filming has moved to **Spoleto** (see p. 330).

Essentials

ARRIVING If you're **driving,** follow the scenic SS298 for the 45-minute trip. A handy place to park is **Parcheggio Via della Repubblica** (www.gubbioculturamultiservizi.it; ✆ **075/922-2027**), where you'll pay about 1.10€ an hour and .40€ each successive hour between 8am and 8pm. Gubbio is not served directly by **train,** though Fossato di Vico, 18km (11 miles) south, is on the Rome–Ancona line, with trains arriving about every 2 hours. Buses operated by **BusItalia** (www.fsbusitalia.it; ✆ **075/963-7001**) run from the station for the 35-min. trip to Gubbio usually at least hourly. Eight or nine daily BusItalia also runs between Gubbio and Perugia (70 min.); buses arrive at Piazza 40 Martiri, named for citizens killed by the Nazis for aiding partisans during World War II. From here it's an easy level walk to an elevator that will take you up to Piazza Grande.

VISITOR INFORMATION The **tourist office,** Via della Repubblica 15 (www.comune.gubbio.pg.it; ✆ **075/922-2027**), is open daily 9am to 7pm. Staff hands out maps and, for 1€, sells a brief but handy walking guide to the town.

SPECIAL EVENTS Aside from the springtime Corso dei Ceri (see Monte Igino, p. 317), Gubbio's biggest event is lighting the **world's largest Christmas tree** on the slopes in December. Lights are laid out to form a shape 2,130 feet high and 1,100 feet wide at the base. The pope often does the honors of lighting the tree, using a computer in the Vatican palace. The town seems especially medieval the **last weekend in May,** when Eugubian *balestrieri,* or crossbow competitors, line up in Piazza Grande to face off with competitors from Sansepolcro in Tuscany.

Exploring Gubbio

Start your explorations on hillside **Piazza Grande** (to avoid the climb, take the free elevator at the junction of Via Repubblica and Via Baldassini, which runs daily 9am–7:30pm). After marveling at the airy view over the valley below, turn around to admire the rambling **Palazzo Ranghiasci** behind you, on the north side. That the facade resembles an 18th-century neoclassical British country house is no accident: A nobleman of the time married an English lady and brought her back to Gubbio, where she languished in homesickness before fleeing. To lure his wife back, the heartbroken duke commissioned an architect to rebuild the front of his palace in the latest British fashion, but to no avail—his bride never returned. Note that one of the Greek-style columns has been clumsily replaced with bricks, a patch job after the Allies lobbed a shell into the piazza to dislodge Nazi occupiers at the end of World War II. Next head for the **Fountain of the Madmen** in Largo Bargello, a short walk west of the piazza along Via Consoli, but approach with care—it's said that if you circle the monument three times you are sure to go mad.

Festa dei Ceri celebrations outside the Palazzo dei Consoli in Gubbio.

Steep, narrow lanes switchback up the hill to Gubbio's sturdy **Duomo** and fortresslike **Palazzo Ducale** at the top of the town, where church and state could keep an eye on the citizens below (you may also reach the Duomo and palazzo on another elevator off the east side of Piazza Grande). In 1472 Duke Federico da Montefeltro commissioned for his palace the **Gubbio Studiolo,** a glorious room decorated with wood inlay; to see this treasure nowadays, however, you'd have to go to the Metropolitan Museum of Art in New York City. What remains in the formal, painting-hung salons is less inspiring, though the classically proportioned Renaissance courtyard is beautiful (Tues–Sun 8:30am–7:30pm; 12€, 8€ seniors, includes guided tour). As you approach the palace on Via Federico da Montefeltro, through a gate you'll see the **Botte dei Canonici** (Canon's Barrel), a humongous vessel capable of holding more than 5,000 gallons of wine. Monks in the monastery above, or so the story goes, could serve themselves by dipping a ladle through a trapdoor in the ceiling.

Monte Igino ★★ PARK/GARDEN On an open-air funicular, **Funivia Colle Eletto** (www.funiviagubbio.it; ✆ **075-927-3881**), you hop into a moving basket to be whisked about 6 minutes to the top of this 908m (2,980-ft.) summit for stupendous Umbrian views. In the May 15 **Corso dei Ceri** (www.ceri.it), teams race up the mountainside on foot carrying 15-foot-long wooden battering rams called *ceri,* or "candles." The race is part of festivities honoring St. Ubaldo, the bishop who allegedly smooth-talked Frederick Barbarossa out of sacking the town in the 1150s. Ubaldo's corpse is up here, too, in a glass casket at the Basilica di Sant'Ubaldo, a 5-minute walk from the funicular stop.

Funicular leaves from Via San Girolamo. Roundtrip 6€ adults, 4€ ages 4–13. June daily 9:30am–1:15pm and 2:30–7pm; July–Aug daily 9am–8pm; early Sept daily 9:30am–7pm; late Sept Mon–Sat 9:30am–1:15pm and 2:30–7pm, Sun 9am–7pm; Oct daily 10am–1:15pm and 2:30–6pm; Nov–Feb Thurs–Tues 10am–1:15pm and 2:30–5pm; Mar daily 10am–1:15pm and 2:30–5:30pm (until 6pm Sun); Apr–May daily 10am–1:15pm and 2:30–6:30pm (until 7pm Sun).

Museo del Palazzo dei Consoli ★★ MUSEUM The former home of the town government is a solidly Gothic-looking palace, with crenellations, a tower, and an imposing stone staircase that sweeps up from Piazza Grande. The main hall, where the medieval commune met, houses the town museum, where one prize stands out amid old coins and pottery: The seven **Eugubine Tables,** inscribed on bronze from 200 to 70 B.C., is ancient Umbria's Rosetta Stone, the only existing record of the Umbri language transposed in Etruscan and Latin letters. A local farmer turned up the tablets while plowing his fields in 1444; city officials convinced him to sell them for 2 years' worth of grazing rights. ***Tip:*** Look for the secret corridor from the back of the ceramics room to the Pinacoteca upstairs, via the medieval toilets.

Piazza Grande. www.palazzodeiconsoli.it. ✆ **075/927-4298.** 7€ adults; 5€ seniors and ages 6–25; free for children under 5. Mon–Fri 10am–1pm and 3–6pm (closes 5:30pm Nov–Mar); Sat–Sun 10am–6pm.

Where to Stay & Eat in Gubbio

Grotta dell'Angelo ★ ITALIAN/UMBRIAN A barrel-vaulted dining room where locals have been gathering for the past 700 years or so is the place to sit in winter, while warm-weather dining is on a vine-shaded terrace. Wherever you eat, enjoy homemade gnocchi and other pastas, followed by sausages and other meats roasted over the open fire—the whole roast chicken stuffed with fennel is especially delicious. Hotel rooms upstairs are similarly homey (55€–70€ double, breakfast 6€).

Via Gioia 47. www.grottadellangelo.it. ✆ **075/927-1747.** Entrees 9€–14€. Wed–Mon 12:30–2:30pm and 7:30–11pm. Closed Jan 7–Feb 7.

Hotel Relais Ducale ★★★ What were once the palace annexes of the Montefalco dukes, the great Renaissance powerbrokers, open off Piazza Grande and now house extremely comfortable guest rooms that are scattered over several levels, with highly polished floors and well-tended traditional furnishings befitting the royal surroundings. Some have barrel vaulting and a few open to terraces, though all are within easy reach of delightful patios and shady nooks. Proprietors Daniela and Sean offer lots of personal attention; they'll even pick you up at the train station in Fossato di Vico.

Via Galeotti 19. www.relaisducale.com. ✆ **075/922-0157.** 30 units. 95€–110€ double. Rates include breakfast. **Amenities:** Bar; room service; free Wi-Fi.

Taverna del Lupo ★★ UMBRIAN Around 1220, or so the story goes, a ferocious wolf *(lupo)* menaced the good people of Gubbio, devouring them the moment they stepped outside the town gates. St. Francis, then living a monkish life of contemplation in Gubbio, went to the beast's lair, tamed him, and led him back into the marketplace, where townsfolk agreed to feed him in return for good behavior. A charming fresco depicting Francis and the wolf is one of many artworks on the stone walls of these former cellars, where legend says the animal often popped in to eat. These days diners count on the refined surroundings for specialties like homemade tagliatelle with truffles or the kitchen's famous *faraona al ginepro,* guinea hen roasted with juniper berries.

Via Ansidei 21. www.tavernadellupo.it. ✆ **075/927-4368.** Entrees 10€–22€. Daily noon–3pm and 7–10pm. Closed Jan 7–Feb 7.

A Side Trip to Urbino ★

One of the steepest hill towns in Italy, Urbino is a time capsule of the Renaissance, a storybook compilation of towers, domes, and red-tile roofs. Though the glory days wound down 500 years ago, this remote hill town is still prosperous and lively, thanks to Urbino's prestigious university. The 66km (40-mile) drive or bus trip (www.autolineecurcio.it) northeast from Gubbio through mountainous terrain on the SP3 takes a leisurely hour at best, and the landscape en route is stunning: Rippling hills carpeted with fields and forests, topped with the occasional walled village.

Stash your car in the large parking lot at Borgo del Mercatale (1.20€ per hr.), and then hit the steep cobblestone streets on foot.

Aside from the scenic hills, Urbino's main draws are all about art: It's the birthplace of Raphael, Renaissance painter of glorious frescos, and home to the outstanding art collection of Duke Federico da Montefeltro.

Galleria Nazionale delle Marche Palazzo Ducale di Urbino ★★★ MUSEUM Wise and worldly Duke Federico da Montefeltro (1422–82) paced the halls of this palace and contemplated his vast holdings from the study window, all the while dreaming up some of the most enlightened ideals of the Renaissance. One of the palace's most enchanting rooms is that study, beautifully paneled with intarsia depicting classical and humanistic writers as well as great religious thinkers. The duke famously came up with the concept of *sprezzatura,* the ideal of maintaining grace under pressure. Duke Federico and his son, Guidobaldo, oversaw a court so enlightened that Baldassare Castiglione set his 1507 bestseller, *Book of the Courtier,* in the palace's Hall of Vigils. Father and son were patrons of some of the great artists of their day, whose works now hang in the salons and staterooms. "Ideal City," attributed to Piero della Francesca, perfectly evokes the dukes' enlightened ideas; della Francesca's "Flagellation," another palace treasure, is one of the Renaissance's finest accomplishments in perspective. Another achievement in perspective, Paolo Uccello's "The Profanation of the Host" reveals 15th-century anti-Semitic propaganda in its depiction of a Jewish pawnbroker attempting to cook the sacred communion wafer (believed to transform into the body of Christ during the Eucharist), as blood seeping under his door attracts bailiffs.

Piazza Duca Federico. www.gallerianazionalemarche.it. ✆ **0722/322625.** 10€. Tues–Sun 8:30am–7:15pm.

Raphael's Birthplace ★ MUSEUM One of the great artists of the High Renaissance (you can see his work at Cappella di San Severo in Perugia, p. 308, and his best efforts at the Vatican, p. 75) was born here in 1483. His earliest known work, a modest boyhood fresco, "Madonna and Child," hangs on one of the walls here in his childhood home. Compare this modest effort to his "Portrait of a Young Woman," in the nearby Palazzo Ducale (see above), which shows the genius of his mature style. The museum also holds works by Raphael's lesser-known father, Giovanni Santi, a court painter to the duke.

Via Rafaello 57. www.casaraffaello.com. 3€. Mon–Sat 9am–1:30pm; Sun 10am–12:30pm and 3–5:30pm.

WHERE TO EAT IN URBINO

Taverna degli Artisti ★★ ITALIAN These vaulted underground rooms, one with colorful frescoes, are the place to try an Urbino favorite, *Strozzapretti con salmone, asparagi, e funghi:* thick, elongated pasta (the name means "priest choker") with a creamy sauce of salmon, asparagus, and mushrooms. The other pastas and pizzas are excellent, too.

Via Bramante 52. ✆ **0722/2676.** Entrees 8€–15€. Tues–Sun 12:30–2:30pm and 7:30–11pm.

ASSISI ★★★

27km (17 miles) E of Perugia, 175km (109 miles) SE from Florence, 175km (109 miles) NE from Rome

St. Francis is still working miracles: His birthplace remains a transporting Umbrian hill town, despite a steady onslaught of visitors. Many pilgrims come to pay homage to Francis at the Basilica di San Francisco; almost as many are drawn by Giotto's frescoes celebrating the life of the saint. You'll find a blend of romance and magic in Assisi's honey-colored stone, quiet lanes, and mists that rise and fall over the Val di Spoleto below town. With this saintly presence and pleasing ambience, Assisi is an essential stop on any Umbrian tour.

Essentials

ARRIVING About 20 trains run daily from **Perugia** (25–30 min.). From **Florence** (2–3 hr.), trains run almost hourly, though some require a transfer at Terontola; hourly trains run from Rome, many requiring a change in

The Basilica di San Francesco, resting place of St. Francis of Assisi.

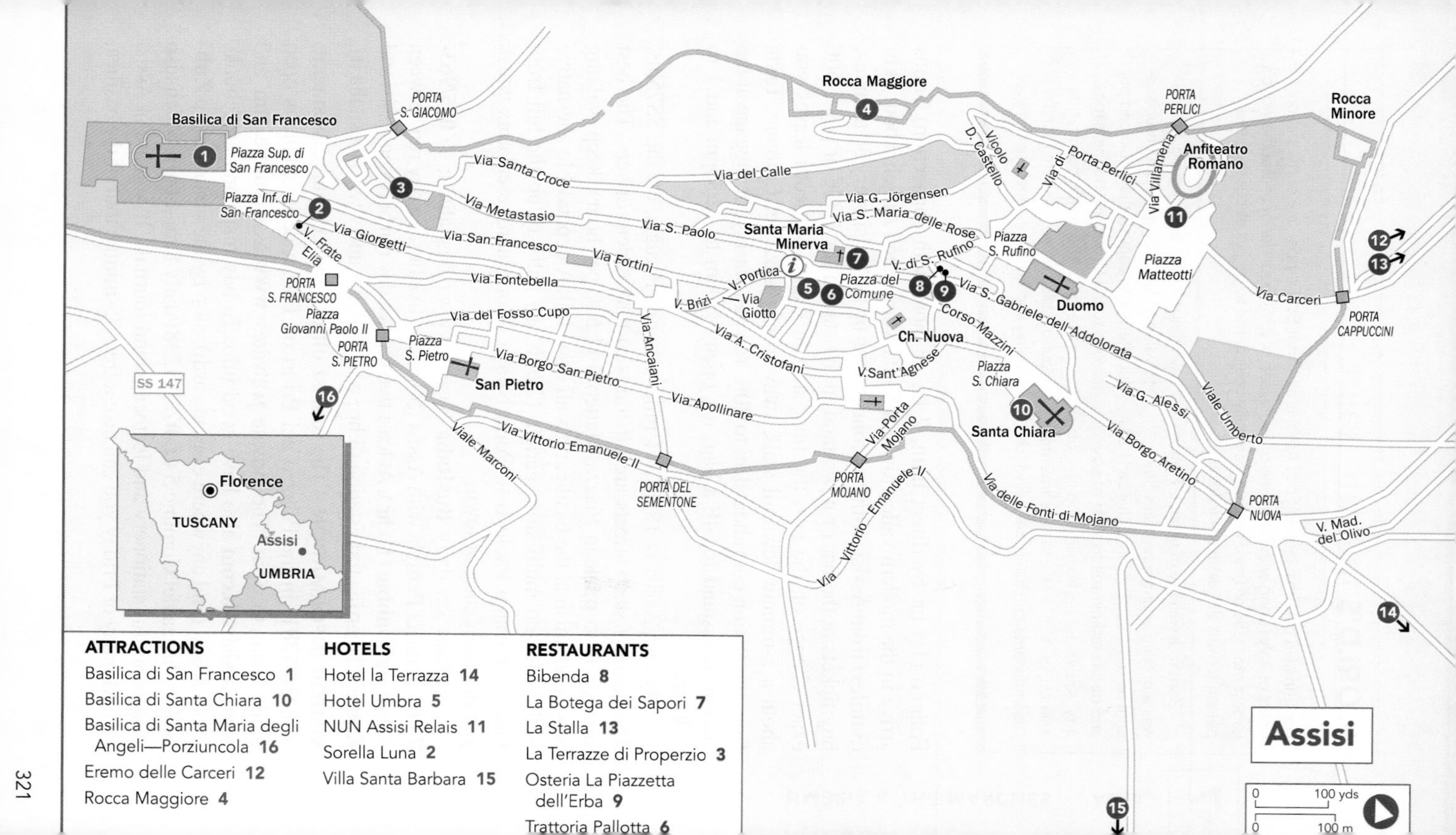
Assisi
Basilica di San Francesco
Piazza Sup. di San Francesco
Piazza Inf. di San Francesco
V. Frate Elia
PORTA S. FRANCESCO
Piazza Giovanni Paolo II
PORTA S. PIETRO
SS 147
PORTA S. GIACOMO
Via Santa Croce
Via Metastasio
Via Giorgetti
Via San Francesco
Via Fontebella
Via del Fosso Cupo
Piazza S. Pietro
San Pietro
Via Borgo San Pietro
Viale Marconi
Via Vittorio Emanuele II
PORTA DEL SEMENTONE
Via Ancaiani
Via Apollinare
Via A. Cristofani
V. Brizi
Via Giotto
V. Portica
Via Fortini
Via S. Paolo
Via del Calle
Rocca Maggiore
Santa Maria Minerva
Piazza del Comune
V. di S. Rufino
Via G. Jörgensen
Via S. Maria delle Rose
Vicolo D. Castello
Via di Porta Perlici
PORTA PERLICI
Via Villamena
Anfiteatro Romano
Rocca Minore
Piazza S. Rufino
Piazza Matteotti
Duomo
Via S. Gabriele dell'Addolorata
Corso Mazzini
Ch. Nuova
V. Sant'Agnese
Piazza S. Chiara
Santa Chiara
Via Porta Mojano
PORTA MOJANO
Via Vittorio Emanuele II
Via delle Fonti di Mojano
Via Borgo Aretino
Via G. Alessi
Viale Umberto
Via Carceri
PORTA CAPPUCCINI
PORTA NUOVA
V. Mad. del Olivo
Florence
TUSCANY
Assisi
UMBRIA
0 100 yds
0 100 m
ATTRACTIONS
Basilica di San Francesco 1
Basilica di Santa Chiara 10
Basilica di Santa Maria degli Angeli—Porziuncola 16
Eremo delle Carceri 12
Rocca Maggiore 4
HOTELS
Hotel la Terrazza 14
Hotel Umbra 5
NUN Assisi Relais 11
Sorella Luna 2
Villa Santa Barbara 15
RESTAURANTS
Bibenda 8
La Botega dei Sapori 7
La Stalla 13
La Terrazze di Properzio 3
Osteria La Piazzetta dell'Erba 9
Trattoria Pallotta 6

WORLD'S favorite saint

For Christian pilgrims, the magic of Assisi is all about **St. Francis,** one of the patron saints of Italy (along with Catherine of Siena, see p. 236). Founder of one of the world's largest monastic orders, Francis is generally considered to be just about the holiest person to walk the earth since Jesus.

Born to a wealthy merchant, Francis was a spoiled young man of his time, until he did an about-turn in his early 20s and dedicated himself to a life of poverty. Known for his humility and love of animals, he also is said to have invented Christmastime crèche scenes, all which have helped ensure his legend. Francis traveled as far as Egypt (in an unsuccessful attempt to convert the sultan and put an end to the Crusades), but he is most associated with the gentle countryside around Assisi, where he spent months praying and fasting in lonely hermitages.

Foligno (1¾ hr. by direct train, 2 hr. or more with connection) Trains arrive in the modern valley town of Santa Maria degli Angeli, about 5km (3 miles) from Assisi, with bus connections up to Assisi every 30 minutes; buy tickets at the bar or newsstand in the station for 1.30€ or pay 1.50€ exact change on the bus; the final stop in Piazza Matteotti leaves you about a 5-minute downhill walk away from Piazza del Comune. **Taxis** from the station cost about 15€ to 20€. You can stash your luggage at the station newsstand for 4€ a bag; it's open 6:30am to 12:30pm and 1 to 7:30pm.

By **car,** Assisi is 18km (11 miles) east of Perugia, off the SS75bis. The center's steep streets are off-limits to nonresident drivers. The best strategy is to **park** in Piazza Matteotti (1.50€ per hour), keep walking west, and finish at the basilica; it's all downhill. A dependable alternative is the Mojano multi-story garage (2.50€ hr.) halfway up the hill from Piazza Giovanni Paolo II to Porta Nuova. From there, escalators whisk you into the center of town.

At least six daily **BusItalia** buses (www.fsbusitalia.it; ✆ **075/963-7001**) connect Perugia with Assisi (50 min.); five buses a day run between Assisi and **Gubbio** (1¾ hr.). At least two buses a day run between Assisi and **Rome's** Tiburtina train station (3 hr.; www.sulga.it and www.fsbusitalia.it).

VISITOR INFORMATION The **tourist office** (www.comune.assisi.pg.it; ✆ **075/81381**) in the Palazzo dei Priori on Piazza del Comune is open daily 10am to 5pm. The private websites **www.assisionline.com** and **www.assisiweb.com** also have good info. To buy maps and guidebooks about Assisi (and anywhere else on earth), stop by the vintage shop **Zubboli** at Piazza del Comune 5 (✆ **075/81238;** daily 8am–8pm), which also sells beautiful stationery and leather-bound journals. If you are in Assisi on a Monday or Friday you can take a free, 75-minute tour of the basilica, in English, with a friar. Sign up in advance at info@sanfrancescoassisi.org.

Exploring Assisi

Assisi's geographical and civic heart is **Piazza del Comune,** with its 13th-century Palazzo del Capitano and the stately Corinthian columns of the Roman Tempio di Minerva guarding its northern fringe. The most atmospheric route to the basilica goes downhill from here along medieval Via Portica, which becomes Via Fortini and Via San Francesco before arriving at the main event.

Some pilgrims like to end a visit with a walk or drive out to the **Eremo delle Carceri,** a series of caves on the forested slopes of Monte Subasio where St. Francis would retire to pray and commune with nature; one of the grottos is equipped with a stone bed on which the saint slept. The hermitage is 4km (2½ miles) east of town

Basilica di San Francesco ★★★ RELIGIOUS SITE One of the most popular pilgrimage sites in Christendom combines homage to eternally popular St. Francis, masterworks of medieval architecture, and beloved works of Western art. The basilica is actually two churches, lower and upper; the lower church is dark and somber, a place of contemplation, while the upper church soars into light-filled Gothic vaults, instilling a sense of celebration. This assemblage was begun soon after the saint's death in 1226, under the guidance of Francis's savvy and worldly colleague Brother Elias. Set on a steeply sloping site just outside the city walls, previously used for executions and known as the Hill of Hell, the lower church was completed in 1230, the upper church in 1280. Today the presence of Francis, patron saint of Italy, and his credo "For it is in giving that we receive," still seems to permeate the soft gray stones. These frescoed spaces move the devout to tears and art lovers to fits of near-religious ecstasy.

THE LOWER CHURCH Entered off Piazza Inferiore di San Francesco (the lower of the two squares abutting the church), the basilica's bottom half is first and foremost a crypt, housing the stone **sarcophagus of St. Francis,** surrounded by four of his disciples. An almost steady stream of the faithful files past the monument, many on their knees. Inside is the saint's remarkably intact skeleton. Most saints of the Middle Ages fell victim to the purveyors of relics, who made enormous profit dispensing bones, a finger here, a toe there. Brother Elias, however, apparently had the foresight to seal Francis's coffin in stone, so his bones remained undetected, and thus undefiled. The dimly lit atmosphere is enlivened by many rich frescoes, including Simone Martini's action-packed "Life of St. Martin" in the **Cappella di San Martino** (1322–26). Martini displays a flair for boldly patterned fabrics and familiarity with detailed manuscript illumination. Martini was, like St. Martin, a knight, which may have influenced his depictions of the saint—a Roman soldier—being invested, ripping his cloak to share it with a beggar, and renouncing chivalry and weaponry in favor of doing good deeds. The imagery is not out of keeping with Francis, who as a youth dreamed of being a soldier. Giotto and his assistants frescoed the **Cappella della Santa Maria Maddalena** with the "Life of St. Mary Magdalene" (1303–09). An incredibly moving cycle of "Christ's Passion" (1316–19) by Pietro Lorenzetti includes a hauntingly humane "Deposition," in which the young Sienese artist depicts a gaunt Christ and sorrowful Mary, displaying a naturalism and emotion not before seen in painting.

THE UPPER CHURCH Entering the light-filled interior of the Upper Church, you'll first encounter **scenes of the New Testament** by Cimabue, the last great painter of the Byzantine style. Some critics say only the faded, vaguely surreal "Crucifixion" (1277) is his, the rest being by his assistants. In any case, it's ironic he's here at all: The artist was infamous for his stubborn, difficult character (in the *Divine Comedy,* Dante places him in Purgatory among the proud, adding that "Cimabue thought to hold the field of painting, and now Giotto hath the cry.") And it's Giotto who famously holds court in this church, with his 28-part fresco cycle **"The Life of St. Francis,"** completed in the 1290s. Even nonreligious viewers love the scenes of the saint removing his clothing to renounce material possessions, marrying poverty (symbolized by a woman in rags), and preaching to the birds (the subject of ubiquitous postcards on sale). Assisi itself stars in the panel in which a humble man spreads his cloak before Francis—the sturdy palaces of Piazza del Comune are a recognizable backdrop.

Piazza Superiore di San Francesco. www.sanfrancescoassisi.org. ✆ **075/819001.** Free. Lower Church daily 6am–6:30pm; Upper Church daily 8:30am–5:45pm.

Basilica di Santa Chiara ★★ CHURCH One of the first followers of St. Francis was a young woman, Chiara (Clare, in English), daughter of a count and countess, who was so swept away by the teachings of the zealot that she allowed him to cut her hair and dress her in sackcloth. She founded the order of the Poor Dames (now known as Poor Clares), whose members continue to renounce material possessions. Her remains lie in this vast, stark church on full view, her face covered in wax. Also in this church, the **Oratorio del Crocifisso** houses the venerated 12th-century crucifix from which the figure of Christ allegedly spoke to St. Francis, asking him to rebuild his church (the institution had by then become mired in corruption and warfare). As Clare lay ill on Christmas

Dress Appropriately

San Francesco and Santa Chiara have a strict dress code. Entrance is *forbidden* to those wearing shorts or miniskirts or showing bare shoulders. You also must remain silent and cannot take photographs in the Upper Church of San Francesco.

Eve 1252, she allegedly voiced regrets that she would not be able to attend services in the new Basilica di San Francisco. Suddenly, in a vision, she saw and heard the Mass clear as a bell and in color, a miracle for which in 1958 she was named the patron saint of television.

Piazza Santa Chiara. www.assisisantachiara.it. ✆ **075/812282.** Free. Daily 9am–noon and 2–6pm (7pm in summer).

Basilica di Santa Maria degli Angeli—Porziuncola ★★ CHURCH The seventh-largest church in Christendom sits on the plains below Assisi, on ground that's been hallowed since St. Francis died in 1226 in a simple infirmary cell, the Cappella del Transito, to one side of the present-day basilica. Beginning in 1569, pilgrim huts and friar cells were cleared to make room for this massive edifice, a century in the making. A soaring domed nave surrounds the well-preserved and heavily frescoed **Porziuncola** ("little portion"), a chapel that's been on this site since the 9th century, where Francis renounced his worldly goods to live among the poor, establishing the Franciscan order. Outside is the **rose garden** where Francis communed with turtle doves and asked them to be one with God.

Piazza della Porziuncola, Santa Maria degli Angeli. ✆ **075/805-1430.** Admission to basilica free, 3€ crypt, chapels, and museum. Daily 6:15am–12:30pm (until 12:45pm on Sun) and 2:30pm–7:30pm.

Rocca Maggiore ★★ CASTLE This civic show of might built of bleached yellow stone perches atop a steep hillside very high above Assisi. Some claim that a sharp-eyed observer can see all the way to the Mediterranean on a clear day. Hyperbole aside, views across the Umbrian plain below are wonderful, and you can enjoy them from the grounds without paying the admission fee to see the dull displays of costumes and weapons in the restored keep and soldiers' quarters.

Piazzale delle Libertà Comunali, at the ends of Via della Rocca, Via del Colle, and Vicolo San Lorenzo off Via Porta Perlici. www.umbriatourism.it. ✆ **075/8138680.** 6€ adults; 4€ ages 8–18 and over 65; free for ages 7 and under. Mid-Mar and Oct daily 10am–5:30pm; Apr–May and Sept daily 10am–7:30pm; June–Aug 9am–8pm; Nov–Feb 10am–4:30pm.

Where to Stay in Assisi

Especially from Easter to fall, never show up in Assisi without a hotel reservation. Don't even *think* of showing up without a reservation on **church holidays** or the **Calendimaggio,** a spring celebration the first weekend (starting Thursday) after May 1, which features processions and medieval contests of strength and skill, all in 14th-century costume. At these times you may wind up stuck overnight in one of the bus-pilgrimage facilities 4km (2½ miles) away in Santa Maria degli Angeli.

Hotel la Terrazza ★★ The best of two worlds come together here in the countryside just outside the town walls—the basilica and other sights are a 20-minute walk away, while a pool, garden, and green surroundings provide a break from Assisi's stony streets and squares. The nicest rooms are in a low-slung outbuilding facing lawns on one side and balcony views of the valley on the other, but those in a hotel section also open to gardens or balconies. Room decor is functionally comfortable, enlivened with colorful reproductions of Giotto's basilica murals over the beds to instill dreams of doing saintly deeds.

Via Fratelli Canonichetti 1. www.laterrazzahotel.it. ✆ **075/812368.** 40 units. 85€–130€ double. Rates include breakfast. **Amenities:** Restaurant; bar; pool; spa; free Wi-Fi.

Hotel Umbra ★★★ Assisi lodgings just don't get any homier than the Laudenzi family's traditional little inn, down a tiny alley from Piazza del Comune. A gate opens into a shady patio, and beyond are comfortable, if a bit outdated, guest rooms with vaulted ceilings, fresco fragments, and other historic remnants here and there, all nicely furnished with old-fashioned armoires and dressers. Views over rooftops to the valley below unfold through the tall windows, from airy public terraces, and a few private ones.

Via Degli Archi 6 (off west end of Piazza del Comune). www.hotelumbra.it. ✆ **075/812240.** 24 units. 110€–145€ double. Rates include breakfast. Closed mid-Jan to Easter. **Amenities:** Babysitting; concierge; room service; free Wi-Fi.

NUN Assisi Relais ★★ A contemporary redo of a centuries-old convent offers a break from Assisi's heavily medieval aura in handsome guest quarters with all-white surfaces and bursts of color, accented with stone walls and arches and boldly turned out with Eames chairs, laminate tables, and high-tech lighting. A two-level suite with a hanging sleeping loft is focused on a massive 13th-century fresco of saints in the wilderness. Downstairs are pleasures the former tenants could never have dreamed of: two pools, sauna and steam room, and a state-of-the-art spa.

Eremo delle Carceri 1A. www.nunassisi.com. ✆ **075/815-5150.** 18 units. 450€–550€ double. Rates include breakfast. Closed Jan to mid-Feb. **Amenities:** Restaurant; bar; concierge; indoor pools; room service; sauna; steam room; spa; free Wi-Fi.

Sorella Luna ★★ Renovators have given this 15th-century palace a contemporary slant, with a flower-filled terraced garden and glassed-in atriums. In the bright guest rooms, stone walls and wood beams offset the modern furnishings and tiled baths. The name refers to Clare (Sorella Luna), the follower of St. Francis whose church is on the other end of town. The Basilica di San Francisco is just down the street.

Via Frate Ella 5. www.hotelsorellaluna.it. ✆ **075/816194.** 13 units. 80€–95€ double. Rates include breakfast. Closed Jan–Feb. **Amenities:** Free Wi-Fi.

Villa Santa Barbara ★★★ If you have a car, consider visiting Assisi from smaller nearby towns, like the appealing wine village of Montefalco (see box p. 329), about 20 minutes south and a nice place to relax while touring the region. This old estate from the 16th century will make you feel like a guest in a gracious Italian villa and puts you up in airy, light-filled bedrooms comfortably equipped with armchairs, king-size beds, nice antiques, and big marble-sheathed bathrooms. Palm-shaded gardens surround the pool, and welcoming lounges are filled with books and pottery. Dinners are served in a vaulted room glistening with terra-cotta tiles.

Locanda San Luca (just E of Montefalco). www.hotelvillasantabarbara.com. © **0742/399-402.** 34 units. 165€–195€ double. Rates include breakfast. Closed Nov–Mar. **Amenities:** Restaurant; bar; pool; free Wi-Fi.

Where to Eat in Assisi

Assisi's restaurants serve a local flatbread called *torta al testo,* often grilled and split and stuffed with cheeses, sausages, and vegetables (spinach is popular). Another Umbrian classic is *porchetta,* roasted pork stuffed with garlic and herbs; it's often served from sidewalk stands with *torta al testo.* **La Botega dei Sapori,** a wine and food shop on Piazza del Comune (no. 34; © **075/812204**), serves platters of local meats and cheese and a delicious *porchetta* sandwich, accompanied by excellent wines. Seating is limited, but if you wish, they'll fix a snack plate for you to take back to your hotel. They also ship wines. **Bibenda,** an atmospheric wine cellar off Piazzetta dell'Erba at Vicolo Nepis 9 (www.bibendaassisi.it; © **075/815-5176**), pairs Umbrian wines with small plates of local cheeses and salami. Popular in these parts are Grechettos, full-bodied, honey-colored whites from the nearby Montefalco vineyards (see p. 329).

La Stalla ★★ GRILL/UMBRIAN A 15-minute walk into the countryside will work up an appetite for a hearty meal in these rustic, stone-walled rooms, converted from livestock stalls. Begin with the *assaggini di torta al testo,* samplers of flatbread stuffed with cheese, meat, and vegetables, then move through a selection of pastas to simple servings of grilled steak, chicken, pork, and sausage skewers, accompanied by grilled potatoes. House wines complement the meals; you can dine on a terrace in good weather.

Santuario della Carceri 24, 1.5km (about 1 mile) from center, direction Eremo. www.fontemaggio.it. © **075/813636.** Entrees 8€–13€. Thurs–Mon 12:30–2:30pm and 7:30–10pm; Tues–Wed 7:30–10pm. Closed Jan–Feb.

La Terrazze di Properzio ★★ UMBRIAN Award for best view goes to these attractive stone-walled rooms opening onto a terrace that seems to float above the valley. This is Assissi's most romantic warm-weather dining experience. Lofty as the setting is, the menu focuses on such down-to-earth classics as fried artichokes, pasta carbonara, and boar stew. Reserve for a terrace table.

Via Metastasio 13. © **075/816868.** Entrees 9€–16€. Daily 12:15–2:30pm and 7:20–9:30pm. Closed Jan–mid-Feb.

Osteria La Piazzetta dell'Erba ★★ UMBRIAN The arched room and flower-filled terrace facing a market square seem in keeping with this postcard-perfect hill town, but the kitchen breaks from tradition with Asian takes on Umbrian classics. Even a stalwart Umbrian *costolette di maiale* (baked pork ribs) gets a fresh twist with a honey yogurt sauce, while tartares of salmon and tuna, *tataki di tonno* (a Japanese method of quick searing marinated tuna), and sushi, *maki* rolls, and poke bowls break from the meat-heavy local cuisine with a taste of the sea. Via San Gabriele dell'Addolorata 15b. www.osteriapiazzettadellerba.it. ✆ **075/815352.** Entrees 8€–18€. Tues–Sun 12:30–2:30pm and 7:30–10pm.

Trattoria Pallotta ★★ UMBRIAN All the warmth of Assisi comes to the fore in these beamed, tiled, and charmingly furnished rooms tucked under the arches off Piazza del Comune. The food is satisfyingly Umbrian, too—homemade pastas with rich sauces, roasted rabbit, and grilled filets. Piazza del Comune. www.trattoriapallotta.it. ✆ **075/815-5273.** Entrees 12€–20€. Wed–Mon noon–3pm and 7–9:30pm.

A Side Trip to Spello ★

14km (9 miles) S of Assisi

There are a couple of compelling reasons to make the short trip down SS75 from Assisi to this hill town of pink and honey-colored stone on the flanks of Monte Subasio. For one thing, it's beguilingly pretty, unspoiled, and relatively undiscovered, with fewer tourists than its more famous

The flower-lined streets of Spello.

CLIMBING HIGHER: more hill towns

For sheer picturesqueness, few Umbrian hill towns can match proud **Todi ★★**, 45km (28 miles) southwest of Spello. At the top of the town is the finest square in Umbria, an assemblage of 12th- to 14th-century palaces and the Duomo, with belvederes that provide soaring views of the rolling Umbrian countryside and Tiber Valley below.

Montefalco ★, 18km (11 miles) southwest of Spello on SR316, tops a hill above the Valle Umbra, with the five-sided Piazza del Commune at the highest point in town. Surrounding vineyards yield Sagrantino reds; the **Strada del Sagrantino** wine trail office, Piazza del Comune 17 (www.stradadelsagrantino.it; ✆ **0742/378490**), can set you up with maps and winery-tour info. Art lovers come here for a charming mid-15th-century fresco cycle of the life of St. Francis by Florentine master Benozzo Gozzoli, in the **Museo di San Francesco,** Via Ringhiera Umbra 6 (www.museomontefalco.it; ✆ **0742/379598;** 7€; Apr–Oct daily 10:30am–6pm [to 7pm June–Aug]; Nov–Mar Wed–Sun 10:30am–1pm and 2:30–5pm).

Rather than clinging to a hillside, **Bevagna ★★**, 8km (5 miles) north of Montefalco on SP443, nestles on the floor of the Valle Umbra beside the River Teverone. Inside sturdy gates, Bevagna seems firmly locked into the Middle Ages, with the simply ornamented churches of **San Michele Arcangelo** and **San Silvestro** facing each other across Piazza Silvestri (both usually open 9am–1pm and 4–7pm). The mosaic floor of a ruined bath complex on Via Terme Romana, with a swirl of octopi and other sea creatures, is a reminder of the town's prosperity as a Roman outpost on the Via Flaminia; the ruins are part of the **Museo Civico,** Corso Giacomo Matteotti 70 (www.sistemamuseo.it; ✆ **0742/360081;** 7€; Apr–Jan daily 10am–1pm and 3–6pm; Feb–Mar Thurs–Sun 10am–1pm and 2:30–5:30pm).

neighbor. Then there's Pinturicchio—"The Little Painter"—who created one of Umbria's great masterpieces, color-saturated frescoes of the life of Christ in the Cappello Baglioni (see below). The **tourist office** in Piazza Matteotti (www.comune.spello.pg.it; ✆ **0742/301009**) is open daily 9:30am to 12:30pm and 3:30 to 5:30pm.

Cappella Baglioni ★★★ CHURCH/MUSEUM Spello's powerful Baglioni family decided to use this side chapel in the Santa Maria Maggiore church to generate some good press, and maybe some goodwill with the Almighty. Troilo Baglioni commissioned Pinturicchio to paint scenes from the boyhood of Christ after the Red Wedding in June 1500, when one branch of the family turned against the other in a murderous bloodbath (inspiration for a *Games of Thrones* episode). The color-filled frescoes are enchanting, filled with rich architectural detail and Umbrian landscapes, with some sly cynical commentaries (note the church treasurer with bursting money bags witnessing the Annunciation). Pinturicchio himself appears in a portrait in the Annunciation scene, and Troilo Baglioni shows up in the Disputation in the Temple.
Piazza Matteotti. Free. Daily 9:45am–12:30pm and 3:30–5pm.

WHERE TO STAY & EAT IN SPELLO

Hotel Palazzo Bocci ★★ If rooms at the inns in Assisi are full, consider settling into Spello in style at the palace of a 15th-century merchant, converted in the 18th and 19th centuries to its fairly splendid current state. The vaulted salons are suitably regal, filled with antiques and trompe l'oeil detailing, while guest rooms retain all the character you'd expect from historic surroundings in which frescoes and marble mantelpieces are standard-issue. Views from rooms in the rear are especially refreshing, overlooking a large garden and terrace to the valley below.
Via Cavour 17. www.palazzobocci.com. ✆ **0742/301021.** 100€–115€ double. Rates include breakfast. Closed Jan–Mar. **Amenities:** Restaurant; bar; free Wi-Fi.

SPOLETO ★★

63km (39 miles) SE of Perugia

Spoleto feels like the center of the cultured world in June, when the **Festival dei Due Mondi** (aka **Spoleto Festival**) draws performers and audiences from all over the world. For most of the year, though, Spoleto is just another appealing Umbrian hill town, a pleasant warren of steep streets and airy piazzas lined with artifacts from the Roman past and prosperous Middle Ages, including one of Italy's most beautifully situated cathedrals.

Essentials

ARRIVING Spoleto is a main **rail** station on the Rome-Ancona line, and 16 daily trains from **Rome** stop here (about 1½ hr.). From **Perugia,** take one of the 20 daily trains to Foligno (25 min.) to transfer to this line for the final 20-minute leg. From outside the station, you can take bus AC or B to the Posterna stop, where you can get on the moving walkway (see below); or from the station it's a level 10-minute walk to Piazza della Vittoria on the edge of the old town. Buses from the station run about every 20 to 20 minutes and the fare is 1.30€; buy a ticket at a *tabacchi* or newsstand.

By **car,** approach town on the old Roman Via Flaminia, now the SS3. Three lots/garages are at the base of the hill: Spoletosfera, Posterna, and Ponzianina are all connected to sights in the old town above via escalators, moving sidewalks, and elevators. Parking is about 1€ per hour; take a ticket upon entering and pay in a machine upon leaving. Hotels will help you arrange long-term parking.

VISITOR INFORMATION The **information center** is at Largo Francesco Ferrer 7 (www.visitspoleto.it; ✆ **0743/220773;** Mon–Sat 9am–1:30pm and 2:30–6pm, Sun 9am–1pm. The office hands out useful booklets on the town's sights and an excellent map. You'll find good information online at www.comune.spoleto.pg.it/turismoecultura/en. The **Spoleto Card,** valid for 7 days, provides admission to the Casa Romana, Rocca, Teatro Romana, and several other sights; the cost is 9.50€, 8€ seniors, while separate

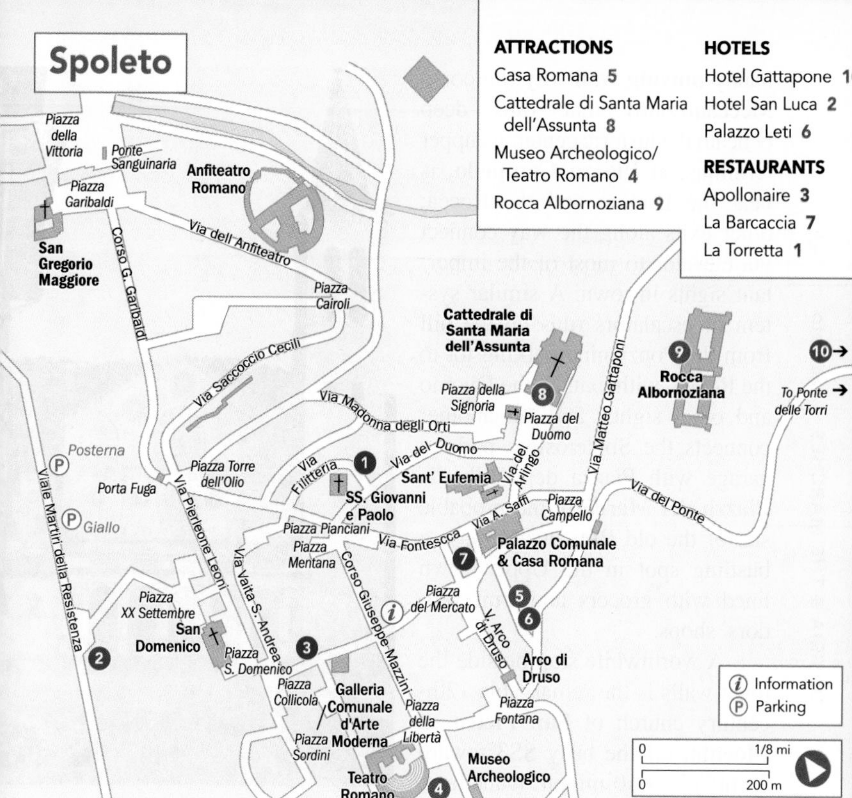

admission to just the three sights mentioned here would come to 14.50€; the card is available at participating sights.

Exploring Spoleto

While the upper town is the main attraction, before you head uphill, stop by the imposing 11th-century Romanesque church of **San Gregorio di Maggiore,** Piazza della Vittoria (© **0743/44140;** free admission; daily 8am–noon and 4–6pm). The church's namesake saint was killed at the nearby amphitheater in A.D. 304, along with some 10,000 other lesser-known martyrs; their bones reside beneath the altar. Pop into the Cappella degli Innocenti, on the left side of the portico, to see a fresco depicting Spoleto as it looked in the 16th century (little has changed since then). Across the piazza, a gated staircase, open most mornings, leads down to a platform where you can view **Ponte Sanguinario,** a massive 1st-century travertine bridge 24m (79 ft.) long, and 4.5m (15 ft.) wide, which over the centuries was buried in sediment from the stream it once crossed. It's an easy 5-minute walk south from San Gregorio Maggiore along Via Interna delle Mura to the Posterna parking garage, where you can get on the handy **moving walkway** (Percorso Meccanizzato) that runs deep beneath the historic center. Its upper terminus, at **Piazza Campello,** is near the Duomo and the Rocca; other exits along the way connect via elevator to most of the important sights in town. A similar system of escalators runs up the hill from the Ponzianina parking lot to the Rocca, with exits at the Duomo and other sights, and yet another connects the Spoletosfera parking garage with Piazza della Libertà. **Piazza del Mercato,** the probable site of the old Roman forum, is a bustling spot in the Upper Town lined with grocers and fruit vendors' shops.

Cattedrale di Santa Maria Assunta in Spoleto.

A worthwhile stop outside the town walls is the remarkable 12th-century church of **San Pietro ex Moenia,** off the busy SS3 toward Terni; it's a 10-minute walk from the Spoletosfera parking garage (reached by moving walkway from Piazza della Libertà in the Upper Town). The interior is sparse (usually open 9am–6pm), but spend your time contemplating New Testament scenes and a complex catechism of Christian symbols on the remarkable Romanesque facade—Christ washing the feet of his disciples, deer and snakes, foxes and crows, holy men in little boats, all charmingly rendered by medieval sculptors.

Casa Romana ★ HISTORIC HOME As a stop on the busy Via Flaminia route and an important wine supplier, Spoletium was fairly prosperous in the Roman world. Enough of this patrician's home remains, including frescoes and mosaics, to give an idea of what the good life was like for a Roman occupant in the A.D. 1st century. The resident was obviously well-to-do, though there's no proof for the claim that she was Vespasia Polla, the mother of the Emperor Vespasian.

Via di Visiale. ✆ **0743/40255.** 3€ adults; 2€ ages 15–25; free for children 14 and under. Included with the Spoleto Card. Wed–Mon 10am–1:30pm and 2–5:30pm.

Cattedrale di Santa Maria dell'Assunta (Duomo) ★★ CATHEDRAL Spoleto's almost playfully picturesque cathedral was consecrated in 1098, barely 40 years after Frederick Barbarossa, Holy Roman

Emperor, razed the entire town in retaliation for the citizens' lack of support in his ongoing wars against the papacy. The church seems to defy the brutality of that catastrophe, set in a broad piazza at the bottom of a long, leisurely cascade of steps. White marble and golden mosaics on the dazzling facade are framed against a gentle backdrop of a forested hill. Inside, the apse is graced with frescoes of the "Life of the Virgin," largely from the brush of Filippo Lippi, one of the more colorful characters of his time. An ordained priest, Filippo shirked his duties and was eventually given permission to paint full-time. Though he worked frequently and was a favorite of the Medicis, he was chronically impoverished, supposedly because he spent so much money on women. The commission to come to Spoleto must have been a plum for the artist, then close to 60. His engaging scenes of the Virgin being visited by the Archangel and holding her sweet-looking infant betray nothing of the turbulence in his life—he was fighting to get dispensation to marry a young nun, Lucrezia Buti, who had borne his son, Filippino Lippi (who would soon match his father's greatness as a painter). Both Lippis appear in the Dormition of the Virgin scene, Filippo wearing a white habit with young Filippino, as an angel, in front of him. Filippo died before he completed the frescoes; his assistants finished the task. The cause of his death was suspected to be poison, perhaps administered by Lucrezia's family or yet another paramour. He is buried beneath a monument on the right side of the transept, which his son Filippino designed. The **Cappella delle Reliquie** (Reliquary Chapel), on the left aisle, holds a rare treasure—a letter written and signed by St. Francis. (Assisi has his only other bona-fide signature.) An Art of the Spirit audioguide tour also visits the nearby Church of Sant'Eufemia and Diocesan Museum, and in season (Apr–Oct) explores the cathedral's upper galleries and campanile.

Piazza del Duomo. www.duomospoleto.it. ✆ **0743/218620.** Free. Art of the Spirit Tour 9€. Mon–Sat 10:30am–7 pm (Nov–Feb until 5pm); Sun 12:30–6pm (Nov–Feb until 5pm).

Museo Archeologico/Teatro Romano ★ MUSEUM/RUINS Spoleto had the good fortune to flourish through the Dark Ages and the Middle Ages—which meant that most of the Roman city was quarried or built over. In 1891 it was discovered that the monastery of St. Agata had been built atop this splendid ancient theater. Thoroughly restored in the 1950s, the theater is an evocative performance venue, often used during the Spoleto Festival. Much of the original orchestra flooring is intact, as is an elaborate drainage system (installed for flushing out the blood of slain animals and martyrs). Busts and statuary that once adorned the theater are on display in the adjoining Museo Archeologico. ***Tip:*** You can view the theater for free from the east end of Piazza della Libertà.

Via di Sant'Agata 18A. www.musei.umbria.beniculturali.it. ✆ **0743/223277.** 4€ adults; 2€ ages 18–25; free for ages 17 and under. Included with the Spoleto Card. Thurs–Sun 8:30am–1:30pm.

Rocca Albornoziana ★★ CASTLE Cardinal Albornoz, a power-hungry zealot tasked with rebuilding and strengthening the papal states, arrived in Spoleto in the mid-14th century and commissioned the Umbrian architect Matteo Gattapone to build a fortress. The site was perfect—atop a high hill above the town and virtually impregnable. The walled-and-moated castle became famous in the 20th century as one of Italy's most secure prisons, where members of the Red Brigades terrorist organization were routinely incarcerated. (The fortunate ones might have had a view through their cell windows of the majestic **Ponte delle Torri**—see "A Walk Above Spoleto," p. 336.) The current occupant of the fortress is the **Museo Nazionale del Ducato di Spoleto** (✆ **0743/223055**), a somewhat numbing collection of sarcophagi, mosaics, and statuary. (There's also a highly reputed school here that trains students in the craft of restoring books and manuscripts, but that's off-limits to the public.) You can walk around the Rocca grounds, no admission fee required, to enjoy spectacular views of the town and Umbrian countryside—and it's an easy trip up to these heights, via a series of escalators and elevators.

Spoleto's Big Bash

Over 3 weeks from the end of June through early July, the **Spoleto Festival dei Due Mondi** (www.festivaldispoleto.com) stages world-class drama, music, and dance in such evocative spaces as the open-air restored Roman theater and the piazza fronting the Duomo. A secondary **Spoleto d'Estate** season (www.comune.spoleto.pg.it) runs from just after the festival through September.

Piazza Campello. ✆ **0743/224952.** 7.50€ adults; 2€ ages 15–25; free for ages 17 and under. Included with the Spoleto Card. Daily 9:30am–7:30pm.

Where to Stay in Spoleto

Accommodations are tight during the Spoleto Festival; reserve by March if you want to find a room. Whether arriving by car or public transport, ask for explicit directions on how to reach your hotel—navigating the Upper Town, built on many different hillside levels, can be a challenge.

Hotel Gattapone ★ From the street, this hideaway beneath the Rocca Albornoziana looks like a relatively modest 19th-century villa. But step inside and there's a 1960s Antonioni-film feel to the place: polished wood, free-floating staircases, and leather couches facing windows overlooking the Ponte delle Torre and green Monteluco hillsides. Guest rooms have slightly dated but well-maintained contemporary furnishings mixed with traditional pieces, and large, view-filled windows. Some guests comment that the air-conditioning is vintage, too. Travelers with mobility issues should know there's no elevator, and rooms and lounges are set on several levels.

Via del Ponte 6. hotel-gattapone-spoleto.booked.net. ✆ **0743/223447.** 15 units. 75€–85€ double. Rates include breakfast. **Amenities:** Bar; free Wi-Fi.

Hotel San Luca ★★★ A 19th-century tannery at the far edge of the city next to the Roman walls lends itself well to its current incarnation. A book-lined lounge, where canaries chirp in an antique cage and a fire crackles in cold months, faces a large courtyard, and so do many rooms; others overlook a rose garden to the side. The unusually large quarters are all different, a mix of traditional and contemporary pieces with a smattering of antiques, plus extremely large and well-equipped marble bathrooms. Sights and restaurants are about a 5-minute walk away, and the attentive staff will map out a route that involves the least amount of climbing. The easy-to-reach in-house garage is a real rarity in Spoleto.

Via Interna delle Mura 21. www.hotelsanluca.com. ✆ **0743/223399.** 35 units. 90€–120€ double. Rates include breakfast. Closed Jan–Feb. **Amenities:** Bar; babysitting; bikes; concierge; room service; garage (15€); free Wi-Fi

Palazzo Leti ★★★ An entrance through a Renaissance garden that opens to the Tessino gorge announces that this beautifully restored 13th-century palace of the Leti family is a rather special place. Views of the gorge and green Monteluco hills are the focal point of most rooms, though a few overlook a medieval alley that has its own charm; all have period furniture and rich fabrics, plus couches and armchairs in the larger rooms and wood beams, granite hearths, and vaulted ceilings throughout. Anna Laura and Gianpaolo, who restored the palace from a dilapidated pile, are a friendly presence and provide all sorts of helpful advice.

Via degli Eremiti 10. www.palazzoleti.com. ✆ **0743/224930.** 12 units. 120€–150€ double. Rates include breakfast. Closed Feb to early Mar. **Amenities:** Bar; bikes; spa; free Wi-Fi.

Where to Eat in Spoleto

Norcia, 40km (25 miles) east of Spoleto in the Apennine mountains, famously produces pork sausage, salami, prosciutto, and other cured meats that show up in shops and restaurants in Spoleto and throughout Umbria. Many dishes are prepared *alla Norcina,* meaning with pork in some variation. A nice spot for an aperitivo is **Caffè degli Artisti,** Piazza del Mercato 32, where your drink will come with a heaping platter of appetizers (✆ **0743/225071**). **Prosciutteria del Corso,** near Piazza della Libertà at Corso Mazzini 73, makes delicious sandwiches from these ingredients (✆ **0743/224014;** daily noon–3pm and 7pm–midnight). **Gelateria Crispini,** Viale Trento e Trieste 29, serves some of Umbria's best gelato, notably the pistachio and "bread and chocolate" flavors (www.gelaticrispini.it; ✆ **0743/235015;** daily 1–8pm, from 3pm Sun).

Apollonaire ★★ UMBRIAN The low wood ceilings, stone walls, and beams are traditional holdovers from a 12th-century Franciscan monastery, while the adventurous menu puts a fresh twist on fresh local ingredients and traditional recipes: *Strangozzi* (the local long, rectangular wheat pasta) is topped with a pungent sauce of cherry tomatoes and mint;

herb-roasted rabbit is served with black olive sauce; and pork filet mignon is topped with a sauce of pecorino cheese and pears soaked in Rosso di Montefalco.

Via Sant'Agata 14 (near Piazza della Libertà). www.ristoranteapollinare.it. ✆ **0743/223256.** Entrees 12€–24€. Wed–Mon 12:30–2:30pm and 7:30–10:30pm. Closed Feb.

La Barcaccia ★★ UMBRIAN Despite the name (the "Old Boat"), these brightly lit rooms are set on dry land near the top of the town—and, except for some Adriatic fish choices, the menu is firmly landlocked in Umbrian classics. This is the place to strangle the priest, that is, enjoy the *strangozzi alla spoletina* (with peppery tomato sauce), named for rebellious clergy who broke with the papacy in the 14th century. A good choice of vegetarian dishes includes *scamorza,* a cow's milk cheese similar to mozzarella, baked with radicchio.

Piazza Fratelli Bandiera 4. www.ristorantelabarcaccia.it. ✆ **0743/225082.** Entrees 9€–18€. Wed–Mon 11am–3pm and 6–10pm.

La Torretta ★★★ UMBRIAN In two welcoming rooms in a medieval tower, brothers Stefano and Elio Salvucci extend a genuine welcome and a nice selection of Umbrian dishes. Delicious starters such as *tris di antipasti al tartufo estivo* (trio of truffle-based appetizers) and *zuppa di farro* (spelt soup with sausage) pave the way for beautifully seasoned pork or beef grilled over a wood fire. The kitchen also makes a light-as-air truffle omelet, a memorable break from heavier *secondi.*

Via Filitteria 43. www.trattorialatorretta.com. ✆ **0743/44954.** Entrees 10€–20€. Mon, Wed–Sat 12:30–2:30pm and 7:30–10pm; Sun 12:30–2:30pm.

Osteria Del Matto Di Proietti Filippo ★★★ UMBRIAN You'll put yourself in the hands of friendly Filippo Proietti when you walk in the door of this charmingly eclectic and old-fashioned room off the market square. He brings you whatever the kitchen is preparing that day, five or six courses, always including a pasta or two and many appetizers, along with a meat or fish course, and dessert. House wine is a little extra, and excellent, and grappa usually follows. The total will rarely be more than 30€ a person.

Piazza del Mercato 3, Spoleto. ✆ **0743/225506.** Set price menu 25€. Daily 11am–4pm and 7–11pm.

A Walk Above Spoleto

Climbing Spoleto's steep streets is exercise in itself, but if you want to stretch your legs a bit more, try the fairly easy, well-marked scenic walk that makes a circuit from Piazza Campello around the base of the **Rocca** (p. 334). Views over the town and countryside include a closeup look at the **Ponte delle Torri,** a 232m- (760-ft.) long aqueduct built in the 13th century on Roman foundations. its arches spanning a deep, verdant gorge 90m (295 ft.) down to the Tessino river. From there the trail crosses a forested hillside, then descends through olive groves into the valley. The only gear you'll need for this trek are comfortable walking shoes and a camera.

ORVIETO ★★

87km (54 miles) W of Spoleto, 86km (53 miles) SW of Perugia

Walking through the streets of Orvieto, you might be pleased to discover that nothing much has changed in the past 500 years. Adding to the magic is what might be Italy's most beautiful cathedral, with a facade covered in dazzling mosaics and statuary and rising above an airy piazza. The final coup de grace is the fact that the entire town is set atop a volcanic outcropping some 315m (1,033 ft.) above the green countryside. This impenetrable perch ensured that Etruscan "Velzna" was among the most powerful members of the *dodecapoli* (Etruscan confederation of 12 cities). The lofty setting continues to make Orvieto seem a world apart.

Essentials

ARRIVING Fourteen **trains** on the main **Rome-Florence** line stop at Orvieto daily (1 hr., 45 min. from Florence; 1 hr., 20 min. from Rome). From **Perugia,** take the train to Terontola (16 trains daily) to transfer to this line heading south toward Rome, for a total trip time of 1½ hours. From **Spoleto**, hourly trains connect through **Orte,** for a total trip time of just over 2 hours. Orvieto makes a convenient stopover on a train trip between Rome and Florence; you can store bags at the Welcome Point (www.orvietoviva.com) behind the train station in the Piazza della Pace (3€ per large bag for 4 hr., 15€ for 24 hr.; open 9am–6pm). Orvieto's **station** is in the valley, in Orvieto Scalo, but right across the street from the station, a **funicular** (www.orvietoviva.com; 1.30€; every 10 min. from 7:15am–8:30pm [from 8am holidays]) ascends to hilltop Orvieto. It's an easy, level 10-minute walk from the upper terminus to the Duomo and other sights in the historic center, and a free shuttle bus runs to and from Piazza Duomo.

Orvieto is easy to reach by **car:** It's right off the A1. A main link to the rest of Umbria is the SS448 to Todi (40 min.) for the E45 between Perugia and Terni. You can drop off your car at the large free parking lot behind the train station off Piazza della Pace and take the funicular up to town, but if you want to get a bit closer, a lot and garage at Campo della Fiera, just outside the Porta Romana, is connected by an elevator/escalator system up to Piazza San Giovanni or Piazza Ranieri. Parking here and at lots on the perimeter of the upper town costs 1.50€ an hour.

VISITOR INFORMATION The **tourist office** is opposite the Duomo at Piazza Duomo 24 (www.comune.orvieto.tr.it; © **0763/341772**). It's open Monday to Friday 9am to 1pm and 3 to 6pm, Saturday and Sunday 10am to 7pm.

Exploring Orvieto

Life in Orvieto transpires on and around animated **Corso Cavour,** cutting through the center of town. If you take the funicular up from the lower town, you'll begin your walk through Orvieto at the eastern end of the street. In the very center of town rises the **Torre del Moro,** a 13th-century show of civic might that provides views across all the territory the medieval city controlled, stretching east to the Apennines and west to the Mediterranean. To enjoy those views today, you'll take an elevator and then climb up 171 steps (3.80€, 2€ seniors; open daily May–Aug 10am–8pm, Mar–Apr and Sept–Oct 10am–7pm, Nov–Feb 10:30am–4:30pm). Locals have been setting their time by the clock for the past 700 years. Just to the north is **Piazza del Popolo,** where the Capitano del Popolo (Captain of the People) ruled from the formidable, crenellated Palazzo del Popolo. The square is filled with market stalls on Thursday and Saturday mornings. **Via del Duomo** leads south from the tower to Orvieto's masterwork, one of the most celebrated cathedrals in Italy.

Orvieto's other great wonder is the volcanic plug upon which it sits. To look at the city's tufa foundations, take a hike along the ***rupe,*** a path that encircles the base of the cliff. (The tourist office can supply a map.) A landmark along the north side of the path is the **Necropoli Etrusca di Crocifisso del Tufo** (Etruscan Necropolis), where ancient Etruscan tombs

The richly decorated facade of Orvieto's Duomo.

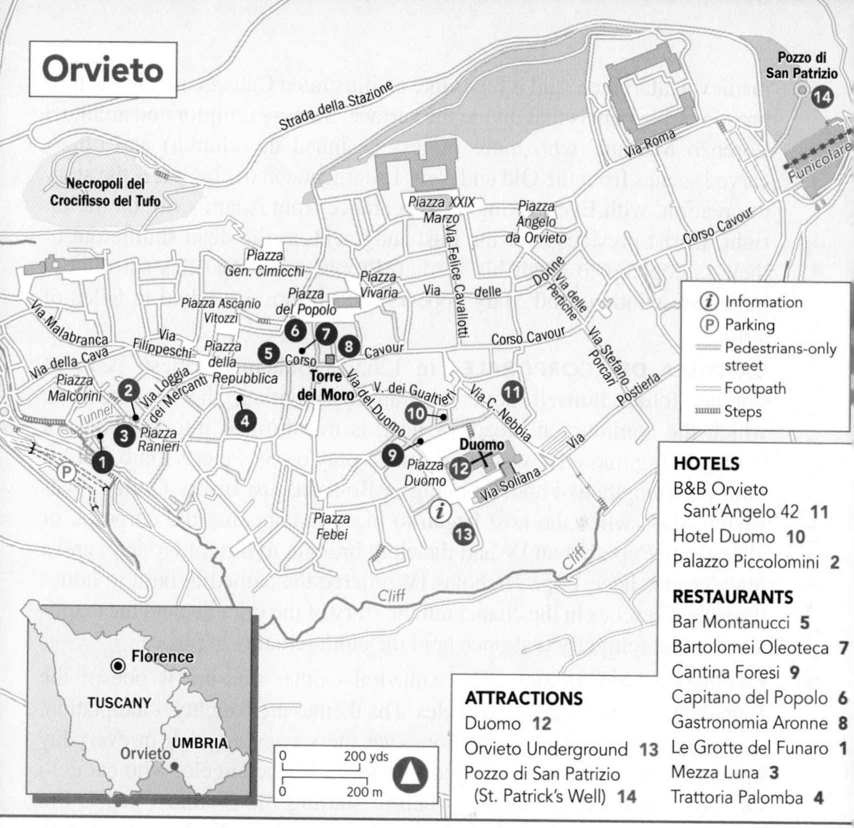

lie in a gridlike pattern in subterranean caverns (www.musei.umbria.beniculturali.it; ✆ **0763/343611;** 3€; Wed and Fri 9am–6pm, Thurs and Sat 9am–3pm, second and third Sun of the month 9am–6pm). Many of the jewelry, ceramics, and other finds are in the town's two small archaeological collections on Piazza Duomo: The **Museo Archeologico Nazionale** (www.musei.umbria.beniculturali.it; ✆ **0763/341039**) is open Tuesday through Sunday 8:30am to 7:30pm, and admission is 4€; the **Museo Claidio Faina di Orvieto** (museofaina.it; ✆ **0763/341511**) is open Wednesday through Monday 9:30am to 6pm (10am–5pm Jan–Feb), and admission is 6€. You can also stroll along the high ramparts that fringe the edges of town. Some of the most accessible are on the west side, just past Sant'Agostino church.

Duomo ★★★ CATHEDRAL Orvieto's pièce de résistance is a mesmerizing assemblage of spikes and spires, mosaics and marble statuary—and that's just the facade. The rest of the bulky-yet-elegant church is banded in black and white stone and seems to perch miraculously on the edge of the cliffs that surround the town. The church is wider at the front than at the back, designed to create the optical illusion upon entering that the nave is longer than it actually is. The facade has been compared to a medieval altarpiece, and it reads like an illustrated Catechism. On the four broad marble panels that divide the surface, Sienese sculptor and architect Lorenzo Maitani (who more or less designed the church) and others carved scenes from the Old and New Testament. On the far left is the story of creation, with Eve making an appearance from Adam's rib; on the far right, Christ presides over the Last Judgment, as the dead shuffle out of their sarcophagi to await his verdict. Prophets and apostles surround a huge rose window, and Mary appears in lush mosaics inlaid in fields of gold.

CAPPELLA DEL CORPORALE In 1263, a Bohemian priest, Peter of Prague, found himself doubting transubstantiation, the sacrament in which the communion bread, or host, is transformed into the body of Christ during mass. He went to Rome to pray on St. Peter's tomb that his faith be strengthened and, stopping in Bolsena, just below Orvieto, was saying Mass when the host began to bleed, dampening the corporal, or altar cloth. Pope Urban IV had the cloth brought to him in Orvieto, and a few decades later, Pope Nicholas IV ordered the cathedral built to house the relic. Frescoes in the chapel tell the story of the miracle, and the exquisite enamel reliquary that once held the cloth remains in place.

CAPPELLA SAN BRIZIO The cathedral's other treasure is one of the Renaissance's greatest fresco cycles. The themes are weighty—temptation, salvation, damnation, resurrection—yet the scenes are rich in everyday humanity. These frescoes allegedly inspired Michelangelo, who came to Orvieto and filled sketchbooks before starting the Sistine Chapel. Fra Angelico (the "Angelic Friar") began the series in 1447; Luca Signorelli completed the works, which are considered his masterpiece, in 1504. Both artists appear, dressed in black in the lower left corner, in a magnificent panel of the "Sermon of the Antichrist," in which the devil coaxes a Christ impostor to lure the faithful to damnation. Signorelli looks handsome and proud, with his long blonde hair; a mistress who jilted him is shown receiving funds from a money lender (for prostitution services, some conject). To the right of the altar is "The Entrance to Hell" and "The Damned in Hell," in which devils torment their victims, bodies writhe in agony, and a man raises his fists to curse God as he sees Charon crossing the Styx for him. Signorelli gets revenge on his ex-mistress again here—she's the terrified blonde on the back of a leering winged devil. For something a little more uplifting, look at the "Elect in Heaven," where the saved look quite content in their assurance of eternal salvation.

Piazza del Duomo. www.opsm.it. ✆ **0763/341-167.** 5€; free for children 10 and under. Apr–Sept Mon–Sat 9:30am–7pm, Sun 1–5:30pm; Mar and Oct Mon–Sat 9:30am–6pm, Sun 1–5:30pm; Nov–Feb Mon–Sat 9:30am–5pm, Sun 1–4:30pm.

Orvieto Underground ★★ HISTORIC SITE More than 1,200 artificial and natural caverns have been found in the *pozzolana* (a volcanic stone powdered to make cement mix) and *tufa* rock upon which Orvieto rests. Guided tours explore 15m (45 ft.) below Santa Chiara convent, reached by a steep climb up and down 55 steps, along a narrow rock-hewn passage. Over centuries the caverns have been used as Etruscan houses, water wells, ceramic ovens, pigeon coops, and cold storage (the temperature is a constant 14°C/58°F). Medieval citizens considered the tunnels safe refuges in times of siege, and residents took shelter in them during World War II Allied bombings, but most unwisely—a direct hit would have annihilated the soft rock. For a quicker look at the city's underside, step into **Pozzo della Cava,** where a self-guided tour reveals a series of caverns beneath a medieval house.

Piazza Duomo 23. www.orvietounderground.it. ✆ **0763/344-891.** Guided tours only: 7€ adults, 5€ students and seniors. Tours (45 min–1 hr.) daily; timing of English-language tours varies, but usually 11am, 12:30, 2:30, and 5:30pm. **Pozzo della Cavo:** Via della Cava 28 (www.pozzodellacava.it; ✆ **0763/342373**). 4€; 2.50€ seniors and children 6 and under. Tues–Sun 9am–8pm.

Pozzo di San Patrizio (St. Patrick's Well) ★ HISTORIC SITE

Orvieto's position atop a rocky outcropping made the city a perfect redoubt in time of siege, but with one big drawback—a lack of water. When Pope Clement VII holed up in Orvieto in 1527 to avoid turbulence in Rome, he hired Antonio Sangallo the Younger to dig a new well. Sangallo's design was unique: a shaft 53m (175-ft.) deep and 14m (45-ft.) wide, accessible via a pair of wide spiral staircases that form a double helix, lit by 72 internal windows. Mule-drawn carts could descend on one ramp and come back up the other. You can climb down, too, though it's a 496-step trek down and back up, and there's nothing at the bottom but, well, a well. A few steps up and down is all you need to get the idea. The name refers to St. Patrick's Purgatory, a pilgrimage site in Ireland where Christ allegedly showed St. Patrick a cave and told him it was an entrance to hell.

Viale San Gallo (near funicular stop on Piazza Cahen). ✆ **0763/343768.** 5€ adults; 3.50€ seniors, students, and ages 17 and under. May–Aug daily 9am–8pm; Mar–Apr and Sept–Oct daily 9am–7pm; Nov–Feb daily 10am–4:30pm.

Where to Stay in Orvieto

The upper town has few places to stay, so book ahead—especially on weekends, when Romans flock to Orvieto for a small-town getaway.

B&B Orvieto Sant'Angelo 42 ★★★ From the moment you step into the stone-floored foyer you'll feel right at home in Giulia Donato's pretty house on a narrow street off the Corso. In a lounge/breakfast room, a couch and chairs surround a huge hearth, and up a stone staircase are high-ceilinged guest rooms, two large doubles and a suite-size triple. Bathrooms are spacious (with deep tubs in the larger rooms), beds are luxurious, and handsome traditional pieces complement highly polished floors and mellow old beams and stones. Top-floor rooms come with a perk: little step-out balconies looking across rooftops to the distant hills.

Via Sant'Angelo 42. www.bborvieto.com. ✆ **0763/341-959.** 3 units. 85€–95€ double. Rates include breakfast. **Amenities:** Lounge; free Wi-Fi.

Exploring Orvieto's narrow cobbled lanes.

Hotel Duomo ★★ These quarters just a few steps from the Duomo (viewable from some rooms with a lean out the window) have lots of modern built-in wood furnishings and excellent lighting and plenty of quirky decor. A local artist, Livio Orazio Valentini, hung his surrealistic paintings in the hallways, lounges, and rooms, complementing them with colorful upholstery and carpets. He also created the sculptural light fixtures hanging over many of the desks. The bohemian yet homey ambience is topped off nicely with a pleasant garden to one side of the hotel.

Vicolo dei Maurizio 7. www.orvietohotelduomo.com. ✆ **0763/341-887.** 18 units. 85€–120€ double. Rates include breakfast. **Amenities:** Free Wi-Fi.

Palazzo Piccolomini ★★ In a 16th-century *palazzo,* resurrected from a dilapidated wreck in the 1980s, the stone and vaulted subterranean breakfast room and a couple of frescoed salons whisk you into the past, but most of the guest rooms are done with contemporary chic: wood and tile floors, dark furnishings, and crisp white walls with soothing neutral-tone accents. Some rooms have sitting areas or open to terraces, or are two-level; rooms on the upper floors have a countryside view.

Piazza Ranieri 36. www.palazzopiccolomini.it. ✆ **0763/341-743.** 32 units. 120€–140€ double. Rates include breakfast. **Amenities:** Restaurant; babysitting; concierge; room service; Wi-Fi (free in public areas).

Where to Eat in Orvieto

Orvieto's favorite pasta is *umbrichelli,* a slightly chewy spaghetti rolled out unevenly by hand, similar to the *pici* of southern Tuscany. To sample a glass of Orvieto Classico (accompanied by a *panino*), drop by the **Cantina Foresi,** Piazza Duomo 2 (✆ **0763/341-611**). Ask to see the small, moldy cellar carved directly into the *tufa*. **Bar Montanucci** (Corso Cavour 23; www.barmontanucci.com; ✆ **0763/341262**), is a popular spot for snacks and drinks, with fun wooden sculptures, a large rear terrace, and a huge selection of chocolates, some house-made. **Bartolomei Oleoteca,** Corso Cavour 49 (www.oleificiobartolomei.it; ✆ **0763/344540**), sells its own olive oils and such specialties as roasted artichokes in oil and olive paste. You can taste local meats and sheep's milk cheeses at **Drogheria Le Chicche degli Svizzeri,** Piazza della Repubblica 32 (www.drogheria orvieto.com; ✆ **349/494-8359**). **Gastronomia Aronne,** Corso Cavour 101 (✆ **0763/340014**), elevates a light meal into a gourmet indulgence, with excellent meat and cheese platters, sandwiches, pastas, and other well-prepared fare in a light-filled shop/dining room. Orvieto restaurants do a brisk business in summer and on weekend evenings, when it's best to reserve a table.

Capitano del Popolo ★★★ UMBRIAN Chef/proprietor Valentina Santanicchio grew up on a farm just outside Orvieto, and she combines a passion for cooking with a commitment to locally grown ingredients. In a dining room with vintage '50s cabinets and tables topped with crisp linens and fresh flowers, Valentina presents her *carbonara* and other pastas, along with spicy boar ragùs, roast duck, and many other Umbrian classics that landed her a segment on *Stanley Tucci: Searching for Italy.*
Piazza del Popolo 7–9. www.capitanodelpopolo.com. ✆ **320/928-7474.** Daily noon–3pm and 7–10pm (from 7:30pm on Tues). Entrees 10€–22€.

La Mezza Luna ★★ UMBRIAN When booking your Orvieto hotel room, ask them to reserve a table for you at this small vaulted room behind a vine-covered entrance on a side street. Reserving in advance is the only way you're likely to eat here. Don't expect even a smile from grumpy proprietor Averino. Still, for more than 40 years he's been serving what many consider the best carbonara they've ever eaten—and that attracts customers from the ends of the earth. The kitchen also prepares other pastas and grilled meat, but you're only here for the standout attraction.
Via Ripa Serancia 5. ✆ **0763/341-234.** Entrees 7€–10€. Mon–Sat 12:30–2pm and 7:30–8:30pm.

Orvieto's Liquid Gold

The plains and low hills around Orvieto grow the grapes—verdello, grechetto, and Tuscan varietals trebbiano and malvasia—that produce one of Italy's great wines, a pale straw-colored DOC white called simply **Orvieto Classico.** Well-rounded and fragrant (often with a hint of crushed almonds), it goes well with lunch or a light dinner. Most Orvieto Classico is *secco* (dry), but you can also find *abboccato* (semidry/semisweet), *amabile* (medium sweet), and *dolce* (sweet) varieties. To visit a winery, pick up the "Strada dei Vini" brochure at the Orvieto tourist office.

Le Grotte del Funaro ★ UMBRIAN A thousand years ago, a *funaro* (ropemaker) had his workshop in these grottoes carved into the cliff's *tufa;* you can almost see him at work in the shadowy recesses of the rooms. Take a seat outside in good weather or better yet—so you don't miss the ambience inside—ask for one of the few window seats; most are in atmospheric subterranean chambers. You'll dine well on grilled meats, the house specialty (try a *grigliata mista* of suckling pig, lamb, sausage, and yellow peppers), or excellent pizzas.

Via Ripa Serancia 41 (near Porta Maggiore). www.grottedelfunaro.it. ✆ **0763/343-276.** Entrees 10€–22€; pizza 6€–8.50€. Tues–Sun noon–3pm and 7pm–10:30pm. Closed 1 week in July.

Trattoria La Palomba ★★★ UMBRIAN This is the kind of place where you'll want to linger, for a long lunch after a morning of sightseeing or a comfy evening dinner. Black Umbrian truffles top many of the homemade pastas, most notably *umbrichelli al tartufo,* tossed with egg yolk and parmigiano. The signature dish, *palomba* (wild dove), is roasted in a delicious sauce of capers, rosemary, olives, and a hint of anchovies. Any of the meat dishes, including beef in a red wine sauce, are similarly satisfying. It's essential to reserve, especially on weekends.

Via Cipirano Menente 16. ✆ **0763/343395.** Entrees 10€–22€. Thurs–Tues 12:30–2:15pm and 7:30–10pm.

Orvieto Shopping

Orogami (Via del Duomo 14/16; www.orogami.com; ✆ **0763/344206**) sells a distinctive line of gold jewelry, including playful pieces like a medallion replicating the Duomo's rose window. The showroom of internationally acclaimed ceramicist **Marino Moretti** at Via del Duomo 55 (www.marinomoretti.it; ✆ **0763/361663**) sells tiles, dinnerware, and other modern takes on traditional designs. Gifted shoemaker **Federico Badia** hand-fashions made-to-order shoes, purses, bags, and belts in his workshop at Via Garibaldi 27 (federicobadiashoes.com).

8

BOLOGNA & EMILIA-ROMAGNA

By Stephen Brewer

A lot of travelers zip through this northernmost stretch of central Italy as they hurry along the well-worn path between Florence and Venice. That's good news for anyone wishing to slow down long enough to visit—you will find appealing towns and cities that are a little less crowded and more engaged in everyday Italian life than more popular stops on the Italian tourism circuit. The region has treasure troves of art and culture, along with an almost hedonistic devotion to fine food.

Each of the region's main towns has its own distinct character and appeal. Bologna is one of Europe's largest remaining medieval enclaves, with art-filled palaces and stony piazzas, yet it also has an animated street life revved up by students at Europe's oldest university. Ferrara is a time capsule of the Renaissance, and Ravenna seems to be entirely covered in glittering Byzantine mosaics. Parma proudly shows off its famous hams and cheeses, its musical traditions, and its art.

It's easy to get from one place to the other by train—Bologna makes a handy base for exploring the entire region—and once you reach these old cities, the preferred ways to get around are walking and biking.

DON'T LEAVE BOLOGNA & EMILIA-ROMAGNA WITHOUT . . .

Immersing Yourself in the Middle Ages. Bologna is one of the world's best-preserved medieval holdovers, an atmospheric set piece with palaces, towers, and 25 miles of centuries-old porticos.

Enjoying Some of the Best Food in Italy. Even other Italians agree: Emilia-Romagna is the culinary heart of the country, with Parma's hams and cheeses setting a delectable gold standard.

Biking Around Ferrara. The city's palace- and convent-lined streets are delightfully flat for easy pedaling, and you can even ride atop the old city walls.

Marveling at Ravenna's Mosaics. Saturated in color, the intricate mosaics blanketing Ravenna's churches and mausoleums have awed travelers since the city's 5th-century heyday.

PREVIOUS PAGE: **Piazza Maggiore in Bologna.**

BOLOGNA ★★

151km (94 miles) SW of Venice, 378km (234 miles) N of Rome

It's easy to love a city so enamored of food that it's nicknamed *La Grassa* (the Fat); so devoted to scholarship (home of Europe's oldest university, founded in 1088) that it's called *La Dotta* (the Learned); and so noted for its fiery liberal politics that it's known as *La Rossa* (the Red). There are plenty of other reasons to like Bologna. The lively city of more than a million residents is built around one of the Europe's largest and best-preserved medieval cores, an attractive swath of palaces, towers, quirky museums, and art-filled churches, and its grand piazzas and narrow lanes are easily traversed on foot. In the Quadrilatero, the medieval town center, shop windows brim with the region's famous hams and cheeses. You don't even have to carry an umbrella in Bologna, because 25 miles of sidewalks are covered with handsome loggias.

Essentials

ARRIVING

BY PLANE The international **Aeroporto Guglielmo Marconi (BLQ;** www.bologna-airport.it; ✆ **051/647-9615)**, 6km (3¾ miles) north of the city center, is served by many of the main European airlines, including British Airways and EasyJet (both from London-Gatwick) and Ryanair

The Quadrilatero, Bologna's medieval heart.

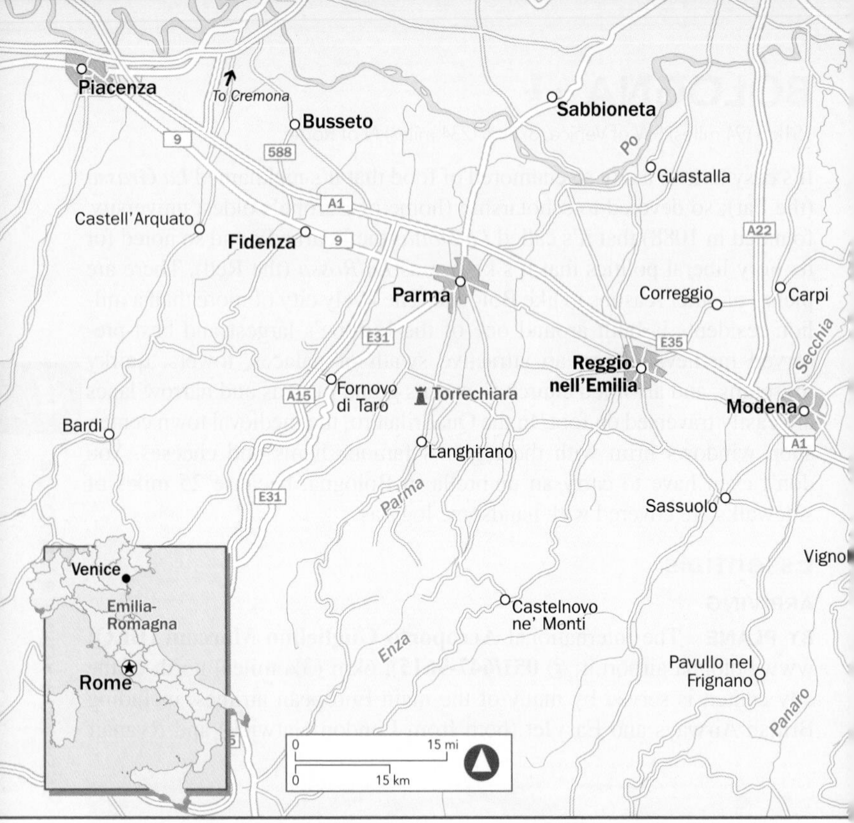

(London-Stansted). The airport does not accommodate transatlantic flights, so travelers from the U.S. will make connections in London or another European hub. The **Marconi Express** automated tram (www.marconiexpress.it) links the airport and main rail station (Stazione Centrale) in just 7 minutes and runs daily every 7 minutes between 5:40am and midnight. One-way fare is 9.20€, payable with tickets dispensed from machines near the platform. A taxi from the airport into the city center costs about 20€.

BY TRAIN Bologna is well connected to nearby cities by train, making it easy to explore the region without a car. Frequent high-speed trains operated by **Trenitalia** (www.trenitalia.com) and **Italo** (www.italotreno.it) from Florence (trip time about 30 min.), Milan (about 1 hr.), Venice (1 hr., 40 min.), Rome (2 hr., 20 min.), and Naples (3 hr., 10 min.) arrive at **Stazione Centrale,** Piazza Medaglie d'Oro 2 (✆ **892-021**). Slower and less expensive trains also run on these routes. A staffed luggage storage facility operated by **KiBag** (www.kibag.it) on the ground floor, open daily 7am to 9pm, stores baggage for 10€ per piece a day; it also has a porter service for 6€ a bag.

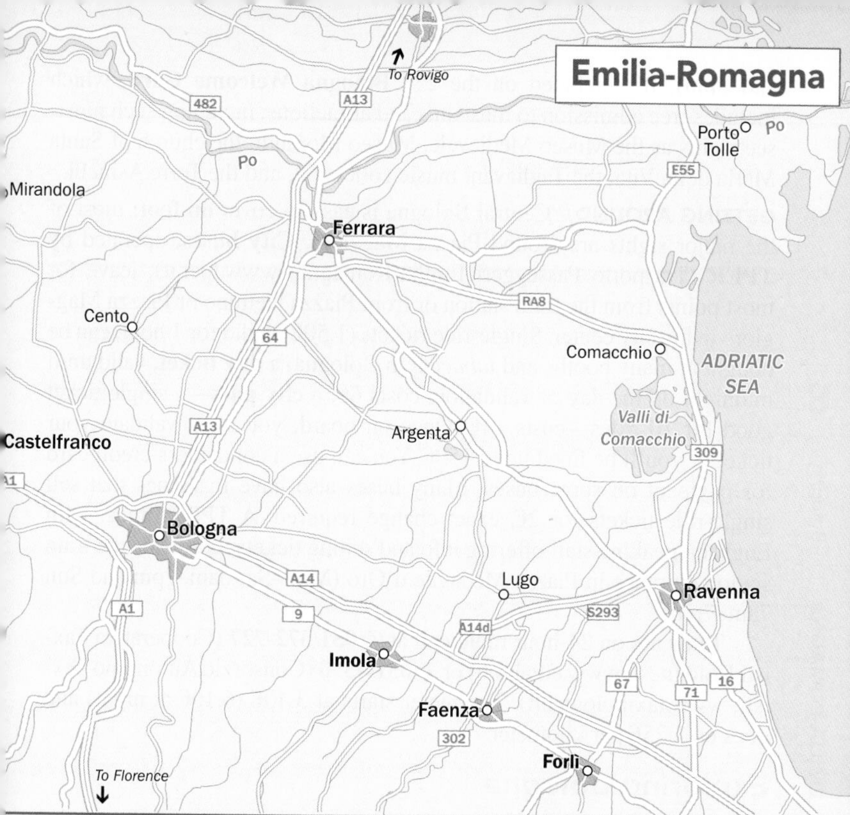

Bus nos. A, 25, and 30 run between the station and Piazza Maggiore, Bologna's historic center; taxi trips into the center cost around 6€. However, it's an easy and level 15-minute walk from the station to Piazza Maggiore down Via Indipendenza, most of the way under covered loggias.

BY CAR If you're driving from Florence, head north on A1 until you reach the outskirts of Bologna, where signs direct you to the city center. From Milan, take A1 southeast. From Venice or Ferrara, follow A13 southwest. From Rimini, Ravenna, and towns along the Adriatic, cut west on A14. See the note on p. 358 about driving and parking in Bologna; if you have a choice, it's much easier to visit Bologna without a car.

VISITOR INFORMATION The **Bologna Welcome tourist office** (www.bolognawelcome.com; ✆ **051/658-3111**), on Piazza Maggiore in the Palazzo del Podestà, is open Monday through Saturday 9am to 7pm and Sunday 10am to 5pm. Helpful staff hands out free city maps, bus maps, and guides to what's happening around the city. The office's daily 2-hour **walking tour** around the historic center is an excellent, informative introduction to the city (15€; leaves from Bologna Welcome Office in Piazza Maggiore Mon–Wed 10:30am, Thurs and Fri 3pm, and Sat and Sun 10am and 3pm); it's included on the 25€ **Bologna Welcome Card,** which includes free admission to museums and attractions, including such must-see sights as the Museo Medievale, Museo Morandi, the church of Santa Maria della Vita, the Tagliavani music collection, and the Torre Asinelli.

GETTING AROUND Central Bologna is easy to cover **on foot;** most of the major sights are around Piazza Maggiore. **City buses,** operated by **TPER** (Trasporto Passeggeri Emilia-Romagna; www.tper.it), leave for most points from the train station or from Piazza Nettuno or Piazza Maggiore in the city center. Single-ride rickets (1.50€), valid for 1 hour, can be bought at many booths and *tabacchi* in Bologna; a **day ticket,** valid until midnight on the day of validation, costs 6€; a **city pass**—a single ticket good for 10 rides—costs 14€. Once on board, you must validate your ticket or you'll be fined up to 150€. You can use a contactless credit card for payment on some buses. Many buses also have machines that sell single-ride tickets for 2€, exact change required. A TPER office, with English-speaking staff offering info and selling tickets, is outside the train station entrance in Piazza Medaglie d'Oro (Mon–Sat 6am–7pm and Sun 7am–7pm).

Taxis are on 24-hour radio call at ✆ **051/372-727** (Cooperativa Taxisti Bolognesi; www.cotabo.it) or ✆ **051/4590** (Consorzio Autonomo Taxisti; www.taxibologna.it). The meter starts at 3.40€ (6.10€ at night) and goes up 1.25€ per kilometer.

Exploring Bologna

A huge statue of a virile Neptune presides over the center of Bologna, the sweeping expanse of **Piazza Maggiore.** At one end looms the enormous, though never completed, **Basilica di San Petronio** (see p. 352); crenellated 12th- and 13th-century *palazzi* occupy the other sides, including, on the northeast, the **Palazzo di Rei Enzo.** In the long-running feud between the Ghibellines (who supported the Holy Roman Empire) and the Guelphs (supporters of the Pope), Enzo—the illegitimate son of German Emperor Frederick II, and king of Sardinia—sided with the Ghibellines at the wrong time. He was imprisoned in this grim-looking palace for 23 years until his death, though he didn't exactly languish in a dungeon—he was known for his lavish feasts and romantic conquests, and almost escaped once (his blond hair, protruding from a basket, gave him away).

Rising high above the square is the **Torre dell'Orologio,** an impressive cap atop the formidable **Palazzo d'Accursio,** seat of Bologna's municipal offices. An ascent to the parapet provides a bird's-eye view over the city's towers, domes, and medieval rooftops and comes with a look at frescoed salons filled with the city's art collections. It's open daily 10am to 7pm; admission is 8€.

Most of the city's sights are within an easy walk from the piazza. Just to the east of the square rise the **Due Torri** (p. 354), Bologna's iconic leaning towers, presiding over the atmospheric **Piazza della Mercanzia,**

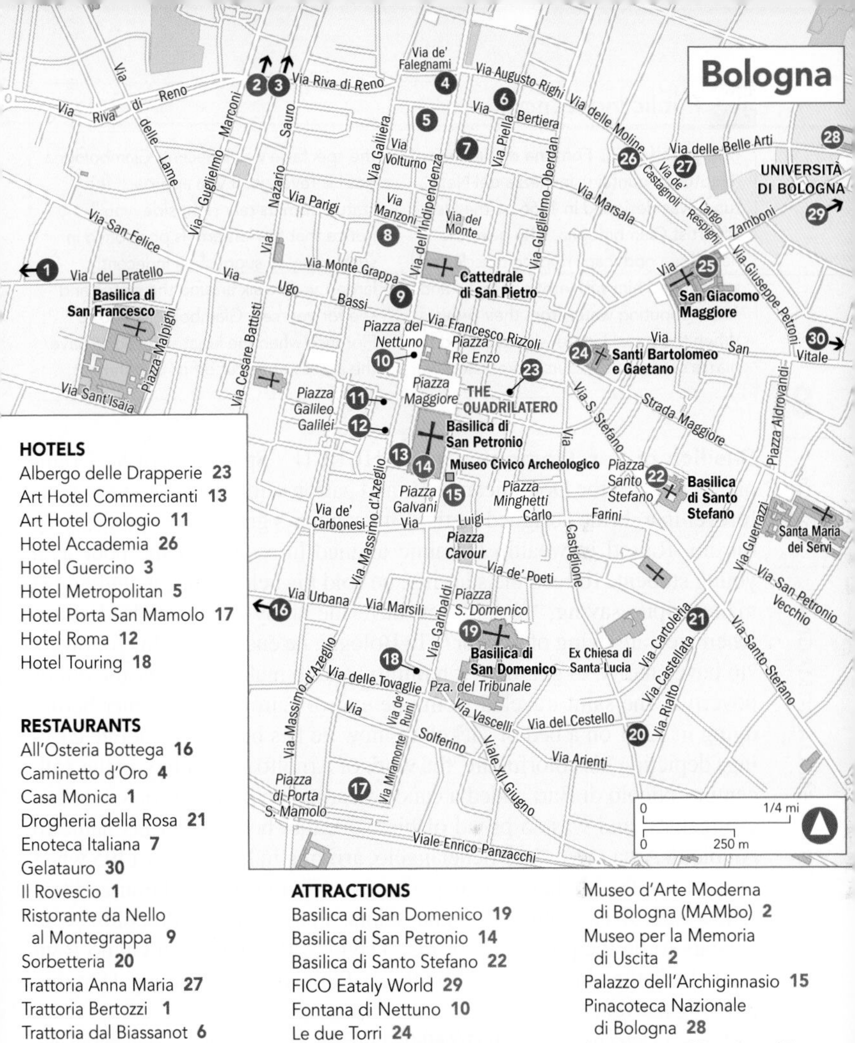

a marketplace from Roman times through the Middle Ages. The poet Dante, exiled from his native Florence, sat in cafes on this piazza and watched beautiful women stroll by. From the square, little lanes dive southwest into the **Quadrilatero,** the old quarter of food shops (see p. 362); Via Santo Stefano leads south to the basilicas of **Santo Stefano** (p. 353) and **San Domenico** (p. 352), and Via Zamboni heads northeast into the **university district.** In your wanderings, keep an eye out for windows on Via Piella, Via Oberdan, and Via Malcontenti that open to the remaining stretches of the many **canals** that once coursed through the city to power silk works and mills, along with providing transport for goods and people.

Public Indecency

Bologna's famous **Fontana di Nettuno** (Neptune Fountain), in Piazza del Nettuno, was designed in 1566 by the Flemish artist Giambologna, who gave the naked sea god many rippling muscles and surrounded him with erotic cherubs and sirens spouting water from their breasts. When the papal legate who occupied the piazza's Palazzo d'Accursio protested that the spectacle was indecent, Giambologna got his revenge: If you approach the statue from its rear right side, you'll notice that the left arm is positioned in such a way to suggest an indecently large...well, walk around the statue and see for yourself. Giambologna fled to Florence when the legate vowed to have the artist's arms cut off as punishment.

Basilica di San Domenico ★★ CHURCH Spanish-born St. Dominic, founder of the Dominican order and patron saint of astronomers, rests forever in a shrine designed by the 13th century's greatest sculptor, Nicola Pisano. Raised in wealth, Dominic aligned himself with the poor as a young student. To feed the starving, he sold his belongings, including his manuscripts, saying, "Would you have me study off these dead skins, when men are dying of hunger?" In Bologna he encouraged his followers "to have charity, to guard their humility, and to make their treasure out of poverty." The saint traveled from one end of Europe to the other before dying in 1221 on a bed of sackcloth; now he lies beneath elaborate carvings depicting his colorful life, the work of Arnolfo di Cambio. In the 15th century Nicolo di Bari added a canopy, carved with images of saints and evangelists, and was so proud of his work that he changed his name to Nicolo di Arca. A young Michelangelo, arriving in Bologna in 1495 when his patrons, the Medici, were expelled from Florence, added transcendent renderings of two other Bologna saints, Petronius and Proculus (who appears to be the prototype for his "David"). Bologna-born Guido Reni topped off the shrine in 1615 with a ceiling fresco depicting Dominic entering heaven.

Piazza San Domenico 13. ✆ **051/640-0411.** Free. Mon–Sat 9am–noon and 3:30–6pm; Sun 3:30–5pm. Bus: A, 16, 30, 38, 39, 59.

Basilica di San Petronio ★ CHURCH The massive church honoring Bologna's patron, the 5th-century bishop Petronio, was begun in 1390, designed to be larger than St. Peter's in Rome. Then papal powers cut off funding and the basilica remains unfinished—the formidable brick walls were never sheathed in marble as intended and transepts are severely truncated (look down either side of the church to see where extensions end abruptly in the surrounding streets). Among the few flourishes are a magnificent **central doorway** surrounded by Old Testament figures rendered in marble by Jacopo della Quercia of Siena (where he designed the Fonte Gaia for the Campo; see p. 233). He was a well-regarded artist in his fifties when he came to Bologna in 1425 to undertake the commission; he finished just before his death in 1438. Michelangelo claimed that della

Nave in the Basilica di San Petronio.

Quercia's rendering of the Creation of Adam here inspired his Genesis in the Sistine Chapel. In the **Cappella dei Magi** (also known as Cappella Bolognini), the fourth on the left as you enter, Giovanni da Modena's fresco cycle, painted between 1408 and 1420, depicts the life of Petronio. Scenes of Hell from Dante's Inferno include a startling image of Satan eating and excreting doomed souls and Mohammed being devoured by devils (Al-Qaeda operatives and other terrorists in recent years have tried to blow up the church in retaliation). If you visit the church around noon, look for a shadow falling on a meridian line in the left aisle, indicating the day of the year; it's the world's longest sundial, 70m (231 ft.) long, designed by famed 17th-century astronomer Giovanni Domenico Cassini.

Piazza Maggiore. www.basilicadisanpetronio.org. ✆ **051/231415.** Free; 5€ for Cappella dei Magi. Basilica: daily 8:30am–1pm and 2:30–6pm. Cappella dei Magi: daily 9:30am–12:30 and 2:30–5:15pm. Bus: A, 11, 13, 14, 17, 18, 19, 20, 25.

Basilica di Santo Stefano ★★★ CHURCH Bologna's most storied religious site is actually five churches, a stone maze of medieval apses, romantic porticos, and courtyards awash in legend. Petronio, the 5th-century bishop of Bologna, allegedly founded the church on the remains of a Roman temple to the earth goddess Isis. He was originally laid to rest here in the **Church of the Sepulcher,** where pregnant Bolognese women would circle his tomb 33 times—once for every year of Christ's life—stopping at every turn to crawl through a low door to say a prayer before the saint's remains (his body has been since been reunited with his head in the Basilica di San Petronio; see above); prostitutes were allowed to perform the same ritual as an act of purification once a year at Easter. The mothers-to-be moved on to the **Church of the Trinity** to pray before a fresco depicting a very pregnant Madonna stroking her belly. The **Church of Vitale and Agricola** is devoted to two other popular Bolognese saints and the city's first Christian martyrs, the 4th-century nobleman Agricola and his devoted slave; a cross near the tomb is said to be the one Agricola was holding when he was crucified, though it dates from much later. Similarly, a marble basin in the **Cortile di Pilato** (Courtyard of Pilate), alleged

Sidewalk Porticos: Staying Dry in Bologna

Almost 40km (25 miles) of porticos cover the sidewalks of Bologna, providing the Bolognese with a venue to stroll during the evening *passeggiata*, no matter how inclement the weather. Most are high enough to accommodate a man on horseback, as mandated by a 14th-century city ordinance. They also allowed residents to extend the upper stories of their homes over the sidewalks, helping ease a medieval housing crunch. Showiest is the 3.5km (2-mile) stretch of porticos that climb a green hillside to the **Santuario della Madonna di San Luca.** As you tackle the seemingly endless steps, note that this stretch of arcades is supported by 666 arches, a number associated with the devil—and you might believe there's a diabolical presence afoot as you huff and puff your way toward your reward, heavenly views of the city and countryside from the church's front steps. You can save yourself the climb (though that defeats the purpose of a pilgrimage, doesn't it?) by hopping aboard the **San Luca Express** (cityredbus.com), a tourist train that operates from Piazza Maggiore daily from March through December, with 5 trips a day Tuesday to Thursday and 10 trips Friday to Monday; round-trip fare is 12€, 6€ children 6–10, and 3€ 5 and under. Check the website for limited hours of operation in January and February.

to be the one in which Pontius Pilate washed his hands after condemning Christ to death, actually dates to the 8th century; a statue atop a nearby column pays homage to the rooster who crowed three times when Peter denied knowing Jesus. It's said that Dante used to sit in the Romanesque **cloister** and reflect during his exile in Bologna. Dante might have found inspiration for the hellish scenes of the *Divine Comedy* while looking at the carved capitals atop the pillars, with their grotesque imagery of swiveling heads and men crushed beneath boulders.

Via Santo Stefano 24. www.santostefanobologna.it. ✆ **051/223-256.** Free. Tues–Sun 9:30am–12:30pm and 2:30–7pm (until 7:30pm Sat–Sun). Bus: 11, 13, 90, 96.

Le Due Torri ★★ MONUMENT It's been estimated that in the 12th and 13th centuries as many as 180 stone towers rose above Bologna's rooftops, reaching heights of up to 100m (330 ft.). Probably built as places of refuge in times of war, they were also proof of a family's wealth—it took enormous expense to erect such towers, carefully crafted with successively thinner layers of masonry on the upper levels. Some 22 towers remain; the most famous are these two slender medieval skyscrapers just east of Piazza Maggiore. The **Garisenda** rises 49m (162 ft.) and leans about 3m (10 ft.) from perpendicular; the **Asinelli** stands 102m (334 ft.) tall and inclines almost 2.5m (8 ft.). Garisenda is off-limits, but a climb up Asinelli's 500 steps reveals Bologna's finest aerial panorama, a sea of red-tile roofs and the green hills beyond.

Piazza di Porta Ravegnana. www.duetorribologna.com. Buy tickets at tourist office or online for timed entry: 5€ adults, 3€ under 12 and over 65. Included with Bologna Welcome Card. Daily Jan and Nov–Dec 10am–4:30pm; Mar and Oct 10am–6pm; Apr–Oct 10am–7pm (until 8:15pm Thurs–Sun); entry at 15-min. intervals. Bus: 11, 13, 14, 19, 25, 27.

Le Due Torri, near Piazza Maggiore.

Museo Civico Medievale ★★ MUSEUM Displayed in the salons of the magnificently medieval Palazzo Ghisilardi, the treasures in this museum bring to life the Bologna of the Middle Ages. You'll find rare illuminated manuscripts and intriguing artifacts such as a courtesan's dainty shoe, but most illuminating are the statues showing off the haircuts and clunky headgear of the times, and the ordinary funeral slabs that provide such telling glimpses as a relief of a supine professor with his hands resting on a book, as if he has fallen asleep while reading.

Via Manzoni 4. www.museibologna.it/arteanticaen. ✆ **051/219-3930.** 6€ adults; 3€ over 65 and 18–25; 2€ 12–18. Included with Bologna Welcome Card. Tues and Thurs 10am–2pm; Wed and Fri 2–7pm; Sat–Sun 10am–7pm. Bus: A, 11, 20, 27, 28.

Museo d'Arte Moderna di Bologna (MAMbo) ★★ MUSEUM This is the city's showcase for the avant-garde, with an emphasis on post–World War II art. The standout is a museum within a museum, the **Museo Morandi ★★★**, exhibiting a collection of works by Bolognese painter/printmaker Giorgio Morandi (1890–1964), who once said, "What interests me most is expressing what's in nature, in the visible world"—an understatement given his deceptively straightforward still lifes, which seem almost abstract in their minimalism. Morandi's studio has been reconstructed here, and you can also visit his **apartment** at Via Fondazza 36 (✆ **051/649-6653;** by appointment; free admission), converted to stark galleries where his personal effects and the vases, utensils, and other objects he painted are on view. In the larger museum, one standout piece is Renato Guttuso's "I Funerali di Togliatti" (1972), awash in red flags, which depicts the funeral of the leader of the communist party, surrounded by images of left-wing luminaries.

Via Don Minzoni 14. www.mambo-bologna.org. ✆ **051/649-6611.** 6€ adults; 4€ students and ages 6–17; free for children 5 and under. Included with Bologna Welcome Card. Tues–Wed 2–7pm; Thurs 2–8pm; Fri–Sun 10am–7pm. Bus: A, 11, 20, 27, 28.

Palazzo dell'Archiginnasio ★★ HISTORIC SITE It's no accident that one of the grander buildings of Bologna University, completed in 1563, is adjacent to the basilica of San Petronio. Pope Pius IV ordered this central hall for the university faculties to be built here for a reason: to prevent the basilica from expanding and surpassing in size St. Peter's in Rome. Corridors and staircases decorated with family crests lead to the **Teatro Anatomico,** a handsome spruce-paneled lecture hall with tiers of wood benches surrounding a marble slab for med-school dissections. Apollo, god of medicine, gazes down from the ceiling, and statues of Hippocrates and other august physicians line the walls; the doctor holding a nose is Gaspare Tagliacozzi, a pioneer of rhinoplasty (aka "nose job"), a procedure much in demand in an era when noses were routinely cut off for punishment. Look for the secret panel, where a church inquisitor spied on classes to make sure dissections followed church protocol—in cold weather, dissections had to take place in one continuous session (often 2 full days) to preserve the bodies, and all organs had to remain *in situ* and intact, ready for Judgment Day.

Piazza Galvani. www.archiginnasio.it. ✆ **051/276811.** 3€. Mon–Sun 10am–6pm. Bus: A or 29B.

Pinacoteca Nazionale di Bologna ★★ MUSEUM Beginning in the late 18th century, the former St. Ignatius monastery began to house altarpieces and other works gathered from religious institutions throughout Bologna. Among the great works is Raphael's "St. Cecilia in Ecstasy" (Gallery 15), in which the saint, patron of music, is portrayed holding a lute, rapturously listening to a heavenly choir. **Guido Reni** (1575–1642), born and buried in Bologna, dominates Gallery 24 with his "Massacre of the Innocents," in which two muscular, knife-wielding soldiers set upon a group of screaming women and children. Gallery 23 features Bologna's **Carracci family**—brothers Agostino and Annibale and their cousin Lodovico—who opened a famous academy in Bologna in the 1580s. Agostino's masterpiece is "The Communion of St. Jerome," but the work for which he became best known was his copy of "I Modi" (The Way), a highly erotic series of engravings (not here). Annibale was the greater and more passionate painter, known for his realistic renderings of human features, as you'll see in his darkly moving "Mocking of Christ." He was famous for his photographic memory: When still a child, he and his father were set upon by robbers, and young Annibale drew the thieves with such precision that they were soon apprehended and the Carraccis' money returned.

Via delle Belle Arti 56. www.pinacotecabologna.beniculturali.it. ✆ **051/420-9411.** 6€ adults; 2€ ages 18–25; free for ages 17 and under. Included with Bologna Welcome Card. Tues–Wed 9am–2pm, Thurs–Sun 9am–7pm. Bus: 20, 28, 36, 37, 89, 93, 94, 99 (to Porta San Donato).

San Giacomo Maggiore ★ CHURCH This Romanesque landmark, facing one of Bologna's most welcoming squares and graced with an elegant Renaissance portico, in its present form was largely funded by Bologna's most powerful 15th-century family, the Bentivoglios, who were constantly plotting and being plotted against. Many are laid to rest in the

beyond THE GREATEST HITS

The Carraccis are the stars of the Pinacoteca Nazionale (p. 356), but their masterpiece, the *Founding of Rome* fresco cycle, is in the **Palazzo Magnani-Salem,** Via Zamboni 20 (✆ **051/296-2503;** free; hours vary but usually Wed 10am–1:30pm and 2:30–6pm and second Sat of month). The Carraccis also decorated the first floor of **Palazzo Fava,** Via Manzoni 2 (genusbononiae.it; ✆ **051/1993-6305;** 10€, included with Bologna Welcome Card; usually Tues–Sun 10am–7pm), with colorful renditions of Jason and the Argonauts and other mythical scenes. A gentle portrait of Medea bathing next to a stream is considered to be the first female nude since classical times.

Aside from his carvings on the tomb of St. Dominic (p. 352), Niccolò dell'Arca's other great work in Bologna is "Compianto sul Cristo Morto" in the **Church of Santa Maria della Vita,** Via Clavature 8 (genusbononiae.it; ✆ **051/230260;** 5€, included with Bologna Welcome Card; Tues–Sun 10am–6:30pm). These life-size terracotta figures depicting Christ being taken from the cross are some of the most humane and moving religious images you'll ever see, the expressions on the faces of the lamenters etched in grief—even though they're clumsily shored up with wood to prevent earthquake damage.

Of more recent vintage is a haunting installation by Christian Boltanski, **Museo per la Memoria di Ustica,** at Via di Saliceto 3/22 (www.museomemoriaustica.it; ✆ **051/377-680;** free; Tues–Fri 9:30am–1:30pm and Sat–Sun 10pm–6:30pm), commemorating the crash of a Bologna–Palermo flight off the Sicilian island of Ustica on June 27, 1980. Wreckage of the DC-9, allegedly shot down by an Italian military missile when mistaken for a Libyan spy plane, is accompanied by lighting and sound effects—victims are represented by 81 lights blinking off and on against the black ceiling while from 81 speakers come snippets of heartbreakingly ordinary conversation.

Cappella Bentivoglio, decorated in vivid frescoes by Lorenzo Costa, who came to Bologna in the 1480s before moving on to great fame in Mantua (see p. 497). "Madonna Enthroned" depicts Giovanni II Bentivoglio—who was eventually excommunicated and imprisoned in Rome—kneeling with his wife next to the Madonna, as his family gives thanks for the unmasking of a conspiracy against them. Anton Galeazzo Bentivoglio, who fell out of favor with the papacy and was beheaded in 1435, lies in a tomb designed by Jacopo della Quercia. For an eerie thrill, follow the left-side chapels about halfway down until you come to a terrifyingly realistic effigy of the corpse of Christ, complete with lash marks, oozing wounds, and plenty of blood.

Piazza Rossini, Via Zamboni. ✆ **051/225-970.** Free. Daily 7:30am–12:30pm and 3:30–6:30pm. Bus: C.

Where to Stay in Bologna

Bologna normally hosts four to six major trade fairs a year, which dramatically affect hotel room rates; check the calendar at www.bolognafiere.it to see if anything's scheduled for the time you wish to visit. Rate ranges

CABINETS OF curiosity

Life was precarious in the Middle Ages, and the medieval mindset never forgot that we are, in the end, just flesh and blood. For a grisly reminder of this, head to **Chiesa della Santa,** Tagliapietre 19, where the body of St. Catherine—a 15th-century nun who's the city patron and protector of artists—sits on a golden throne in a side chapel. The faithful claim Catherine has remained miraculously intact since her death; the blackened, leathery flesh stretched over skeletal features suggests otherwise. To join the faithful in the little sanctuary, adorned with the saint's violin and other relics, ring the bell next to a wooden door on the left in the church vestibule (daily 9am–noon and 3–7pm). There's a similarly creepy vibe at the University of Bologna's **Museo di Palazzo Poggi,** Via Zamboni 33, a wonderful 16th-century assemblage of what was thought to be all the living organisms on earth. Along with fossils and an (alleged) unicorn tusk, you'll see anatomically correct wax models of humans in various states of flaying, as well as remarkably lifelike models of infants in the womb. Gruesome, yes, but remember that these helped medieval physicians advance medicine from folk practice to science (www.sma.unibo.it; ✆ **051/20-99610;** 7€, 4€ over 65 and 19–26, free for 18 and under; Tues–Fri 10am–4pm, Sat–Sun 10am–6pm). On a lighter note, the frescoed salons of the Palazzo Sanguinetti, Strada Maggiore 34, are home to the **Museo Internazionale e Biblioteca della Musica,** filled with scores, libretti, and musical instruments from the 16th century on, including an utterly charming re-creation of a lute-maker's studio (www.museibologna.it/musica; ✆ **051/275-711;** 5€, included with Bologna Welcome Card; Tues–Thurs 11am–1:30pm and 2:30–6:30pm, Fri 10am–1:30pm and 2:30–7pm, Sat–Sun 10am–7pm). Music lovers should also check out the harpsichords, pianos, and other early instruments that fill the beautiful former church of St. Colombano, Via Parigi 5, all part of the **Collezione Tagliavani** (genusbononiae.it; ✆ **051/1993-6366;** 7€; Wed–Sun 11am–6pm; included with Bologna Welcome Card).

below do not reflect the sky-high prices that might be in effect during fairs, when you're better off staying elsewhere in Emilia-Romagna. Bologna has many short-term rental apartments, many appearing on **Airbnb.com** and **Vrbo.com**.

An important note on driving and parking: Parts of central Bologna (Via Ugo Bassi, Via Rizzoli, and Via Indipendenza) are closed to cars almost entirely, and large parts of the central city are entirely off-limits to traffic on Sundays, when you will have to park outside the center. Other areas are closed to cars without special permits from 7am to 8pm daily (including Sun and holidays). If your hotel is in a limited traffic zone, you will be allowed to drive in to unload your bags and park, but only if you've first registered with the police. When booking a room, present your car registration number, which the hotel will then provide to the police to ensure that you are not fined for driving in a restricted area. If you're planning to drive into Bologna, ask about these restrictions when booking, and also ask where to find nearby parking facilities. Best yet, come to this easily walkable city without a car.

EXPENSIVE

Art Hotel Orologio ★★ This tall, narrow old house has been an inn for a couple of centuries and takes its name from the adjoining clock tower. The comfy surroundings are full of nooks and crannies, and no two guest rooms are the same. Most of the traditionally furnished rooms have soothing, deep-hued wall coverings, and many have nice touches like little writing nooks. The higher you get, the more likely your room or suite has a glimpse of nearby Piazza Maggiore, or at least a tower and dome or two. Most of the sights and the lively market streets of the Quadrilatero (see p. 362) are just steps away.

Via 4 Novembre 10. www.art-hotel-orologio.it. ✆ **051/745-7411.** 33 units. 250€–300€ double. Rates include breakfast. Parking 28€ per day. Bus: 11, 13, 20, 30. **Amenities:** Bar; room service; free Wi-Fi.

MODERATE

Art Hotel Commercianti ★★ You can't stay any closer to San Petronio than this atmosphere-rich *palazzo*—in the best rooms and suites you can lie in bed, sit on a leafy terrace, or even soak in a deep tub while admiring the church's exquisite brickwork and statuary. Exposed timbers and fresco fragments lend a medieval aura to the decor, though many of the furnishings are plush and contemporary, with armchairs and couches that invite you to relax after forays to the surrounding sights. A morning buffet is served beneath vaulted arches that show off the hotel's 13th-century origins.

Via de' Pignattari 11. www.art-hotel-commercianti.it. ✆ **051/745-7511.** 34 units. 130€–160€ double. Rates include breakfast. Parking 30€ per day. Bus: 11, 13, 20, 30. **Amenities:** Bar; babysitting; bikes; room service; free Wi-Fi.

This deluxe double room at the Art Hotel Commercianti comes with a terrace that looks directly onto San Petronio.

Hotel Metropolitan ★★★ Just a few steps off Via Indipendenza, this stylish haven is a world removed, an oasis of calm and comfort. Soothing whites and neutral shades offset Indonesian antiques and other Asian pieces. All rooms have large mosaic-tiled bathrooms, many have small sitting rooms, and several have terraces. In addition to a rooftop terrace, five airy two-room suites open off a leafy roof garden planted with olive trees; they're some of the most restful accommodations in the city center. Piazza Maggiore and most city sights are an easy walk away. The hotel also rents out modern and well-equipped apartments nearby; rates range from 100€ to 400€ per day.

Via Dell'Orso 6. www.hotelmetropolitan.com. ✆ **051/229-393.** 50 units. 160€–200€ double. Rates include breakfast. Parking 20€ a day. Bus: A, 11, 20, 27, 28. **Amenities:** Restaurant; bar; babysitting; room service; free Wi-Fi.

Hotel Porta San Mamolo ★★ Most of these rather romantic rooms surround a leafy courtyard, bringing the sense of a country retreat to the heart of Bologna—Piazza Maggiore is only a 15-minute walk away. Nice-sized, tile-floored rooms are done in soothing creams and warm golds and reds, with stylishly contemporary furnishings offset by exposed beams, vaulted ceilings, and other architectural details. A few rooms have large terraces; others open directly into the garden. Breakfast is served in an airy, greenhouse-like pavilion that seems summery even during the gray Bolognese winter.

Vicolo del Falconi 6–8. www.hotel-portasanmamolo.it. ✆ **051/583056.** 43 units. 120€–190€ double. Rates include breakfast. Parking 20€ per day. Bus: 29B or 52. **Amenities:** Bikes; room service; free Wi-Fi.

Hotel Roma ★★ What this old Bologna fixture lacks in chic style it makes up for with plenty of old-school charm and hospitality and a wonderful location just off Piazza Maggiore. Downstairs lounges and a small bar are gracious and welcoming, and the no-nonsense guest rooms upstairs are large and pleasantly done with brass beds and gleaming wooden floors; many open to small terraces overlooking the surrounding streets, and many of the large, tiled bathrooms are windowed. The excellent in-house restaurant, **C'era Una Volta**—which translates as "Once Upon a Time"—offers Bolognese classics served by crisply uniformed waiters.

Via Massimo d'Azeglio 64. www.hotelroma.biz. ✆ **051/226-322.** 86 units. 135€–160€ double. Rates include breakfast. Parking 20€ per day. Bus: 11, 13, 20, 30. **Amenities:** Restaurant; bar; bikes; room service; free Wi-Fi.

Hotel Touring ★★ A rooftop terrace overlooking tile roofs and domes to the hills that surround Bologna is perfect for a few hours of quiet relaxation, an *aperitivo,* or even a soak in the hot tub. Guest rooms are all geared to quiet comfort, too, done in soothing cream colors and functional furnishings, and those on the third and fourth floors have a great amenity: city-view terraces or balconies. A ground-floor reading room warmed by a fireplace is a perfect hideout in cooler weather.

Via De' Mattuiani 1/2. www.hoteltouring.it. ✆ **051/584-305.** 140€–220€. Rates include breakfast. Parking 25€. **Amenities:** Bar; free Wi-Fi.

INEXPENSIVE

Albergo delle Drapperie ★★ This centuries-old guesthouse is smack in the middle of the bustling market streets and steps from Piazza Maggiore. Top-floor rooms, the largest and best, have vaulted ceilings, wooden beams, gables, window seats that double as extra beds, and other atmospheric touches. Lower-floor rooms are smaller and furnished with not much more than beds, though they're enlivened with homey iron bedsteads and the occasional fresco or coffered ceiling. You'll have to do some climbing to reach any of these rooms, as well as the lobby and breakfast room. The Drapperie also rents out apartments in a nearby building; call for rates.

Via Drapperie 5. www.albergodrapperie.com. ✆ **051/223-955.** 21 units. 110€–125€ double. Rates include breakfast. Bus: A, 11, 20, 27, 28. **Amenities:** Free Wi-Fi.

Hotel Accademia ★ The neighborhood is a bit scruffy, but one of the few hotels in the university district is surrounded by lively clubs, bars, and affordable student-oriented *osterie.* Large guest rooms have high ceilings and are spiffily up to date, with polished wooden floors, blond furniture, muted colors, and shiny bathrooms—many with that ever-so-rare fixture in less-expensive Italian hotels, a bathtub. The colorful street life can be a late-night curse for some—if this bothers you, ask for a room facing the courtyard.

Via delle Belle Arte 6. www.hotelaccademia.com. ✆ **051/232-318.** 28 units. 110€–140€ double. Rates include breakfast. Parking 15€ per day. Bus: A, 11, 20, 27, 28. **Amenities:** Bikes; free Wi-Fi.

Hotel Il Guercino ★★s A welcoming courtyard off a busy street in the Bolognina neighborhood sets the mood that extends into the colorful lounges, hung with prints by the namesake artist, and guest rooms that are similarly bohemian and comfortable; the superiors on the top floor come with a terrace. The location behind the train station is a plus for exploring the region, and the surrounding bars and restaurants lend a friendly vibe that can be a nice break from the busier tourist areas. Those are a half-hour walk away, or an easy ride on one of the bikes the hotel provides.

Via Luigi Serra 7, Bologna. www.guercino.it. ✆ **051/369893.** 100€–120€ double. Rates include breakfast. **Amenities:** Fitness room; spa; free bikes; free Wi-Fi.

Where to Eat in Bologna

As capital of Italy's most productive agricultural region, Bologna has been a food center for centuries. Specialties include locally raised beef, exquisitely cured pork (especially prosciutto, salami, and mortadella), fresh pastas, and hearty sauces—and Bologna denies any association with the Americanized sandwich meat that was named after the city. See p. 362 for details on the food shops of the **Quadrilatero** neighborhood.

Artisan gelato is another Bologna mainstay. Run by three brothers, **Gelatauro,** Via San Vitale 98 (www.gelatauro.com; ✆ **051/230049**), is known for its organic gelato, including a divine concoction made from Sicilian oranges. **Sorbetteria** (www.lasorbetteria.it) makes more than 100 decadently rich flavors as well as some classic tastes without milk and sugar, dispensing them from shops at Via Castiglione 44 (✆ **051/095-0772**) and Via Saragozza 83 (✆ **051/093568**).

A moveable feast IN THE QUADRILATERO

On a warren of medieval lanes behind Piazza Maggiore, the **Quadrilatero** is the gastronome epicenter of Bologna, full of venerable gourmet shops. At **Tamburini,** Via Caprarie 1 (www.tamburini.com; ✆ **051/234726**), a selection of pastas, meats and fish, soups and salads, vegetables, and sweets is sold to be taken away or enjoyed in-house, accompanied by 200 wines by the glass. **La Baita Vecchia Malga,** Via Pescherie Vecchie 3A (✆ **051/223940**), lets you choose from a dizzying selection of hams and cheeses and enjoy them in a busy mezzanine dining room. At **Salumeria Simoni,** Via Drapperie 5/2A (www.salumeriasimoni.it; ✆ **051/231880**), you can stock up (or dine in) on cheese and meat, sandwiches, and other dishes, while next-door **Gilberto,** Via Drapperie 5 (www.drogheriagilberto.it; ✆ **051/223925**), sells balsamic vinegars, oils, chocolates, and other local specialties. Founded in 1880, nearby **Atti,** Via Caprarie 7 (www.paoloatti.com; ✆ **051/220425**), is renowned for pasta and pastries.

Bologna Eataly, Via degli Orefici 19 (www.eataly.it; ✆ **051/095-2820**) sells cookbooks, cheeses, hams, and other products, as well as prepared foods and wine that can be consumed picnic-style at indoor and outdoor tables. The covered marketplace across the way has been converted into the **Mercato di Mezzo,** Via Clavature (✆ **051/232919**), a food hall housing small bars and food stands; in the evenings many offer snacks to accompany drinks. **Osteria del Sole,** Vicolo Ranocchi 1D (osteriadelsole.it; ✆ **348/225-6887;** closed Sun), is an invitingly rundown room with a provenance (serving since 1465) and a novel twist on the BYO policy—you bring the food from neighboring shops; they supply the wine for 2.50€ a glass.

Venture a few blocks west of the Quadrilatero to find Bologna's central food market, **Mercato delle Erbe,** at Via Ugo Bassi 25 (www.mercatodelleerbe.eu; stores Mon–Sat 7am–7:30pm; restaurants Mon–Sat noon–2:30pm and 7pm–midnight, Sun 11am–3pm). Aside from produce, fish, and other food vendors, the hall has fast-food outlets with a couple of clamorous dining areas.

Just a short walk north from the Quadrilatero, **Sfoglia Rina,** Via Castiglione 5b (www.sfogliarina.it; ✆ **051/9911710**), offers a changing menu of the city's traditional tagliatelle and tortellini, freshly made and topped with ragù and other signature sauces, served at communal tables or packaged for takeaway.

Bologna Eataly, one of many food shops in the Quadrilatero.

EXPENSIVE

Caminetto d'Oro ★★ BOLOGNESE/ITALIAN Despite the sleekly contemporary look of the formal dining room and more casual bistro to the side, the Carrati family has been feeding Bologna for 80 years, from premises that were once a bakery. A decades-old oven is still used to bake their own delicious breads, which are all made, along with the pasta, using wheat flour from a mill near Modena. The *tagliatelle al ragù* here is renowned—and a favorite of many performers and theatergoers from nearby Arena del Sole. This is also the best place in town for a steak; T-bones from local Romagnola cattle are seared on soapstone.
Via de'Falegnami 4. www.caminettodoro.it. ✆ **051/263494.** Entrees 10€–28€. Tues–Sat noon–2:30pm and 7–10:30pm. Bus: C.

Ristorante da Nello al Montegrappa ★★ BOLOGNESE Occupying several cozily paneled subterranean rooms just off Piazza Maggiore, this Bologna institution has been serving since 1948. Crisply uniformed waiters lead you through the specialties, which include the house signature dish, *tortellini Montegrappa,* served in a cream-and-meat sauce. *Funghi porcini* and truffles appear in many of the classics, including a fragrant veal scallopine in truffle sauce. Daily specials offer some surprising variations of Bolognese standards, such as spinach tortellini with chicken filling. Meals should begin with a platter of buttery prosciutto and end with a selection of cheeses, all washed down with one of the fine wines from local vineyards. To ensure a table in the cheerful rooms downstairs, reserve for dinner.
Via Montegrappa 2. www.ristorantedanello.com. ✆ **051/236331.** Entrees 10€–22€. Tues–Sun noon–2:30pm and 7–10:30pm (until 11pm Fri and Sat). Closed 2 weeks in Jan/Feb and all of Aug. Bus: A, 11, 20, 27, 28.

A Street of Cheap Eats

For an inexpensive meal, head to **Via del Pratello,** west of Piazza Maggiore near the basilica of San Francesco; the narrow street is lined with low-cost osterias, bars, and no-frills take-out shops. **Capra e Cavoli,** at number 58c (capraecavolibologna.it; ✆ **342/775-7553**), and **Pasta Fresca Naldi,** at number 69 (www.pastafrescanaldi.it; ✆ **051/523288**), prepare delicious pastas, including *tortellini alla panna,* to match those from the finest kitchens in town. **MozzaBella-Pratello,** at number 65 (✆ **051/550506**), transforms pizza slices into gourmet concoctions.

MODERATE

Casa Monica ★★ BOLOGNESE/VEGETARIAN Tucked away in a converted workshop at the western edge of the historic center, this pleasant, low-key dining room is an oasis of calm and refinement. Deep rose hues and warm lamplight give the contemporary surroundings a welcoming glow, and the cuisine can be a welcome break from heavier Bolognese fare. Many choices are vegetarian, including creamy risottos and an airy flan *di zucca* (squash), and several main courses are fish. Even the desserts are deceptively light. This transporting spot is only a 15-minute walk or a short cab or bus ride away from Piazza Maggiore.

Via San Rocco 16. www.casamonica.it. ✆ **051/522522.** Entrees 10€–18€. Mon–Sat 8pm–1am. Bus: 13 or 96.

Drogheria della Rosa ★★★ BOLOGNESE/ITALIAN In premises that once dispensed medicines, wine bottles are now mixed in among the old-fashioned jars on the wooden shelves, while chef/owner Emanuele Addone dishes out down-to-earth Bolognese cooking, with an emphasis on market-fresh ingredients. There's no menu, but a waiter—often Emanuele himself—will guide you through the daily offerings and suggest wines to match. A meal usually begins with a plate of prosciutto and a glass of Prosecco. Tortellini are stuffed with zucchini blossoms or eggplant puree and the lasagna is a house classic. Filet mignon is roasted to perfection and drizzled with balsamic vinegar from Modena; guinea fowl is done beautifully with a honey sauce. Desserts include a mascarpone with chocolate shavings.

Via Cartoleria 10. www.drogheriadellarosa.it. ✆ **051/222-529.** Entrees 10€–18€. Tues–Sat 1–2pm and 8–11pm, Sun 1–2:30pm. Closed 2 weeks in Aug and 1st week of Jan. Bus: C, 11, 13.

Il Rovescio ★★ BOLOGNESE/VEGETARIAN The name of this rustic-looking little room just off bar- and *osterie*-lined Via del Pratello (see p. 363) translates roughly as "upside down" or "backwards"—a clue that you're likely to find some unusual takes on traditional Bolognese cuisine. All the food is locally sourced; the menu changes frequently to reflect what's in season, and—a rarity in Bologna—includes many vegetarian choices, like grilled radicchio on a bed of polenta, or crepes filled with caramelized squash. Meat presentations, such as little ginger-laced meatballs on a bed of pureed peas, can be surprising. Rovescio operates an evenings-only **bio-pizzeria** next door, where only organically grown ingredients are used.

Via Pietralata 28. www.rovescio.it. ✆ **051/523-545.** Entrees 10€–20€. Tues–Sun 12:30–2:30pm (until 3pm Sat and Sun) and 7:30pm–10:30pm (until 11pm Sat and Sun). Bus: C, 11, 13.

Trattoria Bertozzi ★★ BOLOGNESE An unassuming neighborhood favorite just west of the historic center enjoys citywide acclaim for friendly service, overseen by on-the-scene patrons Fabio and Alessandro and their close-to-perfection takes on *tortellini in brodo, tagiliatelle al ragù,* braised lamb chops, and other classic dishes. Homemade cakes are just as winning.

Via Andrea Costa 84/2. www.trattoriabertozzibologna.it. ✆ **051/614-1425.** Entrees 10€–22€. Fri, Sat, and Mon 12:30–2:30pm and 7:30–10:30pm; Tues–Thurs 7:30–10:30pm. Bus: 14, 21, 61, 89.

Trattoria dal Biassanot ★★★ EMILIAN The wood beams, lace tablecloths, warm service, and other grace notes of this welcoming bistro

(the name roughly means "night owl") do justice to the expertly prepared Bolognese classics that emerge from the kitchen. Light-as-a-feather *tagliatelle* with ragù has a reputation as one of the best in a city that's famous for the dish, but all of the handmade pastas and succulent sauces are excellent; even the bread is house-made and delicious. For a taste of the city's famous pastas, try three on Biassanot's Tris Bologna offering.
Via Piella 16a. www.dalbiassanot.it. ✆ **051/230644.** Entrees 10€–19€. Daily noon–2:15pm and 7–10:15pm. Closed Aug. Bus: 19, 27, 94.

Trattoria da Me ★★★ MODERN BOLOGNESE Chef Elisa Rusconi became a TV star with her cooking show *4 Ristoranti,* then returned to her Bologna roots to revamp the simple trattoria her grandparents opened in the 1930s. Warm and welcoming shabby-chic surroundings do the old-fashioned premises justice, while Elisa's menu puts a slight twist on Bolognese favorites, including pumpkin tortellini with beets and bacon, a cheese board that includes some memorable cheese gelati, and the town's best Bolognese, a pounded veal chop with prosciutto and Parmigiano Reggiano. Many regulars would dine nowhere else, so reserve for dinner.
Via San Felice 50. www.trattoriadame.it. ✆ **051/555486.** Entrees 13€–22€. Tues–Sun 12:30–2:30pm and 7:30–10pm. Bus: 36, 37, 39.

INEXPENSIVE

All'Osteria Bottega ★★★ BOLOGNESE/ITALIAN In this unassuming storefront, the simple tables are covered with butcher paper, and pride of place belongs to the bright red meat slicer and the meats and

Diving Deeper into the Local Food Scene

A visit to **FICO Eataly World,** the 25-acre food shopping mall on the city outskirts, Via Paolo Canali 8 (www.eatalyworld.it; ✆ **051/0029001**), lacks the appeal of an authentic shopping experience in the Quadrilatero (see p. 362) but delivers a quick look into local gastronomy: mortadella, Parmigiano, gelato, and pasta are produced in glassed-in workshops with detailed descriptions of the processes, while dozens of vendors and restaurants sell a vast selection of food from every corner of Italy. The park is open Thursday through Sunday 11am to 10pm, and entry fee is 10€; free shuttle bus from stop near the train station on Saturdays (must show entrance ticket). **Italian Days** (www.italiandays.it; ✆ **338/421-6659**) ventures into the countryside to visit top producers of Parmigiano Reggiano, prosciutto, and balsamic vinegar on 10-hour tours that include breakfast, lunch, many tastings, discourses on the aging and certification processes, and hospitality as delectable as the food; from 150€. At **Salotto di Penelope,** Via San Felice 116 (ilsalottodipenelope.it; ✆ **051/649-3627**), the engaging Barbara and Valeria lead half-day workshops in preparing gnocchi, tagliatelle, and tortelloni as well as the city's classic ragù, in which carrot, onion, and celery are combined with minced beef, wine, and a dab of tomato paste and simmered for hours. Lessons and the accompanying meal are laced with lively tips on techniques and shopping and dining in Bologna. Classes are about 120€.

cheeses on display. These find their way into *affettati misti* and delicious pastas, followed by roast rabbit and other hearty main courses. On hand to enthuse about the daily offerings, owner Danielle Minarelli will guide you through one of your most memorable meals in Italy. Reservations recommended, especially for dinner.
Via Santa Caterina 51. ✆ **051/585111.** Entrees 8€–16€. Tues–Sat 12:30–2:30pm and 8–10:30pm. Bus: 11 or 13.

Trattoria Anna Maria ★ BOLOGNESE Photographs of Sophia Loren, Marcello Mastroianni, and legions of other celebrities line the walls of these high-ceilinged, welcoming rooms, but everyone in Bologna knows that the real star is Anna Maria, who has been serving her freshly made pasta for 30 years. *Tortellini in brodo,* parcels of pasta filled with minced pork and floating in chicken broth, and tagliatelle with a hearty ragù sauce are her signature dishes, but the lasagnas are memorable, too. Anna Maria will likely find her way to your table at some point during your meal to make sure you've eaten every bite, but that won't be an issue.
Via Bella Arti 17/A. www.trattoriannamaria.com. ✆ **051/266894.** Entrees 10€–15€. Tues–Sun 12:30–3pm and 7:30–11pm. Bus: 11, 13, 20, 29B, 30, 38, 39.

Shopping

Shopping in Bologna often revolves around food; see p. 362 for some recommended gourmet stops. U.S. travelers should keep in mind that you are allowed to bring Parmigiano and other hard cheese home with you, as long as it's wrapped and labeled from the shop, but not prosciutto or most other meats. Olive oil and vinegar are okay, too, but any container over 3.5 ounces will have to go into your checked luggage. See p. 362 for more info.

Maybe it's not unexpected that Bologna has many famous chocolatiers. **Majani,** Via de' Carbonesi 5 (www.majani.it; ✆ **051/234302**), claims to be Italy's oldest sweets shop, making confections since 1796. **Roccati,** Via Clavature 17A (www.roccaticioccolato.com; ✆ **051/261964**), is run by a husband-and-wife team that makes the *gianduja* (hazelnut and cognac-filled chocolate) their ancestors once concocted for the princes of Savoy.

It also only stands to reason that this youth-oriented city is awash in bohemian chic, and the place to seek out some stylish vintage fashion is **La Leonarda,** Via San Leonarda 2/2A (✆ **340/936-8884**), with a well-chosen, ever-changing selection of secondhand fashions; proceeds go to an organization that aids the homeless.

Entertainment & Nightlife

The 200-plus-year-old **Teatro Arena del Sole,** Via Indipendenza 44 (bologna.emiliaromagnateatro.com; ✆ **051/291-0911**), stages theater and dance productions. **Teatro Comunale,** Largo Respighi 1 (www.tcbo.it;

✆ **051/529995**), inaugurated in 1763, is the city's main venue for opera and classical music.

Bologna's large student population keeps bars, clubs, and *osterie* busy. Many are clustered near the university on Via Zamboni and Via delle Belle Arti. Bolognese of all stripes, even those who plan to turn in early, stop at bars all over town for an *aperitivo,* when a glass of wine or a cocktail comes with snacks.

Camera a Sud ★ Three shabby-chic rooms in the Jewish ghetto are part coffeehouse, part wine bar, and popular any time of day. Via Valdonica 5. www.cameraasud.net. ✆ **051/095-1448.** Daily noon–1am (until midnight Sun and Mon).

Cantina Bentivoglio ★★ You'll hear some of the best jazz in Bologna in the cellars of this 16th-century *palazzo* near the university. Select from one of more than 500 labels that fill the wine racks. Via Mascarella 4B. www.cantinabentivoglio.it. ✆ **051/265-416.** Daily 8pm–2am.

PULLING INTO THE fast lane

Prosperous **Modena,** 40km (25 miles) northwest of Bologna, lies in the center of what's known as La Terra dei Motori, the "Land of Motors." A car enthusiast who's been patiently traipsing through museums and churches might be delighted to learn that all of Italy's famed sports-car manufacturers are located here—and open to the public. **Maserati,** founded in Bologna in 1914, is now based in Modena, and 20 vintage models are parked permanently at the **Museo Panini** in the Modena suburb of Cittanova (on the SS9). Highlights include a rare Maserati Tipo 6CM from the 1930s and a Maserati A6G/54 from the 1950s (www.paninimotormuseum.it; visits by written request only [use form on website]; free; Mon–Fri 9am–1pm and Sat 9am–1pm; closed mid-Dec to Feb).

In Maranello, 18km/11 miles from central Modena, **Museo Ferrari,** Via Dino Ferrari 43, pays homage to the magnificent cars that Enzo Ferrari began turning out in 1929; vintage and current models are on display. Tours run at 12:30pm and 1:30pm; buy tickets in advance on the website. More Ferraris, and the engines that power them, are on display at the **Museo Enzo Ferrari,** Via Paolo Ferrari 85, Modena. Both museums have the same website and phone (musei.ferrari.com; ✆ **0536/943-204**); each museum charges 22€, 18€ senior, 9€ under 19; a combined ticket costs 30€. Both are open April to October daily 9:30am to 7pm and October to March daily 9:30am to 6pm.

A visit to the **Museo Lamborghini,** at Via Modena 12 in the company's hometown of Sant' Agata Bolognese, between Bologna and Modenacan, costs 18€, 14€ seniors; and with a guide, 23€, 19€ seniors. A museum visit with a tour of the factory is 80€, 76€ seniors. Reserve visits on the website (www.lamborghini.com; ✆ **051/681-7611;** daily 9:30am–6pm).

It's possible to make the pilgrimage by public transport, but not easily, and you certainly couldn't do the whole circuit in a day. Besides, a car buff will probably want to rent a car anyway, right? As an alternative, **MotorStars** (motorstarstour.com; ✆ **059/921-667**) provides a full day of touring, with transport from Bologna plus lunch from 285€.

Enoteca Italiana ★★★ No place in Bologna serves a better selection of regional and Italian wines, accompanied by ham, cheese, and a wide choice of gourmet goods to eat on the premises or take away. Via Marsala 2/B. www.enotecaitaliana.it. ✆ **051/235-989.** Mon–Sat 9am–9:30pm.

Le Stanze ★ Cocktails are served in the heavily frescoed salons and 17th-century chapel of an aristocratic palace. Via del Borgo di San Pietro. www.lestanzecafe.it. ✆ **051/228-767.** Tues–Sun 11am–1am.

Nu Lounge Bar ★★ Hip young professionals check out each other (and themselves in the huge mirrors) while enjoying martinis under the porticos in the Quadrilatero. Via dei Musei 6. www.nuloungebar.com. ✆ **051/222-532.** Mon–Fri 6:30–11pm; Sat–Sun 3:30–11pm.

Side Trip to Modena ★★

45km (28 miles) NW of Bologna

By all appearances, residents of this elegant little city, only a half-hour train ride from Bologna, excel at whatever pursuit they undertake. The city is famous for cars (see box p. 367); for hams and cheeses, like its neighbors in Emilia-Romagna; and for balsamic vinegar, *aceto balsemico,* made from grape must. You will taste the dark, intense elixir at just about any meal around town, and sample a wide variety at such specialty shops as **La Consertia 1966,** Piazza Giuseppe Mazzini 9 (✆ **393/802-7841**) or on a walk through **Mercato Albinelli,** the covered market at Via Albinelli 13.

At the city center is the showiest creation of all, the 12th-century **Duomo,** probably the finest creation of Romanesque architecture, above which towers a slightly leaning bell tower, the **Ghirlandina** (Duomo; www.visitmodena.it; ✆ **059/216078;** free admission; Tues–Sun 7:30am–7pm, Mon 7am–12:30pm and 3:30–7pm). The sculptor Wigilemo surrounded the main Duomo entrance with a fearsome medieval bestiary depicting the temptation-ridden perils of our mortal journey, offset with poignant depictions of Adam and Eve, Noah's Ark, and other scenes from the Old Testament to suggest the path to redemption. On the northern side, the Porta della Pescheria (Fish Market doorway) is framed with an utterly charming assemblage of scenes of the 12 months (an old crone huddles in front of a fire in February) and knights-on-steeds tales from Arthurian legend.

A treasure trove of Italian painting (including a transcendent Madonna and Child by Botticelli) is in the **Galleria Estense,** Largo Porta Sant'Agostino 337, the legacy of the Este dukes who ruled the city from the 14th through 18th centuries (www.gallerie-estensi.beniculturali.it; ✆ **059/439-5711;** Tues–Sat 8:30am–7:30pm, Sun 10am–6pm; 6€).

FERRARA ★★

52km (32 miles) N of Bologna, 100km (62 miles) SW of Venice

It's not that quiet, elegant Ferrara hasn't had some big moments. For almost 4 centuries, the powerful Este family controlled this city on the Po River, and painters, composers, and poets under their patronage made Ferrara one of Europe's great capitals of culture. Lucrezia Borgia, notorious femme fatale of the Renaissance, arrived by ceremonial barge in 1502 to marry Prince Alfonso Este, and they and the other Estes built pleasure pavilions and gardens and expanded their holdings into the Addizione, a model Renaissance city crisscrossed with straight palace-lined avenues. By the end of the 16th century, however, the Estes were gone—and Ferrara has looked pretty much the same ever since. That, of course, is its appeal. It's essentially a time capsule, with the Estes' castle, palace, and encircling walls, along with proud old convents and churches, serving as a backdrop for everyday life in this attractive provincial city.

Essentials

ARRIVING Ferrara is on the main **train** line between Bologna and Venice, with service to and from both cities twice an hour (30–45 min. from Bologna; 1–1½ hr. from Venice). Ravenna is an hour away, with hourly departures all day. From the train station it's an easy 20-minute walk to the Duomo, but you can also take the frequent no. 1 or 9 bus to Piazza Travaglio (1.30€; buy your ticket at the bus office inside the train station or at a tobacco shop; www.tper.it). You may also rent a **bike** at the station and get around the way most locals do (see box below).

If you have a **car** and are coming from Bologna, take A13 north. From Venice, take A4 southwest to Padua and continue on A13 south to Ferrara. A convenient parking spot close to the historic center is Parcheggio Centro Storico off Via Darsena, where daytime rates are .80€ an hour

From Streets & Squares to the Po Delta

Ferrara is known in Italy as a *città della bicicletta,* because just about everyone in town, regardless of age, gets around on two wheels. The flat streets and squares lend themselves to easy pedaling, and the medieval walls are topped with trees, lawns, and a wide path that's ideal for cycling. Many hotels offer guests free use of bikes, or you can rent them from the lot outside the train station (2.50€ an hour, 10€ a day). If you want to go farther afield, well-marked bike paths lead into the Po Delta Park. At the heart of the delta is **Comacchio,** 42km (25 miles east of Ferrara; frequent bus connections at www.tper.it), a small town laced with canals lined with some impressive landmarks that include the Tre Ponti, a massive brick bridge that crosses the intersection of several canals. Comacchio is a base for excursions by boat and bike through lagoons and salt flats and is adjacent to a string of Adriatic beaches; info on excursions at www.ferrarainfo.com.

up to a maximum of 3.20€ for the day between 7:30am and 8pm, and .25€ up to a maximum of 1€ between 8pm and 7:30am.

VISITOR INFORMATION The helpful **tourist office** is inside the Castello Estense, Piazza del Castello (www.ferrarateraeacqua.it; ✆ **0532/419190**). It's open Monday to Saturday from 9am to 6pm, Sunday 9:30am to 5:30pm.

Exploring Ferrara

The **Castello Estense** is pretty much the center of town, with the **Cattedrale San Giorgio Martire** and twisting lanes of the medieval town just to the southeast. (The cathedral, known for its fearsome carvings of the damned, is currently closed for restoration and may reopen in time for Christmas 2023.) South of Castello lies the city's most atmospheric medieval lane, narrow cobblestoned **Via delle Volte,** darkened with arched, upper-story passageways that once linked merchants' houses with their riverside warehouses. North from the Castello, **Corso Ercole I d'Este,** flanked by beautiful *palazzi,* leads into the Renaissance city and past **Palazzo dei Diamanti** to the city walls.

The **Ferrara Tourist Card** gives access to the attractions listed here, with the exception of MEIS and the Monastero di Sant'Antonio in Polesine, so provides a substantial savings over individual admissions. The

Cyclists on Via Giuseppe Mazzini in Ferrara, during an Umbrella Project installation.

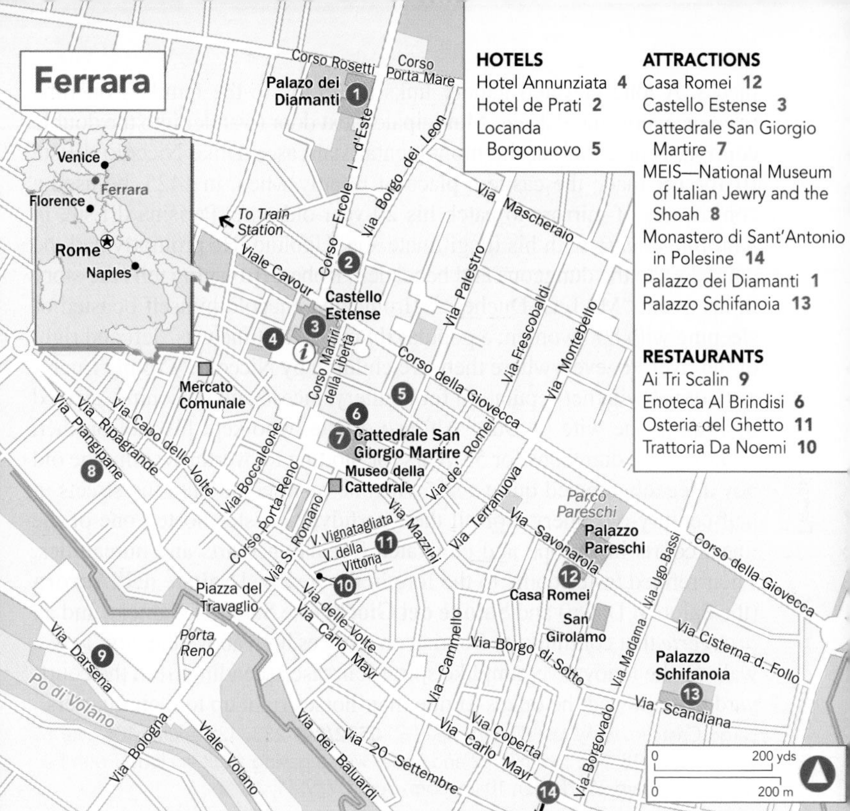

card costs 20€ for 2 days, 22€ for 3 days, and 25€ for 6 days and is available from the tourist office and most museum ticket offices.

Casa Romei ★★ PALACE Ambitious 15th-century financier Giovanni Romei worked his way up in the Este administration, capping off his rise by marrying the daughter of an Este duke. He built this palatial townhouse between 1440 and 1450, commissioning lavish frescoes for salons surrounding a vast interior courtyard. Though the Estes carted off most of the furnishings when they left Ferrara in 1598, the Sala delle Sibille, with its original terracotta fireplace, coffered wooden ceiling, and images of the sibyls (classical Greek prophetesses) provides an idea of the comfortable lifestyle the occupants enjoyed. Scattered about the place are frescoes and sculptures from churches and chapels around the city.
Via Savonarola 30. www.ferraraterraeacqua.it. ✆ **0532/234130.** 5€. Included with Ferrara Tourist Card. Sun–Wed 8:30am–2pm; Thurs–Sat 2–7:30pm. Bus: 11.

Castello Estense ★★ CASTLE With its moat, hefty brick walls, drawbridges, heavy gates, and four sturdy towers, the domain of the Este family still suggests power and might. Niccolò II d'Este ordered the castle built in 1385 as a place of refuge when his subjects, becoming restless after a series of tax increases, quite literally tore one of his officials to pieces. A long elevated gallery links the castle to the family's onetime residence, now the Palazzo Municipale, next door (wander into the double courtyard for a look at the monumental staircase). Duke Niccolò d'Este III forever made the castle a place of infamy when, in 1425, he used a contrivance of mirrors to catch his 20-year-old wife, Parisina d'Este, *in flagrante delicto* with his illegitimate son, Ugolino. He promptly had the pair taken to the dungeons and beheaded; Robert Browning tells the story in his poem "My Last Duchess." (Ironically, Niccolò himself boasted of sleeping with 800 women; a popular rhyme of the time was "left and right of the river Po, everywhere there are children by Niccolò.") Young Lucrezia Borgia, with her reputation for adultery, incest, and poisoning, arrived in 1502 as the wife of Duke Alfonso d'Este, who kept his half-brother, Giulio, in the dungeons for 53 years for plotting to overthrow him; the old boy allegedly created quite a stir when he re-emerged onto the streets in half-century-old finery. For all their perfidy, the Estes hosted one of the finest courts in Europe and cultivated Renaissance arts and humanities. Their refined tastes come to the fore in the frescoed **Salone dell'Aurora** (the Salon of Dawn) and **Salone dei Giochi** (the Salon of Games), and an *orangerie* that continues to flourish on terraces high above the city. Take a walk up the innovative ramplike spiral staircase ascending from the courtyard that allowed the dukes to ride their horses right up to their quarters. Largo Castello. www.castelloestense.it. ✆ **0532/299-233.** 12€ adults; 10€ over 65 and ages 13–18; free for child 12 and under with a paying adult. Included with Ferrara Tourist Card. Wed–Mon 10am–6pm. Bus: 1, 7, 9, 11, 21.

Monastero di Sant'Antonio in Polesine ★★ CHURCH The Estes weren't all about worldly goods and power. In the early 13th century the aristocratic lady who would become Saint Beatrice d'Este entered this tranquil convent near the city walls when her groom-to-be died of battle wounds just before their wedding day. Over the years Este money paid for improvements that included a colorful fresco cycle by the school of Giotto in the nun's chapel—the charming images include an exuberant Christ climbing a ladder onto the cross, where two spike-wielding tormentors await, and a gentle-looking Virgin fluttering her hands to ascend to Heaven. Ring the bell to enter, and a nun will emerge to show off the frescoes (in Italian). She'll also invite you to return for 5pm vespers, where you'll hear the cloistered order sing Gregorian chants from behind a grill. Vicolo del Gambone. www.ferraraterraeacqua.it. ✆ **0532/64068.** Free (donations welcome). Mon–Sat 9:30–11:30am and 3:15–4:45pm. Bus 2 to XX Settembre Ghisiglieri stop.

Palazzo dei Diamanti ★★ MUSEUM The facade of the Estes' most remarkable residence—8,500 spiky diamond-shaped white marble blocks—creates an architectural spectacle, shimmering in the light and seemingly constantly in movement. The *palazzo* stands at the intersection of two monumental avenues that were the main thoroughfares of the

Addizione that Ercole d'Este laid out in the late 15th century, doubling the size of Ferrara and making the city a Renaissance showplace. On the first floor of the *palazzo,* the **Pinacoteca Nazionale** provides a handy overview of the School of Ferrara, especially the trio of old masters who flourished under the Estes—Cosmé Tura, Francesco del Cossa, and Ercole de' Roberti. Pride of place belongs to Tura's "Martyrdom of St. Maurelius," in which the saint, an early bishop of Ferrara, calmly kneels as his executioner swings a sword above his neck and some nattily attired soldiers gather cheerfully around.

Corso Ercole d'Este 21. gallerie-estensi.beniculturali.it. ✆ **0532/244949**. Pinacoteca 8€ adults; 2€ 18–25; free for ages 17 and under. Included with Ferrara Tourist Card. Tues–Sun 10am–7:30pm. Bus: 3C or 4C.

Palazzo Schifanoia ★★★ PALACE The Estes retreated for leisure to this pleasure palace enlarged by Duke Borso d'Este between 1450 and 1471. Schifanoia translates roughly as "chasing away tedium," and the concept comes to the fore in the **Salone dei Mesi** (Salon of the Months), where a mesmerizing cycle of frescoes once represented the 12 months. Only a few remain intact, each divided into three horizontal bands: The lower bands show scenes from the daily life of courtiers and people, with Duke Borso frequently making an appearance astride a horse; the middle bands illustrate signs of the zodiac; and upper sections depict gods and goddesses associated with the sign. A collaboration by the masters of the Ferrarese school of painting—Francesco del Cossa, Ercole dei Roberti, and Cosimo Tura—the frescoes' characters seem to come alive and step out of the scenes (one figure actually does, and perches on the edge of the frame as if he's about to jump into the room). Men ride horses and run footraces, harvesters pick grapes, women do needlework and play lutes. The artists even dug some skeletons out of the Este closet: In a mythical scene depicting Mars and Venus caught in a net as they make love, their clothing laid beside the bed suggests a decapitated man and woman—a sly reference to the fate of Ugolino and Parisina d'Este (see Castello Estense, p. 371).

Via Scandiana 23. www.artecultura.fe.it. ✆ **0532/244949.** 10€ adults; 9€ seniors and ages 18–30; free for ages 17 and under. Included with Ferrara Tourist Card. Tues–Sun 10am–7pm. Bus: 1, 7, 9, or 21.

Where to Stay in Ferrara

Hotel Annunziata ★★ The setting, across from Castello Estense, is medieval, and Casanova spent the night here when the place was a simple inn. But once inside the doors, you'll feel like you've been transported from old Ferrara into a Milanese showroom for contemporary style. The white color scheme strays into grays and beige here and there, even the occasional burst of red or orange, but for the most part this place is all about sleek lines, soothing neutrals, and minimalist calm. In large and bright guest rooms (the best with castle views), high-tech lighting and snowy linens contrast with wood floors and the occasional timbered

ceiling, and bathrooms are luxurious. Six stylish apartments with kitchenettes are located in a 14th-century annex.
Piazza Repubblica 5. www.annunziata.it. ✆ **0532/201111.** 27 units. 100€–150€ double. Rates include breakfast. Bus: 1, 7, 9, 11, 21. **Amenities:** Restaurant; bar; babysitting; bikes; room service; free Wi-Fi.

Hotel de Prati ★★ This welcoming inn is nicely appointed with polished antiques and wrought-iron bedsteads in bright, quiet rooms enlivened with colorful paintings by local artists. Timbered beams and old archways show off the house's centuries-old origins. The refined old-world air extends to the gracious service provided by the de Prati family, who have been running the place for three generations.
Via Padiglioni 5. www.hoteldeprati.com. ✆ **0532/241905.** 28 units. 85€–90€ double. Rates include breakfast. Bus: 3C or 4C. **Amenities:** Bikes; free Wi-Fi.

Locanda Borgonuovo ★★★ This lovely old house, converted from a 17th-century convent and just down a cobblestone street from the *castello,* could set the gold standard for B&Bs everywhere. The four rooms are furnished with family pieces, including some serious antiques, and share a flowery courtyard; one especially large double has an extra bed and a kitchenette. An excellent breakfast is served in the family living room, and the gracious hosts lend bikes and dispense advice about the best ways to enjoy their beloved Ferrara. They also rent a few one- and two-bedroom apartments in an adjoining building.
Via Cairoli 21. www.borgonuovo.com. ✆ **0532/211100.** 85€–100€ double. Rates include breakfast. Bus: 4C or 7. **Amenities:** Bikes; free Wi-Fi.

Where to Eat in Ferrara

You'll get a good intro to Ferrara's iconic foods, many dating from the Renaissance, on a stroll down **Via Cortevecchia,** a narrow brick lane near the cathedral, and through the food stalls of the **Mercato Comunale,** at the corner of Via Santo Stefano and Via del Mercato. Traditional *salumerias* sell the city's famous *salama da sugo,* handmade sausages of pork

Lucrezia Borgia, a Woman Misjudged?

Five hundred years after their Renaissance heyday, the Borgias are still one of history's most dysfunctional families. Lucrezia, born into the clan in 1480, was the illegitimate daughter of Cardinal Rodrigo Borgia (soon to be Pope Alexander VI). By the time she was 20, she had a child, allegedly fathered by her brother Cesare, and had been married twice—one husband fled for his life when the Pope decided Lucrezia needed a more politically useful alliance, another was strangled as he lay recovering from knife wounds (both attacks arranged by Cesare). No wonder Lucrezia got a chilly reception when she arrived in Ferrara in 1500 as the new bride of Duke Alfonso d'Este. However, she proved herself a brilliant conversationalist and patron of the arts; while she is said to have carried on a passionate affair with the poet Pietro Bembo, she was also a loving wife and attentive mother, dying just before her 39th birthday after giving birth to her fifth child.

and spices that are often boiled for 8 hours and served atop mashed potatoes or pumpkin. This sausage and mash was a favorite of Lucrezia Borgia, whose golden locks are said to have inspired *coppia ferrarese,* sourdough bread stretched into intertwining rolls; the name derives from that fact the bread resembles two sets of legs ("the couple"). The pastas to try are *cappellacci di zucca,* round pasta stuffed with pumpkin or squash and served *al burro e salvia* (with butter and sage sauce) or *al ragù* (with meat sauce), and *pasticcio,* also known as *maccheroni alla ferrarese;* this favorite of the d'Este family is a rich pie with a sweet or salty crust filled with short, macaroni-like pasta, pork and liver ragu, wild mushrooms, and a creamy, nutmeg-infused bechamel sauce.

Enoteca Al Brindisi ★★ FERRARESE It would be easy for this atmospheric little place—probably the oldest wine bar in the world, dating from 1435—to rest on its laurels. Titian was a regular, Copernicus is said to have lived upstairs while studying for his degree in 1503, and it looks like some of the dusty bottles stacked above the cramped tables have been around ever since. Locals (some of whom look like they've been around awhile, too) still pack the place, and waiters take earnest pride in recommending Italian wines, accompanied by a short menu of *cappellacci di zucca* (squash ravioli) and a few other local specialties.

Via Adelardi 11. www.albrindisi.net. ✆ **0532/473744.** Entrees 7€–12€. Wed–Sun 11am–11pm. Bus: 11.

I Tri Scalin ★ FERRARESE Locals pack into this simple, half-paneled room near the city walls at mealtimes (best to reserve for dinner) to enjoy the ages-old dishes their grandmothers used to make. Grilled *salama da sugo,* the city's famed sausages, are the preferred starters, followed by *pasticcio.* By now you may have figured out that the Ferrarese are shameless carnivores: *Cotechino,* boiled sausage, is served with a rich salami sauce, and lamb chops or steaks are seasoned with green peppercorns and grilled to perfection. The dessert of choice is *tenerina,* the city's own version of chocolate cake, similar to a brownie, with a crunchy crust and creamy interior.

Via Darsena 50. ✆ **0532/760331.** Entrees 9€–18€. Tues–Sun noon–2:30pm and 7:15–10:45pm. Bus: 2.

Osteria del Ghetto ★★ FERRARESE/SEAFOOD From a simple storefront on the narrow cobblestone lanes of Ferrara's centuries-old Jewish ghetto, a staircase leads to two homey upstairs rooms enlivened with colorful murals. Dishes show off traditional Ferrarese cuisine and some Middle Eastern and Jewish influences, as well as a passion for fish—including rich fish soup, *spaghetti alle vongole,* grilled octopus, pan-fried anchovies, a fresh catch of the day, and other choices to tempt you away from the region's meat-heavy staples.

Via Vittoria 26/28. www.osteriadelghetto.it. ✆ **0532/764936.** Entrees 8€–16€. Tues–Sun noon–2:30pm and 7:30–10:30pm. Bus: 2.

The Jews of Ferrara

Ferrara's Jewish heritage dates to the Middle Ages, when a Jewish community flourished under the Este control of the city. The sad fate of Ferrara's socially prominent 20th-century Jews is the subject of Giorgio Bassani's novel *The Garden of the Finzi-Contini*, brought evocatively to the screen in director Vittorio de Sica's 1970 film. **MEIS—National Museum of Italian Jewry and the Shoah,** in a former prison at Via Piangipane 81, displays manuscripts and other artifacts from Ferrara and elsewhere in Italy, as well as video and multimedia exhibits on the Jewish-Italian experience from the Roman era through the rise of Christianity; on Jews in the Renaissance; and on the Holocaust experience in Italy (www.meisweb.it; ✆ **0532/769-137;** 10€; Tues–Sun 10am–6pm).

Trattoria Da Noemi ★★★ FERRARESE The surroundings date to 1400, with a pleasant old-world decor that befits the provenance and gracious service. The menu leans to Ferrarese classics—some residents say no one does them better. This is the place to become acquainted with *cappellacci di zucca,* the city's signature dish, little pockets of light egg pasta stuffed with roasted butternut squash with hints of nutmeg and Parmigiano. Most of the meat-heavy *secondi* feature local beef grilled over a wood fire. The house *semifreddo,* a delicious half-frozen custard with pistachio and walnuts or mint, is the perfect finish.

Via Ragno 31. www.trattoriadanoemi.it. ✆ **0532/769070.** Entrees 8€–24€. Thurs–Mon 12:30–2:30pm and 7:30–10:30pm; Wed 12:30–2:30pm. Bus: 2 or 11.

RAVENNA ★★

74km (46 miles) E of Bologna, 145km (90 miles) S of Venice, 130km (81 miles) NE of Florence

It's hard to believe that Ravenna was the epicenter of the Western World for a brief spell, when it was the capital of the Western Roman Empire from A.D. 402 to A.D. 476. Those rulers and the fathers of the early Christian church, and then the Goths and Byzantines who followed them, blanketed Ravenna's churches and monuments in glittering mosaics to create an artistic legacy that rivals the splendors of Venice and Istanbul. The poet Dante, who's buried here, described Ravenna's mosaics as "the sweet color of Oriental sapphires." Set amid the marshy landscapes of Emilia-Romagna's coastal plain, this once powerful city is a bit off the beaten path but well worth the effort to reach.

Essentials

ARRIVING With hourly **trains** that take only 1 hour, 20 minutes from Bologna, Ravenna can easily be visited on a day trip. There's also frequent service from Ferrara (1 hr., 15 min.), which has connections to Venice. The train station is a 10-minute walk from the center at Piazza Bernini

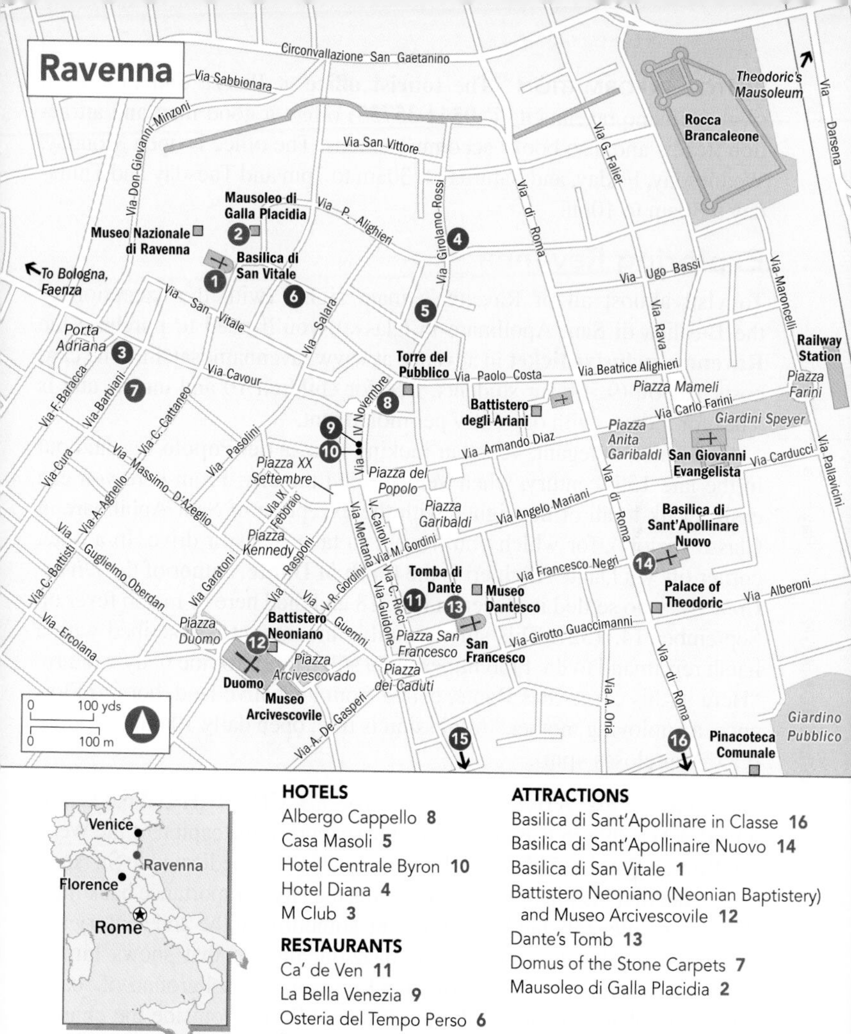

(✆ **892-021**). If you have a **car** and are coming from Bologna, head east along A14. From Ferrara, take the S16.

GETTING AROUND If you need to take a local **bus** (as you will to visit the Basilica di Sant'Apollinare in Classe; see p. 378), buy tickets (1.50€; www.startromagna.it) in advance from bars or *tabacchi.* Ravenna is flat and well-suited to biking, and many hotels offer **bikes** for guests to use. You can pedal farther afield to the beaches around Marina di Ravenna (12km/7 miles) or into the Po Delta Park (see p. 369). Among many shops that rent bikes and e-bikes is V.E.R.A. Bike Rental, Piazza Farini 1 (velostazione.ra.it; ✆ **345/718-7028**).

VISITOR INFORMATION The **tourist office** at Piazza San Francesco (www.turismo.ravenna.it; ✆ **0544-35755**) offers a good map and attraction tickets and also books accommodations. The office is open Monday, Wednesday, Friday, and Saturday 8:30am to 7pm and Tuesday and Thursday 9:30am to 10pm.

Exploring Ravenna

To visit almost all of Ravenna's main sights (with the exception of the Basilica di Sant'Apollinare in Classe), you'll need to purchase the **Ravenna inclusive ticket** in advance at www.ravennamosaici.it. The card costs 10.50€ (9.50€ for students, free for children 10 and under) and is valid for 7 days, with one entry per monument.

Ravenna's elegant, Venetian-looking **Piazza del Popolo** was laid out in the late 15th century, when Venice ruled the city. From here you can easily walk to all of the sights, with the exception of Sant'Apollinare in Classe (below), for which you'll want to take a bus or drive. In a quiet corner off Via Dante Alighieri is the **tomb of Dante,** author of the *Divine Comedy,* who settled in Ravenna in 1318 and died here of marsh fever on September 14, 1321. This simple marble monument is inscribed with a harsh reprimand to the Florentines, who still clamor for the body's return: "Here in this corner lies Dante, exiled from his native land, born to Florence, an unloving mother." Admission is free; open daily 10am to 6:30pm (Oct–Mar closes 4pm).

Basilica di Sant'Apollinare in Classe ★★ CHURCH What is now a landlocked suburb was at one time the seaport of the capital of the Western Roman Empire. This huge 6th-century church—dedicated to St. Apollinare, the first bishop of Ravenna—befits the city's importance back then. Apollinare allegedly landed in Ravenna sometime in the 2nd century and converted the locals; look for the dazzling mosaic that shows him in prayer, surrounded by lambs (his flock) against a background of rocks, birds, and plants, including the pines that still grow outside the church. (Lord Byron used to ride here with his Ravennese mistress, Teresa Guiccioli.) Above Apollinare is a scene of the Transfiguration, when Christ became radiant with light; he is represented as a golden cross on a starry blue background, while Peter, James, and John, the three disciples who witnessed the event, are shown as lambs. Some especially touching mosaics on the right of the church shows three Old Testament figures who made sacrifices to God: Abel, Melchizedek, and Abraham. The church is in the town of Classe, about 6km (3¾ miles) south of Ravenna.

Via Romea Sud 224, Classe. www.musei.emiliaromagna.beniculturali.it. ✆ **0544/473-569.** 5€ adults; free for ages 17 and under. Mon–Sat 8:30am–7:30pm; Sun 1:30–7:30pm. Bus: 4 from train station or Piazza Caduti.

Basilica di Sant'Apollinare Nuovo ★★ CHURCH The church that Emperor Theodoric built in the first part of the 6th century for followers

Ravenna's Piazza del Popolo with Orologio tower and Palazzo del Governo.

of Arianism, a Christian sect, seems to be in perpetual motion. On the left side of the nave, reserved for women, 22 female saints and martyrs approach Mary and the Christ child as they receive gifts from the Three Magi. On the right side, 26 male martyrs led by St. Martin approach a bearded Christ. Above these processions are 26 charmingly rendered scenes from the life of Christ, including one of Christ standing on the shore and calling to Peter and Andrew in their small fishing boat, asking them to be his disciples. Mosaics near the door provide a picture-postcard view of the old city, including Theodoric's palace and the port city of Classe. Look for the detached hand and forearm wrapped around a column of Theodoric's palace—it was once part of a portrait of Theodoric's court that was removed when the church became a Catholic basilica. Via di Roma. www.ravennamosaici.it. ✆ **0544/541-688.** Included in Ravenna inclusive ticket (see p. 378). Mar–Oct daily 9am–7pm; Nov–Feb daily 10am–5pm.

Basilica di San Vitale ★★★ CHURCH The emperor Justinian (who never visited Ravenna and ruled instead from Constantinople) completed this octagonal church—richly ornamented with intensely green, blue, and gold mosaics—in 540 as a symbol of his power. Endowed with a halo to indicate his role as head of church and state, Justinian is portrayed standing next to a clean-shaven Christ, perched atop the world, flanked by saints and angels. Looking on are Justinian's two most important adjuncts, his empress, Theodora, and a bald Maximianus, bishop of Ravenna. Theodora's presence suggests her immense influence and rapacious rise to power. Born into the circus, she became a famous actress and courtesan known for her beauty. As Justinian's wife, she wielded such power that in 532, not long before this church was completed, she ordered that 30,000 insurgents be gathered up, brought to the Hippodrome in Constantinople, and slaughtered.

Via San Vitale 17. www.ravennamosaici.it. ✆ **0544/215-193.** Included in Ravenna inclusive ticket (see p. 378). Mar–Oct daily 9am–7pm; Nov–Feb daily 10am–5pm.

Battistero Neoniano (Neonian Baptistery) ★ CHURCH Ravenna's oldest monument was erected by Bishop Ursus around 400, to accompany a basilica (long since destroyed) on the site of an ancient Roman bath. The eight sides of this octagonal structure represent the 7 days of the week, as set out in Genesis, plus the day of the Resurrection, when Christ gave mankind eternal life. Bishop Neon embellished the structure at the end of the 5th century, adding the intensely colored blue, green, and gold mosaics that spread over the dome, showing John the Baptist baptizing Christ in the River Jordan, surrounded by the 12 Apostles carrying crowns as a sign of celestial glory. Many of the marble panels in the walls were taken from the Roman bathhouse. Note that the baptistery was originally at street level, which has risen more than 3m (10 ft.) over the intervening centuries. Adjacent is the **Museo Arcivescovile,** set in what was the private oratory of the 5th-century bishops of Ravenna. A mosaic in its chapel portrays Christ in a way he is rarely seen elsewhere—as a victorious warrior in battle garb standing on a snake. The museum is a warren of cramped little galleries, but make sure you locate one item in particular: a 6th-century bishops' throne that just may be the finest bit of ivory work in the world.

Piazza del Duomo. www.ravennamosaici.it. ✆ **0544/215-201.** Included in Ravenna inclusive ticket (see p. 378). Mar–Oct daily 9am–7pm; Nov–Feb daily 10am–5pm.

Mausoleo di Galla Placidia ★★ MONUMENT One of the most powerful women of the Byzantine world, Galla Placidia was the daughter

underground **TREASURES**

In 1993, archeologists found a small Roman palace beneath the church of Sant'Eufemia—14 rooms and 3 courtyards carpeted in colorful mosaics, with scenes of dancers, lute players, and frolicking forest animals. The so-called **Domus of the Stone Carpets** (Via Barbiani 16; www.domusdeitappetidipietra.it; ✆ **0544/32512**) evokes a lavish lifestyle at the very end of the Roman empires. The mosaics are on view year-round daily 10am to 6:30pm; visitors are asked to reserve online in advance. Descend into the 5th-century crypt of the **Basilica of San Francesco** (Piazza San Francesco; free; daily 8am–1pm and 4–7pm) for an eerie sight: As groundwater has seeped into the crypt, mosaics on the submerged floor can be seen shimmering in the light.

Pedestrian streets of Ravenna.

and granddaughter of Roman emperors, sister of one ruler of the Western Roman Empire and widow of another. Captured by the Visigoths during the sack of Rome in 410, she married King Athaulf, moved with his barbarian hordes to Barcelona, was traded back to the Romans for grain when Athaulf was murdered, and then married co-emperor Constantius, with whom she had a son, Valentinian III. When Constantius died and Valentinian became emperor at the age of 6, Galla acted as regent, ruling the Western world for 12 years. Though she's most likely buried in Rome, her mausoleum here is spectacular, crowned with a dome decorated with mosaics in vivid hues of peacock blue, moss green, Roman gold, eggplant purple, and burnt orange. Their simple spirituality is striking—doves drink from fountains, as the devout are nourished by God; a purple-robed Christ is surrounded by lambs, as the Heavenly king is surrounded by the faithful; and 570 tiny gold stars, suggesting life eternal, twinkle in the cupola. Soft light filtered by alabaster infuses everything with other-worldly luminosity.

Via Fiandrini Benedetto. www.ravennamosaici.it. ✆ **0544/541-688.** Included in Ravenna inclusive ticket (see p. 378). Daily Mar–Oct 9am–7pm, Nov–Feb 10am–5pm.

Where to Stay in Ravenna

Albergo Cappello ★★ An old palace in the center of town retains enough damask, Murano chandeliers, stone fireplaces, and impressive old

furnishings to make any guest feel like an aristocrat. (One former high-born inhabitant was Francesca da Polenta, whose story Dante told in his *Divine Comedy*—her husband caught her with her lover and strangled them both.) Most of the seven large, high-ceilinged rooms are suites that open off salons on the piano nobile, while a few less grand but similarly character-filled quarters are tucked into a wing in the rear. Breakfast is served in a morning room downstairs amid a charming bestiary of forest creatures; a handsome wood-beamed **wine bar** serves well into the night.
Via IV Novembre 41. www.albergocappello.it. ✆ **0544/212-114.** 7 units. 140€–150€ double. Rates include breakfast. **Amenities:** Wine bar; restaurant; free Wi-Fi.

Casa Masoli ★★★ An 18th-century *palazzo* near the city center exudes a familial and slightly bohemian ambience, like the home of your favorite aunt and uncle, the arty ones. Two splendid suites at the front of the house are especially grand and cavernous—one retains the original brick vaulting, another frescoes and a marble tub—but high ceilings, tall windows, and wood-veneered bathrooms lend all the rooms a dose of grandeur; those in the back face a garden. Scattered antiques, comfy lounge chairs and couches, and framed lithographs are friendly touches, as is the generous breakfast buffet with lots of homemade fare served in a frescoed salon.
Via Girolamo Rossi 22. www.casamasoli.it. ✆ **0544/217-682.** 7 units. 70€–130€ double. Rates include breakfast. **Amenities:** Free Wi-Fi.

Hotel Centrale Byron ★ From 1819 to 1821 Lord Byron shared a nearby palace with his lover, Contessa Teresa Guiccioli, her husband (who was 40 years her senior), and a bestiary of pets that included peacocks and ducks; Ravenna has been milking the story ever since. One of several establishments in town named for the Romantic poet is a lot less evocative than its name suggests, but it is wonderfully located, a stone's throw from most sights, a few steps from Piazza del Popolo, and an easy stroll from the train station. Constant updating has given the rooms a contemporary patina geared more toward comfort than character, with welcome touches such as soundproofing and excellent lighting.
Via IV Novembre 14. www.hotelsravenna.it. ✆ **0544/212-225.** 54 units. 85€–100€ double. Most rates include breakfast. Closed part of Jan. **Amenities:** Bar; room service; free Wi-Fi.

Hotel Diana ★★ Tucked away slightly off the beaten path at the edge of the city center, but an easy stroll from the sights, these large, light, and eclectically homey rooms are enlivened with bright colors and attractive prints (and many have extremely large windowed bathrooms). Downstairs, an English-speaking staff dispenses recommendations with genuine enthusiasm, and a generous buffet breakfast is served on a large, glass-enclosed patio. This is a handy base for motorists, with several easy-to-reach garages nearby.
Via Girolamo Rossi 47. www.hoteldiana.ra.it. ✆ **0544/39164.** 33 units. 80€–90€ double. Rates include breakfast. **Amenities:** Bikes; free Wi-Fi.

M Club ★★★ Keeping in step with the quiet elegance of old Ravenna, these bright quarters at the edge of the historic center are stylish and welcoming, crisscrossed with heavy beams and filled with a tasteful mix of antiques, oil paintings, French and Italian prints, and family memorabilia. Large windows open to Hadrian's Gate across the square out front or a quiet garden in back. While the six distinctively decorated rooms are set up for relaxing in private (the suite has a monastery table long enough to host a banquet), lounges are inviting as well.

Via Baracca. www.m-club.it. ✆ **333/955-6466.** 5 units. 100€–120€ double. Rates include breakfast. Closed 2 weeks in late Jan/early Feb**. Amenities:** Bikes; free Wi-Fi.

Where to Eat in Ravenna

Ravenna's **Mercato Coperto** (near the center of town on Piazza Andrea Costa) houses shops, bars, and restaurants. **Gastronomia Marchesini,** an elegant food store at Via Mazzini 2/6 (www.ristorantemarchesiniravenna.it; ✆ **0544/212309**), is a good place to buy regional hams and cheeses; it operates a reasonably priced self-service restaurant upstairs and a full-service restaurant above that. **Profumo di Piadina,** 24 Via Cairoli (www.profumodipiadina.it; ✆ **333/292-8079**), tops warm-from-the oven *piadina* (flatbread) with prosciutto, creamy *squacquerone* (cheese), and other locally produced ingredients that you can eat on the go or enjoy at one of the few tables.

Ca' de Ven ★★ ROMAGNOLA A 16th-century guesthouse and former spice warehouse with frescoed ceilings and lots of paneling and exposed timbers makes a character-filled stop for lunch or a light dinner. Heavier food is offered, but the emphasis here is on *piadina,* the local flatbread, served with a dozen or so fillings or, even better, by itself warm from the oven with a selection of cured meats and *squacquerone,* a delicate soft cheese. There's also a huge selection of wine by the glass. At lunch and in early evening you'll rub elbows at communal tables with what seems like half the population of Ravenna, so enjoy the atmosphere and ignore the often-brusque service.

Via Corrado Ricci 24. www.cadeven.it. ✆ **0544/30163.** *Piadine* about 4€; entrees 11€–15€. Tues–Sun 11am–2:30pm and 6:30–10pm.

La Bella Venezia ★★ ROMAGNOLA Cream-colored walls and light, starched tablecloths in this small room off the Piazza della Popolo create the scene for elegant dining. Despite the name, the menu is typically and deliciously Romagnolese. The kitchen is much respected for its *cappelletti alla romagnola* (cap-shaped pasta stuffed with ricotta, roasted pork loin, chicken breast, and nutmeg, and served with meat sauce) and other homemade pastas, including simple ravioli with butter and sage, and risotto with fresh seasonal vegetables. An abundance of old-world flair keeps a local clientele coming back.

Via IV Novembre 16. www.bellavenezia.it. ✆ **0544/212-746.** Entrees 10€–17€. Mon–Fri 11am–3pm and 7pm–midnight. Closed part of late Jan.

Osteria del Tempo Perso ★★ SEAFOOD/ROMAGNOLA Ravenna is no longer a port, but the sea is close enough to supply fresh seafood for an innovative menu, accompanied by soft jazz in warm-hued rooms lined with books and wine bottles. It would be a shame not to indulge in at least one seafood course, maybe the *spaghetti con bocconcini di spade,* with savory chunks of swordfish, or a hefty *fritto misto,* though *tortelloni di zucca,* pumpkin-filled pasta, and other land-based favorites are expertly done, too.

Via Gamba 12. www.osteriadeltempoperso.it. ✆ **0544/215-393.** Entrees 12€–22€. Mon–Fri 7:30pm–11pm; Sat–Sun 12:30–2:30pm and 7:30pm–11pm.

Ristorante Alexander ★ ITALIAN/SEAFOOD In this former church that was later converted to a movie house, vintage film posters hang beneath ancient beams in a vast, double-height hall—a blend of sacred and profane that makes a sophisticated setting for refined cooking. Ravenna's proximity to the sea comes to the fore in fresh fish and in nice combinations like fusilli with tuna and pork or calamari couscous; meat dishes lean toward roasted game birds and some unusual local preparations, such as veal cheeks with potato and lemon puree. Service is friendly and attentive, as soft jazz and mellow renditions of movie themes float through the space.

Via Bassa del Pignataro 8. www.ristorantealexander.it. ✆ **0544/212-967.** Entrees 15€–28€. Five-course set menu: fish 53€, meat 50€. Tues–Sun 12:30–2:30pm and 7:30–11:30pm.

PARMA ★

457km (283 miles) NW of Rome, 97km (60 miles) NW of Bologna, 121km (75 miles) SE of Milan

This prosperous little city on the Roman Via Emilia, about an hour north of Bologna, delivers a slice of the good life. Residents are surrounded by art-filled palaces and churches bestowed upon them by the Renaissance Farnese family and later Marie-Louise, wife of Napoleon. They enjoy the music of their own Giuseppe Verdi in a grand opera house, and when it comes to food, elegant Parma has given the world some of the finest hams and cheeses ever. You can easily fill a very satisfying day or two here, enjoying beautiful monuments, listening to music, stepping in and out of tempting food shops, and sitting down to some memorable meals.

Essentials

ARRIVING Parma is served by the Milan-Bologna **rail** line, with hourly trains arriving from Milan (trip time: 1 hr. on frequent fast trains, 1½ hr. on less-expensive slower trains). From Bologna, trains depart for Parma every 30 minutes or so (a little under an hour). There are a few direct trains a day from Florence (2 hr.); most journeys require a change in Bologna. For information and schedules, go to www.trenitalia.com. You might also pass through Parma to connect with a train to La Spezia on the west

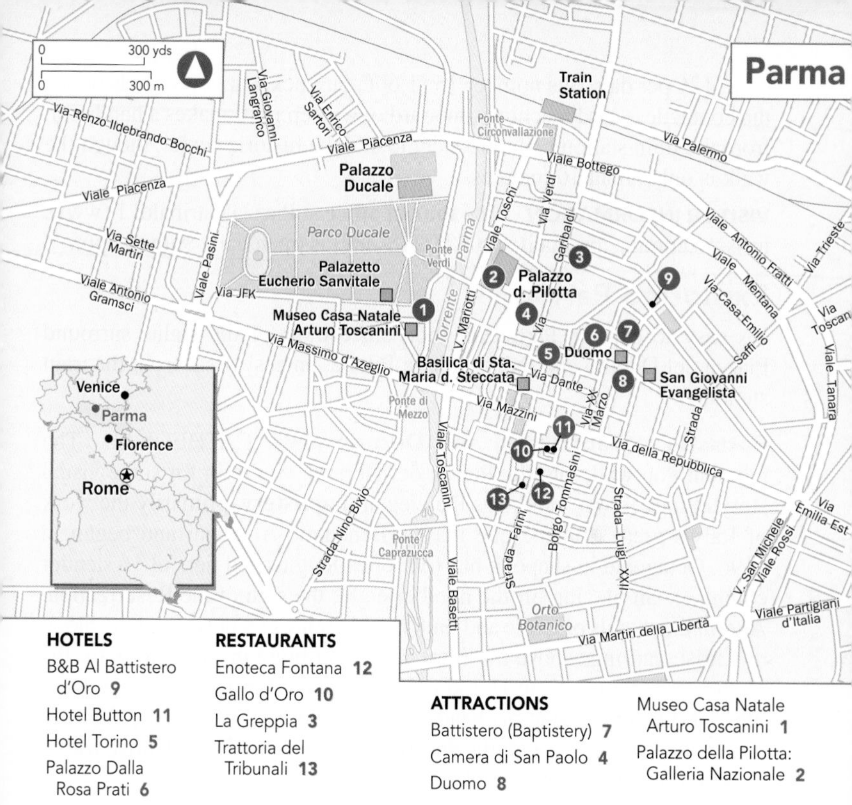

coast, and from there to the Cinque Terre and other places along the Italian Riviera. Whatever your destination, hop off the train long enough to see the beautiful Duomo and Baptistery. Stash your bags in one of the luggage storage lockers (1€ an hour or 5€ a day) just outside the station in Piazzale Carlo Alberto Dalla Chiesa (www.parmawelcome.it; ✆ **366/502-1899;** Mon–Sun 8am–9pm).

If you are coming by **car** from Bologna, drive northwest along A1. Note that **driving in the historic center is restricted**—from October through March it's off-limits to cars entirely on Thursdays, and cars are not allowed within the ring roads on the first Sunday of the month, December excluded. Don't drive into the old city without first contacting your hotel—without a special pass you'll be fined 90€. Outside the restricted area, you can park on the street wherever you see blue lines (not blue-and-white lines; for those, purchase a ticket from curbside machines) or aim for the official parking lots: Goito, Toschi, Duc, Dus, and Via Abbeveratoia (around 1€–1.70€ per hour), with free shuttle service to the city center.

GETTING AROUND Parma is bike-friendly, with rentals available from the large stand outside the train station in Piazzale Carlo Alberto dalla Chiesa (www.infomobility.pr.it; ✆ **0521/281-979**). Rates are 1.50€ an hour, 12€ per day. Bus number 15 (1.60€, buy ticket at newsstands or use the contactless card machines onboard; www.tep.pr.it) makes a handy run from the train station to Teatro Reggio and the historic center, though the walk is only about 10 minutes.

VISITOR INFORMATION The **tourist office** at Piazza Garibaldi 1 (www.turismo.comune.parma.it; ✆ **0521/218-889**) is open daily 9am to 7pm.

Exploring Parma

It's easy to explore Parma on foot, since most of the sights surround Piazza del Duomo and Palazzo della Pilotta, an easy walk from the train station.

Battistero (Baptistery) and Duomo ★★★ CATHEDRAL The moment you walk into the Piazza del Duomo, you're in for some visual storytelling. To one side rises the elegant **baptistery,** primarily the work of Italy's great Romanesque master Benedetto Antelami and begun in 1196. Octagonal in shape, it has four open loggias and tiers of 16 slender columns—all playing off the number eight, the sign of the Resurrection. Alternating bands of white and pink marble represent purity and the blood of Christ; carvings above the entrance are scripture in stone (look for the sequence depicting King Herod pulling his beard in rage, Salome dancing, and St. John losing his head). Inside, colorful 13th-century frescoes depict the zodiac, the months and seasons, and the life of Christ with a wealth of medieval iconography.

Two stone lions guard the entrance to the adjacent **Duomo,** one crushing a serpent (the devil), the other a lamb (symbol of sacrifice) under their paws. Inside are two of Parma's greatest treasures. Correggio, the master of light and color, spent 8 years painting the cupola; after finishing in 1530, he took his payment in a sack full of small change, went home, and died of fever at the age of 40. His "Assumption of the Virgin" is a sea of free-floating angels and billowing clouds; a leggy Christ tumbles out of the celestial light to meet the outstretched arms of his ascending mother. A contemporary compared the effect to a "hash of frogs' legs," and Charles Dickens commented that this was a scene that "no operative surgeon gone mad could imagine in his wildest delirium." Church authorities supposedly approached Titian to redo the dome; he replied that the work was so masterful, they should have filled the structure with gold and presented it to Correggio. The other highlight is in the transept to the right: a somber bas-relief of "The Deposition from the Cross" by Antelami, creator of the baptistery next door. A melancholy Christ stretches his elongated arms over two groups—Mary and pious converts to one side, and the unenlightened on the other, including a group of Roman soldiers playing cards.

Piazza del Duomo 1. www.cattedrale.parma.it. ✆ **0521/235-886.** Cathedral: free. Battistero: 12€ with Museo Diocesano, 10€ students, 8€ under 18. Cathedral: daily 7:30am–noon and 3–7:30pm; Battistero and Museo Diocesano: daily 10am–6pm.

Camera di San Paolo ★★ CONVENT San Paolo was one of many well-endowed convents where wealthy women who did not marry could spend their lives in relative comfort. When, around 1519, the cultured abbess Giovanna di Piacenza wanted to fresco her private dining room, she had the means to hire Correggio, who created vivid mythological scenes, cherubs, astrological references, and an image of Diana, goddess of the hunt. The frescoes may have sparked conversation for the intellectuals who frequently gathered at the abbess's table, though the significance of the images remains a mystery. Church authorities later sealed off the chamber—with no religious subjects and so many bare-bottomed *putti,* it was deemed profane.

Via Melloni 3 (off Strada Garibaldi). ✆ **0521/533-221.** 5€ adults; 3€ ages 18–25; free ages 17 and under. Mon, Thurs, and Fri 9:30am–5:30pm; Sat and Sun 9:30am–6:30pm.

Palazzo della Pilotta: Galleria Nazionale ★★ MUSEUM Like many Italian cities, Parma became a great center of the Renaissance under one ruling family—in this case, the Farneses, whose members included popes, cardinals, and the dukes of Parma. They began their fortresslike Palazzo della Pilotta in the 1580s and remained there until the last heiress, Elisabetta, married King Philip of Spain and decamped for Madrid in 1714. The Hapsburg princess Marie-Louise (1791–1847)—Napoleon's second wife and a great-niece of Marie Antoinette—was awarded the duchy a century later, and she set about gathering art treasures from the city in the palace the Farneses had left empty; she also collected works from villas and churches throughout Italy, confiscated when her husband marched down the peninsula. Badly bomb-damaged in World War II, the restored palace now houses the Galleria Nazionale. It's not surprising that the Vienna-born duchess's collection would include such northern artists as Hans Holbein, Brueghel, and Van Dyck, but Parma artists steal the show. Correggio's "Madonna della Scodella (with a Bowl)" portrays Joseph as an elderly man and Mary as a young woman gazing adoringly at her infant son; his "St. Jerome with the Madonna and Child" also represents age, youth, and love—a gentle ode to tenderness. (Napoleon supposedly wanted to cart these off to the Louvre, but Marie-Louise insisted they remain in Parma.) The alluring "Turkish Slave," by the city's own Parmigiano, portrays a well-kept young woman dressed in gold-threaded finery; everything about her—turban, cheeks, eyes, breasts—is beautifully rounded. "La Scapigliata" (aka the "Female Head") is one of the most celebrated works by Leonardo da Vinci. The palace's other treasure is the **Teatro Farnese,** a wooden theater the Farneses had built, along the lines of Palladio's theater at Vicenza, to impress the Medicis. It's been used only a few times, including during an inaugural event in 1639 when the section in front was flooded for mock naval battles.

Piazzale della Pilotta 15. pilotta.beniculturali.it. ✆ **0521/233-309.** 12€ adults; 5€ ages 18–25; 3€ ages 5–17; free for children under 5; includes Teatro Farnese. Daily 10:30am–6:30pm.

NEAR PARMA

Castello di Torrechiara ★★ CASTLE One of Italy's most beautiful castles is on a hilltop above the lush agricultural valleys outside Parma. Soldier and courtier Count Pier Maria Rossi built the castle as a fortress, installing massive walls, tower, and a drawbridge, and also as a love nest where he could rendezvous with his mistress, Milanese noblewoman Bianca Pellegrini. The two sojourned on view-filled loggias and in heavily frescoed salons, all beautifully intact to provide a glimpse at a late-medieval/early Renaissance luxe lifestyle. A hamlet clustered around the walls has a couple of shops and eateries. Buses run from Parma's station almost hourly, with a stop at Torrechiara (fare 3.40€). From there it's a 10- to 15-minute uphill climb to the main gate.

Beautiful Teatro Reggio, the main venue for Parma's annual Verdi Festival.

Torrechiara, 18km (11 miles) S of Parma on SP665. www.castellidelducato.it. ✆ **0521/355-821.** 5€. Apr–Sept Tues–Sat 9am–7pm, Sun 9:45am–7pm; Oct–Mar Tues–Sat 9am–5pm, Sun 9:30am–5pm.

Where to Stay in Parma

B&B Al Battistero d'Oro ★★★ It's easy to slip into the Parma good life in this elegant 19th-century house just behind the Duomo, where Patrizia Valenti's sprawling and tasteful apartment surrounds a courtyard. The hostess puts up her guests in a delightful ground-floor room with a private entrance and two large bedrooms off a back corridor, welcoming them also into her bright and handsomely furnished living room and polished dining room, where she serves a delicious breakfast. Patrizia is on hand to dispense advice on getting the most out of her native Parma.

Strada Sant'anna 22. www.albattisterodoro.com. ✆ **338/490-4697.** 3 units. 110€–120€ double. Rates include breakfast. **Amenities:** Free Wi-Fi.

Hotel Button ★★ The Cortesa family has been welcoming guests to this 17th-century *palazzo* for more than 40 years, providing lots of advice and dispensing excellent coffee from the small lobby bar. You might be charmed by the extra-large rooms and old-fashioned ambience in the public areas (as we are) or find the place to be a bit stuffy and out of date, but you can't quibble with the excellent location in the heart of old Parma just off Piazza Garibaldi.

Borgo delle Salina 7. hotelbutton.it. © **0521/208039.** 40 units. 90€–105€ double. Rates include breakfast. **Amenities:** Bar; babysitting; free Wi-Fi.

Hotel Torino ★ A couple of handsome lounges off the lobby and a sprightly, patio-like breakfast room do justice to one of Parma's best lodging locations, just down the street from Piazza del Duomo. Guest rooms are soothing with muted tones and neutral furnishings and range in size. Standard doubles are small (and some of the singles feel like ship cabins) but streamlined with lots of handy built-ins for stashing gear. Parking in a small garage beneath the hotel is 15€ a night.

Borgo Angelo Massa. www.hotel-torino.it. © **0521/281046.** 39 units. 120€–150€ double. Rates include breakfast. **Amenities:** Bar; free Wi-Fi.

Palazzo Dalla Rosa Prati ★★★ The Marquis Dalla Rosa Prati and his family have converted one wing of their palace to seven sprawling, handsomely furnished suites, all with kitchenettes; another section is broken into 10 large apartments. In the suites, huge wooden bedsteads, massive armoires, and other polished antiques complement the largely 18th-century surroundings. Apartments have one or two bedrooms, generous space to spread out, and full kitchens.

Strada al Duomo 7. www.palazzodallarosaprati.it. © **0521/386429.** 17 units. 100€–160€ double. Rates include breakfast. **Amenities:** Free Wi-Fi.

Where to Eat in Parma

Via Farini, cutting a swath through the old town south of Piazza Garibaldi, is lined with bars and cafes. The top stop for a quick meal is **Enoteca Fontana,** Via Farini 24 (© **0521/286037**) for morsels of Parmigiano

HITTING THE high NOTES

Besides collecting art in the Palazzo della Pilotta (see p. 387), Duchess Marie-Louise also enriched Parma's cultural life in 1829 by building the **Teatro Reggio,** Via Garibaldi 16, near Piazza della Pace (www.teatroregioparma.it; © **0521/203-911**). Still considered one of the world's finest music theaters, the house hosts an opera season that rivals Milan's. Particularly favored are the operas of **Giuseppe Verdi,** composer of *Il Trovatore* and *Aïda,* who was born outside Parma in 1813 and later lived with his mistress, soprano Giuseppina Strepponi, in nearby Busseto. Their villa, set on lush parklike grounds, is owned by descendants and only occasionally open to the public; check with the tourist office in Parma for details. Each October, Parma celebrates the **Verdi Festival,** with concerts and performances in the Teatro Reggio and other venues.

Parma's other musical genius, **Arturo Toscanini,** the great 20th-century orchestral conductor, was born in Parma in 1867. His birthplace, **Museo Casa Natale Arturo Toscanini,** Via Rodolfo Tanzi 13, now displays his scores, photos, and other personal effects (www.museotoscanini.it; © **0521/031769;** free; Wed–Sun 10am–6pm).

WELCOME TO THE food valley

Parma has been distinguished as a UNESCO Creative Center of Gastronomy, a nod to the Parmigiano cheese, hams and other cured meats, and balsamic vinegar produced in surrounding farms and factories in what is known as the Food Valley. Among cured meats, pride of place belongs to *culatello di Zibello,* the haunch of the pig that is slightly salted, stuffed in a pig bladder, and cured in drying rooms in low-lying plains near the Po and Parma rivers. Paying homage to the region's gastronomic output are 25 so-called **Museums of Taste** (www.winefoodemiliaromagna.com) that include the **Museo del Parmigiano Reggiano** in Soragno, the **Museo del Prosciutto di Parma** in Langhirano, and the **Museo del Balsamico** in Spilamberto. You can visit local producers on tours with **Maestro** (www.maestrotravelexperience.com), from 95€. The **Consorzio del Parmigiano Reggiano** (www.parmigianoreggiano.com; ✆ **0521/292-7000**), at Via Gramsci 26, can help you plan visits to local producers. Among them is **Caseificio San Pier Damiani,** Strada Gazzano 35/A (www.sanpierdamiani.com; ✆ **521/645181**), where in a 2-hour visit (20€) you can see cheese production from curd to ready-to-age wheel. You may also see and taste local products in town at the attractive and aromatic **Salumeria Garibaldi,** Via Garibaldi 42 (www.specialitadiparma.it; ✆ **0521/235606**), and **La Prosciutteria,** Strada Farini 9 (www.silvanoromaniparma.it; ✆ **0521/234-188**).

drizzled with balsamic vinegar from Modena, slices of prosciutto, and *crostini,* pieces of bread topped with everything from pesto to chicken livers (Tues–Sat noon–2:30pm and 8–10:30pm).

Gallo d'Oro ★ PARMIGIANA Parma's formidable food scene becomes decidedly relaxed at this bric-a-brac-filled trattoria just off Piazza Garibaldi. A local crowd appreciates the old traditions: Lambrusco, a slightly sparkling red, is the wine of choice, and *cavallo* (horse) and *coniglio* (rabbit) are served a few different ways. Less adventurous eaters can enjoy *tortelli ripieni* (pasta stuffed with cheese and vegetables), *ravioli alla zucca* (pumpkin), and a long list of other homemade pastas.
Borgo della Salina 3. www.gallodororistorante.it. ✆ **0521/208-846.** Entrees 9€–18€. Daily noon–2:30pm and 7:30–10:45pm.

La Greppia ★★ PARMIGIANA/ITALIAN Looking toward the window at one end of the simple dining room, you'll see into the kitchen and notice that the kitchen crew is mostly female. In their hands you'll be treated to exquisite dishes, some of which you may never have encountered before. Pears poached in red wine with a dense cream sauce is the house antipasto; handmade pastas are often filled with the freshest local vegetables; and the *secondi* menu features duck breast, fillets of beef and sucking pig, and other regional favorites. The homemade *tortas,* filled with marmalade and a miraculous mélange of other ingredients, are irresistible.
Via Garibaldi 39. ✆ **0521/233-686.** Entrees 10€–20€. Daily noon–2:30pm and 7–10:30pm.

Trattoria del Tribunali ★★★ PARMIGIANA/ITALIAN In two floors of dining rooms, stretching beyond counters hung with hams, menu choices range from delicious pastas, such as *tortelli* (pasta pockets) stuffed with pumpkin or ricotta, to steaks with Barolo and veal stuffed with Parmigiano. You may even find such distinctly local fare as horsemeat hash. A veteran staff never seems too flustered to be friendly. It's a good idea to reserve, especially on weekend nights.

Vicolo Politi 5. www.trattoriadeltribunale.it. ✆ **0521/285-527.** Entrees 8€–18€. Daily noon–3pm and 7–11pm.

NEAR PARMA

Al Vedel ★★★ EMILIA-ROMAGNAN A simple village tavern established in 1780 has expanded into several elegant dining rooms, and below them are the cellars of Podere Cadassa, where some of the region's most prized *culatello di Zibello* (from the haunch of the pig) is aged. That delicacy is the starter of choice, along with other cured meats and local cheeses. Chef-proprietor Enrico Bergonzi proudly shows off the culatello operation to his guests, and he and his staff produce many seasonal variations of local favorites, such as wintertime tortellini filled with *mostarda.* The menu also features local fowl, truffles, and produce.

Via Vodele 68, Colorno (about 20km/12 miles N of Parma). www.poderecadassa.it. ✆ **0521/816169.** Entrees 9€–22€. Wed–Sun noon–2:30pm and 7:30–10:30pm.

Hostaria d'Ivan ★★★ EMILIA-ROMAGNAN A trip out to this welcoming inn, in a farm hamlet near the River Po, is an immersion course in all that's good about the region's cooking. *Culatello,* the choicest cut of prosciutto, and Parmigiano, aged for several years, are produced on nearby farms; the duck, roasted with herbs, comes from marshes along the river banks. On request, you can dine in the "salametherapy room," where cured meats hang from the ceiling, but a meal in the simply furnished dining room, overlooking a small garden, is just as memorable. Four cozy bedrooms are tucked under the eaves at the top of the house (100€ double).

Via Villa 24, Fontanelle di Roccabianca (25km/15 miles NW of Parma via SP10). www.hostariadaivan.it. ✆ **0521/870-113.** Entrees 10€–18€. Daily noon–11:45pm.

VENICE

By Stephen Keeling

9

No other place in the world looks quite like Venice. This vast, floating city of grand palazzi, elegant bridges, gondolas, and canals is a magnificent spectacle, truly magical when approached by sea for the first time, when its golden domes and soaring bell towers seem to rise straight from the sea. While it can sometimes appear that Venice is little more than an open-air museum where tourists always outnumber locals—by a large margin—it is still surprisingly easy to lose the crowds. Indeed, the best way to enjoy Venice is simply to get lost in its labyrinth of narrow, enchanting streets, stumbling upon a quiet campo (square), market stall, or cafe far off the beaten track, where even the humblest medieval church might contain masterful work by Tiepolo, Titian, or Tintoretto.

The origins of Venice—known as "La Serenissima" for centuries—are as muddy as parts of the lagoon it now occupies, but most histories begin with the arrival of refugees from Attila the Hun's invasion of Italy in the mid–5th century (though the official foundation date is A.D. 421). The mudflats were gradually built over and linked together, channels and streams eventually becoming canals. By the 11th century, Venice had emerged as a major independent trading city, and by the 13th century its seaborne empire (which included Crete, Corfu, and Cyprus) was held together by a huge navy and commercial fleet. Despite being embroiled with wars against rival Italian city Genoa and the Turks, the next few centuries were golden years for Venice, when booming trade with the Far East funded much of its grand architecture and art. Although it remained an outwardly rich city, by the 1700s the good times were over, and in 1797 Napoleon dissolved the Venetian Republic without a shot (handing it over to the Austrians shortly afterwards). You'll gain a sense of some of this history touring **Piazza San Marco** and **St. Mark's Basilica,** or by visiting the **Accademia,** one of Italy's great art galleries. But only when you wander the back *calli* (streets) will you encounter the true, living, breathing side of Venice, still redolent of those glory days.

FACING PAGE: **Rio Marin Canal in Venice.**

DON'T LEAVE VENICE WITHOUT . . .

Getting Lost. So sublime is the city's lineup of architectural eye candy that Venice simply invites aimless wandering. If you stick to the areas congested with tourists (which are surprisingly small), you'll never discover the real Venice.

Cruising the Waters of the Grand Canal. Hop aboard a gondola or *vaporetto* no. 1 (see p. 397) for a complete lap of Venice's primary marine highway, adorned with views of the city's most jewel-like *palazzi.*

Exploring St. Mark's Basilica. This Byzantine gem may be one of the city's busiest tourist attractions, but that doesn't make it any less wondrous (see p. 406).

Snacking on *Cicchetti* (Appetizers) at a *Bàcaro.* Eating tapas-style with an *ombra* (glass of local Veneto wine) in age-old *bàcari,* the small bars where locals mingle, is an essential Venice experience.

Experiencing Art, Art, and More Art. The Accademia Gallery (p. 417) has the greatest collection of classic Venetian art on earth, while the nearby Peggy Guggenheim Collection (see p. 419) displays some of the best of Western Modernism. All around the city are churches and *scuole* (schools) stuffed with compelling masterpieces.

Safe Travels in Venice

In 2020 the Covid-19 pandemic shuttered businesses in Venice and devastated the tourist industry. The city fared better than other areas of Italy, however, and by the end of the year Venice had largely reopened for business. At the time of writing, it is no longer mandatory to wear a face mask on public transport, but its use indoors and in all cases of crowded outdoor events is highly recommended. Masks are still likely to be required in hospitals and health clinics, so bring some just in case. Check with your hotel or the Venezia Unica website for the latest.

ESSENTIALS

Arriving

BY PLANE From North America, the cheapest flights to Venice tend to route through Rome or Milan via **ITA,** though **Swissair** (via Zurich), **Lufthansa** (via Frankfurt), **KLM** (via Amsterdam), and **Air France** (via Paris) usually offer cheap fares in low season (code-sharing with U.S. carriers). If traveling in the peak spring and summer seasons, however, it's worth considering far more convenient seasonal nonstop flights, which are often priced competitively (assuming you buy far enough in advance): **Delta Airlines** (www.delta.com) flying from Atlanta (late June–Aug only) New York-JFK (Apr–Sept only), **United Airlines** (www.united.com) from Newark (June–late Sept), and **American Airlines**

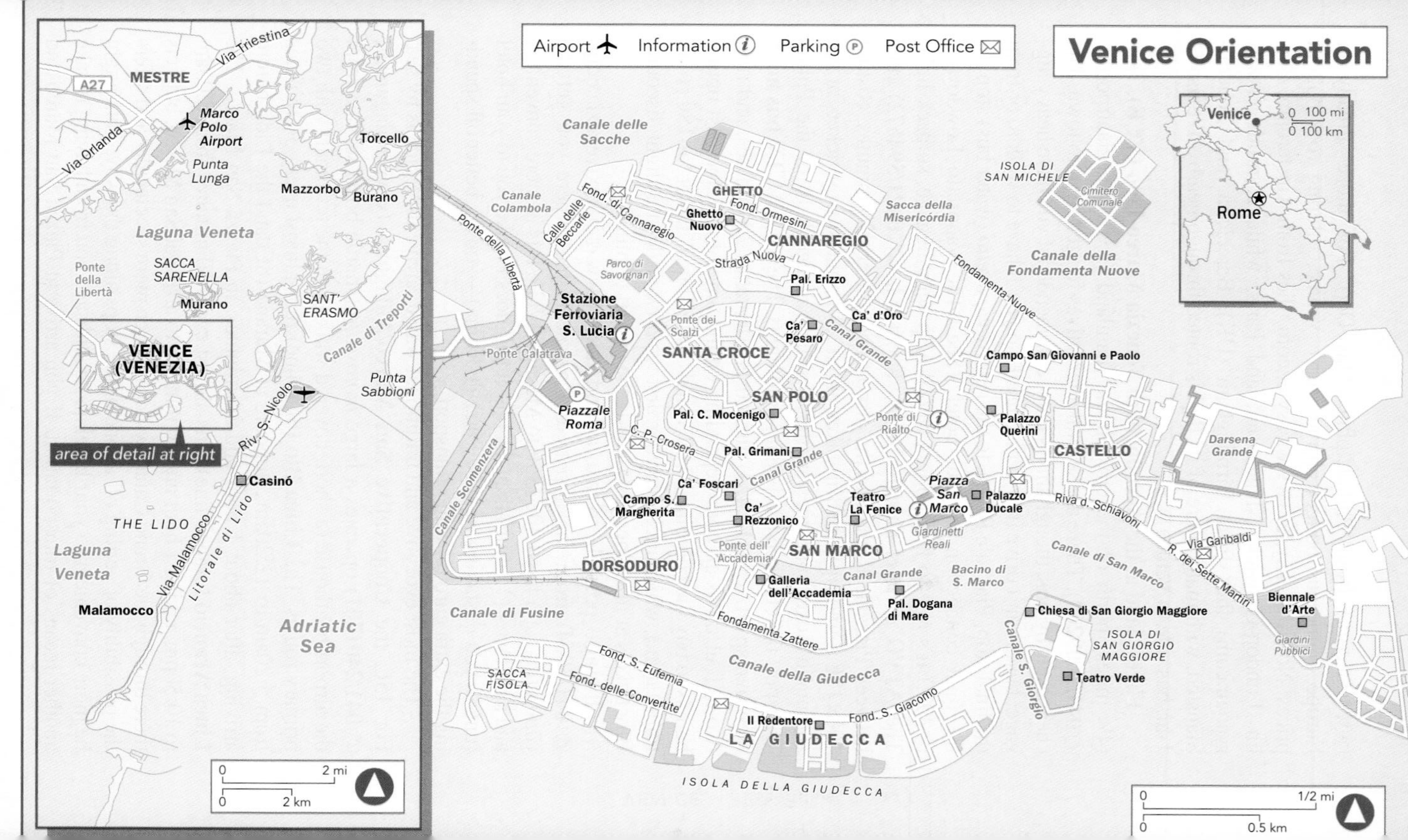

Venice Orientation
Airport
Information
Parking
Post Office
Venice
Rome
0 100 mi
0 100 km
A27
MESTRE
Via Triestina
Via Orlanda
Marco Polo Airport
Punta Lunga
Torcello
Mazzorbo
Burano
Laguna Veneta
Ponte della Libertà
SACCA SARENELLA
Murano
SANT' ERASMO
Canale di Treporti
VENICE (VENEZIA)
Punta Sabbioni
Riv. S. Nicolo
area of detail at right
Casinó
THE LIDO
Laguna Veneta
Via Malamocco
Litorale di Lido
Malamocco
Adriatic Sea
0 2 mi
0 2 km
Canale delle Sacche
Canale Colambola
Calle delle Beccarie
Fond. di Cannaregio
Ponte della Libertà
GHETTO
Ghetto Nuovo
Fond. Ormesini
CANNAREGIO
Sacca della Misericórdia
ISOLA DI SAN MICHELE
Cimitero Comunale
Canale della Fondamenta Nuove
Parco di Savorgnan
Strada Nuova
Pal. Erizzo
Fondamenta Nuove
Stazione Ferroviaria S. Lucia
Ponte dei Scalzi
Ca' Pesaro
Ca' d'Oro
Canal Grande
Ponte Calatrava
SANTA CROCE
Campo San Giovanni e Paolo
SAN POLO
Piazzale Roma
Pal. C. Mocenigo
Ponte di Rialto
Palazzo Querini
C. P. Crosera
Pal. Grimani
Canal Grande
CASTELLO
Darsena Grande
Canale Scomenzera
Ca' Foscari
Campo S. Margherita
Ca' Rezzonico
Teatro La Fenice
Piazza San Marco
Palazzo Ducale
Riva d. Schiavoni
Giardinetti Reali
Ponte dell' Accademia
SAN MARCO
Canale di San Marco
Via Garibaldi
R. dei Sette Martiri
DORSODURO
Galleria dell'Accademia
Canal Grande
Bacino di S. Marco
Pal. Dogana di Mare
Canale di Fusine
Fondamenta Zattere
Chiesa di San Giorgio Maggiore
Biennale d'Arte
Giardini Pubblici
ISOLA DI SAN GIORGIO MAGGIORE
Canale S. Giorgio
Teatro Verde
SACCA FISOLA
Fond. S. Eufemia
Fond. delle Convertite
Canale della Giudecca
Il Redentore
Fond. S. Giacomo
LA GIUDECCA
ISOLA DELLA GIUDECCA
0 1/2 mi
0 0.5 km

(www.aa.com) from Philadelphia (May–Oct). For those already in Europe, numerous budget airlines serve Venice, offering rock-bottom prices. No-frills **easyJet** (www.easyjet.com) flies from Amsterdam, Berlin, London-Gatwick, Manchester, and Paris, while **Ryanair** (www.ryanair.com) flies from Birmingham (UK), Barcelona, and London-Stansted, with many more of its flights routed through nearby **Treviso** (a 1-hr. bus ride to Venice).

Flights land at the **Aeroporto di Venezia Marco Polo (VCE)**, 7km (4¼ miles) north of the city on the mainland (www.veneziaairport.it; ✆ **041/2609260**). There are several alternatives for getting into town. The cheapest is by **bus,** though this is not recommended if you have heavy luggage; buses can't drive into Venice itself, so you'll have to walk to or from the final stop, Piazzale Roma, to the nearby ***vaporetto*** (water bus) stop for the final connection to your hotel. (See "The Vaporetto Lowdown," p. 397.) It's rare to find porters who'll help with luggage, so pack light. The **ATVO airport shuttle bus** (www.atvo.it; ✆ **0421/594672**) runs between Piazzale Roma and the airport about every 20 minutes, costing 10€ (18€ roundtrip); the trip takes about 20 minutes. Buy tickets at the automatic ticket machines in the arrivals baggage hall, or the Public Transport ticket office (daily 8am–midnight). The local **ACTV bus no. 5** (actv.avmspa.it; ✆ **041/2424**) also costs 10€, takes 20 minutes, and runs two to four times an hour depending on the time of day; the best option here is to buy the combined ACTV and "Rete Unica" ticket for 18€ (valid for 90 min.), which includes your first *vaporetto* ride at a slight discount. Buy tickets at machines just outside the airport terminal.

It's also possible to take a **land taxi** (www.radiotaxivenezia.com; ✆ **041/5964**) from the airport to Piazzale Roma (where you get the *vaporetto*) for a fixed 40€ (35€ to Mestre). While this is more convenient and a bit faster (15 min.) than the bus, it still doesn't take you to your hotel (unless you're staying right by Piazzale Roma)—you are better off spending the extra euro on water transport.

The most evocative and traditional way to arrive in Venice is by sea. For 15€, the **Cooperative San Marco/Alilaguna** (www.alilaguna.it; ✆ **041/2401701**) operates a large *motoscafo* (shuttle boat) service from the airport boathouse (a short, covered walk from the terminal) with two primary routes. The **Linea Blu** (blue line) runs almost every 30 minutes from 5:20am to 12:20am, stopping at Murano (8€) and the Lido before arriving, after about 1 hour and 30 minutes, in Piazza San Marco. The **Linea Arancio** (orange line) runs almost every 30 minutes from 8:05am to 10:50pm, taking 1 hour and 20 minutes to arrive at San Marco, but gets there through the Grand Canal, which is much more spectacular and offers the possibility of getting off at one of the stops along the way. This might be more convenient to your hotel and could save you from having to take another means of transportation. If you arrive at Piazza San Marco and your hotel isn't in the area, you'll have to make a connection at the *vaporetto* launches. (If you're booking a hotel in advance, be sure to get specific advice on how to get there.)

A good alternative is **Venice Shuttle** (www.venicelink.com; daily 4am–11pm; minimum 2 people for reservations), a shared water taxi (carrying 6–8 people) that will whisk you from the airport directly to many hotels and most major locations in the city for 32€ (add 6€ after 8pm). You must reserve online in advance.

A **private water taxi** (20–30 min. to/from the airport) is the most convenient option but costly—there is a 122€ fee (discounted rates of 50€–70€ at www.venicelink.com) for up to four passengers with one bag each (plus 10€ more for each extra person up to a maximum of 10, 5€ for each extra suitcase, and another 10€ for 10pm–7am arrivals). It's worth considering if you're pressed for time, have an early flight (taxis run 24 hr.), are carrying a lot of luggage (a Venice no-no), or can split the cost

THE VAPORETTO lowdown

Whether you're arriving by train, bus, or car, your first challenge upon arriving in Venice will be to take a *vaporetto* (water bus) on to your final destination. The *vaporetto* is the seagoing streetcar of Venice, going to all parts of the city. Here's how to do it right.

Finding the right boat is a little easier if you're arriving by bus or car, because you'll be in Piazzale Roma, the route **no. 1** *vaporetto* terminus, and all these boats will be going the right direction. (See "By Vaporetto," p. 403, for information on tickets). Exiting the train station, however, you'll find the Grand Canal immediately in front of you, with the docks for a number of *vaporetti* lines to your left and right. Head to the booths to your left, near the bridge, to buy tickets, then head for the docks farther to your right.

The most useful routes are the two lines plying the Grand Canal: the **no. 2 express** (from bay "B"), which stops only at the San Marcuola, Rialto Bridge, San Tomà, San Samuele, and Accademia before hitting San Marco (30 min. total); and the slower **no. 1** (from bay "E"), which makes 13 stops before arriving at San Marco (a 36-min. trip). Both leave every 10 minutes or so, but before 9am and after 8pm, the no. 2 sometimes stops short at Rialto, meaning you'll have to disembark and hop on the next no. 1 or 2 that comes along to continue to San Marco.

Word to the wise: The *vaporetti* go in two directions from the train station. Those heading left go down the Grand Canal toward San Marco—which is the (relatively) fast and scenic way. The no. 2 route heading right also eventually gets you to San Marco (at the San Zaccaria stop), but takes more than twice as long because it goes the long way around Dorsoduro (this line serves mainly commuters). As for the no. 1 line going to the right from the train station, it will go only one more stop before it hits its terminus at Piazzale Roma. **Make sure the *vaporetto* you get on is heading to the left.** Departing from **Piazzale Roma, make sure no. 2 is going to the right** (no.1 will only go right).

with a friend or two. The taxi may be able to drop you off at the front (or side) door of your hotel, or as close as it can maneuver given your hotel's location (check with the hotel before arriving). Your taxi captain should be able to tell you before boarding just how close you can get. Try **Corsorzio Motoscafi Venezia** (www.motoscafivenezia.it; ✆ **041/5222303**) or **Venezia Taxi** (www.veneziataxi.it; ✆ **041/723112**).

BY TRAIN Trains from Rome (4 hr.), Milan (2½ hr.), Florence (2¼ hr.), and all over Europe arrive at the **Stazione Venezia Santa Lucia.** To get there, all must pass through a station marked Venezia-Mestre. Don't be confused: Mestre is a charmless industrial city that's the last major stop on the mainland (some trains also stop at the next station, Venezia Porto Marghera, before continuing to Venice proper). Occasionally trains end in Mestre, in which case you have to catch one of the frequent 10-minute shuttles connecting with Venice; it's inconvenient, so when you book your ticket, confirm that the final destination is Venezia Santa Lucia.

BY BUS Although rail travel is more convenient and commonplace, Venice is serviced by long-distance buses from all over mainland Italy and some international cities. The final destination is Piazzale Roma, where you'll need to pick up *vaporetto* no. 1 or no. 2 (see box p. 397) to connect

Vaporetti (water buses) ply Venice's main canals.

tourist tax: **NEW START FOR VENICE?**

Pre-Covid, Venice was attracting an astounding 30 million visitors a year or around 80,000 visitors per day—dwarfing the population of just 50,000. The 2020 lockdown resulted in less pollution and crystal-clear canals for the first time in decades. Though most Venetians recognize the importance of tourism to the local economy, few want to return to the pre-lockdown bad old days of over-tourism. Organizations such as the **Venetian Heritage Foundation** (www.venetianheritage.org) and **Save Venice** (www.savevenice.org) have called for restrictions on Airbnb apartments in Venice and support for cheaper long-term rentals to encourage locals to move back from the mainland. In a move widely applauded, **cruise ships were banned** from the inner lagoon in August 2021 (with ships diverted to the ports of Monfalcone or Marghera, or eventually to a new permanent passenger terminal at the Lido). They'd also like for tourists to stay longer—what's been dubbed "slow tourism," as opposed to *"mordi e fuggi"* or "hit-and-run" tourism, with day-trippers who spend generally low amounts of money. As a result, the city plans to charge **entry fees for day-trippers.** The plan has been delayed many times, but should be in place sometime in 2023, when even diverted cruise-ship passengers will pay a flat 5€ fee (eventually rising to 7€). For everyone else, the rate will vary according to season and demand, ranging from 3€ to10€ per day. Day-trippers will also have to make an online booking just to *enter* Venice (entry will be monitored via electronic turnstiles). Check the city's information website for the latest.

you with stops in the heart of Venice and along the Grand Canal. Eurolines (www.eurolines.eu) buses drop off on the adjacent island of **Tronchetto,** which is a much longer walk from the action. Buses stop at the Tronchetto **People Mover** station where a light railway takes you to Piazzale Roma in just 3 minutes (1.50€ one-way), though you will most likely need onward transportation from there. *Vaporetto* line 2 does stop at Tronchetto: Facing the water, boats depart left to the train station and Grand Canal, right to San Marco.

BY CAR The only wheels you'll see in Venice are those attached to luggage. **No cars are allowed,** or more to the point, no cars could drive through the narrow streets and over the footbridges—even the police, fire department, and ambulance services use boats. You can drive across the Ponte della Libertà from Mestre (on the mainland) to Venice, but you can go no farther than Piazzale Roma at the Venice end, where many garages eagerly await your euro (and in high season are often full). The **Autorimessa Comunale garage** (avm.avmspa.it; ✆ **041/2727301**) charges 35€ for a 24-hour period (30€ online), while **Garage San Marco** (www.garagesanmarco.it; ✆ **041/5232213**) costs 45€ for 24 hours. From Piazzale Roma, you can catch *vaporetti* lines 1 and 2 (see box p. 397), which go down the Grand Canal to the train station and, eventually, Piazza San

Marco. Cheaper (and in some cases free) parking is available on the adjacent island of **Tronchetto** (see "By Bus," above), first right as you cross the Ponte della Libertà.

Visitor Information

TOURIST OFFICES The most central **Venezia Unica information office** lies in the arcade at the western end of Piazza San Marco (Calle Larga de l'Ascensione 71F), near Museo Correr (daily 7am–7pm; ✆ **041/2424**). There are also offices at Piazzale Roma (kiosk near Ponte della Costituzione; daily 7am–8pm), the train station (opposite platforms 2 and 3; daily 7am–9pm), and in the arrivals hall at Marco Polo Airport (daily 8:30am–7pm). These offices do not offer free maps—they cost 3€. See also **www.veneziaunica.it**.

The monthly magazine ***Un Ospite di Venezia*** (www.unospitedivenezia.it) is a useful source of information (published in Italian and English); most hotels have free copies. Also very useful is ***VeNews*** (www.venezianews.it), published monthly (3€) and sold at newsstands all over the city (also in English and Italian).

City Layout

Even armed with the best map or a hefty smartphone data plan, expect to get a little bit lost in Venice, at least some of the time (GPS directions are notoriously unreliable here). View it as an opportunity to stumble upon Venice's most intriguing corners. Keep in mind as you wander hopelessly among the *calli* (streets) and *campi* (squares) that Venice wasn't built to make sense to those on foot, but rather to those plying its canals.

Venice lies 4km (2½ miles) from terra firma, connected to the mainland at Mestre by the Ponte della Libertà, which leads to Piazzale Roma. Snaking through the city like an inverted *S* is the **Grand Canal,** the wide main artery. Central Venice refers to the built-up block of islands in the lagoon's center, the six main *sestieri* (districts) that make up the bulk of the tourist city. Greater Venice includes all the inhabited islands of the lagoon—central Venice plus Murano, Burano, Torcello, and the Lido.

A Note on Addresses

Within each *sestiere* is a most original system of numbering the *palazzi,* using one continuous string of 6,000 or so numbers. The format for addresses in this chapter is, where possible, the number with the actual street or *campo* on which you'll find that address. But official mailing addresses (and what you'll see written down in most places) are simply the *sestiere* name followed by the building number, which isn't especially helpful—for example, San Marco 1471 may not necessarily be found close to San Marco 1473. Many buildings aren't numbered at all.

Venice Neighborhoods in Brief

SAN MARCO The most visited, and most central, *sestiere* is anchored by the magnificent Piazza San Marco and St. Mark's Basilica to the south and the Rialto Bridge to the north. This has been the commercial, religious, and political heart of the city for more than a millennium. Unfortunately, ever-rising rents have persuaded most locals to look for housing in other neighborhoods, but the area is laced with first-class hotels—see p. 434 for suggestions on where to stay in the heart of Venice without going broke.

CASTELLO Just east of Piazza San Marco, Castello's tony waterside esplanade Riva degli Schiavoni follows the Bacino di San Marco (St. Mark's Basin), skirting Venice's most congested area to the north and east. Riva degli Schiavoni is often thronged, but if you head farther east in the direction of the Arsenale or inland away from the *bacino,* the crowds thin out. Here you'll find such major sights as Campo SS. Giovanni e Paolo and the Scuola di San Giorgio.

DORSODURO Residential Dorsoduro, the largest of the *sestieri,* lies across the Accademia Bridge from San Marco. Home to the Accademia and Peggy Guggenheim museums, it was known as an artists' haven until rising rents forced many residents to relocate. Come here for good neighborhood restaurants, a charming gondola boatyard, lively Campo Santa Margherita, and the sunny canalside quay of le Zattere.

SAN POLO This mixed bag of residential corners and tourist sights stretches northwest of the Rialto Bridge to the church of Santa Maria dei Frari. At the foot of the bridge, you'll find the bustling Rialto Market. Some of the city's best restaurants flourish here alongside some of its worst tourist traps. Spacious Campo San Polo is the main piazza.

SANTA CROCE North and northwest of the San Polo district and across the Grand Canal from the train station, Santa Croce stretches all the way to Piazzale Roma. Less lively than San Polo but just as authentic, it feels light-years away from San Marco; its little-visited eastern section is a great place for curious visitors to explore. Quiet, lovely Campo San Giacomo dell'Orio is its heart.

CANNAREGIO On the same side of the Grand Canal as San Marco and Castello, Cannaregio stretches north and east from the train station to include the old Jewish Ghetto. One-quarter of Venice's ever-shrinking population of 50,000 lives here. Many one-star hotels are clustered about the train station—not a dangerous neighborhood but not known for its charm, either. Strada Nova is Cannaregio's main thoroughfare, leading to the Rialto bridge.

LA GIUDECCA Across the Giudecca Canal from Piazza San Marco and Dorsoduro, tranquil La Giudecca is a residential island where you'll find a youth hostel and a few hotels (including the deluxe Cipriani).

LIDO DI VENEZIA This slim, 11km-long (6¾-mile) island, the only spot in the Venetian lagoon where cars circulate, is the city's beach, fronting the open sea. It's also home of the annual Venice Film Festival.

Getting Around Venice

Aside from traveling by boat, the only way to explore Venice is by walking—and by getting lost repeatedly. You'll navigate many twisting streets whose names change constantly and don't appear on any map, and streets that may very well simply end in a blind alley or spill abruptly into a canal. You'll also cross dozens of footbridges. Treat getting bewilderingly lost in Venice as part of the fun, and budget more time than you'd think necessary to get wherever you're going.

STREET MAPS & SIGNAGE The map sold by the tourist office (3€) and free maps provided by most hotels don't always show—much less name or index—all the *calli* (streets) and pathways of Venice. Pick up a more detailed map (ask for a *pianta della città* at news kiosks—especially those

Getting away from the tourist center is one of the best ways to get to know Venice—but you'll definitely need a good map.

at the train station and around San Marco or most bookstores). The best is the highly detailed **Touring Club Italiano map,** available in a variety of forms (folding from 8.50€) and scales. If using your phone, note that GPS directions are often unreliable in Venice, though Google Maps has definitely improved in recent years (and has added its "streetview" option to the city).

Still, Venice's confusing layout confounds even the best navigators. You're better off just stopping every couple of blocks and asking a local to point you in the right direction (always know the name of the *campo*/square or major sight closest to the address you're looking for, and ask for that).

As you wander, look for the yellow signs (well, *usually* yellow) whose destinations and arrows direct you toward five major landmarks: **Ferrovia** (the train station), **Piazzale Roma** (the parking garage), **Rialto** (one of four bridges over the Grand Canal), **San Marco** (the city's main square), and the **Accademia** (the southernmost Grand Canal bridge).

BY VAPORETTO The various *sestieri* are linked by a comprehensive *vaporetto* (water bus/ferry) system of about a dozen lines operated by the **Azienda del Consorzio Trasporti Veneziano (ACTV;** actv.avmspa.it; **✆ 041/5287886**). Transit maps are available at the tourist office and most ACTV ticket offices. It's easier to get around the center on foot; the *vaporetti* mostly serve the Grand Canal, outskirts, and outer islands. The crisscross network of small canals is the province of delivery vessels, gondolas, and private boats.

A ticket for 75 minutes of travel (after validation) on a *vaporetto* is a steep 9.50€, while a 24-hour travel card is 25€. Most lines run every 10 to 15 minutes from 7am to midnight, and then hourly until morning. Most *vaporetto* docks have timetables posted. You can buy tickets at Venezia Unica offices, authorized retailers that display the ACTV/Venezia Unica sticker in town, and usually at the dock itself, though not all of these have machines or kiosks that sell tickets. If you haven't bought a travel card (see "Venice Discounts," p. 414) or tickets beforehand, you'll have to settle up with the conductors onboard. Look for them immediately on boarding—they won't come looking for you—or you risk a stiff on-the-spot fine of at least 61€. No excuses accepted. Also available are travel cards for 48 hours (35€), 72 hours (45€), and 1 week (65€). If you're planning to stay in Venice for a week or more and intend to use the *vaporetto* service a lot, it makes sense to pick up a **Venezia Unica city pass** (see "Venice Discounts," p. 414), with which you can buy *vaporetto* tickets for just 1.50€. You **must validate** (stamp) all tickets in the yellow machines at the docks before getting aboard.

BY TRAGHETTO Just four bridges span the Grand Canal, and to fill in the gaps, *traghetti* skiffs (oversize gondolas rowed by two standing *gondolieri*) cross the Grand Canal at several intermediate points. Stations

CRUISING THE canals

A leisurely cruise along the **Grand Canal** ★★★ (p. 410) from Piazza San Marco to the train station (Ferrovia)—or the reverse—is one of Venice's must-dos. It's the world's most unusual Main Street, a watery boulevard whose *palazzi* have been converted into condos. Lower water-lapped floors are now deserted, but the higher floors are still coveted by the city's titled families, who have inhabited these glorious residences for centuries; others have become the dream homes of privileged expats, drawn as irresistibly as the romantic Venetians-by-adoption who preceded them—Richard Wagner, Henry James, Robert Browning, and Lord Byron among them.

As much a symbol of Venice as the winged lion, the **gondola** ★★★ is one of Europe's great traditions, incredibly expensive but truly as romantic as it looks (detractors who write it off as too touristy have most likely never tried it). The official, fixed rate is 80€ for a 30-minute gondola tour for up to five passengers. The rate bumps up to 100€ from 7pm to 8am (for 35 min.), and it's 40€ for every additional 20 minutes (50€ at night). That's not a typo: 150€ for a not-quite-1-hour evening cruise. ***Tip:*** Although the price is fixed by the city, a good negotiator at the right time of day (when business is slow) can sometimes grab a small discount for a shorter ride. And at these ridiculously inflated prices, there is no need to tip the gondolier. You might also find **discounts online.**

Aim for late afternoon before sundown, when the light does its magic on the canal reflections (and bring a bottle of Prosecco and glasses). If the price is too high, ask visitors at your hotel or others lingering about at the gondola stations if they'd like to share it. Though the price is "fixed," before setting off you should establish with the gondolier the cost, time, and route (back canals are preferable to the trafficked and often choppy Grand Canal). They're regulated by the **Ente Gondola** (www.gondolavenezia.it; ✆ **041/5285075**); call if you have questions or complaints.

And what of the **serenading gondolier** immortalized in film? Frankly, you're better off without, but if warbling is de rigueur for you, here's the scoop: An ensemble of accordion player and tenor is so expensive that it's shared among several gondolas traveling together. A number of tour operators (and online brokers such as www.viator.com) book evening serenades for around 50€ per person.

Venice has 12 gondola stations, including Piazzale Roma, the train station, the Rialto Bridge, and Piazza San Marco. There are also a number of smaller stations, with *gondolieri* in striped shirts standing alongside their sleek 11m (36-ft.) black wonders looking for passengers. They all speak enough English to communicate the necessary details. Remember, if you just want a quick taste of being in a gondola, you can take a cheap *traghetto* across the Grand Canal.

were traditionally located at the end of streets named Calle del Traghetto, and indicated by a yellow sign with the black gondola symbol. These days only a handful operate regularly, primarily at San Tomà, Santa Maria del Giglio, and Santa Sofia (check with a local if in doubt). The fare is 2€, which you hand to the gondolier when boarding. Most Venetians cross standing up. Try the Santa Sofia crossing (Mon–Sat 7:30am–7pm, Sun 9am–7pm; Oct–Mar last crossing 6:30pm), which connects the Ca' d'Oro and the Pescheria fish market, on the Grand Canal just north of the Rialto Bridge—the gondoliers expertly dodge water traffic at this point of the canal, where it's the busiest and most heart-stopping.

BY WATER TAXI *Taxi acquei* (water taxis) charge high prices and aren't for visitors watching their euro. Trips in town are likely to cost at least 50€ to 90€, depending on distance, time of day, and whether you've booked in advance or just hired on the spot. Each trip includes allowance for up to four to five pieces of luggage—beyond that there's a surcharge of 3€ to 5€ per piece (rates differ slightly according to company and how you reserve your trip). Plus there's a 20€ supplement for service from 10pm to 7am, and a 5€ charge for taxis on-call. Those rates cover up to four people; if any more squeeze in, it's another 5€ to 10€ per extra passenger (maximum 10 people). Taking a water taxi from the train station to Piazza San Marco or any area hotels costs around 90€ (the Lido is around 100€), while fixed fees to the airport range from 120€ to 130€ (for up to four people). Taxis to Burano or Torcello will be at least 140€. Note that only taxi boats with a yellow strip are the official operators sanctioned by the city. You can book trips with **Consorzio Moscafi Venezia** online at **www.motoscafi venezia.it** or call ✆ **041/5222303.** Six water-taxi stations serve key points in the city: the Ferrovia, Piazzale Roma, the Rialto Bridge, Piazza San Marco, the Lido, and Marco Polo Airport.

[FastFACTS] VENICE

Doctors & Hospitals The **Ospedale Civile Santi Giovanni e Paolo** (✆ **041/5294111**), on Campo Santi Giovanni e Paolo in Castello, has English-speaking staff and provides 24/7 emergency service (*vaporetto* Ospedale).

Emergencies For general emergency, call ✆ **112.** To call the local police, dial ✆ **113;** for an ambulance, ✆ **118;** for a fire ✆ **115.**

Internet Access Venice offers citywide Wi-Fi through the **Wi-Fi Venezia** (www.veneziaunica.it) network of 200 hotspots. Buy packages online (5€/24 hr., 15€/3 days, or 20€/7 days); access codes are then sent via e-mail.

Mail The most convenient post offices are: **Venezia Centro** at Calle de la Acque, San Marco (✆ **041/2404149;** Mon–Fri 8:25am–7:10pm and Sat 8:25am–12:35pm); **Venezia 4** at Calle de l'Ascension 1241, off the west side of Piazza San Marco (✆ **041/2446711;** Tues–Fri 8:25am–1:35pm and Sat 8:25am–12:35pm); and **Venezia 3** at Campo San Polo 2012 (✆ **041/5200315;** same hours as Venezia 4).

Police Dial ✆ **113.**

Safety Generally speaking, Venice is one of Italy's safest cities. Be aware of pickpocketing on crowded *vaporetti,* particularly on tourist routes where passengers are more intent on the passing scenery than on watching their bags. Venice's often deserted back streets are virtually crime-free, though occasional tales of theft have circulated.

EXPLORING VENICE

Venice is notorious for changing and extending the opening hours of its museums and, to a lesser degree, its churches (often due to special events). Before you begin your exploration of Venice's sights, check online or ask at the tourist office for the season's list of museum and church hours.

San Marco

Basilica di San Marco (St. Mark's) ★★★ CATHEDRAL One of the grandest, and certainly the most exotic of all cathedrals in Europe, **Basilica di San Marco** is a treasure heap of Venetian art and all sorts of booty garnered from the eastern Mediterranean. Legend has it that **St. Mark,** on his way to Rome in the A.D. 1st century, was told by an angel his body would rest near the lagoon that would one day become Venice. Hundreds of years later, the city fathers were looking to replace their original patron St. Theodore with a saint of high stature, someone more in keeping with their lofty aspirations. In 828 the prophecy was fulfilled when Venetian merchants stole the remains of St. Mark from Alexandria in Egypt (supposedly the body was packed in pickled pork to avoid the attention of the Muslim guards). Today the high altar's green marble

The exotic exterior of Basilica di San Marco.

canopy on alabaster columns is believed to cover the remains of St. Mark and continues to be the focus of the basilica, at least for the faithful.

Modeled on Constantinople's Church of the Twelve Apostles, the original shrine of St. Mark was consecrated in 832, but in 976 the church burned down. The present incarnation was completed in 1094, then extended and embellished over the years; it served as the doge's personal church. Today, San Marco looks more Orthodox cathedral than Roman Catholic church, with a cavernous interior gilded with Byzantine mosaics added over 7 centuries, covering every inch of ceiling and pavement.

For a closer look at the most remarkable ceiling mosaics and a better view of the Oriental carpet–like patterns of the pavement mosaics, it's worth it to pay the admission to go upstairs to the **Museo di San Marco** (enter in the atrium at the principal entrance); this was originally the women's gallery, or *matroneum,* and includes access to the outdoor **Loggia dei Cavalli.** Here you can admire a panoramic view of the piazza below and replicas of the celebrated ***Triumphal Quadriga,*** four gilded bronze horses dating from the 2nd or 3rd century A.D.; the Roman originals were moved inside in the 1980s for preservation. (The word *quadriga* actually refers to a car or chariot pulled by four horses, though in this case there are only the horses.) The horses were transported to Venice from Constantinople in 1204, along with lots of other loot from the Fourth Crusade.

Know Before You Go

Always check the Basilica website for the latest opening times and regulations. Normally, www.venetoinside.com offers "Skip the Line" entry April through October for an additional 3€ fee; check to see if this perk is available again. At all times the guards at St. Mark's entrance are serious about forbidding entry to anyone in **inappropriate attire**—shorts, sleeveless shirts, cropped tops, and skirts above the knee. Note also that you cannot enter the basilica with luggage; photos and filming inside are forbidden.

The basilica's greatest treasure is the altarpiece known as the **Pala d'Oro** (Golden Altarpiece), a Gothic masterpiece encrusted with over 2,000 precious gems and 83 enameled panels. It was created in 10th-century Constantinople and embellished by Venetian and Byzantine artisans between the 12th and 14th centuries. Second to the Pala d'Oro in importance is the 10th-century **"Madonna di Nicopeia,"** a bejeweled icon also purloined from Constantinople and exhibited in its own chapel. Worth a visit as well is the **Tesoro** (Treasury), a collection of crusaders' plunder from Constantinople and other relics amassed over the years. Much of the loot has been incorporated into the interior and exterior of the basilica in the form of marble, columns, capitals, and statuary.

Guided tours (1 hr.) normally run Monday to Saturday (at least one daily, at 10:45am; guides speak English) and are well worth considering if you'd like to get a better understanding of the Basilica's treasures. Book

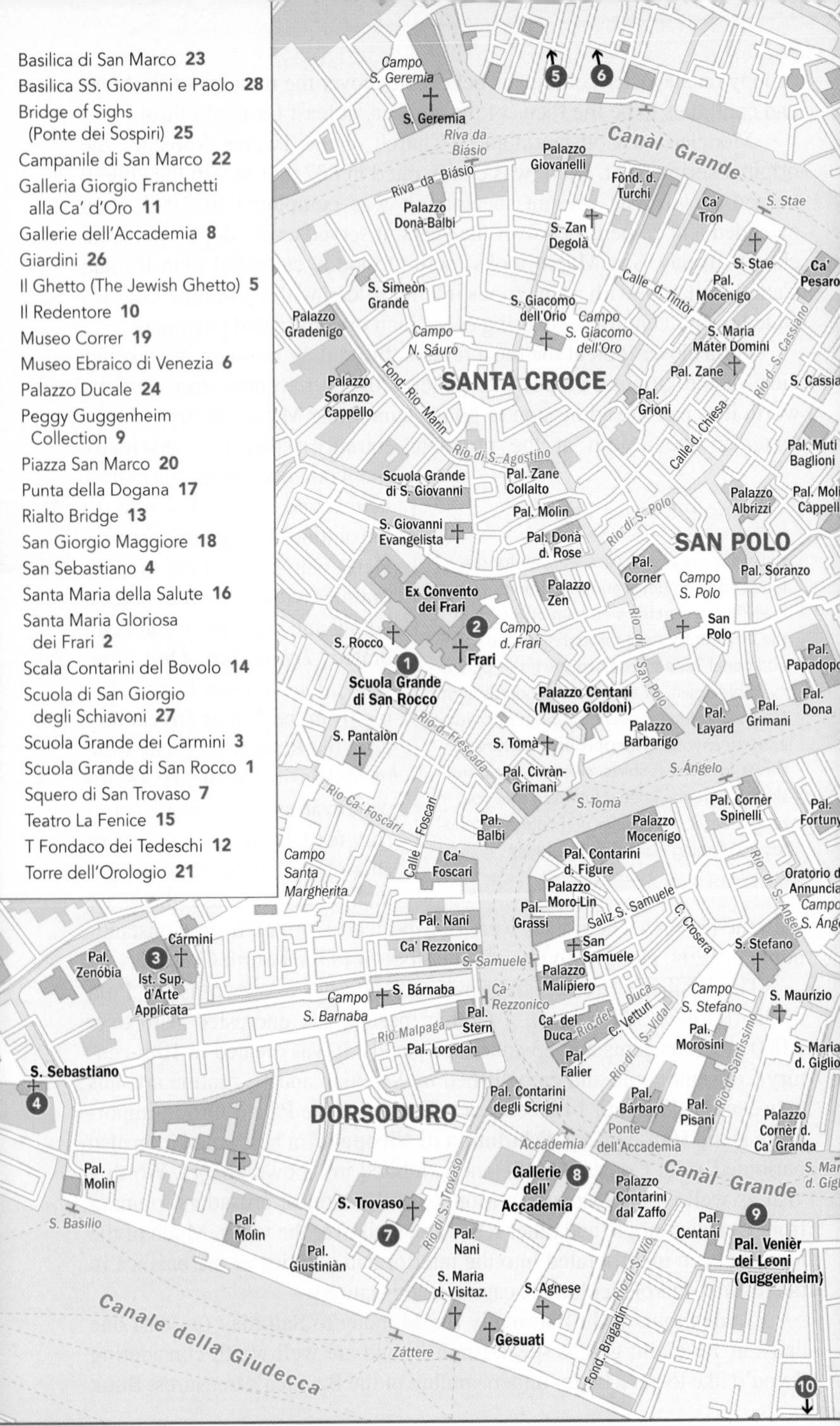
Basilica di San Marco 23
Basilica SS. Giovanni e Paolo 28
Bridge of Sighs (Ponte dei Sospiri) 25
Campanile di San Marco 22
Galleria Giorgio Franchetti alla Ca' d'Oro 11
Gallerie dell'Accademia 8
Giardini 26
Il Ghetto (The Jewish Ghetto) 5
Il Redentore 10
Museo Correr 19
Museo Ebraico di Venezia 6
Palazzo Ducale 24
Peggy Guggenheim Collection 9
Piazza San Marco 20
Punta della Dogana 17
Rialto Bridge 13
San Giorgio Maggiore 18
San Sebastiano 4
Santa Maria della Salute 16
Santa Maria Gloriosa dei Frari 2
Scala Contarini del Bovolo 14
Scuola di San Giorgio degli Schiavoni 27
Scuola Grande dei Carmini 3
Scuola Grande di San Rocco 1
Squero di San Trovaso 7
Teatro La Fenice 15
T Fondaco dei Tedeschi 12
Torre dell'Orologio 21
Campo S. Geremia
S. Geremia
Riva da Biásio
Canàl Grande
Palazzo Giovanelli
Fònd. d. Turchi
Ca' Tron
S. Stae
Palazzo Donà-Balbi
S. Zan Degolà
Calle d. Tintòr
Ca' Pesaro
Pal. Mocenigo
S. Simeòn Grande
S. Giacomo dell'Orio
Campo S. Giacomo dell'Oro
Palazzo Gradenigo
Campo N. Sáuro
S. Maria Máter Domini
Rio d. S. Cassiano
Pal. Zane
S. Cassia
Palazzo Soranzo-Cappello
Fond. Rio Marin
SANTA CROCE
Pal. Grioni
Calle d. Chiesa
Rio di S. Agostino
Pal. Muti Baglioni
Scuola Grande di S. Giovanni
Pal. Zane Collalto
Palazzo Albrizzi
Pal. Moli Cappell
Pal. Molin
Rio di S. Polo
S. Giovanni Evangelista
Pal. Donà d. Rose
SAN POLO
Pal. Corner
Campo S. Polo
Pal. Soranzo
Ex Convento dei Frari
Palazzo Zen
Campo d. Frari
San Polo
S. Rocco
Frari
Rio di San Polo
Pal. Papadopo
Scuola Grande di San Rocco
Palazzo Centani (Museo Goldoni)
Pal. Layard
Pal. Grimani
Pal. Dona
Palazzo Barbarigo
Rio d. Frescada
S. Pantalòn
S. Tomà
Pal. Civràn-Grimani
S. Ángelo
Rio Ca' Foscari
Calle Foscari
S. Tomà
Pal. Cornèr Spinelli
Pal. Fortuny
Pal. Balbi
Palazzo Mocenigo
Campo Santa Margherita
Ca' Foscari
Pal. Contarini d. Figure
Rio di S. Ángelo
Oratorio d Annuncia
Campo S. Áng
Palazzo Moro-Lin
Pal. Grassi
Saliz S. Samuele
C. Crosera
Pal. Nani
Cármini
Ca' Rezzonico
S. Stefano
Pal. Zenóbia
Ist. Sup. d'Arte Applicata
S. Samuele
San Samuele
Palazzo Malipiero
Campo S. Stefano
S. Maurízio
Campo S. Barnaba
S. Bárnaba
Ca' Rezzonico
Pal. Stern
Ca' del Duca
Rio del Duca
C. Vetturi
S. Vidal
Rio Malpaga
Pal. Loredan
Pal. Morosini
Rio d. Santissimo
S. Maria d. Giglio
S. Sebastiano
Pal. Falier
Rio di
Pal. Contarini degli Scrigni
Pal. Bárbaro
Pal. Pisani
Palazzo Cornèr d. Ca' Granda
DORSODURO
Ponte dell'Accademia
Accademia
Pal. Molìn
Gallerie dell' Accademia
Palazzo Contarini dal Zaffo
S. Mar d. Gigl
S. Trovaso
Rio di S. Trovaso
Pal. Centani
Pal. Venièr dei Leoni (Guggenheim)
S. Basílio
Pal. Molìn
Pal. Nani
Pal. Giustiniàn
Rio di S. Vio
S. Maria d. Visitaz.
S. Agnese
Canale della Giudecca
Gesuati
Fond. Bragadin
Zàttere

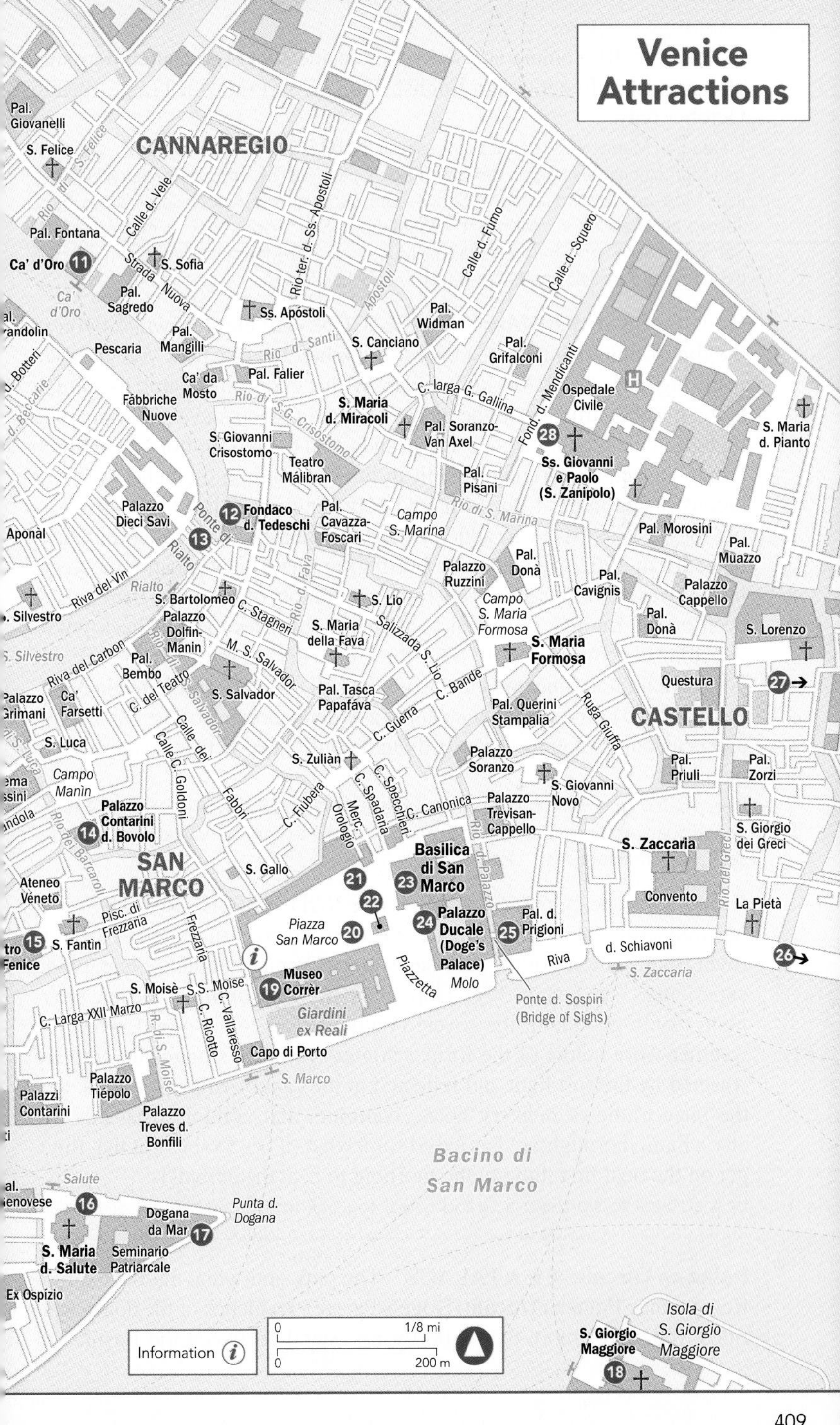
Venice Attractions
CANNAREGIO
CASTELLO
SAN MARCO
Pal. Giovanelli
S. Felice
Pal. Fontana
Ca' d'Oro 11
S. Sofia
Strada Nuova
Pal. Sagredo
Pescaria
Pal. Mangilli
Ss. Apóstoli
Rio ter. d. Ss. Apostoli
Calle d. Fumo
Calle d. Squero
Pal. Widman
S. Canciano
Pal. Grifalconi
Fond. d. Mendicanti
Ospedale Civile
Ca' da Mosto
Pal. Falier
Fábbriche Nuove
C. larga G. Gallina
S. Maria d. Miracoli
Pal. Soranzo-Van Axel
28
Ss. Giovanni e Paolo (S. Zanipolo)
S. Maria d. Pianto
S. Giovanni Crisostomo
Teatro Málibran
Pal. Pisani
Rio di S. Marina
Palazzo Dieci Savi
12 Fondaco d. Tedeschi
Pal. Cavazza-Foscari
Campo S. Marina
Pal. Morosini
Pal. Muazzo
Aponàl
13
Ponte di Rialto
Riva del Vin
Rialto
Palazzo Ruzzini
Pal. Donà
Pal. Cavignis
Palazzo Cappello
S. Bartolomeo
C. Stagneri
S. Lio
Campo S. Maria Formosa
S. Silvestro
Palazzo Dolfin-Manin
S. Maria della Fava
Salizzada S. Lio
S. Maria Formosa
Pal. Donà
S. Lorenzo
Riva del Carbon
Pal. Bembo
M. S. Salvador
Questura
27
Palazzo Grimani
Ca' Farsetti
C. del Teatro
S. Salvador
Pal. Tasca Papafava
C. Bande
Pal. Querini Stampalia
Ruga Giuffa
S. Luca
Calle dei Fabbri
Calle C. Goldoni
C. Guerra
Campo Manìn
S. Zuliàn
Palazzo Soranzo
S. Giovanni Novo
Pal. Priuli
Pal. Zorzi
Palazzo Contarini d. Bovolo
14
C. Fiubera
C. Spadaria
C. Specchieri
Merc. Orologio
C. Canonica
Palazzo Trevisan-Cappello
S. Giorgio dei Greci
S. Zaccaria
Rio d. Palazzo
Rio dei Barcaroli
Basilica di San Marco
23
21
Ateneo Véneto
S. Gallo
Convento
La Pietà
22
Pisc. di Frezzaria
Piazza San Marco
20
24 Palazzo Ducale (Doge's Palace)
25 Pal. d. Prigioni
Rio del Greci
15
S. Fantìn
Frezzaria
Riva d. Schiavoni
26
Piazzetta
Molo
S. Zaccaria
Museo Corrèr 19
S. Moisè
S.S. Moise
C. Vallaresso
C. Ricotto
Ponte d. Sospiri (Bridge of Sighs)
C. Larga XXII Marzo
Giardini ex Reali
R. di S. Moisè
Capo di Porto
S. Marco
Palazzo Tiépolo
Palazzi Contarini
Palazzo Treves d. Bonfili
Bacino di San Marco
Salute
16
Dogana da Mar 17
Punta d. Dogana
S. Maria d. Salute
Seminario Patriarcale
Ex Ospízio
Isola di S. Giorgio Maggiore
S. Giorgio Maggiore
18
Information
0 1/8 mi
0 200 m

tours (from 40€) online at www.venetoinside.com. The church normally also organizes free tours, in English Monday to Friday at 11am, April to October only.

Piazza San Marco. www.basilicasanmarco.it. ✆ **041/2708311.** Basilica 3€; Museo di San Marco (includes Loggia dei Cavalli) 7€; Pala d'Oro 5€; Tesoro (Treasury) 5€. Basilica: Mon–Sat 9:30am–5:15pm, Sun 2–5pm (Nov to mid-Apr closes 4:30pm Sun). Tesoro and Pala d'Oro: Mon–Sat 9:45am–5pm, Sun 2–5pm (Nov to mid-Apr Mon–Sat 9:45am–4:45pm, Sun 2–4:30pm). Museo di San Marco: daily 9:30am–5:15pm (Nov to mid-Apr 9:45am–4:45pm). *Vaporetto:* San Marco.

Campanile di San Marco ★★★ ICON An elevator whisks you to the top of this 97m (318-ft.) brown brick bell tower where you get awe-inspiring views of St. Mark's cupolas. With a gilded angel atop its spire, it is the highest structure in the city, offering a pigeon's-eye panorama that includes the lagoon, neighboring islands, and the red rooftops and church domes of Venice. Originally built in the 9th century, the bell tower was reconstructed in the 12th, 14th, and 16th centuries, when the pretty marble loggia at its base was added by Jacopo Sansovino. It collapsed unexpectedly in 1902, miraculously hurting no one except a cat. Nine years later it was rebuilt exactly as before, using most of the same materials—even one of the five historical bells that it still uses today. Check www.venetoinside.com to see if "Skip the Line" tickets are available. ***Tip:*** If you have limited time, the view from the bell tower of **San Giorgio Maggiore** (p. 425) is much better (you get a wider panorama of the whole city) and is a couple of euro cheaper, though you'll need to take a *vaporetto* to get there.

Piazza San Marco. www.basilicasanmarco.it. ✆ **041/2708311.** 10€. Daily mid-Apr to Sept 9:30am–9:15pm; Oct–Mar 9:30am–5pm; Apr 1 to mid-Apr 9:30am–5:30pm (closes Jan for maintenance). *Vaporetto:* San Marco.

Canal Grande (Grand Canal) ★★★ NATURAL ATTRACTION A leisurely cruise along the "Canalazzo" from Piazza San Marco to the Ferrovia (train station), or the reverse, is one of Venice's (and life's) must-do experiences (see box, p. 397). Hop on the **no. 1 *vaporetto*** in the late afternoon (try to get one of the coveted outdoor seats in the prow), when the weather-worn colors of the former homes of Venice's merchant elite are warmed by the soft light and reflected in the canal's rippling waters, and the busy traffic of delivery boats, *vaporetti,* and gondolas that fills the city's main thoroughfare has eased somewhat (if it's too busy at that time, get on the boat first thing in the morning to beat the crowds).

Best stations to start/end a Grand Canal tour: Ferrovia (train station) or Piazzale Roma on northwest side of canal; Piazza San Marco in southeast. Tickets 9.50€.

Palazzo Ducale ★★★ PALACE The pink-and-white marble Gothic-Renaissance **Palazzo Ducale** (Doge's Palace), residence of the doges who ruled Venice for more than 1,000 years, stands between the Basilica di

San Marco and the sea. A symbol of prosperity and power, the original was destroyed by a succession of fires, with the current building started in 1340, extended in the 1420s, and redesigned again after a fire in 1483. If you want to understand something of this magnificent place, the history of the 1,000-year-old maritime republic, and the intrigue of the government that ruled it, take the **Secret Itineraries tour** ★★★ (see box p. 412). Failing that, at least download the free iPhone/Android app (see the website) or shell out for the audioguide tour (available at entrance for 5€) to help make sense of it all. Unless you can tag along with an English-speaking tour group, you may otherwise miss out on the importance of much of what you're seeing.

The 15th-century **Porta della Carta** (Paper Gate) opens onto a splendid inner courtyard with a double row of Renaissance arches (today visitors enter through a doorway on the lagoon side of the palace). The self-guided route through the palace begins in the main courtyard, where the **Museo dell'Opera** contains assorted bits of masonry preserved from the palazzo's exterior. Beyond here, the first major room you'll come to is the spacious **Sala delle Quattro Porte** (Hall of the Four Doors), with a worn ceiling by Tintoretto. The **Sala dell'Anticollegio,** where foreign ambassadors waited to be received by the doge and his council, is covered in four works by Tintoretto, including "Mercury & the Three Graces" and **"Bacchus and Ariadne"** ★★, the latter deemed one of his best by some critics. The Tintorettos are outshone, however, by Veronese's **"Rape of Europa"** ★★, one of the palazzo's finest paintings. The highlight of the adjacent **Sala del Collegio** (the Council Chamber itself) is the spectacular cycle of **ceiling paintings** ★★, a Veronese masterpiece completed between 1575 and 1578. Next door lies the most impressive of the interior rooms, the richly adorned **Sala del Senato** (Senate Chamber), with Tintoretto's ceiling painting "The Triumph of Venice." After passing again through the Sala delle Quattro Porte, you'll enter the Veronese-decorated **Stanza del Consiglio dei Dieci** (Room of the Council of Ten), where justice was dispensed and decapitations ordered by the Republic's dreaded security police. Formed in the 14th century to deal with emergency situations, the Ten became more powerful than the Senate. In the **Sala della Bussola** (Compass Chamber), notice the **Bocca dei Leoni** (Lion's Mouth), a slit in the wall into which secret denunciations and accusations of enemies of the state were placed for quick action by the much-feared Council.

The main sight on the next level down—indeed, the main sight in the entire palace—is the **Sala del Maggior Consiglio** (Great Council Hall). This enormous space is animated by Tintoretto's huge **"Paradiso"** ★ at the far end of the hall above the doge's seat. Measuring 7×23m (23×75 ft.), it is said to be the world's largest oil painting; together with Veronese's gorgeous **"Il Trionfo di Venezia"** ★★ ("The Triumph of Venice") in the

secrets **OF THE PALAZZO DUCALE**

The **Itinerari Segreti** ★★★ (Secret Itineraries) guided tours of the Palazzo Ducale are a must-see for any visit to Venice of more than 1 day. The tours offer an unparaleled look into the world of Venetian politics over the centuries and are the only way to access the otherwise restricted quarters and hidden passageways of this enormous palace, such as the doges' private chambers and the torture chambers where prisoners were interrogated. The tour must be reserved in advance online (muve.vivaticket.it), by phone (✆ **041/4273-0892**) or in person at the ticket desk. Tours often sell out at least a few days ahead, especially from spring through fall. Tours in English are daily at 10am, 11:30am and 1pm, and cost 32€ adults, 20€ ages 6 to 14, seniors, and students 15 to 25. There are also tours in Italian at 11am and 12:30pm, and French at 10:30am and noon. The tour lasts about 75 minutes.

oval panel on the ceiling, it affirms the power emanating from the council sessions held here. Tintoretto also did the portraits of the 76 doges encircling the top of this chamber; note that the picture of the Doge Marin Falier, who was convicted of treason and beheaded in 1355, has been blacked out—Venice has never forgiven him. Tours culminate at the enclosed **Ponte dei Sospiri** (Bridge of Sighs), built in 1600, which connects the Ducal Palace with the grim **Palazzo delle Prigioni** (Prison). The bridge took its current name in the 19th century—Lord Byron popularized it in his epic poem *Childe Harold's Pilgrimage,* romantically imagining the prisoners' final breath of resignation upon viewing the outside world one last time. Some cells still have the original graffiti of past prisoners, many of them locked up interminably for petty crimes.

San Marco, Piazza San Marco. www.palazzoducale.visitmuve.it. ✆ **041/2715911.** 30€ (reduced to 25€ if purchased 30 days in advance online), 15€ students and seniors (or 13€ in advance). Included in **Museum Pass** (see p. 414). For **Secret Itineraries** guided tour in English, see box above. Daily 9am–6pm (last entrance 5pm). *Vaporetto:* San Marco.

Rialto Bridge ★★ ICON This graceful arch over the Grand Canal, linking the San Marco and San Polo districts, normally teems with tourists and overpriced boutiques. Until the 1800s, it was the only bridge across the Grand Canal, originally built as a pontoon bridge at the canal's narrowest point. The 1444 incarnation was the first to include shops, interrupted by a drawbridge in the center. In 1592, the current graceful stone span was finished to the designs of Antonio da Ponte, who beat out Sansovino, Palladio, and Michelangelo with plans that called for a single, vast, 28m-wide (92-ft.) arch in the center to allow trading ships to pass.

Ponte del Rialto. *Vaporetto:* Rialto.

Scala Contarini del Bovolo ★★ VIEW Part of a palazzo built in the late 15th century, this multi-arch spiral staircase was artfully restored in

The Rialto Bridge at sunset.

2016, featuring a belvedere with fabulous views of Venice. Halfway up, the **Sala del Tintoretto** (Tintoretto Room) contains the rare portrait of Lazzaro Zen, an African who converted to Christianity in Venice in 1770, as well as a preparatory painting by Tintoretto of his monumental "Paradise" (the final version is in the Palazzo Ducale). You can buy **timed entry tickets** in advance at www.ticketlandia.com.

Corte Contarini del Bovolo 4299. www.gioiellinascostidivenezia.it. ✆ **041/309-6605.** 8€. Daily 10am–6pm (Nov–Feb 9:30am–5:30pm). *Vaporetto:* Rialto.

Teatro La Fenice ★★★ OPERA HOUSE One of Italy's most famous opera houses (it ranks third after La Scala in Milan and San Carlo in Naples), La Fenice was originally completed in 1792 but has been rebuilt twice after devastating fires in 1837 and in 2004. Self-guided tours take in the opulent main theater, ornate side rooms, the gilded "royal box," and a small exhibit dedicated to soprano Maria Callas. For tickets to performances, see p. 453.

Campo San Fantin 1965, San Marco. www.teatrolafenice.it (buy tour tickets on site or in advance at festfenice.com). ✆ **041/2424.** 12€. Daily 9:30am–6pm. *Vaporetto:* Giglio.

VENICE discounts

Venice offers a somewhat bewildering range of passes and discount cards. For short stays, we recommend buying an **ACTV travel card** (p. 403) and combining that with one of the first two passes listed below. The more complex Venezia Unica card scheme is recommended if you intend to stay up to 7 days and do a lot of sightseeing. The **Venezia Unica website** (www.veneziaunica.it) is a one-stop shop for all the passes listed below.

The **Museum Pass** (MUVE) grants admission to all city-run museums over a 6-month period, and also lets you skip ticketing lines, a useful perk in high season. The pass covers the museums of St. Mark's Square (Palazzo Ducale, Museo Correr, Museo Archeologico Nazionale, the Biblioteca Nazionale Marciana), as well as the Museo di Palazzo Mocenigo (Costume Museum), Ca' Rezzonico, Ca' Pesaro, the Museo del Vetro (Glass Museum) on Murano, and the Museo del Merletto (Lace Museum) on Burano. The Museum Pass is available online (for an extra 1€), or at any participating museum. It costs 40€ adults and 22€ students under 26, kids ages 6–14, and seniors over 65. It's a good deal, as the Doge's Palace alone will set you back 30€; visit two more of the larger museums (for example Palazzo Mocenigo, 10€, and Ca' Pesaro, 10€) and you've made a decent savings.

The **Chorus Pass** (www.chorusvenezia.org) grants admission to almost every major church in Venice, 18 in all, for 12€ (8€ for students under 30), for up to 1 year. For 24€, the **Chorus Pass Family** gives you the same perks for two adults and their children up to 18 years old. Most churches charge 3€ admission, which means you'll need to visit more than four to make this pass worthwhile.

The **Venezia Unica card** (www.veneziaunica.it) combines the above passes, transport, discounts, and even Internet access on one card via a "made-to-order" online system, where you choose the services you want. Of these, the 7-day passes (if available) are the best value. You can also buy various transportation packages from Venezia Unica (1, 2, 3 and 7-day ACTV passes (25€–65€), for example, which cover all *vaporetto* and bus travel, or just Wi-Fi access (from 5€ for 24 hr.).

For visitors between ages 6 and 29, the **Rolling Venice** card (also available at www.veneziaunica.it) costs just 6€. Valid through the end of the year in which you buy it, it entitles the bearer to significant (20%–30%) discounts at participating restaurants (cardholder's meal only) and discounted ACTV travel cards (27€ for 3 days), along with discounts in museums, stores, hotels, and bars across the city (it comes with a thick booklet listing everywhere you're entitled to get discounts).

T Fondaco dei Tedeschi ★★ PALAZZO/STORE This 16th-century palazzo was converted into a posh department store in 2016, centered on an elegant courtyard and the **Rooftop Terrace,** with quite possibly Venice's greatest view—the Rialto, Grand Canal, and all the city's bell towers laid out before you. You need to make reservations for the terrace in advance (up to 21 days), on the store website.

Calle de Fontego dei Tedeschi, Ponte di Rialto, San Marco. www.dfs.com/en/venice. ✆ **041/3142000.** Daily 10am–7:30pm (roof deck free; daily 10:15am–7pm; visits limited to 15 min.). *Vaporetto:* Rialto.

Torre dell'Orologio ★ MONUMENT As you enter the magnificent **Piazza San Marco,** this Renaissance clock tower is one of the first things you see, standing on the north side, the centerpiece of the stately white **Procuratie Vecchie** (the ancient administration buildings for the Republic). With its distinctive blue face ringed by astrological symbols, the tower was built between 1496 and 1506; the clock mechanism still keeps perfect time. On the top, two bronze figures, known as "Moors" because of the dark color of the bronze, pivot to strike the hour. Visits inside are by guided tour only (included in admission), recommended only for those interested in the clock's history.

Piazza San Marco. www.torreorologio.visitmuve.it. ✆ **848/082000** or 041-42730892. 14€; 11€ ages 6–14 and students 15–25. Ticket also good for Museo Correr, Museo Archeologico Nazionale, and Biblioteca Nazionale Marciana (but not Palazzo Ducale). Tours in English at: 11am (Mon, Fri, Sun); noon (Tues, Wed, Thurs); 2pm (Mon–Wed, Fri, Sat); 4pm (Fri, Sat); must be reserved in advance online. Tours start at Museo Correr ticket office. *Vaporetto:* San Marco.

The colorful Renaissance Torre dell'Orologio on Piazza San Marco still keeps perfect time.

Castello

While the highlight of this neighborhood is the huge **Santi Giovanni e Paolo** (see below), within a few minutes' walk from here are two more magnificent Renaissance churches: **Santa Maria Formosa** (3€; Mon–Sat 10:30am–1:30pm and 2:30–5pm), on Campo Santa Maria Formosa, and **San Zaccaria** (free; Mon–Sat 10am–noon and 4–6pm, Sun 4–6pm), at Campo San Zaccaria, which contains Giovanni Bellini's exceptional **San Zaccaria Altarpiece** ★★. Pay 3€ to enter San Zaccaria's side chapels for Tintoretto's "Birth of Saint John the Baptist" and the creepy flooded crypt, which houses the bodies of eight doges. Several attractions lie on the far eastern side of Castello. The sprawling **Museo Storico Navale di Venezia** (Riva San Biasio 2148; marina.difesa.it) is worthwhile for folks with a deep interest in maritime history, but can be skipped by most others. Nearby is the **Ponte del Paradiso** and the famous twin-towered entrance to the **Arsenale** (only open during the Biennale).

COME HELL OR high water

During the tidal *acqua alta* (high water) floods, Venice's lagoon rises until it engulfs the city, leaving up to 1.5 to 1.8m (5–6 ft.) of water in the lowest-lying streets. Piazza San Marco, as the lowest point in the city, goes first. As many as 60 floods a year have been recorded since they first started keeping track in the late 1700s. One of the most devastating was in 1966, though the second-highest occurred in November 2019, and they seem to be getting worse—in 2021 flooding affected the city in August, much earlier than usual.

The good news is that the long-delayed **Modulo Sperimentale Elettromeccanico,** or **MOSE** project (www.mosevenezia.eu), began operating in October 2020. A complex system of hydraulic gates, MOSE was built out in the lagoon to cut off the highest of these high tides, though it won't be fully complete until 2025. It's controversial because of its environmental impact—keeping the gates closed for long periods could result in parts of the lagoon becoming stagnant, for example—but in the short run, key sights such as St. Mark's Square will be spared the worst of the flooding. Note however, MOSE is only activated to block tides of more than 110cm (3 ft., 7 in.), which means light flooding is still likely to occur.

Significant *acqua alta* can begin as early as late September or October, but usually takes place November to March (there is no way to predict them in advance). The waters usually recede after just a few hours—there is no need to get wet and the city doesn't shut down. Walkways are set up along the main routes, but if you intend to wander around, do as the locals do and buy rubber wading boots, available from most stores from 20€ (for about 10€, souvenir shops and stands in Piazza San Marco also sell disposable knee-high plastic waterproof slippers, good for a couple of days).

Basilica SS. Giovanni e Paolo ★ CHURCH Built by the Dominican order from the 13th to the 15th century, this massive Gothic church is an unofficial Pantheon where 25 doges are buried (a number of tombs are part of the unfinished facade). The church, commonly known as Zanipolo in Venetian dialect, is also home to many artistic treasures. The brilliantly colored **"Polyptych of St. Vincent Ferrer"** (ca. 1465), attributed to a young Giovanni Bellini, is in the right aisle. You'll also see the mummified foot of St. Catherine of Siena—considered a holy relic—encased in glass near here. Visit the **Cappella del Rosario ★**, through a glass door off the left transept, to see three restored ceiling canvases and one oil painting by Paolo Veronese, particularly "The Assumption of the Madonna."

Anchoring the large and impressive *campo* outside the church, a popular crossroads for this area of Castello, is the **statue of Bartolomeo Colleoni ★★**, the Renaissance *condottiere* (mercenary) who defended Venice's interests at the height of its power until his death in 1475. The

15th-century sculpture by the Florentine Andrea Verrocchio is considered one of the world's great equestrian monuments.

Campo Santi Giovanni e Paolo. santigiovanniepaolo.it. ✆ **041/5235913.** 3.50€. Daily 7:30am–7pm; open to tourists Mon–Sat 9am–6pm, Sun noon–6pm. *Vaporetto:* Rialto.

Scuola di San Giorgio degli Schiavoni ★★ MUSEUM One of the most mesmerizing spaces in Europe, the tiny main hall of this *scuola* once served as a meeting house for Venice's Dalmatian community (Dalmatia is a region of Croatia—*schiavoni* means "Slavs"). Venetian *scuole,* or schools, were guilds that brought together merchants and craftspeople from certain trades or similar religious devotions. Built beside its sister church, San Giovanni di Malta, in the early 16th century, the scuola is most famous for the awe-inspiring **cycle of paintings** on its walls, created by Renaissance master Vittore Carpaccio between 1502 and 1509. The paintings depict the lives of the Dalmatian patron saints George (of dragon-slaying fame), Tryphon, and Jerome; in the upper hall (Sala dell'Albergo) is Carpaccio's masterful "Vision of St. Augustine."

Calle dei Furlani 3259A. www.scuoladalmatavenezia.com. ✆ **041/5228828.** 6€, cash only. Mon & Wed–Sun 10am–5:30pm (last entry 5pm); Reservations required in advance at segreteria@scuoladalmatavenezia.com. *Vaporetto:* Rialto.

Dorsoduro

Art aficionados should head to the eastern tip of Dorsoduro and the 17th-century Dogana di Mare (Customs House), transformed by architect Tadao Ando into a beautiful exhibition space dubbed the **Punta della Dogana** (Fondamenta della Dogana alla Salute 2; www.palazzograssi.it).

Gallerie dell'Accademia ★★★ MUSEUM Along with San Marco and the Palazzo Ducale, the Accademia is one of the city's highlights, a magnificent collection of European art and Venetian painting from the 14th to the 18th centuries. Visitor numbers are always capped, so online

The Biennale

Venice hosts the latest in contemporary art and sculpture from dozens of countries during the prestigious **Biennale d'Arte** ★★★ (www.labiennale.org; ✆ **041/5218711**), one of the world's top international art shows. It fills the pavilions of the **Giardini** (public gardens) at the east end of **Castello,** and at the **Arsenale,** as well as other spaces around the city from April to November on even years. (The next Biennale should take place in 2024, 2026, and so on.) It's usually open Tuesday through Sunday 10am to 6pm; tickets cost around 25€ (20€ seniors, 16€ students and ages 26 and under). The **Biennale Architettura** (international architecture exhibition) takes place in alternate years (2025, 2027, and so on).

advance reservations are essential. In general, the least crowded times are at opening in the morning and around 2 hours before closing.

There's a lot to take in here, so buy a catalog in the store, as these contain detailed descriptions of the core paintings and plenty of context—the audioguides are a little muddled and not worth 6€. Note also that one of the museum's prize holdings, Da Vinci's iconic **Vitruvian Man ★★★** ("L'Uomo Vitruviano"), is an extremely fragile ink drawing and rarely displayed in public; check the website before you visit, as exhibitions featuring the work are rare but well-publicized.

Rooms are laid out in rough chronological order, though renovations and closures mean some rooms may be off-limits when you visit (call ahead to check on specific paintings or check the website, updated monthly). Work began on the second-floor galleries in 2018—rooms 12 to 17 and 22 to 24 are likely to be closed at some point before the work is complete in 2024 or 2025. The following artworks should be on display somewhere in the museum, though locations will change (again, check the website for the latest).

Visits normally begin upstairs on the second floor, where room 1 (the grand meeting room of the Scuola Grande della Carità) displays a beautifully presented collection of lavish medieval and early Renaissance art, primarily religious images and altarpieces dating from 1300 to 1450. The giant canvases in room 2 include Carpaccio's "Presentation of Jesus in the Temple," and works by Giovanni Bellini (Bellini is also the focus of rooms 4 and 5). Room 7 features the unsettling, surreal paintings of Hieronymus Bosch, while Giorgione's "The Tempest" and "The Old Woman" are displayed in Room 8. Room 9 showcases Venetian heavyweights Titian and Lorenzo Lotto, while Room 10 is dominated by Paolo Veronese's mammoth **"Feast in the House of Levi" ★★**. Other vast Veronese canvases make up the rest of the room. Room 11 contains work by another Venetian legend, Tintoretto, including **"The Miracle of the Slave" ★★**, along with several paintings by Tiepolo, the master of 18th-century Venetian art, and Titian's last painting, a "Pietà" intended for his own tomb.

Room 20 is usually filled by Gentile Bellini's cycle of **"The Miracles of the Relic of the Cross" ★**, painted around 1500. Room 21 normally contains a monumental cycle of nine paintings by Carpaccio illustrating the **Story of St. Ursula ★★**; most of these continue to undergo restoration, with "Arrival in Cologne" the only one likely to be displayed for some time.

While renovations are ongoing, room 23 will contain some of the museum's most famous paintings—check with the museum information desk (or online) if there's a particular work you want to see. Finally, room 24 is adorned with Titian's **"Presentation of the Virgin,"** actually created to hang in this space between 1534 and 1538.

Downstairs, the renovated ground-floor galleries cover the late 18th to 19th centuries, a far more mediocre collection of baroque and romantic works, though delicate paintings by Tiepolo share space with his large tondo **"Feast of the Cross"** in gallery 2, along with Veronese's **"Venice Receives Homage from Hercules and Ceres."** Sculpture galleries (featuring the work of Canova) should also be open on this level.

Campo della Carità 1050, at foot of Accademia bridge. www.gallerieaccademia.it. ✆ **041/5200345.** 12€ adults (plus 1.50€ booking fee); 2€ ages 18–25; kids 17 and under free (price may change during temporary exhibitions). Daily 8:15am–7:15pm (Mon closes 2pm). *Vaporetto:* Accademia.

Peggy Guggenheim Collection ★★ MUSEUM It's one of the best museums in Italy covering American and European art of the 20th century, but you might find the experience a little jarring, given its location in a city so heavily associated with the High Renaissance and the `baroque. Nevertheless, art aficionados will find some fascinating work here, and the main galleries occupy Peggy Guggenheim's wonderful former home, the 18th-century "unfinished" Palazzo Venier dei Leoni, right on the Grand Canal. Guggenheim purchased the mansion in 1949 and lived here, on and off, until her death in 1979 (the history of this once

The sculpture garden at the Peggy Guggenheim Collection.

derelict palace is wonderfully brought to life in Judith Mackrell's *The Unfinished Palazzo*). Today the entire villa has been converted into galleries. Highlights include Picasso's extremely abstract "Poet" and his more gentle "On the Beach," several works by Kandinsky ("Landscape with Red Spots No. 2" and "White Cross"), Miró's expressionistic "Seated Woman II," Klee's mystical "Magic Garden," and some unsettling works by Max Ernst ("The Kiss," "Attirement of the Bride"), who was briefly married to Guggenheim in the 1940s. Also look for Magritte's "Empire of Light," Dalí's "Birth of Liquid Desires," and a couple of gems from Pollock (who was especially championed by Guggenheim): his early "Moon Woman," which recalls Picasso, and "Alchemy," a more typical "poured" painting. The Italian Futurists are also well represented here, with a rare portrait from Modigliani ("Portrait of the Painter Frank Haviland"). Adjacent buildings added later to the complex (serving as temporary exhibition space, a cafe, and shop) are connected to the main building by the pleasantly shady **Nasher Sculpture Garden;** Guggenheim is buried in the corner, marked by a simple headstone. Free presentations on aspects of the collection are given daily in the museum galleries or garden (check the website for times). Guided tours can be arranged in advance and cost 95€, for a group of up to 20 people. ***Tip:*** It's not a good idea to visit the Guggenheim and St. Mark's on the same day—it's a fairly long walk between the two. We also don't advise seeing it on the same day as the Accademia, even though they're only 10 minutes apart; the artistic overload is likely to prove too much for even the most avid art aficionado.

Fondamenta Venier dai Leon 704. www.guggenheim-venice.it. © **041/2405411.** Tickets (advance purchase online recommended) 16€ adults, 14€ 65 and over, 9€ students 10–26. Audioguide 7€. Wed–Mon 10am–6pm. *Vaporetto:* Accademia (walk around left side of Accademia, take 1st left, and follow signs).

San Sebastiano ★★ CHURCH Lose the crowds as you make a pilgrimage to the parish church of **Paolo Veronese,** home to some of his finest work. Veronese painted the coffered nave ceiling with the florid "Scenes from the Life of St. Esther." In the 1560s he also decorated the organ shutters and panels in the chancel with scenes from the life of St. Sebastian. Although Veronese is the main event here, don't miss Titian's sensitive "St. Nicholas" (just inside the church on the right). Veronese's sepulchral monument (with bust by Mattia Carneri) is to the left of the altar. The real highlight is the sacristy (go through the door under the organ), a tiny jewel box of a room adorned with more wonderful Veronese paintings of the "Coronation of the Virgin" and the "Four Evangelists."

Campo San Sebastiano. © **041/2750462.** 3€. Mon–Sat 10:30am–1:30pm and 2:30–5pm. *Vaporetto:* San Basilio.

Santa Maria della Salute ★ CHURCH The church of the Virgin Mary of Good Health, known as "La Salute," is a jewel of baroque architecture, proudly reigning over a landmark point almost directly across from the Piazza San Marco, where the Grand Canal empties into the lagoon. The first stone was laid in 1631 after the Senate decided to honor the Virgin Mary for delivering Venice from a plague that had killed around 95,000 people. It was built from the revolutionary plans of a young, relatively unknown architect, Baldassare Longhena, who dedicated the next 50 years of his life to overseeing its progress (he would die 5 years before its completion). Today the dome of the church is an iconic presence on the Venice skyline, recognized for its exuberant exterior of volutes, scrolls, and more than 125 statues. The most revered image inside is the **Madonna della Salute,** a rare black-faced sculpture of Mary brought back in 1670 from Candia in Crete as war booty. The otherwise sober interior is enlivened by the **sacristy** (6€ entry), with a number of important ceiling paintings and portraits by **Titian.** On the right wall of the sacristy is Tintoretto's **"Marriage at Cana"** ★, considered one of his best paintings. It's also now possible to climb 150 steps up the dome ("Cupola") for 8€ (mostly Fri–Sun only but check the website), for a unique panorama of the city from the south.

Campo della Salute 1. www.basilicasalutevenezia.it. ✆ **041/5225558.** Church free; sacristy 6€. Daily Apr–Oct 9am–noon and 3–5:30pm; Nov–Mar 9:30am–12:30pm and 3–5:30pm. **Sacristy:** Apr–Oct Tues 2–3:30pm and 4:40–5:30pm, Wed–Fri 10am–12:30pm, 2–3:30pm, and 4:40–5:30pm, Sat 10am–12:30pm and 2–5:30pm, Sun 10–10:30am and 2–5:30pm; Nov–Mar Mon–Fri 10am–noon, 3–3:30pm and 4:40–5:30pm, Sat 10am–noon and 2–5:30pm, Sun 10–10:30am and 2–5:30pm. *Vaporetto:* Salute.

Entrance to Santa Maria della Salute church.

Scuola Grande dei Carmini ★★ CHURCH The former Venetian base of the Carmelites, finished in the 18th century, is now a shrine of sorts to **Giambattista Tiepolo,** who painted the ceiling of the upstairs hall between 1739 and 1744. It's a magnificent sight. Tiepolo's elaborate rococo interpretation of "Simon Stock Receiving the Scapular" is now fully restored, along with various panels throughout the building.

Campo San Margherita 2617. www.scuolagrandecarmini.it. ✆ **041/5289420.** 7€. Daily 10am–5pm. *Vaporetto:* San Basilio.

Squero di San Trovaso ★★ HISTORIC SITE One of the most intriguing sights in Venice is this small *squero* (boatyard), which first opened in the 17th century on the narrow Rio San Trovaso (not far from the Accademia Bridge). It is surrounded by Tyrolean-looking wooden structures (a rarity in this city of stone) that are home to the multigenerational owners and original workshops for traditional Venetian boats. Aware that they themselves have become a tourist sight, the gondoliers don't mind if you watch them at work from across the narrow Rio di San Trovaso, but don't try to invite yourself in.

Dorsoduro 1097 (on the Rio San Trovaso). *Vaporetto:* Zattere.

Gondolas are built and repaired at the Squero di San Trovaso boatyard in Dorsoduro.

San Polo & Santa Croce

Santa Maria Gloriosa dei Frari ★★ CHURCH Known simply as "i Frari," this immense 14th-century Gothic basilica built by the Franciscans is the largest church in Venice after San Marco. It houses a number of important artworks, including two Titian masterpieces: the **"Assumption of the Virgin"** ★★ over the main altar, painted when the artist was in his late 20s, and "Virgin of the Pesaro Family" in the left nave, for which Titian's wife posed for the figure of Mary (she died soon afterward in childbirth). Don't miss Giovanni Bellini's **"Madonna & Child"** ★★ over the altar in the sacristy, of which novelist Henry James wrote, "It is as solemn as it is gorgeous." The grand **mausoleum of Titian** is on the right as you enter the church, opposite an incongruous pyramid-shaped

18th-century monument to sculptor **Antonio Canova**—designed by Canova himself, this was originally supposed to be Titian's tomb.

Campo dei Frari. www.basilicadeifrari.it. ✆ **041/2728611.** 5€; 3€ 65 and over; 2€ students under 30. Audioguide 2€. Mon–Sat 9am–6pm; Sun 1–6pm (extended hours June–Sept; see website). *Vaporetto:* San Tomà (walk straight on Calle del Traghetto, turn right and immediately left across Campo San Tomà; walk straight on Ramo Mandoler then Calle Larga Prima, turn right at beginning of Salizada San Rocco).

Scuola Grande di San Rocco ★★★ MUSEUM Like many medieval saints, French-born San Rocco (St. Roch) died young, but thanks to his work healing the sick in the 14th century, his cult became associated with the power to cure the plague and other serious illnesses. When his body was brought to Venice in 1485, this *scuola* began to reap the benefits, and by 1560, the current complex was completed. Work soon began on more than 50 paintings by **Tintoretto,** and today the *scuola* is primarily a shrine to the masterful Venetian artist. You enter at the **Sala Terrena** (Ground Floor Hall), where the paintings were created between 1583 and 1587, led by one of the most frenzied "Annunciations" ever made. The "Flight into Egypt" here is undeniably one of Tintoretto's greatest works. Upstairs is the **Sala Superiore** (Great Upper Hall), where Old Testament scenes cover the ceiling. The paintings around the walls, based on the New Testament, are generally regarded as a master class of perspective, shadow, and color. In the **Sala dell'Albergo,** an entire wall is adorned by Tintoretto's mind-blowing "Crucifixion" (as well as his "Glorification of St. Roch," on the ceiling, the painting that actually won him the contract to paint the *scuola*). Way up in the loft, the **Tesoro** (Treasury) is a tiny space dedicated primarily to gold reliquaries containing venerated relics such as the fingers of St. Peter and St. Andrew, and one of the thorns that crowned Christ during the crucifixion.

Campo San Rocco 3052, adjacent to Campo dei Frari. www.scuolagrandesanrocco.org. ✆ **041/5234864.** 10€ adults; 8€ ages 18–26 and over 65; 18 and under free. Audioguide 3€. Daily 9:30am–5:30pm. *Vaporetto:* San Tomà (walk straight on Calle del Traghetto, turn right and immediately left across Campo San Tomà; walk straight on Ramo Mandoler, Calle Larga Prima, and Salizada San Rocco, which leads into the *campo* of the same name—look for crimson sign behind Frari Church).

Cannaregio

Galleria Giorgio Franchetti alla Ca' d'Oro ★★ MUSEUM A magnificent palazzo overlooking the Grand Canal, the "golden house" was built between 1428 and 1430 for the noble Contarini family. Baron Giorgio Franchetti bought the place in 1894, and it now serves as an atmospheric gallery for his exceptional art collection (mostly early Renaissance Italian and Flemish). The highlight is Paduan artist Andrea Mantegna's **"St. Sebastian" ★★**, displayed in its own marble side chapel. Mantegna's third and final painting of the saint, created around 1490,

it's quite different from the other two (in Vienna and Paris); this bold, deeply pessimistic work has none of Mantegna's usual background details to detract from the saint's suffering. Don't miss the three panels from Carpaccio's "Stories of the Virgin" series on the second floor.
Strada Nuova 3932. polomusealeveneto.beniculturali.it. ✆ **041/520-0345.** 6€; free audioguide available online. Tues–Sun 9am–7pm. *Vaporetto:* Ca' d'Oro.

Museo Ebraico di Venezia ★ MUSEUM/SYNAGOGUE In the heart of the Ghetto Nuovo, the Jewish Museum contains a small but precious collection of artifacts related to the long history of the Jews in Venice. The museum closed for a major restoration in 2021 that should be complete in 2023 or 2024. Until then, tours of the Scuola Levantina synagogue (and the Luzzatto midrash) will depart a temporary location from the Campo del Ghetto Nuovo (ladies must have shoulders covered and men must have heads covered; no photos). The new museum is slated to expand into three new buildings on the campo, and will include space for temporary exhibits as well as the permanent collection that includes historic chandeliers, goblets, and spice holders used to celebrate Shabbat, Shofàrs (ram's horns), and a Séfer Torà (Scroll of Divine Law). But for many, the real highlight will be the chance to tour the area's historic synagogues (all hidden from view on the top floor of otherwise normal-looking Venetian tenements): **German** (Scuola Grande Tedesca), founded in 1528; **Italian** (Scuola Italiana), founded in 1575; **Sephardic** (Scuola Levantina), founded in 1541 but rebuilt in the 17th century; **Spanish** (Scuola Spagnola), rebuilt in the first half of the 17th century; and the baroque-style **Scuola Canton,** established in 1532 (likely by French

il ghetto & THE JEWS OF VENICE

Jews began settling in Venice in great numbers in the 15th century, and the Republic soon came to value their services as moneylenders, physicians, and traders. In 1516, however, fearing their growing influence, the Venetians forced the Jewish population to live on an island with an abandoned foundry (*ghetto* is old Venetian dialect for "foundry"), and drawbridges were raised to enforce a nighttime curfew. By the end of the 17th century, as many as 5,000 Jews lived in the Ghetto's cramped confines. Napoleon tore down the Ghetto gates in 1797, but it wasn't until the unification of Italy in 1866 that Jews achieved equal status. Il Ghetto remains the spiritual center for Venice's ever-diminishing community of Jewish families, with two synagogues and a Chabad House; it's said that anywhere from 450 to 2,000 Jews live in all of Venice and Mestre, though very few now live in the Ghetto. Aside from its historic interest, this is also one of the less touristy neighborhoods in Venice and makes for a pleasant and scenic place to stroll. Venice's first kosher restaurant, **Gam Gam,** opened here in 1996, at 1122 Ghetto Vecchi on the canal (www.gamgamkosher.com; ✆ **366/2504505**), close to the Guglie *vaporetto* stop. Owned and run by Orthodox Jews, it is open Sunday to Thursday noon to 10pm, Friday noon to 2 hours before Shabbat (sunset), and Saturday from 1 hour after Shabbat until 11pm (excluding summer).

Provençal Jews) but largely rebuilt in the 18th century. The Canton, German, and Italian synagogues are undergoing various stages of restoration that should also be complete by 2024 (depending on funding) and will be part of the new museum experience. The Levantina and Spanish synagogues are used regularly for services, but will also be open for tours at certain times.

Campo del Ghetto Nuovo. www.facebook.com/culturaebraicavenezia. ✆ **041/715359.** Museum/tour 10€ adults, 8€ kids and students ages 6–26. For tour times and the latest on the museum, check the website. Closed Jewish holidays. *Vaporetto:* Guglie.

Giudecca

Il Redentore ★★ CHURCH Perhaps the greatest masterpiece of Andrea Palladio, the great Renaissance architect from nearby Padua, Il Redentore was commissioned by Venice to give thanks for being delivered from the great plague (1575–77), which claimed over a quarter of the population (some 46,000 people). The doge established a tradition of visiting this church by crossing a long pontoon bridge made up of boats from the Dorsoduro's Zattere on the third Sunday of each July, a tradition that survived the demise of the doges and remains one of Venice's most popular festivals ("Festa del Redentore"). The interior is done in austere but elegant Palladian style. Artworks tend to be workshop pieces (from the studios or schools of Tintoretto and Veronese), but a fine "Baptism of Christ" by Veronese himself is in the sacristy (accessed through a door in the last chapel on the right).

Campo del Redentore. ✆ **041/523-1415.** 3€. Mon–Sat 10:30am–1:30pm and 2:30–5pm. *Vaporetto:* Redentore.

San Giorgio Maggiore

Sitting on the little island of San Giorgio Maggiore across from Piazza San Marco are a handful of intriguing sights, not least its namesake church, another Palladio masterpiece. Next door to the church and designed by Selldorf Architects, the stylish **Stanze del Vetro** (lestanzedel vetro.org; usually free) hosts traveling exhibitions dedicated to the art of glassmaking (it's usually closed between shows, so check the website for the latest). You can also tour the galleries of the nearby **Fondazione Giorgio Cini** (www.visitcini.com; from 15€) in the old San Giorgio Monastery, plus the foundation's Borges Labyrinth, its 10 "Vatican Chapels," and the 1950s Teatro Verde.

San Giorgio Maggiore ★★ CHURCH Palladio designed this magnificent church in 1565 and it was completed in 1610. To impose a classical front on the traditional church structure, Palladio designed two interlocking facades, with repeating triangles, rectangles, and columns harmoniously proportioned. The main altar is flanked by two epic paintings by Tintoretto, "The Fall of Manna," to the left, and the more noteworthy **"The Last Supper"** ★★ to the right, famous for its chiaroscuro.

Accessed by free guided tour only (usually Apr–Oct only; times vary), the adjacent **Cappella dei Morti** (Chapel of the Dead) contains Tintoretto's "Deposition," and the upper chapel contains Carpaccio's "St. George Killing the Dragon." To the left of the choir is an elevator that you can take to the top of the 1791 campanile—for a charge of 8€—to experience an unforgettable view of the island, the lagoon, and the Palazzo Ducale and Piazza San Marco across the way.

San Giorgio Maggiore. ✆ **041/5227827.** Free. Daily Apr–Oct 9am–7pm; Nov–Mar 8:30am–6pm. *Vaporetto:* Take Giudecca-bound *vaporetto* no. 2 on Riva degli Schiavoni (San Marco/San Zaccaria) and get off at 1st stop, San Giorgio Maggiore.

Exploring Venice's Islands

Venice shares its lagoon with four other principal islands: **Murano, Burano, Torcello,** and the **Lido.** Guided tours of the first three are available (30€–45€ for 3–4 hr.), but while these can be informative, unless you are very short of time you'll enjoy exploring the islands in far more leisurely fashion on your own, easily done using the *vaporetti.* Line nos. 4.1 and 4.2 make the journey to **Murano** from Fondamente Nove (north side of Castello). For **Murano, Burano,** and **Torcello,** Line no. 12 departs Fondamente Nove every 30 minutes; for Torcello, change to the Line 9 shuttle boat from Burano, timed to match arrivals from Venice (it zips between the two islands every 15 min. or so). The islands are small and easy to navigate, but check the schedule for island-to-island departures and plan your return so that you don't spend most of your day waiting for connections.

Vaporetto line nos. 1, 2, 5.1, 5.2, and LN cross the lagoon to the **Lido** from the San Zaccaria–Danieli stop near San Marco. Note that the Lido becomes chilly, windswept, and utterly deserted from October to April.

MURANO ★★

The island of Murano has long been famous throughout the world for the products of its glass factories. The illuminating **Museo del Vetro** ★ (Museum of Glass), Fondamenta Giustinian 8 (www.museovetro.visitmuve.it; ✆ **041/739586**), charts the history of the island's glassmaking and is definitely worthwhile if you intend to purchase a lot of glassware, providing plenty of background so you know what you're buying in the stores outside. It's normally open daily 10am to 5pm (last entry 4pm); admission is 10€ adults, 7.50€ ages 6 to 14 and students 25 and under; it's also included in the Museum Pass (p. 414).

Dozens of *fornaci* (kilns) offer free (or cheap) shows of mouth-blown glassmaking, almost invariably hitched to a hard-sell tour of the factory outlet store. Once you're on the island, you can't miss these places; they're pretty much of equal quality. A dependable choice is **Original Murano Glass** ★ (Feb–Oct normally open daily 10am–3pm; reserve 5€ tours and demonstrations at www.visitmuranoglassfactory.com), at the Ellegi Glass *fornaci,* Fondamenta San Giovanni dei Battuti 4, a few minutes' walk from the Murano Faro *vaporetti* stop. Almost all shops will ship their goods, although that often doubles the price. On the other hand, these pieces are instant heirlooms.

Murano is also graced with two worthy churches (both free admission): the largely 15th-century **San Pietro Martire** ★ (Mon–Sat 9am–5:30pm, Sun noon–5:30pm), with paintings by Veronese and Giovanni Bellini, and the ancient **Santa Maria e Donato** ★ (Mon–Sat 9am–6pm, Sun 12:30–6pm), with its intricate Byzantine exterior apse, 6th-century pulpit, stunning mosaic of Mary, and fantastic 12th-century inlaid floor.

BURANO ★★★

Lace is the claim to fame of tiny, historic Burano, a craft kept alive for centuries by the wives of fishermen waiting for their husbands to return from the sea. Sadly, most of the lace sold on the island these days is made by machine elsewhere. The local government continues its attempt to keep Burano's centuries-old lace legacy alive with subsidized classes. It's still worth a trip to stroll the back streets of the island, whose canals are lined with the brightly colored, simple homes of the Buranesi fishermen—quite unlike anything in Venice or Murano. **Butter biscuits,** known as *buranelli,* are another famous island product—expect to be offered them in almost every store. While you're here, visit the **Museo del Merletto** (Museum of Lace Making), Piazza Galuppi 187 (www.museomerletto.visitmuve.it; ✆ **041/730034**), to understand why something so exquisite should not be

Colorful fishermen's homes on the island of Burano.

allowed to fade into extinction. It's normally open Tuesday to Sunday 10am to 5pm (Nov–Mar to 4pm); admission is 5€ adults, 3.50€ ages 6 to 14 and students 25 and under; it's included in the Museum Pass (p. 414).

TORCELLO ★★

Torcello is perhaps the most charming of the islands, though today it consists of little more than one long canal leading from the *vaporetto* landing to a clump of buildings at its center (a 10-min. walk). Hard to imagine this was once a thriving city in its own right, with at least 20,000 inhabitants in the 16th century. Torcello boasts the oldest Venetian monument, the **Basilica di Santa Maria dell'Assunta ★★★**, whose foundation dates from the 7th century (✆ **041/2702464**). It's famous for its spectacular 11th- to 12th-century Byzantine mosaics—a "Madonna and Child" in the apse and a monumental "Last Judgment" on the west wall—rivaling those of Ravenna's and St. Mark's basilicas. Note that taking photos inside is forbidden. The cathedral is open daily 10:30am to 6pm (Nov–Feb to 5pm), and admission is 5€ (audioguide 2€). The bell tower, which is separate and closes 15 to 30 minutes earlier than the Basilica, is 5€, or 9€ combined with the Basilica. Also of interest is the adjacent 11th-century **Santa Fosca** (free admission; closes 30 min. before Basilica), a Byzantine brick chapel with a plain interior, and the **Museo di Torcello** (✆ **041/730761;** 3€; Tues–Sun 10:30am–5:30pm, Nov–Feb 10am–5pm), showcasing archaeological artifacts from the Iron Age to the medieval era, many found on the island. Buy tickets at the basilica entrance (all three attractions 12€).

Peaceful Torcello is now uninhabited except for a handful of families, and is a favorite picnic spot. You'll have to bring the food from Venice—there are no stores on the island and only a handful of bars/trattorias along the canal plus one fabulous destination restaurant, the **Locanda Cipriani** (www.locandacipriani.com; ✆ **041/730150;** Wed–Mon noon–3pm and 7–9pm; closed Jan to mid-Feb), of Hemingway fame; Queen Elizabeth II, Winston Churchill, and Princess Diana all dined here too. Opened in 1935 by Giuseppe Cipriani (it's still owned by the family), this spot is definitely worth a splurge (reservations recommended). Once the tour groups have left, the island offers a very special moment of solitude and escape.

THE LIDO

Although a convenient 15-minute *vaporetto* ride away from San Marco (see transport details, p. 397), Venice's **Lido beaches** are not much to write home about and certainly no longer a chic destination (the Grand Hotel des Bains depicted in Thomas Mann's *Death in Venice* closed in 2010). For swimming and sunbathing there are much better beaches nearby—in **Jesolo,** to the north, for example. But the parade of wealthy Italian and foreign tourists and Venetian families who still frequent the Lido is an interesting sight indeed—in summer it feels more like the south of France than Venice.

The Lido has two main beach areas. **Blue Moon** (Piazzale Bucintoro) is at the opposite end of Gran Viale Santa Maria Elisabetta (the main drag, referred to as the Gran Viale) from the *vaporetto* station Santa Elisabetta. It's a 10-minute stroll; walk straight ahead along Gran Viale to reach the beach (Gran Viale is lined with seafood restaurants and bars). **San Nicolò,** about 1.5km (1 mile) north, can be reached by bus B from Santa Elisabetta. The beaches tend to get narrower to the south, though **Alberoni** at the southern tip is a wilder, less developed stretch backed by dunes. At the main beach areas, loungers and parasols can be rented for 10€ to 20€ per person (per day) depending on the time of year (it's just 1€ to use the public showers and bathrooms). Keep in mind that if you stay at any of the hotels on the Lido, most have some kind of agreement with the different *bagni* (private beach establishments). Also note that the restored **Ancient Jewish Cemetery** (Antico Cimitero Ebraico) on the Lido (established in 1386) is open to the public but best appreciated on a tour from the **Museo Ebraico** (p. 424).

The Film Festival

The **Venice International Film Festival ★**, in late August and early September, is the most respected celebration of celluloid in Europe after Cannes. Films from all over the world are shown primarily in the **Palazzo del Cinema** and **Palazzo del Casinò** on the Lido. Ticket prices vary, but those for the less-sought-after films are usually modest. Visit www.labiennale.org/en/cinema for details.

Organized Tours

Because of the sheer number of sights to see in Venice, some first-time visitors like to start out with an organized tour. Although few things can really be covered in any depth on these overview tours, they're somewhat useful for getting your bearings. **Avventure Bellissime** (www.tours-italy.com; ✆ **041/970499**) coordinates a plethora of tours (in English), by boat and gondola, though the walking tours are the best value, covering all the main sights around Piazza San Marco in 2 hours for 45€ (includes "Skip the Line" tickets to St Mark's Basilica).

For those with more energy, learn to "row like a Venetian" (yes, standing up) at **Row Venice** (www.rowvenice.org; ✆ **347/7250637**), where 1½-hour lessons take place in traditional, hand-built "shrimp-tail" or *batele coda di gambero* boats for 85€ for up to two people. Or you could abandon tradition altogether and opt for a **Venice Kayak** tour (www.venicekayak.com; ✆ **346/4771327**), a truly enchanting way to see the city from the water. The company offers a variety of tours from April to early November, from 2-hour loops to a full day (110€–160€). **SUP in Venice** (www.supinvenice.com; ✆ **389/9851866**) offers guided SUP ("stand-up paddleboard") tours in Venice (Apr–Oct), with 1-hour, 40-minute sessions starting at 70€.

carnevale A VENEZIA

Carnevale traditionally was the celebration preceding Lent, the period of penitence and abstinence prior to Easter; its name is derived from the Latin *carnem levare,* meaning "to take meat away." In Venice, the heyday of Carnevale was the 18th century; it was outlawed in 1797 and only revived in 1979 to boost winter tourism. Today Carnevale in Venice builds for a whole month until the big blowout, Shrove Tuesday, when fireworks illuminate the Grand Canal and Piazza San Marco becomes a giant open-air ballroom for the masses. The festival is a harlequin patchwork of cultural events, many free of charge, appealing to all ages, tastes, nationalities, and budgets. Musical events from reggae and zydeco to jazz and baroque are staged in dozens of *piazze.* Book your hotel months ahead, especially for the 2 weekends prior to Shrove Tuesday. Check **www.carnevale.venezia.it/en** for details.

Especially for Kids

It goes without saying that a **gondola ride** (p. 404) will be the thrill of a lifetime for any child (or adult). If that's too expensive, consider the far cheaper alternative: a **ride on the no. 1 *vaporetto*** (p. 397).

Judging from the squeals of delight, **feeding the pigeons in Piazza San Marco** could be the high point of your child's visit to Venice, and it's the ultimate photo op. Purchase a bag of corn and you'll be draped in fluttering and flapping pigeons in a nanosecond.

A jaunt to the neighboring **island of Murano** (p. 426) can be as educational as it is recreational—follow the signs to any *fornace* (kiln), where a glassblowing performance of the island's thousand-year-old art is free entertainment. But be ready for the sales pitch that follows.

Take the elevator to the **top of the Campanile di San Marco** (p. 410) for a scintillating view of Venice's rooftops and cupolas, or get up close and personal with the four bronze horses on the facade of the **Basilica di San Marco** (p. 406). The view from its outdoor loggia is something you and your children won't forget. Scaling the **Torre dell'Orologio** (p. 415) or the bell tower at **San Giorgio Maggiore** (p. 425) is also lots of fun.

The **winged lion,** said to have been a kind of good luck mascot to St. Mark, patron saint of Venice, was the very symbol of the Serene Republic and to this day appears on everything from cafe napkins to T-shirts. Keep a running tab of who can spot the most flying lions—you'll find them on facades, atop columns, over doorways, as pavement mosaics, on government stamps, and on the local flag.

WHERE TO STAY IN VENICE

Few cities boast as long a high season as that of Venice, which begins with the Easter period—for most hotels it runs mid-March through November, includes weekends year-round, Christmas and New Year, and carnival. This leaves the few weeks between late November and late December,

January, and the week or so after Carnevale in early March to capture the low season rates. May, June, and September are the best months weather-wise, and therefore normally the most crowded. July and August are hot (few of the one- and two-star hotels offer air-conditioning; when they do, it usually costs extra). Hotels are normally more expensive here than in any other Italian city, with no apparent upgrade in amenities—and since the end of the COVID-19 pandemic, rates have skyrocketed. The least special of those below are clean and functional; at best, they're charming and thoroughly enjoyable, with the serenade of a passing gondolier thrown in for good measure. Some may even be your best stay in all of Europe. You'll need to reserve lodging as far in advance as possible, even in the off-season.

Self-Catering Apartments

Anyone looking to get into the local swing of things in Venice should opt for a short-term **rental apartment.** For the same price or less than a hotel room, you could have your own one-bedroom apartment with a washing machine, air-conditioning, and a fridge to keep your Prosecco cold. Properties of all sizes and price ranges are available for stays of 1 night to several weeks.

In terms of **location,** San Marco is the most convenient part of the city, though anywhere near the Grand Canal will give you easy access to the best of Venice. Apartments in the farther reaches of Santa Croce, Cannaregio, Giudecca, and Castello may be slightly cheaper and allow a glimpse of residential life in the city, but getting to and from the main sights will take a lot of time.

For those renting apartments, rather than staying in hotels, secure **luggage storage facilities** are available through Radical Storage from 5€ per day (radicalstorage.com). Radical Storage coordinates a network of various businesses throughout Venice prepared to look after your bags—check for the most convenient option on the website.

RECOMMENDED AGENCIES **Airbnb** (www.airbnb.com), **VRBO.com**, and **Homeaway.com** are now major players in Venice, each with hundreds of properties listed. On Airbnb you can rent a room in someone's home from just 30€ per night. **Couchsurfing** (www.couchsurfing.com) is also popular and generally safe in Venice, though take the usual precautions (for those who don't know the company, it allows locals to offer free rooms to travelers). **Cities Reference** (www.citiesreference.com; ✆ **06/48903612**) is the best traditional rental agency for Venice, with around 50 properties listed. The company's no-surprises property descriptions come with helpful information and lots of photos. **Cross Pollinate** (www.cross-pollinate.com; ✆ **06/99369799**) is a multi-destination agency with a decent roster of personally inspected apartments and B&Bs in Venice, created by the American owners of the Beehive hotel in Rome (p. 135). **Rental in Venice** (www.rentalinvenice.com; ✆ **041/718981**) has an

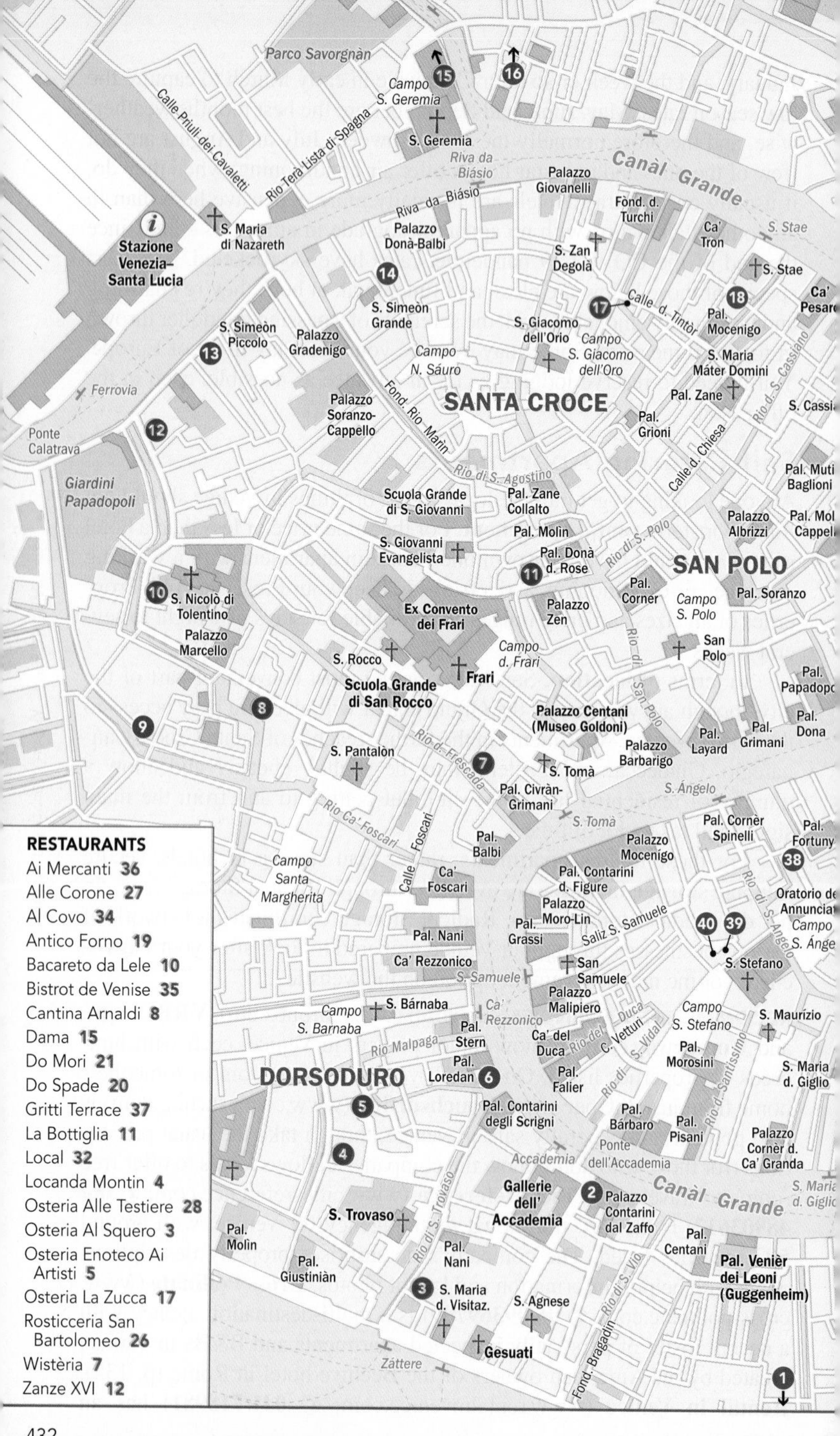
Parco Savorgnàn
Campo S. Geremia
S. Geremia
Calle Priuli dei Cavaletti
Rio Terà Lista di Spagna
Riva da Biásio
Palazzo Giovanelli
Canàl Grande
Fònd. d. Turchi
S. Stae
Ca' Tron
S. Maria di Nazareth
Stazione Venezia–Santa Lucia
Palazzo Donà-Balbi
S. Zan Degolà
S. Simeòn Grande
Calle d. Tintòr
Pal. Mocenigo
Ca' Pesaro
S. Simeòn Piccolo
Palazzo Gradenigo
Campo N. Sàuro
S. Giacomo dell'Orio
Campo S. Giacomo dell'Oro
S. Maria Máter Domini
Ferrovia
Fond. Rio Marìn
SANTA CROCE
Pal. Zane
Rio d. S. Cassiano
S. Cassiano
Palazzo Soranzo-Cappello
Pal. Grioni
Ponte Calatrava
Calle d. Chiesa
Giardini Papadopoli
Rio di S. Agostino
Pal. Muti Baglioni
Scuola Grande di S. Giovanni
Pal. Zane Collalto
Palazzo Albrizzi
Pal. Molin Cappello
Pal. Molìn
S. Giovanni Evangelista
Pal. Donà d. Rose
Rio di S. Polo
SAN POLO
S. Nicolò di Tolentino
Pal. Corner
Campo S. Polo
Pal. Soranzo
Ex Convento dei Frari
Palazzo Zen
Palazzo Marcello
Campo d. Frari
San Polo
S. Rocco
Frari
Rio di San Polo
Pal. Papadopoli
Scuola Grande di San Rocco
Palazzo Centani (Museo Goldoni)
Pal. Dona
Pal. Layard
Pal. Grimani
Palazzo Barbarigo
S. Pantalòn
Rio d. Frescada
S. Tomà
Pal. Civràn-Grimani
S. Ángelo
Rio Ca' Foscari
Calle Foscari
Pal. Cornèr Spinelli
Pal. Fortuny
Pal. Balbi
Palazzo Mocenígo
Campo Santa Margherita
Ca' Foscari
Pal. Contarini d. Figure
Oratorio dell'Annunciata
Palazzo Moro-Lin
Rio di S. Angelo
Campo S. Ángelo
Pal. Grassi
Saliz S. Samuele
Pal. Nani
Ca' Rezzonico
San Samuele
S. Stefano
S. Samuele
Palazzo Malipiero
Campo S. Bárnaba
S. Bárnaba
Ca' Rezzonico
Campo S. Stefano
S. Maurízio
Pal. Stern
Ca' del Duca
Rio del Duca
C. Vetturi
Rio S. Vidal
Rio Malpaga
Pal. Morosini
DORSODURO
Pal. Loredan
Pal. Falier
Rio di S. Vidal
S. Maria d. Giglio
Rio d. Santissimo
Pal. Contarini degli Scrigni
Pal. Bárbaro
Pal. Pisani
Palazzo Cornèr d. Ca' Granda
Accademia
Ponte dell'Accademia
Gallerie dell' Accademia
Palazzo Contarini dal Zaffo
S. Maria d. Giglio
S. Trovaso
Rio di S. Trovaso
Pal. Molin
Pal. Nani
Pal. Centani
Pal. Venièr dei Leoni (Guggenheim)
Pal. Giustiniàn
S. Maria d. Visitaz.
S. Agnese
Rio di S. Vio
Gesuati
Fond. Bragadin
Záttere
RESTAURANTS
Ai Mercanti 36
Alle Corone 27
Al Covo 34
Antico Forno 19
Bacareto da Lele 10
Bistrot de Venise 35
Cantina Arnaldi 8
Dama 15
Do Mori 21
Do Spade 20
Gritti Terrace 37
La Bottiglia 11
Local 32
Locanda Montin 4
Osteria Alle Testiere 28
Osteria Al Squero 3
Osteria Enoteco Ai Artisti 5
Osteria La Zucca 17
Rosticceria San Bartolomeo 26
Wistèria 7
Zanze XVI 12

Venice Hotels & Restaurants
0 1/8 mi
0 200 m
Information
CANNAREGIO
Pal. Giovanelli
S. Felice
Rio di S. Felice
Calle d. Vele
Pal. Fontana
Ca' d'Oro
S. Sofia
Strada Nuova
Pal. Sagredo
Ca' d'Oro
Pal. Brandolin
Pal. Mangilli
Pescaria
Calle d. Botteri
Rio d. Beccarie
Fàbbriche Nuove
Ca' da Mosto
Pal. Falier
Rio d. Santi Apostoli
Rio ter. d. Ss. Apóstoli
Ss. Apóstoli
S. Canciano
Pal. Widman
Calle d. Fumo
Calle d. Squero
Pal. Grifalconi
Fond. d. Mendicanti
Ospedale Civile
S. Maria d. Pianto
Rio di S.G. Crisostomo
S. Giovanni Crisostomo
S. Maria d. Miracoli
C. larga G. Gallina
Pal. Soranzo-Van Axel
Teatro Málibran
Pal. Pisani
Ss. Giovanni e Paolo (S. Zanipolo)
Palazzo Dieci Savi
Fóndaco d. Tedeschi
Pal. Cavazza-Foscari
Campo S. Marina
Rio di S. Marina
Pal. Morosini
Pal. Muazzo
Ponte di Rialto
Aponàl
Rio d. Fava
S. Lio
Palazzo Ruzzini
Pal. Donà
Pal. Cavignis
Palazzo Cappello
Rialto
Riva del Vin
S. Bartolomeo
C. Stagneri
S. Silvestro
Palazzo Dolfin-Manin
S. Maria della Fava
Salizzada S. Lio
Campo S. Maria Formosa
S. Maria Formosa
Pal. Donà
S. Lorenzo
S. Silvestro
Riva del Carbon
M. S. Salvador
Pal. Bembo
C. del Teatro
Rio di S. Salvador
S. Salvador
Pal. Tasca Papafava
C. Bande
Questura
Palazzo Grimani
Ca' Farsetti
Rio di S. Luca
Calle dei Fabbri
C. Guerra
Pal. Querini Stampalia
Ruga Giuffa
CASTELLO
S. Luca
Calle C. Goldoni
S. Zulian
Palazzo Soranzo
Cinema Rossini
Campo Manin
C. Fiubera
C. Spadaria
C. Specchieri
Merc. Orologio
C. Canonica
Palazzo Trevisan-Cappello
S. Giovanni Novo
Pal. Priuli
Pal. Zorzi
Mandola
Rio dei Barcaroli
Rio d. Palazzo
S. Giorgio dei Greci
S. Zaccaria
SAN MARCO
S. Gallo
Torre d. Orologio
Basilica di San Marco
Ateneo Véneto
Convento
Rio del Greci
La Pietà
Pisc. di Frezzaria
Campanile
Piazza San Marco
Palazzo Ducale (Doge's Palace)
Pal. d. Prigioni
S. Fantin
Frezzaria
Teatro La Fenice
Piazzetta
Riva d. Schiavoni
S. Zaccaria
Molo
S. Moisè
S.S. Moise
Museo Corrèr
C. Larga XXII Marzo
R. di S. Moise
C. Ricotto
C. Vallaresso
Giardini ex Reali
Ponte d. Sospiri (Bridge of Sighs)
Capo di Porto
S. Marco
Palazzi Contarini
Palazzo Tiépolo
Palazzo Treves d. Bonfili
Salute
Pal. Genovese
Punta d. Dogana
Dogana da Mar
S. Maria d. Salute
Seminario Patriarcale
Ex Ospízio
Bacino di San Marco
HOTELS
Ai Due Fanali 14
Al Piave 29
Al Ponte Antico 25
Al Ponte Mocenigo 18
Antiche Figure 13
Arcadia 16
B&B San Marco 31
Bloom B&B 39
Ca'Barba B&B 22
Casa Verardo 30
Combo, Venezia 24
Corte Di Gabriela 38
Galleria 2
Generator Venice 1
Locanda Fiorita 40
Metropole 33
Moresco 9
Pensione Accademia 6
Pensione Guerrato 23

alluring website—with video clips of the apartments—and the widest selection of midrange and luxury apartments in the prime San Marco zone (plus less expensive ones, too).

It's standard practice for local rental agencies to collect 30% of the total rental amount upfront to secure a booking. When you check in, the balance of your rental fee is normally payable in cash only, so make sure you have enough euro in hand. Upon booking, the agency should provide you with detailed check-in procedures. Most apartments provide a list of nearby shops and services; beyond that, you're on your own, which is what makes an apartment stay a great way to do as the Venetians do.

San Marco

EXPENSIVE

Bloom B&B ★★★ Right in the heart of San Marco, just off one of its most interesting squares, this relatively new boutique hotel is a romantic hideaway blending classical Venetian style and modern design. Each room is uniquely decorated in lavish color schemes that range from crimson to purple and includes exposed brick, baroque wallpaper, and lots of silky curtains—look at rooms carefully online if you have a preference. All rooms are air-conditioned and feature a minibar and LCD TV. The best feature is the rooftop terrace, with sensational views of the city, and the adjacent reading room. Note, however, that there is no elevator.

Campo Santo Stefano 3470. www.bloom-venice.com. ✆ **340/1498872.** 6 units. 180€–300€ double. Rates include breakfast. *Vaporetto:* Sant'Angelo (walk to tall brick building and go around it, turn right into Ramo Narisi; at small bridge turn left and follow Calle del Pestrin to Campiello Novo on your right—the hotel is opposite the church of Santo Stefano). **Amenities:** Concierge; room service (limited hours); free Wi-Fi.

Corte Di Gabriela ★★★ This gorgeous boutique hotel, just a short walk from Piazza San Marco, combines contemporary design with classical Venetian style—ceiling murals, marble pillars, and exposed brick blend with designer furniture and appliances (including free use of iPads, strong Wi-Fi, and satellite TV). The fully renovated property dates from 1870, once serving as the home and offices of Venetian lawyers. Breakfast is one of the highlights and well worth lingering over: fresh pastries made by the owners the night before, decent espresso, and crepes and omelets cooked on request.

Calle degli Avvocati 3836. www.cortedigabriela.com. ✆ **041/5235077.** 10 units. 270€–920€ double. Rates include breakfast. *Vaporetto:* Sant'Angelo. **Amenities:** Bar; babysitting; concierge; room service (limited hours); free Wi-Fi.

MODERATE

Locando Fiorita ★★ Hard to imagine a more picturesque location for this little hotel, a charming, quiet *campiello* draped in vines and blossoms—no wonder it's a favorite of professional photographers. Most of the standard rooms are small (bathrooms are tiny), but all are furnished in an elegant 18th-century style, with wooden floors, shuttered windows, and richly patterned fittings (air-conditioning and satellite TV included). The helpful staff more than make up for any deficiencies, and breakfast is a real pleasure, especially when taken outside on the *campiello.*

Campiello Novo 3457a. www.locandafiorita.com. ✆ **041/5234754.** 10 units. 145€–240€ double. Rates include breakfast. *Vaporetto:* Sant'Angelo (walk to tall brick building and go around it, turn right into Ramo Narisi; at small bridge turn left and follow Calle del Pestrin to Campiello Novo on your right). **Amenities:** Babysitting; concierge; room service; free Wi-Fi.

Castello

EXPENSIVE

Metropole ★★★ This behemoth with a waterfront location is part luxury hotel, part eclectic art museum, with antiques, Asian artworks, and tapestries dotted throughout. But this is no dusty grand dame; on the contrary, it's a chic boutique hotel with rooms opulently furnished in white, red, and gold color schemes. It began life in the Middle Ages as the Ospedale della Pietà, a charitable institution for orphans and abandoned girls, and later became the music school where Vivaldi taught violin in the early 1700s. After it was converted into a hotel in 1895, Sigmund Freud was an early guest, along with Thomas Mann, who allegedly wrote parts of *Death in Venice* here.

Riva degli Schiavoni 4149. www.hotelmetropole.com. ✆ **041/5205044.** 67 units. 320€–701€ double. Rates include breakfast. *Vaporetto:* San Zaccaria (walk along Riva degli Schiavoni to right; hotel is next to La Pietà church). **Amenities:** Restaurant; bar; babysitting; concierge; room service; free Wi-Fi.

MODERATE

Al Piave ★★ Al Piave is a cozy, old-fashioned family-run hotel just 5 minutes from Piazza San Marco. Rooms are simply but attractively furnished with richly woven rugs, marble floors, and some of the original wood beams exposed (some come with a terrace). Family suites are a good value for groups. Bathrooms are relatively big, and the air-conditioning is a welcome bonus in the summer, but there are no elevators, so be prepared if you get a higher floor. Outside of peak months (May, July, Sept), Piave offers exceptionally good value, given its proximity to the *piazza.*

Ruga Giuffa 4838. www.hotelalpiave.com. ✆ **041/5285174.** 20 units. 145€–300€ double. Rates include breakfast. Closed Jan 7 to Carnevale. *Vaporetto:* San Zaccaria (find Calle delle Rasse beyond Palazzo Daniele; walk to end of street; turn left and then immediately right; continue to Ponte Storto, cross and continue to Ruga Giuffa—hotel is on left). **Amenities:** Babysitting; concierge; free Wi-Fi.

Casa Verardo ★★★ Tucked away across a small bridge in the warren of central Castello, this enchanting property occupies a 16th-century *palazzo,* converted to a hotel in 1911. Rooms sport an old-fashioned Venetian style, with Florentine furniture, hand-painted beds, and colorful textiles (antiques and paintings are scattered throughout), but updated with

Guest room at the Casa Verardo.

air-conditioning and satellite TV. Some rooms have a view over a canal, others over the shady courtyard and the city.

Calle Drio La Chiesa 4765. www.casaverardo.it. ✆ **041/5286138.** 25 units. 135€–220€ double. Rates include breakfast. *Vaporetto:* San Zaccaria (walk straight on Calle delle Rasse to Campo SS. Filippo e Giacomo; cross *campo* to Calle della Sacrestia, then Calle Drio La Chiesa to Ponte Storto; look for hotel on left). **Amenities:** Bar; babysitting; concierge; room service; free Wi-Fi.

INEXPENSIVE

B&B San Marco ★★★ With just three double rooms, this exquisite B&B in a peaceful residential neighborhood fills up fast, so book ahead. It's a comfortable, charming, yet convenient option, not too far from the main sights. Your hosts are the bubbly Marco and Alice Scurati, who live in the attic upstairs and are always happy to provide help and advice. Rooms overlook the Scuola di San Giorgio degli Schiavoni and offer wonderful views of the canal. Two rooms share a bathroom; the third has private facilities. Breakfast is self-service in the shared kitchen, offering yogurts, pastries, espresso, cappuccino, juice, and tea.

Fondamenta San Giorgio dei Schiavoni 3385. www.realvenice.it. ✆ **041/5227589.** 3 units. 75€–130€ double. Rates include breakfast. Closed Aug and Jan 7–Carnevale. *Vaporetto:* San Zaccaria (walk on Calle delle Rasse to Campo SS. Filippo e Giacomo; cross *campo* to Calle della Sacrestia, cross canal; turn left at Campo S Provolo on Fondamenta Osmarin; turn left at canal's end, walk to bridge that connects to Calle Lion; at street's end turn left along canal onto Fondamenta San Giorgio dei Schiavoni). **Amenities:** Babysitting; free Wi-Fi.

Dorsoduro

EXPENSIVE

Moresco ★★★ An incredibly attentive staff, a decadent breakfast that includes Prosecco (to mix with orange juice, ahem), and lavish 19th-century Venetian decor away from the tourist hubbub make this a popular choice. Rooms seamlessly blend Venetian style with modern design. Some have a terrace (with canal or garden views), while others have spa bathtubs; all have flatscreen TVs. If the weather cooperates, take breakfast in the courtyard garden to really soak up the ambience. The hotel is a 5- to 10-minute walk from Piazzale Roma and the train station, but you'll have a number of bridges and stairs to negotiate along the way.

Fondamenta del Rio Novo 3499, Dorsoduro. www.hotelmorescovenice.com. ✆ **041/2440202.** 23 units. 170€–450€ double. Rates include breakfast. *Vaporetto:* Ferrovia/Piazzale Roma (from train station walk SW along Fondamenta Santa Lucia, cross Ponte della Costituzione and turn left onto Fondamenta Santa Chiara; cross Ponte Santa Chiara and turn right onto Fondamenta Papadopoli, continue across Campiello Lavadori then along Fondamenta del Rio Novo). **Amenities:** Bar; concierge; free trips to Murano; room service; free Wi-Fi.

MODERATE/EXPENSIVE

Galleria ★★ Just around the corner from the Accademia, right on the Grand Canal, this hotel occupies a 19th-century *palazzo* in one of the city's most inviting locations. It's been a hotel since the 1800s, hosted poet Robert Browning in 1878, and maintains an 18th-century theme in the rooms, with wood furniture and rococo decor. Hosts Luciano and Lucio serve a simple breakfast in your room. The smallest rooms here really are tiny, and there is no TV or air-conditioning (rooms are supplied with fans when it gets hot), but the fridge of free water and sodas is a lifesaver in summer. Choose from Grand Canal (more expensive) or Accademia Bridge views.

Dorsoduro 878a. www.hotelgalleria.it. ✆ **041/5232489.** 10 units. 100€–290€ double. Rates include breakfast. *Vaporetto:* Accademia (with Accademia Bridge behind you, hotel is just to your left). **Amenities:** Babysitting; concierge; room service; free Wi-Fi.

Pensione Accademia ★★ This spellbinding hotel with a tranquil blossom-filled garden has a fascinating history. The Gothic-style Villa Maravege was built in the 17th century as a family residence, but served as the Russian Embassy between World Wars I and II before becoming a hotel in 1950. If that's not enticing enough, rooms are outfitted with Venetian-style antique reproductions, wood furnishings, handsome tapestries, and air-conditioning, with views over the Rio San Trovaso or the garden. Breakfast is served in your room, in the dining hall, or on the patio.

Fondamenta Bollani 1058. www.pensioneaccademia.it. ✆ **041/5210188.** 27 units. 145€–370€ double. Rates include breakfast. *Vaporetto:* Accademia (turn right down Calle Gambara, which becomes Calle Corfu, which ends at a side canal; walk left over bridge, then turn right back toward Grand Canal to the hotel). **Amenities:** Bar; babysitting; concierge; room service; free Wi-Fi.

San Polo

MODERATE/INEXPENSIVE

Ca'Barba B&B ★★ What you'll remember most about Ca'Barba may well be the host, Alessandro, who usually meets guests at the Rialto *vaporetto* stop; inspires daily wanderings with tips, maps, and books, and provides fresh breads and pastries from the local bakery for breakfast. Of the four rooms (reservations are essential), no. 201 is the largest and brightest, with a Jacuzzi tub (no. 202 also has one). All rooms have antique furniture, 19th-century paintings, wood-beamed ceilings, LCD TVs, air-conditioning, and strong Wi-Fi.

Calle Campanile Castello 1825. www.cabarba.com. ✆ **041/5242816.** 4 units. 95€–140€ double. Rates include breakfast. *Vaporetto:* Rialto (walk back along Grand Canal, turn left at Calle Campanile Castello). **Amenities:** Concierge; free Wi-Fi.

Pensione Guerrato ★★★ Dating, incredibly, from 1227, this is definitely one of the city's most historic places to stay. The building's long history—it was once the "Inn of the Monkey," run by nuns, with the original structure mostly destroyed by fire in 1513—is worth delving into (the owners have all the details). Rooms are simply but classically furnished, with wood floors, exposed beams, air-conditioning, and private baths—many with original frescos that may date from the medieval inn. Note that the cheapest rooms have shared bathrooms, and some are on the seventh floor—and there's no elevator.

Calle Drio La Scimia 240a (near Rialto Market). www.hotelguerrato.com. ✆ **041/5227131.** 20 units. 125€–170€ double. Rates include breakfast. Closed Dec 22–26 and Jan 8–early Feb. *Vaporetto:* Rialto (from north side of Ponte Rialto, walk through market to corner with UniCredit Banca; go 1 short block and turn right on Calle Drio La Scimia). **Amenities:** Babysitting; concierge; free Wi-Fi.

Santa Croce

EXPENSIVE

Antiche Figure ★★★ The most convenient luxury hotel in Venice lies directly across the Grand Canal from the train station, a captivating 15th-century *palazzo* adjacent to an ancient gondola workshop. History aside, this is a very plush choice, its rooms decorated in neoclassical Venetian style with gold leaf, antique furniture, red carpets, silk tapestries, and Murano glass and chandeliers, but also LCD satellite TVs and decent Wi-Fi. There is an elevator, just in case you were wondering.

Fondamenta San Simeone Piccolo 687. www.hotelantichefigure.it. ✆ **041/2759486.** 22 units. 142€–420€ double. Rates include breakfast. *Vaporetto:* Ferrovia (from train station cross Scalzi Bridge on left and take a right). **Amenities:** Restaurant; bar; babysitting; concierge; room service; free Wi-Fi.

MODERATE/INEXPENSIVE

Ai Due Fanali ★ Originally a wooden oratory frequented by fishermen and farmers (later rebuilt), this beguiling hotel features small but artsy rooms, even for Venice: Headboards have been hand-painted by a local artist, exposed wood beams crisscross the ceiling, vintage drapes add a cozy feel, and work by 16th-century Mannerist painter Jacopo Palma the Younger adorns the public areas. Bathrooms are embellished with terra-cotta tiles and Carrera marble. The location is close to the train station, and the roof terrace is the best place to soak up a city panorama (breakfast is served here). It's incredibly popular—book months ahead.

Campo San Simeon Profeta 946. www.aiduefanali.com. ✆ **041/718490.** 16 units. 85€–165€ double. Rates include breakfast. Closed most of Jan. *Vaporetto:* Ferrovia (cross Scalzi Bridge over Grand Canal; continue straight, take 2nd left to Campo San Simeon Profeta). **Amenities:** Bar; concierge; room service; free Wi-Fi.

Al Ponte Mocenigo ★★★ This gem of a hotel shows it is possible to live that Golden Age Venetian fantasy without breaking the bank (rates are a real bargain in the low season). The especially spacious rooms here are pure 18th-century Venice with big beds, Murano glass chandeliers, and varnished furniture in pastel greens, creams, and golds. Traditional ceiling beams (in the second-floor rooms) and original Venetian wood and stone floors complete the effect. Breakfasts—served in an enchanting interior courtyard when weather allows—are substantial, with bacon, scrambled eggs, and sausage in addition to all the usual cheeses, fruits, and cold cuts. Another huge plus: it's steps away from the Stan Stae *vaporetto* stop, meaning easy transfers to/from the airport and elsewhere along the Grand Canal. Advanced reservations highly recommended. Note that there is usually a discount for paying in cash.

Fondamenta Mocenigo 2063. alpontemocenigo.com. ✆ **041/5244797.** 10 units. 100€–225€ double. Rates include breakfast. *Vaporetto:* San Stae. **Amenities:** Bar; babysitting; concierge (24 hr.); free Wi-Fi.

Cannaregio

EXPENSIVE

Al Ponte Antico ★★★ Yes it's expensive, but this is one of the most exclusive hotels in Venice, steps from the Rialto Bridge, with a private wharf on the Grand Canal—to indulge your James Bond fantasy, look no further. Part of the attraction is its relatively small size; with just seven rooms, it feels far more intimate than most hotels in this price range, and service is always superior. Rococo wallpaper, rare tapestries, elegant beds, and Louis XV–style furnishings make this place seem like Versailles on the water. The building was originally a 16th-century *palazzo;* one of the many highlights is the charming balcony where breakfast is served, and where Bellinis are offered in the evenings.

Calle dell'Aseo 5768. www.alponteantico.com. ✆ **041/2411944.** 7 units. 250€–620€ double. Rates include breakfast. *Vaporetto:* Rialto (walk up Calle Large Mazzini, take 2nd left to cross Campo San Bartolomeo; walk north on Salizada S.G. Grisostomo to Calle dell'Aseo on left). **Amenities:** Bar; concierge; room service; free Wi-Fi.

MODERATE

Arcadia ★★★ This sensational boutique hotel set in a 17th-century *palazzo* has an appealing blend of old and new: The theme is Byzantium east-meets-west, a mix of Venetian and Asian style, but rooms are full of cool modern touches: rainfall showers, air-conditioning, flatscreen TVs, bathrobes, and posh toiletries, with a lobby crowned with a Murano glass chandelier. It's a 5-minute walk from the train station.

Rio Terà San Leonardo 1333. www.hotelarcadia.net. ✆ **041/717355.** 17 units. 119€–360€ double. Rates include breakfast. *Vaporetto:* Guglie (turn left into Rio Terà San Leonardo; Arcadia is 30m [98 ft.] on left). **Amenities:** Bar; concierge; room service; free Wi-Fi.

INEXPENSIVE

Combo Venezia ★★ This excellent hostel is tucked away at the northern end of Cannaregio in the restored Ex Convento dei Crociferi. It's a quiet spot a little out the way, but only a 10- to 15-minute stroll from the Rialto and the Grand Canal. The elegant, cloistered courtyard is a tranquil place to hang out, while the on-site bar-restaurant usually offers good deals (especially on *cicchetti*). When it comes to the rooms, it's more like a budget boutique hotel than a traditional hostel. All of the rooms (twins, doubles, and apartments) have individual beds and an en-suite bathroom with shower, while some also have their own kitchenettes (it does have dorms, but these have been closed since the COVID epidemic—check the website for the latest).

Campo dei Gesuiti 4878. thisiscombo.com/it/location/venezia. ✆ **041/5286103.** 130 units. 85€–178€ double. Rates include breakfast. *Vaporetto:* Fondamente Nove (walk straight up Campo dei Gesuit and it's on the left). **Amenities:** Bar; concierge; self-service laundry; shared kitchen; free Wi-Fi.

Giudecca

INEXPENSIVE

Generator Venice ★ It's worth the trek over to the tranquil island of Giudecca to stay in one of the city's best hostels. Set inside an old warehouse on the waterfront, Generator offers relatively stylish dorms with bunks (one dorm is female-only), as well as comfy en suite doubles with air-conditioning and canal views. There are also private three-bed and four-bed rooms, with shared bathrooms, that work out a bit cheaper. The bar, restaurant, and waterside terrace are great places to hang out, with happy hour daily 6:30 to 8:30pm.

Fondamenta Zitelle 86. staygenerator.com. ✆ **041/8778288.** 26 units. 80€–250€ double; 15€–56€ dorm. Rates include breakfast. *Vaporetto:* Zitelle (walk right along the canal side, Fondamenta Croce/Zitelle, for about 525ft./160m, and the hostel will be on the left, overlooking the water). **Amenities:** Bar; restaurant; concierge; free Wi-Fi.

WHERE TO EAT IN VENICE

Eating cheaply in Venice is not easy, though it's by no means impossible. The city's reputation for mass-produced menus, poor service, and overpriced food is, sadly, well warranted, and if you've been traveling in other parts of the country, you may be a little disappointed here. Having said that, everything is relative—this is still Italy, after all—and you'll find plenty of excellent dining options in Venice. As a basic rule, value for money tends to increase the farther you travel away from Piazza San Marco, and anything described as a *menù turistico,* while cheaper than à la carte, is rarely any good in Venice (exceptions noted below). Note also that compared with Rome and other points south, Venice is a city of early meals: You should be seated by 7:30 to 8:30pm. Most kitchens close at 10 or 10:30pm, even though the restaurant may stay open later.

San Marco

EXPENSIVE

Bistrot de Venise ★★★ VENETIAN It may look a bit like a wood-paneled French bistro, but the menu here is old-school Venetian, specializing in rare wines and historical recipes from the 14th to 18th centuries. It's gimmicky but it works; think fennel soup, homemade pasta with goose sauce and pine nuts, and almond-crusted sturgeon in a black grape sauce, with a yellow garlic and almond pudding. The four-course "classic and historic" tasting menu is a splurge, but we recommend it as the best introduction.

4685 Calle dei Fabbri. www.bistrotdevenise.com. ✆ **041/5236651.** Entrees 26€–42€; 4-course tasting menu 94€; 7-course tasting menu 150€. Daily noon–3pm and 7pm–11:30pm (bar 11am–11pm). *Vaporetto:* Rialto (turn right along canal, cross footbridge over Rio San Salvador, turn left onto Calle Bembo, which becomes Calle dei Fabbri; Bistrot is about 5 blocks ahead).

Gritti Terrace ★★ ITALIAN/VENETIAN One of the city's most famous restaurants remains one of its most magical experiences, despite the high prices. First-time Venice visitors in particular should not miss the chance to dine on this venerable deck overlooking the Grand Canal on a sunny day (now part of the year-round Club del Doge restaurant). The view across to Santa Maria della Salute is spectacular (the signature

BÀCARI & CICCHETTI

One of the essential culinary experiences of Venice is trawling the countless neighborhood bars known as ***bàcari,*** where you can stand or sit with *tramezzini* (small, triangular white-bread half-sandwiches filled with everything from thinly sliced meats and tuna salad to cheeses and vegetables) and ***cicchetti*** (tapas-like finger foods, such as calamari rings, fried olives, potato croquettes, or grilled polenta squares), traditionally washed down with a small glass of wine, Veneto Prosecco, or a spritz (a cocktail of Prosecco and orange-flavored Aperol). All of the above will cost approximately 1.50€ to 6€ if you stand at the bar, as much as double when seated. Bar food usually sells out by late afternoon, so while it can make a great lunch, don't rely on it for dinner. A concentration of popular, well-stocked bars can be found along the **Mercerie** shopping strip that connects Piazza San Marco with the Rialto Bridge; on the always lively **Campo San Luca** (look for Bar Torino, Bar Black Jack, or the character-filled Leon Bianco wine bar); and on **Campo Santa Margherita.**

"Basil-i-ca" cocktail was inspired by the church). The menu features light salads, pasta, risotto, and platters of seasonal seafood. A sumptuous afternoon tea is also served, along with the usual selection of Champagne, Bellini, and Negroni cocktails. Reservations required.

Campo Santa Maria del Giglio 2467 (Gritti Palace Hotel). www.clubdeldoge.com. ✆ **041/794611.** Entrees 24€–60€. Apr–Oct daily noon–10:30pm; closed Nov–Mar. *Vaporetto:* Santa Maria del Giglio.

MODERATE

Ai Mercanti ★★★ VENETIAN/INTERNATIONAL Nadia Locatello's lauded restaurant pioneered the "gastrosteria" concept (based on the French "bistronomie"), where gourmet dishes are created from relatively simple (and cheap-ish) ingredients. Though it's not a budget restaurant, you'll definitely get your money's worth here, with creative dishes—such as croaker fish with cauliflower and candied lemon, cod in coconut and lemongrass spicy soup, and the signature "apparently crispy" egg—a little cheaper than they'd be at similarly feted spots. Dinner is served in two shifts: Tables are available at 7pm and 7:30pm for 2 hours, with a second sitting at 9pm and 9:30pm (reservations required online). Another plus: They offer excellent wines by the glass, not just the "house" pours.

Corte Coppo 4346/a (off Calle dei Fuseri). www.aimercanti.it. ✆ **041/5238269.** Entrees 14€–28€. Tues–Sat 12:30–3pm and 7–10pm (closed Jan). *Vaporetto:* Rialto.

Rosticceria San Bartolomeo ★ DELI/VENETIAN Also known as Rosticceria Gislon, this no-frills spot is incredibly popular with locals, with a handful of small tables and bar stools, plus bigger tables in the upstairs dining room (which tends to be quieter). Don't be fooled by appearances. The food here is excellent, with a range of grilled fish and cheap seafood pastas and a tasty "*mozzarella in carrozza*" (fried cheese sandwich; 2.50€). Note that food displayed on the countertop is reheated to order but still tastes good. Otherwise just sit at the counter and soak up the animated scene, as cooks chop, customers chat, and people come and go.

Calle della Bissa 5424. ✆ **041/5223569.** Entrees 11€–20€ (pasta downstairs 7€–11€, *cicchetti* 2€–4€). Daily 9am–9:30pm. *Vaporetto:* Rialto (with bridge at your back on San Marco side, walk straight to Campo San Bartolomeo; take underpass to your left marked sottoportego della bissa; *rosticceria* is at 1st corner on right; look for gislon above the entrance).

Castello

EXPENSIVE

Al Covo ★★ SEAFOOD/VENETIAN For years, this high-quality Venetian restaurant from Diane and Cesare Benelli has been deservingly popular with American food writers and TV chefs. It features two cozy dining rooms adorned with art (plus some outdoor seating in summer), but it's the food that takes center stage here: fresh fish from the lagoon or the Adriatic, fruits and vegetables from local farms, and meat sourced from the esteemed Falaschi butchery. The pasta, desserts, and sauces are

tours FOR FOODIES

While it's relatively easy to explore Venice's culinary scene solo, it can be fun and enlightening to enlist the services of a local guide. Indie outfit **The Roman Guy** (the romaguy.com; ✆ **06/94804747**) offers more focused evening food tours in Cannaregio (85€ for 2½ hr.), while **Food Tours of Venice** (foodtoursofvenice.com; ✆ **393/1670961**) offers Rialto and Jewish Ghetto culinary tours (from 89€). **Cesarine** (cesarine.com), Italy's oldest network of home cooks, runs excellent cooking classes in Venice, as well as lunches in local homes, market tours, and wine tastings.

all homemade. Begin with Venetian *saor* (sweet-and-sour fish and shellfish) or fried zucchini flowers, followed by fresh monkfish with pancetta on a celeriac fondue, or deep-fried scampi, calamari, and baby sole. Diane's desserts might include rustic pear and prune cake with a grappa-cinnamon sauce or green apple sorbet with Calvados.

Campiello della Pescheria 3968. www.ristorantealcovo.com. ✆ **041/5223812.** Reservations required. Entrees 22€–31€. Thurs–Mon 12:30–3:30pm (kitchen closes 2pm) and 7:30pm–midnight (kitchen closes 10pm). Closed usually Jan and 10 days in Aug. *Vaporetto:* Piazza San Marco (walk along Riva degli Schiavoni toward Arsenale, and take 3rd narrow street on left, Calle della Pescaria, after Hotel Metropole).

Alle Corone ★★★ SEAFOOD/VENETIAN This is one of Venice's finest restaurants, an elegant 19th-century dining room inside the Hotel Ai Reali and overlooking the canal. Start with grilled artichokes with blueberry gel and chicory (26€) before moving on to risotto with saffron, pigeon, and coffee powder (28€) or main courses such as turbot fillet in pistachio crust with cauliflower cream, or guinea fowl leg with red onion, Roman cabbage, and tangerines. To finish, the homemade tiramisu or crème brulée is spectacular. Reservations recommended.

Campo della Fava 5527 (Hotel Ai Reali). www.ristoranteallecorone.com. ✆ **041/2410253.** Entrees 26€–35€; 6-course tasting menu 100€. Daily noon–2:30pm and 7–10:30pm (closed Wed and Jan). *Vaporetto:* Rialto (walk east along Calle Larga Mazzini, turn left on Merceria, then right on Calle Stella to the hotel).

Local ★★★ SEAFOOD/VENETIAN One of several newish, contemporary restaurants in Venice serving inventive menus. In an elegant space with mint green walls and original timbered ceilings, Chef Salvatore Sodano serves a seven-course (110€) or nine-course seasonal menu (150€) that might feature traditional *cicchetti,* sushi, blue crab. and entrees such as risotto with smoked butter, eel and herring caviar, or duck with black cabbage and persimmon.

Salizzada dei Greci 3303. www.ristorantelocal.com. ✆ **041/2411128.** Tasting menus: 7-course 110€, 9-course 150€. Mon and Fri–Sat noon–2pm and 7–10:30pm; Thurs and Sun 7–10:30pm (closed Tues and Wed). *Vaporetto:* S. Marco-San Zaccaria A (walk north along Calle de la Pietà then Calle Bosello and turn right on Salizzada dei Greci—the restaurant is on the left just before the canal).

Osteria Alle Testiere ★★★ ITALIAN/VENETIAN This tiny restaurant (with only nine tables) is the connoisseur's choice (and an alleged favorite of Meryl Streep, Emily Blunt, and Stanley Tucci) for fresh fish and seafood, with a menu that changes daily. Dinner is served at two seatings (reservations are essential), where you choose from appetizers such as swordfish carpaccio or clams that seem to have been plucked straight from the sea. Fresh fish fillets with aromatic herbs are always an exceptional main choice, but the pastas—like smoked ravioli with prawns and curry, or spaghetti with clams—are superb. Top things off with homemade peach pie or chestnut pudding. In peak season, make reservations at least 1 month ahead, and note that the second seating offers a less-rushed experience.

Calle del Mondo Novo 5801. www.osterialletestiere.it. ✆ **041/5227220.** Entrees 25€–55€; many types of fish sold by weight. Tues–Sat 12:30–1:30pm, dinner seatings 7 and 9:30pm; closed Jan. *Vaporetto:* Rialto or San Marco. Look for Salizada San Lio (west of Campo Santa Maria Formosa), and from there ask for Calle del Mondo Novo.

Dorsoduro

EXPENSIVE

Locanda Montin ★★ VENETIAN Montin was the famous ex-hangout of Peggy Guggenheim in the 1950s, and has been frequented by Jimmy Carter, Robert De Niro, and Brad Pitt, among many other celebs. Is the food still any good? Well, yes. Grab a table in the wonderfully serene back garden (completely covered by an arching trellis), itself a good reason to visit, and sample Venetian classics like sardines in *saor* (a marinade of vinegar, wine, onion, and raisins), and an exquisite *seppie in nero* (cuttlefish cooked in its ink). For a main course, it's hard to beat the crispy sea bass *(branzino)* or legendary monkfish, while the lemon sorbet with vodka is a perfect tart conclusion to any meal.

Fondamenta di Borgo 1147. www.locandamontin.com. ✆ **041/5227151.** Entrees 21€–30€. Daily 12:15–2:30pm and 7:15–10pm (usually closed Nov–Feb). *Vaporetto:* Ca'Rezzonico (walk straight along Calle Lunga San Barnaba, then turn left along Fondamenta di Borgo).

Osteria Enoteca Ai Artisi ★★★ VENETIAN This unpretentious, family-owned *osteria* and *enoteca* is one of the best dining experiences in Venice, with a menu that changes daily according to market offerings (the fish market is closed Mon, so no fish is served that day). Grab a table by the canal and feast on octopus salad, swordfish steak, and an amazing buttery beef cheek with corn polenta, or opt for one of the wonderful pastas (such as fettuccine with spider crab). It's a tiny place, so reservations are recommended.

Fondamenta della Toletta 1169A. www.enotecaartisti.com. ✆ **041/5238944.** Entrees 25€–29€. Tues–Sat 12:45–2:45pm, dinner seatings 7–9pm and 9:30–11pm. *Vaporetto:* Accademia (walk around Accademia, turn right on Calle Gambara; at Rio di San Trovaso, turn left on Fondamenta Priuli; take 1st bridge onto road leading into Fondamenta della Toletta).

Canalside dining at Osteria Enoteca Ai Artisi.

INEXPENSIVE

Osteria Al Squero ★★★ WINE BAR/VENETIAN This enticing *osteria* with perhaps the most beguiling view in Venice is opposite the Squero di San Trovaso (p. 422). Sip coffee or wine and nibble *cicchetti* while observing the activity at the medieval gondola boatyard and workshop, on the other side of the Rio di San Trovaso (drinks served in glasses inside, but in plastic cups if you want to stand outside). It's essentially a place for a light lunch or *aperitivi* rather than a full meal. Snack on delights such as Carnia smoked sausage, *baccalà* (cod) crostini, anchovies, blue cheese, tuna, and sardines in *saor* for a total of around 13€ to 16€ per person. Spritz from 2.50€.

Fondamenta Nani 943–944. ✆ **335/6007513.** *Cicchetti* 1.50€–2.80€ per piece. Thurs–Tues 11am–8:30pm. *Vaporetto:* Zattere (walk west along water to Rio di San Trovaso and turn right up Fondamenta Nani).

San Polo

EXPENSIVE

Wistèria ★★★ VENETIAN One of the city's newer batch of Michelin-starred restaurants, Wistèria was established by partners Andrea Martin and Massimiliano (Max) Rossetti in 2019, with Chef Valerio Dallamano in the kitchen, and an outdoor space enhanced by blossoming wisteria in the spring. The menu is known for experimentation and innovation—expect lots of unusual shapes, colors, and ingredients and incredible flavors. For dinner there's usually a choice of two menus: the signature "Serendipity" eight-course menu and a slightly cheaper six-course tasting menu. Lunch (even cheaper) includes two courses, chosen by the chef, a glass of wine, and a bottle of water. Menus change seasonally but usually have a Venetian theme, with riffs on traditional *cicchetti* and *castradina* (a classic mutton soup) and creative dishes like "liquid ravioli Milanese style"; pink oyster and pomegranate; capon, hazelnut and calamansi; and boiled salami, red chicory, and horseradish—you get the picture.

Fondamenta del Forner 2908. www.wisteria-restaurant.com. ✆ **041/5243373.** Lunch menu (2 courses) 50€. Tasting menu (6 courses) 150€; Serendipity menu (8 courses) 180€. Mon and Tues 7–9pm; Fri–Sun noon–1:30pm and 7–9pm (usually closed Jan). *Vaporetto:* San Tomà (with your back to Grand Canal, walk up Calle del Traghetto Vecchio, and turn left on Calle del Campanile; at the canal turn right on Fondamenta del Forner, and the restaurant will be ahead on the right).

MODERATE

Do Spade ★ VENETIAN It's tough to find dining this authentic so close to the Rialto Bridge these days, but Do Spade ("Two Swords") has been around since 1448 (Casanova ate here). Most locals come for the *cicchetti,* small plates such as fried calamari, its famed *polpetta di spianata calabra* (meatballs of Calabrian sausage, smoked cheese and potatoes), and salted cod (1.50€–3.50€), and decent Italian wines (3€ a glass). The more formal restaurant section is also worth a try, with seafood highlights including a delicately prepared monkfish, scallops served with fresh zucchini, and rich seafood lasagna. The seasonal pumpkin ravioli is one of the best dishes in the city.

Calle de le Do Spade 859. www.cantinadospade.com. ✆ **041/5210574.** Entrees 15€–24€. Daily 10am–3pm and 6–10pm. *Vaporetto:* Rialto Mercato (with your back to Grand Canal, walk up Ruga Vecchia San Giovanni, turn right on Ruga dei Spezieri; at end turn left on Calle de le Beccarie O Panataria, then take 2nd right onto covered Sottoportego do Spade).

INEXPENSIVE

Antico Forno ★★★ ITALIAN/PIZZA Venice is not known for pizza, partly because fire codes restrict the use of traditional wood-burning ovens, but the big, fluffy-crusted pies here are the best in the city. Little more than a hole-in-the-wall (takeout only), Antico Forno has been selling pizza by the slice since 2001, both thick- and thin-crust (as well as excellent craft beers). Its "La Pizzaccia-style" pizza is a soft focaccia topped with fresh chopped tomatoes, *mozzarella fior di latte* (from Treviso farms), and everything from Trevisan sausage to gorgonzola and mushrooms.

Ruga Rialto 973. www.anticofornovenezia.it. ✆ **041/5204110.** Pizza slices 5.50€–9€. Daily 11am–10pm (usually closed Jan). *Vaporetto:* Rialto Mercato (walk into Campo de la Pescaria, follow Ruga Vecchia San Giovanni for around 300m/984 ft., just beyond Calle del Paradiso).

Do Mori ★★★ WINE BAR/VENETIAN Serving good wine and *cicchetti* since 1462, Do Mori is above all a fun place to have a genuine Venetian experience, a small, dimly lit *bàcari* that can barely accommodate 10 people standing up. Sample the baby octopus and ham on mango, lard-smothered *crostini,* and pickled onions speared with salty anchovies, or opt for the *tramezzini* (tiny sandwiches). Local TV (and BBC) star Francesco Da Mosto is a regular, but note that this institution is very much on the well-trodden tourist trail—plenty of *cicchetti* tours stop by in the early evening. Local wine is 3€ to 5€ per glass. Cash only.

Calle Do Mori 429 (also Calle Galeazza 401). ✆ **041/5225401.** *Tramezzini* and *cicchetti* 2€–3.50€ per piece. Mon–Fri 8am–7:30pm; Sat 8am–5pm (June–Aug closed daily 2–4:30pm). *Vaporetto:* Rialto Mercato (with your back to Grand Canal, walk up Ruga Vecchia San Giovanni, turn right on Calle Galeazza).

La Bottiglia ★★ WINE BAR/VENETIAN This more contemporary *bàcari* features wonderful cheese and meat boards, a well-curated wine list (exceptional Amarone red wine is served here), and excellent panini sandwiches stuffed with prosciutto and cheeses. As you might expect, it's a tiny place, with a few tables outside near the Rio San Stin and just five bar stools inside (most visitors stand).

Campo San Stin (Calle de la Chiesa) 2537. ✆ **041/4762426.** Sandwiches from 7€. Daily 10am–11pm. *Vaporetto:* Ferrovia or San Toma.

Santa Croce

EXPENSIVE

Zanze XVI ★★★ ITALIAN/VENETIAN Contemporary *osteria* with a simple but elegant dining room featuring exposed wood beams and wood-block tables. It's helmed by Chef Nicola Dinato, whose dishes are created daily depending on fresh ingredients available at local markets and gardens. The menu usually includes fresh fish, with dishes such as pilchard tortelli with chard and pecorino cheese; risotto with oysters and prosecco; and sea bass in black squid ink.

Fondamenta dei Tolentini 231. zanze.it. ✆ **041/715394.** Entrees 25€–40€. Tasting menus: 5-course 110€, 7-course 130€. Tues–Sun noon–2pm and 7:30–10pm. *Vaporetto:* Piazzale Roma (turn left and walk along the Grand Canal, crossing two bridges before turning right on Fondamenta dei Tolentini).

MODERATE

Osteria La Zucca ★★ ITALIAN/VEGETARIAN Though not specifically a vegetarian restaurant, the romantic, canal-side dining room of La Zucca (aka "the pumpkin") does offer a huge range of high-quality vegetable dishes, from the signature pumpkin-and-ricotta flan and potato cakes to zucchini-and-almond lasagna. The seasonal menu (Italian only, but the staff speak English) also includes plenty of meat dishes, such as succulent rabbit with white wine and lamb with spices. End with one of the homemade cakes—pear cake with ginger or the "spices tart" with red wine and raspberry.

Calle dello Spezier 1762. lazucca.it. ✆ **041/5241570.** Reservations recommended by phone 11am–noon and 6–7pm, up 20 days in advance. Entrees 9€–24€. Mon–Sat 12:30–2:30pm and 7–10:30pm. *Vaporetto:* San Stae (walk down Salizada San Stae, turn right on Calle del Tentor; turn left at Calle Del Meglio and follow it as it turns right).

EATING cheaply IN VENICE

You don't have to eat in a fancy restaurant to enjoy good food in Venice. Prepare a picnic, and while you eat alfresco you can observe life in the city's *campi* or the aquatic parade on its main thoroughfare, the Grand Canal.

Mercato Rialto Venice's principal open-air market has two parts, beginning with the **produce section,** with many stalls unfolding north on the San Polo side of the Rialto Bridge. Vendors are here Monday to Saturday 7am to 1pm (some stay later). Behind these stalls a few permanent food stores sell cheese, cold cuts, and bread. At the market's farthest point, the covered **fish market** is still redolent of the days when it was one of the Mediterranean's great fish bazaars. The fish merchants take Monday off and work mornings only.

Campo Santa Margherita Every Tuesday through Saturday from 8:30am to 1pm open-air stalls set up on this spacious Dorsoduro *campo*, selling fresh fruit and vegetables. A conventional supermarket, **Conad City** (Mon–Sat 7:30am–8:30pm; Sun 9am–2pm and 4–7:30pm) is just off the *campo* in the direction of nearby Campo San Barnaba, at no. 3017.

San Barnaba Venice's heavily photographed **floating market** (mostly fruit and vegetables) now operates from just one boat moored off San Barnaba at the Ponte dei Pugni in Dorsoduro. This market is open daily 8am to 1pm and 3:30 to 7:30pm, except Wednesday afternoon and Sunday.

The Best Picnic Spots Given its aquatic roots, you won't find much in the way of green space in Venice (if you are desperate for green, walk 30 minutes past San Marco along the water to the **Giardini Pubblici,** Venice's only green park). An easier alternative is to find one of the larger *campi* that have park benches, such as **Campo San Giacomo dell'Orio,** in the quiet *sestiere* of Santa Croce. The two most central are **Campo Santa Margherita** in Dorsoduro and **Campo San Polo** in San Polo.

Near La Salute Church in Dorsoduro, the **Punta della Dogana** (Customs House) is a prime viewing site at the mouth of the Grand Canal. Perch on the embankment here and watch the water activity against a canvaslike backdrop deserving of the Accademia Museum. In this same area, **Campo San Vio** (near the Guggenheim) is another superb spot directly on the Grand Canal; it boasts two benches and the option of sitting on an untrafficked small bridge.

A bit farther afield, you can take the *vaporetto* to Burano and then a 5-minute ride on no. 9 to the near-deserted island of **Torcello.** Bring a basketful of bread, cheese, and wine to reenact the romantic scene between Katharine Hepburn and Rossano Brazzi from the 1955 film *Summertime.*

INEXPENSIVE

Bacareto da Lele ★★★ WINE BAR/VENETIAN This tiny hole-in-the-wall *bacaro* is worth seeking out for its cheap, fresh snacks, sandwiches, and *cicchetti.* Tiny glasses *(ombras)* of wine and Prosecco are just 1€ to 1.70€—there are no seats, so do as the locals do and grab a space by the canal while you sip and nibble. Opt for a tiny porchetta or bacon and artichoke panini (1€–2.50€), antipasti plates (cheese and salami; from

1.50€) or a freshly baked crostini for 1.60€ to 2.50€. Expect long lines here in peak season—the secret is definitely out.

Campo dei Tolentini 183. No phone. *Cicchetti* 1.60€–2.50€ per piece. Mon–Fri 6am–8pm; Sat 6am–2pm. *Vaporetto:* Piazzale Roma (walk left along Grand Canal past Ponte della Costituzione into Giardino Papadopoli; turn right on Fonadmenta Papadopoli then left. Cross park at 1st bridge; next canal is Rio del Tolentini, with the campo across the bridge and Da Lele on SW corner).

Cantina Arnaldi ★★★ WINE BAR/VENETIAN This welcoming *bàcari* offers some of the freshest snacks in the city, washed down with quality wines, spritz, and Prosecco (3€–7€). The thing to order is the delicious board of cheese and cold cuts, all sourced from the region and enhanced with fresh fruits, fig jam, local bread, and a small pot of roasted potatoes. It's a small place, so reservations are recommended if you want a table (there are also a handful of barstools).

Salizada San Pantalon 35. www.cantinaarnaldi.com. ✆ **041/718989.** *Cicchetti* 2€–6€ per piece, focaccias 18€–22€. Thurs–Tues 11:30am–midnight. *Vaporetto:* San Toma' (walk up Calle Traghetto Vecchio Galeazza, turn left at Calle del Campanile and right on Fondamenta del Forner; turn left and cross canal on Calle Gozzi, follow to Calle Crosera; turn right and walk straight, crossing Rio de San Pantalon and on to Salizada San Pantalon).

Cannaregio

EXPENSIVE

Dama ★★★ VENETIAN/SEAFOOD Overlooking the busy Canale di Cannaregio in the historic Hotel Ca' Bonfadini (and a less than 10-min. walk from the station), this contemporary Venetian kitchen is one of the best in the city. Chef Lorenzo Cogo focuses on local seafood, using modern techniques and creative combinations; think langoustine with hazelnuts miso and sesame to start, black macaroni and spiked squid with ginseng and buffalo stracciatella for first course, and confit mullet with sweet and sour sauce, vermouth and plum and rosemary for an entree. The long tables inside have been fashioned from old Venetian mooring posts.

Fondamenta Savorgnan 461. www.damavenice.com. ✆ **041/0986297.** Entrees 25€–40€; tasting menus 90€–140€. Daily 12:20–2:30pm and 7:30–10pm. *Vaporetto:* Crea (walk left along the canal, with the water on your left, and the restaurant is around 200m/750 ft. on the right).

La Giudecca

MODERATE

La Palanca ★★ SEAFOOD/VENETIAN For simple, no-frills Venetian cuisine with a stellar view across to the spires of Dorsoduro, this Giudecca spot, well off the tourist trail, is hard to beat. Grab a table on the waterside for coffee and cake (most locals take breakfast standing at the bar), or have a sandwich, a more substantial lunch, or sunset spritz (meals usually served noon to 2:30pm; it's just *cicchetti* and drinks thereafter).

Fondamenta Sant'Eufemia 448. ✆ **041/5287719.** Entrees 9€–20€. Mon–Sat 7am–9pm. Reserve for lunch. *Vaporetto:* Palanca (restaurant is 80m/262 ft. along canal to left).

Murano & Burano

The glass-making island of **Murano** isn't especially known for its food, though there are plenty of decent trattorias scattered along the main streets. For a real treat, make for **La Fornace ★★** (Fondamenta Manin 1; lafornacemurano.it; ✆ **041/5275408;** Mon and Wed noon–6pm, Thurs–Sun noon–5:30pm and 6:30–10pm), a spacious contemporary restaurant in a restored glass furnace, with gorgeous views of the lagoon. It's best known for traditional Venetian dishes and fresh seafood.

The island of **Burano** makes a wonderful culinary excursion for its seafood restaurants, notably **Trattoria al Gatto Nero ★★**, the "Black Cat" (Fondamenta della Guidecca 88; www.gattonero.com; ✆ **041/730120;** Tues–Sat 12:30–3pm and 7–9:30pm, Sun 12:30–3pm; usually closed Nov), around since the 1960s. Signature dishes include Burano-style risotto (made with *ghiozzi,* a small, long-bodied fish from the lagoon), local turbot and seabass, and tagliolini with spider crab. Another favorite is **Trattoria da Romano ★★** (Via Baldassarre Galuppi 221; daromano.it; ✆ **041/730030;** Mon and Wed–Sat noon–3pm and 6:30–11:30pm, Sun noon–3pm), its dining room adorned with over 400 art-works donated by visiting artists since the 1940s.

Gelato

Is the gelato any good in Venice? Italians might demur, but by international standards, the answer is most definitely yes. As always, gelato parlors aimed exclusively at tourists are notorious for poor quality and extortionate prices. Avoid places near Piazza San Marco altogether. Below are two of our favorite spots in the city.

Il Doge ★★ GELATO Contender for best gelato in Venice, Il Doge has a convenient location at the southern end of Campo Santa Margherita. These guys use only natural, homemade flavors and ingredients, from an exceptional spicy chocolate to the house specialty, Crema de Doge, a rich mix of eggs, cream, and oranges. Try a refreshing *granita* in summer.

Campo Santa Margherita 3058, Dorsoduro. ✆ **041/5234607.** Cones and cups 2€–6€. Daily 11am–10pm (usually closed late-Dec to Jan). *Vaporetto:* Ca'Rezzonico.

La Mela Verde ★★ GELATO The popular rival to Il Doge for best scoop in the city, with sharp flavors and all the classics done sensationally well: pistachio, chocolate, *nocciola,* and the mind-blowing lemon and basil. The overall champions: *mela verde* (green apple), like creamy, frozen fruit served in a cup, and the addictive tiramisu.

Fondamenta de L'Osmarin 4977, Castello. ✆ **349/1957924.** Cones or cups from 2€. Daily 11am–11pm (usually closed mid-Nov to mid-Feb). *Vaporetto:* Zaccaria.

VENICE SHOPPING

In a city that for centuries has thrived almost exclusively on tourism, remember this: **Where you buy cheap, you get cheap.** Venetians, centuries-old merchants, aren't known for bargaining. You'll stand a better chance of getting a good deal if you pay in cash or buy more than one item. In our limited space below, we've listed some of the more reputable places to stock up on classic Venetian items.

Shopping Streets & Markets

A mix of low-end trinket stores and mid-market-to-upscale boutiques lines the narrow zigzagging **Mercerie** running north between Piazza San Marco and the Rialto Bridge. More expensive boutiques make for great window-shopping on **Calle Larga XXII Marzo,** the wide street that begins west of Piazza San Marco and wends its way to the expansive Campo Santo Stefano near the Accademia. The narrow **Frezzaria,** just west of Piazza San Marco and running north-south, offers a grab bag of bars, souvenir shops, and tony clothing stores like Louis Vuitton and Versace. The non-produce part of the **Rialto Market** is as good as it gets for basic souvenirs, such as cheap T-shirts, glow-in-the-dark plastic gondolas, and tawdry glass trinkets. The 3-day professional antiques market **Mercatino dell'Antiquariato** (www.mercatinocamposanmaurizio.it) takes place four to five times a year (usually Mar–Apr, May, Sept, Oct, and Dec; check website for dates) in Campo San Maurizio, San Marco.

Arts & Crafts

Venice is famous for local crafts that have been produced here for centuries and are hard to get elsewhere: the **glassware** from Murano, the **delicate lace** from Burano, and the *cartapesta* (papier-mâché) **Carnevale masks** you'll find in endless *botteghe* (shops), where you can watch artisans paint amid their wares.

Glassblower making a vase in Murano.

Now here's the bad news: There's such an overwhelming sea of cheap glass gewgaws that buying Venetian glass can become something of a turnoff (shipping and insurance costs make most things unaffordable; the alternative is to hand-carry anything fragile). Plus, there are so few women left on Burano willing to spend countless hours keeping alive the art of lacemaking that any pieces not produced by machine in China are sold at stratospheric prices; ditto the truly high-quality glass (although trinkets can be cheap and fun). The best place to buy glass is Murano itself—the **"Vetro Artistico Murano"** trademark guarantees its origin, but expect to pay as much as 60€ for just a wineglass.

Atelier Segalin di Daniela Ghezzo ★★ Founded in 1932 by master cobbler Antonio Segalin and his son Rolando, this old leather shoe store is now run by Daniela Ghezzo (the star apprentice of Rolando), maker of exuberant handmade shoes and boots, from basic flats to crazy footwear designed for Carnevale (custom footwear from 650€–1,800€). Calle dei Fuseri 4365, San Marco. www.danielaghezzo.it. ✆ **041/5222115.** Mon–Fri 10am–1pm and 3–7pm; Sat 10am–1pm. *Vaporetto:* San Marco.

Il Grifone ★★★ Toni Peressin's handmade leather briefcases, bound notebooks, belts, and soft-leather purses have garnered quite a following, and justly so—his craftsmanship is magnificent (he makes everything in the workshop out back). Items start at around 25€. Fondamenta del Gaffaro 3516, Dorsoduro. www.ilgrifonevenezia.it. ✆ **041/5229452.** Tues and Fri 10am–6pm; Wed, Thurs, Sat 10am–1pm and 4–7pm. *Vaporetto:* Piazzale Roma.

Kartaruga ★★ Remember the creepy orgy scenes in Stanley Kubrick's film *Eyes Wide Shut*? The ornate masks used in the movie were made by the owners of this vaunted store. All manner of traditional, feathered, and animal masks are knocked out of their on-site workshop. Calle delle Bande 5369 (near Campo Santa Maria Formosa), Castello. kartaruga.it. ✆ **041/5210393.** Daily 10am–7pm. *Vaporetto:* San Zaccaria.

La Bottega dei Mascareri ★★ High-quality, creative masks—some based on Tiepolo paintings—have been crafted by brothers Sergio and Massimo Boldrin since 1984. Basic masks start at around 20€, but you'll pay over 75€ for a more innovative piece. The smaller, original branch lies at the foot of the Rialto Bridge (San Polo 80; ✆ **041/5223857**). Calle dei Saoneri 2720, San Polo. www.mascarer.com. ✆ **041/5242887.** Both locations daily 9am–6pm. *Vaporetto:* Rialto.

Marco Polo International ★ This vast showroom, just west of the Piazza San Marco, displays quality glass direct from Murano (although it's more expensive than if you buy on the island yourself), including plenty of easy-to-carry items such as paperweights and small dishes. Frezzaria 1644, San Marco. www.marcopolointernational.it. ✆ **041/5229295.** Daily 10am–7pm. *Vaporetto:* San Marco.

Books

Libreria Acqua Alta ★★★ Like a set on a Harry Potter movie, this venerable bookshop has become a tourist attraction as much for its museum-like atmosphere, its gondola filled with paperbacks, and its friendly cats as its books, though it's a great place to pick up rare and used tomes (especially in Italian). Get here early to avoid long lines. Calle Longa Santa Maria Formosa 5176b. ✆ **041/2960841.** Daily 9am–7:30pm. *Vaporetto:* San Marco or Ospedale.

ENTERTAINMENT & NIGHTLIFE

If you're looking for serious nocturnal action, you're in the wrong town—Verona and Padua are far livelier. Your best bet is to sit in moonlit **Piazza San Marco** and listen to the cafes' outdoor orchestras, with the floodlit basilica before you—the perfect opera set—though this pleasure comes with a hefty price tag. Other popular spots include **Campo San Bartolomeo,** at the foot of the Rialto Bridge (a zoo in high season), and **Campo San Luca.** For low prices and low pretension, the absolute best place to go is **Campo Santa Margherita,** a huge open *campo* between the train station and the Accademia Bridge.

Visit one of the tourist information centers for current English-language schedules of the month's special events. The monthly *Un Ospite di Venezia* is distributed free or online at **www.unospitedivenezia.it** and is extremely helpful but usually available only in the more expensive hotels.

Performing Arts & Live Music

Venice has a long and rich tradition of classical music; this was, after all, the home of Vivaldi. People dressed in period costumes stand around in heavily trafficked spots near San Marco and Rialto passing out brochures advertising classical music concerts, so you'll have no trouble finding up-to-date information.

Santa Maria della Pietà ★★ The so-called "Vivaldi Church," built between 1745 and 1760, holds concerts throughout the year, mostly performed by lauded ensemble **I Virtuosi Italiani;** check the website for specific dates. Tickets are usually 28€ to 35€ (with discounts online). Riva degli Schiavoni 3701, Castello. www.ivirtuositaliani.eu/chiesa-di-vivaldi. ✆ **041/5221120.** *Vaporetto:* San Zaccaria.

Teatro La Fenice ★★★ The opera season runs late November through June, but there are also classical concerts and ballet. Tickets are expensive for the major productions (110€–210€ for the gallery and 190€–240€ for a decent seat); budget travelers can opt for obstructed-view seats (from 35€). Campo San Fantin 1965, San Marco. www.teatrolafenice.it. ✆ **041/2424.** *Vaporetto:* Giglio.

Cafes

For tourists and locals alike, Venetian nightlife mainly centers on the many cafes in one of the world's most beautiful public squares: Piazza San Marco. It is also a most expensive and touristed place to linger over a spritz (the Venetian classic cocktail of Prosecco and orange-flavored Aperol), but it's a splurge that should not be dismissed too readily.

Caffè dei Frari ★★★ Established in 1870, this inviting bar and cafe overlooking the Frari church has walls still adorned with the original Art Nouveau murals, an antique wooden bar, and cozy upstairs. The whole

Interior of Teatro La Fenice.

place morphs into **Il Mercante Cocktail Bar** in the evenings (Sun 6pm–midnight; Tues–Thurs 6pm–1am; Fri–Sat 6pm–2am). Fondamenta dei Frari 2564, San Polo. www.ilmercantevenezia.com. ✆ **041/5241877.** Tues–Sat 9am–5pm. *Vaporetto:* San Tomà.

Caffè Florian ★★ Occupying prime *piazza* real estate since 1720, this is one of the world's oldest coffee shops, with a florid interior of 18th-century mirrors, frescoes, and statuary. Sitting at a table, expect to pay 11.50€ for a cappuccino, 22€ for a Bellini (Prosecco and fresh peach nectar in season), and 16€ for a spritz—add another 6€ per person if the orchestra plays (Mar–Nov). Standing at the bar is much cheaper (5.50€ for a cappuccino, 11.50€ for a Bellini, and so on). Piazza San Marco 57. www.caffeflorian.com. ✆ **041/5205641.** Mon–Thurs 10am–9pm; Fri–Sat 9am–11pm; Sun 9am–9pm. *Vaporetto:* San Marco.

Il Caffè (Caffè Rosso) ★★★ Established in the late 19th century, Il Caffè has a history almost as colorful as its clientele—a mix of students, aging regulars, and lost tourists. This old-fashioned, no-nonsense cafe/bar has reasonably priced drinks (spritz 3.50€) and sandwiches, and lots of seating on the *campo* (plus a small seating area inside). Cash only. Campo Santa Margherita 2963, Dorsoduro. www.cafferosso.it. ✆ **041/5287998.** Mon–Sat 7am–1am. *Vaporetto:* Ca'Rezzonico.

Pasticceria Tonolo ★ This tiny bakery has enjoyed a cult following since 1886 thanks to its deep-fried sweet treats (*frittelle,* Italian-style doughnuts, plus a vast range of sumptuous cakes and cookies; *frittelle*

1.30€–1.80€). Coffee is served in charming, antique blue German porcelain cups (standing room only). Calle San Pantalon 3764, Dorsoduro. ✆ **041/5237209.** Tues–Sat 7:30am–8pm; Sun 7:30am–1pm; often closed through Aug. *Vaporetto:* San Tomà.

Birreria, Wine & Cocktail Bars

Venice has never been a late-night clubbing hotspot. Evenings are better spent lingering over a late dinner, having a pint in a *birreria,* or nursing a glass of Prosecco in one of the pricey outdoor bars and cafes in Piazza San Marco or Campo Santa Margherita.

Al Prosecco ★★ Get acquainted with all things bubbly at this smart *enoteca,* a specialist, as you'd expect, in Veneto Prosecco. It features tasty *cicchetti* and plenty of outdoor tables from which to observe the laid-back Campo San Giacomo da l'Orio. Most drinks run 3€ to 5€. Campo San Giacomo da l'Orio 1503, Santa Croce. www.alprosecco.com. ✆ **041/5240222.** Mon–Sat 10am–10:30pm (closes 8pm in winter; closed Aug and Jan). *Vaporetto:* San Stae.

Bar Dandolo ★★ Doge Dandolo built his glorious Venetian Gothic palace three doors down from the Palazzo Ducale in the 14th century, and current occupier Hotel Danieli has been one of the most sumptuous hotels in Venice since 1822. Nestled amid marble columns on the ground floor, this classic Venice bar serves everything from velvet-capped cappuccinos and a traditional afternoon tea (daily 3–6pm) to a decadent Vesper Martini cocktail. You can also opt for an alfresco drink on the rooftop **Bar Terrazza Danieli** (Apr–Oct daily 3–11pm). Riva degli Schiavoni 4196, Castello. ✆ **041/5226480.** Daily 6:30am–1am (pianist plays daily 7pm–12:30am); usually closed Jan. *Vaporetto:* San Zaccaria.

Bar Longhi ★★★ The Gritti Palace Hotel really was the 16th-century palace of Doge Andrea Gritti, whose portrait graces one of the antiques-filled lounges (it remains the city's most expensive hotel since opening in 1895). Bar Longhi is the quintessential Venetian watering hole, with lavish decor (hand-sculptured mirrors, Murano glass appliqués, and a marble bar counter) plus paintings belonging to the school of the celebrated 18th-century Venetian artist Pietro Longhi. Afternoon tea, cocktails and champagne are served. Campo Santa Maria del Giglio 2467 (Gritti Palace Hotel), San Marco. www.marriott.com. ✆ **041/794611.** Daily 11am–1am. *Vaporetto:* Santa Maria del Giglio.

Harry's Bar ★ Possibly the most famous bar in Venice (and now a global chain), Harry's was established in 1931 by Giuseppe Cipriani and frequented by the likes of Ernest Hemingway and Charlie Chaplin. The Bellini was invented here in 1948 (along with *carpaccio* 2 years later); you can sip the signature concoction of freshly squeezed peach juice and Prosecco for a mere 22€. Go for the history but don't expect a five-star experience—most first-timers are surprised just how ordinary it looks inside (though the bow-tied waitstaff still look the part). It's more a restaurant than a bar these days, serving very expensive food (main courses 40€–45€), but just stick to the drinks. Calle Vallaresso 1323, San Marco. www.cipriani.com. ✆ **041/5285777.** Daily 10am–midnight; usually closed Jan. *Vaporetto:* Vallaresso.

Il Santo Bevitore ★★ Beer aficionados will be pleased to learn that Italy has a growing **craft beer** scene, and this local spot showcases the best brews from all over the country (many on tap). Sample brews from Milan's Birrificio Lambrate and Birrificio Extraomnes, Parma's Birra Toccalmatto, Udine's Borderline Brewery, and Veneto's very own Mesh Brewery. The small bar overlooks the Rio de Servi just off the main drag (Strada Nova), with a few benches outside for warmer weather. Fondamenta Diedo 2393, Cannaregio. www.ilsantobevitorepub.com. ✆ **335/8415771.** Daily 4pm–2am. *Vaporetto:* San Marcuola.

DAY TRIPS FROM VENICE

If you only have 3 days or so, you will probably want to spend them in the center of Venice. However, if you are here for a week—or on your second visit to the city—head over to the mainland to see some of the old towns that lie within the historic Veneto region.

Padua ★★★

40km (25 miles) W of Venice

Tucked away within the ancient heart of Padua lies one of the greatest artistic treasures in all Italy, the precious Giotto frescoes of the **Cappella degli Scrovegni.** Although the city itself is not especially attractive (it was largely rebuilt after bombing during World War II), don't be put off by the urban sprawl that now surrounds it; central Padua is refreshingly bereft of tourist crowds, a workaday Veneto town with a large student population and a small but intriguing ensemble of historic sights.

ESSENTIALS

ARRIVING The most efficient way to reach Padua is to take the **train** from Venice's Santa Lucia station. Trains depart every 10 to 20 minutes, and take 26 to 50 minutes depending on the class (4.70€–19€ one-way). Padua ("Padova" in Italian) station is a short walk north up Corso del Popolo from the Cappella degli Scrovegni and the old city.

VISITOR INFORMATION The **tourist office** at Vicolo Pedrocchi 9 is usually open Monday to Saturday 9am to 7pm and Sunday 10am to 4pm (www.turismopadova.it; ✆ **049/5207415**).

EXPLORING PADUA

The one unmissable sight in Padua is the **Cappella degli Scrovegni ★★★** (www.cappelladegliscrovegni.it; ✆ **049/2010020;** daily 9am–7pm) at Piazza Eremitani, an outwardly unassuming chapel commissioned in

A tranquil scene in Padua.

1303 by Enrico Scrovegni, a wealthy banker. Inside, however, the chapel is gloriously decorated with a cycle of frescoes by Florentine genius **Giotto,** depicting the lives of the Virgin Mary and Jesus and culminating in the Ascension and Last Judgment. Seeing Giotto's work in the flesh is spine-tingling; this is where he makes the decisive break with Byzantine art toward the realism and humanism that would define the Italian Renaissance.

Entrance to the chapel is limited, involving small groups of visitors spending 15 minutes in a climate-controlled airlock, used to stabilize the temperature, before going inside for another 15 to 20 minutes. To visit the chapel, you must **make a reservation at least 24 hours in advance** and arrive 45 minutes before the time on your ticket. Tickets cost 14€ (5€ for kids ages 6–17 and students under 27).

If you have time, try to take in Padua's other historic highlights. The vast **Palazzo della Ragione** on Piazza del Erbe (7€; Tues–Sun 9am–7pm, closes 6pm Nov–Jan) is an architectural marvel, a cavernous town hall completed in 1219 and decorated by frescoes by Nicola Miretto in the 15th century. The **Basilica di Sant'Antonio** (www.santantonio.org; **✆ 049/8225652;** free admission; daily 6:15am–7:30pm) on the Piazza del Santo, is the stately resting place of **St. Anthony of Padua,** the Portuguese Franciscan best known as the patron saint of finding things or lost people. While the exterior of the church is a bizarre mix of Byzantine, Romanesque, and Gothic styles, the interior is richly adorned with statuary and murals. Don't miss **Donatello**'s stupendous equestrian statue of the Venetian *condottiere* Gattamelata (Erasmo da Narni) in the piazza outside, the first large bronze sculpture of the Renaissance.

WHERE TO EAT

Padua offers plenty of places to eat and drink (Aperol was created here in 1919), and you'll especially appreciate the overall drop in prices compared to Venice. It's hard to match the location of **Bar Nazionale ★★**, Piazza del Erbe 40 (Mon and Sat 7am–10:30pm; Tues, Thurs, Fri 7am–11:30am; Wed 7am–midnight; Sun 9am–9:30pm), on the steps leading up to Palazzo della Ragione, but it's best for drinks and snacks (excellent *tramezzini* from 3€, panini from 4.50€, spritz 3.50€, and glasses of wine 3.50€–4€) rather than a full meal. For that, make for **Belle Parti ★★★**, Via Belle Parti 11, a short walk from Piazza dei Signori (www.ristorantebelleparti.it; ✆ **049/8751822;** Mon–Sat 12:30–2:30pm and 7:30–10:30pm), one of Padua's best restaurants. Set within the historic Palazzo Prosdocimi, it serves classic Veneto dishes and seafood (entrees 18€–28€).

Verona ★★

115km (71 miles) W of Venice

The affluent city of Verona, with its handsome red- and peach-colored medieval buildings and Roman ruins, is one of Italy's major tourist draws, though its appeal owes more to William Shakespeare than real history. He immortalized the city in his (totally fictional) *Romeo and Juliet, The Two Gentlemen of Verona,* and partly, *The Taming of the Shrew.* In spite of its popularity with visitors, Verona is not Venice; it's a booming commercial center with vibrant science and technology sectors.

ESSENTIALS

ARRIVING The best way to reach Verona from Venice is by **train.** Direct services depart every 30 minutes and take anywhere from 1 hour and 10 minutes to 2 hours and 20 minutes, depending on the type of train you catch (one-way tickets cost 10€–28€). From Verona station (Verona Porta Nuova), it's a 15-minute walk to the historic center.

VISITOR INFORMATION The **tourist office** at Via Leoncino 61 (Palazzo Barbieri) in Piazza Bra (www.visitverona.it; ✆ **045/8068680;** Mon–Sat 9am–5pm, Sun 10am–4pm) has maps and tour information.

EXPLORING VERONA

"Two households, both alike in dignity, in fair Verona…" So go the immortal opening lines of *Romeo and Juliet,* ensuring that the city has been a target for lovesick romantics ever since. Though Verona is crammed with genuine historic goodies, one of the most popular sites is the ersatz **Casa di Giulietta,** Via Cappello 23 (6€; Tues–Sun 9am–7pm, also open Mon June–Sept; reserve tickets at museiverona.com), a 14th-century house (with balcony, naturally), said to be the Capulets' home. In the courtyard, the chest of a bronze statue of Juliet has been polished to a gleaming sheen, thanks to a legend claiming that stroking her right breast brings good fortune. **Juliet's Wall,** at the entrance, is quite a spectacle,

Verona
Information
0 1/4 mi
0 250 m
Via Farinata
Piazza Vittorio Veneto
Via dei Millie
Ponte Catena
Piazza del Duomo
Ponte Pietra
Ponte Garibaldi
Via Pigna
Via Garibaldi
Via Forti
Via S. Chiara
Lungre Teodorico
Via Giusti
Via da Vico
Via Risorgimento
Via IV Novembre
Lungre Matteotti
Adige
Via Rosa
Sant'Anastasia
Via Sottoriva
Via della Repubblica
Ponte Risorgimento
Via Arsenale
Via Pontida
Via E. Corso
Piazza dei Signori
Via Arche Scaligeri
Ponte Nuovo
Corso Milano
San Zeno Maggiore
Via Carducci
Muro Pardi
Lungadige B. Rubele
Piazza delle Erbe
P. Bosari
Ponte Vittoria
Piazza Arsenale
Piazza S. Zeno
Via Rosmini
Regaste San Zeno
Via San Marco
Via Mazzini
Via Cappello
Via Stella
Corso Cavour
Ponte Scaligero
Cir. ne Maroncelli
Via S. Bernardino
Museo di Castelvecchio
Via S. Paolo
Ponte Navi
Arena
L. Leoncino
Via Mazza
Stradone A. Provoeo
Piazza Brà
Via Filippini
Via Campofiore
Via Saffi
Stradone Porta Palio
Via Manin
Via Alpini
Stradone S. Fermo
Via C. Scalzi
Via Pallone
Verona
Porta Palio
Via G. Marconi
Via Valverde
Via Montanari
Via del Pontiere
Lungre Capuleti
Rome
Via della Casa
Corso So. P. ta Nuova
Via Battisti
Via del Lanciere
Ponte Aleardi
Zoological Garden
To Stazione Porta Nuova Train Station
ATTRACTIONS
Arena di Verona 5
Basilica di San Zeno Maggiore 1
Casa di Giulietta 4
RESTAURANTS
Antica Bottega del Vino 3
Caffè Monte Baldo 2

covered with the scribbles of star-crossed lovers (though the corridor is periodically scrubbed clean of graffiti and gum); love letters placed here are taken down and, along with 5,000 letters annually, answered by the Club di Giulietta (locally based volunteers). There's not much to see inside the house (period bedrooms, costumes "worn" by Romeo and Juliet), though plenty of visitors line up for a chance of a selfie on the balcony.

Statue of Juliet with love notes, Casa di Giulietta.

Once you've made the obligatory Juliet pilgrimage, focus on actual historic sights. The 1st-century **Arena di Verona ★** (10€; Mon 1:30–7:30pm and Tues–Sun 8:30am–7:30pm), in the spacious Piazza Bra, is the third largest classical arena in Italy after Rome's Colosseum and the arena at Capua—it could seat some 25,000 spectators and still hosts performances today (www.arena.it).

To the northwest on Piazza San Zeno, the **Basilica di San Zeno Maggiore ★★** (www.basilicasanzeno.it; 4€, includes audioguide; Mar–Oct Mon–Fri 9:30am–6pm, Sat 9am–6pm, Sun 1–6pm; Nov–Feb Mon–Fri 10am–5pm, Sat 9am–6pm, Sun 1–6pm) is the greatest Romanesque church in northern Italy. The present structure was completed around 1135 over a 4th-century shrine to Verona's patron saint, St. Zeno (who died in 380). The church's massive rose window represents the Wheel of Fortune, while lintels above the portal represent the months of the year. The highlight of the interior is Mantegna's "Madonna and Saints" above the altar.

WHERE TO EAT

Even in chic Verona, you'll spend less on a meal than in Venice. The most authentic central restaurant is **Antica Bottega del Vino ★**, Via Scudo di Francia 3 (bottegavini.it; ✆ **045/8004535;** daily 11am–midnight; restaurant Mon–Fri 12:30–2:40pm and 6:30–10:40pm, Sat and Sun 12:30–10:40pm), open since 1890. Dishes range from risotto with Amarone wine and tortellini with black truffle and crispy Parmesan to pigeon with broccoli and Venetian-style veal liver with toasted polenta (14€–26€). Open since 1909, **Caffè Monte Baldo ★**, Via Rosa 12 (www.osteriamontebaldo.com;

✆ **045/8030579;** Mon, Wed, Thurs 11am–3pm and 6–11:30pm, Fri 11am–midnight, Sat and Sun 10am–midnight), an old-fashioned cafe transformed into a trendy *osteria,* serves classic pastas and scrumptious *crostini* with wine in the evenings.

Treviso ★★

30km (19 miles) N of Venice

Long overshadowed by Venice, **Treviso** is a small, prosperous city of narrow medieval streets, Gothic churches, and an enchanting network of canals, replete with weeping willows and waterwheels (it's known as "piccola Venezia" or "little Venice"). Giotto's follower **Tomaso da Modena** (1326–79), one of northern Italy's lesser-known artistic geniuses, frescoed many of its churches, and its maze of back streets makes for pleasant, often tourist-free exploring. Fashion giant Benetton was founded here in 1965; the city also claims to have invented tiramisu.

ESSENTIALS

ARRIVING The fastest way to reach Treviso from Venice is by **train** from Santa Lucia station (30–40 min.). Trains run two to four times an hour, and tickets start at 3.80€ one-way. From Treviso Centrale station it's an easy 10- to 15-minute walk to Piazza dei Signori, north across the River Sile (follow signs to "Centro"). Note also that most Ryanair budget flights to Venice actually arrive at Treviso airport (p. 396).

VISITOR INFORMATION The **tourist office** at Via Fiumicelli 30 (www.visittreviso.it; ✆ **0422/547-632**) is open Monday from 10am to 1pm, Tuesday to Saturday 10am to 5pm, and Sunday 10am to 4pm.

EXPLORING TREVISO

The **Piazza dei Signori** ★ is the historic heart of Treviso. The square is anchored by the **Palazzo del Podestà,** rebuilt in the 1870s with a tall clock tower, and the **Palazzo dei Trecento,** the 13th-century town council hall, now home to chic Bar Beltrame beneath the arches. Just beyond the square, on adjacent Piazza San Vito, sits a handsome pair of medieval churches: **Santa Lucia** ★ (www.santaluciatreviso.it; ✆ **0422/5457200**), with a superb Tomaso da Modena fresco of the "Madonna del Pavegio" in the first shrine on the right, and **San Vito** ★, with its Byzantine-style frescoes from the 13th century. Both are open daily 9am to noon, and Saturday and Sunday 3:30 to 6pm; admission is free. Historic **Via Calmaggiore,** lined with posh boutiques, runs northwest from Piazza dei Signori towards the cathedral. The relatively dull neoclassical facade of the **Duomo** ★ (free admission; Mon–Sat 7:30am–noon and 3:30–7pm, Sun 8am–1pm and 3:30–8pm) is from 1836, but it's flanked by Romanesque lions that, along with its seven Venetian-Byzantine-style green copper domes, are remnants of the cathedral's 12th-century origins. The crypt is the most compelling part of the interior, with the tombs of the city's bishops amid

A chic shopping street near Treviso's Piazza dei Signori.

a forest of columns and fragments of 14th-century frescoes and mosaics. The highlight in the main body of the cathedral is a fine altarpiece, the "Malchiostro Annunciation" by Titian, from 1520.

A short stroll southwest from the Duomo, the massive brick 13th- to 14th-century Italian Gothic church of **San Nicolò ★** (free admission; daily 8am–noon and 3:30–6pm) houses some intriguing Gothic frescoes. Tomaso da Modena and his school decorated the huge round columns with a series of saints, notably St. Jerome, St. Agnes, and St. Romuald. Antonio da Treviso painted the absolutely gargantuan St. Christopher—his .9m-long (3-ft.) feet strolling over biting fish—in 1410.

East of Piazza dei Signori, across the **Buranelli,** the most attractive of Treviso's canals, lies the wide Canale Cagnan Grande, whose island hosts a **pescheria** (fish market) Monday to Saturday.

Farther east on Piazzetta Mario Botter is a deconsecrated church that's now an enjoyable museum: **Museo di Santa Caterina** (www.museicivicitreviso.it; ✆ **0422/658442;** 6€; Tues–Sun 10am–6pm). Its highlight is another fresco cycle by Tomaso da Modena, the "Story of the Life of Saint Ursula" (detached from a now-destroyed church and preserved here). There's also a cache of local archaeological finds plus minor works by Titian, Lorenzo Lotto, and Francesco Guardi.

To the south, the 15th-century church of **Santa Maria Maggiore** (free admission; daily 8am–noon and 3:30–6pm) houses a venerated image of Mary (the "Madonna Granda"), a frescoed "Madonna and Child" originally painted in Byzantine style (probably pre–9th century), and later touched up by Tomaso and members of his school.

WHERE TO EAT

Treviso has some excellent restaurants, but its real claim to fame is as the home of **tiramisu.** Legend has it that the addictive dessert was first served at restaurant **Le Beccherie ★★** Piazza Ancilotto 9 (www.lebeccherie.it; **✆ 0422/540871;** Wed–Mon 12:20–2:15pm and 7:20–10:15pm), in 1972. The claim has been disputed over the years, but the restaurant is still open and still knocks out an exceptional tiramisu (the "classico" is 9€). In fact, just about every menu in town features tiramisu, as well as Treviso's other culinary specialty, **radicchio** (bitter red lettuce).

The bars and cafes around the **pescheria,** particularly along Via Palestro, are always buzzing, and perfect for sampling good-value local cuisine. For atmosphere it's hard to beat the **Hosteria Dai Naneti ★★**, Vicolo Broli 2 (**✆ 3403/783158;** Mon–Sat 9am–2:30pm and 5:30–9pm, Sun 11am–2pm and 5–9pm; closed Sun May–Sept), a cozy tavern, deli, and cheese shop where you can grab a delicious baguette and glass of wine, or just snack at the bar for around 6€ (standing room only).

For a full meal in the center, reserve a table at **Trattoria All'Antico Portico ★★**, overlooking the church at Piazza Santa Maria Maggiore 18 (www.anticoportico.it; **✆ 0422/545259;** Mon 9am–4pm, Wed–Sun 9am–11pm), which serves local specialties such as radicchio risotto and *baccalà alla veneziana* (salt cod); main courses are 11€ to 22€.

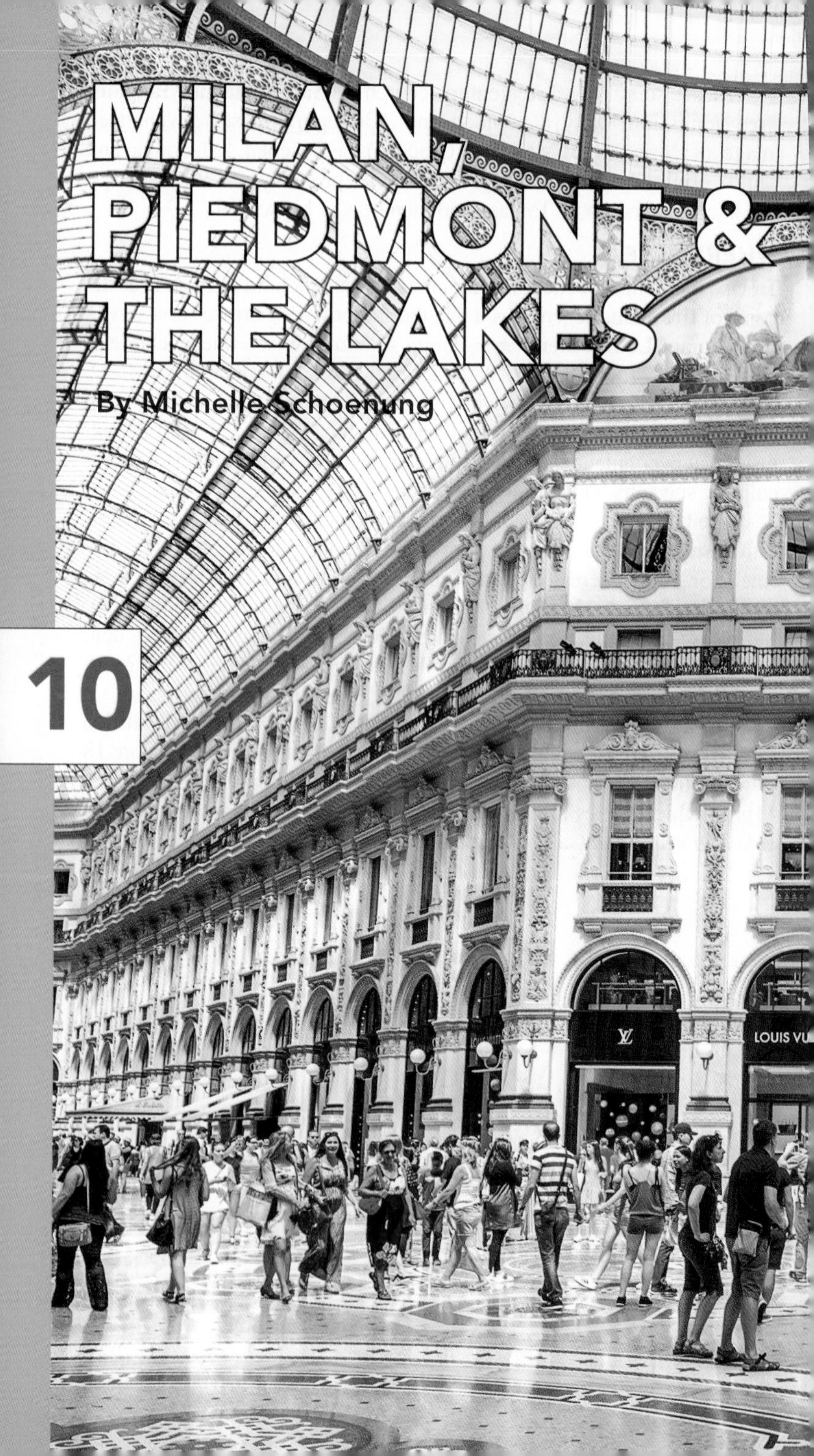

MILAN, PIEDMONT & THE LAKES

By Michelle Schoenung

10

Milan is the glitzy capital of Lombardy (Lombardia), Italy's most prosperous region. Its companies largely fuel the Italian economy, and its attractions—high fashion, fine dining, hopping dance clubs, and da Vinci's "Last Supper"—have much to offer the visitor. But Lombardy is much more than one sophisticated city. To the north, the region bumps up against craggy mountains in a romantic lake district, and the south spreads into fertile farmlands fed by the Po and other rivers.

Lombardy feels different from the rest of Italy. The *Lombardi* descended from one of the Germanic tribes that overran the Roman empire, and have over the centuries been ruled by feudal dynasties from Spain, Austria, and France, so they tend to be a bit more Continental than their neighbors to the south—fast-talking, faster-paced, and more business-oriented. They even dine differently, with butter often used alongside olive oil, and polenta and risotto as common as pasta—though these days the Milanese are equally enamored of sushi and other ethnic foods.

Backed by the Alps and ringed by lush gardens and verdant forests, the Italian lakes have entranced writers from Catullus to Ernest Hemingway. While each lake has its own distinct charm, they are all ideal for short retreats: Lake Maggiore and Lake Como are both less than an hour from Milan, and Lake Garda is tantalizingly close to Venice.

DON'T LEAVE MILAN & THE LAKE DISTRICT WITHOUT . . .

Paying Homage to Michelangelo & da Vinci. You'll find "The Last Supper" in Santa Maria delle Grazie (p. 481) and the "Pietà," Michelangelo's first work, inside the medieval Castello Sforzesco (p. 471).

Climbing to the Roof of Milan's Gothic Duomo. Wander amid the buttresses and statue-topped spires for a citywide panorama. See p. 474.

Taking a Window Shopping Spin. Browse the high-end boutiques in Milan's Golden Rectangle, then go on a budget-shopping spree on Corso Buenos Aires. See p. 491.

Ferrying Among Lake Maggiore's Borromean Islands. You can tour the palaces of one of Lombardy's last remaining Renaissance-era noble families, and watch the peacocks wander their exotic gardens. See p. 509.

FACING PAGE: **Galleria Vittorio Emanuele II in Milan.**

Visiting Lake Garda's Picturesque Sirmione. Despite plenty of summer tourists, this historic town—which has attracted visitors since the Romans discovered hot springs here—hasn't lost its charm. See p. 515.

Safe Travels in Lombardy & the Piedmont

Lombardy was hit hard by the pandemic, and locals have become well drilled in all the protocols of mask-wearing and social distancing. Depending on when you visit, museums and indoor establishments may still require mask-wearing, social distancing, and occupancy limits. Proof of vaccination (see p. 820) is likely to be required for entry to museums and restaurants. Advance reservations are more important than ever, and essential for some attractions (particularly DaVinci's "The Last Supper," p. 481). Check ahead to make sure that a site you want to visit has not temporarily curtailed its hours. See p. 820 for more information, and check the updated Covid pages at www.italia.it.

MILAN ★★★

552km (342 miles) NW of Rome, 288km (179 miles) NW of Florence, 257km (159 miles W of Venice) 140km (87 miles) NE of Turin, 142km (88 miles) N of Genoa

Milan—or Milano, as the Italians say it—is elegant, chaotic, and utterly beguiling. Traffic chokes the streets, and it can be bitterly cold in winter and stiflingly hot in summer, but it more than compensates with majestic architecture and robust Northern Italian cuisine. It's a world-class stop on the international fashion stage, the banking capital of Italy, and a wealthy city of glamorous people and stylish shopping streets. Milan also is rich in history, from its Roman ruins and soaring Duomo to a host of ancient churches, medieval castles, and Renaissance palaces.

The World's Fair in 2015, known as Expo Milano, rode in on a wave of urban revitalization, bringing a whole new energy to this northern Italy city along with ultra-modern skyscrapers, expanded parks, bike-sharing lanes, and a wider range of bars, restaurants, and hotels; this sense of transformation continues today as Milan gears up to hold the 2026 Winter Olympics along with Cortina d'Ampezzo.

Essentials

ARRIVING

BY PLANE **Milan Malpensa (MXP)**, 45km (28 miles) northwest of the city, is Milan's major international airport. The **Malpensa Express** train (www.malpensaexpress.it; ✆ **02-7249-4949;** 13€ one-way, 20€ roundtrip) leaves from both Terminal 1 and Terminal 2 with a 30-minute run half-hourly to Cadorna train station, or hourly to Stazione Centrale (45 min.). Buses run directly to Stazione Centrale, a 50-minute journey, with five trips per hour, for 10€ one-way or 16€ round-trip; they're operated by

Malpensa Shuttle (www.malpensashuttle.it; ✆ **02-5858-3185**) or **Autostradale** (www.autostradale.it; ✆ **02-3008-9000**). By **taxi,** the trip into town costs a wallet-stripping 100€ and takes the same amount of time as the bus—50 minutes. We don't recommend it, but it's the only option after midnight. Keep in mind that the two terminals are several miles apart; a shuttle bus between them runs 24 hours a day and takes about 15 minutes. Terminal 1 is the larger, newer terminal; most travelers will leave in and out of here. Older, smaller Terminal 2 mainly serves low-cost airline easyJet for flights within Europe.

Milan Linate (LIN), 7km (4.5 miles) east of the center, handles European and domestic flights. The city's **subway line** now reaches Linate. The blue line (also known as **M4**) goes from the city center to this nearby airport for the cost of a regular ticket (2.20€). City bus no. 73 leaves about every 10 minutes during the day (less frequently after about 7pm) for the city center and takes 25 minutes. Tickets cost 2.20€. A trip into town by taxi costs roughly 25€.

Malpensa Shuttle buses also connect Malpensa and Linate airports with five daily runs between 9:30am and 6:20pm. The trip takes 90 minutes and costs 13€ (roundtrip 26€).

BY TRAIN Milan is one of Europe's busiest rail hubs. Trains travel every half-hour to Bergamo (1 hr.), Mantua (2 hr.), and Turin (1 hr. by the AV high-speed train). Stazione Centrale is a half-hour walk northeast of the center, with easy connections to Piazza del Duomo by Metro, tram, and bus. The Metro stop is called Centrale F.S. To buy train tickets, use the multilingual automatic ticket machines, which accept cash, credit cards, and ATM cards (they even have a reader for contactless cards). Keep in mind that the credit-card and ATM functions are sometimes out of order; however, there are typically attendants to help (look for official attendants wearing a vest with the Trenitalia logo, and don't let "volunteers" help you—they will often badger you for a tip at the end of the transaction). You may need to validate your ticket in the machines at the beginning of the track as you get on your train, especially if you don't have an e-ticket.

While Stazione Centrale is Milan's major station, trains also serve **Stazione Cadorna** (Como and Malpensa airport) and **Porta Garibaldi** (Lecco and the north). All these stations are on the green Metro Linea 2; Cadorna is also on the red Metro Linea 1.

BY BUS Long-distance buses are useful for reaching the ski resorts in Valle d'Aosta. Most bus services depart from the Lampugnano bus terminal (metro Lampugnano), although some originate in Piazza Castello (metro Cairoli). **Autostradale** (www.autostradale.it; ✆ **02-3008-9000**) operates most of the bus lines and has ticket offices in front of Castello Sforzesco on Piazza Castello (daily 9am–6pm), and in front of the Duomo in Passageway 2 next to the TIM mobile phone store (weekdays

8:30am–6pm; weekends 9am–4pm). **Arriva** (www.arriva.it; ✆ **035/289-000**) runs five daily buses (sometimes more in winter) between Milan Lampugnano and Aosta (2½ hr.; 17€) or Courmayeur (3½ hr.; 19.50€).

BY CAR The A1 autostrada links Milan with Florence (3 hr.) and Rome (6 hr.), while the A4 connects Milan with Verona (2 hr.) and Venice (2½ hr.) to the east and Turin (1 hr.) to the west. That being said, we don't recommend trying to drive around Milan. It's a huge hassle. See below for more.

GETTING AROUND

BY TRAIN Milan's most famous sights are within walking distance of one another, but the public transport system, an integrated system of **Metro, trams,** and **buses,** run by **ATM** (www.atm.it; ✆ **02-48-607-607**), is a cheap and effective alternative to walking. The Metro closes at midnight (Sat at 1am), but buses and trams run all night. Metro stations are well-signposted; trains are speedy, safe, and frequent—they run every couple of minutes during the day and about every 5 minutes after 9pm. Tickets for 90 minutes of travel on Metro, trams, or buses cost 2.20€. A 24-hour unlimited travel ticket is a decent value at 7.60€. Tickets are available at newsstands and Metro stations (all machines have English-language options; the 24-hr. ticket option is listed under "Urban"). Stamp your ticket when you board a bus or tram—there is a 35€ fine (more if not paid on the spot) if you don't.

Lines 1 (red, with stops at Cairoli for Castello Sforzesco and Duomo for Galleria Vittorio Emanuele II and the Duomo) and **3** (yellow, with a stop at Via Montenapoleone) are the most useful for sightseeing.

BY CAR Driving and parking in Milan are not experiences to relish. First of all, you'll have to pay the Area C congestion charge of 5€ to enter the *centro storico* Monday to Friday 7:30am to 7:30pm. On top of that, the one-way system is complicated, some streets are reserved for public transport only, and there are many pedestrianized areas. Hotels will make parking arrangements for guests—take advantage of that.

Milano Discount Card

The **MilanoCard** (www.milanocard.it) offers a great deal on sightseeing at 13.50€ for 24 hours, 19€ for 2 days, or 21€ for 3 days. You get quite a bit for your buck, including a 5€ credit toward taxi travel, free travel on all public transport, discounts in some stores and restaurants, a free drink in a bar in the city, discounted luggage storage, and free or reduced entry to some of the best attractions in Milan. Cards can be purchased online with a credit card, and you will receive instructions for how to make use of it and activate it for the public-transportation system. You have 12 months from the time of purchase to use it.

BY TAXI While you can't hail a taxi on the street, taxi stands can be found in major *piazze* and by major Metro stops. There is a taxi stand in Piazza del Duomo and outside Castello Sforzesco; a journey between the two will cost around 8€. Hotel reception staff can call a taxi for you; otherwise, a reliable company is **Taxiblu** at ✆ **02-4040.** Meters start at 3.50€ during the day (6.80€ at night), and prices increase by 1.14€ per kilometer. Expect surcharges for waiting time, luggage, late-night travel, and Sunday journeys. At press time, Uber was still operating legally in Milan.

BY BIKE With the streets of the *centro storico* largely pedestrianized, Milan is a good city for cycling, with a handy bike-sharing program, **BikeMi,** which is so popular you can't always find bikes at some stations. The tariff for the pass is very convoluted: For 4.50€ a day or 9€ a week, you can buy a pass that allows 30 minutes of free travel between one station and the next. If you keep the bike longer, you are charged .50€ per 30 minutes (or part of it) up to 2 hours; thereafter you are charged 2€ per hour (or part of it). Once you return a bike, you have to wait 5 minutes before starting another rental. There are bike racks outside Castello Sforzesco and the Duomo as well as at tram, bus, and Metro stops. Buy your pass online (www.bikemi.com), by phone (✆ **02-48-607-607**) or at the ATM Points at Centrale, Cadorna, Garibaldi, and Duomo stations (Mon–Sat 7:45am–8pm).

ON FOOT The attractions of the *centro storico* are all accessible on foot. From Piazza del Duomo, Via Montenapoleone is a 10-minute walk through Piazza della Scala and along Via Manzoni, and it is a 10-minute walk to Castello Sforzesco. Santa Maria delle Grazie and "The Last Supper" are a 30-minute stroll from Piazza del Duomo.

VISITOR INFORMATION

The main **tourist office** (called **IAT,** for Informazione e Accoglienza Turistica) is in Galleria Vittorio Emanuele on the corner of Piazza della Scala (✆ **02-8845-5555**). It's open Monday to Friday 9am to 7pm, Saturday 9am to 6pm, and Sunday 10am to 6pm.

CITY LAYOUT

Milan developed as a series of circles radiating out from the central hub, **Piazza del Duomo.** Within the inner circle are most of the churches, museums, and shops of the *centro storico.* **Parco Sempione** and Leonardo's "The Last Supper" are to the west in a posh neighborhood. The slightly grungy yet hip cafe-filled districts of **Porta Ticinese** and **Navigli** lie directly south, with genteel **Brera** and its classy stores, galleries, and restaurants slightly to the north. The mecca of Milanese fashion, the **Quadrilatero d'Oro** (Golden Quadrilateral), is northeast of the Duomo. North of the center, there's a burgeoning **financial district** between Porta Garibaldi and Centrale stations, while the modern towers of the **CityLife** development rise northwest of Castello Sforzesco.

[Fast FACTS] MILAN

ATMs/Banks Banks with multilingual ATMs are all over the city center. Bank hours are roughly Monday to Friday 8:30am to 1:30pm and 3 to 4pm; major branches open Saturday morning for a couple of hours.

Business Hours Most stores in central Milan are open Tuesday to Saturday 9:30am to 7:30pm, with a half-day Monday (3:30–7:30pm). Most shops close on Sundays, and some still close for lunch between 12:30pm and 3:30pm.

Doctors/Dentists The **Centro Medico Santagostino** has several reasonably priced clinics throughout the city and a team of doctors and dentists with many different specialties. Call or make an appointment online; the website lists prices for most types of visits (www.cmsantagostino.it/en; ✆ **02/8970-1701**). You can also reserve via WhatsApp by sending a message to ✆ **345/398-8236.**

Drugstores Pharmacies rotate 24-hour shifts. Signs in most pharmacies post the schedule. In Stazione Centrale, the **Farmacia Stazione Centrale** (✆ **02/669-0735**) keeps longer hours and is often open overnight; the staff speaks English.

Emergencies All emergency numbers are free. Call ✆ **112** for **police, medical, or fire emergencies.**

Hospitals The **Ospedale Maggiore Policlinico** (✆ **02/55-031**) is a 5-minute walk southeast of the Duomo at Via Francesco Sforza 35. Some of its medical staff speak English.

Internet The city purports to offer free Wi-Fi, but logging in can be a frustrating process involving codes sent to your mobile phone (not super-helpful if your phone is on airplane mode to avoid roaming charges). Many hotels, bars, and cafes offer free Wi-Fi, but the **Starbucks Reserve Roastery** (www.starbucksreserve.com/en-us/locations/milano) is probably the best place in the city for free Wi-Fi and clean public bathrooms.

Police For police emergencies, dial ✆ **112.** There is a police station in Stazione Centrale; the **Questura** is at the main station, just west of the Giardini Pubblici at Via Fatebenefratelli 11 (✆ **02/62-261;** metro Turati).

Post Office The main post office, **Poste e Telecommunicazioni,** is at Via Cordusio 4 (✆ **02/7248-2508;** metro Cordusio). It's open Monday to Friday 8:20am to 7:05pm and Saturday 8:30am to 12:35pm. The post office in Stazione Centrale is open Monday to Saturday 8:20am to 7:05pm. Other branches are open Monday to Saturday 8:30am to 1:30pm.

Safety Milan has generally low levels of street crime, although public parks and the area around Stazione Centrale are best avoided at night.

Exploring Milan

The **Piazza del Duomo** has been the beating heart of Milan since the Romans took over in 222 B.C., naming it Mediolanum. This vast traffic-free piazza sees local life passing to and fro daily, while tourists peer up at the majestic **Duomo** (p. 474) and street sellers push cheap souvenirs. From here a tangle of narrow streets branch off in all directions through the city's *centro storico* (historic center). The square took on its present form following the Unification of Italy in 1861, when its medieval buildings were replaced by splendid neoclassical buildings designed by Giuseppe Mengoni (1829–77), also architect of the **Galleria Vittorio Emanuele II** (see p. 475). Located around the piazza are the superb **Museo del Duomo** (p. 476), temporary art exhibitions in the **Palazzo**

Reale (www.palazzorealemilano.it; ✆ **02/8844-5181**), and 20th-century Italian art in the **Museo del Novecento** (p. 477).

Note: Dress modestly when visiting Milan's churches: no short shorts for either sex, women must have their shoulders covered, and skirts must be below the knee. The dress code at the Duomo is particularly strict.

Castello Sforzesco ★ MUSEUM Although it has lived many lives under several different occupiers and been restored many times, this fortified castle is the masterpiece of Milan's two most powerful medieval and Renaissance dynasties, the Visconti and the Sforza. The Visconti built the castle (as well as the Duomo) in the 14th century; after the Sforzas married into the Visconti clan and eclipsed their power, they took the castle in the 1450s, transforming it into one of the most gracious palaces of the Renaissance. Sforza *capo* Ludovico il Moro and his wife, Beatrice d'Este, helped make Milan one of Italy's Renaissance centers by commissioning works by Bramante and Leonardo.

The castle was extensively restored by architect Luca Beltrami at the end of the 19th century, and restoration is always ongoing. It opened as a museum in 1905; today it contains a dozen museums, known collectively as the Musei del Castello Sforzesco. Many Sforza treasures are on view in the castle's labyrinthine courtyards and corridors, including a *pinacoteca* (painting gallery) with works by Bellini and Correggio plus Mannerists

The skyline of Milan.

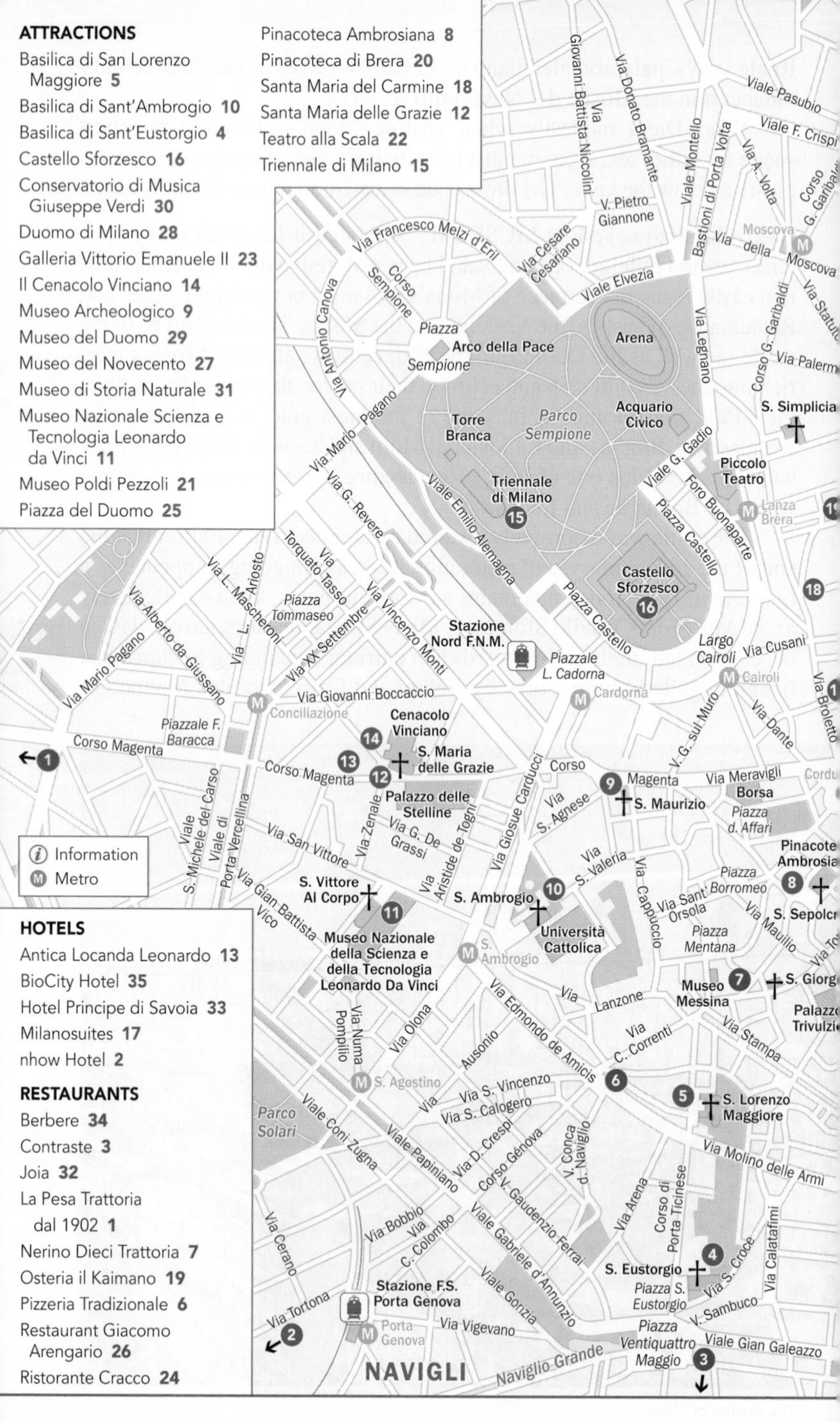
ATTRACTIONS
Basilica di San Lorenzo Maggiore 5
Basilica di Sant'Ambrogio 10
Basilica di Sant'Eustorgio 4
Castello Sforzesco 16
Conservatorio di Musica Giuseppe Verdi 30
Duomo di Milano 28
Galleria Vittorio Emanuele II 23
Il Cenacolo Vinciano 14
Museo Archeologico 9
Museo del Duomo 29
Museo del Novecento 27
Museo di Storia Naturale 31
Museo Nazionale Scienza e Tecnologia Leonardo da Vinci 11
Museo Poldi Pezzoli 21
Piazza del Duomo 25
Pinacoteca Ambrosiana 8
Pinacoteca di Brera 20
Santa Maria del Carmine 18
Santa Maria delle Grazie 12
Teatro alla Scala 22
Triennale di Milano 15
Information
Metro
HOTELS
Antica Locanda Leonardo 13
BioCity Hotel 35
Hotel Principe di Savoia 33
Milanosuites 17
nhow Hotel 2
RESTAURANTS
Berbere 34
Contraste 3
Joia 32
La Pesa Trattoria dal 1902 1
Nerino Dieci Trattoria 7
Osteria il Kaimano 19
Pizzeria Tradizionale 6
Restaurant Giacomo Arengario 26
Ristorante Cracco 24
Arco della Pace
Piazza Sempione
Arena
Acquario Civico
Torre Branca
Parco Sempione
Triennale di Milano
Castello Sforzesco
Piccolo Teatro
Stazione Nord F.N.M.
Piazzale L. Cadorna
Largo Cairoli
Cenacolo Vinciano
S. Maria delle Grazie
Palazzo delle Stelline
S. Maurizio
Borsa
Piazza d. Affari
S. Vittore Al Corpo
S. Ambrogio
Università Cattolica
Museo Nazionale della Scienza e della Tecnologia Leonardo Da Vinci
Museo Messina
S. Lorenzo Maggiore
S. Eustorgio
Piazza S. Eustorgio
Stazione F.S. Porta Genova
Piazza Ventiquattro Maggio
Parco Solari
NAVIGLI
Naviglio Grande
S. Simpliciano
Moscova
Lanza Brera
Cairoli
Cardorna
Conciliazione
S. Ambrogio
S. Agostino
Porta Genova
Piazzale F. Baracca
Piazza Tommaseo
Piazza Borromeo
Piazza Mentana
S. Sepolcro
Corso Sempione
Via Francesco Melzi d'Eril
Viale Elvezia
Via Legnano
Corso Magenta
Via XX Settembre
Via Vincenzo Monti
Via Giovanni Boccaccio
Via San Vittore
Via Edmondo de Amicis
Via Molino delle Armi
Corso di Porta Ticinese
Viale Gabriele d'Annunzio
Viale Papiniano
Viale Coni Zugna
Corso Genova
Via Torino
Viale Gian Galeazzo
Via Vigevano
Via Tortona
Via Dante
Via Meravigli
Via Cusani
Viale Pasubio
Viale F. Crispi

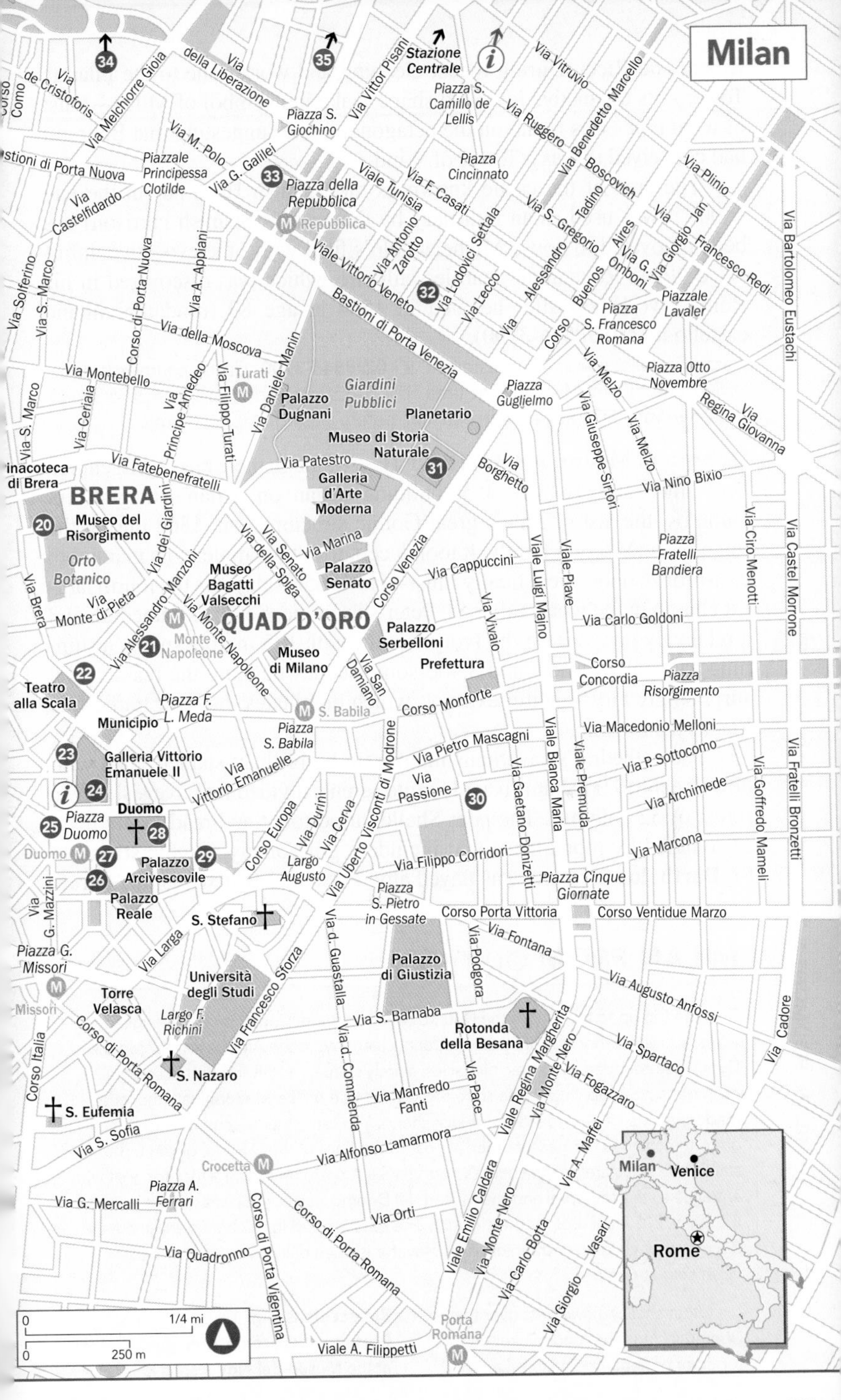
Milan
Stazione Centrale
Piazza S. Camillo de Lellis
Via Vitruvio
Via della Liberazione
Via Melchiorre Gioia
Via de Cristoforis
Corso Como
Piazza S. Giochino
Via Vittor Pisani
Via Ruggero Boscovich
Via Benedetto Marcello
Via M. Polo
Bastioni di Porta Nuova
Piazzale Principessa Clotilde
Via G. Galilei
Piazza della Repubblica
Repubblica
Viale Tunisia
Via F. Casati
Piazza Cincinnato
Via Plinio
Via Castelfidardo
Via S. Gregorio
Via Alessandro Tadino
Via Francesco Redi
Via Giorgio Jan
Via G. Omboni
Aires
Buenos
Corso
Via Bartolomeo Eustachi
Via Solferino
Via S. Marco
Corso di Porta Nuova
Via A. Appiani
Viale Vittorio Veneto
Via Antonio Zarotto
Via Lodovici Settala
Via Lecco
Piazzale Lavaler
Piazza S. Francesco Romana
Bastioni di Porta Venezia
Via della Moscova
Via Daniele Manin
Via Melzo
Piazza Otto Novembre
Via Regina Giovanna
Via Montebello
Via Principe Amedeo
Via Filippo Turati
Turati
Giardini Pubblici
Palazzo Dugnani
Planetario
Piazza Guglielmo
Via S. Marco
Via Ceriaia
Museo di Storia Naturale
Via Patestro
Via Borghetto
Via Giuseppe Sirtori
Pinacoteca di Brera
Via Fatebenefratelli
Galleria d'Arte Moderna
Via Nino Bixio
BRERA
Museo del Risorgimento
Via dei Giardini
Via Senato
Via della Spiga
Via Marina
Orto Botanico
Museo Bagatti Valsecchi
Palazzo Senato
Corso Venezia
Via Cappuccini
Viale Luigi Majno
Viale Piave
Piazza Fratelli Bandiera
Via Ciro Menotti
Via Castel Morrone
Via Brera
Via Monte di Pietà
Via Alessandro Manzoni
Via Monte Napoleone
Monte Napoleone
QUAD D'ORO
Palazzo Serbelloni
Via Vivaio
Via Carlo Goldoni
Museo di Milano
Via San Damiano
Prefettura
Corso Concordia
Piazza Risorgimento
Teatro alla Scala
Piazza F. L. Meda
S. Babila
Corso Monforte
Municipio
Piazza S. Babila
Via Macedonio Melloni
Viale Bianca Maria
Galleria Vittorio Emanuele II
Via Vittorio Emanuele
Via Uberto Visconti di Modrone
Via Pietro Mascagni
Viale Premuda
Via P. Sottocomo
Via Fratelli Bronzetti
Via Passione
Via Gaetano Donizetti
Via Archimede
Via Goffredo Mameli
Duomo
Piazza Duomo
Corso Europa
Via Durini
Via Cerva
Via Marcona
Palazzo Arcivescovile
Largo Augusto
Via Filippo Corridori
Piazza Cinque Giornate
Palazzo Reale
Via G. Mazzini
Piazza S. Pietro in Gessate
Corso Porta Vittoria
Corso Ventidue Marzo
S. Stefano
Via Fontana
Piazza G. Missori
Via Larga
Via d. Guastalla
Palazzo di Giustizia
Via Podgora
Università degli Studi
Via Francesco Sforza
Via Augusto Anfossi
Missori
Torre Velasca
Largo F. Richini
Via S. Barnaba
Rotonda della Besana
Via Cadore
Corso di Porta Romana
Via Spartaco
Corso Italia
S. Nazaro
Via d. Commenda
Via Pace
Viale Regina Margherita
Via Monte Nero
Via Fogazzaro
Via Manfredo Fanti
S. Eufemia
Via S. Sofia
Via A. Maffei
Via Alfonso Lamarmora
Crocetta
Milan
Venice
Piazza A. Ferrari
Via G. Mercalli
Corso di Porta Vigentina
Via Orti
Viale Emilio Caldara
Via Monte Nero
Via Carlo Botta
Via Vasari
Rome
Via Quadronno
Via Giorgio
0
1/4 mi
0
250 m
Porta Romana
Viale A. Filippetti
34
35
33
32
31
20
21
22
23
24
25
26
27
28
29
30

Ribera and Ricci. During recent cleaning and work done to the Filarete Tower—its distinctive look and shape make it a symbol of Milan—a list of wind types was found on the octagonal dome suggesting that Beltrami had conceived this as a Tower of Wind.

The area of the castle known as the Spanish Hospital (in the late 1500s it was used as an infirmary by the castle's Spanish garrison) has been renovated to house Michelangelo's final work: the evocative unfinished "Pietà Rondanini" marble sculpture, which was discovered in his Roman workshop after he died in 1564 at age 89 (rondanini.milanocastello.it; ✆ **02/8846-3700**).

Piazza Castello. www.milanocastello.it. ✆ **02/8846-3700.** Castle courtyards: Free. Daily 7am–7:30pm. Museums: 5€ (free Tues 2–5:30pm and Wed–Sun 4:30–5:30pm). Tues–Sun 9am–5:30pm (last entry 30 min. before closing). Metro: Cairoli.

Duomo di Milano ★★★ CHURCH Although there has been a church here since at least A.D. 355, building began on Milan's magnificent Duomo—the last of Italy's great Gothic structures—in 1368 during the reign of the Visconti family. It took 5 centuries to complete; its mammoth cast-bronze doors were finally finished in 1965. Today it is the fourth largest church in the world (after St. Peter's in Rome, Seville's cathedral, and a relatively new one on the Ivory Coast), with 135 marble spires, a stunning triangular facade, and 3,400-some statues flanking the massive yet surprisingly airy, fanciful exterior, which dominates the vast, traffic-free Piazza del Duomo.

The cathedral's cavernous interior, lit by brilliant stained-glass windows, seats 40,000 but is usually quite serene, divided into five aisles by a forest of 52 columns. The poet Shelley used to sit and read Dante here, surrounded by monuments that include a gruesomely graphic **statue of St. Bartholomew** (who was flayed alive). Another British visitor, Alfred,

MILAN FROM on high

Take the trip up to the roof of the Duomo (www.duomomilano.it) for spine-tingling views across the rooftops of Milan and, on a clear day, to the Alps beyond. Atop the Duomo, surrounded by Gothic pinnacles, saintly statues, and flying buttresses, you even get a close-up view of the spire-top gold statue of **"La Madonnina"** (the little Madonna), the city's beloved good-luck charm. You can either ascend by elevator (14€; go to the church's northeast corner, almost to the back of the Duomo) or climb the stairs (10€; stairs are on the church's north flank). A pass combining a roof-top visit with entrance to the cathedral and the Museo del Duomo (see p. 476) costs 15€ if you take the stairs, 20€ if you opt for the elevator. The pass is good for 72 hours, and there are discounts for children and seniors. The elevator is open daily 9am to 6:30pm (last ticket sold at 6pm).

Other sneaky viewpoints over the Duomo include the food market on the top floor of department store **La Rinascente** (see p. 492) and the posh **Restaurant Giacomo Arengario** (p. 488) at the **Museo del Novecento** (p. 477).

Lord Tennyson, rhapsodized about the view from the roof (see box above). In the crypt, the **Battistero di San Giovanni alle Fonti** reveals remains of the octagonal 4th-century foundations of an earlier church that stood here, which is almost certainly where Sant'Ambrogio—patron saint and bishop of Milan in A.D. 374—christened the great missionary St. Augustine. Pride of place in the crypt goes to the ornate gilded **tomb of San Carlo Borromeo,** archbishop of Milan and leader of the Counter-Reformation, who died in 1584. Entrance to the crypt is included in admission to the Museo del Duomo (see p. 476), though opening times may be different.
Piazza del Duomo. www.duomomilano.it. ✆ **02/7202-2656.** Variety of ticket options starting at 6€. Daily 9am–7pm for visitors. Metro: Duomo.

Galleria Vittorio Emanuele II ★★ SHOPPING MALL The best place from which to admire the Duomo facade is from the cafe at the entrance of the Galleria, Milan's late-19th-century prototype of the modern shopping mall. No modern malls even come close to matching the Galleria for style and flair, however; this wonderful steel-and-glass-covered, cross-shaped arcade is a neoclassical beauty, with ornate marble flooring and a massive octagonal glass dome. Inside, the arcade is lined with grand cafes such as Biffi and Savini, where the local elite gather to dine after a night at the opera. Designer stores here include Gucci, Versace, Prada, Louis Vuitton, and Swarovski. Its span links the Piazza del Duomo with Piazza della Scala, site of the famous opera house.

Galleria Vittorio Emanuele II was the masterpiece of Bolognese architect Giuseppe Mengoni, who designed it in the 1870s to mark the unification of Italy under King Vittorio Emanuele II; mosaic and fresco decorations incorporate the patriotic symbols and coats of arms of various Italian cities. Mengoni never saw his magnus opus flourishing—he died in a fall from scaffolding the day before it opened in 1878. Today giggling visitors gather under the dome to spin around on one heel on the private parts of a little mosaic bull in the floor, a legendary good-luck ritual.
Piazza del Duomo. Open 24 hr. Metro: Duomo.

Museo Archeologico ★★ MUSEUM Milan's expertly curated archaeology museum is set in a series of airy galleries housed among the cloisters, towers, and courtyards of the 8th-century convent of Monastero Maggiore of San Maurizio. As was common at the time, the convent was constructed atop an older structure, so part of the museum is built around the remains of an ancient villa and a section of 4th-century Roman walls, which fortified Milan—then called Mediolanum—in its heyday as capital of the Western Roman Empire. A 3rd-century defense tower has traces of medieval frescoes on its rounded walls portraying Jesus showing his stigmata to St. Francis. The inner cloister leads from the former convent to a more modern extension with Milanese, Greek, and Etruscan artifacts, many of which were excavated locally. Highlights of the collection include a 1st-century-B.C. mosaic pavement unearthed nearby in 1913; the

MILAN'S time-travel CHURCHES

Milan has been an important center of Christianity since Emperor Constantine sanctioned the faith in A.D. 313. The city has more than 100 churches, and, like the Duomo, many of them lie on pagan foundations. In these, layer upon layer of history can be stripped back to their early remains.

Two such churches are on Corso di Porta Ticinese. The **Basilica di San Lorenzo Maggiore** was built in the 4th century, using rubble removed from an ancient amphitheater (the row of 16 Corinthian columns outside are relics of the theater). The church now has a 16th-century facade, but inside, fragments of the original building survive: The octagonal Cappella di Sant'Aquilino retains pieces of the 4th-century gold mosaic that once covered all the walls, and to the right of this, stairs lead down to the foundations of the first basilica. Down the street, the **Basilica di Sant'Eustorgio** has undergone many face-lifts. The present Neo-Romanesque facade dates from 1865, but foundations of the original 4th-century church are behind the altar, and the ornate Cappella Portinari, a memorial to St. Peter of Verona, dates from the 15th century.

In Piazza Sant'Ambrogio, the sublime Lombard Romanesque **Basilica di Sant'Ambrogio** was built over a Roman cemetery and extensively remodeled from the 8th to 11th centuries. The remains of Milan's patron saint, Ambrogio, are housed here in the great gold altar, constructed in the 9th century; scenes from the saint's life are depicted in glittering mosaics in the apse and wall frescoes in the side chapels.

The church of **Santa Maria del Carmine** in Brera was built over the remains of a Romanesque basilica and partly remodeled in 1400; most of its present incarnation dates from 1447. Its baroque presbytery was added in the 17th century and the Gothic-Lombard facade in 1880, making the church a true stylistic mishmash.

stunning, gleaming 4th-century Trivulzio Diattreta Cup, made of the finest hand-blown glass and featuring the inscription Bibe Vivas Multis Annis (drink so you can live many years); the Parabiago plate, an ancient Roman silver serving plate depicting mythological figures; and busts of various emperors from Caesar on.

Corso Magenta 15. www.museoarcheologicomilano.it. ✆ **02/8844-5208.** 5€ adults; free after 2pm 1st and 3rd Tues of month. Tues–Sun 10am–5:30pm. Metro: Cadorna.

Museo del Duomo ★★★ MUSEUM Beguiling treasures from the Duomo are displayed in this museum, which is actually located across the piazza from the Duomo, on the ground floor of Palazzo Reale (as you face the palace with the Duomo behind you, the entrance is to the left). Pop in here before viewing the cathedral to gain a full understanding of the Duomo. An imaginatively constructed exhibition leads visitors on a chronological journey through the life of both Milan and its cathedral. Highlights among the carved cherubs, angels, and Renaissance Madonnas displayed include a room full of startling gargoyles, ethereal 15th-century stained-glass works, scale models of the cathedral, and the original supporting structure of "La Madonnina" (see p. 474), which has adorned the

Duomo rooftop since 1774. The standout piece is "Christ Disputing in the Temple" by Tintoretto, rediscovered by happy accident in the Duomo sacristy after World War II.

Piazza del Duomo 12. www.duomomilano.it. ✆ **02/7200-3768.** 7€; 3€ seniors and ages 26 and under (ticket includes cathedral admission). Tues–Sun 10am–6pm. Metro: Duomo.

Museo del Novecento ★ MUSEUM Next door to the Palazzo Reale, Milan's museum of 20th-century art begins with a circular passageway, which winds up to the entrance on an upper floor The collection showcases Italian modern art from the Futurist movement to Pop art, trying to make the case that Italy's contribution to the world of art did not end with the Renaissance. While that claim is only partially successful, you will see some brilliant bursts of genius like works by Amedeo Modigliani, such as The Portrait of Beatrice Hastings (1915), which marked his definitive return to painting after a period of working on sculpture, and the moving "Thirst" (1934) by sculptor Arturo Martini. One of the best things about this museum? The views of the Duomo and its famous square. Even if you don't visit the museum, it is free to walk up the circular passageway, which offers some nice views of the cathedral from a different angle.

Via Marconi 1. www.museodelnovecento.org. ✆ **02/8844-0461.** 5€ adults; 3€ seniors over 65 or EU citizens 18–25; free for kids under 18. Tues–Sun 10am–7:30pm (Thurs, Sat until 10:30pm). Metro: Duomo.

Museo Nazionale Scienza e Tecnologica Leonardo da Vinci ★★ MUSEUM The cavernous science museum occupies not only the former Benedictine monastery of San Vittore Olivetan but also three modern additions and outdoor spaces. While the museum is continuously being updated to make the exhibits more fun and interactive, the floor plan can be confusing; pick up a brochure at the entrance so you don't miss the highlights. Parts of the museum seem a bit dated, but modern installations in the new Leonardo da Vinci galleries, showcasing more than 170 historical models, works of art, and ancient documents, bring the exhibition's narrative to life—and make this the largest permanent exhibition in the world dedicated to da Vinci, the man, inventor, and humanist. The monastery and its beautiful cloister are also filled with planes, trains, carriages, sewing machines, typewriters, optical devices, and other exhibits. There's even a mini-submarine to visit (tickets cost an extra 10€ for adults and 7.50€ for those 3–17; buy at the museum or online at www.museoscienza.org/toti). The museum often holds interactive science workshops and has a tinkering zone and maker space for kids, but most activities are held in Italian.

Via San Vittore 21. www.museoscienza.org. ✆ **02/485-551.** 10€ adults; 7.50€ under 25; 5€ seniors. 1-hr guided tour in English 65€. Tues–Fri 9:30am–5pm; Sat–Sun 9:30am–6:30pm. Metro: Sant'Ambrogio.

Museo Poldi Pezzoli ★★ MUSEUM This wonderfully eclectic art collection was the life's work of aristocrat Gian Giacomo Poldi Pezzoli,

Naviglio Grande canal in Milan.

who donated his cache of art and decorative arts to the city in 1879. It is now elegantly displayed in his luxurious 17th-century *palazzo,* one of Milan's several "house museums," giving visitors insight into how the upper class lived in previous centuries. The ornate rooms of the ground floor feature Oriental rugs, ancient armor, and rare books. Up the carved marble stairs the riches continue, through extravagant rooms adorned with family portraits, Murano glass, and Limoges china. Scenes from *The Divine Comedy* are featured in stained glass, and gilded pistols sit beside precious jewelry. Highlights include the Armillary Sphere, crafted by Flemish clockmaker Gualterus Arsenius in 1568 to illustrate contemporary theories of planetary movement, and Renaissance paintings by Botticelli and Piero della Francesca in the Golden Room. The clock and watch collection boasts more than 500 pieces from the Renaissance to the late 1800s.

Via Manzoni 12. www.museopoldipezzoli.it. ✆ **02/794-889.** 14€ adults; 10€ seniors, 6€ students 11–18; free for children under 10. Audioguide 5€. Wed–Mon 10am–6pm; closed Tues. Metro: Montenapoleone.

Pinacoteca Ambrosiana ★★ MUSEUM Founded in 1609 to display the collections of the pious Cardinal of Milan Federico Borromeo, this gallery is housed in Europe's second-oldest public library (after the Bodleian in Oxford). The gallery, which mostly features Italian art from the 15th to 20th centuries, has a confusing layout—a maze of courtyards, passageways, stairwells, and any number of tiny exhibition rooms—but it's worth persisting to find four outstanding artworks: the cartoon for "The School of Athens" by Raphael (1510), back in public viewing after a 4-year restoration and on display in room 5; Caravaggio's charming "Basket with Fruit," from around 1599; and Titian's "Adoration of the Magi" (ca. 1550). The fourth, the haunting "Portrait of a Musician," has been attributed to Leonardo da Vinci (1490), although many scholars question that provenance. If it is indeed a da Vinci, however, it's his only painting hanging in any Italian museum. You can hit most of the major works in the first eight rooms of the museum (there are about 24 in total).

Leonardo's original **"Codex Atlanticus"** is in the Biblioteca Ambrosiana next door along with other rare manuscripts. Drawings from the "Codex," which consists of 1,750 drawings and jottings the master did between 1478 and 1519, can be seen in the Sacristy of Bramante in Santa Maria delle Grazie (p. 480). Leonardo's entire life as an artist and scientist can be found in this extraordinary collection.

Piazza Pio XI. www.ambrosiana.eu. ✆ **02/806-921.** Pinacoteca 10€; Pinacoteca plus Codex Atlanticus 15€ adults, 10€ ages under 18 and over 65, free for kids 14 and under. Tues–Sun 10am–6pm. Metro: Duomo or Cordusio.

Pinacoteca di Brera ★★★ MUSEUM Milan's, and indeed Lombardy's, premier art collection resides in a 17th-century Jesuit college, wrapped around a two-story arcaded courtyard. This peerless collection leads the visitor on a circular tour through Italian art from medieval to Surrealism in 38 roughly chronological rooms. Along the way are splendid Renaissance altarpieces, Venetian School and baroque paintings, gloomy Mannerist works, and the odd piece by Carlo Carrà and Umberto Boccioni.

cruising **THE CANALS**

Milan's **Navigli** area (*navigli* means canals) is the perfect spot for a relaxed drink, people-watching, and a late-night supper. (To get there, take Metro Line 2 to Porta Genova.) Its streets are refreshingly casual in ambience after the dressy obsession of the city center—it's one of the few places in Milan where you will see punks, hippies, and Goths, and where you will find vintage-clothing stores.

Construction of the canals started in the late 13th century, initially to transport marble slabs from quarries along Lake Maggiore (see p. 508) to build the Duomo. The Naviglio Grande was Europe's first major canal and remains an engineering marvel of the medieval era. Used to import food, commodities, and trade goods, the canals were crucial to Milan's infrastructure until the 1970s, when road transport won out. Take a boat tour of the canals to peek into Milan's industrial heritage; **Navigami** (www.navigami.com; ✆ **02/867-131**) runs frequent tours, though lack of rain in recent years, especially during the summer, has led to low water levels in the canals. Check to make sure boats are running.

The elegant galleries of the Pinacoteca di Brera.

Although the collection is not immense, it is of exquisite quality; highlights include Piero della Francesca's sublime **Montefeltro Altarpiece** (1474); the ethereal **"Dead Christ"** by Andrea Mantegna (1480); Caravaggio's superb, mournful **"Supper at Emmaus"** (1601); and Raphael's **"Marriage of the Virgin"** (1504), expertly kept in glass-walled, temperature-controlled restoration rooms here, which are also open to the public. More modern standouts include Francesco Hayez's **"The Kiss"** (1859) and artist Giovanni Fattori's pastoral scenes, which paved the way for the late-19th-century Macchiaioli School of Italian Impressionists. Moving the collection up to the present day are works by the Italian playboy artist Amedeo Modigliani and sculptor Marino Marini. Even if you don't visit the collection, you can enter the courtyard for free (many visitors come here merely to take photos of the statue of "Napoleon as Mars the Peacemaker") or have a coffee or bite to eat at the gorgeous **Caffè Fernanda,** a space that reflects the artistic and historical context of the palazzo.

Via Brera 28. pinacotecabrera.org. ✆ **02/722-632-30.** 15€ adults; 2€ ages 18–25; free for kids under 18; 1€ seniors Tues–Wed. Tues–Sun 8:30am–7:15pm (until 10:15pm 3rd Thurs of month). Free every 1st Sun of month. Metro: Lanza.

Santa Maria delle Grazie ★★ CHURCH The delightful Lombard Renaissance church of Santa Maria delle Grazie is often ignored in the mad scramble to see Leonardo da Vinci's world-renowned "Last Supper" (see p. 481) in the *cenacolo* (refectory) of the Dominican convent attached to the church. Started in 1465–82 by Guiniforte Solari (ca. 1429–81), the church was enlarged when the Sforza duke Ludovico il Moro (see p. 471) decided to make it his family mausoleum. He commissioned Leonardo da Vinci to paint the "Last Supper," and asked Donato Bramante, the leading architect of the Lombard Renaissance—who also helped design St. Peter's in Rome—to add the terracotta-and-cream-colored choir in 1492. Inside the church itself, note the clash of styles between Solari's frescoed Gothic nave and Bramante's airy, somber apse.

Piazza Santa Maria delle Grazie. ✆ **02/467-6111.** Free. Mon–Sat 7am–noon and 3–7:30pm (4–7:30pm summer); Sun 7:30am–12:30pm and 4–9pm. Metro: Cadorna or Conciliazione.

Santa Maria delle Grazie, Il Cenacolo Vinciano (The Last Supper) ★★★ CHURCH Milan's greatest art treasure is also one of the most famous on earth, in part thanks to Dan Brown's blockbuster novel *The Da Vinci Code.* Painted for Ludovico il Moro by Leonardo da Vinci between 1495 and 1497, "The Last Supper" adorns the back wall of the refectory in the Dominican convent attached to Santa Maria delle Grazie. Leonardo's masterpiece depicts Christ revealing that one of his disciples will soon betray him; horror and disbelief are etched into every face, while Jesus remains calm and resigned. As we look at the fresco, Judas sits to the left of Jesus, leaning away from him with the bag of silver clearly

seeing "THE LAST SUPPER"

Unsurprisingly, Leonardo's "The Last Supper" is on almost every tourist's itinerary of Milan. And with a maximum of 30 people allowed into the Cenacolo Vinciano at a time (as few as 18 at a time when the space first reopened after the coronavirus emergency), it is a challenge to get a ticket if you don't book well in advance. Try the official website first, www.cenacolovinciano.net, or call ✆ **02/9280-0360** (tickets are 15€ from the website, plus a 2€ booking fee; children under 18 enter free but still pay the 2€ fee) **3 months** or more before you are due to visit. If you have purchased your tickets online (maximum of 5 tickets per order), go to the booking office outside the Cenacolo in Piazza Santa Maria delle Grazie at least 20 minutes before your allotted time slot. You will need to show identification that matches the name on the reservation. And remember that the Cenacolo is not in the church of Santa Maria delle Grazie itself, but in the refectory behind it, with a separate entrance of its own.

If you've missed the opportunity to snag a ticket in advance, many tour companies guarantee admission to "The Last Supper" as part of their guided tours of the city, which range from 40€ to 70€ (see "Organized Tours," p. 483). It also doesn't hurt to go directly to the ticket office at the refectory and ask if last-minute tickets are available for the same day.

Don't miss **Leonardo's Vineyard Museum** across the street in the Casa degli Atellani, where da Vinci lived while he was painting "The Last Supper." It is said that he would go back to the house at the end of the day and, given he came from a family of winemakers, tend to his vines in the garden to unwind (www.vignadileonardo.com; ✆ **02/481-6150**). The small vineyard has been revived today, and visitors can tour it and the noble *palazzo.* Tickets are 10€ adults and 8€ ages 6 to 18.

visible in his right hand. Is that Mary Magdalene sitting between him and Jesus? (Most historians think it's St. John, who was typically depicted as a beautiful youth.) Wherever you stand on the issue, there's no doubt that "The Last Supper" is one of the world's most poignant works of art.

In experimenting with his painting technique, Leonardo applied tempera straight on to the walls of the refectory. As a result, his work began to deteriorate virtually as soon as it was completed. It suffered several hamfisted restoration attempts in the 18th and 19th centuries and survived target practice by Napoleon's troops, not to mention a period exposed to the open air after Allied bombing in World War II. The latest cleanup of the fresco was completed in 1999, and while the colors are muted, they are thought to resemble Leonardo's original. The famous fresco is now climate-controlled for preservation; groups of only 30 at a time are allowed in to view it, in pre-allocated periods of 15 minutes.

Piazza Santa Maria delle Grazie 2. www.cenacolovinciano.net. ✆ **02/9280-0360.** 15€ adults; 2€ ages 18–25; free for kids under 18; 2€ booking fee for all tickets. Reservations essential. Tues–Sun 8:15am–7pm. Metro: Cadorna or Conciliazione.

Triennale di Milano ★★★ MUSEUM Located at the north end of Parco Sempione by the Torre Branca, this sleek temple of contemporary design has been around since 1923, featuring on-trend temporary exhibitions of modern craftsmanship, fashion, theater, and photography. Some of the exhibitions are more interesting than others, but the garden and terrace restaurant (when open) are worth a visit.

Viale Alemagna 6. www.triennale.org. ✆ **02/724-341.** Depending on the exhibition, tickets start at around 5€ adults; free for kids under 16. Tues–Sun 11am–8pm. Metro: Cadorna or Cairoli.

Outlying Attractions

Autodromo Nazionale Monza ★★ RACING CIRCUIT Located along the River Lambro, 15km (10¼ miles) northeast of Milan, Monza is an appealing city with a photogenic central core and a sprawling park that is famous throughout Europe. Sadly, the *centro storico* is usually bypassed in favor of this 10km (6.2-mile) Formula One racetrack, the epicenter of car-mad Italy's hopes and dreams. The home of the Italian Grand Prix since 1922, Monza track is now open to any and all who fancy being a racing driver for the day. Race-training sessions are held daily, with half-hour slots available for would-be champions to try out their skills on the track. Rallies, races, and special events take place all year round. Check the website for tickets and event details.

Via Vedano 5, Monza. www.monzanet.it. ✆ **039/24-821.** Trains to Monza take about 15 min. from Centrale or Garibaldi station; park is a 15-min. walk from the town center.

Certosa di Pavia ★★★ CHURCH Located a few miles north of the town of Pavia, this awe-inspiring Carthusian monastery was originally commissioned in 1396 as a mausoleum for Milan's ruling Visconti family (see p. 471). After their dynastic downfall, the Sforza family took over, refurbishing per their exorbitant tastes. The highly intricate Renaissance facade is the swan song of 15th-century master architect Giovanni Antonio Amadeo, who also worked on Bergamo's Basilica di Santa Maria Maggiore (p. 494). The monastery contains the ornate tomb (but not the bodies) of Ludovico del Moro and his wife, Beatrice, who together shaped the Milanese Renaissance. A tour takes in the peaceful cloisters, monks' cells, and refectory, but the highlight is the church, with its swaths of frescoes, the *pietra dura* altar, and the massive mausoleum of Gian Galeazzo Visconti. Via Del Monumento 4, Certosa di Pavia. www.museo.certosadipavia.beniculturali.it. ✆ **0382/925-613.** Admission and guided tours by donation. Tues–Sun 9–11:30am and 2:30–6pm (closes 5:30pm Apr and Sept, 5pm Mar and Oct, 4pm Nov–Feb). Metro Line 3 to Certosa, then a 10-min. walk.

Organized Tours

Among the scores of companies offering guided tours of Milan and Lombardy, here are a few of the best. **Zani Viaggi** (www.zaniviaggi.it; ✆ **02/867-131**) leads specialist tours to the revered turf of San Siro Stadium (see p. 484) and the shopping outlets of northern Lombardy. **Opera d'Arte** (www.operadartemilano.it; ✆ **02/4548-7400**) offers guided tours of exhibitions, museums, and historic sites, including a special Castello Sforzesco tour with access to the battlements and underground areas that typically are not open to the public. Italy-based **Do Eat Better** (doeatbetterexperience.com/italy-food-tour/what-to-do-in-milan; ✆ **329/179-0647**) offers food tours with locals. You can choose from among an aperitivo tour in the Navigli district, a pastry tasting experience, or a gourmet food tour.

Outdoor Activities

Milan is a densely populated urban sprawl where green space is rare and precious, though the city has worked hard in recent years to plant more trees and build and expand parks. The largest park is the 47-hectare (116-acre) **Parco Sempione** behind Castello Sforzesco, a favorite place for well-heeled Milanese to walk their dogs along shady pathways sheltered by giant chestnuts; lovers come here to moon around the ornamental lakes. The **Giardini Pubblici** at Porta Venezia is another haven, a firm favorite with families on the weekend for its little fair. Joggers circuit the park, and in winter there's ice-skating on its ponds. **Parco Solari** and **Acquatica Waterpark** (p. 485) have swimming pools, and **Idroscalo** (p. 484) near Linate offers every outdoor activity from sailing and swimming to climbing or tennis. The 1930s-era **Villa Necchi Campiglio** (fondoambiente.it/villa-necchi-campiglio-eng) is probably the most famous "house museum" in the city, especially considering it has been the setting for various films, including *House of Gucci* (though nobody in the Gucci family ever actually lived here). The lush gardens and outdoor swimming pool make it an oasis of tranquility right in the heart of the city, between Porta Venezia and the Duomo. Sit in the garden and catch your breath from a busy day sightseeing or come here for *aperitivo* and watch the sun go down poolside. It is free to enter the gardens. For sports fans, the **San Siro** football (soccer) stadium (www.sansiro.net; ✆ **02/4879-8201**) and **Monza F1 racetrack** (p. 482) are open for tours.

Especially for Kids

Despite being world-renowned as a hub of high finance, fashion, and design, Milan is after all an Italian city—and all Italians dote on children. The city's rather formal facade belies its many family-friendly attractions, museums, *gelaterie,* and play parks, and everywhere you go, your *bambini* will be worshipped, hugged, and multilaterally adored.

Where to start? Chief among attractions that all kids will love is the ride up to the **Duomo rooftop** (see p. 474) for views of the city's red rooftops and the new skyscraper district, all the way to the Alps. The **Museo Nazionale Scienza e Tecnologica Leonardo da Vinci** (p. 477) is stuffed full of fun interactive activities for kids. Children ages 4 to 11 can enjoy workshops (usually in Italian) at the Sforzinda children's area in the 14th-century dungeons of **Castello Sforzesco** (p. 471) while parents explore the decorative arts upstairs. A picnic lunch and a run in adjoining **Parco Sempione** is a welcome respite from cultural overload.

The **Museo dei Bambini** (Via Enrico Besana 12; www.muba.it; ✆ **02/4398-0402**) doesn't have a permanent collection, but offers creative and educational workshops for children ages 2 and up. Opening times vary, as do the costs of workshops, which tend to run around 10 euro.

Another great green public space is the **Giardini Pubblici Indro Montanelli** (see p. 483), which has playgrounds, roundabouts, and a little electric train that chugs around the park. On the Corso Venezia side of the park, you can take the kids to the **Museo di Storia Naturale** (museodistorianaturalemilano.it; ✆ **02/8846-3337;** Tues–Sun 9am–5:30pm; admission 5€, children under 18 free) to see dinosaur skeletons and the carcasses of massive bugs. Near Porta Romana, the **Bagni Misteriosi** (www.bagnimisteriosi.com; ✆ **02/8973-1800;** Via Carlo Botta 18) is an outdoor swimming pool from the 1930s that was abandoned for decades and has been brought back to life. It's a great place to beat the heat in the torrid summer months, but make sure to arrive early to get a chair or a spot in the grass. Whatever you do, bring a swim cap (standard practice in most pools in Italy) or you'll be charged around 8€ for one.

The newly restored **Darsena,** the historic port of the canal network in the Navigli area, is a great place to sit down with a picnic or gelato and watch boats go by, either in one of the seating areas or at waterside cafes.

Near Linate airport, just east of the city center, the **Idroscalo** park (Via Circonvallazione Idroscalo 29, Segrate; www.idroscalo.info; no phone) features a manmade lake that was originally created for seaplanes to land. This area has now been turned into a park and is open daily (summer 7am–9pm; winter 7am–5pm).

FUN IN THE theme parks

Italy's version of Disneyland, **Gardaland,** is located a couple of hours from Milan in Castlenuovo del Garda (see p. 516), but plenty of other options lie closer to the city.

If you're looking to beat the summertime heat, the **Acquatica** waterpark (Via Gaetano Airaghi 61; www.acquaticapark.it; ✆ **02/4820-0134**) on the far western outskirts of town has splashy waterslides, rides, and picnic areas. It opens at the end of May and closes the end of August. To get there, take the subway's lilac line (also called MM5) to the San Siro stop, then either bus 80 (toward Quinto Romano) or bus 423 (toward Settimo Milanese), both of which stop directly in front of the water park. The park is open daily 10am to 7pm. An all-day ticket costs 19€ adults (23€ on weekends), 13€ for kids under 12. Children under 100cm (3 ft., 3 in.) tall enter for free. Enter after 2:30pm for slightly reduced tickets. Parking is 2€.

About 30 minutes northeast of Milan in the direction of Bergamo, the **Leolandia** amusement park (Via Vittorio Veneto 52, Capriate San Gervasio; www.leolandia.it) has rides and games for kids of all ages, as well as the delightful Minitalia, a replica of major cities and monuments in Italy. More compact and manageable than Gardaland, it may be better suited to smaller children, with features such as Peppa Pig World and Thomas the Tank Engine. Tickets purchased at the park cost 39.50€, but can be half that online. Children up to 89cm (about 3 ft.) enter free. Leolandia opens in late March and stays open through Halloween. In early spring and fall, it's open weekends only; in June and July it's open Wednesday to Sunday; in August it's open daily. The Z301 Milan-Bergamo bus, managed by **Nord Est Trasporti** (www.nordesttrasporti.it; ✆ **800/905-150**), stops near Leolandia, at Capriate San Gervasio.

Most restaurants will happily rustle up a child's portion of pasta and tomato sauce, and if all else fails, it's usually easy to bribe any child with a visit to one of Milan's delicious ice cream shops; try **Biancolatte** (Via Turati 30; ✆ **02/6208-6177**), for baked goods and ice-cream cakes, or **Rinomata Gelateria** (Ripa di Porta Ticinese 1; ✆ **02/5811-3877**) in the Navigli area for one of the most traditional ice-cream cones in town.

Where to Stay in Milan

Milan is northern Italy's largest commercial center, big on banking and industry, and for years its hotels have tended to chase expense-account customers, often to the detriment of tourists and families. The winds of change are blowing, however. A recent wave of cozy, independent *locandas* and *albergos,* as well as design-conscious boutique hotels, have come along to complement the grand old institutions.

Note that prices are often higher during the week than on the weekend, and room rates really soar when the fashion and design crowd hits town (in normal years, late Feb, mid-May, and late Sept).

SELF-CATERING ROOMS & APARTMENTS

If you want to live like a real Milanese, self-catering rooms and apartments can be a great option, allowing you to shop at local markets, try your hand at cooking the local cuisine, or at least have a refrigerator where you can keep water, wine, and cheese. Some properties even have washing machines (thanks to high electricity costs, don't expect most to have dryers).

EXPENSIVE

Hotel Principe di Savoia ★★ At this grand Beaux Arts institution, part of the Dorchester Collection of hotels, every conceivable guest whim is impeccably addressed. A stay here is truly a respite from the bustling city outside; guests have access to serene gardens, a soothing top-floor spa, a quality restaurant, an elegant bar, and opulent rooms and suites. The presidential suite even has its own indoor swimming pool (those traveling with children can ask for private swim lessons). This luxury comes at a price, but for a bit of old-fashioned glamour, there's nowhere else like it. It's strategically located near both Stazione Centrale and the modern Piazza Gae Aulenti, representing the new face of the city. Across the street, stroll along Piazza Lina Bo Bardi (Milan's version of New York's High Line) to reach tony Corso Como. If you are in Milan to hit the stores, ask for the VIP Shopping Card, which grants exclusive access to select boutiques.

Piazza Della Repubblica 17. www.dorchestercollection.com/en/milan/hotel-principe-di-savoia. ✆ **02/623-01.** 301 units. 300€–900€ double. Metro: Repubblica. **Amenities:** Restaurant; bar; concierge; room service; babysitting; spa; gym; indoor pool; free Wi-Fi.

Milanosuites ★★★ The elegant, light-filled Milanosuites property is located on a cobblestoned street between the Duomo and the castle, with the La Scala opera house smack in the middle of those two monuments. Set in a charming 18th-century townhouse, one- and two-bedroom suites have parquet floors and sleek white furnishings that add a note of glamour. All have separate living rooms; some have kitchenettes, but no laundry facilities. The property also has a lounge and communal breakfast area, though breakfast usually costs an extra 10€ or so.

Via San Tomaso 6. www.milanosuites.it. ✆ **02/805-1023.** 5 units. 250€–395€ double. Metro: Cordusio or Cairoli. **Amenities:** Concierge; room service; free Wi-Fi.

MODERATE

Antica Locanda Leonardo ★★★ Just a few doors down from where "The Last Supper" hangs in Santa Maria delle Grazie church, this lovely *albergo* in a 19th-century building overlooks a surprisingly tranquil courtyard garden. It's like stepping into a family home, thanks to the hospitality offered by owners Martina and Camilla. Rooms retain a wonderfully traditional feel, with heavy antique headboards and dressers, gilt mirrors, and elegant draperies. Like any historic home, it has its quirks—in colder months, it can get a bit drafty, for example, and sometimes electrical outlets are not in the most convenient locations for charging multiple devices. Fortunately, bathrooms have been brought into the 21st century. The cozy lounge and breakfast room remain delightfully of a former age but with modern touches here and there. The more expensive courtyard-facing rooms, many with tiny wrought-iron balconies, are buffered from the noise of trams rumbling down Corso Magenta. Check the website for the most competitive rates.

Corso Magenta 78. www.anticalocandaleonardo.com. ✆ **02/4801-4197.** 16 units. 130€–350€ double. Rates include breakfast. Metro: Conciliazione, Cadorna. **Amenities:** Concierge; free Wi-Fi.

nhow Milan ★★ This boutique hotel in the Navigli area is popular with the fashion and design set who flock here during Milan's fashion weeks and the Salone del Mobile furniture fair. A sleek reception area sets the scene with an orange color scheme straight from the 1960s. nhow seeks to wow with what it calls "unconventional spaces": colorful corners for having a drink or admiring the temporary art exhibitions. Glass elevators whiz guests up to rooms decorated in white and bright solid colors; standard rooms are compact, however, with walk-in showers. Chic loft-style suites on the fourth floor have views over Milan's Zona Tortona fashion district along with quirky details like transparent glass tubs with portholes that offer plays of light to the floor below.

Via Tortona 35. www.nhow-milan.com. ✆ **02/489-8861.** 246 units. 150€–289€ double. Rates include breakfast. Metro: Porto Genova. **Amenities:** Restaurant; bar; spa; gym; free Wi-Fi.

INEXPENSIVE

BioCity Hotel ★★★ This fab little "organic city hotel" housed in a villa from the 1920s offers great value and is only a few minutes' walk from Stazione Centrale (though the train station has been spruced up, it is still a not good idea to linger too long on the streets here at night). BioCity is all a budget hotel should be: small and pristine, with a miniscule bar and breakfast room (serving a basic continental breakfast of cheeses, cold cuts, pastries, and yogurt) and a tiny terrace out back—*and* it's eco-friendly. Guest rooms are stylish with big bathrooms almost fit for a four-star hotel. The minimal reception area manages to squeeze in a little lounge furnished with funky pieces. This gem of a hotel is close to both metro line 2 and metro line 3, which can take you to the city's major sites. A small wellness area with sauna, aromatherapy showers, a relaxation zone, and herbal teas is available for 45€ an hour, which is incredibly private given that only one room is able to gain access at a time; robes and slippers are provided. The only time of year you won't find good value for money here is during the city's fashion weeks or the Salone del Mobile furniture fair in the spring.

Via Edolo 18. www.biocityhotel.it. ✆ **02/6670-3595.** 17 units. 85€–199€ double. Rates include breakfast. Metro: Sondrio. **Amenities:** Bar; free Wi-Fi.

Where to Eat in Milan

Milan has thousands of eateries, from pizzerias to grand old cafes, Michelin-starred restaurants in highfalutin surroundings to corner bars with a great selection of *aperitivo*-time tapas, *gelaterie,* and traditional *osterie.* Avoid obvious tourist traps—any place that has a menu showing photos of the dishes.

Cocktail hour starts around 6:30pm, all over town, as the Milanese magically appear from shopping or work to meet up for cocktails, a bitter Campari, or a glass of Prosecco. By the time *aperitivo* hour is over, thoughts turn towards supper and restaurants start to fill up. Sadly, the lavish *aperitivo* spreads of the past—where you could fill up on olives, crudités, cold pasta dishes, rice, salads, salamis, and breads—were suspended during the pandemic and may never return.

If you find yourself tiring of Italian cuisine, Milan now has quite a variety of ethnic restaurants; sushi and Chinese food are especially popular, and Via Paolo Sarpi, the main street of Milan's thriving Chinatown neighborhood, offers a variety of options.

EXPENSIVE

Contraste ★★★ ITALIAN FUSION Set behind a graffiti-covered wall, the "contrasts" are evident here from outside this restaurant, with the only signage a small gold plate next to a residential gate.. It's hard to believe you're about to enter a Michelin-starred restaurant that offers "wow factor" for both the eyes and the taste buds, serving innovative, playful dishes in an intimate all-white space. Various tasting menus offer intriguing specialties such as a "donut" alla Bolognese (actually a circular lasagna with a hole), crème brûlée with foie gras, and gnocchi with smoked eel and burrata cheese. The chefs here don't believe in being held to a set menu, which also means that you tell the waitstaff what you're in the mood for, and the kitchen may just make it for you. If you are feeling more adventurous, just ask to be surprised and the kitchen will put out the best of what's in season in their signature playful way.

Via G. Meda 2. www.contrastemilano.it. ✆ **02/4953-6597.** Entrees 20€–50€. Daily 7:30pm–midnight; Sat–Sun 12:30–3pm. On Tram 3, it's 7 stops from the Duomo.

Joia ★★★ VEGETARIAN Milan is not all bone-marrow risotto and *osso buco,* and this fine-dining vegetarian restaurant (the first in Europe to earn a Michelin star) is a local institution. The decor, with light wood-paneled walls, is meant to be a nod to understated Eastern minimalism, but the real draw is Swiss chef Pietro Leemann's creative vegan and vegetarian food. He's known for whimsical and philosophical presentations: A savory red-lentil tart with baby turnips and a tangerine sauce is cryptically named "There Once Was a King," while "Oh My Dear Planet" is a vegan take on *foie gras.* An interesting interpretation of risotto called "The Navel of the World" contains delica pumpkin and nutmeg, cashew soft cheese, sweet black salsify with turnip tops, and a green sauce made from capers. Reservations recommended.

Via P. Castaldi 18. www.joia.it. ✆ **02/2952-2124.** Entrees 28€–42€. Tues–Sat noon–2:30pm and 7:30–11pm. Closed Sun and Mon. Metro: Repubblica.

Restaurant Giacomo Arengario ★★★ MODERN ITALIAN Deserving three stars just for its Duomo views, this restaurant is a top choice for a business lunch among well-heeled Milanese. Set on the top floor of the Palazzo dell'Arengario, which also houses the Museo del Novecento (p. 477), it has a smart little bar for early-evening *aperitivos,* but the real point is to get a table near those plate-glass windows to gawk at the Duomo. The menu offers creatively presented Milanese classics like veal cutlet—risotto in particular is prepared to perfection—along with gourmet takes on dishes from around Italy, such as *tortelli cacio e pepe* served with red prawns. Finish off your meal with the house specialty dessert, the "Bomba," an artfully presented explosion of puff pastry, Chantilly cream, mascarpone, and wild strawberries. Not in the mood for a full meal? Come for coffee and dessert (or a cocktail) after a visit to the museum downstairs or the Duomo.

Via Guglielmo Marconi 1. giacomomilano.com. ✆ **02/72-093-814.** Entrees 20€–55€. Daily noon–midnight. Metro: Duomo.

Ristorante Cracco ★★ MODERN ITALIAN Celebrated chef Carlo Cracco has realized his dream of opening in the Galleria, with a multilevel space that includes a cafe, a fine-dining restaurant, a wine cellar, smoking room, and a private lounge for special occasions. Patrons enter from the elegant cafe downstairs (which, in the mornings, serves up excellent brioches put out by the master pastry chefs here, for about the same price as those offered by anonymous coffee bars around town), to reach the first-floor restaurant set up like a welcoming and elegantly appointed historic home. Like the space, Cracco's cuisine is both traditional and innovative, and given that even appetizers can run up to 70€ (lobster served with Sicilian avocado, kiwi, and caviar), a meal here is certainly a splurge. Some of the dishes give a nod to local tradition, such as Milanese veal served with broccoli, taggiasca olives, and grapes or the classic saffron risotto with grilled bone marrow. If you get a chance, check out the wine cellar for a tasting—with more than 2,000 labels to choose from.

Galleria Vittorio Emanuele II. www.ristorantecracco.it. ✆ **02/876-774.** Entrees 40€–60€. Tues–Fri lunch and dinner; Mon and Sat dinner only; closed Sun. Metro: Duomo.

MODERATE

La Pesa Trattoria dal 1902 ★★ LOMBARDY/NORTHERN ITALIAN With Milan being the most international city in Italy, in some neighborhoods it is easier to find Asian fusion or Lebanese cuisine than traditional Milanese dishes. La Pesa Trattoria—located to the east of the city center not far from San Siro stadium—has been around since 1902 and serves up all of the classics, including saffron risotto, osso buco, Milanese tripe soup, and breaded veal cutlet. Start off with *sciatt,* crunchy fritters filled with taleggio cheese, or the house specialty meatballs served with a special mustard sauce. The atmosphere here is intimate and rustic, with moss green walls, beamed ceilings, and checked tablecloths. It is about a 15-minute walk from the nearest subway station.

Via Fantoni 26. www.trattorialapesa1902.it. ✆ **02/3651-4525.** Entrees 12€–23€. Mon–Sun noon–3pm and 7pm–midnight. Metro: Segesta, Bande Nere.

Osteria il Kaimano ★★ ITALIAN This casual, pleasantly chaotic *osteria* is a reliable choice in the artsy, cobblestoned Brera district. Strong choices include zucchini flowers stuffed with ricotta, ravioli with smoked ham and radicchio, or the Neapolitan-style pizzas that continually slide out of the wood-burning oven. First courses *(primi)* are reasonably priced but the second-course meat dishes *(secondi)* can be on the pricey side. Milanese favorites like veal cutlet and saffron risotto are on offer here along with dishes from around Italy, ranging from spaghetti in Bolognese sauce to Sicilian-style swordfish. Despite the translated menu posted outside, an abundant local clientele proves this is no tourist trap. **Nabucco** (Via Fiori Chiari 10; www.nabucco.it; ✆ **02/860-663**) is another good Brera option with a similar menu and slightly higher prices, but Kaimano wins for its cozy atmosphere and warm service.

Via Fiori Chiari 20. www.il-kaimano.it. ✆ **02/8050-2733.** Entrees 15€–40€. Daily noon–2:30pm and 6–11:30pm. Metro: Lanza Brera.

INEXPENSIVE

Berberè ★★ PIZZERIA Traditionally, Milan has not been a pizza town—Milanese pies are typically simple, flat, and crispy—but a wave of Neapolitan-style pizzerias is changing that, thanks to topnotch ingredients, a special sourdough starter, and long-rising dough. Berberè, which was started by two brothers in Bologna since expanding to other cities in Italy, serves "artisanal pizzas" in a light and bright space in the funky Isola neighborhood (and several other locations in the city: near Stazione Centrale, near Porta Roma, and in the Navigli district). Most of the pizzas are made from stone-ground, semi-whole-wheat flour (there are other dough options as well). Not too thick or too thin, each pizza is perfectly chewy and airy, with interesting seasonal toppings—many of them organic—like beets, Salina capers, spicy Calabrian 'nduja sausage, roast pumpkin, *mozzarella di bufala,* or *fiordilatte mozzarella.* Pair your pizza with a craft beer or an organic wine.

Via Sebenico 24. www.berberepizza.it. ✆ **02/3670-7820.** Entrees 6€–12€. Mon–Fri 7–11:30pm; Sat–Sun 12:30–2:30pm and 7–11:30pm. Metro: Isola.

Nerino Dieci Trattoria ★★ MEDITERRANEAN Call at least a month in advance for dinner reservations at this wildly popular family-run trattoria near the *centro storico,* offering solid seasonal Italian cuisine at reasonable prices for the quality of food and sophisticated presentation. The restaurant is laid out with plenty of cozy little corners, well-suited for a romantic dinner or even business lunch. Service is attentive. The menu changes with the seasons—seafood is one specialty here—with creative twists on traditional dishes, such as taglioni pasta with clams and spicy salami or sous-vide pork with apple chutney, fondant potatoes, and beurre noisette.

Via Nerino 10. www.nerinodieci.it. ✆ **02/3983-1019.** Entrees 12€–22€. Mon–Fri noon–2:30pm and 7:30–11pm; Sat 7:30–11pm. Metro: Missori.

Pizzeria Tradizionale ★★ PIZZERIA This canalside pizzeria in the Navigli neighborhood is nothing fancy (think checked tablecloths), but it's always busy and buzzing; you may want to reserve ahead of time. Happy patrons devour enormous and reasonably priced crispy pizzas piled with local cold cuts and mozzarella, as well as vast bowls of garlic-infused spaghetti alle *vongole* (clams). It bills itself as a "pizzeria and fish restaurant," so the menu offers Neapolitan-style seafood dishes as well. Service is usually fast and friendly. The location on the canals is great, and you can eat outside when weather permits.

Ripa di Porta Ticinese 7. www.pizzeriatradizionale.com. ✆ **02/839-5133.** Entrees 8.50€–18€. Daily noon–2:30pm and 7pm–1am (no lunch Wed). Metro: Porta Genova.

Milan Shopping

Milan is known worldwide as a temple of high fashion, with the hallowed streets **Montenapoleone** and **Spiga** in the **Quadrilatero d'Oro** being the most popular places of wallet-stripping worship. Here D&G, Prada, Gucci, Hermès, Louis Vuitton, Armani, Ralph Lauren, Versace, and Cavalli all jostle for Milan's fashionistas. The area around Porta Nuova (at the top of Corso Como) is also starting to become a luxury-shopping district. More reasonable shopping areas include **Via Torino** and **Corso Buenos Aires,** where midrange international brands proliferate; if you're clever you can snag a designer bargain at outlet store **Il Salvagente** (Via Fratelli Bronzetti 16; ✆ **02/7611-0328**). Milan is also a design hub; if you want to take home a unique piece, stop in the three-story **Fornasetti Store** (Corso Venezia 21A; ✆ **02/8416-1374**), which sells bold, whimsical

Upscale shopping in Milan.

creations (everything from coasters to ceramics to furnishings) based on the "practical madness" of the late Milanese designer Piero Fornasetti.

Fashion is one Milanese obsession; food is another, and the *centro storico* has many superb delis where you can purchase the purest of olive oils and the finest cheeses. **Peck** (Via Spadari 9; ✆ **02/802-3161**), still the number-one gourmet spot, has expanded to include several locations; it has keen competition in the **Eataly** megastore in Piazza XXV Aprile (www.eataly.it) for all Italian comestibles. The top floor of the **La Rinascente department store** in Piazza del Duomo is another haven for foodies, with its Obicà mozzarella bar, Moët & Chandon Champagne bar, a sushi corner, a mini steak restaurant, and fine selection of packaged Italian goods (as an added bonus, you get a close-up view of the Duomo).

English-language books are sold at **Feltrinelli Librerie** (corner of Piazza del Duomo and Via Ugo Foscolo 1/3), **Mondadori Megastore** (Piazza del Duomo 1), **Rizzoli** (inside the Galleria Vittorio Emanuele II, see p. 475), and the Feltrinelli Express inside Stazione Centrale. English-language newspapers can be found on most major newsstands around the *centro storico.*

MILANO MARKETS

Everybody loves a bargain, and there's no better place to find one than at the colorful **Viale Papiniano market** (metro Sant'Agostino). Its sea of stalls is open Tuesday and Saturday; some flog designer seconds, others leather basics. **Flea markets** spring up on Saturdays along the Alzaia Naviglio Grande and Fiera di Sinigaglia (metro Porta Genova for both), and on Sundays at San Donato Metro stop. During the Christmas season, **holiday markets** (complete with ice skating) pop up in different parts of the city, from Piazza Gae Aulenti (metro Garibaldi) to the Castello Sforzesco (metro Cairoli) to the area behind the Museum of Natural History (metro Palestro) in the Giardini Pubblici Indro Montanelli. A large **food market** at the Piazza Wagner metro is open every morning except Sunday. A two-level food hall in Stazione Centrale known as **Mercato Centrale** (www.mercatocentrale.com/milan) has around 24 stalls and ample seating upstairs. Here you can find everything from empanadas to risotto to pizza to Chinese dumplings. You can also come here for a relaxing cocktail or to buy bread or focaccia to take with you on the train.

Nightlife & Entertainment

Unless you're heading for the Ticinese and Navigli, Milan is a dressy city and generally looks askance at scruffy jeans and sneakers after dark. When many people don't dine until well after 10pm, it's not surprising that clubs and bars stay open until the very wee hours.

A couple of spots unique to Milan include the vine-covered cocktail terrace at **10 Corso Como** (www.10corsocomo.com; ✆ **02/2901-3581**) and **Ceresio 7 Pools & Restaurant**, Via Ceresio 7 (www.ceresio7.com; ✆ **02/310-392-21**), which offers a novel setup: a chic, sleek rooftop lounge with two pools where one can enjoy a cocktail while enjoying amazing views of the city.

A venerable Milan institution, the **Conservatorio di Musica Giuseppe Verdi** has two stages for classical concerts, at Via Conservatorio 12 (www.consmilano.it; ✆ **02/762-110**). Check the website for the latest schedules.

Milan is forever associated with the grand old dame of opera, **Teatro alla Scala ★★**, perhaps the world's favorite opera house, decked out with sumptuous red seats, boxes adorned with gilt, and chandeliers dripping crystal. It's a good idea to book well in advance of the opera season (Dec–late July and early Sept–Nov). Book online at teatroallascala.vivaticket.it or at the ticket office in Largo Ghiringhelli, Piazza della Scala (in between the theater entrance and the entrance to the La Scala Museum). ***Tip:*** Two hours before each performance, unsold seats are sold at a discounted price online at www.teatroallascala.org, and you can also check the box office 1 hour before to see if any seats remain unsold. There are also a limited number of obstructed-view balcony seats available for most performances, but you must get on the list for these seats, which can be a somewhat complicated, ever-changing process. Keep in mind that to pick up tickets or be put on the list, you must bring a form of identification with you. For updated information, go to www.teatroallascala.org/en/box-office.

BERGAMO ★★

47km (29 miles) NE of Milan

Bergamo is a city of two distinct characters. The ancient **Città Alta** is a beautiful medieval and Renaissance town perched on a green hill. **Città Bassa,** mostly built in the 19th and 20th centuries, sits at the feet of the upper town and concerns itself with 21st-century life. Visitors tend to focus on the historic upper town, a place for wandering, soaking in the rarified atmosphere, and enjoying the lovely vistas from its belvederes.

Essentials

ARRIVING **Trains** arrive from and depart for Milan Stazione Centrale hourly (50 min.; 5.80€). If you are **driving,** Bergamo is linked to Milan via the A4. The trip takes under an hour if traffic is good. ***Note:*** It's difficult to park in the largely pedestrianized Città Alta—park instead in Città Bassa and take the **funicular** (see below) up to the historic area.

VISITOR INFORMATION The Città Bassa tourist office is close to the train and bus stations at Viale Papa Giovanni XXIII 57 (✆ **035/210-204**); it's open daily 9am to 12:30pm and 2 to 5:30pm. The Città Alta office is at Via Gombito 13 (✆ **035/242-226**), right off Via Colleoni, and is open daily 9am to 5:30pm. The **Visit Bergamo** official tourism website is www.visitbergamo.net.

GETTING AROUND Bergamo has an efficient bus system that runs throughout the Città Bassa and to points around the Città Alta; tickets are 1.50€ for 75 minutes of travel and are available from machines at the bus stops outside the train station or at the bus station opposite. To reach the Città Alta from the train station, take bus no. 1 or 1A (clearly marked Città Alta on front) and make the free transfer to the Funicolare Bergamo Alta, run by ATB Bergamo (Largo Porta Nuova; www.atb.bergamo.it), connecting the upper and lower cities. It typically runs every 7 minutes from 7am to 1:20am.

Exploring the Città Bassa

Most visitors scurry through Bergamo's lower, newer town on their way to the Città Alta, but you may want to pause long enough to explore the main thoroughfare, **Corso Sentierone,** with its mishmash of architectural styles (16th-century porticos, the Mussolini-era Palazzo di Giustizia, and two mock Doric temples); it's a pleasant place to linger over espresso at a sidewalk cafe. The **Accademia Carrara** (Piazza Giacomo Carrara 82, www.lacarrara.it; ✆ **035/234-396**) is worth a peek for its fine collection of Raphaels, Bellinis, Botticellis, and Canalettos. Città Bassa's 19th-century **Teatro Gaetano Donizetti** (Piazza Cavour 15) is the hub of Bergamo's lively cultural scene, with a fall opera season and a winter-to-spring season of dramatic performances; for details, contact the theater at ✆ **035/4160-601** (www.teatrodonizetti.it).

Exploring the Città Alta

Crammed with *palazzi,* monuments, and churches, the Città Alta centers on two hauntingly beautiful adjoining squares, **piazzas Vecchia** and **del Duomo.** The Città Alta is dissected by delightful cobblestoned **Via Colleoni** (named for Bergamasco strongman Bartolomeo Colleoni; see p. 496), which is so narrow that in places you can almost touch the buildings on either side at once. It's lined with swank shoe shops, posh delis, and classy confectioners.

Piazza Vecchia (a 5-min. stroll from the funicular station along Via Gombito) looks like a set for one of local son Gaetano Donizetti's operas. This hauntingly beautiful square was the hub of Bergamo's political and civic life from medieval times. The 12th-century **Palazzo della Ragione** (Court of Justice) was built by the Venetians; its graceful arcades are embellished with the Lion of Saint Mark, symbol of the Venetian Republic, visible above the tiny 16th-century balcony and reached by a covered staircase to the right of the palace. Across the piazza is the **Biblioteca Civica** (Public Library).

Walk through the archways of the Palazzo della Ragione to reach **Piazza del Duomo** and the **Basilica di Santa Maria Maggiore ★★** (www.fondazionemia.it; ✆ **035/211-355**). You'll enter the basilica through an ornate portico supported by Venetian lions; the interior is a masterpiece of baroque giltwork hung with Renaissance tapestries. Bergamo native Gaetano Donizetti, the famed composer, is entombed here in a marble sarcophagus that's as excessive as the rest of the church. The oft-forgotten **Tempietto di Santa Croce,** tucked to the left of the basilica entrance, is

Lombardy & the Lake District

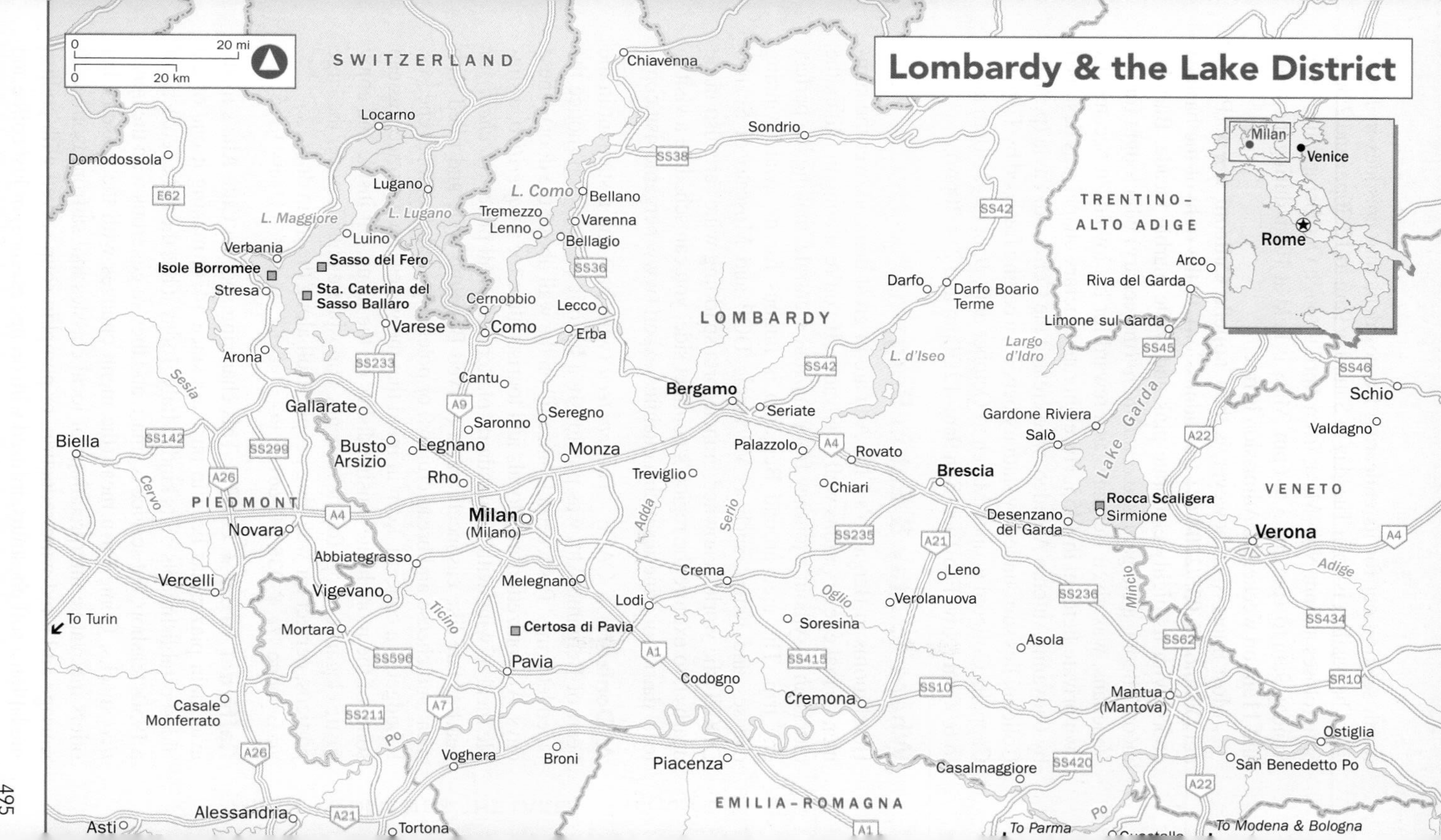

worth seeking out for its endearing frescos depicting episodes in Jesus' life. The basilica is open Tuesday to Saturday 9am to 12:30pm and 2:30 to 6pm (closes at 5pm Nov–Mar); from April through October it's also open Sunday 9am to 1pm and 3 to 6pm. Mass is held at 10am during the week and 11am on weekends. Admission is free.

Most impressive, however, is the **Cappella Colleoni ★★★** (Piazza del Duomo; ✆ **035/210-061;** free admission), to the right of the basilica doors, with its highly elaborate pink-and-white marble facade. Bartolomeo Colleoni, a Bergamasco *condottiero* (mercenary) who fought for the Venetians, was given Bergamo as a reward for his loyalty; it became his own private fiefdom in 1455. His elaborate funerary chapel was designed by Giovanni Antonio Amadeo, who created the Certosa di Pavia (p. 482). Colleoni lies surrounded by statuary beneath a ceiling frescoed by Tiepolo. Cappella Colleoni is open March to October daily 9am to 12:30pm and 2 to 6:30pm (Nov–Feb Tues–Sun 9am–12:30pm and 2–4:30pm).

Where to Stay & Eat in Bergamo

Hotel rooms in Bergamo's Città Alta are in great demand over the summer, so make reservations well in advance. If you're staying in Milan, the city is an easy hour's journey from Stazione Centrale, making it a perfect day trip. The area around Bergamo is famous for its award-winning cheeses and wines, such as Valcalepio DOP and Moscato di Scanzo DOCG (the world-renowned Franciacorta sparkling wines are also made nearby); to explore the region's gourmet side, you can schedule a visit to local dairies or wineries with a qualified expert (www.bergamovisit.com).

Al Donizetti ★ CAFE This *enoteca* (wine bar) and restaurant in the heart of Bergamo Alta was previously a historic pastry shop (notice the faded lettering "Pasticceria Donizetti" on the wall above the door). These days, Al Donizetti draws locals and tourists alike for an *aperitivo,* a simple meal of wine with a charcuterie platter and small plates (*cicchetti*), or heartier fare like casoncelli pasta (served Bergamo style and filled with meat and cheese and bread crumbs) or polenta served with local cheeses. If budget is a concern, keep in mind that the wines can get pricey, as can some of the more haute-cuisine dishes on the menu. Sit inside and enjoy rustic elegance or opt for the romantic atmosphere outside under the large porticos, perfect for watching people stroll along the main drag.
Via Gombito 17a. ✆ **035/242-661.** Entrees 14€–32€. Wed–Mon 11am–11pm.

Caffè del Tasso ★ CAFE This charming spot on Città Alta's medieval main piazza has been in business since 1476, making it one of the oldest establishments of its kind in Italy. Today it has the rather cozy air of a 1950s teashop, but service is smart, and they're generous with the *aperitivo* snacks. Come for a meal (the menu changes with the seasons, but offers innovative interpretations of local classics like saffron risotto with sausage and a red-wine reduction, or pumpkin soup served with codfish medallions, soft chestnuts, infused with orange essence) or just coffee and a pastry. An early evening drink at one of its outdoor tables on a warm night is truly heavenly; if you're in the mood for a cold treat, the gelateria next door does a brisk trade in summer.

Piazza Vecchia 3. www.caffedeltasso.com. ✆ **035/237-966.** Entrees 13€–20€. Daily 8am–midnight.

Hotel Le Funi ★★ Located in the shadow of the Venetian Walls in the Città Alta, this property in a historic building is well located for visiting the major sites of the old town. Recently renovated rooms offer modern conveniences along with wonderful views of the nearby hills. In warm weather, a breakfast of pastries, croissants, and local specialties, like cheeses and cured meats, is provided on the panoramic terrace (otherwise, it is served indoors in the lounge). The ground floor of the hotel is home to **Casual,** a stylish fine-dining restaurant from Michelin-starred chef Enrico Bartolini serving contemporary Italian cuisine. There's a nice room in the hotel's annex with its own private terrace with views of an orchard, but if you are sensitive to noise, it's important to know that the funicular runs right behind it.

Via S. Virgilio1. www.lefunihotel.it. ✆ **035/250-043.** 16 units. 120€–260€ double. Rates include breakfast. **Amenities:** Private parking (15€ per day); free Wi-Fi.

MANTUA ★★★

158km (98 miles) E of Milan, 62km (38 miles) N of Parma, 150km (93 miles) SW of Venice

One of Lombardy's best-kept secrets, Mantua (Mantova in Italian) lies in the eastern reaches of the region, making it a fairly easy side trip from Milan. Like its neighboring cities in Emilia-Romagna, Mantua owes its handsome Renaissance monuments to one family, in this case the Gonzagas, who conquered the city in 1328 and ruled benevolently until 1707. Avid collectors, the Gonzagas ruled through the greatest centuries of Italian art, and today you can encounter their treasures in the **Palazzo Ducale;** in their summer retreat, the **Palazzo Te;** and in the churches and piazzas that grew up around their court.

Essentials

ARRIVING Six direct **trains** depart daily from Milan Stazione Centrale (1 hr. 50 min.; 12€). There are nine daily trains from Verona (30–40 min.; 4.50€).

The speediest **highway** connections from Milan are via the A4 autostrada to Verona, then the A22 from Verona to Mantua (about 2 hr.).

VISITOR INFORMATION The tourist office at Piazza Mantegna 6 (www.turismo.mantova.it; ✆ 0376/432-432) is open on weekends from 9am to 5pm; during the week, hours are 9am to 1:30pm and 2:30 to 5pm (until 6pm in spring and summer). It's just to the right of the basilica of Sant'Andrea.

CITY LAYOUT Mantua is tucked onto a fat finger of land surrounded on three sides by the Mincio River, which widens into a series of lakes, prosaically named Lago Superiore, Lago di Mezzo, and Lago Inferiore. Most sights are within an easy walk of one another in the compact center, a 15-minute walk northwards from the lakeside train station.

Exploring Mantua

Mantua is a place for wandering along arcaded streets and through cobbled squares with handsomely proportioned churches and *palazzi.*

The southernmost of these squares is **Piazza delle Erbe** ★ (Square of the Herbs), so named for its produce and food market. Mantua's civic might is clustered here in a series of late-medieval and early Renaissance structures that include the **Palazzo della Ragione** (Courts of Justice) and **Palazzo del Podestà** (Mayor's Palace) from the 12th and 13th centuries, and the **Torre dell'Orologio,** topped with a 14th-century astrological clock. Also on this square is Mantua's earliest religious structure, the **Rotonda di San Lorenzo,** a miniature round church from the 11th century. The city's Renaissance masterpiece, **Basilica di Sant'Andrea** (see below), is off to one side on Piazza Mantegna.

To the north, Piazza delle Erbe transforms into **Piazza Broletto** through a series of arcades; here a statue honors the poet Virgil, who was born in Mantua in 70 B.C. The next square, vast cobbled **Piazza Sordello,** is lined with medieval *palazzi* and the 13th-century Duomo. Most notable is the massive hulk of the **Palazzo Ducale** (see p. 499), which forms the piazza's eastern wall. To enjoy lakeside views and walks, follow Via San Giorgio from Piazza Sordello and turn right onto Lungolago dei Gonzaga, which leads back along the lakeshore to the town center.

Tip: If you're spending more than a few hours in Mantua, consider getting the **Mantova Sabbioneta Card** (www.cittadimantova.it/en-ww/infopoint.aspx), which allows discounted or free access to 17 city museums plus several others in outlying Sabbioneta, as well as free bus transportation and bike sharing. Valid for 72 hours, it costs 20€ (8€ for ages 12–18). Just about all of the museums listed in this guide honor the card.

Basilica di Sant'Andrea ★★ CHURCH A graceful Renaissance facade fronts this 15th-century church by architect Leon Battista Alberti. The grandest church in Mantua, it is topped by a dome added by Filippo Juvarra in the 18th century. Inside, the vast, classically proportioned space is centered on the church's single aisle. Light pours in through the dome, highlighting the carefully crafted *trompe l'oeil* painting of the coffered ceiling. The Gonzagas' court painter Andrea Mantegna—creator of the Camera degli Sposi in the Palazzo Ducale (see below)—is buried in the first chapel on the left. The crypt houses a reliquary containing the blood of Christ, which was allegedly brought here by Longinus, the Roman soldier who thrust his spear into Jesus's side; this is processed through town on March 18, the feast of Mantua's patron, Sant'Anselmo.

Piazza Mantegna. Free. Daily 8am–noon and 3–7pm.

Museo di Palazzo Ducale ★★ PALACE The massive power base of the Gonzaga dynasty spreads over the northeast corner of Mantua, incorporating Piazza Sordello, the Duomo, Castello San Giorgio, and the Palazzo Ducale. Together they form a private city connected by corridors, courtyards, and staircases filled with Renaissance frescoes and ancient Roman sculptures. Within the walls of this fortress-cum-palace lies the history of Mantua's most powerful family and what's left of the treasure trove they amassed over centuries. Between their skills as warriors and a knack for marrying into wealthier houses, the Gonzagas acquired power, money, and the services of some of the top artists of the time, including Pisanello, Titian, and Mantegna. The most fortunate union was in 1490 between Francesco II Gonzaga and aristocratic Isabella d'Este from Ferrara, who commissioned many of the complex's art-filled apartments. In this glorious maze of gilded, frescoed, marbled rooms, passageways, and secret gardens, here are some standouts: the Arthurian legends adorning the Sala del Pisanello, painted by Pisanello between 1436 and 1444; the **Sale degli Arazzi** (Tapestry Rooms) hung with copies of Raphael's Vatican tapestries; the **Galleria degli Specchi** (Hall of Mirrors); **Appartamento dei Nani** (Apartments of the Dwarfs), with its miniature replica of the Vatican's Holy Staircase; and the **Galleria dei Mesi** (Hall of the Months). In the north tower of the Castello San Giorgio, don't miss the incomparable **Camera degli Sposi,** the masterpiece of Andrea Mantegna,

Basilica of Sant'Andrea in Piazza Mantegna Square in Mantua.

who took 9 years to complete it. Commissioned by Ludovico III Gonzaga, it features portraits of his family members, providing an intriguing glimpse into late-15th-century court life. (***Tip:*** Admission to the Camera degli Sposi is limited, so reserve a time slot for visiting it when you buy your tickets.)

Piazza Sordello 40. www.mantovaducale.beniculturali.it. ✆ **0376/224-832.** 15€ for Castello San Giorgio, Corte Vecchia, Camera degli Sposi, and archaeological museum; 9€ without Camera degli Sposi and archaeological museum; free for 17 and under. All free 1st Sun every month. Tues–Sun 8:15am–7:15pm; last entry 6:20pm.

Palazzo Te ★★ PALACE A 20-minute walk from the historic center along Via Principe Amedeo, this glorious Renaissance summer palace, designed by Giulio Romano between 1525 and 1535, was built for Federico II Gonzaga, the sybaritic son of Isabella d'Este. As his retreat from court life, it was designed to indulge his obsessions. A series of lavishly adorned apartments, decorated by the best artists of the day, reveal Gonzaga's enthusiasms for love and sex, astrology, and horses, from the almost 3-D effect in the Hall of the Horses to erotic frescoes by Romano in the elaborate Chamber of Amor and Psyche. The greatest room in the palace, however, is a metaphor for Gonzaga power: In the **Sala dei Giganti** (Room of the Giants), Titan is overthrown by the gods in a dizzying display of *trompe l'oeil* painting that surrounds the viewer on all sides (and overhead!). The Palazzo Te is also home to the Museo Civico, whose collections include the Gonzaga family's coins, medallions, 20th-century portraits by Armando Spadini, and a few Egyptian artifacts.

Viale Te 13. ✆ **0376/323-266.** 15€ adults; 11€ seniors; 7€ ages 12–18 and students; free for ages 11 and under. Mon 1–6:30pm; Tues–Sun 9am–6:30pm (hours may be extended in summer).

MORE MANTUA MUSEUMS

En route from the center of town to Palazzo Te, you'll pass **Casa del Mantegna ★**, the house and studio of Andrea Mantegna, now an art gallery (Via Acerbi 47, ✆ **0376/360-506;** free admission; Tues–Sun 10am–1pm, Tues–Wed and Sat–Sun 3–6pm).

Just to the left of Palazzo Ducale's main entrance, in the old market hall at the corner of Piazza Sordello, the **Museo Archeologico Nazionale di Mantova** houses in one giant space all sorts of local discoveries of Bronze Age, Greek, Etruscan, and Roman pottery, glassware, and utensils (www.museoarcheologicomantova.beniculturali.it; ✆ **0376/320-003;** adults 15€ including admission to Palazzo Ducale with the Camera degli Sposi, 9€ including Palazzo Ducale but not the Camera degli Sposi; ages 17 and under free; Tues–Sun 8:30am–7pm, Sun 2–7pm).

The lovely baroque interior of the **Teatro Bibiena ★★** is also worth a peek for its rows of luxurious theater boxes. Find it at Via Accademia 47 (✆ **0376/327-653;** adults 3€, ages 17 and under free; Tues–Sun 10am–1pm and 3–6pm, plus Sat–Sun 10am–6pm mid-Mar to mid-Nov).

For a change of pace, the **Galleria Storica dei Vigili del Fuoco ★** (Fire Engine Museum) at Largo Vigili del Fuoco 1 (www.museovigilidelfuoco.it; ✆ **0376/364-124;** free admission) has plenty of historic engines on display. Call beforehand to check opening hours, which are usually on weekends.

Where to Stay in Mantua

Like Milan, Mantua sees mainly expense-account business travelers during the week, with families and tourists flocking in for the weekends and over summer, so book rooms in the town center well ahead of time.

Casa Poli ★★★ Located about 15 minutes on foot from the center, this bijou boutique hotel hidden behind the facade of a 19th-century mansion is popular with both business and leisure travelers. Spotless guest rooms have a chic minimalist style, with parquet floors, funky lights, and equally cool bathrooms. Superior rooms are slightly larger, and triple rooms are available. The hotel aims to offer the "comfort of a home and the elegance of a hotel," with a lounge full of arty books and a summer courtyard that's a great spot for an evening *aperitivo*. But it's the staff that really makes this place shine; they're chatty and informal and willing to go the extra mile to please guests. This is a good solution for those traveling by car since there is parking (15€ per day), and it lies outside the restricted traffic zone for residents and those with a special permit; entering this area unauthorized can lead to heavy fines.

Corso Garibaldi 32. www.hotelcasapoli.it. ✆ **0376/288-170.** 27 units. 115€–170€ double. Rates include breakfast. **Amenities:** Bar; concierge; free Wi-Fi.

Residenza Bibiena ★★ Located on a pretty corner of Mantua's *centro storico* minutes from the Palazzo Ducale, this cozy B&B in a traditional terracotta townhouse has a pleasing old-school charm. Warm color schemes and pretty linens enliven simple rooms with wooden furniture and tile floors. Two rooms geared to families boast especially large bathrooms for Italian standards. Four additional rooms at the **Residenza Bibiena Deluxe,** a few doors down at Piazza Arche 8, have slightly more modern accommodations. Some rooms in both properties have terraces and even lake views. Note that the properties are located at one of the main streets leading into the city (right outside the restricted traffic zone, a plus for motorists), so traffic noise may be an issue.

Piazza Arche, 5. www.residenzabibiena.it. ✆ **331/508-0876.** 8 units (incl. both properties). 80€ double. Rates include breakfast. **Amenities:** Free Wi-Fi.

Where to Eat in Mantua

Caffè Modi ★ ITALIAN Named for the artist Amedeo Modigliani, this cafe is a friendly stop on the tourist circuit around Piazza Sordello and the San Giorgio castle. Chill music, gramophones, and threadbare armchairs lend a bohemian charm to the place. There are a few local pastas (like pumpkin tortellini in a butter sage sauce) on the menu, but *insalatone* (big salads), panini, and charcuterie dishes dominate. The cafe also often has live music. In warm weather, grab a table outside where you can glimpse views of the water. You can also get food to go.

Via San Giorgio 4. ✆ **0376/181-0111.** Entrees 10€–17€. Wed–Mon noon–midnight, sometimes later on weekends.

Lo Scalco Grasso ★★ MODERN ITALIAN This contemporary bistro with minimalist decor likes to push boundaries. It's a sophisticated choice, offering beautifully crafted dishes featuring vegetables—local pasta stuffed with squash, delicate risotto, or perhaps a superb chickpea soup flavored with squid—alongside heartier menu items like duck breast served with sweet-and-sour radicchio, braised beef cheek with polenta, or bigoli pasta (like a thick spaghetti) with a sardine sauce. Lovely wines are available by the glass or bottle, and little bites of specialties are happily produced for guests to sample before ordering. It is small and tables can be a bit close together, but it offers some of the best food in town. The restaurant is about a 10-minute walk from the center. Reservations recommended.

Via Trieste 55. www.loscalcograsso.it. ✆ **349/374-7958.** Entrees 15€–24€. Tues–Sat noon–2pm and 7:30–10pm (later on weekends); Sun noon–2pm; Mon 7:30–10pm.

Osteria dell'Oca ★★★ LOMBARDY The Badalucco family's "restaurant of the goose" is crammed nightly with locals enjoying vibrant cooking at excellent prices. This is a rustic Italian *osteria* at its very best: noisy, happy, joyous, and with the menu printed right on the paper placemats. Start off sharing some *peccati di gola* ("delectable delights"), local salamis and pancetta with a wedge of creamy polenta and beetroot salsa. Looking for true local specialties? Try the Mantua sliced beef served with arugula and parmesan; "drunken" risotto with Lambrusco wine and toasted pancetta (this restaurant has been voted as having the "best risotto in Mantua"); or *tagliatelle alla baffo,* pasta with beans and sausage, based on a family recipe. Only three wines are served, in thick carafes; opt for the white, from local vineyards, rather than the *Lambrusco,* which is quite sweet. The generous outpouring of food ends with complimentary coffee and a thick hazelnut liqueur. Book ahead, especially on weekends. The restaurant is about a 10-minute walk from the center along a busy road that leads out of town.

Via Trieste 10. www.osteriadelloca.it. ✆ **0376/327-171.** Entrees 12€–18€. Wed–Sat and Mon 12:15–2:30pm and 7:15–11:30pm; Sun 12:15–2:30pm.

Mantua Shopping & Entertainment

The favored shopping streets in Mantua radiate off Piazza delle Erbe, a delightful cluster of cobbled and arcaded streets sheltering delis stuffed with local cheeses, hams, fresh pasta, and olive oils. **Corso Umberto, Via Verdi,** and **Via Oberdan** are lined with posh boutiques, smart shoe shops, and bookstores. There's a **farmers' market** on Lungorio IV di Novembre on Saturday, perfect fodder for a picnic in the lakeside gardens along Lungolago dei Gonzaga.

Mantua is a cultured city with ample theater and classical concerts; there are regular recitals at **Teatro Bibiena** (see p. 500) and a full program of films and concerts at **Mantova Teatro,** Piazza Cavallotti (www.teatrosocialemantova.it); a **chamber-music festival** is held every May; and the **Festivaletteratura** (www.festivaletteratura.it) literature festival is a popular draw in September.

LAKE COMO ★★★

Como (town): 65km (40 miles) NE of Milan; Menaggio: 35km (22 miles) NE of Como and 85km (53 miles) N of Milan; Varenna: 50km (31 miles) NE of Como and 80km (50 miles) NE of Milan

Life is slower around the northern Italian lakes than in fast-paced Milan. The city of Como is an ideal base for drawing breath and kicking back. Sitting on the southwestern tip of Lake Como, the city is essentially a center of commerce with a miniscule medieval quarter and a pretty waterfront. Tourists flock to Como for its ancient heritage, fine churches, and lake views. From here, frequent ferry service hops around the lake, visiting its many romantic lakeshore villas and villages.

Essentials

ARRIVING Frequent **trains** from Milan take 1 hour and cost 5€. Trains from Stazione Central and Porta Garibaldi arrive at Como San Giovanni; trains from Milan Cadorna arrive at Como Nord Lago, just off the lakefront promenade near the ferry point.

VISITOR INFORMATION The regional tourist office at Via Albertolli 7 (www.lakecomo.com; ✆ **031/449-3068**) has info on hotels, restaurants, and campgrounds around the lake. The office is open Monday to Saturday 9am to 1pm and 2 to 6pm. You'll also find tourist offices open in summer in several small towns around the lake; in Tremezzo at Via Regina 3 (✆ **0344/40-493**); in Varenna at Via IV Novembre 7 (www.varennaturismo.com; ✆ **0341/830-367**), though it is usually closed in January and February; and in Bellagio at Piazza della Chiesa 14 (www.bellagiolakecomo.com; ✆ **031/951-555**).

GETTING AROUND Como is the jumping-off point for most adventures on Lake Como, which is crisscrossed by regular ferry routes: It takes 4 hours to travel from one end to the other, with many stops along the way. The most popular are Tremezzo, Menaggio, Bellagio, and timeless Varenna. Single fares from Como are 10.40€ to Bellagio; a day pass costs 23.30€. Tickets cannot be purchased online. The ferry terminal, run by **Navigazione Lago di Como,** is on the esplanade at Via per Cernobbio 18 (www.navigazionelaghi.it; ✆ **800/551-801**).

Exploring Como ★★

Como's tiny *centro storico* is dominated by the flamboyant **Duomo ★★** (Piazza Duomo; www.cattedraledicomo.it; ✆ **031/331-2275**), which combines Gothic and Renaissance architecture for two very different facades; long, narrow windows and a Gothic stained-glass rose window mark the western end, with an apse and baroque dome added in 1744 by architect Filippo Juvarra at the eastern end. The Duomo is free and open daily 7:30am to 7:30pm (Sun until 9:30pm).

Two blocks south of the Duomo, the 12th-century **San Fedele ★** basilica (www.parrocchiasanfedelecomo.it; free admission; daily 8am–noon 3:30–7pm) stands above a charming square of the same name. Parts of the five-sided church, including the altar, date from the 6th century, and there are some fine frescoes along the right-hand side aisle.

Como's main street, **Corso Vittorio Emanuele II,** cuts through the medieval quarter and has plenty of upmarket boutiques and classy delis. If you have time, take the 10-minute **funicular ride** from Lungo Lario Trieste up to hilltop **Brunate ★★**, which has a cluster of excellent restaurants and bars. The funicular runs up a steep cliffside, with glorious views of Lake Como glinting below; at the top are wooded hiking trails that lead north to Bellagio. The funicular ticket office is at Piazza de Gasperi 4 (www.funicolarecomo.it; ✆ **031/303-608;** daily 6am–10:30pm; funicular runs until midnight on Sat and in summer). Tickets are 3.30€ adults, 2.20€ for kids under 12 (children under 110cm/3 ft., 7in. in height travel free). Trains depart from both ends of the line every 30 minutes.

Exploring Around Lake Como

The romantic waterfront villages of Lake Como, with their cute clusters of yellow and pink houses, majestic *palazzos,* and lush lakeside gardens, are easily explored by ferry (see p. 503) or by car. Here are a few of the highlights, going clockwise round the lake from Como.

Lenno ★★★ For centuries Lake Como was the playground of privileged Lombardian aristocrats, and quite honestly, not much has changed. **Villa del Balbianello** at Lenno (Via Comoedia 5; fondoambiente.it/villa-del-balbianello-eng; ✆ **0344/56-110**) is one of the best-known of their fabulous villas, with ornate landscaped gardens and a 16th-century palace sitting high on a peninsula over the lake. (You may recognize it from *Star Wars: Episode II – Attack of the Clones* or the Bond movie *Casino Royale.*) The interior is full of priceless French furniture complemented by eclectic artwork from the travels of its former owner, explorer Guido Monzino, who died in 1988 and left the villa to the Italian National Trust. Garden entrance is 12€ adults, 9€ children 4 to 12; garden and villa (with compulsory 60-min. tour) is 23€ adults, 15€ children 4 to 12. It's open mid-March to mid-November 10am to 6pm (closed Mon and Wed). It is a bit of a walk to reach the villa from the center of Lenno, but you can take a taxi boat from Lenno and be let out right at the villa's dock, for about 7€ round-trip.

Tremezzo ★★ On the western side of Lake Como, Tremezzo was the 19th-century retreat of the Italian aristocracy; today it is lorded over by the exceptionally expensive **Grand Hotel Tremezzo** (www.grandhotel tremezzo.com; ✆ **0344/42-491**) and its wonderfully stylish beach. The plush gardens, museum, and rich art collections of the ornate 17th-century **Villa Carlotta** are open to the public (Via Regina 2; www.villacarlotta.it; ✆ **0344/404-05;** 15€ adults, 13€ seniors, 6€ students; late Mar to mid-Oct 9am–7:30pm [last entry 6pm] and late Oct to mid-Mar 10am–6pm [last entry 5pm]; hours can vary over holiday weekends).

Bellano ★ Most people stop in Bellano on the eastern shore of Lake Como to visit the **Orrido** (www.discoveringbellano.eu/it/orrido-di-bellano; 5€ adults, 3€ seniors and ages 6–12, children under 6 free), a deep gorge cut out of the cliffs by the River Pioverna as it tears down the hillside. A nighttime trip down the floodlit gorge is a rare and eerie treat, and one that appears to be under threat from hydroelectric plans expected to reduce the flow of the torrent. Opening times vary seasonally but are roughly July through August 10am to 7pm and 8:45 to 10pm, April through June and September 10am to 1pm and 2:30 to 7pm.

Varenna ★★★ Adorable Varenna gives Bellagio a run for its money as the prettiest village on Lake Como, a tumble of pink and terracotta houses in a labyrinth of narrow, cobbled streets, with smart villas

Varenna, one of Lake Como's charming villages.

clustered around the shoreline. Its winding lakeside path hangs over the water, with bars, shops, and art galleries looking over the lake. Linger a while over a glass of Prosecco and watch the sun go down over the glittering water.

Bellagio ★★★ Photogenic Bellagio is the most popular destination around Lake Como yet has so far avoided becoming too overtly touristic. The shady lakefront promenade is lined with chic hotels, bars, and cafes. Pretty medieval alleyways ascending steeply from the lake are lined with souvenir stores selling pricey handmade leather accessories. Regardless of the multitude of tourists, this is still a lovely place to linger for lunch overlooking the lake.

The colorful streets of Bellagio.

Where to Stay & Eat Around Lake Como

For such a popular destination, Como town suffers from a shortage of decent moderately priced hotels, although there are still plenty of options around the lake. If you're looking for a splurge, Cernobbio is home to one of Italy's most exclusive and expensive hotels, the **Villa d'Este** (p. 508). The local cuisine draws heavily from the lake.

Hotel du Lac ★★ With one entrance on Varenna's charming waterfront and the other hidden away in its equally photogenic tangle of alleyways, the Hotel du Lac is housed in an elegant 19th-century villa offering prized views across Lake Como. The inside of the property has an understated romantic flair, with marble pillars and wrought-iron staircases. Each of the 16 rooms has been individually decorated and is quite spacious (for Europe), with modern bathrooms. Not all have lake views, and some have only partial views. Enjoy creative Italian cuisine on the restaurant's outdoor terrace—chef Alessandro changes the menu weekly based on what is in season.

Via del Prestino 11, Varenna. www.albergodulac.com. ✆ **0341/830-238.** 16 units. 200€–335€ double. Rates include breakfast. Closed mid-Nov to Feb. **Amenities:** Restaurant; bar; free Wi-Fi.

Hotel Paradiso sul Lago ★★★ This great family-run property is one of the first eco-hotels around Lake Como (thanks to its use of solar panels and a "green policy" for low energy consumption). Located in a little piazza at the top of the village of Brunate above Como town and near the famous Volta lighthouse (Faro Voltiano), it offers amazing hilltop views from the breakfast room and a panoramic terrace with swimming pool and Jacuzzi. Guest rooms are clean and functional with improvements constantly being made and little touches like Nespresso machines; some have great lake views, and there are triple and quadruple rooms for larger groups. The drive up the hill on a narrow road is tricky, but you can always take the cable car and then contact the hotel's owners for a ride (it's a challenging uphill walk from the funicular). Try the Mama Gina cafe/bistro for a full meal or a sunset cocktail and snacks.

Via Scalini 7, Brunate. www.hotelparadisocomo.com. ✆ **031/364-099.** 13 units. 120€–169€ double. Rates include breakfast. **Amenities:** Restaurant; cafe; bar; outdoor pool; shuttle service; free Wi-Fi.

La Polenteria ★★★ REGIONAL ITALIAN This out-of-the-way spot above Como in Brunate near the Faro Voltiano lighthouse has some of the best polenta around these parts. La Polenteria aims to highlight whatever is in season, such as chestnuts and porcini mushrooms in fall, or snails and fresh fish from the lake in spring. The menu also has a few pasta dishes. Vegetarians may have a hard time here beyond the polenta, an occasional soup, or pasta with tomato sauce. All desserts are homemade. Only open on weekends, the restaurant is often full, so reserve in advance before you make the trek up. It's quite the uphill walk from the funicular; be sure to map out your route before coming if you don't have a car (the old San Maurizio mule track leading up here from the funicular makes for a good 30-min. hike); buses also run from the funicular, but they don't always follow a frequent schedule. Reservations highly recommended.

Via Scalini, 66, Brunate. www.lapolenteria.it. ✆ **031/336-5105.** Entrees 10€–30€. Fri 7:15–10:30pm; Sat–Sun 12:15pm–2:30pm and 7:30–10:30pm.

Locanda Barbarasso ★★★ MEDITERRANEAN/PIZZERIA This cozy *locanda* on a side street off of medieval Piazza San Fedele in Como's *centro storico* serves seafood dishes and regional specialties—including typical dishes from the nearby mountains like *pizzoccheri,* a flat-ribbon buckwheat pasta cooked with potatoes and greens and then layered with different cheeses—as well as crispy pizzas. The inside is light and bright with graceful arches and gray stone walls. Try the red-white-and-green risotto with cherry tomatoes, stracciatella cheese, and pesto. Reservations are recommended.

Via Odescalchi 10/12, Como. www.locandabarbarossa.it. ✆ **031/275-3421.** Entrees 9€–25€. Tues–Sun 12:30–2:30pm and 7–11:30pm; closed Mon.

Nest on the Lake ★★ This gem of a B&B on the shores of Lake Como is in Lezzeno, a tranquil town just down the road from Bellagio. This old fisherman's house from the early 1800s has rooms in shades of calming pastels, some with four-poster beds, and all have patios or wrought-iron balconies. Continental breakfast is served in a delightful stone-walled room on the ground floor, and owners Raffa and Costantino are always on hand to recommend restaurants and organize activities. The location midway up the lake makes it a great base for hiking, waterskiing, and wakeboarding; guests can access a small beach with canoes that can be taken out on to the water. In summer there's a 3-night minimum stay. A self-catering apartment for up to four people is also available, but breakfast is not included.

Via Sostra 17/19, Lezzeno. www.nestonthelake.com. ✆ **031/914-372.** 5 units. 130–170€ double; around 200€ apartment. Room rates include breakfast. **Amenities:** Solarium; free Wi-Fi.

Splendide Ristorante ★★★ REGIONAL ITALIAN You would be hard-pressed to find a prettier spot on the whole of Lake Como than the geranium-filled terrace of the Hotel Excelsior Splendide in Bellagio. Perched over the shimmering waters of the lake, the restaurant is a perfect place to watch boats pull into port while enjoying everything from light salads and pasta to fresh lake trout and prawns sizzled in garlic. The **Lounge Bar** also now serves as a pizzeria (you can also ask to sit on the panoramic terrace to enjoy the views) with gourmet pizzas, boasting premium ingredients and low-gluten dough that is left to rise overnight. Service can be a bit harried, so keep that in mind if you don't have time to sit back and relax.

Via Lungo Lario Manzoni 28, Bellagio. www.hsplendide.com. ✆ **031/950-225.** Entrees 12€–42€. Mar–Nov noon–2:30pm.

Villa d'Este ★★ Princes, princesses, and sultans have passed through the gates of this ornate Renaissance *palazzo* dating from 1568 (though it's been a hotel since 1873, recently celebrating 150 years in business); today a constant procession of major celebs and minor royalty arrive by speedboat or helicopter to luxuriate in what this resort has to offer. Villa d'Este is quintessential Lake Como, overlooking the water amid verdant parklands. It boasts an array of sports facilities, a selection of fine-dining options (guests are expected to dress elegantly for dinner), and refined rooms furnished with priceless antiques. As befits one of the most exclusive hotels in the world, four large private villas (entire homes) guarantee complete seclusion from the masses.

Via Regina 40, Cernobbio. www.villadeste.com. ✆ **031/3481.** 152 units. 700€–1,000€ double. Rates include breakfast. Closed mid-Nov to mid-Mar. **Amenities:** 3 restaurants; 3 bars; nightclub; indoor and outdoor pools; spa; concierge; free Wi-Fi.

LAKE MAGGIORE ★★

Stresa: 90km (56 miles) NW of Milan

West of Como lies Maggiore, a long, thin wisp of a lake protected by mountains and fed by the River Ticino, which flows on to Milan. Roughly a quarter of the northern section of the lake is in Switzerland, including the city of Locarno and its delightful satellite resort of Ascona. **Stresa** is the largest town on the Italian side, a timeless resort on the western shoreline, famed for its setting opposite the **Isole Borromee** islands (see below). Regular **ferries** span Maggiore, with frequent stops on the way from **Arona,** south of Stresa; two of the most popular stops are at **Luino,** known for its massive street market every Wednesday, and **Laveno,** which offers cable-car rides up to mountain peaks. Note that the cable car in Stresa may still be temporarily closed after an accident in May 2021 killed 14 people.

Essentials

ARRIVING Stresa is linked with Milan Stazione Centrale by 20 **trains** a day. Journeys take about an hour and cost 8.60€. **Boats** arrive at and depart from Piazza Marconi, Stresa. Many lakeside spots can be reached from Stresa, with most boats on the lake operated by **Navigazione Laghi** (www.navlaghi.it; ✆ **800/551-801**). The main ferry office, however, is at the lake's southern tip in Arona, at Viale Baracca 1; from there, ferries to Stresa take 40 minutes and cost 6.20€.

By **car,** take the A8 west from Milan to Sesto Calende, near the south end of the lake; from there, follow Route SS33 up the western shore to Stresa. The trip takes just over an hour, but can be much longer in summer traffic.

VISITOR INFORMATION Stresa's **tourist office,** at the ferry dock on Piazza Marconi (www.stresaturismo.it; ✆ **0323/-301-50**), is open daily 10am to 12:30pm and 3 to 6:30pm (mid-Oct to mid-Mar closed Sat afternoons and Sun).

Exploring Stresa & the Islands

The biggest town on the Italian side of Maggiore, elegant Stresa is the springboard to the Isole Borromee (Borromean Islands), the tiny baroque jewels of the lake. Now a genteel tourist town, Stresa captured the hearts of 19th-century aristocracy, who settled in grandiose villas strung along the promenade. Just back into the tangle of medieval streets, **Piazza Cadorna** is a mass of restaurants that spill out into the center of the square in summer. There's a food and craft market on summer Thursday afternoons on the promenade, and a lido and beach club on the lakefront.

The three **Isole Borromee** (www.isoleborromee.it) are named for the aristocratic Borromeo family (see box p. 510), who've owned them since the 12th century. Public **ferries** leave for the islands every half-hour from Stresa's Piazza Marconi.

ISOLA DEI PESCATORI ★★ Pescatori is stuck in a medieval time warp, with ancient fishermen's houses clustered together on every inch of the tiny island. As you wander the cobbled streets, you'll discover tiny churches, art galleries, souvenir shops, pizza and pasta restaurants, and, at every turn, a glimpse of the lake beyond. It's an entrancing place to explore, but be warned: The prices are extortionate and it gets plenty of tourist traffic.

Isola Bella on Lake Maggiore, with Stresa on the distant shore.

ISOLA BELLA ★★★ The minute islet of Bella is dominated by the massive baroque **Palazzo Borromeo** with its formal Italianate gardens. The *palazzo* makes for an absorbing tour, with conspicuous displays of wealth evident in the rich decor and exquisite furnishings. Terraced gardens dotted with follies have spectacular views across Maggiore. Of special interest are the ornate grottoes where the Borromeos went to stay cool, and a painting gallery hung with 130 of the most important works the Borromeos collected over the centuries. Admission (20€ ages 16 and older, 11€ ages 6–15) includes entry to the gardens and the painting gallery. It's open mid-March through the end of October 9am to 5:30pm (it closes slightly earlier in spring and fall).

ISOLA MADRE ★★ The largest and most peaceful of the islands is Isola Madre (30 min. from Stresa), overspread with exquisite flora in the 3.2-hectare (8-acre) **Orto Botanico.** Pick up a map at the ticket office to identify all the rhododendrons, camellias, and ancient wisteria. Many a peacock and fancy pheasant stalk across the lawns of another 16th-century **Borromeo palazzo,** this one filled with family memorabilia and some interesting old puppet-show stages. Admission to the garden and

ITALY'S MEDIEVAL oligarchs

The all-powerful Borromeo family were Lombardian aristocrats who loomed large in Milanese politics and religion for 200 years. They regarded the vast tracts of land around the southern end of Lake Maggiore as their personal fiefdom, where they built castles, monuments, and palaces. The family spawned several archbishops of Milan, including Federico (1564–1631) and Carlo (1538–84), a singularly wily individual who was canonized in 1610 for his support of the Counter-Reformation against papal infallibility. A great bronze statue of Carlo stands in Arona, looking out across the lake to his former family home, **Rocca Borromeo** at Angera (www.isoleborromeo.it), an imposing fortress that now offers visitors a medieval garden, a toy and doll museum, and exhibits of contemporary art. Like the other Borromeo properties, it's open mid-March through late October.

palace is 17€ adults and 10€ ages 6 to 15. It's open March to late October 9am to 5:30pm (it closes slightly earlier in spring and fall).

Exploring Around Lake Maggiore

Beyond Stresa, Maggiore offers natural beauty and architectural wonders as well as lively towns, markets, and cable-car rides into the mountains.

Arona ★★ As well as having the lake's main ferry office (see p. 509), this sophisticated town at the southern end of Lake Maggiore is a shopping magnet, with its charming **Via Cavour** lined with elegant boutiques and expensive delicatessens. The giant bronze **statue of Carlo Borromeo** (see p. 475), who was born in Arona in 1538, is located just outside of town. It's so huge you can even climb inside and gaze out at the lake through Carlo's eyes (www.statuasancarlo.it; ✆ **0322/249-669;** admission 10€ for the terrace and inside the statue, 5€ for terrace only). It's open mid-March through October daily 9am to noon and 2 to 6pm (on Sun it stays open continually 9am–6pm).

Luino ★★ On the western shore of Lake Maggiore just a few miles from the Swiss border, Luino is home to one of northern Italy's most popular **street markets,** with more than 350 stalls taking over the town every Wednesday. Here you'll find spices, piles of salami, grappas, and olive oils, as well as the hand-tooled leather belts and bags for which the region is famous. Extra ferries (www.navlaghi.it) serve the town every Wednesday, and many shoppers visit Luino directly by train from Milan's Stazione Centrale (2 hr.; 8.30€).

A massive 17th-century bronze statue of San Carlo Borromeo stands in Arona.

Sasso del Fero ★★★ Northeast of Laveno, Laveno Mombello is the terminus for a 16-minute **cable-car** ride (www.funiviedel lagomaggiore.it; ✆ **0332/668-012;** 12€ roundtrip) up the lush Val Cuvia to the Poggia Sant'Elsa viewpoint atop **Sasso del Ferro,** towering 1,062m (3,484 ft.) over Lake Maggiore. Each car is for one or two people. The truly breathtaking panoramas look west to the snow-capped Alps or south over the lakes

Varese, Monate, and Comabbio. If the conditions are right, there'll be plenty of paragliders, and the hills are traversed with hiking trails. Leave time to relax over a Prosecco in the **Ristorante Albergo Funivia** (see below). Times vary according to weather and season, but the cable car generally runs March to November (Mon–Fri 11am–6:30pm; Sat–Sun 11am–10:30pm).

Santa Caterina del Sasso Ballaro ★★★ Just south of Reno on the southeastern leg of Maggiore, beneath an inconspicuous car park in Piazza Cascine del Quiquio, take an elevator or a 268-step staircase down to the magical hermitage of **Santa Caterina del Sasso Ballaro** (Via Santa Caterina 13, Leggiuno; www.santacaterinadelsasso.com; ✆ **0332/647-172**). Founded in the 13th century, this Dominican monastery sits photogenically against a sheer rock face, clinging to an escarpment 15m (49 ft.) above the lake. The serene complex of soft-pink stone is embellished with Renaissance arches and pretty cobbled courtyards. Don't miss the chapel's 14th-century frescoes of biblical scenes, which were hidden under lime during the Italian suppression of the monasteries in the 1770s and only rediscovered in 2003. The gift shop sells honey, candles, and soaps made by the monks. It costs 5€ to enter, and the elevator costs 1€ (Apr–Oct 9am–noon and 2:30–6pm; Nov–Mar Sat–Sun 9am–noon and 2–5pm).

Where to Stay & Eat Around Lake Maggiore

There are many hotels scattered around Maggiore eager to grab the tourist dollar: some good, some bad, many indifferent. The two listed here, at opposite ends of the price spectrum, are exceptional. Similarly, food quality in the area varies wildly; in touristy Stresa, pick restaurants with care.

Albergo Funivia ★★ This basic hotel located on the Poggia Sant'Elsa belvedere is only accessible by the Sasso del Ferro cable car (see p. 511), and free parking is available in the lot down below. What Albergo Funivia lacks in charm, it makes up for in beautiful views over Lake Maggiore towards the Alps from the balconies in every room (where you can also choose to take breakfast). Rooms are a bit dated, but they are clean, and the staff is friendly and helpful. Summer is the best time, with good weather almost guaranteed, though winters are milder than might be expected here "on top of the world." A restaurant/bar offers a simple local menu, but the real draw is the terrace, where tables are at a premium on sunny days; at night, it's a delight to sit here watching the lights around the lake glittering in the distance. The rooms closest to the cable car can be a bit loud.

Via Tinelli, 15, Località Poggio Sant Elsa, Laveno Mombello. www.funiviedellagomaggiore.it. ✆ **0332/610-303.** 18 units. 120–140€ double. Rates include breakfast. **Amenities:** Restaurant; bar; free Wi-Fi.

Grand Hotel des Iles Borromee ★★★ This majestic old hotel—a vast, over-the-top example of Belle Epoque architecture, in Stresa—wows upon arrival with exquisitely manicured and landscaped gardens. The interior is just as impressive; all is tastefully ornate and gilded, like a mini-Versailles. Doubles with garden views are decorated in a (relatively) discreet manner, with bathrooms luxuriously outfitted in marble. Quirky "attic rooms" are slightly smaller (meaning they also cost less) and can be accessed from the sixth floor via a small staircase. These rooms with sloped ceilings and dormer windows are the most budget-friendly option here. The fabulously glitzy Hemingway Suite (the famous writer actually stayed here twice, once right after World War II and again in 1948) includes three bedrooms, a living room, four bathrooms, and a terrace overlooking the lake. The enormous **Des Iles** wellness area has a spa, two pools (indoor and outdoor), a medical and beauty lab, and gym and offers everything from a Turkish bath and hammam to traditional Chinese medicine.

Corso Umberto I 67, Stresa. www.borromees.it. ✆ **0323/938-938.** 172 units. 200€–430€ double. Rates include breakfast. **Amenities:** Restaurant; bar; concierge; spa; sauna; indoor pool; 2 outdoor pools; personal trainer; gym; helicopter pad; free Wi-Fi.

Il Verbano ★★ SEAFOOD While many restaurants on the Isole Borromee are overpriced and underwhelming, the fine food and sublime position of Hotel Verbano's restaurant on Isola Pescatori can't be beat. It offers breathtaking views of Isola Bella's Palazzo Borromeo (see p. 510) and the nearby mountains, while lake waters lap around the terrace. Chef Marco Sacco (2 Michelin stars) offers a variety of tasting menus that focus on delicacies from the lake and nearby mountains, along with a "tour of Italy." Try smoked marbled trout with beech and juniper in a raspberry vinegar sauce served with crispy seaweed or beef cheek braised in Barolo wine served with Parmesan mashed potatoes and crispy vegetables. The restaurant does serve lunch (as well as aperitif), but dinner—after the tourists have left the island—is quieter and more romantic. If you don't come over by ferry, contact the restaurant to find out how you can zip here and back via private taxi boat like something out of a James Bond movie.

Via Ugo Ara 2, Isola Pescatori. www.ilverbano.com. ✆ **0323/312-26.** Entrees 20€–40€. Daily noon–2:30pm and 7–10pm. Closed Jan and sometimes Feb.

Ristorante Piemontese ★★ NORTHERN ITALIAN Among the many anonymous pizza/pasta places in Stresa's town center, this restaurant, which now also goes by the name Bistrot 76, is certainly a cut above. It is still owned by members of the Bellossi family, who are serious about food and wine. The menu boasts classic dishes like tagliolini with black truffle alongside creative additions like black rice with perch in a curry sauce. Dine in the elegant wood-paneled main restaurant or, in warmer months, outside in a courtyard shaded by trellis vines.

Via Mazzini 25, Stresa. www.ristorantepiemontese.com. ✆ **0323/302-35.** Entrees 13€–30€. Tues–Sun 7:30–10:30pm. Closed Dec–Jan.

LAKE GARDA ★★

Sirmione: 130km (81 miles) E of Milan, 150km (93 miles) W of Venice; Riva del Garda: 170km (105 miles) NE of Milan, 199km (123 miles) NW of Venice

Lake Garda is the largest and easternmost of the northern Italian lakes, with its western flanks lapping against the flat plains of Lombardy and its southern extremes in the Veneto. In the north, its deep waters are backed by Alpine peaks. Garda's shores are green and fragrant with flowery gardens, groves of olives and lemons, and forests of pines and cypress.

Essentials

ARRIVING Regular **trains** run from Milan Stazione Centrale, stopping at Desenzano del Garda (fares start at 9.60€). From here it's a 20-minute bus ride to Sirmione; buses make the trip every half-hour for 2€.

Hydrofoils and ferries operated by **Navigazione Laghi** (www.navlaghi.it; ✆ **800/551-801**) ply the waters of the lake. One to two hourly ferries connect Sirmione with Desenzano del Garda in season (20 min. by ferry, 3€); less frequently October to April.

Sirmione is just off the A4 between Milan and Venice. From Venice the trip takes about 1½ hours, and from Milan a little over an hour. There's ample parking in Piazzale Monte Baldo (though it can fill up early on weekends in spring and summer), which is about a 15-minute walk into the heart of town.

Lake Garda and the Sarca River.

VISITOR INFORMATION **Sirmione**'s tourist office is at Viale Marconi 8 (visitsirmione.com; ✆ **349/818-3452**). There is also a tourism kiosk across the street at Viale Marconi 2 just before the bridge into the old part of town. In **Riva del Garda,** the tourist office is on the lakefront at Largo Medaglie d'Oro 5 (www.gardatrentino.it/en; ✆ **0464/554-444**). There's also a tourist office in **Gardone Riviera** at Corso Repubblica 8 (✆ **030/3748-736**). For all, hours vary depending on the season.

GETAWAY TO gardone RIVIERA

Halfway up the western shore of Lake Garda, this little resort—easily accessible by ferry or bus from Desenzano del Garda—offers visitors a gorgeous backdrop for a little relaxation. Oleanders dot the paved promenade, and the charming *centro storico* (Gardone Sopra) is filled with enticing bars and restaurants.

Uphill from the Gardone Riviera lakefront, the **Heller Garden** (Via Roma 2; www.hellergarden.com; ✆ **0336/410-877**) is a tropical paradise founded by Arthur Hruska, a botanist who was also dentist to the ill-fated Tsar Nicholas II of Russia. Hruska planted this botanical haven in the 1900s, and 8,000 rare palms, orchids, and tree ferns now thrive here, thanks to the town's mild, sheltered climate. Today the gardens are curated by Austrian artist André Heller, whose sculptures can be found scattered among the water features, cacti, and bamboo copses. The garden is open March to October daily 9am to 7pm; admission is 12€, 5€ for ages 6 to 11.

Gardone Riviera's other highlight is the **Vittoriale degli Italiani** (Via Vittoriale 12; www.vittoriale.it; ✆ **0365/296-511**), the wildly ostentatious and bizarrely decorated villa home of Gabriele d'Annunzio, the notorious Italian poet and sometime war hero. He bought this hillside estate in 1921 and died here in 1936; a visit pays tribute to d'Annunzio's hedonistic lifestyle rather than his fairly awful poetry. The claustrophobic rooms of this madcap mansion are stuffed with bric-a-brac and artifacts from his colorful life, including mementos of his long affair with actress Eleonora Duse. The patrol boat D'Annunzio commanded in World War I, a museum containing his biplane and photos, and his hilltop mausoleum are all found in the formal gardens that cascade down the hillside. The villa is open daily 9am until 8pm in summer, 5pm in winter. Admission ranges from 12€ to 18€, depending on which parts you visit. Children 6 and under enter for free, and there are reduced prices for seniors and ages 7 to 18.

Sirmione

Perched on a promontory swathed in cypress and olive groves on the southernmost edge of Lake Garda, photogenic Sirmione has been a popular spot since the Romans first discovered hot springs here. Despite the onslaught of summer visitors, this historic town manages to retain its charm. Sirmione has lakeside promenades and pleasant beaches and is small enough for everything to be accessible on foot. It is chiefly famous for its thermal springs, castle, and northern Italy's largest Roman ruins.

Built on the peninsula's narrowest point, the moated, fortified **Rocca Scaligera ★★★** (✆ **030/916-468**) dominates the *centro storico.* Built in the late 13th century by the Della Scala family, who ruled Verona and many of the lands surrounding the lake, the castle is worth a visit for its sweeping courtyards, turreted towers, dungeons, and views across Lake Garda. It's open Tuesday to Saturday 8:30am to 7:30pm, Sunday 8:30am to 1:30pm; admission is 6€ adults, 3€ ages 18 to 25, seniors and kids under 18 free.

From the castle, it's a 15-minute walk (or take the open-air tram from Piazza Piatti) along Via Vittorio Emanuele from the town center to the tip of Sirmione's peninsula and the **Grotte di Catullo ★★** (✆ **030/916-157**), romantically placed ruins with views across the lake. Built around A.D. 150, the remains are thought to represent two sizeable aristocratic villas. A small museum of Roman artifacts from the site includes jewelry and mosaic fragments (Piazzale Orti Manara 4; 8€ adults, 4€ 18–25; free first Sun of month); hours are generally Tuesday to Saturday 8:30am to 7:30pm and Sunday 9:30am to 6:30pm, with shorter hours October to March.

Rocca Scaligera castle in Sirmione.

The massive amusement park **Gardaland** (www.gardaland.it; ✆ **045/6449-777**) is half an hour's drive east of Sirmione at Castelnuovo del Garda. This huge resort includes several hotels, an aquarium, and the newly added LEGOLAND water park and is generally busy during summer and school vacation periods.

Riva del Garda

The northernmost settlement on Lake Garda is a thriving Italian town with medieval towers, Renaissance churches and *palazzi,* and narrow cobblestone streets where everyday business proceeds in its alluring way. Note that Riva del Garda becomes a cultural mecca in October, when the town hosts the international **Lago di Garda Musica Festival** (www.mrf-musicfestivals.com). If you want to see amateur choirs and orchestras perform classical music in magnificent villas and palazzos, with the lake as a breathtaking backdrop, make hotel reservations well in advance. Riva del Garda's **Old Town** is pleasant, although it has only two notable historic attractions. The 13th-century **Torre d'Apponale** (2€, ages 16 and under free) in Piazza III Novembre is open in summer for visitors to climb its 165 steps for views across the lake. The town's moated lakeside castle, **La Rocca,** houses an unassuming civic museum (www.museoaltogarda.it; ✆ **0464/573-869;** 2.50€ adults, kids 14 and under free; Tues–Sun 10am–6pm, typically closes Dec–Jan and sometimes Feb).

Where to Stay & Eat Around Lake Garda

Sirmione and Riva del Garda have a choice of pleasant, moderately priced hotels, all of which book up quickly in July and August, when rates go up. The local cuisine features fish from the lake and lots of pasta.

Hotel du Lac et du Parc ★★★ The vast, lush gardens are one of the best parts of this massive, family-friendly Riva del Garda resort, which also boasts swimming pools, a modern spa, and every conceivable luxury. The grounds lead down to a little lakefront beach where you can windsurf, paddle-board, take sailing lessons, or take part in many other water sports at the **Sailing Du Lac** sailing school (see box below). Accommodation options include bungalows, luxurious suites in the villas, or rooms in the hotel in the heart of the resort. Despite the size of the property, service still feels personal, and attention to detail can be seen everywhere. The gym, spas, and pools are spotless, hotel rooms are cheery and tasteful, and the breakfast is topnotch. If you don't want to eat in one of the resort's three restaurants (two upscale options and a more casual bistro/lounge), there are plenty of restaurants in Riva del Garda itself, just a 15-minute walk away. For much of the year, the Paolino miniclub is open to kids aged 3 to 10; professional staff lead a variety of children's activities throughout the day, offering parents a bit of time to relax on their own.

Via Rovereto 44, Riva del Garda. www.dulacetduparc.com. ✆ **0464/566-600.** 159 units in main hotel. 180€–259€ double. Rates include breakfast. Closed Dec–Apr. **Amenities:** 3 restaurants; 3 bars; 2 outdoor pools; indoor pool; gym; spa; sauna; babysitting; kids' club; water sports; concierge; room service; free Wi-Fi.

out & about ON LAKE GARDA

Riva del Garda's main attraction is the lake, lined with plush hotels and a waterside promenade that stretches for several miles past parks and pebbly beaches. The water is warm enough for swimming May to October, and air currents fanned by the mountains make Riva and neighboring Torbole the windsurfing capitals of Europe. Kitesurfing, kayaking, and sailing are all popular pastimes.

A convenient point of embarkation for a lake outing is the beach next to **La Rocca** castle, where from March through October you can rent rowboats or pedal boats for about 10€ per hour; the concession is open daily 8am to 8pm.

Check out the sailing and windsurfing at **Sailing du Lac** (www.sailingdulac.com) at the luxurious **Hotel du Lac et du Parc** (see above), where windsurf equipment can be rented for 65€ per day or 30€ per hour. Lessons start at 72€ for 3 hours. A catamaran for two to four people can be rented for 65€ per hour; you must leave a 200€ deposit and show identification such as a passport. Catamaran lessons start at 85€ per 2-hour session. The school is open mid-April to mid-October from 8:30am to 6:30pm.

Lake Garda is also renowned for mountain biking; there are more than 80 routes around the lake and up into the Alpine foothills. At **Happy Bike,** Viale Rovereto 72 (www.happy-bike.it; ✆ **347/943-1208;** daily 9am–7pm), you can rent a city bike for 16€ per day, a mountain bike for around 25€ per day.

Hotel Eden ★ Once home to American poet Ezra Pound, today this pink-stucco palazzo on the lake is a modernized hotel in the heart of Sirmione's *centro storico* mere steps from the castle. Common areas are bright and feature vivid wallpaper and touches. A breakfast room leads to a terrace overlooking the lake, with a pier that juts out over the water. The focus on modernity and bright colors continues in the guest rooms, where splashy touches here and there liven up simple furnishings. Guests of the Hotel Eden now have access to the spa and wellness area at nearby partner property, Hotel Olivi, about an 8-minute walk away. Ask for a lakeview room, as it can be somewhat noisy at night on the other side of the hotel. The hotel can set up a private boat tour, which departs right from the dock outside.

Piazza Carducci 19, Sirmione. www.hoteledensirmione.it. ✆ **030/916-481.** 30 units. 105€–190€ double. Rates include breakfast. Closed Nov–Mar. **Amenities:** Restaurant; bar; concierge; room service; free Wi-Fi.

Osteria Al Torcol ★★ ITALIAN Located at the top of a little hill on a quiet side street, Torcol is consistently regarded as *the* standout restaurant in Sirmione and among the best on Lake Garda. The wood-beamed interior is packed with bottles of local wines (many available by the glass). This high-end *osteria* is known for interesting flavor combinations and artful presentation. Start off with a selection of locally sourced *salumi* or cheeses served with pickled fruit preserves. Signature dishes include homemade *bigoli* (like a thicker spaghetti) with Garda tench fish and capers, or local perch in a matcha-tea tempura batter served with zucchini flowers and chive yogurt. Meat dishes include lamp chops served over a cabbage salad with a coconut and black sesame sauce. If you have your heart set on views of the lake, this isn't the restaurant for you, but the courtyard is quite an oasis if you can get a table outside. Make sure to book in advance.

Via San Salvatore 30, Sirmione. ✆ **030/990-4605.** Entrees 16€–30€. May–Dec daily 12:30–3pm and 7:30–10:30pm; Oct–Jan Sat–Sun 12:30–3pm and 7:30–10:30pm; Feb–Apr Sat–Sun 7:30–10:30pm.

Trattoria Riolet ★ ITALIAN If you make the uphill trek to the Trattoria Riolet (about 25 min. on foot from the center of Gardone Riviera, or a 5-min. drive), you will be rewarded with unsurpassed views over Lake Garda. This unpretentious hilltop spot is as popular with locals as it is with summer visitors. The big draw here is the grilled meat and fish cooked over an open fire—*coregone* (a type of white fish) fresh from the lake or marinated spareribs—but there are also a few options for vegetarians like a vegetable lasagna, eggplant parmigiana, or gnocchi in tomato sauce. There's not always a set menu and options can be limited, so follow your waiter's advice in ordering—and be sure to enjoy a carafe or two of local wine. Call ahead to reserve a table, especially when the weather is nice.

Via Fasano Sopra 47, Gardone Riviera. ✆ **0365/205-45.** Thurs–Tues 7–10:30pm. Entrees 12€–25€.

TURIN ★★★

669km (415 miles) NW of Rome, 140km (87 miles) E of Milan

It's often said that Turin (Torino in Italian) is the most French city in Italy. The reason is partly historical and partly architectural. From the late 13th century until Italy's unification in 1861, Turin was the capital of the **House of Savoy.** These wealthy aristocrats were as French as they were Italian, with estates that extended into the present-day French regions of Savoy and the Côte d'Azur. Under the Savoys, Francophile 17th- and 18th-century architects razed much of the city and its Roman foundations, replacing them with broad avenues and grandiose buildings. As a result, Turin is one of Europe's great baroque cities, befitting a one-time capital of the nation. These days, thanks in part to the 2006 Winter Olympics and another makeover in 2011 for the 150th anniversary of Italian unification, Turin has transformed itself from an industrial power into a go-to destination—a vibrant, sophisticated city of museums, enticing cafes, beautiful squares, and designer shops.

Essentials

ARRIVING Domestic and international **flights** land at **Turin Airport** (**TRN;** www.aeroportoditorino.it; ✆ **011/567-6361**), about 13km (8 miles) northwest of Turin. Direct **trains** (www.gtt.to.it; ✆ **011/57-641**) run from the airport to GTT Dora commuter rail station every 30 minutes between 5am and 11pm; the 4€ trip takes 19 minutes. **Arriva buses** (torino.arriva.it) serve the airport and Turin's main train stations, Porta Nuova and Porta Susa (40 min.; 7.50€ from the ticket office, 8.50€ on board, though if you pay on board with a contactless credit card, the cost is still 7.50€). **Taxis** into town take about 30 minutes and cost 30€ to 50€, depending on the time of day.

Turin's main **train** station is **Stazione di Porta Nuova** on Piazza Carlo Felice. There is regular daily **Trenitalia** (www.trenitalia.com; ✆ **892-021**) service from Milan. The fastest trains take 1 hour, with fares averaging 29€. Slower trains take up to 2 hours, with fares of 12€ to 17€. **Stazione di Porta Susa** connects Turin with local Piedmont towns and is the terminus for the **TGV service to Paris;** four trains a day make that trip in under 6 hours for around 98€, but there are sometimes specials for as low as 29€ each way. To get a better fare, try to book well in advance.

Turin's main **bus terminal** is **Autostazione Bus,** Corso Vittorio Emanuele II 131 (www.autostazionetorino.it). Buses connect Turin to Courmayeur, Aosta, Milan, and many small towns in Piedmont. A 2-hour **Arriva** (torino.arriva.it) bus service to Milan Malpensa Airport costs 22€ each way.

Turin is at the hub of the autostrade grid. The A4 connects Turin with Milan in 90 minutes. Journey time on the A5 to Aosta is around 90 minutes.

See Turin's Top Sights & Save

If you're planning to visit three or more attractions, you can save money by buying the **Torino+Piemonte Card** (www.turismotorino.org/card), which grants access to over 180 museums, monuments, castles, and royal palazzos, as well as offering discounts on public transportation and at attractions throughout the Piedmont region. All of the attractions covered below are included. A variety of passes are available; a 24-hour pass valid for one adult costs 29€. There are cheaper passes for families or individually for those under the age of 18. Passes can be bought online or at the Piazza Castello tourist office or Stazione Porta Nuova.

GETTING AROUND All the main sights of Turin are well within walking distance of each other. There's also a vast network of **GTT** trams and buses as well as one metro line (www.gtt.to.it; ✆ **011/57-641**). The historic Linea 7 tourist tram, known as a "museum on the move," trundles around a circular route from Piazza Castello. Public transport tickets, available at newsstands, cost 1.70€ for 100 minutes of travel; all-day tickets cost 4€ and are valid until the end of service that day. There is no need to drive in the city center.

You can find **taxis** at stands in front of the train stations and around Piazza San Carlo and Piazza Castello. To call a taxi, you can dial **Taxi Torino** at ✆ **011/5730** or 011/5737, but all hotel reception desks will order a taxi for you. Meters start at around 4€ and increase by 1.50€ per km up to 10€, after which the per-km rate decreases based on how long you travel; there are surcharges for waiting, luggage, late-night travel, and Sunday journeys.

VISITOR INFORMATION The **tourist office** on the corner of Via Garibaldi and Piazza Castello (www.turismotorino.org; ✆ **011/535-181**) is open daily 9am to 6pm. There is also a branch across from Stazione Porta Nuova in Piazza Carlo Felice (same phone; same hours).

CITY LAYOUT Turin's glamorous spine is the arcaded Via Roma, lined with designer shops and grand cafes. Via Roma runs northwards through a series of ever-lovelier baroque squares until it reaches Piazza Castello and the palaces of the Savoy nobility. From here, a walk west on Via Garibaldi leads to the square-shaped Quadrilatero Romano, a mellow jumble of narrow streets that's the oldest part of the city. Or turn east from Piazza Castello along Via Po to one of Italy's largest squares, the Piazza Vittorio Veneto, and at the end of this elegant expanse, the River Po and Parco del Valentino.

Exploring Turin

The stately arcades of **Via Roma,** Turin's premier shopping street, were designed in 1714 by Filippo Juvarra. Starting at the Porta Nuova train station, this chic thoroughfare runs from **Piazza Carlo Felice,** an ellipse of

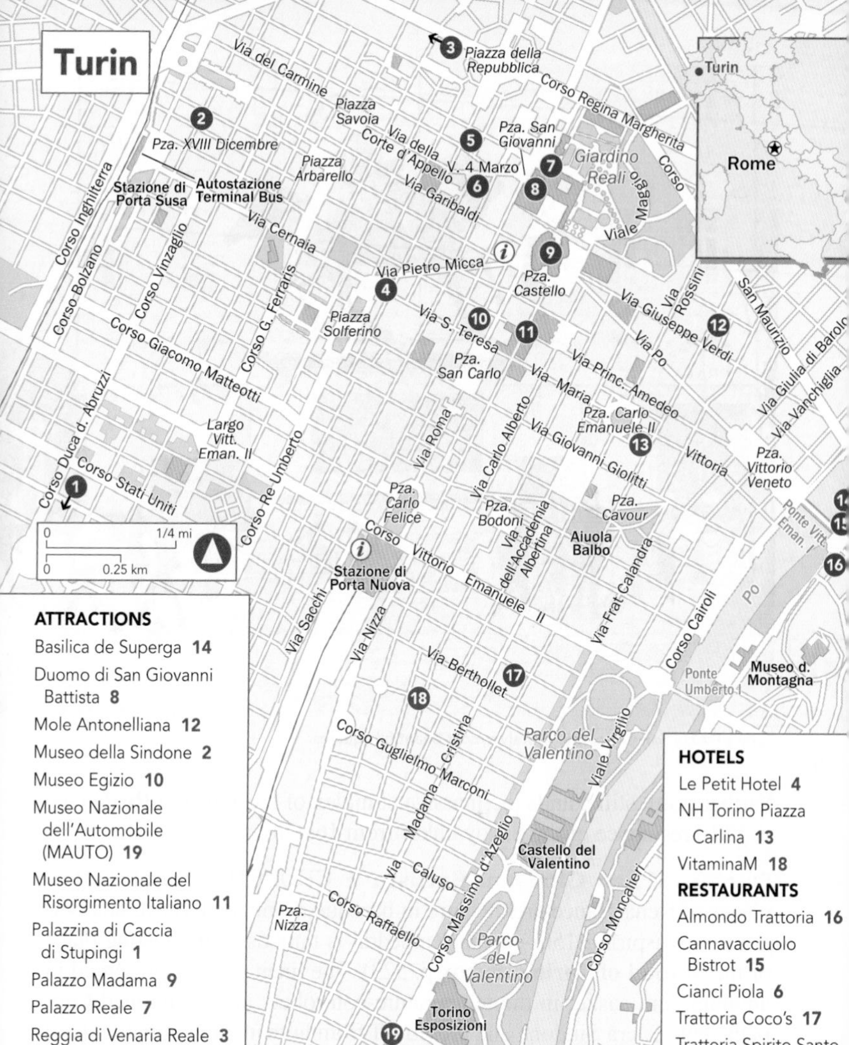

formal gardens ringed with outdoor cafes, north into **Piazza San Carlo,** quite possibly Italy's most beautiful square. In summer, harmonious Piazza San Carlo is Turin's outdoor *salone,* its arcaded sidewalks lined with big-name fashion stores and elegant cafes, including the genteel **Caffé Torino** (✆ **011/545-118**). In the center of the piazza prances a 19th-century equestrian statue of Duke Emanuele Filiberto of Savoy. Two 17th-century churches**, San Carlo** and **Santa Cristina,** face each other like bookends at the southern entrance to the square.

At the far north end of Via Roma, the **Piazza Castello** is dominated by **Palazzo Madama** (see p. 526), named for its 17th-century inhabitant, Christine Marie of France, who married into the Savoy dynasty in 1619.

Turin's Piazza San Carlo, one of Italy's most beautiful squares.

Farther north still stands the massive complex of the **Palazzo Reale** (see p. 527), residence of the Savoy dukes from 1646 to 1865.

Duomo di San Giovanni Battista ★ CHURCH One of the few pieces of Renaissance architecture in baroque-dominated Turin, this otherwise uninspiring 15th-century cathedral is famous as the resting place of the **Shroud of Turin** (see box p. 523). The linen cloth is preserved in an aluminum casket in the temperature-controlled, air-conditioned Cappella della Sacra Sindone and closed off from human contamination (and public view) with bulletproof glass. The casket is adorned with a crown of thorns; the faithful come in droves to worship at the chapel, which is the last one in the left-hand aisle. To learn about the history of the shroud, head for the **Museo della Sindone** (see p. 524).

Piazza San Giovanni. ✆ **011/436-1540.** Free. Mon–Fri 7am–12:30pm and 3–7pm; Sat–Sun 8am–12:30pm and 3–7pm. Bus: 11, 12, 51, 55, 56, 61, 68. Trams: 4, 13, 15, 18.

Mole Antonelliana & Museo Nazionale del Cinema ★★★ MUSEUM Turin's most peculiar building, dominating the skyline from all directions, was once the tallest in Europe. Building started in 1863 on what was originally meant to be a synagogue; later, city fathers decided to make it a monument to Italian unification (at the time, Italy was ruled by the House of Savoy from its power base in Turin). Set on a squat brick base, the Mole rises through layers of windows and pseudo-Greek columns to a huge ribbed cupola and needlelike spire, all of it looming 167m (548 ft.) above the streets.

The Mole is now home to Italy's National Film Museum, which houses more than 2 million objects, enhanced with interactive displays and hands-on activities. The first galleries track the intriguing development of moving pictures, from shadow puppets to risqué peep shows and flickering images of galloping horses filmed by Edward Muybridge in 1878. Other exhibits use clips, stills, posters, and props to illustrate aspects of movie production, such as the creepy steady-cam work in *The Shining;* a section of movie memorabilia includes jewels and shoes worn by Marilyn Monroe and Darth Vader's mask from *The Empire Strikes Back.* Throughout the year, the museum hosts various film festivals, the foremost being the Torino Film Festival, which usually takes place in late November, plus other events focused on themes such as environmental movies and LGBTQ themes in cinema.

A major highlight of a visit includes a panoramic elevator ride through the roof of the museum's vast atrium and up 85m (279 ft.) inside the tower to the 360-degree observation platform at the top. The view of Turin and the surrounding countryside, backed by the Alps, is stunning. ***Note:*** You can bypass the museum and only do the panoramic elevator for a cost of 9€ (7€ with the **Torino+Piemonte Card,** see p. 520). Lines form

MYSTERY OF THE shroud of turin

One of the Christian world's most revered relics, the Shroud of Turin—displayed in Turin's **Duomo di San Giovanni Battista** (p. 522)—is said to be the very same piece of fabric in which Christ was wrapped when he was taken from the cross, which miraculously became imprinted with his image.

The image on the cloth does shows a bearded face—remarkably similar to the depiction of Christ in Byzantine icons—and a body marked with bloodstains, in spots that match where a crown of thorns, a spear slash in the rib cage, and nail holes in the wrists and ankles would be, along with scourge marks on the back from flagellation.

So is the Shroud real? Carbon dating results are confusing; some suggest that the shroud was manufactured around the 13th or 14th centuries, while other tests imply that those results were thrown off by a fire that all but destroyed the shroud in December 1532.

But the mystery remains, at least in part because no one can explain how the haunting image appeared on the cloth. Debunkers have attempted to create replicas using lemon juice and the sun, mineral pigments, even aloe and myrrh (which were used in funerary traditions of Jesus' time). A 2015 study of DNA in the shroud's dust particles further confused the picture: It was shown to contain genetic material from plants across the globe—perhaps not surprising, considering how many people have come into contact with it over the years.

on weekends, so try to come early or reserve your spot ahead of time by buying tickets online.

Via Montebello 20. www.museocinema.it. ✆ **011/8138-563.** Museum & elevator: 17€, 14€ seniors and students up to age 26, 10€ ages 6–18, free for children under 5. Museum only: 12€, 10€ seniors and students up to age 26, 4€ ages 6–18, free for children under 5. Elevator only: 9€, 7€ students, seniors, ages 6–18. Wed–Mon 9am–8pm; Sat 9am–11pm. Bus: 18, 55, 56, 61, 68. Tram: 13, 15, 16.

Museo della Sindone ★★ MUSEUM Despite the fact that the shroud isn't actually kept here and there are no special effects, the endearing Holy Shroud Museum is still a hit, fully representing the Shroud of Turin's status as one of the world's most famous religious relics (see box, p. 523). A visit starts with a 15-minute film (offered in five languages) about the shroud, its provenance, and the various theories and mysteries surrounding it. Visitors then wander through a series of rooms chronicling the shroud's history, from its first mention in 1204 to the fire that nearly destroyed it in Chambéry in 1532 to its arrival in Turin with the House of Savoy in 1578 to modern-day carbon-testing efforts. The last stop is the richly ornamented chapel of Santo Sudario—a private place of worship for the Savoy dukes—where a copy of the shroud is displayed over the gleaming, gilded altar. Each of the displays is well marked in both English and Italian, and more information is available via QR code that can be scanned with a digital device.

The **shroud** itself is kept nearby, in the royal chapel of the Duomo, usually out of public view (see p. 523). It is, however, typically taken out for public viewing every few years, most recently for a few days in late 2020 for the meeting of Europe's Youth Pilgrimage; the decision to do so is usually made by the reigning pope. Log on to www.sindone.org to find out when the shroud will next be taken out; advance reservations are required to see the shroud during these brief public displays.

Via San Domenico 28. www.sindone.it. ✆ **011/436-5832.** 8€ adults; 6€ seniors; students, and kids over the age of 6; free under age 6. Daily 9am–noon and 3–7pm.

Museo Egizio ★★ MUSEUM Even before the massive renovation that doubled the exhibition space, people came from all around Italy and beyond to visit Turin's magnificent Egyptian Museum. It is one of the world's largest—no surprise, considering it was also the world's *first* Egyptian museum, thanks to the Savoy kings and their explorers Bernardino Drovetti and Ernesto Schiaparelli, who voraciously hoarded Egyptian ephemera until the early 1900s, when attitudes about cultural plundering changed. Some say this is the most important collection of Egyptian artifacts outside of Cairo, so it's definitely a must-visit when in Turin. Not only have Egyptian cultural and funereal elements been reconstructed down to the smallest details, the museum also tells the history of the archaeological expeditions. Artifacts from all eras of ancient Egypt include a papyrus "Book of the Dead." One of the most captivating exhibits is the exquisitely painted wooden sarcophagi and mummies of Kha and Merit, an aristocratic couple whose tomb was discovered in 1906. Powerful X-ray technology has been used to digitally "unwrap" the mummies, with the images on display showing how they are adorned with amazing jewels (which have been re-created via 3-D printing). A visit to the museum finishes with the monumental statues in the spectacular "Gallery of Kings" designed by world-renowned production designer, costume designer, and art director Dante Ferretti. It's definitely best to reserve your visit ahead of time online (you can also reserve themed tours in English), choosing from among various itineraries. Bags larger than a purse are not allowed in the museum and will have to be left in the coat check on floor -1.

Via Accademia delle Scienze 6. www.museoegizio.it. ✆ **011/440-6903.** 18€ adults; 3€ ages 15–18; 1€ ages 6–14; free for children 5 and under. Mon 9am–2pm; Tues–Sun 8:30am–7:30pm. Bus: 55, 56. Tram: 13.

Museo Nazionale dell'Automobile (MAUTO) ★★★ MUSEUM
Considering that Turin spawned auto giant Fiat, it is only fitting that the city would have a museum where the car is king. This innovative museum, located just south of Parco del Valentino, is a perfect place to bring kids who've traipsed around one too many dusty palazzos. A visit here will

Vintage cars at the Museo Nazionale dell'Automobile.

take about 2 hours. Visitors enter through a futuristic covered courtyard that leads into the venue; a cafe and bookshop are off to the left as you come in. Alfa Romeos and lots of bright-red Ferraris feature heavily among the displays, which start with vintage cars from the days when road travel was only for the very wealthy. Exhibits also highlight the social, financial, and environmental impact that combustion engines have had on the planet. Different areas of the museum include "The Car and the 20th Century," "The Car and Man," and "The Car and Design." There's also a simulator where (for an additional cost of around 20€) you can enjoy the thrill of "driving" a Ferrari or a rally car.

Corso Unità d'Italia 40. www.museoauto.it. ✆ **011/677-666.** 14€ adults; 5€ ages 6–18 and seniors; free for kids under 6. Mon 10am–2pm; Tues 2–7pm; Wed–Thurs, Sun 10am–7pm; Fri–Sat 10am–9pm. Metro: Lingotto.

Museo Nazionale del Risorgimento Italiano ★★★ MUSEUM

Located on majestic Piazza Carignano, the equally handsome redbrick *palazzo* of the same name acquired huge national importance as the occasional home of Italy's first king after the country's unification in 1861. Originally built between 1679 and 1685 by baroque maestro Guarino Guarini, the palace now houses the Museo del Risorgimento (Risorgimento, meaning "resurgence" or "revival," is the name given to Italy's unification movement). At its heart is the ornate circular chamber where Italy's first parliament met. Despite the museum's focus on the past, the displays are quite innovative for an Italian museum, with multilingual signage and labeling, audioguides, video guides, and interactive touchscreens. History buffs could easily spend hours here, but if time is of the essence, much of the museum's collections are online with Google Arts & Culture (artsandculture.google.com), where you can virtually visit multiple rooms, exploring in 360 degrees. A cinema room shows films that illustrate the importance of this building and of Turin during the era. More than 30 richly furnished rooms detail the military campaigns that led to unification; even non-Italians can easily appreciate the stirring drama of these years. Uniforms, paintings, weapons, maps, and correspondence testify to feats of great bravado, tracing a course through the Italy of the 19th century from Napoleon to Garibaldi. There are other museums in Italy dedicated to the Risorgimento, but this is the largest and most important.

Via Accademia delle Scienze 5. www.museorisorgimentotorino.it. ✆ **011/562-1147.** 10€ adults; 8€ seniors; 5€ students; 2.50€ primary schoolers; free ages 6 and under; free with the Torino + Piemonte Card (p. 520). Tues–Sun 10am–6pm. Bus: 11, 12, 27, 51, 51, 55, 56, 57. Tram: 13, 15.

Palazzo Madama—Museo Civico di Arte Antica ★ MUSEUM

Don't be misled by the baroque facade on the Palazzo Madama, which was added by architect Filippo Juvarra in the 18th century—walk around this massive structure and you'll see that it also incorporates a medieval castle, a Roman gate, and several Renaissance additions. A visit here is also about learning about the history of the building and its multiple styles while enjoying the collections from the Civic Museum of Ancient Arte from past eras, over four mammoth floors (stop to admire the monumental marble staircase, another Juvarra touch). Works from the medieval and Renaissance periods show off well against the building's austere, stony interior; on the top floor you'll also find one of Italy's largest collections of ceramics. Still, it can be rather disorganized—you'll have to hunt for the star of the show, Antonello da Messina's sublime "Portrait of a Man," which is hidden away in the Treasure Tower at the back of the building on the ground floor where art from the Middle Ages and the Renaissance is displayed.

Piazza Castello. www.palazzomadamatorino.it. ✆ **011/443-3501.** 10€ adults; 8€ student and seniors; free under 18. Mon, Wed–Fri 10am–6pm; Sat 11am–7pm; Sun 10am–7pm. Free admission 1st Wed of month (excluding holidays). Bus: 11, 12, 51, 55, 56, 61, 68; Trams: 4, 13, 15, 18.

Palazzo Reale ★ PALACE Overshadowing the north side of the Piazza Castello, the residence of the House of Savoy was begun in 1646; the family lived here until 1865. Designed by the architect Amedeo di Castellamonte, the palace reflects the ornate tastes of European ruling families of the time, while its sheer size proves their wealth. This Savoy palace gives the flamboyant frippery of Versailles a run for its money, its throne rooms, ballrooms, and apartments lavishly adorned with priceless Gobelins tapestries, silk walls, sparkling chandeliers, ornate wooden floors, and gilded furniture.

The east wing of the *palazzo* houses the **Armeria Reale,** one of the most important arms and armor collections in Europe, especially of weapons from the 16th and 17th centuries. It also has a unique collection of stuffed horses, which look ready to leap into battle at any moment. Behind the palace are the formal **Giardini Reali** (Royal Gardens), laid out in part by André Le Nôtre, who designed the Tuileries in Paris and the gardens at Versailles.

The Savoy royal family had an even keener eye for paintings than for baroque decor, amassing a collection of 8,000 works of art. The collection's highlights are on display in the **Galleria Sabauda** in the Palazzo Reale's New Wing (a few minutes' walk from the main *palazzo*). The exhibition kicks off with early Piedmont and Dutch religious works, plus a moody Rembrandt self-portrait and two massive paintings by van Dyck: "The Children of Charles I" (1637) and a magnificent equestrian portrait of Prince Thomas of Savoy (ca. 1634). In the basement beneath the Galleria Sabauda, the **Museo Archeologico**'s thoughtfully designed exhibition tells the story of Turin's development from Roman through medieval times. Incorporated into its displays are a section of Roman wall, remnants from a theater nearby, and a mosaic only discovered in 1993.

The **Biblioteca Reale** (Royal Library) is also part of the Palazzo Reale complex; it's free to enter, and you'll find it on the right of the main entrance. Founded in 1831, it houses 200,000 rare volumes as well as ancient maps and prints. On the opposite side of the gates is the fine **church of San Lorenzo,** designed by master architect Guarino Guarini in 1666. Its plain facade belies a lacy dome and frothy interior.

Warning: Security rules prohibit visitors from bringing in large bags (backpacks, duffel bags, and luggage), and the *palazzo* currently offers no place to check these items for safekeeping (at press time, they were working on a new wardrobe service).

Piazzetta Reale 1. www.ilpalazzorealeditorino.it. ✆ **011/436-1455.** Palazzo and all exhibitions: 15€ adults, 2€ ages 18–25, free for children and seniors. Free admission 1st Sun of month. Tues–Sun 9am–7pm; last admission 6pm. Museo Archeologico closed Sun morning. Bus: 11, 51, 55, 56, 68; Trams: 4, 13, 15, 18.

A Glimpse into Roman Turin

Close to Turin's Duomo (see p. 522) and partly incorporated into the Museo Archeologico (see p. 475) stand two landmarks of Roman Turin: the remains of a theater and fragments of wall, as well as the **Porta Palatina,** a Roman-era city gate, flanked by twin 16-sided towers on Piazza Cesare Augusto. The **Area Romana** west of the Piazza Castello is the oldest part of the city, a charming web of streets occupied since ancient times.

Outlying Attractions

Basilica di Superga ★★ CHURCH Half the fun of a visit to this lovely basilica is the 6.5km (4-mile) journey northeast of the city center on a narrow-gauge railway through the lush countryside of the Parco Naturale della Collina di Superga. The church was built as thanksgiving to the Virgin Mary for Turin's deliverance from the French siege of 1706. Prince Vittorio Amedeo II commissioned Filippo Juvarra, the Sicilian architect who designed much of Turin's elegant center, to build the magical baroque confection on a hill high above the city. The eye-catching exterior, with its beautiful colonnaded portico, elaborate dome, and twin bell towers, is actually more appealing than the ornate but gloomy interior, a circular chamber ringed by six chapels. Many scions of the House of Savoy are buried here in the Crypt of Kings beneath the main chapel.

Strada della Basilica di Superga, 73, www.basilicadisuperga.com. ✆ **011/899-7456.** Basilica admission free; 5€ to visit Royal Tombs or Royal Apartment; 3€ to climb dome. Mon–Fri 9am–noon and 3–6pm; Sat–Sun 9am–noon and 3–7pm (closes 1 hr. earlier in winter). Tram: Tranvia a Dentiera from Stazione Sassi (6€ round-trip) to Superga stop. Bus: 61 from side of Ponte Vittorio Emanuele I opposite Piazza Vittorio Veneto.

Palazzina di Caccia di Stupinigi ★ PALACE Yet another Savoy family home is found at Stupinigi, just a few miles southwest of Turin. More great work commissioned in 1729 from the architect Filippo Juvarra resulted in a sumptuous hunting lodge surrounded by royal forests. Built on a humungous scale, the palace's wings fan out from the main house, topped by a domed pavilion. Every bit as lavish as the apartments in the Savoys' city residence, **Palazzo Reale** (p. 527), the interior is stuffed with furniture, paintings, and bric-à-brac assembled from myriad Savoy residences; it's now the **Museo dell'Arte e Ammobiliamento** (Museum of Art and Furniture). Wander through the acres of apartments to understand why Napoleon chose this palace for his brief sojourn in Piedmont in 1805 while en route to Milan to be crowned emperor. Outstanding among the many, many frescoes are the scenes of a deer hunt in the King's Apartment and the triumph of Diana in the grand salon. The elegant gardens and surrounding forests provide lovely terrain for a jaunt. One quirky thing about this palace is that you may find the ticket office closed for lunch between 1 and 2pm.

Piazza Principe Amedeo 7, Stupingi, Nichelino (8.5km/5¼ miles SW of city center). www.ordinemauriziano.it/palazzina-di-caccia-stupinigi. ✆ **011/620-0634.** 12€; 8€ seniors and ages 6–18; free for kids under 6. Tues–Fri 10am–5:30pm; Sat 10am–6:30pm.

Reggia di Venaria Reale ★★★ PALACE Completing the triumvirate of glitzy Savoy households around Turin, the Venaria was constructed in the mid-17th century to a design by Amedeo di Castellamonte, but sure enough Filippo Juvarra also had a hand in it. This massive complex, its stables, and the awesome formal gardens are now a UNESCO World Heritage Site. Venaria offers a great family-oriented day out with loads of outdoor summer activities as well as a glimpse into the extraordinarily privileged lives of the Savoy family. The Fountain of the Stag dances to music in the lake outside the *palazzo;* on the grounds are follies aplenty and the mock-Roman Fountain of Hercules.

Piazza della Repubblica 4, Venaria Reale (10km/6¼ miles NW of city center). www.lavenaria.it. ✆ **011/499-2333.** Prices range from 20€ for palace, gardens & activities to 5€ for gardens only (full range of options may not be available in winter). Tues–Fri 9am–5pm; Sat–Sun 9:30am–6:30pm (last admission 1 hr. before closing). Bus: 11 from Piazza Repubblica. A Venaria Express bus runs Tues–Sun (40 min.), with stops at Stazione Porta Nuova, Via XX Settembre, and Stazione Porta Susa.

Organized Tours

The nonprofit organization **Free Tour Turin** (www.freetourturin.com) offers a free 2½-hour guided tour of the city center (in English and Italian) Thursday through Monday at 10:30am. Tour groups meet outside the Porta Nuova metro station in Piazza Carlo Felice near the Sambuy Garden (look for the guide holding a sign or umbrella).

Especially for Kids

There's plenty for kids to do in Turin. The **Parco del Valentino** (see p. 533) has lots of open spaces to run around in, plus free admission to the open-air **Borgo Medievale,** a mock-Piedmontese village built for the Italian General Exposition in 1884 (Viale Virgilio 107; www.borgo medievaletorino.it; ✆ **011/4431-701;** daily 9am–7pm [8pm in summer]). Most youngsters will be intrigued by the **Museum of Cinema** at the Mole Antonelliana (p. 522), or at least the trip up the Mole's tower to see the city far below. The **Museo Nazionale dell'Automobile** (p. 525) provides an antidote to Turin's baroque attractions. **Zoom Torino** (www.zoom torino.it) is an immersive zoo—no bars or cages—located about 35 minutes southwest of the city center by car in the town of Cumiana. You can also get there by train, getting out at the Piscina di Pinerolo station and taking the Zoom shuttle, which costs 5€ (for those 3 and over), and you must reserve online on the www.zoomtorino.it site.

If all else fails, pop into **Caffè Fiorio** (Via Po 8; ✆ **011/8173-225**) for some delicious gelato or, in cooler months, Turin's famous hot chocolate.

Where to Stay in Turin

In recent years, Turin has seen an influx of boutique hotels, giving travelers an alternative to the faceless frumpery of many of the city's older hotels.

SELF-CATERING ROOMS & APARTMENTS

If **VitaminaM** (see p. 530) is booked up, the charming **Cute** apartment (www.airbnb.com/rooms/17945654), in the heart of the action mere steps from Piazza Castello, averages about 75€ a night for two people. It has one bedroom, one bath, and a full kitchen; its historic beams blend well with the modern amenities.

Le Petit Hotel ★★ This great budget option in the center of the city lies in a strategic location—it is 10 minutes' walk from both the Porta Nuova and Porta Susa train stations, and very close to Palazzo Madama and the Egyptian museum. You won't find luxury here, but simple rooms with spotless, functional bathrooms. A colorfully furnished breakfast room offers a selection of breads, cheeses, fruit, and pastries. There are plenty of dining options in the vicinity, but the hotel's restaurant, Marechiaro, is a solid option if you don't feel like straying too far. It serves up Mediterranean cuisine, including traditional dishes from the Piedmont region along with pizza. When it's warm, you can sit outside and people-watch on the pedestrian-only street. The hotel also has some slightly more modern self-catering apartments.

Via San Francesco d'Assisi 21. www.lepetithotel.it. ✆ **011/561-2626.** 79 units. 90€–140€ double; 180€–220€ apartment. Rates include breakfast. **Amenities:** Restaurant; free Wi-Fi.

NH Hotels Torino Piazza Carlina ★★★ Located in the heart of most of the major attractions in Turin and near the Po River, this hotel in a 17th-century palazzo is just off of a busy city *piazza.* Modern rooms come in muted shades of beige, cream, and rose, and some offer views of the square down below or the nearby Mole Antonelliana. There are even Family XL rooms for up to eight people and a selection of suites with contemporary touches, terraces, and some of the best views. Hotel guests can make use of two large terraces (including an herb garden) off of the fifth floor, which is also home to a spacious gym. The sophisticated Restaurant Carlina is open for lunch and dinner, offering up modern Mediterranean cuisine with international flair.

15 Piazza Carlo Emanuele II. www.nh-hotels.com/hotel/nh-collection-torino-piazza-carlina. ✆ **011/860-1611.** 160 units. 165€–225€ double. Rates include breakfast. **Amenities:** Restaurant; bar; concierge; gym; free Wi-Fi.

VitaminaM ★★★ With just two rooms, this B&B near Porta Nuova train station is more like staying in a short-term apartment rental, a particularly special one. The funky interiors make it feel like the sophisticated city home of a modern art lover, with a library open to all featuring books on Turin, Piedmont, and design, along with light-flooded rooms and bathrooms that are surprisingly luxurious. The Roberta room is slightly larger, while the Leslie room has a small terrace. The charming hosts provide little touches like chocolates on your pillow and homemade jams at breakfast. The neighborhood is quite bustling—good news for travelers who want to be surrounded by shops and restaurants, but it's hard to find parking if you come by car (during the day, street parking costs 1.5€ per hour), and it can also be quite loud on weekend nights. The B&B is four floors up with no elevator, though someone is usually available to help with your bags. Book well ahead; this is one of the hottest tickets in town.

Via Belfiore 18. www.vitaminam.com. ✆ **347/1526-130.** 2 units. 100€–120€ double; additional bed 30€. Rates include breakfast. **Amenities:** Free Wi-Fi.

Where to Eat in Turin

Turin's gourmet reputation outshines other Italian cities renowned for their gastronomy. Many restaurants are strong advocates of the Slow Food movement, and a glance at a menu will tell you whether ingredients are local; look for porcini mushrooms and truffles in season. Wine lists feature Barolo, Barbera, and Barbaresco reds and sparkling Asti whites. Turin is also home to the world's largest food and wine fair, the **Terra Madre Salone del Gusto** (www.salonedelgusto.com), which runs every 2 years in September or October. If you would like to enjoy Turin's cuisine while keeping the calorie count down, local guide Roberto leads gourmet bike tours via **EasyTorino** (www.easytorino.com). A variety of tours are available—cycle through the city along the Po River or take to the hills where you can taste wine and products from small farms.

Almondo Trattoria ★ MODERN ITALIAN This contemporary establishment just over the Vittorio Emanuele I bridge on the other side of the Po River (about a 15-min. walk from the center) has a sort of clean Italo-Scandinavian industrial aesthetic but with welcoming archways and green plants hanging decoratively from the ceiling. Almondo serves up bright plates of Italian specialty dishes from north to south—*pizzoccheri* pasta from the mountains, Roman *cacio e pepe,* Venetian-style liver, Sicilian orange salad with fennel—but with a wine list that focuses on local vintages from the nearby Piedmont hills. The staff is cheerful, and pricing is fair. Almondo is right across the street from the Gran Madre di Dio church, built to celebrate the defeat of Napoleon and quite impressive in all of its Neoclassic splendor.

Piazza Gran Madre di Dio 2/L. almondotrattoria.it. ✆ **011/411-9684.** Entrees 10€–18€. Daily 12:30–2:30pm and 7:30–11:30pm.

Cannavacciuolo Bistrot ★★ ITALIAN Just across the Po River, this is one of the hottest fine-dining experiences in town. The elegant yet minimalist space of Italian celebrity chef Antonio Cannavacciuolo sets the stage for lighter Piedmontese dishes with influences from southern Italy (Cannavacciuolo is from near Naples). Fassona beef tartare comes with a hazelnut mayonnaise, black truffle, and Parmesan; tagliatelle with shrimp and orange is more of a nod to the Mediterranean, while Genoese spaghetti with sausage from the town of Bra is a mix of land and sea. There are a variety of tasting menus (120€–130€) for those wanting to try a bit of everything. Desserts are definitely a highlight here—meals often end with a selection of Neapolitan pastries, a nod to the chef's origins.

Via Umberto Cosmo 6. www.cannavacciuolobistrot.it/torino. ✆ **011/839-9893.** Entrees 20€–40€. Mon–Sat 12:30–3pm and 7–11pm; closed Sun.

Cianci Piola ★★ ITALIAN REGIONAL With its in-your-face attitude (the slogan is "for many but not for all") and spirited decorations on the brick walls, this isn't your usual *piola* (a local term for an establishment serving authentic Piedmontese cuisine at good prices). Tables spill out on to a charming square mere blocks from the Royal Palace. For a location right in the city center, prices are quite low and portions are large, but the waitstaff aims to turn tables over quickly here, so this isn't the place to linger when it's busy (thus the reason it may not be "for all"). Creative and classic interpretations of *Piemontese* dishes are on the menu, with tajarin pasta prepared a variety of ways (with a rabbit ragout, say, or with sausage and radicchio) and mustard-roasted pork is served with an apple salad. Finish off with *bunet* for dessert, an ancient regional specialty, sort of like a chocolate pudding with *amaretti* biscuits. Call or pop by to reserve a table.

Via Largo IV Marzo 9/b. www.ciancipiola.it. ✆ **353/342-6322.** Entrees 6€–10€. Daily noon–midnight.

Trattoria Coco's ★★ ITALIAN Locals flock to this unassuming trattoria for the down-home cooking. With its wood-paneled walls and vintage sports photos on the wall, time seems to have stood still at this quintessential *piola* in the heart of the San Salvario neighborhood, about a 5-minute walk from Porta Nuova station. Coco's still makes things the way *nonna* used to—Italian comfort food like *pasta e fagioli,* Milanese cutlet, *vitello tonnato* (veal in creamy tuna sauce), homemade tortellini filled with herbs and cheese and topped with butter and hazelnuts, and risotto with saffron and toma cheese, all presented with flair and at incredibly reasonable prices. The restaurant doesn't take reservations, so you may have to wait in line outside, especially on weekends.

Via Bernardino Galliari 28. ✆ **011/657-465.** Entrees 9€–11€. Mon–Wed 7am–8pm; Thurs–Sat 7am–midnight; closed Sun.

Trattoria Spirito Santo ★★ SEAFOOD Thanks to its prime location in a quaint piazza in the heart of the Quadrilatero Romano, this trattoria could be mistaken for a tourist trap. But Spirito Santo is well-loved by locals and tourists alike for its seafood and fast, friendly service. This trattoria has been serving up vast platters of mussels, tuna carpaccio, simply grilled fish, and delicious fettucine with lobster for decades now. Portions can be huge—and the prices do reflect that to some extent—so don't be tempted to over-order. People come here for home cooking, with fresh ingredients (try the smoked-fish appetizer, porcini mushroom ravioli, linguine with squid ink, or the special "Spirito Santo" grilled fish plate). In summer, tables spread onto the piazza; in winter a cozy fire blazes inside and heaters warm the enclosed patio. Space can be tight, and they aim to turn tables fast, so call ahead for a reservation.

Largo IV Marzo 11. www.trattoriaspiritosanto.com. ✆ **011/4360-877.** Entrees 11€–35€; tasting menus 40€. Daily 12:30–3:30pm and 7:30pm–midnight.

Shaken, Not Stirred

Turin gave the world the aperitif vermouth, which was invented in 1786 by Antonio Benedetto Carpano; the brands Martini and Cinzano are still made in the Piedmont region. Order a glass at the gorgeous Art Nouveau **Caffè Mulassano** at Piazza Castello 15 (www.caffemulassano.com; ✆ **366/194-9539**), or come early to enjoy coffee and tempting cannoli or dainty fruit tarts at the ornate marble counter.

Outdoor Activities

Turin's beautiful playground is **Parco del Valentino,** which cradles the left bank of the River Po between the Ponte Umberto I and the Ponte Isabella. Its first incarnation was in 1630, when it was the private garden of the Savoy dukes, but the park was much extended in the 1860s and opened to the public. It's a romantic place to stroll among botanical gardens, flowerbeds, and manicured lawns. The park's massive **Castello del Valentino,** built in 1660, was once the pleasure palace of Christine Marie of France (see p. 521); it is closed to the public. The castle forms an incongruous backdrop to the **Borgo Medievale** (see p. 530), a riverside replica of a 15th-century Piedmontese village. It's a pleasant walk from the city center along Corso Emanuele Vittorio II, or you can hop Tram 9.

Rowing on the Po is a popular pastime in Turin, with half a dozen rowing clubs, the oldest being Reale Società Canottieri Cerea. You can watch boats plying the water as you follow **jogging** and **cycling** routes along the riverside pathways.

The city of Turin manages the **TOBike** (www.tobike.it) bike-sharing platform, with more than 140 bike stations throughout the city. You have to register on the site. Of the various plans, 4YOUflat gives you 4 hours of bike time over 24 hours and costs 8€.

Shopping & Nightlife

Turin's high-end shopping area is quite simply one of the most beautiful in the world. The arcaded **Via Roma** does full justice to the exquisite fashions of Gucci, Armani, Ferragamo, Max Mara, and so on. At the end of Via Roma, the glass-roofed **Galleria Subalpina** (Piazza Castello 27), which links Piazza Castello with Piazza Carlo, competes with Milan's Galleria Vittorio Emanuele II for sheer opulence in its three levels of art galleries, antiquarian bookstores, and cafes. For those whose pockets may not be quite so deep, **Via Garibaldi, Corso XX Settembre,** and their surrounding streets offer midrange brands at reasonable prices.

The windows of Italian food shops are always a thing of joy, and the specialist delis and confectioners of Turin are no exceptions. **Confetteria Stratta** (Piazza San Carlo 191; www.stratta1836.it; ✆ **011/547-920**) and **Pasticceria Gerla** (Corso Vittorio Emanuele II 88) are known for their extravagant pastries, cakes, and *gianduiotti* (chocolate with hazelnuts). Turin is famous for its quality confectionery—the city produces 40% of Italy's **chocolate.** Turin has two branches of the **Eataly** chain, the current mecca for gourmet Italian fare, one in the center in Via Lagrange 3 and another one in the Lingotto area at Via Nizza 230.

Most news agents in Turin have English-language newspapers, and the two branches of **Feltrinelli** (Piazza Castello 19, ✆ **011/541-627;** or Stazione Porta Nuova, ✆ **011/563-981**) sell multilingual books.

Nightlife in the city that invented the vermouth *aperitivo* is sophisticated and, as in Milan, starts in the cafes and bars and finishes very, very late. Squeeze in with the Torinese at **Caffè Platti** (Corso Vittorio Emanuele II 72; ✆ **011/454-6151**) for a vermouth, and pick from the plates of enticing little pizzas made on the premises.

Dance, opera, theater, and musical performances (mostly classical) are on the agenda all year long—check www.visitatorino.com—but

The Markets of Turin

The **produce market** in and around Porta Palazzo takes over the gigantic Piazza della Repubblica Monday to Friday 7am to 2pm and Saturday until 7pm. A bustling **flea market** takes place in the warren of streets behind the Porta Palazzo every Saturday, among the antique shops on Via Borgo Dora. The second Sunday of every month, the same spot is the scene of an **antiques market,** the continuously expanding **Gran Balon** (www.balon.it), with more than 300 dealers from across northern Italy; a smaller version (called Balon) occurs every Saturday. Come December, a **Christmas market** sets out its stalls in Via Borgo Dora. Turin has many stores specializing in rare books and old prints, and these sell their wares from stalls along the Via Po.

Outdoor market in Turin.

September is the month to really enjoy classical music in Turin, when more than 60 concerts are staged around the city during the month-long **Settembre Musica** festival (www.mitosettembremusica.it), hosted jointly with the city of Milan. Beyond the festivals you'll find classical concerts at **Auditorium della RAI,** Via Rossini 15 (www.raicultura.it/orchestrarai; ✆ **011/810-4653**) and dance performances and operas staged at the city's venerable **Teatro Regio** (www.teatroregio.torino.it; ✆ **011/8815-557**).

THE PIEDMONT WINE COUNTRY ★★

South of Turin, the Po valley rises into the rolling hills of Langhe and Roero, flanked by orchards and vineyards. You'll recognize the region's place names from the labels of its first-rate wines, among them **Asti Spumanti, Barbaresco,** and **Barolo.** And vines are not all that flourish in this fertile soil—truffles top the list of the region's gastronomic delights, along with rabbit, game, and excellent cheeses.

Asti ★★★

60km (37 miles) SE of Turin, 127km (79 miles) SW of Milan

The Asti of sparkling-wine fame is a bustling working city, but it has many treasures to uncover in its history-drenched *centro storico*—medieval towers (there were about 120 at one time), Renaissance palaces, and piazzas provide the perfect setting in which to sample the town's most famous product, which flows readily in the local *enoteche* and cantinas.

ESSENTIALS

ARRIVING Up to four **trains** per hour link Asti with Turin Porta Nuova (35 min; 5.80€) via **Trenitalia** (www.trenitalia.com; ✆ **892-021**). By car, Asti can be reached in less than an hour from Turin via Autostrada 21.

VISITOR INFORMATION The APT tourist office is near the train station at Piazza Alfieri 34 (✆ **0141/530-357**). It's open Monday to Saturday 9am to 1pm and 2:30 to 6:30pm and Sunday 9am to 1pm and 1:30pm to 5:30pm.

EXPLORING ASTI

Asti's historic heart is centered on three adjoining squares: **Piazza Libertá,** the vast **Campo del Palio,** and the grand arcaded **Piazza Alfieri.** Each year, in early September, the area is mobbed for the **Palio,** Asti's annual horse race (visit.asti.it; ✆ **0141/399-482**), now held in Piazza Alfieri (originally it was in Campo del Palio) and throughout the town's streets. Like the similar race in the Tuscan city of Siena (see p. 234), Asti's Palio begins with a colorful medieval pageant through the town and ends with a wild bareback ride around the triangular piazza. First staged around 1275, the race coincides with Asti's other great festival, the **Douja d'Or** (www.doujador.it), a weeklong bacchanal celebrating the grape harvest.

Behind Piazza Alfieri stands the Romanesque-Gothic **Collegiata di San Secondo** (✆ **0141/530-066;** daily 7:30am–7pm). This redbrick church has two distinctions: it houses the Palio Astigiano, the prestigious banner awarded to the winning jockey at the Palio; and it also contains the tomb of St. Secondo, patron saint of both the race and the town. A Roman

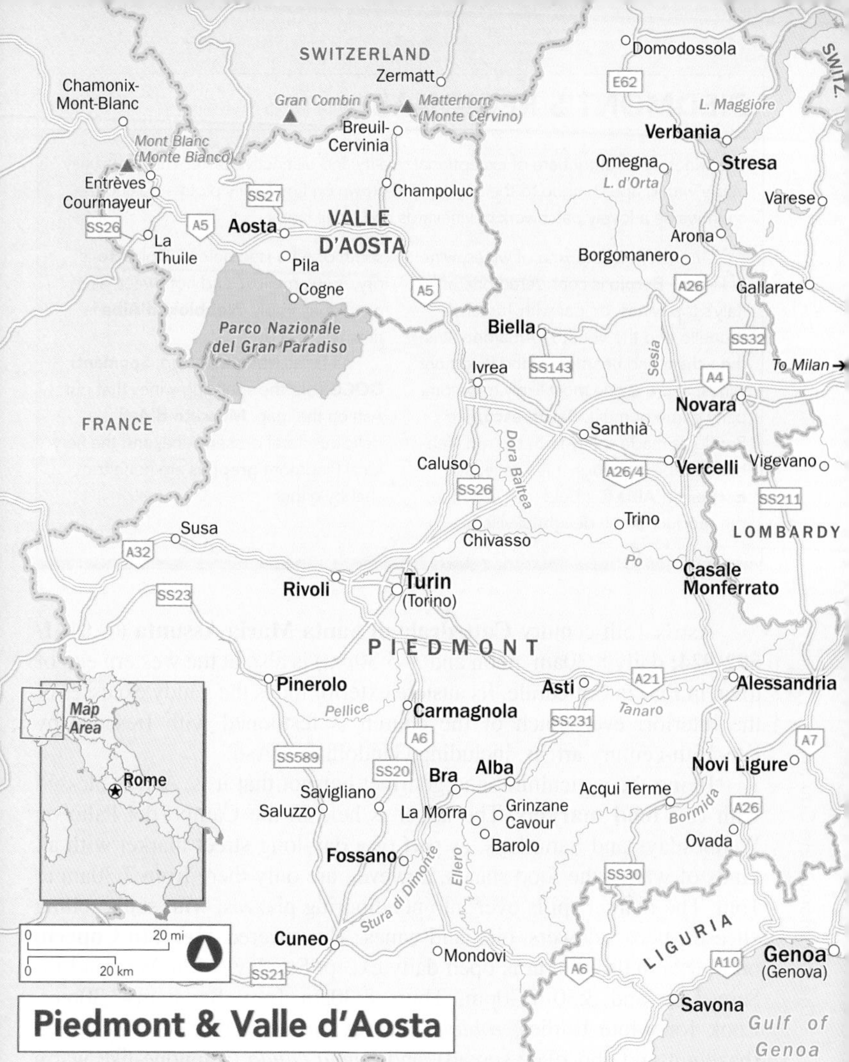

officer who converted to Christianity in A.D. 119, Secondo was martyred for his faith, beheaded in roughly the spot where his tomb now stands.

From Piazza Alfieri, the charming and largely pedestrianized **Corso Alfieri** bisects the old town and is lined with Renaissance *palazzi.* At the eastern end is the church of **San Pietro in Consavia (© 0141/530-403;** Tues–Sun 10am–1pm and 3–6pm, until 7pm in summer), with a 10th-century Romanesque baptistery that was once a place of worship for the Knights of the Order of St. John. At the western extreme of Corso Alfieri, you'll find the rotund **church of Santa Caterina,** abutting the medieval red-and-white brick-topped **Torre Rossa.**

PIEDMONT'S REGIONAL wines

The wines of Piedmont are of exceptional quality and distinctive taste. They're usually made with grapes unique to the region, and grown on tiny family plots—making the countryside a lovely patchwork of vineyards and small farms.

Often called "the king of wines, wine of kings," **Barolo** is considered one of Italy's top wines, on par with Tuscany's Brunello and the Veneto's Amarone. It is the richest and heartiest of the Piedmont wines, and the one most likely to accompany game or meat. **Barbaresco,** like Barolo, is made solely from the red Nebbiolo grape, although it is less tannic. **Barbera d'Alba** is a bold, rich red wine, the product of the delightful villages south of Alba (see below). **Dolcetto** is dry, fruity, mellow, and not sweet, as its name may imply. **Nebbiolo d'Alba** is rich, full, and dry.

As far as white wines go, **Spumanti DOCGs** are the sparkling wines that put Asti on the map. **Moscato d'Asti** is a delicious floral dessert wine, and the fiery local Piedmont **grappas** are none too shabby either.

Asti's 15th-century **Cattedrale di Santa Maria Assunta (✆ 0141/592-924;** daily 8:30am–noon and 3–5:30pm) is also at the western end of town in Piazza Cattedrale. Its austere exterior hides the gaudy excesses of the interior; every inch of the church is festooned with frescoes by late-15th-century artists, including Gandolfino d'Asti.

Being the agricultural and gourmet hotspot that it is, Asti is blessed with two **food markets.** The larger is held in the Campo del Palio on Wednesdays and Saturdays, as part of a day-long street market with all kinds of wares; the food stands, however, are only there from 7:30am to 1pm. The market spills over into neighboring piazzas, with stalls selling cheeses, herbs, flowers, oils, and wines. The covered **Mercato Coperto** on Piazza della Libertà is open daily except Sunday (Mon–Wed and Fri 8am–1pm and 3:30–7:30pm; Thurs 8:30am–1pm; Sat 8am–7:30pm). Look for white truffles, *robiola* cheeses, *amaretti* biscuits, *nocciolata* (hazelnut and chocolate spread), and *bagna cauda* (a fondue-like warm dip made with ingredients like olive, oil, butter, garlic, and anchovies). The region's famous Asti Spumante DOCG sparkling wines can be bought from *cantinas* and *enoteche* in the town center and direct from some vineyards—a list is available from the **tourist office** at Piazza Alfieri 34 (see p. 536).

The Piedmont Wine Villages

Gastro-destination **Alba ★★** (60km/37 miles south of Turin) is the jumping-off point for visiting the many vineyards of the Barolo wine-producing region. While it's a pleasure to walk along Via Vittorio Emanuele and the narrow streets of the old town center, wine and food are what Alba's all about. Wherever you go, you'll end up peering into store windows to admire displays of wines, truffles, and the calorific but exquisite *nocciolata* cake made of hazelnuts and chocolate. The streets are crammed with enough enticing restaurants to make gourmands very happy indeed (see p. 540).

Just to the south of Alba lie some of the Piedmont's most enchanting wine villages, sitting on hilltops among orderly rows of vines. The best way to see these villages is to drive; hire cars in Turin from **Avis,** Via Giuseppe Giusti 1 (www.avisautonoleggio.it; ✆ **011/440-9231**), or **Hertz,** at Corso Turati 37 (www.hertz.it; ✆ **011/502-080**). Before you head out on the small country roads, get a list of vineyards from the tourist office in Asti (see p. 536). A detailed map is also a good idea, in case you lose the satellite signal for your GPS.

Precious white truffles from Alba.

The main road through the wine region is the SS231, which runs between Alba and Asti. It is, however, a fast, busy, and unattractive highway; you'll want to turn off it to explore Piedmont's rustic backwaters among hazelnut groves and vineyards.

One such enchanting drive heads south from Alba to the wine villages of the **Langhe hills** (follow signs out of town for Barolo on the SP3). After 8km (5 miles), take the right turn for **Grinzane Cavour,** a hilltop village built around a castle harboring the **Enoteca Regionale Piemontese Cavour** (www.castellogrinzane.com; ✆ **0173/262-159**), which is open daily 9:30am to 7pm (until 6pm Nov–Mar). Here you can sample local wines from over 300 labels; the fine restaurant is perfect for lunch.

Return to the main road, turn left, and after 4km (2½ miles) south, take the right fork to **La Morra,** perched among vineyards with panoramic views over the rolling, vine-clad countryside. La Morra has several cafes and restaurants in which to taste the local vintages. The **Cantina Comunale di La Morra** at Via Alberto 2 (www.cantinalamorra.com;

The village of Barolo and Castello Falletti, surrounded by vineyards.

(✆ **0173/509-204**) represents local growers, selling Barolo, Nebbiolo, Barbera, and Dolcetto. It's open daily (except Tues) 10am to 12:30pm and 2:30 to 6:30pm. La Morra's tourist office (Piazza Martiri 1; www.lamorra turismo.it; ✆ **0173/500-344**) is open on Monday and Tuesday 9:30am to 1:30 p.m. and Thursday through Sunday 10am to 6pm.

Barolo is a handsome little village dominated by two ancient castles; it's 5km (3 miles) along the SP58 from La Morra. Here, too, you'll find a choice of restaurants and shops selling world-renowned red wines from local vineyards. Among these is the **Enoteca del Barolo** (www.enoteca delbarolo.it; ✆ **388/626-2864**), with a wine bar offering tastings in its cavernous cellars. They even offer Barolo and chocolate pairings.

WHERE TO STAY & EAT IN THE PIEDMONT WINE COUNTRY

As well as a few decent urban hotels, the Barolo region is the land of the *agriturismo,* with options to stay on wine estates in the hills of Langhe. You can find properties on www.agriturismo.it; search on the Piedmont region or search for specific town names. As for restaurants, they don't come much classier than the best of the Piedmont. If you are looking for food and wine tours in the region, California native Anna Savino (www.italianna.com) is based locally and can organize wine tours, cheese tours, cooking classes, and truffle hunts.

La Cascina del Monastero ★★★ Perfectly situated for exploring the Barolo wine region, this beautiful 16th-century family-run estate is part rustic B&B and part winery, all just minutes away from La Morra. Converted from an outbuilding of soft stone and arcading, the suites and apartments are beautifully furnished in a rustic way with Italian antiques and brass beds. Exposed stone walls (like in the unique Autunno Suite), beams, wooden floors, and homey personal touches add to the ambience. Guest facilities include a large pool surrounded by vineyards, and the unusual wellness area has a sauna in a massive wine barrel. Don't miss out on a chance to taste the estate's wines (you can even have bottles of your favorites shipped home). An abundant farm-to-table breakfast with local specialties (from cheeses from the Langhe area to homemade cakes) is served, allowing you to fuel up before setting out to discover the area.

Cascina Luciani 112A, Frazione Annunziata, La Morra. www.cascinadelmonastero.it. ✆ **0173/509-245.** 10 units. 170€–190€ double; 180€–195€ apartment. Rates include breakfast. Closed Jan and sometimes Feb. **Amenities:** Playground; spa; outdoor pool; room service; sauna; free Wi-Fi.

Palazzo Finati ★★ Just around the corner from Alba's Piazza del Duomo and some of the town's best shops and gourmet restaurants, this historic *palazzo* offers a taste of old-fashioned luxury. The Finati has nine individually designed rooms and suites; some have romantic touches, frescoed ceilings, and terraces overlooking the inner courtyard. A breakfast of fresh pastries, fruit, local cheeses, and cured meats is served in an elegant brick-ceilinged, barrel-vaulted dining room with details that go back to Roman times. Parking can be an issue—if you're coming by car, make sure to request access to the enclosed parking area.

Via Vernazza 8, Alba. www.palazzofinati.it. ✆ **0173/366-324.** 9 units. 150€–180€ double; 170€–250€ suite. Rates include breakfast. **Amenities:** Free Wi-Fi.

Ristorante Marc Lanteri ★★★ GOURMET Michelin-starred chef Marc Lanteri used to run a restaurant inside the Grinzane Cavour castle but relocated into a space of his own about 10 miles away in the town of Castagnito, north of Alba. A French chef born to Italian parents, he considers his food to be a mix of the best of Piedmont and Provence, with influences from throughout the Mediterranean. To truly get into the Piedmontese spirit, try the Fassona beef rump steak served with sautéed greens, roasted shallot, and black truffles; other creative dishes might include mugnolo broccoli risotto with escargot and local black garlic or spiced glazed duck breast served with wilted greens and apple confit. The chef's American wife, Amy, is the restaurant's sommelier.

Via Serra 21/d, Castagnito. www.marclanteri.it. ✆ **0173/262-172.** Entrees 27€–38€. Wed–Sun noon–1pm (till 2pm Sun) and 5:30–9pm. Closed Jan and sometimes Feb.

AOSTA ★★ & VALLE D'AOSTA ★★★

Aosta: 113km (70 miles) N of Turin, 184km (114 miles) NW of Milan; Courmayeur: 35km (22 miles) W of Aosta, 148km (92 miles) NW of Turin

Tucked up against the French and Swiss borders in northwest Italy, the Aosta Valley is a land of harsh snow-capped peaks, lush pastures, thick forests, waterfalls cascading into mountain streams, and romantic castles clinging to wooded hillsides. A year-round stream of skiers, hikers, cyclists, and nature lovers flocks to this tiny Alpine region north of Turin for the scenery, outdoor adventure, and rustic gastronomy.

Aosta

ESSENTIALS

ARRIVING Aosta is served by 20 **trains** a day to and from Turin (2 hr., change in Ivrea or Chivasso; tickets 9.45€) aboard **Trenitalia** (www.trenitalia.com; ✆ **892-021**). **Bus service** to Aosta is much less handy: Only a few buses travel from Turin Porta Nuova per day (most change in Ivrea), and even the direct trip takes 2 hours, the indirect route more than 3. However, an **Arriva** (aosta.arriva.it) bus conveniently connects Aosta hourly to **Courmayeur** (1 hr.; 3.50€, 4€ if bought on board) and other popular spots in the valley.

Autostrada A5 from Turin shoots up the length of Valle d'Aosta en route to France and Switzerland via the Mont Blanc tunnel; there are numerous exits in the valley. The trip from Turin to Aosta normally takes about 90 minutes, but traffic can be heavy on weekends in ski season.

VISITOR INFORMATION The tourist office in Aosta (Piazza Porta Praetoria 3; www.lovevda.it; ✆ **0165/236-627**) dispenses a wealth of information on hiking trails, ski lifts and passes, bike rentals, and rafting trips. It's open daily 9am to 7pm.

EXPLORING AOSTA

An appealing mountain town with an ancient heart, Aosta—nicknamed "the Rome of the Alps"—is surrounded by snowcapped peaks and steeped in a history that goes back to Roman times. Although you're not going to find much pristine Alpine quaintness here in the Valle d'Aosta's busy tourist center, you will find Roman ruins, medieval bell towers, and chic shops. Aosta's **weekly market** day is Tuesday, when stalls selling food, clothes, and crafts fill the Piazza Cavalieri di Vittorio Veneto.

Well-preserved city walls date from the days when Aosta was one of Rome's most important trading and military outposts. A **Roman bridge** spans the River Buthier, and two Roman gates arch gracefully across the Via San Anselmo. The **Porta Pretoria** forms the western entrance to the Roman town and the **Arco di Augusto** the eastern entrance. The **Teatro Romano** and the ruins of the **amphitheater** are north of the Porta

Pretoria; the ruins of the **forum** are in an adjacent park. The theater and forum are open generally from 9am to 6pm (typically closed for a few hours in the afternoon in the winter), and admission is free. Architectural fragments from these monuments that were found during excavations are displayed in Aosta's **Archaeological Museum** at Piazza Roncas 12 (✆ **0165/ 275-902;** summer daily 9am–7pm, fall and winter Tues–Sun 10am–1pm and 2–5pm). The 7€ ticket is valid for a year and allows for visiting four other sites of archaeological importance in the region.

The Valle d'Aosta

Most visitors to the Valle d'Aosta come here for outdoor activities rather than sightseeing; the region has some of Italy's best hiking trails and is a major skiing destination.

The little town of **Cogne** is the gateway to the untamed **Parco Nazionale del Gran Paradiso ★★**, one of Europe's finest parcels of unspoiled wilderness. This national park, Italy's oldest, was once the hunting grounds of King Vittorio Emanuele II; it encompasses the jagged peaks of **Gran Paradiso** (4,061m/13,323-ft. high), five valleys, and some 703 sq. km (271 sq. miles) of forests and pastureland. Many Alpine beasts roam wild here, including the ibex (curly-horned goat) and the elusive chamois (small antelope), both of which are nearly extinct in Europe. Humans can roam these wilds via a vast network of well-marked hiking trails. The park's main **visitor center** is at Via Alpetta, Ronco Canavese (www.pngp.it/en; ✆ **0124/ 817-377**). Admission is free. In winter, the meadows and Alpine forests around Cogne boast 80km (50 miles) of challenging **cross-country (Nordic) skiing trails;** check www.cogneturismo.it for details.

Summer Alpine hiking in the Valle d'Aosta.

In winter, most visitors head for the **downhill skiing** and **snowboarding** destinations of **Courmayeur, Breuil-Cervinia,** and **Monte Rose,** a ski area around the resort towns of Champoluc and Gressoney. There are trails for all levels, from gentle nursery slopes to black diamond runs and mogul fields. Expert

UP & OVER mont blanc

Riding high over Mont Blanc—Europe's tallest mountain at 4,811m (15,784 ft.)—has to be one of the most awe-inspiring experiences in the Italian Alps. It's an enchanted journey passing over glaciers and steep ravines, mountain lakes, and snowy peaks on the Italian side of the Vallée Blanche.

For years, this trek involved three changes of cable car, starting from the little ski village of **La Palud** (3km/1¾ miles above Courmayeur) and ascending through **Le Pavillon** and **Rifugio Torino** to the viewing terrace at **Punta Helbronner** (3,462m/11,358 ft.), in the heart of the Mont Blanc Massif. From here it was possible to take the cable car down to **Aiguille de Midi** on the French side of Mont Blanc, and then the Panoramic Mont-Blanc Gondola on into the party-loving resort of **Chamonix.**

But all that changed in 2015 when a new, vastly improved cable-car service, **Skyway Monte Bianco** (www.montebianco.com), launched. Run by Funivie del Monte Bianco, the system has sleek rotating gondolas departing from a swish station at **Pontal d'Entrèves** (near the entrance to the Mont Blanc tunnel) on a high-speed connection up to Punta Helbronner for a bird's-eye view of Monte Bianco and the surrounding peaks of Gran Paradiso and Monte Cervinia (Matterhorn).

The Skyway Monte Bianco ascends Mont Blanc.

Be prepared to pay for these breathtaking views: A roundtrip ticket from Pontal to Punta Helbronner is 55€, free for ages 7 and under; a one-way ticket costs 42€. If you want to enjoy the views but may suffer from altitude sickness at the very top, you can opt to go just to the midway point, Pavillon du Mont-Fréty, which has a restaurant and shopping area; that ticket costs 23€ adults (17€ one-way).

You can still continue on from Punta Helbronner to Chamonix via cable car—and if you do so, you can return to Courmayeur via France's **SAT bus service** through the Mont Blanc tunnel. Buses run daily each way, and the journey takes 45 minutes (www.sat-montblanc.com; tickets 15€, discounts available for children under age 12).

skiers are best off at high-altitude **La Thuile** for excellent off-trail powder and heli-skiing. Depending on conditions, the ski season kicks off in early November and runs through April. Altogether there are 800km (500 miles) of ski runs available under the **Valle d'Aosta ski pass.** In low season, multi-day passes range from a 3-day pass for 170€ to a 2-week pass for 584€; in high season, rates increase to 184€ for 3 days up to 641€ for 2 weeks. One child under age 8 skis free with each adult who buys the pass. For details, go to www.skilife.ski. Meanwhile, if you're looking for something a bit different, consider **dog sledding** (www.dogsledman.com) near Courmayeur.

Where to Stay & Eat in the Valle d'Aosta

In ski season, many Valle d'Aosta hotels expect guests to eat on premises and stay 3 nights or more, but they're more flexible outside busy tourist times.

The Valle d'Aosta is the land of mountain food—hams and salamis, creamy polenta—and buttery Fontina is the cheese of choice.

Hostellerie du Cheval Blanc ★★ It's no traditional wood-paneled chalet, but if family comforts and town-center convenience are what you're after, the Cheval Blanc (meaning "white horse") fits the bill, and you'll still get some Alpine views. The contemporary-style hotel in the ancient Roman heart of Aosta is designed around a massive atrium with stylish leather sofas and has two restaurants: the fairly expensive Le Petit and the more casual Brasserie, which is well-suited to early dinners with kids. Rooms are tastefully decorated in neutral shades, but bathrooms are fitted out in ornate marble, most with bathtubs as well as showers. Skiers will appreciate a winter shuttle to the cable car up to Pila (about a half a mile away), and the pool and sauna provide perfect après-ski relaxation before a night of fun in the bars of Aosta. Guests have access to a gym and wellness center with pools, Jacuzzi, and two saunas.

Rue Clavalité 20, Aosta. www.chevalblanc.it. ✆ **0165/239-140.** 55 units. 119€–190€ double. Rates include breakfast. **Amenities:** 2 restaurants; bar; children's playroom; indoor pool; gym; sauna; spa; room service; free Wi-Fi.

Osteria da Nando ★★ FONDUE This cheery *osteria* with terra-cotta-colored walls and rustic touches has been run by the Scarpa family since 1957. Over the years, it has become one of Aosta's most popular restaurants for its hearty yet surprisingly sophisticated seasonal fare. Try different types of fondue, from *bourguignonne* served with tender beef filet to *raclette* served with creamy Fontina cheese and chunks of chewy bread, alongside the classic Piedmontese *bagna cauda* (anchovy fondue). Tasting menus start at around 40€ (wine pairings are extra) and include favorite dishes like fresh spaghetti in a citrus sauce, braised beef cheek, or the signature polenta with fontina fondue and a fried egg. Desserts are playfully presented (like panna cotta with licorice and cinnamon), and the wine selection is impressively local.

Via Sant'Anselmo 99. Aosta. www.osterianando.com. ✆ **0165/44-455.** Entrees 12€–27€. Wed–Mon noon–2pm and 7:30–10pm. Closed 2 weeks late Jun–early July.

Ristorante La Palud ★★ PIZZA/SEAFOOD Impressive Monte Bianco and glacier views make this pizzeria/restaurant a perpetual favorite. Thanks to its proximity to the tunnel into France, it is a popular stop-off point. Decorated to look like a sophisticated mountain chalet, La Palud keeps diners coming back for enormous thin-crust pizzas, dishes typical of the Valle d'Aosta like gnocchi in a fondue made from local cheese, and fresh fish brought up from the Ligurian coast on Fridays. In summer, sit outside on the flower-filled terrace; in winter, huddle around the open fire and admire the drifts of snow piled up outside. Try the mille-feuille for dessert.

Strada la Palud 17, Courmayeur. www.lapalud.it. ✆ **0165/89-169.** Entrees 12€–25€. Daily noon–3:30pm and 7:30–10:30pm.

GENOA & THE CINQUE TERRE

11

By Michelle Schoenung

Hugging the Mediterranean coastline from the French border to the tip of Tuscany lies a crescent-shaped strip of land that makes up the region of Liguria. The pleasures of this area are no secret. Since the 19th century, world-weary travelers have been heading for Liguria's resorts, such as San Remo and Portofino, to enjoy balmy weather and a sapphire-blue sea. Beyond the beach, fishing villages, small resort towns, and proud old port cities bake in the sun, and hillsides are fragrant with the scent of bougainvillea and pines.

Liguria is really two coasts. First, the "white sand" stretch west of Genoa known as the **Riviera di Ponente** (Riviera of the Setting Sun) is studded with fashionable resorts, many of which, like San Remo, have seen their heydays fade but continue to entice visitors with palm-fringed promenades and a gentle way of life. The rockier, more rugged, but also more colorful stretch southeast of Genoa, known as the **Riviera di Levante** (Rising Sun), extends past the posh harbor of Portofino to the ever-popular villages of the Cinque Terre.

The province's capital, Genoa, is Italy's busiest port, an ancient center of commerce, and one of history's great maritime powers. Despite its rough exterior, it is an underrated gem filled with architectural delights, Italy's largest historic center, and a sense of "real Italy" that has become hard to come by in many of the country's more popular cities.

DON'T LEAVE GENOA & THE CINQUE TERRE WITHOUT . . .

Getting Lost in Genoa. It's been more than 170 years since Charles Dickens enthused on the wonders of losing yourself in the labyrinth of Europe's largest preserved medieval city, but it's still enthralling.

Toasting the Setting Sun. The Riviera di Levante is famous for its sunsets, and justifiably so. Its sheer cliffs afford huge, humbling views of this blazing show. Raise a glass of the region's golden Sciacchetrà wine in tribute.

Seeing the Jewel of the Cinque Terre. Vernazza is the quintessential postcard-perfect seaside village, with tall, colorful houses (known as *terratetti*) clustered around a natural harbor where you can swim among the fishing boats. Best way to get here? Hike from Monterosso, along the most scenic, if arduous, leg of the famed Cinque Terre trail.

PREVIOUS PAGE: **Hiking near Manarola village in the Cinque Terre.**

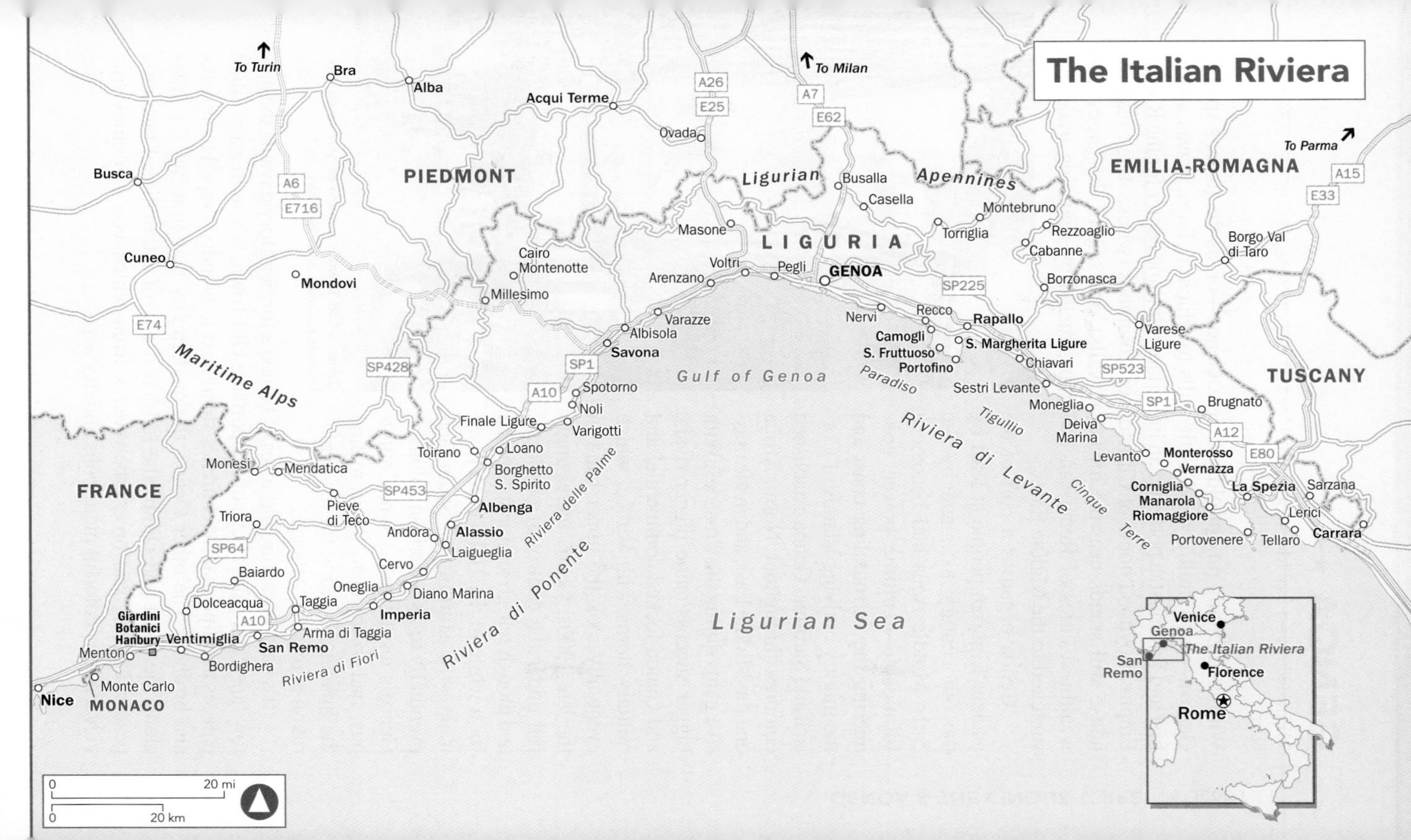

The Italian Riviera
To Turin
To Milan
To Parma
Bra
Alba
Acqui Terme
Ovada
A26
E25
A7
E62
A15
E33
Busca
A6
E716
PIEDMONT
Ligurian
Apennines
Busalla
Casella
Montebruno
Torriglia
Rezzoaglio
Cabanne
Borzonasca
EMILIA-ROMAGNA
Borgo Val di Taro
Masone
LIGURIA
Cuneo
Mondovi
Cairo Montenotte
Millesimo
Voltri
Pegli
GENOA
Arenzano
SP225
Varazze
Albisola
Savona
Nervi
Recco
Rapallo
Camogli
S. Margherita Ligure
S. Fruttuoso
Portofino
Chiavari
Varese Ligure
E74
Maritime Alps
SP428
SP1
Gulf of Genoa
Paradiso
SP523
TUSCANY
A10
Spotorno
Noli
Varigotti
Sestri Levante
Moneglia
Deiva Marina
SP1
Brugnato
A12
Finale Ligure
Toirano
Loano
Borghetto S. Spirito
Tigullio
Riviera di Levante
Levanto
Monterosso
Vernazza
E80
Monesi
Mendatica
FRANCE
SP453
Pieve di Teco
Albenga
Riviera delle Palme
Corniglia
Manarola
Riomaggiore
La Spezia
Sarzana
Lerici
Cinque Terre
Portovenere
Tellaro
Carrara
Triora
Andora
Alassio
Laigueglia
SP64
Cervo
Baiardo
Riviera di Ponente
Oneglia
Diano Marina
Dolceacqua
Taggia
Imperia
Giardini Botanici Hanbury
A10
Arma di Taggia
Ligurian Sea
Ventimiglia
San Remo
Menton
Bordighera
Riviera di Fiori
Monte Carlo
Nice
MONACO
Venice
Genoa
The Italian Riviera
San Remo
Florence
Rome
0
20 mi
0
20 km

GENOA ★★

142km (88 miles) S of Milan, 501km (311 miles) NW of Rome, 194km (120 miles) E of Nice

With its dizzying mix of old and new, Genoa—or, as the Italians spell it, Genova—is as multilayered as the hills to which it clings. It was and is, first and foremost, a port city: an important maritime center for the Roman Empire, boyhood home of Christopher Columbus (whose much-restored house still stands near the medieval walls), and one of the largest and wealthiest cities of Renaissance Europe, fueled by seafaring trade that stretched to the Middle East.

Genoa began as a port of the ancient Ligurian people at least by the 6th century B.C., and by the early Middle Ages had become a formidable maritime power, conquering the surrounding coast and the mighty outlying islands of Corsica and Sardinia. Genoa established colonies throughout North Africa and the Middle East, and made massive gains during the Crusades. With bigger success came bigger rivals, and Genoa locked commercial and military horns with Venice, which eventually took the upper hand in the late 1300s. Genoa increasingly fell under the control of outsiders, and though self-government returned for a while in the 16th century, sea trade was shifting to Spain and eventually to its American colonies. Genoa's most famous son, Columbus, had to travel to Spain to find the financial backing for his exploration across the Atlantic.

Genoa's Old Town is a maze of narrow streets, historic palaces, and churches.

It's easy to capture glimpses of Genoa's former glory days on the narrow lanes and dank alleys of the portside Old Town, where treasure-filled palaces and fine marble churches stand next to laundry-draped tenements and brothels. The other Genoa, the modern city that stretches for miles along the coast and climbs the hills, is a city of international business, peaceful parks, and breezy belvederes from which you can enjoy fine views of this colorful metropolis and the sea.

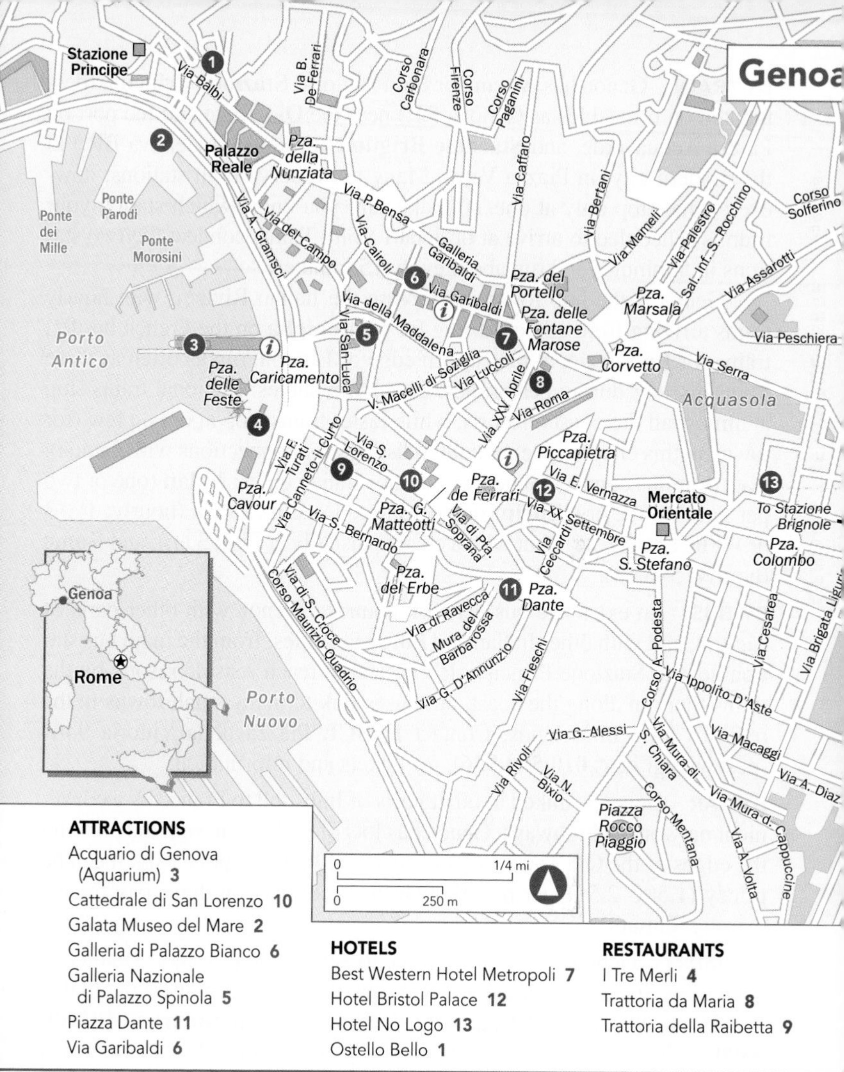

Essentials

ARRIVING

BY PLANE Flights to and from most European capitals serve **Cristoforo Colombo International Airport (GOA),** just 6.5km (4 miles) west of the city center (www.airport.genova.it; ✆ **010/60-151**). **Volabus** (www.amt.genova.it; ✆ **010/558-2414**) connects the airport with the Principe and Brignole train stations, with buses running the 30-minute trip once or twice an hour from 5am to 10pm; buy tickets on the bus (6€; includes a transfer to or from the city transportation network).

BY TRAIN Genoa has two major train stations: **Stazione Principe** (designated on timetables as Genova P.P.) near the Old Town and the port on Piazza Acquaverde, and **Stazione Brignole** (designated Genova BR.) in the modern city on Piazza Verdi. Many trains serve both stations; however, some stop only at one, so make sure you know which station your train is scheduled to arrive at or depart from. Trains connect the two stations in 5 minutes and run about every 15 minutes.

Genoa is the hub for trains serving the Italian Riviera, with hourly trains arriving from and departing for **Ventimiglia** on the French border; trains for **La Spezia,** at the eastern edge of Liguria, run as often as three trains an hour during peak times. Check timetables: Regional trains stop at almost all the coastal resorts, while faster trains stop at only a few (for towns in this chapter, see individual listings for connections with Genoa). Lots of trains connect Genoa with major Italian cities: **Milan** (one or two per hour; 1½–2 hr.), **Turin** (one per hour; 1¾–2 hr.), **Pisa** (hourly; 1½–3 hr.), **Florence** (hourly but with a change, usually at Pisa; 3 hr.), and **Rome** (hourly; 5–6 hr.).

BY BUS An extensive bus network connects Genoa with other parts of Liguria, and with other Italian and European cities, from the main bus station next to Stazione Principe. It's easiest to reach seaside resorts by the trains that run along the coast, but buses link to many small towns in the region's hilly hinterlands. Contact **PESCI,** Piazza della Vittoria 94/R (pesciviaggi.it; ✆ **010/564-936**), for tickets and information.

BY CAR Genoa is linked to other parts of Italy and to France by a convenient network of highways. Genoa has lots of parking around the port and the edges of the Old Town, so you can usually find a spot easily. It can be pricey (1.50€–2.50€ per hr.), though in some lots you don't pay for the overnight hours.

BY FERRY Genoa connects by ferry to several other major Mediterranean ports, including Barcelona, Sardinia, and Sicily (www.traghettitalia.it). Most boats leave and depart from the **Stazione Marittima** (✆ **010/089-8300**), which is on a waterfront roadway, Via Marina D'Italia, about a 5-minute walk south of Stazione Principe. For service to and from the **Riviera Levante,** check with **Tigullio** (www.traghettiportofino.it; ✆ **0185/284-670**) or **Golfo Paradiso** (www.golfoparadiso.it; ✆ **0185/772-091**); there's almost hourly service from 9am to 5pm daily in July and August.

VISITOR INFORMATION

The **main tourist office** is on **Via Garibaldi 12/R** across from the beautiful city hall (www.visitgenoa.it; ✆ **010/557-2903**), open daily 9am to 6:20pm. There are also branches near Porto Antico in **Via al Porto Antico 2,** open daily from about 9am to 6pm with longer hours in summer; and at **Cristoforo Colombo airport,** open daily 9am to 1pm and 1:30 to 5:30pm.

GETTING AROUND

Given Genoa's labyrinth of small streets (many of which cannot be negotiated by car or bus), the only way to traverse much of the city is on foot—and you'll need a good map. The tourist office gives out terrific maps, but you can also buy an audioguide with map that really helps you navigate the small *vicoli,* or alleyways. Genovese are usually happy to direct visitors, but given the geography with which they are dealing, their instructions can be complicated.

BY BUS Bus tickets (1.50€) are available at newsstands and at ticket booths, *tabacchi* (tobacconists, marked by a brown and white t sign), and at the train stations; look for the symbol **AMT** (www.amt.genova.it; ✆ **010/558-2414**). Otherwise, tickets cost 2.50€ on board on nights and weekends. You must stamp your ticket when you board. Bus tickets can also be used on the funiculars and public elevators that climb the steep hills surrounding the ancient core of the town. Tickets good for 24 hours cost 4.50€; 9€ for four people (two people travel for free).

BY TAXI A metered taxi, which you can find at cabstands, is your best bet for getting around Genoa at night. For instance, you may well want to consider taking one from a restaurant in the Old Town to your hotel or to one of the train stations (especially Stazione Brignole, which is a bit farther out). Cabstands at Piazza della Nunziata, Piazza Fontane Marose, and Piazza de Ferrari are especially convenient to the Old Town, or call **Radiotaxi** at ✆ **010/5966.** The meter starts at 5€ and adds .90€ every kilometer (or every minute if the taxi is traveling less than 30 kph). Additional fees are added at night or if one needs to leave city limits.

Genoa Takes to the Sea

Every June, an ancient tradition continues when Genoa takes to the sea in the **Regata delle Antiche Repubbliche Marinare,** rowing against crews from its ancient maritime rivals, Amalfi, Pisa, and Venice. Each city takes turns hosting the event, so it's not in Genoa every June, but there's another spectacular—though more modern—regatta every September: the **Millevele,** or Thousand Sails, when Genoa's bay is carpeted with the mainsails and spinnakers of nautical enthusiasts from around the world.

BY SUBWAY The city's nascent subway system is a work in progress, with only eight stops on a single line between the new Brignole station and a suburb to the northwest called Certosa (there are convenient stops in between at Stazione Principe and at Dinegro close to the ferry port). The tickets are the same as those used for the bus.

CITY LAYOUT

Genoa extends for miles along the coast, with neighborhoods and suburbs tucked into valleys and climbing the city's many hills. Most sights of interest are in the **Old Town,** a fascinating jumble of old *palazzi,* shabby tenements, cramped squares, and tiny lanes and alleyways clustered on the eastern side of the old port. **Via Garibaldi,** lined with a succession of majestic *palazzi,* forms the northern flank of the Old Town and is the best place to begin your explorations. Many of the city's most important museums and monuments are on and around this street, and from here you can descend into the warren of little lanes, known as ***caruggi,*** that lead through the heart of the city and down to the port. ***Note:*** These very small alleyways of the Old Town can be sketchy at night; wait for other pedestrians, preferably locals, before entering them.

The city's two train stations are located on either side of the Old Town; wherever you are in the Old Town, you are only a short walk or bus or taxi ride from one of these two stations. **Stazione Principe** is the closest, just to the west; from Piazza Acquaverde, in front of the station, follow **Via Balbi** through **Piazza della Nunziata** and **Via Bensa** to **Via Cairoli,** which runs into Via Garibaldi (the walk will take about 15 min.). From **Stazione Brignole,** walk straight across the broad, open space to Piazza della Vittoria/Via Luigi Cadorna and turn right to follow broad **Via XX Settembre,** one of the city's major shopping avenues, due west for about 15 or 20 minutes to **Piazza de Ferrari,** on the eastern edge of the Old Town. From here, **Via San Lorenzo** will lead you past Genoa's cathedral and to the port, or follow **Via XXV Aprile** north to Piazza delle Fontane Marose, the eastern end of Via Garibaldi.

Exploring Genoa

Acquario di Genova ★★★ AQUARIUM Genoa boasts the largest aquarium in Europe, and it is undoubtedly the city's biggest draw, in 2022 celebrating its 30th anniversary. Like a huge freight ship, it presides over a pier in the Old Port, about a 15-minute walk from Stazione Principe and 10 minutes from Via Garibaldi. After entering the Blue Planet room, which offers an overview of marine life from all bodies of water, you can wander past more than 50 aquatic displays. There are huge tanks re-creating Red Sea coral reefs, pools in the tropical rainforests of the Amazon River

A Cumulative Ticket

Admission to Genoa's major palaces and art galleries is grouped together on the **Card Musei** (15€ for 1 day, including unlimited use of Genoa public transport). The card includes entrance to 28 city museums—the main palaces, the cathedral treasury of San Lorenzo, the Galleria di Palazzo Bianco, the Galleria Nazionale di Palazzo Spinola, and a handful of other museums around town, plus discounts to the aquarium, the Galata museum, and movie theaters. Pick it up at any city museum, the airport tourist office, or in one of several bookstores downtown (www.visitgenoa.it). The new **Genova City Pass** (www.genovacitypass.it) includes free public transportation and can be personalized to visitors' interests (culture and heritage, edutainment, active, and so on) with specific itineraries over 24, 48, or 72 hours. It starts at around 20€.

basin, and other marine ecosystems that provide a home for sharks, seals, dolphins, penguins, piranhas, and just about every other kind of water creature. Afterward you can easily spend a day around the old harbor by also visiting the nearby **Galata Museo del Mare** (see p. 556), flying high over the harbor on the **Bigo Panoramic Lift,** and walking through endangered tropical forests in the great glass globe of the **Biosphere.** Buying tickets online is the most economical option, and there are also packages that combine the various attractions for a lower price. Another great attraction on the port is the children's museum, **Città dei Bambini** (www.cittadeibambini.net), a great option for families if the aquarium is too busy. It reopened in late 2022 as an "experience museum" with interactive attractions for children ages 2 to 12, with a focus on the "5 Senses."

Ponte Spinola (at the port). www.acquariodigenova.it. ✆ **010/23451.** 22€ and up adults, 18€ and up seniors, and 14€ and up children 4–12; prices vary depending on season or day of week. Mon–Fri 9am–6pm; Sat–Sun 8:30am–7pm (July–Aug daily until 10:30pm). Bus: 1-8 and 12-15. Metro: Darsena.

Cattedrale di San Lorenzo ★ CATHEDRAL Genoa's main cathedral has its own austere dignity, its black-and-white-striped 12th-century facade enlivened by fanciful French Gothic carvings over the main doorway and a pair of stone lions guarding the steps. A later addition is the bell tower, completed in the 16th century. In the frescoed interior, chapels house two of Genoa's most notable curiosities: Beyond the first pilaster on the right is a still-unexploded shell fired through the roof from a British ship during World War II; and in the **Cappella di San Giovanni** (left aisle), a 13th-century crypt contains what crusaders returning from the Holy Land claimed to be relics of John the Baptist. The adjoining treasury **(Museo del Tesoro)** seems to specialize in sacred tableware of doubtful provenance: the plate upon which Saint John's head was supposedly served to Salome, a bowl allegedly used at the Last Supper, and a bowl thought at one time to be the Holy Grail. Less storied but nonetheless magnificent gold and bejeweled objects reflect Genoa's medieval prominence as a maritime power. You can visit the treasury

Genoa's Gothic Cattedrale di San Lorenzo.

only by a half-hour guided tour in Italian, but it's still worth seeing what is inside, even if the extent of your Italian is *gelato* and *pizza*.

Piazza San Lorenzo. ✆ **010/254-1250.** Cathedral: Free. Treasury: 6€ adults, 5€ seniors and students. Included in Card Musei (p. 554). Mon–Sat 9am–noon and 3–6pm. Bus: 1, 7, 8, 17, 18, 19, 20.

Galata Museo del Mare ★★ MUSEUM Visiting the Galata—billed as the largest and most innovative maritime museum in Europe—is like embarking on a voyage right from the port along what is now known as "museum row." Despite the modern appearance, the building itself is the oldest surviving construction of the dockyard from the old Republic, where Genovese galleys were built during the 17th century. Visitors enter through a gallery dedicated to the old port, with paintings and artifacts of the period, then it's on to a full-scale reproduction of a Genovese "attack ship," with fun artifacts and props that will engage all ages. An interesting section of the museum called **MEM (Memory and Migrations)** focuses on the places Italians have immigrated to over the centuries as well as the more recent phenomenon of immigrants from other countries arriving on Italian shores, an especially timely topic. Certain exhibits (like the submarine *Nazario Sauro* docked in the waters alongside the museum) require an additional cost. There is now an "open air" section of the museum right out on the docks where visitors can learn more about the history of the shipyards and watch fisherman roll in with their fresh catches to be sold at the market right on the port.

Ponte Parodi (at the port). www.galatamuseodelmare.it. ✆ **010/234-5655.** 17€ adults; 12€ seniors and students ages 7–17. Mar–Oct daily 10am–7:30pm; Nov–Feb Tues–Fri 10am–6pm, Sat–Sun 10am–7:30pm (last entry 1 hr. before closing). Bus: 1-8 and 12-15. Metro: Darsena.

Galleria di Palazzo Bianco ★★ MUSEUM The White Palace is one of a string of magnificent *palazzi* along ritzy Via Garibaldi, the Strada Nuova built by the Genovese aristocracy during the Renaissance (and a UNESCO World Heritage Site). Although it was built during the mid-16th century by Luca Grimaldi, a scion of one of the most important Genovese families, the gorgeous white facade was reconstructed in the 18th century. Maria Durazzo Brignole-Sale de Ferrari donated the palace and her art collection to the city in 1884 to create Genoa's first public gallery. The collection is heavy on painters of the Spanish and Flemish schools, including Van Dyck, Rubens, Filippino Lippi, Veronese, and Caravaggio. One of the museum's most notable holdings is the "Portrait of a Lady" by Lucas Cranach the Elder.

Via Garibaldi 11. www.museidigenova.it/it/content/palazzo-bianco. ✆ **010/557-2193.** 9€ adults; includes entrance to Palazzo Rosso and Palazzo Tursi. Included in Card Musei (p. 554). Mar 28–Oct 8 Tues–Fri 9am–7pm, Sat–Sun 10am–7:30pm; Oct 11–Mar 26 Tues–Fri 9am–6:30pm, Sat–Sun 9:30am–6:30pm. Bus: 18, 20, 35, 37, 39, 40, 41, 42.

Galleria Nazionale di Palazzo Spinola ★ MUSEUM Another prominent Genovese family, the Spinolas, donated their palace and magnificent art collection to the city in 1958. Not only is the art collection something to behold, but the circa-1593 palace, on historic Piazza Pellicceria, is a wonderful example of how Genovese aristocrats really lived, among frescos and mirrored galleries. Lower floors fortunately escaped damage during World War II, though the two upper floors had to be completely rebuilt (and now host what is known as the National Gallery of Liguria with paintings, porcelain objects, and furnishings from over the centuries). As in Genoa's other art collections, you will find masterworks ranging from native artists like Strozzi, da Messina, Reni, Giordano, and de Ferrari to van Dyck and other painters of the Dutch and Flemish schools, whose commissioned portraits were once such a status symbol among Genoa's wealthy.

Piazza Pellicceria 1. www.palazzospinola.beniculturali.it. ✆ **010/270-5300.** 10€ adults; 2€ ages 18–25; free for seniors and kids under 18; includes admission to the National Gallery of Liguria and the museums of the Royal Palace. Included in Card Musei (p. 554). Free 1st Sun of month. Tues–Sat 8:30am–7:30pm; Sun 1:30–7:30pm. Bus: 1, 18, 20, 34.

Piazza Dante ★ Though most of this square just south of Piazza de Ferrari is made up of 1930s-era office buildings, one end is bounded by the reconstructed **Porta Soprana** ★★, a twin-towered town gate built in 1155. The main draw, though, is the small **house** (rebuilt in the 18th century), standing a bit incongruously in a tidy little park below the gate, said to have belonged to **Christopher Columbus's father,** a weaver and gatekeeper (whether young Christopher lived here is open to debate).

Bus: 14, 35, 42, 44.

Via Garibaldi ★★ Many of Genoa's museums and other sights are clustered on and around this street, also known as Strada Nuova, one of the most beautiful in Italy. Here Genoa's wealthy families built palaces in the 16th and 17th centuries that were the envy of all of Europe. Besides the **Galleria di Palazzo Bianco** (p. 556), the **Palazzo Podesta,** at no. 7, hides a beautiful fountain in its courtyard, and the **Palazzo Tursi** (no. 9), which now houses municipal offices, displays artifacts of famous locals: letters written by Columbus and a violin of Nicolo Paganini (still played on special occasions).

Palazzo Tursi entrance included in admission to Galleria di Palazzo Bianco; open same hours as Palazzo Bianco. Bus: 20, 32, 33, 35, 36, 41, 42.

Where to Stay in Genoa

Despite the draw of the aquarium and its intriguing Old Town, Genoa is still geared more to business travelers or conference-goers. A pleasant boom of new quality accommodations has sprouted up, however, as the city becomes more tourist-friendly. Keep in mind that Genoa books up

A Market Cornucopia

The sprawling **Mercato Orientale,** Genoa's boisterous indoor food market, evokes the days when ships brought back spices and other commodities from the ends of the earth. An excellent place to stock up on olives, herbs, fresh fruit, and other Ligurian products, it is held Monday through Wednesday 7:30am to 1pm and 3:30 to 7:30pm, and Thursday through Saturday 7:30am to 7:30pm. Entrances are on Via XX Settembre and Via Galata (about halfway between Piazza de Ferrari at the edge of the Old Town and Stazione Brignole). The district just north of the market (especially Via San Vincenzo and Via Colombo) is a gourmand's dream, with many bakeries, *pasticcerie* (pastry shops), and stores selling pasta and cheese, wine, olive oil, and other foodstuffs.

solid during its annual boat show, the world's largest, when hotel prices can jump as much as 25%. The boat show is normally held in September or October.

SELF-CATERING ROOMS & APARTMENTS

If you want to feel like more of a local, self-catering apartments are definitely a great option. For example, **Virginia's Rooms** (which can be reserved via Booking.com for an average price of 100€ per night for a two-person deluxe room) are private rooms in a residential area not far from the center. This property not only offers convenient parking but also features flatscreen televisions and swish modern bathrooms along with colorful bedrooms with traditional furnishings.

EXPENSIVE

Hotel Bristol Palace ★ This 19th-century *palazzo* has maintained its opulent elliptical staircase (it's said that Alfred Hitchcock—twice a guest here—drew inspiration from this Art Nouveau masterpiece in making *Vertigo*) and exquisite stained-glass dome, making it one of Genoa's most regal hotels. Located in the middle of the city's shopping district and steps from Genoa's most famous museums, historic palazzos, and the opera house, it is surprisingly quiet and perfectly located for exploring the sights. **Ristorante Giotto** serves sophisticated local cuisine at lunch and dinner most days of the week in a room with elegant frescoed ceilings; an outdoor dining terrace adds even more appeal to this oasis-like lodging in the city center.

Via XX Settembre 35. www.hotelbristolpalace.com. ✆ **010/592-541.** 138 units. 140€–480€ double. Rates include breakfast. **Amenities:** Restaurant; bar; babysitting; bikes; concierge; room service; free Wi-Fi.

MODERATE

Best Western Hotel Metropoli ★★ Hotel Metropoli is located in the center of the action on one of the most beautiful squares in town, surrounded by *palazzos* from the 16th century. It offers very good lodging with modern amenities, a robust breakfast buffet, and helpful service. Guest rooms are soundproofed, clean, and comfortable, with refurbished bathrooms. Family rooms have bunk beds and game consoles (strollers, bottle warmers, and changing tables can also be provided for free). Come here if location is key but you are not necessarily seeking old-world charm or peace and quiet.

Piazza delle Fontane Marose. www.hotelmetropoli.it. ✆ **010/246-8888.** 48 units. 97€–246€ double. Rates include breakfast. **Amenities:** Bar; room service; free Wi-Fi.

INEXPENSIVE

Hotel No Logo ★★ No Logo, which is low on frills but full of flair, is conveniently located near Brignole train station in a bustling neighborhood full of bars, restaurants, and nearby shopping on Via XX Settembre. The brightly colored rooms at the No Logo all have music themes ("Rock," "Pop," "Reggae," "Blues"), and family rooms are big enough for up to six people. A basic breakfast is available for 4.50€ per person, though there are also plenty of coffee bars nearby if a hotel breakfast isn't your thing. A 3-night stay at the hotel comes with a free 72-hour Genova City Pass, which includes free public transportation and access to a wide variety of museums and attractions.

Via Sauli 5. www.hotelnologo.it. ✆ **010/089-8060.** 56 units. 60€–90€ double. **Amenities:** Bar; free Wi-Fi.

A bounty of fresh vegetables in Genoa's Mercato Orientale.

Ostello Bello ★★ Located a stone's throw from Genoa's Principe train station, this hostel in a recently renovated historical building is crisp and clean, offering dormitory beds in shared rooms as well as private rooms with en-suite bathrooms. It boasts a bar, a common kitchen, a large terrace with a grill, and hammocks. Given that this hostel is fairly new (though Ostello Bello is actually a chain of hostels throughout Italy), it has modern amenities like Wi-Fi throughout the property and USB plugs next to beds. This is not only perfectly positioned for the train station, it's also a mere 10-minute walk to the city's famous alleyways and 15 minutes on foot from the Porto Antico and world-renowned aquarium. A continental breakfast of coffee, tea, juice, cold cuts, and the local focaccia is available for 5.90€.
Via Balbi 38/A. www.ostellobello.com. ✆ **010/247-0800.** 20€ and up dormitory bed; 86€ and up twin room; 100€ and up triple room; 126€ and up family room. **Amenities:** Bar; luggage storage; free Wi-Fi.

Where to Eat in Genoa

I Tre Merli ★★ LIGURIAN This stylish restaurant located right on the old port is all high ceilings, black-and-white columns, and exposed stone walls, nicely in line with the local architecture. Grab a table outside on the large patio to get a front-row seat to the action on the Porto Antico. This is a convenient spot for those with children, given all of the family-friendly attractions right here on the port. Local seafood features heavily in dishes, such as *fritua* (fried fish, squid, and shrimp with crisp vegetables and fried

FAST...& OH, SO good

All over Genoa you'll find shops selling **focaccia,** Liguria's answer to pizza, a thick flatbread often stuffed or topped with cheese, herbs, olives, onions, vegetables, or prosciutto. Many of these *focaccerie* also sell **farinata,** a chickpea fritter that usually emerges from the oven in the shape of a big round pizza. Just point and make a hand gesture to show how much you want. Prices are by weight, and in most cases a piece of either will cost about 1.50€ to 3€. Most focaccia (especially the ones with cheese) and all *farinata* are better warm, so if the piece you are getting looks like it's been there a while, ask them to warm it up (*"scaldarla,"* in Italian).

A favorite spot for both snacks, near Stazione Principe, is **La Focacceria di Teobaldo ★**, Via Balbi 115r (daily 8am–8pm), which also has a crunchy *(croccante)* focaccia that doesn't need to be warmed up and is great for taking on the go. In the heart of the Old Town, **Focacceria di Via Lomellini ★**, Via Lomellini 57/59 (Mon–Sat 8am–7:30pm), has great *focaccia di Recco* (also called *focaccia al formaggio*), a super-thin focaccia filled with cheese and the specialty of the nearby town of Recco. Follow up with something sweet at **Fratelli Klainguti** (Piazza di Soziglia 98). At the Porto Antico, get your focaccia fix (you *will* be addicted after your first taste) at **Il Localino,** Via Turati 8r (Tues–Mon 8am–8pm; closed Wed). You can also get pretty good focaccia at the **Eataly** on the old port near the aquarium.

sage) or Ligurian fish with potatoes, black olives, and pine nuts. Cheese *focaccia* comes with artichokes or arugula and Parma ham, and the wood-burning oven also churns out thin, crispy pizzas. There are quite a few options for vegetarians here. I Tre Merli also operates a small **wine bar** and *affittacamere* (rooms for rent) in Camogli (see p. 568).

Calata Cattaneo 17. www.itremerli.it. ✆ **010/246-4416.** Entrees 16€–20€. Daily noon–3pm and 7:30–11pm.

Trattoria da Maria ★★ LIGURIAN Located in a nondescript alleyway near Piazza delle Fontane Marose, this simple trattoria might not look like one of Genoa's most famous eateries, but it's been a draw for over 100 years. Here, you dine elbow-to-elbow with lawyers, construction workers, students, and tourists. Maria is no longer around, but the third and fourth generations of the family are carrying on the tradition. With Maria's grandson, a trained chef, in the kitchen, this spot continues to offer flavorful, no-nonsense dishes, such as the near-perfect pesto, stuffed anchovies, and fish sautéed in white wine. Pay no mind to the generic decor (red-and-white checkered tablecloths) and concentrate on the great dishes this authentic Genovese institution has to offer, with a handwritten menu that changes daily.

Vico Testadoro 14r (just off Via XXV Aprile). ✆ **010/581-080.** Entrees 6€–10€. Mon–Sat noon–3pm and 7–9:15pm.

Trattoria della Raibetta ★ GENOVESE Located in the alleyways not far from the port, this cozy and historic trattoria—one of the oldest restaurants in the city—serves up Genovese favorites like *trenette al pesto patate e fagiolini* (a type of long, flat noodle with pesto, potatoes, and green beans), *pansotti* (a homemade ricotta-filled pasta) in walnut sauce, and sea bream with potatoes. The wine list is equally impressive, with hundreds of labels, many of them local to the area. For a simple local dessert, try the *canestrelli* shortbread cookies served with sweet Moscato wine. The atmosphere here is warm and rustic, with sunny yellow walls and brick archways.

Vico Caprettari 12r. www.trattoriadellaraibetta.it. ✆ **010/246-8877.** Entrees 8€–18€. Tues–Sun noon–2:30pm and 7:30–10:30pm.

Entertainment & Nightlife

The Old Town, some parts of which are sketchy in broad daylight, is even more risky after dark. This is an area where petty crimes take place at night and pickpockets linger in the shadows. Confine late-hour prowls in this area to the well-trafficked streets such as Via San Lorenzo and Via Garibaldi. On the edges of the Old Town, good places to walk at night are around the waterfront, Piazza delle Fontane Marose, Piazza de Ferrari, and Piazza delle Erbe, where many bars and clubs are located.

Genoa has two major culture venues: the restored **Teatro Carlo Felice,** Piazza de Ferrari (www.carlofelice.it; ✆ **010/538-1432**), home to Genoa's opera company, and the **Teatro Nazionale di Genova,** formerly called the Teatro Stabile (teatronazionalegenova.it; ✆ **010/53-421**), which hosts concerts, dance, and other programs in locations around the city.

THE RIVIERA DI PONENTE: SAN REMO ★★

140km (87 miles) W of Genoa, 56km (35 miles) E of Nice

Gone are the days when Tchaikovsky and the Russian empress Maria Alexandrovna joined a well-heeled mix of *nobili* strolling along San Remo's palm-lined avenues. They left behind an onion-domed Orthodox church, a few grand hotels, and a casino, but **San Remo** is a different sort of town these days. It's still the most cosmopolitan stop on the Riviera di Ponente, as the coastal stretch west of Genoa is called, but now it caters mostly to sun-seeking Italian families in summer and, in winter, Milanese who come to escape the fog and chilly temperatures of their city.

If you've got a few extra days, base yourself in San Remo and explore farther along the coast, all the way to the French border. Train connections are good, and the coastal SS1 road links several charming towns. Highlights include the quiet resort town of **Bordighera** (12km/7½ miles west of San Remo); one of Europe's finest gardens, **Giardini Botanici Hanbury** (28km/20 miles west of San Remo, just past Ventimiglia); and the inland village of **Dolceacqua** (23km/14 miles northwest of San Remo), with its well-preserved medieval core and abandoned castle.

Essentials

ARRIVING **Trains** run hourly between San Remo and Genoa (about 2 hr.). If you're arriving by train, note that San Remo's newer rail station is a bit of a hike from the center of town and the old port. Trains from Genoa continue west for another 20 minutes to Ventimiglia on the French border. Some trains continue on into France; at Ventimiglia you can change onto one of the frequent trains across the border to **Nice,** 50 minutes west.

The fastest **driving route** in and out of San Remo is Autostrada A10, which follows the coast from Genoa (about 45 min. away) to the French border (20 min. away). The slower coast road, SS1, cuts right through the center of town.

A Day at the Beach

The pebbly strand below the **Passeggiata dell'Imperatrice** is lined with beach stations, where many visitors choose to spend their days: It's easy to linger here, because most provide showers, snack bars, beach chairs, lounges, and umbrellas. Expect to spend up to 15€ for a basic lounge, and 20€ for a more elaborate sun-bed arrangement with umbrella. ***Note:*** As is standard at most European resort towns without "public" sections of beach (which are usually not very nice anyway), you cannot go onto the beach in the main part of town without paying for at least a lounge chair in high season.

FESTIVALS Since the 1950s, the **Sanremo Festival** (mid- to late February; www.sanremo.rai.it) has been Italy's premier music fest, sort of an Italian Grammy Awards. Spread out over several days, it features live performances by Italian pop stars, international headliners, and plenty of up-and-comers. Hotels up and down the coast (and into France) get booked up months in advance.

Exploring San Remo

San Remo's two main thoroughfares are **Via Roma** and **Corso Matteotti.** Corso Matteotti runs east-west between **Piazza Colombo,** with its flower market, and the **casino** (see below), passing through the heart of the bustling, pedestrian-only business district. Here you can shop, sit in cafes, and do a bit of Italian people-watching. Midway along Corso Matteotti, turn north on **Via Feraldi** to reach the charming older precincts of town. From **Piazza Mercato,** Via Montà leads into the medieval quarter, **La Pigna,** set on a hill shaped like a pinecone (*la pigna* in Italian). Aside from a few restaurants, La Pigna is a residential quarter, with tall old houses overshadowing narrow lanes that twist and turn up the hillside, with the park-enclosed ruins of a **castle** at the top.

VISITING THE CASINO

San Remo's white palace of a **casino** (www.casinosanremo.it; ✆ **0184/5951**) is the hub of the local nightlife scene, set intimidatingly atop a long flight of steps just uphill from the old train station; Corso degli Inglesi curves up from Corso Matteotti to its entrance. You can't set foot inside

San Remo's elegant Art Nouveau casino.

without being properly attired (jacket for gents Oct–June; in general, avoid track suits, shorts, T-shirts, and flip-flops for the entire casino). You must show your passport to enter, and you must be 18 or older. Some of the poker tables start at just a few euro, but the more serious tables attract high rollers from the length of the Riviera. Gaming rooms are open 2:30pm to 2:30am (Fri–Sat 3pm–3:30am). Things are more relaxed in the rooms set aside for slot machines, where there is no real dress code. It's open Sunday to Thursday 10am to 2:30am and Friday and Saturday 10am to 3:30am.

Where to Stay & Eat in San Remo

Most restaurants and hotels in the "City of Flowers" are concentrated either along the promenade leading into town or in the streets and alleyways around the famous **Ariston Theater,** where the annual Sanremo music festival (see p. 563) is held. Seafood specialties are featured in local restaurants, such as **Paolo & Barbara** (Via Roma 47), a San Remo favorite.

Hotel Villa Maria ★★ Originally three separate villas, the spacious, almost regal hotel and its many salons recall the golden eras of the 1920s, '30s, and '40s; several public rooms open to a nicely planted terrace. This hotel offers comfort and quality on the hillside just above the casino, and it is not far from the beach. The Empress's Promenade, with its biking and walking path right along the beach, is also nearby. Many of the guest rooms are somewhat dated, but the hotel's reasonable rates and the setting more than make up for this. Room sizes and styles can vary, so ask what's available when booking or ask to see a few upon arrival. Some rooms have balconies with sea views.

Corso Nuvoloni 30. www.villamariahotel.it. ✆ **0184/531-422.** 38 units, 2 w/shared bath. 60€–360€ double. Rates include breakfast. **Amenities:** Restaurant; concierge; room service; Wi-Fi (free in common areas).

Ristorante L'Airone ★ LIGURIAN/PIZZA Located in a quaint piazza halfway between the landmark Ariston Theater and the casino, this cute restaurant serves consistently good food at decent prices, which is why it is almost always busy. The ever-changing menu focuses on creative Mediterranean dishes, such as baked swordfish with asparagus; calamari stuffed with couscous and vegetables; or tuna tartare with ginger and walnuts. There is also excellent thin-crust pizza (always available at dinner, but only served at lunchtime on Tues and Sat) and various menus for children. Tables can be a bit close together inside, but in nice weather you can also dine in the small back garden or on the piazza in front. Reservations are recommended, especially for dinner.

Piazza Eroi Sanremesi 12. www.ristorantelairone.it. ✆ **0184/531-469.** Entrees 7.50€–17€. Fri 7:30–11:30pm; Sat–Wed noon–2:30pm and 7:30–11:30pm.

Royal Hotel ★★★ Having just celebrated its 150th anniversary, this sprawling seafront resort on the edge of Old Town mixes old-world charm and luxury. It is not a modern boutique hotel, but what it lacks in contemporary touches in some areas, it makes up for with impeccable service. Most rooms have sea views and are tastefully decorated. Along with the five-star luxury designation, however, come jaw-dropping prices, even in the off-season. Families traveling in the warmer months will appreciate the kids' club, where children can play while parents relax or take advantage of the many activities offered. The modern wellness center is an oasis of calm, and the outdoor seawater pool, designed in 1948 by famed architect Giò Ponti, is the centerpiece of the spectacular gardens. The main restaurant serves seasonal cuisine from Liguria and other regions of Italy; the breakfast is particularly abundant. The hotel closes for a few months in late fall and winter, usually reopening in February.

Corso Imperatrice 80. www.royalhotelsanremo.com. ✆ **0184/5391.** 126 units. 248€–665€ double. Rates include breakfast. **Amenities:** 3 restaurants; bar; 24-hr. room service; babysitting; kid's club; concierge; room service; free Wi-Fi.

THE RIVIERA DI LEVANTE: CAMOGLI, SANTA MARGHERITA LIGURE & PORTOFINO ★★

Camogli: 26km (16 miles) E of Genoa; Santa Margherita Ligure: 31km (19 miles) E of Genoa; Portofino: 38km (24 miles) E of Genoa; Rapallo: 37km (23 miles) E of Genoa

Hugged by mountains that plunge into the sapphire-colored seas, the coast east of Genoa, the **Riviera di Levante** (Riviera of the Rising Sun), is more ruggedly beautiful and less developed than the Riviera Ponente. Three of the coast's most appealing towns are within a few kilometers of one another, clinging to the shores of the Monte Portofino Promontory east of Genoa: **Camogli, Santa Margherita Ligure,** and little **Portofino.**

Essentials

ARRIVING One to three **trains** per hour ply the coastline, connecting Genoa with Santa Margherita (25–30 min.) and Camogli (30–45 min.); the trip between Camogli and Santa Margherita takes 5 minutes by train. To get to **Portofino,** take the train to Santa Margherita and then take a taxi or bus sometimes known as 782 and other times merely as 82 (www.atpesercizio.it; ✆ **848-000-030**), a 25-minute ride via a beautiful coastal road (bus service every 30 min. to 1 hr.). The one-way fare is 4€ on board, 3€ if you buy beforehand—ask for the Portofino Pass at any newsstand or the IAT office in Piazza Vittorio Veneto. Roundtrip fare is 5€ if bought ahead of time and 6€ if bought on board. Some buses and bus stops now have a credit-card reader, making purchasing tickets that much easier.

In summer, **boats** operated by Golfo Paradiso (www.golfoparadiso.it; ✆ **0185/772-091;** roundtrip tickets 6€–35€ depending on route) run from Camogli to Portofino and Genoa. **Tigullio ferries** (www.traghettiportofino.it; ✆ **0185/284-670**) make hourly trips from Santa Margherita to

Portofino (15 min.; 16€ roundtrip). In summer, a boat runs several days a week to the Cinque Terre (30€–40€). Hours of service vary considerably with the season; schedules are posted on the docks at Piazza Martiri della Libertà.

The fastest **car** route into the region is Autostrada A12 from Genoa (exit at Recco for Camogli), which takes about 40 minutes to either Camogli or Santa Margherita. Route SS1 along the coast from Genoa is much slower but more scenic. ***Note:*** Parking is a challenge in Camogli and Portofino in the summer, and traffic quickly gets clogged on the tiny road between Santa Margherita and Portofino. If you're coming by car, park in Santa Margherita and take the bus or boat to Portofino.

VISITOR INFORMATION **Camogli**'s tourist office is across from the train station at Via XX Settembre 33 (www.welcomecamogli.it; ✆ **0185/771-066**). In **Santa Margherita,** the tourist office is in Piazza Vittorio Veneto (www.livesanta.it; ✆ **0185/287-485**). The **Portofino** tourist office is at Via Roma 35 (✆ **0185/215-037**). All are open daily in summer (Portofino's office is closed Mon); expect shorter hours in winter, and a lunchtime closure between noon and 3pm.

Camogli ★

Camogli remains delightfully unspoiled, an authentic Ligurian fishing port with tall houses in pastel colors facing the harbor and a nice swath of beach. Given its excellent accommodations and eateries, Camogli is a lovely base for exploring the Riviera Levante. It's also a restful retreat from which to visit Genoa, which is only 30 minutes away. Some say Camogli's name comes from Genovese dialect and means "low lands." Others say it is derived from *"Ca de Mogge,"* or "House of the Wives" in the local dialect, so-named for the women who held down the fort while their husbands went to sea. Another possibility is that it comes from *"Ca a Muggi,"* or "clustered houses"—particularly apt when you're out swimming in the sea and turn to look up at the town's wonderful mass of colorful buildings.

EXPLORING CAMOGLI

Camogli is clustered around its delightful waterfront, from which the town ascends via steep, staircased lanes to Via XX Settembre, one of the few streets in the town proper to accommodate cars (this is where the train station, tourist office, and many shops and other businesses are located). Adding to the setting's charm is the fact that the oldest part of Camogli juts into the harbor on a picturesque point (once an island). Here ancient houses cluster around the little **Castello del Dragone** and the **Basilica di Santa Maria Assunta** (✆ **0185/770-130**), originally built in the 12th century but much altered through the ages; its overwhelming baroque interior is open daily 7:30am to noon and 3:30 to 7pm.

Most visitors, though, are drawn to the pleasant **seaside promenade ★** that runs the length of the town. You can swim from the pebbly beach

Camogli's annual Festa della Stella Maris.

below, and you can rent a lounge chair from one of the few beach stations for about 15€—highly recommended in the summer months, when finding even a small piece of pebbly sand is nearly impossible.

WHERE TO STAY & EAT IN CAMOGLI

Bar Primula/Boccondivino Ristorante ★ CAFE/RESTAURANT Having been a bar—and Camogli institution—for many years, this establishment has expanded to be a bit more of a restaurant as well, with the main draw still its prime position along the *lungomare* (promenade). Inside, the tables are a little close together; if weather permits, try to sit outside to enjoy the people-watching. Patrons fill the front terrace day and night. Pasta and main courses are served at lunch and dinner—there's a focus on fish here, and you can even choose what you want from the cart with the catch of the day—but Primula may be best for simple foods like panini, salads, gelato, and the classic *aperitivo*.
Via Garibaldi 140. ✆ **0185/770-351.** Entrees 12€–22€. Daily 8am–1am.

Hotel Canobie dei Dogi ★★ The amazing position of this resort, combined with the beautifully manicured grounds and old-world charm of the main building, make this one of the most popular (and most expensive) hotels along the Riviera Levante. The fact that it sits perched over the Gulf of Camogli doesn't hurt either—make sure to grab a meal or a drink on the terrace or the **Playa** restaurant, offering amazing views and Ligurian specialties (you can also ask for a special romantic "table for two on the pier"). Rooms come in various shapes and sizes and, for the most part,

Getting Festive in Camogli

Camogli throws a well-attended annual party, the **Sagra del Pesce ★★**, on the second Sunday of May, when the town fries up thousands of sardines in a 3.6m-diameter (12-ft.) pan and passes them around for free.

The first Sunday of August, Camogli stages the lovely **Festa della Stella Maris ★**, during which a procession of boats sails to Punta Chiappa, a spot of land about 1.5km (1 mile) down the coast, and releases 10,000 burning candles. Meanwhile, the same number of candles is set afloat from the Camogli beach. If currents are favorable, the burning candles will come together at sea, signifying a year of unity for couples who watch the spectacle.

are tastefully decorated in a mix of traditional style and Mediterranean flair. The large, heated saltwater pool is especially inviting, as is the private beach: one part terraced stone, one part pebbles, which is typical of the area. The **Doge Beauty Spa** is a small but welcoming space offering manicures, pedicures, facials, and various massages.

Via Cuneo 34. www.cenobio.it. ✆ **0185/7241.** 108 units. 129€–480€ double. Rates include breakfast and beach facilities. Free parking. **Amenities:** 2 restaurants, 2 bars; babysitting; concierge; outdoor saltwater pool; tennis courts; watersports rentals; free Wi-Fi.

La Camogliese ★★ La Camogliese may be basic, but it's affordable and perfectly positioned: at one end of the promenade, by the entrance of the old village, with easy access to the beach and to the bus and train stations. Its large, bright rooms have simple furniture and comfortable beds; a few have balconies that require a slight twist of the head to get a sea view (the best views are from rooms 3 and 16B). Some bathrooms are small even by Italian standards, but they are adequate. The property also has a few apartments with kitchenettes (daily cleaning and breakfast not included in rates). Keep in mind that this family-run hotel fills up fast, especially on weekends and in the summer, so book early. This property stands out for its attention to detail and an optimal location.

Via Garibaldi 55. www.lacamogliese.it. ✆ **0185/771-402.** 21 units. 50€–130€ double. Rates include breakfast. 2- to 4-night required min. stay. **Amenities:** Babysitting; concierge; exercise room; outdoor pool; room service; free Wi-Fi.

Locanda I Tre Merli ★ This tiny property right on Camogli's charming harbor is a wine bar with five cozy, brightly colored guest rooms, each of which has views over the water. Breakfast includes things like freshly baked focaccia along with yogurt and other sweet and savory options; in warm weather, it's served outside—a slice of true Italian seaside life, with boats coming and going, fishermen unloading the day's catch, and families and small children playing along the walkway. A small wellness area with a hot tub offers a wonderful port view, but be aware that the large window also allows those on the outside to peer in, but it can be reserved in a more private fashion, including use of the Turkish bath and massage services. The rooms have TVs and Wi-Fi. If you come by car, parking is available at the top of a very big hill in a tiny lot that can be a tight squeeze. Via Scalo 5. www.locandaitremerli.com. © **0185/770-592.** 5 units. 95€–250€ double. Rates include breakfast. **Amenities:** Bar; free Wi-Fi.

Vento Ariel ★★ SEAFOOD We love the old port setting of this popular restaurant almost as much we love the food. Seafood is done right here; succulent dishes include *patè di seppie* (cuttlefish mousse), "sea-to-table" *acciughe* (anchovies served a variety of ways—with lemon juice, fried, in a sweet-and-sour sauce), and *pennette Vento Ariel* (kamut pasta with octopus, anchovies, and olives). Flavors are simple yet sophisticated. The wine list is extensive and contains some local, hard-to-find bottles of Pigato along with other wonderful whites from the region. If you can, grab a table outside to drink in the local ambience as well. Reservations are highly recommended. The rustic-looking restaurant is through the medieval archway leading from the main part of town to the old port, nestled in a corner facing the *gozzi* (traditional fishing boats). Calata Porticciolo 1. www.ventoariel.it. © **0185/771-080.** Entrees 12€–25€. Daily noon–2:30pm and 8–11pm.

Focaccia by the Seaside

It might be the perfect seaside setting, or perhaps there is something in the water, but no matter the reason, Camogli has some of the best focaccia in all of Liguria. Along Via Garibaldi, the promenade above the beach, are many *focaccerie* to choose from. It's hard to go wrong with any of them, but **Revello** (www.revellocamogli.com), at no. 183 (closest to the church), stands out. There, Tino carries on the tradition passed down by his uncle, who first began pulling focaccia out of the oven here in 1964. Revello is open daily 10am to 6pm (later in summer). You can enjoy your loot on one of the few benches outside.

Santa Margherita Ligure ★

Santa Margherita had one brief moment in the spotlight at the beginning of the 20th century, when it was an internationally renowned resort. Fortunately, the seaside town didn't let fame spoil its charm, and now that it's no longer as well-known as its glitzy neighbor Portofino, it could be the Mediterranean retreat of your dreams. A palm-lined harbor, a decent beach, and a friendly ambience make Santa Margherita a fine place to settle down for a few days of sun and relaxation.

EXPLORING SANTA MARGHERITA

Life in Santa Margherita centers on its palm-fringed **waterfront,** a pleasant string of marinas, docks for pleasure and fishing boats, and pebbly beaches, in some spots with imported sand of passable quality. Landlubbers congregate in the cafes that spill out into the town's two seaside squares, Piazza Martiri della Libertà and Piazza Vittorio Veneto.

The train station is above the waterfront, with a staircase in front of the entrance leading down into the heart of town. Santa Margherita's landmark of note is its namesake **Basilica di Santa Margherita** (daily 7:30am–noon and 3–6:30pm), on Piazza Caprera. It's well worth a visit to view the church's extravagant, gilded, chandeliered interior.

One of the more interesting daily spectacles in town is the **fish market** on Lungomare Marconi from 8am to 12:30pm. On Friday, Corso Matteotti, Santa Margherita's major street for food shopping, becomes an open-air **food market.**

WHERE TO STAY & EAT IN SANTA MARGHERITA LIGURE

Grand Hotel Miramare ★★★ An impressive example of Art Nouveau architecture, this once-private villa is pure Riviera elegance. Just a 10-minute walk from the town center along the (heavily-trafficked) road to Portofino, the Grand Hotel Miramare—known merely as "Mira" to those who frequent it—is all sleek class, featuring carefully restored antique furniture and crystal chandeliers while still managing to feel somewhat contemporary. Guest rooms are large, most with parquet floors, antique rugs, and charming stucco decorations on the walls and ceilings. Fifth-floor suites are larger and a bit more modern, and have balconies overlooking the Gulf of Tigullio. Two junior suites in a small building known as "the cottage" can be connected to give guests an entire standalone property to themselves. A lovely (but steep) park with terraced gardens rises behind the hotel toward Mount Portofino; it includes a pleasant hiking trail to Portofino with fantastic views of land and sea. You can relax at the small, private pebble beach across the busy road or opt for a beauty or wellness treatment in the E'SPA'CE center. Valet parking costs 40€ a day; reserve parking ahead of time, as space is limited.

Via Milite Ignoto 30. www.grandhotelmiramare.it. ✆ **0185/287-013.** 84 units. 220€–600€ double. Rates include breakfast. **Amenities:** Restaurant, 3 bars; babysitting; concierge; outdoor saltwater pool; room service; spa; watersports rentals; free Wi-Fi.

Hotel Metropole ★★ This popular, family-run hotel is just above the port and a 5-minute stroll from the town center. Some accommodations are in the modern main building, while others are in the more appealing Villa Porticciolo, a dusty-red manor house right on the beach; rooms in the villa are smaller, but they're graced with 19th-century stuccoes and hand-carved furniture, and the sea practically laps up against the building. All rooms, most of which have been recently renovated, have large terraces or balconies, but some standard rooms have small bathrooms. Other amenities include a small private beach, a sunbathing terrace, a kids' club, and a private boat launch. The panoramic beach club restaurant serves typical Ligurian cuisine as well as dishes with an international flair. An indoor swimming pool and wellness center on the lower levels of the main building make this property an option even in the off-season.

Via Pagana 2. www.metropole.it. ✆ **0185/286-134.** 57 units. 120€–360€ double. Rates include breakfast. **Amenities:** 2 restaurants; bar; babysitting; exercise room; swimming pool; sauna; watersports rentals; free Wi-Fi.

La Paranza ★★ GENOVESE/LIGURIAN This recently renovated, family-run restaurant near the port is all white walls with nautical details, but locals have come here for years for the food, not the ambience. The menu is filled with delicious, innovative dishes, from the *bianchetti fritti* (fried baby sardines) to prawns served on a bed of fennel-scented polenta to grilled-to-perfection fresh fish. Pesto, a true Ligurian specialty, is available with a variety of pastas, including lasagna. There is also a raw-fish menu. Tables on the glass-enclosed veranda offer sea views.
Via Jacopo Ruffini 46. www.laparanzasantamargherita.it. ✆ **0185/283-686.** Entrees 19€–30€. Daily 12:30–2:20pm and 7:30–10:30pm. Closed Nov.

Portofino ★★★

Portofino is almost too beautiful for its own good. In practically any season, you'll be sharing Portofino's harborside quays with day-trippers, Italian industrialists, international celebrities, and rich-but-not-so-famous folks who consider this little town the epicenter of the good life. But if you

AN excursion TO SAN FRUTTUOSO

Much of the **Monte Portofino Promontory** can be approached only on foot or by boat (see below), making it a prime destination for hikers. If you want to combine excellent exercise with magnificent glimpses of the sea through a lush forest, arm yourself with a map from the tourist offices in Camogli, Santa Margherita Ligure, Portofino, or Rapallo, and set out. You can explore the upper reaches of the promontory or aim for the **Abbazia di San Fruttuoso** (✆ **0185/772-703**), a medieval abbey surrounded by a tiny six-house hamlet and two beaches. It is about a 90-minute hike from Portofino.

Once you reach San Fruttuoso, you may well want to relax on the pebbly beach and enjoy a beverage or meal at one of the seaside bars. You can tour the stark interior of the abbey for 8.50€ (June to mid-Sept daily 10am–5:45pm; May Tues–Sun 10am–5:45pm; Mar–Apr and Oct Tues–Sun 10am–3:30pm; and Nov–Feb Sat–Sun 10am–3:45pm). Despite these official hours, the abbey tends to close whenever the last boat leaves. Should you have scuba or snorkeling gear along, you can take the plunge to visit **Christ of the Abyss,** a statue of Jesus erected 15m (49 ft.) beneath the surface to honor sailors lost at sea. If you don't want to get wet, there are boats that will take you close to it so you can view it from the surface.

Boats run almost every hour during the summer months from Camogli. A round-trip costs 15€ (10€ one-way) and takes about 30 minutes. For details, contact **Golfo Paradiso** (www.golfoparadiso.it; ✆ **0185/772-091**). Hourly (in summer) **Tigullio boats** (www.traghettiportofino.it; ✆ **0185/284-670**) run to San Fruttuoso from Portofino (20 min.; 10€–15€ roundtrip), Santa Margherita (35 min.; 13€–10€ roundtrip), and Rapallo (50 min.; 15€–22€ roundtrip). Bear in mind that the seas are often too choppy to take passengers to San Fruttuoso, because docking there can be tricky. In that case, there are private boats you can take—smaller, rubber crafts capable of bad-weather landings—though these are expensive. From Portofino, you will likely be charged at least 100€ for up to 12 people.

make an appearance in the late afternoon when the promenades begin to empty a bit, you are sure to experience what remains so appealing about this enchanting place—its indelible beauty.

EXPLORING PORTOFINO

The one thing that won't break the bank in Portofino is the spectacular scenery. Begin with a stroll around the stunning **harbor,** lined with expensive boutiques, eateries, and colorful houses set along the quay with steep green hills rising behind them. One of the most scenic walks takes you uphill for about 10 minutes along a well-signposted path from the west side of town just behind the harbor to the **Chiesa di San Giorgio,** built on the site of a sanctuary Roman soldiers dedicated to the Persian god Mithras. It's open daily 9am to 7pm.

Colorful, exclusive Portofino.

From there, continue uphill for a few minutes more to Portofino's 15th-century **Castello Brown** (www.castellobrown.com; ✆ **375/791-8926**), which has a lush garden and great views of the town and harbor below. It costs 5€ (kids up to age 12 enter free) and is open daily 10am to 6pm in the spring and fall, and often open until 7pm in summer; the rest of the year it's open Saturday and Sunday from 10am to 5pm. For more scenic views of this stretch of coast, go even higher up through lovely pine forests to the ***faro*** (lighthouse).

From Portofino, you can also set out for a longer hike on paths that cross the **Monte Portofino Promontory** to the Abbazia di San Fruttuoso (see "An Excursion to San Fruttuoso," p. 571). The tourist office provides maps.

WHERE TO STAY & EAT IN PORTOFINO

Portofino's charms come at a price. Its few hotels are expensive enough to put them in the "trip of a lifetime" category, and the harborside restaurants can take a serious chunk out of a vacation budget as well. A smart alternative strategy is to enjoy a light snack at a bar or one of the many shops selling focaccia, and wait to dine in Santa Margherita or one of the other nearby towns.

Belmond Hotel Splendido ★★★ Over the years, the rich and famous—Bogart and Bacall, Taylor and Burton—have flocked to what has been the top resort on the Italian Riviera for more than a century. This former monastery turned five-star luxury hotel is right in the heart of Portofino, surrounded by verdant gardens. Nearly all of the guest rooms, including 35 suites, have balconies with scintillating views across the picturesque harbor. The **La Terrazza** restaurant not only boasts high-end regional cuisine, but its vine-covered terrace offers breathtaking bay views (the **Pool Grill** is a more casual dining option). If you are looking to really pamper yourself, the signature Portofino Dream treatment in the spa includes a full body exfoliation with sea salt and essential oils and a ylang-ylang body massage, finishing off with almond tea and basil cookies. The Splendido's sister hotel, the **Belmond Hotel Mare,** is closer to the water and more intimate, with just 14 rooms, some of which offer views of the harbor and famous piazzetta, and two magnificent suites. Be warned: The hotel's room rates may make your heart stop momentarily.

Salita Baratta 16. www.hotelsplendido.com. ✆ **0185/267-801.** 67 units. 500€–4,500€ double. Rates include breakfast. Closed mid-Dec to Mar or Apr. **Amenities:** 3 restaurants; piano bar; concierge; room service; wellness center; saltwater pool; tennis court; access to hotel's motorboat; free Wi-Fi.

Hotel Nazionale ★★ It isn't often that a hotel in the best spot in town (in this case, right on the most famous square) is also relatively affordable, but this family-run property offers a great location at a decent price. Rooms are fairly basic with not much in the way of decoration, but you are right on the harbor and paying less than most of the other options in the village. Several of the rooms are lofted suites with bedrooms upstairs; we highly recommend splurging for one of the five junior suites, as they are a bit more colorful and offer harbor views. In warm weather, breakfast, which is quite basic, is served on the wonderful veranda. Though the hotel has no elevator, luggage service is provided. The hotel restaurant, **Da Nicola,** offers delightful views of the *piazzetta* and water, and serves up typical Ligurian cuisine and pizza.

Via Roma 8. www.nazionaleportofino.com. ✆ **0185/269-575.** 12 units. 250€–400€ double. Rates include breakfast. Closed mid-Dec to Mar. **Amenities:** Restaurant; bar; concierge; room service; free Wi-Fi.

Ristorante Puny ★★ LIGURIAN Although the famously gregarious "Puny" (owner Luigi Miroli) has since passed away, his family still runs this harborfront restaurant, a favorite haunt of well-heeled locals and tourists for decades. People go wild for the *pappardelle al portofino* (large flat noodles served with a mix of tomato and pesto sauce; note that you can request gluten-free pasta), but the freshness of its seafood is also well-known—try the heavenly *pesce al forno* baked in bay leaves, or the famed *orata alla genovese* (sea bream served Genovese-style with potatoes). The restaurant has a welcoming, cozy feel and especially accommodating staff, which keeps people coming back. Be prepared to pay for the location,

RIVIERA runners-up

While Portofino and the Cinque Terre get their accolades, it would be a shame to overlook some other lovely seaside destinations that also make a great base for exploring the area. When the Cinque Terre is drowning in tourists (a common occurrence May–Sept), these alternatives offer as much beauty, a bit more breathing room, and more options in terms of accommodations.

Set on opposites sides of the stunning Gulf of Poets lie the picturesque seaside medieval villages of **Portovenere** (tourist info: ✆ **0187/790-691**) and **Lerici** (tourist info: ✆ **0187/969-164**). Once archrivals—Portovenere belonged to Genoa and Lerici to Pisa—both built imposing fortresses to protect themselves from the enemy (and pirates). These incredible edifices still remain along with charming, colorful homes backing up to olive tree–covered hills. The beautiful harbors hold local fishing boats and yachts alike. One can easily take the spectacular ferry ride up to the Cinque Terre in less than an hour.

To the north of the Cinque Terre and only a 5-minute train ride from Monterosso is the sunny seaside town of **Levanto** (tourist info: www.levanto.com; ✆ **0187/808-125**), with its large sand beach, lovely historic center, and lodging options ranging from campsites to four-star hotels. Heading west on the coast toward Santa Margherita Ligure, you'll also find nice beaches and colorful town centers at **Bonassola, Moneglia,** and **Sestri Levanto** (tourist info: www.sestri-levante.net; ✆ **0185/478-530**). The beach along Sestri's breathtaking "Bay of Silence" is considered one of Italy's most beautiful strands.

view, food, and being part of the scene (Kourtney Kardashian and Travis Barker held one of their wedding events here in 2022). Despite having a social-media presence now, the restaurant still keeps it old school for reservations: telephone only.

Piazza Martiri dell'Olivetta 5. punyportofino.it. ✆ **0185/269-037.** Entrees 20€–30€. Fri–Wed 12:30–3:30pm and 7:30–11pm. Closed Jan–Feb.

THE CINQUE TERRE ★★★

Monterosso: 93km (58 miles) E of Genoa

Rocky coves, dramatic cliffs, and Apennine ridges are the spectacular backdrop to the Cinque Terre (Five Lands), a region that consists of five fishing and wine-making villages dramatically perched along an 11-mile stretch of Italy's Ligurian coast. Terraced vineyards and olive groves climb slopes that are largely inaccessible by road but have become a hiker's haven, stretching southeast from Monterosso al Mare to Vernazza, Corniglia, Manarola, and Riomaggiore.

Not too surprisingly, these charms have not gone unnoticed. From May to October (weekends are worst), you are likely to find yourself in a long procession of like-minded, non-Italian-speaking trekkers making their way down the coast, including day-trippers from cruise ships. Two of the most popular trails now require you to buy a ticket during high season from about late March until November.

Essentials

ARRIVING Cinque Terre towns are served only by local **train** runs. Coming from Florence or Rome, you will likely have to change trains in nearby La Spezia, which has one or two local trains per hour (6–8 min. to the smaller towns). From Pisa, there are about six daily trains to La Spezia (1¼ hr.); from Genoa, there are one or two direct trains per hour to La Spezia, stopping in Monterosso (1 hr., 40 min. from Genoa) and sometimes Riomaggiore (15 min. farther south).

The fastest **driving** route is via Autostrada A12 from Genoa. Get off at the Corrodano exit for Monterosso. The drive from Genoa to Corrodano takes less than an hour, while the much shorter 15km (9¼-mile) trip from Corrodano to Monterosso (via Levanto) follows a narrow road and can take half an hour. Coming from the south or Florence, get off Autostrada A12 at La Spezia and follow cinque terre signs.

Navigazione Golfo dei Poeti (www.navigazionegolfodeipoeti.it; ✆ **0187/732-987**) runs a **ferry service** from the Riviera Levante towns, April to November, though these tend to be day cruises stopping for anywhere from 1 to 3 hours in Vernazza before returning.

GETTING AROUND The best way to see the Cinque Terre is to devote a whole day and hoof it along the trails. See "Exploring the Cinque Terre," p. 576, for hiking details.

Local **trains** make frequent runs (two or three per hour) between the five towns; some stop only in Monterosso and Riomaggiore, so check the posted *partenze* schedule at the station first to be sure you're catching a local. One-way tickets (from around 2€ to 5€ depending on whether it is high or low season) between any two towns are available—or you can buy a day ticket good for unlimited trips for 18.20€, meaning you can use it to town-hop as well as access the pay trails (from Monterosso to Vernazza and from Vernazza to Corniglia during high season from late March to Nov). During low season (from about Dec until early March), it makes more sense to buy train tickets individually and not get the day ticket, as the trails are all also free during that period.

From the port in Monterosso, **Navigazione Golfo dei Poeti** (www.navigazionegolfodeipoeti.it; ✆ **0187/732-987**) makes eight to ten **boat** trips a day between Monterosso and Riomaggiore (25-min. trip), all stopping in Vernazza and half of them stopping in Manarola as well. A daily ticket for all of the Cinque Terre is 30€, so that you can take as many boats as you like over the course of a day. One-way tickets tend to cost between 7€ and 13€, but it seems they are really pushing for visitors to buy a pass; an afternoon pass for all of the Cinque Terre costs 23€. Children 6 to 11 get a bit of a discount depending on the type of ticket.

A narrow, one-lane coast road hugs the mountainside above the towns, but all the towns' centers are closed to cars. Parking is difficult and, where available, expensive. Some people park along the side of the road, and there are areas where parking is free for a few hours (you will need to have a "parking disk" to show the time you arrived), but if you overstay your time, you risk a hefty fine. Riomaggiore and Manarola both have small **public parking facilities** just above their towns and minibuses to carry you and your luggage down. In Monterosso, try to find parking in the Loreto garage, located where Strada Provinciale 38 meets Via Roma just before the beginning of the pedestrian zone (there is another lot in an area of town called Fegina, but it's farther away); the price is 2.50€ per hour or 25€ per day, though prices go down for longer stays and are somewhat cheaper in the off-season between November and March.

VISITOR INFORMATION The Cinque Terre **tourist office** is underneath the train station of Monterosso, Via Fegina 38 (www.prolocomonterosso.it; ✆ **0187/817-506**). It's open Easter through September daily 9am to 5pm; hours are reduced the rest of the year. Even when it's closed, you will usually find a display of phone numbers and other information, from hotels to ferries, posted outside the office.

Additional useful websites for the region include **www.cinqueterre.it** and **www.parconazionale5terre.it**. Both sites are especially helpful in getting updated information about which trails are open and which may be closed for maintenance or because of landslides or bad weather.

Exploring the Cinque Terre

Aside from swimming and soaking in the atmosphere of unspoiled fishing villages, the most popular activity in the Cinque Terre is **hiking from one village to the next ★★★** along centuries-old goat paths, which are now

The Cinque Terre Card

Depending on the time of year, to access the trails of the Cinque Terre national park, you will need to buy a **Cinque Terre Card,** available at park welcome centers in each town. There are two versions of this card. The **Cinque Terre Trekking Card** (7.50€ adults; 4.50€ children under 12) offers 1-day access to all of the trails, along with free use of pay bathrooms along the trails, bus service between towns, reduced-price admission to local museums, and use of Wi-Fi at public hotspots. In low season, all trails are free, so the Trekking card is actually not necessary. The **Cinque Terre Treno Card** (18.20€ adults; 11.40€ children under 12) offers all of the above in addition to unlimited second-class train travel between towns. The Treno card is really only worth the extra money during high season because it also offers access to the two pay trails (again, all trails are free during low season). In low season, it is better to just pay to travel town to town if you choose to go by train, with tickets averaging around 2.20€ each way. Train ticket prices go up during high season, which is another reason the Treno card works out to a better deal from March to November. Check www.parconazionale5terre.it for updated info.

Walking path above Manarola in the Cinque Terre.

maintained as a national park (see "The Cinque Terre Card," p. 576), and two of the five trails require payment during high season. Trails plunge through vineyards and groves of olive and lemon trees, hugging seaside cliffs and affording heart-stopping views of the coast and romantic little villages in the distance. The well-signposted walks from village to village range in difficulty and length, but as a loose rule, they get longer and steeper—and more rewarding—the farther north you go.

Depending on your pace, and not including eventual stops for focaccia and *Sciacchetrà,* the local sweet wine, you can make the trip between **Monterosso,** at the northern end of the Cinque Terre, and **Riomaggiore,** at the southern end, in about 4½ hours. You should decide whether you want to walk north to south or south to north. Walking south means tackling the hardest trail first, which you may prefer, because you'll get it out of the way and things will get easier as the day goes on. Heading north, the trail gets progressively harder between towns—a route you might prefer if you want to walk just until you tire and then hop on the train.

The walk from **Monterosso to Vernazza** is the most arduous and takes 1½ hours, on a trail that makes several steep ascents and descents (on the portion outside Monterosso, you'll pass beneath funicular-like cars that transport grapes down the steep hillsides). The leg from **Vernazza to Corniglia** is also demanding and takes another 1½ hours, plunging into some dense forests and involving some lengthy ascents, but it's probably the prettiest and most rewarding stretch. Part of the path between **Corniglia** and **Manarola,** about 45 minutes apart, follows a level grade above a long stretch of beach, tempting you to break stride and take a dip. From **Manarola** to **Riomaggiore,** it's easy going for about half an hour along a partially paved path known as the Via dell'Amore, so named for its romantic vistas (great at sunset).

Because all the villages are linked by rail, you can hike as many portions of the itinerary as you wish and take the train to your next destination. Trails also cut through the forested, hilly terrain inland from the coast, much of which is protected as a nature preserve. The tourist office in Monterosso can provide maps.

Monterosso ★★★ The Cinque Terre's largest village seems incredibly busy compared to its sleepier neighbors, but it's not without its charms. Monterosso is actually two towns—a bustling, character-filled Old Town behind the harbor, and a relaxed resort that stretches along the Cinque Terre's only **sand beach.** This is where you'll find the train station and the tiny regional tourist office (upon exiting the station, turn left and head through the tunnel for the Old Town; turn right for the newer town).

The region's most famous art treasure is here, housed in the **Convento dei Cappuccini,** perched on a hillock in the center of the Old Town: a "Crucifixion" by Anthony van Dyck, the Flemish master who worked for a time in nearby Genoa (convent open daily 9am–noon and 4–7pm). You will find the most modern conveniences in Monterosso, but you'll have a more "rustic" experience if you stay in one of the other four villages.

The beach at Monterosso.

Vernazza surrounds a natural harbor.

Vernazza ★★★ Vernazza may just be the quintessential, postcard-perfect seaside village. Tall, colorful houses (known as *terratetti*) cluster around a natural harbor, where you can swim among the fishing boats; above them a castle stands high atop a rocky promontory that juts into the sea (the **Doria Castle,** which is nothing special, though it offers great views; open Mar–Oct daily 10am–6:30pm; admission 1.50€). The center of town is waterside **Piazza Marconi,** itself a sea of cafe tables. The only Vernazza drawback is that too much good press has turned it into the Cinque Terre's mecca for tourists from around the world.

Corniglia ★ The quietest village in the Cinque Terre is isolated by its position midway down the coast, a hilltop location high above the open sea, and the hard-to-access harbor. Whether you arrive by boat, train, or the trail from the south, you'll have to climb some 300 steps to reach the village proper (arriving by trail from the north is the only way to avoid these stairs), an enticing maze of little walkways shadowed by tall houses.

Once there, though, the views over the surrounding vineyards and up and down the coastline are stupendous—for the best outlook, walk to the end of the narrow main street to a belvedere that seems perched between the sea and sky. Corniglia is the village most likely to offer a glimpse into life in the Cinque Terre the way it was decades ago.

Manarola ★ Manarola is a near-vertical cluster of tall houses that seem to rise piggyback up the hills on either side of the harbor. In fact, in a region with no shortage of heart-stopping views, one of the most amazing sights is the descent into the town of Manarola on the path from Corniglia: From this perspective, the hill-climbing houses seem to merge into one another to form a row of skyscrapers. Despite these urban associations, Manarola is a delightfully rural village where fishing and winemaking are big business. The region's major **wine cooperative,** Cooperativa Agricoltura di Riomaggiore, Manarola, Corniglia, Vernazza e Monterosso, made up of 300 local producers, is here; check www.cantinacinqueterre.com or call ✆ **0187/920-435** for information about tours of its modern (established 1982) facilities or walking tours of the vineyards. Try to reserve at least 3 days before your visit.

Riomaggiore ★ Riomaggiore clings to the rustic ways of the Cinque Terre while making some (unfortunate) concessions to the modern world. The old fishing quarter has expanded in recent years, and Riomaggiore now has some sections of new houses and apartment blocks. This blend of old and new is a bit of a shame. The village center still looks like something from 50 years ago, bustling and prosperous in a charming setting, while the "new side" of town feels like a half-effort at maintaining the old mostly in color. A credit to both sides is that many of the lanes end in seaside belvederes.

From the parking garage, follow the main street down; from the train station, exit and turn right to head through the tunnel for the central part of town (or, from the station, take off left up the brick stairs to walk the Via dell'Amore to Manarola). That tunnel and the main drag meet at the base of an elevated terrace that holds the train tracks; from there, a staircase leads down to a tiny fishing harbor. At the left of the harbor, a rambling path leads to a pleasant little **beach** of large pebbles.

Where to Stay in the Cinque Terre

If you'd like to base yourself nearby but not technically in the five Cinque Terre villages, there are reasonably priced options in Portovenere (see "Riviera Runners-Up," p. 574), offering easy access to all of the Cinque Terre via boat. For example, **La Calata** (Via Capellini 57; affittacamerelacalata.com; ✆ **380-450-9997**) is a small B&B right in the heart of town (and very close to the ferry port) renting out double, triple, and quadruple rooms with private bathrooms starting at around 119€. All rooms have a sea views.

SELF-CATERING ROOMS & APARTMENTS

There have always been quite a few *affittacamere* (room rentals) in the various Cinque Terre towns, but getting information on them meant having local contacts and relying on word of mouth. Now that local room and apartment owners have gotten more Internet savvy, finding rentals online has become much easier, even aside from **www.airbnb.com**, which does have many listings in each of the five towns. For a room with private bathroom for two people, expect to pay anywhere from 70€ to 150€ per night depending on the season and the amenities offered. **L'Ancora** (appartamenticinqueterre.net) in Riomaggiore has three rooms (with private bath) in an ancient Ligurian building, with traditional elements like wood beams and exposed bricks, but very modern bathrooms. The agency that rents out the rooms also has larger apartment rentals; check the website for details. In the heart of Vernazza, **Memo Rooms** (www.memorooms.com) are two simple yet elegant rooms with private bath above the gelateria on the main drag. **Albergo Barbara** (www.albergobarbara.it) in Vernazza also has rooms to rent—some with harbor views—but they are on the third and fourth floor of a building without an elevator, so keep that in mind before booking.

MANAROLA

La Torretta ★★★ Located in an ancient tower in the center of Manarola, this charming "boutique lodge" has chic flair (similar to **La Mala** in Vernazza). The property has a range of lovely rooms and suites that mix contemporary and traditional furnishings along with quirky details and wild patterns. Several rooms have sea or vineyard views and balconies, and all have nice in-room amenities, such as Nespresso machines, charging stations, luxurious toiletries, and a selection of wines. Our favorite rooms are the Design Suite in the main building and the Panoramic Suite in the annex, just a short walk from the main building. If you really want to splurge, go for the duplex suite with a "cave" bathroom with exposed stone walls and an amazing private terrace with sea views. Despite the fairly steep prices (and position on the hill), rooms book up quickly here in high season, so reserve way ahead of time. Fortunately, a luggage transfer service means guests don't have to lug their own bags up the hill from the train station. Breakfast is served on a panoramic terrace (aperitif is often offered here as well).

Vico Volto 20, Manarola. www.torrettas.com. ✆ **0187/920-327.** 11 units. 400€–600€ double. Rates include breakfast. Closed Nov. **Amenities:** Solarium; free Wi-Fi.

MONTEROSSO

Hotel Porto Roca ★★ This four-star hotel is the Cinque Terre's one real resort, spectacularly positioned upon a cliffside overlooking the village, cemetery, and blue sea below. Most guest rooms are in need of an update (and some of the common areas are also a bit dated), but once you step out onto your private balcony suspended above the Mediterranean, it's easy to forget any shortcomings. Prices are high even for a room in the back without sea views; we suggest splurging on a better room to enjoy the full experience. If you tire of the infinity pool and Jacuzzi, there's a section of beach for hotel guests, with free umbrellas and deck chairs. The restaurant serves typical Ligurian dishes, and in nice weather, the cliffside patio offers the best seat in town. When it's warm, breakfast is also served on the panoramic terrace. The hotel is located in a pedestrian-only area where only taxis can enter. The hotel promotes booking directly on its site by offering free taxi shuttle to and from the train station or local parking lot and a 15% discount at the **La Terrazza** restaurant. It also runs a shuttle service to the historic part of town.

Via Corone 1, Monterosso al Mare (SP). www.portoroca.it. ✆ **0187/817-502.** 43 units. 240€–695€ double. Rates include breakfast. Closed Nov–Mar. **Amenities:** Restaurant; bar; concierge; spa; pool; room service; free Wi-Fi.

Il Giardino Incantato ★★ This "Enchanted Garden" makes for a tranquil and relaxing refuge in the Cinque Terre's most bustling town. If you are looking for sea views or balconies, this charming family-run B&B in a converted 16th-century villa isn't the property for you. However, it will suit you well if you want to be in a prime location just off Via Roma in Monterosso's old village, a stone's throw from the town beach and the boat pier. The four guest rooms have been lovingly decorated with terra-cotta tiles, wood-beamed ceilings, and wrought-iron beds. Three rooms overlook the pedestrian street outside the property while the fourth opens on to a courtyard. The villa sits opposite a lovely garden with lemon trees, lavender, and colorful flowers, lovingly tended by owner Mariapia. This is where breakfast (including Ligurian favorites like focaccia along with more classic options like cereal and eggs) is served in nice weather. The house is full of antiques and other precious objects, so the property does not accept guests under the age of 14.

Via Mazzini 18, Monterosso al Mare (SP). www.ilgiardinoincantato.net. ✆ **0187/818-315.** 4 units. 200€–230€ double. Rates include breakfast. Closed Nov–early Apr. **Amenities:** Garden; free Wi-Fi.

VERNAZZA

Gianni Franzi ★★ This small guesthouse offers 23 rooms to rent in three different buildings; some have excellent views over the water. When you arrive in town, stop by the trattoria of the same name **(Gianni Franzi)** or call the numbers listed below. Though the restaurant is closed on Wednesdays, there is usually someone there in the afternoons to take care of new arrivals. Breakfast is served on a rooftop deck designed like the bow of an ocean liner, offering wonderful views of the sea. Keep in mind that most rooms require a steep climb up stairs, and luggage service is no longer provided. Wi-Fi can also be spotty.

Restaurant address: Piazza G. Marconi 5, Vernazza (SP). www.giannifranzi.it. Restaurant ✆ **0187/812-228.** To book a room, call ✆ **393/900-8155.** 23 units. 100€–180€ double (some w/shared bath). Rates include breakfast. Closed early Jan to mid-Mar. **Amenities:** Restaurant; bar; garden/terrace; free Wi-Fi.

La Mala ★★★ This stylish four-room property (a converted Ligurian-style home) has a chic, beachy feel. Rooms are not large, but they are well appointed and sunny, boasting gorgeous views of the sea, village, harbor, or Doria castle; bathrooms are clean and modern. Room 26 has a small living area that can accommodate a third bed, making it ideal for families. Room 31 is especially large and bright, seemingly suspended in air between sea and sky. The other two rooms are slightly smaller, with limited harbor views. La Mala is quite central, but it is set back a bit so it really feels like a retreat, if you don't mind the sound of bells chiming from a nearby church. The communal seaside terrace is the perfect spot for a relaxing sunset *aperitivo.* You can ask for special in-room services like a personalized wine tasting, a selection of local food specialties, or prosecco and flowers upon your arrival. There is no reception area—just call (or find) the owner, Gian, when you get to town, and someone will meet you to help with your bags. There's no breakfast area either, though rooms have a machine for making coffee and tea; in high season, rates include vouchers for a typical Italian breakfast (such as a cappuccino and brioche) at a local coffee bar, while in low season a bottle of local wine is offered instead.

Via San Giovanni Battista 29, Vernazza. www.lamala.it. ✆ **334/287-5718.** 4 units. 110€–250€ double. Closed Jan 10–Mar. **Amenities:** Free Wi-Fi.

Where to Eat in the Cinque Terre

CORNIGLIA

Osteria a Cantina de Mananan ★★ LIGURIAN Locals and tourists alike seek out this tiny eatery carved out of an old wine cellar in an ancient stone house. This unique and lively restaurant has very few tables—be prepared to share one with other diners—and there's often only one seating per meal (sometimes up to two), so be sure to call ahead. Though it has a rustic feel with paper placemats and a cluttered collection of quirky artwork on the walls, the food is the real standout, with vegetables sourced from nearby terraced gardens and seafood provided by the town's fishermen. Highlights of the simple yet tasty menu include *pansotti* (a sort of Ligurian ravioli usually stuffed with herbs and cheese), lemon anchovies, and *testaroli* (a crepe-like pasta that is said to date back to the times of the Etruscans) served with traditional pesto sauce. Seasonal specialties are listed on the big board on the wall.

Via Fieschi 117, Corniglia. ✆ **0187/821-166.** Entrees 12€–20€. Wed–Mon 12:30–2:30pm and 7:30–9:30pm; closed Tues. Closed Mon–Fri in Dec, and part of Jan–Feb.

MONTEROSSO

Ristorante Miky ★ SEAFOOD This family-run restaurant in Monterosso is considered one of the best—and most expensive—in the Cinque Terre, with friendly service and artfully presented food. On warm days, you can dine in a lovely garden with the smell of lemon and rosemary in the air. House specialties include the famous Monterosso anchovies, an excellent seafood sampler platter, monkfish ravioli, and *pesce al sale,* fresh fish covered in coarse salt and slowly cooked in a wood-burning oven. One of the most unique pasta dishes is homemade spaghetti (made from locally milled flour), fresh Monterosso anchovies, Taggiasche olives, capers, and pine nuts encased in a thin sheet of dough to concentrate all of the flavors. An extensive wine list (about 250 labels) focuses on local producers, and homemade *limoncello* is offered at the end of your meal. Miky certainly isn't cheap, but the inventive food, elegant ambience, and overall experience make it worthwhile. Reservations are highly recommended. The owners also have a wine bar and cafe just a few doors down (at Via Fegina 90; ✆ **0187-802-525**), known as the **Cantina di Miky,** which offers more casual seaside dining as well as a bit of nightlife.

Via Fegina 104, Monterosso al Mare. www.ristorantemiky.it. ✆ **0187/817-608.** Entrees 20€–40€. Daily noon–3pm and 7:30pm–late. Closed Nov–Mar.

VERNAZZA

Ristorante Belforte ★★★ LIGURIAN Perched on a medieval watchtower overlooking the Mediterranean, this upscale restaurant has been around for half a century and boasts a unique and fantastic setting. Run by local families since its inception, it serves up traditional Ligurian cuisine, such as local anchovies offered in a variety of ways. Other notable dishes include *antipasto misto di pesce,* a selection of five or six small bites of seafood (hot and cold delicacies); lobster tagliatelle, and Belforte-style baked fish (depending on what the catch of the day is) served with vegetables. The award-winning taglioloni pasta with squid ink and shrimp is a must try. Desserts include traditional Italian favorites like panna cotta and tiramisu as well as the house specialty: gelato served with sautéed strawberries. You'll need to reserve ahead of time and be persistent (there's an online form for reserving, but it's a better idea to call)—if you are able to nab the single table on a small balcony at sunset, you are in for a romantic treat!

Via Guidoni 42, Vernazza. www.ristorantebelforte.it. ✆ **0187/812-222.** Entrees 16€–30€. Wed–Mon noon–3:30pm and 7–10pm. Closed Nov to mid-Mar.

NAPLES & POMPEII
12
By Stephen Brewer

B*ienvenuti al sud*—welcome to the south. Your first encounter with southern Italy will probably be Naples. If you've enjoyed the grandeur of Venice, the elegance of Florence, and the awesomeness of monumental Rome, be prepared for a bit of a jolt: Everything seems a bit more intense in Italy's third-largest city, the capital of the south. Though decidedly rundown in places, the city delights with its residents' energy and genuine warmth, and surprises with the sophistication of the monuments, museums, and cultural and culinary scenes. A visit to this noisy, crowded, chaotic city can be overwhelming, but that's part of the city's allure. And Naples is just the beginning.

There's even more around Naples—some of the most extensive remains of the ancient world in Herculaneum and Pompeii, and the natural ominous wonders of Mt. Vesuvius and the Campi Flegrei. You might want to think of the Naples area as Italy on overdrive. Hang on and enjoy the ride.

DON'T LEAVE NAPLES & POMPEII WITHOUT . . .

Prowling Around the Attic of Antiquity. Among the prizes in the National Archaeology Museum, you'll find touchingly human statues of gods and goddesses, frescoes and mosaics from Pompeii and Herculaneum, even some titter-inducing pornography.

Plunging into Neapolitan Street Life. Lively Via Tribunali provides a good taste of the city's color and clamor, from the magnificent church of San Lorenzo Maggiore to the pizzas emerging from the ovens at Sorbillo.

Soaking in Soothing Views. Hit the airy heights by riding the funicular up to the Certosa di San Martino. Admire the vista of Mt. Vesuvius looming over the bay from Castel dell'Ovo or the gardens of the Villa Communale.

Stepping Back into Ancient Times in Herculaneum and Pompeii. It's eerily easy to imagine everyday life as it was 2,000 years ago along the streets of these accidentally preserved seaside towns.

Sampling Naples' Greatest Contribution to World Cuisine. You haven't eaten pizza until you've eaten it in Naples, the city where pizza was born. And that's just a start when it comes to enjoying the local cuisine.

PREVIOUS PAGE: **Columns and statue in Pompeii.**

Safe Travels in Naples

You won't easily avoid crowds in the big, boisterous city of Naples, and be forewarned that the narrow streets of the old quarters tend to be crowded with maskless mobs. Naples' subterranean attractions (see "Underground Naples," p. 602) remain open, despite less-than-optimal ventilation. Outside the city, the ruins of Herculaneum and Pompeii are open-air sites where social distancing is less of a problem, though you may want to reach them on the less-crowded Campania Express rather than the jam-packed Circumvesuviana train.

Depending on when you travel, pandemic restrictions may apply in terms of indoor mask-wearing, social distancing, and occupancy limits. Few museums in Naples require timed entry tickets, although Pompeii may require advance reservations for Saturdays and bank holidays. Advance reservations are advised, however, especially for popular attractions such as the Cappella Sansevero and the National Archaeological Museum. Proof of vaccination (see p. 820) may be required for entry to museums, restaurants, and concert venues; at press time, Pompeii was offering free onsite Covid tests for visitors who show up without proof of vaccination. Check ahead to make sure that a site you want to visit has not temporarily curtailed its hours. See p. 820 for more information, and check updated Covid pages at www.italia.it.

NAPLES ★★

219km (136 miles) SE of Rome

In Naples, Mt. Vesuvius looms to the east, the fumaroles of the Campi Flegrei hiss and steam to the west, and the isle of Capri (see p. 683) floats phantomlike across the gleaming waters of the bay. For all the splendor and drama of this natural setting, one of Italy's most intense urban concoctions is the real show. Naples shoots out so many sensations that it takes a while for visitors to know what's hit them. Dark brooding lanes open to palm-fringed piazzas. Laundry-strewn tenements stand cheek by jowl with grand palaces. Medieval churches and castles rise above a grid of streets laid out by ancient Greeks. There's no denying that parts of the city are squalid, yet the museums are packed with riches.

It seems that most of life here transpires on the streets, so you'll witness a lot. The pace can be leisurely in the southern way, and amazingly hectic. When you partake—in a meal, in a *passeggiata,* or just in a simple transaction—you'll notice the warmth, general good nature, and a sense of fun. In more than a few places, you may be reminded of scenes from Elena Ferrante's bestselling quartet of Neapolitan novels. You get the idea—but you won't really, until you experience this fascinating, perplexing, and beguiling city for yourself.

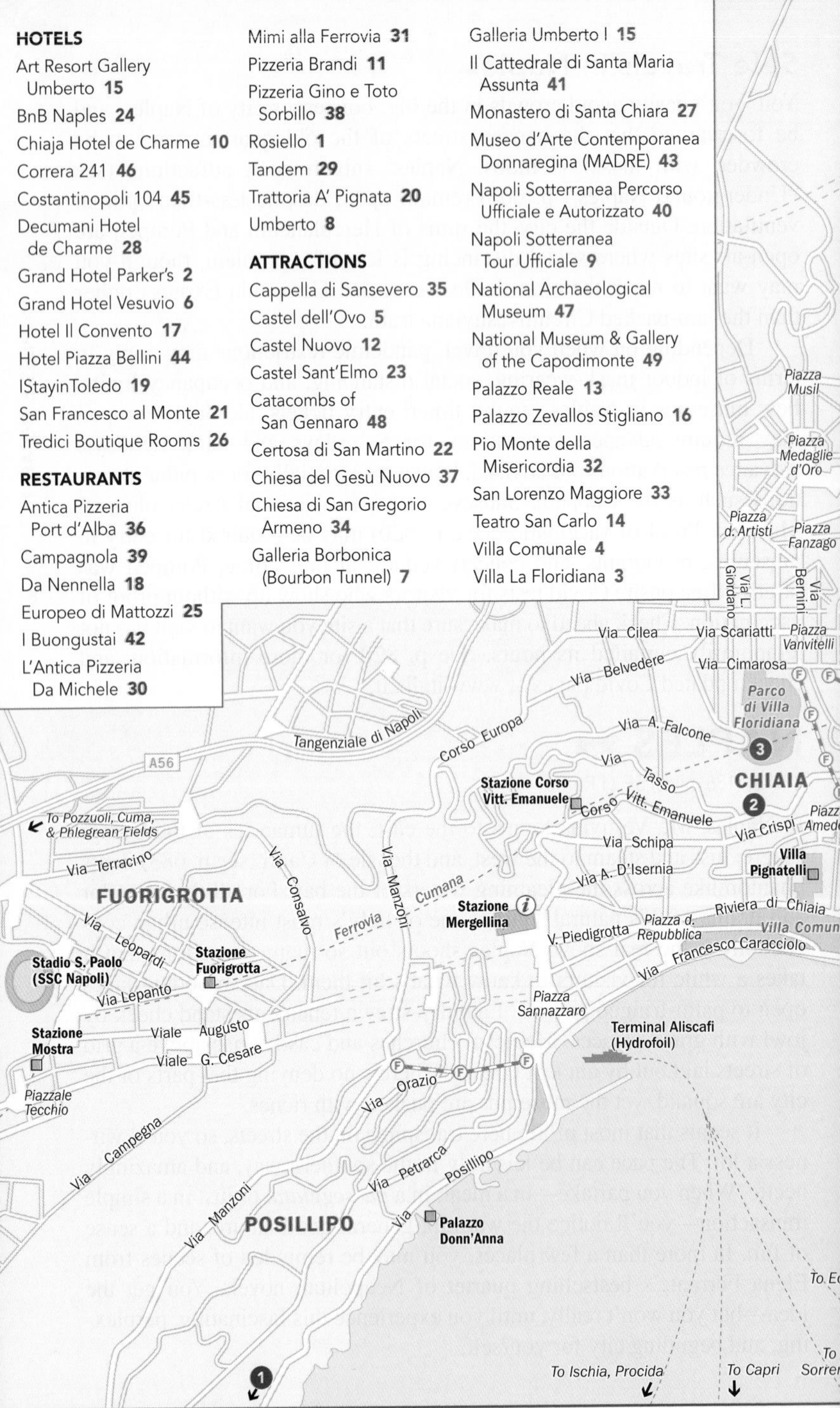

HOTELS
Art Resort Gallery Umberto 15
BnB Naples 24
Chiaja Hotel de Charme 10
Correra 241 46
Costantinopoli 104 45
Decumani Hotel de Charme 28
Grand Hotel Parker's 2
Grand Hotel Vesuvio 6
Hotel Il Convento 17
Hotel Piazza Bellini 44
IStayinToledo 19
San Francesco al Monte 21
Tredici Boutique Rooms 26
RESTAURANTS
Antica Pizzeria Port d'Alba 36
Campagnola 39
Da Nennella 18
Europeo di Mattozzi 25
I Buongustai 42
L'Antica Pizzeria Da Michele 30
Mimì alla Ferrovia 31
Pizzeria Brandi 11
Pizzeria Gino e Toto Sorbillo 38
Rosiello 1
Tandem 29
Trattoria A' Pignata 20
Umberto 8
ATTRACTIONS
Cappella di Sansevero 35
Castel dell'Ovo 5
Castel Nuovo 12
Castel Sant'Elmo 23
Catacombs of San Gennaro 48
Certosa di San Martino 22
Chiesa del Gesù Nuovo 37
Chiesa di San Gregorio Armeno 34
Galleria Borbonica (Bourbon Tunnel) 7
Galleria Umberto I 15
Il Cattedrale di Santa Maria Assunta 41
Monastero di Santa Chiara 27
Museo d'Arte Contemporanea Donnaregina (MADRE) 43
Napoli Sotterranea Percorso Ufficiale e Autorizzato 40
Napoli Sotterranea Tour Ufficiale 9
National Archaeological Museum 47
National Museum & Gallery of the Capodimonte 49
Palazzo Reale 13
Palazzo Zevallos Stigliano 16
Pio Monte della Misericordia 32
San Lorenzo Maggiore 33
Teatro San Carlo 14
Villa Comunale 4
Villa La Floridiana 3
Piazza Musil
Piazza Medaglie d'Oro
Piazza d. Artisti
Piazza Fanzago
Via L. Giordano
Via Bernini
Via Cilea
Via Scariatti
Piazza Vanvitelli
Via Belvedere
Via Cimarosa
Parco di Villa Floridiana
Tangenziale di Napoli
Corso Europa
Via A. Falcone
A56
Via Tasso
CHIAIA
Stazione Corso Vitt. Emanuele
Corso Vitt. Emanuele
To Pozzuoli, Cuma, & Phlegrean Fields
Via Crispi
Via Schipa
Villa Pignatelli
Via Terracino
Via Consalvo
Via Manzoni
Via A. D'Isernia
FUORIGROTTA
Ferrovia Cumana
Stazione Mergellina
Riviera di Chiaia
Villa Comun
Via Leopardi
V. Piedigrotta
Piazza d. Repubblica
Stadio S. Paolo (SSC Napoli)
Stazione Fuorigrotta
Via Francesco Caracciolo
Via Lepanto
Piazza Sannazzaro
Stazione Mostra
Viale Augusto
Viale G. Cesare
Terminal Aliscafi (Hydrofoil)
Via Orazio
Piazzale Tecchio
Via Campegna
Via Petrarca
Via Posillipo
Via Manzoni
POSILLIPO
Palazzo Donn'Anna
To Ischia, Procida
To Capri
To Sorre

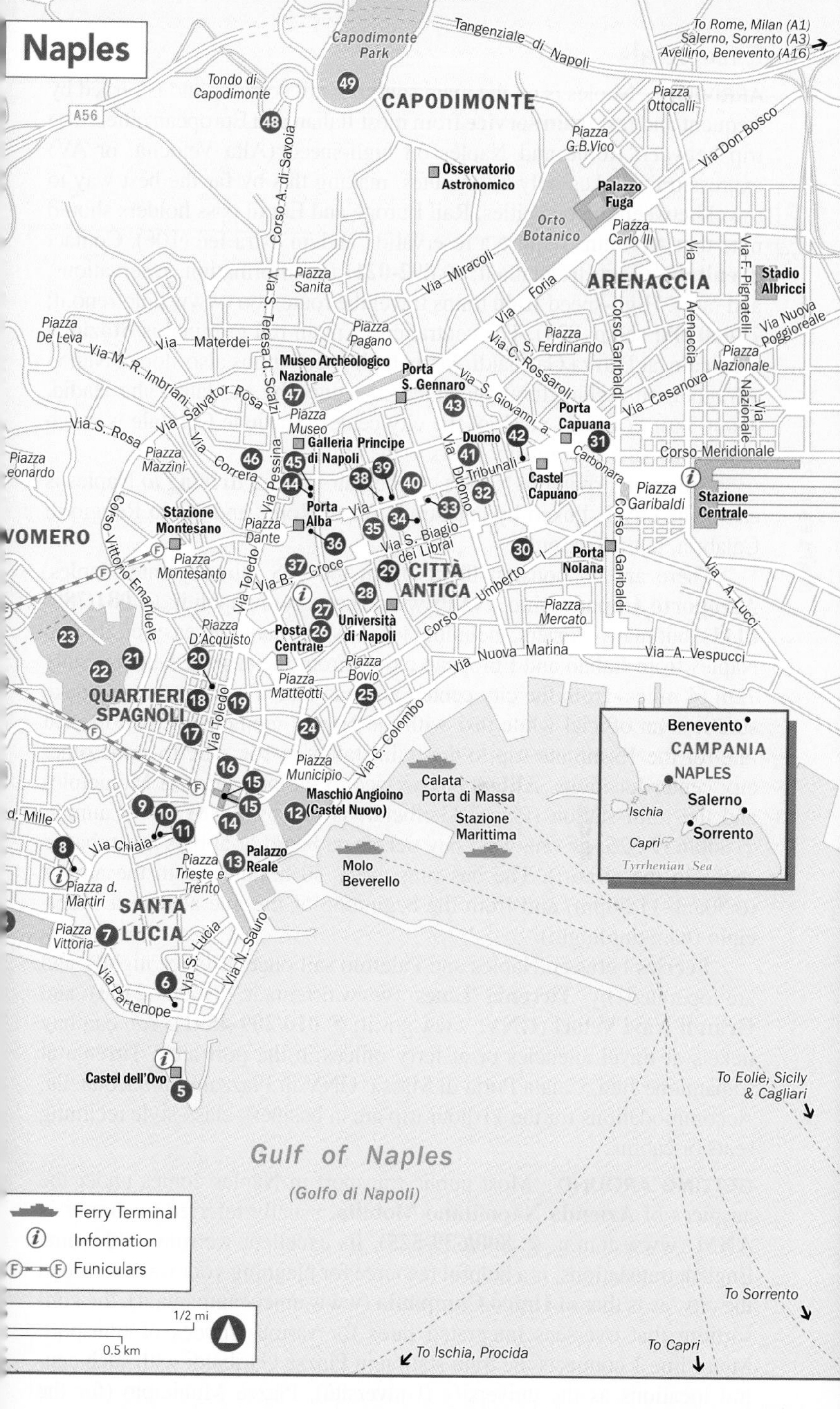

Naples
Capodimonte Park
Tangenziale di Napoli
To Rome, Milan (A1)
Salerno, Sorrento (A3)
Avellino, Benevento (A16)
Tondo di Capodimonte
CAPODIMONTE
A56
Piazza Ottocalli
Piazza G.B.Vico
Via Don Bosco
Osservatorio Astronomico
Palazzo Fuga
Corso A. di Savoia
Orto Botanico
Piazza Carlo III
Via Miracoli
Piazza Sanita
Via Foria
ARENACCIA
Stadio Albricci
Via S. Teresa d. Scalzi
Via Arenaccia
Via F. Pignatelli
Via Nuova Poggioreale
Piazza De Leva
Via Materdei
Piazza Pagano
Piazza S. Ferdinando
Corso Garibaldi
Piazza Nazionale
Via M. R. Imbriani
Museo Archeologico Nazionale
Porta S. Gennaro
Via C. Rossaroli
Via Salvator Rosa
Via S. Giovanni a Carbonara
Via Casanova
Via Nazionale
Piazza Museo
Porta Capuana
Via S. Rosa
Galleria Principe di Napoli
Duomo
Piazza Mazzini
Via Correra
Via Pessina
Via Duomo
Tribunali
Corso Meridionale
Piazza Leonardo
Castel Capuano
Piazza Garibaldi
Stazione Centrale
Porta Alba
Via
Corso Vittorio Emanuele
Stazione Montesano
Piazza Dante
Via S. Biagio dei Librai
VOMERO
Piazza Montesanto
Via Toledo
Via B. Croce
CITTÀ ANTICA
Porta Nolana
Via A. Lucci
Corso Umberto I
Piazza Mercato
Piazza D'Acquisto
Posta Centrale
Università di Napoli
Via Nuova Marina
Via A. Vespucci
Piazza Bovio
QUARTIERI SPAGNOLI
Piazza Matteotti
Via C. Colombo
Benevento
CAMPANIA
NAPLES
Ischia
Salerno
Capri
Sorrento
Tyrrhenian Sea
Piazza Municipio
Calata Porta di Massa
Maschio Angioino (Castel Nuovo)
Stazione Marittima
d. Mille
Via Chiaia
Palazzo Reale
Piazza Trieste e Trento
Molo Beverello
Piazza d. Martiri
SANTA LUCIA
Piazza Vittoria
Via S. Lucia
Via N. Sauro
Via Partenope
Castel dell'Ovo
To Eolie, Sicily & Cagliari
Gulf of Naples
(Golfo di Napoli)
Ferry Terminal
Information
Funiculars
1/2 mi
0.5 km
To Sorrento
To Ischia, Procida
To Capri

Essentials

ARRIVING Naples is on the main southern rail corridor and is served by frequent and fast **train service** from most Italian and European cities. The trip between Rome and Naples on high-speed (Alta Velocità, or AV) express trains takes only 87 minutes, making this by far the best way to travel between the two cities. Rail Europe and Eurail pass holders should note that AV trains require a reservation and an extra fee (10€). Contact **Trenitalia** (www.trenitalia.it; ✆ **892-021**) for information, reservations, and fares. High-speed **Italo** trains travel the route, too (www.italotreno.it; ✆ **060708;** see p. 824). The central city's main rail terminal is **Stazione Centrale,** at Piazza Garibaldi. Many high-speed trains also stop at Napoli Afragola, an architectural showpiece designed by the late Zaha Hadid, about 3km (2 miles) north of the city center; Stazione Centrale is much more convenient for most visitors to the city.

Although driving *in* Naples can be hair-raising, **driving** *to* Naples is easy. The city is linked by autostrada A2 to Rome and A3 to Reggio di Calabria, in the far south.

There are no nonstop flights from the U.S. directly into Naples' **Aeroporto Capodichino** (**NAP;** www.aeroportodinapoli.it; ✆ **081/789-6111**), but many carriers, including low-cost Ryanair and easyJet, fly into Naples from Italian and European cities. From the airport, which is only 7km (4 miles) from the city center, you can take a taxi into town (make sure it is an official white taxi with the Naples municipal logo); the flat rate for the 15-minute trip to the train station is 16€, 18€ to some other city center locations. **Alibus** bus service to the port (Piazza Municipio) and the train station (Piazza Garibaldi) is run by **ANM** (www.anm.it; ✆ **800/639-525;** 5€ one-way; buy tickets on board or at bars and tobacco shops in the airport). The bus runs every 30 minutes from the airport (6:30am–11:50pm) and from the beginning of the line at Piazza Municipio (6am–midnight).

Ferries between Naples and Palermo sail once or twice nightly and are operated by **Tirrenia Lines** (www.tirrenia.it; ✆ **089-2123**) and **Grandi Navi Veloci** (**GNV;** www.gnv.it; ✆ **010/209-4591**). You can buy tickets at travel agencies or at ferry offices in the port area: Tirrenia at Capannone Juta, Calata Porta di Massa; GNV in Piazzale Immacolatella. Accommodations for the 11-hour trip are in business-class-style reclining seats or cabins.

GETTING AROUND Most public transport in Naples comes under the auspices of **Azienda Napolitano Mobilta,** usually referred to simply as **ANM** (www.anm.it; ✆ **800/639-525**). Its excellent website, with some English translations, is a helpful resource for planning your travels around the city, as is that of **Unico Campania** (www.unicocampania.it), the consortium that oversees integrated fares for various modes of transport. Metro line 1 connects the train station in Piazza Garibaldi with such central locations as the university (Università), Piazza Municipio (for the port), Via Toledo, Piazza Dante, Duomo, and the archaeological museum (Museo stop); Metro line 2 (a commuter line operated by Trenitalia) runs from Pozzuoli in the western suburbs through the city, with stops that include Mergellina, Piazza Amadeo, Montesanto, the archaeological museum (Museo stop), and Piazza Garibaldi. Several new stations have opened in recent years, with more on the way, including a planned expansion of line 1 to the airport. As you ride the system, you'll notice many stations decorated with art installations. Mosaic tiles and lights in the Toledo station are in shades of blue that become deeper and more intense as you descend; psychedelic colors and shapes in the Università station are intended to immerse you in the digital age.

There are also two urban railway networks that can be handy for getting to major attractions. The **Circumvesuviana train** leaves from a station adjacent to the main train station in Piazza Garibaldi and runs southeast around the Bay of Naples to Pompeii and Herculaneum (p. 625) and Sorrento (p. 640). The **Ferrovia Cumana** runs from Piazza Montesanto to Pozzuoli and other towns in the Campi Flegrei (p. 617).

Handy **bus** routes include the R lines (R1, R2, R3, R4), with frequent stops at major tourist attractions (the R4, for example, connects the archaeological museum and Catacombs of San Gennaro), and the electric minibuses (marked e) that skirt the historic district.

Four **funiculars** take passengers up and down the steep hills of Naples. The **Funicolare Centrale,** one of the world's longest (about a mile) and busiest funiculars, connects the central city to Vomero. Daily departures (6:30am–12:30am) are from the Augusteo station on the Piazzetta Duca d'Aosta just off Via Toledo.

One-way fare for subways, buses, and funiculars is 1.20€; daily tickets (Biglietto Giornaliero) cost 4.20€, valid until midnight the day they are validated; weekly tickets (Biglietto Settimanale) are 12.50€. You can buy tickets at some newsstands and tobacco shops, from machines in most Metro and funicular stations, and at some bus stops. Some Metro stations are equipped with terminals that allow you to tap a contactless credit card for entrance. When riding the bus, you must validate tickets in the electronic ticket machines on board.

Be Prepared

It's a good idea to **carry some extra transport tickets** with you when exploring the city. Lines at ticket-vending machines at Metro stations are often long (especially at Piazza Garibaldi), machines are commonly out of service (*fuori servizio*), and it can be hard to find ticket vendors near bus stops.

Metro stops are not announced and are poorly marked. Keep a close eye out for signs and keep track of stations along the route so you have a clear idea of when you might be approaching your stop. Don't be shy about asking other riders for help.

Taxis are an excellent, relatively inexpensive way to get around the city and are very reliable and strictly regulated. Official taxis are painted

> ### See the Sights for Less
>
> The confoundingly complex **Campania Card** (www.campaniartecard.it; ✆ **800/600-601** or 06/3996-7650) can save you money if you plan to make the rounds of churches, museums, and archaeological sites. For most visitors, the most basic versions will suffice: the **Napoli 3 Giorni** card (21€), good for 3 days, gives you free admission to three attractions, a discount of 50% at others, and free use of public transport; the **Campania 3 Giorni** (32€) card provides free admission to two attractions and a 50% discount at others and includes Pompeii and Herculaneum, so it delivers a substantial discount if, for instance, you plan to see those two sites and the National Archaeological Museum. Cards are for sale at participating sites and at tourist information offices.

white and marked comune di napoli. Inside a sign lists official flat rates to the seaports, central hotels, and top attractions; don't fret if your driver doesn't use the meter—*not* using the meter is legal for all rides with established flat rates. Taxis don't cruise for street hails, but can be found at many taxi stands around town; for an extra 1€ surcharge, you can request a taxi by phone (✆ **081/8888** or 081/2222).

As for **driving** around Naples, we have one word: *Don't.* If you're tempted, take a look at the cars on the street. In the rest of Italy, even the simplest models are kept in pristine condition; here, cars look like they've been used in demolition derbies. Car theft is common—some rental companies won't extend theft protection coverage if you'll be driving in Naples. If you do bring a car into the city, a convenient place for long-term parking is **Parcheggio Brin,** Via Benedetto Brin at Via Volta (www.anm.it; ✆ **081/763-2855**) at the eastern edge of the center, easily reached from the Via Marina exit off the A3 autostrada. Parking costs 1.30€ for the first 4 hours, 0.30€ each additional hour to a maximum of 7.20€.

Walking is the best way to get around the city center, where sights are fairly close together, but remember: For Neapolitan drivers, red lights are mere suggestions; cross busy streets carefully. Always look both ways, too, since many drivers scoff at the notion of a one-way street. Zebra stripes (white lines) in the street, indicating where pedestrians have the right of way, mean absolutely nothing here.

VISITOR INFORMATION The **tourist office** in Stazione Centrale (incampania.it; ✆ **081/268-779;** Metro: Piazza Garibaldi) is open daily 9am to 6pm. Other **tourist information points** are located in Piazza del Gesù (✆ **081/551-2701**) and in the tourist port in Varco Immacolatella, both open daily (Mon–Sat 9:30am–6:30pm; Sun 9:30am–2pm). These offices can give you a free map, an essential piece of gear when navigating Naples, and advise on bus and subway routes.

Exploring Naples

Large as Naples is, it's easy to get to the sights you want to see on foot, letting you experience one of the city's greatest allures: its street life.

From **Piazza Trieste e Trento,** with the magnificent Teatro San Carlo (p. 616) and Galleria Umberto I (p. 595), **Via Toledo** leads north. To the left is the **Quartieri Spagnoli,** a neighborhood of narrow, tightly packed lanes, while to the right, just beyond Piazza Dante, is the atmospheric **historical center** of the city, where many of the churches you want to see face airy piazzas. At the northern end of Via Toledo, about a 10-minute walk beyond Piazza Dante, is Naples' celebrated archaeological museum.

A colorful souvenir stand in Naples' historic center.

You'll probably be safe just about anywhere you wander along the well-worn tourist trail; the crime rate in Naples, despite the city's bad rap, is a lot lower than it is in many American cities. It's best to avoid the darker corners of the Spagnoli neighborhood at night, however, and pickpockets and purse-and-jewelry snatchers can be a menace, especially around the train station and in the Porta Nolana market; on **Via San Gregorio Armeno** (see p. 614), people gawking at shop windows filled with nativity scenes are easy targets.

SANTA LUCIA & THE SEAFRONT

Not surprisingly, some of the city's most magnificent squares and public monuments are clustered near the seafront. **Piazza del Plebiscito ★★**, the most beautiful square in Naples, is surrounded by an elegant assemblage of neoclassical landmarks. Among them is the **Palazzo Reale ★** (Royal Palace), with 30 grandiose yet strangely vacuous rooms where Neapolitan royalty ruled and entertained in the 18th and 19th centuries. Among the more interesting objects on display are the gramophones, sheet music, recordings, and other mementos honoring Neapolitan-born tenor Enrico Caruso (palazzorealedinapoli.org; ✆ **081/580-8255;** 10€; Thurs–Tues 9am–8pm; gardens close at sunset Sept–Apr; bus R2 or R3). In the piazza two Neapolitan kings survey the cobblestones on horseback: the forward-thinking Carlo III (1716–1788) and the treacherous Ferdinando I (1423–1494). It's said you will be blessed with good fortune if you face the Palazzo Reale, close your eyes, and walk backwards across the square between the two kings (much harder to do than you might

Getting to Know Napoli

A good way to get to know the city is on a free walking tour with **Napoli That's Amore** (www.napolithatsamore.org). Local professional guides lead highly informative and personalized walks: through the Old Town from Piazza Dante and a Best of Naples circuit beginning at Piazza Municipio. Go to the website to book; tour times vary throughout the year. There's no fee, but tips are appreciated and well deserved.

think—local lore has it that condemned prisoners were once blindfolded and made to perform this feat, and few succeeded).

A short walk up the seafront, the airy **Piazza Municipio** is the best place to view the towers and crenellations of **Castel Nuovo ★** (New Castle; castelnuovo.comune.napoli.it; ✆ **081/795-7701**), with the white-marble Triumphal Arch of Alfonso I of Aragon squeezed between two of its turrets. You can forgo a visit to the castle's fairly uninspired staterooms and art collection, and simply admire this medieval sea-girt beauty from the outside. (If you do want to step inside, the salons and galleries are open Mon–Sat 8:30am–5pm; admission 6€.) Gazing at the castle, you might consider the plight of former prisoners who shared their dungeons with crocodiles imported from Egypt to snack on the doomed souls. In Piazza Municipio you'll also see the water-spouting lions and sea monsters of the **Fontana del Nettuno ★★**, a 17th-century marble showpiece originally installed in front of the Palazzo Reale and carted around the city to several locations since then. It was partly the work of Pietro Bernini, whose greatest creation is the Fontana della Barcaccia at the bottom of the Spanish Steps in Rome (his more famous son, Lorenzo, designed the Fontana dei Quattro Fiumi in Rome's Piazza Navona).

Head south along the Santa Lucia seafront to see the city's outrageously picturesque **Castel dell'Ovo ★★** (Castle of the Egg), on Borgo Marinari (off Via Partenope). As every Neapolitan knows, the ancient Roman poet Virgil placed an egg under the foundations of the castle; when it breaks, a great disaster will befall the city. Considering earthquakes, eruptions of nearby Mt. Vesuvius, plague outbreaks, and wars, it's probably safe to assume the egg is no longer intact. The castle is enchanting even without such legends, squeezed onto a tiny island the Greeks first settled almost 3 millennia ago and a royal residence from the 13th through 20th centuries (www.comune.napoli.it/casteldellovo; ✆ **081/795-6180;** free admission; Mon–Sat 9am–6:30pm, Sun 9am–6pm). The little lanes beneath the thick walls are lined with the fishermen's houses of Borgo Marinaro, now occupied by bars and pizzerias. For Neapolitans, a walk across the stout bridge onto the island is a favorite Sunday afternoon outing. Just behind the waterfront stretches the quirkily elegant **Chiaia** district, once the fashionable address for Bourbon nobility. Many palaces and villas from those days are slowly moldering, with the exception of wonderful **Villa Pignatelli,** Riviera di Chiaia 200, its salons furnished in 19th-century gilded finery (www.beniculturali.it; ✆ **081/761-2356;** open Wed–Mon 9:30am–5pm; 5€).

Galleria Umberto I ★★ SHOPPING MALL Shopping malls have only gone downhill since the late 19th century, when elegant glass-and-iron landmarks like this were all the rage. The cafe- and shop-lined gallery modeled after Milan's Galleria Vittorio Emanuele II (p. 475) saw its best days in the years before World War I, but Neapolitans are once again enjoying the pleasures of shopping beneath its glass dome and vaulted wings. If the place works its magic on you, dip into *The Gallery,* a poignant 1947 novel by John Horne Burnes about American GIs in Naples after World War II. Much of its action transpires in the Galleria.
Entrances off Via Toledo, Via Giuseppe Verdi, Via Santa Brigida, and Via San Carlo. Bus: R2 or 151 to Piazza Trieste e Trento. Metro: Municipio.

The airy atrium of the Galleria Umberto I shopping arcade.

Villa Comunale ★★ PARK/GARDEN Time was the public was only allowed into the seaside gardens of the royal family once a year, on September 8, the Festa di Piedigrotta. That changed with the proletarian sentiments that swept in with the unification of Italy in 1869, and a good thing, too. One of the city's great delights is to follow the paths through greenery and past statues and fountains for a kilometer (½ mile) or so from Piazza Vittoria on the east to Piazza della Repubblica on the west. The Bay of Naples shimmers to the south, and many of its denizens—octopi, squid, and sea urchins—now reside in tanks at the Naples Aquarium of the **Anton Dohrn Zoological Station** (fondazione dohrn.it/home/aquarium; ✆ **081/583-3442;** daily 10am–1pm and 4:15–8pm; 7€). A popular **antiques market** takes over a corner of Villa Comunale on the 3rd and 4th weekends of each month from 8:30am to 1pm; contact the tourist office (p. 592) for info.
Piazza Vittoria. Daily 7am–midnight. Bus: C82 or R2.

CENTRO STORICO/SPACCANAPOLI

This warren of narrow lanes and boisterous piazzas is best known as Spaccanapoli (literally, "Naples Splitter," after the street that runs straight through the center of the neighborhood, as it has ever since the Greeks established a colony here). Roughly, the heart of Naples extends north from seaside Castel Nuovo to the Museo Archeologico Nazionale, and east from Via Toledo to the Porta Nolana Fish Market. West of Via Toledo, the Quartieri Spagnoli is a maze of laundry-strung lanes named for the Spanish troops once garrisoned here to subdue the rebellious population.

Cappella Sansevero ★★ MUSEUM Only in Naples would a room as colorful, fanciful, mysterious, beautiful, and macabre as this exist. Prince Raimondo di Sangro of Sansevero remodeled his family's funerary chapel in the 18th century, combining the then-fashionable baroque style with his own love of complex symbolism and intellectual quests. Neapolitan sculptor Giuseppe Sanmartino crafted "Christ Veiled Under a Shroud," in which a thin transparent covering seems to make Christ's flesh look even more tormented. (When Venetian sculptor Antonio Canova came to Naples a century later, he said he would give 10 years of his life to have created something so beautiful.) The prince's father lies beneath a statue of "Despair on Disillusion," in which a man disentangling himself from a marble net suggests a troubled soul seeking relief—provided by the winged boy who represents intellect. Prince Raimondo's mother, who died at age 20, lies beneath a statue of "Veiled Truth," in which a woman holds a broken tablet, symbol of an interrupted life. Raimondo himself is surrounded by colorful floor tiles arranged in a complex maze, symbol of the quest to unravel the secrets of life. Downstairs are the skeletal forms of a man and a woman in which the circulatory systems and musculature are brightly colored, allegedly with the injection of a substance the prince devised. Despite legend, the figures are not the prince's

On a lane in Spaccanapoli, a statue honors the commedia character Pulcinella, a city mascot.

unwilling servants, scarified in the interest of science—they were fashioned from human skeletons and beeswax.

Via Francesco De Sanctis 19 (near Piazza San Domenico Maggiore). www.museosansevero.it. ✆ **081/551-8470.** 8€, 5€ ages 10–25. Wed–Mon 9am–7pm. Audioguide 3:50€. Closed May 1 and Easter Mon. Metro: Dante.

Il Cattedrale di Santa Maria Assunta (Duomo) ★★ CATHEDRAL Three times a year—the first Saturday in May, September 19, and December 16—all of Naples squeezes into the great cathedral that King Carlo I d'Angiò dedicated to San Gennaro, the city's patron saint, in the 13th century. On these dates the saint's dried blood is supposed to liquefy, though sometimes it doesn't—thus foretelling terrible events for Naples, such as an outbreak of the plague in 1528 or the 1980 earthquake that killed 2,000 residents. The rest of the year his blood is kept in a vault inside an altar in the **Cappella di San Gennaro,** the baroque masterpiece of priest-architect Francesco Grimaldi, where a reliquary also houses Gennaro's head, severed from his body around 305. Decorating the chapel was a prize that set Neapolitan artists against one another, with Guido Reni fleeing the city when his assistant was stabbed and Domenichino dropping dead after a poisoning. The Spaniard Jusepe de Ribera (see p. 603), a master of capturing human cruelty, survived to paint "St. Janarius Emerges Unscathed from the Furnace," depicting another of San Gennaro's travails (he was also allegedly thrown to lions, who refused to eat him). Within the cathedral are Naples' two oldest places of worship: The **Cappella di Santa Restituta,** the city's 4th-century basilica, heavily renovated but still supported by a forest of columns from a Greek temple; and the **Cappella di San Giovanni in Fonte,** a 5th-century baptistery; if you crane your neck and squint (binoculars or a telescopic lens come in handy) you can make out the extensive remnants of mosaic scenes in the dome.

Via del Duomo 147. ✆ **081/449097.** Free. Mon–Sat 8:30am–1pm and 3:30–7:30pm; Sun 8:30am–1pm and 4:30–7:30pm. Bus R1. Metro: Cavour or Duomo.

Chiesa del Gesù Nuovo ★ CHURCH The princes of Salerno built what was once their palace in 1470, requesting that the facade be done in *bugnato a punta di diamante,* with stone blocks elaborately cut to create a pattern of projecting points, like cut diamonds. The princes lost the palace a century later thanks to political intrigues, and the Jesuit order bought the property and converted its stately salons into a church. In due time they, too, were evicted, but not before enlivening the interior with opulent frescoes and marble work. Above the doorway inside is a dramatic fresco by Francesco Solimena (1657–1747), a mediocre baroque painter who compensated for his lack of genius with flamboyance—his "Expulsion of Heliodorus from the Temple" is a colorful swirl of flowing draperies and churning robes. The altar of the chapel of the Visitation is the final resting place of Naples' most popular modern saint, Giuseppe Moscati (1880–1927), a devout physician and biochemist famous for his ability to heal impossible cases. The so-called Holy Physician of Naples is believed to still be working miracles: His shrine is often thronged with the ill and injured seeking his help, and it's said that many have been cured on the spot.

Piazza del Gesù. www.gesunuovo.it. ✆ **081/557-8111.** Free. Daily 9am–12:30pm and 5–7:15pm; Sun 8:30am–1:30pm and 4:30–7:30pm. Bus: R1, R2, R3, or R4. Metro: Dante.

Chiesa di San Gregorio Armeno ★★ CHURCH When nuns fleeing persecution in Asia Minor came to Naples in the 8th century, they brought with them the relics of St. Gregory, an Armenian bishop. Over the centuries they built suitable surroundings for the saint, who now rests in a sumptuous baroque church bursting at the seams with gold leaf and elaborate marble carvings. Stepping into the church, described as "a room of paradise on earth," is like walking into one of the elaborate nativity scenes, *presepi,* that vendors sell up and down the street outside (see box p. 614). Seventeenth-century master of the baroque Luca Giordano tells the story of the nuns' flight with their precious cargo in a series of dramatic frescoes. Gregory, however, is upstaged by one of the nuns, Santa Patrizia, whose dried blood is said to liquefy every Tuesday. The beautiful cloisters are an oasis of tranquility; seek them out when the *centro storico* gets to be overwhelming.

Via San Gregorio Armeno 44. ✆ **081/552-0186.** Church free; cloisters 4€. Church 9am–noon (until 1pm on Sun); cloisters Mon–Fri 9:30am–1pm, Sat–Sun 10am–1pm and 3-7pm. Metro: Cavour.

Monastero di Santa Chiara ★★★ CHURCH/GARDEN It's not a good sign in a marriage when a wife's only desire is to become a nun, but that's what Queen Sancha wanted, so Robert of Anjou founded Santa Chiara as a place for his wife to retreat. Their granddaughter, Joan, was crowned queen here in 1343, launching an enlightened reign nonetheless marred by plotting, intrigue, the murder of a husband, and her own demise at age 56, when she was smothered with pillows. Her body was thrown into a deep well on the grounds, and once retrieved, buried in an unmarked grave beneath the church floor. During World War II Allied bombers laid waste to most of the church's frescoes, but a few fragments remain, including biblical scenes by Giotto. Other frescoes line the walls of the delightful lemon-scented cloisters, where columns and benches are covered in colorful Mallorca tiles depicting landscapes, hunting parties, dancers, and other snippets of the good life in 18th-century Naples—surprisingly worldly and frivolous, considering that for 200 years or so the cloisters were enjoyed only by cloistered nuns. This is one of the most refreshing corners of Naples, and well worth the admission fee if you've been walking around the city and need a little peace and quiet.

Via Santa Chiara 49. ✆ **081/797-1235.** Church free; cloisters 6€. Church Mon–Sat 8am–12:45pm and 4:30–8pm; cloisters Mon–Sat 9:30am–5:30pm, Sun 10am–2:30pm. Metro: Dante.

BAD BOY WITH A brush

The painter Caravaggio arrived in Naples in 1606, fleeing authorities in Rome after he killed a man in a fight over a debt. With his taste for gambling, prostitutes, young boys, rowdiness, and drunkenness, the tempestuous artist must have felt right at home in Naples. The city was then the second largest in Europe after Paris, with 350,000 inhabitants, more than a few of whom shared Caravaggio's reckless disposition. His sumptuous canvases, with their realistic human figures and dramatic use of light, have become emblematic of the city's emotion-filled baroque style.

Three major Caravaggio works are in Naples. The dark, moody, and chaotic "Seven Acts of Mercy" altarpiece is in the chapel of the **Pio Monte della Misericordia,** Via Tribunali 253 (www.piomontedellamisericordia.it; ✆ **081/446-944;** Metro: Dante), a fraternity founded by nobles in 1601 to loan money to the poor. Try to identify the various acts of mercy—St. Martin in the foreground giving his cloak to the beggar is easy (clothing the naked)—and you'll probably only detect six. But look again at the scene of the old man sucking at the breast of the young woman: That counts as two, visiting prisoners and feeding the hungry. (Classicists identify the pair as the Roman Cimon, who was sentenced to death by starvation, and his daughter, Pero, who secretly suckled him, an act of family honor that won him his release.) While you're here, look at the painting gallery upstairs: It features works by the so-called Cabal of Naples, a notorious trio of painters—Belisario Corenzio, Jusepe de Ribera, and Battistello Caracciolo—who were known to harass or even poison their competitors and destroy the works of rivals who won commissions they thought were rightfully theirs. Admission to the chapel and gallery is 9.50€ (Mon–Sat 10am–6pm, Sun 9am–2:30pm; last admissions 1 hr. before closing).

In the **Capodimonte gallery** (p. 604), Caravaggio's "Flagellation of Christ" depicts two brutish tormentors whipping a nearly naked Christ; a third one in the foreground is preparing his scourge to join in the action. Lighting emphasizes the flailing arms and Christ's twisted, suffering body; it's a visceral depiction of cruelty in action, and one of two flagellation scenes Caravaggio painted while in Naples.

The "Martyrdom of St. Ursula" hangs in the **Palazzo Zevallos Stigliano** (Via Toledo 185; www.gallerieditalia.com; ✆ **800/454-229;** Metro: Montesanto), today the lavish headquarters of the Banco Intesa Sanpaolo. Ursula appears unfazed as the king of the Huns—whose marriage proposal she has just refused—shoots an arrow into her breast at point-blank range. (As legend has it, the 11,000 virginal handmaidens accompanying Ursula had just been beheaded, so she couldn't have been too surprised that her jilted suitor was displeased). Caravaggio himself looks on from the background. This was his last painting and the last image we have of him—he died of fever while returning to Rome a couple of months later. Admission to the Palazzo is 7€ (Tues–Fri 10am–6:30pm; Sat–Sun 10am–7:30pm).

Museo d'Arte Contemporanea Donnaregina (MADRE) ★ ART MUSEUM In the middle of medieval and baroque Naples, the **Palazzo Regina** provides a dramatic counterpoint with works by contemporary artists such as Anish Kapoor and Richard Serra. Painter Francesco Clemente, who was born in Naples, decorated two rooms in colorful tile floors and frescoes replicating ancient symbols of the city. Conceptual sculptor Kapoor transformed a room into a white cube with rich blue pigments on the floor that seem to draw you into the bowels of the earth; he also designed the entrance to the Monte S. Angelo subway station to resemble Dante's entrance to the underworld (perhaps sympathizing with riders that commuting can be hell). Across town, the **Palazzo delle Arti Napoli** (**PAN;** Via dei Mille 60; www.comune.napoli.it; ✆ **081/795-8604**) houses rotating exhibits of contemporary art.

Via Settembrini 79. www.madrenapoli.it. ✆ **081/1931-3016.** 8€. Mon and Wed–Sat 10am–7:30pm; Sun 10am–8pm. Bus: E1. Metro: Cavour.

National Archaeological Museum (Museo Archeologico Nazionale) ★★★ MUSEUM The echoey, dusty, gloomy galleries of the rundown Palazzo degli Studi provide one of the world's great time-travel experiences, back to the ancient world. Two treasure troves in particular should not be missed.

The Ercole (Hercules) Farnese.

On the mezzanine and upper floors are **mosaics, frescoes, and bronzes excavated from Pompeii and Herculaneum.** Seeing these everyday objects from villas and shops hauntingly brings the ruined cities to life. Some, such as baking equipment and signage, are quite mundane, touchingly so; many, such as the bronze statues of the "Dancing Faun" (on the mezzanine), the "Drunken Faun" (top floor), and five life-size female bronzes known as "Dancers" (top floor) show off sophisticated artistry. Most of the mosaics, on the mezzanine, are from the House of Faun, one of the largest residences in Pompeii. The million-plus-piece floor mosaic, "Alexander Fighting the Persians," depicts the wavy-haired king of Macedonia astride Bucephalos, the most famous steed in antiquity, sweeping into battle against King Darius III of Persia, who's looking a bit concerned in his chariot. The **Gabinetto Segreto** (Secret Room; also on the mezzanine) displays some of the erotica that was commonplace in Pompeii. Some works are from brothels, among them frescoes that show acts lively yet predictable and some bestial, and others include phallus-shaped oil lamps and huge phalluses placed at doorways to bring fertility and good fortune. We might titter at the bulges under togas, but they weren't necessarily intended to be pornography and rather suggest the libertine attitudes of the time.

The superb **Farnese Collection** of Roman sculpture shows off the pieces snapped up by the enormously wealthy Roman Cardinal Alessandro Farnese, later Pope Paul III (1543–1549), who was at the top of the Renaissance game of antiquity hunting. His remarkable collection was inherited by Elisabetta Farnese, who married Philip V of Spain and whose son and grandson became kings of Naples and brought the collection here in the 18th century. Among Cardinal Farnese's great prizes was the **Ercole Farnese,** a huge statue of Hercules unearthed at the Baths of Caracalla in Rome. The superhero son of Zeus looks tuckered out, leaning on his club after completing his eleventh labor, and who can blame him? After slaying monsters and subduing beasts, he's just learned he has to go back into the fray, descend into Hell, and bring back Cerberus, the three-headed canine guardian. It's a magnificent piece, powerful and wonderfully human. Carved out of one piece of marble, the colossal **Toro Farnese,** 4m (13-ft.) high, the world's largest-known sculpture from antiquity, was also unearthed at the Baths of Caracalla. Cardinal Farnese hired a team of Renaissance masters, Michelangelo among them, to restore it. The intricate and delicate work depicts one of mythology's most satisfying acts of revenge, when the twin brothers Amphion and Zethus tied Dirce—who had imprisoned and mistreated their mother, Antiope—to the horns of a bull that will drag her to her death.

Piazza Museo 19. www.museoarcheologiconapoli.it. ✆ **081/4422111.** 18€; under 18 2€. Daily 9am–7:30pm. Metro: Museo or Cavour.

San Lorenzo Maggiore ★★ CHURCH The most beautiful of Naples' medieval churches seems to inspire great literature. Petrarch, the medieval master of Italian verse, lived in the adjoining convent in 1345, and it was here on Holy Saturday 1338 that Boccaccio (author of *The Decameron*) supposedly first laid eyes on his muse, Maria d'Aquino. The daughter of a count (but rumored to have been the illegitimate daughter of Robert of Anjou, king of Naples), Maria was married but preferred refuge in a convent to life with her debauched husband. For Boccaccio, it was love at first sight; he nicknamed her La Fiammetta (Little Flame), wooed her with his romantic epic *Filocolo,* and eventually convinced her to become his mistress (she jilted him for another man a few years later). Ponder 14th-century romance as you stroll the delightful cloisters, then descend a staircase to witness more of the city's multilayered history: Excavations have unearthed streets from the Greco-Roman city Neapolis, lined with bakeries and shops, a covered market, and an early Christian basilica.

Piazza San Gaetano, Via Tribunali 316. www.laneapolissotterrata.it. ✆ **081/211-0860.** Church free. Daily 9:30am–5:30pm. Excavations 9€, 7€ over 65, 6€ under 18. Daily guided tours in English at 11am, 1:15, 3:15, and and 5pm. Metro: Cavour.

underground NAPLES

Beneath Naples' city streets is a labyrinth of tunnels, age-old cisterns, and Greek and Roman ruins that you can explore on four tours. The **Galleria Borbonica ★★** (Bourbon Tunnel), usually entered through a parking garage at Via Morelli 61 (www.galleriaborbonica.com; ✆ **366/248-4151**) was engineered for mid-19th-century Bourbon royals as an escape route from the Palazzo Reale to military barracks near the port, maneuvering around ancient and medieval waterworks. The 1½-hour guided tour costs 15€ (10€ ages 10–13; children under 10 not admitted) and runs Friday to Sunday at 10am, noon, 3pm, and 5pm. See website for any other tour times and prices**. Napoli Sotterranea Tour Ufficiale ★★**, usually leaving from the Gran Caffè Gambrinus on Piazza Trieste e Trento (www.lanapolisotterranea.it; ✆ **081/400-256**), explores the huge cisterns Romans dug beneath the city, which were used well into the 19th century, until cholera outbreaks necessitated purer sources. Parts of the cistern network were used as quarries and as World War II bomb shelters (some wartime furnishings and graffiti remain). Tours last about 1 hour and include English commentary. Exit points vary, but usually you climb out of the dark up a long staircase and emerge into the courtyard of an ordinary-looking apartment house—a good illustration of this city's age-spanning layers. Aside from climbing stairs, you'll also be asked to squeeze through a very tight passage (not recommended for the claustrophobic or the overweight). The guided tour, which is usually in English, costs 10€ (8€ children under 10) and takes place daily at 10am, noon, 2pm, and 4:30pm (plus 6pm Sat). **Napoli Sotterranea Percorso Ufficiale ★★**, Piazza San Gaetano 58 (www.napolisotterranea.org; ✆ **081 296944**), shows off the diverse city that lies beneath the streets of the historic center with a tour of Greek waterworks, a Greco-Roman theater, and more World War II air-raid shelters. The guided tour costs 15€ (10€ children under 10), with tours in English at 10am, noon, 2pm, 4pm, and 6pm. Across the square, more ruins of Greco-Roman Neapolis can be explored beneath the church of **San Lorenzo Maggiore** (see p. 601).

VOMERO

Life in Naples never really becomes *too* gentrified, but it calms down a bit in the hilltop enclave of the Napoli *bene* (the city's middle and upper classes). The trip up here from the center is on the Centrale and Montesanto funiculars.

Certosa e Museo di San Martino (Carthusian Monastery) ★★

The Carthusian monks who took up residence high atop the Vomero hill in 1368 obviously knew something of the good life. Their view is still the best in Naples, across the city and the bay to Mt. Vesuvius. Over the centuries they hired the city's best artists to embellish their environs. Foremost among them, the fractious architect and sculptor Cosimo Fanzago (1591–1678) created the pièce de la resistance, an enormous central courtyard/cloisters that is a masterpiece of the baroque, a grand assemblage of statue-lined porticoes facing a broad lawn. Lest the monks got too comfortable in their earthly surroundings, a gallery of skulls reminded them of their inevitable fate. As if to reinforce the point, in surrounding chapels the Spanish painter Jusepe de Ribera (1591–1652) executed ghoulish scenes of martyrdom and suffering, so realistically portrayed with wounds, wrinkles, and writhing agony that he's been said to partake in "the poetry of the repulsive." As you wander the vast monastery, now housing the **Museo Nazionale di San Martino ★★**, it's easy to see why royal administrators were so appalled by the monks' lavish lifestyle that they threatened to cut off state subsidies.

The museum is a repository of all things Neapolitan: paintings, prints, sculpture, artifacts, and the *presepi* (Nativity scenes) for which the city has an undying affection (see box p. 614). None outshine the 750-piece Cuciniello Presepe, equipped with a lighting system that simulates the cycle of a day from dusk to nightfall. Even larger is the full-size model of the Great Barge used by King Charles of Bourbon in the 1700s, housed amid models and artifacts that honor the city's role as a maritime power. The Gothic cellars are filled with sculpture, including an astonishing St. Francis of Assisi by Giuseppe Sanmartino, who so artfully crafted "Christ Veiled Under a Shroud" in the Cappella Sansevero (p. 596).

An elaborately decorated ceiling at the Certosa di San Martino, once a monastery, now a museum.

Largo San Martino 8. cultura.gov.it/luogo/certosa-e-museo-di-san-martino. ✆ **081/578-1769.** 6€. Thurs–Tues 8:30am–7pm; ticket booth closes 1 hr. earlier. Closed Jan 1 and Dec 25. Metro: Vanvitelli and then bus V1 to Piazzale San Martino. Bus: C28, C31, or C36 to Piazza Vanvitelli. Funicular: Centrale to Piazza Fuga or Montesanto to Morghen.

Villa La Floridiana & Museo Nazionale della Ceramica Duca di Martina ★★ MUSEUM When King Ferdinand I returned to Naples in 1815 after 10 years of exile, he brought with him an Italian/Spanish wife, Lucia Migliaccio, the duchess of Floridia. Their wedding, just months after the death of Ferdinand's first wife, Queen Marina Carolina of Austria, created an international scandal. The duchess did not care for court life or for Naples, and Neapolitans didn't care for her, so Ferdinand bought her this magnificent retreat on the Vomero hill with gardens and views that would make anyone surrender to the city's charms. The villa now houses the 6,000-plus ceramics collection of another noble Neapolitan, Placido de Sangro, the duke of Martina. Items of interest include King Ferdinand's walking stick, with a glass top that contains a portrait of Lucia; it was said this was the only way the queen would ever appear in court.

Admission to the gardens is free, and though a bit ramshackle these days, they're green and luxuriant and you can follow a path through them from the villa to a viewpoint overlooking the city.

Via Cimarosa 77. www.beniculturali.it/luogo/museo-della-ceramica-duca-di-martina-in-villa-floridiana. ✆ **081/578-8418.** Museum 4€; gardens free. Wed–Mon 9:30am–5pm. Bus: C28, C32, or C36. Funicular: Chiaia to Cimarosa. Metro: Vanvitelli.

FARTHER AFIELD

Catacombs of San Gennaro ★ RELIGIOUS SITE Naples' popular patron San Gennaro (St. Januarius) was once buried here, forever lending his name to this multistory underground cemetery, used from the 2nd through 11th centuries. Some of the city's earliest frescoes include one depicting a haloed San Gennaro with Mt. Vesuvius on his shoulders, and a charming 2nd-century scene with Adam and Eve. Guides (most speak English) will lead you past the frescoed burial niches and early basilicas carved from the tufa rock, providing fascinating insights into the city's long past—with a special nod to Sant'Agrippino, a 3rd-century bishop once interred here, who is almost as popular among Neapolitans as San Gennaro. As you emerge from the lower level of this city of the dead you'll be in the lively Rione Sanità quarter, very much a world of the living. In the 16th and 17th centuries, Neapolitans who became ill were banished to this neighborhood to protect the health of those living within the city walls. Later it was home to early-18th-century architect Ferdinando San Felice, who built the elegant Palazzo dello Spagnolo at 19 Via Vergini; step inside the courtyard for a look at his magnificent double staircase.

Via Capodimonte 13. www.catacombedinapoli.it. ✆ **081/744-3714.** 11€; 7€ students and over 65; 5€ under 18; free for children under 6. Tours (in English) daily on the hour 10am–5pm. Bus: 168, 178,C63, or R4 (from the Archaeological Museum).

National Museum & Gallery of the Capodimonte ★ MUSEUM Italy has many better art collections, but there's plenty to lure you out to this former hunting preserve of the Bourbon kings—the *bosco reale* (royal woods) is one of the few parks in Naples, and sharing the greenery with picnicking families can be refreshing. The core of the collection is from Elisabetta Farnese, duchess of Parma, who handed down the family's paintings to her children and grandchildren after she became Queen of Spain; they in turn brought them back to Italy when they became kings of Naples. By the time the works got here, however, many of the best had found their way into other collections; what's left tends to be secondary works by a roster of Italian and Northern masters. In fact, the museum's two standout pieces have nothing to do with the Farneses: Caravaggio's dramatic "Flagellation of Christ" (see p. 599), which was brought here in the 1970s, and in the contemporary galleries, Andy Warhol's "Mount Vesuvius," a comic-book-like depiction of an eruption in gaudy modern colors. In the Royal Apartments there's enough Sèvres and Meissen china to serve a royal feast of epic proportions. Capodimonte ceramics were fired right here on the grounds throughout the 18th century.

Palazzo Capodimonte, Via Miano 1; also through the park from Via Capodimonte. www.museocapodimonte.beniculturali.it. ✆ **081/749-9111.** 12€. Thurs–Tues 8:30am–7:30pm. Bus: 168, 178, C63, R4 (from the Archaeological Museum).

Reggia di Caserta (Royal Palace of Caserta) Museum & Gallery of the Capodimonte ★★★ PALACE The 18th-century Bourbon kings of Naples intended their royal residence to impress, and the largest palace in the world still awes visitors. The Royal Apartments in the 1,200-room showplace are reached by sweeping staircases and awash in marbles and frescoes, but the pièce de résistance lies beyond the tall windows: Versailles-like gardens stretching for 3km (2 miles) and laced with pools, fountains, and forests of rare trees, the perfect setting for an easy day out from Naples.

Piazza Carlo di Borbone, Caserta, 35km (21 miles) N of Naples. reggiadicaserta.cultura.gov.it. ✆ **0823/448084.** 14€. 9€ park only, 10€ Royal Apartments only. Wed–Mon 8:30am–7pm (Royal Apartments until 7:30pm); gardens until 3:30pm Dec and Jan, 4:30pm in Feb and Nov, 5pm in Mar, 5:30 in Oct. Frequent train service from Naples Central Station to Caserta; the station is just outside the palace gates.

Where to Stay in Naples

Where you stay in Naples makes a difference. You want a safe neighborhood close to the sights, and our suggestions below meet that criterion.

EXPENSIVE

Grand Hotel Parker's ★★ Naples' oldest grand hotel has been welcoming guests since 1870, when Prince Grifeo decided to transform his palace into a posh stopover where travelers on the Grand Tour could enjoy a bit of Neapolitan luxury. The name comes from British naturalist George Bidder Parker, who bought the enterprise in 1899 while working on the gardens in the Villa Comunale (see p. 595). Through wars, earthquakes, and other ups and downs the tradition continues, and this gracious old place on a hillside above the bay is still all about quiet refinement. Lounges are floored with rich marble and hung with a museum-worthy art collection, while the stylish guest rooms all open to balconies and are soothingly done with both traditional and contemporary touches. Choicest rooms overlook the bay, but all guests can enjoy the views from an airy top-floor lounge and dining area and an expansive roof terrace.

Corso Vittorio Emanuele 135. www.grandhotelparkers.it. ✆ **081/761–2474.** 82 units. 310€–370€ double. Rates include breakfast. Garage parking 25€. Bus: 128. Metro: Amedeo. Montesanto or Centrale funiculars to Corso Vittorio Emanuele. **Amenities:** Restaurant; 2 bars; room service; spa; roof terrace; free Wi-Fi.

Grand Hotel Vesuvio ★★ Old-world glamour holds sway in this famed waterfront hostelry, which pampers the rich and famous with a Grand Tour–worthy experience plus all the 21st-century amenities, including a spiffy spa. Expanses of shiny parquet, handsome old prints, fine

Balcony view of the Castel dell'Ovo from the Grand Hotel Vesuvio.

linens on firm beds, and classic furnishings give the large, very comfortable rooms sophisticated-yet-understated polish. The big perk, though, is the view of the bay, the Castel dell'Ovo, and Mt. Vesuvius through glass doors that open to balconies off many rooms. You'll get the same eyeful from the rooftop restaurant and the bright lounge where a lavish breakfast buffet is served.

Via Partenope 45 (off Via Santa Lucia by Castel dell'Ovo). www.vesuvio.it. ✆ **081/764-0044.** 160 units. 375€–430€ double. Most rates include breakfast. Bus: 152, 140, or C25. **Amenities:** 2 restaurants; bar; fitness center; indoor pool (fee); room service; spa; free Wi-Fi.

MODERATE

Art Resort Gallery Umberto ★ The location is already dramatic enough, but this upper floor of accommodations in the city's 1890s Art Nouveau–style glass shopping arcade (see p. 595) adds plush, over-the-top interiors. The painted headboards, swag draperies, and gilded furniture may not be for minimalists, but it's hard to beat the theatricality and location. Many of the rooms face the interior of the *galleria,* just below the glass roof, so they are quite bright; others look out over an adjoining piazzetta, while a choice few have little balconies. All guests can enjoy the large interior terrace high above the tile-floored arcades.

Galleria Umberto 1. www.artresortgalleriaumberto.com. ✆ **081/497-6224.** 16 units. 120€–170€ double. Rates include breakfast. Bus: R2. **Amenities:** Bar; concierge; free Wi-Fi.

Chiaja Hotel de Charme ★★ With its bright shops and bars, spiffy, pedestrian-only Via Chiaia may be the city's friendliest address, and this warmly decorated inn in an old noble residence does the location justice. Some smaller rooms face interior courtyards and have snug, shower-only bathrooms, while many larger ones on the street side (with double panes to keep the noise down) have large bathrooms with Jacuzzi tubs. Decor throughout is sufficiently traditional and regal to suggest the *palazzo's* aristocratic provenance, and services are more wholesome than they were when the place was an upscale brothel. Pastries and snacks are laid out in the sitting room in the afternoon and evening, the buffet breakfast is generous, and the staff is adept at recommending restaurants and providing directions. Via Chiaia 216. www.chiaiahotel.com. ✆ **081/415-555.** 33 units. 90€–135€ double. Rates include breakfast. Bus: R2. **Amenities:** Bar; concierge; Wi-Fi (free in lobby and some rooms).

Costantinopoli 104 ★★ Set in a palm-shaded courtyard, this 19th-century Art Nouveau palace is mere steps from the archaeological museum but a world away from the noisy city—it even has a small swimming pool. Contemporary art and some stunning stained glass grace a series of salons; some rooms are traditionally done with rich fabrics and dark wood furnishings, others are breezily contemporary. The choicest are on the top floor and open onto a sprawling roof terrace—a magical retreat above the rooftops and definitely what you should ask for when booking. Via Santa Maria di Costantinopoli 104 (off Piazza Bellini). www.costantinopoli104.it. ✆ **081/557-1035.** 19 units. 135€–220€ double. Rates include breakfast. Metro: Museo. **Amenities:** Pool; room service; free Wi-Fi.

Decumani Hotel de Charme ★★ The heart-of-Naples neighborhood beyond the grand entrance can be gritty, but these are sprucely regal lodgings, on the piano nobile of the *palazzo* of the last bishop of the Bourbon kingdom, Cardinal Sisto Riario Sforza. Guest rooms surround a vast, frescoed ballroom-cum-breakfast room; all have plush draperies and fabrics and a few antiques complementing hardwood floors and timbered ceilings. Larger rooms include sitting areas and face the quiet courtyard, while many of the smaller, street-facing doubles share small terraces. Via San Giovanni Maggiore Pignatelli 15 (off Via Benedetto Croce, btw. vias Santa Chiara and Mezzocannone). www.decumani.com. ✆ **081/551-8188.** 22 units. 100€–135€ double. Rates include breakfast. Metro: Dante. **Amenities:** Free Wi-Fi.

Decumani Hotel de Charme's elegant breakfast room.

Hotel Piazza Bellini ★★★ The archaeological museum and lively Piazza Bellini are just outside the door of this centuries-old palace, but a cool contemporary redo softens the edges of city life. An outdoor living room fills the cobbled courtyard, and the rooms, which range across several floors, are minimalist chic with hardwood floors, neutral tones and warm-hued accents, sleek surfaces, and plenty of space for storage, plus Philippe Starck chairs and crisp white linens. Some of the rooms have terraces and balconies, a few are bi-level, and some with limited views are set aside as "economy"—but rates for any room in the house are a good value.

Via Costantinipoli 101. www.hotelpiazzabellini.com. ✆ **081/451-732.** 48 units. 90€–145€ double. Rates include breakfast. Metro: Dante or Cavour. **Amenities:** Bar; concierge; free Wi-Fi.

San Francesco al Monte ★★ This ex-Franciscan convent just above the Spanish quarter and halfway up the San Martino hill makes the monastic life seem pretty appealing. The friars left behind a chapel, a refectory, secret stairways, and lots of atmospheric nooks and crannies, while their cells have been combined into large tiled guest rooms and sprawling suites. Views from all rooms and several airy lounges sweep across the city to the bay. The hillside location is a handy refuge above the fray but an easy walk or funicular ride away from the sights. In the sprawling rooftop garden, vine-shaded walkways are carved out of the cliff side; a swimming pool and outdoor bar on these heights are welcome perks in summer.

Corso Vittorio Emanuele 328. www.sanfrancescoalmonte.it. ✆ **081/423-9111.** 45 units. 145€–210€ double. Rates include breakfast. Metro: Amedeo. Montesanto or Centrale funiculars to Corso Vittorio Emanuele. **Amenities:** Restaurant; bar; pool; room service; free Wi-Fi.

INEXPENSIVE

BnB Naples ★★ Native Neapolitan Elia has gone into the hospitality business with flair, converting his law offices on two upper floors of an old palace near the port into a welcoming little inn. His seven rooms are large and bright, with high ceilings, huge windows opening to balconies in some, and plenty of fine old woodwork and finishes; contemporary furnishings are sparse but comfortable and geared to convenience, with good work spaces, ample lighting, and plenty of room to spread out and lounge. Bathrooms are crisp and up to date. The location, just off Piazza Municipio, is prime for sightseeing, with the port, historic center, and Santa Lucia seafront all an easy walk away, and Elia is pleased to suggest ways to go about taking it all in. Modern conveniences aside, an old Neapolitan institution remains—the cage elevator operates on .10€ coins, so arrive with change in your pocket.

Via Medina 17. www.bnbnaples.com. ✆ **081/551-9978.** 7 units. 70€–110€ double. Rates include breakfast at a nearby bar. Metro: Municipio. **Amenities:** Free Wi-Fi.

Correra 241 ★ Follow a narrow side street, enter the rear courtyard of an old palazzo, and walk up a ramp into a former factory tucked into a tufa cliff. Old workrooms and storage lofts have been converted into cheery lodgings furnished with contemporary flair. Yellow concrete floors, rock walls, colorful artwork, even an Etruscan-Greco aqueduct leading off the lobby, befit a city legendary for its quirky pockets. There's no such thing as standard accommodations here: Some rooms are lit by skylights only, others by windows high on double-height walls, and still others are two-story—ask about your room's distinct features when you book. You'll be only steps from the archaeological museum, but that rear courtyard setting lets you enjoy a rare amenity in Naples: quiet.

Via Correra 241. www.correra.it. © **081/1956-2842.** 21 units. 80€–130€ double (2-night minimum stay required some periods). Rates include breakfast. Parking 20€. Metro: Dante or Museo. **Amenities:** Bar; free Wi-Fi.

Hotel Il Convento ★★ If you want to experience a slice of Neapolitan life—as in laundry flapping outside your window—but also enjoy creature comforts, this is the place for you. While the narrow Spagnoli streets outside teem with neighborhood color and bustle, a 17th-century former convent provides cozy ambience, with lots of wood beams, brick arches, and terra-cotta floors. Two rooms have their own planted rooftop terraces, and two others spread over two levels. Main artery Via Toledo is just 2 short blocks away, taking the edge off of comings and goings at night. An eager staff will steer you to neighborhood restaurants and shops. Small pets are allowed.

Via Speranzella 137/A. www.hotelilconvento.it. © **081/403-977.** 14 units. 80€–130€. Rates include breakfast. Metro: Toledo or Municipio. **Amenities:** Bar; fitness room and sauna; room service; free Wi-Fi.

IStayinToledo ★★★ Fabio and Dario's light-filled apartment- turned-guesthouse is a welcome retreat smack dab in the center of Naples, right above the stunningly designed Toledo metro station. This location puts you a short subway ride away from the main train station and much of what you want to see within easy walking distance. The brick 1920s-era Rationalist-style apartment and office block is itself a landmark, and the commodious, light-filled rooms are immaculately kept and chicly furnished, each one named for its distinctive color scheme and all surrounding an airy lounge that opens to a corner balcony overlooking the comings and goings on Via Toledo. Breakfast, included in some rates, is served at a friendly cafe downstairs.

Via Amando Diaz 8. istayintoledo.it. © **339/187-2920**. 6 units. 90€–110€ double. Most rates include breakfast. **Amenities:** Free Wi-Fi.

Tredici Boutique Rooms ★★★ Brothers Andrea and Mattia Tredici fashioned their welcoming and luxurious guesthouse from an old apartment in the historical center, paying attention to every arch and beam to create comfortable and distinctive lodgings. The large, attractive rooms are equipped with minibars, excellent beds topped off with down comforters and pillows, soothing lighting, plenty of storage, and spiffy bathrooms equipped with walk-in showers; one room sports a soaking tub. The brothers treat their guests with the same care they've lavished on the premises, and they are on hand with advice on dining, transport, sights, and anything else you need to know.

Via dei Carrozzieri a Monteoliveto 29. tredici-boutique-rooms. ✆ **339/ 694-0525.** 3 units. 65€–95€ double. Most rates include breakfast. **Amenities:** Free Wi-Fi.

Where to Eat in Naples

What's not to like about a cuisine in which pizza is closely entwined with city history? **Antica Pizzeria Port d'Alba,** Via Port Alba 18 (anticapizzeriaportalba.com; ✆ **081/459713**), where ovens are lined with rocks from Mt. Vesuvius, claims to be the world's first pizzeria, established in 1738. D'Alba was once known for its generous (alas, erstwhile) *pizza a otto* payment system, by which patrons could pay 8 days after eating—making it *the* place to enjoy a free last meal, provided you died before payment was due. **Pizzeria Brandi,** Salita S. Anna di Palazzo 1/2 (www.brandi.it; ✆ **081/416928**), is famously the birthplace of the pizza Margherita, created in 1889 for Margherita, Queen of Savoy; topped with mozzarella, tomato sauce, and basil, its colors mimicking the Italian flag.

Other iconic Neapolitan dishes include *mozzarella in carrozza* (fried mozzarella in a "carriage"), in which mozzarella is fried between two pieces of bread and topped with a sauce of the chef's design, often with

Campania is famous for its pizza.

The Wines of Campania

The wines produced in the harsh, hot landscapes of Campania seem stronger, rougher, and, in many cases, more powerful than those grown in gentler climes. Ones to try are *Lacryma Christi* (Tears of Christ), from grapes that grow in the volcanic soil on the slopes of Mt. Vesuvius; *Taurasi,* a potent, full-bodied red also known as *Aglianico;* and *Greco di Tufo,* a pungent white laden with the odors of apricots and apples. *Falanghina,* one of the most popular white wine varieties, is produced from the famed Falernian grapes favored by the ancient Romans. Another varietal of special interest is fruity *Piedirosso,* a dark red grape that is famously grown on the slopes of Vesuvius and the isle of Capri.

tomatoes and capers; *gnocchi alla sorrentina,* pockets of potato pasta filled with mozzarella and topped with tomato sauce; *ragu,* a meat sauce cooked for hours and served atop pasta; *parmigiana di melanzane* (eggplant parmesan), the ubiquitous dish of fried eggplant, tomato sauce, mozzarella, *parmigiano,* and basil; *crocchè di patate* (fried potatoes), mashed with herbs, cheese, sometimes salami, lightly coated in breadcrumbs and fried; and *pasta e fagioli,* beans and pasta—nothing could be more Neapolitan. *Cozze* (mussels), often served *alla marinara* (simmered in tomato sauce), and *polpette,* succulent little meatballs, abound.

EXPENSIVE

Rosiello ★★★ NEAPOLITAN/SEAFOOD It's a cab ride or long bus trip out to this retreat on a hilltop above the sea in swanky and leafy Posillipo, but ask your hotel to make reservations and help arrange transport, because a meal on the terrace here is one of the city's great treats. Everything comes from the sea at your feet or the restaurant's extensive vegetable plots on the hillside; even the cheese is local. These ingredients find their way into feasts that might include risotto *alla pescatora* (with seafood) and *pezzogna all'acquapazza* (fish in a light tomato broth), but even a simple pasta here, such as *scialatielli con melanzane e provola* (fresh pasta with local cheese and eggplant), is elegant and simply delicious.
Via Santo Strato 10. www.ristoranterosiello.it. ✆ **081/574-2341.** Entrees 10€–25€. Thurs–Tues noon–4pm and 7pm–midnight. Closed 2 weeks Jan and Aug. Bus: C3 to Mergellina (end of line), and then 140.

MODERATE

Europeo di Mattozzi ★★ NEAPOLITAN/PIZZA/SEAFOOD Many Neapolitans rank this attractive center-of-town eatery as a favorite, and the walls covered with copper pots, framed photos, and oil paintings suggest that a meal here is a carefully curated experience. Pizzas are traditional starters, while some excellent alternatives include *zuppa di cannellini e cozze* (bean and mussel soup) or *pasta e patate con provola* (pasta and potatoes with melted cheese). Seafood *secondi* are the house specialties, including *ricciola all'acquapazza* (a local species in a light tomato and herb broth) and *stoccafisso alla pizzaiola* (dried codfish in a tomato, garlic, and oregano sauce). Reservations are a must on weekends.

Via Marchese Campodisola 4. www.ristorantemattozzi.it. ✆ **081/552-1323.** Entrees 12€–18€. Mon–Sat 12:30–3:30pm and 7:30–11pm (until 11:30pm Sat). Closed 2 weeks Aug. Bus: R2 or R3 to Piazza Trieste e Trento. Metro: Municipio or Dante.

Mimi alla Ferrovia ★★★ SEAFOOD/NEAPOLITAN Emilio (Mimi) Giugliano must have been an optimist, opening what is now a beloved institution in 1943, when Naples was in the grips of World War II. Paintings from that time still adorn the elegantly plain rooms on a gritty side street near the train station, where a fourth generation now prepares variations of the original dishes, many of them almost legendary—ravioli with sea bass, a succulent *bacala,* and to start any meal, roasted peppers stuffed with ham and cheese and lightly fried.

Via Alfonso D'Aragona 19–21. www.mimiallaferrovia.it. ✆ **081/553-8525.** Entrees 8€–16€. Mon–Sat noon–3:30pm and 7–11pm. Metro: Garibaldi.

Tandem ★★ NEAPOLITAN Take a seat in the simple room or on the pleasant little terrace on the lane outside and linger over the house specialty, *ragù.* A lot of locals stop by this friendly, funky little spot for their fix of the city staple, which comes with meat (three or four kinds, slow-cooked) or vegetarian (including a delicious version with smoky eggplant), served over a choice of pastas or by itself with thick slices of bread for dunking, along with carafes of the house wine. If there's a long wait, as there often is, you might have better chances of getting a table at the Tandem outlet a few blocks away on Piazza del Gesù Nuovo.

Via Paladino 51. tandemnapoli.it. ✆ **081/1900-2468.** Entrees 8€–18€. Daily 11–11pm. Metro: Dante.

Umberto ★★★ NEAPOLITAN This Chiaia neighborhood favorite has been going strong for a century. Founder Umberto Di Porzio is commemorated in one of the many dishes his heirs continue to serve—*tubettoni 'do tre dita* ("three-finger") pasta with octopus, tomato, olives, and capers (Umberto lost two fingers in a hunting accident). The family atmosphere befits such other homey classics as eggplant *parmigiana* and spaghetti

THE BEST pizza IN NAPLES

According to about half the residents of Naples, no-frills, zero-ambience **L'Antica Pizzeria Da Michele ★★★**, Via Sersale 1 (www.damichele.net; ✆ **081/553-9204;** Metro Piazza Garibaldi), serves the best pizzas in town—they come in just two varieties, *margherita* or *marinara* (toppings are for snobs, say the guys behind the counter). The other half would vote for **Pizzeria Gino e Toto Sorbillo ★★★,** Via Tribunali 32 (www.sorbillo.it, ✆ **081/446-643;** Metro Dante), where a long menu of pizzas with toppings is accompanied by a palatable house wine. At both, prepare to wait for a table, but not for long, as pizzas emerge from the ovens in a mere 20 seconds, an act of wizardry that keeps the tables turning quickly. At both, pizzas are 5€ to 7€; Michele is closed on Sunday.

GO OFF YOUR diet

To eat like a Neapolitan, you just may have to set healthy habits aside. Clam-shaped *sfogliatelle*, filled with ricotta cream, is the city's unofficial pastry, available at bars and bakeries all over the city. *Il baba* are little cakes soaked in rum or limoncello syrup and often filled with cream; *delizia al limone* is sponge cake soaked with lemon or limoncello syrup, filled with lemon pastry cream, and iced with lemon-flavored whipped cream. Dark, flourless *torta* Caprese, topped with powdered sugar, is the chocolate cake of choice. For the classic coffee-and-a-pastry experience, try **Scaturchio,** Piazza San Domenico Maggiore 19 (www.scaturchio.it; ✆ **081/551-7031**); **Sfogliatella Mary** in the Galleria Umberto I (✆ **081/402-218**); and **Il Vero Bar del Professore** at Piazza Trieste e Trento 46 (www.ilverobardelprofessore.com; ✆ **081/403-041**).

For some of Italy's best gelato, **Gelateria della Scimmia,** Piazza della Carità 4 (www.gelateriadellascimmia.it; ✆ **081/5520272**), is a mandatory stop. Naples' elegant temple of chocolate, **Gay-Odin** (www.gay-odin.it), sells chocolate *cozze* (mussels) and chocolate-wrapped coffee beans at shops throughout the city; a convenient central location is at Via Benedetto Croce 61 (✆ **081/551-0794**).

Friggatorie shops focus on delicious deep-fried snacks, like *panzarotti* (potato croquettes), *arancini* (fried rice balls), and *pizza fritte* (deep-fried pizza dough topped with sauce and cheese). Top stops are **Friggitoria Vomero,** near the Vomero funicular stop at Via Domenico Cimarosa 44 (✆ **081/578-3130**), and **1947 Pizza Fritta,** in the historic center at Via Pietro Colletta 16 (1947-pizzafritta.business.site; ✆ **333/400-8562**). **Di Matteo,** a venerable pizzeria in the historic center at Via Tribunali 94 (www.pizzeriadimatteo.com; ✆ **081/455-262**), also sells fried food from a street-side counter. You'll sample many of these foods, accompanied by lively commentary, on a walk through the historic center on 2½-hour **Naples Street Food Tours,** about 40€, from Viator (www.viator.com) and other companies; **Streaty** tours (www.streaty.com; ✆ **0351/5133552**) add a stop in the outdoor Pignasecca market and some drinks (55€). Whatever tour you take, show up with an empty stomach, as the pizza, fried snacks, and sweets you'll sample add up to a hearty meal.

con vongole, while waistcoated waiters and exhibitions of contemporary art elevate a comfortable meal to a fine dining experience.

Via Alabardieri 30. www.umberto.it. ✆ **081/418555.** Entrees 7€–15€. Tues–Sun 12:15–3:45pm and 7:15pm–midnight; Mon 7:15pm–midnight. Metro: Piazza Amedeo.

INEXPENSIVE

Campagnola ★★ NEAPOLITAN Many of the students, professors, and neighborhood regulars eat at this plain, homey wine shop/trattoria almost every day, or at least stop by for a glass of the house wine and a plate of fried artichokes. The chalkboard menu changes daily, ranging through Neapolitan home-style favorites like *parmigiano di melanzane* and *vitello limone.* Pizzas are perfect starters, and a meal usually ends with *zeppole* (fried doughnuts), courtesy of the house.

Via Tribunale 47. ✆ **081/457-663.** Entrees 7€–10€. Daily 12:30pm–3:30pm (Sun until 4pm) and 7:30–11pm. Metro: Dante.

Da Nennella ★★ NEAPOLITAN The guys at this Spagnoli favorite will make you feel like one of the regulars as you grab a seat on the covered terrace or in the plain white dining room for satisfying home cooking. Stick to the specials, listed on a board and recited by the busy waiters—*pasta e patate* (pasta and potatoes), maybe some fried fish or roasted pork, and salads of fresh greens. Even with wine, a meal here won't cost more than 12€ or 15€.
Vico Lungo Teatro 103–105. ✆ **081/414338.** Entrees 6€–8€. Mon–Sat noon–3pm and 7–11pm. Metro: Toledo.

I Buongustai ★★ NEAPOLITAN/PIZZA To get away from the crowds on Via Tribunali, walk towards its eastern end, where a neighborhood vibe takes over. This local, no-frills lunchtime favorite is always busy, with a takeaway counter out front and a small dining room in the rear. A huge selection of pizzas, including one that can be made with your choice of toppings, is served alongside *fritturina* (fried vegetables and other bits), *bruschetti,* and choices from a *tavola calda* (hot table), with grilled sausages, meatballs, and whatever else the chef is making that day.
Via Tribunali 201. ✆ **081/446-768.** Pizzas and entrees 4€–8€. Mon–Sat 9am–5pm.

Trattoria A' Pignata ★★★ NEAPOLITAN This indoor/outdoor spot on a crowded alley in the Spanish Quarter, just off Via Toledo, is justly popular with Neapolitans and their visitors alike, and no one seems to mind waiting for a table while taking in the street life. A busy and friendly staff serves heaping plates of nicely done *gnocchi alla sorrentina,*

EVERY DAY IS christmas

Among the many delights of Naples are the *presepi,* nativity scenes that you can find everywhere, any time of the year, although they really come out in force around Christmas. St. Francis of Assisi is said to have commissioned the first *presepe* in the 13th century, but it was here in Naples that the scenes became elevated to high art, bolstered by the patronage of King Charles III in the 18th century. City craftsmen still go all out, carving figures in wood, firing them in ceramics, even fitting them with tailored clothing. Besides mainstays like Mary, Joseph, and the baby Jesus, the Neapolitan cast of characters often includes soccer stars and other celebrities, and settings can be a lot more elaborate than a humble manger: medieval town squares, rusticated villages with thatched cottages, elaborate caves that look like some troglodyte fantasy. On **Via San Gregorio Armeno,** dozens of shops sell figures beginning at about 15€. You can buy a complete scene for anywhere from 100€ to well into five digits, or have one made with figures of your own family and favorite celebrities (as many Neapolitans do). Be aware that pickpockets flock to the street like sheep to a Bethlehem hillside to prey on distracted window-shoppers. Among the most reputable shops are **Gambardella Pastoria** ★, Via San Gregorio Armeno 40 (www.gambardellapastori.com; ✆ **081/551-7107**); **Giuseppe e Marco Ferrigno** ★, Via San Gregorio Armeno 10 (www.arteferrigno.it; ✆ **081/552-3148**); and **Petrucciani** ★, Via San Gregorio Armeno 51 (www.petruccianisangregorioarmeno.it; ✆ **081/551-2496**).

eggplant *parmigiana,* and other homey staples typical of the city's back-street trattorias. Here the choices also include several pasta dishes topped with fresh-from-the market seafood.

Vico Lungo del Gelso. www.trattoriapignata.it. ✆ **081/413-526.** Entrees 7€–12€. Tues–Sun noon–3:30pm and 7–11:30pm.

Naples Shopping

Via Toledo and Galleria Umberto I hold their own as mainstays of Naples shopping, though the clothing and accessories shops in Chiaia tend to be a little more elegant these days. There, big Italian fashion names have outlets along the Riviera di Chiaia, Via Calabritto, Via dei Mille, Via Filangieri, Via Poerio, and Piazza dei Martiri.

Nativity figurines in the workshops of Via San Gregorio Armeno.

Handmade **Marinella ties,** a symbol of luxurious quality for more than a century and worn by the likes of Bill Clinton and Aristotle Onassis, are showcased at the main store and workshop at Via Riviera di Chiaia 287 (www.emarinella.com; ✆ **081/764-3265**). The city is justly famous for other handcrafted goods as well. Heading the list are *presepi,* the nativity scenes crafted and sold along **Via San Gregorio Armeno** (see box, p. 614). Another shop selling handcrafted figurines is **La Scarabatto,** in the historic center at Via die Tribunali 50 (www.lascarabattola.it; ✆ **081/291-735**), where the output includes traditional folk figures and contemporary ceramics.

The lively **Mercato di Porta Nolano** food market stretches around Piazza Nolano, south of the train station. Stalls burst with seafood and local produce and all manner of other foodstuffs; they operate daily until 6pm Monday to Saturday and 2pm on Sunday (pickpockets have a field day here, so watch your effects). Every third Saturday and Sunday of each month from 8am to 2pm (except in Aug), a *fiera antiquaria* **(antiques fair)** is held in the Villa Comunale on Viale Dohrn.

Opening hours for stores in Naples are generally Monday to Saturday from 10:30am to 1pm and from 4 to 7:30pm.

Entertainment & Nightlife

Neapolitans make the best of balmy evenings by passing the time on cafe terraces. Top choice is the oldest cafe in Naples, with a Liberty-style interior from the 1860s, the elegant **Gran Caffè Gambrinus,** Via Chiaia 1, in Piazza Trieste e Trento (grancaffegambrinus.com; ✆ **081/417-582**). Jean-Paul Sartre and Ernest Hemingway were among the luminaries who have lingered over coffee and drinks here, and the cafe observes the city's long-standing Suspended Coffee tradition—patrons who buy a coffee may pay for another and leave the receipt in an antique coffee pot so someone less fortunate can retrieve it and enjoy a cup, too.

OPERA & CLASSICAL MUSIC The great Naples-born tenor Enrico Caruso (1873–1921) appeared only once at his hometown's sumptuous opera house, in 1901—he was booed off the stage and vowed never to return. The venerable **Teatro San Carlo,** Via San Carlo 98 (www.teatrosancarlo.it; ✆ **081/797-2412** or 081/797-2331), has been kinder to other performers and composers. The world's oldest opera house, inaugurated on November 4, 1737, has welcomed Rossini, Bellini, Verdi, Puccini, and a veritable who's who of opera greats. The house still stages world-class opera, along with dance and orchestral works, Tuesday through Sunday, December through June. Tickets cost between 30€ and 100€. Guided tours (9€) are available daily in English at 11:30am and 3:30pm.

The **Centro di Musica Antica Pietà dei Turchini** music conservatory, Via Santa Caterina da Siena 38, at the base of the Vomero hill near the Vittorio Emanuele funicular stop (www.turchini.it; ✆ **081/402-395**), is well known for concerts of early music, though the repertoire extends to other music as well. Concerts are held in the church of Pietà dei Turchini, beneath paintings by some of Naples' great baroque masters, and in a hall that was once an orphanage where young charges were instructed in singing and musical composition. Star pupils included Alessandro Scarlatti (1660–1725) and Giovanni Pergolesi (1710–36).

The **Associazione Alessandro Scarlatti,** Piazza dei Martiri 58 (www.associazionescarlatti.it; ✆ **081/406-011**), stages chamber music concerts at Castel Sant'Elmo and other locales; ticket prices range from 15€ to 25€. Student concerts are frequently staged at **San Pietro a Majella** (www.sanpietroamajella.it; ✆ **081/544-9255**), a former monastery and now a conservatory, at Via San Pietro a Majella 35, just off Via San Sebastiano, known for its many music shops.

Trianon Viviani, near the Piazza Garibaldi train station at Piazza Vincenzo Calenda 9 (www.teatrotrianon.org; ✆ **081/225-8285**), focuses on traditional Neapolitan song and theater; the concert season usually starts in April, with performances Thursday through Sunday.

BARS & CLUBS **Piazza Bellini,** near the university at the edge of the historical center, is an especially lively destination. With a lush terrace and rooms full of books and old photos, the deservedly popular **Intra**

Moenia, Piazza Bellini 7 (www.intramoenia.it; ✆ **081/290–988;** daily morning to late), is a gathering spot for coffee, light meals, and drinks. **Cammarota Spritz,** Vico Lungo Teatro Nuovo 31, might be Naples' most popular bar, with outside service only for ridiculously inexpensive drinks served in plastic cups. **Archeobar,** Via Mezzocannone 101/B (✆ **081/1917-8862**), is friendly to students and sightseers alike, with a lively downstairs room and a quieter, book-lined room upstairs where patrons chat quietly and, gasp, even read.

Enoteche, or wine bars, provide wines by the glass and the bottle, along with some food and often a relaxed atmosphere. Among the best are **Enoteca Belledonne,** Vico Belledonne a Chiaia 18 (www.enoteca belledonne.it; ✆ **081/403-162;** closed Sun), with a local vibe, and **Barril,** Via Giuseppe Fiorelli 11 (www.barril.it; ✆ **081/4362**), serving wine in chic rooms and a garden. In Vomero, **Archivo Storico,** Via Alessandro Scarlatti 30 (www.archiviostorico.com; ✆ **375/608-9682**), mixes classic cocktails in refined surroundings.

AROUND NAPLES

To the west of Naples are the weird volcanic landscapes and evocative ancient ruins of the **Campi Flegrei,** the Phlegraean Fields. To the southeast are two of the world's most famous and well-preserved ancient cities, **Herculaneum** and **Pompeii,** and the volcano that doomed them, **Vesuvius.** You can visit any of these fabled places easily on a day trip and be back in Naples in time for a *passeggiata* and dinner.

Campi Flegrei (Phlegraean Fields) ★★

On this seaside peninsula just west of Naples, volcanic vents steam and hiss, and ruined villas testify to ancient hedonism. Our alphabet was invented here, when the Latin language officially adopted the characters used for written communication in Cuma. Nero murdered his mother, Agrippina, outside Baiae, the Palm Beach of the ancient world; here Caesar relaxed and Hadrian breathed his last. Away from Pozzuoli and other busy seaside towns, moonlike lava landscapes are interspersed with lush hillsides carpeted in olive groves and orange and lemon orchards, adding an eerie beauty to the mix.

ARRIVING & GETTING AROUND

A day exploring this strange, mythic landscape begins in seaside Pozzuoli, reached from Naples by Line 2 of the Metropolitana (subway) or via the **Cumana Railroad** (www.unicocampania.it; ✆ **800/053-939**), starting from Piazza Montesanto. The Metropolitana station in Pozzuoli is above the main town, near the Anfiteatro Flavio; the Cumana Railroad station is near the seafront and town center, just around the corner from the Serapeo ruins. From Pozzuoli, **EVA** (formerly SEPSA) **buses** (www.eavsrl.it; ✆ **081/735-4965**) run to the Solfatara. The Cumana Railroad and bus connections will get you to Baia (change buses at Lucrina), Lago d'Averno, and Cuma (change buses in Torregaveta). Getting around the Campo Flegrei requires some logistics, but you can get a good sense of the area in just a day at Pozzuoli. Tip: If you plan to see several area sights, for just 10€ you can get a **Campi Flegrei** combined ticket, valid for 2 days, which includes the Anfiteatro Flavio, Castello di Baia, Zona Archeologica in Baia, and Scavi di Cuma. Admission to any of these costs 5€, so if you visit more than two, it'll save you money.

POZZUOLI ★★

23km (14 miles) W of Naples

Screen legend Sophia Loren was born in this seaside town in 1934, contributing more color to a place already steeped in lore. The Greek colony of Dicearchia, founded in 530 B.C., became the Roman Puteoli in 194 B.C. You will soon sniff out the origin of the name—from the Latin putere, "to stink," from the sulfurous springs surrounding the town. (More kindly, the name may also come from the Greek pyteolos, or "little well." Roman emperors preferred this harbor to the one at Partenope [Naples]). Among them was Caligula, who performed a famous stunt at Puteoli: He rode his horse across a floating bridge of boats to Baia, defying the soothsayer who said he had "no more chance of becoming Emperor than of riding a horse across the Gulf of Baiae."

Puteoli was also a hub for cargo ships from all over the Roman world—dockworkers unloaded grain from Egypt, Sicily, and other outposts of the empire and reloaded them with marble, mosaics, and other exports. Among the voyagers who disembarked here was St. Paul, sometime around A.D. 60. He'd sailed across the Mediterranean from Caesarea, in present-day Israel, where he'd been imprisoned. From Puteoli he traveled up the Appian Way to Rome to stand trial for alleged crimes in Asia Minor and was later freed.

The town also became famous for *pozzolana,* volcanic ash that reacts with water to form a substance like concrete that allowed engineers to build the huge dome of Rome's Pantheon.

The barbarian Alaric destroyed the Roman town in A.D. 410, but the acropolis, on a tufa-stone promontory pushing into the sea, continued to be inhabited throughout the Dark Ages. A modern town grew up around and on top of the hill in the following centuries. With its storied past, ancient monuments, volcanic landscapes, and sweeping views over the sea and the islands of Ischia and Procida, Pozzuoli is a lot more interesting and appealing than an otherwise scrappy suburban town has any right to be.

Anfiteatro Flavio ★★ RUINS More than 20,000 spectators could squeeze into the many rows of seats in the late-1st-century Flavian Amphitheater, the third-largest arena in the Roman world. So much remains that it seems as if a crowd is about to mill in for the next gladiatorial show. The theater's engineers, who also built the Colosseum in Rome, devised sophisticated subterranean staging areas with "mechanics" that hoisted wild beasts up to the field of slaughter and pumped in water to flood the arena for mock naval battles. Among the unfortunate victims of the spectacles staged here was Januarius, or San Gennaro, the patron saint of Naples. A painting by Artemisia Gentileschi (1593–1656), a surprisingly successful female artist of the Neapolitan baroque, shows the bishop calmly withstanding the attacks of a ferocious boar. (You can see Gentileschi's painting in Naples' Museo Nazionale di Capodimonte, p. 604.) According to legend, however, the beasts released to devour him fell submissively at his feet. Alas, Gennaro was later beheaded on the crater floor of the nearby Solfatara volcano.

Via Nicola Terracciano 75. www.pafleg.it. ✆ **081/526-6007.** 5€ (10€ Campi Flegrei combined ticket, see p. 618). Hours vary but generally Wed–Mon 9am–8pm.

Rione Terra ★★ ARCHAEOLOGICAL SITE The Greek city that the Romans renamed Puteoli sits on a promontory above the sea. Built up over millennia, the area was inhabited until the 1980s, when "bradyseism," a settling and rising of unstable volcanic ground, rendered living in the district unsafe, especially after sewer lines burst, creating a public health issue. Excavations beneath crumbling houses from the 16th and 17th centuries have revealed the ancient town, and visitors can now walk down gridlike Roman streets past the foundations of shops, taverns, houses, and slave quarters. It's easy to envision day-to-day life in ancient Puteoli: Grooves in the pavement in front of doorways are tracks on which wooden screens were pulled shut at night; the remnants of lead pipes are from a sophisticated water system fed by aqueducts. The showpiece is a magnificent Greek/Roman temple, incorporated into the baroque Duomo.

Access from Via Duomo. www.beniculturali.it. ✆ **081/1993-6286.** By guided tour only, often in English, 5€. Hours vary (check website), but often weekends 9am–noon and 1:30–4:30pm.

Solfatara ★★ PARK The ancients called this dormant volcano just 1km (½ mile) above the Anfiteatro Flavio "Forum Vulcani," believing it to be the residence and workshop of the god Vulcan and an entrance to Hades. It's easy to see why: Lunar landscapes hiss, steam, bubble, and spew sulfurous clouds, and the ground beneath your feet can feel as hot as, well, hell. Despite the heavy stench of sulfur, the volcano has not erupted since 1198, and visitors can walk around the caldera floor on well-marked paths, observing steaming fumaroles and lakes of gassy mud sizzling at 250°C (482°F).

Via Solfatara 161. www.solfatara.it. ✆ **081/526-2341.** 8€, 15€ with guide. Apr–Oct daily 8:30am–7pm; Nov–Mar daily 8:30am–4:30pm. Closed at times of increased volcanic activity, so check website ahead of visit. Bus: P9 from Anfiteatro Flavio entrance.

Temple of Serapis ★★ RUINS The name refers to a statue of the Greco-Egyptian god Serapis, which once stood in a niche of this magnificent marketplace with a marble-floored arcaded courtyard; in the middle rose a *tholos,* a raised meeting hall decorated with sea creatures. In the 19th century, antiquarians noticed that columns in the marketplace were riddled with holes drilled by mollusks; subsequent investigations revealed that the culprit was bradyseism, where unstable ground settled under sea level for periods of time then rose above sea level again, shifting as much as 6 feet in a decade—making living in Pozzuoli a shaky business. (A series of uplifts in the 1980s forced much of the town to be evacuated, damaged 8,000 buildings, and raised the seabed to the point that the harbor can no longer accommodate large craft.) As you circle around the site, try to spot the little holes in the marble columns once submerged in water. Pozzuoli center. www.archeoflegrei.it. ✆ **081/526-6007.** Free. Viewed from surrounding sidewalk.

BAIA ★

6km (4 miles) SW of Pozzuoli

Many of the villas and thermal baths of this ancient spa town are now underwater, though enough remains on terra firma to suggest the grandeur of **Ancient Baiae** (the modern town dropped the last "e"). Julius Caesar, Nero, and others of the Roman elite once relaxed and debauched in Baiae's large villas, equipped with swimming pools and other luxuries. Seneca the Younger, the 1st-century philosopher and man of letters, called the place a "vortex of luxury." The poet Ovid said it was "a favorable place for love-making," while Horace chimed in, "No bay on Earth outshines pleasing Baiae." The town—which takes its name from Baio, the navigator of Odysseus, said to be buried somewhere in Baia—was famed for its thermal baths, fed by sulfur springs believed to have medicinal properties.

Baiae had its share of salacious moments. According to legend, this is where emperor Nero tried to kill his mother, the ambitious and villainous Agrippina, by contriving to have a ceiling crash down on her bed. When that didn't work, he arranged to have her boat rammed at sea, but she swam ashore. The thwarted emperor finally sent a henchman to Baiae to stab the doomed woman. Poster girl for the town's debauchery may have been Messalina, third wife of the emperor Claudius, who was said to be sexually insatiable—gossip claimed she snuck out of her Baiae villa in disguise at night to work at the town's brothel under the name She Wolf.

Ruins of temples, villas, and bathing establishments litter three grassy terraces above the bay in the **Complesso Archeologico di Baia.** The ruins are not especially well marked nor well preserved. It's believed that a pile of stones near the top may have been the villa of Julius Caesar, who popped from here up to Rome for a meeting of the senate on the Ides of March 44 B.C. (the rest is history). His houseguest at the time was

Cleopatra. Enough remains of the Terme di Baiae to show just how elaborate the bathing complexes were. Admission is free weekdays; on weekends 5€ (or 10€ Campi Flegrei combined ticket, see p. 618). The park is open Wednesday to Monday 9am till 7:30pm.

Much of the ancient town is underwater, preserved as the **Parco Archeologico Sommerso di Baiae ★★** (Via Sella di Baia 22, Bacoli; www.parcoarcheologicosommersodibaia.it; ✆ **848/800-228**). Mosaic flooring, statuary, fishponds, and other ruins litter the seabed amid bubbling geysers and flourishing flora. You can view this undersea world on dives, by snorkeling, or on trips on glass-bottom boats. Dive centers and boat tours operate out of the port and Via Lucullo in Baia; expect to pay about 10€ for a boat trip, 20€ for a snorkeling tour, and 35€ for a guided dive. The office of the **Area Protteta di Baia** (Via Lucullo 94, ✆ **081/523-2739**) can provide a list of tour operators.

Castello di Baia ★★ HISTORIC SITE/MUSEUM One of the most impressive landmarks in a town steeped in legend is the work of the Aragonese kings of Naples of the 16th century. Their massive complex of thick walls and defensive moats rises from a wave-buffeted headland that was once topped with a villa of Emperor Nero. The sea-facing battlements were meant to deter Barbary pirates from North Africa, who would pillage coastal towns and take captives to sell into the Ottoman slave market. More important, the unassailable stronghold with its sweeping views of the bay also ensured protection against the French navy, whose ships didn't stand a chance of sailing past the lookouts to invade Naples. Some of the vast rooms now house the **Museo Archeologico dei Campi Flegrei ★**, showing off statuary and other artifacts from Baia and the surrounding region. Most enchanting are the two *nymphaeums,* delightful statue-lined porches that were once equipped with lavish fountains; one, rescued from the sea floor, is said to have been from the villa of Emperor Claudius.

Via Castello 39. www.pafleg.it. ✆ **081/523-3797** or 848/800-288. 5€ (10€ Campi Flegrei combined ticket, see p. 618). Tues–Sun 9am–2:20pm

CUMA ★

7km (4½ miles) NW of Lago d'Averno

The Greeks founded their first colony on mainland Italy at Cuma in the 8th century B.C., and Cuma grew into an important center of Greek farming operations in Campania. The settlers soon discovered they had a helpful neighbor: the Cumaean Sibyl, who, according to legend, passed on messages from Apollo. The god told the Sibyl he would grant her one wish. She took a handful of sand and said she wanted to live as many years as the number of grains she held. Then came the catch: Apollo wanted her virginity in return. Sibyl refused, so Apollo gave her long life but not eternal youth. Over the centuries she withered away, eventually becoming so small she could be kept in a jar, then only her voice remained—handy for uttering a last request, "I want to die." The **Sibyl's chamber**—a big draw for advice-seekers from around the ancient world—sits at the end of a long, narrow tunnel cut through volcanic stone, 131.5m (432 ft.) long, some 5m (16.5 ft.) high, and as wide as 2.4m (8 ft.) across. That impressive entrance most likely assured supplicants they were about to hear something gravely important; it can still send chills down the spine.

The cave of the Cumaean Sibyl still has an air of mystery.

The Sibyl is said to have ferried Aeneas, son of Aphrodite, across nearby **Lago d'Averno,** where he discovered the River Styx, the gateway to Hades. Legend claims that the lake's vaporous waters were once so lethal (possibly from gas-emitting underwater vents) that it was named after a Greek word meaning "without birds," because winged creatures flying over the waters would plunge to their deaths. In the 1st century B.C., Emperor Agrippa had a canal dug to connect the lake with the sea, providing safe harbor for Roman ships. He also ordered construction of the Grotta di Cocceio (Cocceio's Cave), a straight tunnel between the lake and Cuma, 1km (½ mile) long and wide enough for a chariot to pass. The tunnel was passable for almost 2,000 years, until World War II bombs caused a section to collapse.

Via Montecuma. www.pafleg.it. ✆ **081/854-3060.** 5€ (10€ Campi Flegrei combined ticket, see p. 618). Wed–Mon 9am–7:30pm.

PROCIDA ★★★

15km (9 miles) W of Pozzuoli

The third of the trio of islands in the Bay of Naples is separated from Pozzuoli and other seaside suburbs only by a narrow channel. While not as glamorous as Capri nor as lush as Ischia, and less visited than these popular neighbors, the tiny island is a quiet beauty. The jumble of pastel-colored houses is a pleasure to explore on foot, wandering up and down the narrow alleys of Marina Grande into the old fishing village of Marina di Corricella. At the island's height is Terra Murrata, a medieval enclave rimmed with sea-facing viewpoints. Back at sea level are some much-appreciated beaches, including the sands around Marina di Chiaolella, and a pristine nature preserve, Isola di Vivara. Free electric buses make a circuit of the island. Frequent ferry service operated by **SNAV** (www.snav.it; ✆ **081/428555**) and **Caremar** (www.caremar.it; ✆ **081/189–66690**) connects Procida with Naples and Pozzuoli; go to www.ferryhopper.com for schedules.

Vesuvius ★★

Towering, pitch-black Mount Vesuvius looms menacingly over the Bay of Naples. The volcano has erupted periodically since A.D. 79, when it buried Pompeii and Herculaneum in explosions that released 100,000 times the thermal energy of the Hiroshima bomb. Less violent eruptions occurred in 1631, in 1906, and 1944. Mount Vesuvius is the only active volcano on mainland Europe, though another formidable volcanic peak, Mount Etna, is only 560km (335 miles) away, on the east coast of Sicily (see p. 776).

The mountain still puffs steam every once in a while, just to keep everybody on their toes. Volcanologists and geologists say that, given the historic record, a major eruption is likely in the relatively near future—it's a question of *when* rather than *if* the mountain will blow its top again. With 3 million people living around the Bay of Naples, that makes Vesuvius one of the most potentially deadly volcanoes in the world.

ARRIVING The most convenient way to visit Vesuvius by public transportation from Naples or Sorrento is on the Circumvesuviana **train** (www.eavsrl.it; ✆ **800/211388** toll-free within Italy) to the Ercolano Scavi. From the Ercolano Scavi, you can catch **Vesuvio Express** (www.vesuvioexpress.info) vans to the parking lot below the summit. Fares are 10€ round-trip; you'll pay another 10€ for admission to the park. Vans run every 45 minutes daily from 9:30am; the last bus departs 2 hours before the park closes. **Busvia del Vesuvio** (www.busviadelvesuvio.com; ✆ **340/935-2616**) offers rides on a bumpy back road up the mountain from Pompeii in a 4x4 vehicle that drops you at the summit parking lot; round-trip fare is 22€, including park admission. The service runs April to October daily 9am to 3pm (sometimes later in July and Aug). Buy tickets at a booth just to the right as you exit the Pompei Scavi train station.

Funiculì, Funiculà

One way you won't be making the ascent up the mountain is on the Mt. Vesuvius Funicular, which once climbed to the summit from Pugliano, near Ercolano. It opened to great fanfare in 1880, when the song "Funiculì, Funiculà" was written to celebrate the event. Everyone from Connie Francis and the Grateful Dead to Luciano Pavarotti recorded the jaunty tune. The eruption of 1944 wiped out the tracks and sealed the railway's fate; the ascent by road was by then more practical.

By **car,** take the Torre del Greco exit from the A3 autostrada and follow the signs to Vesuvio. The road ends in the parking lot below the summit, where you'll pay 2.50€ to park. A taxi from Naples costs a flat rate of 90€ round-trip, including a 2-hour wait.

VISITOR INFORMATION The **Parco Nazionale del Vesuvio** (www.parconazionaledelvesuvio.it; ✆ **081/865-3911**) maintains trails and other visitor facilities. All transportation arrives at the park entrance at 1,017m (3,337 ft.) in altitude; you'll pay 10€ to continue on a fairly steep trail to the summit or explore the mountainside on other trails, none of them wheelchair accessible. The entrance fee also includes admission to an observatory, the world's oldest seismological/volcanological institution, dating from 1841. The park opens daily at 9am, closing at 6pm July to August, 5pm April to June and September, 4pm March and October, and 3pm November through February. The trail to the crater closes in extreme weather.

EXPLORING VESUVIUS

The historic peak is the centerpiece of 8,482-hectare (20,959-acre) **Parco Nazionale del Vesuvio ★★★** (Vesuvius National Park), where nine

KEEPING UP WITH THE pompeiians

All around the shores of the Bay of Naples, various towns reveal the good life wealthy Romans once enjoyed here. **Oplontis,** a swanky seafront suburb of Pompeii (the very name means "opulence"), was wiped out in Vesuvius's eruption and subsequently buried beneath the highways, apartment blocks, and factories of grimy Torre Annunziata. You can still visit Oplontis' showplace, **Villa Poppea,** a huge spread that was the retreat of Poppea Sabina, second wife of Emperor Nero and an infamous schemer and plotter. Here she bathed in a milk-filled pool beneath a fresco of Hercules and entertained in mosaic-floored rooms, sea-view gardens, and a massive swimming pool. (Her slaves, meanwhile, labored in a primitive kitchen and slept in cubicles.) Poppea allegedly met a gruesome end when her husband jumped on her stomach in a fit of rage and caused her to miscarry. Entrance to the villa is at Via Seplocri 12, Torre Annunziata (pompeiisites.org; ✆ **081/857-5347;** 5€). April through October, the villa is open daily 9am to 7pm, and November through March daily 9am to 5pm. It's a short walk from the Circumvesuviana station.

Stabia was another beautiful seafront enclave, long buried beneath **Castellammare del Stabia,** an industrial suburb known for shipbuilding. Excavations there include lavish **Villa di Arianna** and **Villa San Marco,** where you can view frescoed halls and atria, and at Villa San Marco, a massive swimming pool, a long colonnade, and a dining hall that could seat 125 guests. Entrances are off SS14; admission is free and the villas are open daily 9am to 7:30pm (until 5pm Nov–Mar). Take the Circumvesuviana train to Castellammare di Stabia and get a taxi for the trip out to the villas; it's possible to walk from one to the other. A visit to Castellammare comes with a perk: From the station a *funivia* (funicular) climbs the 1,100m (3,609-ft.) summit of Monte Faito, for sensational views across the Bay of Naples.

summit trails highlight the lava flows and other geology underfoot. Placards along the way explain the unique micro-environment of the volcanic summit, including many species of orchids and other amazingly tenacious vegetation. The ticket office hands out route maps (short versions are also on the website), which range from easy 1-hour strolls to strenuous 8-hour hikes. The number 5 trail, **Gran Cono,** is the classic ascent to the top: a moderately difficult uphill walk of about half a mile from the parking area and ticket office to the 230m (754-ft.)-deep crater. The walk takes about 20 minutes, but forego any notions of being alone in empty volcanic landscapes—cafes and souvenir stands line the route. A guide will lead you around the rim, but make sure the guide who approaches you is a bona-fide ranger and not a shill looking for a tip; guide service is free with the price of admission and mandatory. Wear sneakers—the lava underfoot can be hard on the feet—and bring a sweater, because it can be surprisingly chilly in the heights. The mesmerizing view across Naples and the bay might just make you forget how menacing Vesuvius really is. As a reminder, consider that before the A.D. 79 eruption, the mountain was more than twice as tall as its current 1,282m (4,206 ft.).

POMPEII & HERCULANEUM ★★★

On one fateful day in A.D. 79 the people of Pompeii, a prosperous fishing town, and Herculaneum, a resort just down the coast, watched Mount Vesuvius hurl a churning column of gas and ash high into the sky. It was only a matter of time before flows of superheated molten rock coursed through the streets of Herculaneum and ash and pumice buried Pompeii. In Herculaneum, volcanic debris quickly hardened into a layer of rock that fossilized everything—furniture, wooden beams, clothing, skeletons, graffiti, mosaics; in Pompeii, ash and rock fragments buried structures under a layer as deep as 12m (20 ft.), preserving everything beneath it through the centuries.

Pompeii is much more extensive than Herculaneum, with more to see, but Herculaneum provides an easier-to-manage experience. With its gridlike streets, Pompeii provides an overview of a large Roman town; Herculaneum's better-preserved houses and artifacts give an evocative glimpse into day-to-day life. It's possible to see both in one day, but get a good rest the night before, because seeing the sights involves lots of walking and possible sensory overload—you'll be taking in an enormous amount of information. If you have to choose between the two, Pompeii provides the more sensational experience.

Essentials

ARRIVING **Circumvesuviana** trains (www.eavsrl.it; ✆ **800/211-388** toll-free in Italy) run between Naples Piazza Garibaldi and Sorrento every half-hour, with stops in Herculaneum and Pompeii. For Herculaneum, get off at **Ercolano Scavi** (*scavi* means "archaeological excavation"). Herculaneum is 20 minutes from Naples and 50 minutes from Sorrento; the entrance is about 10 blocks, an easy downhill walk, from the station. For Pompeii, exit the train at **Pompei Scavi** (note that the modern spelling drops the last "i" of the ancient name). The entrance is about 45m (150 ft.) from the station. Pompeii is about 40 minutes from Naples and 30 minutes from Sorrento. The **Campania Express,** which runs between Naples Piazza Garibaldi and Sorrento four times a day from mid-March to mid-October, offers express service to the excavations; the trip from Naples to Herculaneum is only 10 minutes and the trip to Pompeii 30 minutes. **High-speed trains** are scheduled to begin running directly between Rome and Fiumicino Airport and Pompeii some time in 2024; check **www.trenitalia.com** for updates.

To reach either by **car** from Naples, follow the *autostrada* A3 toward Salerno. If you're coming from Sorrento, head east on SS 145, where you can connect with A3 (marked napoli). Then take the signposted turnoffs for Pompeii and Herculaneum.

LOGISTICS The **Herculaneum** excavations are open daily 9:30am to 7:30pm (closing at 5pm Nov-Mar), last admission 90 minutes before closing. Admission is 13€. The **Pompeii** excavations are open daily 9am to 7pm (closing at 5pm Nov-Mar), last admission 90 minutes before closing. Under Covid restrictions, Pompeii required online purchase for Saturday and bank holiday tickets at **www.ticketone.it** (tickets for other days can be booked in advance on the site as well; check pompeiisites.org for current information on entry requirements). Admission is 18€;. you can purchase tickets in advance online at www.ticketone.it for a 1.50€ fee but that's not really necessary.

Both sites are busiest in the mornings, especially when tour groups arrive in the summer. Ticket offices provide free maps and rent audio guides (8€, 5€ kids' version, 6.50€ for 2 people, though sharing is not a particularly good idea). Inside the entrances, bookstores sell guidebooks to the ruins (available in English), and licensed English-speaking guides await visitors. Guides are generally qualified and reliable, but establish a price before setting out (generally about 20€ a person, depending on the size of the group). Their services, or an audioguide, are a welcome asset, since labeling at both sites is extremely limited. An app, **MyPompeii,** provides a lot of background on stops within the excavations marked with QR codes, and also has updates on the number of visitors at any time so you can avoid crowds. Pompeii has a **cafeteria** inside the archaeological zone that's handy for sandwiches and drinks. At Herculaneum there's a picnic area with vending machines, and several **cafes** are just outside the entrance. You can store your luggage at both sites (also at the train station in Pompeii), making it possible to work in a visit if you're en route between Naples and Sorrento or the Amalfi Coast. If you're visiting the sites on a sunny day, wear sunscreen and bring a bottle of water.

VISITOR INFORMATION For more information about Herculaneum, visit ercolano.beniculturali.it, or call ✆ **081/777-7008;** for Pompeii, visit www.pompeiisites.org (an especially rich source of information that includes news of ongoing excavations) or call ✆ **081/857-5111.**

Herculaneum (Ercalano)

10km (6 miles) SE of Naples

Excavations began at Herculaneum in the early 18th century and continue to this day, with the fairly recent discovery of a beached boat full of desperate souls trying to escape by sea. Another 300 skeletons were found in vaulted stone boathouses on what would have been the town's beach; huddled there waiting to board boats and sail to safety, they were killed instantly by the poisonous vapors of a wall of heated gas and rock sweeping through the town at 100mph. Although many questions about Herculaneum remain unanswered, it's known for certain that this glitzy seaside resort for elite Romans was about a third the size of Pompeii, with a

Mosaic of Neptune and Amphitrite in the ruins of Herculaneum, once a seaside resort for the Roman elite.

population of about 4,000. Herculaneum had little commerce or industry, and its streets were lined with elegant villas, along with a few apartment blocks for poor laborers and fishermen.

EXPLORING HERCULANEUM'S ARCHAEOLOGICAL AREA ★★★

The ruins of Herculaneum give the unsettling impression of a ghost town from which residents have only recently walked away. Many of the houses retain their second floors, making them seem more like residences than ruins. The volcanic mud that covered Herculaneum during the eruption of Vesuvius in A.D. 79 quickly hardened to a rocklike material. While making excavations difficult, this semi-rock protected the structures underneath, and rather remarkably preserved wooden beams and floors along with furnishings, clothing, and other household objects. The ruins provide a wealth of intriguing detail about building techniques, architecture, and domestic decoration in Roman times, and, of course, about daily life. The charred wood, staircases, and double-height houses here instill the sense of being in a real town, unlike the remote detachment you might experience in Pompeii and other ancient ruins.

The excavations stretch from the town's main street, Via IV Novembre, to what was once the shoreline (now a kilometer to the west); the rest of the Roman town remains inaccessible beneath the buildings of modern Ercolano. From the Ercolano-Scavi station, follow the signs for Scavi di Ercolano for 10 blocks down Via IV Novembre; the entrance is about a 10-minute walk from the station. Plan to spend at least 2 hours.

DECUMANUS MAXIMUS Decumanus Maximus is a street lined with shops, some of them still sporting advertisements and price lists. One of the discoveries along this street was a crucifix, proof that Christianity had already come to Herculaneum by the time of the eruption.

TERME DEL FORO Elegant mosaics of fish, dolphins, and other sea creatures decorate the town's largest and grandest bath complex, with several entrances that include, of course, separate ones for men and women. Enough of the men's section, the **Terme Maschili,** remains to show the range of facilities: a latrine, a changing room lined with benches and shelves for stashing personal effects, and an exercise room. You can still make out the *frigidarium* (cold bath), to the left, and the *tepadarium* (tepid bath), to the right. Once patrons had gone through these ablutions, they could settle into the *caldarium* (hot bath) for a long, soothing soak. In the smaller but similarly elaborate **Terme Feminili,** a mosaic of a naked Triton decorates the floor of the changing rooms.

SEDES DEGLI AUGUSTALI (HALL OF THE AUGUSTALS) The Augustals were priests of a cult to Augustus, founder and first emperor of the Roman empire. These rooms with marble floors and elaborate wall paintings did

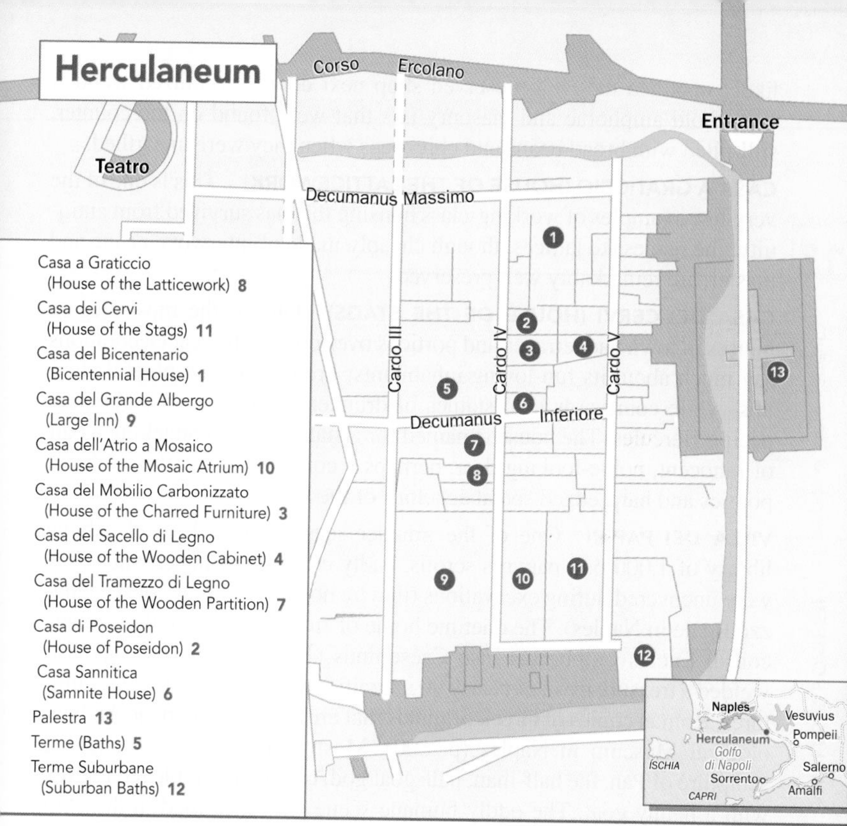

justice to their elite status. Their custodian died in his sleep, in a small room that's still furnished with the bed where his skeleton was found.

CASA DEL TRAMEZZO DI LEGNO (HOUSE OF THE WOODEN PARTITION) Behind a perfect facade is a rarity in Roman houses, a double atrium. It probably just means that at some point the owner scraped together enough money to buy adjoining houses and merge them. He obviously worked hard: The house is named for a well-preserved wooden screen that separated part of the atrium from the *tablium,* a little room that served as an office.

CASA DEL BELLA CORTILE (HOUSE OF THE BEAUTIFUL COURTYARD) The namesake courtyard seems almost medieval, with a wide stone staircase ascending to a landing on the second floor. Three skeletons that have been placed here are presumed to be those of a mother, father, and daughter trapped on the beach as they tried to flee.

CASA DEL MOSAICO DI NETTUNO E ANFITRITE (HOUSE OF THE NEPTUNE AND ANFITRITIS MOSAIC) A bright blue mosaic of the sea god and his nymph is just one of many decorations in this house, whose owner likely operated the well-preserved shop next door. Carbonized wooden racks hold amphorae and masonry jars that were found on the counter, still filled with broad beans and chickpeas when they were unearthed.

CASA A GRATICCIO (HOUSE OF THE LATTICEWORK) This is one of the very few examples of working-class housing that has survived from antiquity; the namesake lattices, though cheaply made of interwoven cane and plaster, are remarkably well preserved.

CASA DEI CERVI (HOUSE OF THE STAGS) One of the most elegant houses in town had terraces and porticos overlooking the sea. Decorations say much about its fun-loving inhabitants: Frescoes depict playful cherubs, while courtyards held statues of drunken satyrs and an inebriated, peeing Hercules. The house is named for a statue of dogs attacking a pair of innocent, noble-looking deer, perhaps a commentary on the cutthroat politics and hard-edged social echelons of the Roman era.

VILLA DEI PAPIRI One of the grander seaside villas housed a huge library of 1,000-odd papyrus scrolls, badly charred but intact when they were uncovered during excavations (they're now in the library of the Palazzo Reale in Naples). The onetime home of Julius Caesar's father-in-law, consul Lucius Calpurnius Piso Caesoninus (100 B.C.–43 B.C.), has also yielded a treasure trove of nearly 90 magnificent bronze and marble sculptures, Roman copies of Greek originals that are now housed in the Archaeological Museum in Naples (p. 600). Most famous among them is a sculpture of Pan, the half-man, half-goat god, caught in marble having sex with a nanny goat. The oddly humane scene was unearthed in the 18th century but was thought to be so licentious that it was locked away in the cellars of a royal palace. Fortunately, since the early 19th century randy Pan has been one of the Archaeological Museum's most cherished prizes.

TERME SUBURBANE (SUBURBAN BATHS) Another bath complex shows off state-of-the art sophistication, with marble floors and benches and an elaborate under-floor heating system in which heat generated by wood fires circulated through a maze of conduits. In the *caldarium* (hot bath), a few stucco friezes still look down on visitors as they did on bathers.

Pompeii

19km (11 miles) SE of Herculaneum, 30km (18 miles) SE of Naples

A visit to Italy's second-most popular archaeological site (after the Colosseum in Rome) is a journey into a world locked in an ancient time. The 4m-to-6m (13-20-ft.) layer of volcanic ash with which Vesuvius buried the city preserved shops, civic buildings, and private houses. Excavations began in 1748 and are still ongoing—in Regio V, a section north of the current ruins, recent finds have included the remains of a horse being saddled for flight, an elaborately decorated ceremonial chariot, and an erotic fresco of Leda and the Swan. While most of the section is closed to

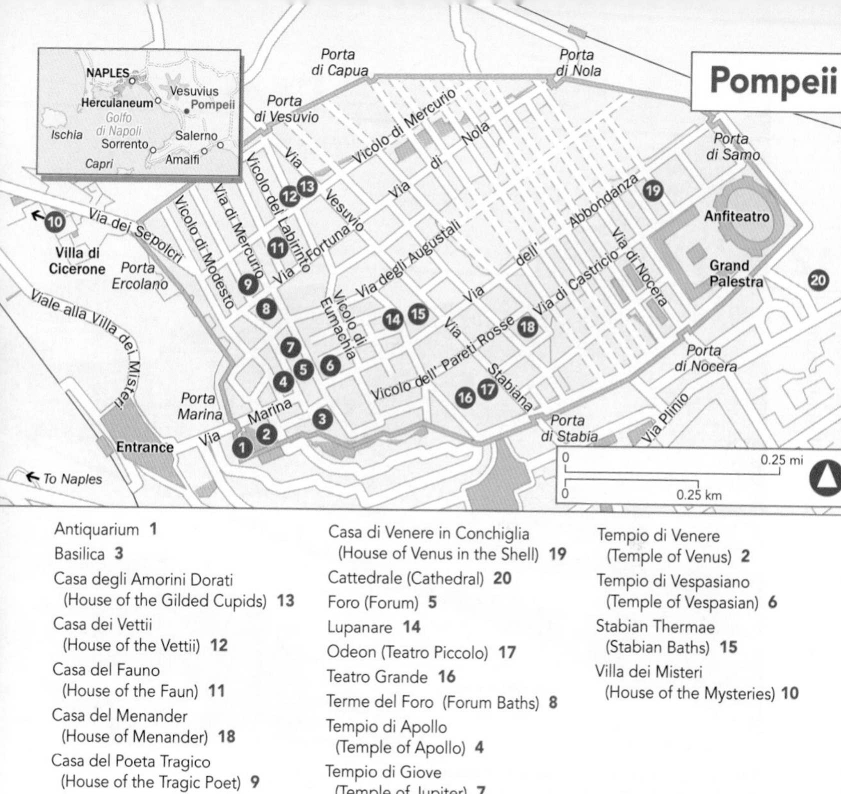

visitors, a recently excavated Thermopolium, or snack bar, is open at limited times (check www.pompeiisites.org). The thermopolium, one of 80 such establishments unearthed in Pompeii, has a counter elaborately painted with images of the animals customers could likely consume there.

How many people were living in Pompeii at the time of the eruption is not known, nor is the exact date—based on ancient writings, it was long thought to be August 24, A.D. 79, but recent findings (the seeds of autumn fruits, an inscription apparently dated in mid-Oct) suggest the event occurred later. A major earthquake in A.D. 62 had recently rocked the city, destroying temples, houses, and public works, and repairs were still underway in A.D. 79; many of the city's 11,000 recorded inhabitants had probably resettled elsewhere. The unfortunate Pompeiians who remained behind are the most haunting presence at the site. Their decaying bodies often left a mold inside the ash and lava that buried them, empty spaces that excavators filled with plaster. These eerie, lifelike casts lie in the Garden of the Fugitives and other spots around town.

The entrance to the site is almost directly across from the train station. Allow at least 4 hours for even a superficial visit.

The ruined streets of Pompeii evoke everyday life, circa A.D. 79.

EXPLORING POMPEII'S ARCHAEOLOGICAL AREA ★★★

Pompeii was a workaday town, and what stands out amid the ruins is a remarkable evocation of everyday life—streets, shops, bakeries, brothels, baths. Unlike Herculaneum, with its seafront district of lavish villas, in Pompeii the wealthy usually lived among the working classes. Houses are interspersed with shops, which were often combined with dwellings.

The first thing you'll notice is the typical Roman plan of gridlike streets, with stepping stones at every intersection. These were laid down to allow residents to cross the pavement even when the streets were being flushed with water, as they were at least once a day. Stones are spaced exactly to allow chariot wheels to roll past them. Also notice the remains of 25 street fountains, fed by a system of aqueducts, cisterns, and lead pipes that kept baths, businesses, and homes supplied with fresh water. Raised sidewalks conceal water and sewage pipes, while glittering bits of marble mixed in with the volcanic pavement reflected light to make walking easier at night.

PORTA MARINA The site's main entrance is an impressive seafront gate, one of seven portals in the walls that surrounded the ancient city. Pompeii's docks did a brisk business importing and exporting goods that were often transported to and from Rome on the nearby Appian Way. The shimmering sea that once lapped the shoreline in front of the gate is nowhere to be seen: the sprawl of modern Pompei (one "i" in the modern spelling) now lies between the excavations and the sea, which has receded by about .5km (¼ mile) over the centuries. The **Tempio de Venere** (Temple of Venus), to the right of the entrance, has not fared as well as the gate; a lone column is all that attests to its onetime grandeur.

FORO (FORUM) Pompeii's marketplace, damaged in the A.D. 62 earthquake, had not been repaired when the final destruction rained down. Columns still line the portico that surrounded a large, rectangular open space on three sides and opened to a covered meat and fish market, the **Macellum.** Facing the Forum are the **Basilica** (the city's largest single structure), a law court, exchange, and civic hall. The **Temple of Apollo,** with its columned portico, was the city's most important religious building. The **Granai del Foro** (Forum Granary) is now the repository for many of the plaster casts of victims made by 19th-century excavators.

LUPANARE GRANDE (LARGE BROTHEL) Pompeii's most titter-inducing sight and prime photo op is just northeast of the forum off Via degli Augustali. Graphic wall paintings reveal what certainly appears to be a libertine attitude toward sex. It's easy to see why, correctly or not, the city is often associated with easy virtue. In the nearby Basilica, where many travelers stopped on a visit to Pompeii, a bit of graffiti loosely read, "If anyone is looking for some tender love in this town, keep in mind that here all the girls are very friendly." A list of prices is inscribed on the wall near the brothel. It's believed that Pompeii may have had dozens of these establishments. Many of the graphic works that once covered the walls of this one, the city's grandest pleasure palace, have been carted off to the Archaeological Museum in Naples (p. 600), though many remain in place in these 10 small rooms equipped with stone beds.

VIA DELL'ABBONDANZA The town's main commercial street is rightfully named: surrounding fields and vineyards kept Pompeii supplied with an abundance of goods, as did a brisk trade with other Roman cities. This street was lined with shops, including **Fullonica Stephani** (Stephen's Laundry), and eateries where pots full of daily offerings were kept on counters that are still in place. In most houses on the street, a shop is on the ground floor and the owner's apartment is on the second level. Many of the painted signs for bars and shops remain; some have revealed the world's first known bit of advertising punditry, hawking Vesuvinum—a clever combo of Vesuvius and "vinum," the word for wine.

TRIANGULAR FORUM This large open area was the heart of the theater district. The beautiful **Teatro Grande,** carved out of a hillside of volcanic rock in the 2nd century B.C., could seat an audience of 5,000, while the smaller 1st-century-B.C. 1,000-seat **Odeion,** or Small Theater, was used for music and mime shows. Audiences could step out between acts for a stroll along the columned **Quadriportico dei Teatri,** though the breezy walkway was later enclosed to serve as a barracks for gladiators. Nearby is the **Tempio di Iside** (Temple of Isis), one of the best-conserved temples to this goddess to survive from antiquity.

CASA DEGLI AMANTI The House of the Lovers, recently reopened after sustaining damage in a 1980 earthquake, is named for a motto over the entrance ("Lovers like bees pass a sweet life like honey. I wish it were so."). The large dwelling at the edge of the theater district is built around a garden surrounded on the ground floor by a colonnaded portico, and has many frescoes of landscapes and domestic scenes.

TERME STABIANE One of Pompeii's many public baths, the Stabian Baths' arrangement of cold, tepid, and hot baths is a typical floor plan for such places, mainstays of all Roman towns, where people could cleanse, relax, and socialize. The vaulted *apodyterium* (changing room) was the showpiece here, with fanciful wall paintings of playful nymphs. Looking at them must have been a welcome perk for slaves as they waited for their masters in the vast chamber, with orders to keep an eye on their belongings.

The Villa dei Misteri's remarkable frescoes.

CASA DI LOREIUS TIBURTINUS Election placards painted on the facade—"Vote for Loreius" and "Vote for Tiburntinus"—gave this large house its name. The owner, the well-off Octavius Quartio, entertained his guests in a gardenlike *triclinium,* or dining room, where a delightful fresco depicts Pyramis and Thisbe, the lovely maiden and handsome youth of myth who belonged to feuding families; centuries later their doomed love inspired *Romeo and Juliet.*

GRANDE PALESTRA Sports events were held on this track and on the surrounding sports fields, while onlookers could escape the sun in the shade of an impressively long portico. A grandiose swimming pool was surrounded by plane trees (you can see the plaster casts of the stumps).

ANFITEATRO The oldest Roman amphitheater in the world (built in 80 B.C.) could seat 1,000 people and was the first to be built of stone. Especially enlightened were the entrances designed for crowd control, and the state-of-the-art latrines. The theater became known for its gladiatorial contests, and the ancient counterparts of soccer hooligans packed in for events. Games were banned for 10 years after an A.D. 59 brawl between Pompeians and visitors from nearby Nuceria left 10 dead.

TERME SUBURBANE Among Pompeii's bathhouses—some of the finest to survive from antiquity—this one is unusual in that men and women shared the facilities. Vividly colored frescoes in the changing rooms depict graphic sex acts, a point of ongoing controversy: Were they simply amusing decorations or did they advertise sexual services available on the upper floors? These scenes and other so-called pornography from Pompeii shocked Francis I, king of the Two Sicilies. Coming across erotic artifacts on an 1819 visit to the Archaeological Museum in Naples with his wife and daughter, he ordered many of them to be locked away in the museum's Gabinetto Segreto (Secret Cabinet), open only to "people of mature ages and respected morals."

CASA DEI VETTII Pompeii's most elegant patrician villa was the ultimate bachelor pad, the home of wealthy merchants, the Vettii brothers. The huge phallus resting on a pair of scales at the entrance was a sign of good fortune—which the black-and-red Pompeian dining room with its frescoes of delicate cupids and colonnaded garden show the brothers had plenty of. Strongboxes embedded in the floor suggest that they might have made at least part of their fortune as money lenders.

CASA DEL FAUNO The sumptuous decor here is ancient proof that money and good taste can go together. Two of the great treasures of the Archaeological Museum in Naples (p. 600) come from this huge spread, covering an entire city block, the biggest house in town. A bronze statue of a dancing faun decorated the *impluvium,* rain tank, used to collect water for the household, and a much-celebrated "Battle of Alexander the Great" battle scene is one of many mosaics decorating the lavish rooms.

VILLA DEI MISTERI A layer of ash ensured that this 90-room villa near the Porto Ercolano, just outside the walls (follow Viale alla Villa dei Misteri), retained its remarkable frescoes, the best still in place in Pompeii. Set against a background of a deep hue that's now known as Pompeian red, figures in the Dionysiac Frieze are busy with elaborate rituals that, scholars say, may have been wedding preparations or initiation into a sect of Dionysus (Bacchus), one of many cults that flourished in Roman times.

SORRENTO & THE AMALFI COAST

By Stephen Brewer

13

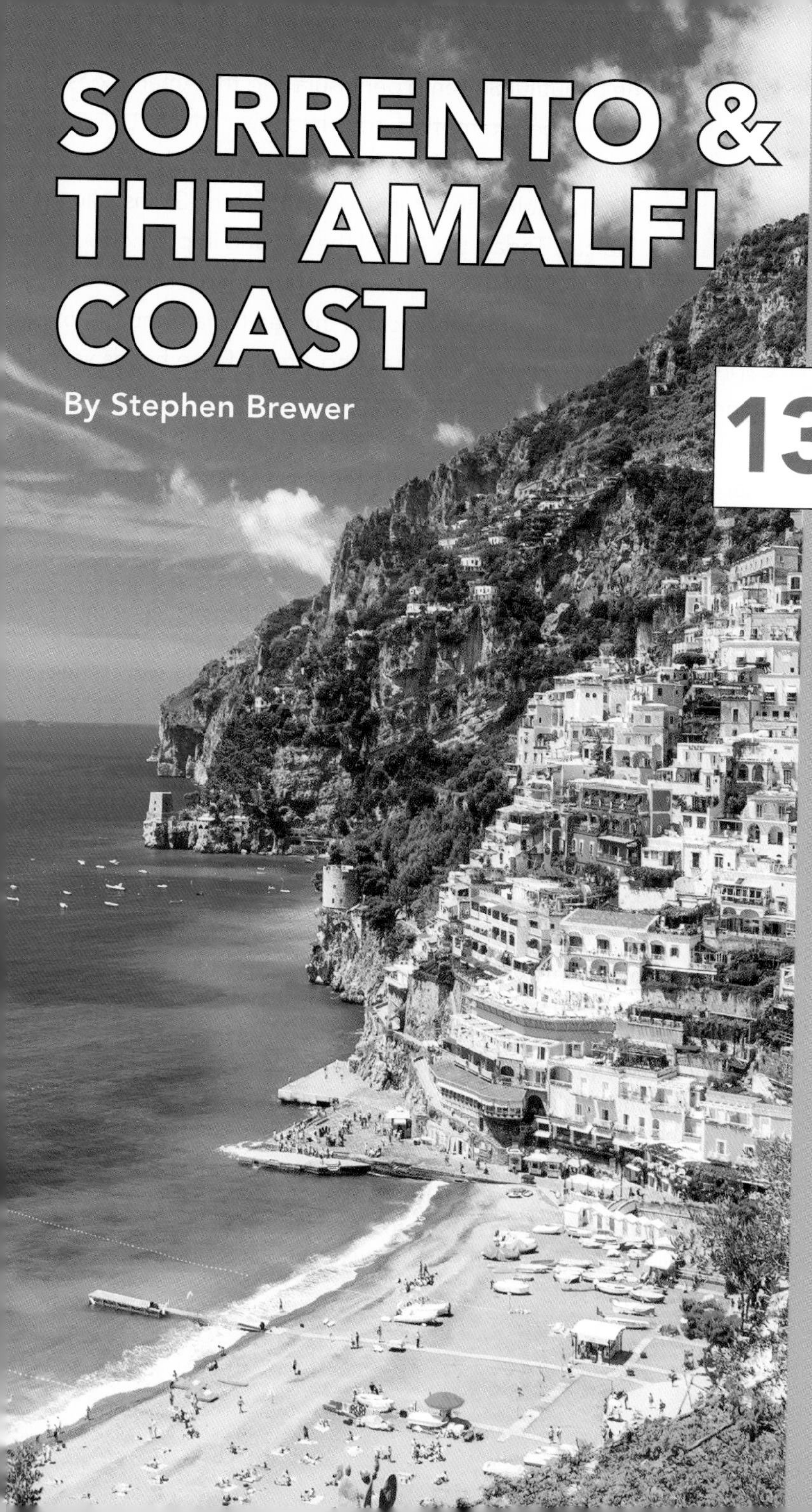

The beautiful Sorrento peninsula and the Amalfi Coast have been tempting travelers ever since Ulysses sailed by, having filled his sailors' ears with wax and tied himself to the mast to withstand the Sirens' alluring call. Today, the pull of the sea and imposing rock-bound coast remain just as compelling. Graceful old Sorrento is perched high atop a cliff gazing across the sea toward the isle of Capri. The spectacular but nerve-racking Amalfi Drive heads vertiginously east, clinging to cliffs and rounding one bend after another until it comes to Positano, a tile-domed village hugging a near-vertical rock, then to Amalfi, a little seaside town that was once the center of a powerful maritime republic.

With transporting green hillsides, azure seas, and the enticing scent of lemon and frangipani, the charms of Sorrento and the Amalfi Coast are no secret. You'll do yourself a favor if you schedule a visit for the early spring or fall, before and after the peak summer season, and even then accept the fact that you will not have this slice of paradise to yourself.

DON'T LEAVE SORRENTO & THE AMALFI COAST WITHOUT . . .

Floating Between Heaven and Earth in the Belvedere Cimbrone. In the gardens of Ravello's Villa Cimbrone, this coastal panorama of the shimmering Mediterranean meeting the blue sky just may be the most beautiful view in the world.

Strolling Along Capri's Via Tragara. With the sea twinkling far below, a warm breeze rustling the pines, and the legendary Faraglioni rock formations rising from the waves, you'll think you've found heaven on earth.

Taking a Bus Down the Famed Amalfi Drive. Transport by public bus may not seem as glamorous as handling the hairpin curves in an Alfa Romeo, but the views are just as spectacular and you won't have to worry about keeping your eyes on the road.

Soaking on Ischia. Hot, mineral-rich waters bubble up everywhere on this beautiful island—on beaches, into the sea, and most hedonistically, in pleasure-geared thermal parks where luxuriant gardens are laced with soothing pools.

PREVIOUS PAGE: **Positano on the Amalfi Coast.**

Campania & the Amalfi Coast

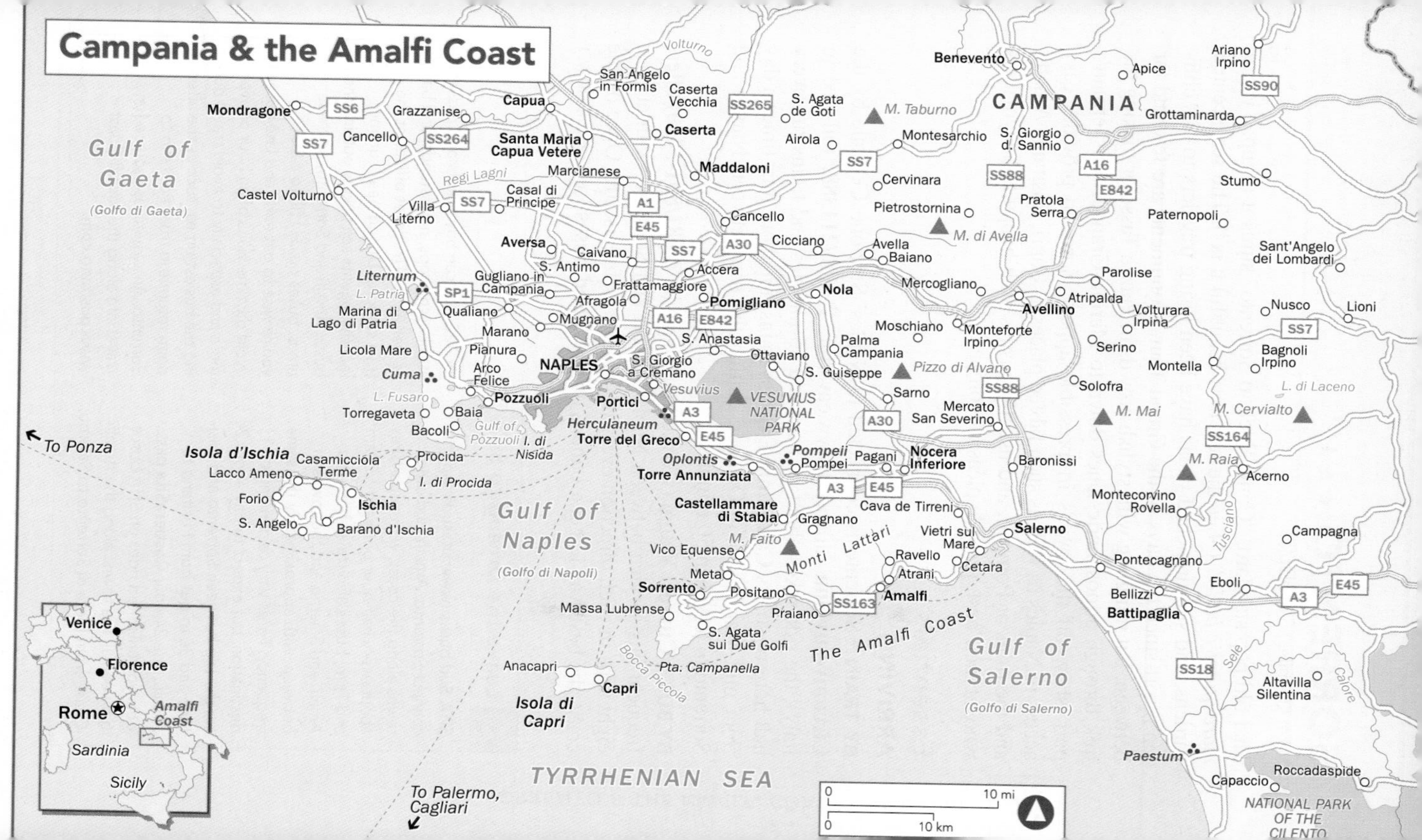

SORRENTO ★★★

50km (31 miles) S of Naples

That old pop standard, "Come Back to Sorrento" sums it all up: *"Vir 'o mare quant'è bello"* ("See the sea, how beautiful it is"). The sea, scented gardens, and sun-drenched vistas have been luring travelers to this cliff-top resort since the days of the Grand Tour. Monuments are few and far between, but mingling with stylish crowds in Piazza Tasso or making the trek through atmospheric lanes down to Marina Grande, a fisherman's port, show off the town's irrepressible appeal. Sorrento provides easy access to Naples as well as such fabled places as Capri, Positano, Amalfi, and the ruins at Pompeii, and usually bustles with happy holidaymakers who, at their best, provide pleasant company.

Essentials

ARRIVING

BY TRAIN Sorrento is connected to Naples' Stazione Centrale by the **Circumvesuviana** railway (www.eavsrl.it; ✆ **800/211388,** toll-free in Italy); the ride takes about an hour and 15 minutes and trains run every half hour or so. Its **Campania Express** trains run about four times a day from mid-March to mid-October, cutting the trip between Naples and Sorrento to less than 50 minutes.

BY BUS **Curreri Viaggi** (www.curreriviaggi.it; ✆ **081/801-5420**) offers frequent bus service between Naples airport and Sorrento, with at least eight trips in each direction every day; one-way fare is 10€. Once on the coast, the best way to get around is on **SITA Sud buses** (see box below.)

Leave the Driving to SITA Sud

SITA Sud buses (www.sitasudtrasporti.it) connect Sorrento, Amalfi, and other towns along the coast, with departures about every half-hour between 6:30am and 7pm; buses also travel between Amalfi and Salerno and the towns in between, with approximately the same frequency. Fares vary depending on destination, but expect to pay about 2€ for the trip between Sorrento and Positano and 3€ to get from Positano to Amalfi. The 24-hour **CostieraSita** pass gets you unlimited rides on SITA buses between all the towns along the Amalfi Coast, from Meta di Sorrento to Salerno, for 12€. You can buy tickets and passes at tobacco shops, newsstands, and bars, as well as at SITA ticket offices at the train stations. During peak summer months, agents sell tickets outside the bus in Amalfi and Sorrento. At these times, buses quickly fill to capacity—you're wise to get early and late buses to avoid daytime waits of an hour or even more and especially to avoid travel during the busiest times, such as the afternoon return trip from Positano to Sorrento. An easy-to-use source for travel info along the Amalfi Coast is **www.positano.com**.

ATTRACTIONS
Chiesa di San Francesco **13**
Largo Dominova **10**
Marina Grande **3**
Museo Correale di Terranova **26**
Villa Comunale **14**

HOTELS
Artis Domus **6**
Grand Hotel Cocumella **25**
Hotel Antiche Mura **20**
Hotel Rivoli **15**
La Badia **1**
M Suites **23**
Masseria Astapiana Villa Giusso **25**
Palazzo Marziale **12**
Parco di Principe **25**
Sorrento Relais **25**
Ulisse Deluxe Hostel **5**

RESTAURANTS
A'Marenna **9**
Davide **11**
Il Bagni Delfino **2**
Inn Bufalito **8**
Kebab Ciampa **19**
La Cantinacci del Popolo **24**
Leone Rosso **22**
Pizzeria del Franco **24**
Primavera **18**
Ristorante Museo Caruso **17**
Ristorante o'Parruchiano La Favorita **7**
Ristorante Pizzeria Tasso **21**
Star Pub **16**
Trattoria da Emilia **4**

BY BOAT In summer, ferries and hydrofoils operated by **NLG-Navigazione Libera del Golfo** (www.navlib.it; ✆ **081/552-0763**) and **Linee Lauro** (www.alilauro.it; ✆ **081/497-2206**) make daily runs to and from Sorrento, Naples, Ischia, Capri, Positano, and Amalfi, with limited service between Sorrento and Naples off-season. Boats not only provide a scenic ride, but traveling by sea is also a welcome alternative to the traffic-choked coastal roads in high season. The trip between Naples and Sorrento takes only 40 minutes, faster than on the train.

BY CAR By **car** from Naples, take the A3, and exit at Castellammare di Stabia for the SS145 to Sorrento. Allow about 1 hour and 10 minutes for the drive. The trip from Naples to Sorrento by **taxi** costs about 90€. The ride is metered, but drivers will usually establish a price before you set off. Taxis within Sorrento are exorbitant, so it's best to avoid using them when possible; hotels will advise you on the many options for traveling by bus and boat.

VISITOR INFORMATION Sorrento's **tourist office** is at Via Luigi de Maio 35, off Piazza Tasso (✆ **081/807-4033;** daily 8:30am to 7pm in summer, Mon–Fri 8:30am–4pm rest of year). An **information office** outside

choosing A TOWN

Just about everyone who visits Sorrento and the Amalfi Coast comes away with a favorite town to which they yearn to return. It's hard to go wrong in this beautiful part of the world, but you may want to take some practical considerations into account. **Sorrento** is best situated as a base for exploring, given its excellent train, bus, and boat connections to Capri, Naples, Pompeii, Herculaneum, and other towns. **Positano** is the most picturesque and resortlike, with the best (and most easily accessible) beaches, though getting in and out of town in high season on the traffic-choked coast road can be a nightmare (boats are a pleasant alternative). **Amalfi** provides small-town charm and gives you a two-fer—its beautiful neighbor **Ravello.** You can also avoid the worst of the coastal traffic by approaching and leaving Amalfi on buses through Salerno, with its excellent train connections to Naples.

the train station (daily 10am–1pm and 3–7pm) is run by a private company whose interest is to book tours, but they are helpful with advice on transportation and other matters. The station newsstand sells bus tickets to points all along the Amalfi Coast. An informative web source is **www.sorrentoinfo.com**.

Exploring Sorrento

Sorrento is long and narrow, strung out along the top of seaside cliffs. Just about everything you want to see is an easy walk from the train station, with the exception of the two ports, which many residents opt to reach by the town's little minibuses (1.30€). **Marina Piccola,** below Piazza Tasso, is the commercial port where ferries and hydrofoils dock; **Marina Grande,** below the town's western edge, is the old fishing port. An elevator descends from Villa Comunale to the seaside next to Marina Picola (1.10€ each way).

The center of town is sunny **Piazza Tasso.** Amid the piazza's cafes and glossy shops stands a statue of the namesake poet, Tarquato Tasso, who was born into a noble family in Sorrento in 1544 and died in a madhouse at the age of 51. The piazza dramatically spans a deep gorge; the north end overhangs a steep hillside that descends

Sant'Antonio Sabate monument in Piazza Tasso, in the heart of Sorrento town.

to Marina Piccola, while to the south you can follow a walkway and look down into a verdant valley where a settlement flourished by a stream as early as the 5th century B.C. Work is underway on a path into the gorge.

The old town is bisected by busy **Corso Italia** (closed to car traffic). Along the Corso a few blocks west of the square, at Via Santa Maria della Pieta, is Sorrento's **cathedral** (www.cattedralesorrento.it; ✆ **081/878-2248;** free admission; daily 8am–12:30pm and 4:30–8:30pm). Frequent rebuilding has rendered the facade rather bland, except for an intriguing arcaded three-story campanile with embedded Roman columns; inside are doors inlaid with scenes of Sorrento life, a map of the town, and an enormous *presepe* (nativity scene), set on the streets of Naples with Mt. Vesuvius looming behind the manger. North of here are the quieter precincts around the gardens of the **Villa Comunale and Piazza della Vittoria,** both opening to sweeping views of the bay. A filling way to get to know the town is with **Secret Walks of Sorrento,** from Tour Guide Naples (tourguidenaples.com; ✆ **338/888-4282**); you'll tour artisan workshops and quiet neighborhoods in the company of a native while stopping for coffee, gelato, and limoncello. The fee is 40€.

Chiesa di San Francisco ★★ CHURCH Top choice for the most charming spot in Sorrento goes to the 14th-century Moorish and Romanesque cloisters of this church and convent, where an old pepper tree shades tufa-rock arches interspersed with elaborately capped columns. Inside the church, Francis is shown above the altar in a transcendent moment when, after weeks of fasting and praying, wounds opened on his hands, sides, and feet, bringing him close to the suffering Christ in body as well as in spirit.

Piazza Francesco Saverio Gargiulo. ✆ **081/878-1269.** Free. Daily 8am–8pm.

Largo Dominova ★★ SQUARE For Sorrentines, this little square in the old quarter at the intersection of Via San Cesareo and Via P. R. Giuliani is the real heart of town. The town council used to meet in the 16th-century Sedile Dominova, an arched loggia with a green-tile cupola; its richly frescoed interior of trompe l'oeil columns and scenes of aristocratic life is now a gathering spot for retired workers. The old gents are used to visitors popping in to admire their opulent surroundings, so don't be shy.

Marina Grande ★★ NEIGHBORHOOD Walking past a row of narrow houses squeezed along the quays between the steep hillside and the sea, you'll get a sense of Sorrento as an old-time fishing port. Even so, you'll have to contend with shills trying to lure you into restaurants with multi-language menus (a few restaurants here are excellent; see p. 649). It's a nice walk from Sorrento down to the port; just follow the well-marked road from Piazza Vittoria, which eventually becomes a staircase and passes beneath a Greek gate—a reminder that Marina Grande was once a separate town that was vulnerable to pirate raids, a much riskier

Colorful Marina Grande in Sorrento.

place to live than fortified Sorrento. You can take a dip here, but the small, pebbly beach is less than inviting; for better options, see p. 645. The scene is quite romantic in the evening, with moonlight illuminating a harbor full of bobbing boats. Should you have one *limoncello* too many while taking in the spectacle, hop on the minibus to get back up the hill.

Museo Correale di Terranova ★ MUSEUM Counts Alfredo and Pompeo Correale donated the collection their family had amassed since 1500; the randomness of the assortment is its charm. Neapolitan paintings from the 17th through 19th centuries capture the scenic Sorrento views that have been inspiring travelers since the days of the Grand Tour. Inlaid intarsia furniture is from studios right here in Sorrento, and much of the porcelain was fired in kilns on the grounds of the Capodimonte palace in Naples. It's all housed in the salons of an elegant 18th-century villa set into another star attraction, an enormous palm-shaded garden through which paths wind to a clifftop viewpoint that affords stunning vistas up and down the coast.

Via Correale 50. www.museocorreale.it. ✆ **081/878-1846.** 5€; free for children 10 and under. Hours and fees are subject to change and may be reduced as the museum undergoes ongoing restorations. Mon–Sat 9am–2pm.

Villa Comunale ★★ PARK/GARDEN Views from one side of this delightful, palm-studded patch of greenery take in the port far below and a broad sweep of the bay of Naples. A statue of St. Francis stands amid the cliffside gardens, looking contented to be in such pleasant surroundings. From the far side of the gardens you can take an **elevator** (1.10€) or follow a well-marked lane and stairway down to Marina Piccola and some so-called beach clubs, where pier-like platforms are lined with sun loungers.

Beaches

You can swim from pebbly patches at Marina Grande or Marina Picola, or rent a sunbed at one of the many beach clubs to the west of Marina Picola, where umbrellas extend along piers onto the breakfront. These include **Leonelli's** (www.leonellisbeach.com) and **Marameo** (www.marameobeach.com). Sunbed rentals are about 18€ a day, and food is served. The nicest close-to-town beach is **Marinella,** below the cliffs in Sant'Agnello, an attractive seaside community that adjoins Sorrento to the east. You can use the facilities at **Spiaggia la Marinella** (www.lamarinellasorrento.com), or perch for free on a concrete platform that extends onto a jetty; the water and views are lovely. For real sand, take the Circumvesuviana train

Villa Comunale is a lovely green place to stroll and drink in sweeping bay views.

or the EAV bus (www.eavsrl.it; 2.20€; leaves from in front of the Sorrento train station) to the beach at **Meta,** popular among Neapolitans out for a day in the sun. A slightly less-crowded beach west of town, also reachable on the EAV bus from the station, is **Bagno della Regina Giovanna** (Queen Giovanna's Bath) at Punta del Capo, the northwestern tip of the Sorrento Peninsula. Here a small rock-sheltered cove of clear water, reached on a path through citrus and olive groves, was once the private harbor of the ancient Roman Villa of Pollio Felice. Step through the ruins at the top of the cliff, where cultured man of letters Pollio Felice once entertained guests with readings of Virgil and Horace. Just beyond, also reached by the A bus, is **Marina di Puolo,** a little fishing port where you can swim from a sandy beach.

Set Sail

You can spend a pleasant day exploring the region on a boat tour, either cruising along the coast with stops in Positano and Amalfi, or sailing over to Capri, with time on the island. Rates are 50€ for the Amalfi tour, 55€ for the Capri tour, including hotel pickup, on a boat that accommodates about 50 passengers. Among many companies offering the trip is **Jolly Rent,** Corso Italia 3 (www.jollyrent.com; ✆ **081/877-3450**).

Where to Stay in Sorrento

EXPENSIVE

Grand Hotel Cocumella ★★★ Of all Sorrento's grand hotels, this magically converted monastery is the most serene, set amid lush gardens above the sea in Sant'Agnello, a residential enclave at the eastern end of town. Rooms created from combined monk's cells are chic and sophisticated, mixing antiques with nice contemporary touches, offset with gleaming white tile floors. Some have sea-view terraces while others hang over orange-scented gardens, where a pool is tucked into the greenery. An elevator descends to the sea and a swimming platform.

Via Cocumella 7, Sant'Agnello. www.cocumella.com. ✆ **081/878-2933.** 48 units. 300€–500€ double. Rates include breakfast. Closed Nov to mid-Apr. **Amenities:** Restaurant; bar; concierge; pool; beach; free Wi-Fi.

Palazzo Marziale ★★★ You can't help but feel a bit privileged in this character-filled old *palazzo* in the heart of town, as if you're visiting aristocratic relatives. In fact, this is the ancestral home of the proprietors, who've turned a stone-arched entrance court into a glassed-in lounge and furnished the huge guest rooms with old family prints and antiques, adding designer touches with deep colors and rich fabrics. All have queen- or king-size beds, sofa beds, and enormous marble bathrooms.

Piazza Francesco Saverio Gargiulo 2. www.palazzomarziale.com. ✆ **081/807-4406.** 7 units. 175€–280€ double. Rates include breakfast. Closed Dec to mid-Jan. **Amenities:** Restaurant; bar; parking (18€); free Wi-Fi.

Parco di Principe ★★ On grounds where Jesuit friars once grew aphrodisiac plants, in the early 19th century Prince Leopold, Count of Syracuse commissioned a villa in which he could lead a life wholeheartedly devoted to pleasure away from his fanatically religious wife. Tsar Nicholas II of Russia didn't make it in time to see the *dacha* built on the grounds for his visit a century later. In the 1960s, architect Gio Ponti (designer of Milan's Pirelli Tower) redid the place, creating stunning surroundings that are also an artistic statement that's all about blue: blue sky and blue sea beyond the terraces and huge windows, blue tiles covering the floors—even the upholstery on the impeccable Modernist chairs and couches is a blue that Ponti calibrated. The restful effect is to make you feel, as Ponti intended, that you're floating between sea and sky.

Via Rota 44, Sant'Agnello. www.royalgroup.it/parcodeiprincipi. ✆ **081/878-4644.** 96 units. 150€–550€ double. Rates include breakfast. Closed early Jan–Feb. **Amenities:** 2 restaurants; bar; pool; beach; spa; gym; free Wi-Fi.

MODERATE

Hotel Antiche Mura ★★★ This elegant Art Nouveau–style palazzo built atop the town's former defensive walls reveals many surprises, including a huge garden filled with lemon trees surrounding a pool, as well as precipitous views from many rooms into the deep gorge that runs through Sorrento. Attractive public lounges flow over a couple of floors and include a conservatory-like breakfast room. Guest quarters are bright and cheerful, with colorful Vietri tile floors; many have balconies facing the gorge or town, while some are tucked into the garden. Service is as gracious and welcoming as the surroundings.

Via Fuorimura 7 (entrance on Piazza Tasso). www.hotelantichemura.com. ✆ **081/807-3523.** 46 units. 130€–250€ double. Rates include breakfast. Closed Jan to mid-Mar. **Amenities:** Bar; concierge; garage; pool; free Wi-Fi.

Hotel Rivoli ★ Convenience comes with high style at this strikingly revamped convent right in the center of town. A dramatic glass staircase floats up to airy, smartly decorated guest rooms and a rooftop breakfast room and terrace. Cozy, antiques-filled reading nooks open off the landings (there's also an elevator). You'll trade a pool and sea views for a center-of-town location—pedestrian-only town lanes are just outside the soundproofed windows, and the train station, port, and bus stops are nearby, making this a very handy base for exploring the coast.

Via Santa Maria delle Grazie 16. www.sorrentorivoli.com. ✆ **081/365-4089.** 8 units. 70€–220€ double. Rates include breakfast. Discounts for longer stays. Closed Jan–Mar. **Amenities:** Free Wi-Fi.

La Badia ★★ A centuries-old monastery perched high on a hilltop is an idyllic getaway retreat, where extensive gardens of olive trees and pines are filled with sea views, and guest quarters, many opening to balconies, are soothingly done with colorful tiles and light furnishings. A huge panoramic terrace serves as a bar and outdoor living/dining room, and a pool is set amid the greenery. A footpath winds down the hillside to the center of Sorrento, a 10-minute descent, and buses stop just outside the gates.

8 via Capodimonte. www.hotellabadia.it. ✆ **081/878-1154.** 28 units. 145€–175€ double. Rates include breakfast. Min. stay required at peak times. Closed Nov to mid-Apr. **Amenities:** Restaurant; bar; pool; free Wi-Fi.

M Suites ★★ You might be tempted to settle in for the whole season in these fashionable apartments carved out of a private villa on a hillside above town. Each of the roomy one-bedroom units sleeps four and has a kitchen, terrace, and large bathroom with Jacuzzi tub. Antiques, Vietri tile floors, and paintings create rich surroundings inside, while extensive gardens and terraces are pillowed in flowers and lush foliage. Views extend across the peninsula to the sea. Guests can use the pool and facilities at the Hotel Mediterraneo, down the hill in seaside Sant'Agnello.

Via Rubinacci 5. www.msuitesorrento.com. ✆ **081/350-9956.** 3 units. Doubles 125€–185€; longer-stay rates available; min. stays sometimes required. **Amenities:** At nearby Hotel Mediterraneo: 2 restaurants, 2 bars, pool; free Wi-Fi.

INEXPENSIVE

Masseria Astapiana Villa Giusso ★★ An ancient monastery turned noble residence perched at the top of a hill outside Vico Equense is surrounded by parkland, olive groves, and vineyards, all set on 14 hectares (35 acres) overlooking the sea and the coast. Salons-turned-guest-rooms in the atmospheric old house are comfortably done with plump armchairs, antiques, and wrought-iron beds, with a smattering of original frescoes and arched ceilings throughout. Breakfast with lemons, walnuts, apples, and other bounty from the farm is served in a vast tiled kitchen, and the grounds are laced with woodland paths, sunny terraces, and other quiet hideaways. Sorrento is 10km (6 miles) west, making a car a necessity in this out-of-the way spot.

Via Camaldoli 51. www.astapiana.com. ✆ **081/802-4392.** 15 units. 90€–120€ double, discounts for longer stays and half-board available. Rates include breakfast. Closed Nov–Mar. **Amenities:** Restaurant; pool; free Wi-Fi.

Sorrento Relais ★★ No sea views, no balconies, no grand hotel atmosphere—but this small, comfortable inn on the lower levels of an apartment house across from the Museo Correale di Terranova is appealing and an extremely good value. Compact, contemporary-style rooms have excellent beds and good lighting (both a rarity in lower-priced Italian hotels) and are artfully decorated with striped fabrics, bright colors, and quirky wall coverings. Mood lighting in the showers changes with the touch of a remote control, adding an extra splash to the sleek bathrooms. Rooms on the ground floor are bright despite the lack of views—those in the rear are blissfully quiet—though some less desirable accommodations are in the basement, where a decent breakfast is served in a large, convivial space.

Via Bernardino Rota 5. www.sorrentorelais.com. © **081/1892-0834.** 7 units. 70€–130€ double. Rates include breakfast. **Amenities:** Lounge; free Wi-Fi.

Ulisse Deluxe Hostel ★★ Hostel life takes on a glossy sheen in these chic, sprawling lounges and large, handsomely furnished guest rooms. A few quadruples remain true to the dormlike hostel image, but for the most part the emphasis is on quiet, hotel-standard comfort. Rooms lack thrills—no balconies or sweeping sea views—but white-tile floors shine, wood furnishings are polished to a high gloss, beds are firm (many are king-size), and extras include minibars and a luxury spa with steam room, sauna, and large pool. The hillside perch is nicely located on the road down to Marina Grande, just west of the historic center.

Via del Mar 22. www.ulissedeluxe.com. © **081/877-4753.** 50 units. 50€–140€ double. Discounts for longer stays. Rates include breakfast. **Amenities:** Bar; spa; pool; free Wi-Fi.

Where to Eat in Sorrento

For a quick meal, try the veal or chicken kebabs at **Kebab Ciampa,** Via Pieta 23 (© **081/807-4595**), which also serves falafel and meatballs. **Star Pub,** Via Luigi de Maio 17 (© **081/877-3618**), satisfies a hamburger craving, and also makes excellent salads that are meals in themselves, washed down with a well-curated selection of wine and beer. **A'Marenna,** Via Tasso 23 (leggimenu.it/menu/amarennasorrento; © **081/1849-5183**), serves excellent sandwiches, many made with *panuozzo,* bread baked from pizza dough. **Pizzeria del Franco,** Corso Italia 265 (© **081/877-2066**), is a local institution that serves calzones, *piadine* (stuffed sandwiches), and pizzas in many varieties. Pizza aficionados head 11km (7 miles) down the bay toward Naples to cliff-hugging Vico Equenese (a 10-min. train ride), where **Pizza a Metro** (www.pizzametro.it; © **081/879-8309**) has been turning out pizzas by the meter since the 1930s.

The beautiful garden of **Artis Domus,** a spa and small hotel at Vico III Fuoro 2 on the western edge of town above Marina Grande (www.artisdomusrelais.com; © **081/877-0670**), is an idyllic daytime retreat (bar closes at 7pm) for a glass of wine and light lunch; for 20€ you can stay all day and use the pool.

Two gelato shops vie for the title of best in town: **Davide,** Via Padre Reginaldo Giuliani 39 (© **081/807-2092;** closed Wed in winter), and **Primavera,** Corso Italia 142 (© **081/807-3252**); flavors at both include deliciously creamy *noci di Sorrento* (Sorrento walnuts) and *delizia al limone* (a lemon cream).

EXPENSIVE

Il Bagni Delfino ★★ SORRENTINE A meal here comes with a perk, the chance to swim off the adjoining pier. That's a good incentive to eat lightly from the snack food menu, though the heaping platters of fresh seafood pastas are tempting. It's a popular Sunday afternoon lunch choice, when locals come down to take in the sun and indulge in excellent cooking and polished service.

Western end of port off Via Marina Grande. www.ristoranteildelfinosorrento.com. ✆ **081/878-2038.** Entrees 12€–24€. Daily noon–2:30pm and 6:30–9:30pm. Closed Nov–Mar.

Ristorante Museo Caruso ★★ NEAPOLITAN/SORRENTINE The great tenor Enrico Caruso lived in Sorrento shortly before he died in his native Naples in 1921, and he's remembered in these shrine-like rooms by hundreds of photos and posters, while tasting menus show off the Neapolitan and Sorrentine classics he loved, with an emphasis on seafood. Ravioli is stuffed with octopus, and shrimp risotto and simple spaghetti with clams are seasoned with local lemons. Meals are accompanied by a soundtrack of Caruso standards.

Via San Antontino 12. www.ristorantemuseocaruso.com. ✆ **081/807-3156.** Entrees 18€–60€; tasting menus 55€ and 65€. Daily noon–11pm.

MODERATE

Inn Bufalito ★ SORRENTINE The approach here is to use only local products, especially buffalo meats and cheeses (buffalo-milk mozzarella is one of the region's most prized specialties). The brown-toned room gives off a rustic vibe, even though the menu and service are decidedly urbane. Enjoy buffalo steaks or pasta with a heavy sauce of buffalo *ragu,* while a platter of cheeses and salamis is a nice light meal.

Vico I Foro 21. www.innbufalito.com. ✆ **081/365-6975.** Entrees 10€–22€. Thurs–Tues noon–midnight. Closed Jan–Feb.

Ristorante o'Parrucchiano La Favorita ★★★ SORRENTINE This old-time Sorrento landmark dates back to 1868, when a former priest decided to get into the restaurant business (the name means "Priest's Place"). The vast, multilevel, greenhouse-like space opens to a vine-covered garden planted with potted citrus trees, all guaranteed to give the grumpiest customer a festive dining experience. Tour groups pour in, but there's room for everybody, and the food is consistently good. Some dishes, such as baked pasta crêpes stuffed with ricotta, mozzarella, and minced beef, have been on the menu since the start; more recent innovations include some wonderful seafood pastas, like shrimp ravioli in clam sauce.

Corso Italia 71. www.parrucchiano.com. ✆ **081/878-1321.** Entrees 10€–25€. Daily noon–3:30pm and 7–10:30pm.

Ristorante Pizzeria Tasso ★★ SORRENTINE Sorrento prides itself on fresh seafood, and the catch is the focus in these casually elegant salons and glassed-in veranda that wraps around a large garden. Choices change daily, with two reasonably priced set menus, though you can also dine a la carte or have one of the excellent pizzas.

Via Correale 11d. www.ristorantetasso.com. ✆ **081/878-5809.** Entrees 9€–24€. Daily noon–11:30pm.

INEXPENSIVE

La Cantinaccia del Popolo ★★★ SORRENTINE The hams hanging over your head and deli cases next to your table give you a good idea of what to expect at this town favorite on a back lane: a bounty of house-cured meats and local cheeses paired with garden-fresh vegetables, fresh fish, pasta served right from the pan, and expertly grilled steaks. A front garden and homey, rattan-paneled decor adds to a sense that you've walked into a friend's barbecue party, and the house-made wine and limoncello only enhance the feeling.

Vico Terzo Rota. ✆ **366/101-5497.** Entrees 7€–10€. Tues–Sun noon–3:30pm and 7:30–11:30pm (from 6:30pm Thurs); Fri–Sun only Nov–Mar.

Leone Rosso ★ SORRENTINE/PIZZA Sorrentines fill the terrace and bright, rambling rooms for simple, straightforward seafood dishes, offered in many variations. Put down the huge menu and simply ask one of the friendly, English-speaking waiters to recite the daily specials that will likely include all sorts of fresh catch, expertly grilled, and heaping platters of *risotto alla pescatore* (seafood risotto) and *spaghetti alla vongole* (spaghetti with clams). Non-pescatarians can enjoy *gnocchi alla Sorrentina,* pockets of potato pasta filled with mozzarella and topped with tomato sauce, and other land-based Sorrento classics.

Via Marziale 25. www.illeonerosso.it. ✆ **081/807-3089.** Entrees 7€–12€. Daily noon–11:30pm (until 11pm Sun).

Trattoria da Emilia ★★ SORRENTINE The simple pleasures of this old boat shed in Marina Grande are well-known—even Sophia Loren was once a regular—so getting a table during the summer rush may require a long wait. Patience pays off with old-time classics such as *gnocchi alla Sorrentina* (potato dumplings with cheese and tomato sauce) along with

An Acquired Taste?

Lunch and dinner in Sorrento and on the Amalfi Coast often ends with a *limoncello,* usually homemade and often complimentary. Almost every family in Campania has its own recipe, passed on for generations, for this potent and sweet liqueur. True *limoncello* is made from *sfusato di Amalfi,* a particular lemon that has obtained D.O.P. recognition (the stamp of controlled origin for produce, similar to D.O.C. for wine). The Amalfi lemon is large and light in color, with a sweet and very flavorful aroma and taste, almost no seeds, and a very thick skin.

their own variation with seafood, *gnocchi al frutti di mare.* The best tables, of course, are on the pier outside.

Via Marina Grande 62. www.daemilia.it. ✆ **081/807-2720.** Entrees 9€–18€. Daily noon–10pm (closed Tues in winter). Closed Dec–Feb.

Shopping

For a bottle of the town's ubiquitous *limoncello* liqueur, walk out to the touristic-yet-charming **Giardini di Cataldo,** just off Corso Italia near the train station (www.igiardinidicataldo.it; ✆ **081/878-1888**); in a fragrant lemon and orange grove you can taste and buy *limoncello,* marmalade, and other products made on the premises. **Limonoro,** Via San Cesareo 49 (✆ **081/878-5348**), sells chocolate-covered limoncello balls, other candies, and, of course, their own limoncello, with ample tastings on offer. For a more rural experience, head into the hills to the lemon-scented grounds of a former 14th-century Franciscan monastery, **Il Convento,** at Via Lapurlo 12 outside the town of Massa Lubrenese (www.ilconvento.biz; ✆ **081/878-9380**), where the Pollio family makes award-winning limoncello, along with *digestivi* from walnuts and fennel. It's open daily 9am to 6pm in season; tastings 15€.

Lemon-flavored treats abound in the shops of Sorrento.

For centuries, Sorrento craftspeople have been known for producing the beautiful inlaid wood designs known as intarsia. You can see fine examples at the **Museo-bottega della Tarsialignea,** Via San Nicola 28 (www.museomuta.it; ✆ **081/877-1942**), and even order a custom-made piece of furniture if you're tempted. The 19th-century prints of old Sorrento are equally enticing. **Gargiulo & Jannuzzi,** Piazza Tasso 1 (www.gargiulo-jannuzzi.it; ✆ **081/878-1041**), sells fine intarsia, and you can visit the workshops for a demonstration.

Libreria Tasso, Via San Cesareo 96 (✆ **081/807-1639**), stocks a good selection of English-language titles, from the latest thrillers to guidebooks.

Sorrento Nightlife

Epicenter of nightlife in Sorrento is the lively terrace of the **Fauno Bar,** Piazza Tasso 13 (www.faunobar.it; ✆ **081/878-1135**), popular for an *aperitivo* and people-watching throughout the day until late into the evening. **Guarracino,** on Via Sant'Antonino 19 (www.guarracinosorrento.it; ✆ **081/878-1728**), a quiet little back lane off Piazza Tasso, is an especially pleasant place for a cocktail and snacks near the center of town. **Fuoro Caffè,** Via Fuoro 19 (✆ **081/922-5971**), will introduce you to the limoncello spritz and a potent lemon granita infused with limoncello, served in a little alleyway opposite the shop. **La Bottega della Birra,** via San Nicola 13 (✆ **340/591-6221**), stocks hundreds of beers from Italy and all over Europe, and **Officina Wine Bar 82,** in a residential area east of the center at Viale Nizza 17 (✆ **340/069-8477**), serves from an extensive list assembled by its knowledgeable and affable owner Giacomo.

The **cloister of San Francesco,** Piazza Francesco Saverio Gargiulo, is the evocative setting for summertime concerts. Contact the tourist office (p. 641) for a schedule of events, including others staged at many restaurants and taverns in town.

THE SORRENTO PENINSULA

When Sorrento seems a little too crowded, you only need to travel a few miles south into the southwestern stretches of the Sorrento peninsula, where the steep hillsides are carpeted in lemon and olive groves.

Essentials

ARRIVING By **car,** SS145 leads west from Sorrento, then south for access to the peninsula. Both **EAV** and **SITA Sud buses** (see p. 640) serve towns on the Sorrento Peninsula. EAV buses run more frequently, and fares (1.30€) are the same on both, but be sure to specify which line you are using when you buy your ticket. ***Tip:*** To get the best views on the dramatic drive from Sorrento east along the coast, get a seat on the right-hand side of the bus.

VISITOR INFORMATION The **tourist office** in Sorrento (see p. 641) has information on towns and activities, including hiking, on the Sorrento Peninsula. Another good source is the **tourist office** in the center of Massa Lubrense at Viale Filangieri 11 (www.massalubrenseturismo.it; ✆ **081/533-9021**), where the staff will provide info on hiking routes and help you sort out bus schedules for moving around the rest of the peninsula; it's open daily 9:30am to 1pm.

Sant'Agata sui Due Golfi ★★

7km (4½ miles) S of Sorrento

It won't take you too long to figure out where this hilltop village (at 300m/990 ft., you could almost say mountaintop) got the "two gulfs" part of its name. Look to the south, and you'll see the Gulf of Sorrento; turn your head to the north, and there's the Gulf of Naples. It's also easy to see why the town was already famous in the days of the Roman Empire as the junction of trading routes across the peninsula. Artisans working on the 17th-century church of **Santa Maria delle Grazie** matched the views with a ridiculously sumptuous altar of marble, mother of pearl, and lapis lazuli (daily 9am–1pm and 4pm–7pm). Nuns desiring less ostentatious surroundings settled in the **Monastero di San Paolo,** on a hillside 1km (half a mile) outside town; follow Corso Sant'Agata from the center to the pine-shaded drive. Few visitors are invited inside the formidable convent, but the attraction is the **view** from the terrace atop a long staircase: You'll be able to see all the way to Ischia in the northwest and down the coast to Paestum in the east. Before the road to Positano and Amalfi opened in the late 1830s, this was a major stop on the Grand Tour, as far along the coast as view-seekers could get by land. The terrace is generally open April through September daily 8am to noon and 5 to 7pm; and October through March weekends 10am to noon and 3 to 5pm.

Marina del Cantone ★

5km (3 miles) S of Sant'Agata Sui Due Golfi

This cove cut into the cliffs was known to the ancient Greeks as Hyeros Anthos, meaning "Sacred Flower." From Sant'Agata, follow the road down through Metrano then on to hillside Nerano and from there down to Marina del Cantone. The beach (mostly pebbles) is the longest for miles around, packed solid in summer with sunbeds (any number of beach clubs rent them for about 15€ a day) and backed by houses and bars and cafes. Looming just offshore are **Li Galli,** an archipelago of tiny islets (see p. 659).

Massa Lubrense ★★

5km (3 miles) W of Sant'Agata Sui Due Golfi

Quiet hillside Massa Lubrense was once a powerful rival to Sorrento for dominance over this coast. These days its off-the-beaten-track position, along with considerable natural beauty, are the town's great assets. You'll want to pause long enough on Largo Vescovado to take in the dead-on view of the shimmering profile of Capri, just across the bay at this point, then step into the church of **Santa Maria delle Grazie** for a look at its colorful majolica floor; it's open daily 7am to noon and 5 to 7pm.

Massa's port, **Marina della Lobra,** is about 1km (half a mile) below town, reached on foot by following Via Roma until it ends at a centuries-old stone path that cuts through lemon and olive groves down to the sea (you might want to make the ascent by bus). With its pebbly beach and several low-key beach clubs, Marina della Lobra is one of the most pleasant seaside spots on the peninsula.

Punta Campanella ★★

9km (6 miles) S of Massa Lubrense

Lands End on the Sorrento Peninsula is this rocky point where a lighthouse guides ships through the treacherous Capri Narrows, the 3km (2 miles) of swift-moving waters between the peninsula and Capri. The name Punta Campanella refers to the "small bell" that once warned of pirate incursions from atop **Torre Minerva,** a 14th-century watchtower built next to the ruins of a temple dedicated to Athena (called Minerva by the Romans). With luck and divine guidance from the goddess of wisdom, ancient sailors could just make it through the rock-strewn narrows.

Hiking in Punta Campanella.

Hiking Around the Sorrento Peninsula

The peninsula is traversed by a network of 22 well-maintained **hiking** paths that crisscross valleys, meander atop seaside cliffs, and descend hillsides to secret coves for a total length of 110km (68 miles). The **tourist office** in Sorrento (see p. 641) can provide you with maps.

One of the most scenic walks is from the village of **Torca** (2km/1 mile southeast of Sant'Agata sui Due Golfi), where Via Pedara becomes a dirt path that descends a cliff past the ruins of the 12th-century abbey of San Pietro, ending in a quiet cove. Just offshore are the Li Galli islets.

Another walk descends from the village of **Termini** (5km/3 miles southwest of Sant'Agata sui Due Golfi) into the Vallone della Cala di Mitigliano, carpeted with olive groves and *macchia mediterranea,* typical Mediterranean vegetation that includes the beautifully scented *mirto.* The trail then crosses a plateau with large boulders and the ruins of Torre di Namonte, a medieval watchtower, before descending steeply toward the sea, with the profile of Capri looming ahead.

On the southwestern side of the peninsula, the seashore and offshore waters are protected as a marine park, **Area Marina Protetta di Punta Campanella** (www.puntacampanella.org; ✆ **081/808-9877**). A good way to see this unspoiled coast is on a snorkeling cruise with **Punta Cam-**

Leave the Car in the Garage

Driving along the Amalfi Drive, with its many twists and turns, bumper-to-bumper traffic, and near-to-impossible parking, is never a good idea, and at times it's even illegal. Only cars with license plates ending in odd numbers may use the 22-mile stretch between Positano and Vietri sul Mare on odd-numbered dates, those with even-numbered plates other days. Taxis, buses, and residents' vehicles are exempt, as are those of visitors enroute to hotels where they've prebooked parking arrangements. Rules are in affect weekends from mid-June through September, all of August, and Easter week. Check with your hotel for updates, and be prepared to take advantage of the region's many public transport options.

panella Diving, on Via Fontanella in Massa Lubrense (www.puntacampanelladiving.com; ✆ **338/471-2360;** 3-hr. tours, including pickup in Sorrento, from 80€). **Masticiello Boat Service** (www.masticiello.com; ✆ **081/808-1443**) is one of many outfits in Marina del Cantone that rents motor launches on which you can explore the shoreline; prices begin at about 150€ a day for a motorized rubber boat that accommodates six.

Where to Eat Around the Sorrento Peninsula

Don Alfonso 1890 ★★ CREATIVE SORRENTINE The Iaccarino family has won international fame for their charming dining rooms, poolside terrace, and local flavors that infuse their dishes: Breads and pasta are made in-house and almost everything else comes from the family garden or a network of local suppliers. Owner and former chef Alfonso Iaccarino grows the vegetables, shops, and orders; his wife, Livia, oversees the dining room. Homegrown tomatoes infuse a bouillabaisse with freshly caught fish and ravioli filled with farmhouse cheese. If you wish to prolong the experience, **Don Alfonso 1890 Relais** has nine elegant guest rooms, many with a glimpse of the sea and furnished with antiques (from 400€).

Corso Sant'Agata 11, Sant'Agata sui Due Golfi. www.donalfonso.com. ✆ **081/878-0026.** Entrees 35€–45€; tasting menu from 140€. Tues–Fri 8–10:30pm; Sat–Sun 12:30–2:30pm and 8–10:30pm. Closed Nov–Mar.

POSITANO ★★

16km (10 miles) E of Sorrento

Hugging a semi-vertical rock formation, the first town of any size on the Amalfi Drive heading east from Sorrento is the very essence of picturesque, an enticing collection of pastel-colored houses and majolica domes that spill down a ravine to the sea. Novelist John Steinbeck, after a visit in 1953, described it in words that still ring true: "It is a dream place that isn't quite real when you are there and becomes beckoningly real after you have gone." It's not surprising that Positano was the retreat for *la dolce vita* set in the 1960s and '70s. In midsummer, visitors can seem like an invading horde, much like those that attacked the little kingdom back in the 9th to 11th centuries, when it was part of the powerful Republic of the Amalfis, rival to Venice as a sea power.

Essentials

ARRIVING If you're driving down from Naples, take the A3 and exit at Castellammare di Stabia for the SS145 to Sorrento. The SS163 branches off the SS145 before you get to Sorrento and heads over the peninsula to Positano; drive time from Naples is about 2 hours. **SITA Sud** buses (see box p. 640) connect Positano with other towns along the coast. In summer, ferries and hydrofoils operated by **NLG-Navigazione Libera del Golfo** (www.navlib.it; ✆ **081/807-552-0763**) and **Linee Lauro** (www.alilauro.it; ✆ **081/497-2206**) make daily runs to and from Sorrento, Naples, Ischia, Capri, Positano, and Amalfi.

VISITOR INFORMATION The **tourist office** is at Via Regina Giovanna 13 (www.aziendaturismopositano.it; ✆ **089/875067**), open Monday to Saturday 8:30am to 2pm, and also from 3:30 to 8pm in July and August.

Positano's idyllic cityscape and shoreline.

Exploring Positano

Whether you arrive by boat or bus, you're in for an uphill or downhill climb along narrow lanes and steep lanes (wear comfortable walking shoes). At some point you'll want to stay put, probably along the sea at **Marina Grande,** where the town's few fishermen still haul up their boats and ferries arrive and depart. Most of the pebbly shoreline is taken up with a beach, backed by restaurants and bars in what were once shipyards and storehouses when Positano was a naval power. From Marina Grande, **Via Positanesi d'America,** a cliff-side pedestrian promenade, stretches along the shore past the cape of **Torre Trasita** and a 13th-century lookout to the smaller and more relaxing beach of **Fornillo.**

If you wander up the steps from Marina Grande you'll soon find yourself amid a souklike sprawl of shops shaded by bougainvillea-laced trellises. The majolica-domed **Collegiata di Santa Maria Assunta ★★**, Piazza Flavio Gioia (✆ **089/875480;** daily 9:30am–noon and 4–8pm), is Positano's main church, founded as a Benedictine monastery in the 13th century. The "Madonna Nera" (Black Madonna), a Byzantine-style icon above the altar, allegedly gave the town its name when a 12th-century pirate ship carrying the icon sailed into a violent storm. Sailors heard the Madonna on the icon saying "Posa, Posa" ("Put me down") and they took their ship to safety in what would become the harbor of Positano. The icon is carried through the streets on August 15th, the feast of the Assumption of Mary, and in the evening illuminated boats come ashore to commemorate the fateful landing. A relief on the campanile outside shows a wolf nursing seven fish, a clue to how the town once made its living. SITA buses stop twice in Positano: just above Piazza dei Mulini near the center of town and higher up, at the **Chiesa di Nuova** (this will be the first stop if you're coming from Sorrento, the second from Amalfi). To get a sense of this hill-clinging town, get off at the Chiesa Nuova stop and, after taking a look at the church's colorful majolica tile floor, wander down from here. Stepped lanes lined with tiny houses stacked one atop the other will bring you down to the beach at Fornillo, where you can follow the waterfront into the main part of town.

BEACHES & BOATING

Positano has two beaches, **Spiaggia Grande** and the slightly quieter **Fornillo.** You can swim for free at either, or rent a lounger and umbrella for about 10€. Both are backed by open-air beach bars and casual eateries. To reach more idyllic settings, board any of the tour boats that set off from Spiaggia Grande for stops at coves along the coast, or rent a rowboat and poke along the rocky shoreline at your own pace. Boats can be rented from **Lucibello** (www.lucibello.it; ✆ **089/875032**) for 35€ and 60€ per hour, without a skipper, depending on the kind of boat and the duration of the rental.

Many day sailors set their sights on **Li Galli ★★** (The Roosters), the four small islands visible to the west of Marina Grande. According to Homer, Sirens—birdlike creatures with human faces and the bodies of fish—who lived on the rocky outcroppings lured mariners to their deaths on the rocky shoals with their enchanting songs; the islands are also known as the Isole Sirenuse. If the light is right and you've had some wine on the voyage, it's easy to see how the rooster-shaped islets might have appeared to be Sirens rising out of the sea mist. The island to head for is **Gallo Lungo,** where a medieval watchtower rises above a little beach. This is where Russian dancer Rudolph Nureyev settled a few years before his death of AIDS in 1993, transforming a villa built for another Russian ballet star, Léonide Messine (1896–1979), into an Aladdin's cave filled with rich mosaics and kilims. The public is not allowed to step ashore but may swim in the surrounding waters.

HIKING

The 8km-long (5-mile) **Il Sentiero degli Dei** (Path of the Gods) clings to a hillside above Positano, descending from Bomerano, part of the community of Agerola, to Nocelle. The relatively easy, well-signposted trail meanders through cultivated terraces and citrus groves and follows view-filled, vertigo-inducing heights for much of the way. To avoid the strenuous ascent from the coast, take the Sita Sud bus to Amalfi and switch there for a bus to Bomerano. From the village square there, it should take about 3 hours to make the gradual descent.

Where to Stay in Positano

Small, guesthouse-style rooms offer a way to beat Positano's sky-high lodging prices. The **tourist office** (see p. 657) has a full list of bed-and-breakfasts, home stays, and other moderately priced accommodations.

EXPENSIVE

Hotel Buca di Bacco ★ This former fisherman's hut, much expanded and glorified over the years, is right on Marina Grande. The beachfront perch puts you in the center of the action, so convenience comes with a bit of noise, along with endless sea views from colorfully tiled balconies and terraces. Even rooms with partial or no sea views are a bit of a treat, with handsome antiques and comfy upholstered pieces set on tile floors to create a casual, gracious elegance that's typical of the Amalfi Coast. Three generations of the Rispoli family look after guests with care that extends to excellent meals in a sea-facing dining room and an informal snack bar just off the beach below, a good stop for nonguests as well.

Via Rampa Teglia 4. www.bucadibacco.it. ✆ **089/875699.** 46 units. 220€–450€ double (2-night min. stay for some summer dates). Rates include breakfast. Closed Nov–Mar. **Amenities:** Restaurant; bar; beach (public); babysitting; concierge; room service; free Wi-Fi.

Palazzo Murat ★★ Gioacchino Murat, Napoleon's brother-in-law and king of Naples, built this enticing and vaguely exotic 18th-century baroque palace near Positano's small port as a summer getaway. It's still a retreat of royal magnitude, set amid a vast garden and orchard swathed in flowering vines and scented with lemons and jasmine. Five especially large rooms, filled with handsome antiques, are in the original palace; others are in a new but extremely tasteful addition, where tile floors and traditional furnishings adhere to the historical ambience. Most rooms have balconies, some with sea views; others overlook the surrounding greenery and the tile-domed church of Santa Maria Assunta. Buffet breakfast is served in the garden in good weather.

Via dei Mulini 23. www.palazzomurat.it. ✆ **089/875177.** 31 units. 700€–1,000€ double (3-night min. stay for some summer dates). Rates include breakfast. Closed Jan to week before Easter. **Amenities:** Restaurant; concierge; pool; room service; free Wi-Fi.

San Pietro ★★★ One of the world's most fabled getaways perches on its own promontory above the sea, providing the vacation experience of a lifetime. Opulently tiled terraces cascade down the cliff face, laced with shaded nooks and crannies, perfectly poised for hours of relaxation (and the best setting in Positano for a cocktail, expensive but memorable). Facing the sea through huge windows and private terraces, the large accommodations are a gracious mix of antiques, stylishly informal pieces, and elaborate tiles and artwork. The pièce de résistance is the private beach, reached by an elevator that descends through the cliff. For those who want to venture farther, the hotel's private yacht takes guests on complimentary coast cruises, and a free shuttle plies the 2km (1 mile) to town. Many guests, however, choose to stay put in the hedonistic surroundings, relying on the glorious, view-filled terrace of **Il San Pietro** restaurant for exceptional sustenance.

Via Laurito 2. www.ilsanpietro.it. ✆ **089/812080.** 60 units. 790€–2,600€ double. Rates include breakfast. 3-night min. stay in high season. Closed Nov–Mar. **Amenities:** 2 restaurants; 2 bars; concierge; health club; pool; room service; sauna; spa; tennis court; free Wi-Fi.

MODERATE

Hotel Dormira Fornillo ★★ It's hard to imagine a more dreamlike spot than this promontory several hundred feet above the same-named beach. The simple decor and basic comforts don't match the grandeur of the setting, but rooms are large and airy and cheerfully decked out with bright tiles. Many guests will be happy to forgo luxuries in a perch like this, with sweeping views over town and sea from all the rooms, which open to patios and the pine-shaded, edge-of-the-cliff garden beyond. Reaching this spot requires maneuvering steps and narrow lanes, so notify the staff before you arrive to plan logistics and get help with your bags.

Via Fornillo 27. www.hoteldimorafornillo.it. ✆ **089/811422.** 7 units. 150€–250€. Rates include breakfast. Closed Nov–Mar. **Amenities:** Garden; free Wi-Fi.

Hotel Savoia ★ You won't find a lot of luxe amenities, but a great location right in the heart of Positano, steps from the beach and easy to reach by car, is coupled with pleasant decor—bright tile floors, comfortable beds, and attractive traditional furnishings. Some rooms have sea views, and others take in the sweep of the old town climbing the hillside. The old-fashioned ambience comes with a provenance: The D'Aiello family has been running this place since 1936, when Positano was a getaway for a select few, and that's how they treat their guests still.

Via Cristoforo Colombo 73. www.savoiapositano.it. ✆ **089/875003.** 39 units. 130€–240€ double. Rates include breakfast. **Amenities:** Bar; babysitting; concierge; room service; free Wi-Fi.

Hotel Villa Yiara ★★★ Imara and Silvio have converted their sun-drenched 18th-century villa into a welcoming bed-and-breakfast that combines the warmth of an artfully bohemian home with features found in more expensive Positano hotels: flower-filled terraces, endless sea views, and stylish decor awash in white furnishings set against colorful tiles. The town and beach are a 10-minute walk down the hillside—a little bus makes the climb back up—and this privileged hillside locale seems a world removed from the bustle below.

Viale Pasitea 193. www.villayiara.it. ✆ **089/8122379.** 8 units. 230€–290€ double. Rates include breakfast. **Amenities:** Free Wi-Fi.

INEXPENSIVE

La Fenice ★★★ All the charm and beauty of Positano comes to the fore in this little parcel of heaven clinging to a cliff on the outskirts of town. A stay requires a bit of walking and climbing, to and from the town center (about a 10-min. stroll) and on the gorgeous property itself, along shaded walkways and stone stairways through gardens to the pool and private beach below—an amenity found in only a few much more expensive retreats along the coast. Simple whitewashed rooms, most with tiled terraces overlooking the sea, are tucked into villas and cottages that descend the hillside amid lemon groves and grapevines. Owner Constantino Marino and his family live on the property and make guests feel at home, carting bags up and down the stairs and serving informal meals made with produce from the garden (meals served on request).

Via Giuglielmo Marconi 4. lafenicepositano.com. ✆ **089/875513.** 14 units. 140€–170€. Rates include breakfast. Closed Dec–Feb. **Amenities:** Pool; beach; free Wi-Fi.

La Rosa dei Venti ★★ Each of the humbly furnished, tile-floored rooms in this house high on a hillside in a quieter part of Positano comes with a big perk: a large planted terrace with a sea view. It's tempting to settle in here and stay put, but moving around town and the coast is easy to do; the beach at Fornillo is at the bottom of many flights of steps, shops and restaurants are nearby, and it's an easy climb up to the bus stop or along lanes into the heart of town and the harbor.

Via Fornillo 40. www.larosadeiventi.net. ✆ **089/875252.** 150€–220€ double. Rates include breakfast. **Amenities:** Free Wi-Fi.

Where to Eat in Positano

EXPENSIVE

Next 2 ★★ AMALFITAN Step through iron gates into this softly lit courtyard with knockout sea views and a contemporary room of dazzling white linens and bright cushions. You'll dine on refined takes on local favorites, many made with fresh ingredients from the restaurant garden. Fried ravioli stuffed with ricotta and mozzarella are set on a bed of tomatoes plucked from the vine minutes before, while *fiori di zucchini* (zucchini flowers) are filled with ricotta, mozzarella, and basil and served with pesto sauce. Fresh fish is a specialty, paired with the same homegrown ingredients.

Via Pasitea 242. https://next2.it. ✆ **089/8123516.** Reservations recommended. Entrees 16€–25€. Daily 6:30pm–11:30pm. Closed Jan–Mar and Wed in off-season.

MODERATE

Da Adolfo ★★ AMALFITAN/SEAFOOD One of Positano's old-time favorites, tucked away in a secluded cove east of town, is part beach club and part restaurant. The kitchen focuses on local specialties such as mozzarella *alla brace* (grilled on fresh lemon leaves), followed by a beautifully seasoned *zuppa di cozze* (mussel stew). Come for lunch and spend the afternoon, making use of the adjacent changing rooms, showers, and chair and umbrella rentals. Sooner or later, though, you'll have to face the 450 rugged steps up the hillside to the road—unless you take the free water-shuttle service back to town. Free boat service for customers leaves from Positano beginning at 10am; return trips begin at 4pm.

Via Spiaggia di Laurito 40. www.daadolfo.com. ✆ **089/875022.** Reservations (by phone only) recommended. Entrees 10€–18€. Daily 10am–8pm. Closed mid-Oct to early May.

Hostaria di Bacco ★★ SEAFOOD/AMALFITAN In 1948, director Roberto Rossellini and actress Anna Magnani, known affectionately as la Nannarella, lived in a simple fisherman's hut on the beach in Furore (see p. 665). The couple dined regularly in what's still a local gathering spot, where one evening Rossellini broke the news to his lover that he was leaving her for Swedish actress Ingrid Bergman. The fiery Magnani replied by

Photo Op

If you're traveling by car or taxi, just west of Positano on SS 163 (that is, as you approach from Sorrento) keep an eye out for the renowned **Belvedere dello Schiaccone,** the best lookout point on the Amalfi Drive, 200m (656 ft.) above sea level. The view extends across palm and citrus groves to the archipelago of Li Galli and Capo Sottile, with the splendid summit of Monte Sant'Angelo a Tre Pizzi in the background. According to the legend of Monte Sant'Angelo, the devil challenged the Virgin Mary to see who could pierce the rock face. The devil could only scratch the surface, but at the Virgin's touch the rock crumbled and the large opening that you see in one side of the peak appeared.

throwing a dish at Rossellini that has ever since been known as *Ferrazzuoli alla Nannarella,* pasta with swordfish, raisins, pine nuts, and sun-dried tomatoes. It's one of many straightforward local classics served in the view-filled dining room and on the terrace. Upstairs are four pleasant, simple guest rooms (100€–200€ double).

Via G.B. Lama 9, Furore. www.baccofurore.it. ✆ **089/830360.** Entrees 9€–22€. Daily 8:30am–11pm. Closed some winter periods.

Il Ritrovo ★★ AMALFITAN/PIZZA Just being in this mountainside village above Positano is a treat, far removed from the resort scene 450m (1,500 ft.) below. The airy terrace makes the most of the sea and mountain views, and the menu is inspired by both. *Grigliata mista* (grilled meat medley) and the chicken roasted with mountain herbs are hearty and excellent, as are the excellent pastas laden with fresh seafood. Chef Salvatore might come out and insist you follow up a meal with one of his homemade liqueurs. He shares his considerable skills in year-round cooking classes. You can take the SITA bus up from town, or the restaurant will send a car down for a free pickup.

Via Montepertuso 77, Montepertuso. www.ilritrovo.com. ✆ **089/875453.** Entrees 10€–20€. Thurs–Tues noon–3:30pm and 7pm–11:30pm; open daily Apr to mid-Oct. Closed Jan to mid-Mar.

INEXPENSIVE

Pupetto Cafe ★ PIZZA The Pupetto hotel operates this bar on a shady deck just above the sand and rocks on Fornillo beach, serving sandwiches, salads, snacks, and drinks throughout the day. Service is top-notch and attentive, and the staff encourages their clientele to hang around a long time, shuttle back and forth between the tables and the beach loungers below, and enjoy one of the most pleasant experiences in Positano. Climb the stairs to the hotel's lemon-scented terrace for a more substantial lunch or dinner of grilled fresh fish, seafood pasta, or pizza.

Via Fornillo 37. www.hotelpupetto.it. ✆ **089/875087.** Cafe: sandwiches and salads from 5€; May–Oct daily 9am–sunset. Restaurant: entrees 12€–22€; pizza 7€–10€; daily 12:30–3pm and 7:30–10pm. Closed Nov–Mar.

Positano is famous for handcrafted sandals.

Shopping

Though Positano appears to have sold its soul to the devils of commerce, with a few exceptions the endless rows of shops are curiously unenticing. If you can't resist, consider loungewear, a throwback to the '70s when Moda Positano was all the rage. The excellent **Sartoria Maria Lampo,** Viale Pasitea 12 (www.marialampo.it; © **089/875021**), is a holdover from those days. The town is also famous for handcrafted sandals, often made while you wait. Top shoemakers are **La Botteguccia,** Via Regina Giovanna 19 (www.labotteguccia positano.it; © **089/811824**) and **Safari,** Via della Taratana 2 (www.safaripositano.com).

BETWEEN POSITANO & AMALFI ★★

East of Positano, the famed Amalfi Drive swings into full gear, twisting and turning past a number of charming coastal towns. Parking for nonresidents is limited, however, so except for the winter months, you can't really explore them unless you're traveling by bus. SITA buses make stops at all communities along the Amalfi Drive.

With a profusion of porticos and domes, medieval **Praiano** and its adjacent twin, **Vettica Maggiore** (6km/4 miles east of Positano), sit 120m (394 ft.) above sea level on the slopes of Monte Sant'Angelo, draping seaward over the Capo Sottile promontory. (Urbino Positano minibuses, departing from Positano's Piazza dei Mulini, make regular runs to and from the mountainside center

The beautifully tiled dome of San Gennaro in Praiano.

Steps lead down to the picturesque mouth of the fjord in Furore.

of Praiano.) It's said that "Whoever wants to live a healthy life spends the morning in Vettica and the evening in Praiano," which probably just means that this is a good place to spend an entire day, wandering up and down staired alleyways that meander through olive and lemon groves. The towns were the summer residence of the Amalfi doges, who loved the beautiful views over Positano, Amalfi, and the Faraglioni of Capri. The two settlements merge at a sea-facing, majolica-paved piazza in front of the **church of San Gennaro,** which seems more like a ship deck than a shelf of terra firma. From there, follow signs for "Spiaggia" (beach) on lanes tucked into the hillside to **Gavitella,** a tiny slip of pebbles on a cliff-enclosed cove. East of Praiano, picturesque **Marina di Praia** sits at the bottom of a chasm with a small, pebbly beach and the stout Torre a Mare, a 13th-century watchtower, commands a promontory above.

Residents of gravity-defying **Furore,** 12km (7 miles) farther along the Drive (18km/11 miles southeast of Positano), might have the strongest legs in Italy, since it's a climb of more than 500m (1,600 ft.) from the waterfront to the top of the town. Down at sea level, where you'll probably spend most of your time, is the fjord of Furore, a deep cleft in the cliffs that provides a natural harbor. (From the bus stop, next to the bridge across the fjord, it's 944 steps down to the strip of pebbles along the harbor.) When water roars though the fjord with a fury, it's easy to see how the town got its name. You can sit in one of the little bars above the fjord and consider the perils of coastal life as you sip delicious wines from the highly acclaimed winery **Cantine Marisa Cuomo,** Via Lama 14 (www.marisacuomo.com; ✆ **089/830348**); its tasting room is open daily April through October 9am to 6pm; by appointment the rest of the year.

Rambling little **Conca dei Marini,** 2km (1 mile) east of Furore, is really just a hamlet of houses perched hillside along the coast road. It's hard to believe that the little harbor beneath Capo di Conca once bustled with boatbuilding and provided moorage for 27 galleons, making the town richer than Amalfi. More recently, Conca's views and out-of-the way quiet have lured privacy-seeking celebs, among them Jackie O, Carlo Ponti, Princess Margaret of England, and the Queen of Holland.

Today Conca is best known as the jumping-off point for the touristy **Grotta dello Smeraldo** (Emerald Grotto). Stalactites and stalagmites in this famous sea cave, discovered in 1932, produce transcendent light effects, and an otherworldly blue-green aura envelops the grotto when the sun is high and the sea is calm (it's open daily 9am–3pm [until 2:30pm on Mon], but the light effects are best between noon and 3pm). You can reach the cave from the Amalfi Drive (SS 163) via an elevator or a long series of steps, after which you climb into a rowboat for an all-too-short glide through the spectacle. You can also take a boat from Amalfi, just 5km (3 miles) down the coast (trips usually 17€, including admission to the grotto). Admission is 7€, including the rowboat ride through the grotto. The grotto often closes due to inclement weather and rough seas.

While you're in Conca, take time to try Sfogliatella di Santa Rosa, a delicious pastry invented by 17th-century nuns at the local **Convento di Santa Rosa.** The enterprising sisters replaced the traditional ricotta-cheese filling of the popular Neapolitan *sfogliatella* with cream and a dash of *amarene,* candied sour cherries in syrup. And mamma mia!—the creation was a hit that you can still taste in pastry shops all along the coast.

AMALFI ★★

19km (12 miles) E of Positano

From the 9th to the 11th century, the seafaring Republic of Amalfi rivaled the great maritime powers of Genoa and Venice. Nowadays, Amalfi is prominent mostly as an alluring resort town, set among lemon groves and olive trees on the slopes of the Lattari Mountains and the Bay of Salerno. Despite its popularity, Amalfi doesn't seem crushed by tourism as Positano does—at least not in the early morning and evening hours before and after the tour buses and boats descend. The town is within easy reach of some the best stretches of sand and pebbles on the coast.

Evening stroll along Via Amalfi.

Essentials

ARRIVING If you're coming from Positano by land, you'll follow the famous Amalfi Drive (SS 163) by car or take a **SITA Sud bus** (see box p. 640). If you're driving directly from Naples, take *autostrada* A3 to Vietre sul Mar, then head west on SS 163 from there; total travel time is about 1½ hours. **Taxis** offer a flat rate of 130€ to Amalfi from Naples Airport. By public transport from Naples, take the high-speed **train** to Salerno (see p. 712) and from there head west up the coast on the SITA Sud bus (about 90 min. faster than taking the Circumvesuviana train to Sorrento and the SITA bus from there). There is a SITA Sud express bus between Naples and Amalfi, but its schedules are geared to locals: Buses operate mornings and late afternoons on some days, but the return bus to Naples from Amalfi travels in the wee hours of the morning.

In summer, **ferries** and **hydrofoils** operated by **NLG-Navigazione Libera del Golfo** (www.navlib.it; ✆ **081/552-0763**) and **Linee Lauro** (www.alilauro.it; ✆ **081/497-2206**) make daily runs to and from Sorrento, Naples, Ischia, Capri, Positano, and Amalfi.

VISITOR INFORMATION The **tourist office** (www.amalfitouristoffice.it; ✆ **089/871107**) is on the waterfront east of the harbor in Palazzo di Città,

Corso delle Repubbliche Marinare 19. It's open Monday to Friday 9am to 1pm and 2 to 6pm, Saturday 9am to noon (open only in the mornings in winter). Staff hands out some useful booklets on walks in and around town, which you can also download from the website.

Exploring Amalfi

Right by the ferry pier in the center of town, **Piazza Flavio Gioia** opens onto the harbor. The square commemorates the local navigator who some say invented the compass around 1300 (a dubious claim, since sailors used rudimentary compasses, likely introduced by Arab navigators, long before; he might have perfected the compass for marine use). It is fact that Amalfi sailors provided material for some of the first nautical charts of the Middle Ages and also developed a maritime code, the **Tavole Amalfitane,** which was followed in the Mediterranean for centuries, with guidelines for everything from terms for haulage to conditions for the crew. This document is on view in the **Arsenale della Repubblica** (see below).

Amalfi's former role as one of the most important ports and maritime powers in the world is illustrated in a pair of tile panels created by artist Renato Rossi in the 1950s; they're embedded in a wall along the harborfront by the **Porta della Marina.** To the east, on **Corso delle Repubbliche Marinare,** a 1970s-era ceramic piece tells more of Amalfi's history, from its founding by Romans to the arrival of the body of St. Andrew, Amalfi's patron saint.

The medieval heart of Amalfi, a maze of covered walks and narrow streets, stretches from **Piazza Duomo,** a lively cathedral square near the seafront, into an increasingly narrow ravine. You can walk the length of town in 10 minutes or so, along Via Amalfi from Piazza Duomo up to the **Paper Museum** (see p. 669). For much of the town's history, Via Amalfi was a rushing stream; you can still hear water gurgling beneath the pavement. To navigate the town as medieval residents once did, walk up the Ruga Nova Mercatorum, a tunnel-like alleyway east of Via Amalfi that ends in Piazza Santa Spirito. A fountain in the square, **Capo di Ciuccio** (Donkey's Head), is so called because the hard-working beasts could pause here and dip their muzzles into the cool water. A local family decorates every inch of the wall behind the basin with a year-round nativity scene. From another tunnel, this one modern and off Piazza Municipio behind the cathedral (leading to the town's parking garage and Atrani, see below), an elevator whisks you to the top of town for a bird's-eye view over the cathedral's tiled dome, the pastel-hued houses climbing steep mountainsides, and the sea beyond; the easy descent is along stepped lanes.

Arsenale della Repubblica ★★ HISTORIC SITE The Republic of Amalfi's power in the Mediterranean was maintained in this medieval shipyard, where galleys up to 40m (131 ft.) long were built, to be powered by 120 oarsmen. The stone-vaulted boatsheds now house the solid-looking gold coins *(tari)* that Amalfi once minted and the documents with which the republic wielded its considerable legal clout. The spotlight here is on the 66-chapter **Tavole Amalfitane,** a maritime code that more or less established the laws of the high seas from the 13th to 16th centuries. Storms have erased much of the complex, but 10 of 22 piers retain some semblance of their former appearance.

Largo Cesareo Console 3. 2€ (fees vary with exhibitions on display). Summer Tues–Sun 10am–8pm; winter Tues–Sun 10am–1pm and 3–7pm.

Duomo ★★★ CHURCH This monument to Amalfi's rich past, covered in black-and-white marble and rich mosaics, sits atop a monumental staircase just inland from the sea. The **Chiostro del Paradiso** (Cloister of Paradise) is decidedly Moorish, with a whitewashed quadrangle of interlaced arches and brightly colored geometric mosaics. Amalfi's medieval nobles are entombed in sarcophagi set around this exotic enclosure. The **Crypt** houses the remains of St. Andrew, Amalfi's protector saint. It was important for Amalfi to have a famous patron, just as Venice had St. Mark, so soldiers brought the remains of Andrew back from Constantinople at the end of the 4th Crusade, in 1206. Legend has it that Andrew has been working miracles ever since—such as in 1544, when the pirate Ariadeno Barbarossa's fleet, after attacking Amalfi, suddenly sank in a giant sea surge. Andrew's miraculous thick ooze, reverentially called "manna," appears on this tomb every once in a while. An 18th-century baroque restoration of the interior added lots of marble and mundane frescoes, but it's a disappointment after that wonderfully fanciful facade and cloisters. An austere medieval basilica next door holds a museum of gold chalices and other treasures.

Piazza del Duomo. ✆ **089/871059.** Free. Museum and cloister (✆ **089/871324**): 3€. July–Sept daily10am–7:30pm; Oct–Feb daily 10am–1pm and 2:30–4:30pm; Mar–June 9am–6:45pm.

Museo della Carta ★ HISTORIC SITE Among the many goods Amalfi's sailors and merchants brought back from their voyages was paper, a popular commodity throughout the Middle East. From the 13th through the mid-19th centuries, Amalfi was one of Europe's largest exporters of paper, produced in waterwheel-powered factories whose ruins dot the Valle dei Mulini (Valley of the Mills) at the end of town. In the remains of one of the mills a guide shows off vintage machinery and paper that's still sold in Amalfi shops. A path through the valley (see "Hiking" below) takes you past several evocative factory ruins.

Palazzo Pagliara, Via delle Cartiere 24. www.museodellacarta.it. ✆ **089/830-4561.** 4.50€. Mar–Oct and Dec 27–Jan 6 daily 10am–7pm; Nov–Jan Tues–Sun 10am–5pm.

BEACHES & BOATING

Amalfi's **beaches** are two pebbly strips on either side of the harbor. However, the tiny town of **Minori,** 4km (2½ miles) east of Amalfi, has an asset that's the envy of almost every town on the Amalfi Coast: a long, sandy beach surrounded by citrus groves. **Maiori,** separated from Minori by a rocky headland, has an even longer beach, backed by a palm-lined promenade. **Pasticceria Napoli,** in Maiori at Corso Regina 64 (✆ **089/853182**), serves ricotta-filled *sfogliatelle* and other pastries to savor on the beach. SITA Sud buses (see box p. 640) and ferries from Amalfi serve both towns.

From the harbor at Amalfi's **Marina Grande** you can rent **boats**—with or without a skipper—to explore the coast. **Cooperativa Sant'Andrea** (www.coopsantandrea.it; ✆ **089/873190**) offers regular service to the beaches of Duoglio and Santa Croce, only a few minutes away; in summer, boats leave every 30 minutes between 9am and 5pm.

HIKING

A popular **hike** from Amalfi is the walk along **Valle dei Mulini** (Valley of the Mills). Follow Via Amalfi through town until you come to a series of steps to the right as you head away from town; these climb the hillside to a well-signposted trail through lush countryside along the banks of the River Canneto to the **Mulino Rovinato** (Ruined Mill), about 1 hour away. Flour mills once thrived here, as did the paper mills. If you continue to climb the hill, you'll come into the **Vallone delle Ferriere,** where now-ruined *ferriere* (iron mills) operated into the 19th century. At the top of the valley is a waterfall; allow 1½ hours to reach the falls from Amalfi. If you're really ambitious and have another 2 hours, continue from here up to Ravello (see p. 675).

Paths crisscross **Capo d'Orso,** a wild, 1,235-acre headland near Maiori, just east of Amalfi. In Maiori, set off along Via Casale Alto, which becomes a flight of steps, then a mule path leading through vineyards, orchards, and meadows. An uphill trek of about 5km (3 miles) brings you to the Santuario di Maria Santissima Avvocata and sweeping coast views.

Where to Stay in Amalfi

EXPENSIVE

Hotel Luna Convento ★★ St. Francis himself founded this seaside monastery in 1222. The beautiful cloisters and transformed monks' cells and chapel also have a history of hospitality, as one of the first grand hotels on the Amalfi Coast, receiving guests since 1822. American playwright Tennessee Williams spent time here, as did heads of state Otto von Bismarck and Benito Mussolini. Norwegian playwright Henrik Ibsen wrote *A Doll's House* here in 1879. Adding even more luster to the surroundings is a 15th-century Saracen watchtower, now housing a bar and standing guard over a private beach and large seawater pool. Most of the plain-yet-chic guest rooms, many carved out of former monks' cells, have sea views; some have terraces. All are embellished with nice art and antiques to enhance the historic provenance. Lounging in the sunny gardens that

Lemon tree terraces descend to the sea at the clifftop Hotel Santa Caterina.

once supplied the monks' kitchens is yet another experience to savor at this unusual retreat.

Via Pantaleone Comite 33. www.lunahotel.it. ✆ **089/871002.** 48 units. 420€–490€ double. Rates include breakfast. Closed some winter months. **Amenities:** 2 restaurants; bar; babysitting; concierge; outdoor pool; room service; free Wi-Fi.

Hotel Santa Caterina ★★★ One of the world's fabled getaways not only delivers the stay of a lifetime, but also makes guests feel right at home. Rooms and suites are wonderfully luxurious yet unpretentious, set in gardens and citrus groves hovering above the water. Colorful Vietri tiles and handsome antiques add notes of elegance, while balconies and terraces make the most of a cliffside location with the sea twinkling below. A glass elevator and winding garden path descend to a private beach and saltwater swimming pool, and memorable meals are served in a vine-covered, glassed-in dining room or on a seaside terrace. Several private bungalows with private pools tucked into citrus groves provide the ultimate hideaways.

Via Nazionale 9. www.hotelsantacaterina.it. ✆ **089/871012.** 66 units. 350€–1,800€ double. Rates include breakfast. Closed Nov to mid-Apr. **Amenities:** 2 restaurants; 2 bars; beach; concierge; gym; pool; room service; spa; free Wi-Fi.

MODERATE

Hotel Lidomare ★ One of Amalfi's few bargains is set on a small square just beyond the main street, providing pleasant, old-fashioned ambience in a 13th-century *palazzo*. You might find the enormous, high-ceilinged, tile-floored guest rooms either charmingly authentic or a bit ramshackle, but many have sea views, and all are furnished with antiques and comfy old furnishings. Amalfi's beach is just steps away.

Largo Piccolomini 9. www.lidomare.it. ✆ **089/871332.** 15 units. 120€–170€ double. Rates include breakfast. **Amenities:** Free Wi-Fi.

Residenza Luce ★★★ These attractive and comfortable rooms near the town center top the list for an affordable stay in Amalfi. Half of the handsomely decorated, tile-floored units have sleeping lofts tucked above living areas; many have balconies. All have large windows opening onto medieval lanes and squares. A sunny rooftop breakfast room overlooks surrounding hills, while the beach and port are close at hand.

Via Fra Gerardo Sasso. www.residenzaluce.it. ✆ **089/871537.** 10 units. 130€–175€ double. Rates include breakfast. Closed Jan–Feb. Parking available for 20€. **Amenities:** Wi-Fi (free).

Where to Eat in Amalfi

Amalfi is well suited to cafe sitting. On Piazza Duomo, the elegant **Bar Francese** (✆ **089/871049**) serves excellent pastries. Another sweet stop on the piazza is **Pasticceria Pansa** (✆ **089/871065;** closed Tues), concocting delicious pastries since 1830; try the *torta caprese* or sticky, lemon-flavored *delizia al limone.* **Gelateria Porto Salvo,** Piazza Duomo 22 (✆ **089/871636;** closed Jan–Mar), is one of the best *gelaterie* on this part of the coast—try the *mandorla candita* (candied almond) flavor. **Gran Caffè di Amalfi,** Corso Repubbliche Marinare (✆ **089/871047**), overlooks the sea, making it a prime spot for an *aperitivo.*

EXPENSIVE

Da Gemma ★★ SEAFOOD/AMALFITAN Amalfi's old-time classic, in warm-hued rooms tucked behind the cathedral, has been in the hands of the Grimaldi family for several generations, and they hold high standards for the seafood they serve to a loyal and discerning clientele. The house *zuppa di pesce* is a meal in itself, prepared only for two. Equally memorable is the special pasta *paccheri all'acqua pazza,* with shrimp and monkfish. The dessert of choice is *crostata* (pie with jam), made with pine nuts and homemade marmalades of lemon, orange, and tangerine. Reservations, especially on weekends, are a must.

Via Frà Gerardo Sasso 11. www.trattoriadagemma.com. ✆ **089/871345.** Entrees 16€–40€. Daily noon–2:30pm and 7–10:30pm (closed Fri Nov to mid-Apr). Closed 6 weeks Jan–early Mar.

La Caravella ★★★ MODERN AMALFITAN You'll leave today's world behind when you step into this 12th-century palazzo in medieval Amalfi. In romantic dining rooms, candlelight plays off stucco walls adorned with colorful frescoes—a stage-like setting for some of the best food on the coast. This was the first restaurant in Italy to earn a Michelin star, way back in 1967, and ever since, the *dolce vita* set has flocked to these linen-covered tables for Amalfi classics as simple as *scialatelli alla caravella* (handmade pasta in a tomato-seafood sauce) or *pezzogna* (fresh local fish), enlivened with local lemons and mountain herbs. Reservations are a good idea, especially in summer. Refined as the food and setting are, smart informal attire is acceptable; after all, this place is playful enough to embellish its tables with ceramic donkeys.

Via Matteo Camera 12. www.ristorantelacaravella.it. ✆ **089/871029.** Entrees 25€–35€; tasting menus from 60€ (lunch) or 100€ (dinner). Wed–Mon noon–2:30pm and 7–10pm. Closed Nov and Jan.

Ristorante Al Mare ★ PIZZA/AMALFITAN The bamboo-roofed, alfresco dining terrace just above the beach at the Hotel Santa Caterina (see p. 671) is an alluring spot for a seaside lunch. The menu offers a nice choice of pizzas, grilled fish, and pastas that include the hotel specialty, *tagilolini limone,* homemade noodles with a lemon cream sauce. Prices aren't exactly in the beach-shack category, but it's hard to beat the magnificent surroundings for a dash of informal glamour.

Via Nazionale 9. www.hotelsantacaterina.it. ✆ **089/871012.** Entrees 20€–35€, pizzas from 20€. May–Oct daily 12:30–3:30pm.

MODERATE

'a Paranza ★★ SEAFOOD/AMALFITAN The walk between Amalfi and Atrani (see below) is an excellent way to begin and end a meal, especially when the feast is as memorable as those served in this old-fashioned room off Atrani's main piazza. Any meal should include the antipasti, from heavenly Seafood reigns here, right from the start with antipasti of slices of fresh tuna, stewed octopus, and grilled razor clams. Other local favorites include *sarchiapone,* a long gourd stuffed with meat, or *melanzane con la cioccolata*—eggplant with chocolate, deep-fried and topped with walnuts and dried fruit.

Via Dragone 1–2, Atrani. www.ristoranteparanza.com. ✆ **089/871840.** Entrees 12€–23€. Wed–Mon 12:30–3pm and 7–11pm.

Il Tari ★ AMALFITAN/PIZZA The name (after the coin used in the days of the Amalfi Republic) and the setting (an old stable chicly redone with white walls and colorful artwork) harken back to older times in Amalfi, as does the simple menu of traditional favorites. *Scialatielli* (long, fettuccine-like noodles) comes laden with mussels and other seafood (a trio of pastas with various sauces is served as a starter), and the fish soup with pasta and beans is an old Amalfi recipe. Excellent pizza is served at lunch and dinner, and set menus are a very good value.

Via P. Capuano 9. www.amalfiristorantetari.it. ✆ **089/871832.** Entrees 8€–19€. Tasting menus 50€. Daily noon–3pm and 6:30–10:30pm.

L'Abside ★★ SEAFOOD/AMALFITAN This delightful place deserves to be called a temple of gastronomy—after all, it occupies part of a former church. As it is, the arched whitewashed room adds casual charm to a delicious meal (also served on a terrace out front in good weather). Seafood and vegetables are so fresh that even a simple bruschetta with anchovies is memorable, as are the homemade pastas and garden-fresh salads.

Piazza dei Dogi. www.ristorantelabside.it. ✆ **089/873586.** Entrees 9€–20€. Wed–Mon noon–3pm and 7–10pm.

Around Amalfi: Atrani ★★ & Beyond

Pretty little Atrani is just 1km (half a mile) east along the coast, an easy 15-minute stroll. Leaving town, follow the main road around the headland until you come to a staircase signposted for Atrani; the stairs descend to a road leading to the town's beach and harbor. (To avoid walking on the busy road out of Amalfi, take the pedestrian tunnel from Piazza Municipio behind the Duomo; it leads to the town parking garage and will deposit you near the Atrani staircase.) From Atrani's beach, a maze of vaulted alleys and stepped streets leads through a labyrinth of white houses to **Piazza Umberto I,** where more than a few window boxes put the final flourishes on the charming tableau. M.C. Escher (1898–1972), the Dutch artist who depicted scenes filled with intricate geometric patterns and complex perspective, loved Atrani and sketched the town; looking at the layer upon layer of connected whitewashed houses, it's easy to see Atrani's influence on his work.

The sandy beach at Atrani, just east of Amalfi.

By the 12th century, Atrani had become the preferred residence of Amalfi aristocrats, and Amalfi doges were crowned and buried in the 10th-century **church of San Salvatore de Bireto.** Inside, beyond bronze doors pillaged from Constantinople, a plaque shows off two peacocks, signs of vanity and pride, something this rich little town once had aplenty.

The coast road continues east toward Salerno, after about 15km (9 miles) coming to **Cetara.** The name refers to a tuna fishing net, and boats still return here, one of the few remaining fishing ports on this coast, with holds full of fresh tuna and anchovies. **Delfino Battista,** Via Rossini 1/3 (www.delfinobattistasrl.it; ✆ **0828/351028**), specializes in oil-packed tuna and *colatura,* an anchovy sauce the ancient Romans concocted. *Colatura* is made by layering anchovies and salt in wooden barrels and, after aging, applying a press to extract an amber-colored juice that's drizzled on fish, pasta, and vegetables. The specialty in **Vietri sul Mare,** another 7km (4 miles) east, is ceramics, made here since the 16th century, with massive furnaces firing pieces in bright Mediterranean colors. The most distinctive of Vietri's many china shops is **Ceramica Artistica Solimene,** Via Madonna degli Angeli 7 (www.ceramicasolimene.it; ✆ **089/210243**), built in the 1950s by architect and Frank Lloyd Wright disciple Paolo

Soleme, who fashioned the extraordinary-looking workshop out of glass and ceramics, arranged in conelike shapes. The wares are beautiful as well.

RAVELLO ★★★

7km (4 miles) N of Amalfi

Clinging to a mountainside high above Amalfi, Ravello can seem a world removed from the clamor below. This sense of escape, along with views and some of the world's most splendid gardens, has long made this aerie 1,000 feet above the coast a refuge for the rich and famous, including composer Richard Wagner, writers D.H. Lawrence and Gore Vidal, and actress Greta Garbo. Like they did, you'll come here to do not much else but stroll in the gardens, gaze at the coastline, and maybe relax for a few days in one of many villas converted into luxury hotels. Ravello is simply a beautiful, beautiful place, maybe more so than any other town in Italy.

Essentials

ARRIVING The most convenient way up to Ravello from Amalfi is the **SITA Sud bus** (see box p. 640). If you're going directly to Ravello from Naples, the quickest route is via high-speed train to Salerno (as quick as half an hour) and then the **SITA Sud** bus up the coast. If you're driving from Naples, take the A3 to a well-marked exit near Angri, then climb over the mountains on SP2b and SP1 before dropping into Ravello on the Valico di Chiunsi; total drive time is about 2½ hours. ***Tip:*** If you're driving, park as you approach town in a large public parking lot at Piazza Duomo (1.50€ an hour); this is not an easy town to drive in.

VISITOR INFORMATION Ravello's **tourist office,** Piazza Fontana Moresca (✆ **089/857096**), is open daily 9am to 7pm (to 5pm Nov–May).

Exploring Ravello

Ravello is largely pedestrian, with steep lanes and many stairs. The heart of town is **Piazza del Vescovado,** a terrace overlooking the valley of the Dragone, and the adjacent **Piazza del Duomo.** Climb up Via Richard Wagner (behind the tourist office) to reach **Via San Giovanni del Toro,** lined with some of Ravello's grandest medieval palaces, built as hilltop retreats for wealthy Amalfi Republic families and now home to some of Italy's most distinguished hotels. Two pockets of greenery open off the street—the public gardens of the Comune, or Town Hall, and the **Giardini Principessa di Piemonte,** which offers some sweeping views.

Auditorium Niemeyer ★★ LANDMARK Ravello's most controversial landmark was inaugurated in 2010 to critical architectural acclaim but the disdain of many residents and visitors. Naysayers find the sweeping, dazzling-white canopied roof of Brazilian architect Oscar Niemeyer's auditorium sorely out of keeping with Ravello's medieval ambience. It's hard, though, not to admire the way the sinuous curves tuck so naturally into the hillside, and no one can complain about the pleasure of enjoying a concert while viewing the spectacle of sea and sky through the huge eye-shaped window.

Via della Repubblica 12. ✆ **089/857096.** Open for concerts and film screenings (check tourist office for schedules).

Duomo ★★★ CHURCH All the glories of Ravello's past seem to come to the fore in the beautiful cathedral that Orso Papiro, first bishop of Ravello, founded in 1086. The 54 embossed panels of the 12th-century bronze doors, cast in Constantinople, were designed to delight the faithful with stories of Christ's miracles and other familiar Bible stories. Another piece of scripture comes to life in the beautiful mosaics of the **Ambone dell'Epistola** ★★★, a pulpit dating from 1130, depicting Jonah being swallowed by the whale. Opposite, another pulpit rests atop twisting columns that in turn rise out of the backs of two regal-looking lions, with a mighty eagle perched atop the whole affair. Add to that a wonderful collection of Roman sarcophagi and columns, bits of medieval frescoes, and a floor that tilts gently toward the entrance, enhancing the perspective and visually enlarging the space. The **Cappella di San Pantaleone** honors the cathedral's patron, a physician saint who was beheaded in Nicomedia (in present-day Turkey) on July 27, 305; the blood in his reliquary is said to liquefy and come to a boil every year on the anniversary of his death.

Piazza del Vescovado. ✆ **089/85831.** Duomo: Free. Museum: 3€. Daily 10am–6pm. Guided tours available.

Museo del Corallo ★ MUSEUM/SHOP For centuries, craftspeople around the Bay of Naples carved precious cameos and other objects out of coral and shell. In fact, the earliest object in this stunning private collection is an A.D.-3rd-century Roman amphora with a coral formation inside it. The 600 pieces here are the possessions of cameo craftsman Giorgio Filocamo, whose Camo workshops are attached to the museum; the gallery testifies to his love for the art, with antique pieces, such as a 17th-century coral Christ on the Cross, that are coveted by museums around the world. Filocamo has carved cameos for Hilary Clinton, Pope John Paul II, and Princess Caroline of Monaco; you can pick up one of his creations for yourself in the adjoining shop.

Piazza Duomo 9. www.museodelcorallo.com. ✆ **089/857461.** Free. Mon–Sat 9:30am–noon and 3–5:30pm.

Villa Cimbrone ★★★ GARDEN Englishman Lord Grimthorpe—dilettante, gardener, and erstwhile banker—created this grand villa in 1904, embellishing a crumbling 14th-century farmhouse with towers, turrets, and exotic Arabesque details (the villa is now a hotel). The lavish salons and gardens soon became associated with the 20th-century elite, few more elusive than Swedish actress Greta Garbo, who hid out here in 1937—not to be alone, but to be with her lover, the conductor Leopold Stokowski. The high point of the lavish gardens, quite literally, is the **Belvedere Cimbrone,** where you'll have the dizzying sensation of being suspended between sea and sky. Writer Gore Vidal, who for many years lived in a villa clinging to the cliff just below the gardens, called the outlook "the most beautiful view in the world."

Via Santa Chiara 26. ✆ **089/857459.** Gardens 10€. Daily 9am–sunset. Last admission 30 min. before close.

Villa Rufolo ★★ GARDEN The 14th-century poet Boccaccio was so moved by this onetime residence of 13th-century merchant prince Landolfo Rufolo that he included it as background in one of his tales. In the mid-19th century, Scotsman Sir Francis Reid transformed the house into an exotic fantasy, with Moorish cloisters. The palace's most famous visitor was Richard Wagner, who composed an act of *Parsifal* here in 1880 and used the surroundings for his Garden of Klingsor, home of the Flower Maidens; the Norman tower was renamed Klingsor's Tower in his honor. Paths wind through beds of rare plantings to lookout points high above the coastline, where the surreal scene of sea meeting sky is as transporting as the house and gardens. The lower garden, known as the Wagner Terrace, is the setting for the Ravello Festival's **Concerti Wagneriani.**

Piazza Duomo. www.villarufolo.it. ✆ **089/857621.** 7€; 5€ children 5–12; under 5 free. Daily 9am–5pm. Last admission 30 min. earlier.

A sweeping view from the Villa Rufolo garden.

HIKING

Hikers can take heart in the fact that from Ravello it's all downhill—or mostly, since one popular hike goes up to the **Monastery of Saint Nicholas,** 486m (1,594 ft.) high. From the center of Ravello, take the road to Sambuco for 1km (half a mile) and from there the trail up to the monastery. Plan on 2 hours for the 9km (6-mile) round-trip. For a downhill hike, from the town center take another footpath—actually, a series of steps and alleys—that descends to seaside **Minori** (see p. 669). Start from the alley to the left of Villa Rufolo, next to the small fountain. It will take you past the 13th-century Annunziata church, then the church of San Pietro, before you reach the hamlet of Torello. From there the path descends through olive trees to Minori. The hike down takes about an hour, the return trip at least double that (you may opt to take a bus back up!).

Where to Stay in Ravello

EXPENSIVE

Hotel Rufolo ★★ Your postcards home might be a little more florid while staying at this ages-old villa in the heart of town, converted to a *pensione* for an arty set more than a century ago. D.H. Lawrence hid away in room 423 while writing *Lady Chatterley's Lover,* leading a monklike life despite the scenes erupting on his pages. It's hard to live here like a monk these days: Rooms and suites are filled with fine old furnishings set on gleaming Vietri tile floors; a large pool sparkles in the verdant garden; and a hedonistic spa pampers guests. Then, too, of course, there are all those glorious views.

Via San Francesco 1. www.hotelrufolo.com. ✆ **089/857133.** 34 units. 240€–440€ double. Rates include breakfast. Closed Nov–Mar. **Amenities:** Restaurant; bar; pool; spa; free Wi-Fi.

Palazzo Avino ★★★ A 12th-century patrician palace strikes just the right balance between comfort and opulence, with enough antiques, Vietri ceramic floors, and fine linens to satisfy the most discerning guest. Views extending for miles up and down the coast make the most of Ravello's aerie-like position. They're enjoyed through huge windows in just about every room, on a rooftop terrace with two Jacuzzis, from sumptuous gardens and pool that cascade partway down the cliff, and from the hotel's double-Michelin-starred, dinner-only **Rossellinis** (see p. 679). A free shuttle takes guests to the **Clubhouse by the Sea** (open May–Sept), the hotel's beach club, with a small outdoor pool, a waterside terrace with lounge chairs and umbrellas, and a casual restaurant.

Via San Giovanni del Toro 28. www.palazzoavino.com. ✆ **089/818181.** 43 units. 360€–1,200€ double. Rates include breakfast. Closed late Oct–Mar. **Amenities:** 2 restaurants; bar; concierge; gym; pool; room service; spa; free Wi-Fi.

MODERATE

Giordano Hotel ★★ Plenty of old-world charm, albeit slightly faded, prevails at this fine villa set right in the middle of town, with faux antiques and upholstered armchairs resting on tile floors and pretty gardens surrounding a swimming pool. Most of the rooms open to private or shared terraces, though none have sea views. For those you need only step outside the door and into one of the nearby scenic overlooks.

Via Trinità 14. www.giordanohotel.it. ✆ **089/857255.** 33 units. 150€–220€ double. Rates include breakfast. Closed Nov–Apr. **Amenities:** Bar; pool; free Wi-Fi.

Hotel Parsifal ★★ A monastery-turned-holiday-getaway is hardly a rarity on the Amalfi Coast, but few offer good-value accommodations like these in such charming architectural surroundings. The cloisters, tiled hallways, fishpond, and flower-filled patios still exude contemplative peace, just as the original 13th-century residents intended. Whitewashed rooms fashioned from former monks' cells are plain and frugal enough to suit their former occupants, and the slightly rickety old-fashioned aura is enhanced with colorful tile floors and, from some rooms, sensational views. Meals in the friendly sea-view dining room may remind you of the days when rooms came with board.

Via Gioacchino D'Anna. www.hotelparsifal.com. ✆ **089/857144.** 17 units. 90€–225€ double. 2-night min. stay in high season. Rates include breakfast. **Amenities:** Restaurant; bar; concierge; free Wi-Fi.

INEXPENSIVE

Cecco Rooms ★ With Ravello's most lavish pleasure palace hotels as neighbors, these simple, lower-level rooms may seem a bit humble. Then again, they place you in the best part of town at a fraction of the price of the luxury lodgings that line the street, and the prime real estate comes with views over the town and surrounding valleys. Gardens and the town center are just steps away, and the low-key accommodations open to pleasant outdoor spaces.

Viale Giocchino d'Anna 6. ceccorooms.com. ✆ **389/545-8477.** 5 units. 95€–150€ double. Rates include breakfast. **Amenities:** Kitchens; high-speed Internet access.

Where to Eat in Ravello

In the delightful little **Babel Wine Bar, Deli, and Art,** Via Santissima Trinità 13 (www.babelravello.com; ✆ **089/858-6215**), ceramics and paintings by Amalfi artists are a backdrop for a selection of local wines and snacks, including bruschetta with creamy local *burrata* cheese. The garden-bar of the **Hotel Rufolo** (see p. 678) is a choice spot to sit back, relax, and soak in Ravello's getaway ambience.

The mountains behind Ravello are aptly named Monti Lattari, or "rich in milk" in Latin. Goats, sheep, and cows grazing the heights yield milk from which farmers make mozzarella, ricotta, provolone, and other cheeses, all scented with mountain herbs. In shops and restaurants along the coast look for *treccione,* a creamy mozzarella twisted into a braid, or hearty *caciocavallo,* the region's teardrop-shaped mountain cheese. About 15km (9 miles) north of Ravello off SP1, you can taste them at family-run dairy and shop **Antica Latteria di Tramonti,** in Gete on the flanks of Monte Finestre (www.anticalatteriaditramonti.it; ✆ **089/876920**).

EXPENSIVE

Rossellinis ★★★ CREATIVE AMALFITAN Meals in this elegant dining room and view-filled terrace come with a reputation as one of

Italy's best, with two Michelin stars. Service is impeccable, and the menu showcases creative takes on local cuisine. Even the bread, with ham baked into it, is exceptional, as are such sublime creations as ravioli stuffed with squid or cod in an olive crust. Meals are paired with local wines and followed with mountain cheeses and sweets that, like everything else here, satisfy without being overwhelming.

Via San Giovanni del Toro 28 (in the Palazzo Avino, p. 678). www.palazzoavino.com. ✆ **089/818181.** Entrees 28€–40€; tasting menus from 120€. Daily 7:30–11pm. Closed Nov–Mar.

MODERATE

Cumpa' Cosimo ★★ AMALFITAN Netta Bottone runs the restaurant her family started back in 1929, serving generous portions of pastas (including an extravaganza with seven types of noodles topped with seven different sauces) and big platters of *frittura di pesce* (fish fry) along with some very well-done lamb and veal dishes (Netta also runs the butcher shop next door). Artichokes and other vegetables are right out of nearby garden plots. Whatever you order, Netta herself may well serve it with a flourish and a kiss on the cheek.

Via Roma 44. ✆ **089/857156.** Entrees 11€–22€; pizza 6€–10€. Daily noon–3:30pm and 6–10:30pm. Closed Mon Nov–Feb.

INEXPENSIVE

Pizzeria Vaccaro ★★ PIZZA Lemon groves and vineyards have long occupied residents of **Tramonti,** about 12km (8 miles) inland from Ravello, and in their spare time they invented a quick bite called pizza (a claim made by many others, for sure). The pizzas here, once baked in communal bread ovens, are undeniably delicious and make the village quite a culinary outpost. Local nuns added to the offerings when they came up with *concierto,* a bitter-sweet digestive liquor concocted from nine different mountain herbs and spices. Try these specialties at what many fans consider to be the best pizzeria on the Amalfi Coast. Delectable crusts are topped with ingredients from nearby farms: Salami and mozzarella are homemade, vegetables are homegrown, olive oil is from local groves, and the bread is oven-fresh.

Via Vaccaro, Tramonti. ✆ **089/876140.** Entrees 8€–15€; pizza from 7€. Daily noon–3:30pm and 6:30–midnight.

Pizzeria Vittoria ★★ PIZZA It's refreshing to know that life in Ravello can come down to earth, too, as it does in this friendly pizzeria near the Duomo. Thin-crust pies with a huge variety of toppings are the draw; even the classic Margherita seems like perfection, given that everything is fresh—tomatoes and basil from the garden, mozzarella from nearby farms, herbs from the mountains. The simple pasta dishes are similarly delicious. The tile-floored rooms fill up quickly.

Via dei Rufolo 3. www.ristorantepizzeriavittoria.it. ✆ **089/857947.** Entrees 10€–15€; pizza from 7€. Daily 12:30–3pm and 7:30–10:30pm. Closed Nov–Mar.

Beautiful ceramics in Ravello.

Shopping

In addition to the cameo handiwork that might tempt you at the **Camo** workshops at the Museo del Corallo (see p. 676), you'll encounter some beautiful ceramics at **Ceramiche d'Arte Carmella,** Via die Rufolo 16 (www.ceramichedarte carmela.com; ✆ **089/857303**). **Profumi della Costiera,** Via Trinita 37 (www.profumidellacostiera.it; ✆ **089/858167**), carries a remarkable selection of limoncello and other sweet liqueurs.

Nightlife

Ravello's entertainment scene ramps up considerably from July through September, when the town hosts the internationally famous **Festival di Ravello** (www.ravellofestival.com; ✆ **089/858422**). The focus is on classical music and includes concerts of Wagnerian works in the garden of **Villa Rufolo ★★** (p. 677). Tickets run from 15€ to 130€.

THE RUINS OF PAESTUM ★★★

35km (22 miles) S of Salerno; 100km (62 miles) SE of Naples

South of Salerno, three honey-colored temples, some of the best-preserved remains of the ancient world, rise from the wide agricultural plain. The dramatic scene is especially picturesque in spring and early summer, when poppies and wildflowers surround the ruins. Adding to a sense of timelessness are huge Italian water buffalo, who have grazed the low-lying grasslands for the past 1,000 years or so, producing milk that yields the region's deliciously creamy *mozzarella di bufala.*

Essentials

ARRIVING **Trains** stop at two stations near the ruins: **Capaccio-Roccadaspide** and **Paestum,** only 5 minutes from each other. Either station is only about a 10- to 15-minute walk from the archaeological area, with Paestum being more convenient. Via Porta Sirena leads from Paestum station to Via Magna Grecia, which cuts through the middle of the archaeological site. The trip to either is about 30 minutes from Salerno, 90 minutes from Naples; to shorten the time from Naples, take the high-speed train to Salerno and connect to a local train there.

Paestum is well connected to Salerno by bus, via **BusItalia Campania** (www.fsbusitaliacampania.it; ✆ **089/252228** or 800/016659, toll-free within Italy), with regular service to Paestum from Naples and Salerno.

By **car,** take autostrada A3, exit at Battipaglia onto SS 18, and follow the brown signs for Paestum.

Exploring the Ruins

While the forum and other parts of the town have been reduced to rubble, Paestum's three magnificent **temples,** excavated around 1750, are remarkably intact. So are parts of the circuit of massive defensive **walls,** 5m (16½ ft.) thick on average, 15m (50 ft.) high, and 4,750m (15,584 ft.) in length, with 24 square and round towers along their length. At the monumental western gate, **Porta Marina,** you can climb the walls and walk on the patrol paths, enjoying excellent views over the ruins and coast. Wear comfortable shoes and bring a hat and water. Allow at least an hour to see the temples and another hour for the museum (see below).

Archaeological Area of Paestum ★★★ The enclosed site contains the three temples (all built facing east) and a number of other ruins that were part of the sacred area at the center of the ancient Greek town. The **Via Sacra** (Sacred Street) runs arrow-straight through the length of the site, connecting all three temples, its Roman pavement laid over the original Greek road. When it was built, the road continued for about 12km (7½ miles) to connect the Greek town of Poseidonia with the Sanctuary of Hera, on the river Sele about 9km (5 miles) up the coast.

Tempio di Hera ★★★ The oldest of Paestum's temples, the Temple of Hera was built in 550 B.C. with a massive portico that's still supported by 50 columns. Worshippers attended rites in front, gathering around a sacrificial altar (now partially ruined) and a square *bothros,* a sacrificial well where the remains were thrown. The temple is believed to have been part of a huge complex dedicated to Hera, wife and sister of Zeus and the goddess of fertility and maternity.

Tempio di Nettuno ★★★ The world's best example of a Doric temple, the Temple of Neptune, which dates from around 450 B.C., is lined in travertine stone that glows a magical gold hue when struck by the sun's rays. Perfect proportions lend a slender elegance, while thick, closely spaced columns give the temple a sturdy, almost forceful presence. This is the best preserved of Paestum's temples: only the roof and internal walls are missing. In front are two sacrificial altars; the smaller one is a Roman addition from the 3rd century B.C.

Tempio di Cerere ★★ The smallest of the three temples, at the northern end of the site, was built at the end of the 6th century B.C., probably in honor of the goddess Athena. Under the Romans it was dedicated to Ceres, their goddess of agriculture and fertility; Christian tombs in the portico suggest later use as a church.

Main entrance Via Magna Grecia 917; secondary entrance Porta della Giustizia (Justice Gate) off Via Nettuno, for ticket holders only. www.museopaestum.beniculturali.it. ✆ **0828/722654.** Mar–Nov 13.50€, family ticket 21.50€ (2 adults plus children under 25), under 18 3.50€; Dec–Feb 6€, family ticket 11€ (2 adults plus children under 25), under 18 2€; includes admission to museum. May–Sept daily 10am–7:30pm; Oct–Jan daily 10am–4pm; Feb–Apr 10am–5:30pm (last entry 40 min. earlier).

National Archaeological Museum of Paestum ★★ MUSEUM
Star of the show in modern galleries near the entrance to the ruins is the fresco of a young man taking a swan dive into a rushing stream, from the so-called Tomb of the Diver, probably dating to around 470 B.C. The meaning of the simple, powerful image has long been debated, though a good guess is that the diver is gracefully making the transition from earth into the other world. The young man was clearly an athletic sort—flasks filled with the oil he used to prepare himself for wrestling matches were found next to a skeleton assumed to be his. Four other frescoes from the same tomb complex depict scenes of a symposium—more or less a drinking bash—probably to give the deceased a good send-off. These images are unique, the only tomb frescoes from the ancient period that depict human figures.

A frieze from the nearby Sanctuary of Hera includes some mythological scenes that would have delighted a 6th-century-B.C. audience, such as the comical story of Hercules and the Kerkopes. As legend has it, the hero had fallen asleep when these two scamps snuck up and stole his weapons. Hercules awoke, captured the miscreants, and tied them upside down to a pole that he carried over his shoulder. The Kerkopes started laughing and Hercules demanded to know why. They told him they were laughing at his hairy backside, so he started laughing, too, and set the boys free (Zeus was less amused by their antics and later turned them into monkeys). Another delightful scene depicts two lithe and gleeful maidens running, their finely sculpted robes flowing around them—the joy of these images suggests just how light-hearted ancient Greek religion could be.

Via Magna Grecia 918. www.museopaestum.beniculturali.it. ✆ **0828/811023.** For admission and times, see Archaeological Area.

CAPRI ★★★

5km (3 miles) W off the tip of the Sorrentine peninsula

Rugged, mountainous Capri (pronounced *Cap*-ry, not Ca-*pree*), just off the tip of the Sorrentine Peninsula, is one of the most glamorous and beautiful islands in the world. The legend-steeped, gossip-soaked outcropping of limestone, a mere 4 square miles in size, has beguiled a long list of admirers. Emperor Tiberius ruled the Roman Empire from these pine- and rosemary-scented cliffs, British music-hall star Gracie Fields belted out tunes for the likes of Maria Callas and Liz Taylor at her seaside hideaway on Marina Piccola, and poets Pablo Neruda and Rainer Maria Rilke took inspiration from the magical landscapes. The island is still a magnet for the rich, the famous, artists, eccentrics, and just plain folks. All delight in the same pleasures: stark-white villas, garden walls draped with bougainvillea and hibiscus, azure seas lapping rugged coasts, a chorus of birdsong, and a heady taste of the good life. Emperor Augustus was onto something when he called the island Apragopolis, or "City of Sweet Idleness." Capri's popularity can sometimes make it hard to soak in the island's beauty. An overnight stay lets you better enjoy the quiet that descends when summer day-trippers have sailed away. To see the island at its best, you might want to visit in spring or early fall. Note that the island shuts down almost entirely from November to May.

Beachgoers flock to Marina Grande, Capri.

Essentials

ARRIVING You can easily reach Capri from either Naples or Sorrento, and in summer there's also regular ferry service from Amalfi and Positano. Don't let the profusion of companies confuse you: At tourist offices, docks, and most hotels along the Amalfi Coast you'll find simplified listings of ferry schedules. From Naples' Molo Beverello dock (take bus or taxi from the train station), the **hydrofoil** *(aliscafo)* takes just 45 minutes and departs several times daily (some stop at Sorrento). Regular **ferry** *(traghetto)* service departing from Porta di Massa is cheaper but takes longer (about 1½ hrs. each way). Many companies operate in the Bay of Naples, all of similar quality; the main thing is to figure out which boat is going where you want to go, when it departs, and how long the trip will take. **Alilauro** (www.alilauro.it; ✆ **081/837-0819**) connects Capri with Salerno, Positano, Amalfi, and Ischia; **NLG-Navigazione Libera del**

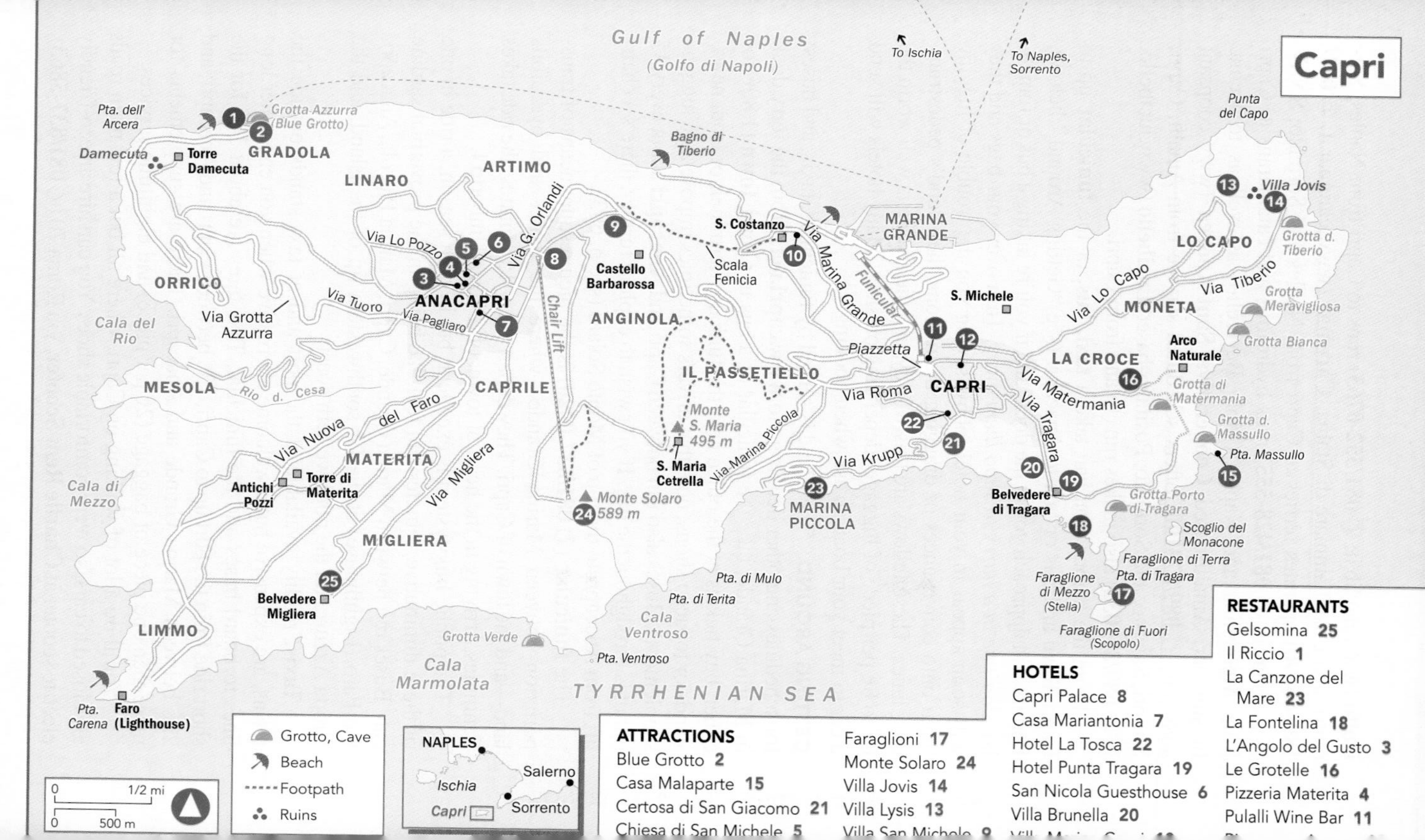

Capri
Gulf of Naples
(Golfo di Napoli)
To Ischia
To Naples, Sorrento
Punta del Capo
Pta. dell' Arcera
Grotta Azzurra (Blue Grotto)
Damecuta
Torre Damecuta
GRADOLA
LINARO
ARTIMO
Bagno di Tiberio
Villa Jovis
MARINA GRANDE
LO CAPO
Grotta d. Tiberio
Via Lo Pozzo
Via G. Orlandi
Castello Barbarossa
S. Costanzo
Scala Fenicia
Via Marina Grande
Funicular
ORRICO
ANACAPRI
Via Tuoro
Via Pagliaro
Via Grotta Azzurra
Cala del Rio
Chair Lift
ANGINOLA
S. Michele
Via Lo Capo
Via Tiberio
MONETA
Grotta Meravigliosa
Grotta Bianca
Arco Naturale
Piazzetta
LA CROCE
IL PASSETIELLO
MESOLA
Rio d. Cesa
CAPRILE
Via Roma
CAPRI
Via Matermania
Grotta di Matermania
Monte S. Maria 495 m
Via Tragara
Grotta d. Massullo
Via Nuova del Faro
Via Marina Piccola
Pta. Massullo
MATERITA
Via Migliera
S. Maria Cetrella
Via Krupp
Cala di Mezzo
Antichi Pozzi
Torre di Materita
Monte Solaro 589 m
MARINA PICCOLA
Belvedere di Tragara
Grotta Porto di Tragara
Scoglio del Monacone
MIGLIERA
Faraglione di Terra
Pta. di Mulo
Faraglione di Mezzo (Stella)
Pta. di Tragara
Belvedere Migliera
Pta. di Terita
LIMMO
Cala Ventroso
Faraglione di Fuori (Scopolo)
Grotta Verde
Pta. Ventroso
Cala Marmolata
TYRRHENIAN SEA
Pta. Carena
Faro (Lighthouse)
Grotto, Cave
Beach
Footpath
Ruins
0 1/2 mi
0 500 m
NAPLES
Ischia
Capri
Salerno
Sorrento
ATTRACTIONS
Blue Grotto 2
Casa Malaparte 15
Certosa di San Giacomo 21
Chiesa di San Michele 5
Faraglioni 17
Monte Solaro 24
Villa Jovis 14
Villa Lysis 13
Villa San Michele 9
HOTELS
Capri Palace 8
Casa Mariantonia 7
Hotel La Tosca 22
Hotel Punta Tragara 19
San Nicola Guesthouse 6
Villa Brunella 20
RESTAURANTS
Gelsomina 25
Il Riccio 1
La Canzone del Mare 23
La Fontelina 18
L'Angolo del Gusto 3
Le Grotelle 16
Pizzeria Materita 4
Pulalli Wine Bar 11

Golfo (www.navlib.it; ✆ **081/552-0763**) runs to Capri from Naples, Sorrento, and Castellammare di Stabia. **Caremar** (www.caremar.it; ✆ **081/189–66690**) operates ferries to Capri from Naples and Sorrento; **SNAV** (www.snav.it; ✆ **081/428-555**) runs hydrofoils and catamarans to Capri from Mergellina and Naples (Molo Beverello) as well as to Ischia. In summer, Amalfi-based **Cooperativa Sant'Andrea** (www.coopsantandrea.it; ✆ **089/873190**) offers scheduled service from Amalfi, Capri, Minori, Salerno, and Sorrento; Positano-based **Lucibello** (www.lucibello.it; ✆ **089/875032**) also makes runs to and from Capri.

From the harbor, you can take a **taxi, bus,** or the **funicular** up to Capri Town and bus or taxi to Anacapri (see "Getting Around," below). Porters will approach you at the dock, and if you're taking a bus or funicular, *don't be in a hurry to shoo them away.* Turn over your bags and they will soon appear in your hotel lobby, saving you the trouble of lugging them onto conveyances or dragging them along the island's pedestrian-only lanes. These fellows are trustworthy, and the charge is well worth the 6€ to 8€ per piece of luggage (depending on size). Many hotels will send a car to meet your boat, so ask when booking.

GETTING AROUND The island is served by funiculars, taxis, and buses; for schedules and other details go to **www.capri.net**. From the ferry dock in Marina Grande, take the funicular or a bus to **Capri Town** (1.80€ for either, buy tickets at the office near the funicular terminal, or from newsstands or tobacco shops; note that drivers sometimes impose a 2€ luggage supplement). Buses also run between Capri and **Anacapri** about every 15 minutes throughout the day. If you wish to explore further, there's a chairlift from Anacapri to the top of Monte Solaro (see p. 693).

The **funicular** (✆ **081/837-0420**) is the picturesque means of transportation between Marina Grande—where the ferries and hydrofoils land—and the town of Capri. They depart every 15 minutes; the ride takes 5 minutes, arriving in the heart of town, off Piazza Umberto I.

The public **bus** system is excellent, but in high season, a ride in one of these diminutive vehicles can feel like being in the proverbial sardine can. Buses run between Marina Grande, Capri, Marina Piccola, Anacapri, the Faro (Lighthouse) at the far southwestern tip of the island, and the Grotta Azzurra on the northwestern coast.

Taxis, readily available at the port and at taxi stands outside the towns, are expensive but a welcome alternative when you encounter long lines to board buses and the funicular. Taxi fares are about 17€ for the short ride from the port up to Capri; 15€ between Capri and Anacapri; and 23€ between Marina Grande and Anacapri. There are supplements for more than one piece of baggage (2€ per piece) and nighttime services.

You'll do a lot of walking on Capri, where all but a few main roads are closed to cars, so wear comfortable shoes. You can hire an eco-friendly electric scooter at **Charlie Rent Scooter,** Via Roma 70 (✆ **081/837-5863**),

50€ a day, and the many outlets clustered around the port in Marina Grande.

VISITOR INFORMATION The **tourist office** is in Capri Town on Piazzetta Italo Cerio (www.capritourism.com; ✆ **081/837-5308**) with a branch in Marina Grande. They are generally open Monday to Saturday 8:30am to 8:30pm and Sunday 8:30am to 2:30pm (Nov–Mar Mon–Sat 9am–1pm and 3:30–6:30pm). The website is a gold mine of information on the island, including bus, funicular, and boat schedules.

Exploring Capri

You'll soon discover that life on the island, quite literally, has its ups and down. From **Marina Grande,** the main harbor, you'll go up, via road or funicular, to Capri Town. The white houses of the island's main settlement rise and dip across hilly terrain on a saddle between the twin peaks of Monte Tiberio and Monte Solaro. **Anacapri,** the island's other town, is even higher, tucked onto the slopes of Monte Solaro. Getting down to the sea from these towns, and elsewhere on the island, often means descending the formidable, grotto-laced cliffs that ring the shoreline. More often than not you do so via paths and steps, hundreds of them, that often lead to viewpoints where you can catch your breath and take in views. The easiest, and often only, way to get around is on foot, and it would be hard to find a more inviting place on the planet to walk.

CAPRI TOWN ★★

Most visitors approach Capri's mountainside main town on the funicular railway that climbs steep slopes just behind the harbor. A traffic-choked road also makes the ascent, as does a footpath for the hearty. However you make the climb, as soon as you step into the enticing warren of narrow lanes lined with walled villa gardens, you'll realize you're in a rather exotic place. Town life radiates from the **Piazzetta,** a small square that draws such a stream of visitors, it's called the "world's living room." While the Gucci-dressed beauties and suave Lotharios suggest a certain see-and-be-seen glamour, you can escape the scene by popping into medieval **Palazzo Cerio** to visit the archaeology and natural history exhibits of the **Museo Caprense Ignazio Cerio** (www.centrocaprense.org; ✆ **081/837-6681;** 3€; Mon 10am–1pm, Tues–Sat 10am–4pm). Overlooking the square, the pleasantly plain **Torre dell'Orologio** rises above the old city gateway; next to it is the homey **church of Santo Stefano.**

If the square's collection of celebrities, obscure royals, and poseurs starts to get on your nerves, remember that the island has attracted a jaded set for centuries. Early-20th-century novelist D.H. Lawrence grumpily described Capri as "a gossipy, villa-stricken, two-humped chunk of limestone, a microcosm that does heaven much credit, but mankind none at all." It may also help to recall that not too many centuries ago, the hilly uplands that cradle the pretty town were grazing land for the goats, *caprerae,* which gave the island its name. And it's easy to escape the fray—from the Piazzetta, the old town's narrow streets lead west past glittering shops along vista-filled, pine-scented walkways to the more sedate **Certosa di San Giacomo** (see below). Just beyond are the **Giardini di Augusto ★★**, terraced public gardens (daily 10am–8pm [till 5pm Oct–Mar]; admission 1.50€) with panoramic views toward Monte Solaro, the Faraglioni, and Marina Piccola. German steel manufacturer and longtime visitor Friedrich Alfred Krupp (1854–1902) laid out the gardens to show off the island's rich flora. An unexpected presence amid the flowerbeds is a statue of Vladimir Lenin (1870–1924), the first leader of the Soviet Union. In 1908 the great revolutionary was a guest of Russian writer Maxim Gorky, who lived here from 1906 to 1913. Gorky, a novelist and political activist, began his *Encyclopedia of Russian History* on the island and lived in the villa opposite the gardens, now the Villa Krupp hotel.

Certosa di San Giacomo ★ RELIGIOUS SITE The island's most imposing architectural landmark is this former monastery built in the 14th century by Count Giacomo Arcucci as a place to retire from the world. Arcucci's former employer, Queen Joanna I of Naples, provided the prime parcel of land and the funds, and the count became a Carthusian

Dining alfresco on Piazza Umberto in Capri Town.

monk, ending his days in solitary contemplation. The monks were not popular with the islanders, who showed up at their gates seeking refuge from the plague of 1653 and were locked out. The suffering populace retaliated by throwing plague victims' corpses over the monastery walls.

Ironically, the complex, perched poetically above the sea, is quite community-oriented these days, housing the island's public library and a high school. Its cloisters make an evocative setting for concerts, and the garden that looks out into azure infinity is a favorite spot for romantic tête-à-têtes. Also on the premises is the quirky **Museo Diefenbach,** which shows the works of painter Karl Wilhelm Diefenbach, an advocate of peace, free love, and nudism who lived on Capri from 1900 to 1913. He was a bit of an attraction himself, walking the paths barefoot in a white robe, his long gray hair flowing behind him.

Via Certosa. www.musei.campania.beniculturali.it. ✆ **081/837-6218.** 3€. Tues–Sun May 10am–6pm, June–Aug 10am–7pm, Sept–Oct 10am–5pm, Nov–Dec 10am–2pm.

Villa Jovis ★★ ARCHAEOLOGICAL SITE From Capri Town, a comfortable 45-minute stroll of about 2.5km (1½ miles) ends with a steep climb to the northeastern tip of the island and the most sumptuous and best-preserved of the 12 villas the Roman emperor Tiberius (ruled A.D. 14–37) built on Capri. The emperor spent the final 10 years of his reign on the island, partly because he was fond of the scenery and the views, but also because the sheer waterside cliffs and few closely guarded harbors made the island unassailable to assassins—an antidote to his increasing paranoia. Even then, the emperor had his bread imported from Positano, afraid the islanders would poison him. Eight levels of walls and many staircases remain to suggest the size of the villa, probably covering about 1½ acres, with vast terraces and floors of reception halls and living quarters clinging to the craggy summit of Monte Tiberio. Architects devised an ingenious way to collect rainwater for the elaborate baths. The covered Loggia Imperiale follows the cliff edge to the Salto di Tiberio, a 330m-high (1,083-ft.) precipice from which it was said Tiberius would hurl lovers who'd fallen out of favor with him. Whether or not you believe this—many historians consider it nothing more than grisly gossip—you can enjoy the views across the island and over the straits to the Sorrento Peninsula.

Via Tiberio. www.capri.com. ✆ **081/837-0381.** 6€. Daily June–Sept 10am–7pm, Apr–May and Oct Wed–Mon 10am–6pm, Nov–Dec and Mar Wed–Mon 10am–4pm. Hours subject to change, so check with tourist office before making the trek up the hill.

Villa Lysis ★ ARCHITECTURAL SITE Of the many eccentric foreigners who have sought refuge on Capri, Baron Jacques d'Adelsward-Fersen (1880–1923) might be the most colorful character of all. When a scandal involving French schoolboys (and a subsequent prison stint) forced the dissolute baron to leave France in 1905, he came to Capri with his lover, Nino Cesarini, a famous young Roman model of erotic photographs. The house Fersen built on the heights just below Villa Jovis (see above) is a neoclassic fantasy of marble, columns, tile work, and gilt mosaics, with a motto etched in stone above the entrance proclaiming the premises to be a "shrine to love and sorrow." (The name Lysis, from the Socratic dialogues, is a reference to homosexual love.) The furnishings have long since been removed, but the blue-and-white majolica-tile lounge, the huge bedroom with three windows facing the Bay of Naples and three facing Monte Tiberio, and the many terraces all suggest that Fersen drowned his sorrows in the good life. And more than that: In the Chinese room in the basement, specially built for smoking opium, he succumbed to an overdose of cocaine while sipping Champagne.

Via Lo Capo. www.capritourism.com. ✆ **081/838-6111.** 2€. Thurs–Tues June–Aug 10am–7pm, late Mar–May and Sept–Oct 10am–6pm.

MARINA PICCOLA ★★

The island's largest beach, on the southern shore, is nothing much, just a pebbly strip tucked picturesquely amid the rocky shorelines, but the water is clean and crystal clear. The pretty cove has been a focus of island life since the Romans harbored their boats here. In recent centuries fishermen have shared the space with beachgoers, who arrive in droves on summer weekends to frequent the many little bathing establishments perched on the rocks. It's said that the outcropping that divides Marina Piccola neatly into halves is the very rock from which the Sirens tried to lure Ulysses and his crew onto the shoals and wreck their ships, a tale that adds even more romance to an already idyllic setting.

While buses make frequent runs between Capri Town and Marina Piccola, the classic approach is on Via Krupp, a steep path that descends the cliffs in a series of giddy switchbacks from the Giardini di Augusto at the edge of Capri Town. Friedrich Alfred Krupp had the walkway built at the turn of the 20th century so he could easily travel between his two yachts at Marina Piccola and his suite at the Quisisana Hotel in Capri Town. Word leaked out that Krupp also used the path to access the notorious Grotta di Fra Felice, a cave at the base of the cliff where gentlemen enjoyed the sexual favors of island youth, and he was eventually forced to leave Italy and committed suicide soon after. ***Note:*** Falling rocks can render passage unsafe and the path is often closed.

FARAGLIONI ★★★

Among Italy's most famous natural sights are these three rock stacks rising as high as 100m (330 ft.) from the sea off of Capri's southeast coast. The outermost rock is home to a type of bright blue lizard, the *Podarcis sicula coerulea,* found nowhere else on the planet. It's believed that the blue color serves as camouflage that allows the little reptiles to blend in with the surrounding sky and water. Records suggest that ancient Roman aristocrats imported the colorful creatures from Greece to brighten up their island gardens. The middle stack, Faraglioni di Mezzo, is punctured with a poetic little archway where waves have worn away part of the base. It's a popular game for anyone at the helm of a boat to navigate the opening. A shale ledge connects the rock closest to shore, Stella, to the island, and the base shelters two famous beaches with bathing establishments, **La Fontelina** (see p. 700) and **Da Luigi.** Boats ferry customers back and forth to Marina Piccola, but a far more sporting way to reach the base of the rocks is on the hundreds of steps that descend from Punta Tragara.

PUNTA TRAGARA ★★★

Just 10 minutes beyond the Piazzetta, on pine-shaded paths, is a world far removed from the clamor and bling. The island's most dazzling walks are along this stretch of coastline on Via Tragara and its eastward continuation, Via Pizzolungo, skirting lush vegetation on the top of the cliffs and affording glimpses of spectacular seascapes through the trees. The enchanting paths intersect at the Punta Tragara lookout, a perch high above the sea and the Faraglioni. Among those who admired the views was Chilean poet-in-exile Pablo Neruda, who in 1953 stayed in a villa on Via Tragara as a guest of Edwin Cerio (see **Museo Caprense Ignazio Cerio,** p. 687). Steps leading down to the Faraglioni from the viewpoint are informally known as the Neruda path; a plaque honors the poet at the top.

Isolated beyond Via Tragara atop Punta Massullo is **Casa Malaparte,** a boxlike villa that seems to grow out of the rock, with steps in the shape of an inverted pyramid leading to a rooftop terrace. It's the creation of freethinking, outspoken Curzio Malaparte, who curried favor with Fascists, communists, and even Italy's Allied liberators during the 1930s and World War II years. The house, still vilified by islanders for its harsh intrusion on protected lands, is the star of Jean-Luc Goddard's 1963 film *Contempt.* Its cold, vast spaces and vertigo-inducing perch high above the sea reflect the estrangement and sense of looming disaster between the couple, played by Brigitte Bardot and Michel Piccoli. The film might afford your only look at the interior; the house is now owned by the Ronchi Foundation and is open only occasionally for cultural events.

BLUE GROTTO (GROTTA AZZURRA) ★★★

Italy's tourist-trap extraordinaire can be beguiling, despite all the hassle a visit entails—the frenzy of climbing off a motorboat into a small rowboat, waiting for your turn to be rowed in, lying back, squeezing through a narrow opening, and being rowed out again just as you are beginning to enjoy the experience. The magical colors of the water and walls of this huge grotto are extraordinary, even more so than they appear in countless photographs. Little wonder that postcard writers have rhapsodized about the cave since it became part of the tourist circuit in the 19th century. (Actually, a small, ancient Roman dock and some statues retrieved from the sea floor suggest this outlet of a vast system of shoreline caverns was known long before then.) It's open daily 9am to 5pm (www.capri.com). In summer, boats leave frequently from the harbor at Marina Grande, transporting passengers to the grotto's entrance for 17€ round-trip (that includes the fee for the rowboat that takes you inside). If you get to the entrance to the Blue Grotto under your own steam (via bus from Anacapri), you'll still pay 15€ to be rowed in. The boat trip out from Marina Grande is well worth a couple extra euro, delivering sea-level views of the island's spectacular cliffs and rugged shoreline.

ANACAPRI ★★★

Capri's second town, perched on heights surrounded by vineyards, is a pleasant place where, once away from the main square, life transpires like you might have hoped it would on a small island in the Mediterranean.

Your first impression, as you arrive at the main squares, Piazza Della Pace and Piazza Vittoria, might be otherwise. This is where folks gather to board buses down to the Blue Grotto, get onto the chairlift to be whisked up Monte Solaro, and make the short walk out to **Villa San Michele** (see p. 692). And you might already be a bit shell-shocked by your ride up here in the noisy little orange bus that zips along the island's narrow main road from Capri Town, grinding around switchbacks in first gear. You may well wonder where all those glamorous habitués of the Piazzetta cafes have gone, as elderly housewives jab you with sharp elbows and knock you around with huge bags full of mysterious foodstuffs. Time was, the only way to get between Capri's two towns was on the **Scala Fenicia** (Phoenician Staircase), a steep path (with no authenticated connection to the ancient peoples of its name) of 881 steps—and many superb views.

Wander off the square onto Via Orlandini and you'll soon be passing tailor shops and shoemakers. Villagers sit on benches in front of the **church of Santa Sofia,** and from there you can meander along narrow lanes lined with vineyards, lemon groves, and flower-filled gardens. An easy 20-minute walk along Via Migliara takes you to **Philosophers Park ★**, a parcel of hillside carpeted in scrub and broom, where winding paths are lined with 60 ceramic plaques bearing inscriptions from the great philosophers (www.philosophicalpark.org; free admission; dawn–dusk). Just beyond the garden, the **Belvedere Migliara** overlooks the southern coast. Or follow Str. Faro di Carena out to Punta Carena, about 2km (1 mile) beyond Anacapri at the southwestern tip of the island, with its landmark **Faro** (lighthouse). A coastal path, the **Sentiero die Fortini,** or Path of the Forts, makes for some good hiking out here (see Hiking, p. 694), and the little cove beneath the Faro is one of the nicest places on the island for a swim. From there, a bus takes you back to Anacapri.

Chiesa di San Michele ★★ CHURCH The 18th-century builders of this octagonal church made a wise decision when they decided to install a delightful **majolica floor,** now one of the island's most colorful manmade sights. Francesco Solimena (1657–1747), the undisputed master of Neapolitan baroque painting, did the design, full of his typical flamboyance, and Naples' finest ceramics master, Leonardo Chiaiese, executed the hand-painted tile work. Their minutely detailed assemblage re-creates the drama-filled moment when Adam and Eve are expelled from the Garden of Eden, as a unicorn, a goat, and other unlikely creatures look on. The final effect of the piece is so pleasing that no one's ever felt comfortable treading on the floor, creating some logistical problems. Pews were never installed, and worshippers and visitors are relegated to a wooden walkway around the perimeter. Those in the know head up the spiral staircase for a bird's-eye view of the multicolor scene.

Piazza San Nicola. ✆ **081/837-2396.** 2€. Daily Apr–Sept 9am–7pm, Oct–Mar 10am–3pm.

Monte Solaro ★★★ NATURAL WONDER Capri's highest peak soars to 590m (1,932 ft.), a magnet for view seekers who "ooh" and "ahh" at the island and the Bay of Naples unfolding at their feet. You can hike up along fairly easy paths in about an hour (the easiest is a well-marked route that begins next to Villa San Michele). The chairlift **Seggiovia Monte Solaro** (www.capriseggiovia.it; ✆ **081/837-1428**) departs from Anacapri's Piazza Vittoria and whisks you to the top in just 12 minutes. Tickets cost 9€ one-way, 12€ round-trip, free for ages 8 and under; it runs daily May through October 9:30am to 5pm, March through April 9:30am to 4pm, and November through February 9:30am to 3:30pm. Emperor Augustus greets you at the top, right arm outstretched as if he's claiming everything in the name of the Roman Empire, while also ushering you into the bustling, poetically named **Canzone del Cielo** (Song of the Sky) cafe.

Villa San Michele ★★★ HISTORIC HOUSE Swedish doctor and writer Axel Munthe built this remarkable, gracious house in the 19th century on the ruins of one of Tiberius's villas. He had the funds and inspiration to fulfill his wish that "My home shall be open for the sun and the wind and the voices of the sea—like a Greek temple—and light, light, light everywhere!" Perched on a ledge at the top of the Scala Fenicia entrance to Anacapri (see p. 692), the spacious, airy house is filled with Munthe's art and antiques. An arbor-lined path leads to panoramic views across the bay. A sphinx looks out to sea—touching its well-worn hindquarters is said to bring good luck.

Munthe preferred San Michele to his residences in England and Sweden, though a devastating eye condition forced him to forgo the bright light of Capri for a time in the 1920s. In his absence he rented San Michele to the eccentric heiress Luisa Casati (1881–1957), who famously said, "I want to be a living work of art," and shocked the locals by walking around the island with leashed cheetahs and wearing live snakes as jewelry. Her lavish lifestyle at Villa San Michele and elsewhere left her $25 million in debt; she ended her days in relative poverty in London. After successful eye surgery, Munthe returned to Capri, living many happy years here before returning to Stockholm during World War II as a guest of the royal family.

Viale Axel Munthe 34. www.villasanmichele.eu. ✆ **081/837-1401.** 10€. Daily May–Sept 9am–6pm, Apr and Oct 9am–5pm, Mar 9am–4:30pm, Nov–Feb 9am–3:30pm.

Beaches

Inviting as Capri's waters are, getting into them can be bit of a challenge. The most convenient place to get wet is **Marina Piccola,** where the pebbly beaches are accessible by bus from Capri Town. Also near Capri Town is **Bagni di Tiberio,** a nice, sandy stretch on the north side of the island about 1km (a half-mile) east of Marina Grande. Getting down (and especially back up) from the cliff path requires a bit of a climb, though you can also get there and back in a little boat from Marina Grande for about 3€ each way. Other beaches are **next to the Blue Grotto** (Via Grotta Azzurra), accessible by bus from Anacapri; below the Faro (lighthouse) at **Punta Carena,** at the southwest tip of the island, also reached by bus from Anacapri; and at the base of the **Faraglioni,** reached by hundreds of steps from Via Tragara or by boat from Marina Piccola. You can bring a towel and lounge on the beach and rocks at any of these places. Most are lined with **beach clubs** *(stabilimenti balneari)*, usually open mid-March to mid-November 9am to sunset, which charge about 20€ a day for use of a changing room, chair or lounge, and towels; you'll find snack bars at most, excellent restaurants at some (see "Where to Eat on Capri," p. 697), and pools at a few.

Hiking

Capri is heaven for walkers. The island is laced with paths that beckon anyone with a good pair of walking shoes, a sun hat, and a bottle of water. Paths are indicated on most maps of the island, including those from the tourist office; you can also download them from the office's website, **www.capritourism.com**. Some especially enticing routes just outside Capri Town take you across handsome, view-filled landscapes around Punta Tragara and to some of the island's most famous sights, including the Faraglioni and Villa Jovis. A less-traveled but no less exhilarating route is on the western side of the island, the **Sentiero die Forini** (Path of the Forts). This 5km (3-mile) walk between the Blue Grotto and Faro (lighthouse) at Punta Carena passes four small coastal fortresses erected over the centuries to keep pirates and foreign powers at bay. However busy the island might be, here you'll find yourself amid Mediterranean countryside and an almost inexhaustible supply of sparkling sea views.

You may opt to take the chairlift to the summit of Monte Solaro (see p. 693) and hike down back to Anacapri through wooded countryside into the **valley of Cetrella.** You'll be following paths once used by the Carthusian monks of the Certosa di San Giacomo (see p. 688), who came out here to check on their herds. The route passes the aptly named **Villa Solitaria,** the former home of British novelist Compton Mackenzie (1883–1972), who lived with his wife, Faith, on Capri from 1913 to 1920 and intermittently thereafter. The island's famous tolerance of homosexual foreigners, along with Faith's affair with the classical pianist Renata Borgatti, inspired Mackenzie's lesbian-themed 1928 *Extraordinary Women.* A less secular landmark is just down the path, where the little **hermitage of Cetrella** and its **church of Santa Maria** nestle in a verdant copse. The church is not often open, so check with the tourist office before setting out if you'd like to take a look inside at its unusual double nave.

Where to Stay on Capri

EXPENSIVE

Capri Palace ★★★ At this delightful getaway in Anacapri on the slopes of Monte Solaro, everything is geared to soothing relaxation. An expanse of green lawn surrounds the swimming pool, chic lounges are quiet and welcoming, and guest rooms are done in restful creams with rose-colored tile floors and white linens. Some suites have private pools, and some rooms look across the sea all the way to Vesuvius, but even the outlooks from rear rooms over the green flanks of Monte Solaro are relaxing. A shuttle bus runs to the port, Capri Town, and a beach club with platforms that make it easy to dip into the Mediterranean.

Via Capodimonte 2, Anacapri. www.capripalace.com. ✆ **081/978-0111.** 79 units. 700€–1,100€ double. Rates include breakfast. Closed mid-Oct to mid-Apr. No children under 10 June–Aug. **Amenities:** 2 restaurants; bar; beach club; pool; room service; spa; free Wi-Fi.

Hotel Punta Tragara ★★ French architect le Corbusier designed this multilevel villa in the 1920s, and Winston Churchill and Dwight Eisenhower are among those who've enjoyed falling asleep to the sound of waves lapping on the shore far below. Each of the stylish quarters is different, some strikingly contemporary, others comfortingly traditional; all are luxurious without being pretentious and open onto terraces, most offering views of the Faraglioni. You can descend to the sea via hundreds of steps outside the gate, or take a dip in the two pools tucked into gardens.

Via Tragara 57, Capri Town. www.hoteltragara.com. ✆ **081/837-0844.** 45 units. 800€–1,200€ double. Rates include breakfast. Closed mid-Oct to mid-Apr. **Amenities:** Restaurant; bar; concierge; gym; 2 pools; room service; spa; free Wi-Fi.

Villa Marina Capri ★★ On its view-filled perch above Marina Grande, this late-19th-century villa has been converted into a romantic island getaway, set amid lush gardens and sunny terraces. Quietly glamorous rooms are named for artists and bohemians who have landed on Capri over the years, with decor firmly geared to soothing contemporary comfort. Most rooms open to the outdoors and sea views. Among the pampering amenities are a spa, restaurant, and notably attentive service, as well as free shuttle service to the port and Capri Town.

Via Prov, Marina Grande 191, Capri. www.villamarinacapri.com. ✆ **081/837-6630.** 21 units. 600€–1,400€ double. Rates include breakfast. Closed late Oct–Apr. **Amenities:** Restaurant; bar; pool; spa; free shuttle; free Wi-Fi.

MODERATE

Casa Mariantonia ★★ A gracious old villa near the Church of San Michele commands some of the best real estate in Anacapri—a shady lemon grove, lawns, gardens, and a big swimming pool all right in the center of town. Four generations have been welcoming guests to the family home, which mixes traditional island architecture with contemporary touches for a relaxed but luxurious ambience. The family claims that great-grandmother Mariantonia invented *limoncello,* which may be a bit of a stretch, but sipping the house-made elixir on a terrace next to the trees from whence it comes is a great Capri experience.

Via Guiseppe Orlandi 180, Anacapri. www.casamariantonia.com. ✆ **081/837-2923.** 10 units. 140€–230€ double. Rates include breakfast. Closed Jan–Mar. **Amenities:** Bar; pool; free Wi-Fi.

Villa Brunella ★★ Flower-filled terraces spilling down the hillside from Via Tragara pull you right into the magic of Capri, with eye-popping sea views from each of the airy, tile-floored guest rooms. Ambience hovers between cozy old-fashioned Italian hospitality and romantic getaway, with some nice antiques and overstuffed armchairs in the bright rooms and plenty of bougainvillea-filled nooks on pine-shaded grounds. A pool sparkles on a patio, and guests have access to a beach club at Marina Piccola. **Terrazza Brunella** provides excellent food in an elegant setting for times when even the short walk to town seems an effort.

Via Tragara 24, Capri Town. www.villabrunella.it. ✆ **081/837-0122.** 20 units. 200€–450€ double. Rates include breakfast. Closed Nov–Apr. **Amenities:** Restaurant; bar; pool; room service; free Wi-Fi.

INEXPENSIVE

Hotel La Tosca ★ You don't have to break the bank to stay on the island or even sacrifice style at this pretty little retreat on the quiet side of Capri Town, near the Gardens of Augustus. Many of the bright, whitewashed rooms have sea views, some have terraces, and all look out over lush gardens. Arches, vaulted ceilings, and tile floors help create the ambience of a simple-yet-tasteful island house. Breakfast is served on a breezy sea-view terrace.

Via Dalmazio Birago 5, Capri Town. www.latoscahotel.com. ✆ **081/837-0989.** 11 units. 125€–225€ double. Rates include breakfast. **Amenities:** Free Wi-Fi.

San Nicola Guesthouse ★★★ Large, airy tile-floored rooms tucked away on a little lane in Anacapri provide a quiet getaway and plenty of warm hospitality. Stylish contemporary furnishings are bright and comfortable, and bathrooms are commodious and up-to-date. Don't expect a view—high windows let the light stream in but have no outlooks—but a two-tiered shared terrace, well set up for outdoor lounging, looks over surrounding rooftops.

Via Prima Traversa Timpone 3A, Anacapri. www.sncapri.com. ✆ **338/831-8635.** 4 units. 120€–240€ double. Rates include breakfast. Closed mid-Oct to Apr. **Amenities:** Terrace; free Wi-Fi.

Where to Eat on Capri

EXPENSIVE

Le Grottelle ★★ CAPRESE A trek along the southern side of the island is rewarded with a stop at this out-of-the-way lair on a ledge above the Arco Naturale. A cave etched out of limestone cliffs and a panoramic terrace provide plenty of ambience, perhaps more memorable than the meal itself, though simple dishes like *zuppa di fagioli* (bean soup) and *spaghetti con pomodoro e basilica* (with fresh tomatoes and basil) are perfectly fine accompaniments to the views that extend across the sea to the Amalfi Coast. To find this delightful spot, wander east from Punta Tragara; it's about a 20-minute walk from the Piazzetta.

Via Arco Naturale 13, Capri Town. ✆ **081/837-5719.** Entrees 15€–30€. Daily noon–11:30pm. Closed Nov–Mar.

Ristorante Aurora ★ CAPRESE You'll get a taste of Capri's high life at the island's oldest eatery, where photos of celebrities hang above the white banquettes. A few may also be sitting around you in the minimalist main dining room or on the terrace facing Capri Town's main thoroughfare. Despite all the glitz, the third generation of the D'Alessio family sticks to the basics, serving island classics like the trademark thin-crust *pizza all'acqua,* with mozzarella and hot peppers, *sformatino alla Franco* (rice pie in prawn sauce), and spaghetti *alle vongole* (clams).

Via Fuorlovado 18, Capri Town. ✆ **081/837-0181.** Entrees 12€–22€. Apr–Dec daily noon–2:45pm and 7–11pm.

MODERATE

Gelsomina ★★ CAPRESE The sparkling swimming pool is a tempting draw on a warm summer day at this countryside retreat outside Anacapri. Come for the day, to swim, have lunch, and maybe walk to the

Belvedere della Migliera just down the road. It's also a popular evening spot, with dining on a sea-view terrace. The food is a perfect complement to the low-key setting, with many ingredients plucked straight from the surrounding gardens. Homemade *ravioli di caprese* is light as a feather and stuffed with delicious ricotta from a local producer. Anacapri is about 15 minutes away on foot, on lanes that slice through vineyards and gardens; a free shuttle is available. Five modest **guest rooms** (115€–190€ double) are above the restaurant, under the same management as the pleasant, reasonably priced **Villa Ceselle** hotel (www.villaceselle.com; 120€–180€ double), with a pool and garden near the center of Anacapri.

Via Migliara 72, Anacapri. www.dagelsomina.com. ✆ **081/837-1499.** Entrees 10€–18€. Daily noon–3:30pm and 7–11pm (from noon Fri and Sat; no dinner mid-Oct to Nov). Closed Nov to mid-Mar.

L'Angolo del Gusto ★★★ CAPRESE/SEAFOOD Village life seems pretty idyllic when observed from this attractive terrace on a piazza in Anacapri, and not much dispels the mood—certainly not the excellent service, the delicious preparations of fish grilled to perfection, or the risotto with shrimp and just-plucked lemons. A simple whitewashed stone room is amply atmospheric when the terrace fills up, and you'll be encouraged to linger over dessert and limoncello.

Via Boffe 2, Anacapri. ✆ **081/837-3467.** Entrees 8€–18€. Daily noon–3pm and 6:30–10:30pm.

Pulalli Wine Bar ★★ CAPRESE To find a hideaway in the always-busy Piazzetta, just look up to this little terrace next to the clock tower. The bird's-eye view from this perch comes with wine, a selection of cheeses, or a full meal—the *risotto al limone* (lemon-flavored risotto) is especially transporting, served in a hollowed-out lemon. To secure one of the seven tables in this coveted spot, it's best to reserve well ahead.

Piazza Umberto I 4, Capri Town. ✆ **081/837-4108.** Entrees 10€–25€. Wed–Mon noon–3pm and 7pm–midnight. Closed Nov–Mar.

INEXPENSIVE

Pizzeria Materita ★ PIZZERIA/CAPRESE All the warmth of little Anacapri comes to the fore in this busy local favorite on an animated square overlooking the church of Santa Sofia. Pizzas from the wood-fired oven and the palatable house wine are crowd pleasers, though the simple pastas are solidly tasty, too. Busy waiters often come around with fresh fish that soon reappear perfectly grilled with island herbs.

Via Giuseppe Orlandi 140, Anacapri. ✆ **081/837-3375.** Entrees 8€–18€. Daily noon–3pm and 7–11pm.

Beach Clubs

Some of Capri's most beloved institutions are the *stabilmenti balneari*, beach clubs, where you can eat well and begin or end a meal with a swim and some lounging. A day at one of these places is, like so much else about Capri, a simple pleasure with a glamorous twist.

Il Riccio ★★★ SEAFOOD The cliffside pavilion that serves as the informal beach bistro of the Capri Palace hotel (see p. 695) is done in soothing shades of blue and crisp white and hangs just above the Grotta Azzurra, bathed in the same mesmerizing light. The setting is so delightful you won't want to leave after feasting on a fish lunch, and you don't have to—the top level is a sunning platform, filled with lounges and umbrellas, while stairs and a path descend to wave-washed swimming platforms below. Lunch draws patrons even from the mainland, and dinner is also served in summer, making this the prime spot on the island for a romantic splurge. The kitchen transforms what's said to be the freshest seafood on Capri into such creations as turbot baked in a salt crust, and a spaghetti with urchin roe that's so good you'll wonder why you've been missing out on this treat all your life. Buses from Anacapri to the Grotta Azzurra stop just outside the door, as do shuttles from the Capri Palace. Via Gradola 4, Grotta Azzurra. www.capripalace.com. ✆ **081/837-1380.** Entrees 40€–50€. Daily 12:30–3:30pm and 7:30–10:30pm; lounge open throughout the day. Closed Nov to mid-Apr.

La Canzone del Mare ★ SEAFOOD/CAPRESE The British music-hall star Gracie Fields came to Capri in the 1930s and decided she would be the happiest woman on earth if "one small blade of grass on this wonderful, gentle place could belong to me." She eventually bought Il Fortino,

Beach club on Capri.

a house fashioned out of a ruined fort at Marina Piccola. Over the years she carved bathing platforms out of the rocks, installed a saltwater pool shaped like the island, and built terraces and lounges that would accommodate a restaurant, an American bar, and a few guest rooms, as well as living quarters that served as an informal retreat from life at her villa in Anacapri. Fields died of pneumonia after performing on the Royal Yacht anchored offshore, but her bathing establishment and restaurant still flourish. A meal of fresh vegetables and seafood pastas is a lot more expensive than you might expect from the simple surroundings, but the atmosphere is fun and eccentric, and Fields is still a presence. Five rooms named after famous former guests (like Elizabeth Taylor) provide sleeping quarters about as close to the sea as you'll find on Capri.

Via Marina Piccola 93. www.lacanzonedelmare.com. ✆ **081/837-0104.** Entrees 20€–40€. Daily noon–6pm; beach club daily 8:30am–7pm, entry 70€ May to mid-June, 80€ mid-June to Sept, includes bar and restaurant credit. Closed Oct–Apr.

La Fontelina ★★ CAPRESE/SEAFOOD Many travelers spend the winter months dreaming of a summertime lunch on the rocks at the base of the Faraglioni, where a meal comes with a swim in one of Europe's most legendary seaside settings. A fruit-loaded Sangria is the house drink, the Caprese salad—with *mozzarella di bufala* and just-off-the-vine tomatoes—is legendary, and the fish is so fresh you might think it jumped right out of the sea onto your plate. Lunch is the only meal served, and it's necessary to reserve for either of the two seatings, at 1 and 3pm. Most guests come early and hang around long after a meal to lounge on the rocks and dip into the crystalline waters. You can reach this spot by following the Punta Tragara paths from Capri Town (see p. 691) or take a launch from and to Marina Piccola, for 6€ a person each way.

Via Faraglioni. www.fontelina-capri.com. ✆ **081/837-0845.** Entrees 20€–40€. Daily noon–4pm; beach club only entry from 36€. Closed Oct–late Apr.

ISCHIA ★★

30km (18 miles) NW of Capri; 42km (26 miles) SW of Naples; 20km (13 miles) W of Pozzuoli

While Capri is swathed in glamor and sophistication, Ischia (pronounced EES-kee-a) is scented with sulfur, rising off hundreds of hot springs. These wellsprings have been the island's calling card ever since ancient Romans stepped ashore and discovered the pleasures of a long, soothing soak. **Monte Epomeo,** the island's 788m-high (2,585-ft.) dormant volcano, still has enough life in it to feed the mineral hot springs, producing therapeutic muds that supply the island's 150 spas. As a result, Ischia is often called the "island of eternal youth," a moniker that more aptly describes the young Neapolitans who peacock around cafes and bronze themselves on the many beaches. Ischia is also known as the Isola Verde

(Green Island), not, as some assume, for its verdant slopes, but for the green-tinged karst (limestone) that underlies much of the landscape. Yet Ischia *is* refreshingly green, with forests, orchards, and vineyards, and the towns along its 37km (23 miles) of shoreline are laidback, pleasant places. If they lack the sophistication of Capri, for many admirers they are all the better for that.

Essentials

ARRIVING Ischia's three main harbors—**Ischia Porto** (the largest), **Forio,** and **Casamicciola**—are well connected to the mainland, with most ferries leaving from Pozzuoli and Naples' two harbors (Mergellina Terminal Aliscafi and Stazione Marittima). Both **ferry** and **hydrofoil** *(aliscafi)* services are frequent in summer but slow down during the winter, when the hydrofoil is sometimes suspended because of rough seas. **Caremar** (www.caremar.it; ✆ **081/189–66690**), **Medmar** (www.medmargroup.it; ✆ **081/333-4411**), and **SNAV** (www.snav.it; ✆ **081/428-555**) offer ferry service from Naples, Pozzuoli, Capri, and Procida to Ischia Porto and Casamicciola. **Alilauro** (www.alilauro.it; ✆ **081/497-2222**) runs hydrofoils from Naples (Molo Beverello) to Ischia Porto and to Forio. ***Note:*** In high season, car access to the island is restricted and car slots are limited; if you plan to bring your car, make your reservations well in advance.

GETTING AROUND Public transportation on Ischia is excellent, with a well-organized **bus** system, **EAV** (www.eavsrl.it; ✆ **800/0539-309** toll-free in Italy). One line circles the island in a clockwise direction (*circolare destra* marked cd), and the other counterclockwise (*circolare sinistra,* marked cs). A number of other numbered lines crisscross the island. Tickets cost 1.50€ from a bar, tobacco shop, or news kiosk, 2€ on the bus (daily pass 4.50€). The ticket office at the main bus station next to the harbor in Ischia Porto can provide bus schedules and tell you which bus goes where, or you can find the schedules online at **www.ischiareview.com**.

Taxis wait at stands strategically located around the island, including Piazza degli Eroi (✆ **081/992550**) and Piazzetta San Girolamo (✆ **081/993-720**) in Ischia Porto; Piazza Bagni (✆ **081/900881**) in Casamicciola; and Piazza Girardi in Lacco Ameno (✆ **081/995113**).

You can **rent motor scooters, bicycles,** and **cars** on the island from a number of agencies, including **Calise** at Via Mazzella 116 in Forio (www.autonoleggio-ischia.com; ✆ **081/989486**) and **Island Center,** Via V. Di Meglio 161 in Barano (www.islandcenterischia.it; ✆ **081/902525**).

VISITOR INFORMATION The main **tourist office** (www.infoischia procida.it; ✆ **081/984-163**) is at Via Iasolino 7, Ischia Porto, where you'll find free maps as well as information and brochures. The office is open June through September Monday through Saturday 9am to 1:30pm and 3 to 8pm, and Monday through Saturday 9am to 1:30pm at other times. Another good source of information is **www.ischia.it**.

Exploring Ischia

Ischia is large as far as its neighbors in the Bay of Naples go, about 46 sq. km (18 sq. miles). Most of its main settlements—Ischia Porto, Casamicciola, and Lacco Ameno—are on the north shore, with Forio on the west coast. Boats call at **Ischia Porto,** with the island's one great historic landmark, the **Castello Aragonese,** in adjoining Isola Ponte. The busy harbor of Ischia Porto is a volcanic crater that was landlocked until 1854, when Bourbon King Ferdinand II had a channel cut to the sea. He created one of the most thrilling sea entrances anywhere, as ferries and yachts navigate the impossibly narrow cut and emerge into a becalmed lake surrounded by colorful waterside cafes and green hillsides carpeted with the island's distinctive white, flat-roofed houses. **Casamicciola,** to the west of Ischia Porto, is a famous spa town, devoted to the healing arts since the 17th century (in late 2022 it made news for a devastating landslide). Among the arthritic, gouty, and otherwise ailing travelers who've stayed here, Norwegian playwright Henrik Ibsen came for a cure in the 1860s, writing his famous verse drama *Peer Gynt* between treatments. He's honored with a plaque in Piazza Marina, near a statue of King Vittorio Emanuele II. The island's most sophisticated resort, **Lacco Ameno,** is just west of Casamicciola and became famous in 1963 when Richard Burton and Elizabeth Taylor arrived to shoot the barge scenes from the blockbuster film *Cleopatra;* the quiet little backwater became a jet-set hotspot when newspapers around the world ran paparazzi photos of the adulterous lovers yachting and swimming. Looming just offshore is the **Fungo,** a

Massive Castello Aragonese dominates Isola Ponte, a tiny island attached by causeway to Ischia.

mushroom-shaped lump of wave-sculpted tufa that is as iconic to Ischia as the Faraglioni are to Capri. On the west coast, **Forio** compensates for its lack of beauty with spectacular stretches of sand, a lively resort scene, and some extremely palatable wines from the surrounding vineyards. Wherever you settle, you won't be too far from the sights. A road follows the coast much of the way around the island, and buses make it easy to get from one town to the other.

Castello Aragonese ★★★ HISTORIC SITE Greeks settled this rocky islet as early as the 5th century B.C., building watchtowers to keep an eye on enemy fleets. Alfonso I gave the walled complex its present form in the mid-15th century as a defense against pirate raids, shoring up watchtowers and walls and installing churches, terraces, and squares that give the compound a village-like air. At one time some 17,000 people sheltered within the walls, among them nuns, monks, and soldiers. The British shelled the citadel during the Napoleonic Wars, and did a pretty good job of it, though enough remains to give an idea of its onetime might. Many churches still stand, in various states of repair. The frescoed crypt is about all that remains of the **Cattedrale dell'Assunta,** while the **Chiesa dell'Immaculata** and hexagonal **San Pietro a Pantaniello** are fairly intact. A somber if not downright macabre presence is the small **Cimitero delle Monache Clarisse,** attached to the island's convent. When the inhabitants breathed their last, they were left sitting on stone chairs as a reminder of what becomes of our earthly presence—the spooky-looking seating arrangement is still in place, minus the bones.

You can ponder all this as you make a circuit of the breezy ramparts, a vertigo-inducing lookout hundreds of feet above the crashing waves. An elevator whisks visitors up to the castle entrance, though the climb up the stairs and ramps provides a more authentic experience.

Piazzale Aragonese, Ischia Ponte. www.castelloaragoneseischia.com. ✆**081/992834.** 12€ adults; 6€ youth 10–14; free for children 9 and under. Daily 9am–sunset (last admission 1½ hr. before closing).

Villa La Mortella ★★★ GARDEN Sir William Walton (1902–83), one of the greatest English composers of the 20th century, and his Argentine wife, Susana Walton (1926–2010), settled on Ischia in 1949. Walton found peace and light conducive to composition, and Susana became enchanted with the idea of creating a garden at their home, La Mortella (the Myrtles) on the west side of the Monte Vico promontory outside Forio. Working with the great landscape designer Russell Page, she created the Valley Garden, filling it with rare Mediterranean and South American species, great sweeps of orchids and other flowers, and fountains, ponds, and brooks. (Walton had valves in his study so he could turn off the jets when the gurgling disturbed him.) Lady Walton designed the sunny, view-filled Hill Garden as a tribute to her husband, working in the soil herself well into her later years. The exotic romance of the gardens are an apt tribute to the Waltons, who married just a few months after meeting in Buenos Aires; in a fit of spite, the bride's father spent his daughter's entire dowry on the Champagne served at the wedding reception. It's customary on a walk along the garden paths to wave at the palms, following Lady Walton's belief that "You have to wave at them when you go by because they think you haven't paid attention."

Via Francesco Calise 39, Forio. www.lamortella.it. ✆ **081/986220.** 12€ adults; 10€ seniors and ages 12–18; 6€ children 5–11. Apr–Nov Tues, Thurs, and Sat–Sun 9am–7pm. Guided tour (15€, includes entry fee) Tues 10:30am and 4pm, Thurs 10:30am and 3:15pm, Sat 10:30am (limited tours offered in winter months); reservations required. Bus CS from Ischia Porto, Casamicciola, and Laco Ameno; CD from Forio.

Beaches

Ischia has a commodity that's the envy of Capri and towns along the Amalfi Coast: long stretches of sand, which draw a mixed lot of islanders, day-tripping Neapolitans, and Germans and Scandinavians. If you're staying in or near Ischia Ponte, your best bet is **Spiaggia dei Pescatori ★**, where local fishermen beach their boats; it's just west of the Aragonese Castle. On the north coast, the scenic beach on the bay of **San Montano ★★** is set on the flanks of the Monte Vico promontory near Lacco Ameno. On the west coast, south of Forio, **Spiaggia Citara ★★** has hot mineral springs that flow out to sea at its southern edge. On the south coast, the island's most beautiful beach is 2km (1¼-mile) long **Spiaggia dei Maronti ★★★**. Also on the south coast, just east of the village of Sant'Angelo, is so-called **Fumarole beach,** where hot underground vapors heat the sand to such temperatures that islanders come to bury chicken and fish in aluminum foil, then take a swim as they wait for their food to cook. The sands are also sought out by arthritis sufferers, who plonk down and let the heat penetrate their aching joints. Just offshore, geysers bubble up to create natural hot-tub-like pools. A flotilla of little boats ferry passengers from the town marina to this otherworldly seascape, about 5€ each way; the pools are also easy to reach on a seaside path.

Spas & Thermo-Mineral Baths

Ischia's elaborate *terme,* or thermal baths, have been popular ever since ancient Greeks soaked their weary bones in the natural hot springs. Most facilities offer slightly lower rates after midafternoon, so opt for a late entrance and a sunset soak. They also offer multi-day passes, for those who want to spend most of their time on Ischia quite literally in hot water.

Parco Termale Castiglione ★★ "Low-key" is not quite the right description for a place that splashes out with 10 pools, but they're set in tastefully designed seaside terraces laced with all sorts of quiet nooks and crannies. If the pool temperatures get to be too relaxing—they range from

82° to 104°F (28°–40°C)—a stone jetty is poised for a dip in the sea. The lack of a beach, and the serious mud and thermal treatments, makes the park more popular with a sedate clientele than with families.

Shore Rd. btw. Ischia Porto and Casamicciola. www.termecastiglione.it. ✆ **081/982551.** From 24€ a day, 17€ after 1pm; 15€ children 2–12. Aug 29€ per day, 25.50€ afternoon. Mid-Apr to Oct 9am–7pm.

Parco Termale Giardini Poseidon ★ Everything about Ischia's largest spa is over the top, with 22 pools, a large private beach, tropical gardens, and several restaurants. The kitsch runs high, including toga-bedecked statues, yet it's hard not to feel like a figure of ancient legend in the complex's nicest feature, an eons-old natural thermal cave etched out of a cliff. It's particularly popular with German and Italian families.

Via Giovanni Mazzella, Citara Beach, near Forio. www.giardiniposeidon.it. ✆ **081/908-7111.** June–July and Sept 40€ a day, 35€ after 1pm; Apr–May and Oct 38€ a day, 33€ after 1pm (after 12:30pm in Oct); Aug 45€ a day, 40€ after 1pm; children 4–11 half price; 3 and under free. Mid-Apr to Oct daily 9am–7pm.

Ischia has long been known for its thermal baths, such as this garden pool at Parco Termale Negombo.

Parco Termale Negombo ★★★ If you have time and/or inclination to visit only one thermal establishment on Ischia, make it this delightful spot on the island's most picturesque cove, San Montano. Gorgeous gardens, laid out by botanist Duke Luigi Camerini, surround 12 pools and facilities that include saunas, steam rooms, and massage cabins. While waterfalls and luxuriant plantings create a transporting getaway, just as alluring is the beach of fine sand. You could happily spend a day shuttling between the warm pools and the refreshing sea, with some naptime in the shade beside one of the garden's beautiful ersatz waterfalls.

San Montano beach, on Monte Vico promontory near Lacco Ameno. www.negombo.it. ✆ **081/986152.** 65€ a day 1 adult, 80€ a day 2 adults; 47€ 1 adult, 58€ 2 adults after 2pm; 40€ 1 adult, 50€ 2 adults after 3:30pm; prices include umbrella and sunbed. Late Apr to mid-Oct daily 8:30am–7pm.

Where to Stay on Ischia

Albergo Il Monastero ★★ The labyrinth of stone-walled, arched passageways, courtyards, and arbor-shaded seaside terraces of this former monastery are enticing in themselves, all the more so since the old premises are set within Ischia's spectacular **Castello Aragonese** (p. 703). Whitewashed guest rooms carved out of former monks' cells are spacious and soberly stylish, with handsome furnishings and knockout sea views from most. A huge panoramic terrace atop the castle walls is the setting for breakfast and delicious dinners, fed by produce from the hotel's garden. Guests have access to the rest of the castle and the castle gardens.

Castello Aragonese, Ischia Ponte. www.albergoilmonastero.it. ✆ **081/992435.** 20 units. 130€–270€ double. Rates include breakfast. Closed mid-Oct to mid-Apr. **Amenities:** Restaurant; free Wi-Fi.

Hotel della Baia ★★ At this delightful little getaway on a myrtle-clad hillside above San Montano Bay, a lounge is shaded by lime trees, and simple-chic rooms open to bougainvillea-filled terraces. Just down the road are two delightful places to swim and lounge, a sandy beach in a lovely cove and **Negombo,** the nicest of Ischia's thermal parks (p. 705).

San Montano beach, on Monte Vico promontory near Lacco Ameno. hoteldellabaia.negombo.it. ✆ **081/986150.** 16 units. 120€–145€ double. Rates include breakfast/brunch. Closed mid-Oct to mid-Apr. **Amenities:** Bar; pool; beach; free Wi-Fi.

Hotel Mandorla ★★ Maronti is the largest and in many views the best beach in Ischia, and the breezy terraces and gardens of this cheerful complex are right above the sands. All of the simply furnished rooms open to outdoor spaces where greenery and patios surrounds pools for soaking in mineral-rich thermal waters. The easygoing ambience and the chance to soothe weary bones and lie in the sun is a big draw with many northern Europeans who return year after year to settle in for a week or so. Beachside restaurants and bars are just outside the door, as is a bus stop for the 20-minute ride to and from Ischia Porto.

Via Provinciale Maronti 57, Maronti. en.hotel-lamandorla.it. ✆ **081/990-046.** 36 units. 90€–170€ double. Rates include breakfast; air-conditioning extra with some rates. Discounts for longer stays. Closed Nov to mid-May. **Amenities:** Bar; pools; private beach; free Wi-Fi.

Mezzatorre Resort & Spa ★★★ A former fortress at the end of a rocky promontory provides a sense of privileged escape and more than a whiff of la dolce vita amid 17 seaside acres of pine-scented gardens. Airy, view-filled accommodations in the dark-coral 15th-century watchtower and bungalows scattered among the garden are stylishly done in bright Mediterranean colors and a chic mix of antiques and contemporary pieces. Thermal pools on seaside terraces, a hot spring and spa, and a private beach ensure you can partake of a wellness regimen without leaving the property.

Via Mezzatorre, Forio. www.mezzatorre.it. ✆ **081/986-111.** 60 units. 350€–650€ double. Rates include breakfast. Free parking. Closed Nov–Apr. **Amenities:** 2 restaurants; bar; babysitting; concierge; health club; 3 pools; room service; thermal spa; outdoor tennis courts; free Wi-Fi.

Where to Eat on Ischia

Da Ciccio ★★★ SEAFOOD A seat on the terrace comes with killer views of the Castello Aragonese (p. 703). That's about as showy as it gets at this little hole in the wall, where Ciccio and son Bruno focus on fresh seafood in memorably delicious preparations: thick mussel soup is steeped with mountain herbs and topped with fried bread; squid is stuffed with breadcrumbs, raisins, and chopped fish; and linguine is laden with clams.

Via Luigi Mazzella 32, Ischia Ponte. ✆ **081/991686.** Entrees 10€–15€. Tues–Sun noon–3pm and 7–11:30pm.

La Cantinola di Zio Jack ★★★ ISCHIAN Not all the island's cuisine is from the sea—much is based on the bounty of the land, and this mountainside wine cave and terrace high above Forio shows just how delicious this can be. Rabbit, an island specialty, is stewed the traditional way, in a terra-cotta pot; another standout is pasta baked with fresh mozzarella and farm-grown potatoes, served in a bowl of baked pizza dough. Wines are from the surrounding hillsides. It's a trek up here on gravel roads, but the restaurant will send a car to pick you up in Forio; make a request for pickup when booking on the website.

Via Santa Maria al Monte, Forio. lacantinoladiziojack.it. ✆ **081/3332585.** Entrees 8€–12€. Daily noon–3pm and 7–11:30pm.

Ottomano ★★ ITALIAN/SEAFOOD A homey dining room and small terrace hang right over the sands of Maronti beach, making this a prime spot for a casual lunch or dinner. The small menu matches the easygoing ambience with a focus on *spaghetti alla vongole* and other nonfussy basics, as well as delicious pizzas from the oven.

Via Maronti, Barano D'Ischia. ✆ **328/902-9773.** Entrees 9€–16€. Daily 9am–10pm.

BASILICATA & PUGLIA

By Stephen Brewer

14

South of Naples, the Mezzogiorno begins in earnest. The name, which literally means "midday," evokes rugged sunbaked landscapes. But that doesn't begin to cover the riches you'll find in Basilicata and Puglia, the heel of the Italian boot. Some of Italy's great architectural marvels are here: *sassi* cave dwellings in Matera, fantastical cone-shaped *trulli* in Alberobello, and Lecce's honey-colored baroque churches and palaces.

Outside the towns, the countryside is a sweep of groves, orchards, vineyards, and fields. It's estimated that more than 6 million olive trees carpet the southeast, yielding almost half the country's oil production, and almost any view may include gnarled trunks growing out of red earth. Where there's good olive oil, there's good wine and good food. Once you've tasted the region's simple, delicious *cucina povera* (peasant cooking), you'll never think of a fava bean with indifference again.

DON'T LEAVE BASILICATA & PUGLIA WITHOUT . . .

Climbing through Matera. One of the oldest continually inhabited places on earth, Matera is a vertical maze of lanes and staircases connecting hill-clinging neighborhoods of *sassi* cave dwellings.

Gawking at the *Trulli.* Hundreds of these round, conical roofed houses line winding lanes in Alberobello, creating a fantasy-like townscape.

Being Dazzled by the White Cities. In the Valle d'Itria, the towns of Cisternino Locorotondo, Martina Franca, Ostuni, and Ceglie Messapica are so blindingly bright, you'll need sunglasses to wander their streets.

Going for Baroque in Lecce. The city is a showplace of extravagance from the 17th century, when craftsmen carved saints and sinners, gods and goddesses, and entire scenes into limestone as if it were butter.

MATERA ★★★

254km (158 miles) SE of Naples, 73km (44 miles) SW of Bari, 136km (82 miles) W of Brindisi

In Matera, it's all about caves: A vast honeycomb of thousands of caverns riddle the chalk cliffs above the gorge of the Gravina River. It's estimated that these caves have been inhabited for at least 9,000 years, making Matera one of the oldest continuously inhabited places on earth. The rugged landscapes appear to have sheltered hunters and gatherers even long before then—the remains of a 150,000-year-old hominid have been found

FACING PAGE: **Beach in Gargano National Park.**

Interior of a traditional cave house in Matera.

in a nearby cave. Excavations around the cathedral have unearthed successive waves of occupation: 3,000-year-old ceramics, Greek and Byzantine coins, Roman houses, and the coffins of early Christians.

By the mid-20th century, however, some of Italy's poorest residents lived in Matera's caves, as many as 20,000 troglodytes eking out a miserable existence in what had become a vast, unsanitary underground slum. Man and beast shared the dank caves, a breeding ground for disease. As Carlo Levi observed in his 1945 autobiographical novel *Christ Stopped at Eboli,* "I have never in all my life seen such a picture of poverty."

Eventually the Italian government moved the cave dwellers to more sanitary housing on the ridge above the cliffs in modern Matera. By the mid-1980s, the rock-cut settlement was attracting attention for its unique beauty, a delightful warm-hued jumble of steep "streets" and meandering staircases running right over the rooftops of underlying houses. The unique cave city, now a UNESCO World Heritage Site, is so richly evocative of ancient Mediterranean civilization that it's been a location for many films, including Pier Paolo Pasolini's *The Gospel According to St. Matthew* (1964), Mel Gibson's *The Passion of the Christ* (2004), and the James Bond film *No Time to Die* (2020).

You can get a good sense of Matera and see the main sights in a full day, and the city makes a good overnight stop on the circuit south from Naples into Puglia.

Basilicata & Puglia
Milan
Venice
Rome
ADRIATIC SEA
Gulf of Manfredonia
Gulf of Taranto
Gulf of Salerno
MOLISE
PUGLIA
CAMPANIA
BASILICATA
CALABRIA
Gargano Peninsula
Salentine Peninsula
Le Murge
Appennino Campano
Appennino Lucano
Lago di Varano
Lago di Lesina
Ofanto
Bradano
Basento
Peschici
Vieste
Rodi Garganico
San Nicandro Garganico
Monte Sant'Angelo
Lesina
Apricena
San Giovanni Rotondo
San Marco in Lamis
Manfredonia
Torremaggiore
San Severo
Margherita di Savoia
Barletta
Trani
Bisceglie
Giovinazzo
Bari
Mola di Bari
Polignano a Mare
Monopoli
Egnazia
Trinitapoli
Foggia
Lucera
San Ferdinando di Puglia
Andria
Molfetta
Bitonto
Triggiano
Rutigliano
Orta Nova
Cerignola
Canosa di Puglia
Corato
Ruvo di Puglia
Castel del Monte
Bitetto
Grumo Appula
Castellana Grotte
Fasano
Ostuni
Carovigno
Brindisi
Cisternino
San Vito dei Normanni
Alberobello
Locorotondo
Martina Franca
Ceglie Messapica
Mesagne
San Pietro Vernotico
Cassano delle Murge
Gioia del Colle
Santeramo in Colle
Altamura
Gravina in Puglia
Lavello
Melfi
Venosa
Rionero in Vulture
Ariano Irpino
Benevento
Avellino
Salerno
Campagna
Sala Consilina
Capaccio
Agropoli
Sorrento
Sapri
Lauria
Avigliano
Potenza
Volo dell'Angelo
Matera
Laterza
Ginosa
Montescaglioso
Bernalda
Policoro
Castellaneta
Mottola
Crispiano
Massafra
Palagiano
Grottaglie
Taranto
Oria
San Pancrazio Salentino
San Giorgio Ionico
Manduria
Sava
Lizzano
Pulsano
Lecce
Copertino
Galatina
Nardò
Galatone
Gallipoli
Matino
Taviano
Racale
Taurisano
Ugento
Otranto
Maglie
Santa Cesarea Terme
Tricase
Santa Maria di Leuca
A14
A16
A3
A30
SS89
SS17
SS16
SS655
SR1
SR6
SP231
SS96
SS99
SS379
SS172
SS7
SS87
RA 9
RA 2
RA5
SS691
SS407
SS18
SS106
SP430/a
SP430/b
0
25 mi

Essentials

ARRIVING The closest airports are in Bari and Brindisi (for info on both, go to www.aeroportidipuglia.it). **Buses** operated by Cotrab (www.cotrab.it) make four or five trips between Bari airport and Matera throughout the day; travel time is about 75 minutes. Matera is about an hour's drive south of Bari via SP236; from Brindisi, it's 2 hours northeast via E90 and SS7.

Trains from Rome and other major Italian cities stop at Bari; to continue to Matera, switch to the narrow-gauge train operated by **Ferrovie Appulo Lucane (FAL;** ferrovieappulolucane.it), which runs almost hourly (no service Sun) and takes about 1½ hours. Trains arrive at the new Matera Centrale station, with buses running down to the *sassi* from there.

If you're traveling to Matera from Naples, the easiest way is **by car,** following the A3 south, then the E847 east through Potenza; the drive takes a little more than 2 hours. **Bus** service between Naples and Matera, run by Marino (www.marinobus.it; ✆ **080/3112335**), takes 4½ hours, with six buses a day. **Flixbus** (www.flixbus.it) and other companies operate buses several times a day to connect Matera with Bari in a little over an hour. About a dozen **trains** (www.trenitalia.com) make the 4- to 5-hour run daily (often with a change in Potenza or Salerno) between Naples and the nearby town of Ferrandina-Scalo Matera, where you can catch a bus to Matera (fare around 3€).

GETTING AROUND The only way to get around much of Matera is **on foot,** and be prepared for a lot of climbing. Most of the *sassi* district is closed to car traffic; if you're arriving by car, arrange in advance with your hotel. Most hotels have agreements with lots and garages in the modern town where you can park for about 12€ a day, and garages will usually drop you off and pick up at a point near your hotel for about 5€. At times it's possible to drive to the bottom of Sasso Barisano and continue along Via Madonna delle Virtù into the bottom of Sasso Caveoso, though this should be only to drop off bags; your hotel must give your license plate number to the police in advance. Even so, it's best to avoid this hair-raising trip and leave the car above. The dispatch number for **Matera taxi** is ✆ **334348.**

A Crash Course on Cave Life

For some background on Matera, step into **Casa Noha,** Recinto Cavone 9 (www.fondoambiente.it/luoghi/casa-noha; ✆ **0835/335-452**), where visual projections onto cave walls and a good soundtrack trace the city's history and its unique social and architectural heritage. It's open daily except Tuesday April through October 10am to 7pm (Feb–Mar and Nov–Dec 10am–5pm); admission is 6.50€, 3€ ages 6 to 18, 17€ families of 2 adults and 2 children. On weekends Casa Noha staff also include tours of the *sassi* and the adjacent Parco della Murgia; tours cost 24€ adults, 12€ ages 6 to 18, 70€ families of two adults and two children, kids under 5 free.

VISITOR INFORMATION The municipal **Matera Welcome tourist office** in the modern town across from the train station on Viale Aldo Moro (www.materawelcome.it; ✆ **0835/241340**) is open Monday to Friday 9am to 2pm and Tuesday and Thursday 4 to 6pm. The website is a good source for tours, events, and other information. Your hotel will most likely provide you with a map, and beware, navigation apps go crazy in Matera. Private agencies abound, most in business to sell walking tours of the *sassi.* A good online source for tours is www.getyourguide.com, with 2½-hour excursions (from 25€) that shed light on life as it once was in the *sassi* and point out such details as charming frescoes by local artisans in the churches.

Exploring Matera

Matera is essentially divided into three districts. At the top of the ridge is the center of the modern town, or **Civita,** where the Duomo (p. 714) stands amid squares and palaces. Below Via Duomo spread the ***sassi*** (literally, "stones"), the cliff-hugging districts of cave dwellings. **Sasso Barisano,** to the north, has seen the most restoration, with many cave dwellings converted to hotels, restaurants, shops, and Airbnb rentals. **Sasso Caveoso,** to the south, is more authentically derelict, though renewal has begun.

The best way to appreciate the *sassi* is to plunge in and wander, following one of the well-marked stone staircases off Via Duomo. At the foot of the cliff in each *sasso* is one street with shops and cafes—in Sasso Barisano it's **Via dei Fiorentino,** in Sasso Caveoso, **Via Bruno Buozzi.** Along the way down are wonky staircases, blind alleys, crumbling stone courtyards with bursts of greenery, and many remarkable vistas.

Overlooking the Civita, or medieval heart of Matera.

Trying to find a specific address in the *sassi* can be challenging, but a few sights are worth seeking out. In Sasso Caveoso, besides the **Casa Grotta di Vico Solitario** (see below), you'll be able to see some cave rooms in the **Museum of Contemporary Sculpture Matera** ★ (Via San Giacomo, www.musma.it; ✆ **0835/330-582**), housed in the Palazzo Pomarico, a 16th-century palace with frescoed salons displaying works by an international roster of artists. Admission is 7€; it's open daily 10am to 6pm. Also in Sasso Caveoso are the ancient underground passages of **La Raccolta delle Acque** ★ (www.museimatera.it/raccolta-delle-acque; ✆ **329/063-1517;** enter at Via Purgatorio Vecchio), which carried the city's often-unhealthy water supply, channeling rainwater collected from streets and roofs into deep cisterns. Since streets were littered with human and animal waste, cholera and typhoid were rampant. The Raccolta is open daily 10am to 4pm. Admission is 2.50€.

One of Matera's best-preserved rock church complexes, **Santa Lucia alle Malve** ★★, also in Sasso Caveoso (www.oltrelartematera.it; ✆ **327/980–3776**), was a refuge for monks fleeing 8th-century persecution in the Middle East; it later became a convent for Benedictine nuns, who in the 13th century frescoed the caves in colorful scenes that include a breast-feeding Madonna. The church is open daily 10am to 4pm; admission is 4€.

Some of the best views of the *sassi* are from the **Parco della Murgia Materana** ★★ (www.parcomurgia.it; ✆ **0835/336166**), covering 70 sq. km (27 sq. miles) along the gorge of the Gravina River just below town. High ground affords sweeping views, while the ravines are riddled with caves that have been used as rock churches, stables, and shepherds' shelters. Enter the park on trails off Via Madonna delle Virtù. Confusingly, this park is also known as Parco Archeologico Storico Naturale delle Chiese Rupestri del Materano, and the names are used interchangeably.

Casa Grotta di Vico Solitario ★ MUSEUM The past is brought to life in this re-created dwelling from the 1950s, when the government cleared out the *sassi* and moved residents up to modern Matera. The crude authentic furnishings include a ridiculously high bed that kept folks up off the frigid stone floor and provided storage space beneath. It's not as filthy as it must've been when residents shared the space with pigs and donkeys, but accompanying film footage conveys the district's former squalor.

Off Via Bruno Buozzi, Sasso Caveoso. www.casagrotta.it. ✆ **0835/310118.** 5€. Daily 9am–9pm.

Duomo ★ CHURCH The residents of the *sassi* are never out of sight of the city's soaring cathedral, completed in 1270 on high ground at the side of the cliff just above them. Carvings on the facade deliver a morality lesson to the faithful: A mermaid warns of the passions likely to steer us off a path of righteousness; an eagle is poised to devour meeker animals, just as we are always prey to sin; the Archangel Michael battles a dragon (representing the forces of evil) before an audience of the town's medieval elite. Most of the similarly moralistic frescoes that once covered the interior

The *sassi* district in Matera.

were destroyed in renovations, but a terrifying 13th-century "Last Judgment" remains, to the right of the entrance, with Archangel Michael wielding his sword in hell as serpents attack the damned—among them popes, monks, and kings, proof that no one escapes the final judgment. An antidote is the charming 16th-century nativity scene in a side chapel, where shepherds and their flocks are set against a re-creation of Matera, looking just like it does today.

Piazza del Duomo. Free (audioguide 2€). Mon–Sat 9am–7pm; Sun 12:30–7pm.

Madonna delle Virtù e San Nicola dei Greci ★★★ HISTORIC SITE In Sasso Barisano, this intriguing maze of 10th- and 11th-century frescoed chapels and living quarters once held a community of nuns on one level, monks on another. At one point the low-slung caverns open to an almost majestic apse with a domed ceiling.

Via Madonna delle Virtù, Sasso Barisano. www.caveheritage.it. ✆ **0377/444-8885.** 5€. Daily 10am–6pm.

Museo Nazionale d'Arte Medievale e Moderna della Basilicata-Palazzo Lanfranchi ★ MUSEUM Among the paintings and religious objects in this converted monastery are colorful canvases by artist Carlo Levi (1902–1975), who was exiled to this region in the 1930s for antifascist activities. Levi's autobiographical novel, *Christ Stopped at Eboli,* brought the area's poverty and squalid living conditions to world attention, and these hard-hitting paintings capture the hardship of peasant life in the *sassi.*

Piazzetta Giovanni Pascoli, in the Civita. www.museonazionaledimatera.it. ✆ **0835/310058.** 5€. Thurs–Tues 9am–8pm.

Where to Stay in Matera

Many Materani have converted caves into rentals, and many of them are available through **Airbnb** (www.airbnb.com). Typical of the unique Sassi accommodations available is the view-filled double room with a balcony that Marghertia Albanese rents near her delightful jewelry shop, **Arterego,** at Via Rosario 48 (www.arterego.it; ✆ **338/295-5845**).

Alle Malve Bed & Breakfast ★ No one says a cave dwelling can't have a chipper vibe, and this ancient house dug into the hillside at the foot of Sassi Caveoso is downright cheerful. Contemporary touches in the bright lounge and guest rooms include a floating staircase, a sunken sitting area in front of a crackling fire, and large state-of-the-art bathrooms. Papevero is an especially appealing room, with high wooden ceilings and a large terrace.

Via Bruno Buozzi 102. www.allemalve.com. ✆ **0835/312-816.** 5 units. 95€–170€ double. Rates include breakfast. **Amenities:** Free Wi-Fi.

Fra I Sassi Residence ★★★ At this beautiful enclave at the bottom of Sasso Barisano, well-designed and comfortably furnished cave rooms (some with sunken tubs) open onto a bright terrace—a front-row seat for a spectacular vista of dwellings clinging to the surrounding hillsides. Welcoming outdoor spaces are well supplied with loungers, the perfect perch for a drink, a nap, or just soaking in the views. The breakfast room does double duty as a bar/cafe.

Via D'Addozio 102. www.fraisassiresidence.com. ✆ **0835/336-020.** 18 units, plus 8-bed hostel. 110€–155€ double; hostel rates on request. 2- to 3-night minimum stay required some periods. Rates include breakfast. **Amenities:** Bar; free Wi-Fi.

San Giorgio Hotel ★★ You will feel like a bona-fide troglodyte—albeit a high-living one—in one of these well-equipped dwellings scattered throughout Sassi Barisano. Most have one or two bedrooms; many are multilevel and, given their unusual settings, rich in arches, vaults, and other architectural details, including fireplaces and terraces in some. An accommodating staff serves breakfast in a pleasant room in the main house.

Via Fiorentini 259. www.sangiorgio.matera.it. ✆ **0835/334583.** 11 units. 100€–150€ double. 2-night minimum stay required some periods. **Amenities:** Free Wi-Fi.

Sextantio le Grotte della Civita ★★ If the Flintstones had hired a big-name decorator, they might have been treated to a design-magazine-worthy abode like these luxurious cave sanctuaries overlooking the Gravina River gorge. Furnishings are rustic chic, with authentically old pieces scattered around cavernous spaces where soft light flickers off stone walls.

Luxuries include freestanding tubs, fireplaces, and (in many rooms) terraces overlooking green, rock-studded countryside. The attempt to re-create the look of a primitive cave dwelling without sacrificing creature comforts is quite dramatic, and it's hard to quibble with the luxury of stepping out of bed onto a cave floor heated underneath. Breakfast, drinks, and some meals are served in an ancient church hewn out of the rock.

Via Civita 28. be www.sextantio.it/en/legrottedellacivita/matera. ✆ **0835/332-744.** 20 units. 165€–350€ double. Rates include breakfast. **Amenities:** Bar; cafe; spa; free Wi-Fi.

Where to Eat in Matera

In restaurants around town, favored pastas are ear-shaped *orecchiette* and *lagane* (similar to *tagliatelle*); sauces often use local **pork** and are seasoned with *pepperoni* cruschi (fried red peppers) and fried breadcrumbs. **I Vizi degli Angeli Laboratorio di Gelateria Artigianale,** Via Domenico Ridola 36 (✆ **0835/310637**), serves organic *gelati* and *sorbetti.*

La Talpa ★★ BASILICATESE Matera's caves don't get any more inviting than these snug, white-walled rooms hung with old cooking implements and filled with gingham-topped tables. The homey setting is suited for such local dishes as *purea di fave con cicorielle di campo* (broad-bean puree with chicory) or *cavatelli* with chickpea puree, arugula, porcini mushrooms, and tomatoes. Lamb and veal are grilled to perfection, and pizzas emerge from a wood oven at the back of the cave.

Via dei Fiorentini 167. www.latalparistorante.it. ✆ **0835/335-086.** Entrees 9€–18€. Daily noon–3:30pm and 7–11pm. Closed late Jan and early Feb and for lunch in Feb.

Oi Mari ★★ BASILICATESE/NEAPOLITAN This convivial spot in Sasso Barisano took its name from a famous Neapolitan serenade—and

The Bread of Life

Matera is known for its delicious breads, stuffed and topped with cheese and meat fillings: bakeries around the city make *strazzata,* a type of focaccia, from local durum wheat, as well *pucce,* a sandwich bread based on pizza dough, and *panzerotti,* a crescent-shaped turnover that's like a calzone only thinner. **Panifico Perone il Forno di Gennaro,** Via Nazionale 52 (www.ilfornodigennaro.com; ✆ **0835/385-656**), a long-standing Matera institution, moved out of the Sassi into the new town 60 years ago but still bakes its delicious bread, including focaccia, in wood-fired ovens; the bakery also offers 4-hour breadmaking workshops, from about 70€. **Pasticceria Schiuma,** near the Duomo at Via XX Settembre 10 (www.pasticceriaschiuma.com; ✆ **0835/331-862**), is another venerable favorite, serving snacks and sandwiches in polished surroundings, alongside an irresistible selection of cakes and pastries. **Panificio Paoluccio,** Via del Corso 22 (✆ **0334/185-9799**), tops house-made focaccia with tomatoes, potatoes, garden vegetables, and other local ingredients, while **Pucceria Quatroquarti,** Via Ascanio Persio 25 (www.quattroquarti matera.it; ✆ **393/966-2961**) stuffs *pucce* with pork sausage, local onions and eggplants, and smoked cheeses.

that's not the only way in which this cheery candlelit cave takes inspiration from Naples. The pizzas are the best in town, filling the cavernous space nightly with eager diners. You can nicely stretch out a meal with heaping platters of *antipasto di mare,* with octopus, squid, and *baccala,* or choose from a wide array of seafood pastas and meat dishes.
Via dei Fiorentini 66. www.oimari.it. ✆ **0835/346-121.** Entrees 8€–18€. Fri–Tues 12:30–3pm and 7:30pm–midnight; Thurs 7:30pm–midnight.

Ristorante Francesca ★★★ BASILICATESE Simple contemporary furnishings and chic lighting highlight the atmosphere of a millennia-old dwelling, where a meal in soothing cave rooms or on a warm-weather terrace is steeped in Matera traditions. That means local *burratina* cheeses, herb-infused sausages and grilled lamb, and hand-rolled *orecchiette* and *cavatelli* with fava beans and fresh vegetables, all to be washed down with Aglianico, the inky local red wine.
Via Bruno Buozzi 9. ✆ **083/531-0443.** Entrees 8€–18€. Thurs–Sun 7:30–10pm; Sun 12:30–3pm.

Trattoria del Caveoso ★ BASILICATESE Bold contemporary art decorates this convivial multilevel cave in Sasso Caveoso, but it's all about old-fashioned cuisine: wholesome, straightforward preparations that don't pretend to be anything other than *cucina povera,* poor man's grub. Fresh local produce brightens dishes like *strascinate con rape mollica fritta* (pasta topped with broccoli, chili peppers, and breadcrumbs) or lamb fried with onions, tomatoes, mushrooms, and wild onions.
Via Bruno Buozzi 21. www.ristorantedelcaveoso.it. ✆ **0835/312-374.** Entrees 8€–16€. Thurs–Tues 12:30–3pm and 7:30–11pm. Closed late Jan–early Feb.

The Maratea

Basilicata dips down to the Tyrrhenian sea only briefly, but quite dramatically so, along the Maratea coast, 200km (120 miles) southwest of Matera. It's a 2½ hour drive and 8-hour bus ride through the mountains to this slip of seashore, but the beaches and turquoise waters are only 2 hours by car

fly LIKE AN ANGEL

To add some zip to a Matera visit, travel about 80km (49 miles) west via SS7 and E847 to Castelmezzano and Pietrapertosa, picturesque villages perched on adjacent mountainsides. The neighbors have linked themselves via the **Volo dell'Angelo** (Flight of the Angel) zipline, making it possible to get from one village to the other at a top speed of 120kph (74mph) along cables almost a mile long. You may also traverse the gorge between the two on the 2km (1¼-mile) **Percorso delle Sette Pietre** ("Walk of the Seven Stones"). The zipline operates May through early November and every day from mid-July through August; check the website for days outside that period; a round-trip costs 35€, 63€ for couples, 45€ and 78€ on weekends. For reservations and information, go to www.volodellangelo.com.

or train from the Amalfi Coast (see chapter 13), providing a pleasant alternative for beachgoers willing to forgo the glamor, polish, and crowds. The **Via Nazionale,** the local equivalent of the Amalfi Drive, winds past sand-fringed coves at Acquafredda and Grotta della Scala, and above it all is the beautiful main town, **Maratea Superiore,** where 44 churches and chapels cling to the mountainside. Higher still is the statue of Christ the Redeemer atop **Monte San Biagio.** If approaching by car from points north, take A2 through Salerno toward Reggio-Calabria and exit at **Sapri,** near the northern gateway to the region. Frequent north–south trains stop at Sapri, from which local trains and buses travel along the coast to Acquafredda and Maratea (from the Amalfi Coast, board a Sapri-bound train at Salerno).

PUGLIA'S NORTH COAST ★★

The beautiful city of **Trani** is a jumping-off point for the remarkable **Castel del Monte** (p. 721) and the **Gargano peninsula** (p. 722). **Bari** (see box p. 720) is the gateway to the region: **Trains** operated by Trenitalia and Italo (www.italotreno.it) make the trip from Rome in about 4 hours, **buses** from Naples in about 4 hours (many operated by Marino, www.marinobus.it). Bari's **airport** (www.aeroportidipuglia.it) handles flights to and from cities throughout Europe. For bus and train travel around Puglia, check schedules with **Ferrovie del Sud Est** (www.fseonline.it) or go to the Puglia tourism website, www.viaggiareinpuglia.it.

Trani

85km (51 miles) N of Matera

A bit off the beaten track, this once-thriving medieval seaport has twisting lanes and airy piazzas lined with palaces and churches, all hewn from golden limestone that glows with a tinge of pink when the sun hits it. Sooner or later the maze untangles alongside the shimmering blue waters of the Adriatic, where one of Italy's most dramatic cathedrals seems to rise out of the waves.

ESSENTIALS

ARRIVING Trani is just off the A14 autostrada, which follows the Adriatic coast between Bari and Rimini. If you're driving from Matera, head north to Altamura, then follow signs through Corato to Trani. Trani is 40 minutes by train from Bari; for schedules and tickets, go to www.trenitalia.com. The closest airports are in Bari and Brindisi (www.aeroportidipuglia.it).

GETTING AROUND Stash the car as soon as possible and navigate the old city on foot. You'll find park-and-display parking near the seafront next to the Duomo and Castello Svevo.

VISITOR INFORMATION Visit **www.viaggiareinpuglia.it** for information about the region. Trani's **tourist office** is at Piazza Trieste 10 (www.agenziapugliapromozione.it; ✆ **0883/588830**).

Bari: Gateway to Puglia & Home to Santa Claus

A 4th-century bishop of Myra, Turkey, St. Nicholas—whose gift-giving habits gave rise to the Santa Claus tradition—lay at peace in his hometown until 1076, when pirates stole his bones and brought them to Bari, now the largest city in Puglia. Nicholas was a big prize, a top draw for pilgrims from all over Christendom, and Bari zealously built the almost fortress-like, twin-towered **basilica of San Nicola** to house him. St. Nick's feast day, December 6, is a big event in Bari, especially the ceremony in which a flask is lowered into the crypt to extract a miraculous liquid said to be emitted by the saint's remains (they even sell it in little bottles). The basilica, on Largo Abate Elia (© **080/5737111**), is open Monday through Saturday 7:15am to 8:30pm and Sunday 7:15am to 10pm; admission is free. Around the basilica are the lanes and squares of **Bari Vecchia,** an intriguing old quarter that juts into the sea. Cafe-lined **Piazza del Ferrarese** is the liveliest corner; along atmospheric Arco Basso and Arco Alto, women sell homemade *orecchiette* and other goods from tables in front of their doors. Modern Bari, laid out in a grid around the historic quarter and a massive 12th-century castle (now government offices), is quite pleasant, inspiring the saying "if Paris had the sea, it would be a little Bari."

EXPLORING TRANI

For most of Trani's history, travelers approached the city by sea. Today you'll likely enter town through its scruffy outskirts, but you'll still want to head to the port. The enormous 13th-century seafront **Castello Svevo** is proof of Trani's onetime power, street names like Via Synagoga testify to a large medieval Jewish population, and Via Cambio (Street of the Moneychangers) reveals Trani's role as a major Mediterranean trading center. During the Crusades, Trani was an embarkation port for Christian forces heading to the Middle East; soldiers of the elite Knights Templar order received blessings in the courtyard of the splendid **church of Ogisanti,** on Via Ogisanti (Fri 6–8pm and Sat 9:30am–12:30pm and 6–8pm).

Duomo ★★ CATHEDRAL For your first glimpse of this gleaming Romanesque-style masterwork, head for the east side of Trani harbor: You'll see the **campanile** (bell tower) stretching 59m-high (194-ft.) toward the sky, while the church's sheer limestone walls seem to be rooted not in the ground but in the sea. This dramatic union of sea and sky lifts the spirit, an effect no doubt intended by the architects and craftsmen who began work in 1097. Their singular mission was to outdo Bari, their neighbor just down the coast, which had just snatched the relics of St. Nicholas (see box above) and was building a basilica to house them, sure to draw crowds of pilgrims. Trani had a new saint of its own to promote, San Nicola Pellegrino (St. Nicholas the Pilgrim), an extremely pious Greek shepherd boy who, after a long sea voyage, collapsed and died from exhaustion in front of the 7th-century church of Santa Maria, which formerly occupied this site. (Nicola reputedly spent all his waking hours chanting the phrase "Kyrie Eleison"—"Lord, have mercy," a habit that may have annoyed his companions but nevertheless won him almost instant sainthood). The foundations of the Santa Maria church are still in the crypt, where the saint's tomb rests among a forest of columns. The main church is a soaring display of arches, columns, and vaults luminously fashioned from golden limestone. The heavy bronze doors (created by Barisano da Trani, whose most famous work is the doors in Monreale, Sicily, see p. 767) depict familiar biblical figures as well as dragons, lions, archers, and jugglers—look for the panel where the artist portrays himself, humbly at the feet of San Nicola.

Piazza Duomo 9. www.cattedraletrani.it. ✆ **0883/500-293.** Free. Apr–Oct daily 9am–12:30pm and 3:30–7pm (4–8:30pm Sun); Nov–Mar daily 9am–12:30pm and 3:30–6pm (4–8pm Sun).

Castel del Monte

34km (21 miles) S of Trani

Topping a small mount above the fertile Puglian plains, this majestic castle comes into sight from miles away, just as the enlightened Frederick II, Holy Roman Emperor and King of Sicily, intended when he ordered it built in 1237. The distinctive octagonal shape may look familiar—it's reproduced on every 1-cent euro printed in Italy. What's not clear, however, is what this castle was built for. It has no moat or walls, so it wouldn't have been practical for defense, despite the strategic hilltop position (certainly no enemy could approach without being spotted). Frederick's passion for science and mathematics is reflected in the precision of the octagonal shape with eight octagonal towers, blending Islamic and Gothic

One of the eight octagonal towers in Castel del Monte, Trani.

influences. Large trapezoidal rooms on two floors are warmed by fireplaces, implying a certain degree of luxury and suggesting the castle might have been built for entertaining or as a hunting lodge. A few fragments of mosaics, frescoes, and marble work remain, and it's known that an ingenious plumbing system fed by rainwater supplied baths and latrines. Frederick's successors converted the castle to a prison, where convicts languished in cold chambers. To get here from Trani, head southwest on SP130 to Andria, then south toward Spinazzola. From Matera, head to Altamura, then Gravina, and follow signs to Spinazzola. The **castle** (www.casteldelmonte.org; ✆ **0883/569997**) is well sign-posted off Strada Statale 170, outside Andira. It is open daily April to September 10am to 6:45pm and October to March 9am to 5:45pm, and entrance is on the hour. Admission is 7€, 2€ ages 18 to 25.

Promontorio del Gargano

About 90km (55 miles) NW of Trani

The spur of the Italian boot is this thumb-shaped promontory northwest of Trani, mostly now protected as the **Parco Nazionale del Gargano.** Much of the peninsula's mountainous interior is carpeted with an ancient oak and beech forest, the Foresta Umbra, which once covered much of Central Europe; the coast is a magical seascape of cliffs, rock formations, caves, islets, and sandy beaches. Come August, Italian families head to low-key summer resorts around the whitewashed towns of **Vieste** and **Peschici.** In centuries past, both towns continually fended off pirates and other

Rock outcroppings protect lovely sandy beaches along the coast of the Gargano peninsula.

invaders—in Vieste in 1554 the Turks beheaded more than 5,000 men, women, and children.

The ever-popular **cave of St. Michael the Archangel** in hilltop Monte Sant'Angelo (www.santuariosanmichele.it) is the oldest shrine in Western Europe, founded in the 7th century (the archangel is believed to have appeared there three times). Admission to the chapels and rock-hewn sanctuary is free. It's open Monday to Saturday 7am to 1pm and 2:30 to 8pm (closes 7pm Nov–Mar), Sunday 7:30am to 12:30pm and 2:30pm to 7pm; July through September it stays open with no midday break and until 8pm on Sunday. Even more popular is the sanctuary of **Padre Pio** (www.conventosantuariopadrepio.it) in San Giovanni Rotondo, where the beloved mystic saint (canonized in 2002) served as priest from 1916 to 1968. Padre Pio's shrine includes architect Renzo Piano's stunning **Chiesa San Pio Da Pietrelcina** (www.conventosantuariopadrepio.it; daily 7am–8pm), built in 2004 and the second-most-visited Catholic pilgrimage site in the world, after Mexico City's Our Lady of Guadalupe, with 7 million pilgrims a year.

From Trani, the Gargano gateway city is Manfredonia, about 80km (50 miles) northwest via SS16 and SP77. From there, SS89 skirts the peninsula; expect at least half a day of slow driving to make the circuit. You'll find **tourist offices** at Vieste (Piazza J.F. Kennedy, ✆ **0884/708806**) and Peschici (Via Magenta 3, ✆ **0884/915362**). **Park headquarters** is in Monte Sant'Angelo, 90km (55 miles) NW of Trani (www.parks.it/parco.nazionale.gargano).

Where to Stay & Eat on the North Coast

B&B Palazzo Paciotti ★★★ A restored palace in Trani's old quarter near the cathedral oozes with history, but beyond the rich stone facade, large, high-ceilinged spaces on the third floor (with elevator) are spruce and modern. Low-slung chairs are upholstered in white, beds are framed in white steel, and modern bathrooms gleam with mosaic tiles. Breakfast is served in an upper-floor sunroom with terrace, shared with the slightly snazzier **Le Dimore del Re** (✆ **393/019-2208**) on another floor of the palace.

Via della Giudea 41. ✆ **340/238-8121.** 5 units. 60€–100€ double. Rates include breakfast. **Amenities:** Free Wi-Fi.

Corteinfiore ★★★ SEAFOOD A few outdoor rooms meander through the courtyard of an old palace near Trani's port, covered in winter and full of greenery offsetting chic white furnishings. The short, simple menu is a fish fancier's delight, with antipastos of fresh sashimi and sushi or a cooked chef's choice selection, depending on what's fresh; follow-ups are a few grilled choices and perfectly prepared seafood pastas and risottos.

Via Ognissanti 18. www.corteinfiore.it. ✆ **0883/508-402.** Entrees 12€–25€. Tues–Sun 12:30–2:15pm and 8–10:30pm.

Hotel Seggio ★★ The former 17th-century town hall of Vieste provides a picturesque clifftop perch for soaking in the drama and beauty of the Gargano region. Many of the basic but comfortable rooms take in the views from private balconies, while an elevator descends to a pool and private beach. The intriguing old town is just outside the door.
Via Vesta 7, Vieste. www.hotelseggio.it. ✆ **0884/708123.** 25 units. 200€–250€ double. Weeklong stays may be required in summer. Rates include breakfast. Closed Dec–mid-Apr. **Amenities:** Bar; snack bar; pool; garage; free Wi-Fi.

THE VALLE D'ITRIA: TRULLO COUNTRY ★★

The Valle d'Itria feels like a magical place, where cone-shaped stone *trulli* houses poke above olive groves. While *trulli* are sprinkled over farms and fields throughout this part of Puglia, in the town of Alberobello, at the heart of the Valle d'Itria, more than 1,600 beehive houses line the hilly winding lanes, earning UNESCO World Heritage Site status. As if this weren't enough, the road heading south through the Valle d'Itria leads to a string of hilltop towns built of gleaming white stone.

Alberobello ★★

69km (43 miles) NE of Matera, 55km (34 miles) SE of Bari, 80km (50 miles) NW of Brindisi

Alberobello has 1,620 *trulli,* and the effect is whimsical, even a bit weird. Walking through the narrow streets you can't help but feel you've stepped into the pages of a fairy tale or a scene from *The Hobbit.* You'll be forgiven for making a crack or two, in the vein of "These are *trulli* charming." Just don't think you're clever—the residents of Alberobello have heard it all.

Most of Alberobello's *trulli* (from the Greek *troulos,* "dome") date from the mid-16th century to the 19th century, when they proliferated for two reasons: They were easy to build, with stones put in place without mortar, and their design was flexible. At first the conical-roofed stone huts were shelters for farmers in the fields, but in Alberobello the *trullo* became the standard house type. Local lore has it that the technique became popular because when tax inspectors came around, residents could swiftly dismantle their *trulli;* more likely is that since no mortar was used, the structures didn't qualify for full taxation. With thick stone walls supporting a conical roof, *trulli* could only be single-room structures—each roof corresponds with a single room below—but many *trulli* are clustered together to create multi-room residences.

ESSENTIALS

ARRIVING From Bari by **car,** head south on S100 and then east (signposted) on S172. A parking lot off Largo Martellotta charges about 2€ an hour; a machine dispenses a ticket to place on your dashboard. From Bari

The trulli district in Alberobello looks like a fairy-tale stage set.

by **bus** and **train,** Ferrovia del Sud Est (FSE; www.fseonline.it) runs hourly (every 2 hr. Sun), taking about 1¾ hours; most trips are by bus, though some require a change to a train in Putignano.

VISITOR INFORMATION For many travelers, Alberobello offers a first taste of the Puglia region (for regional info, visit **www.viaggiareinpuglia.it**). Alberobello's small municipal **tourist** office, in Via Brigata Regina, just off Largo Martellotta (www.comunealberobello.it; ✆ **080/432-1200**) is open daily 10am to 5:30pm (Sun until 8:30pm), with a midday closure from 1pm to 2:30pm.

EXPLORING ALBEROBELLO

To find the *trulli,* follow Via Mazzini, which turns into Via Garibaldi, to Piazza del Popolo. Turn left on Largo Martellotta, which takes you to the edge of the popular tourist area; the *trulli* are well signposted. You need an hour or two to tour the *trulli,* starting from **Largo Martellotta,** an airy square that separates the two *trulli* zones. **Rione Monti,** to the south, is the larger and busier of the two; many of its *trulli* are now coffee bars and, of course, gift shops. It's hard to resist leaving Alberobello without a small-scale replica of a *trullo,* crafted in the same type of stone that the town's builders used. Once you've adjusted to the whimsy, cross the square and walk northeast up the hill into quiet, residential **Rione Aia Piccola,** which seems much more like a quaint village. From Aia Piccola's hillside, you'll get a great view across the valley to the spectacle of Monti's hundreds upon hundreds of densely packed *trulli.*

The most monumental house in town is the **Trullo Sovrano,** on the far northern edge of modern Alberobello at Piazza Sacramento 10 (www.trullosovrano.eu; ✆ **080/432-6030**). From Largo Martellotta, walk north into Piazza del Popolo and then follow Via Vittorio Emanuele north to Piazza Sacramento. This rare two-story *trullo* comprises 16 separate, joined structures surrounding a central *trullo* with a cupola. A prominent family built the compound, complete with stables, barns, and a farm court, in the late 18th century. It later became headquarters for a religious confraternity and today shows off *trulli* domestic life, with a bread-baking oven and quaintly furnished rooms. It's open daily 10am to 12:45pm and 3:30 to 6:30pm (until 6pm Nov–Mar). Admission is 2€.

As you walk around town, notice the sculpted pinnacles, or finials, atop many *trulli.* These probably advertised which *trullaro* (*trulli* craftsman) built the house. Some *trulli* have artwork on the sides of their roofs, often traditional pagan, Jewish, and Christian symbols—look for a radiant orb, representing the sun and Christ, or a heart with an arrow through it, depicting the heartache of the Virgin Mary.

WHERE TO STAY & EAT IN ALBEROBELLO

While it's easy to see the appeal of staying in a setting as unique as the *trulli* zone, remember that you will essentially be stepping onto a Disney-like stage set, with thousands of selfie-taking gawkers trooping up and down the narrow streets. On the other hand, once the day-trippers leave, having the strange townscape almost to yourself is a magical experience.

Alberobello is an evocative setting in which to enjoy *cucina povera,* literally poor kitchen, based on whatever ingredients are on hand. This often means pasta made with local durum wheat, sauces based on fresh vegetables, and a garnish of fried breadcrumbs instead of more expensive Parmigiano. For a hands-on experience with cucina povera, take a 1½-hour cooking class with Nonna Maria at **Trulli del Bosco** (www.trullidelbosco.com; ✆ **338/423-9369**), in the pleasant countryside just outside of town; classes are from 60€. The property also has accommodation in four *trulli,* each sleeping two to three people, set amid gardens equipped with a swimming pool (35€–80€ per person, breakfast included).

For a quick bite on the main square, step into **La Fontana 1914** at Largo Martellotta 55 (✆ **380/369-6969**), a butcher shop that also grills meat to order and serves *bombette,* pork shoulder wrapped around melted cheese and spiced with herbs. It's open daily 8am to 11pm.

La Cantina ★★ PUGLIESE The Lippolis family has been satisfying local appetites since 1958. Their homey, stone-walled eatery just outside the *trulli* district is such an institution that the street out front is named for them. Owner-chef Francesco usually sends out some delicious *bruschetta,* on thick local bread with rich olive oil and fresh tomatoes and mozzarella, perhaps followed by local *salumi* and *burrata.* The pork from nearby Martina Franca is grilled to perfection. La Cantina has only seven tables, so booking is essential, even in the winter.

Vico Lippolis 8. www.ilristorantelacantina.it. ✆ **080/432-3473.** Entrees 9€–15€. Wed–Mon 12:30–3pm and 8–11:30pm. Closed 2 weeks in Feb and 2 weeks in July.

Masseria Torre Coccaro ★★★ You can jump from one architectural experience to another with a 45-minute drive northeast from Alberobello over to the coast, where this centuries-old *masseria,* a fortified farm compound, offers an experience as transporting as the *trulli.* Accommodations are tucked into haylofts and towers, and in the case of the cavernous Orange Garden suite, carved out of a rocky hillside. All surround citrus-scented gardens and a lake-like swimming pool. Dining is in an elegantly transformed stable block; cooking lessons are available.

Contrada Coccaro 8, Savelletri di Fasano. www.masseriatorrecoccaro.com. ✆ **080/482-9310.** 39 units. 310€–620€ double. Rates include breakfast. **Amenities:** Restaurant; bar; babysitting; bikes; exercise room; pool; room service; spa; free Wi-Fi.

Trulli e Puglia B&B ★ A cluster of well-restored *trulli* in the heart of the Monti district shows off the stonework and conical beehive ceilings that make these dwellings so distinctive. Several are two stories, with sleeping lofts atop spiral staircases, and all sport rustic furnishings and wood finishes for a cozy atmosphere. All units have fridges and a few have kitchenettes, plus such modern conveniences as air-conditioning (not really necessary, given the thick walls and stone roofs) and surprisingly spacious, nicely appointed bathrooms. Innkeeper Mimmo and his staff provide a welcome that's as memorable as the architecture.

Via Monte San Michele 58. www.trulliepuglia.com. ✆ **080/432-4376.** 6 units. 120€–170€ double. Rates include breakfast. 2-night min. stay. Closed Nov–Dec. **Amenities:** Bar; free Wi-Fi.

Trullo d'Oro ★★★ PUGLIESE In a suite of warmly decorated *trulli,* chef Davide Girolamo presents a fresh take on *cucina povera.* His menu uses local seasonal ingredients, elevating the fava bean in many variations, and showcases such simple specialties as *burrata pugliese,* a soft, creamy mozzarella cousin encased in a skin of velvety curd, and *orecchiette* with a ragu of donkey. Seafood also comes into play, with a creamy baccalà and *puree di fave bianche con polpo,* steamed octopus served atop fava beans.

Via Felice Cavallotti 27. www.ristorantetrullodoro.com. ✆ **080/432-1820.** Entrees 12€–32€. Tues–Sat noon–2:30pm and 8–10:30pm; Sun noon–2:30pm.

A SIDE TRIP TO THE GROTTE DI CASTELLANA

Just 17km (11 miles) north of Alberobello via SS172 and SS237, the **Grotte di Castellana** is a vast network of caves, 3,350m (11,050 ft.) long and 125m (412 ft.) deep, carved out over centuries by water streaming through the limestone that underlies this part of Puglia. The caves' vastness and eerie light have given rise to all sorts of legends of demons and lost souls floating through the depths. A series of paths winds through underground rooms with names like the **Grave, Corridoio del Serpent,** and **Corridoio del Deserto,** filled with stalagmites and stalactites, and lead to the majestic **Grotta Bianca,** where walls gleam with white alabaster and the rock formations are translucent. Visits are only by guided

A guided tour inside the limestone caves of the Grotte di Castellana.

tours, offered in Italian, English, French, and German; hours vary from 9am to noon in winter to 9am to 7pm in summer (www.grottedicastellana.it; ✆ **080/4998221**). From November to February, the caves are open by reservation only. Admission is 18€ for a 2-hour tour (15€ ages 6–14, free for 5 and under), 15€ for a 1-hour tour (12€ ages 6–14, free for 5 and under); the shorter tour does not include the Grotta Bianca. Bring an extra layer: It's 16° to 18°C (61°–64°F) in the caves year-round.

The White Cities

South of Alberobello lie a string of hill towns hewn out of light-colored stone, so glaringly bright in the sun that they're collectively known as the "white cities." It's easiest to reach them **by car,** heading south through the Valle d'Itria along SS172 to Locorotondo and Martina Franca, with short detours to Cisternino, Ostuni, and Ceglie Messapica; the towns are all well signposted and you can easily visit all five in a couple of days. Ostuni is on the Adriatic **railway** line (www.trenitalia.com), while Locorotondo and Martina Franca are connected to Bari and Alberobello by frequent Ferrovie del Sud Est **bus** service (www.fseonline.it). Ceglie Messsapica and Cisternino are both on the Martina Franca–Lecce train line. Service throughout the region is frequent and the Ferrovie del Sud Est website makes planning fairly easy. Be forewarned, however, that various bus companies may use different bus stops, and finding the right one is not always easy. Bars and *tabacchi* that sell tickets can direct you to the right place, and tourist offices are also usually helpful in sorting out stops and schedules.

LOCOROTONDO ★★★

8km (5 miles) SE of Alberobello

As you approach this cheerful little town you might think you're seeing a mirage: A ring of bright white houses with pointed gable roofs (called *cummerse*) crown the top of a hill. From a distance the scene looks a little like a rimrock canyon from the American West, or a Hanseatic port on the Baltic Sea—except, of course, for the baroque church domes rising above the rooftops. Locorotondo means "round place," and once inside the gates you'll see why: Streets of light-colored stone are flanked by white houses that hug the contours of the hilltop in near-perfect concentric circles. Surrounding them are the old protective walls, skirted by a ring road from which you can see far across the plains below—a view that earns Locorotondo the nickname "balcony of the Valle d'Itria."

Locorotondo is famous for its white wine, which you can sample in any of the restaurants and bars in town. The town's **tourist office,** at Piazza Vittorio Emanuele 27 (✆ **080/431-3099**), is usually open Tuesday through Sunday 9am to 1pm and 4 to 7pm.

MARTINA FRANCA ★★

6km (4 miles) S of Locorotondo, 14km (9 miles) S of Alberobello

This lively hill town with its baroque finery and whitewashed back alleys was founded in the 10th century by coastal residents fleeing Saracen attacks along the Adriatic and Ionian coasts. The *centro storico* is an intriguing tangle of medieval lanes that lead from one piazza to another—a layout deliberately planned to confuse plunderers.

The **tourist office** at Piazza XX Settembre no. 3 (www.viaggiarein puglia.it; ✆ **080/411-6554**) is usually open Monday through Friday 10am to 1pm and 5 to 8pm, and Saturday and Sunday 9:30am to 1pm and 4:30 to 8:30pm. You can't drive in Martina Franca's *centro storico,* but you can park a few blocks away on Via Giuseppe Aprile, Via Gabriele d'Annunzio, Piazza Francesco Crispi, Piazza Umberto, or Via Verdi.

At the center of town are two adjoining squares, Piazza Plebiscito and Piazza Immacolata. Rising above **Piazza Plebiscito** is the **Basilica di San Martino ★★** (✆ **080/4306536;** free; daily 8am–9pm), its facade richly adorned with baroque relief sculptures depicting episodes from the life of St. Martin. The most famous scene shows the saint, a Hungarian soldier in the Roman legions, meeting a poor beggar on a chilly November night and cutting his military cloak in half with his sword to keep the beggar warm. Martin's feast day on November 11th coincides with the grape harvest, earning him the honor of patron saint of wine. Also in the square is the **municipal clock tower,** erected in 1734, with a *meridiana* (sundial) inscribed on an eye-level plaque. In pretty **Piazza Immacolata,** the landmark is century-old **Caffè Tripoli** (Via Garibaldi 10; ✆ **080/480-5260**), where the specialty is *granita di caffè* (espresso with whipped cream). **Via Cavour,** leading south from Piazza Immacolata, is the main street of the

Piazza Plebiscito and the Basilica di San Martino, Martina Franca.

Lama, the old quarter. Lining the handsome street are baroque *palazzi,* with fanciful arches and balconies, often loaded with stone cherubs. On and off Via Cavour (and also north of the two piazzas) is a maze of whitewashed back streets, impossibly narrow passageways, and blind alleys.

The town's culinary specialty is *capocollo di Martina Franca,* cured pork cut from the top of the neck where it meets the shoulder, and dried with local wine, herbs, and wood smoke. Butcher/deli **Romanelli,** just off Piazza XX Settembre at Via Valle d'Itria 8–12 (www.macelleriaromanelli.it; ✆ **080/480-5385**), usually gives a tasting of its *capocollo,* and you can buy it sliced by the *etto* (100 grams).

CISTERNINO★★

10km (6¼ miles) E of Locorotondo, 12km (7 miles) NE of Martina Franca

Like its near neighbor Locorotondo, this sunny whitewashed hilltop town is smaller and quainter than Martina Franca or Ostuni, without their modern outskirts. Before plunging into the labyrinth of medieval lanes that converge in central Piazza Vittorio, stop to enjoy the views over the Valle d'Itria from the base of the **Torre Normanna Sveva,** at the edge of the ridge on which the town is built.

Cisternino is famous for its Fornelli Pronti—literally, "ready ovens," holdovers from the times when butchers operated communal ovens where meat was grilled upon purchase. Shops all over town still do the honors, grilling *bombetti*—veal crusted in breadcrumbs and Parmigiano and rolled around caciocavallo cheese—and serving them, alongside other grilled meats and carafes of local red wine, at outside tables. One popular spot is **Zio Pietro,** Via Duca d'Aosta 3 (© **080/444-8300**).

OSTUNI ★★

16km (10 miles) E of Martina Franca

Other nearby towns may bill themselves as "white cities," but they're positively beige compared to Ostuni. Practically blinding in summer, perched atop a commanding hill 8km (5 miles) above the Adriatic coast, Ostuni makes it clear you're close to Greece. Ancient Greeks, in fact, are among the many invaders and occupiers who came here over the past 2,500 years, though the town's mazelike streets and arched steps tumbling down hillsides are mostly medieval. Especially beneficent to Ostuni over the ages were two female rulers, Isabella of Aragon and her daughter, Bona Sforza, who in the 16th century made the city a cultured outpost and added walls and lookout towers along the coast, where beacon fires were lit to warn of approaching pirates.

Whitewashed facades in the "white city" of Ostuni.

In **Piazza della Libertà,** at the foot of the hill where the oldest part of town clings, look for the statue of Sant'Oronzo high atop La Colonna di Sant'Oronzo. The patron saint of nearby Lecce, Oronzo is honored here for allegedly saving Ostuni from the plague twice in 1657 and 1771. Below the saint, on a warm weekend night everyone from miles around gathers in the piazza to chat, stroll, and sit in the cafes. From Piazza della Libertà, **Via Cattedrale** winds up through *la città Bianca* to the hilltop Gothic **Duomo,** with its marble facade swooping into a gracious curve on one side; it's open daily 8:30am to 12:30pm and 4:30 to 7:30pm (admission 1€). Above a doorway to the left of the main entrance, Oronzo appears again, this time cradling Ostuni in his protective arms.

The **tourist office** at Corso Mazzini 6 (www.comune.ostuni.br.it; © **083/339627**) is open daily 10am to 1pm and 3pm to 6pm, keeping longer hours in summer.

CEGLIE MESSAPICA ★★

13km (8 miles) SW of Ostuni

A bit farther afield, this quiet town is older than the other White Cities, having been founded by seafaring Greeks in the 7th century B.C. The town flourished again in the 16th century under the kingdom of Naples, and a large hilltop castle, **Castello Ducale,** was enlarged, with the old town encircling it in a maze of narrow lanes. Surrounded by miles of rich farmland, vineyards, and olive groves, the town today is a prosperous-looking ensemble of three elegant squares surrounded by narrow streets lined with cubical whitewashed houses that look almost Moorish. The local bounty shows up in market stalls and restaurants around town; a staple is the *biscotto cegliese,* a biscuit made with almond paste and a hint of lemon. The helpful **tourist office** is in the oldest part of town, near the castle, at via G. Elia 16 (www.viaggiareinpuglia.it; ✆ **0831/371003**); it's open daily in summer 9am to 1pm and 4 to 9pm, with shorter hours the rest of the year.

WHERE TO STAY IN THE WHITE CITIES

A good source for stays in *masserie,* farmhouses near the White Cities and scattered around Puglia, is **www.masseriedimoresalento.com**.

La Sommità Relais ★★★ A 16th-century fortified palazzo on a lane behind Ostuni's Duomo is full of hidden charms within thick stucco walls. On the ground floor, stylish lounges and an elegant restaurant occupy a maze of high arched rooms opening to a walled garden; upstairs a sea-view terrace, a perfect perch for cocktails, sits on the ramparts. Sleek contemporary-styled guest rooms are full of perks; some have terraces facing the plain and seashore below, others surround interior courtyards and have deep soaking tubs and other luxuries (one has a fireplace).

Via Scipione Petrarolo 7, Ostuni. www.lasommita.it. ✆ **0831/305925.** 15 units. 230€–370€ double. Rates include breakfast. Closed Nov–Mar. **Amenities:** Bar; restaurant; spa; free Wi-Fi.

Masseria Salinola ★★★ A centuries-old walled olive estate welcomes guests into stylish rooms and suites fashioned from an old salt warehouse; they're full of arches, stonework, and old beams, enhanced with luxurious beds and well-curated family pieces. A former stable is now a character-filled, hearth-warmed lounge and dining room that spills onto a terrace in warmer months; a pool is set in lush gardens full of palm-shaded nooks. Though Ostuni is just a short drive away, a family-style dinner of local favorites made with garden-fresh ingredients, served most evenings, will tempt you to stay put in such relaxing surroundings.

3km (2 miles) S of Ostuni off SP 29. www.masseriasalinola.it. ✆ **0831/308330.** 7 units. 180€–340€ double. Rates include breakfast. **Amenities:** Restaurant; bar; pool; free Wi-Fi.

Sotto le Cummerse ★★★ In welcoming Locorotondo, visitors can live like a local in distinctive lodgings tucked into houses around the old town. All are different, ranging from simple ground-floor studios to multilevel suites; all are nicely furnished in traditional style and make the most of stone walls, fireplaces, and other vintage details. Many have terraces, and all have up-to-date bathrooms, some equipped with Jacuzzis. Breakfast is served in a welcoming room near the reception, where the accommodating staff is on hand well into the evening hours.

Via Vittorio Emanuele 138, Locorotondo. www.sottolecummerse.it. ✆ **080/431-3298.** 13 units. 80€–180€ double. Rates include breakfast. Closed Jan. **Amenities:** Free Wi-Fi.

WHERE TO EAT IN THE WHITE CITIES

La Tavernetta ★★ PUGLIESE Step down off the busy street into this arched, white-walled cellar and you're transported to old Puglia, where veteran waiters dispense one traditional Pugliese classic after another, at decidedly old-fashioned prices. House specialties include *fave e cicoria* (pureed fava beans with sautéed chicory), *orecchiette al ragu* (handmade ear-shaped semolina pasta with a robust sauce), and *braciole* (sliced veal stuffed with parsley, cheese, and garlic, simmered in tomato sauce).

Via Vittorio Emanuele 30, Martina Franca. ✆ **080/430-6323.** Entrees 7€–15€. Tues–Sun 12:30–2:45pm and 7:30pm–11:30pm.

Osteria del Tempo Perso ★★ PUGLIESE Even in its former guise as a bakery, the *osteria* "of lost time" must have been charming, its rough-hewn walls carved out of a cave. Today, linen-topped tables spread into an atmospheric adjoining room, hung with old farm implements and beautiful local ceramics. In this colorful setting, just around the corner from Ostuni's Duomo, the food sticks close to local tradition, with lots of Adriatic seafood. Try the house special casserole, *tegamino di funghi,* with bread, mushrooms, and zucchini flowers. The kitchen shares its passion for local cuisine in frequent cooking classes.

Via G. Tanzarella Vitale 47, Ostuni. www.osteriadeltempoperso.com. ✆ **0831/304819.** Entrees 9€–28€. Tues–Sun 12:30–3pm and 7:30–10:30pm.

Pizzeria Casa Pinto ★★★ PIZZERIA It's probably not much of an exaggeration to say that on weekend nights most of Locorotondo fills these tiny rooms, one of them taken up by a huge pizza oven. Tables are tucked into a cavelike vaulted cellar and a rooftop terrace, and the pizzas are almost as distinctive, made with organic products. Some are topped so lightly with olive oil and cheese that they seem more like savory baked bread than pizza. Other toppings are more traditional, and any choice should be washed down with the town's signature white wine.

Via Aprile 23, Locorotondo. www.pizzeriacasapinto.it. ✆ **346/431-7510.** Pizzas 6€–12€. Wed–Mon noon–3pm and 7pm–midnight; Sun 7pm–midnight.

The Seacoast from Bari to Brindisi

Just to the east of the Valle d'Itria, the Adriatic washes up onto a long stretch of appealing beaches, strung along the coastal highway. One of the most picturesque seaside towns in Italy is **Polignano a Mare,** 39km (24 miles) southeast of Bari (on the Bari–Ostuni train line), where seaside cliffs are etched with coves and topped by the tall white houses of the intriguing old town; native son Domenico Modugno, who wrote the 1950s hit song "Volare," is honored with a statue on the seaside promenade named after him. **Monopoli,** 9km (5½ miles) southeast of Polignano a Mare and on the same Bari–Ostuni train line, has a beautiful and evocative seaside old quarter packed with churches, palaces, and a 16th-century castle built around a string of harbors. Another 12km (7½ miles) down the coast, outside Fasano, lie the ruins of **Egnazia,** a trading center that was settled around 1500 B.C. and flourished under the Romans. A well-preserved segment of the Trajan Way bisects the ancient city, where the Tomb of the Pomegranates (symbol of eternal life) is entered through huge doors on which handles and hinges still function (open only on special occasions). The site (musei.beniculturali.it) is open daily 8:30am to 1pm; the museum is open daily 8:30am to 7:30pm. Admission to the park and museum is 6€.

East of Fasano, **Parco Naturale Regionale Dune Costiere** (www.parcodunecostiere.org) follows the coast for 8km (5 miles), its sandy beaches backed by dunes and centuries-old olive groves. Another half hour down the coast, the **Torre Guaceto** nature preserve (www.riservaditorreguaceto.it), 24km (13 miles) east of Ostuni, has miles of pristine sands, dunes, and marshes; its offshore coral formations are a lure for snorkelers.

LECCE ★★

113km (68 miles) SE of Alberobello, 40km (25 miles) SE of Brindisi

Sophisticated Lecce combines baroque architecture and urbane elegance with typical southern Italian radiance. The handsome old city center is clad almost entirely in warm golden limestone, amplified by *il barocco leccese*—a particularly ebullient version of 17th-century Italy's fondness for architectural decoration. Because the local limestone is fairly soft and easy to chisel, sculptors covered church facades and civic palaces with saints, angels, and intricate details as if they were drawing on paper. While it's tempting to describe the stone as "buttery," "milky" is more apt—milk was applied to the final work, to seep into the stone's pores and harden it.

Founded by Greeks more than 2,200 years ago, Lecce has a Roman theater and amphitheater and the bastions of the 16th-century Castello Carlo V (Castle of Charles V, the Habsburg Holy Roman Emperor). Lecce is often promoted as the "Florence of the South," but the city's identity is southern Italian through and through, devoted to agriculture—especially olive oil and wine—more than tourism. Lecce is a pleasant base for day trips around the rest of the Salento peninsula.

Essentials

ARRIVING High-speed Frecciargento **trains** connect Lecce with Rome in 5½ hours, 8½ hours by regular service. Lecce also has frequent train

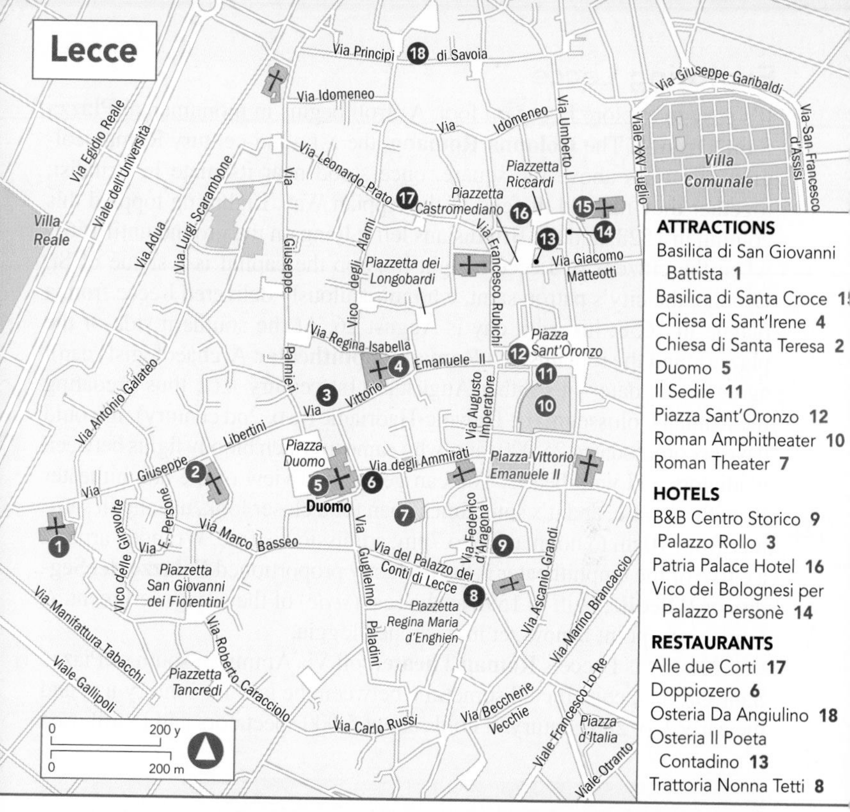

service to Bari (1½ hr.) and Brindisi (30 min.). Visit www.trenitalia.com for schedules and information. Note that Lecce's train station is about 2km (1¼ miles) from the heart of the old quarter; from the train station, buses 11, 12, and 14 run to Porta Napoli at the edge of the *centro storico*. The fare is 1.50€ and you can purchase tickets at newsstands; for more information, go to www.sgmlecce.it. If you want to store your bags at the station, make arrangements with radicalstorage.com, 5€ a bag per day.

If you're traveling by **car** from the north, follow signs to Brindisi, then take state highway SS613 south to Lecce (38km/24 miles). Most of the center is closed to car traffic and parking is extremely limited; it's best to leave your car in one of the large lots in Piazza Muratore or Piazza Giuseppe Libertini. You can most likely make parking arrangements with your hotel for one of these lots in advance.

VISITOR INFORMATION A **tourist office** is at Piazza Duomo 2 (www.infolecce.it; ✆ **0832/521877**); it's open daily 9am to 10pm. The office also operates an **info-point** in the Sedile, on Piazza Sant'Oronzo, open the same hours.

Exploring Lecce

It's easy to explore Lecce on foot. A stroll begins in monumental **Piazza Sant'Oronzo.** The **Colonna Romana,** the A.D.-2nd-century Roman column that rises above the square, once stood near its mate in Brindisi; together they marked the end of the Appian Way. Lightning toppled this column in 1528, and the Brindisians left it lying on the ground until 1661, when the citizens of Lecce bought it. Atop the capital is a statue of St. Oronzo, the city's patron saint, who miraculously delivered Lecce from a plague in 1658; his saint day is August 26. At the southern side of the piazza stand the remains of a **Roman amphitheater.** Archaeologists can't agree on its date—it's either Augustan (1st century B.C., thus predating the Roman Colosseum) or Trajanic-Hadrianic (A.D. 2nd century). It would have accommodated 25,000 fans, who came to watch bloody fights between gladiators and wild beasts. You can get a good view of the amphitheater from the square, and it's sometimes open for a closer look, usually in summer from 10am to noon and 3 to 7pm; admission is free. Wrapped around a curve of the amphitheater is the perfectly proportioned **Palazzo del Seggio, or Il Sedile,** built in 1592 as the seat *(sede)* of the city government. A tourist info-point is now set in its arched loggia.

Nearby is Lecce's **Roman Theater,** off Via Ammirati south of Piazza Sant'Oronzo, constructed sometime between the late 1st century B.C. and the early A.D. 2nd century. It holds about 5,000 spectators and is still used

Piazza Sant'Oronzo, Lecce's principal square.

for plays and concerts. You can step into the theater as part of a visit to the adjacent **Museo del Teatro Romano** (www.itersalento.it/museo-teatro-romano; ✆ **0832/279196;** Mon–Sat 9am–2pm; admission 3€).

To the west of Piazza Sant'Oronzo is a string of extravagantly baroque churches. To get an eyeful of them, follow Via Vittorio Emanuele and its continuation, Via Giuseppe Libertini, past the Duomo to the 18th-century Porta Rudiae. The first church you come to on Via Vittorio Emanuele, the **Chiesa di Sant'Irene,** dates to 1591; priest-architect Francesco Grimaldi designed it with the same flair he showed with his baroque landmarks in Naples and Rome, adorning the facade with columns, niches, statues, and a wolf from the town's coat of arms. St. Irene, who stands above the portal, was Lecce's patron saint before Oronzo. Lecce's first telegraph station was installed in the tower in the mid-19th century, while the nave became a community meeting hall during the unification of Italy. Farther up on Via Libertini, the 17th-century **Chiesa di Santa Teresa** (✆ **0832/332699**) has also served multiple humble purposes, as a police barracks, a school, and a tobacco warehouse, despite its fanciful facade by master sculptor Giuseppe Zimbalo (see the Duomo and Santa Croce, below). The facade, though unfinished, features an exuberance of columns and statuary, among them the two Saint Johns, the Baptist and the Evangelist. Inside is what might be the town's most macabre work of art, a lifelike statue of a bloodied, emaciated Christ lying in a coffinlike glass box. By comparison, the **Basilica di San Giovanni Battista,** a few steps up Via Libertini (✆ **0832/308540**), is a joyful place, where cherubs float through the light-filled interior. Admission to most of Lecce's churches is free, and they're generally open daily from 7am to 1pm and 3:30 to 7pm.

For more layers of Lecce's history, descend through **Museo Faggiano** (Via Ascanio Grande; ✆ **0832/300528**), privately run by a family who bought a modest building and beneath it found ancient tombs, a Roman granary, and the embalming rooms of a Franciscan convent, now displaying a wealth of found artifacts. It's open daily 9:30am to 8pm; admission is 5€, 3€ ages 8 to 16, under 8 free.

Basilica di Santa Croce ★★ CHURCH The *barocco leccese* hits fever pitch at Santa Croce (Holy Cross) basilica, where sculptors crammed the facade with lions, angels, sea creatures, goddesses—hundreds of figures in all, crowding the columned tiers. Most significant might be the turbaned Turks, whose forces menaced Lecce and the rest of southern Europe for centuries before being defeated at the Battle of Lepanto in 1571. Beasts and figures on the lower tiers represent the Christian forces that conquered the Turks (the griffon stands for the Republic of Genoa; Hercules represents the dukes of Tuscany). It's okay if you don't understand much of the iconography—just stand out front and soak in the spectacle. The facade is the work of three generations of local masons; most notable is master Giuseppe Zimbalo (1620–1710), also known as Lo Zingarello, the "Tiny Gypsy." His son, Francesco, did the portals and some beautiful work in the interior, including his richly carved tomb of local saint Francesco di Paolo, an animal-loving hermit friar much like St. Francis of Assisi. You'll see scenes of his most acclaimed miracles, include restoring life to a roasted lamb and a fried trout; the envy of sailors, he could hoist up his robes to catch a breeze and sail across the sea. Via Umberto I. basilicasantacrocelecce.it. ✆ **0832/241957.** Admission 6€, 9€ with Duomo. Daily 9am–9pm.

Duomo ★ CHURCH Lecce's cathedral stands in an almost completely enclosed square, a setting both dramatic and practical. In times of siege, residents would take refuge in the huge piazza, with its narrow entrances that could be completely closed off. Giuseppe Zimbalo, one of the creators of Santa Croce (above), also reworked the facade of the 12th-century cathedral, embellishing it with sculpted saints and other figures. High above the entrance is Lecce's patron St. Oronzo. Zimbalo also designed the adjacent **campanile,** which towers 64m (210 ft.) above the piazza, ascending in tiers like a wedding cake. The **seminary,** across the square, has a chiseled facade that could have been squirted out of a pastry tube, the work of Giuseppe Cino, a student of Zimbalo. The exuberant **Bishop's Palace** (Palazzo Vescovile), with its arches and saint-filled niches, is still home to Lecce's archbishops. The extravagance continues north up **Via Palmieri,** past a long line of sculpted palace facades to the triumphal arch of **Porta Napoli,** the main city gate, built in 1548 to honor a state visit from Holy Roman Emperor Charles V.

St. Oronzo, Lecce's patron saint, presides over the Duomo's ornate facade.

Piazza del Duomo. Via Vittorio Emanuele. www.cattedraledilecce.it. ✆ **0832/308557.** Admission 6€, 9€ with Santa Croce. Daily 9am–9pm.

Where to Stay in Lecce

B&B Centro Storico ★★★ Every inch of this beautifully restored lodging, on one floor of a baroque palace, is carefully tended by the two proprietor brothers, Filippo and Alberto, who offer their guests the same attention. Centuries-old stone window frames were sculpted to capture maximum sunlight; baroque ceilings form *volte a stella,* star-shaped vaults; sleeping lofts rise above gleaming wood floors in salons-turned-suites. A mix of antiques and modern pieces add to the appeal of these character-filled, very comfortable spaces. Above is a rambling roof deck with a hot tub and a cottage-like guest room with private terrace. Breakfast is served in a nearby cafe.

Via A. Vignes 2. www.centrostoricolecce.it. ✆ **0832/242-727.** 6 units. 85€–110€. Rates include breakfast. **Amenities:** Roof terrace; hot tub; free Wi-Fi.

Palazzo Rollo ★★ Stepping into the vine-covered courtyard of this 17th-century palace is like entering a world unto itself, the private domain of the Rollo clan for more than 200 years. In its current guise the old palace houses guests in a warren of suites that are more homey than luxurious, with tile floors, old-fashioned furnishings, and lots of nooks and crannies. Four ground-floor apartments off the courtyard were originally stone-vaulted storerooms. A luxuriant roof garden offers plenty of shade and a view over the adjacent bell tower and the *centro storico* rooftops.

Via Vittorio Emanuele II 14. www.palazzorollo.it. ✆ **0832/3017152.** 4 suites, 4 apartments. 110€–130€ double. Rates include breakfast. **Amenities:** Free Wi-Fi.

Patria Palace Hotel ★★ Lecce's bastion of luxury has been pampering guests since 1797, and these days does so in richly upholstered and chicly appointed rooms to create a clublike lair that's especially popular with traveling business folk. Some windows of the old *palazzo* catch a glimpse of its flamboyant neighbor, the remarkably ornamented Santa Croce basilica. A few rooms have private terraces, while a roof garden is a perfect spot to enjoy a bottle of wine while admiring the baroque surroundings.

Piazzetta Riccardi 13. patriapalace.com. ✆ **0832/245111.** 67 units. 280€–340€ double. Rates include breakfast. Closed Jan–Mar. **Amenities:** Restaurant; bar; concierge; room service; free Wi-Fi.

Vico dei Bolognesi per Palazzo Personè ★★★ These wonderful rooms surround the courtyard of a palazzo and occupy parts of a former synagogue in the heart of the old quarter, displaying a mix of details—fireplaces, high beamed ceilings, gently time-worn wood and tile, mid-century furniture, and contemporary touches. Breakfast is served in a pleasant cafe facing the lane out front.

Viale Umberto I 5. www.palazzopersone.it. ✆ **0832/279968.** 6 units. 170€–300€ double. 2-night min. stay. Rates include breakfast. Closed late Jan–Feb. **Amenities:** Bar; cafe; free Wi-Fi.

Where to Eat in Lecce

An almost mandatory stop in Lecce is **Natale,** at Via Trinchese 7A (www.natalepasticceria.it; ✆ **0832/202462**), for the town's best gelato and pastry. At **Mamma Elvira Enoteca,** Via Umberto I 19 (✆ **0832/169-2011**), an especially welcoming bar/shop, you can introduce yourself to the wines of the southeast. Lecce's large student population frequents the wildly popular pizzeria **La Succursale,** Viale dell'Università 15 (✆ **391/497-7749**), open Tuesday through Sunday 12:30 to 3:30pm and 6 to midnight and Monday 6pm to midnight. Two local foods to look for are *puccia,* an oval sandwich stuffed with tuna, capers, and dried tomatoes that originated as a snack for Roman legionnaires, and *mariati,* pasta dressed with fresh tomato sauce and strong ricotta. The **Awaiting Table** (awaitingtable.com; ✆ **347/676970**) offers daylong classes in Pugliese cooking, including a market visit and some sightseeing; from 145€.

Alle Due Corti ★★ PUGLIESE These simple whitewashed rooms off two courtyards are a perfect backdrop for Pugliese cooking. The standout is *ciceri e tria,* a combination of pasta and chickpeas in which the pasta is lightly fried, a throwback to times when the added crunchiness compensated for a lack of meat. These days the kitchen, under the guidance of local gastronome Rosalba De Carlo, adds fresh seasonal vegetables and often seafood, and follows up with such simple concoctions as chicken baked in white wine and mussels with rice and potatoes.

Corte dei Giugni 1. ✆ **0832/242223.** Entrees 8€–14€. Mon–Sat 12:30–2pm and 7:45–11pm.

Doppiozero ★★ PUGLIESE Lecce shows off its hip, urbane side in this cafe/deli where repurposed bottles light long communal tables and local wines are stacked to the ceiling, alongside hams, long salamis, wheels of cheese, and vats of olive oil. These and other market-fresh ingredients, also available for takeaway, find their way into sandwiches, deli boards, crostini, salads, soups, and a few daily pastas. The light fare is a hit with a crowd that doesn't seem to mind the pleasant but rushed service.

Via Paladini 2. ✆ **0832/521-052.** Entrees 8€–14€. Daily 8:30am–12:30am (closes at 4:30pm Mon in winter).

Osteria Da Angiulino ★★ PUGLIESE These brightly tiled, vaulted rooms are Lecce's traditional outpost for *cucina povera.* Many of the dishes are vegetarian, including an appetizer of green beans and fava beans, parboiled to perfect crunchiness. The *melanzane alla parmigiana* is a perfect meatless main-course follow-up. On the carnivorous side of the menu is horsemeat prepared in every way imaginable—as meatballs, chopped, filleted, and topped with a green sauce, or in a savory stew. The house wine is as hearty and affordable as the cuisine.

Via Principe di Savoia 4. ✆ **0832/245146.** Entrees 6€–9€. Mon–Sat 12:45–3pm and 7:45–11pm (until 11:30pm Thurs).

Osteria Il Poeta Contadino ★ PUGLIESE/SEAFOOD You'll be reminded that Lecce is almost on the Adriatic in this comfy little room with big glass windows facing Piazza Sant'Oronzo. The freshest seafood shows up in a few well-done preparations each day, from sandwiches generously filled with fillets of swordfish and fresh vegetables to *spaghetti alla vongole* (with clams). The name means "poet farmer," and true to that

idea, there's a nice selection of meat-and-vegetable-topped *bruschetta* and pastas with fresh vegetables, all accompanied by good local wines.
Piazzetta Castromediano 8. www.facebook.com/osteriailpoetacontadino. ✆ **392/540-2344.** Entrees 8€–16€. Fri, Sat, and Mon noon–3pm and 6:30pm–11pm; Sun noon–5:30pm.

Trattoria Nonna Tetti ★★ PUGLIESE Warm and inviting, with lots of tile and stone, this is another outpost for local cooking. The big menu also expands into the rest of Italy, but the standouts are strictly Leccese, like *ricciarelle* pasta with cherry tomatoes, garlic, and cheese, or wild chicory with a purée of boiled fava beans.
Piazzetta Regina Maria 17. ✆ **0832/246036.** Entrees 8€–12€. Mon–Sat noon–3pm and 7:30pm–midnight.

Lecce Shopping

Cartoleria Pantheon Lecce, Via Giuseppe Libertini 69 (www.manufactuslecce.com; ✆ **0832/521312**), offers Florence-worthy leather and paper goods, from iPhone cases and datebooks to briefcases and bags. Papier-mâché is a local craft, and the material is often fashioned into Madonnas and saints. You'll find papier-maché items in shops around town, and to see a true artisan at work, stop in the workshop of Marco Epicochi at Piazza Duomo 18 (✆ **327/282-4185**).

Lecce Beaches

The most popular beach for locals is at **San Cataldo,** 15km (9 miles) east on SP364, where a long stretch of sand borders the **San Cataldo reserve**, formerly malaria-infested swampland that's now green pine and eucalyptus forest. Another 8km (5 miles) south on SP366, the **Cesine nature preserve** (www.riservalecesine.it) has trails that lead across wetlands and through forests to remote beaches.

Side Trips to Otranto & Gallipoli

OTRANTO ★★

45km (28 miles) SE of Lecce

It's said if you look hard enough on a clear day, you can see all the way to Albania from **Otranto,** the easternmost town in Italy. Two colors dominate here: the electric turquoise of the sea and the gleaming white of the old quarter. You can get here by **car** (45 min. from Lecce via SS16) or by **train** (Ferovia Sud Est FSE; www.fseonline.it; travel time a little over an hour, often with a change to a bus at Lecce Via Don Bosco). The **tourist office** is at Piazza Castello 8 (✆ **0836/801436;** daily 9am–noon and 3–6pm).

Castello Aragonese ★ FORTRESS Otranto's 15th-century sea-facing fortress, surrounded in part by a moat filled with fearsome green water, looks mighty enough. But the thick fortifications failed to thwart

Turquoise seas and the gleaming white houses at Otranto.

Mehmet the Conqueror, who in 1480 took the city in just 2 weeks. Most of the garrison and townsfolk fled as the Turkish fleet approached; those who hid in the fortress poured boiling water over the ramparts, to little avail. When the castle and town were overrun, more than 800 captives chose to die rather than renounce Christianity. The skulls of the Martyrs of Otranto are in the Duomo (see below). Don't expect the setting of Horace Walpole's gothic novel *The Castle of Otranto*—the fortress looks nothing like its fictional self, though its underground tunnels are spooky indeed.

Piazza Castello. www.comune.otranto.le.it. ✆ **0836/210094.** 7€. Daily 10am–7pm (until 8pm Sat).

Cattedrale di Otranto ★★★ CHURCH Otranto's formidable 11th-century cathedral was built atop remains of the town's previous inhabitants—a village founded by the Messappi tribe in the 8th century B.C.; a Roman villa; and an early Christian church. The remarkable **Tree of Life floor mosaic,** created in the 1160s by the monk-artist Pantaleone, lies on the floor like a genealogy tree, telling a medieval version of history. Some figures are easy to identify—Adam and Eve, Noah, the goddess Diana, King Arthur—while others are mysterious (mermaids, couples riding fish). The *beati martiri,* the skulls of citizens beheaded after the 1480 Ottoman sack of the Castello (above), are preserved in a side chapel.

Piazza Basilica. www.comune.otranto.le.it. ✆ **0836/802720.** Free. Daily 8am–noon and 3–7:15pm (until 7:45pm summer).

The medieval Tree of Life mosaic on the floor of Otranto Cathedral.

BEYOND OTRANTO

Head south from Otranto on coastal SP87 for 17km (10 miles) to **Santa Cesarea Terme,** a spa town for over 500 years, thanks to the sulfuric waters rising from its underlying rock. Take a soak in thermal pools at the **Terme di Santa Cesarea** spa, Via Roma 40 (www.termesantacesarea.it; ✆ **0836/-944314;** 55€ for treatment cycle; open 6am–6:30pm). At the peninsula's southern tip, **Santa Maria di Leuca** (58km/ 35 miles south of Otranto), you can climb up to the lighthouse and adjacent basilica, **Santa Maria de Finibus Terrae** (End of the World; www.basilicaleuca.it), for a bracing, almost 360-degree panorama of the Adriatic and Ionian Seas. Swing another 12km (7 miles) around the tip to **Pescolus** to enjoy its long white-sand beach. From here it's 55km (33 miles) back to Otranto, or continue up the peninsula's east coast on SS274 to Gallipoli.

GALLIPOLI ★★★

52km (32 miles) E of Otranto, 30km (18 miles) SE of Lecce

The wave-washed old town of Gallipoli is a photogenic concoction of white houses and churches crammed onto a small island, connected by one bridge to the new town on the mainland. Greeks founded the once-thriving port, and Normans built a fortress on the islet's eastern edge. The old town's meandering lanes open into squares lined with baroque palaces and churches; on the north side, a sandy beach stretches beneath 14th-century seawalls. For many visitors the real attractions are the beautiful beaches flanking Gallipoli. To the south, several beaches lie along **Baia Verde,** the least crowded being **Punta della Suina,** part of the **Punta Piazza nature preserve** 10km (6 miles) south of Gallipoli on SS274 and SS239. A long stretch of dune- and pine-backed white sands surround **Punta Prosciutto,** 43km (26 miles) north of Gallipoli on SP112 and SP359.

SICILY

By Stephen Brewer

15

The island of Sicily has been conquered, settled, and abandoned by dozens of civilizations, from the Phoenicians, Greeks, and Carthaginians in antiquity to the Arabs, Berbers, Moors, and Normans in the Middle Ages, to the Spanish and Bourbons in the Renaissance, and finally (at least nominally), modern Italy. It's an intricate story that has left a fascinating legacy. Touring the relics of Sicily's tumultuous past can sometimes make you feel that you're visiting several different countries at once.

Though separated from the mainland only by the Stretto di Messina (Strait of Messina), the 25,708-sq.-km (9,926-sq.-mile) island, the largest in the Mediterranean, has a captivating sense of otherness. Some Sicilians will refer to a trip to the mainland as "going to Italy." The descendants of many conquerors, Sicilians can be welcoming yet suspicious, taciturn yet garrulous, reverent of tradition yet determined not to be shackled by the past. Their warmth can make even everyday transactions memorable.

Sicily offers the full package of Italian travel experiences: evocative towns, compelling art, impressive architecture, ancient ruins, and a robust culinary heritage. Alongside the jewels of Sicily's ancient past (Agrigento, Siracusa, Segesta, Piazza Armerina), you'll see baroque cities rebuilt after devastating earthquakes (Noto and Ragusa) and some hideous postwar concrete monstrosities (modern Agrigento). The island's geography ranges from the arid, chalky southeast to the brooding slopes of Mt. Etna to the brawny headlands of Palermo and the gentle agricultural landscapes of the east, surrounded by cobalt seas and beaches where you can swim from May to October.

In Goethe's words, "The key to it all is here."

DON'T LEAVE SICILY WITHOUT . . .

Wandering Through a Palermo Market. The local bounty, from fresh tomatoes to huge slabs of tuna, is staggering, but the real treat is watching the shills and hagglers in action.

Gazing Skyward in Monreale's Cathedral. Biblical characters, saints, angels, and the heavenly pantheon look down from a sea of colorful mosaics.

Communing with the Ancient World. It's easy to do on an island so richly endowed with relics of the Greek and Roman past. Top stops are the theaters in Taormina and Siracusa, the temples at Agrigento, Segesta, and Selinunte, and the mosaics in Piazza Armerina.

FACING PAGE: **The ancient Teatro Greco in Taormina, Sicily.**

Hitting the Heights. Take in sweeping panoramic views from elegant, mountainside Taormina and aerie-like, medieval Erice. Highest and most dramatic of all: the summit of Mt. Etna.

Going for Baroque. Swaths of Noto, Ragusa, Siracusa, and other towns in the southeast are stage sets of honey-colored limestone fashioned into curvaceous facades and curling staircases.

PALERMO ★★★

233km (145 miles) W of Messina, 721km (447 miles) S of Naples, 934km (579 miles) S of Rome

In Palermo, street markets evoke Middle Eastern souks, and famous monuments bear the exotic artistic signature of the Arab-Norman 12th century, when the city was one of Europe's greatest cultural and intellectual centers. Palermo is Sicily's largest port, its capital, and a jumble of contradictions. Parts of some neighborhoods remain bombed out and not yet rebuilt from World War II while others are rapidly gentrifying; unemployment, poverty, and crime are ever-present. Palermo boasts some of the greatest sights and museums in Italy, pedestrian streets that invite long strolls, and dining options from street food to sophisticated takes on Sicilian classics. Looming over it all is crown-shaped Monte Pellegrino, what Goethe called "the most beautiful headland on earth."

Even the mix of monuments can be baffling: Byzantine mosaics, rococo stuccoes, Islamic red domes, Catalonian-Gothic arches. Yet there is magic in its madness, and those who embrace the city's chaotic charm discover artistic gems and memorable vignettes of street life. You won't love every inch of this alluring yet hectic place, but you'll be swept away by much of the city, and you may come away with the travel experience of a lifetime.

Essentials

ARRIVING

BY AIR Palermo's dramatically situated **Falcone-Borsellino Airport (PMO,** aka Punta Raisi; www.gesap.it; ✆ **800/541880**) is on the sea among tall headlands 25km (16 miles) northwest of the city center. Palermo is well served by flights from all over Italy and many European cities, though there are no nonstop flights from the U.S. All the major rental car companies have desks here (if you drive into Palermo with a rental car, get clear directions and parking information from your accommodation). An easier way to reach the center is on a **Prestia e Comandè** shuttle bus (www.prestiaecomande.it; ✆ **091/586351**), which run every half-hour from 5am to 12:30am (service from Palermo begins at 4am and ends at 9:30pm)—the trip takes 45 minutes and costs 6€ one-way, 10€ roundtrip; get tickets from a desk in the arrivals hall or on the bus. In central Palermo, buses stop at several points along Via Libertà, Teatro Politeama, the

Sicily
Venice
Florence
Rome
Sicily
TYRRHENIAN SEA
IONIAN SEA
MEDITERRANEAN SEA
Aeolian Is.
Stromboli
Panarea
Salina
Lípari
Vulcano
Filicudi
Alicudi
Ustica
Egadi Is.
Marettimo
Levanzo
Favignana
Straits of Messina
Gulf of Catania
Gulf of Avola
Gulf of Castellammare
Parco Nazionale dell' Aspromonte
Parco Regionale dei Nebrodi
Parco Regionale delle Madonie
Mt. Etna
Villa San Giovanni
Reggio di Calàbria
Messina
Milazzo
Barcellona Pozzo di Gotto
Taormina
Castelmola
Randazzo
Acireale
Aci Trezza
Aci Castello
Catania
Adrano
Paternò
Augusta
Lentini
Siracusa (Syracuse)
Buccheri
Avola
Noto
Íspica
Módica
Ragusa
Cómiso
Vittória
Caltagirone
Gela
Piazza Armerina
Capo d'Orlando
S. Stéfano di Camastra
Castelbuono
Nicosia
Gangi
Petralias
Enna
Caltanissetta
Canicattì
Licata
Agrigento
Porto Empédocle
Cefalù
Isnello
Polizzi Generosa
Caltavuturo
Alia
Bagheria
Palermo
Mondello
Monreale
S. Cipirello
Corleone
Prizzi
Chiusa Sclafani
Sambuca di Sicilia
Sciacca
Marinella
Selinunte
Castelvetrano
Salemi
Segesta
Érice
Trápani
Birgi
Marsala
Mazara d. Vallo
A3
A18
A19
A29
S113
S114
S115
S117
S120
S121
S122
S186
S189
S192
S194
S284
S286
S514
S640
0
40 mi
40 km

main train station, and Via Emerico Amari (port). A **train service,** the **Trinacria Express,** connects the airport with the main train station, but the "express" part is a bit of hyperbole: The train can take more than an hour, and the line is often nonoperational. Scheduled service from the airport begins at 5:30am and ends 10:10pm; service operates every half-hour throughout most of the day and the fare is 5.90€ each way. You can purchase tickets at desks in the station and airport or from machines near the platform. **Taxis** are plentiful; expect to pay about 40€ from the airport to town, but be sure to settle on a price before you set off. You can share a cab for about 10€—drivers depart from a well-marked "shared taxi" area outside the terminal. This is a safe and reliable option, though you will have to slip the driver a little extra to take you all the way to your destination rather than dropping you at an intersection nearby.

Street market in Palermo.

BY TRAIN Trains to Palermo from mainland Italy come down through Calabria and across the Strait of Messina on ferries equipped with railroad tracks on the cargo deck. It's a novel way to arrive in Sicily, but takes some time (the Rome–Palermo trip is at least 11 hours, Naples–Palermo 9–10 hours). Night trains between Palermo and Rome and other mainland cities usually have sleeping accommodations. All trains come into **Palermo Stazione Centrale,** at the edge of the historic center. Passenger rail service around the island is generally spotty and slow, but there's decent service on routes between Palermo and Messina, Catania, and Agrigento. For information, go to www.trenitalia.com or call © **89/2021.**

BY BUS **Buses** from the mainland and elsewhere in Sicily arrive at a depot adjacent to the train station. Bus service in Sicily is excellent, with good connections between cities and even smaller towns. Coaches are clean and modern, with comfortable, upholstered seats, air-conditioning, and smooth suspensions. The main bus companies include **Interbus** (www.interbus.it; © **06/164-160;** also known as **Etna Trasporti, Segesta,** or **Sicilbus,** depending on which part of Sicily you're in), and **Cuffaro** (www.cuffaro.info; © **091/616-1510**), which operates buses between Palermo and Agrigento.

BY CAR The northeastern tip of Sicily is separated from mainland Italy by the 5km- (3-mile) wide Stretto di Messina (Strait of Messina), which

ATTRACTIONS

Catacombe dei Cappuccini **37**
Chiesa della Martorana/San Cataldo **25**
Duomo **33**
Galleria d'Arte Moderna **22**
Galleria Regionale della Sicilia/ Palazzo Abatellis **11**
Il Castello della Zisa **38**
Museo Archeologico Regionale Antonino Salinas **2**
Museo d'Arte Contemporanea della Sicilia **29**
Oratorio del Rosario di San Domenico **4**
Oratorio del Rosario di Santa Cita **3**
Oratorio di San Lorenzo **20**
Palazzo Chiaromonte Steri/ Museo dell'Inquizione **8**
Palazzo dei Normanni and Cappella Palatina **35**
Palazzo Mirto **17**
San Giovanni degli Eremiti **34**
Stanza al Genio **15**

HOTELS

Ariston Petit Hotel **1**
Butera 28 **10**
Eurostars Centrale Palace **28**
Grand Hotel Piazza Borsa **24**
Hotel Porta Felice **9**
Il Giardino di Ballarò **32**
Palazzo Brunaccini **31**

is crossed by regular car ferries between the Calabrian port of Villa San Giovanni (just north of Reggio Calabria, essentially the "toe" of the Italian peninsula's boot) and the Sicilian city of Messina. From Messina, which lies on the well-maintained A20 and A18 *autostrade,* it's a straight shot west to Palermo (233km/145 miles; about 2 hr.). If you're planning to drive down from Naples or Rome, prepare yourself for a long ride: 721km (448 miles) south from Naples or 934km (580 miles) south from Rome.

BY SEA Palermo's large port is served by passenger ferries from the Italian mainland ports of Naples, Civitavecchia (near Rome), Livorno, and Genoa, and from the Sardinian city of Cagliari. Nearly all are night-time crossings, departing between 7pm and 9pm and arriving the next morning between 6am and 8am. Some of these ferries are tricked out like miniature cruise ships, with swimming pools, beauty salons, discos, and cabins in many configurations, from four-bunk dorms to private rooms. Ferries from Naples are the most numerous, operating daily year-round. The Naples–Palermo route is run by **Tirrenia Lines** (www.tirrenia.it; **✆ 02/760-28132**) and **Grandi Navi Veloci** (**GNV;** www.gnv.it; **✆ 010/209-4591**). The trip takes 11 hours. **GNV** also operates overnight ferries to Palermo from Civitavecchia (the cruise ship port for Rome).

GETTING AROUND PALERMO

Walking is the best way to get around Palermo, as distances are never great within the historic center. Buses run by **AMAT** (amat.pa.it; **✆ 091/350111**) charge 1.40€ per ride and 3.50€ for an all-day ticket; they run from 5:30am to 11:30pm. Bus tickets are sold at *tabacchi,* some newsstands, and kiosks near some stops; if you buy them on board, you will pay 1.80€. Four tram lines, with the same fare, service outlying districts; tickets are available from machines on the platforms. A free shuttle bus runs around the historic center, from Porta Felice near the waterfront up Via Allora to Via Maqueda.

VISITOR INFORMATION

Municipal **tourist information offices** (turismo.comune.palermo.it) are located at the airport (**✆ 091/591-698;** Mon–Sat 8:30am–7:30pm) and in the city center at Piazza Castelnuovo 35, behind the Teatro Politeama (**✆ 091/6058351;** Mon–Fri 8:30am–1:30pm and 2:30–5:30pm; afternoon hours only on Tues. and Thurs. in winter). Other city-run tourist-office locations include Piazza Bellini and Piazza Marina. **Wonderful Italy** at Via Torremuzza 15 in the Kalsa district (wonderfulitaly.eu; **✆ 091/783-8185;** Mon–Sat 10am–1pm and 2:30–5:30pm, Sun 10am–2pm) rents bikes and arranges kayaking, hiking, and other excursions, as well as off-beat tours, such as walks showing off sites in Palermo where anti-Mafia activity has centered.

SAFETY

Palermo is quite safe for tourists, though the city is home to some of the most skilled pickpockets on the continent. Police squads operate mobile centers throughout the town to help combat street crime, but **your best**

defense is common sense. Don't flaunt expensive jewelry, cameras, or wads of bills, and be especially careful in busy street markets and on buses; routes to Monreale and Mondello, popular sightseeing destinations, are fertile ground for pickpockets. Thieves on scooters are adept at snatching jewelry and handbags. Do not carry a wallet anywhere accessible, even in an inside jacket pocket, where someone (or a pair, as is often the case) brushing against you can easily get to it. When traveling around Sicily, don't leave documents, cash, credit cards, expensive electronics, and other valuables in an unattended car, even out of sight in the trunk. Stash them safely at your hotel or, if you're on the move and stopping at an attraction en route, carry them with you.

Neighborhoods in Brief

Palermo is divided into four historical districts, or *mandamenti,* that spread out from **Quattro Canti,** or Four Corners. (Time was, and not too long ago, that it was unthinkable for Palermitani from one district to marry someone from another.) The actual name of the square is Piazza Vigliena, after the viceroy who commissioned it; it marks the intersection of north-south **Via Maqueda** and east-west **Corso Vittorio Emanuele.** The square is also known as Theater of the Sun, because at any given time of day, the sun is shining on one of its four corners. Each corner of the square is decorated with a three-tiered niche: The first tier of each holds a fountain and a statue representing one of the four seasons; the second tier displays a statue of one of the Spanish Habsburg kings; and the third tier has a statue of the patron saint of whichever neighborhood adjoins the niche.

ALBERGHERIA Southwest of the Quattro Canti, the oldest of the four *mandamenti* is also referred to as Palazzo Reale because the royal palace was set here, in the highest part of the city. The Albergheria is filled with narrow, dimly lit alleyways and decaying buildings. Still, there are some exquisite corners—especially the splendid **Piazza Bologni,** with its noble palaces and statue of Charles V, and the historic market **Il Ballarò** extending from Piazza Bologni to Corso Tukory.

IL CAPO The northwestern neighborhood, enclosed within Via Maqueda, Corso Vittorio Emanuele, Via Papireto, and Via Volturno, is a warren of tiny winding streets and alleyways spread out behind the Teatro Massimo. At its heart is the largest of Palermo's markets, **Il Capo** (see p. 766), once the headquarters of the secret society of the Beati Paoli, who robbed from the rich and gave to the poor. Pickpockets still adhere to this age-old principle, so watch your wallet.

CASTELLAMMARE Named after the castle that once overlooked the sea, this northeastern quadrant is bordered by Corso Vittorio Emanuele, Via Cavour, Via Roma, and Via Crispi. Though heavily bombed in World War II, the neighborhood still has some spectacular palazzi and churches, such as the **Oratorio del Rosario di Santa Cita** and the **Oratorio di San Lorenzo** (p. 756). The centuries-old market **La Vucciria,** once the beating

Baroque Piazza Pretoria lies just off Quattro Canti, where Palermo's four historic districts meet.

heart of Palermo, is here (see p. 766), with a few remaining butcher shops, fishmongers, and hole-in-the-wall eateries; it's now a nightlife scene, too.

LA KALSA Settled a thousand years ago by Arabs, this southeast quadrant, bounded by Via Lincoln, Via Roma, Corso Vittorio Emanuele, and the Foro Italico, still has an exotic aura. Some patches were never rebuilt after 1943 air raids, and the never-completed church **Santa Maria dello Spasimo** (Via dello Spasimo; ✆ **091/616-1486**) is a skeleton of broken Gothic vaults. Even 10 years ago, walking down La Kalsa's narrow lanes was risky business (it's still wise to avoid empty areas after dark), but a rash of hip restaurants and bars have recently opened in old *palazzi.* The excellent **Galleria Regionale della Sicilia** (p. 755) is here, as is a shady park in the middle of Piazza Marina, cooled by breezes off the nearby sea. At the southern end of the neighborhood, off Via Lincoln, you'll find the city's lush botanical garden, **Orto Botanico di Palermo.**

NEW CITY The monumental **Teatro Massimo** at Piazza Verdi roughly marks the division between the Old City and the New City. Head northwest up Via Ruggero Séttimo to the massive double squares at Piazza Politeama, site of the **Teatro Politeama Garibaldi.** North of there, swanky **Via della Libertà** runs up to the Giardino Inglese (the English Gardens). This is Palermo's Art Nouveau quarter, though many streamlined beauties were torn down to make way for ugly cement behemoths, marring the neighborhood's elegance.

Exploring Palermo

Most of everything you want to see is within walking distance of the Quattro Canti, where Via Maqueda, running north–south through the city, meets Corso Vittorio Emanuele, running east–west. The seaside entrance to Corso Vittorio Emanuele is the Porta Felice and the landside entrance, near the Duomo and Palazzo dei Normanni, is the Porta Nuova.

Il Castello della Zisa ★ PALACE Few places in Palermo evoke the Arab past as evocatively as this palace of pleasure-loving Norman king William I. Arriving in Palermo, the 12th-century ruler went gloriously native, hiring craftsmen to create his summer retreat—Zisa translates as "splendid"—in Moorish style. Arches, niches, fountains, towers, and ingenious cooling systems (contrived from breezes flowing over pools and through interior vents) were all geared to creating an exotic retreat. Despite a rather clumsy recent restoration, just enough remains of the once-derelict palace to suggest its original glory.

Piazza Gugliemo il Buono (near Piazza Camporeale at end of Via Dante). ✆ **091/652-0269.** 6€. Tues–Sat 9am–7pm, Sun and Mon 9am–1:30pm. Bus: 106, 124, or 134.

Catacombe dei Cappuccini ★ CEMETERY In 1599, the occupants of the adjoining Capuchin monastery discovered that the bodies of the brothers they placed in their catacombs soon became naturally mummified (albeit with the aid of chemical infusions), and Sicilians began demanding to be buried along with them. Which is why the corpses of some 8,000 people in various stages of preservation now hang from walls and recline in open caskets. Wearing their Sunday best, the dead are grouped according to sex and rank—men, women, virgins, priests, nobles, professors (possibly including the painter Velasquez), and children. This last grouping includes the most recent resident, 2-year-old Rosalia Lombardo, who died in 1920 and whom locals have dubbed "Sleeping Beauty."

Piazza Cappuccini 1. www.palermocatacombs.com. ✆ **091/212-117.** 3€. Daily 9am–1pm and 3–6pm. Closed Sun afternoons late Oct–late Mar. Bus: 327 from Piazza Indipendenza.

Chiesa della Martorana/San Cataldo ★★ CHURCH These two Norman churches stand side by side, separated by a little tropical garden. George of Antioch—Sicilian king Roger II's Greek admiral—founded Santa Maria dell'Ammiraglio in 1141; the church was later renamed **Chiesa della Martorana** for Eloisa Martorana, who established a nearby Benedictine convent. The nuns earned the everlasting appreciation of Palermitans when they invented marzipan, and *frutta di Martorana*—in which marzipan is fashioned into the shape of little fruits—has outlived the order. George of Antioch, for his part, loved Byzantine mosaics and hired North African craftsmen to cover the church's walls, pillars, and floors with stunning mosaics. Christ crowns Roger II, George appears in a Byzantine robe, and Christ appears again in the dome, circled by angels. The Arab geographer/traveler Ibn Jubayr visited Palermo in 1166 and called the church "the most beautiful monument in the world." In 1266 Sicilian nobles met here and agreed to offer the crown to Peter of Aragon, ending a bloody uprising against French rule known as the Sicilian

Colorful mosaics in della Martorana church in Palermo.

Vespers. A baroque redo has rendered the interior a little less transporting than it was then, but it's still beautiful.

Maio of Bari, chancellor to William I, began the tiny **Chiesa di San Cataldo** next door in 1154; after he died in 1160, the church was left unfinished. The red domes and the lacy crenellation around the tops of the walls are decidedly Moorish, while the stone interior, with three little cupolas over the nave, evoke the Middle Ages.

Piazza Bellini 2, adjacent to Piazza Pretoria. La Martorana: ✆ **345/828-8231,** San Cataldo ✆ **091/782-9684.** La Martorana: free; Mon–Sat 9am–1pm and Sun 11am–1pm. San Cataldo: 2.50€; Tues– Sun 10am–1pm and 3–7pm. Bus: 101 or 102.

Duomo ★★ CATHEDRAL All those who came, saw, and conquered in Palermo left their mark on this cathedral, a remarkable architectural pastiche. Neapolitan architect Ferdinando Fuga began a restoration in 1771 in an all-encompassing neoclassical style, adding a cupola that rises impressively but incongruously above the original Norman design. Some original elements remain: four impressive bell towers from the 14th century; the middle portal from the 15th century; and the south and north porticos from the 15th and 16th centuries. The church is the final resting place of Roger II, the first king of Sicily, who died in 1154, and other Norman–Swabian royalty.

Piazza Cattedrale. ✆ **091/334373.** Duomo free; royal tombs 2€; crypt and treasury 6€. Church: Mon–Sat 7am–7pm, Sun 8am–1pm and 4–7pm. Crypt and Treasury: Mon–Fri 9:30am–2:30pm, Sat 9am–6pm, and Sun 9am–1pm. Bus: 101, 104, 105, 107, 139.

Galleria Regionale della Sicilia/Palazzo Abatellis ★★★ MUSEUM Competing for attention with this fine art collection is the late-15th-century *palazzo* that houses it, built around two courtyards and beautifully restored in the 1950s. On display is an array of Sicilian art from the 13th to the 18th centuries. You can't miss the gallery's most celebrated work, the **"Trionfo della Morte"** ("Triumph of Death"), prominently displayed in a two-story ground-floor gallery (climb the stairs to the balcony for an overview). Dating from 1449 and of uncertain attribution, this huge study in black and gray depicts Death as a fearsome skeletal demon astride an undernourished steed, brandishing a scythe as he leaps over his victims (allegedly members of Palermo aristocracy, who were none too pleased with the portrayal); the poor and hungry look on, having escaped this gruesome fate for now. The precision of this astonishing work, including details of the horse's nostrils and the men and women in the full flush of their youth, juxtaposed against such darkness, suggests the Surrealism movement that arose 400 years later.

The second masterpiece of the gallery, in room 4, is a refreshing antidote, and also quite modern-looking: the white-marble, slanted-eyed bust of **Eleonora di Aragona** by Francesco Laurana, who captured this likeness of Eleanor, daughter of King Ferdinand I of Naples, shortly before she married Ercole d'Este in 1468 and became the duchess of Ferrara. In room 11, Antonello da Messina's **"Annunciation"** is probably the artist's most famous work, completed in 1476 in Venice. He depicts the Virgin as an adolescent girl, sitting at a desk with a devotional book in front of her, clasping her cloak modestly to her chest. She raises her hand, seemingly to us viewers but probably to Gabriel, who has just announced that she is to be mother to the son of God. Considering that news, her expression is remarkably serene. It's one of the most calming, lovely works anywhere. Via Alloro 4, Palazzo Abatellis. ✆ **331/658-1788.** 8€ adults; 4€ children. Tues–Sat 9am–7pm; Sun 9am–1:30pm. Bus: 103, 105, 139.

Museo Archeologico Regionale Antonino Salinas (Regional Archaeological Museum) ★★★ MUSEUM A head-spinning repository of artifacts from Sicily's many inhabitants and invaders—Phoenicians, Greeks, Saracens, Romans—is set in the former convent of

The Fountain of Shame

In front of Chiesa della Martorana in Piazza Pretoria, naked nymphs, gods, and goddesses romp over the 16th-century **Fontana Pretoria,** created by Florentine sculptor Francesco Camilliani for the garden of a Tuscan villa then sold to Palermo as a centerpiece of the city's new waterworks. Palermitans call the nude-encrusted fountain the "Fountain of Shame," and nuns from a nearby convent used to clothe the statues. They went so far as to lop off the noses off the naked males (you can still see some clumsy reattachments)—the sisters could not bring themselves to touch the members that really offended them.

THE oratories OF GIACOMO SERPOTTA

Some of Palermo's most delightful places of worship are oratories, private chapels funded by societies and guilds and usually connected to a larger church. As you explore Palermo, seek out these three oratories, decorated in the early 18th century by Giacomo Serpotta, a native master of sculpting in stucco.

Serpotta was a member of the Society of the Holy Rosary, and he decorated the society's **Oratorio del Rosario di San Domenico,** Via dei Bambinai, with delightfully expressive putti (cherubs), who are locked forever in a playground of happy antics. His 3-D reliefs depict everything from the Allegories of the Virtues to the Apocalypse of St. John to a writhing "Devil Falling from Heaven." The Dutch master Anthony van Dyck, who spent time in Palermo in the 1620s, did the "Madonna of the Rosary" over the high altar (www.ilgeniodipalermo.com; ✆ **091/332779;** 6€; daily 10am–5:30pm). The same 6€ ticket also gets you into the all-white **Oratorio del Rosario di Santa Cita,** Via Valverde 3; which houses Serpotta's crowning achievement: a detailed relief of the 1571 Battle of Lepanto, in which a coalition of European states defeated the Turks, more or less preventing the expansion of the Ottoman Empire into Western Europe. Serpotta's cherubs, oblivious to international affairs, romp up and down the walls and climb onto window frames (www.ilgeniodipalermo.com; ✆ **091/332779;** 4€, or 6€ with San Domenico; daily 10am–5:30pm).

Serpotta also worked on the **Oratorio di San Lorenzo,** Via dell'Immacolatella, creating what critics have admiringly called "a cave of white coral." In his panels on the lives of St. Francis and St. Lawrence, some of the most expressive stuccoes depict the martyrdom of Lawrence, who, being roasted to death, nonchalantly told his tormentors, "I'm well done. Turn me over." Caravaggio's last large painting, a Nativity, once hung over the altar, but it was stolen in 1969 and never recovered (www.amicimuseisiciliani.it; ✆ **091/611-8168;** 3€; daily 10am–6pm).

the Filippini. The most important treasures are *metopes* (temple friezes) from Selinunte (see p. 812), sumptuous, detailed marbles depicting Perseus slaying Medusa, the Rape of Europa by Zeus, Actaeon being transformed into a stag, and other scenes that bring these myths vividly to life. Among the other artifacts—anchors from Punic warships and mirrors used by the Etruscans—is a rare Egyptian find: The **Pietra di Palermo** (Palermo Stone), a black slab dating from 2700 B.C. that is known as the Rosetta stone of Sicily. Discovered in Egypt in the 19th century, it was in transit for the British Museum in London when it was shuffled off to the corners of a Palermo dock. Hieroglyphics reveal the inscriber's attention to detail: a list of pharaohs, details of the delivery of 40 shiploads of cedarwood to Snefru, and flood levels of the Nile.

Piazza Olivella 24. www.regione.sicilia.it/beniculturali/salinas. ✆ **091/611-6805.** 8€. Tues–Sat 9am–5:30pm; Sun 9am–1pm. Bus: 101, 102, 103, 104, 107.

Palazzo Chiaramonte Steri/Museo dell'Inquisizione ★ PALACE/MUSEUM The Inquisition held sway in Sicily from about 1600 to 1780, allowing the Roman Catholic church to stifle the aristocracy and control the populace. Accused were held in this palace, built in 1307 for the powerful Chiaramonte family, when it was headquarters of the Aragonese/Spanish viceroys of Sicily. The lower floors housed prisoners from all levels of society in miniscule cage-like cells that were left untouched through the centuries, preserving a wealth of graffiti: hearts, caricatures, maps, initials, and verse inscribed by the hapless souls who were left here to rot or, worse, tortured and hung. An antidote to all this misery is a bright gallery housing *Le Vucciria,* an exuberant scene of the nearby market saturated with color and realism, by Palermitano painter Renato Guttuso (1912–1987). Even more refreshing are views of the sea and the old city from the top-floor **Sala Magna,** with its elaborately painted ceiling depicting scenes from the Bible and mythology. You can only visit on guided tours, offered in English.

Piazza Marina 61. www.musei.unipa.ithttp:/www.musei.unipa.it/steri.html. ✆ **091/607-5306.** 8€; 5€ seniors over 70 and ages 10–17. Mon–Fri 3pm–8pm and Sat–Sun 10am–8pm.

Palazzo dei Normanni ★★ and Cappella Palatina ★★★ PALACE The cultural influences of Sicily collide in this palace dating back to the 8th century B.C., when Punic administrators set up an outpost in the highest part of the city. In the A.D. 9th century, the Arabs built a stronghold here for their emirs and their harems, and in the 12th century the Normans turned what was essentially a fortress into a sumptuous royal residence. Here Frederick II presided over the early-13th-century court of minstrels and literati that founded the Scuola Poetica Siciliana, marking the birth of Italian literature. In 1555, Spanish viceroys moved in, and today most of the vast maze of rooms houses Sicily's regional government.

Courtyard of Palazzo dei Normanni, in Palermo.

Arab–Norman cultural influences intersect most spectacularly in the **Cappella Palatina,** a chapel covered in glittering Byzantine mosaics from 1130 to 1140. Work was finished in time for the coronation of Roger II, who proved to be not only the most powerful European king but also one of the most enlightened. High in the cupola at the end of the apse is Christ Pantocrator (holding the New Testament in his left hand and making the blessing with his right hand), surrounded by biblical characters, some interpreted a little less piously than usual—an unremorseful Adam and Eve happily munch on the forbidden fruit and greedily reach for a second piece. (Shame prevails in the next scene, when God steps in reproachfully and the naked couple cover themselves.) The mosaics are vibrant in the soft light, an effect especially powerful in scenes depicting water—in the flood and the Baptism of Christ, the water actually appears to be shimmering.

Scenes on the wooden ceiling were done in a 3-D technique using small sections of carved wood, known in Arabic as *muqarnas.* A team of Egyptian carpenters and painters created the playfully secular scenarios of dancers, musicians, hunters, drinkers, and banqueters in a harem. They're best seen with binoculars or a telephoto lens.

The **Royal Apartments** are open to the public when the Sicilian parliament is not in session. Tuesdays through Thursdays, legislators meet in the **Salone d'Ercole,** named for its mammoth 19th-century frescoes of the twelve labors of Hercules (an apt emblem for legislators wading through government bureaucracy). Rooms from the years of Spanish rule are fairly pompous, but remnants of earlier eras are fascinating. The **Sala dei Presidenti,** a stark medieval chamber hidden in the bowels of the palace for centuries, was completely unknown until it was exposed by a 2002 earthquake. The **Torre Gioaria** (Tower of the Wind) provided a 12th-century version of air-conditioning: A fountain in the middle of the tower (since removed) spouted water that cooled the breezes coming from the four hallways. Much less hospitable are the **Segrete,** or dungeons, where cold stone walls are etched with primitive scenes of Norman warships. The otherwise enlightened Frederick II allegedly took his interest in science to perverse lengths in these chambers, shutting prisoners in casks to see if their souls could be observed escaping through a small hole at the moment of death. Frederick was also fascinated by the stars and brought many astronomers and astrologers to his court. His Bourbon successors shared the interest and in 1790 added a still-active astronomical observatory at the top of the **Torre Pisana.** From these heights in 1801 the priest Fra Giuseppe Piazza discovered Ceres, the first asteroid known to mankind.

Piazza del Parlamento. www.federicosecondo.org. ✆ **091/626-833.** Cappella Palatina and Royal Apartments 19€, 17€ seniors and ages 14–17; Cappella Palatina only 15:50€, 13.50€ seniors and ages 14–17. Mon–Sat 8:30am–4:30pm; Sun 8:30am–12:30pm. Bus: 104, 105, 108, 109, 110, 118, 304, 309.

Palazzo Mirto ★★ HISTORIC SITE The streets of old Palermo are lined with palaces, and though some are decrepit and/or abandoned, many are still the homes of aristocrats. Few are as beautifully maintained as the home of the princes of Lanza Filangieri, one of Sicily's oldest families. The last of the princes bequeathed his 17th-century home to the city in the 1980s, leaving behind the trappings of his privileged lifestyle: furnishings, statues, rococo fountains that splash on hidden patios, and elaborate

State-of-the-Art Art

Palermo also has a rich contemporary art scene, with a beachhead in the beautiful 18th-century Palazzo Riso, home to the **Museo d'Arte Contemporanea della Sicilia** and its permanent collection and rotating exhibitions of contemporary artists, Via Vittorio Emanuele 365 (www.museoartecontemporanea.it; ✆ **091/778-3343;** 6€; Tues–Sat 9am–6:30pm, Sun 9am–1pm). Works by late-19th and 20th-century Sicilian artists fill a 15th-century Franciscan convent and an adjoining church housing the **Galleria d'Arte Moderna (GAM),** in the Kalsa at Via Sant'Ana 21 (www.gampalermo.it; ✆ **091/843-1605;** 10€, 8€ seniors; Tues–Sun 9:30am–6:30pm). The excellent English-language audio guides will enhance your experience.

tableware (including plates given away as party favors, decorated with images of the costumed nobs who once danced the night away in the over-the-top ballroom). It's hard to imagine that life in the grandiose, tapestry-hung salons was very comfortable or relaxed, especially for the 20th-century princes and princesses whose photos appear casually on ornate side tables. Then again, it would have been transporting to while away an evening in the smoking room, decorated in painted-silk scenes of everyday life in China as a 19th-century artisan imagined it.

Via Merlo 2. ✆ **331/661-6927.** 6€; 4€ 18–25; free for under 18. Tues–Sat 9am–7pm; Sun 9am–1:30pm. Bus: 103, 105, 139.

San Giovanni degli Eremiti ★ CHURCH Palermo's most romantic landmark is a simple affair, part Arab, part Norman, with five red domes atop a portico, a single nave, two small apses, and a squat tower. As befits the humble Spanish recluse it honors, St. John of the Hermits, the church is almost devoid of decoration, though surrounding citrus blossoms and flowers imbue the modest structure with an otherworldly aura. Adding to the charm of the spot is a Norman cloister, part of a Benedictine monastery that once stood here.

Via dei Benedettini 3. arabonormannaunesco.it. ✆ **091/651-5019.** 6€ adults. Mon–Sat 9am–6pm; Sun–Mon 9am–1:30pm. Bus: 109 or 318.

Where to Stay in Palermo

Palermo has some excellent hotels, with rates much lower than those in Rome or Florence. For convenience and atmosphere, don't stay too far beyond the neighborhoods in the old center (see p. 751).

EXPENSIVE

Grand Hotel Piazza Borsa ★★ This conglomeration of three historic buildings takes in the banking floor and grand offices of the old stock exchange, a monastery, and a centuries-old *palazzo,* combined into atmospheric surroundings that include a cloister, open-roofed atrium, paneled dining rooms, and frescoed salons. Guest rooms are a bit more

House of Tiles

One of Palermo's delightful hidden treasures is the **Stanza al Genio ★**, a collection of 2,300 historic tiles of Neapolitan and Sicilian manufacture, covering every inch of a private apartment on the *piano nobile* of an old palace in the Kalsa district. An informative guide will walk you through the kitchen, dining room, and living room, explaining the glorious ceramics carpeting the walls and floors. The museum is at Via Garibaldi 11 (www.stanzealgenio.it; ✆ **340/097-1561**); tours in English and Italian are led Tuesday through Friday at 4, 4:40, and 5:20pm and Saturday and Sunday at 10, 10:40, and 11:20am. Admission is 10€.

businesslike, though large and plushly comfortable, with hardwood floors and furnishings that cross tradition with contemporary style; the best have balconies overlooking nearby churches and palaces. A spa and exercise area includes a sauna and steam room.

Via dei Cartari 18. www.piazzaborsa.com. ✆ **091/320075.** 103 units. 120€–240€ double. Rates include breakfast. Bus: 103, 104, 105, 118, 225. **Amenities:** Restaurant; bar; babysitting; concierge; spa; free Wi-Fi.

Hotel Porta Felice ★ A sign of the old Kalsa district's gentrification, this elegant and subdued retreat has risen amid a once-neglected block of buildings just off the seafront. Marble-floored public areas are coolly soothing, while guest rooms are sleekly contemporary, with just enough antique pieces and expanses of hardwood to suggest traditional comfort. A rooftop bar and terrace is a welcome refuge, while the downstairs health spa is geared to ultimate relaxation.

Via Butera 35. www.hotelportafelice.it. ✆ **091/617-5678.** 33 units. 110€–130€ double. Rates include breakfast. Bus: 103, 104, 105, 118, 225. **Amenities:** Bar; spa; free Wi-Fi.

MODERATE

Butera 28 ★★★ The 17th-century Lanza Tomasi palace, facing the seafront, is the home of Duke Gioacchino Lanza Tomasi, adopted son of Prince Giuseppe Tomasi di Lampedusa, author of one of the greatest works of modern Italian literature, *The Leopard.* The gracious duke and his charming wife, Nicoletta, have converted 12 apartments of their *palazzo* to short-stay apartments, filling them with family pieces and all the modern conveniences, including full kitchens and, a traveler's dream come true, washing machines. Apartments have one or two bedrooms; some have sea views and terraces, others are multilevel, and all have beautiful hardwood or tile floors and other detailing. The duchess also offers cooking classes, and she, the duke, and their hospitable assistants are on hand to provide a wealth of advice to help you get the most out of their beloved Palermo.

Via Butera 28. www.butera28.it. ✆ **333/316-5432.** 12 units. 85€–200€ double. Bus: 103, 104, 105, 118, 225. **Amenities:** Kitchens; free Wi-Fi.

Eurostars Centrale Palace ★★ A wonderful location steps from the Quattro Canti puts this much-redone yet still grand *palazzo* within easy reach of most sights. Public rooms, including a vast frescoed salon where breakfast is served, evoke the 1890s Belle Epoque when the 17th-century *palazzo* was first converted to a hotel. The good-size guest rooms are comfortably functional, with rich fabrics, mosaic-tiled bathrooms, and other luxe touches; double-pane windows in the front rooms keep the street noise at bay. A rooftop terrace with an airy dining room has views extending to Monte Pellegrino. It's a great spot for cocktails on a warm summer night.
Via Vittorio Emanuele 327 (at Via Maqueda). www.eurostarshotels.co.uk. ✆ **091/336666.** 104 units. 90€–230€ double. Breakfast included in most rates. Bus: 103, 104, 105. **Amenities:** 2 restaurants; bar; exercise room; sauna; room service; babysitting; free Wi-Fi.

Il Giardino di Ballarò ★★★ The stables of the Palazzo Conte Federico were converted to a bakery more than a century ago, and now they've been revamped in the style of a casually luxurious country house, steps from the Ballarò market. In the downstairs lounges, plump couches surround a fireplace against a backdrop of old brick, arches, and columns, while a breakfast lounge and several guest rooms face a rear garden filled with banana trees and other exotic plantings. Two rooms are tucked under the eaves beneath huge skylights, and the large family rooms have two bathrooms. The distinctive decor is enhanced with splashes of color, kilims, and contemporary art, all reflecting the refined taste of proprietor Annalise Correnti, whose two daughters are gracious and capable hosts.
Via Porta di Castro 75/77. www.ilgiardinodiballaro.it. ✆ **091/212215.** 7 units. 100€–140€. Rates include breakfast. Bus: 104, 105, 108, 109, 110, 118. **Amenities:** Bar; garden; Jacuzzi (use by arrangement); free Wi-Fi.

Palazzo Brunaccini ★★ Princess Lucrezia Brunaccini probably wouldn't recognize the home from which she reigned over 18th-century Palermo society, but her dignified old *palazzo* still commands a beautiful and tranquil piazza just steps from the madness of the Ballarò market. Salons and the airy guest rooms are a pleasant mix of traditional grandeur and clean-lined contemporary touches, with oil paintings, wall hangings, and antiques thrown into the mix. Many of the high-ceilinged rooms overlook the piazza and surrounding neighborhood from small terraces.
Piazza Lucrezia Brunaccini. www.palazzobrunaccini.it. ✆ **091/586904.** 18 units. 100€–220€ double. Rates include breakfast. Bus: 104, 105, 108, 109, 110, 118. **Amenities:** Restaurant; bar; free Wi-Fi.

INEXPENSIVE

Ariston Petit Hotel ★★ The sixth floor of an apartment building near Teatro Massimo houses bright, airy rooms spread along a corridor off a comfortable lounge. Furnishings are of the basic wood-veneer modular variety and luxuries don't extend much beyond free coffee and tea, but the premises are spotless, owner/manager Giuseppe is a welcoming host, and a smattering of modern art hits just the right tasteful notes—all making this terribly pleasant place an excellent value.

Via Mariano Stabile 139. www.aristonpalermo.it. ✆ **091/332-2434.** 8 units. 40€–65€ double. Bus: 101. **Amenities:** Free Wi-Fi.

Where to Eat in Palermo

The opulent **Antico Caffè Spinnato**, Via Principe di Belmonte 115, established in 1860, is the place to linger over a pastry and coffee (www.spinnato.it; ✆ **091/329220**). In the Kalsa quarter, **Ciccolateria Lorenzo**, Via Quattro Aprile 7 (✆ **091/840846;** closed Mon), has a wonderful selection of cakes and the best hot chocolate in Palermo. For a huge selection of elaborate pastries, head to the corner of Via Lincoln and Via Nicolo Cervello, across from the botanical gardens, where neighboring **Bar Touring,** 38 Via Lincoln (✆ **091/616-7242**), and **Bar Rosanero,** Piazzetta Porta Reale 6 (✆ **091/616-4229**), outdo each other with their displays of homemade sweets. The Riso di Paradise, a concoction of chocolate, rice, and whipped cream, will bring you back daily to **Antica Gelateria Patricola**, on the waterfront at Foro Umberto 1 (✆ **091/851223**). Next to the cloisters of the Monastero San Caterina d'Alessandria, the treats at **I**

Fast Food, Palermo Style

The *cucina povera* (literally "poor man's cuisine") sold by street vendors and simple eateries is a delicacy in itself. For a flavorful introduction, take a fun and wonderfully informative food tour with **Streaty** (www.streaty.com; ✆ **351/513-3552**), which includes a market visit, many tastings, and a picnic of local delicacies from shops along the route; daily, from 49€. Among the street classics are *cazzilli* (potato croquettes), *panelle* (chickpea fritters), and *arancini* ("little oranges"), saffron-flavored rice balls, usually filled with meat ragu or ham and mozzarella, rolled in breadcrumbs, and fried. A venerable stop for arancini is **Sfrigola,** just outside the Porta Nuova at Corso Calatafimi 11 (www.sfrigola.it; ✆ **091/271-0460;** daily 11am–3pm and 6–10pm).

Commanding a side of Piazza Kalsa, **Panineria Friggitoria Chiluzzo,** Piazza della Kalsa 10 (✆ **329/061-5929;** daily 8am–5pm), is Palermo's go-to spot for street food. Even in the heat of summer, a big vat of boiling oil turns out *panelle* and *pane e panelle* (in which the fritter is tucked between heavenly pieces of sesame bread), eaten at shared tables overlooking the palm-studded square and the wonderfully Arabesque 16th-century Greek Gate. **Nini Franco U' Vastiddaru,** Via Vittorio Emaneule 21 (✆ **091/325987**), masters the art of deep frying and also serves *pani ca meusa* (bread roll stuffed with slices of boiled spleen and melted cheese) from a takeout window or in a bare-bones room and terrace overlooking Piazza Marina; the buzzing spot is open daily 9am to 1am, to 11pm on Tuesdays. Another popular spleen-stop is **Pani câ Meusa Porta Carbone,** facing the marina at Via Cala 62 (✆ **091/323433;** Mon–Fri 7:30am–10pm, until midnight on Sat). The master of *pani ca meusa*, though, is Rocky Basile, a longtime fixture of the Vucciria market, where most days he sells sandwiches from a cart.

DINE LIKE A duke

The best lunch in Palermo is a banquet in the Palazzo Lanza Tomasi, following a morning spent **Cooking with the Duchess** (www.butera28.it; ✆ **333/316-5432**). The duchess—the charming Nicoletta Lanza Tomasi—introduces students to the art of Sicilian cookery in the colorfully tiled kitchens of the palace that she and her husband, the duke of Palma, have restored in the Kalsa (the duke is the adopted son of Giuseppe Tomasi di Lampedusa, author of the modern classic *The Leopard,* who lived here at the end of his life). Sessions include a market visit and a stop on the palace's seaside terrace to pick herbs; participants are guided through preparations of such typical dishes as *panelle,* pasta with creamy pistachio pesto, or swordfish filled with anchovies, pine nuts, and parsley sauce. After a meal served by footmen in the regal dining room, a stroll through stately rooms includes a stop in the library where Lampedusa's original manuscript for *The Leopard* enjoys pride of place. Classes are 180€.

Segreti del Chiostro, Piazza Bellini 1, are based on recipes gathered from convent bakeries throughout Sicily and made with the purest ingredients; many of them, including marzipan fruits and many types of *cassata,* are almost too beautiful to eat, but you should. While there, step into the exquisite baroque church and climb to the rooftop terrace for views over Palermo (www.isegretidelchiostro.com; ✆ **0327/588-2302;** daily 10am–6pm; 7€).

EXPENSIVE

L'Ottava Nota ★★★ SICILIAN "New Sicilian" is in full force at the most exciting of the restaurants that have opened in recent years in the once-derelict Kalsa district, where a sleek, black-on-gray decor is the setting for creative takes on Sicilian classics. Tuna tartare is served with avocado, risotto is laced with leeks and tuna caviar, and eggplant meatballs are topped with tomato cream. Duck, beef, and fish are market-fresh and beautifully prepared, but you may not want to go beyond the pastas with fresh seafood—linguine with scallops, risotto with shrimp, tagliatelle with sea urchins. Despite the chic vibe, the friendly, attentive service is strictly old-school; a meal often begins with a complimentary glass of Prosecco.

Via Butera 55. www.ristoranteottavanota.it. ✆ **091/616-8601.** Entrees 22€–28€. Mon–Sat 7:30–11pm. Bus: 103, 104, 105, 118, 225.

Osteria dei Vespiri ★ SICILIAN In a quiet corner of the Kalsa, several small, simple rooms occupy the lower floor of the beautiful Palazzo Valguarnera-Gangi (film buffs take note: The ballroom scene in *The Leopard* was filmed upstairs). Menus change frequently but always focus on fresh seasonal ingredients, featuring some house creations—ravioli stuffed with potato cream, gnocchi topped with mussels, cuttlefish couscous—as well as such Sicilian classics as softly roasted tuna and pasta with sea urchins. In summer, the main dining scene moves to the romantic terrace out front.

Piazza Croce dei Vespiri. www.osteriadeivespri.it. ✆ **091/617-1631.** Entrees 28€–32€; tasting menus 85€–105€. Mon–Sat 12:30–2:45pm and 7:30–10:45pm. Bus: 103, 104, 105, 118, 225.

Palazzo Sambuca ★★ SEAFOOD/SICILIAN While the beautifully restored Palazzo Sambuca in the Kalsa quarter is one of Palermo's great baroque landmarks, this ground-floor namesake is white and chicly contemporary, with a couple of small, intimate dining rooms. A mother-and-son team oversees the kitchen while father and daughter tend to guests, serving Sicilian classics on a daily-changing menu. Lightly fried baby squid, seafood risotto, simply grilled and baked fresh fish, and other seafood is the focus, but land-based classics, including a perfectly grilled steak, are given the same reverence, and all are part of a warm and elegant experience.

Via Alloro 26. ✆ **091/507-6794.** Entrees 14€–24€. Mon–Sat noon–3pm and 7–11pm. Bus: 103, 104, 105, 118, 225.

MODERATE

Casa del Brodo ★★ SICILIAN With two plain rooms on the edge of the diminished Vucciria market, this century-plus-old institution serves vintage Sicilian specialties that you might not encounter outside of home kitchens, such as *fritelle di fava,* fava beans fried with vegetables and cheese; *carni bollite*, a tantalizing assortment of tender, herb-flavored boiled meats; and *macco di fave* (meatballs and tripe), a carnivore's delight. The namesake *brodo* (broth) is served several ways, best as tortellini in brodo, with house-made pasta.

Corso Vittorio Emanuele 175. www.casadelbrodo.it. ✆ **091/321655.** Entrees 10€–16€. Wed–Mon 7:30–11pm. Bus: 103, 104, 105, 118, 225.

La Cambusa ★ SICILIAN/SEAFOOD Palermitani come to this Kalsa outpost to enjoy Sicilian favorites, in good weather enjoying the beautiful Piazza Marina from the terrace out front and at other times dining in one of two plain dining rooms warmly decorated with paintings by local artists. The city's ties to the sea come to the fore in such classics as *zuppe di cozze* (mussels soup) and *buccatino fresco con le sarde* (homemade buccatini with fresh sardines), though land-based dishes include excellent vegetarian choices, such as a memorable *ravioli ricotta e pistachi* (ricotta and pumpkin ravioli), served in a mushroom sauce.

Piazza Marina. www.lacambusa.it. ✆ **091/584574.** Entrees 9€–18€. Tues–Sun 12:30–3pm and 7:30–11pm; shorter hours Jan–Feb. Bus: 103, 104, 105, 118, 225.

Quid Gusto Siciliano ★★★ SICILIAN Classic Sicilian recipes are given a modern twist in a memorably Palermo setting, a terrace shadowed by the huge banyan tree in atmospheric Piazza Marina. The handsomely sparse white interior is welcoming, too, as are such dishes as *mezzemaniche* (half sleeves) pasta with clams in a white bean sauce and squid served Palermitana-style, in red anchovy sauce.

Piazza Marina 52. quidgustosiciliano.com. ✆ **091/729-6996.** Entrees 15€–22€. Daily noon–3pm and 7–11pm.

INEXPENSIVE

Antica Focacceria San Francesco ★ SICILIAN/SNACKS If you've shied away from buying a *panino con la milza* (bread roll stuffed with slices of boiled spleen and melted cheese) from a street vendor, you might want to initiate yourself to the Palermo specialty in this atmospheric, marble-floored institution founded in 1834. You can also snack or lunch on *panelle* (deep-fried chickpea fritters), *arancini di riso* (rice balls stuffed with tomatoes and peas or mozzarella), *focaccia farcita* (flat pizza with fillings), or sandwiches, curtly dispensed from a busy counter.

Via A. Paternostro 58. www.afsf.it. ✆ **091/321655.** Sandwiches 4€–6€; entrees 5€–8€. Daily 11am–11pm. Bus: 103, 105, 225.

Arte e Tradizione ★★ PIZZA One of the city's favorite pizza parlors is the liveliest spot in the Kalsa quarter. In the large, bright room, and on the terrace facing a scrappy patch of greenery, you'll likely dine with students and extended families. Aside from some appetizers, you won't find much but pizza, with choices running to the dozens, including some decadent dessert concoctions. Reservations are essential on weekends, when you're unlikely to get a table without one.

Via Santa Teresa 2. arteetradizione.it. ✆ **091/252-4451.** Pizzas 6€–14€. Daily 7pm–11pm. Bus: 107, 224.

Bisso Bistrot ★★★ SICILIAN It's a sign of Palermo's renewal that you can now sit down and enjoy a fine meal right on the Quatro Canti, in character-filled rooms that were once the Libreria Dante bookstore. Pastas, including a classic alla Norma (with eggplant), swordfish *involtini,* and other Sicilian classics are served at communal tables that are always bustling, from morning coffee to late-night snacks.

Via Maqueda 172a. bissobistrot.it. ✆ **328/131-4595.** Entrees 7€–11€. Daily 9am–11pm.

Ferro di Cavallo ★★★ SICILIAN Bright red walls seem to rev up the energy to high levels in this ever-busy favorite, but the buzz is really about the good, simple food served at very reasonable prices. A decent *antipasti* platter offers a nice sampling of *panelle* (fried chickpea fritters) and other street food, but go with the daily specials to get the full flavor of the kitchen. The preference is for beans and celery, broad beans and vegetables, meatballs in tomato sauce, boiled veal, and other classics. Service hovers between nonchalant and brusque, but the jovial atmosphere compensates, and you'll pay very little for your homey meal.

Via Venezia 20. www.ferrodicavallopalermo.it. ✆ **091/331835.** Entrees 7€–9€. Mon–Tues noon–3:30pm; Wed–Sat noon–3pm and 7:30–11pm. Bus: 103, 104, 105, 118, 225.

Do Some Market Research

You can't do justice to Palermo without swinging through one of its street markets. Nowhere is Palermo's multicultural pedigree more evident than at the stalls of the **Ballarò** (in Piazza Ballarò), **Capo** (from Via Porta Carini south toward the cathedral), and even the sadly declined **La Vucciria** (on Via Argenteria, north of Via Vittorio Emanuele and east of Via Roma). These open-air souks go on for blocks, hawking everything from spices to seafood to handicrafts to electronics. Delve even deeper into Palermo's market culture at the neighborhood **Borgo Vecchio** market (along Via Ettore Ximenes to Via Principe di Scordia) in the newer part of the city, northwest of Piazza Politeama. Antiques vendors with many unusual buys congregate at the **Mercato delle Pulci** (Flea Market) along the Piazza Peranni, off Corso Vittorio Emanuele.

Moltivolti ★★★ MIDDLE EASTERN/NORTH AFRICAN/ECLECTIC The name means "many faces," and these colorful, mural-decorated rooms in the Ballarò neighborhood function as an all-day cafe, bar, restaurant, and shared workspace for humanitarian groups, creating a vibrant cultural hub that focuses on Palermo's migrant culture. The international staff, many from North Africa and the Middle East, prepare a similarly eclectic and excellent menu of couscous, *mafe* (a stew of lamb in peanut sauce), moussaka, and some Sicilian classics, accompanied by dips, salads, and a few desserts.

Via Giuseppe Mario Puglia. moltivolti.org. ✆ **091/271-0285.** Entrees 10€–12€. Daily 9am–midnight. Bus: 104, 105, 108, 109, 110, 118.

Palermo Entertainment & Nightlife

Palermo is a cultural center of some note, with an opera and ballet season running from November to July. The principal performance venue is the restored **Teatro Massimo ★★**, Piazza G. Verdi (www.teatromassimo.it; ✆ **091/605-3111**), which boasts the third largest indoor stage in Europe. (Francis Ford Coppola shot the climactic opera scene here for *The Godfather: Part III.*) Built between 1875 and 1897 in a neoclassical style, the theater was restored in 1997 to celebrate its centennial. Tickets range from 10€ to 125€. The box office is open Tuesday to Sunday 10am to 3pm. Guided tours in English are given daily 9:30am to 5:30pm and cost 10€. Watch your step on the monumental staircase leading up to the entrance: Legend has it that the ghost of a nun whose convent was displaced to build the theater takes her revenge by tripping operagoers.

The old **Vucciria market,** no longer the lively shopping souk it once was, is remerging as a nightlife scene. **Via Chiavettieri,** leading into the neighborhood off Via Vittorio Emanuele, is lined with bars where your aperitivo comes with free *cicchetti* (snacks). The decrepit old market square and lanes surrounding it are also lined with street-food outlets and bars, and the square fills with tables on weekends and during soccer matches, broadcast on a huge outdoor screen. **Via Maqueda,** in the blocks just north of the Quattro Canti, is also a nightlife strip with many bars and restaurants.

Side Trips from Palermo

The popular summertime escape from Palermo is **Mondello Lido,** 12km (7½ miles) west, where Belle Epoque Europeans once came to winter. Their Art Nouveau villas face a sandy beach that stretches for about 2km (1¼ miles), though there's little or no elbow room in July and August. Bus no. 806 makes the 30-minute trip from Piazza Mordini and along Via Libertà. Many other sights are within easy reach of Palermo.

MONREALE ★★★

10km (6 miles) S of Palermo

On Monte Caputo overlooking the fertile Conca d'Oro (Golden Valley), this hilltop village would be just another of the many that dot this area if it weren't for its majestic Duomo, one of Italy's greatest medieval treasures, sheathed in shimmering mosaics. The locals even have a saying, "To come to Palermo without having seen Monreale is like coming in like a donkey and leaving like an ass."

Interior of the Cathedral of Monreale.

ARRIVING **AMAT bus 389** (www.amat.pa.it; © **091/350111**) leaves approximately every 1 hour and 15 minutes throughout the day from a stop near Palazzo dei Normanni, on Piazza Indipendenza. If you are **driving** (it's about a 30-min. drive), leave your vehicle at the car park at Via Ignazio Florio. From there walk up the 99 steps that lead to the cathedral.

Exploring the Duomo

Duomo ★★★ CATHEDRAL Legend has it that the idea for this cathedral came to William II in a dream when, during a hunting expedition, he fell asleep under a carob tree. In his slumber, the Virgin Mary appeared to him, indicating where a treasure chest was located—and with this loot he was to build a church in her honor. Legends aside, William's ambition to leave his mark was the force behind the last and greatest of Sicily's Arab-Norman cathedrals. The cathedral in Monreale never underwent any such "improvements" as were applied to the cathedral of Palermo, so its original beauty has been preserved.

Mosaics carpet the vast interior and comprise 130 individual scenes depicting biblical and religious events, covering some 6,400 sq. m (68,890 sq. ft.), and utilizing some 2,200 kg (4,850 lb.) of gold. The shop in the arcade outside the entrance sells a plan of the mosaics with a legend detailing what's what, a mandatory aid to enjoying the spectacle; binoculars are also handy.

Episodes from the Old Testament are in the central nave (a particularly charming scene shows Noah's Ark riding the waves) while the side aisles illustrate scenes from the New Testament. Christ Pantocrator, the Great Ruler, looks over it all from the central apse; actually, he gazes off to one side, toward scenes from his life. Just below is a mosaic of the Teokotos (Mother of God) with the Christ child on her lap, bathed in light from the window above the main entrance. Among the angels and saints flanking Teokotos is Thomas à Becket, Archbishop of Canterbury, who was murdered on the order of William's father-in-law, Henry II (he is the second from the right). William is buried here and honored with a mosaic showing him being crowned by Christ.

The cloisters adjacent to the cathedral are an Arabesque fantasy, surrounded by 228 columns topped with capitals carved with scenes from Sicily's Norman history. A splendid fountain in the shape of a palm tree adds to the romance of the place.

Piazza Guglielmo il Buono. © **091/640-4413.** Free; 6€ north transept, cloisters, and treasury; 2€ roof. Duomo: Mon–Sat 9am–12:45pm and 2:30–4:30pm; Sun 2:30–4:30pm. Cloisters: Daily 9am–7pm.

CEFALÙ ★★

81km (50 miles) E of Palermo

If you saw the Oscar-winning film *Cinema Paradiso,* you've already been charmed by the former fishing village of Cefalù, now a popular resort. The filmmakers wisely left out the swarm of white-fleshed northern

Europeans who roast themselves on its crescent-shaped **beach,** one of the best along the northern coast, which stretches beneath the tall white houses of the old town. Towering 278m (912 ft.) above the beach and town is **La Rocca,** a massive and much-photographed crag. The Greeks thought it evoked a head, so they named the village Kephalos, which in time became Cefalù. It's a long, hot, sweaty climb up to the top of La Rocca, but once there, the view is panoramic, extending all the way to Palermo's skyline in the west, Capo d'Orlando in the east, and across the Madonie mountains to the south.

ARRIVING From Palermo, some three dozen **trains** (www.trenitalia.com; ✆ **892021**) head east to Cefalù (trip time: 1 hr.). By **car,** follow Route 113 east from Palermo to Cefalù; count on at least 1½ hours of driving time. Once in Cefalù, park along either side of Via Roma for free, or pay 1€ per hour for a spot within one of the two lots signposted from the main street; both are within an easy walk of the town's medieval core.

VISITOR INFORMATION The **Cefalù tourist office,** Piazza Duomo 9 (✆ **327/196-5559**), is open Wednesday to Saturday 9am to 1pm, Sunday and Tuesday 9am to 1pm (longer hours in summer).

Exploring Cefalù

Getting around Cefalù on foot is easy, and no cars are allowed in the historic core. The city's main street, **Corso Ruggero,** starts at Piazza Garibaldi,

Duomo di Cefalù.

one of four historic gateways to the town. Well-marked off Via Vittorio Emanuele in the town center is a reminder of everyday life for centuries: The river Cefalino flows through a series of large basins in the communal laundry, with a channel carrying dirty rinse water into the sea below. On the north end of town, remains of medieval bastions skirt a rocky shoreline.

Duomo ★★★ CHURCH Anchored on a wide square at the foot of towering La Rocca, the twin-towered facade of Cefalù's Duomo forms a landmark visible for miles around. Legend has it that Roger II ordered the construction of this mighty church in the 12th century after his life was spared in a violent storm off the coast. In reality, he probably built it to flex his muscle with the papacy and show the extent of his power in Sicily. This being a Norman church, shimmering mosaics in the apse depict Christ as a blonde, not a brunette. In his hand is a Bible, a standard fixture in images of Christ the Pantocrator (the Ruler), with the verse, "I am the light of the world; he who follows me shall not walk in darkness." A guided tour (6€–8€, depending on what parts of the church are included) is the only way to get a close-up look at the mosaics. Columns in the nave are said to be from the ruined Temple of Diana halfway up La Rocca.
Piazza del Duomo. duomocefalu.it. ✆ **0921/926366.** Duomo free. Apr–Oct daily 8am–12:45pm and 3:30–7:30pm.

Museo Mandralisca ★ MUSEUM There is only one reason to step into this small museum, and it's a compelling one: "Ritratto di un Uomo Ignoto" ("Portrait of an Unknown Man"), a 1470 work by the Sicilian painter Antonello da Messina. Seeing this young man with a sly smile and twinkling eyes—some say he was a pirate from the island of Lipari—is an experience akin to seeing the "Mona Lisa," and you won't have to fight your way through camera-wielding crowds to do so.
Via Mandralisca 13. www.fondazionemandralisca.it. ✆ **0921/421-547.** 6€; 4€ ages 11–15; 2€ ages 6–10. Daily 9am–7pm (to 11pm July and Aug).

Where to Eat in Cefalù

Osteria del Duomo ★★ SICILIAN/SEAFOOD A prime spot across from the Duomo with great views of La Rocca makes this a worthy stop, and the fresh seafood does justice to the locale. Seafood salads are a perfect choice for lunch on a summer's day, and piscivores will love the *carpaccio de pesce* (raw, thinly sliced fish). Carnivores can tuck into the similarly excellent carpaccio of beef. Reserve on weekends.
Via Seminario 3. ✆ **0921/421838.** Entrees 8€–16€. Daily 10:30am–11:30pm. Closed mid-Nov to mid-Dec.

SEGESTA ★★★

75km (47 miles) SW of Palermo

The **Tempio di Segesta,** one of the best-preserved ancient Doric temples in Italy, proves yet again that the Greeks had a remarkable eye for where

The Greek Temple of Segesta.

to build. Part of the ruined ancient city of Segesta, for millennia this beautiful structure in a lonely field overlooking the countryside has been delighting those lucky enough to gaze upon it. The temple was especially popular with 18th-century artists traveling in Sicily, whose paintings usually included flocks of sheep and herds of cattle surrounding the temple.

ARRIVING By **car,** take the autostrada (A29) running between Palermo and Trapani. The exit at Segesta is clearly marked. The journey takes a little under an hour from Palermo. The only easy way to visit the temple by public transportation is by bus from Trapani (see p. 803). **Tours of Sicily** (www.tourofsicily.com; ✆ **091/626-9685**) and numerous other tour companies include Segesta on their itineraries.

Exploring the Archaeological Park

The archaeological site, which is outside the modern town of Calatafimi, is still the subject of study by archaeologists from around the world. There's a small, canopied eating area opposite the only cafe, where visitors can unwind or rest during their visit.

Area Archeologico Segesta ★★★ RUINS The **Tempio di Segesta** (Temple of Segesta) stands on a 304m (997-ft.) hill, on the edge of a deep ravine carved by the Pispisa River. Built in the 5th century B.C., the temple was never finished, its columns left unfluted and its roof missing. It's been

AEOLIAN ISLAND escapes

The **Aeolian Islands** can seem like exotic getaways, even as close as they are to Sicily's civilized north coast (they're reached by ferries and hydrofoils from the port of Milazzo, a 45-minute drive west of Messina, 2½ hours east of Palermo). The seven islands share sparkling waters and lava-etched landscapes, and each has its own devotees. Especially popular are **Vulcano,** a stomping ground for summertime partiers and known for black-sand beaches and thermal baths, and **Stromboli,** whose volcano sends red-hot lava tumbling down its slopes to meet the sea with a loud hiss.

suggested that the temple was actually a ruse, begun to impress diplomats from Athens who, it was thought, would see the project as a sign of the city's wealth and therefore ally with Segesta against Selinunte. Construction halted as soon as the delegation left town. Segesta's other great sight is the perfectly preserved **Teatro** (Theater), hewn out of rock at the top of 431m (1,414 ft.) Mount Barbaro (accessible by a hike of 4km/2½ miles, or by buses that run every half-hour; 1.50€ round-trip). The *cavea* of 20 semicircular rows could seat 4,000 spectators, who enjoyed views across the surrounding farmland to the Gulf of Castellamare. Those stunning views surely competed with any performance—and still do, during summertime stagings of operas, concerts, and plays.

Parco Archaelogico Segesta. www.parcodisegesta.com. ✆ **0924/952-356.** 6€ adults; 3€ ages 18–25. Apr–Sept daily 9am–7:30pm; Mar 9am–6:30pm; Oct–Feb 9am–5pm. Ticket office closes 1 hr. before park closes.

TAORMINA ★★★

53km (33 miles) N of Catania, 53km (33 miles) S of Messina, 250km (155 miles) E of Palermo

Guy de Maupassant, the 19th-century French short-story writer, played the tourist shill and wrote, "Should you only have one day to spend in Sicily and you ask me 'what is there to see?' I would reply 'Taormina' without any hesitation. It…seems to have been created to seduce the eyes, the mind and the imagination." Lots of visitors have felt the same way. The Roman poet Ovid loved Taormina, and 18th-century German man of letters Wolfgang Goethe put the town on the Grand Tour circuit when he extolled its virtues in his widely published diaries. Oscar Wilde was one of the gentlemen who made Taormina, as writer and dilettante Harold Acton put it, "a polite synonym for Sodom," and Greta Garbo is one of many film legends who have sought a bit of privacy here. A recent depiction in the television series *White Lotus* as an enchanted playground for the rich and entitled and those who prey on them has put Taormina in the spotlight yet again.

With its beauty and sophistication, Taormina has a surfeit of star quality. The town seems more international than Sicilian, with visitors

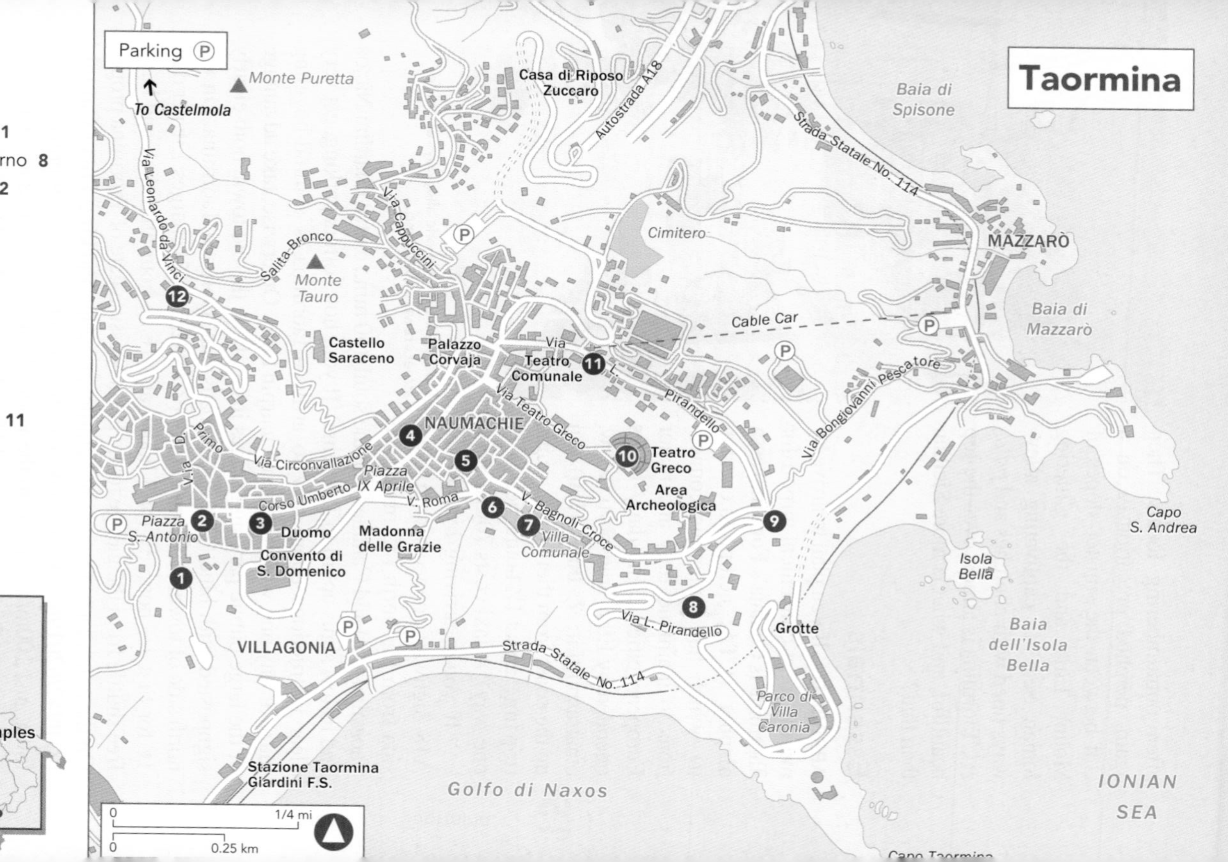

Taormina
Parking
To Castelmola
Monte Puretta
HOTELS
Excelsior Palace 1
Hotel Bel Soggiorno 8
Hotel del Corso 2
Villa Carlotta 9
Villa Ducale 12
Villa Paradiso 6
RESTAURANTS
Il Duomo 3
Osteria da Rita 5
Tischi Toschi 4
Trattoria da Nino 11
ATTRACTIONS
Teatro Greco 10
Villa Comunale 7
Milan
Venice
Florence
Rome
Naples
Sardinia
Sicily
Taormina
Casa di Riposo Zuccaro
Autostrada A18
Strada Statale No. 114
Baia di Spisone
MAZZARÒ
Baia di Mazzarò
Cimitero
Cable Car
Via Leonardo da Vinci
Via Cappuccini
Salita Bronco
Monte Tauro
Castello Saraceno
Palazzo Corvaja
Via Teatro Comunale
L. Pirandello
Via Bongiovanni Pescatore
NAUMACHIE
Via Teatro Greco
Teatro Greco
Area Archeologica
Via D. Primo
Via Circonvallazione
Piazza IX Aprile
Corso Umberto
V. Roma
V. Bagnoli Croce
Villa Comunale
Piazza S. Antonio
Duomo
Convento di S. Domenico
Madonna delle Grazie
Capo S. Andrea
Isola Bella
Baia dell'Isola Bella
Grotte
Via L. Pirandello
VILLAGONIA
Strada Statale No. 114
Parco di Villa Caronia
Stazione Taormina Giardini F.S.
Golfo di Naxos
IONIAN SEA
0
1/4 mi
0
0.25 km

often outnumbering locals. Then again, perched precariously on a cliff between the sinister slopes of Mount Etna and the glittering Ionian Sea, its captivating alleyways lined with churches and *palazzi,* Taormina is almost over-the-top beautiful, and what is more Sicilian than that?

Taormina's atmospheric alleyways and side streets reward exploring.

Essentials

ARRIVING If you plan to arrive by **air,** the most convenient airport for Taormina is Catania's **Fontanarossa airport (CTA;** aeroporto.catania.it), which has numerous connections to mainland Italy and major European cities. Nine daily **buses** operated by Etna Transporti (www.etnatrasporti.it; ✆ **06/164160**) run up the coast from there to Taormina (trip time: about 1½ hours; tickets 7€ one-way). A taxi costs 70€ to 80€.

If you're arriving by **car,** the A18 highway connects with Messina from the north (45 min.; take Taormina exit) and Catania from the south (50 min.; exit at Giardini Naxos and follow signs uphill to Taormina). If your hotel offers parking, get very clear instructions about how to arrive—Taormina is a mind-boggling maze of tiny one-way streets and hairpin turns. Otherwise, take advantage of the large public parking garages just outside the old town, both clearly signposted with blue "P"s on all roads that approach Taormina. On the north side of town, **Parking Lumbi** (✆ **0942/24345**) charges 13€ per day, 1€ for first 1½ hour, 3€ for 3 hours, and 1€ an hour after that, and has a free shuttle from the garage to the Porta Messina gate of Taormina proper. On the south end of town, the multilevel garage **Parking Porta Catania** (✆ **0942/620196;** 14€ per day) has the advantage of being practically in town, just 100m/328 ft. from the Porta Catania city gate, and charges 1€ for first hour, 5€ for 2 hours, and 1€ an hour after that. Down by the beach at Mazzarò, in the vicinity of the lower cable-car station, is **Parking Mazzarò** (17€ per day, 5€ for 3 hours, and 1€ an hour after that). For more info on parking, go to **www.taorminaservizipubblici.it**.

Taormina is well served by **buses** from the rest of Sicily, usually connecting through Catania (visit www.etnatrasporti.it for schedules). Taormina's bus station is on Via Pirandello, near Porta Messina, on the north end of town. **Trains** to Taormina run on a line between Messina and Catania, each between 40 minutes and 1½ hours away, depending on the speed of your train. Go to www.trenitalia.com (✆ **89/2021**) for schedules; service on Sundays is infrequent. Taormina's train station is shared with the seaside town of Giardini-Naxos, so it's 1.6km (1 mile) away from town—you'll have to take a taxi (about 15€–20€) or a bus up the hill to Taormina (buses run infrequently 9am–9pm; 1.10€ one-way; www.taorminaservizi pubblici.it for schedules).

VISITOR INFORMATION The **tourist office** is in Palazzo Corvaja, Piazza Santa Caterina (✆ **0942/23243;** Mon–Thurs 8:30am–2pm and 4–7pm; Fri 8:30am–2pm). Here you can get a free map, hotel listings, bus and rail timetables, and a schedule of summer cultural events staged at the **Teatro Greco** (Greek Theater; see below).

Exploring Taormina

Just about everything to see in Taormina unfolds from the main drag, **Corso Umberto I,** which slices through town from Porta Messina, in the north, to Porta Catania, in the south. It only takes 15 minutes to walk the length of the Corso. Taormina is also a handy base for trips to Mount Etna—the high-altitude visitor areas are only about 1 hour away by car.

Teatro Greco (Teatro Antico) ★★★ RUINS With their penchant for building in beautiful settings, the Greeks perched the second-largest ancient theater in Sicily (after Siracusa's, see p. 787) on the rocky flanks of Mount Tauro. The backdrop of smoldering Mount Etna and the sea crashing far below certainly provided as much drama as any theatrical production. Romans rebuilt much of the theater, adding the finishing touches on what we see today in the A.D. 2nd century, and put the arena to use for gladiatorial events. In ruin, but with much of the hillside *cavea,* or curved seating area, intact, the theater is still the setting for performances and film screenings, greatly enhanced by columns and arches framing the sea and volcano in the background. Check with the **TaorminaArte** headquarters, Corso Umberto 19 (www.taoarte.it; ✆ **391/746-2146**), or at the tourist office for dates and ticket info.

Via del Teatro Greco. www.parconaxostaormina.com. ✆ **0942/21142.** 10€; audioguide 5€; guided tours 11€. Daily 9am–7pm (closes 6:30pm Apr and early Sept, 6pm late Sept, 5:30pm late Mar and early Oct, 5pm early Mar and late Oct, 4:30pm late Feb, 4pm Nov to mid-Feb).

Villa Comunale ★★★ PARK/GARDEN Of all the colorful characters who have spent time in Taormina, the one leaving the biggest mark may have been Lady Florence Trevelyan, who in the late 19th century created these beautiful gardens, now also known as Parco Duca di Cesarò. Lady Trevelyan allegedly was asked to leave Britain after an entanglement with Edward, Prince of Wales, son of Queen Victoria. She settled in Taormina, married, and lived quite happily in the lovely adjacent villa,

MEET mighty MOUNT ETNA

Warning: Always get the latest report from the tourist office before setting out for a trip to Mount Etna, one of the world's most active volcanoes, with sporadic gas, steam, lava, and ash emissions from its summit. Adventurers have been killed by the occasional surprise "belch" (volcanic explosions).

Looming menacingly over the coast of eastern Sicily, Mount Etna is the highest and largest active volcano in Europe. The peak changes in size over the years, but it currently soars some 3,324m (10,906 ft.). Etna has been active in modern times: In 1928, the little village of Mascali was buried under lava, and powerful eruptions in 1971, 1992, 2001, and 2003 caused extensive damage to facilities nearby. Throughout the year, episodes of spectacular but usually harmless lava fountains, some hundreds of meters high, are not uncommon, providing a dramatic show for viewers in Taormina.

Etna has figured in history and in Greek mythology. Empedocles, the 5th-century-B.C. Greek philosopher, is said to have jumped into its crater in the belief that he would be delivered directly to Mt. Olympus to take his seat among the gods. It was under Etna that Zeus crushed the multiheaded dragon Typhoeus, thereby securing domination over Olympus. Hephaestus, god of fire, made his headquarters in Etna, aided by the single-eyed Cyclops. The Greeks warned that when Typhoeus tried to break out of his prison, lava erupted and earthquakes cracked the land. That must mean that the monster nearly escaped on March 11, 1669, when one of the most violent eruptions ever destroyed Catania, about 27km (17 miles) away.

Etna is easy to reach by car from Taormina. The fastest way is to take the E45 *autostrada* south to the Acireale exit. From here, follow the brown etna signs west to Nicolosi, passing through several smaller towns along the way. From Nicolosi, keep following the etna signs up the hill toward **Rifugio Sapienza** (1,923m/6,307 ft.), the starting point for all expeditions to the crater. The faux-Alpine hamlet here has tourist services and cheap and ample parking, and is the base station of the **Funivia del Etna** cable car (www.funiviaetna.com; ✆ **095/914141;** daily 8:30am–4:10pm), which takes you to the **Torre del Filosofo** (Philosopher's Tower) station at 2,900m (9,514 ft.). You can also hike up to the station, but it's a strenuous climb and takes about 5 hours. The final ascent to the authorized crater areas at about 3,000m (9,843 ft., as close to the summit as visitors are allowed) is via *Star Wars*-ish off-road vehicles over a scrabbly terrain of ash and dead ladybugs (dead ladybugs are everywhere on Mount Etna). Conditions at the crater zone are thrilling, but the high winds, exposure, and potential sense of vertigo are not for the faint of heart.

The round-trip cost of getting to the top of Etna, including the cable car ride, the off-road vans, and the requisite authorized guide at the crater zone, is about 55€. Etna is not a complicated excursion to do on your own, but if you'd prefer to go with a tour, Taormina is chock-full of agencies that organize Etna day trips.

now the hotel **Villa Paradiso** (see p. 778). Her liaison with a farmer, much of it conducted amid these groves and terraces, supposedly inspired D.H. Lawrence's *Lady Chatterley's Lover.* Lady Trevelyan built stone and brick pavilions in the park for birdwatching and entertaining, and 3 hectares (7½ acres) of groomed terraces are filled with luxuriant vegetation, cobblestone walkways, picturesque stone stairways, and a sinuous path lining the park's eastern rim with superb views over the sea.

Via Bagnoli Croce. No phone. Free. Daily 8:30am–7pm (6pm in winter).

Where to Stay in Taormina

Hotels in Taormina are some of the best in Sicily. Quite a few close in the winter, but those that remain open offer rates at a fraction of summertime tariffs. If you're driving to Taormina, call ahead to see what arrangements can be made for your car. A good source for apartment rentals and other info about Taormina is **www.gotaormina.com**.

EXPENSIVE

Villa Carlotta ★★ Tucked away at the edge of town, this castellated 1920s stone villa is another creation of Andrea and Rosaria Quartucci, who work their magic at **Villa Ducale** (below). A wall of Byzantine catacombs adds an air of mystery, but what wins you over is the classic-yet-contemporary style and wonderful sense of privacy and comfort. Most of the warm-hued, stylish rooms have terraces and sea views, and many overlook the luxuriant rear gardens, with a swimming pool amid the greenery. Service is personalized and attentive. Villa Carlotta also houses guests in luxury apartments up the street.

Via Pirandello 81. www.hotelvillacarlottataormina.com. ✆ **0942/626-058.** 23 units. 425€–500€ double. Rates include breakfast. 2-night minimum stay. Parking 30€. Closed Nov–early Mar. **Amenities:** Restaurant; concierge; health club; pool; free Wi-Fi.

Villa Ducale ★★★ Andrea and Rosaria Quartucci have fashioned a family villa into a warm and stylish getaway perched high on a hillside above the town, with flower-planted terraces, Mediterranean gardens, and extraordinary eagle's-nest views that extend as far as Calabria. Distinctive rooms and suites, in the villa and a house across the road, are done in Sicilian chic, with extremely comfortable furnishings set against warm hues that play off terra-cotta floors; they're enlivened with beams, arches, and other architectural details, equipped with luxurious baths, and fitted out with fine linens and works by local artists. Service is warm and personal. A lavish buffet breakfast and complimentary sunset cocktails, accompanied by a spread of Sicilian appetizers, are served on a living-room-like terrace; lunch and dinner are available on request. A shuttle runs to and from town.

Via Leonardo da Vinci 60. www.villaducale.com. ✆ **0942/28153.** 15 units. 240€–420€ double. Rates include buffet breakfast. Parking 20€. Closed Jan–Mar. **Amenities:** Bar; pool; Jacuzzi; room service; free Wi-Fi.

MODERATE

Excelsior Palace ★ Though this sprawling pink landmark behind the Duomo, welcoming guests since 1904, is often filled with groups, service is attentive and old-world, with waiters in ties and jackets serving cocktails in frumpy lounges full of overstuffed couches and armchairs. Rooms

are conventionally comfortable and well maintained, and all have views, many of Mt. Etna and the coastline; several have tiny balconies with just enough room for two chairs. The best amenity is the magnificent garden, draped over a view-filled promontory with a superbly perched swimming pool, making this a top summertime choice.
Via Toselli 8. www.excelsiorpalacetaormina.it. ✆ **0942/23975.** 85 units. 110€–200€ double. Rates include breakfast. **Amenities:** Restaurant; bar; concierge; pool; Wi-Fi in public areas (free).

Hotel Bel Soggiorno ★★ You could be nowhere but Sicily in this rather grand old villa surrounded by lush gardens that tumble down a hillside, filled with lemon and orange trees, exotic flowers, and sweeping coastal vistas. Tile-floored guest rooms are plain but comfortable, with handsome iron bedsteads and simple wooden furniture. All open through French doors to balconies and, in many cases, huge terraces. A friendly staff serves breakfast, with some cooked choices, in a beautiful orangerie and on an adjoining patio. As bucolic as the surroundings are, the center of town is an easy 10-minute walk away.
Via Luigi Pirandello 60. www.belsoggiorno.com. ✆ **0942/23342.** 100€–160€ double. Rates include breakfast. **Amenities:** Bar; gardens; free Wi-Fi.

Villa Paradiso ★★ Lady Florence Trevelyan, who created the beautiful gardens that are now the Villa Comunale (see p. 775), lived in this villa until her death in 1907. The elegant house then passed to the Martorana family, three generations of whom have proven to be outstanding hoteliers and avid renovators, adding entire floors to the original house. Family antiques, comfy armchairs and couches, and paintings (many presented by guests over the years) fill lounges and bright, handsomely decorated guest rooms, where balconies and sun-drenched sitting alcoves face the sea. Breakfast and dinners are served in a top-floor, glassed-in restaurant, **Settimo Cielo** (Seventh Heaven), which it really seems to be. Between June and October, the hotel offers shuttle service and free entrance to the Paradise Beach Club, about 6km (4 miles) to the east, in the seaside resort of Letojanni.
Via Roma 2. www.hotelvillaparadisotaormina.com. ✆ **0942/23921.** 37 units. 130€–240€ double. Rates include breakfast. Parking 20€. **Amenities:** Restaurant; bar; room service; free Wi-Fi.

INEXPENSIVE

Hotel del Corso ★ You'll forgo spas, pools, and other chic luxuries in these basic lodgings right in the heart of town, on Corso Umberto near the Duomo, but you won't give up views of the sea and Mt. Etna. They fill the windows of many of the rooms and spread out below the top-floor lounge, breakfast room, and sun terrace; some rooms have less dramatic but pleasing views of the town. Black-and-white terrazzo floors, iron bedsteads, and soothing neutral colors add a lot of spark to the comfortable guest rooms, a few of which have small balconies. Book well in advance, especially on weekends, when this good-value property fills up fast.

Corso Umberto 328. del-corso.taorminahotelsweb.com. ✆ **0942/628-698.** 15 units. 90€–110€ double. Rates include breakfast. **Amenities:** Free Wi-Fi.

Where to Eat in Taormina

The ultimate Sicilian summer refreshment, sorbet-like *granita,* is perfect at **Bam Bar,** not far from the Grand Hotel Timeo at Via di Giovanni 45 (✆ **0942/24355**). Specialties are the almond *(mandorla)* or white fig *(fico bianco)*, but it usually has a dozen or more flavors to choose from.

Il Duomo ★★ SICILIAN Take a table near the large window overlooking the Duomo or, in good weather, on the side terrace. Then enjoy traditional Sicilian cooking with some well-conceived modern twists. This is the best place in town to try pasta *con sarde* (with sardines and breadcrumbs); the fish is fresh and nicely enlivened with capers, tomatoes, and olives.

Vico Ebrei (at Piazza Duomo). ✆ **0942/625656.** Entrees 10€–18€. Daily noon–3pm and 7–11pm.

Osteria da Rita ★★ SICILIAN/PIZZA Taormina needs more easygoing eateries like this pleasant little place tucked away between the Corso and Villa Comunale. Pizzas, sandwiches, salads, omelets, and a few pasta dishes—including heaping platters of spaghetti carbonara and *pasta alla Norma*—are served in a small, plain room and on a picture-perfect piazzetta out front. Service is friendly and prices are reasonable.

Via Calapitrulli 3. ✆ **0942/681051.** Entrees 7€–13€. Daily 11am–11pm.

Tischi Toschi ★★★ SICILIAN/SEAFOOD A warm-hued yellow room facing a little piazza and decorated with old ceramics is the setting for creative takes on old Sicilian classics. Even *pasta alla Norma* (with eggplant and ricotta) seems like a work of art here, topped with grilled eggplant. Venture further and sample some dishes you might not find many other places, such as *insalata di pesce stocco,* a salad made from dried cod, raw fennel, and tomato dressed with olive oil and parsley, or *sarde a beccafico,* sardines stuffed with pine nuts and fennel and served with lemon and orange. Don't miss the delicious fried artichokes, and end a meal with the heavenly, refreshing lemon jelly.

Via F. Paladini 3 (off Corso Umberto). www.tischitoschitaormina.com. ✆ **339/364-2088.** Entrees 12€–20€. Daily 7–11pm.

Trattoria da Nino ★★ SICILIAN Good, no-nonsense Sicilian *cucina casalinga* (home cooking) is the recipe for success in this unpretentious, brightly lit room (with an airy terrace in warm weather) across from the upper station of the cable car. Pastas are house-made (deliciously delicate gnocchi, little potato dumplings, are served *alla Norma,* with eggplant and ricotta), and the fish is served simply grilled. Nino's is a local institution, a 50-plus-year veteran of the Taormina dining scene, and it's always busy. They don't take reservations for groups of fewer than six. Via Pirandello 37. www.trattoriadaninotaormina.com. ✆ **0942/21265.** Entrees 8€–18€. Tues–Sun noon–2:30pm and 7–10:30pm; Mon 7–10:30pm.

Beaches Near Taormina

You can reach Taormina's best and most popular beach, **Lido Mazzarò,** via a cable car (www.taorminaservizipubblici.it; ✆ **0942/23906**) that in theory but not always in practice leaves from Via Pirandello every 15 minutes (3€ each way; 10€ day ticket; 50€ weekly ticket for nonresidents; spring and summer only) between 7:45am and 8pm (from 8:45am on Monday). The soft, finely pebbled beach is one of the best equipped in Sicily, with bars, restaurants, and hotels. You can rent beach chairs, umbrellas, and watersports equipment at kiosks from April to October. South of Lido Mazzarò, past the Capo Sant'Andrea headland, is the region's prettiest cove, where twin crescents of beach sweep out to the minuscule **Isola Bella** islet. South of Isola Bella, the large resort beach of **Giardini** can get crowded. North of Mazzarò, you'll find fewer people at the long, wide beaches at **Spisone** and **Letojanni.** A local bus leaves Taormina for Mazzarò, Spisone, and Letojanni; another heads down the coast to Giardini.

Taormina Shopping

Shopping is all too easy in Taormina—just walk along **Corso Umberto I.** Ceramics are one of Sicily's most notable handicrafts, and Taormina's shops are among the best places to buy them on the island, as the selection is excellent. **Di Blasi Ceramiche,** Corso Umberto I 103 (✆ **0942/24671**), has a nice range of designs and specializes in the highly valued "white pottery" from Caltagirone. Mixing the new and the old, **Carlo Panarello Antichità,** Corso Umberto I 122 (✆ **0942/23910**), offers Sicilian ceramics (from pots to tables) and also deals in eclectic antique furnishings, paintings, and engravings.

Side Trips from Taormina

CASTELMOLA ★★

Taormina gets high praise for its gorgeous views, but for connoisseurs of scenic outlooks, the real show takes place in the village of Castelmola, 3km (2 miles) northwest of Taormina, and about 300m (1,000 ft.) feet higher. The Ionian Sea seems to stretch to the ends of the earth from up here, and you'll be staring right into the northern flanks of Mt. Etna. For the full experience, make the trip up on foot, following routes that begin at Taormina's Porta Catania and Porta Messina (the tourist office or any hotel desk can give you directions); the Porta Messina trail passes a section of the Roman aqueduct and the Convento dei Cappuccini, where you can pause for a breather. Either route involves an hour or so of fairly strenuous walking. Once at the top, stop at Castelmola's **Bar Turrisi** (Piazza Duomo 19; ✆ **0942/28181;** daily 10am–11am, until 6pm Mon–Thurs in winter) for a glass of *vino alla mandorla* (almond wine) and a look at its peculiar art collection. If that's more walking than you care to do, you can also drive up to Castelmola (park below the village and walk in) or take an orange bus that runs more or less hourly from Porta Messina (1.10€ one way).

GOLE DELL'ALCANTARA ★★

In a series of narrow gorges *(gole)* on the Alcantara (Al-*cahn*-ta-rah) river, rushing ice-cold water fed by Mt. Etna snowmelt dashes over fantastically twisted volcanic rock, creating a scenic spectacle that's especially refreshing on a hot day. The gorges are now protected as **Parco Fluviale dell'Alcanta** (www.parcoalcantara.it; ✆ **0942/985010**), though ticket booths, turnstiles, and elevators into the gorge lend an amusement-park aura. Get away from the crowds with a hike along the riverbed, stopping now and then to lounge on flat riverside rocks and wade and even swim in the chilly water. From October to April, only the upper area of the park, with an overlook trail above the gorge, is open. It costs 13€ to enter the park in summer, from 7€ to 10€ other times (daily 8am–7pm; shorter hours in winter). Amenities include a gift shop, cafeteria, picnic areas, and toilets. You can reach the Gole dell'Alcantara by car from Taormina in 35 minutes, or you can take **Interbus** (www.interbus.it; ✆ **0942/625301**), a 1-hour trip with several daily runs from Taormina (5€ roundtrip). Organized excursions (from 25€) are also offered by tour operators in Taormina, often in conjunction with a visit to Mount Etna.

SIRACUSA ★★★

This small, out-of-the-way southern city packs a one-two punch. Siracusa was one of the most important cities of Magna Graecia (Greater Greece), rivaling even Athens in power and influence. The still-functioning Teatro Greco, where Aeschylus debuted his plays, is one of many landmarks of this ancient metropolis. Ortigia, the quaint historical center spreading over its own island, belongs to a much later time, when palaces and churches were built in baroque style after the earthquake that destroyed much of the southeast in 1693.

Siracusa might seem far removed from most of Europe, but in visiting the southeast coast you'll follow the illustrious footsteps of the scientist Archimedes, statesman Cicero, evangelist St. Paul, martyr St. Lucy, painter Caravaggio, and naval hero Admiral Lord Horatio Nelson, all of whom left a mark on this remarkable place. According to myth, Leto gave birth here to Artemis, one of the twins she conceived with Zeus, before continuing on to deliver Apollo on the Greek island of Delos.

Essentials

ARRIVING The most convenient airport for Siracusa is Catania's **Fontanarossa airport (CTA;** aeroporto.catania.it), which has numerous connections to mainland Italy and many European cities. **Interbus buses** (www.etnatrasporti.it) run almost hourly for the 45-minute trip from the airport to Siracusa.

By **car,** Siracusa is 1½ hours south of Taormina on the A18, and about 2 hours south from Messina. Driving time to Palermo or Agrigento is about 3 hours. Siracusa is well connected with the rest of Sicily by **bus,** 3½ hours from Palermo and 2 hours from Taormina (www.interbus.it). It's 5 to 6 hours from Palermo and 2 hours from Taormina by **train,** usually with a change in Catania (www.trenitalia.com; ✆ **89/2021**); bus service throughout the south is more efficient and frequent than train service. Both trains and buses arrive in Siracusa at the station on Via Francesco Crispi, between the archaeological park and Ortigia Island.

GETTING AROUND You won't need a car, just your own two feet and perhaps a few bus or cab rides to see the best of Siracusa proper. **Buses** (www.astsicilia.it) run between the train station and Ortigia (a fairly easy 15-min. walk), and also serve the archeological park; tickets, from newsstands and tobacco shops, are 1.20€ (1.50€ on board), day ticket 5€. An easy way to tour the sights is on electric **minibuses** operated in the summer by Siracusa d'Amare (www.siracusatravel.com), which travel from the train station to Ortigia, around Ortigia, and from Ortigia and the train station to the archaeological park; fare is 1€, 3€ for a day ticket, payable on board or from *tabacchi.*

If you're traveling by car, ask your hotel before arriving about the best place to park. Ortigia Island is ringed with public lots, including the large **Talete** complex at the northern end, near the bridge to the mainland. Parking is 1.50€ an hour, 15€ a day, payable in machines. These lots use a computerized camera system in which you enter your license number when leaving and pay the appropriate amount. Much of Ortigia, with the exemption of a few main thoroughfares, is off-limits to nonresidents' cars and monitored with cameras, so pay close attention to signs.

VISITOR INFORMATION A **tourist office** near the archeological park at Via San Sebastiano 43 (✆ **0931/481232**) is open Monday to Friday 8:30am to 1:30pm and 3 to 6pm, Saturday 8:30am to 1:30pm (closed in winter). There's another office in Ortigia at Via Santi Coronati 4 (✆ **0931/65201**); it's open Monday to Friday 8:30am to 1:30pm and Wednesday 2:45 to 5:45pm. A good online source for information on what to see and do is **www.siracusaturismo.net**.

Exploring Siracusa

Ortigia Island is Siracusa's *centro storico,* a mostly pedestrian zone where narrow alleys lined with romantic 18th-century *palazzi* spill onto Piazza

Siracusa's Ortigia Island.

del Duomo. The ancient ruins are a good half-hour walk north of Ortigia along Corso Gelone.

ORTIGIA ISLAND ★★★

The historic center of Siracusa is an island only about 1 sq. km (¾ sq. mile), with breezy, palm-shaded seaside promenades fringing its shores. Although Ortigia was settled in ancient times, most of the island today is baroque, with grandiose palaces and churches lining narrow lanes and flamboyant piazzas.

The first landmark you'll come to after you cross Ponte Umbertino from the mainland is the **Temple of Apollo,** the oldest Doric temple in Sicily. The Apollonion would have measured 58m×24m (190×79 ft.) when it was built in the 6th century B.C. It later served as a Byzantine church, then a mosque, then a church again under the Normans; it's now an evocative ruin, with the temple platform, a fragmentary colonnade, and an inner wall rising in the middle of Piazza Pancali.

The **Piazza del Duomo,** certainly one of the most beautiful squares in Italy, is all about theatrics—a sea of white marble softened by pink oleander, surrounded by flamboyant palaces with elaborate stone filigree work and wrought-iron balconies. Similarly fanciful are the frothily baroque **Duomo** and the pretty church of **Santa Lucia alla Badia,** where the facade is equipped with a wrought-iron balcony from which cloistered nuns once watched goings-on in the piazza. Also on Piazza del Duomo is an entrance to the **Hypogeum,** a network of underground chambers and corridors dug as air-raid shelters in World War II (✆ **349/427-3064;** 5€; daily 10am–8pm, closed Jan–Mar).

South of Piazza del Duomo, on the waterfront, is the **Fonte Aretusa,** a basin where papyrus grows in a shallow pool that supplied Siracusa with fresh water for millennia. Classical myth, however, tells a different story: The nymph Aretusa was bathing in a river in Greece when the river god Alpheus took a liking to her. She asked the goddess Artemis, protectress of young women, for help in avoiding his advances; Artemis turned Aretusa into a river that emerged here. Not to be thwarted, Alpheus followed suit, and the two of them bubble forth for eternity.

A short walk east on Via Capodieci, stop in the **Galleria Regionale Palazzo Bellomo,** set in an elegant 13th-century palace, to see one of Siracusa's greatest artworks, Antonello da Messina's "Annunciation" (1474), damaged yet still poignant, an intricate study in light and detail (Via Capodieci 16; ✆ **0931/69511;** 8€; Tues–Sat 9am–7pm, Sun 9am–1pm).

Duomo ★★ CHURCH Despite a frothy baroque facade, Siracusa's main church has ancient roots. Two tiers of Doric columns that define the entrance were once part of the 5th-century-B.C. Temple of Athena, one of the best-known sights of the ancient world, built to mark a Greek victory

SIRACUSA'S virgin SAINT

St. Lucia, a plucky 4th-century Siracusan virgin, is the city's patron. Born of wealth, from an early age Lucy decided to give her worldly goods to the poor. Her piety and generosity so annoyed the young man to whom she'd been betrothed that out of spite he denounced her to Roman authorities. Lucia was condemned to prostitution, but refused to be dragged off to a brothel. Authorities tied her to a pillar and lit a fire beneath her, and she proved to be flame-resistant. Finally, a soldier plunged a sword into her throat. Later embellishments have Lucy gouging her eyes out to defy a lustful brute who admired them or soldiers removing them—these details have earned her a place as the patron saint of those suffering from eye ailments. You'll see depictions of the saint and her gruesome martyrdom throughout Siracusa and the rest of Sicily, often holding her eyes on a plate. She is the subject of Siracusa's prize painting, Caravaggio's **"Burial of St. Lucia,"** commissioned in 1608 when the artist had escaped prison in Malta and fled to Sicily. The masterpiece now hangs above the altar in the **Basicilica Santuario Santa Lucia al Sepolcro,** off of Ortigia on the site of the saint's 4th-century martyrdom off Piazza Santa Lucia (www.basilicasantalucia.com; ✆ **0931/67946**). With his characteristic lighting, Caravaggio highlights the muscular gravediggers, showing their brute strength, while the mourners seem small and meek in the background. A shaft of light falling on Lucia's face and neck highlights the stab wound that killed her; she is a study in serenity, having entered the heavenly kingdom. Lucia's sepulcher is next to the church, though a few centuries ago her remains were spirited away to Venice and remain there. The complex is open daily 9am to 12:45pm and 3:30 to 7pm; admission is free.

A Gigantic Teardrop Runs Through It

The tallest building in Siracusa is the bizarre **Santuario della Madonna delle Lacrime** (Our Lady of Tears Sanctuary, Via Santuario 33; ✆ **0931-21446;** free admission; Mon–Sat 7:30am–12:30 and 3:30–7:30pm, Sun 7:30am–1pm and 3:30–8:45pm), a monstrous cone of contemporary architecture (built in 1993) halfway between Ortigia and the archaeological zone. Meant to evoke a sort of angular teardrop and rising 74m (243 ft.) with a diameter of 80m (262 ft.), the showy edifice houses a statue of the Madonna that supposedly wept for 5 days in 1953. Alleged chemical tests showed that the liquid was similar to that of human tears. Pilgrims flock here, and you'll see postcards of the weepy Virgin around Siracusa. In the interior, vertical windows stretch skyward to the roof. A charlatan TV evangelist and his congregation would not look out of place here.

over the Carthaginians. Cicero, the Roman orator and traveler, reported that the temple was filled with gold, the doors were made of gold and ivory, and a statue of Athena atop the pediment was visible for miles out to sea. Romans made off with much of the gold, alas, and 9th-century Arab marauders took the rest. The church was first fashioned from the temple around the 7th century; a statue of the Virgin now stands atop the pediment as Athena once did. Other ancient columns line the aisle in the church's strikingly simple interior, while a silver statue in a side chapel protects an important Christian relic—an arm of Santa Lucia, Siracusa's patron saint (see p. 784).

Piazza Duomo. ✆ **389/550-3267.** 2€. Apr–Sept Mon–Sat 9am–6:30pm; Oct–Mar Mon–Sat 9am–5:30pm.

THE ANCIENT RUINS ★★★

Of all Sicily's Greek cities of antiquity, Siracusa was the most important, a formidable competitor of Athens. In its heyday, the city dared take on Carthage and even Rome. To reach the sprawling ruins, walk north along Corso Gelone; take a minibus or cab from Ortigia's Piazza Pancali or bus 1, 2, or 3 from Siracusa's central train station. In summer, you can make the trip by electric minibus from Piazza Pancali and other stops (see p. 782).

Castello Eurialo ★ RUINS Part of a massive, 27km-long (16-mile) defense system, this 4th-century-B.C. fortress is surrounded by three trenches, connected by underground tunnels. These supposedly impregnable defenses were never put to the test: Siracusa fell to the Romans in 212 B.C. without a fight, because the entire garrison was celebrating the feast of Aphrodite. It was here, legend has it, that the Greek mathematician Archimedes famously cried "Eureka!" having discovered the law of water displacement while taking a bath. The evocative ruin overlooking the Siracusan plain is the best-preserved Greek castle in the Mediterranean. The defenses are at the far end of the archaeological zone, about

5km (3 miles) outside the city center near a village called Belvedere; buses 25 and 26 pass the entrance.

Piazza Eurialo 1, off Viale Epipoli. ✆ **0931/481111.** 5€. Mon 2:30–6pm; Tues–Sun 8:30am–1:30pm (hours vary, verify with tourist office before making the trip).

Catacombe di San Giovanni ★★ RUINS Spooky subterranean chambers, installed in underground aqueducts that had been abandoned by the Greeks, contain some 20,000 ancient Christian tombs. They are entered through the Church of San Giovanni, now in ruin but holy ground for centuries; this was the city's cathedral until the church was more or less leveled by an earthquake in 1693. St. Paul allegedly preached here when he stopped in Siracusa around A.D. 59, and a church was erected in the 6th century to commemorate the event. The Cripta di San Marciano (Crypt of St. Marcian) honors a popular Siracusan martyr, an A.D.-1st-century bishop who was tied to a pillar and flogged to death on this spot.

Piazza San Giovanni, at end of Viale San Giovanni. ✆ **0931/64694.** 8€ adult; 5€ seniors and under age 16. Daily 9:30am–12:30pm and 2:30–5:30pm (Nov–Mar until 4:30pm, July–Aug until 6pm). Closed Jan.

Museo Archeologico Regionale Paolo Orsi ★★★ MUSEUM One of Italy's finest archaeological collections shows off artifacts from southern Sicily's prehistoric inhabitants through the Romans, showcasing pieces in stunning modern surrounds. Amid prehistoric tools and sculptures are the skeletons of a pair of dwarf elephants, as intriguing to us as they were to the ancients: It's believed that the large central hole in these skeletons' faces—actually a nasal passage—inspired the myth of the one-eyed Cyclops. Look for the often-reproduced grinning terra-cotta Gorgon, originally part of the frieze of the Greek temple of Athena (see Duomo, p. 784), where it was placed to ward off evil. You'll also see votive cult statuettes devoted to Demeter and Persephone, mother and daughter goddesses linked to fertility and the harvest. Legend has it that Hades, god of the underworld, abducted Persephone in Sicily and carried her down to his realm; her angry mother Demeter fought for her return, and the gods struck a deal—Persephone could return to Earth every spring and summer, making nature bloom, but she had to resume her duties as queen of the underworld in fall and winter, causing the lands above to wither and die. The museum's most celebrated piece is the **Landolina Venus,** a Roman copy of an original by the great classical Greek sculptor Praxiteles. The graceful and modest goddess, now headless, rises out of marble waves; French writer Guy de Maupassant called her "the perfect expression of exuberant beauty."

In the gardens of Villa Landolina in Akradina, Viale Teocrito 66. aditusculture.com. ✆ **0931/464-022.** 10€; 18€ with archaeological park. Tues–Sat 9am–7pm; Sun 9am–2pm.

Parco Archeologico della Neapolis ★★★ RUINS Many of Siracusa's ancient ruins are clustered in this archaeological park at the western edge of town, immediately north of Stazione Centrale.

The **Teatro Greco ★★★** (Greek Theater) was hewn out of bedrock in the 5th century B.C., with 67 rows that could seat 16,000 spectators. It was reconstructed in the 3rd century B.C., appears now much as it did then, and is still the setting for ancient drama in spring and early summer.

Gladiators sparred in the **Anfiteatro Romano,** created around 20 B.C. A square hole in the center of the arena suggests that machinery was used to lift wild beasts from below. Historical evidence also suggests that the arena could be flooded for mock sea battles called *naumachiae;* pumps could also have flooded and drained a reservoir in which crocodiles are said to have fed on the corpses of victims killed in the games. The Spanish carted off much of the stonework to rebuild city fortifications when they conquered Siracusa in the 16th century, but some seats remain—the first rows would have been reserved for Roman citizens, those right above for wealthy Siracusans, and the last rows for the hoi polloi.

What is now a lush grove of lemon and orange trees, the **Latomia del Paradiso** (Quarry of Paradise) was at one time a fearsome place, vast, dark, and subterranean—until the cavern's roof collapsed in the great earthquake of 1693. Originally prisoners were worked to death here to quarry the stones used in the construction of ancient Siracusa. What is certainly the most storied attraction in the park is here: the **Orecchio di Dionisio** (Ear of Dionysius), a tall and vaguely ear-shaped cave dug into the cliff by the Greeks to expand the limestone quarry for water storage. Something about this huge cavern always inspired more dramatic accounts, such as the legend (completely unfounded) that the cave was once a prison for Athenians captured by Dionysus' mercenaries in the Peloponnesian Wars; supposedly he liked how the cave's acoustics amplified their screams as they were tortured. Almost as fascinating is the well-documented purpose of the **Ara di Ierone** (Altar of Heron): 5th-century-B.C. Greeks built the altar, 196m (636 ft.) long and 23m (75 ft.) wide and approached by gigantic ramps, to sacrifice 450 bulls at one time.

Via Del Teatro (off intersection of Corso Gelone and Viale Teocrito), Viale Paradiso. aditusculture.com. ✆ **0931/66206.** 13€; 18€ with archaeological museum. Daily Apr–Sept 9am–7:45pm (until 4:30pm on performance evenings in summer), Mar 9am–6pm, Oct–Feb 9am–4:30pm. For performance tickets (30€–70€), contact **INDA,** Corso Matteotti 29, Siracusa (www.indafondazione.org; ✆ **0931/487248**).

Where to Stay in Siracusa

The choice place to stay in Siracusa is Ortigia, with enough character, charm, and comfortable accommodations to keep the most discerning traveler happy. For villas, **The Thinking Traveler** (www.thethinkingtraveller.com) has a carefully edited list of well-equipped properties in and around Siracusa, and elsewhere in Sicily.

EXPENSIVE

Algilà Ortigia Charme Hotel ★ A slightly exotic air pervades this old stone palace at the edge of the sea. Interiors surrounding a peaceful inner courtyard with a splashing fountain are accented with carefully restored stonework and wooden beams, offset by multicolor tiles and other rich details. Rooms combine conventional luxury with all the modern amenities, plus a surfeit of four-poster beds, antiques, and tribal kilims; many have sea views. The in-house restaurant serves Sicilian classics and seafood beneath a beautiful wooden ceiling.

Via Vittorio Veneto 93. www.algila.it. ✆ **0931/465-186.** 30 units. 175€–300€ double. Rates include breakfast. Closed mid-Jan to late Feb. **Amenities:** Restaurant; room service; free Wi-Fi.

Henry's House ★★★ The namesake Henry, a now-departed friend of the owners, could not have a nicer legacy than this distinctive seaside palazzo at the southern edge of Ortigia. Several terraces, including a few private spaces off some rooms, look over the sea, while salons filled with antiques and artifacts are homily atmospheric. Guest quarters set on several floors have beams, tile floors, and character-filled furnishings that further enhance the sense that you're staying with a cultured Sicilian uncle.

Via del Castello Maniace 68. www.hotelhenryshouse.com. ✆ **0931/21361.** 14 units. 200€–230€. Rates include breakfast. Closed Jan–Feb. **Amenities:** Bar; room service; free Wi-Fi.

Staying at Henry's House is like visiting a Sicilian uncle's seaside palazzo.

MODERATE

Approdo delle Sirene ★★ This bright, stylish little inn occupies two floors of a seaside apartment house, beautifully refashioned as light-filled quarters with a slightly nautical flair, as befits the sparkling blue water just beyond the tall windows. In the contemporary guest rooms, polished wood floors offset handsome furnishings, striped fabrics, and bold colors. Several rooms have French doors opening to small balconies, though some rooms are sky-lit only—flooded with light but without views. The sunny breakfast room/lounge and terrace provide plenty of panoramas, however. The hosts, mother Fiora and son Friedrich, are a hospitable on-the-scene presence and can arrange all kinds of tours and excursions. Free bikes are available for guests' use.

Riva Garibaldi 15. www.apprododellesirene.com. ✆ **0931/24857.** 8 units. 100€–140€ double. 2-night min. stay required at some times. Rates include breakfast. Closed Jan–Feb. **Amenities:** Bikes; free Wi-Fi.

Domus Mariae Benessere Guest House ★★ The Ursiline sisters who still occupy a wing of this seaside convent have found their calling as innkeepers. The large, bright rooms border on vaguely luxurious, with plush headboards on extremely comfortable beds, attractive rugs on tile floors, and lots of counter and storage space in the large bathrooms. Some rooms have sea views, while others face an atrium-like courtyard. Surprising indulgences, given the surroundings, include a lovely roof terrace and a lower-level spa, with a small pool and Jacuzzi. An in-house restaurant serves a rather monastic buffet breakfast as well as a well-prepared dinner of healthful Mediterranean fare.

Via Veneto 89. www.domusmariaebenessere.com. ✆ **0931/60087.** 21 units. 110€–150€ double. Rates include breakfast. Closed Jan–Feb. **Amenities:** Bikes; pool; spa; free Wi-Fi.

INEXPENSIVE

Apollo Suite ★★★ At this extremely attractive guesthouse on the upper floor of an old apartment house (reached by an elevator), the large, high-ceilinged, light-filled rooms open to small balconies, most of them overlooking the ruins of the temple of Apollo. Stylish furnishings include comfortable beds, and bathrooms are very well done with large showers. Friendly service extends to a small but ample breakfast of pastries, eggs, and fruit, accompanied by fresh-squeezed orange juice.

Via Salvatore Chindemi 7. www.apollosuiteortigia.it. ✆ **0347/665-4399.** 6 units. 60€–110 double. Rates include breakfast. **Amenities:** Free Wi-Fi.

Hotel Gutkowski ★★ Two old houses facing the sea at the edge of Ortigia are warm and hospitable, and capture the essence of southern Italy: Sicilian hues on the walls, colorful floor tiles, and views of the blue water or sun-baked roofs of the old city. Each room is different, some with balconies, some with terraces; furnishings are functional but chosen to provide restful simplicity, with old Sicilian and vintage midcentury pieces offset by contemporary tables and bedsteads. A rooftop terrace becomes an outdoor living room for much of the year, and the bar serves regional wines and one or two well-prepared dishes in the evenings.

Lungomare Vittorini 26. www.guthotel.it. ✆ **0931/465861.** 25 units. 90€–110€ double. Most rates include breakfast. 2-night (or more) minimum stay required at some times. Closed Jan–Feb. **Amenities:** Bar; restaurant; free Wi-Fi.

Where to Eat in Siracusa

Caseificio Borderi, tucked in among piles of fresh fish in Ortigia's morning market at 6 Via die Benedictis (www.caseificioborderi.eu; ✆ **329/985-2500**), is a required stop on the food circuit for its huge selection of house-made cheeses, cured meats, olives, and wine. The staff hands out samples and makes delicious sandwiches (4€), paired with excellent wines by the glass; it's open Monday through Saturday 7am to 4pm. Another market stop is **Fratelli Burgio,** Piazza Cesare Battista 4 (www.fratelliburgio.com; ✆ **0931/60069**), where a *tagliere* (platter of cheeses and other antipasti) is a meal in itself; it's open Monday through Friday 7am to 9pm and Saturday 7am to 3:30pm.

Apollonion Osteria da Carlo ★★★ SEAFOOD Though the bustling rooms are on an inland street, the emphasis is on the bounty of the sea: Huge platters of fish *capriccio,* orecchiette topped with shrimp and other sea creatures, many kinds of fish fried, baked, and grilled—all fresh from boats docked nearby and deftly prepared. Meals are served in a six-course set menu that includes at least one pasta and many variations of seafood, accompanied by house wine or another beverage.

Via Carmelo Campisi 18. www.facebook.com/osteriapollonion. ✆ **0931/483362.** Set menu from 35€. Mon–Sat 12:30–2:30pm and 6:30–10:30pm. Closed Feb–early Mar.

Darsena da Ianuzzo ★★ SEAFOOD "Darsena" means dock, and the town piers line the harbor just across the street from this brightly lit room with a terrace out front. Several generations of Siracusans have counted on Darsena for the freshest fish in town, displayed on ice in cases near the entrance. A waiter will bring some of the just-caught offerings around for your inspection, then take it back to the kitchen to be grilled or roasted to your preference. *Riccio,* sea urchin, and other local specialties are served raw and in a long, long list of deftly prepared seafood pastas.

Riva Giuseppe Garibaldi. ✆ **0331/342-2000.** Entrees 11€–22€. Wed–Mon 12:30–3:30pm and 7:30–11pm.

Don Camillo ★★★ SIRACUSAN/SEAFOOD A longtime Siracusa favorite sports lots of polished antiques offsetting handsomely tiled floors, rows of wines, and vintage photos of Ortigia. House specialties, like spaghetti *delle Sirene* (with sea urchin and shrimp in butter) and *tagliata al tonno* (with sliced tuna), have drawn regulars for years; on weekend evenings the vaulted medieval rooms fill with Siracusan families out for a special meal.

Via Maestranza 96. www.ristorantedoncamillosiracusa.it. ✆ **0931/67133.** Entrees 20€–35€. Tasting menus 75€–100€. Wed–Mon 12:30–3:30pm and 7:30–11pm.

L'Osteria da Seby ★ SIRACUSAN/SEAFOOD Oil paintings, linen tablecloths, and exposed stone create a setting that is warm and inviting, making this friendly place a favorite of guests from hotels on the nearby waterfront. The straightforward *osteria* fare includes seafood pastas and risottos, mixed grills, and well-done standards such as scallopini in lemon sauce.

Via Mirabella 21. www.losteriadaseby.it. ✆ **0931/181-5619.** Entrees 9€–18€. Tues–Sun noon–3pm and 7pm–midnight.

Taberna Sveva ★★ SIRACUSAN/SEAFOOD Escape the urban buzz with a walk out toward the Castello Maniace at the tip of Ortigia, where a breeze-cooled terrace facing a cobbled square is the perfect setting for a summer meal of classic vegetable and seafood pastas and fresh fish. In cooler weather, the hospitality retreats to a simple rich-hued room that sets the stage for perfectly grilled steaks. Indoors or out, land-based or from the sea, meals are served at rough-hewn tables on hand-painted ceramics, just the right homey touch to the honest cooking.

Piazza Federico di Svevia. ✆ **0931/24663.** Entrees 8€–15€. Daily noon–2:30pm and 7–10:30pm.

Beaches Near Siracusa

Some of the best, most unspoiled shoreline in all of Italy is on Sicily's southeastern coast, but you don't even have to leave Ortigia to get into the water: From July into September, the city maintains wooden swimming platforms near the Fonte Aretusa and off the rocks on the east side of the island. **Fontane Bianche** is the closest beach to Siracusa, 15 minutes away by car or frequent train service. It's an almost-square bay with laid-back beach clubs and luxurious deep sand. **Lido di Noto,** 15 minutes from the baroque hill town of Noto (see p. 792), is a lively beach strip with great waterfront restaurants. Half the beach is private beach clubs (where you pay around 10€ for day use of a lounge chair, umbrella, and shower facilities), and half is free public access.

Between Noto and Pachino, the beautiful **Vendicari Nature Reserve,** 11km (7 miles) south of Noto on SP19, is set amid acres of fragrant citrus groves growing behind beaches backed by wetlands, a refuge for exotic migratory birds. Vendicari's most popular beach is **Calamosche,** on an intimate cove framed by rock cliffs and sea caves; from the Calamosche parking area it's about a 15-minute walk along a path to the beach.

Isola delle Correnti ★★, a little over an hour south of Siracusa at Sicily's southeastern tip, is one of the best beaches on the island, though it's a bit windier and wave-swept than the other spots. On a clear day, you can see Malta, just 100km (60 miles) to the south.

Side Trip to Noto ★★

31km (19 miles) SW of Siracusa

Dubbed the "Stone Garden" for its sheer beauty, this little town is like a baroque stage set, with rich-looking buildings of golden stone lining its main street, Corso Vittorio Emanuele. Noto sits on a high plateau surrounded by olive groves and almond trees, and the town heights provide splendid vistas of the Asinaro Valley.

ESSENTIALS

ARRIVING Take the A18 south from Siracusa for 27km (17 miles), then exit and head north up a hill, following blue signs toward Noto. Near town, follow yellow signs to Noto's *centro storico* (brown Noto Antica signs lead to the ruins of the old city, outside town.) It's about a 35-minute drive. Trains run throughout the day from Siracusa, a 35-minute trip, though the station is about a 15-minute walk outside the center. You can also reach Noto from Siracusa by **AST** bus (www.aziendasiciliana trasporti.it; ✆ **0932/681-818**); about 10 buses per day make the 80-minute trip from Siracusa train station, arriving at the edge of the *centro storico.*

VISITOR INFORMATION The **tourist office,** Via Gioberti 13 (✆ **0931/836503**), is open May to September daily 9am to 1pm and 3:30 to 6:30pm; and October to April Monday to Friday 8am to 2pm and 3:30 to 6:30pm.

Built in the early 18th century, Noto is a dazzling set piece of baroque architecture.

EXPLORING NOTO

This hill town on the flanks of Mount Alviria was a flourishing place in the late 17th century, having outgrown its medieval core and expanded into streets lined with palaces and convents. On January 11, 1693, all came tumbling down when the strongest earthquake in Italian history leveled Noto and much of southeastern Sicily. The ruins of that old city can be seen at the **Noto Antica** archaeological site outside town.

The good to come out of such a devastating tragedy is that Noto was rebuilt—not on the same site but on the banks of the River Asinaro, and not haphazardly but in splendid, unified baroque style. Noto is a stage set of honey-colored limestone, with curved facades, curling staircases, and wrought-iron balconies. You will be surrounded by this theatricality on a walk down **Corso Vittorio Emanuele;** things hit an architectural high note on a side street, **Via Nicolaci,** with the beautiful elliptical facade of the **Chiesa di Montevirgine** and playful **Palazzo Villadorata,** where expressive maidens, dwarves, lions, and horses support the balconies.

Almost as stunning as Noto's baroque architecture are the creations at richly atmospheric, old-fashioned **Caffe Sicilia,** Corso Vittorio Emanuele 125, purveyor of Sicily's best granita and gelato (✆ **0931/835013**).

Side Trip to Ragusa ★★★

79km (49 miles) SW of Siracusa

Like Noto (see above), Ragusa was all but obliterated by the powerful earthquake of 1693, and also like Noto, was rebuilt as a planned city in exuberant baroque style. In Ragusa, however, most of the wary residents decided instead to relocate to an adjacent ridge, separated by a deep ravine, the Valle dei Ponti. Today, Ragusa Superiore is the modern center of the sprawling, bifurcated town, while baroque Ragusa Ibla is a place to wander on quiet lanes and through big piazzas overlooked by flamboyant 18th-century churches. Some topnotch dining and lodging options (see below) make Ragusa worth more than a hurried day trip.

ESSENTIALS

ARRIVING Three **trains** a day make the 2-hour trip to Ragusa from Siracusa, and **AST buses** (www.aziendasicilianatrasporti.it; ✆ **091/620-8111**) make the 3-hour run seven times daily. The train and bus stations are in Ragusa Superiore on Piazza del Popolo and adjoining Piazza Gramsci.

By **car** from Siracusa, the quickest route takes you through Noto (p. 792) then southwest along Route 115 to the town of Ispica, at which point the highway swings northwest toward Ragusa. Parking lots ring the old town and include a handy one outside the Giardino Ibleo.

VISITOR INFORMATION Ragusa has two **tourist offices** (www.comune.ragusa.it), one on Piazza San Giovanni in Ragusa Superiore (✆ **0932/676550**), the other in Ragusa Ibia on Piazza Repubblica (✆ **366/874621**); both are open Monday through Friday 9am to 7pm.

Hilltop Ragusa Ibla is like a symphony in ochre-colored stone.

EXPLORING RAGUSA IBLA

The most scenic way to reach historic Ragusa Ibla from modern Ragusa Superiore is by taking the 242 steps of the Salita Commendatore down the hillside. (Otherwise, take city bus no. 3 from Piazza del Popolo.) You can take a breather along the way on a landing in front of **Santa Maria delle Scale** (St. Mary of the Steps), enjoying views of the ochre-colored houses of Ragusa Ibla spreading out at your feet. The path eventually winds down and around to **Piazza del Duomo,** where a dramatically curved staircase leads to the sumptuous facade of **Cattedrale di San Giorgio ★★** (✆ **0932/220085;** daily 10am–12:30pm [Tues until 1pm] and 4 to 6:30pm). The three tiers of columns and balconies are the piéce de résistance of architect Rosario Gagliardi, master of the Sicilian baroque. Gagliardi's second-best work is just east, **Chiesa di San Giuseppe ★**, Via Torre Nuova 19 (✆ **0932/621-779;** daily 12:30–2:30pm and 7:30–9:30pm), with its tall, three-tiered facade embellished with columns and statues of saints. Inside, above a striking floor of black asphalt interspersed with majolica tiles, is one of Ragusa's most beloved paintings, an altarpiece of the Holy Family—see how Mary holds cherries in her apron, offering them to passersby.

Just down the street are Ragusa's beautiful public gardens, **Giardino Ibleo ★★**. The long avenues lined with palms are idyllic places to stroll, with stone benches tucked into shady alcoves. At the edge of the gardens, a terrace opens to views across the Valley of Irminio. The gardens are free and open daily 8am to 8pm.

EXPLORING MARINA DI RAGUSA ★

Ragusa's seaside getaway, 25km (15 miles) southwest, is a pleasant collection of houses facing a sandy beach and marina. Smaller, quieter, and more famous these days is adjacent **Punta Secca,** fictional home to Inspector Montalbano of the popular Italian TV series; fans will recognize his house near the lighthouse. The series is also filmed on location in Ragusa, Modica, Scicli, and other towns in this corner of the southeast.

WHERE TO STAY & EAT IN RAGUSA

Ragusa Ibla is where you will want to stay and probably eat, and options are improving all the time. A sign of a new wave of gentrification sweeping over town is **I Banchi,** Via Orfanotrofio 39, a stylish bakery, food shop, wine bar, and casual eatery that would seem trendy even in Rome (www.ibanchiragusa.it; ✆ **0932/655-000;** daily 10am–2:30pm and 6–11pm; closed Jan and Feb).

Ciccio Sultano Duomo ★★★ NEW SICILIAN/SEAFOOD At this famed spot, the creation of Chef Ciccio Sultano, parlorlike dining rooms, all dark polished wood and red velvet, suggest an extravagant experience, and nothing that emerges from the kitchen dispels that notion. Regional ingredients and age-old Sicilian traditions form the foundation for dishes that combine homemade pastas, local seafood, and fresh garden produce in remarkably innovative ways, such as a *cannolo* of crème fraîche, raw shrimp, and caviar, or in relatively down-to-earth preparations, like fresh pasta with *bottarga* (fish roe). Leave frugality at the door: The best way to indulge in the extravagance is with one of the tasting menus. Reserve well in advance.

Via Capitano Bocchieri 31, Ibla. ✆ **0932/651-265.** Entrees 40€–60€; tasting menus 80€–200€. Tues–Sat 12:30–2pm and 7:30–10:30pm (daily in Aug). Closed Jan–Feb.

Hotel Antico Convento ★★ The Capuchin monks who settled this convent in the 16th century had a good eye for location, at the edge of town atop the Irminio valley, and the setting was later enhanced even more with the addition of the town's beautiful public gardens, the Giardino Ibleo, which now surround the stone walls. The small monks' cells, converted to guest rooms, remain simple though not austere, with bright stone floors and handsome wooden built-ins; they overlook a peaceful cloister, the gardens, or the valley below. A bar/restaurant spills into the cloister in warmer months.

Giardino Ibleo. Via Margherita 41. www.anticoconventoibla.it. ✆ **347/147-2915.** 24 units. 90€–115€. Rates include breakfast. **Amenities:** Restaurant; bar; free Wi-Fi.

La Bettola ★★ SICILIAN The 1940s-era decor suggests simpler times, and Sicilian classic dishes keep that throwback ambience going strong, arriving at tables bedecked with red-checked tablecloths in the homey dining room and large front terrace. Daily offerings are listed on a chalkboard: house-made caponata, octopus salad, platters of spaghetti *alla Norma,* or simple grilled pork cutlets topped with fresh herbs.

Largo Camerina 7. www.trattorialabettola.it. ✆ **0932/081189.** Entrees 9€–15€. Wed–Sun 12:30–2:30pm and 7:30–11pm; Tues 7:30–11pm.

Locanda Don Serafino ★★ Accommodations in two medieval *palazzi* on a narrow lane above Piazza Duomo are reached by a gloriously primitive rock-hewn staircase, and the wonderful quirks continue from there, in poshly outfitted cave rooms and dramatic two-floor vaulted suites. For many guests, the character-filled surroundings amply compensate for the lack of spa and other luxe amenities, even an elevator. Many come to enjoy dining in the locanda's offsite **restaurant** (on Via Avvocato Giovanni Ottaviano), serving memorable meals in a strikingly decorated maze of stone-vaulted rooms and caves at the edge of town (entrees 30€–45€, set menus 130€–165€; ✆ **0932/248778;** Wed–Mon 12:45–2:30pm and 7:45–10:30pm, Tues 7:45–10:30pm; also 1–2:30pm mid-Aug to mid-Sept). The food is innovative yet down-to-earth, relying on a bounty of fresh local ingredients that come to the fore in such signature dishes as *zuppa di pesce don Serafino* (a rich fish soup). The adjoining guest accommodations are the hotel's splashiest, with private gardens and plunge pools.

Via Via XI Febbraio 15. www.locandadonserafino.it. ✆ **0932/22006.** 11 units. 110€–165€ double. Rates include breakfast. Closed early Feb–early Mar. **Amenities:** Restaurant; free Wi-Fi.

Modica: A Sweet Stop in the Southeast

Chocoholics and other sweet-tooths should head to nearby **Modica,** 35km (21 miles) west of Noto, 16km (20 miles) south of Ragusa, noted as much for its chocolatiers as for its baroque architecture. The chocolate here is grainy, made straight from cocoa beans, and is often flavored with vanilla, cinnamon, and pepperoncino. Local Katia Amore teaches chocolate-making techniques, as well as other Sicilian cookery, in **Love Sicily** sessions in her grandmother's kitchen overlooking the town's domes (lovesicily.com; from 85€). You may also taste the local product at nearby **Antica Dolceria Bonajuto,** Corso Umberto I 159, Sicily's oldest chocolate maker (www.bonajuto.it; ✆ **0932/941225**).

PIAZZA ARMERINA ★★★

134km (83 miles) NW of Siracusa, 158km (98 miles) SE of Palermo

Travelers make a big effort to get to this dusty, sunbaked hill town in the center of Sicily, and you should, too. Here is the world's richest collection of Roman mosaics, in a near-miraculous state of preservation, at the **Villa del Casale,** in the countryside 5km (3 miles) outside of town. Piazza Armerina itself is a friendly, handsome, hilly town, well worth walking around from the hilltop Duomo through the 13th-century center. If you're arriving from the southeast, a worthy stop is **Calatarigione,** 30km (18 miles) southeast of Piazza Armerina, famous for its ceramics; check out the 142 steps of the Scalinata di Santa Maria del Monte, all colorfully tiled.

Intricate mosaics at the Villa Romana del Casale in Piazza Armerina.

Essentials

ARRIVING From Taormina, Siracusa, or anywhere in the east, take the A19 west from Catania, exit at Dittaino, and head south following blue signs for Piazza Armerina. From Palermo, take the A19 east and south, exit at Caltanissetta, then immediately look for signs for Piazza Armerina. (The route is SS626 south to SS122 east to SS117bis.) You can reach Piazza Armerina from Palermo (a 2-hr. trip) via **SAIS bus** (www.saisautolinee.it; ✆ **091/616-6026;** five buses a day, three on weekends); coming from Siracusa or other east coast towns, your best bet is to take a bus to Enna and switch there for Piazza Armerina (40 min.; eight buses a day). Once in Piazza Armerina, take local bus B to the site (15 min.; runs daily 9am–noon and 3–6pm); taxis also eagerly await visitors.

Exploring Villa Romana del Casale

Built between 310 and 340, this enormous villa of a rich and powerful landowner was the center of a vast agricultural estate. The villa was almost completely covered by a landslide in the 12th century, but this natural disaster turned out to be a blessing, because the mud preserved almost 38,000 square feet of mosaic flooring. Rediscovered in the 19th century, the villa was excavated and restored starting in the early 20th century.

The place must have been magnificent, more a palace than a mere villa, with 40 rooms, many of them clad in marble, frescoed, and equipped with fountains and pools. Heating the villa were *terme,* or steam baths (rooms 1–7), with steam circulating through cavities in the floors and walls. The ostentation reached its zenith with mosaics of mythology, flora and fauna, and domestic scenes carpeting most of the floors. Given the style and craftsmanship, these were likely the work of North African master artists.

The 40 rooms are arranged around a garden courtyard, or peristyle. Take time as you wander through the rooms on elevated walkways to enjoy the mosaics, noticing the expressions, colors, and playfulness of the scenes. Remember, they were intended to delight visitors, and they are still entertaining, like a film in glorious Technicolor. Of special note:

Peristyle (room 13): A bestiary of birds, plants, wild animals, and more domesticated creatures, such as horses.

Palestra (Exercise Area, room 15): Mosaics depict a chariot race at Rome's Circus Maximus.

Sala degli Eroti Pescatori ★ (Room of the Fishing Cupids, room 24): In what was probably a bedroom, one could drift off to a scene of four boatloads of winged cupids harpooning, netting, and trapping various fish and sea creatures.

Sala della Piccola Caccia (Room of the Small Hunt, room 25): Hunters in togas pursue deer, wild boar, birds, and other small game as Diana, goddess of the hunt, looks on.

Corridoio della Grande Caccia ★★★ (Corridor of the Great Hunt, room 28): Men capture panthers, leopards, and other exotic animals, loading them onto wagons for transport, and finally onto a ship bound for Rome, where they will be part of the games in the Colosseum.

Vestibolo di Ulisse e Polifemo (Vestibule of Ulysses and Polyphemus, room 47): The Homeric hero proffers a *krater* of wine to the Cyclops (here with three eyes instead of one, and a disemboweled ram draped casually over his lap) in hopes of getting him drunk.

Cubicolo con Scena Erotica (Bedroom with Erotic Scene, room 46): a seductress with a side gaze and a nicely contoured rear end embraces a young man.

Sala delle Palestrite (Room of the Gym Girls, room 30): Girls engaged in various exercises—curling dumbbells, tossing a ball, running—are dressed in skimpy strapless bikinis that would fit right in on any 21st-century beach. Ancient literary sources suggest that these were standard workout apparel 1,700 years ago—the bandeau top was called the *strophium,* and the bikini bottom the *subligar.*

Triclinium (room 33): In a large dining room is a magnificent rendition of the Labors of Hercules. In the central apse, mosaics depict the Gigantomachy (Battle of the Giants), in which five mammoth creatures are in their death throes after being pierced by Hercules' poison arrows.

Villa Romana, Strada Provinciale 15. www.villaromanadelcasale.it. ✆ **0935/680036.** 10€. Daily 9am–7pm.

AGRIGENTO & THE VALLEY OF THE TEMPLES ★★★

129km (80 miles) SE of Palermo, 208km (125 miles) W of Siracusa

The evocative skeletons of seven temples of honey-colored stone, arranged on a long ridge with commanding views of the sea, comprise one of the most memorable sights of the ancient world—the embodiment of classical dignity. Colonists from Crete or Rhodes established Akragas in the 7th century B.C., and by the 5th century B.C. the city was one of the great Mediterranean powers, with close to 200,000 residents. The Greek poet Pindar described Akragas as the most beautiful city "inhabited by mortals" but commented that its citizens "feasted as if there were no tomorrow." The city poured part of its enormous wealth into temples erected along a ridge overlooking the sea, their bright pediments becoming well-known landmarks along southern sea routes. Carthage and Rome fought over the city for centuries until Akragas became part of the Roman Empire in 210 B.C. Tumbled by earthquakes, plundered for marble, and overgrown from neglect, today the temples are proud remnants of ancient grandeur.

The Tempio della Concordia, Valley of the Temples, Agrigento.

Essentials

ARRIVING Agrigento is about 2½ hours by **car** from either Palermo or Siracusa. From Palermo, cut southeast on the SS121, which becomes SS189 before it reaches Agrigento. From Siracusa, take the A18 *autostrada* north to Catania and the A19 west toward Enna; just past Enna, exit the A19 and follow signs south through Caltanissetta and down to Agrigento. (The "coastal route" from Siracusa—taking the SS115 all the way—may look more direct on the map but is much more time-consuming, up to 5 hours on an often very curvy two-lane road.) **Parking** is below the temples, near the entrances to the western section (Zeus) and eastern section (Collina dei Templi). A well-marked path leads along the ridge past the temples. A shuttle bus (3€ each way) connects the parking areas with the top of the site, though the walk is not terribly strenuous.

Bus connections between Palermo and Agrigento are fairly convenient: **Cuffaro** (www.cuffaro.info; ✆ **0922/403-150**) runs nine buses per day and drops you right in front of the entrance to the archaeological site; the 2-hour trip costs about 11€ one-way, 17€ round-trip. There's also bus service from Siracusa, but it's at least 4 hours each way.

A **train** from Palermo takes 2 hours; there are 12 trains daily. From Siracusa, trains take 6 hours, with a change in Catania. For information, visit www.trenitalia.it or call ✆ **89/2021.** Agrigento's rail station, **Stazione Centrale,** is at Piazza Marconi; from there, take a cab or local bus (lines 1, 2, or 3) to the temples, 10 minutes away.

VISITOR INFORMATION Ticket offices at the site can provide any info you need on transport and other matters.

Exploring the Ruins

As you enter the valley surrounded by hills planted with olive and almond trees, you'll see that "valley of the temples" is a misnomer, as the temples are perched along a ridge. The park is divided into eastern and western zones, with entrances at each.

Parco Valle dei Templi ★★★ RUINS In the eastern zone are Agrigento's three best-preserved temples. The **Tempio di Ercole** (Temple of Hercules) is the oldest, dating from the 6th century B.C. At one time the temple sheltered a celebrated statue of Hercules, long since plundered. Eight of 36 columns have been resurrected, while the others lie rather romantically scattered in the tall grass and wildflowers; they still bear black sears from fires set by Carthaginian invaders. The **Tempio della Concordia** (Temple of Concord), surrounded by 34 columns, has survived almost intact since its completion in 430 B.C. It was shored up as a Christian basilica in the 6th century, so was never plundered, and its foundations rest upon soft soil that absorbs the shock of earthquakes. The **Temple of Juno,** which had no such structural resiliency, was partly destroyed in an earthquake, though 30 columns and sections of the colonnade have been restored. A long altar was used for wedding ceremonies and sacrificial offerings.

The western zone would have been the setting of the largest temple in the Greek world, if the **Tempio di Giove** (Temple of Jove/Zeus) had ever been completed—and if what was built had not been toppled in earthquakes. A copy of an 8m-tall (26-ft.) telamon (sculpted figure of a man with arms raised) lies on its back amid the rubble; the original is the pride of the site's Museo Archeologico. Several such figures were used as columnlike supports on the temple. The nearby **Tempio di Castore e Polluce** (Temple of Castor and Pollux, also called Tempio di Dioscuri), with four Doric columns intact, honors Castor and Pollux, the twins who were patrons of seafarers; Demeter, goddess of marriage and the fertile earth; and Persephone, the daughter of Zeus and the symbol of spring.

For more detailed explanations, in both Italian and English, of the many artifacts unearthed here, stop by the **Museo Archeologico** (Via dei Templi; ✆ **0922/40111;** Mon 9am–1:30pm, Tues–Sat 9am–7:30pm), between the ruins and Agrigento town. However, after a long and dusty outing at the ruins, this isn't a mandatory stop.

Parco Valle dei Templi. www.parcovalledeitempli.it. ✆ **0922/621-611.** 10€ temples only; 13.50€ combined ticket with museum. Daily 8:30am–8pm; mid-July to mid-Sept also Mon–Fri 7–10pm and Sat–Sun 7pm–midnight. You can purchase timed-entry tickets online in advance.

Where to Stay & Eat in Agrigento

Hotel Villa Athena ★★ An 18th-century villa set in gardens within the Valley of the Temples might be the best-located hotel in all of Italy. Looking at the Temple of Concord illuminated at night is one of Sicily's great travel experiences and can be enjoyed from the balconies and even the beds of many of the rooms, done with smart traditional furnishings and handsome fabrics. The beautiful garden, surrounding a pool, is also a prime spot to enjoy the view while enjoying a glass of wine.

Via Passeggiata Archeologica 33. www.hotelvillaathena.it. ✆ **0922/596-288.** 27 units. 200€–600€ double. Rates include breakfast. Bus: 2. **Amenities:** Dining room; 2 bars; outdoor pool; room service; free Wi-Fi.

L'Ambasciata di Sicilia ★★ SICILIAN One of the few reasons to venture into modern Agrigento is a chance to enjoy a hearty meal at this old-fashioned favorite, a city institution since 1919. True to its name, the kitchen makes a point of being a Sicilian ambassador, introducing diners to the island's finest cuisine, with delicious preparations of fresh fish, along with *linguine al'Ambasciata* (prepared with meat sauce, bacon, calamari, and zucchini). Meals are served in a small dining room crammed to the ceiling with marionettes and other colorful artifacts; a breezy terrace overlooks the surrounding rooftops.

Via Gianbertoni 2, off Via Atenea. www.facebook.com/people/Osteria-LAmbasciata-di-Sicilia/100065089114989. ✆ **0392/976-7278.** Entrees 7€–12€. Wed–Mon noon–3pm and 7–10pm. Closed 2 weeks Nov.

SICILY'S WEST COAST ★★

The coast between Trapani and Marsala, both storied port towns, is lined with dazzling white salt pans, protected as a nature reserve and populated by migratory birds. A winding uphill half-hour drive (or a funicular ride from Trapani), will take you to medieval, mountaintop Erice. At the southern end of the coast is the vast archaeological park of Selinunte, littered with Greek temples and other evocative ruins, while to the north are the beautiful headlands and beaches around San Vito Lo Capo.

Arriving

BY PLANE **Vincenzo Florio Airport (TPS)** at Birgi, 15km (9 miles) from the center of Trapani (www.airgest.it; ✆ **0923/610-111**), is the island's third-largest airport and the main Ryanair hub for Sicily from the U.K. From here, **AST** buses (www.aziendasicilianatrasporti.it; ✆ **091/620-8111**) run hourly into Trapani (fare 3€).

BY CAR From Palermo, the A29 autostrada is the fastest route southwest into Trapani, about a 1½-hour drive. Marsala is another 45 minutes south on Route 115; the drive from Trapani up to Erice takes about half an hour. Selinunte is a 2-hour drive from Palermo via A29 and E90 (exit at Castelvetrano); the drive between Trapani and Selinunte takes a little over an hour.

BY BUS AND TRAIN The train journey from Palermo to Trapani takes as long as 4½ hours, usually with a change, and it's another 30 minutes on to Marsala, so the bus to either is a much better option. From Palermo, **Salemi** (www.autoservizisalemi.it; ✆ **0923/981120**) runs long-distance bus service to Trapani airport (1½ hr.), Marsala (2½ hours), and Selinunte (1¾ hr.; change buses at Castelvetrano for another 20-min. trip to ruins). **Segesta Autolinee** (www.segesta.it; ✆ **06/164160**) operates hourly buses between Palermo and Trapani (70 min.). **AST** buses (www.aziendasiciliana trasporti.it; ✆ **0921/620-8111**) run between Marsala and Trapani (Piazza Montalto) four times a day, a 35-minute journey; they also go from Trapani's Piazza Montalto to historic Erice (daily 6:40am–7:30pm), a winding, uphill 50-minute trip, and to San Vito Lo Capo, with as many as eight buses a day making the 80-minute trip. One convenient **train** route in the region runs hourly between Trapani and Marsala (www.trenitalia.it; ✆ **89/2021**), a 30-minute trip.

BY BOAT Trapani is a major embarkation point for **ferries** and **hydrofoils.** Most depart for the Egadi Islands of Marettimo, Levanzo, and Favignana. Service is also available to the islands of Ustica and Pantelleria and to the mainland ports of Civitavecchia near Rome and Tunisia in North Africa. Ferries depart from the docks near Piazza Garibaldi. Service is offered by **Liberty Lines** (www.libertylines.it; ✆ **0923/022022**) or **Grimaldi** (www.grimaldi-lines.com; ✆ **081/496444**).

Trapani ★★

100km (62 miles) SW of Palermo, 14km (9 miles) SW of Erice, 31km (19 miles) N of Marsala

Wedged between two especially scenic stretches of shoreline, Trapani spreads along the coastal plain below Mount Erice. The historic center, on a sea-girt promontory, is an atmospheric maze of gridlike medieval streets and squares. To the northeast is the dramatic headland at San Vito Lo Capo, with fine beaches and the Zingaro nature reserve. Stretching south of Trapani are coastal salt pans that have been harvested since antiquity.

VISITOR INFORMATION **Trapani Infopoints,** at Via Torrearsa 69 (www.trapanistruzioniperluso.com; ✆ **0923/031701**) and Piazza Garibaldi 120 (✆ **0923/24459**), provide maps and info on exploring Trapani and other places on the west coast; they're open daily 8am to 7pm.

EXPLORING TRAPANI

The old town extends westward out to sea, with a North African feel to the labyrinth of narrow streets that wind toward the **Torre di Ligny,** a watchtower built in 1671 on the tip of the peninsula. Many elegant baroque buildings line **Corso Vittorio Emanuele,** sometimes called Rua Grande, as it extends west from the **Palazzo Senatorio,** the 17th-century pink-marble town hall. Adjacent 18th-century **Via Garibaldi** (also known as

Trapani's main street, Corso Vittorio Emanuele, and Palazzo Senatorio.

Rua Nova, or "New Road") is flanked by palaces and churches. One of them, the 17th-century baroque **Chiesa del Purgatorio,** houses the single greatest treasure in Trapani: The ***Misteri,*** 20 life-size wooden figures from the 18th century depicting Christ's Passion. Every year they are carried through town for Good Friday's **Processione dei Misteri** (Procession of the Mysteries). The church is officially open daily 8:30am to 12:30pm and 4 to 8pm but is often closed. **Via Torrearsa** leads down to a bustling *pescheria* (fish market) where tuna is traded; the valuable commodity is caught in nearby waters and traded with buyers from as far off as Japan. **Villa Margherita,** public gardens stretching between old and new Trapani, is an inviting oasis with fountains, banyan trees, and palms rustling in the sea breeze.

Santuario dell'Annunziata/Museo Regionale Agostino Pepoli ★
CHURCH/MUSEUM The cloisters of a 14th-century convent, about 2km (a mile or so) outside the center on the eastern edge of town, enclose a collection of archaeological finds and art, much of it salvaged by a local aristocrat, Count Pepoli. With his fine eye, the count found the best examples of coral carving, a popular Trapani tradition that local craftspeople pursued up until the early 20th century, when nearby coral beds were depleted. Many of the works, in which coral is often intermingled with silver filigree, are by local artisans Andrea and Alberto Tipa. Among their creations is a spectacularly elaborate *presepe* (nativity scene). Before leaving the premises, step into the convent's **Cappella della Madonna** to see a graceful, sculpted scene of the Virgin and Child, attributed to the 14th-century Tuscan master Nino Pisano.

Via Conte Agostino Pepoli 200. ✆ **0923/553269.** 6€. Tues–Sat 9am–6pm; Sun 9am–1pm. Bus: 224, 225, or 230 from Piazza Vittorio Emanuele.

Erice ★★★

96km (60 miles) SW of Palermo, 14km (9 miles) NE of Trapani, 45km (28 miles) NW of Marsala

Medieval Erice, high atop Mount Erice (743m/2,438 ft.), is all about views. On a clear summer's day, you can see west to the Egadi Islands, east to Mount Etna, and south to Africa, but the town puts on a good show even in the mists and fogs that frequently roll in, with towers and craggy rocks poking through a hazy blanket of gray. Erice is an atmospheric place, where you'll stop to admire an arch, a door, or a bell tower as you wander its steep cobblestone streets, flanked by churches and stone houses with elaborate baroque balconies packed with cascading geraniums. The city is famous throughout Sicily for its pastries, so be sure to sample such delights as tangy *dolci di badia* cakes, made from almond paste and citron juice.

From Trapani, you can either take an AST bus (see p. 802) or choose a more adventurous option: the ***funivia*** (cableway; www.funiviaerice.it; ✆ **0923/560023**). From the station on Via Capua at the eastern edge of

Approaching Erice's 12th-century Castle of Venus.

Trapani, cable cars whisk you up to Erice in about 12 view-filled minutes at a cost of 9.50€ round-trip, 6€ one way (wheelchair accessibility available). To get to the funicular, take **ATM Trapani** bus no. 201 or 203 from Trapani's Piazza Garibaldi, leaving half-hourly (www.atmtrapani.it; ✆ **0923/559575;** fare 1.20€). ***Note:*** The cableway closes Monday mornings for general maintenance, does not operate in inclement weather, and often isn't running when you want it to be; check before going, but generally the service operates Monday 1pm to 8pm, Tuesday to Sunday 8:30am to 8pm, and Saturday and Sunday 9:30am to 8:30; from mid-July to early September, the cableway operates until 1am, 1:30am on weekends, and until 11pm on weekdays and midnight on weekends the rest of September.

EXPLORING ERICE

Whether you come up to Erice by road or cable car, you will arrive at **Porta Trapani,** one of the city's three entrance gates (the other two are Porta Spada and Porta Spagnola, farther north). The 12th-century Porta Trapani is imbedded in the Elymian-Punic walls, an extensive defense barrier laid out by the Elymians (the ancient inhabitants of western Sicily) around 1200 B.C. and later fortified by the Carthaginians from North Africa to guard the city from attackers coming from the west.

Steep, cobblestone **Via Vittorio Emanuele** leads past churches and monasteries to the town's high point and central square **Piazza Umberto I.** From there, Via Guarnotti leads through Piazza San Giuliano to the beautiful **Giardino del Balio,** surrounding the Norman-era **Castello di Venere.** A cliffside promenade beneath the castle affords the most spectacular views in western Sicily, all the way to Tunisia, a distance of 170km (106 miles), on a clear day. The gardens are always open.

Castello di Venere (Castle of Venus) ★ RUINS The Normans who conquered Sicily in the 12th century built a massive mountaintop castle, a majestic show of might, on the site of an ancient temple to Venus, goddess of love. Medieval towers and the ruins of walls still surround the compound, and through defensive slits and other openings you can look out over the plains of Trapani and the Egadi Islands, showing off the site's defensive advantage. Still visible are the foundations of the temple and precincts that housed a cult whose young female devotees serviced male worshippers sexually. This was deemed such an honorable profession that when the women ended their duties at age 21, they were considered especially desirable brides.

East end of Giardano del Balio. www.fondazioneericearte.org. ✆ **366/671-2832.** 4€, 2€ ages 11–16, includes the Chiesa Matrice tower; free for ages 10 and under. July–Sept daily 10am–7pm (Aug until 8pm); Apr–June and Oct 10am–6pm; Nov–Mar Sat–Sun 10:30am–6pm.

Chiesa Matrice (Royal Duomo of Erice) ★ CHURCH Erice's 14th-century Duomo was constructed with stones from the ancient Temple of Venus, and the *campanile* (bell tower) that rises 28m (92 ft.) next to the church also has an ancient past, built in the late 15th century atop a watchtower from the 2nd century B.C. Frederick of Aragon, who eventually lost Sicily to the Spanish, built the campanile so his sentries could watch for invading troops in the sea lanes far below, a view that's still worth the climb. The church's porch, dubbed the "Gibbena" (from the Latin *agi bene,* meaning "act well"), is a later addition, built to accommodate penitents who weren't allowed to partake in the Mass. Inside the church, you'll find a vaulted Arabesque ceiling and an enormous altarpiece of Carrara marble, depicting the life of Christ.

Piazza Umberto I. ✆ **0923/869123.** Church 2.50€; tower 2.50€. Daily Jan–Mar 10am–4pm (Apr, May, June, and Oct to 6pm; July and Sept to 7pm, Aug to 8pm, Nov–Dec to 1:30pm).

Along the West Coast

From the headlands north of Trapani down to Mazara delle Valo, the stunning natural beauty of western Sicily is on full display.

RISERVA NATURALE DELLO ZINGARO & SAN VITO LO CAPO ★★

A 45-minute drive east from Trapani across the island's northwest tip, the tiny town of **Scopello** is the beginning of the most beautiful stretch of

Sicily's Pastry Capital

Erice is renowned throughout Sicily for its pastries, refined by cloistered nuns from the 14th to the 18th century. Maria Grammatico, raised in the nearby San Carlo convent, became famous in Italy when she wrote her autobiography, *Bitter Almonds.* Her famed crunchy almond cookies, rum- or orange-filled marzipan balls, and confections fashioned from chocolate-covered almond paste are sold at **Pasticceria Maria Grammatico** (Via Vittorio Emanuele 14; www.mariagrammatico.it; **✆ 0923/869390**). **Pasticceria San Carlo** (Via S. Domenico 18; **✆ 0923/869586**) may not have the same celebrity status, but its offerings are also beautiful and tempting.

coastline in Sicily, running north for 12km (7½ miles) to the dramatic bluffs around the resort town of **San Vito Lo Capo.** Beaches here can be overly busy in summer, but they're paradisiacal, alternating sand and pebble strands washed by waters as clear and warm as those of the Caribbean. At the edge of Scopello, the **Tonnara di Scopello**—an abandoned 13th-century tuna-processing plant—is an especially idyllic spot to swim, a sparkling cove surrounded by wind-sculpted rocks. Much of the land is set aside as the **Riserva Naturale dello Zingaro** (www.riservazingaro.it; **✆ 0924/35108**), the first designated wildlife area in Sicily, covering nearly 1,600 hectares (3,954 acres) of Mediterranean maquis and coastline. Within the reserve, the **Grotta dell'Uzzo,** a cave that served as a dwelling in Paleolithic times, is now a refuge for six different types of bats (off-limits to all but sanctioned naturalists). Motorized vehicles are prohibited within the reserve—the only transport is by mule.

AST buses (www.aziendasicilianatrasporti.it; **✆ 091/620-8111**) make regular runs between Trapani and San Vito Lo Capo. Excursion boats departing from the dock in San Vito Lo Capo offer the best way to reach Scopello and the Zingaro reserve's coastline.

THE SALT MARSHES ★★★

Stretching from Trapani south to Marsala along route SP21, the salt pans skirting the coast have been harvested since antiquity (see box p. 809). For millennia, salt was used as a preservative for perishable food and for the Romans as payment for mercenaries (the word "salary" is from the Latin *salaries* meaning "soldier's allowance for the purchase of salt"). The area is now protected as the **Riserva Naturale Orientata Saline di Trapani e Paceco** (www.wwfsalineditrapani.it; **✆ 0923/867700**), covering 1,000 hectares (2,471 acres). The horizon is broken by red-and-white stone windmills, and in the late afternoon migrating birds perform spectacular in-flight choreographies. One of these windmills, **Mulino delle Saline Infersa** (www.seisaline.it/; **✆ 0923/733003**), has a museum and salt tasting room and organizes walks through the salt pans. It's open daily 9:30am to 3:30pm in December and March; 9am to 7pm April, May, and October; 9am to 8pm June and September; and by appointment only January and

San Vito Lo Capo and the scenic coastline near Trapani.

February. To get to the reserve from Trapani, take an **AST bus** (www.aziendasicilianatrasporti.it; ✆ **0923/21021**) to Nubia, a village 7km (4 miles) south in the middle of the pans.

MOZIA ★★★

A mere kilometer offshore from the northern outskirts of Marsala, the tiny island of **San Pantaleo** lies in the Stagnone, a lagoon and nature reserve. Owned by the prominent Marsala winemaking family the Whitakers, the islet is a wonderful place to observe pink flamingoes, curlews, and egrets; in summer the sparse landscape is abloom with white sea daffodil and sea lavender. Footpaths meander among the scattered ruins of the ancient city of Motya (today's **Mozia**), a 6th-century-B.C. Phoenician stronghold. In its heyday, the island settlement was surrounded by nearly 2.5km (1½ miles) of defensive walls. In 397 B.C., Dionysius the Elder of Syracuse mounted a massive attack on the inhabitants, who retreated to Lilybaeum (now Marsala). Today, little is left but crumbling low walls. Most intact are the **Casa dei Mosaici** (House of Mosaics), with scenes of animal life dating to the 4th to 3rd centuries B.C., and the **Tophet,** a Phoenician burial ground for victims of child sacrifice, with intricately carved gravestones. The small **Museo Whitaker** (www.isoladimozia.it; ✆ **349/625-6508**) displays excavated artifacts, including a sensual marble statue of a young man in a wet tunic, the **Giovane di Mozia** (Young Man of Mozia), dating to around 440 B.C. Admission to the island, including the museum, is 9€ (5€ students); it's open daily 10am to 7pm (Nov–Mar 9am–3pm).

Ferries operated by **Arini and Pugliese** (www.ariniepugliese.com; ✆ **347/779-0218**) and the **Mozia Line** (www.mozialine.com) run daily year-round to Mozia from docks outside Marsala, reached by infrequent bus service from Piazza del Popolo. A round-trip costs 5€ (2.50€ students and seniors). Be sure to pick up a free island map at the boat landing—it's essential for making sense of the littered ruins and remains.

THE EGADI ISLANDS

Served by ferry and hydrofoil from Trapani and Marsala, the archipelago of Favignana, Levanzo, and Marettimo forms the westernmost point of Sicily. The islands are popular summertime retreats for swimming and scuba diving, but the rest of the year their 4,600 inhabitants are left to live from the fruits of the sea, especially tuna, as they have done for centuries. A pleasant way to enjoy the beauty of the islands is on boat trips operated by **Egadi Boating** (www.egadiboating.com; ✆ **327/677-2824**) and other companies leaving from the Trapani docks. These trips usually include some time ashore and stops for swimming and snorkeling, and cost about 70€ to 90€ for a day's outing.

Marsala ★

124km (77 miles) SW of Palermo, 31km (19 miles) S of Trapani, 48.5km (30 miles) SW of Erice

This thriving little port on Cape Boéo, the western tip of Sicily overlooking the Egadi Islands and Tunisia, is where the world-famous Marsala sweet wine is produced. You can sample some amber yellow Marsala in one of the town's wine shops, or head through the hills along roads lined with prickly-pear cacti to a vineyard nearby. Townspeople sip the dark, vintage Marsala as a dessert wine with hard piquant cheese, fruit, or pastries. Famous product aside, Marsala is an elegant town with baroque

Salt of the Earth

When the Carthaginians first landed in the area from North Africa they saw the potential for salt production and created basins from which to harvest the valuable commodity. The process exploits the high level of salinity in the seawater and the wind and sun that contribute to the evaporation process. In mid- to late winter, water is pumped into the pans through a canal. Over the next few months the water is left to evaporate, when it assumes a reddish color dense with mineral pigment. Around July, just as the water reaches a sluggish consistency, the salt is raked, harvested, and brought onto dry land to complete the exsiccation process. What look like little salt huts line the road, covered in protective terracotta tiles. Once completely dry, the salt is cleansed of debris and packaged.

palaces and churches, Roman ruins, a lively fish market, and a long, sandy coastline stretching to the north and south.

VISITOR INFORMATION The **tourist office,** at Via 11 Maggio 100 (✆ **0923/714097**), is open Monday to Saturday 8am to 1:45pm and 2 to 8pm and Sunday 9am to noon.

EXPLORING MARSALA

Enter the city from the **Porta Garibaldi,** a massive 17th-century arched gateway crowned by an eagle. Garibaldi is honored because it was at Marsala that the 19th-century freedom fighter and his red-shirted volunteers overthrew the Bourbon regime, paving the way for the independence of southern Italy. From the gate, Via Garibaldi leads to busy **Piazza della Repubblica,** the heart of the city. The square's 18th-century Palazzo Senatorio, now the Town Hall, is nicknamed "Loggia" for its flank of elegant arcades. Leading north from Piazza Repubblica, the main thoroughfare **Via 11 Maggio** is flanked by many splendid baroque palaces. One of them, at Via Garraffa 57, houses the **Museo degli Arazzi Fiamminghi** (FlemishTapestry Museum); darkened salons are filled with eight magnificent Flemish tapestries, woven between 1530 and 1550, depicting the wars against the Jews when the Romans occupied Jerusalem (✆ **0923/711327;** admission 4€; Tues–Sun 9am–1pm, also Tues and Thurs 4:30–7:30pm). To the northwest, facing the sea on the **Lungomare Boéo,** the archaeological museum (see p. 811) stands amid old *bagli,* Marsala wine warehouses.

Chiesa Madre ★ CHURCH It's only fitting that Marsala's most imposing church is dedicated to Britain's St. Thomas à Becket, given the English connections that brought the city such wealth over the centuries (see box p. 811). Legend has it that a ship headed for England, carrying materials to build a church dedicated to Becket, was forced by a storm to seek haven at Marsala, and the crew simply built the church here instead. It's more likely that the cultlike popularity of the saint, murdered in Canterbury cathedral in 1170, had spread as far as Sicily by the 13th century, when the church was founded. The most impressive decorative pieces in the three-aisle interior are also by outsiders—the Gaginis, a 15th-century family of Swiss sculptors who worked their way down the Italian boot until they reached Sicily, undertaking commissions in Palermo and elsewhere around the island. Their best work here, by Domenico Gagini, is the lovely "Madonna del Popolo" in the right transept.

Piazza della Repubblica. ✆ **0923/716295.** Free. Daily 9am–7pm.

Museo Archeologico Lilibeo Marsala–Baglio Anselmi ★★ MUSEUM A former wine warehouse *(baglio)* houses gold jewelry from ancient Mozia (see p. 808), as well as the museum's showpiece, a relatively well-preserved **Punic ship** (Punic being the Latin name for Carthage, the ancient kingdom in what is today's Tunisia). It's believed the ship, discovered in shallow waters in 1971, was constructed for the Battle of the Egadi Islands during the First Punic Wars between Rome and Carthage in 241 B.C. and sank on its maiden voyage; some scholars argue that the vessel was not a warship but a cargo ship. Measuring 35m (115 ft.) long, the ship was manned by 68 oarsmen. Large sections remain, enough to suggest the sleekness and power of the wooden shell covered with sheets of lead fixed with bronze nails. They're displayed along with bowls, plates, animal bones, cannabis leaves, and other material carried on board. Behind the museum (included with admission) are the excavations of ancient Lilybaeum, as Marsala was known in Roman times. Among the relics are the remains of a villa with a steam room and still-glittering mosaics.

Lungomare Boéo. www.turismocomunemarsala.com. ✆ **0923/952535.** 4€ adults; 2€ ages 17 and under. Daily 9am–7:30pm.

NEAR MARSALA: MAZARA DEL VALLO

One of the most exotic cities in Sicily, Mazara del Vallo, 25km (15 miles) south of Marsala, is also Italy's largest fishing port, was once a hub of the island's Arab culture, and is now home to a large Tunisian population. A mazelike kasbah clusters near the port, and Norman churches and baroque palaces surround the central Piazza della Repubblica. On the delightfully baroque Piazza Plebiscito, surrounded by domed towers and arched loggias, the Museo del Satiro Danzante in the church of Sant' Egidio (✆ **0923/933917**) displays the namesake "dancing satyr." The bronze from the 4th century B.C., attributed by some scholars to Greek sculptor Praxetelis, catches a young male in a state of ecstatic frenzy, head thrown

A TASTE FOR marsala

On a dark and stormy night in 1770, English trader John Woodhouse was forced to anchor in Marsala. He headed for a tavern, downed some local wine, discovered it tasted similar to the Portuguese "Porto," and realized the commercial potential. Woodhouse began to mass-produce and export the wine, and he got a big break when the famed Admiral Horatio Nelson developed a taste for Marsala and decided that the British Navy should allot sailors a glass per day. Around the same time, Joseph Whitaker, another English entrepreneur, inherited a vast vineyard in Marsala and expanded the wine's reputation by exporting it to the United States. He also bought the island of **Mozia** (p. 808), where he founded an archaeological museum and published important studies of Tunisian birds. One more businessman entered the scene in the mid-19th century: Vincenzo Florio, from Palermo, who purchased the Woodhouse wine empire and refined Marsala grapes. The Florios, who also exported tuna, were one of Sicily's most prominent families well into the 20th century. Sample Marsala at **Enoteca La Ruota** on Via Scipione l'Africano near the archaeological museum (www.enotecalaruota.it; ✆ **0347/925-8451**), while admiring the Stagnone lagoon in front of you.

back and arms wide, and he remained that way on the bottom of the sea for millennia until fishermen dredged him up in their nets in 1998. The museum is open Tuesday to Saturday 9am to noon and Sunday 9am to noon; admission is 6€. Trains make the 25-minute trip between Marsala and Mazara throughout the day, and it's about a 25-minute drive on the SS115.

Selinunte ★★★

122km (76 miles) SW of Palermo, 55km (34 miles) SE of Marsala, 73km (45 miles) SW of Trapani

This Greek colony on Sicily's southwest coast was once one of the most powerful cities in the world. Then the great Carthaginian general Hannibal virtually destroyed the city in 409 B.C. Even in the context of those brutal times the wrath of the Carthaginians was abhorrent—an army of 100,000 men descended on the city with battering rams, and in an orgy of destruction raped, looted, plundered, and butchered, killing most of the inhabitants and enslaving the rest. Hannibal spared only the temples—not out of respect for the deities, but to preserve the loot they housed. Today this vast park comprises 270 hectares (670 acres), making it Europe's largest archaeological site. Selinunte is not just large, it's also a bucolic spot where you can walk amid the ruins, gaze out to sea, and ponder what life was like millennia ago. As you stroll amid the wildflowers and smell the wild herbs, remember that the town name comes from the Greek word *selinon,* meaning parsley.

Tip: Selinunte is entirely doable as a day trip from Palermo—it's about a 2-hour drive via the A29/E90 autostrada (exit at Castelvetrano)—but it's a good idea to leave early in the morning. You'll need at least 4 hours to explore the ruins, and you don't want to do that in the full heat of mid-day.

VISITOR INFORMATION You can enter the park at two points, with ample parking near each: from Via Selinunte in the village of Marinella di Selinunte and from Via Mediterraneo in the village of Triscina di Selinunte.

EXPLORING THE ARCHAEOLOGICAL PARK

Given the enormity of the area, allow yourself at least 4 hours to visit. Bring drinks, as it can get hot under the sun. If you're not up to extensive walking, you can hop on an electric train that makes a circuit through the ruins; tickets cost 6€.

Parco Archeologico Selinunte ★★★ RUINS The archaeological grounds have three designated zones: The East Hill and temples, the Acropolis and ancient city, and the Sanctuary of Demeter Malophoros. You will likely start your visit from the East Hill, adjacent to the main entrance. Archaeologists are still trying to determine which deity each of

Acropolis of Selinunte.

the Doric temples was dedicated to—for now, they are simply denoted by letters of the alphabet.

The **East Hill** was the sacred district of the city, with three temples surrounded by an enclosure. Temple E, which was in all probability dedicated to Hera, was built between 490 and 480 B.C. and has a staggering 68 columns. The Metopes, reliefs that are the pride and joy of the archaeological museum in Palermo, are from this temple. Temple F is the oldest of the trio, built between 560 and 540 B.C.; in its original state, the temple had a double row of six columns at the eastern entrance and 14 columns on either side. Temple G, now an impressive heap of rubble except for a lone standing column, was destined to be of colossal proportions if it had been completed in 480 B.C.

The **Acropolis,** a district of gridlike streets surrounded by defensive walls, was the center of social and political life. Here atop a plateau stood most of Selinunte's important public and religious buildings, as well as the residences of the town's aristocrats. Temple C, the earliest surviving temple of ancient Selinus, was built here in the 6th century B.C. and is still surrounded by 14 of its resurrected 17 columns. From the Acropolis, you cross the now-dry Modione River to the **Sanctuary of Demeter Malophoros,** the ruins of several shrines to Demeter, goddess of fertility. The custom was for worshipers to place stone figurines in the shrines to honor Demeter; as many as 12,000 such figurines have been unearthed.

Via Selinunte. www.visitselinunte.com. ✆ **0349/625-6508.** Admission 6€. Daily 9am–7pm (to 5pm in winter).

Where to Stay & Eat on Sicily's West Coast

ERICE

Hotel Elimo ★★ A 400-year-old palazzo in the heart of Erice's historic core welcomes guests in stone-walled lounges where in the chilly months a fire blazes in a hearth beneath beamed ceilings. Guest quarters are a bit more conventional, though comfortable, and some have views over the plains below, as do the restaurant and terrace.

Via Vittorio Emanuele 75, Erice. www.hotelelimo.it. ✆ **0923/869377.** 22 units. 80€–110€ double. Rates include breakfast. **Amenities:** Restaurant; bar; free Wi-Fi.

Hotel Moderno ★ The "moderno" dates to the conversion of a 19th-century Erice house just after World War II, though old-fashioned charm prevails. Antiques, brass, and wicker pieces lend a homey touch, and about a dozen rooms open onto private balconies or terraces. The view from the terrace, where breakfast is served in warm weather, is stunning, and the restaurant is excellent.

Via Vittorio Emanuele 67, Erice. www.hotelmodernoerice.it. ✆ **0923/869300.** 40 units. 70€–100€ double. Rates include breakfast. **Amenities:** Restaurant; bar; free Wi-Fi.

Il Carmine ★★ This refurbished 15th-century convent in Erice still shows traces of monastic living in simple, no-frills rooms and shower-only bathrooms. Yet the spartan surroundings are loaded with character, and views into the gardens are as soothing as they were intended to be. A separate entrance ensures that you won't disturb convent life.

Piazza del Carmine, Erice. www.ilcarmine.com. ✆ **0923/869069.** 6 units. 75€–85€ double. Rates include breakfast. Closed Jan–Feb. **Amenities:** Restaurant; free Wi-Fi.

Monte San Giuliano ★★★ SICILIAN You'll navigate some steps and stone alleyways to reach this garden hideaway, where a table on the terrace or in the rustic dining room seems, like much of medieval Erice, far away from the modern world. The menu shows off Arab influences in the flavorful seafood couscous, with many nods to such local favorites as lamb with a pistachio crust. Pasta is served with *sarde* (sardines) or *pesto alla Trapanese,* with garlic, basil, fresh tomatoes, and almonds.

Vicolo San Rocco 7, Erice. www.montesangiuliano.it. ✆ **0923/869595.** Entrees 9€–15€. Tues–Sun 12:15–3pm and 7:30–9:30pm. Closed part of Jan.

MARSALA

Grand Hotel Palace ★★ The 19th-century estate of an English wine importer in Marsala has been redone, but the premises retain a luxurious, old-world aura, so hushed and quiet you feel that even the statues might doze off and topple over. The most character-filled rooms are in the old house, but those in the new annex are fine, too. All are spacious and outfitted with traditional furnishings; many have sea views. In the gardens, stately trees are a backdrop for the swimming pool.

Lungomare Mediterraneo 57, Marsala. www.grandhotelpalace.eu. ✆ **0923/719492.** 56 units. 80€–150€ double. Rates include breakfast. **Amenities:** Restaurant; bar; outdoor pool; room service; babysitting; free Wi-Fi.

Trattoria Garibaldi ★★ SICILIAN/SEAFOOD At this 60-year-old institution near Marsala's cathedral, four arched, colorful dining rooms serve local favorites with a well-deserved reputation for freshness. Seafood, simply grilled with spices or served atop couscous, has a decidedly North African flair, while the homemade local pasta *busiati* with fresh fish is a specialty you probably won't find beyond the west coast.

Piazza dell'Addolorata 35, Marsala. ✆ **0923/953-006.** Entrees 7€–13€. Mon–Sat 12:30–2:45pm (until 3:30pm Tues) and 7:30–10:30pm; Sun 12:30–2:45pm.

Villa Favorita ★★ An early-19th-century hunting lodge is a rather exotic retreat, tucked into lush gardens at the edge of historic Marsala. The fanciest guest rooms and suites are on the upper floors of an elegant villa, with wide-oak and tile floors and arched loggias opening onto a courtyard. Others are garden bungalows that resemble stone igloos—they're unusual but attractive, sort of an Italian take on glamping, and divided into small sitting rooms and bedrooms with a cramped bathroom; they're scattered among greenery and shaded lanes surrounding a beautiful swimming pool. The atmosphere is casual and the grounds are full of many corners for relaxing. A pizza oven is fired up in the summer, and the restaurant serves well-done Sicilian dishes. From the center of Marsala, take SS115 north toward Trapani; the hotel is signposted.

Via Favorita 23, Marsala. www.villafavorita.com. ✆ **0923/989-100.** 29 bungalows, 13 units in main building. 60€–110€ double. Rates include breakfast. **Amenities:** 2 restaurants; bar; outdoor pool; tennis court; free Wi-Fi.

TRAPANI

Trapani is a good place to try what's considered to be the oldest handmade pasta in the world, *busiati.* The curly, eggless pasta has a firm texture and mealy taste and is good eaten with pesto sauce made Trapanese-style with cherry tomatoes. For the past 75 years, the favorite stop in town for a quick bite has been **Calvino Pizzeria dal 1946,** Via Nunzio Nasi 71, with slices and pies to take out or eat in, in several atmospheric rooms (✆ **0923/21464;** Wed–Mon 7pm–midnight). **12 Chiavi,** Corso Vittorio Emanuele 74 (✆ **331/925-6610**), serves a good selection of Sicilian wines by the glass; call for hours.

Ai Lumi Tavernetta ★★ SICILIAN The narrow, arched ground floor of a *palazzo,* filled with heavy rustic tables and chairs, is a cool retreat in which to enjoy Trapanese classics. Seafood is plentiful, as are such meat specialties as roast lamb in a citrus sauce and *busiati,* the thick local pasta, topped with *pesto trapanese,* made of tomato, basil, pecorino, and almonds. The front terrace is one of the nicest places in Trapani to spend a summer evening. Upstairs are 12 pleasant, well-furnished rooms, some with kitchenettes (doubles 80€–105€).

Corso Vittorio Emanuele 75, Trapani. www.ailumi.it. ✆ **0923/872-418.** Entrees 8€–18€. Daily 1–3pm and 7:30–11:30pm.

Cantina Siciliana ★★★ SEAFOOD/TRAPANESE Colorful tiles, Sicilian puppets, and welcoming service enliven this Trapani institution on an old street in the Jewish quarter. The kitchen focuses on local classics: Trapani-style fish couscous, swordfish with capers, and *busiata* pasta topped with Trapanese pesto, accompanied by carefully chosen wines and served with polish.

Via Giudecca 36. www.cantinasiciliana.it. ✆ **0923/28673.** Entrees 10€–22€. Thurs–Tues 12:45–3pm and 7:15–11pm.

Ligny Bed and Breakfast ★★ Right at the edge of the sea at the end of Trapani's historic town, an old *palazzo* offers high-ceilinged rooms, each with a panoramic terrace that takes in sweeping views of the gulf and Erice rising above the shores. Beaches, the port, and the town sights are within an easy walk. Iron bedsteads and some old family pieces add a homey touch to the rooms, up two flights of stairs; bathrooms are shower-only, and some are not en suite.

Via Torre Ligny 114, Trapani. ✆ **0923/194-1515.** 5 units. 40€–70€ double. Rates include breakfast. **Amenities:** Free Wi-Fi.

Osteria La Bettolaccia ★★★ SICILIAN Trapani's longtime favorite never disappoints, drawing a steady stream of diners (reserve if you can) to a couple of rambling, tile-floored rooms near the seafront. The kitchen prepares what many regulars claim is the best seafood couscous in Sicily, laden with calamari and a spicy sauce. Another favorite is spaghetti with swordfish, tuna, tomatoes, herbs, and breadcrumbs.

25 Via Enrico Fardella, Trapani. www.labettolaccia.it. ✆ **0923/21695.** Entrees 8€–15€. Mon–Sat 1–3pm and 8–10:30pm.

16

PLANNING YOUR TRIP TO ITALY

By Donald Strachan

This chapter has tips and tools for anyone planning travel to Italy, including information on how to get there, how to get around in safety and comfort, and the inside track on local resources for up-to-date advice. If you do your homework, pick the right place for the right season, and pack for the climate, preparing for a trip to Italy should be as pleasant and uncomplicated as ever. See also "When to Go," p. 35.

ARRIVING

By Plane

If you're flying across an ocean, you'll likely land at Rome's upgraded **Leonardo da Vinci–Fiumicino Airport (FCO;** www.adr.it/fiumicino), 40km (25 miles) from the center, or **Milan Malpensa (MXP;** www.milanomalpensa-airport.com), 45km (28 miles) northwest of central Milan. These are Italy's major intercontinental hubs; it is almost always cheapest to fly long-haul to one or the other.

Rome's much smaller **Ciampino Airport (CIA;** www.adr.it/ciampino) and Milan's **Linate Airport (LIN;** www.milanolinate-airport.com) serve low-cost airlines connecting to European cities and other destinations in Italy. For information on getting to central Rome from its airports, see p. 63; for Milan, see p. 466. Travelers can also board a direct high-speed train from Rome's Fiumicino Airport to Florence or Venice **without** passing through central Rome.

FLYING DIRECTLY TO VENICE, BOLOGNA, PISA, NAPLES, OR PALERMO

If you are arriving in Italy from elsewhere in Europe, it is often cheaper to fly direct on a budget carrier to one of the smaller cities. Among the most convenient are Venice's **Marco Polo Airport (VCE;** www.veneziaairport.it/en), Bologna's **Marconi Airport (BLQ;** www.bologna-airport.it), Pisa's **Galileo Galilei Airport (PSA;** www.pisa-airport.net), **Naples International Airport (NAP;** www.aeroportodinapoli.it), Catania's **Vincenzo Bellini Airport (CTA;** www.aeroporto.catania.it), or Palermo's **Punta Raisi Airport (PMO;** www.aeroportodipalermo.it). For information on getting into central Venice from the airport, see p. 394; for reaching Florence from Pisa airport or Bologna airport, see p. 165; for reaching central Naples from the airport, see p. 590. For information on arriving in Sicily via Palermo's airport, see p. 746.

PREVIOUS PAGE: **Santa Magdalena church in the Dolomites.**

ETIAS: EUROPE'S NEW *entry* REQUIREMENT

Travelers planning to visit Italy anytime from 2024 onward will encounter a new hoop to jump through: the **European Travel Information and Authorization System (ETIAS).** This electronic visa waiver is essentially the European Union equivalent to the USA's Electronic System for Travel Authorization (ESTA). ETIAS registration will be mandatory for travelers who don't otherwise need a visa to enter Europe's Schengen Area, which includes 22 European Union countries plus Iceland, Liechtenstein, Norway, and Switzerland. It applies to the citizens of around 60 visa-exempt countries, including the U.S., Canada, Mexico, the U.K., Australia, Japan, much of the Caribbean, and most of South America.

The online application process includes the following requirements: personal data (including name, date of birth, address); passport info; name of first Schengen country of intended stay; and answers to background questions about criminal record, any past deportations, and past travel to zones experiencing conflict or infectious disease epidemics.

Unless the applicant is flagged on one of the EU's watch lists, e-mail approval of ETIAS should arrive within minutes. As of now, the proposed fee for ETIAS registration is 7€ (about $7) per applicant between the ages of 18 and 70. All travelers, regardless of age, must register with ETIAS, but those under 18 and over 70 are presumably exempt from paying the fee.

Once approved, ETIAS registration is valid for 3 years. However, if your passport expires during that time, you'll need to apply for a new ETIAS waiver. Consistent with current tourist visa rules, ETIAS is intended for stays of 90 days or less within a 180-day period.

When should travelers planning a trip to Italy apply for ETIAS status? While the EU promises nearly instant approval for most travelers, in some cases processing can take up to 30 days. So it's best to play it safe and secure your ETIAS status a few weeks before your trip. And keep in mind: If you show up for your international flight to Italy without a valid ETIAS document, you will be denied boarding or entry.

For complete information, go to **https://travel-europe.europa.eu/etias_en**.

By Train

Italy's major cities are well connected to Europe's rail hubs. You can arrive in Milan on direct trains from **France** (Paris, Lyon) by **TGV** (www.sncf-connect.com) or from **Switzerland** (www.sbb.ch/en). Connect at Milan to Venice, Florence, or Rome (see "Getting Around," p. 468). TGV services also connect France with Turin. Several routes connect **Vienna** with Italy via a comfortable overnight Austrian sleeper train. These **Nightjet** (www.nightjet.com/en) services visit Verona, Bologna, Milan, Florence, Rome, Genoa, and Venice, among other places. Prices start from 30€ per person if you book ahead (up to 180 days is permitted); family couchette cabins *(Liegewagen)* start from around 240€ for 1 to 3 adults and up to 4 children ages 14 and under (6 people max.). Services also

VISITING ITALY today

From the very first wave of the SARS-CoV-2 virus—which hit Italy, especially Lombardy, early and hard—the national government introduced strict measures to tackle infection rates, including compulsory mask-wearing, limited visitor numbers, stringent cleaning protocols, and contact tracing. While many recommendations remain in place, restrictions and requirements to show a Green Pass or vaccination certificate have been removed. In general, it is wise to carry **proof of vaccination** with you, just in case, especially if you are visiting multiple European countries. Also check the dedicated coronavirus page at www.italia.it before you travel for any rules or guidance updates. The U.S. Embassy website also has a dedicated Covid-19 page for citizens traveling to Italy: **it.usembassy.gov/covid-19-information**.

Many Italian pharmacies still offer **antigen and PCR testing,** as well as certificates in English (typically 20€ and 60€, respectively). Check with your airline and embassy in Italy to see whether you need to arrange a test before returning to your home country.

connect Munich, Germany, with Venice, Florence/Bologna/Rome, or Verona/Milan.

Book your rail travel in Italy or online via **Rail Europe** (www.raileurope.com).

GETTING AROUND

By Car

Much of Italy is accessible by public transportation, but to explore vineyards, countryside, and smaller towns, you need a car. You'll get the **best rate** if you book your car far ahead of arrival. Try the website **AutoSlash.com**, which applies any coupons on the market to your rental and then monitors your booking. If the price drops, they'll make you a new reservation. We have found AutoSlash.com to be the best search engine for rentals by far, although it is a bit clunky to use: You must wait for a return e-mail before you can see the options, but thankfully that e-mail usually comes within minutes of your request. Car rental search companies usually report the lowest rates available between 6 and 8 weeks ahead of arrival. Rent the smallest car possible and request a diesel rather than a gasoline engine, to minimize fuel costs. You must be 25 or older to rent from many agencies (although some accept ages 21 and up, at a premium price).

You also must have nerves of steel, a sense of humor, a valid domestic driver's license, and strictly speaking (for non-EU citizens), an **International Driving Permit** (see below). Insurance on all vehicles is compulsory.

Note: If you're planning to rent a car in Italy during high season, you should **book farther in advance than you usually would.** It's not unheard of to arrive at an airport in July to find every agent out of cars, perhaps for the whole week.

It can sometimes be tricky to get to the *autostrada* (fast highway) from a city center or airport, so consider renting or bringing a GPS-enabled device, or installing an offline sat-nav app on your phone. In bigger cities you will first have to get to the *tangenziale,* or beltway, which will eventually lead to your highway of choice. The beltway in Rome is known as the Grande Raccordo Anulare, or "Big Ring Road."

The going can be slow almost anywhere, especially on Friday afternoons leaving the cities and Sunday nights on the way back into town, and rush hour around any city can be epic. Driving long-distance for a day or so on either side of the busy *Ferragosto* (August 15) holiday is to be avoided *at all costs.* See **www.autostrade.it** for live traffic updates and a road-toll calculator.

Autostrada tolls can get expensive, costing just over 1€ for every 15km (10 miles), which means it would cost about 23€ for a trip from

TURNING TO THE internet or apps FOR A HOTEL DISCOUNT OR EXTRAS

You can still get a good deal by calling a hotel in Italy, but you're more likely to snag a discount online or with an app. Here are some strategies:

1. Start at the **hotel's website.** Hotels often give the lowest rate to travelers who book through their site, rather than via a third party or agent. Booking direct, even at small hotels in Italy, may also snag you free extras (late checkout or breakfast). Should you need to cancel or rearrange at short notice, you may get a more sympathetic hearing if you booked direct.
2. Browse extreme discounts on sites where you reserve or **bid for lodgings** without knowing which hotel you'll get. You'll find these on **Priceline.com** and **Hotwire.com**, and they can be money-savers, particularly when booking within a week of travel (when hotels resort to deep discounts). These feature mostly major chains, so you are very unlikely to end up in a dump.
3. Use the right **hotel search engine.** All are not equal, as we at Frommers.com learned by putting the top 20 sites to the test in 20 destinations around the globe. We discovered **Hotels Combined.com** listed the lowest rates for hotels in the city center, and in the under-$200 range, 16 out of 20 times—the best record, by far, of all the sites we tested. And **Booking.com** includes all taxes and fees in its initial results (not all do, which can make for a frustrating shopping experience). For top-end properties, again in the city center, both Priceline.com and HotelsCombined.com came up with the best rates, tying at 14 wins each.

Rome to Florence. Fuel prices have spiked in recent years: Gas cost more than 1.85€ *per liter* at the time of writing. The **PrezziBenzina app** (www.prezzibenzina.it) finds the lowest-priced local gas station. Add in the price of the rental, and it's often cheaper to travel by train, even for two people.

Before leaving home, you can apply for an **International Driving Permit** from the American Automobile Association (AAA; www.aaa.com; ✆ **800/622-7070** or 650/294-7400). You should apply at least a month before travel; the license costs $20. In Canada, the permit is available from the Canadian Automobile Association (CAA; www.caa.ca; ✆ **800/222-4357**). Technically, you need this permit and your actual driver's license to drive in Italy. Traffic police can fine you for driving without an IDP. Visitors from within the EU need only carry a domestic driver's license.

Italy's equivalent of AAA, the **Automobile Club d'Italia** (ACI; www.aci.it), will respond if you place an emergency call to ✆ **803-116** for road breakdowns (✆ **800-116-800** from an overseas cellphone). You'll be charged for this service if you're not a member.

DRIVING RULES Italian drivers aren't all maniacs; most of them only appear to be. Spend any time on a highway and you will have the experience of somebody driving up from behind insanely close, headlights flashing. Take a deep breath and don't panic: This is the aggressive signal for you to move to the right so he (invariably, it's a "he") can pass. Until you do, he will stay mind-bogglingly close. On a two-lane road, the idiot who swerved into your lane to pass someone in oncoming traffic expects you to veer obligingly over toward the shoulder so three lanes of traffic can fit. He would do the same for you. Probably. Many Italians seem to think blinkers are optional, so assume a car in front could be ready to turn at any moment. When traveling outside of towns, it is compulsory to keep your headlights illuminated—set to dip—even during the day.

Autostrade are toll highways, denoted by green signs and prefaced with an *A,* like the A1 from Milan to Florence, Rome, and Naples. A few fast highways aren't numbered and are simply called a *raccordo,* a connecting road between two cities (such as Florence–Siena and Florence–Pisa).

Strade statali (singular: *strada statale*) are state roads, sometimes without a center divider and two lanes wide (although sometimes they can be a divided four-way highway), indicated by blue signs. Their route numbers are prefaced with an *SS,* as in the SS11 from Milan to Venice. On signs, however, these official route numbers are used infrequently. Usually, you'll just see blue signs listing destinations by name with arrows pointing in appropriate directions. It's impossible to predict which of all the towns that lie along a road will be selected to show on a particular sign. Sometimes a sign gives only the first minuscule village past the turnoff. At other times it lists the first major town down that road. Some signs mention only the major city where the road eventually terminates, even if it's hundreds of kilometers away. It pays to study the map before coming to an intersection or to carry a GPS device or download an offline GPS app for your smartphone. A *strada statale* can be frustratingly slow thanks to traffic, traffic lights, and the fact that it bisects countless towns: If you're in a hurry, pay for the autostrada.

The **speed limit** on roads in built-up areas around towns and cities is 50 kmph (31 mph). On two-lane roads it's 90 kmph (56 mph), and on the highway it's 130 kmph (81 mph). Italians have an astounding disregard for these limits. Know that police can ticket you and collect any fine on the spot. The blood-alcohol limit in Italy is .05%, generally achieved with just two regular-size drinks; driving above the limit can result in a fine of up to 6,000€, a driving ban, or jail. The blood-alcohol limit is zero for commercial drivers and for anyone who has held a driver's license for less than 3 years.

Safety belts are obligatory in both front and back seats; ditto child seats or special restraints for minors under 1.5m (5 ft.) in height, although this latter regulation is often ignored. Drivers may not use a handheld cellphone while driving—yet another law that locals often treat as optional.

PARKING Even savvy locals struggle to find convenient parking in Italy's cities. Hotels rarely have parking facilities, but many do negotiate deals with private city lots. Your hotel should be a first point of contact if you plan to park and leave the car for the duration of a stay. Should you prefer driving to the high-speed train, this is the only sensible option in big cities. On streets, **white lines** indicate free public spaces, **blue lines** are pay public spaces, and **yellow lines** mean only residents are allowed to park. Meters don't line the sidewalk; rather, there's usually one machine

INFLATION hesitation?

There's no sugarcoating it: Prices have risen. Like pretty much everywhere else in the world, Italy is experiencing a period of sustained **inflation** unlike anything seen for more than 3 decades. The rate topped 12% in early 2023. However, price rises are not evenly spread and tend to be more obvious in energy-intensive sectors. Yet even this rule of thumb is only a guideline. While some **museum prices** have risen sharply, many hotel rates have not. **Gas** prices have skyrocketed (though are already falling), but the cost of **train travel** is barely changed. On top of this, travelers from the U.S. are shielded from the brunt of inflationary rises by a dollar that remains strong against the euro. Indeed, the price of Italy rail passes (sold in dollars) has fallen over the last couple of editions of this guide. Obviously, Italy's inflation situation is fluid: If you are concerned, use the tools and advice in this chapter to check ahead.

on the block where you punch in coins corresponding to how long you want to park. The machine spits out a ticket to leave on your dashboard.

If you park in an area marked *parcheggio disco orario,* root around in your glove compartment for a cardboard parking disc. With this device, you dial up the hour of your arrival and display it on the dash. You're allowed *un'ora* (1 hr.), *due ore* (2 hr.), or whatever the sign advises. If you do not have a disc, write your arrival time on a sheet of paper and leave it clearly visible.

Parking lots have ticket dispensers, but exit booths are not usually manned. When you return to the lot to depart, first visit the office or automated payment machine to exchange your ticket for a paid receipt or exit token, which you then use to pass the exit barrier.

ROAD SIGNS A **speed limit** sign is a black number in a red circle on a white background. The **end of a speed zone** is just black and white, with a black slash through the number. A red circle on white, a black arrow pointing down, and a red arrow pointing up means **yield to oncoming traffic,** while a red-and-white triangle pointing down means **yield ahead.**

Many city centers are closed to traffic: A simple white circle with a red border, or the words *zona pedonale* or *zona traffico limitato,* denotes a **pedestrian zone** (you can often prearrange to drop off baggage at your hotel inside the zone); a white arrow on a blue background is used for Italy's many **one-way streets;** a mostly red circle with a horizontal white slash means **Do Not Enter.** Any image in black on a white background surrounded by a red circle means that image is **not allowed** (for instance, if the image is two cars next to each other, it means no passing; a motorcycle means no Harleys permitted; and so on). A circular sign in blue with a red circle-slash means **no parking.** You **may be fined for infringements,** including via automatic traffic camera. The fine may be automatically deducted from a credit card you provided to your rental agency—occasionally many weeks later.

Gasoline (gas or petrol), *benzina,* can be found in gas stations along major roads and on the outskirts of town, as well as in 24-hour stations along the autostrada. Almost all stations are closed for the *riposo* and on Sundays (except for those on the autostrada), but most have machines that accept cash. All gas is unleaded. Diesel is *gasolio* (or simply *diesel*).

By Train

Italy, especially its northern half, has one of the best train systems in Europe with most destinations connected by rail. Almost all lines are run by state-owned **Ferrovie dello Stato,** or FS (www.trenitalia.com; ✆ **892021**). A private operator, **Italo** (www.italotreno.it; ✆ **060708** or 892020) serves key stations on a many long-distance routes: the Turin–Milan–Florence–Rome–Naples–Salerno high-speed line; on branches

Travel Times Between the Major Cities

CITIES	DISTANCE	(FAST) TRAIN TRAVEL TIME	DRIVING TIME
Florence to Venice	281km/174 miles	2 hr.	3 hr.
Florence to Milan	298km/185 miles	1 hr., 40 min.	3½ hr.
Milan to Venice	267km/166 miles	2 hr.	3¼ hr.
Milan to Rome	572km/355 miles	2 hr., 55 min.	5½ hr.
Rome to Florence	277km/172 miles	1½ hr.	3 hr.
Rome to Naples	219km/136 miles	1 hr., 10 min.	2½ hr.
Rome to Bari	425km/264 miles	4 hr., 20 min.	5 hr.
Rome to Turin	669km/415 miles	3 hr., 50 min.	6½ hr.
Rome to Venice	528km/327 miles	3hr., 25 min.	5½ hr.

north from Bologna, including to Ferrara–Padua–Venice and Verona–Trento–Bolzano; between Turin and Venice via Milan and Verona; and from Rome southeast to Bari, in Puglia.

Travel durations and ticket prices vary considerably depending on the type of train you choose. The country's principal north–south high-speed line links Turin and Milan to Bologna, Florence, Rome, Naples, and Salerno. Milan to Rome, for example, takes around 3 hours on the quick train, and costs around 90€ in standard class—although you can find tickets as low as 20€ if you buy way in advance and travel in off-peak hours. Rome to Naples takes 70 minutes and costs 48€ (walk-up fare) on the fast train, or you can spend 14€ for a slower train that takes more than twice as long. To bag the cheapest fares on high-speed trains, aim to **book around 100 to 120 days before your travel dates.** Our advice: Book ahead for the best prices, but do not buy until you are certain you will travel. The **Italo newsletter** (and homepage) regularly advertises limited-time promo code discounts of up to 50% off advance fares, making them crazy cheap. You can also book rail travel on both Trenitalia and Italo via **Trainline** (www.thetrainline.com/trains/italy).

TYPES OF TRAIN The speed and overall quality of Italian trains vary widely. The high-speed **Frecciarossa,** along with **Italo**'s rival high-speed service, is the fastest of the fast. These trains mostly operate on the Turin–Milan–Florence–Rome–Naples–Salerno line, and run up to 300 kmph (186 mph); new FS equipment (Frecciarossa 1000) has a potential top speed of 400 kmph (249 mph). Frecciarossa services also run along Italy's east coast (Milan–Rimini–Ancona–Bari–Lecce) and connect Turin with Venice (with stops in Milan, Verona, and Vicenza). The cheapest class on both operators is perfectly comfortable, even on long journeys (although

Business class on the Frecciarossa is well worth the extra cost if you can find a cheap advance fare). These are Italy's premium rail services.

The **Frecciargento** uses lower-grade hardware and travels a little slower; it links Naples, Rome, Florence, and Venice at speeds of up to 250 kmph (155 mph). There are also Rome–Bari–Lecce, Rome–Verona–Bolzano, Rome–Naples–Reggio Calabria, and Rome–Pisa–Genoa Frecciargento services. Frecciargento trains have the usual two classes, First and Second. The less frequent **Frecciabianca** service isn't a genuine high-speed service, merely a slightly upgraded train running on standard track. The most useful route is between Rome and the Adriatic Sea coast.

Speed and cleanliness come at a price: Tickets for these high-speed trains usually cost around three times what you'd pay for a slower "regional" train. With the *Frecce* you **must make a seat reservation** when you buy a ticket. If you are traveling with a rail pass (see p. 827), you pay a 10€ supplementary fee to ride them and reserve a seat. Passes are not accepted on Italo trains.

Intercity (IC) trains are another step down, in both speed and comfort; as with *Le Frecce,* seat reservations are compulsory on IC trains. The slower ***Regionale*** (R) and ***Regionale Veloce*** (RV) make many stops and can sometimes be on the shabby side, but they are also very cheap: A Venice–Verona second-class ticket will put you back only 10€, compared with 29€ on the high-speed service. There is no advantage in booking R or RV services ahead of travel; just turn up, get a ticket, and ride. Old *Regionale* rolling stock is slowly being replaced, and comfort is improving. However, overcrowding has long been a problem on these services on Friday evenings, weekends, and holidays, especially in and out of big cities, or just after a strike.

TRAIN TRAVEL TIPS **Rail apps** for both Italo and Trenitalia offer paperless ticketing and easy in-app payment via credit card or PayPal. These represent the simplest contactless way to buy and carry rail tickets—for both high-speed and regular services. They are available, in English, from the usual app stores. You can also show a copy (paper or electronic) of an online booking confirmation, which has a unique PNR code.

If you carry a paper ticket without a specific service reservation, then you must **validate by stamping it in the yellow box** on the platform before boarding the train. If you board a train without a ticket, or without having validated yours, you have to pay a hefty fine on top of the ticket or supplement, which the conductor will sell you. If you board a train without a ticket or realize once aboard that you have the wrong type of ticket, your best bet is to search out the conductor, who is likely to be more forgiving because you found her and made it clear you weren't trying to ride for free.

Schedules for all trains leaving a given station are printed on yellow posters tacked up on the station wall (a similar white poster lists all the arrivals). These are good for general guidance. Keep your eye on electronic boards and screens, which update with delays and track *(binario)* changes. You can also get official schedules (and more train information, also in English) and buy tickets at www.trenitalia.com or www.italotreno.it, or via an agent such as **Rail Europe** (www.raileurope.com).

In big cities (especially Milan and Rome) and tourist destinations (above all Venice and Florence), ticketing lines in stations can be dreadfully long. Don't be scared of **automatic ticket machines.** They are easy to navigate, provide instructions in English, accept cash and credit cards, and save you the stress of waiting in a slow line. (***Note:*** You can't buy international tickets at automatic machines.) Best of all, however, use the apps.

RAIL PASSES & DISCOUNTS To buy the **Eurail Italy Pass,** available only outside Europe and priced in U.S. dollars, contact **Rail Europe** (www.raileurope.com) or **Eurail** (www.eurail.com). You have 1 month in which to use the train for a set number of days (the base number of days is 3, and you can add up to 5 more). For adults, the first-class pass costs \$181, second-class is \$142. Each additional day costs \$35 to \$40 more for first class, around \$30 for second class. Up to two children ages 4 to 11 are entitled to a child pass free with any adult pass purchase. For youth travelers (27 and under), a 3-day second-class pass is \$118 and additional days about \$20 each.

Buying your rail pass early in the year is sometimes rewarded with an extra day's travel at no additional cost (such as pay for 3 days, get 4) or seasonal discounts (we have seen up to 35% off some Eurail passes). The **Eurail Global Pass** covers rail travel in Italy, all its neighbors, and most of the rest of Europe (33 countries).

Note: Booking every rail journey online ahead of arrival may beat a rail pass on price, especially if you factor in the cost of compulsory seat reservations on Italy's high-speed trains. However, because the cheapest online fares are usually nonrefundable, you gain flexibility with a pass. The electronic **Trenitalia Pass** costs slightly more than a Eurail Pass, but seat reservations are free and you can buy it in Italy or online at www.trenitalia.com.

Children 14 and under ride half-price on Italian trains, while kids under 4 don't pay, although they also do not have the right to their own seat. State railways also sometimes offer free tickets for children 14 and under traveling with an adult; ask about *"Bimbi gratis"* fares when buying (ticket machines offer this option automatically, if it's available). The **Italo Family** fare, available at least 2 days before travel at a station or online, includes free travel for up to three kids ages 14 and under accompanying an adult paying full flexible fare (in Smart class only).

By Bus

Although trains are quicker and easier, you can get just about anywhere in Italy on a network of local, provincial, and regional bus lines. Keep in mind that in smaller towns, buses mainly shuttle workers and schoolchildren, so most runs are on weekdays, early in the morning, and usually again from midafternoon.

In a big city, the **bus station** for intercity trips is usually near the main train station. A small town's **bus stop** is generally in the main square, on the edge of town, or just outside the town gate. You should always try to find the local ticket vendor—if there's no office, this is invariably the nearest newsstand or *tabacchi* (look for a sign with a white t), or occasionally a bar—but you can usually buy tickets on the bus. Buses in cities and on major routes increasingly accept **fare payment via contactless card or mobile phone.** You can sometimes flag down a passing bus on a country road, but try to find an official stop (a small sign, sometimes tacked onto a tree or pole). Tell the driver where you're going and ask politely if he'll let you know when to get off. When he says, *"È la prossima fermata,"* that means yours is the next stop. *"Posso scendere a…?"* is "Can I get off at…?"

For details on urban bus transportation, see individual chapters. Perhaps the only intercity bus you will take in Italy is the efficient **Florence–Siena** service; see "Siena," p. 230. However, if you are traveling on a tight budget, check **FlixBus** (www.flixbus.it) intercity fares. They often significantly undercut train prices. For comparing times and prices across different modes of transport in Italy, **www.rome2rio.com** is useful. A long-distance bus is *un pullman.*

By Plane

These days, the only internal air connection you will likely make is to the island of **Sicily.** Direct Sicily routes from mainland airports are flown by **Ryanair** (www.ryanair.com); **easyJet** (www.easyjet.com); **ITA** (www.ita-airways.com); and **Wizz Air** (www.wizzair.com).

[FastFACTS] ITALY

Area Codes The **country code** for Italy is **39. City codes** (for example, Florence 055, Venice 041, Milan 02, Rome 06) are incorporated into the numbers themselves. Therefore, you must dial the entire number, ***including the initial zero,*** when calling from *anywhere* outside or inside Italy and even within the same town. For example, to call Milan from the United States, you must dial **011-39-02,** then the rest of the phone number. Phone numbers in Italy can range anywhere from 6 to 12 digits in length.

ATMs The easiest and best way to get cash is from

an ATM, referred to in Italy as ***un bancomat.*** ATMs are easy to find in Italian cities; smaller towns usually have one, but it's good practice to fuel up on cash in urban centers before heading to villages or rural areas.

Before traveling, confirm that your card is valid for international withdrawals and that you have a four-digit PIN. (Some ATMs in Italy will not accept any other number of digits.) Also, be sure you know your daily withdrawal limit before you depart. ***Note:*** Many banks impose a fee when you use a card at another bank's ATM, and this fee can be higher for international transactions (up to $5 or more) than for domestic ones. In addition, the bank from which you withdraw cash may charge its own fee, although this is not common practice in Italy.

If at the ATM you get an on-screen message saying your card isn't valid for international transactions, don't panic: It's most likely the bank can't make an electronic connection (occasionally this can be a citywide epidemic). Try another ATM or another town.

Business Hours

Banks tend to be open Monday through Friday 8:30am to 1:30pm and 2:45 to 4:15pm. General opening hours for **stores, offices,** and **churches** are from 9:30am to noon or 1pm, and again from 3 or 3:30pm to 7:30pm. The early afternoon shutdown is the *riposo*, the Italian siesta (in downtown areas of large cities, stores don't usually close for a *riposo*). Most small stores close all day Sunday and some also on Monday (morning only or all day). Some public services and business offices are open only in the morning.

Traditionally, **state museums** are closed Mondays. Most large museums stay open all day long otherwise, although some smaller or private collections close for *riposo* or are only open in the morning (9am–2pm is popular).

Credit Cards

The evolution of international computerized banking has led to the triumph of plastic throughout Italy. It's still a good idea to carry some cash—small businesses may accept only cash or may even claim their machine is broken to avoid paying card fees. **Visa** and **Mastercard** are almost universally accepted, and some businesses, typically at the luxe end, take **American Express. Diners Club** tends not to be accepted in Italy. Be sure to let your bank know you'll be traveling abroad to avoid having your card blocked after a few days of big purchases far from home. ***Note:*** Many banks assess a 1% to 3% "transaction fee" on **all** charges you incur abroad, whether you're using the local currency or your native currency. Research card providers to see which offer better rates for travelers. ***Tip:*** If a store clerk gives you a choice, **pay in local currency** (euro), not your home currency. Their system's exchange rates will invariably be poor compared with your bank or card provider. The same applies at ATMs.

Customs

Foreign visitors arriving by air can bring in most items for personal use, including new merchandise bought duty-free for up to 430€. Returning to the United States, U.S. citizens can bring with them up to $800 of goods, including one liter of alcohol, but no meats or fresh fruits and vegetables. Vinegars, oils, jams, chocolates, and certain cheeses are permissible (vacuum-packed cheeses, yes; raw milk cheese, no).

Disabled Travelers

Most of the top museums and churches have ramps at their entrances, and several hotels have converted ground-floor rooms into accessible units. Other than that, you may find many charming parts of Italy tricky. Builders in the Middle Ages didn't have wheelchairs in mind when they fashioned narrow doorways and spiral staircases, and preservation laws prevent Italians from doing much about this in some places.

Public transportation is improving, however, with better access for passengers in wheelchairs, particularly on high-speed trains, modern local buses, and new transit infrastructure like Florence's tram. There are usually dedicated seats or areas for those with disabilities, and Italians are quick to give up their place for somebody who appears to need it. **Trenitalia** has a special number for disabled travelers to call for assistance on the rail network: ✆ **02/323232. Italo** has dedicated wheelchair spaces on every train: Call ✆ **060708** for station assistance.

Drinking Laws People of any age can legally consume alcohol in Italy, but a person must be 16 years old to be served alcohol in a restaurant or bar. Bars generally close by 2am, although alcohol is often served in clubs after that. Supermarkets sell beer, wine, and liquor.

Electricity Italy operates on a 220-volt AC (50 cycles) system, as opposed to the U.S. 110-volt AC (60 cycles) system. A simple adapter plug makes American flat pegs fit the Italian round holes and, unless your appliance is dual-voltage (as some hair dryers, travel irons, and almost all gadgets are), an electrical converter will be necessary. You can pick up the hardware at electronics stores, travel specialty stores, luggage shops, and airports. Buy **before** you travel.

Embassies & Consulates The **U.S. Embassy** is in Rome at Via Vittorio Veneto 121 (it.usembassy.gov; ✆ **06/46741**). There are also **U.S. Consulates General** in Florence, at Lungarno Vespucci 38 (✆ **055/266-951**); in Milan, at Via Principe Amedeo 2/10 (✆ **02/290-351**); and in Naples, in Piazza della Repubblica (✆ **081/583-8111**).

The **Canadian** Embassy is in Rome at Via Zara 30 (www.italy.gc.ca; ✆ **06/85444-1**).

The **Australian Embassy** is in Rome at Via Antonio Bosio 5 (italy.embassy.gov.au; ✆ **06/852-721**). The **Australian Consulate-General** is in Milan at Via Borgogna 2 (✆ **02/7767-4200**). The **New Zealand Embassy** (www.mfat.govt.nz/italy; ✆ **06/853-7501**) is in Rome at Via Clitunno 44. The **U.K.** Embassy (www.gov.uk/world/italy; ✆ **06/4220-0001**) is in Rome at Via XX Settembre 80a. The **British Consulate-General** is in Milan at Via San Paolo 7 (✆ **02/723-001**).

Emergencies The best number to call in Italy with a **general emergency** is ✆ **112,** which connects you to the ***Carabinieri*** who will transfer your call as needed. For the **police,** dial ✆ **113;** for a **medical emergency** and to call an **ambulance,** the number is ✆ **118;** for the **fire department,** call ✆ **115.** If your car breaks down, dial ✆ **116** for **roadside aid** courtesy of the Automotive Club of Italy. All are free calls, but roadside assistance is a paid service for nonmembers.

Family Travel Italy is a family-oriented society. A crying baby at a dinner table is greeted with a knowing smile, rather than a stern look. Children can almost always request discounted smaller portions, and sometimes even get a special treat from the waiter, but the availability of such accoutrements as child seats for cars and dinner tables is more the exception than the norm. (The former, however, is a legal requirement: Ask your rental car company to provide one.) There are plenty of parks, offbeat museums, markets, ice-cream parlors, and vibrant street-life scenes to amuse even the youngest children. Child discounts apply on public transportation, and at public and private museums.

Health Care Italy offers universal health care to its citizens and those of fellow European Union countries. Others should be prepared to pay medical bills upfront. Before leaving home, find out what medical services your **health insurance** covers. You will be treated in any emergency in Italy, irrespective of whether you have travel insurance. The country's public health care system is generally well regarded. The richer north tends to have better **hospitals** than the south.

Insurance Italy may be one of the safer places you

can travel in the world, but accidents and setbacks can and do happen, from lost luggage to car crashes. We recommend looking at the following online marketplaces for insurance: **SquareMouth.com**, **Insure MyTrip.com**, and **Travel Insurance.com**. All three allow users to quickly and easily compare policies from different, vetted travel insurance companies. We find the user interface at SquareMouth to be the more intuitive, but all three are excellent resources.

Internet Access You will find Wi-Fi in almost every accommodation, but if this is essential for your stay, make sure you ask before booking. Don't always expect to find a connection in a rural *agriturismo*—digital detox is sometimes part of their appeal. In a pinch, hostels, libraries, and many cafes and bars have access. Several spots around Venice, Florence, Rome, and other big cities are covered with free Wi-Fi access provided by the local administration, but at these and any other Wi-Fi spots around Italy, antiterrorism laws make it obligatory to register before you can log on. **High-speed trains** often have free Wi-Fi (but throttle Skype, video streaming, file sharing, and similar data-hungry services).

LGBT Travelers Italy as a whole, and northern Italy in particular, is LGBT-friendly. Homosexuality is legal and the age of consent is 16. Same-sex civil unions became legal in 2016. Italians tend to be more affectionate than North Americans in all their friendships, and even straight men occasionally walk down the street with their arms around each other—however, kissing anywhere other than on the cheeks may draw attention. As you may expect, small towns can be less permissive than cities and beach resorts.

Italy's national associations and support networks for gays and lesbians are **ArciGay** (www.arcigay.it) and **ArciLesbica** (www.arcilesbica.it). Most cities have a local office. See **www.arcigay.it/en/sedi** for a map directory of local affiliates.

Mail & Postage Sending a postcard or letter up to 20 grams, or a little less than an ounce, costs 1.15€ to European countries, 2.40€ to North America, and a whopping 3.10€ to Australia and New Zealand. Full details on Italy's postal services are available at **www.poste.it** (some of it in English).

Mobile Phones Pretty much any phone with **4G/LTE** or **5G** capability will work in Italy, as long as international service is allowed on the account—contact your service provider before leaving. But—and it's a *big* but—using roaming can be expensive, especially if you access the Internet on your phone. It's usually much cheaper, once you arrive, to buy an Italian SIM card. This is a particularly good idea if your stay in Italy is more than a week. You can **buy a SIM card** at cellphone shops in every city: The main service providers are **TIM** (www.tim.it), **Vodafone** (www.vodafone.it), and **WINDTRE** (www.windtre.it). With an Italian SIM card in your phone, local and national calls may be as low as .10€ per minute, and incoming calls are free. Value prepaid data packages are available—usually with data inclusive—as are prepaid data bundles for iPads and other tablets. Not every network allows **tethering**—ask if you need it. ***Note:*** U.S. contract cellphones are often "locked" and only work with a SIM card from your home service provider, so check whether you have an unlocked phone before buying an Italian SIM card.

Buying a phone is another option, and you shouldn't have trouble finding one for about 20€. Use it, then recycle it when you get home. It will save you a fortune versus alternatives such as roaming or using hotel telephones, as will using Wi-Fi with a VoIP calling service like Skype, Zoom, or FaceTime.

Money & Costs Frommer's lists exact prices in the local currency. The currency

WHAT THINGS COST IN ROME (HOTEL PRICES ARE HIGH SEASON)

Bus ticket (from/to anywhere in the city)	1.50€
Double room at Inn at the Spanish Steps (expensive)	200.00€–500.00€
Double room at Lancelot (moderate)	130.00€–205.00€
Double room at Mimosa (inexpensive)	89.00€–150.00€
Continental breakfast (cappuccino and croissant standing at a bar)	3€–4.50€
Dinner for one, with wine, at Glass (expensive)	60.00€–150.00€
Dinner for one, with wine, at La Barrique (moderate)	25.00€–30.00€
Dinner for one, with wine, at Li Rioni (inexpensive)	15.00€
Small gelato at Fatamorgana	2.50€–3.50€
Glass of wine at a bar	3.50€–8.00€
Coca-Cola (standing/sitting in a bar)	2.50€/5.00€
Cup of espresso (standing/sitting in a bar)	1.00€/2.50€
Admission to the Colosseum and Forum	22.00€ online

conversions quoted below were correct at press time. However, rates fluctuate, so before departing, consult a currency exchange website, such as **www.oanda.com/currency/converter**, to check up-to-the-minute rates.

THE VALUE OF THE EURO VS. OTHER POPULAR CURRENCIES

€	Aus$	Can$	NZ$	UK£	US$
1	1.62	1.46	1.73	0.88	1.08

Like many European countries, Italy uses the **euro** as its currency. Euro coins are issued in denominations of .01€, .02€, .05€, .10€, .20€, and .50€, as well as 1€ and 2€; bills come in denominations of 5€, 10€, 20€, 50€, 100€, 200€, and 500€. You'll get the best rate if you **exchange money** at a bank or bank ATM. The rates at "Cambio/change" exchange booths are less favorable but still better than what you'd get exchanging money at a hotel or shop (a last-resort tactic only). **Traveler's checks** have gone the way of the Stegosaurus.

Newspapers & Magazines *The New York Times International Edition* and *USA Today* are available at newsstands in big cities, and sometimes even in smaller towns. At larger kiosks in big cities you may find the *Wall Street Journal Europe, The Economist,* and major European newspapers and magazines.

Pharmacies Italian pharmacies offer essentially the same range of generic drugs available in North America and internationally. Pharmacies are ubiquitous (look for the green cross) and serve almost like mini clinics, where pharmacists diagnose and treat minor ailments with over-the-counter drugs. Carry the generic name of any prescription medicines in case a local pharmacist is unfamiliar with your overseas brand name. Face masks and hand sanitizer are usually available. Pharmacies in cities take turns doing the night shift.

Police For emergencies, call ✆ **112** or ✆ **113.** The *Carabinieri* (✆ **112;** www.carabinieri.it) normally concern themselves only with serious crimes but point you in the right direction. The *Polizia* (✆ **113;** www.poliziadistato.it), whose city headquarters is called the *questura*, is the place for help with lost and stolen property or petty crimes.

Safety Italy is a remarkably safe country in terms of street crime. The worst threats you'll likely face are pickpockets who sometimes frequent touristy areas and public buses: Keep your hands on a camera at all times and your valuables in an inside zip-pocket. Don't leave anything valuable in a rental car overnight and leave nothing visible in it at any time. If you are robbed, you can fill out paperwork at the nearest police station *(questura)*, but this is mostly for insurance purposes or to get a new passport issued—don't expect them to hunt down the perpetrator. In general, avoid public parks at night. Areas around rail stations are often unsavory, but rarely worse than that.

Senior Travel Seniors and older people are treated with deference in Italy, but few specific programs exist. One exception is at museums and sights, where those aged 60 or 65 and older often pay a reduced admission. As a senior in Italy, you're *un anziano*, or if you're a woman, *un'anziana*, "elderly"—it's a term of respect. Let people know you're one if you think a discount may be in order.

Smoking Smoking has been eradicated from inside restaurants, bars, and most hotels, so smokers tend to take outside tables at bars and restaurants. If you're keen for an alfresco table, you are essentially choosing a seat in the smoking section; requesting that your neighbor not smoke may not be politely received.

Student Travelers An **International Student Identity Card** (ISIC) qualifies students for savings on travel tickets, entrance fees, and more. The card is valid for 1 year. You can apply for the card online at **isicusa.com**. If you're not a student but are aged 26 and under, you can get an **International Youth Travel Card** (IYTC) from the same agency, which entitles you to some discounts. Teachers can apply for an **International Teacher Identity Card** (ITIC), although your work I.D. card should suffice at museums and the like. Students will find that many university cities offer ample student discounts and inexpensive youth hostels.

Taxes No sales tax is added onto purchases in Italy, but a 22% value-added tax (in Italy: **IVA**) is automatically included in just about everything, except some foods and a few specific goods and services, where rates of 4% or 10% apply. Local transportation, hotels, and dining are among a group of goods taxed at 10%. For large purchases, non–E.U. residents can get IVA refunded. Several city governments have also introduced an **accommodation tax.** For example, in Florence, you may be charged between 3€ and 5€ per person per night, depending on the government star rating of the hotel, guesthouse, or rental apartment. Children 11 and under are exempt. Venice, Rome, and many other popular localities also levy their own taxes. This tax is not usually included in any published room rate, even rates prepaid online.

Tipping In **hotels,** service is usually included in your bill. In family-run operations, additional tips are unnecessary and sometimes considered rude. In fancier places with a hired staff, however, you may want to leave a 1€ daily tip for the maid and pay the bellhop or porter 1€ per bag. In **restaurants,** a 2€ to 3€ per person "cover charge" is automatically added to the bill, and in some tourist areas, especially Venice, another 10% to 15% is tacked on. Except in the most unscrupulous places, this will be noted on the menu somewhere; if unsure you should ask, è *incluso il servizio*? It is not necessary to leave extra money on the table, although it is not uncommon to leave up to 10€, especially for good service. Locals often leave nothing. At **bars and cafes,** you can leave small change on the counter for the barman (maybe 1€ or 2€ if you have had a few drinks), although it is not expected. There is no need to leave anything extra if you sit at a table, as they are likely already charging you double or triple the price for standing at the bar. It is not necessary to tip **taxi** drivers, although it is common to round up the bill a euro or two.

Toilets Aside from train stations, where they cost .50€ or 1€ to use, and gas/petrol stations, where they are free (with perhaps a basket seeking gratuities for cleaners), public toilets are few and far between. In an emergency, standard procedure is to enter a cafe, make sure the bathroom is not *fuori servizio* (out of order), and then order a cup of coffee before bolting to the facilities. It is advisable to always make use of the facilities in a hotel, restaurant, or museum before a long walk around town. Public toilets—and often those in bars, too—can be dirty, with no seat or toilet paper. It's best to carry a pack of tissues and some hand sanitizer.

Websites Following are some of our favorite sites to help you plan your trip: **www.italia.it/en** is the official English-language tourism portal for visiting Italy, although regional and city tourism websites are usually more comprehensive and up-to-date (see individual chapters); **www.arttrav.com** is excellent for cultural travel, exhibitions, and openings, especially in Florence and Tuscany; **www.summerinitaly.com/traveltips/transport-strikes-in-italy** provides updates on the latest rail, road, and airline strikes; **www.prezzibenzina.it** finds the cheapest fuel close to you (it also has a smartphone app); **www.ansa.it** and **www.thelocal.it** supply you with Italian news in English; and naturally, **www.frommers.com/destinations/Italy** offers more expert advice on the country.

Index

C

G

N

Q

R

S

T

Accommodations

Restaurants

PHOTO CREDITS

Front cover: Jarek Pawlak /Shutterstock; p. i: canadastock / Shutterstock; p. iii: gillmar / Shutterstock; p. 1: Frank Lammel / Shutterstock; p. 3: Kirk Fisher / Shutterstock.com; p. 4: GoneWithTheWind / Shutterstock.com; p. 6: TravnikovStudio; p. 8: Nattee Chalermtiragool / Shutterstock.com; p. 9: kavalenkava / Shutterstock.com; p. 10: ©photogolfer / Shutterstock.com; p. 12: Giuseppe Strafaci / Shutterstock.com; p. 13: Boris Stroujko / Shutterstock.com; p. 14: Viacheslav Lopatin / Shutterstock.com; p. 17: pegasophoto; p. 20: Massan; p. 23: Mikadun; p. 25: essevu; p. 27: ©Mihai-Bogdan Lazar / Shutterstock.com; p. 29: freevideophotoagency / Shutterstock.com; p. 31: Paolo Bona/ Shutterstock.com; p. 34: Antonello Aringhieri / Shutterstock.com; p. 38: elesi / Shutterstock; p. 40: ©Lucian Milasan / Shutterstock.com; p. 42: Mariia Golovianko / Shutterstock.com; p. 46: Meghan Lamb; p. 51: Roman Kybus / Shutterstock; p. 52: Gaspar Janos; p. 56: ©anshar; p. 58: MeanderingMax; p. 61: Kirk Fisher / Shutterstock; p. 68: Boris-B / Shutterstock.com; p. 75: ©Janis Lacis; p. 78: WDG Photo / Shutterstock.com; p. 81: Genevieve Borden / Shutterstock.com; p. 94: Chanclos / Shutterstock.com; p. 99: Phant; p. 108: leventina / Shutterstock.com; p. 110: r.nagy / Shutterstock.com; p. 111: wjarek / Shutterstock.com; p. 126: Courtesy of Mama Shelter Roma / FRANCIS AMIAND; p. 129: Courtesy of Lancelot; p. 136: Courtesy of Arco del Lauro; p. 139: Meghan Lamb; p. 144: Courtesy of Al Ceppo / pikorra.com; p. 152: Northfoto / Shutterstock.com; p. 155: lornet / Shutterstock.com; p. 161: Marina99; p. 163: Alex_Mastro / Shutterstock; p. 168: Umberto Shtanzman; p. 177: TTphoto / Shutterstock.com; p. 181: InnaFelker / Shutterstock.com; p. 184: voe / Shutterstock.com; p. 186: Nataly Reinch / Shutterstock.com; p. 189: salajean; p. 191: marcovarro / Shutterstock.com; p. 194: Joe deSousa; p. 197: AntipinaE / Shutterstock.com; p. 210: Courtesy of Continentale Hotel / Lungarno Collection; p. 213: Courtesy of Riva Lofts / ALESSANDRO MICHELAZZI; p. 216: I Wei Huang / Shutterstock.com; p. 217: Courtesy of Brac / Anna Positano / Studio Campo; p. 220: Anna Pakutina / Shutterstock.com; p. 224: Courtesy of Cantinetta dei Verrazzano; p. 226: Maciej Czekajewski / Shutterstock; p. 233: Migel / Shutterstock.com; p. 237: Eddy Galeotti / Shutterstock.com; p. 245: Marco Bicci / Shutterstock; p. 248: Dmitriy Yakovlev; p. 254: volkova natalia / Shutterstock.com; p. 259: lapas77 / Shutterstock; p. 262: arkanto / Shutterstock.com; p. 267: Maciej Czekajewski / Shutterstock.com; p. 268: marcobrivio.photography / Shutterstock.com; p. 274: Federico Magonio / Shutterstock.com; p. 278: Roberto Cerruti / Shutterstock.com; p. 286: StockPhotoAstur / Shutterstock.com; p. 296: berni0004 / Shutterstock.com; p. 299: muratart / Shutterstock; p. 302: ArtMediaFactory / Shutterstock.com; p. 304: ArtMediaFactory / Shutterstock.com; p. 309: Davide Zanin / Shutterstock.com; p. 310: Maurizio Zanetti; p. 316: Buffy1982 / Shutterstock.com; p. 320: WDG Photo; p. 326: alexandro900; p. 332: Aksenya / Shutterstock.com; p. 338: KirShu; p. 342: canadastock; p. 345: Yasonya / Shutterstock; p. 347: bellena; p. 353: Pierre Aden / Shutterstock.com; p. 355: Catarina Belova; p. 359: Courtesy of Art Hotel Commercianti; p. 362: pio3 / Shutterstock.com; p. 370: Alvaro German Vilela / Shutterstock.com; p. 379: AlexAnton; p. 381: claudio zaccherini / Shutterstock.com; p. 388: Gimas / Shutterstock.com; p. 392: Efired / Shutterstock; p. 398: Aleksandr Stepanov / Shutterstock.com; p. 402: spass; p. 406: Paolo Gallo / Shutterstock.com; p. 413: Rad Radu; p. 415: Pavel Ilyukhin; p. 419: ©Riccardo de Luca; p. 421: Mila Atkovska; p. 422: Arndale / Shutterstock; p. 427: bellena / Shutterstock.com; p. 436: Courtesy of Casa Verardo; p. 445: Courtesy of Osteria Enoteca Ai Artisti; p. 451: Timur Kulgarin; p. 454: EQRoy / Shutterstock.com; p. 457: ©Arseniy Krasnevsky; p. 460: kavalenkava volha; p. 462: arjma / Shutterstock.com; p. 464: Olgysha / Shutterstock; p. 471: s74 / Shutterstock; p. 478: Mihai-Bogdan Lazar; p. 480: KrimKate / Shutterstock.com; p. 491: ValeStock / Shutterstock.com; p. 499: Roman Babakin / Shutterstock.com; p. 505: Gaspar Janos / Shutterstock; p. 506: Anna-Mari West; p. 510: saiko3p / Shutterstock; p. 511: Joaquin Ossorio Castillo / Shutterstock.com; p. 514: Gaspar Janos; p. 516: mikolajn; p. 522: MikeDotta / Shutterstock.com; p. 525: ©Max Bashirov; p. 535: CatwalkPhotos / Shutterstock; p. 539: Red On; p. 540: PHB.cz (Richard Semik); p. 543: Fabio Lamanna / Shutterstock.com; p. 544: © Venturelli Luca / Shutterstock.com; p. 547: el lobo / Shutterstock; p. 550: trabantos / Shutterstock.com; p. 555: trabantos / Shutterstock.com; p. 559: Yulia Grigoryeva / Shutterstock.com; p. 563: Minoli / Shutterstock.com; p. 567: Pavlo Baliukh / Shutterstock.com; p. 572: LianeM; p. 577: ©Kert; p. 578: PhotoFires; p. 579: iryna1; p. 585: arkanto / Shutterstock;

p. 593: mkos83 / Shutterstock.com; p. 595: Juraj Kamenicky / Shutterstock.com; p. 596: Massimo Santi / Shutterstock.com; p. 600: Anna Pakutina / Shutterstock.com; p. 603: edella / Shutterstock.com; p. 606: Courtesy of Grand Hotel Vesuvio; p. 607: Courtesy of Decumani Hotel de Charme/ Nicoletta Diamanti; p. 610: Meghan Lamb; p. 615: marcobrivio.photo / Shutterstock.com; p. 622: Giuma / Shutterstock.com; p. 627: Isabella Pfenninger / Shutterstock; p. 632: Viacheslav Lopatin; p. 634: Alfiya Safuanova / Shutterstock.com; p. 637: leoks / Shutterstock; p. 642: nikolpetr / Shutterstock.com; p. 644: Meghan Lamb; p. 645: Slavko Sereda; p. 652: Meghan Lamb; p. 655: Massimo Buonaiuto / Shutterstock; p. 657: Meghan Lamb; p. 664, top: Meghan Lamb; p. 664, bottom: Adam Zoltan / Shutterstock; p. 665: jackbolla; p. 667: Meghan Lamb; p. 671: Meghan Lamb; p. 674: Neirfy; p. 677: Meghan Lamb; p. 681: Meghan Lamb; p. 684: Meghan Lamb; p. 688: Roman Babakin / Shutterstock.com; p. 699: ElenaAlisha / Shutterstock; p. 702: Balate Dorin; p. 705: AWP76 / Shutterstock.com; p. 708: Maurizio De Mattei / Shutterstock; p. 710: Elefante; p. 713: Littleaom; p. 715: essevu / Shutterstock; p. 721: Cristiano Palazzini; p. 722: arkanto; p. 725: Francesco Bonino / Shutterstock.com; p. 728: Giovanni G / Shutterstock; p. 730: Emi Cristea; p. 731: Pug Girl; p. 736: Eddy Galeotti / Shutterstock.com; p. 738: Piccia Neri; p. 742: leoks; p. 743: Gimas / Shutterstock.com; p. 744: K. Roy Zerloch / Shutterstock; p. 748: Kiev.Victor / Shutterstock; p. 752: Romas_Photo; p. 754: Boris Stroujko; p. 757: Jerome LABOUYRIE / Shutterstock; p. 767: vvoe / Shutterstock.com; p. 769: Yury Dmitrienko / Shutterstock.com; p. 771: robertonencini / Shutterstock.com; p. 774: Zigres / Shutterstock.com; p. 783: Travellaggio / Shutterstock; p. 788: Courtesy of Charme Hotel Henry's House; p. 792: Frog Dares; p. 794: Stefano_Valeri; p. 797: ©lapas77 / Shutterstock.com; p. 799: ©silky; p. 803: Marco Crupi / Shutterstock.com; p. 805: Avillfoto / Shutterstock.com; p. 808: Standret; p. 813: robertonencini; p. 817: fokke baarssen / Shutterstock; back cover: Boris Stroujko / Shutterstock.

Before, During, or After your use of a Frommer's guidebook... you'll want to consult

FROMMERS.COM

FROMMERS.COM IS KEPT UP-TO-DATE, WITH:

NEWS
The latest events (and deals) to affect your next vacation

BLOGS
Opinionated comments by our outspoken staff

SLIDESHOWS
On weekly-changing, practical but inspiring topics of travel

CONTESTS
Enabling you to win free trips

PODCASTS
Featuring experts from around the world

DESTINATIONS
Hundreds of cities, their hotels, restaurants and sights

TRIP IDEAS
Valuable, offbeat suggestions for your next vacation

***AND MUCH MORE!**

Smart travelers consult Frommers.com